Lecture Notes in Computer Science 8374

Commenced Publication in 1973
Founding and Former Series Editors:
Gerhard Goos, Juris Hartmanis, and Jan van Leeuwen

Dieter an Mey Michael Alexander
Paolo Bientinesi Mario Cannataro Carsten Clauss
Alexandru Costan Gabor Kecskemeti
Christine Morin Laura Ricci Julio Sahuquillo
Martin Schulz Vittorio Scarano Stephen L. Scott
Josef Weidendorfer (Eds.)

Euro-Par 2013: Parallel Processing Workshops

BigDataCloud, DIHC, FedICI, HeteroPar, HiBB, LSDVE, MHPC, OMHI, PADABS, PROPER, Resilience, ROME, and UCHPC 2013
Aachen, Germany, August 26-27, 2013
Revised Selected Papers

Springer

Volume Editors

Dieter an Mey, E-mail: anmey@rz.rwth-aachen.de

Michael Alexander, E-mail: michael.alexander@tuwien.ac.at

Paolo Bientinesi, E-mail: pauldj@aices.rwth-aachen.de

Mario Cannataro, E-mail: cannataro@unicz.it

Carsten Clauss, E-mail: clauss@lfbs.rwth-aachen.de

Alexandru Costan, Email:alexandru.costan@inria.fr

Gabor Kecskemeti, E-mail: kecskemeti.gabor@sztaki.mta.hu

Christine Morin, Email: christine.morin@inria.fr

Laura Ricci, E-mail: ricci@di.unipi.it

Julio Sahuquillo, E-mail: jsahuqui@disca.upv.es

Martin Schulz, E-mail: schulzm@llnl.gov

Vittorio Scarano, E-mail: vitsca@dia.unisa.it

Stephen L. Scott, E-mail: scottsl@ornl.gov

Josef Weidendorfer, E-mail: josef.weidendorfer@in.tum.de

ISSN 0302-9743
ISBN 978-3-642-54419-4
DOI 10.1007/978-3-642-54420-0

e-ISSN 1611-3349
e-ISBN 978-3-642-54420-0

Springer Heidelberg New York Dordrecht London

Library of Congress Control Number: 2014931765

LNCS Sublibrary: SL 1 – Theoretical Computer Science and General Issues

Typesetting: Camera-ready by author, data conversion by Scientific Publishing Services, Chennai, India

Printed on acid-free paper

Springer is part of Springer Science+Business Media (www.springer.com)

Preface

Euro-Par is an annual series of international conferences dedicated to the promotion and advancement of all aspects of parallel and distributed computing. Euro-Par 2013 was the 19th edition in this conference series. Euro-Par covers a wide spectrum of topics from algorithms and theory to software technology and hardware-related issues, with application areas ranging from scientific to mobile and cloud computing. Euro-Par provides a forum for the introduction, presentation, and discussion of the latest scientific and technical advances, extending the frontier of both the state of the art and the state of the practice.

Since 2006, Euro-Par conferences have provided a contiguous platform for a number of accompanying, technical workshops. This is a great opportunity for small and emerging communities to meet and discuss focused research topics. In 2012 a more formal management procedure for Euro-Par Workshops was established. A Workshop Chairpersonship was created, with two co-chairs: one from the Organizing Team (this year Dieter an Mey), and one from the Euro-Par Steering Committee (Luc Bougé, as in 2012).

The rationale behind this choice was to achieve a strong connection with the hosting team as in previous editions and furthermore maintain continuity along the years for the interaction with the workshop organizers. In the coordination process, we were assisted by a Workshop Advisory Board consisting of previous workshop co-chairs Ioannis Caragiannis (2012) and Raymond Namyst (2011), and experienced organizers of previous Euro-Par workshops Michael Alexander, Frédéric Desprez, and Jasper Larson Träff. It was very helpful to rely on their experience; we would like to warmly thank them for their help.

A Call for Workshop Proposals was issued, and the proposals were reviewed by the co-chairs, with advice from the Workshop Advisory Board. Overall, the following 13 workshops were selected for the 2013 edition. The list includes seven workshops that had been collocated with Euro-Par in the previous years:

- **BigDataCloud** – Second Workshop on Big Data Management in Clouds
- **HeteroPar** – 11th International Workshop on Algorithms, Models and Tools for Parallel Computing on Heterogeneous Platforms
- **HiBB** – 4th International Workshop on High-Performance Bioinformatics and Biomedicine
- **OMHI** – Second International Workshop on On-chip Memory Hierarchies and Interconnects

- **PROPER** – 6th International Workshop on Productivity and Performance
- **Resilience** – 6th International Workshop on Resiliency in High-Performance Computing with Clusters, Clouds, and Grids
- **UCHPC** – 6th International Workshop on UnConventional High-Performance Computing

There were also six newcomers:

- **DIHC** – Workshop on Dependability and Interoperability in Heterogeneous Clouds
- **FedICI** – First International Workshop on Federative and Interoperable Cloud Infrastructures
- **LSDVE** – First Workshop on Large-Scale Distributed Virtual Environments on Clouds and P2P
- **MHPC** – 2013 Workshop on Middleware for HPC and Big Data Systems
- **PADABS** – First Workshop on Parallel and Distributed Agent-Based Simulations
- **ROME** – First Workshop on Runtime and Operating Systems for the Many-core Era

Furthermore, tutorials on Tools for High-Productivity Supercomputing, on OpenACC Programming on GPUs, and on Advanced OpenMP were collocated with the workshop program, which consisted of five parallel tracks.

Submission deadlines, notification dates, and final/revised version submission deadlines were synchronized between all workshops. The new procedures established with the 2012 edition turned out to be very helpful for putting together a high-quality workshop program. After the conference, the workshop organizers delivered a workshop management report on the key performance indicators to the Workshop Advisory Board and the Steering Committee. These reports will help to improve the procedures for and the quality of the workshop program of future Euro-Par conferences.

The present volume includes the proceedings of all 13 workshops. Each workshop had its own paper-reviewing process. Special thanks are due to the authors of all the submitted papers, the members of the Program Committees, all the reviewers, and the workshop organizers and co-organizers. The workshops were successful because of their hard work. We are also grateful to the Euro-Par general chairs and the members of the Euro-Par Steering Committee for their support and advice regarding the coordination of workshops. Furthermore, we thank Ioannis Caragiannis, the workshop chair of Euro-Par 2012, for sharing his experience with us. We would like to thank Springer for its continuous support in publishing the workshop proceedings.

It was our pleasure and honor to organize and host the Euro-Par 2013 workshops in Aachen. We hope all the participants enjoyed the workshop program and benefited from the ample opportunities for fruitful exchange of ideas.

November 2013

Dieter an Mey
Luc Bougé

Organization

Euro-Par Steering Committee

Chair

Christian Lengauer	University of Passau, Germany

Vice-Chair

Luc Bougé	ENS Cachan, France

European Representatives

José Cunha	Universidade Nova de Lisboa, Portugal
Marco Danelutto	University of Pisa, Italy
Emmanuel Jeannot	LaBRI-Inria, Bordeaux, France
Christos Kaklamanis	Computer Technology Institute, Greece
Paul Kelly	Imperial College, UK
Thomas Ludwig	University of Hamburg, Germany
Emilio Luque	University Autonoma of Barcelona, Spain
Tomàs Margalef	University Autonoma of Barcelona, Spain
Wolfgang Nagel	Dresden University of Technology, Germany
Rizos Sakellariou	University of Manchester, UK
Henk Sips	Delft University of Technology, The Netherlands
Domenico Talia	University of Calabria, Italy

Honorary Members

Ron Perrott	Oxford e-Research Centre, UK
Karl Dieter Reinartz	University of Erlangen-Nuremberg, Germany

Observers

Fernando Silva	University of Porto, Portugal
Felix Wolf	GRS and RWTH Aachen University, Germany

Euro-Par 2013 Organization

Conference Co-chairs

Felix Wolf	GRS and RWTH Aachen University, Germany
Bernd Mohr	Forschungszentrum Jülich, Germany
Dieter an Mey	RWTH Aachen University, Germany

Local Organizing Committee

Vera Kleber	GRS, Germany
Elisabeth Altenberger	GRS, Germany
Michaela Bleuel	Jülich Aachen Research Alliance, Germany
Andre Dortmund	GRS, Germany
Beate Pütz	GRS, Germany
Adrian Spona	GRS, Germany
Andrea Wiemuth	Jülich Aachen Research Alliance, Germany

Euro-Par 2013 Workshops

Workshop Co-chairs

Luc Bougé	ENS Cachan, France
Dieter an Mey	RWTH Aachen University, Germany

Second Workshop on Big Data Management in Clouds (BigDataCloud 2013)

Program Chairs

Alexandru Costan	Inria and INSA Rennes, France
Frédéric Desprez	Inria and ENS Lyon, France

Program Committee

Gabriel Antoniu	Inria, Rennes, France
Luc Bougé	ENS Bruz, France
Toni Cortes	Universitat Politècnica de Catalunya Barcelona, Spain
Kate Keahey	University of Chicago and Argonne National Laboratory Chicago, USA
Bogdan Nicolae	IBM Research Dublin, Ireland
Maria S. Pérez	Universidad Politècnica de Madrid, Spain
Guillaume Pierre	IRISA and Université de Rennes 1, France
Robert Ross	Argonne National Laboratory, Chicago, USA
Osamu Tatebe	University of Tsukuba, Japan
Cristian Zamfir	EPFL Lausanne, Switzerland

Workshop on Dependability and Interoperability in Heterogeneous Clouds (DIHC 2013)

Program Chairs

Christine Morin	Inria, France
Roberto G. Cascella	Inria, France

Thilo Kielmann	VU Amsterdam, The Netherlands
Paolo Mori	CNR, Italy

Program Committee

Benjamin Aziz	University of Portsmouth, UK
Ioana Banicescu	Mississippi State University, USA
Alysson Bessani	University of Lisbon, Portugal
Lorenzo Blasi	HP, Italy
Massimo Coppola	CNR, Italy
Paolo Costa	Imperial College London, UK
Beniamino Di Martino	University of Naples, Italy
Elisabetta Di Nitto	Politecnico di Milano, Italy
Renato Figueiredo	University of Florida, USA
Yvon Jégou	Inria, France
Jens Jensen	STFC, UK
Fabio Martinelli	CNR, Italy
Dana Petcu	West University of Timisoara, Romania
Guillaume Pierre	University of Rennes 1, France
Florin Pop	UP Bucharest, Romania
Thorsten Schuett	ZIB Berlin, Germany
Josh Simons	VMware, USA

First International Workshop on Federative and Interoperable Cloud Infrastructures (FedICI 2013)

Program Chairs

Gabor Kecskemeti	University of Innsbruck, Austria
Attila Kertesz	MTA SZTAKI and University of Szeged, Hungary
Attila Csaba Marosi	MTA SZTAKI, Hungary
Radu Prodan	University of Innsbruck, Austria

Program Committee

Jameela Al-Jaroodi	United Arab Emirates University, United Arab Emirates
Eddy Caron	Parallel Computing Lab, Ecole Normale Superieure de Lyon, France
Salvatore Distefano	Politecnico di Milano, Italy
Gilles Fedak	Inria and University of Lyon, France
Francesc Guim	Intel Corporation, Spain
Eduardo Huedo Cuesta	Universidad Complutense de Madrid, Spain
Daniele Lezzi	Barcelona Supercomputing Center, Spain
Nader Mohamed	United Arab Emirates University, United Arab Emirates

Zsolt Nemeth	MTA SZTAKI, Hungary
Ariel Oleksiak	Poznan Supercomputing and Networking Cener, Poland
Anne-Cecile Orgerie	CNRS, Myriads, IRISA, France
Simon Ostermann	University of Innsbruck, Austria
Dana Petcu	Western University of Timisoara, Romania
Ivan Rodero	Rutgers the State University of New Jersey, USA
Matthias Schmidt	1&1 Internet AG, Germany
Alan Sill	Texas Tech University, USA
Gergely Sipos	European Grid Infrastructure, The Netherlands
Domenico Talia	ICAR-CNR, Italy
Massimo Villari	University of Messina, Italy

Additional Reviewers

Matthias Janetschek	University of Innsbruck, Austria
Vincenzo De Maio	University of Innsbruck, Austria

11th International Workshop on Algorithms, Models and Tools for Parallel Computing on Heterogeneous Platforms (HeteroPar 2013)

Program Chairs

Paolo Bientinesi	RWTH Aachen, Germany
Enrique Quintana-Ortí	Universidad Jaume I, Spain

Program Committee

Rosa Badia	Barcelona Supercomputing Center, Spain
Jorge Barbosa	Faculdade de Engenharia do Porto, Portugal
Olivier Beaumont	Inria Bordeaux Sud-Ouest, France
François Bodin	IRISA, France
Cristina Boeres	Universidade Federal Fluminense, Brazil
Robert L. Clay	Sandia National Labs, USA
Pierre-Francois Dutot	Laboratoire LIG, France
Toshio Endo	Tokyo Institute of Technology, Japan
Edgar Gabriel	University of Houston, USA
Rafael Mayo Gual	Universidad Jaume I, Spain
José R. Herrero	Universitat Politècnica de Catalunya, Spain
Shuichi Ichikawa	Toyohashi University of Technology, Japan
Francisco D. Igual	Universidad Complutense de Madrid, Spain
Emmanuel Jeannot	Inria, France

Helen Karatza Aristotle	University of Thessaloniki, Greece
Hatem Ltaief	KAUST, Saudi Arabia
Pierre Manneback	University of Mons, Belgium
Satoshi Matsuoka	Tokyo Institute of Technology, Japan
Wahid Nasri	Ecole Supérieure des Sciences et Techniques de Tunis, Tunisia
Dana Petcu	West University of Timisoara, Romania
Serge Petiton	Université des Sciences et Technologies de Lille, France
Vladimir Rychkov	University College Dublin, Ireland
Mitsuhisa Sato	University of Tsukuba, Japan
Howard J. Siegel	Colorado State University, USA
Antonio M. Vidal	Universitat Politècnica de València, Spain

Additional Reviewers

Pedro Alonso	Universitat Politècnica de València, Spain
Pablo Ezzatti	Universidad de la República, Uruguay
Diego Fabregat-Traver	RWTH Aachen, Germany
Isaac Gelado	Barcelona Supercomputing Center, Spain
Tareq Malas	KAUST, Saudi Arabia
Enric Morancho	Universitat Politècnica de Catalunya, Spain
Elmar Peise	RWTH Aachen, Germany
Matthias Petschow	RWTH Aachen, Germany
Alfredo Remón	Universidad Jaume I, Spain
Ruymán Reyes	University of Edinburgh, UK
Malek Smaoui	KAUST, Saudi Arabia
Paul Springer	RWTH Aachen, Germany

4th International Workshop on High-Performance Bioinformatics and Biomedicine (HiBB 2013)

Program Chair

Mario Cannataro	University Magna Græcia of Catanzaro, Italy

Program Committee

Pratul K. Agarwal	Oak Ridge National Laboratory, USA
Ignacio Blanquer	Universidad Politecnica de Valencia, Spain
Daniela Calvetti	Case Western Reserve University, USA
Werner Dubitzky	University of Ulster, UK
Ananth Y. Grama	Purdue University, USA
Concettina Guerra	Georgia Institute of Technology, USA
Pietro H. Guzzi	University Magna Græcia of Catanzaro, Italy
Vicente Hernandez	Universidad Politecnica de Valencia, Spain

Marcelo Lobosco	Federal University of Juiz de Fora, Brazil
Salvatore Orlando	University of Venice, Italy
Horacio Perez-Sanchez	University of Murcia, Spain
Omer F. Rana	Cardiff University, UK
Richard Sinnott	University of Melbourne, Australia
Fabrizio Silvestri	ISTI-CNR, Italy
Erkki Somersalo	Case Western Reserve University, USA
Paolo Trunfio	University of Calabria, Italy
Pierangelo Veltri	University Magna Græcia of Catanzaro, Italy
Albert Zomaya	University of Sydney, Australia

Additional Reviewers

Giuseppe Agapito	University Magna Græcia of Catanzaro, Italy
Marco Aldinucci	University of Turin, Italy
Claudia Misale	University of Turin, Italy
Alessia Sarica	University Magna Græcia of Catanzaro, Italy

First Workshop on Large-Scale Distributed Virtual Environments on Clouds and P2P (LSDVE 2013)

Program Chairs

Laura Ricci	University of Pisa, Italy
Alexandru Iosup	TU Delft, The Netherlands
Andreas Petlund	Simula Research Laboratory, Norway
Radu Prodan	Institute of Computer Science, Innsbruck, Austria

Program Committee

Maha Abdallah	University of Paris VI, France
Emanuele Carlini	ISTI CNR, Pisa, Italy
Massimo Coppola	ISTI CNR, Pisa, Italy
Abennour El Rhalibi	Liverpool John Moores University, UK
Shun Yun Hu	Academia Sinica, Taiwan
Alexandru Iosup	TU Delft, The Netherlands
Yevgeny Koucheryavy	Tampere University of Technology, Finland
Raffaele Perego	ISTI CNR, Pisa, Italy
Andreas Petlund	Simula Research Laboratory, Norway
Radu Prodan	Institute of Computer Science, Innsbruck, Austria
Laura Ricci	University of Pisa, Italy
Gregor Schiele	NUI Galway, Ireland

Shervin Shirmohammadi	University of Ottawa, Canada
Fabrizio Silvestri	ISTI CNR, Pisa, Italy
Alexey Vinel	Tampere University of Technology, Finland

Additional Reviewers

Gaetano Anastasi	ISTI CNR, Pisa, Italy
Fabrizio Baiardi	University of Pisa, Italy
Ranieri Baraglia	ISTI CNR, Pisa, Italy
Patrizio Dazzi	ISTI CNR, Pisa, Italy
Vincenzo De Maio	University of Innsbruck, Austria
Hanna Kavalionak	University of Trento, Italy
Matthias Janetschek	University of Innsbruck, Austria

2013 Workshop on Middleware for HPC and Big Data Systems (MHPC 2013)

Program Chairs

Michael Alexander	Vienna University of Technology, Austria
Gianluigi Zanetti	CRS4, Italy
Anastassios Nanos	National Technical University of Athens, Greece
Jie Tao	Karlsruhe Institute of Technology, Germany
Lizhe Wang	Chinese Academy of Sciences, China

Program Committee

Amitanand Aiyer	Facebook, USA
Costas Bekas	IBM, Switzerland
Jakob Blomer	CERN, Switzerland
William Gardner	University of Guelph, Canada
Jose Gracia	High-Performance Computing Center of the University of Stuttgart, Germany
Zhenghua Guo	Indiana University, USA
Marcus Hardt	Karlsruhe Institute of Technology, Germany
Sverre Jarp	CERN, Switzerland
Christopher Jung	Karlsruhe Institute of Technology, Germany
Andreas Knüpfer	Technische Universität Dresden, Germany
Joanna Kolodziej	Cracow University of Technology, Poland
Nectarios Koziris	National Technical University of Athens, Greece
Yan Ma	Chinese Academy of Sciences, China
Rajiv Ranjan	University of New South Wales, Australia

Etienne Riviere	University of Neuchatel, Switzerland
Martin Schulz	Lawrence Livermore National Laboratory, USA
Viral Shah	MIT Julia Group, USA
Dimitrios Tsoumakos	Ionian University, Greece
Zhifeng Yun	Louisiana State University, USA

Second International Workshop on On-chip Memory Hierarchies and Interconnects: Organization, Management, and Implementation (OMHI 2013)

Program Chairs

Julio Sahuquillo	Universitat Politécnica de Valéncia, Spain
María Engracia Gómez	Universitat Politécnica de Valéncia, Spain
Salvador Petit	Universitat Politécnica de Valéncia, Spain

Program Committee

Marcello Coppola	STMicroelectronics, France
Giorgos Dimitrakopoulos	Democritus University of Thrace, Greece
Pierfrancesco Foglia	Università di Pisa, Italy
Crispín Gómez	Universidad de Castilla-La Mancha, Spain
Kees Goossens	Eindhoven University of Technology, The Netherlands
David Kaeli	Northeastern University, USA
Stefanos Kaxiras	Uppsala University, Sweden
Sonia López	Rochester Institute of Technology, USA
Iakovos Mavroidis	Foundation for Research and Technology - Hellas (FORTH), Greece
Orlando Moreira	ST-Ericsson, The Netherlands
Tor Skeie	Simula Research Laboratory, Norway
Rafael Ubal	Northeastern University, USA
Alberto Ros	Universidad de Murcia, Spain

First Workshop on Parallel and Distributed Agent-Based Simulations (PADABS 2013)

Program Chairs

Vittorio Scarano	Università di Salerno, Italy
Gennaro Cordasco	Seconda Università di Napoli, Italy
Rosario De Chiara	Poste Italiane, Italy
Ugo Erra	Università della Basilicata, Italy

Program Committee

Maria Chli	Aston University, UK
Claudio Cioffi-Revilla	George Mason University, USA
Biagio Cosenza	University of Innsbruck, Austria
Nick Collier	Argonne National Laboratory, USA
Rosaria Conte	Consiglio Nazionale delle Ricerche, Italy
Andrew Evans	University of Leeds, UK
Bernardino Frola	The MathWorks, Cambridge, UK
Nicola Lettieri	Università del Sannio and ISFOL, Italy
Sean Luke	George Mason University, USA
Michael North	Argonne National Laboratory, USA
Mario Paolucci	Consiglio Nazionale delle Ricerche, Italy
Paul Richmond	The University of Sheffield, UK
Arnold Rosenberg	Northeastern University, USA
Michela Taufer	University of Delaware, USA

Additional Reviewers

Lorenzo Andolfo	Università di Salerno, Italy
Luca Vicidomini	Università di Salerno, Italy

6th International Workshop on Productivity and Performance (PROPER 2013)

Program Chair

Martin Schulz	Lawrence Livermore National Laboratory, USA

Steering Committee

Andreas Knüpfer	Technische Universität Dresden, Germany
Michael Gerndt	Technische Universität München, Germany
Bettina Krammer	MoRitS, Bielefeld University and University of Applied Sciences Bielefeld, Germany
Shirley Moore	University of Texas at El Paso, USA
Matthias Müller	RWTH Aachen University, Germany
Felix Wolf	German Research School for Simulation Sciences, Germany

Program Committee

Denis Barthou	Inria, France
David Böhme	German Research School for Simulation Sciences, Germany
Karl Fürlinger	LMU München, Germany
Michael Gerndt	Technische Universität München, Germany

Kevin Huck	University of Oregon, USA
Koji Inoue	Kyushu University, Japan
Andreas Knüpfer	Technische Universität Dresden, Germany
Bettina Krammer	MoRitS, Bielefeld University and University of Applied Sciences Bielefeld, Germany
Ignacio Laguna	Lawrence Livermore National Laboratory, USA
John Mellor-Crummey	Rice University, USA
Matthias Müller	RWTH Aachen, Germany
Shirley Moore	University of Texas at El Paso, USA
Nathan Tallent	Pacific Northwest National Laboratory, USA
Jan Treibig	RRZE, Friedrich-Alexander-Universität Erlangen-Nürnberg, Germany
Anh Vo	Microsoft, USA
Brian Wylie	Jülich Supercomputing Center, Germany

Additional Reviewers

Georg Hager	RRZE, Friedrich-Alexander-Universität Erlangen-Nürnberg, Germany
Michael Maier	LMU München, Germany

6th International Workshop on Resiliency in High-Performance Computing in Clusters, Clouds, and Grids (Resilience 2013)

General Co-chairs

Stephen L. Scott	Tennessee Tech University and Oak Ridge National Laboratory, USA
Chokchai (Box) Leangsuksun	Louisiana Tech University, USA

Program Chairs

Patrick G. Bridges	University of New Mexico, USA
Christian Engelmann	Oak Ridge National Laboratory, USA

Program Committee

Vassil Alexandrov	Barcelona Supercomputing Center, Spain
Greg Bronevetsky	Lawrence Livermore National Laboratory, USA
Franck Cappello	Inria/UIUC, France/USA
Zizhong Chen	University of California, Riverside, USA
Andrew Chien	University of Chicago, USA
Nathan DeBardeleben	Los Alamos National Laboratory, USA
Kurt B. Ferreira	Sandia National Laboratories, USA

Cecile Germain	University Paris-Sud, France
Paul Hargrove	Lawrence Berkeley National Laboratory, USA
Larry Kaplan	Cray, USA
Dieter Kranzlmueller	LMU/LRZ Munich, Germany
Sriram Krishnamoorthy	Pacific Northwest National Laboratory, USA
Celso Mendes	University of Illinois at Urbana Champaign, USA
Christine Morin	Inria Rennes, France
Alexander Reinefeld	Zuse Institute Berlin, Germany
Rolf Riesen	IBM Research, Ireland
Mark Hoemmen	Sandia National Laboratories, USA

Additional Reviewers

Vitalian Danciu	LMU Munich, Germany
Scott Levy	University of New Mexico, USA
Nikos Parlavantzas	Inria, France
Florian Wende	Zuse Institute Berlin, Germany

First Workshop on Runtime and Operating Systems for the Many-core Era (ROME 2013)

Program Chairs

Carsten Clauss	RWTH Aachen University, Germany
Stefan Lankes	RWTH Aachen University, Germany

Program Committee

Carsten Clauss	RWTH Aachen University, Germany
Wolfgang Karl	Karlsruhe Institute of Technology, Germany
Stefan Lankes	RWTH Aachen University, Germany
Timothy Mattson	Intel Corporation, USA
Jörg Nolte	BTU Cottbus, Germany
Eric Noulard	ONERA Toulouse, France
Andreas Polze	Hasso Plattner Institute, Germany
Michael Riepen	Intel Labs Braunschweig, Germany
Bettina Schnor	University of Potsdam, Germany
Oliver Sinnen	University of Auckland, New Zealand
Carsten Trinitis	TU München, Germany
Theo Ungerer	Universität Augsburg, Germany
Josef Weidendorfer	TU München, Germany

Additional Reviewers

Christian Bradatsch	Universität Augsburg, Germany
Steffen Christgau	University of Potsdam, Germany
Bernhard Fechner	Universität Augsburg, Germany
Nasser Giacaman	University of Auckland, New Zealand
Ralf Jahr	Universität Augsburg, Germany
Avinash Malik	University of Auckland, New Zealand
Pablo Reble	RWTH Aachen University, Germany
Randolf Rotta	BTU Cottbus, Germany
Luca Santinelli	Scuola Superiore Sant'Anna, Italy
Roopak Sinha	University of Auckland, Germany
Georg Wassen	RWTH Aachen University, Germany

6th International Workshop on UnConventional High-Performance Computing 2013 (UCHPC 2013)

Program Chairs

Jens Breitbart	Heidelberg University, Germany
Anders Hast	Uppsala University, Sweden
Josef Weidendorfer	Technische Universität München, Germany

Steering Committee

Lars Bengtsson	Chalmers University of Technology, Sweden
Jens Breitbart	Heidelberg University, Germany
Anders Hast	Uppsala University, Sweden
Josef Weidendorfer	Technische Universität München, Germany
Jan-Philipp Weiss	COMSOL, Sweden
Ren Wu	AMD, USA

Program Committee

David A. Bader	Georgia Tech, USA
Michael Bader	Technische Universität München, Germany
Denis Barthou	Université de Bordeaux, France
Alex Bartzas	National Technical University of Athens, Greece
Lars Bengtsson	Chalmers University of Technology, Sweden
Jens Breitbart	University of Heidelberg, Germany
Giorgos Dimitrakopoulos	Democritus University of Thrace, Greece
Karl Fürlinger	LMU Munich, Germany
Dominik Goeddeke	TU Dortmund University, Germany

Georg Hager	Friedrich-Alexander-Universität Erlangen-Nürnberg, Germany
Frank Hannig	Friedrich-Alexander-Universität Erlangen-Nürnberg, Germany
Anders Hast	Uppsala University, Sweden
Rainer Keller	Hochschule für Technik, Stuttgart, Germany
Gaurav Khanna	University of Massachusetts Dartmouth, USA
Harald Köstler	Friedrich-Alexander-Universität Erlangen-Nürnberg, Germany
Manfred Mücke	Sustainable Computing Research, Austria
Andy Nisbet	Manchester Metropolitan University, UK
Ioannis Papaefstathiou	Technical University of Crete, Greece
Bertil Schmidt	University of Mainz, Germany
Ioannis Sourdis	Chalmers University of Technology, Sweden
Josef Weidendorfer	Technische Universität München, Germany
Jan-Philipp Weiss	COMSOL, Sweden
Stephan Wong	Delft University of Technology, The Netherlands
Ren Wu	AMD, USA
Yunquan Zhang	Chinese Academy of Sciences, Beijing, China
Peter Zinterhofjun	University of Salzburg, Austria

Additional Reviewers

M. Faisal Nadeem	Delft University of Technology, The Netherlands
Fakhar Anjam	Delft University of Technology, The Netherlands

Table of Contents

Second Workshop on Big Data Management in Clouds (BigDataCloud 2013)

Workshop on Dependability and Interoperability in Heterogeneous Clouds (DIHC 2013)

First International Workshop on Federative and Interoperable Cloud Infrastructures (FedICI 2013)

11th International Workshop on Algorithms, Models and Tools for Parallel Computing on Heterogeneous Platforms (HeteroPar 2013)

4th International Workshop on High-Performance Bioinformatics and Biomedicine (HiBB 2013)

First Workshop on Large Scale Distributed Virtual Environments on Clouds and P2P (LSDVE 2013)

2013 Workshop on Middleware for HPC and Big Data Systems (MHPC 2013)

Second International Workshop on On-chip Memory Hierarchies and Interconnects: Organization, Management and Implementation (OMHI 2013)

First Workshop on Parallel and Distributed Agent-Based Simulations (PADABS 2013)

6th International Workshop on Productivity and Performance (PROPER 2013)

6th International Workshop on Resiliency in High Performance Computing in Clusters, Clouds, and Grids (Resilience 2013)

First Workshop on Runtime and Operating Systems for the Many-Core Era (ROME 2013)

6th International Workshop on UnConventional High Performance Computing (UCHPC 2013)

Second Workshop on Big Data Management in Clouds (BigDataCloud 2013)

Alexandru Costan and Frédéric Desprez

Program Chairs

As data volumes increase at exponential speed in more and more application fields of science, the challenges posed by handling Big Data gain an increasing importance. Large scientific experiments, such as climate modeling, genome mapping, and high-energy physics simulations generate data volumes reaching petabytes per year. Data collected from remote sensors and satellites, dynamic data-driven applications, and digital libraries and are also producing extremely large datasets for real-time or offline processing. Initially designed for powerful and expensive supercomputers, such applications have seen an increasing adoption on clouds, exploiting their elasticity and economical model.

However, running such applications in an efficient fashion on clouds is challenging. One such open challenge is how to handle this data deluge. Sharing, disseminating and analyzing large data sets has become a critical issue despite the deployment of petascale computing systems, and optical networking speeds reaching up to 100 Gbps. While Map/Reduce covers a large fraction of the development space, there are still many applications that are better served by other models and systems. In such a context, we need to embrace new programming models, scheduling schemes, hybrid infrastructures and scale out of single datacenters to geographically distributed deployments in order to cope with these new challenges effectively.

The Workshop on Big Data Management in Clouds was created to provide a platform for the dissemination of recent research efforts that explicitly aim at addressing these challenges. It supports the presentation of advanced solutions for the efficient management of Big Data in the context of Cloud computing. The workshop aims to provide a venue for researchers to present and discuss results on all aspects of data management in Clouds, new development and deployment efforts in running data-intensive computing workloads. In particular, we are interested in how the use of Cloud-based technologies can meet the data intensive scientific challenges of HPC applications that are not well served by the current supercomputers or grids, and are being ported to Cloud platforms. The goal of the workshop is to support the assessment of the current state, introduce future directions, and present architectures and services for future Clouds supporting data intensive computing.

BigDataCloud 2013 follows the joint BDMC / CGWS workshop held in conjunction with EuroPar 2012, and the previous editions of the CGWS workshop (2009 - 2011). Its goal is to aggregate the data management and clouds/grids/ p2p communities built around these workshops in order to complement the data handling issues with a comprehensive system / infrastructure perspective.

D. an Mey et al. (Eds.): Euro-Par 2013 Workshops, LNCS 8374, pp. 1–2, 2014.

The second edition of the workshop was held on August 26, 2013 and gathered around 30 researchers from academia and industry. We received a total of 11 papers, out of which 5 were selected for presentation after one keynote talk. The keynote talk was given by Dr. Goetz Brasche from Microsoft Research and addressed the evolution and benefits of Big Data in the cloud. It provided examples and illustrated experiences with advancing science in the cloud. The talk gave some potential answers to questions frequently asked by researchers porting their scientific applications on clouds: what are the challenges? where are the opportunities? what is needed to make Big Data in the cloud valuable for scientists?

The first paper studies whether it is possible to take advantage of multiple local disks at virtual machine (VM) level in order to speed up big data analytics; to do so, it identifies the best practices to achieve a high virtualized aggregated I/O throughput in the context of I/O intensive MapReduce workloads. The findings show that Hadoop workloads can significantly benefit from striping to multiple virtual disks. Interestingly, the authors also point that Hadoop is better designed for horizontal rather than vertical scalability: its striping ability makes increasingly less use of the overall aggregated I/O bandwidth with increasing number of virtual disks. The second paper introduces a data federating service able to aggregate multiple storage types and frameworks, and present them to the user under a unified namespace. This approach can be useful to the scientific community by reducing the usage complexity of multiple storage resources, and by avoiding vendor lock-in in case of cloud storage. The next paper provides an alternative storage interface to the traditional byte-stream oriented interfaces, in the context of a live system. The authors argue that storage systems should provide a service based on developer workspaces that enforce isolation within the storage system, allowing storage interfaces to safely evolve from development into production, and integrate with existing provisioning abstractions and developer workflow protocols. The fourth paper tackles the I/O performance issues as a way to speed up and accelerate the data analysis. The authors introduce an approach that enables fine-grained reconfigurations of the data organization of files and file fragments to adapt the storage system to changing workloads, while considering the different characteristics of the storage devices (e.g., SSDs and HDDs). The final paper presents a complete solution for data-intensive workloads that includes tools to facilitate workflow descriptions, a runtime system to schedule and run the workflows according to their description and a storage layer to handle data management.

We wish to thank all the authors, the keynote speaker, the PC members and the organizers of EuroPar 2013 for their contribution to the success of this edition of the Workshop.

Understanding Vertical Scalability of I/O Virtualization for MapReduce Workloads: Challenges and Opportunities

Bogdan Nicolae

IBM Research, Dublin, Ireland
bogdan.nicolae@ie.ibm.com

Abstract. As the explosion of data sizes continues to push the limits of our abilities to efficiently store and process big data, next generation big data systems face multiple challenges. One such important challenge relates to the limited scalability of I/O, a determining factor in the overall performance of big data applications. Although paradigms like MapReduce have long been used to take advantage of local disks and avoid data movements over the network as much as possible, with increasing core count per node, local storage comes under increasing I/O pressure itself and prompts the need to equip nodes with multiple disks. However, given the rising need to virtualize large datacenters in order to provide a more flexible allocation and consolidation of physical resources (transforming them into public or private/hybrid clouds), the following questions arise: is it possible to take advantage of multiple local disks at virtual machine (VM) level in order to speed up big data analytics? If so, what are the best practices to achieve a high virtualized aggregated I/O throughput? This paper aims to answer these questions in the context of I/O intensive MapReduce workloads: it analyzes and characterizes their behavior under different virtualization scenarios in order to propose best practices for current approaches and speculate on future areas of improvement.

1 Introduction

Big Data analytics has enabled unprecedented insight into scientific, social and business challenges. Major advances in almost all fields (i.e. meteorology, genomics, complex physics simulations, environmental research, social networking and dynamics, financial forecasting, etc.) were possible thanks to increasing volume and diversity of data gathered and archived form a variety of sources: sensors, experimental data, mobile devices, etc.

Not surprisingly, the rapid rate at which data sizes are growing has prompted the need for bigger and faster systems / techniques capable to perform big data analytics efficiently at an increasingly larger scale. Today, clusters of tens of thousands of nodes are a common occurrence. However, advances that make such systems possible are not homogeneous: while adding more computational power was demonstrated feasible both in terms cost and scalability, the I/O abilities in terms of networking and storage are lagging behind. Given the data-intensive nature of big data workloads, I/O performance is a determining factor in the overall performance of the applications, thus becoming a critical focus area.

D. an Mey et al. (Eds.): Euro-Par 2013 Workshops, LNCS 8374, pp. 3–12, 2014.

An important technique to limit the impact of I/O bottlenecks is to avoid data movements as much as possible, which conserves network bandwidth and thus helps achieve horizontal scalability. Several big data paradigms were developed around this concept, with MapReduce [1] and its open-source implementation Hadoop [2] being widely adopted in both academia and industry. Two key design principles enable MapReduce to avoid data movements. First, it forces the users to think their application in an embarrassingly parallel fashion that transforms the input as much as possible into a digested form (map phase) over which an aggregation is performed (reduce phase). Thus, during the map phase no extra network traffic is generated due to synchronization. Second, it departs from the traditional model of decoupling storage from computation, taking advantage of local storage to schedule the computation close to the data if possible, which again avoids network traffic.

Although avoiding data movements is a powerful concept that helps conserve network bandwidth, at the same time it shifts the burden of I/O on the local storage. With horizontal scalability increasingly difficult to achieve and attention turning to vertical approaches (i.e. more cores per node), the I/O pressure grows large enough to introduce the need for multiple local disks. Thanks to its embarrassingly parallel design and a streaming I/O model that favors adding new data over modifying old data, MapReduce can easily take advantage of multiple disks to achieve a high aggregated I/O throughput, which is a feature already implemented in Hadoop.

As nodes become increasingly complex and expensive to build and maintain in large numbers, big data systems become prohibitively expensive for most users. In this context, IaaS cloud computing emerged as a key technology to enable users to rent computational resources on-demand, paying only for what they have used. Thanks to virtualization, any user can easily create a large virtual big data cluster with the click of a button. However, how to efficiently map virtual resources to physical resources is a difficult challenge, especially when considering the increasing size and complexity of the nodes. In particular, the problem of how to virtualize multiple local disks efficiently to achieve a high aggregated I/O throughput is not well understood yet it is a crucial step in enabling efficient big data analytics on IaaS clouds.

This paper aims to understand the problem mentioned above. What makes it particularly challenging is the multitude of factors that play a role in the I/O virtualization overhead (i.e. how many VMs per node, how many virtual disks per VM, virtual disk placement, etc.) that need to be analyzed. This is further augmented by missing functionality in state-of-art cloud middleware to enable users to express placement constraints for virtual disks. We summarize our contributions as follows:

- We introduce an experimental framework that emulates a cloud middleware and enables fine-grain control over the hypervisor in order to easily express mapping constrains for virtual disks. Using this approach, experimental setups can be easily defined and the experimental conditions can be tightly monitored and controlled.
- We experiment with I/O intensive MapReduce workloads in several virtualization setups. In particular, we analyze how well the striping mechanism implemented in Hadoop scales when using a variable number of VMs per node, virtual disks per VM and different virtual disk placement strategies.
- Based on the results, we identify several potential areas of improvement and comment on the associated research opportunities.

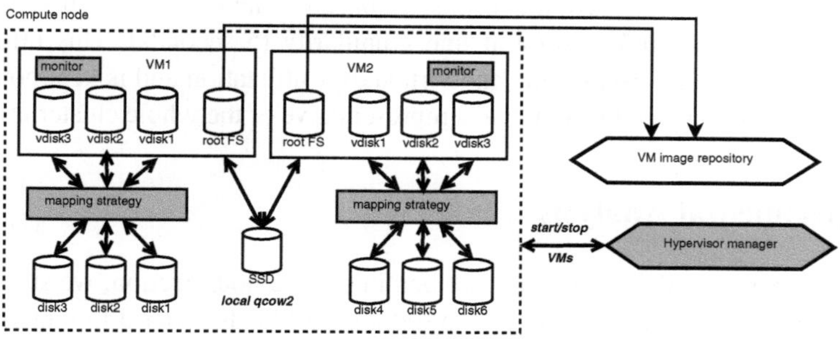

Fig. 1. Architecture of the experimental framework

2 Architecture

To facilitate fine-grain control over the hypervisor and the mapping between virtual and physical resources, we constructed an experimental framework that emulates a typical cloud middleware yet is highly configurable. The simplified architecture of this framework is depicted in Figure 1. For better clarity, the building blocks that are of special interest are emphasized with a darker background.

The *VM image repository* is the storage service responsible to hold the disk image templates for the root file systems of the VM instances. For the purpose of this work, we build our own custom template (based on Debian Sid) with a pre-installed Hadoop environment. All templates are read-only and serve as a base image for locally derived *qcow2* [3] images, where the VM instances are allowed to write into their root file-system. For better performance, the locally derived images are stored on a SSD. Note that Hadoop does not write to the root file-system directly, but uses a separate set of dedicated virtual disks attached to the VM instance.

The *hypervisor manager* is responsible to control all compute nodes and prepare the hypervisors to launch the VM instances in the desired configuration. It can be configured to use a variable number of nodes with a variable number of VMs per node, as well as attach a variable number of virtual disks per VM, according to a *mapping strategy*. For the purpose of this work, we implemented two mapping strategies: (1) *round robin*, which spreads the virtual disks to as many physical disks as possible in order to avoid I/O contention; and (2) *consolidated*, which places as many virtual disks as possible on the same physical disk, thus minimizing the number of required physical disks. Once a configuration was established, the hypervisor manager calculates the number of cores and amount of RAM per VM instance, creates the virtual disks according to the strategy and spawns the VM instances and attaches the virtual disks to them. In a final step, it generates the necessary configuration files for the Hadoop deployment (in particular it, enables striping on the attached virtual disks) and then deploys the Hadoop cluster. Striping is enabled both for HDFS [4], the default storage layer of Hadoop, as well as for the intermediate data that is generated by the mappers and that is used by the reducers as input.

To enable detailed analysis of the results, a *monitor* is deployed on each VM instance to gather performance information at fine granularity (5 seconds). This information includes CPU, memory, networking and virtual disk utilization and is kept both in raw form and in an aggregated fashion that is representative of the whole cluster utilization.

3 Experimental Analysis

Using the experimental framework described in the previous section, we study in this section the behavior of I/O intensive MapReduce workloads under different virtualization scenarios, in order to understand what aspects play an important role with respect to performance and scalability.

3.1 Setup

The platform used to run our experiments is a custom testbed consisting of 6 nodes, each equipped with 32 x86_64 cores with support for virtualization, 96 GB of RAM and several Gigabit Ethernet networking interfaces (one of which is used for the experiments). With respect to local storage, each node is equipped with 12 HDD disks (capacity per disk: 1 TB, measured I/O throughput per disk: 160 MB/s) and 2 SDD disks (capacity per disk: 256GB, measured I/O throughput per disk: 430 MB/s).

The hypervisor running on all compute nodes is QEMU/KVM 1.2.0, while the operating system is a recent Ubuntu distribution. The base image used to deploy the VMs is a recent Debian Sid distribution, on top of which we installed Hadoop 2.0.4. All VM instances share the same base image but write locally into their own derived copy-on-write image (using the *qcow2* format) that is stored on one of the SSDs. All extra virtual disks attached to the VMs that are used by Hadoop in striping mode correspond to *raw* files (256GB) that are stored on the HDDs (according to the mapping strategies presented in Section 2). Each VM formats all its extra virtual disks at boot time using the *ext4* file system. To maximize I/O performance, KVM is configured to run in paravirtualized mode using the *virtio* driver.

3.2 Methodology

We create a series of scenarios that involve a variable number of VMs per node and a variable number of virtual disks per VM using a combination of round robin and consolidated virtual disk mapping strategies.

In all of our experiments, the virtual Hadoop cluster leverages the physical resources of all 6 nodes. More specifically, we reserve 60 GB of RAM and 30 CPU cores for VMs on each node, leaving the rest to deal with jitter and virtualization overhead. These physical resources are leveraged in three configurations: 1 VM / node (using all reserved cores and RAM), 2 VMs / node (each of which is allocated 30 GB of RAM and 15 CPU cores) and 3 VMs / node (each of which is allocated 20 GB of RAM and 10 CPU cores). Thus, we create a virtual Hadoop cluster of 6, 12 and 18 VMs respectively. For each configuration, we vary the number of virtual disks attached to each VM from 1 up to 8. These disks are mapped to physical HDDs using a per-VM round robin policy, i.e. all

VMs on the same node share the same physical disk for their vdisk1, another physical disk for their vdisk2, etc.

The Hadoop deployment itself is performed using YARN. Each VM runs a HDFS *datanode* and a YARN *nodemanager*. As mentioned in Section 2, Hadoop is configured to stripe both its intermediate data and persistent data (i.e. data stored by HDFS). Furthermore, each nodemanager is configured to accept a number of parallel mappers that matches the number of cores allocated to the VM. One of the nodes is chosen as the master and runs the HDFS namespace manager and the YARN resourcemanager, in addition to the datanode and nodemanager.

As a representative workload to perform our study on, we chose the *sort* benchmark, a standard MapReduce workload that is part of the Hadoop distribution. It consists of two phases. In the first phase, a predefined amount of random data is generated using *randomwriter*. This workload writes variable-sized key-value pairs (keys between 10-1000 bytes, values between 0-20000 bytes) directly into HDFS. The mappers do not emit any output and the reduce phase is not used. For the purpose of this work, we configured *randomwriter* to use a total of 180 mappers (i.e. the total number of cores available in the Hadoop cluster), each of which is writing 2GB. After the first phase is complete, all previously generated data is sorted. In this case, the mapper is the predefined IdentityMapper and the reducer is the predefined IdentityReducer, both of which just pass their inputs directly to the output. The sorting itself is achieved thanks to the shuffling that is performed by the MapReduce framework. To parallelize this process as much as possible, we configured *sort* to use a maximum of 180 reducers, which matches the number of mapper slots. Thanks to this minimalist setup in terms of data processing itself, *sort* is heavily data intensive and emphasizes the I/O part, which is the reason why we chose it.

Each experiment consists in fixing the number of VMs per node and the number of virtual disks per VM, then running the *sort* benchmark to completion, while recording cluster-wide monitoring information (using the *monitors* presented in Section 2) and the completion times.

3.3 Results

The completion times for the *sort* benchmark using a variable number of VMs per node and a variable number of disks per VM is depicted in Figure 2(a).

As can be observed, in all three configurations, there is a sharp drop in completion time with an increasing number of virtual disks attached to the VMs. This fact confirms that I/O performance plays a crucial role in the overall application performance: when increasing the number of virtual disks from 1 to 8, a reduction in execution time of up to 70% is observable.

Focusing on the single VM per node scenario, two main factors contribute to the results mentioned above. First, as can be observed in Figure 3(b), an increasing number of virtual disks dramatically lowers the overall I/O pressure in the Hadoop cluster: from an aggregated utilization that tops 100% in the case of 1 virtual disk, a drop to a maximum of 50% and 25% is noticeable in the case of 4 and 8 disks respectively. Figure 3(a) reveals an interesting fact: a lower I/O pressure does not significantly affect the aggregated CPU utilization: all curves follow a similar pattern up to a point when

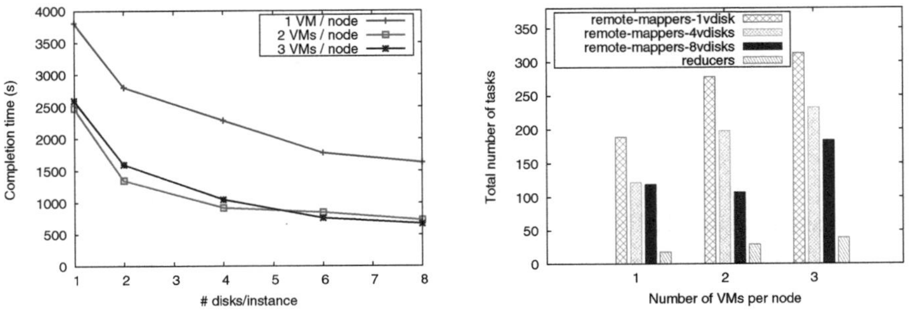

(a) Completion time (b) Statistics on remote mappers and reducers

Fig. 2. Performance results for the *sort* benchmark, using a variable number of VMs per node and a variable number of disks per VM

the CPU utilization drops sharply for the rest of the execution: this is the point when the mappers have finished and only reducers are still running. Thus, I/O is the dominating factor during the reduce phase and it oversaturates the disk bandwidth in the case of 1 vdisk, leading to a longer execution time. This is also confirmed by Figure 3(b): using only 1 vdisk results in 100% disk utilization for a significant portion of the reduce phase.

Second, according to Figure 2(b), a different distribution of map and reduce tasks is observable: increasing the number of virtual disks results in improved locality (less remote mappers, which means more data-local mappers) and thus better performance due to less data movement. However, considering the total number of mappers is around 2800, even for 1 vdisk there are less than 7% of remote mappers. Thus, we suspect the impact of improved locality on the overall application performance is small compared to the impact of lower I/O pressure due to more virtual disks.

What scalability is concerned, there is a noticeable drop in the benefits of adding more virtual disks (i.e. 27% reduction from one to two virtual disks compared to 9% reduction from 6 to 8 virtual disks). This is understandable considering the lower overall I/O utilization and it leads to an important observation: while there is considerable performance improvement due to lower I/O pressure, Hadoop striping does not fully leverage the aggregated I/O bandwidth offered by multiple local virtual disks.

Counter-intuitively, adding more VMs per node also benefits overall performance, despite more virtualization overhead and more data movements due to VMs on the same node being isolated from each other. As can be observed in Figure 2(a), the completion times for 2 and 3 VMs per node follow the same shape as the curve corresponding to 1 VM per node, however they are smaller by a significant near-constant factor.

To explain this effect, notice the better overall CPU utilization in Figure 3(c) and Figure 3(e): from an average of 65% in the case of 1 VM per node, it has risen to 80% and 90% for 2 and 3 VMs respectively, leading to a shorter map phase. Thus, we conclude that the load balancing implemented in Hadoop is currently tuned towards horizontal scalability rather than vertical scalability. This tendency is also confirmed by a shorter reduce phase, for which the explanation is found in Figure 2(b): as the size of

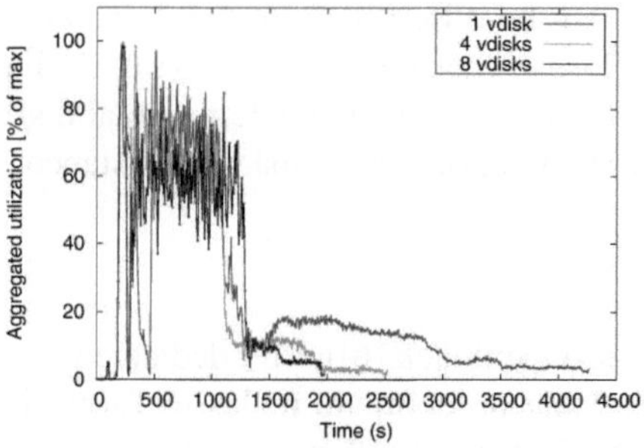

(a) Average CPU utilization for all nodes with 1 VM / node

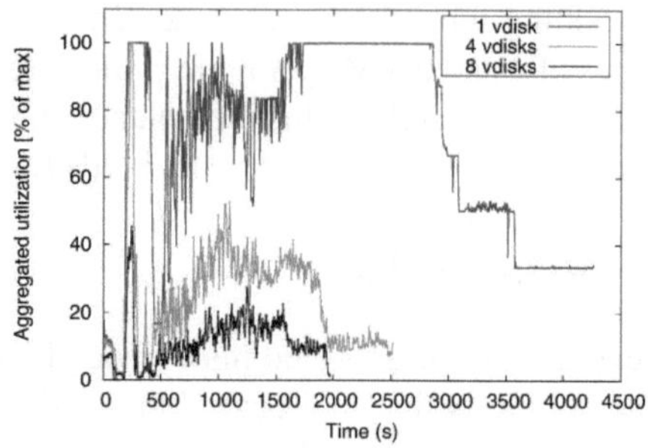

(b) Average disk utilization for all nodes with 1 VM / node

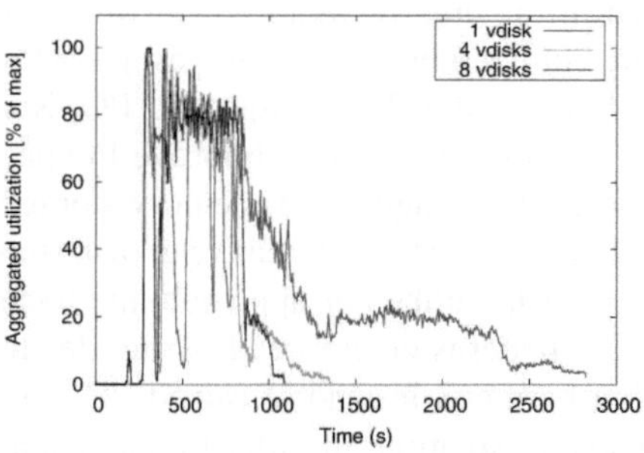

(c) Average CPU utilization for all nodes with 2 VMs / node

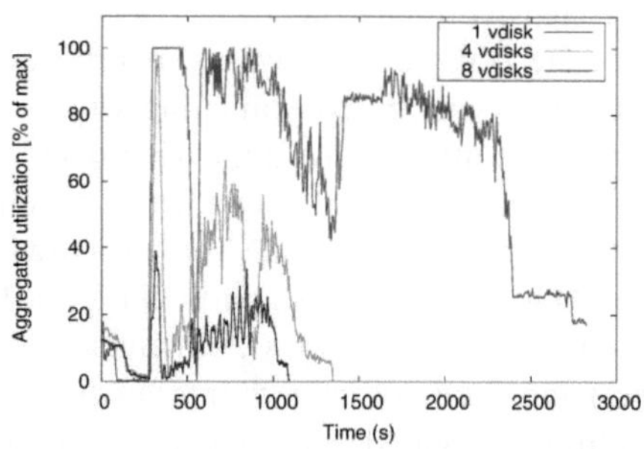

(d) Average disk utilization for all nodes with 2 VMs / node

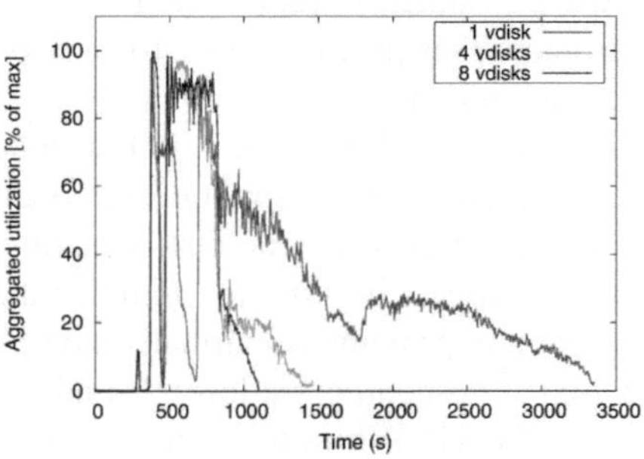

(e) Average CPU utilization for all nodes with 3 VMs / node

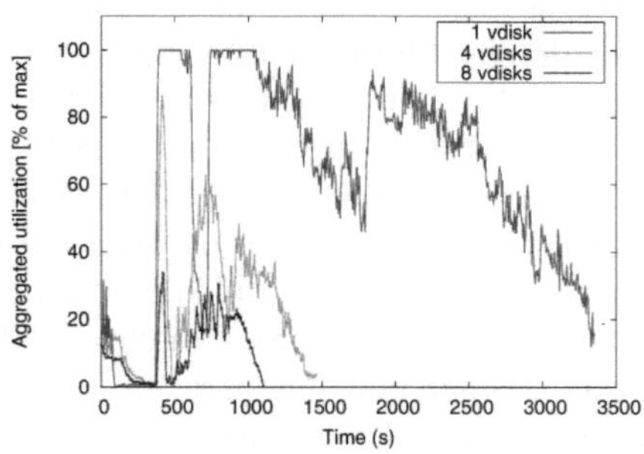

(f) Average disk utilization for all nodes with 3 VMs / node

Fig. 3. Aggregated statistics for overall CPU and disk utilization with a variable number of VMs per node and virtual disks per VM the Hadoop cluster grows, more reducers are used, despite an overall constant number of reducer slots being available in all configurations.

Nevertheless, when the number of VMs that share the same node increases, so does the virtualization overhead, limiting the potential to exploit horizontal scalability simply by adding more VMs per node. This trade-off can be observed from the completion times of 2 and 3 VMs per node, which are very close to each other (Figure 2(a)). Higher I/O pressure slightly tips the balance in favor of 2 VMs per node for few virtual disks per instance, while the opposite holds for higher number of virtual disks per instance.

4 Related Work

Several state-of-art cloud middleware [5] (such as OpenStack [6]) offer dedicated storage solutions that aggregate block storage available on compute nodes to form distributed repositories. However, there is no specific feature or API to control how virtual disks are mapped to physical disks. Thus, we felt the need to contribute with our own experimental framework.

Extensive related work has been undertaken in the area of MapReduce workload characterization. Some works report low resource utilization [7] and suggest potential energy savings by consolidating workloads to fewer nodes. With respect to I/O, Ren et al. [8] conclude that improving data locality has little potential to improve I/O performance, which is also confirmed by our findings. They suggest in-memory storage, potentially in form of a DSM (distributed shared memory) as an alternative to disk storage. Other studies focus particularly on HDFS [9,10]. Unlike our approach, the focus is on HDFS utilization (i.e. metadata, file access patterns create, read, write, delete, etc.) and does not involve intermediate data. Furthermore, instead of mixed I/O from multiple workloads, we analyze single workloads in isolation, in order to understand potential correlations.

Our own previous work [11] explores how to replace HDFS with a new storage layer based on BlobSeer [12], a versioning-based distributed storage system specifically designed for high throughput under concurrency. This previous work focuses on horizontal scalability and does not involve virtualization issues.

Several efforts have acknowledged the need to optimize MapReduce I/O at node level. Themis [13] implements the MapReduce paradigm using different design decisions than Hadoop. In particular, it introduces a centralized per-node disk scheduler that batches together records produced by different mappers in order to minimize the number of I/O operations. Ibrahim et al. [14] focus on improving I/O virtualization by means of smart coupling of the disk schedulers used at host and guest level that adapts to the workload. Unlike our case, the focus in these efforts is on how to optimize I/O for single disks rather than how to efficiently aggregate the bandwidth of multiple disks.

To our best knowledge, we are the fist to explore the problem of efficient virtualization of multiple local disks for data-intensive MapReduce workloads.

5 Conclusions

With increasing data sizes, big data analytics becomes increasingly challenging. In a quest to keep up with scalability, paradigms such as MapReduce were specifically designed to decouple tasks and improve horizontal scalability of big data systems. However, with horizontal scalability increasingly difficult to achieve, vertical scalability has recently gained increasing attention. Although adding more cores per node is a common occurrence, adding more disks per node to improve local I/O capabilities is not. Since big data applications are I/O intensive, doing so is highly desirable in order to remain scalable. Furthermore, given the tendency to virtualize datacenters in order to improve utilization and/or sell cloud computing services, the problem of how to efficiently virtualize multiple local disks for big data analytics is becoming crucial.

In this work we addressed the above problem. Given that this direction is still emerging, current cloud computing middleware is lacking features to guarantee efficient placement of virtual disks. Thus, our first contribution was to build an experimental framework that is able provide control over virtual disk placement, either spreading them over multiple physical disks in order to improve aggregated I/O or consolidating them on few physical disks.

Based on this experimental framework, we analyzed a data-intensive Hadoop workload in various virtualization settings. First of all, we found that Hadoop workloads can significantly benefit from striping to multiple virtual disks, with reductions in overall completion time of up to 70% when aggregating the I/O of 8 disks compared to a single disk.

However, our findings also show that Hadoop is better designed for horizontal rather than vertical scalability: its striping ability makes increasingly less use of the overall aggregated I/O bandwidth with increasing number of virtual disks. Furthermore, its load balancing ability increases with increasing number of VMs, despite sharing the same physical resources. This presents an interesting trade-off: on one side, increasing the number of VMs per node and/or the number of virtual disks per VM increases the virtualization overhead, but on the other hand it enables Hadoop to leverage the infrastructure better.

Thanks to these findings, we propose two interesting directions as future work. The first direction deals with how to improve Hadoop itself in order to enable it to leverage multiple virtual disks efficiently, both at the level of intermediate data and persistent data that needs to be saved in HDFS. In this context, the relationship to virtualization would be interesting to explore: would Hadoop benefit from being virtualization-aware? If so, what optimizations would be possible? Furthermore, does this go both ways (in other words, are there any hints it can give to the virtualization layer so that the latter can perform specific optimizations)?

Second, since Hadoop striping does not fully leverage the aggregated local I/O bandwidth to its full potential, another interesting direction to explore is whether presenting a single virtual disk to the VM and doing striping transparently in the background at hypervisor level can make better use of the aggregated bandwidth. In this context, we propose the concept of *bandwidth-elastic virtual disk*: a virtual disk that stripes to more physical disks under high I/O pressure and consolidates to less physical disks when the I/O pressure is lower, thus improving I/O resource utilization and enabling more efficient multi-tenancy and lower operational costs (e.g. saving energy by powering off disks).

References

1. Dean, J., Ghemawat, S.: MapReduce: simplified data processing on large clusters. Communications of the ACM 51(1), 107–113 (2008)
2. White, T.: Hadoop: The Definitive Guide. O'Reilly Media, Inc. (2009)
3. Gagné, M.: Cooking with Linux—still searching for the ultimate Linux distro? Linux J. 2007(161), 9 (2007)
4. Shvachko, K., Huang, H., Radia, S., Chansler, R.: The Hadoop distributed file system. In: MSST 2010: The 26th Symposium on Massive Storage Systems and Technologies (2010)
5. Zhang, Z., Wu, C., Cheung, D.W.: A survey on cloud interoperability: taxonomies, standards, and practice. SIGMETRICS Perform. Eval. Rev. 40(4), 13–22 (2013)
6. Baset, S.A.: Open source cloud technologies. In: SoCC 2012: Proceedings of the 3rd ACM Symposium on Cloud Computing, pp. 28:1–28:2. ACM, New York (2012)
7. Kavulya, S., Tan, J., Gandhi, R., Narasimhan, P.: An analysis of traces from a production mapreduce cluster. In: CCGRID 2010: Proceedings of the 10th IEEE/ACM International Conference on Cluster, Cloud and Grid Computing, pp. 94–103. IEEE Computer Society (2010)
8. Ren, Z., Xu, X., Wan, J., Shi, W., Zhou, M.: Workload characterization on a production hadoop cluster: A case study on taobao. In: IISWC 2012: Proceedings of the 2012 IEEE International Symposium on Workload Characterization, San Diego, USA, pp. 3–13. IEEE Computer Society (2012)
9. Abad, C.L., Roberts, N., Lu, Y., Campbell, R.H.: A storage-centric analysis of mapreduce workloads: File popularity, temporal locality and arrival patterns. In: IISWC 2012 Proceedings of the 2012 IEEE International Symposium on Workload Characterization, San Diego, USA, pp. 100–109 (2012)
10. Abad, C.L., Luu, H., Roberts, N., Lee, K., Lu, Y., Campbell, R.H.: Metadata traces and workload models for evaluating big storage systems. In: UCC 2012: Proceedings of the 5th International Conference on Utility and Cloud Computing, Chicago, USA, pp. 125–132. IEEE Computer Society (2012)
11. Nicolae, B., Moise, D., Antoniu, G., Bougé, L., Dorier, M.: Blobseer: Bringing high throughput under heavy concurrency to hadoop map/reduce applications. In: IPDPS 2010: Proc. 24th International Parallel and Distributed Processing Symposium, Atlanta, USA, pp. 1–12 (2010)
12. Nicolae, B., Antoniu, G., Bougé, L., Moise, D., Carpen-Amarie, A.: Blobseer: Next-generation data management for large scale infrastructures. J. Parallel Distrib. Comput. 71, 169–184 (2011)
13. Rasmussen, A., Lam, V.T., Conley, M., Porter, G., Kapoor, R., Vahdat, A.: Themis: an i/o-efficient mapreduce. In: SoCC 2012: Proceedings of the Third ACM Symposium on Cloud Computing, San Jose, USA, pp. 13:1–13:14. ACM (2012)
14. Ibrahim, S., Jin, H., Lu, L., He, B., Wu, S.: Adaptive disk i/o scheduling for mapreduce in virtualized environment. In: ICPP 2011: The 2011 International Conference on Parallel Processing, Taipei, Taiwan, pp. 335–344 (2011)

Cloud Data Federation for Scientific Applications

Spiros Koulouzis[1], Dmitry Vasyunin[1], Reginald Cushing[1], Adam Belloum[1], and Marian Bubak[1,2]

[1] Informatics Institute, University of Amsterdam, Amsterdam, The Netherlands
{S.Koulouzis,Dvasunin,R.S.Cushing,A.S.Z.Belloum,M.T.Bubak}@uva.nl
[2] Department of Computer Science, AGH Krakow, Poland
bubak@agh.edu.pl

Abstract. Nowadays, data-intensive scientific research needs storage capabilities that enable efficient data sharing. This is of great importance for many scientific domains such as the Virtual Physiological Human. In this paper, we introduce a solution that federates a variety of systems ranging from file servers to more sophisticated ones used in clouds or grids. Our solution follows a client-centric approach that loosely couples a variety of data resources that may use different technologies such as Openstack-Swift, iRODS, GridFTP, and may be geographically distributed. It is implemented as a lightweight service which does not require installation of a software on the resources it uses. In this way we are able to efficiently use heterogeneous storage resources, reduce the usage complexity of multiple storage resources, and avoid vendor lock-in in case of cloud storage. To demonstrate the usability of our approach we performed a number of experiments that assess the performance and functionality of the developed system.

Keywords: data federation, data sharing, data intensive applications, cloud computing.

1 Introduction

Most *in-silico* experiments in various scientific domains revolve around massive data volumes. Advances in data capture hardware such as telescopes and sequencing machines means that data is being generated at unprecedented rates. The experimental sciences alone are producing more data than ever, for example, the LHC produces 15 PB/year [1] and LOFAR [2] is expected to produce 20 PB in the next 5 years [2]. Scientific data are not only growing in size but are also stored all around the Globe using a variety of storage and access technologies. For this reason, today's research needs advanced storage capabilities to enable collaboration without introducing additional complexity to the way data are accessed and shared [3].

As in many scientific communities, the key challenge within the Virtual Physiological Human (VPH) [4] community is to share and access large datasets that allow the transformation of data to information and information to knowledge.

D. an Mey et al. (Eds.): Euro-Par 2013 Workshops, LNCS 8374, pp. 13–22, 2014.

Workflows are a valuable concept for the transformation of data to knowledge [5]. Most of the workflows within the VPH-Share project [4] consist of three kinds of tasks as shown in Figure 1. The first task obtains biomedical data while complying with privacy and ethics. The next task analyzes the data with some model, and finally the workflow produces the clinical output that provides a treatment strategy. In all these tasks data sharing and access plays a vital role.

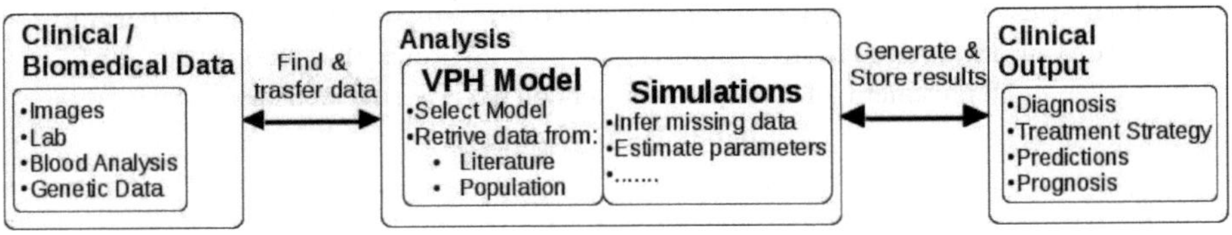

Fig. 1. The components of a generic VPH workflow. The first step always requires access to some dataset that is further analyzed.

Grids and clouds are used to harness geographically distributed resources for data-intensive applications. However, the plethora of data access technologies and distribution of data makes their sharing difficult. The fragmentation of datasets makes their discovery complex and time-consuming. Another problem arises from the need to handle a large set of client implementations in order to consume data from different sources. Furthermore, it is impractical to force storage providers to install and maintain large software stacks on their data storages in order to provide access to a variety of different clients. In the context of VPH-Share, it cannot be assumed that datasets are located in a single storage infrastructure nor that they will be available via a single technology. The vendor lock-in problem is another issue scientific communities have to consider when using clouds [6]. Moreover, a variety of modules of scientific workflows are created from legacy applications that can only access data from a local disk.

A solution that can partly address these problems is a data federation. Our approach is to aggregate a pool of resources in a client-centric manner and present it via a standardized protocol that can be also mounted and presented as a local storage so we can provide a file system abstraction. This can be achieved with the introduction of a common management layer that uses loosely coupled and independent storage resources. Through this common management layer a variety of storage resources such as simple file servers as well as storage clouds and data grids can be aggregated exposing all available storage under a single namespace. As a result, distributed applications have a global shared view of the whole available storage space. This will make the development, deployment and debugging of applications considerably simpler. Applications can be developed locally and then deployed on a distributed environment without changing the data access parameters. Legacy applications that can only read/write files on the local disk can easily become distributed. Moreover, the available storage space is used more efficiently with the copy-on-write strategy. Furthermore, replication of data can be based on efficiency cost measures. Offering a global shared view between applications improves the execution reliability. Experience has shown that a large percentage of execution failures is attributed to missing files [7]. Having a common management layer can help minimize that problem. When using storage clouds we also have a reduced risk of vendor lock-in since no large amount of data will be located on a single provider.

The main objectives of research presented in this paper is to elaborate an architecture that can flexibly federate clouds grids and other storage technologies, without any changes to the existing infrastructure. Existing approach are either tightly coupled with the infrastructure and demand from data owners to use a specific technology, or they are oriented towards a specific environment and implement ad-hoc interfaces making them less interoperable. Our main goal is to provide a large scale virtual file system that can take advantage of all available technologies in order to provide a global shared view of the underling resources. At the same time our approach is easy and intuitive to use as it hides the complexity of federation under a standardized access interface.

The rest of the paper is organized as follows: Section 2 presents an overview of related work. An analysis of the requirements and considerations regarding the system architecture is given in Section 3. Section 4 is devoted to the assessment of our proposed solution, and the paper concludes with Section 5

2 Related Work

Research on data grids, which are inherently distributed in terms of storage and decentralized in terms of administration, has successfully offered solutions for data storage federation. For example in [8] a virtual grid is suggested. In [9] the bases of data grids are described and in [10] the authors describe their approach to data grid federation where they try to combine performance and interoperability within the OGSA-DAI specification. However, these approaches are tightly coupled with a storage infrastructure. Moreover, these solutions often implement "ad-hoc" interfaces that lack interoperability or are specialized for grid environments. Cloud storage systems, on the other hand, apply distributed storage and centralized administration. Numerous architectures have being proposed as a solution for merging providers' infrastructure to meet spike demands. Although these architectures offer a solution for coping with spike demands, they do not address the vendor lock-in problem. There are few approaches aiming at improving cloud storage in a more interoperable client-centric way. In [11] the authors apply RAID-like techniques on the cloud storage level to allow customers to avoid vendor lock-in, reduce the cost of switching providers and to better tolerate provider outages or failures. This approach is limited to Amazon S3 interface.

The authors of [12] propose a unified namespace for removing the complexity of dealing with multiple storage providers. This approach is mostly focused on content delivery networks thus assuming that reading data is more important than writing, whereas in a collaborative scientific environment we can except frequent write operations as well.

In [13], the authors present a solution which is developed with the VPH community in mind, and gives emphasis on sharing and managing medical images, and should support almost any type of biomedical data. However, it uses a custom developed client to make the data available to users. This approach limits the interoperability and adds complexity. Additionally, the proposed solution is isolated in using Storage Resource Broker (SRB) [14].

Our approach tries to cover the needs of data-intensive sciences such as the VPH community by taking advantage all available technologies, so we can offer a large scale collaborative storage environment that is be able to federate multiple storage resources and present them as a unified storage space. Additionally, to make the federation as transparent and as flexible as possible, we loosely couple storage backends. Therefore, there is no need to install specialized software on the storage backends or to limit the type of technologies we can use.

3 Design Considerations

The **L**arge **OB**ject **C**loud **D**ata storag**E** fede**R**ation (LOBCDER) is a storage federation service that aims at making available distributed scientific data stored in various storage framework and independent providers. It is a part of the Data and Compute Cloud Platform of the VPH-Share project [4]. Within that framework, LOBCDER needs to expose large amount of data for the VPH community. At the same time, it is important not to add new software on the data storage. This is so not only because the complexity of managing and maintaining the existing software stack is already high, but also because some storage is outside our administrative domain and we cannot enforce the installation of specialized software that will allow us to federate that resource. Therefore LOBCDER loosely couples a variety of storage resource that may use different technologies such as Openstack-Swift, iRODS [15], GridFTP, and may be geographically distributed.

The LOBCDER service is divided into three main layers. Figure 2 shows a conceptual design of LOBCDER which includes the frontend, the resources and the backend. More specifically, the role of the frontend is to provide access and control as well as authentication and authorization through a standardized interface. LOBCDER's frontend is a WebDAV servlet which provides access to the entire available storage space. To maintain interoperability we chose WebDAV which is an RFC Standard. This enables network transparency[1] for legacy applications through the use of numerous clients that are able to mount WebDAV repositories on the local file system. WebDAV also supports versioning, a feature vital for providing a collaborative scientific framework. Besides versioning, WebDAV offers resource locking which helps in maintaining data consistency. Moreover, WebDAV supports custom properties allowing users to specify grounding[2] and

[1] Network transparency hides the way protocols transmit and receive data over the network, thus any operation that can be performed on a local file can also be performed on a remote file.

[2] Some of the datasets may be subject to legal and ethical restrictions which will require them to be hosted on a specific location

physical location distributions. Authentication and authorization is performed on the frontend layer. However, LOBCDER does not perform authentication by itself; it delegates this to an authentication service (an other component of the VPH-share platform) [16]. This service authenticates user according to a short lived security token. If the authentication service validates the security token, it returns to LOBCDER a set of information about the user (username and the roles associated with this user) where the authorization is performed. When clients want control over properties that depend on the infrastructure, we also have implemented a REST interface. For example, a data integrity application that monitors datasets needs access to the physical data so it may run checksums. To do that it access the RESTfull interface which provides the necessary endpoints to the data.

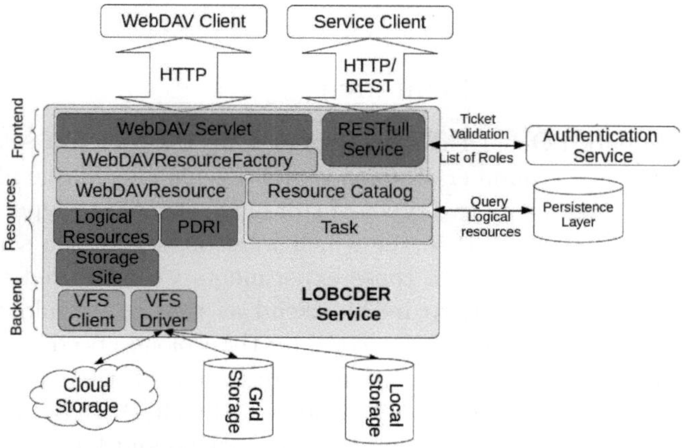

Fig. 2. Conceptual design of LOBCDER. The service is divided into three main layers: The frontend, the resources and the backend.

The purpose of the resource layer is to create a logical representation of the physical storage space and to manage the physical files. The resource layer contains the WebDAV resources, the resource catalog and the task component. The `WebDAVResourceFactory`, and the `WebDAVResource` are responsible for providing a WebDAV representation of the `LogicalResource`. The `ResourceCatalog` is connected to the persistence layer and it queries `LogicalResources`. The `Task` component manages the physical files. LOBCDER currently uses a cache to provide better performance for uploads. When a user uploads a file it is first saved in the local cache and later is replicated onto the available backends. The `Task` component schedules the file's replication. Similarly, when a file is deleted, the catalog removes its entry from the persistence layer and the `Task` component schedules all its physical files for deletion. The resource layer also contains logical resources along with their Physical Resource Identifier or `PDRI` and their Storage Site components. The `LogicalResources` holds basic metadata such as modification date, length, etc. The `PDRI` component represents the physical data and provides methods for replication and deletion. On the same layer the `StorageSite` component provides a description for the storage resources.

The backend layer provides the necessary abstraction to uniformly access physical storage resources. This is a Virtual Resource System API used by VBrowser [17] which was initially developed to access grid resources. The `VFSClient` can perform file system operations on physical data. The last component of the backend layer is the `VFSDriver`. Different driver implementations allow transparent access to storage resources, whether these are cloud, grid, or other resources such as SFTP.

The persistence layer is a relational database which holds the logical data that are represented by the `LogicalResource` and provides Atomicity, Consistency, Isolation and Durability (ACID). These properties are necessary in a multiuser environment for maintaining a synchronized and consistent view of the shared file system.

4 Assessment of Performance

In order to evaluate LOBCDER's performance we conducted a sets of experiments. We performed a number of uploads and downloads of large files (1 GB, 3 GB, 5 GB and 10 GB) using two types of storage backends: an OpenStack-Swift cloud storage and a GridFTP server which were hosted on the same machine at Cyfronet AGH in Krakow. In these experiments we measured the speed of uploads from the LOBCDER to its banckend as well as downloads from the backends to LOBCDER. We did not consider the upload speed from the client to LOBCDER because both applications were hosted on the same machine at the University of Amsterdam (UvA). Moreover, LOBCDER performs uploads in two phases: first, it saves the data on a local cache and later it schedules its replication. Downloads are made directly from the backend, as the mechanisms for managing LOBCDER's cache are still under development. The file sizes we used for measuring LOBCDER are considerably larger than the majority of files used in realistic scenarios. Our analysis of the requests LOBCDER received while deployed on the VPH-Share production environment confirms that in fact file sizes are much smaller than the file we used in our experiments. Figure 3 shows the distribution size of files being uploaded and downloaded during a period of ten days. In Figure 3 we can see 2000 uploaded files were between 0.27 and 0.81 MB while 200 downloaded files had almost the same size. The reason why the majority of files are between 0.27 MB and 0.81 MB is because most of the VPH-Share applications are using DICOM images which size is about 0.6 MB. Figure 4 shows the experimental setup. The UvA host is a 4 core Intel Xeon CPU at 3.00 GHz and 6 GB RAM. The Cyfronet host is a virtual machine on the VPH-Share Cloud Platform with 1 core CPU at 2.5 GHz and 2 GB RAM.

In order to profile the impact of the network on our experiments and be able to better interpret our results we measured the bandwidth between UvA and Cyfronet. We performed a series of experiments using `iperf`[3] by sending data

[3] Iperf is a network testing tool.

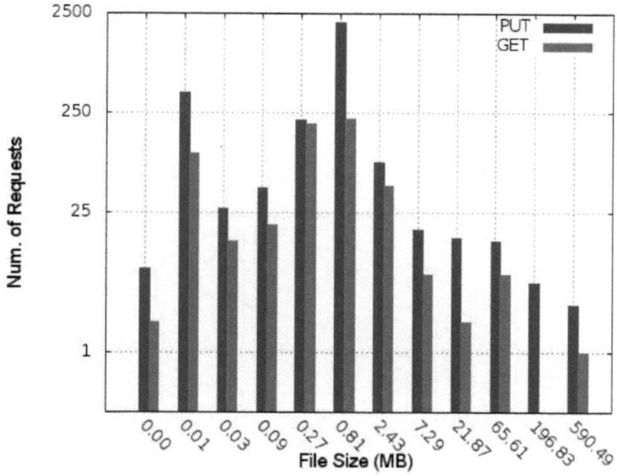

Fig. 3. Uploaded and download requests from the production environment

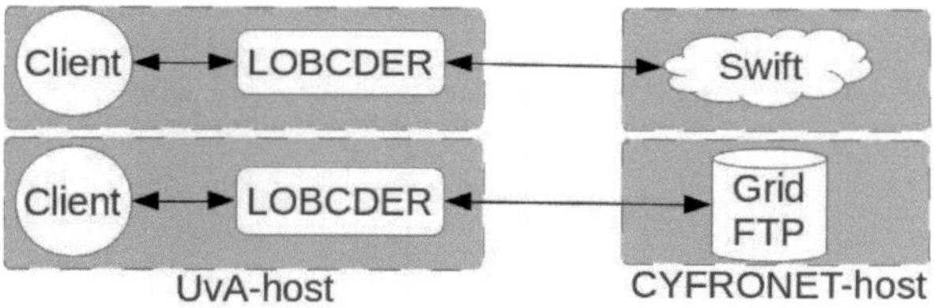

Fig. 4. Experimental setup. LOBCDER and the WebDAV client are located on the same host at UvA and the backends are on a remote host at Cyfronet.

packets via TCP. We measured the network bandwidth for uploads from UvA to Cyfronet and downloads from Cyfronet to UvA and used concurrent threads to evaluate the speedup. Figure 5 shows the results where we can clearly see that when uploading from UvA to Cyfronet we have a linear speedup but low speed. When downloading from Cyfronet to UvA the speedup is limited but the overall speed is much higher that uploading. Figure 6 shows the results obtained for uploading and downloading 1 GB, 3 GB, 5GB and 10 GB files.

Figure 6(a) shows that for a 1 GB file Swift and GridFTP have similar performance. As file size gets larger, Swift performs better. The reason for this performance difference lies in the way most cloud storage services deal with large files. In most cloud storage services it is not possible to upload files larger than 5 GB. Moreover, the cloud API[4] we use was unable to perform multipart requests for files larger than 2 GB. As a consequence we had to use segment upload, where a large file is divided into smaller chunks and uploaded separately. We took advantage of the file segmentation and performed a multi-threaded upload. Hence, we see a speedup when using Swift for file sizes larger than 2 GB. On the other hand, GridFTP performs similarly for all file sizes because the GridFTP was running as a single thread applications. These results can also be explained with the help of Figure 5 where we can see that using a single thread to upload

[4] JClouds API (`www.jclouds.org`)

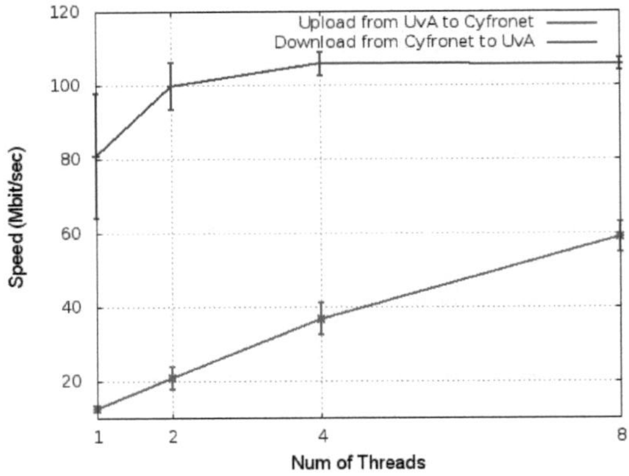

Fig. 5. Bandwidth between UvA and Cyfronet while using up to 8 concurrent threads

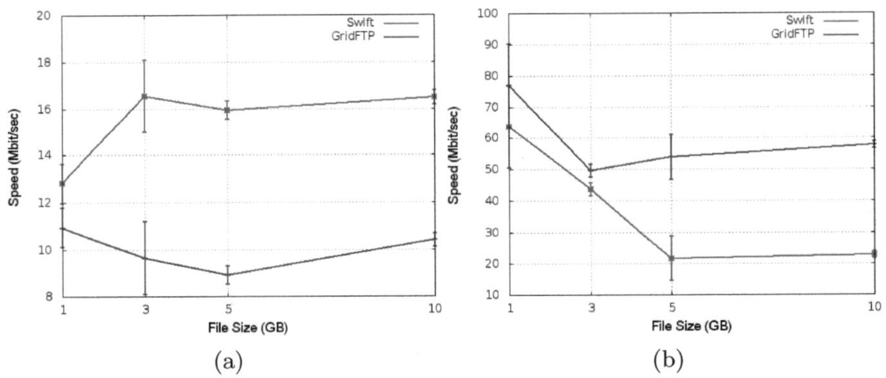

Fig. 6. Upload 6(a) and download 6(b) speeds for a Swift cloud storage and a GridFTP server

limits the speed to approximately 10 Mbit/sec, but when using multiple threads we can achieve a linear speedup.

Figure 6(b) shows the results for downloads where we can see that for a 1 GB file the performance of both backends is similar. However, when downloading larger files, Swift underperforms because files are segmented and the cloud API is single-threaded when downloading file segments. As a consequence, Swift performs worse than GridFTP which utilizes most of the available bandwidth.

Finally, we analyzed the request load LOBCDER is currently handling in the production environment. During 10 days, LOBCDER received in total 673,048 requests. Most of them (669,457) were PROPGET requests followed by PUT (2874). The remaining requests were GET (582) and DELETE (135). This indicates that LOBCDER's current architecture is able to cope with a large number of requests. However, the load from applications and workflows is expected to rise.

5 Conclusions and Future Work

In a collaborative and large scale research environment such as VPH-Share, workflows need access to large datasets which are geographically distributed and located in different storage infrastructures. Many data providers already have in place their own storage infrastructure which often makes the installation of new components impractical. To address these issues we elaborated a new method of data federation and implemented LOBCDER, a data federating service able to aggregate multiple storage types and frameworks, and present them to the user under a unified namespace. In order to provide network transparency, metadata queries, access control, version management and overwrite prevention, a WebDAV repository was developed. The LOBCDER can use cloud and grid infrastructure as well as other technologies as its storage backend. Our performance measures have shown that LOBCDER is able to cope with large data and a large amount of requests. Having verified that the current design is able to meet the demands of the VPH community, we will move further in order to implement efficient and flexible replication algorithms as well as caching mechanisms that will improve performance. Additionally, to increase data availability and performance, we will extend our current architecture into a distributed version that will use per-fetching for more efficient cache usage. When the load on the persistence layer proves to be large for a single database it will be necessary to investigate distributed ACID-compliant solutions.

Acknowledgement. This work was partly funded by the VPH-Share[5] and COMMIT[6] projects. We would also like to thank the Academic Computer Centre Cyfronet[7] for providing the Cloud testbed.

References

1. CERN: Worldwide LHC Computing Grid (March 2012)
2. Begeman, K., Belikov, A.N., Boxhoorn, D.R., Dijkstra, F., Holties, H., Meyer-Zhao, Z., Renting, G.A., Valentijn, E.A., Vriend, W.J.: Lofar information system. Future Gener. Comput. Syst. 27(3), 319–328 (2011)
3. Hey, T., Tansley, S., Tolle, K.: The Fourth Paradigm: Data-Intensive Scientific Discovery. Microsoft (2009)
4. Benkner, S., Bisbal, J., Engelbrecht, G., Hose, R.D., Kaniovskyi, Y., Koehler, M., Pedrinaci, C., Wood, S.: Towards collaborative data management in the VPH-share project. In: Alexander, M., et al. (eds.) Euro-Par 2011, Part I. LNCS, vol. 7155, pp. 54–63. Springer, Heidelberg (2012)
5. Belloum, A., Inda, M., Vasunin, D., Korkhov, V., Zhao, Z., Rauwerda, H., Breit, T., Bubak, M., Hertzberger, L.: Collaborative e-science experiments and scientific workflows. IEEE Internet Computing 15(4), 39–47 (2011)

[5] `http://www.vph-share.eu/`
[6] `http://www.commit-nl.nl/`
[7] `http://www.cyfronet.pl/en/`

6. Kurze, T., Klems, M., Bermbach, D., Lenk, A., Tai, S., Kunze, M.: Cloud federation. In: Proceedings of the 2nd International Conference on Cloud Computing, GRIDs, and Virtualization (CLOUD COMPUTING 2011), IARIA (September 2011)
7. Neokleous, K., Dikaiakos, M., Fragopoulou, P., Markatos, E.: Grid reliability: A study of failures on the egee infrastructure. In: Gorlatch, S., Bubak, M., Priol, T. (eds.) Proceedings of the CoreGRID Integration Workshop 2006, pp. 165–176 (October 2006)
8. Foster, I.: The virtual data grid: a new model and architecture for data-intensive collaboration. In: Proceedings of the 15th International Conference on Scientific and Statistical Database Management, SSDBM 2003, p. 11. IEEE Computer Society, Washington, DC (2003)
9. Rajasekar, A., Wan, M., Moore, R., Kremenek, G., Guptil, T.: Data grids, collections, and grid bricks. In: Proceedings of the 20th IEEE/11th NASA Goddard Conference on Mass Storage Systems and Technologies (MSST 2003), pp. 2–9 (2003)
10. Sánchez, A., Pérez, M.S., Karasavvas, K., Herrero, P., Pérez, A.: Mapfs-dai, an extension of ogsa-dai based on a parallel file system. Future Generation Computer Systems 23(1), 138–145 (2007)
11. Abu-Libdeh, H., Princehouse, L., Weatherspoon, H.: Racs: a case for cloud storage diversity. In: Proceedings of the 1st ACM Symposium on Cloud Computing, SoCC 2010, pp. 229–240. ACM, New York (2010)
12. Broberg, J., Buyya, R., Tari, Z.: MetaCDN: Harnessing Storage Clouds' for high performance content delivery. Journal of Network and Computer Applications 32(5), 1012–1022 (2009) Next Generation Content Networks
13. Testi, D., Quadrani, P., Viceconti, M.: PhysiomeSpace: digital library service for biomedical data. Physical and Engineering Sciences 368(1921), 2853–2861 (2010)
14. Rajasekar, A., Wan, M., Moore, R., Schroeder, W.: A prototype rule-based distributed data management system. In: HPDC Workshop on Next Generation Distributed Data Management (2006)
15. Wan, M., Moore, R., Rajasekar, A.: Integration of cloud storage with data grids. In: Proceedings of ICVCI 2009, 3rd International Conference on the Virtual Computing Initiative, Research Triangle Park, NC, USA (2009)
16. Nowakowski, P., Bartynski, T., Gubala, T., Harezlak, D., Kasztelnik, M., Meizner, M.M.J., Bubak, M.: Cloud platform for vph applications. In: 8th International Conference on eScience 2012 (October 2012)
17. VL-e: VBrowser web site (March 2012), http://www.vl-e.nl/vbrowser

In-vivo Storage System Development

Noah Watkins[1], Carlos Maltzahn[1], Scott Brandt[1], Ian Pye[3], and Adam Manzanares[2]

[1] University of California, Santa Cruz
{jayhawk,carlosm,scott}@cs.ucsc.edu
[2] California State University, Chico
nmtadam@gmail.com
[3] CloudFlare, Inc.
ian@cloudflare.com

Abstract. The emergence of high-performance open-source storage systems is allowing application and middleware developers to consider non-standard storage system interfaces. In contrast to the practice of virtually always designing for file-like byte-stream interfaces, co-designed domain-specific storage system interfaces are becoming increasingly common. However, in order for developers to evolve interfaces in high-availability storage systems, services are needed for *in-vivo* interface evolution that allows the development of interfaces in the context of a *live* system. Current clustered storage systems that provide interface customizability expose primitive services for managing ad-hoc interfaces. For maximum utility, the ability to create, evolve, and deploy *dynamic* storage interfaces is needed. However, in large-scale clusters, dynamic interface instantiation will require system-level support that ensures interface version consistency among storage nodes and client applications. We propose that storage systems should provide services that fully manage the life-cycle of dynamic interfaces that are aligned with the common branch-and-merge form of software maintenance, including isolated development workspaces that can be combined into existing production views of the system.

1 Introduction

The emergence of high-performance open-source storage systems is permitting applications and middleware developers to look beyond traditional file-like interfaces towards co-designed, domain-specific storage interfaces that offer unique opportunities for optimization. However, storage interfaces are inextricably tied to the ability to interpret and access data, elevating the criticality of their preservation and management in storage systems to that of the data artifacts themselves. Despite open-source storage systems paving the way for increased extensibility, systems currently lack any services for managing the life cycle of interface development.

Domain-specific interfaces allow applications to custom tailor data services such as I/O and co-located processing to realize optimizations not possible with

D. an Mey et al. (Eds.): Euro-Par 2013 Workshops, LNCS 8374, pp. 23–32, 2014.

generic file-like interfaces. For instance, structure and data type knowledge exposed through an interface can be used to guarantee data alignment properties and enable low-level data processing such as filtering and data transformation. These types of services, such as filtering, are largely inefficient to perform in middleware compared to a server-side approach, but storage systems deployed today do not offer any type of service for dynamic extensibility. Previous work on active storage systems have shown the benefits of co-locating processing with data, such as reducing data transfer and exploiting I/O and CPU parallelism [1–4]. And more recently, the Rhea [5] system showed that filtering kernels could be extracted from Hadoop jobs using static analysis and applied transparently in cloud storage services such as Microsoft Azure [6]. It is also anticipated that in next-generation exascale systems, array-oriented interfaces and script-based analysis function shipping will be supported natively by storage systems in an effort to circumvent scalability challenges presented by the POSIX file interface [7]. Unfortunately, previous solutions to providing extensibility have focused on architectures in which applications must fully manage interfaces, either by statically installing additional code, or packaging functions into each request. However, applications and storage system interfaces are inherently co-designed—an interface *defines* the data, and must be preserved for continued data access and interpretation. A storage system that allows its interfaces to be dynamically defined presents a challenge for application development, portability, and archival use cases because dynamic storage interfaces tend to be directly managed within the application run-time environment completely decoupled from stored data. We argue in this paper that managing the deployment, consistency, and versioning of interfaces, as well as enforcing isolation between developers and production interfaces is best handled by the storage system itself.

The development of co-designed storage system interfaces is an entirely software-based activity tightly coupled with the development of a driving application. In particular, it is very common for engineering teams to follow a branch-and-merge source-code management style using software such as Git, Mercurial, Perforce, or Subversion, in which feature branches are merged into a production line after some period of insulated feature development and maturation. While application feature development can often take place using, for example small-scale deployments on developer desktops, the same is not true for storage system interface development, where access to distributed resources and the peculiarities of live data are crucial to feature development and testing correctness at scale. One option is to allow developers unconstrained access to the storage system, relying on informal, error prone team guidelines to avoid conflicts such as naming or data format incompatibilities. Yet another option would be to maintain a smaller development cluster, but this leads to increased costs and may not expose the development process to realistic conditions. It would be useful if a storage system provided a development environment for storage interfaces as a first class service akin to the isolated development workflows for application developers using source-code management tools.

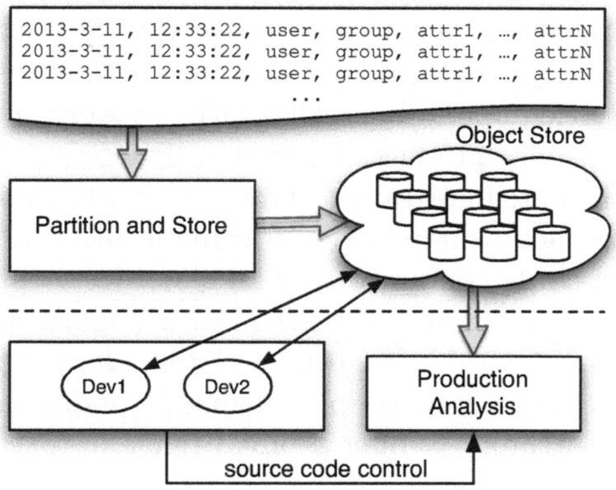

Fig. 1. Log data is stored in objects that are batch analyzed while developers create new features and evolve the system

In the remainder of this paper we present a solution based on the concept of a developer *workspace*. A workspace represents a unit of isolation within the storage system that allows for the independent evolution of interfaces that are dynamically created using a high-performance embedded scripting language. The system fully manages versioned interfaces within a workspace, ensuring a consistent view of interface versions between storage system clients and co-designed interfaces. Developers may merge interfaces from their workspace into production views of the system, providing an evolutionary development path aligned with common software maintenance protocols.

2 Motivation

The collection and analysis of large-scale read-mostly data such as access logs, click streams, and sensor data, as well as scientific simulation output, require scalable, fault-tolerant storage systems. Increasingly, these and other types of data commonly referred to as *big data*, are being maintained with cloud-based solutions using both object and file-based storage abstractions. Figure 1 illustrates a typical architecture in which data, such as time-ordered logs, are partitioned by attributes such as time or data source, and stored within objects in a distributed object-store such as Amazon S3. Shown in the same figure is a production application that interacts with the stored data objects by remotely reading and producing analysis results, or searching for activity patterns. Simultaneously, engineering teams may be developing and testing new features, as well as evolving the production deployment using standard source-code management techniques, workflows, and deployment operations procedures.

While this architecture of decoupling storage from analysis is extremely common, one challenge that arises is the I/O efficiency for data-intensive analysis tasks. For instance, simple filtering or computing statistical summaries are relatively inexpensive to perform, yet generally require transferring all dependent data across the network for analysis. The byte-oriented interfaces exposed by storage systems are a major impediment to offering new extensibility services because structural and type information at a low-level is needed perform these types of semantically rich operations. Alternatively, work in active storage has shown that domain-specific interfaces can be constructed within the storage system, and provide efficient, fine-grained data access. Domain-specific interfaces can provide access to, for example, the arithmetic mean of a single attribute computed over the records contained in a single object, apply a predicate derived from a high-level query, or reorganize data for more efficient access. Such an interface implemented within the storage system allows applications to avoid unnecessary data transfers, complex domain-specific middleware, and allows service providers an opportunity to offer a broad range of services such as offline, best-effort indexing and compression.

Allowing application developers to dynamically construct co-designed storage interfaces as part of the normal development process is a powerful construct for building distributed applications. However, the tight coupling between storage interfaces and applications require that both components can *evolve together* through a standard software development life-cycle, and that storage systems provide services for preserving installed interfaces within a large-scale cluster.

2.1 Storage Interface Evolution

Dynamically created storage interfaces pose a challenge for software development because application software may evolve independently from the deployed storage interfaces, but still require strong version consistency and compatibility between the application and deployed interfaces. Additionally, recall from Figure 1 that multiple developers may evolve an application by first developing and testing features, then integrating the changes into a production deployment. In order for each developer to work on features independently, conflicts that result from customized interfaces must be isolated and handled transparently.

Consider the application life cycle depicted in Figure 2. Developers *Dev1* and *Dev2* are responsible for developing independent, domain-specific interfaces to indvidual objects—arithmetic average, and minimum—that will replace the same per-object operation performed remotely by the production analysis application. Each developer must now evolve the storage-level interfaces, as well as change application-level code to take advantage of the new the features. For instance, both developers begin with a base storage interface exposing the standard byte-oriented interface (ver. A). Each developer evolves the application and storage interfaces with their respective features (ver. B, C). Once the features are complete, they are merged to expose the new interfaces to the production application (ver. D). Two interfaces can conflict if local object resources are not partitioned. For instance, if two interfaces implementing distinct statistical calculations (e.g. *mean* vs *median*) cache their result in a local object attribute to avoid recomputation, but use the same attribute name (e.g. *avg*), data corruption may lead to silent errors and unexpected results. Thus, providing transparent isolation between interfaces is important in order to avoid the type of ad-hoc

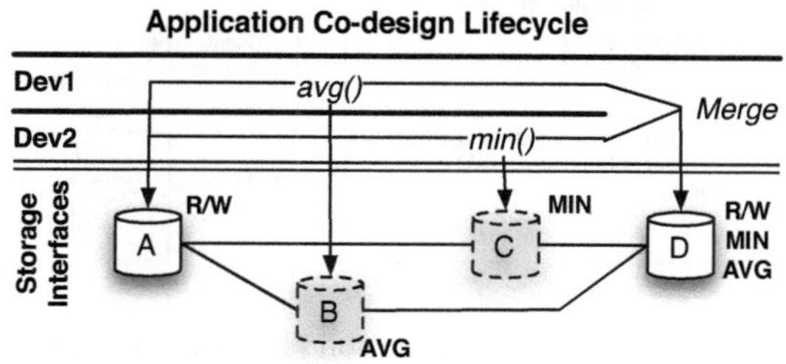

Fig. 2. Developers evolve application software and storage interfaces through a co-design process

coordination among developers that would otherwise be required. Next we discuss dynamic interfaces, the low-level building block for our system.

3 Extensible Object Interfaces

A core building block of our system is a service that allows the dynamic creation of low-level object interfaces using a high-performance embedded scripting language. Note that while our framework assumes the existence of extensible object interfaces, many approaches to providing extensibility should be compatible. In this paper we consider for context a design based on the Ceph distributed storage system, and begin our discussion with a brief overview of Ceph and its object-based storage system called RADOS.

3.1 The RADOS Object Store

The RADOS object store is a highly scalable, fault-tolerant storage service that forms the basis for high-level Ceph services such as the Ceph File System [8, 9]. A RADOS cluster consists of a set object-storage devices that expose a rich object interface including byte-oriented access methods as well extended attributes, indexing, and snapshots. Clients access objects through a library that hides the cluster layout, network, and fault-recovery. In addition to its natively supported interfaces, objects in RADOS can be extended by constructing C++-based plugins that define new methods on objects, analogous to creating a sub-class in an object-oriented language. A method is invoked against a target object remotely by a client and is transparently executed within the storage server process responsible for the object.

The extensibility of RADOS objects is very powerful, can be used to construct a variety of interfaces such as those discussed in Section 2, and is used by Ceph internally, and in several products built on top of Ceph. Unfortunately it is non-trivial to deploy statically compiled, architecture dependent interfaces within a high-availability cluster, making it difficult to integrate rapid interface evolution with the iterative development of applications. What is needed is a mechanism for dynamically constructing new object methods.

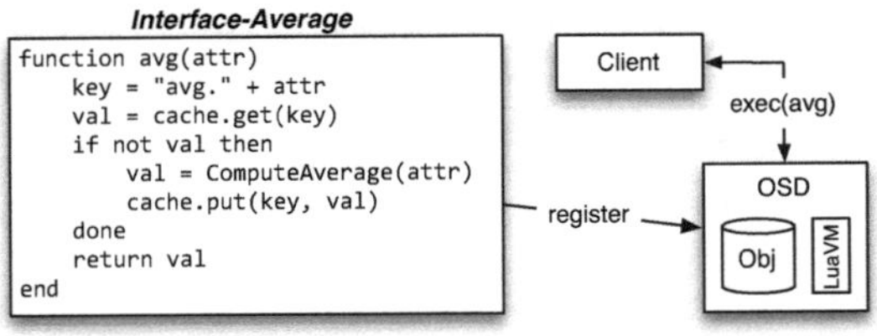

Fig. 3. An interface defining an *average* function is registered with an OSD after which point a client may remotely invoke the method on an object

3.2 Dynamic Interfaces

We have extended the object-storage devices in RADOS to support dynamically defined object interfaces using the Lua language [10], specifically designed as an embedded language for high-performance applications. New interfaces are created by sending to a storage device a Lua script that defines any number of methods, after which point the interfaces are made available through any existing RADOS client library.

Figure 3 illustrates how dynamic interfaces are used. First, a developer authors a Lua script that defines a new object method. Shown in the figure is a script that computes the arithmetic mean of an attribute over the records in a single object. Notice that before computing the average a cached attribute is queried to avoid recomputing results. A client that invokes this method on an object will trigger the method within the OSD process and the results will be returned to the client, potentially avoiding recomputation. Scripts may be pre-registered, or sent along side a client request for completely dynamic behavior.

This basic mechanism of constructing dynamic interfaces using small code fragments allows applications to easily evolve storage interfaces at a fine-granularity. However, two major issues arise. First, when working within a live system, developers should be able to work independently without worrying about causing conflicts. For instance, the author of the interfaced shown in Figure 3 should not be affected by other developers that also cache data with the same name; the system should provide this isolation. And second, in a large, elastic system developers should not have to be involved in the details of ensuring that a consistent view of their deployed interfaces are present on all system devices. To solve these challenges we propose that storage systems provide developers with logically isolated workspaces for interface development, and native services for managing installed interfaces across a cluster.

4 Interface Development Environment

We propose an *interface developer environment* (IDE) for constructing new, native storage interfaces that consist of an isolated *workspace* abstraction that is well-aligned to common software development workflows, and integrates with provisioning and tiering abstractions already present within storage systems.

4.1 Workspaces

A workspace is an entity managed by the storage system which provides isolation between dynamic interfaces. Workspaces can be created, destroyed, and merged through the use of the *interface development environment* (IDE) service, illustrated in Figure 4a. The IDE service exposes an interface similar to that of Git, Mercurial, or Subversion in which a development branch forms the basic unit of isolation. It is expected that the use of a workspace will resemble a developers *working copy* in the traditional sense of source-code control systems, providing a safe environment to construct, test, and refine a line of feature development. The key difference being that a workspace exists within and is managed entirely by the storage system for the purpose of providing server-side interfaces.

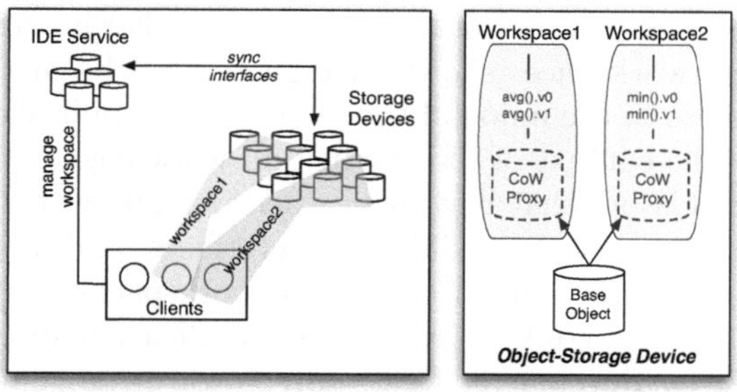

(a) IDE Service (b) Isolation

Fig. 4. In (a) clients use an IDE service to create workspaces that form a context within the storage system. In (b) base data is not duplicated, and CoW provides isolation for interface private data.

Isolation. Providing efficient isolation among workspaces is a challenge. In order to avoid expensive data duplication, the system should allow interfaces to share as much data as possible. For instance, read operations performed by an interface should require no special handling, and be satisfied by base data. However, writes must be carefully handled as to not interfere with state created by interfaces in other workspaces, or blob data associated with the object. For instance, the interface shown in Figure 3 caches a computed *average* value by constructing a key and saving it in an object-local cache. The framework must ensure that other interfaces are unaffected, a problem that could arise if, for example, two interface developers chose identical key names. Write operations that access object services, such as a local index or raw payload data, must be intercepted by the storage device and isolated. Efficient techniques for isolation depend on the type of service. For instance, isolation can be achieved using namespacing when storing key/value pairs, while copy-on-write techniques can be used for data transformations on blob data. Performance isolation is also an important aspect to consider. It is not unreasonable to use existing performance isolation techniques in a system, but we have not considered the need for an entirely new method for performance isolation.

Partitioning. While logical isolation is important to ensure correctness, an organization may want to physically partition its storage in such a way that development workspaces reside on distinct hardware. The logical workspace entity should integrate with existing facilities within the storage system for custom data placement and tiering policies, allowing subsets of data to be placed onto specific sets of nodes. Workspaces can be linked to these physical partitions through existing system abstractions (e.g. a *pool* in Ceph) which ensure that the space of addressed objects is constrained by the physical partitioning.

4.2 Workspace Management

Ultimately, interfaces defined within workspaces as part of application development will be migrated into a production environment. For instance, the interfaces defined in separate workspaces shown in Figure 2 can be merged into production, providing access to the union of the interfaces to applications accessing the storage system in the context of the production workspace.

There are several issues that may arise when merging workspaces. First, at a high-level merging changes the visibility of interfaces, and as a result interface naming conflicts may arise. For instance, two workspaces may define the same interface. These types of conflicts are largely application-specific and must be handled explicitly by developers. Like source-code management systems, the primary responsibility of the storage system is to provide feedback to developers about the changes they are making through the interface development service, and help manage conflict resolution.

Interfaces that utilize private data can be merged without low-level conflicts by migrating the same isolation parameters (e.g. namespacing) used to prevent conflicts between workspaces. However, for interfaces that perform heavy-weight data transforms such as using new data layouts, migrating all interfaces to a use a new layout may be necessary. In order to make format migration easier, workspace merging should optionally specify a transformation routine that the system ensures is applied prior to invoking any interface following a merge operation. Finally, the removal of workspaces will result in lazy deletion of all unmerged interface state created during the lifetime of the workspace.

5 The IDE Service

Interfaces and workspaces are cluster-wide entities that must be managed by the storage system in the face of cluster failures, expansion, and policy changes. For instance, the storage system must ensure that a new storage node has the required interfaces present before it can service requests from applications requiring these interfaces. Further, newly registered versions of interfaces must be propagated to nodes within the system, and properly synchronized with applications expecting the latest version.

Luckily, existing services within distributed storage systems solve similar problems. For instance, a core service often found in distributed systems is a highly available versioned data store commonly implemented using a consensus algorithm, such as Paxos. For instance, Ceph uses *monitor services*, built upon Paxos, to manage cluster membership, service discovery, replicated logs, and authentication. A monitor provides a consistent view of the system state, and clients and OSDs can contact a monitor to synchronize their states. Such existing services are closely related to the requirements of the IDE service, and should be capable of being reused to provide an interface synchronization service within the cluster.

Integration. Finally, a mechanism is needed to associate interface versions managed by the storage system with the versions that applications expect. We are considering two possible solutions to this problem. First, some source-code control systems provide the ability to inject external context information into the managed content (e.g. CVS tags expansion). Extending or exploiting this feature may allow us to automatically generate version macros used to provide context when clients access the system. Similarly, systems such as Git allow external repositories to be seamlessly integrated into existing repositories. By allowing the storage system to export its own virtual Git repository, we can enable the system to present previously registered, versioned code automatically into a higher-level project repository. Providing an easy-to-use and robust integration solution is important for usability, and utilizing other techniques from RPC stub generation may prove to be very valuable.

6 Related Work

Oasis [3] is an active storage framework based on extensions to the T10 standard. Primitive script management associates scripts with *function objects*, but the project does not address high-level management challenges. Runde, et al. [11] use sandboxing virtualization technology to isolate server-side computations, but do not address any type of logical isolation necessary to build the workspace abstraction we have proposed.

GlusterFS [12] translators provide a rich mechanism for adding functionality at different levels of the file system. Translators are statically defined and designed to be a long-lived *permanent* extension.

Building new pNFS striping strategies using the Lua scripting language have been proposed [13]. The script defining a new strategy is embedded in a file inode where script versioning is aligned with inode consistency mechanisms.

The Elephant File System is a versioning file system allowing data to be managed using checkpoints, tags, and other protocols [14]. While this file system is only concerned with payload data, the scalability lessons from this body of work dealing with interface versioning may prove useful.

The Git source-code control library has been integrated into a FUSE-based file system to extend its versioning features to files and directories [15]. We are also considering making use of the Git library for its rich, embeddable interface for managing and versioning textual data such as Lua code snippets, but are interested in mechanisms useful in distributed storage systems.

7 Conclusion

Providing alternative storage interfaces to the traditional byte-stream oriented interface has been the topic of much research. However, little has been done to address the management of co-designed storage interfaces with application development processes. This management is important to address as interest in dynamic interfaces increases. In this paper we have proposed that storage systems provide a service based on developer workspaces that enforce isolation within the storage system, allowing storage interfaces to safely evolve from development into production, and integrate with existing provisioning abstractions and developer workflow protocols.

References

1. Piernas, J., Nieplocha, J., Felix, E.J.: Evaluation of active storage strategies for the lustre parallel file system. In: SC 2007 (2007)
2. Son, S.W., Lang, S., Carns, P., Ross, R., Thakur, R., Ozisikyilmaz, B., Kumar, P., Liao, W.K., Choudhary, A.: Enabling active storage on parallel i/o software stacks. In: MSST 2010 (2010)
3. Xie, Y., Muniswamy-Reddy, K.K., Feng, D., Long, D.D.E., Kang, Y., Niu, Z., Tan, Z.: Design and evaluation of oasis: An active storage framework based on t10 osd standard. In: MSST 2011 (2011)
4. Lim, H., Kapoor, V., Wighe, C., Du, D.H.C.: Active disk file system: A distributed, scalable file system. In: MSST 2008 (2008)
5. Gkantsidis, C., Vytiniotis, D., Hodson, O., Narayanan, D., Dinu, F., Rowstron, A.: Rhea: automatic filtering for unstructured cloud storage. In: NSDI 2013 (2013)
6. Calder, B., et al.: Windows azure storage: A highly available cloud storage service with strong consistency. In: SOSP 2011 (2011)
7. DOE Extreme-Scale Technology Acceleration: Fastforward
8. Weil, S., Leung, A., Brandt, S.A., Maltzahn, C.: Rados: A fast, scalable, and reliable storage service for petabyte-scale storage clusters. In: PDSW 2007 (2007)
9. Weil, S., Brandt, S.A., Miller, E.L., Long, D.D.E., Maltzahn, C.: Ceph: A scalable, high-performance distributed file system. In: OSDI 2006 (2006)
10. Lua language
11. Runde, M.T., Stevens, W.G., Wortman, P.A., Chandy, J.A.: An active storage framework for object storage devices. In: MSST 2012 (2012)
12. Glusterfs clustered file system, `http://www.gluster.org`
13. Grawinkel, M., Suß, T., Best, G., Popov, I., Brinkmann, A.: Towards dynamic scripted pnfs layouts. In: PDSW 2012 (2012)
14. Santry, D.S., Feeley, M.J., Hutchinson, N.C., Veitch, A.C., Carton, R.W., Ofir, J.: Deciding when to forget in the elephant file system. In: SOSP 1999 (1999)
15. Grant, R.: Filesystem interface for the git version control system. Technical report, University of Pennsylvania (2009)

Towards Workload-Driven Adaptation of Data Organization in Heterogeneous Storage Systems

Nikolaus Jeremic[1], Helge Parzyjegla[1], Gero Mühl[1], and Jan Richling[2]

[1] Architecture of Application Systems Group, University of Rostock, Germany
{nikolaus.jeremic,helge.parzyjegla,gero.muehl}@uni-rostock.de
[2] Communication and Operating Systems Group, TU Berlin, Germany
richling@cs.tu-berlin.de

Abstract. Collecting, managing, and analyzing huge data sets (i.e., Big Data) in science and industry poses challenges to current data storage systems in terms of storage capacity, performance, and reliability. In particular, the I/O performance may be a key factor to speed up the data analysis. However, the performance of a storage system significantly depends on its configuration and the access pattern. Designing storage systems always implies making compromises between performance, fault tolerance and net capacity. The decision which compromise is made (e.g., which RAID level is used) has to be taken at deployment time because runtime reconfigurations are usually prohibitively expensive (due to coarse granularity) in current storage architectures.

In this paper, we propose a workload-driven approach to adaptive reconfiguration covering the functionality of the file system, volume manager and RAID. Our approach enables fine-grained reconfigurations of the data organization of files and file fragments to adapt the storage system to changing workloads, while considering the different characteristics of the storage devices (e.g., SSDs and HDDs) in a heterogeneous storage system. We first discuss how our approach decreases the costs of adaptations compared to existing approaches making a continuous and effective adaptation feasible, even for large volumes of data. Then, we present an evaluation based on a prototypical implementation confirming the benefits of our approach.

1 Introduction

The capability to manage, process, and analyze data sets of extreme size, diversity, and complexity is becoming a key requirement in modern business. It enables companies and organizations to mine such sets of Big Data for valuable information in order to faster gain enhanced insight into trends, customers, and markets as well as to better identify opportunities and assess the risks. In this context, storage systems are an essential prerequisite that links the collection of data with its subsequent analysis. First and foremost, a storage system has to provide enough capacity to accommodate Big Data volumes. But beyond that,

D. an Mey et al. (Eds.): Euro-Par 2013 Workshops, LNCS 8374, pp. 33–42, 2014.

the speed with which data can be accessed is particularly important [6] in order to accelerate the processing and analysis of data sets. With the advent of new storage technologies such as flash memory as built into Solid-State Drives (SSDs), more storage alternatives to conventional Hard Disk Drives (HDDs) become available that, on the one hand, promise a significant performance gain and speed up, but on the other hand, currently offer only limited capacities at much higher costs. To profit from both worlds, heterogeneous storage systems provide an elegant solution.

Heterogeneous storage systems often comprise several drive pools each featuring a different technology [2,4] and/or data organization, e.g., RAID scheme [11]. Please note that besides the storage technology, data organization also has a major impact on *performance* (with respect to bandwidth and latency of requests), *reliability* (with respect to drive failures), and *usable storage capacity* [5]. Each data item is, then, stored in the pool which best meets its performance, reliability, and capacity requirements. Moreover, if the access pattern changes, the data item can be migrated to a different pool that better suits the new pattern which renders the storage system adaptive. In general, this is leveraged to maximize the performance for those data items accessed most frequently[1].

However, the coarse granularity of adaptations provided by current storage systems severely limits the effectiveness of this approach. In fact, only logical volumes are often subject to migration although access statistics within the volume may vary widely. Thus, decisions are based on mean values and also affect those portions of the volume that actually do not profit from migration. Even if sub-volume data units are considered [4], as done by more advanced storage systems, these units still have the size of several megabytes. This alleviates the issue, but does not solve the problem. Similarly, adapting the size of the storage pools or changing their RAID policy is usually avoided [11] due to the coarse granularity of the required data reorganization and associated reorganization costs. For instance, removing a drive from one pool and adding it to another with a different RAID configuration, requires a complete data reorganization on the block layer for both pools. In particular for Big Data volumes, it is nearly impossible to accurately estimate whether this huge reorganization effort will pay off in reasonable time.

In this paper, we present a workload-driven approach for an automated fine-grained reconfiguration of storage systems. By adapting the storage configuration in tiny steps, we can capture access patterns much more accurately in large volumes while minimizing the migration and reorganization overhead at the same time. For this purpose, we apply RAID policies at sub-file level and track access patterns at this granularity in order to decide on reorganizations based on the evaluation of benefits and costs. We provide a case study and evaluation that proves the feasibility of the approach and demonstrates its advantages.

[1] Alternatively, caching is often used to speed up access times for frequently used data. Please note, that caching is an orthogonal concept that can be used in addition to data migration and RAID policy adaptation, respectively.

The remainder of this paper is structured as follows: Sect. 2 introduces the background on RAID systems. Based on that, we present our approach in Sect. 3. Sect. 4 describes our case study, followed by the experimental evaluation. Finally, the paper is concluded in Sect. 5.

2 RAID

RAID (Redundant Array of Independent Disks) [9,8] denotes a technique for combining a drive collection into a single logical drive to increase the performance, reliability and storage capacity. This is achieved through data *striping* (declustering), *mirroring* and/or adding *parity*. A *RAID policy* is defined by means of different attributes and their values: the *RAID level*, the number of used drives and configuration parameters specific to the RAID level (e.g., the stripe unit or chunk size, the number of data copies). The RAID level determines the data organization and which of the concepts above are used. Each RAID policy provides a different trade-off between performance, fault tolerance, and usable storage capacity. Thus, an improvement regarding to one of the characteristics often goes along with a degradation in at least one of the others.

A RAID policy can be specified and implemented on different levels within the storage (software) stack, which has major implications for the policy's scope and the reorganization overhead in case of a policy change. Most RAID systems are implemented on the block layer and, thus, allow to specify a policy on a per-volume basis. More advanced implementations additionally subdivide volumes in smaller units in the range of several megabytes and allow to set a RAID policy for a group of such units. Changing the RAID policy requires the reorganization of the complete volume or, in the case of sub-volume units, considerable parts of it causing substantial reorganization overhead. Since on the block level, it cannot be distinguished whether a block contains user data or is actually unused, the overhead is always proportional to the size of the reorganized storage space.

More recently, RAID logic has been integrated into file systems such as *Btrfs* or *ZFS*. Nevertheless, the RAID policy applies to whole volumes, and is eventually implemented on the basis of blocks. Reorganization support is still rudimentary or even missing although it may be implemented in a clever way considering only used blocks. However, when RAID and file system implementations are combined, there is no reason to not allow a more fine-grained specification of the RAID policy, e.g., on the basis of directories or even individual files as proposed by Appuswamy et al. [1]. This increases flexibility but does not always reduce the overhead of potential data reorganizations in case of policy changes because large files may have the size of or may even be bigger than small volumes.

3 Automated RAID Policy Adaptation

As motivated in Sect. 1, automated reconfiguration of the RAID policy is a promising mean to address changes in access pattern. However, reconfiguring large volumes containing assets of Big Data suffers from high costs due to the coarse-grained application of common RAID policies. Therefore, we propose to apply reconfigurations as fine-grained as possible based on the trade-off between cost and benefit that is derived from continuous monitoring of access pattern and requirements (specified by application or user).

The idea is to decompose files into small segments and specify the RAID policy for each segment that can later be individually changed and adapted. The data chunks of each segment are then distributed over available drives according to the segment's RAID policy. Disjoint drives are randomly selected when a new segment is created in order to spread larger requests over multiple drives and balance the load. The exact mapping is stored in metadata and is independent of the chunk's position within the segment. Depending on the modified attributes, this can avoid relocations of the chunks when the RAID policy is changed. Obviously, this approach needs a tight integration into the file system. In this paper, however, we neglect integration details and solely focus on an automated adaptation. In particular, this includes the general concepts to derive an adaptation policy that takes application requirements and reorganization costs into account.

3.1 RAID Reconfiguration Control

The control of RAID reconfigurations is based on the evaluation of system parameters and settings as well as on optimization objectives and priorities between them, thus, basically restricting possible reconfigurations. If, for instance, a particular level of fault tolerance needs to be ensured for certain files, a number of more efficient, but less reliable RAID policies may not be applicable. For the remaining policies, optimization objectives such as performance or storage capacity help weighting the gains of different alternatives. The selection of the RAID policy is based on a generic bonus-malus system which also triggers the execution of corresponding RAID reconfigurations.

To optimize performance, for instance, the data layout of a file segment is adapted to the most frequent access pattern. Thus, if the current layout is well suited for a particular request, a bonus is granted encouraging the current RAID policy, otherwise a malus is taken into account. Bonus and malus are set off against each other, whereby the bonus-malus ratio is maintained for each file segment as score. The score is increased when a malus is taken into account and decreased in the case of bonus. However, the score is reset to 0 when it has dropped below 0 in order to keep the heuristic reactive to pattern changes. If the score reaches a predefined upper bound, the RAID policy is changed and a corresponding reconfiguration is triggered. Hence, when defining the upper bound, a threshold depending on the reorganization overhead needs to be considered. To reduce the latency of the request that triggered the reconfiguration, the reconfiguration can take place after the request has been served.

If optimizing for storage capacity, space-efficient data layouts periodically get a bonus, while others receive a malus. In the meantime, however, the space-inefficient layouts may also score bonus points if data accesses are served performantly. As consequence, primarily cold data gets reorganized first, while performance-oriented RAID policies are kept for hot data as long as possible.

With respect to reliability, we assume that a minimum level of fault tolerance is defined for each data item. Therefore, reconfigurations due to optimization of performance or storage capacity consider only RAID policies meeting this level. If the defined reliability level is low enough, performance optimization may result in striping without redundancy, trading reliability for performance and capacity.

3.2 RAID Reconfiguration Costs

A data layout reorganization in the course of RAID reconfiguration causes additional read and write requests to the drives that dominate the reconfiguration overhead. Hence, we discuss the overhead in terms of such requests. The reconfiguration overhead depends on which changes of the RAID policy are performed. In all cases described below, the number of read requests can be reduced if the affected data is located in the page cache. Changing the RAID level corresponds to switching between striping (either with or without parity) or mirroring. In the event of switching from striping to mirroring, each chunk of a stripe has to be read and replicated multiple times in order to produce the desired number of copies. However, the original chunk can be reused saving one write. Switching from mirroring to striping requires to read the mirrored data and write it to several stripe units. Additionally, in the case of striping with parity, it is required to calculate and write the parities.

Changing the number of drives used in a RAID policy also has a major impact. In the case of mirroring, this translates to increasing or decreasing the number of copies. Adding copies requires reading a chunk once and writing it to each additional drive. Decreasing the number of copies, however, may not require accessing the data at all. In the case of striping, the change of stripe width necessitates to relocate at least a subset of chunks in each stripe of which each must be read and written. If parity is involved, all parities have also to be recalculated and rewritten. Moreover, assigning chunks to drives independently of their position within the stripe can avoid relocations in certain situations, e.g., when parity is added/removed and the stripe width is correspondingly adjusted.

4 Case Study: RAID Level Reconfiguration

This section describes an exemplary instance of the approach proposed in Sect. 3. The objective is to maintain high write throughput by adapting the RAID level based on the request size under the constraint that no data should be lost in the case of up to two arbitrary drives failing simultaneously. Therefore, we consider RAID 10 with triple mirroring and RAID 6 and fix the number of drives to the minimum of six. Furthermore, we also fix and use the same maximum chunk size for both RAID policies. Thus, in case of reconfiguration either a file segment in RAID 6 layout is split into two RAID 10 segments or two adjacent RAID 10 segments are merged into one RAID 6 segment. Both reconfiguration cases do not require a relocation of data chunks, reducing the reorganization overhead.

Table 1. RAID 6 and RAID 10 layout scores for HDDs and SSDs

Affected Chunks	RAID 6 HDDs	RAID 10 HDDs	RAID 6 SSDs	RAID 10 SSDs
1	56	29	30	10
2	55	53	28	20
3	56	72	24	38
4	54	94	21	39

4.1 Reconfiguration Policy

The write throughput depends on the number of affected chunks within a file segment which results from the request size. The reason is that write requests to a file segment translate to different number of subsequent chunk reads and writes depending on the number of affected chunks. The assessment of each RAID layout, with respect to the number of affected chunks and device type (HDD or SSD), is based on measured average throughput (the measurements are described in Sect. 4.2). The considered write overhead is determined by averaged write latency, which is translated into scores summarized in Table 1, where 1 point equals 0.1 ms for HDDs and 0.01 ms for SSDs. For example, according to the first line in Table 1, a write affecting one chunk takes 5.6 ms on HDDs for RAID 6, but only 2.9 ms for RAID 10, saving 2.7 ms when performed in the better suited RAID 10 layout. The considered bonus or malus equals the difference in write latency between the RAID 6 and RAID 10 layout with respect to the device type.

After completing a write request to a segment, its RAID level is switched in the case that its score exceeds a threshold. A reasonable minimum value for the threshold is given by the reconfiguration overhead, but it should be set higher in order to avoid oscillations between the two configurations. The considered reconfiguration overhead is based on measurements and corresponds to the average reconfiguration time (the corresponding measurements are described in Sect. 4.2). Switching from RAID 6 to RAID 10 requires 9.9 ms on HDDs and 0.54 ms on SSDs. The reconfiguration threshold is set to 100 for HDDs and to 55 for SSDs. Switching from RAID 10 to RAID 6 requires 6.5 ms on HDDs (which lies below the average access time of 8.5 ms [10] due to seek time optimizations performed by the HDDs when multiple requests are submitted in parallel) and 0.29 ms on SSDs. Thus, the threshold is set to 66 for HDDs and to 30 for SSDs.

4.2 Experimental Evaluation

A server-class machine (2x Intel Xeon E5-2680, 128 GiB RAM, LSISAS2308 controllers) equipped with Seagate ST91000640SS HDDs and Samsung 830 SSDs served as testbed. On the software side, Linux (kernel 3.7) was used and all measurements were obtained using *fio* 2.0.13 [3]. The workload consisted of synthetically generated file I/O traces. The RAID reconfiguration (explained in Sect. 4.1) was emulated by translating file I/O traces into resulting I/O requests

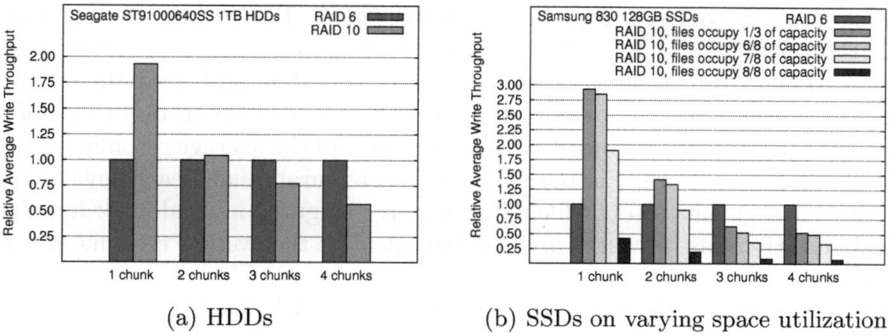

Fig. 1. Average write throughput for RAID 10 compared to RAID 6 considering different number of affected chunks (64 KiB per chunk)

to block devices before measurement. Then, these requests were submitted to drives using *fio* and employing direct, native Linux asynchronous I/O. Furthermore, the *noop* I/O scheduler was used and *NCQ* was enabled for all drives. To minimize the impact of caching, the on-drive caching was disabled on HDDs, however, not on SSDs because read caching cannot be disabled using *hdparm* or *sdparm*. In all experiments, the maximum chunk size was 64 KiB. Each experiment was repeated three times and the mean value was taken as result. In the case of SSDs, the *TRIM command* was applied between runs to discard all data.

The assessment of the considered RAID configurations described in Sect. 4.1 is based on measurements of the average write throughput on varying number of affected chunks, which were performed separately for HDDs and SSDs to consider the different device type characteristics. Write requests were carried out on a set of files on randomly chosen file segments with request sizes based on the intended number of affected chunks: 64 KiB for 1 chunk, 128 KiB for 2 chunks etc. Moreover, to consider the influence of spare capacity on the write performance of SSDs [7], file sets of different sizes were used (Fig. 1(b)). For each RAID layout and device type, the average throughput was measured for writing an amount of data corresponding to 60 GiB.

The measurements for HDDs depicted in Fig. 1(a) show that RAID 10 is more suitable for writes affecting up to 2 chunks, while RAID 6 should be preferred when 3 or 4 chunks are affected due to the higher throughput. The results for SSDs in Fig. 1(b) indicate the same trend, while the differences between RAID 10 and RAID 6 are more pronounced for writes affecting up to 2 chunks. However, the measurements also show that RAID 10 throughput is highly sensitive to the amount of occupied capacity and, hence, of available spare capacity. SSDs perform out-of-place updates, thus, if our data set occupies as much capacity that further write requests will trigger the garbage collection, the write performance drops significantly (cf. [7]). This effect is emphasized in cases where the file set occupies the whole drive capacity, which is represented by the black bars in Fig. 1(b). However, RAID 6 is less sensitive to this effect since its data layout occupies only half of the storage capacity (in our setup) compared to RAID 10.

Therefore, the throughput remains roughly the same. Please note, that we cope with the sensitivity of SSDs to the amount of spare capacity in the remaining experiments by choosing the amount of written data such that the storage capacity of each SSD is not completely utilized. The reconfiguration thresholds mentioned in Sect. 4.1 are based on measurements of the average reconfiguration time on HDDs and SSDs. For both types of reconfiguration and each device type $320,000$ file segments (80 GB file data) were reconfigured in random order. The overall duration was measured and used to calculate the average reconfiguration time.

The proposed heuristic for adaptation of the RAID level to the write request size was compared to an offline algorithm as well as to static RAID 6 and RAID 10 setups. An offline algorithm determines which initial RAID level and reconfigurations lead to the highest write throughput with respect to the empirical cost model described in Sect. 4.1 based on the a priori knowledge of all write requests to each file segment. For the sake of comparing the RAID level adaptation to static setups, the average write throughput was measured based on five synthetically generated workloads (denoted as A, B_1, B_2, C_1, and C_2) with different characteristics that are described in the following. Each workload represents overwriting data in randomly chosen file segments (in a set of files comprising 20 GB data) with different request sizes, which leads to different number of affected chunks. The overall amount of data written to a set of files equals 200 GB for each workload. In workload A, the size of each write request is chosen at random, hence, each number of affected chunks is almost equally likely. Unlike this, in the remaining workloads B_1, B_2, C_1, and C_2, a particular file segment receives a number of recurring writes that last for a certain period, whereby this period is four times longer for B_2 and C_2 than for B_1 and C_1, respectively. Moreover, the request size distribution of B_1 and B_2 is biased to larger requests affecting 3 and 4 chunks. In contrast to this, C_1 and C_2 are dominated by smaller requests, i.e., 1 chunk and 2 chunks.

The results for HDDs depicted in Fig. 2(a) indicate that the RAID level adaptation heuristic leads to a notable performance gain, if a certain write pattern persists for a longer amount of time, which applies to the workload B_2 and C_2. For both workloads, the average write throughput reaches over 95% of throughput achieved by the offline algorithm, whose optimization decisions are based on the a priori knowledge of all performed write requests. However, if the write pattern changes more frequently (as in workload B_1 and C_1), the heuristic can trigger reconfigurations that will not pay off, thus, even leading to lower performance than a static configuration. This applies for workload C_1, where the heuristic reaches a notably lower throughput than RAID 10. However, this advantage seems less when the write pattern changes, e.g., making the RAID 6 setup the better choice. Beside that, the results for workload A indicate a minimal deviation from the empirical cost model, due to approx. 1% higher write throughput in the case of RAID 6 compared to the offline algorithm.

The results for SSDs depicted in Fig. 2(b) show that the heuristic outperforms both static setups for workloads dominated by small requests (C_1 and C_2).

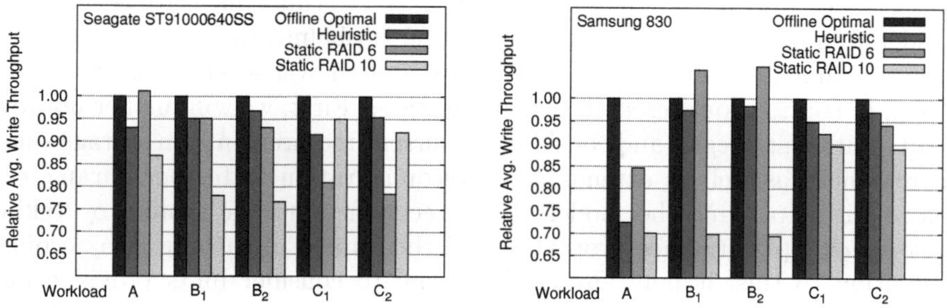

(a) HDDs (b) SSDs

Fig. 2. Relative average write throughput for HDDs and SSDs compared to offline model-optimal RAID level adaptation

However, as C_1 and C_2 are dominated by small requests, RAID 10 is expected to be the better choice according to the write overhead results shown in Fig. 1(b), where RAID 10 clearly outperforms RAID 6, which seems to clash with the results for C_1 and C_2 (where RAID 6 slightly outperforms RAID 10). This stems from the recurring writes to a file segment that increase the temporal locality of reference, which is exploited by the on-drive caching. Please note, that RAID 6 also incurs subsequent chunk reads in the case that writing a file segment affects up to 3 chunks, which does not apply to RAID 10. Thus, when all chunk reads are served from cache the difference between RAID 6 and RAID 10 is evened out if a write affects 1 or 2 chunks. Furthermore, read caching performed by SSDs also widens the performance gap between RAID 6 and RAID 10 for workloads B_1 and B_2, and additionally introduces a remarkable deviation from the empirical cost model (RAID 6 performs better than the offline algorithm). However, for workload A the impact of caching is less pronounced due to lower temporal locality.

5 Conclusion

The performance of secondary storage systems is crucial, in particular, when processing Big Data. It may be the decisive factor to accelerate and speed up the data analysis allowing it to complete within a given time frame. In this paper, we tackled the challenge of adapting the data organization in heterogeneous storage systems to access patterns and storage requirements (e.g., performance, reliability, and capacity). We have proposed a scheme for a workload-driven RAID policy adaptation that was employed in order to increase the performance. To avoid prohibitive reorganization costs due to moving potentially large amount of data, our approach is based on RAID policies that are applied at sub-file level. This permits reacting to fine-grained changes of the workload. We evaluated this approach using a case study and an initial implementation, showing both, its applicability and its advantages. However, our results also make clear that the characteristics of different device types and caching have to be properly considered in order to avoid that optimization turns into the opposite.

As very large data sets have often to be distributed over several storage servers, we plan to continue our research in two directions: First, we will further improve the adaptation strategies and consider the current requirements on storage space and reliability as well as extending the reconfiguration to further parameters. This requires to refine the model of the secondary storage system by taking device-specific performance properties and the impact of caching into account. In addition to this, it may also be beneficial to consider hints provided and requirements posed by applications. Second, we will extend our strategies to scenarios, where data sets are distributed over multiple storage servers. In this case, global information on access patterns, demands, and system state need to be gathered and exploited to improve the overall data organization.

References

1. Appuswamy, R., van Moolenbroek, D.C., Tanenbaum, A.S.: Block-level RAID is dead. In: Proceedings of the 2nd USENIX Conference on Hot Topics in Storage and File Systems, HotStorage 2010, pp. 1–5. USENIX Association, Berkeley (2010)
2. Appuswamy, R., van Moolenbroek, D.C., Tanenbaum, A.S.: Integrating flash-based SSDs into the storage stack. In: Proceedings of the IEEE 28th Symposium on Mass Storage Systems and Technologies (MSST 2012), pp. 1–12. IEEE (2012)
3. Axboe, J.: Flexible I/O tester (2013), http://freecode.com/projects/fio
4. Guerra, J., Pucha, H., Glider, J., Belluomini, W., Rangaswami, R.: Cost effective storage using extent based dynamic tiering. In: Proceedings of the 9th USENIX Conference on File and Storage Technologies, FAST 2011, pp. 1–14. USENIX Association, Berkeley (2011)
5. Jacob, B.L., Ng, S.W., Wang, D.T.: Memory Systems: Cache, DRAM, Disk. Morgan Kaufmann (2008)
6. Jacobs, A.: The pathologies of big data. Commun. ACM 52(8), 36–44 (2009), http://doi.acm.org/10.1145/1536616.1536632
7. Jeremic, N., Mühl, G., Busse, A., Richling, J.: The pitfalls of deploying solid-state drive RAIDs. In: Proceedings of the 4th Annual International Conference on Systems and Storage (SYSTOR 2011), pp. 14:1–14:13. ACM (June 2011), http://doi.acm.org/10.1145/1987816.1987835
8. Katz, R., Gibson, G., Patterson, D.A.: Disk system architectures for high performance computing. Proceedings of the IEEE 77(12), 1842–1858 (1989)
9. Patterson, D.A., Gibson, G., Katz, R.H.: A case for redundant arrays of inexpensive disks (RAID). SIGMOD Rec. 17, 109–116 (1988)
10. Seagate Technology: Product manual Constellation. 2 SAS. Tech. rep., Seagate Technology (April 2012), http://www.seagate.com/files/www-content/support-content/documentation/product-manuals/en-us/Enterprise/Constellation_2_5in/100620418h.pdf
11. Wilkes, J., Golding, R., Staelin, C., Sullivan, T.: The HP AutoRAID hierarchical storage system. ACM Trans. Comput. Syst. 14(1), 108–136 (1996), http://doi.acm.org/10.1145/225535.225539

MapReduce in GPI-Space

Tiberiu Rotaru, Mirko Rahn, and Franz-Josef Pfreundt

Fraunhofer Institute for Industrial Mathematics,
Fraunhofer-Platz 1, 67663 Kaiserslautern, Germany
{tiberiu.rotaru,mirko.rahn,franz-josef.pfreundt}@itwm.fraunhofer.de

Abstract. The computing power of modern high performance systems cannot be fully exploited using traditional parallel programming models. On the other hand, the growing demand for processing big data volumes requires a better control of the workflows, an efficient storage management, as well as a fault-tolerant runtime system. Trying to offer our proper solution to these problems, we designed and developed GPI-Space, a complex but flexible software development and execution platform, in which the data coordination of an application is decoupled from the programming of the algorithms. This allows the domain user to focus on the implementation of its problem only, while the fault tolerant runtime framework automatically runs the application in parallel in complex environments. We discuss the advantages and the disadvantages of our approach by comparison with the most popular MapReduce implementation, Hadoop. The tests performed on a multicore cluster with the wordcount use case showed that GPI-Space is almost three times faster than Hadoop when strictly the execution times are considered, and more than six times faster when the data loading time is also considered.

1 Introduction

Nowadays, clusters with thousands of cores are present in many companies and institutions. At the same time, the price of the data storage has significantly decreased and the companies have now the possibility to stock or to archive big amounts of data related to their businesses, with affordable costs. In this way, they can occasionally or regularly process the backuped data and extract from it valuable information that may contribute to improve their services or to increase their profits. A fundamental question that arises in this context is how to efficiently exploit the full computing power of large multicore clusters when dealing with big amounts of data and which programming model to use for achieving this goal? The MapReduce model, although not perfect, is an answer to this question. Although the MapReduce paradigm existed for a long time in Computer Science, in one form or another, it was first evoked in the form known today by two researchers working at Google, in a paper published in 2004 [3]. Since then, a lot of research studies have been published and a number of different of MapReduce frameworks, written in different languages, have been developed [5].

D. an Mey et al. (Eds.): Euro-Par 2013 Workshops, LNCS 8374, pp. 43–52, 2014.

In this paper we present GPI-Space, a complete software solution for dealing with data intensive computations on multicore clusters. On top of this infrastructure we developed a Petri net workflow for MapReduce computations, giving thus the users that are acquainted with this model the possibility to easily integrate their applications. GPI-Space offers superior performance compared to other tools by using the in-memory storage and sophisticated workflow parallelization and scheduling strategies. While most of the MapReduce implementations are targeted at commodity hardware, GPI-Space relies on the Global Address Space Programming Interface (GPI) middleware [1], which is able to take advantage of the modern network interconnects that enable the Remote Directory Memory Access (RDMA).

1.1 The MapReduce Model

MapReduce represents currently the most successful model that has been applied and has proved its efficiency at large scale [9]. This model tries to ease the task of building large scale data intensive applications, by hiding the details of parallelism, allowing the users to focus on the data processing strategies. The advantages and the limitations of the model are discussed in [7].

The MapReduce programming model is founded on concepts that are rather proper to the functional programming [6]. Generally, in order to build a MapReduce application, the user is required to provide only specific implementation for a reduced number of interface methods, with the signature known in advance. In the first place, the user is required to write the map and the reduce methods. Typically, map takes as input parameter a key-value pair and produces a list of intermediate pairs, while the reduce method takes as input parameters a key and a list of values associated with this key and returns a list of output values:

$$\text{map } (in\_key, in\_value) \longrightarrow \text{list } (out\_key, intermediate\_value)$$
$$\text{reduce } (out\_key, \text{list}(intermediate\_value)) \longrightarrow \text{list } (out\_value)$$

Additionally, the user may provide an implementation for a partitioning method, a compare method and a combine method [9].

Among all the MapReduce implementations, the most important are Google MapReduce [3] and Hadoop [14]. Hadoop is currently an important component of the infrastructure of many web companies, such as Yahoo [12], Facebook [2] and Twitter [8]. Other companies, like eBay, Amazon, IBM, Microsoft, Oracle use or offer services that are based on Hadoop.

2 Fraunhofer GPI-Space

The available computing power of distributed high performance systems, often with several thousands of cores, can hardly be mastered with the conventional programming models. On the other hand, the growing demand for processing huge amounts of data requires a better control of the workflows being executed, an efficient storage management and a fault-tolerant execution of the workflows. Handling these aspects correctly may exceed the capabilities of a normal user, requiring expert knowledge. In order to properly handle this situation and to alleviate the domain specific programmer's mission, a natural idea would be to ensure a separation of the coordination level from the execution level of parallel applications. This requires a more sophisticated programming model and an execution framework that offers support for automatic parallelization and scheduling, a fault-tolerance mechanism and services for the job execution control, monitoring, memory management, etc. Trying to put this concept in practice, we designed and implemented a programming model and an execution framework that clearly realizes this separation. GPI-Space is a complex but flexible software platform, combining several important software components that can also be used either as standalone applications or in combination with other software tools or packages. Each of this components were designed and implemented taking into account the experience accumulated with other important high performance computing projects [11,10]. GPI-Space consists of: a distributed runtime system, a workflow engine and a storage layer.

2.1 The Distributed Run-Time System

The Distributed Run-Time System (DRTS) represents the execution layer of GPI-Space. It is dynamic, fault-tolerant and can dynamically build arbitrary topologies. It relies on a master-slave architecture, where an agent may have multiple masters, event subscribers and workers. On top of such an architecture stays the orchestrator, which is responsible with handling the user requests and scheduling them on the available agents. The agents may have access to the partitioned global address space and thus trigger large data transfers from or to the virtual memory. The agents may dispose of a workflow engine that interprets sub-workflows, creates intermediary tasks and assembles the results. A graphical representation of a DRTS, deployed as a tree topology, is as in the figure 1. In fact, the agents can form logical communication topologies with a much more complex graph structure, allowing thus a straightforward implementation of the parallel algorithms that assume a certain structure of the logical communication graph. The agents implement a Staged Event Driven Architecture [13] and are controlled by finite state machines. The stages are basically thread pools with a shared queue of events and they can asynchronously exchange messages, making thus the agent more flexible and more responsive. The whole distributed run-time system is fault-tolerant and an agent can join and leave the system at any time, without stopping the execution of the submitted workflow. The agent was designed with the bridge pattern in mind, trying to decouple as much as possible the abstract part from the implementation part [4]. An agent is composed of several software components like: a job manager, a scheduler, a worker manager and a backup service. The jobs may be submitted together with a list of requirements and the workers may have different capabilities. Each agent disposes of a scheduler that tries to fairly schedule the jobs on workers whose capabilities are best matching the requirements.

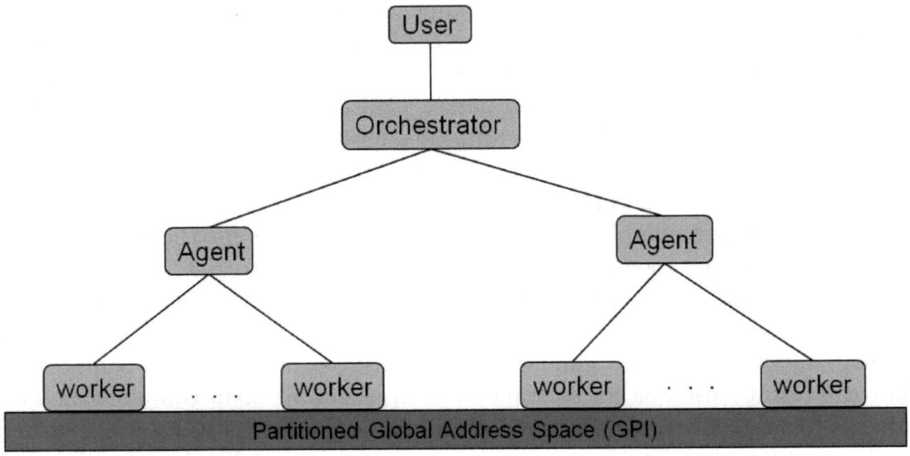

Fig. 1. Distributed run-time system deployed as a tree over a partitioned global address space

2.2 The Workflow Engine

The coordination level consists of a workflow engine, a workflow description language and a set of tools that are intended to help the user to build workflows. The workflows are basically high-level Petri nets, described in a proprietary XML-based language that we defined. We developed also a workflow engine that is capable to concurrently interpret and execute these workflows. The user may either write the workflow directly into the XML-based language or may use an editor (currently under development, but having basic functionality implemented). Apart of the workflow engine, a number of other tools were developed, with the goal to assist the user in the course of the development of a workflow:

- a Petri net compiler which translates the XML description of the workflow into some intermediary format that the workflow engine is capable to understand,
- a verification tool that is able to verify the basic properties of the net,
- a basic visualization tool, based on the Graphviz software package, and
- a graphical editor.

The compiler generates the internal representation of the runtime environment from the XML representation of the Petri net. It checks the semantic validity of the input net, being also able to check other properties like termination, absence of deadlocks, reachability, etc. and to eventually optimize the net. Typically, a user who wants to write an application for GPI-Space should focus on describing the workflow and on how to logically organize the storage layer. In the case of GPI-Space, the Petri nets have a double role: they are used not only for controlling the execution of the generated tasks, but also for controlling the access of the tasks to the partitioned global address space, acting as a transactional mechanism and guaranteeing thus the data integrity. From a global point of view, the execution of a workflow in GPI-Space consists in the following steps:

- The orchestrator receives a job having attached the internal representation of a workflow and assigns it to one of the available agents.
- The agent hands over the attached description of a job received from a master to the workflow engine and this one extracts all the executable activities, some of them being executed locally and the others being sent to available workers.
- When the job completes, the assigned worker or agent sends the result to the corresponding master. This one hands the result over to its workflow engine, which inserts the corresponding output tokens and looks for new active transitions. If new activities were generated, they are sent to the available workers. The process continues until no transition can be fired anymore.
- When no other activities can be generated, the network is considered to be completely processed and the result of the job is sent back to the submitter.

2.3 The Storage Layer

The storage layer within GPI-Space is represented by GPI [1]. This is a middleware that allows for executing parallel applications complying with a Partitioned Global Address Space (PGAS) programming model, developed at our institute [10]. Typically, the memory of the individual nodes in a cluster is aggregated and seen as a single address space, where large objects, often exceeding the capacity of a single cluster node, can be stored. GPI is targeted at RDMA-enabled interconnects such as Infiniband or CRAY Gemini. The main idea here is that the full performance of the RDMA-enabled networks can be delivered to the application directly, without interrupting the CPUs. GPI constitutes an alternative to the traditional message-passing model for the development of parallel applications that are intended to run on modern multicore systems. GPI focuses on one-sided communication and the development of asynchronous algorithms, leveraging the capabilities of modern interconnects to overlap communication with computation.

At the node level, the Manycore Threading Package (MCTP), developed in our department with the goal to better take advantage of new multicore architectures, is used. Within GPI-Space, different applications can be combined into a workflow and executed using the virtual memory as a persistent layer that facilitates the interaction with each-other.

3 MapReduce in GPI-Space

As seen above, GPI-Space is a complex software development and execution platform that allows for writing and executing workflows that rely upon a Petri net semantics. However, writing such relatively complex workflows might be for many users beyond the scope of domain. Therefore, we went one step forward in this direction and we developed a workflow for MapReduce computations in GPI-Space. In this way, the mission of the users that are acquainted to this model is greatly simplified and consists only in overloading a couple of methods.

There are certain similarities between Hadoop and GPI-Space:

- both are focusing on data intensive applications, being able to process large amounts of data,
- both are essentially using a master/slave architecture,
- both of them have their own execution framework,
- both of them use a proprietary storage layer,
- both are addressing important aspects like fault-tolerance, load balancing and data integrity.

However, there are also notable differences like:

- GPI-Space stores the intermediary results into the global space resulted from the aggregation of RAM parts of the cluster nodes and eventually on the local disks, while Hadoop uses for this purpose its own distributed file system.
- In GPI-Space one can write much more complex workflows and the user has the freedom to chose, define and combine his own methods, instead of being restricted to a reduced set of primitives that are to be used for modeling the problem.
- In GPI-Space, the agents can form logical communication topologies with a structure of type graph, allowing thus a straightforward implementation of the algorithms that assume a certain structure of the logical communication graph.

Two important aspects must be taken into consideration when implementing the MapReduce pattern on top of GPI-Space: the organization of the virtual memory and the Petri net scheme that controls the generation and the execution of the tasks and their accesses to the virtual memory. As a graphical or XML description of the workflow is not possible here due to space limitations, we try to sketch out hereafter the main idea behind it. Initially, a configurable number of memory slots is allocated for each operation type (read, map, partition, reduce). The input data is split into chunks of equal sizes, which are then read in binary format, in parallel, and stored into the available read slots. As soon as a map slot becomes free, a nonempty read slot is chosen, its content is parsed and the map function is applied to the found items. The output pairs with the keys in the same partition are grouped together and all the groups are then stored into a map slot. Afterwards, the read slot is freed and can be reused for loading a new data chunk. As soon as a partition slot becomes free, a map slot that contains a contribution to that partition is chosen and the corresponding group of pairs is first sorted and then merged and reduced in one pass with the content of the partition slot. When a partition slot becomes full, its content is merged and reduced in one pass with the content of a free reduce slot, before allowing any other merge and reduce with the corresponding slice of a map slot. If a reduce slot becomes full, its content is reduced on the disk with the corresponding file (typically, one per partition). An invariant of the application is that the partition slots and the reduce slots always contain pairs whose keys are sorted according to a comparison criterion provided by the user. The access to the virtual memory is controlled by the Petri net, which guarantees the mutual exclusion and the data integrity. Typically, to each slot it corresponds a token that may be consumed or released by the transitions corresponding to the MapReduce operations.

One problem that may arise here due to the fact that the data is read in binary format is that some words may be split into pieces that are stored into different data chunks. The Petri net scheme takes care of this aspect, too, and recovers the original words.

We considered as a use case the wordcount example. This is a typical example available with many MapReduce implementations, consisting in determining for each word appearing into a file or a collection of files the number of its occurrences. We performed tests with this use case on both GPI-Space and Hadoop frameworks. For GPI-Space we developed our own workflow, while with Hadoop we used the wordcount example provided in Hadoop-1.1.2, from the Apache incubator. As a hardware setup, we used a set of 12 cluster nodes, each node having 12 Intel Xeon X5660 cores (2.8 Ghz) and disposing of 48 GB RAM. Hadoop was configured to use one DataNode per node, disposing of 800 gigabytes local disk space on each node and using a replication factor of 3. GPI-Space was configured to use a half of the total aggregated RAM for building the partitioned global address space, each worker having reserved one gigabyte shared memory. With Hadoop, we used a block size of 64 megabytes. The figure 2 is a snapshot of the execution monitor of GPI-Space where a MapReduce workflow with the input data size of one terabyte is executed. In the left hand side, the cores and their capabilities are shown. The Gantt diagram illustrates the tasks that are executed and their status. The grey color is used for the created tasks, yellow for the started tasks, green for the finished tasks, red for the failed tasks and magenta for the canceled tasks. The figure shows a good CPU utilization and a fair distribution of the tasks over the cores. The figure 3 illustrates the execution time of the wordcount example with GPI-Space compared to the execution time with Hadoop. Wordcount performs better on GPI-Space than on Hadoop, in terms of execution times. The gap between the two execution times increases with the size of the input data. For 1031 gigabytes (which is approximately one terabyte) of data, the execution time on Hadoop is 9097 seconds while on GPI-Space is 3263 seconds. However, we should note that the data loading into GPI-Space is done at runtime, in parallel with the other MapReduce operations. Moreover, GPI-Space uses RDMA transfers and thus most of the communication overlaps the computation. GPI-Space does not require that all the input data be loaded into the virtual memory before starting the workflow. In the case of Hadoop, data loading and computing are two distinct phases: first the data is loaded into the Hadoop distributed file system (HDFS) and only afterwards the computations are started. The figure 4 shows in comparison the total time for processing input data files of different sizes, including the data loading, on both execution

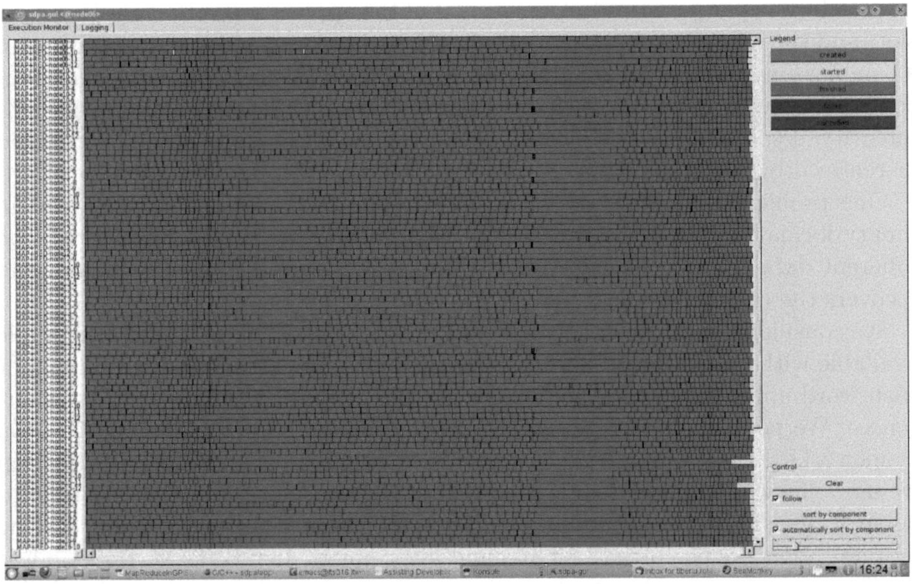

Fig. 2. The task execution monitor of GPI-Space showing the execution of a wordcount job with 1 TB input data

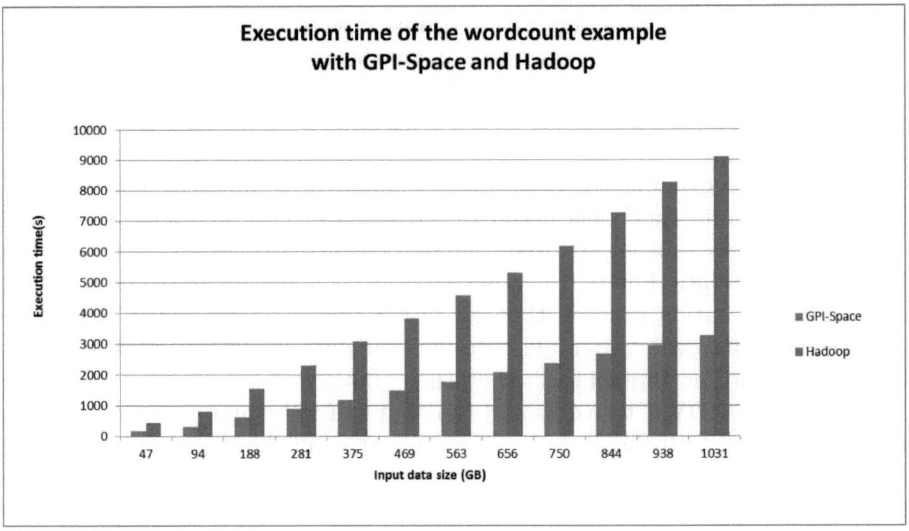

Fig. 3. Execution time of wordcount on GPI-Space and Hadoop

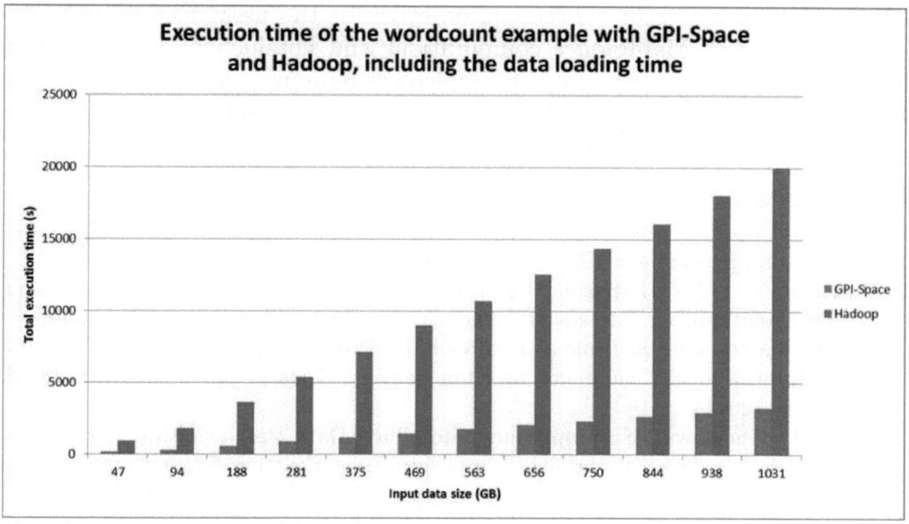

Fig. 4. Total processing time, including data loading, on GPI-Space and Hadoop

frameworks. In this case, processing one terabyte of data with GPI-Space takes 3263 seconds, while with Hadoop, if we count also the data loading time, it takes 20011 seconds. For the users who just want to occasionally use a MapReduce implementation for performing fast analytic operations and not willing to keep or migrate their data on HDFS for different reasons, like security for example, GPI-Space may represent a better option.

4 Conclusions and Future Work

In this paper we presented GPI-Space, a software development and execution platform for multicore clusters and we reported experiments with the construction of a MapReduce workflow on top of this architecture. GPI-Space is fault-tolerant and does automatic parallelization and scheduling, allowing the users to focus on the description of the workflow, primarily. Given the popularity of Hadoop, we considered appropriate to relate to this tool first. Compared to this, GPI-Space is more flexible, offering tools that facilitate the development of more complex workflows than MapReduce. In contrast to Hadoop, which stores the intermediary results on a distributed file system, GPI-Space stores most of the intermediary results into the partitioned global address space resulted from the aggregation of RAM slices of cluster nodes and is able to take advantage of fast RDMA data transfers. The example that we systematically tested, word-count, showed that GPI-Space is faster than Hadoop, when run over the same collection of cluster multicore nodes and using the same sample input data. Our approach has also the advantage that data loading into the virtual memory is carried out in parallel with the computations. Hadoop requires the data to be already on its distributed file system before the computations are started.

GPI-Space may represent a better alternative for the users who want to occasionally run fast MapReduce computations and not having the input data stored on HDFS. Our next goal is to implement more use cases for MapReduce in GPI-Space and to deploy and test the framework at larger scales.

References

1. `http://www.gpi-site.com/gpi2/` (accessed October 2013)
2. Borthakur, D., Gray, J., Sarma, J.S., Muthukkaruppan, K., Spiegelberg, N., Kuang, H., Ranganathan, K., Molkov, D., Menon, A., Rash, S., Schmidt, R., Aiyer, A.: Apache hadoop goes realtime at Facebook. In: Proceedings of the 2011 ACM SIGMOD International Conference on Management of Data, pp. 1071–1080. ACM, New York (2011)
3. Dean, J., Ghemawat, S.: Mapreduce: Simplified Data Processing on Large Clusters. In: Proceedings of the 6th Symposium on Opearting Systems Design and Implementation (OSDI 2004), San Francisco, CA, USA, pp. 137–150 (2004)
4. Gamma, E., Helm, R., Johnson, R., Vlissides, J.: Design Patterns – Elements of Reusable Object-Oriented Software, 1st edn. Addison-Wesley Longman, Amsterdam (1995), 37. Reprint (2009)
5. Jin, H., Ibrahim, S., Qi, L., Cao, H., Wu, S., Shi, X.: The MapReduce Programming Model and Implementations. In: Buyya, R., Broberg, J., Goscinski, A. (eds.) Cloud Computing: Principles and Paradigms, pp. 373–390. John Wiley & Sons, Inc. (2011)
6. Lämmel, R.: Google's MapReduce programming model - Revisited. Sci. Comput. Program. 70(1), 1–30 (2008)
7. Lee, K.H., Lee, Y.J., Choi, H., Chung, Y.D., Moon, B.: Parallel data processing with MapReduce: a survey. SIGMOD Rec. 40(4), 11–20 (2012)
8. Lin, J., Ryaboy, D.: Scaling big data mining infrastructure: the twitter experience. SIGKDD Explor. Newsl. 14(2), 6–19 (2012)
9. Linn, J., Dyer, C.: Data-Intensive Text Processing With MapReduce. Synthesis Lectures on Human Language Technologies Series. Morgan & Claypool Publishers (2010)
10. Machado, R., Lojewski, C., Abreu, S., Pfreundt, F.J.: Unbalanced tree search on a manycore system using the GPI programming model. Computer Science - Research and Development 26(3-4), 229–236 (2011)
11. Rotaru, T., Dalheimer, M., Pfreundt, F.J.: Service-oriented middleware for financial monte carlo simulations on the cell broadband engine. Concurrency and Computation: Practice and Experience 22(5), 643–657 (2010)
12. Shvachko, K., Kuang, H., Radia, S., Chansler, R.: The Hadoop Distributed File System. In: Proceedings of the 2010 IEEE 26th Symposium on Mass Storage Systems and Technologies, MSST 2010, pp. 1–10. IEEE Computer Society, Washington, DC (2010)
13. Welsh, M., Culler, D., Brewer, E.: SEDA: an architecture for well-conditioned, scalable internet services. SIGOPS Oper. Syst. Rev. 35(5), 230–243 (2001)
14. White, T.: Hadoop - The Definitive Guide: Storage and Analysis at Internet Scale, 3rd edn. O'Reilly Media (2012)

Workshop on Dependability and Interoperability in Heterogeneous Clouds (DIHC 2013)

Christine Morin, Roberto G. Cascella, Thilo Kielmann, and Paolo Mori

Program Chairs

The cloud computing market is in rapid expansion due to the opportunities to dynamically allocate a large amount of resources when needed and to pay only for their effective usage. However, many challenges, in terms of interoperability, performance guarantee, and dependability, still need to be addressed to make cloud computing the right solution for companies, research organizations, and universities. The DIHC workshop brought together researchers from academia and industry interested in the design, implementation, and evaluation of services and mechanisms for dependable cloud computing in a multi-cloud environment. This half-day workshop consisted of two sessions; the first one with the accepted submissions, the second consisting of two invited keynote papers.

The paper *Towards Data Interoperability of Cloud Infrastructures using Cloud Storage Services* presents an approach to retrieve and share data of user applications among distinct cloud providers exploiting cloud storage services. The paper includes a simple example where an application for mobile devices exploit cloud services to store and to perform operations on some images, along with some performance tests.

The paper *Multi-Objective Genetic Algorithm for Multi-Cloud Brokering* proposes a cloud broker that selects a set of cloud resources exploiting muti-objective genetic algorithms. In particular, the authors propose to exploit an SLA template and broker policy to request resource, and the NSGA II genetic algorithm to select the set of resources that fit the request.

The paper *Cloud Interoperability via Message Bus and Monitoring Integration* proposes a framework for generic monitoring of cloud services and exchanging this data among multiple cloud providers. The framework adopts a decentralized architecture that requires the deployment of a manager for each cloud and the communication between them are based on a proposed communication bus.

The paper *Reducing VM Startup Time and Storage Costs by VM Image Content Consolidation* presents a detailed study of VM startup time in clouds. After identifying VM image size as the main bottleneck, it proposes a mechanism to minimize the image size by installing the software required to execute the user tasks only.

In addition to these submitted peer reviewed papers, the proceedings includes two invited papers from the keynote speakers. The paper *Clouds-of-Clouds for Dependability and Security: Geo-Replication meets the Cloud* authored by Miguel Correia extracts lessons from some years of research on the notion of using several

D. an Mey et al. (Eds.): Euro-Par 2013 Workshops, LNCS 8374, pp. 53–54, 2014.

clouds instead of a single one with the objective of achieving high dependability and security. It shows with three cases that it is possible for services to continue to operate correctly using a clouds-of-clouds approach. The paper *Towards Standardised SLAs* authored by John M. Kennedy provides an overview of the Service Level Agreement activity in research projects and standardisation.

Multi-objective Genetic Algorithm for Multi-cloud Brokering

Alba Amato, Beniamino Di Martino, and Salvatore Venticinque

Department of Industrial and Information Engineering, Second University of Naples
{alba.amato,beniamino.dimartino,salvatore.venticinque}@unina2.it

Abstract. Cloud computing is a model for enabling ubiquitous, convenient, on-demand network access to a shared pool of configurable computing resources offered by commercial providers according to specific service level agreements. Research effort has been spent to address the lack of Cloud interoperability that is a barrier to cloud-computing adoption because of the vendor lock-in problem. In fact the ability to easily move workloads and data from one cloud provider to another or between private and public clouds can improve performance, availability and reduce costs. In this paper we explore the potential use of multiobjective genetic algorithms in the field of a brokering service, whose aim is to acquire resources from multiple providers on the basis of SLA evaluation rules finding the most suitable composition of Cloud offers that satisfy users' requirements.

1 Introduction

Cloud computing, as defined by the National Institute of Standards and Technology (NIST) [10], is a model for enabling ubiquitous, convenient, on-demand network access to a shared pool of configurable computing resources (e.g., networks, servers, storage, applications, and services) that can be rapidly provisioned and released with minimal management effort or service provider interaction. However users see the lack of cloud interoperability as a barrier to cloud-computing adoption because organizations fear vendor lock-in. In fact the ability to easily move workloads and data from one cloud provider to another or between private and public clouds is often hampered by several factors. Sometimes users are not able to find the most suitable configuration of resources for their applications and to compare it with the several offers of different providers. In fact service options are often not comparable owing to their heterogeneity in terms of resources, technology and service levels. In order to support users in service negotiation we have designed and developed Cloud Agency, a Multi-Agent System (MAS) that have the main task of selecting dynamically a set of Cloud resources, from different vendors, that best fits users requirements. Cloud agency service is compliant with the NIST definition of cloud broker [11], that is an entity that manages the use, performance and delivery of cloud services, and negotiates relationships between Cloud Providers and Cloud Consumers. In previous research [2] [3] we addressed the brokering problem choosing the best offer from a single provider

D. an Mey et al. (Eds.): Euro-Par 2013 Workshops, LNCS 8374, pp. 55–64, 2014.

performing experiments using a single Service Level Agreement (SLA) of a single provider, and the constraints defined on a single service. In this paper we aim at investigating the brokering problem applied to the composition of services from different providers that consists of brokering n services, in a set of m proposals from different providers, which can be composed according to a specific workflow. In this case complexity grows exponentially with n and it will be more difficult to treat because it is necessary to define global criteria among different SLAs and to consider multiple solutions of composition. Here we explore the potential use of multiobjective genetic algorithms in the broker module, whose aim is to acquire resources from providers on the basis of SLA evaluation rules finding the most suitable Cloud provider that satisfy users' requirements. The paper is organized as follows: in Section 2 some relevant works are presented, Section 3 describes the application context and a solution for the brokering problem. Section 4 briefly describes the proposed algorithm; conclusions are drawn in Section 5.

2 Related Work

The current role of multi-objective optimization in various sectors is becoming increasingly relevant. As with most problems, the objectives to be considered are many and often contradict each other. The classical methods of solution are based on the idea of transforming the original problem into one with a single objective function (scalarization) [9]. Although this technique is easy to implement it presents a series of disadvantages, first of all the fact to return a single optimal solution hypothesized. The first problem is constituted by the fact that it is not always clear where this solution is placed compared to the Pareto Front, and in some cases this solution may even prove to be a solution dominated. Besides knowing this variety of solutions on the Pareto Front is extremely useful to have a wider choice available. The Pareto-optimal formulation of the multi-objective problem, in which are not considered scalarization and where all objectives in contrast are kept separate is certainly a more valid and reliable method. Evolutionary algorithms [13] have become some of the main methods for the Exploration of Pareto optimal front in multi-objective optimization problems. This is due not only to the fact that there are few alternatives for finding multiple Pareto optimal solutions in large spaces that could be "intractable". But also to the fact that thanks to parallelization, to their capability to explore the similarity of the solutions with the operation of recombination, these algorithms are able to approximate the Pareto optimal front in a single optimization run. This has resulted in a use of multi-objective evolutionary algorithms in more and more numerous applications and a rapidly growing interest in this type of algorithms. Evolutionary Multi-objective Optimization Methods are based on the principle of natural selection and can be seen as a combination of the evolutionary computation and traditional multiple criteria decision making. A considerable number of evolutionary multi-objective optimization techniques have been developed in recent years [6], [5]. In particular in this paper we discuss the utilization of

NSGA-II (Non-dominated Sorting Genetic Algorithm II) that represents one of the most applied methods in the selection literature. NSGA-II [7] is a computationally fast and elitist MOEA (Multiobjective Evolutionary Algorithm) based on a non-dominated sorting approach that alleviates some difficulties of NSGA and is capable of outperforming many other genetic optimization algorithms. In the first step, NSGA-II constructs a space of solutions, then performs sorting based on non-domination level, and applies the crowded comparison operator to create a new pool of offspring. It applies a fast non-dominated sorting approach which has $O(MN^2)$ computational complexity, where M is the number of objectives and N the population size. NSGA [12] was proposed by Srinivas and Deb. The algorithm modifies the ranking procedure originally proposed by Goldberg [8] based on several layers of classifications of the individuals.

3 The Brokering Problem

The brokering problem consists of choosing the best proposal among the number of offers, which have been received from different providers, who answer to the same call. Here we define Call For Proposal (CFP) the document to be prepared by the customer to specifies his requirements. The CFP includes the list of resources to be acquired and the rules/policies to be used for defining resource brokering strategies, *i.e.* based on prices, availability, etc. As shown in Fig.1, the CFP is composed of two documents. The first one is the *SLA Template* that is described according to the XML SLA@SOI schema (Available at: http://sla-at-soi.eu/). The second document composing the CFP is the *Broker Policy*, containing a set of rules, to be enforced by the brokering algorithm, in order to choose among the different proposals offered by the Cloud market. The *SLA Template* expresses the configuration of resources that are necessary for the user and consists of a set of virtual resources that may include compute, network and storage. In particular the SLA template [1] is composed of *Service Properties*, that define the technical requirements for user's applications; and

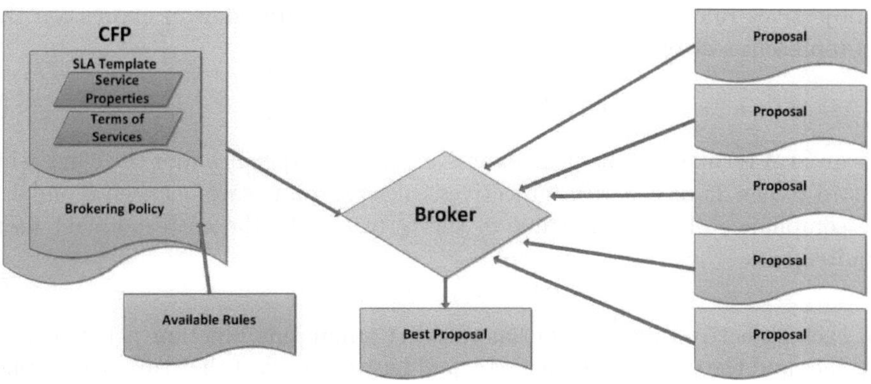

Fig. 1. Architecture of the mOSAIC Broker

the correspondent desired *Service Levels*, such as availability, reliability, performance; *Terms of Service* that include the contract duration, data location and billing frequency, etc. Brokering policy sets *constraints* and *objectives* on multiple parameters such as the best price, the greatest number of cores, the best accredited provider or the minimum accepted availability. We propose a model to formulate the application requirements into constraints that can be architectural constraints and service level constraints. Besides this constraints can be set *hard* or *soft*. Hard constraints refer to the fact that the Cloud offer must have the required condition, otherwise it is to be excluded. Soft constraints refer to desired requirements that can make a provider preferred with respect to another. Simple constraint rules are: exact matches, value in a set, greater/less then, value in a range. Of course not every constraint can be applied to any SLA parameters. For example cpu architecture should match a certain type (x86, amd64) or could match any values in a set. Billing frequency can be set equal to *per_month*, *per_year* or *any*. Price can be set less or equal to a certain value. Availability and Reputation can be set greater or equal to a certain value. The same parameters of the SLA can be considered as input of objectives functions to be optimized. There may be no one single objective for the optimization, and no single optimal solution. For example conflicting goals could be minimization of the cost and maximization of memory. In this case, a multi-objective approach should be adopted and one of the solutions on the Pareto front (that is a set of all those solutions that are considered to be optimal in multi-criteria optimization) should be chosen.

3.1 One-Cloud Evaluation and Brokering

Our broker [3] finds in a set of SLA proposals $\{P_1, \ldots, P_m\}$ the ones that optimize a multi objectives function and satisfy a number of constraints. Each proposal is provided by a Cloud vendor complementing the terms of the SLA template $T = \{t_1, \ldots, t_n\}$, received from the customer, with the correspondent offered values $Pj = \{(t_1; v_{j,1}), \ldots, (t_n; v_{j,n})\}$. In order to evaluate the best proposal the broker can use a set of rules $R = C \cup O$, which can be constraints rules $cr \in C$ or objectives rules $or \in O$ rules. Constraints rules are boolean expression that can represent soft or hard requirements:

$$cr : (t_i, c_i, m_i) \rightarrow [true, false] \quad (1)$$

t_i is an SLA term, c_i is a boolean expression, and m_i specifies that the constraints is hard (when 1) or soft (0). Objectives rules assign a score between 0 and 1 to the compliance of the SLA value of the term t_i with the correspondent user's requirements

$$or : (t_i, f_i, o_i) \rightarrow [0, 1] \quad (2)$$

For each objective rule the user has to select a mapping function f_i between the t_i values and the correspondent score, and has to specify if that rule is an explicit ($o_i = true$) or implicit objective ($o_i = false$). The mapping function change the way to evaluate that objective. For example logarithmic, linear, and exponential function can be used to define the relevance of that objective according to the value $v_{j,i}$ offered by the provider and the one desired by the customer. The broker policy will be a subset of rules $R' \subset R$ that is defined for those terms of the SLA template, which are relevant for the user's requirements. To solve the brokering problem we have to perform the following computation for each received proposal by replacing t_i with the correspondent value $v_{j,i}$:

- $M_j = \prod_{i=1}^{n} \neg(\neg c_i \wedge m_i)\, \forall j = 1, \ldots, m$
  that is used to check if the SLA proposal can be considered as a valid candidate for the SLA , in fact at least a false mandatory constraint invalidates that offer.
- $Opt_j = \sum_{i=1}^{n}(\neg m_i * (c_i = true))\, \forall j = 1, \ldots, m$
  evaluates how many soft constraints are met. It can contribute to the evaluation of the proposal.
- $V_j = \sum_{i=1}^{n}((o_i = false) * f_i(v_{j,i}))\, \forall j = 1, \ldots, m$
  represents an overall evaluation for all those terms which have not to be negotiated independently.

All objectives rules which have $o_i = true$ will be considered independent objectives. In general the best proposals will be the ones which solve the following equations:

$$max_{j=0}^{m}(or_i) : o_i = true\ and\ M_j = 1\, \forall i = 1, n \tag{3}$$

An additional criteria will be:

$$max_{j=0}^{m}(Opt_j) : M_j = 1 \tag{4}$$

All the defined criteria can be grouped if the user set $o_i = false \forall i = 1, \ldots, n$, and $m_i = false\, \forall i = 1, \ldots, n$. In this case the result of brokering will be:

$$max_{j=0}^{m}(V_j) : M_j = 1 \tag{5}$$

that means the best proposal are the ones with the best overall score. The policy edited will be translated in a language supported by programs for symbolic computation like Octave, Matlab or Maple and will be run by replacing t_i parameter with actual values of each proposal.

3.2 Multi-cloud Brokering

In the case of Multi-Cloud brokering problem it needs to define global criteria among different SLAs. Brokering rules defined in the Section 3.1 have to be extended to the entire composition in order to check that the composition still fulfill the consumer's requirements. Moreover, in this case, there is the need to treat the computational complexity that would occur if it were decided to explore all the solutions. In fact several solutions consisting of different combinations of service composition should be evaluated. For this reasons, it is necessary to use algorithms aimed at finding the optimal solution which have a sustainable computational complexity. Some QoS parameters (such as cost, response time, the availability, etc.) can be composed in accordance with a predetermined function, while others may not have a linear dependence on the QoS of each single component. In this preliminary work, given the user service composition, the requirements and their QoS constraint descriptions, we assume that it is possible to express the QoS of n services that make up a composite service as $QoS(composite) = f(QoS(s_1), ..., QoS(s_n))$ where QoS (s) represents the value of the QoS level for a service s, composite is the composite service and s_1, s_2, .. s_n are the services that make up the composite service. As an example, let the negotiation target be a cloud virtual machine service and the parameters of SLA are: Hard Disk, CPU, RAM, Cost, Availability. The approach for computing a the QoS of a composite service is those proposed by [4] but differently from [4] we consider both the indexes of availability promised in the SLA, in the raw **Availability (A)**, and the benchmarking results by a third party (e.g Cloud Harmony available at: www.cloudharmony.com) in the raw **Availability (A_b)**. In the case that different providers will be used as several replicas to increase availability or reliability the aggregation function will be the same of a switch construct shown in Table 1. In the same way if we have a multi-tier Cloud application, that uses services from different providers to optimize the cost or performances the related aggregation function will be equivalent to a sequence. Table 1 shows an aggregation function for each pair work flow construct and QoS attribute.

Table 1. Aggregation functions

QoS Attr.	Sequence	Switch	Flow	Loop
Time (T)	$\sum_{i=1}^{m} T(t_i)$	$\sum_{i=1}^{n} p_{ai} * T(t_i)$	$Max(T(t_i)_{i\in(1...p)})$	k*T(t)
Cost (C)	$\sum_{i=1}^{m} C(t_i)$	$\sum_{i=1}^{n} p_{ai} * C(t_i)$	$\sum_{i=1}^{p} C(t_i)$	$k * C(t)$
Availability (A)	$\prod_{i=1}^{m} A(t_i)$	$\sum_{i=1}^{n} p_{ai} * A(t_i)$	$\prod_{i=1}^{p} A(t_i)$	$A(t)^k$
Availability (A_b)	$\prod_{i=1}^{m} A_b(t_i)$	$\sum_{i=1}^{n} p_{ai} * A_b(t_i)$	$\prod_{i=1}^{p} A_b(t_i)$	$A_b(t)^k$
Reliability (R)	$\prod_{i=1}^{m} R(t_i)$	$\sum_{i=1}^{n} p_{ai} * R(t_i)$	$\prod_{i=1}^{p} R(t_i)$	$R(t)^k$

4 Multiobjective Optimization with NSGA-II

In general, a genetic algorithm allows to find a set of optimal solutions for the problem that is represented by an individual of the space of possible solutions. To operate, the algorithm needs to represent in some way the individuals so to each individual is assigned an appropriate string that represents it, said chromosome: a chromosome is formed by multiple components such genes each of which represents a single feature of the solution. The number of components present in each string is equal to the dimension of the space of solutions. In a multi-objective genetic algorithm, pursuing multiple goals, an individual is considered to be more or less appropriate in relation to most criteria. Besides, as seen before, also the result will be a set of optimal solutions, so the genetics algorithms are used to explore the Pareto front. To determine whether a solution is more suitable than another, a mechanism ranking is needed, different from the value

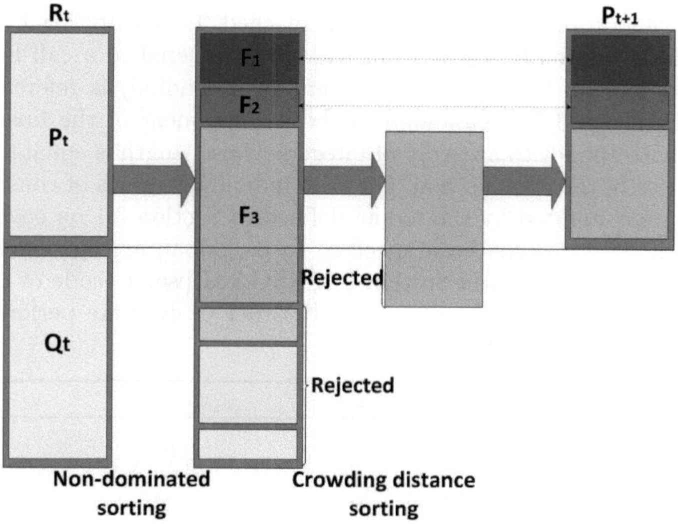

Fig. 2. Structure of NSGA II algorithm

of its own fitness, that have to take into account the presence of more goals. The ranking may be based on dominance, or it can be based on the preference of an objective respect to another, for example by assigning appropriate weights to each objective. In particular NSGA II is based on strict rules of classification of individuals. Before the selection, the population is classified according to the concept of dominance: all individuals that are not dominated, are classified into groups or classes, called rank. In order to maintain the diversity of solutions, individuals classified are shared based on the value that the fitness functions assume in them, and, once formed the first group, it is momentarily ignored for proceed to the creation of other groups of non-dominated lower order. The process continues until all individuals are classified. A key feature of NSGA II is to preserve the diversity among the solutions of the same non-dominated front, in order to maintain a good distribution of solutions. To do this, the NSGA II uses the crowding-distance, a measure of the distance of an individual from its "neighbors", and is used by the algorithm to ensure adequate distribution of individuals, in order to lead the population to adequately explore the whole space of objectives. At first iteration, the usual binary tournament selection, recombination, and mutation operators are used to create a offspring population Q_0 of size N. This population is then combined with the first random generated population P_0 of size N. As shown in Fig. 2 [7], for each iteration a combined population R_t is formed as union of current population Q_t and the previous population P_t. Then, the population R_t, of size $2N$, is sorted according to non domination. After that individuals with the lowest rank are chosen and, in case of equal rank, with a high value of crowding-distance so forming the population P_{t+1}. The new population of size N is then used for selection, crossover, and mutation to create a new population P_{t+1}. The iteration proceeds until the number of generations required has been reached. In our approach we list the SLA templates offered by those providers who answered to a call for proposal for a Cloud service. Each proposal (a gene of individual) is referenced by its index in the list and is a candidate to be a component of the final SLA. An individual corresponds to an array of integers whose length is equal to the number of services of the composition. For each individual values of constraints and objectives are computed by the model defined in Section 3.1 on each proposal. All values, if the rules has been specified to be global, are aggregated according to the function defined in Section 3.2. NSGA II pseudo code of multi-cloud brokering is described in Algorithm 1. In order to evaluate performance and

Algorithm 1. NSGA II for Brokering

Data N individuals, g generation, $f_i(x_i)$
Result N results
  Initialization of Population P of size N
  Evaluation of Constraints
  Evaluation of Objectives
  Ranking Based on Pareto dominance
  Generation of Child generation
  Tournament Selection
  Recombination and Mutation
  for $i = 1 \rightarrow g$ **do**
    for each Parent and Child in Population **do**
      Ranking Based on Pareto
      Dominance Crowing Distance
    end for
    Creation of next generation
    Tournament Selection
    Recombination and Mutation
  end for

feasibility of the proposed approach we used Jmetal, an API that provides an implementation of many genetic algorithms. We developed a multi-cloud broker the actually support the evaluation of general reduction functions on any parameters of a cloud proposal. It supports mean, maximum, minimum value, sum, product reduction operations, but also a number of workflows, which allow to combine services by a switch or sequence operator. In order to test the brokering algorithm with realistic cloud proposals we evaluated 41 different VM offers from Amazon, Rackspace and IBM. For each offer we considered amount of memory, cpu speed, number of cores, availability cost and others. We imagine that a cloud customer want minimize costs and maximize the number of cores of his system by spreading the load of n different machines, possibly allocated in different geographical areas to better support customers in different parts of the world based to geographic jurisdictions. To do this he needs a load balancer to address the tasks to different VM, and a function of ip to redirect the client

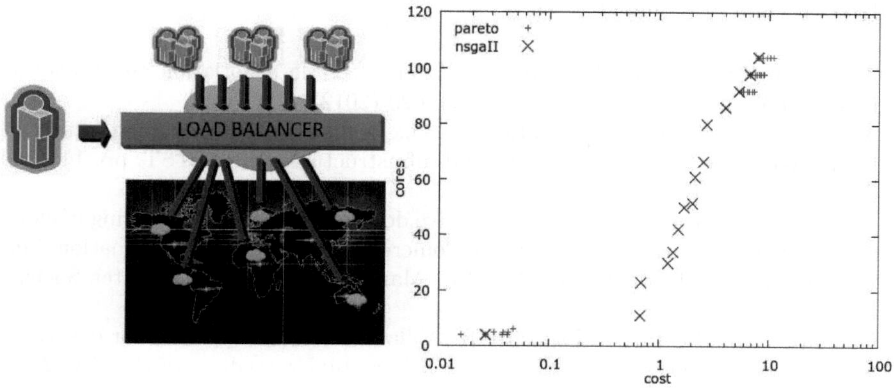

Fig. 3. Example of NSGA II utilization for multiple broker

to the server the corresponding geographical area. So while some tasks may be executed on the same cloud, some others may run on different cloud platforms. The allocation of workloads is used to improve resource utilization and reduce costs. It means that the cloud customer would improve the performance of its composed service. These are really conflicting objectives. Figure 3 shows that in the true Pareto front there are either cheap solutions with few cores or expensive solutions with many cores. We observe a great diversity between solutions that optimize different objectives. In this case the total cost will be computed as: $C_T = \sum_{i=1}^{n} C(t_i)$ and the totalnumber of cores as $CORE_T = \sum_{i=1}^{n} CORE(t_i)$.

5 Conclusion

In this paper we proposed the use of multiobjective genetic algorithms in the field of a Multi-Cloud brokering service, to allow for the evaluation of a composite service by different providers. In particular we proposed the utilization of NSGA II to consider multiple SLAs simultaneously whose composition satisfy the user's requirements. A preliminary example of NSGA II utilization for multiple broker has been shown. The evaluation of the Multi-Cloud brokering service implementation and the discussion of performance results are matter of future work.

Acknowledgments. This work has been supported by PRIST 2009, *Fruizione assistita e context aware di siti archelogici complessi mediante terminali mobile*, founded by Second University of Naples and by the mOSAIC project (EU FP7-ICT programme, project under grant #256910).

References

1. Amato, A., Liccardo, L., Rak, M., Venticinque, S.: Sla negotiation and brokering for sky computing. In: CLOSER, pp. 611–620 (2012)
2. Amato, A., Di Martino, B., Venticinque, S.: Evaluation and brokering of service level agreements for negotiation of cloud infrastructures. In: ICITST, pp. 144–149 (2012)
3. Amato, A., Venticinque, S.: Multi-objective decision support for brokering of cloud sla. In: The 27th IEEE International Conference on Advanced Information Networking and Applications (AINA 2013), March 25-28. IEEE Computer Society, Barcelona (2013)
4. Canfora, G., Di Penta, M., Esposito, R., Villani, M.L.: An approach for qos-aware service composition based on genetic algorithms. In: Proceedings of GECCO 2005, pp. 1069–1075. ACM (2005)
5. Carlos, A.: Comprehensive Survey of Evolutionary-Based Multiobjective Optimization Techniques. Knowledge and Information Systems 1(3), 129–156 (1999)
6. Dastjerdi, A.V., Buyya, R.: A taxonomy of qos management and service selection methodologies for cloud computing. In: Cloud Computing: Methodology, Systems, and Applications, pp. 109–131. CRC Press (2011)
7. Deb, K., Pratap, A., Agarwal, S., Meyarivan, T.: A fast and elitist multiobjective genetic algorithm: NSGA-II. IEEE Transactions on Evolutionary Computation 6(2), 182–197 (2002)
8. Goldberg, D.E.: Genetic Algorithms in Search, Optimization and Machine Learning, 1st edn. Addison-Wesley Longman Publishing Co., Inc., Boston (1989)
9. Marler, R.T., Arora, J.S.: Survey of multi-objective optimization methods for engineering. Structural and Multidisciplinary Optimization 26(6), 369–395 (2004)
10. Mell, P., Grance, T.: The nist definition of cloud computing. Tech. rep., National Institute of Standards and Technology (2011)
11. NIST: NIST cloud computing reference architecture - special publication 500-292 (2011), `http://www.nist.gov/`
12. Srinivas, N., Deb, K.: Multiobjective optimization using nondominated sorting in genetic algorithms. Evol. Comput. 2(3), 221–248 (1994)
13. Van Veldhuizen, D.A.: Multiobjective evolutionary algorithms: classifications, analyses, and new innovations. Ph.D. thesis, Wright Patterson AFB, OH, USA, aAI9928483 (1999)

Cloud Interoperability via Message Bus and Monitoring Integration

Vincent C. Emeakaroha, Philip D. Healy, Kaniz Fatema, and John P. Morrison

Irish Centre for Cloud Computing & Commerce
University College Cork, Ireland
{vc.emeakaroha,p.healy,k.fatema,j.morrison}@cs.ucc.ie

Abstract. In recent years, we have seen the rapid emergence of a plethora of Cloud providers with individual infrastructures, APIs and application description formats. This heterogeneity has resulted in vendor lock-in, which reduces consumer flexibility in terms of negotiation power, reaction to price increases and freedom to change provider. Achieving interoperability between Clouds is a means of addressing this issue. To realise this, the use of open standards has been suggested, but the existing standards are focused mainly on portability instead of interoperability. Besides, this heterogenous nature of Clouds makes inter-Cloud monitoring to facilitate interoperable Cloud management difficult. In this paper, we present a novel integrated approach to achieve interoperability between Clouds and to facilitate the management of service provisioning using multiple Clouds. The approach is based on the integration of a holistic message bus system with monitoring techniques. We present the design and implementation descriptions, and based on a use case scenario, we demonstrate a practical realisation of our approach.

Keywords: Cloud Computing, Interoperability, Interoperable Cloud Management, Message Bus, Data Interchange Format, Monitoring Framework.

1 Introduction

In recent years, many Cloud providers such as Amazon, Google, Microsoft have emerged, each with their own infrastructure, API and application description format [18]. Each promotes its own approach and incompatible implementation, which inhibits the adoption of a particular standard for Cloud service provisioning. Interoperability is a means of addressing these issues, allowing the numerous benefits of Cloud computing, *e.g.*, unlimited resource availability, to be realised. Interoperability embodies the ability to easily exchange information and data between a collection of providers in a usable form. Lack of interoperability is seen as a hinderance to Cloud adoption because enterprises fear vendor lock-in [9]. Once an enterprise chooses a provider, it becomes very costly to change to another. One consequence of vendor lock-in is reduced negotiation power in reaction to price increases.

D. an Mey et al. (Eds.): Euro-Par 2013 Workshops, LNCS 8374, pp. 65–74, 2014.

The use of open standards and co-operation between Clouds are suggested tactics for addressing interoperability [2,4,9]. However, some authors argue that using standards is just one piece of the solution because achieving interoperability also requires sound architecture principles and dynamic negotiation capabilities [10]. However, the reality is that existing standardisation efforts are focused mainly on portability, which is the ability to upload services and data from one provider to another, instead of on interoperability.

Service and resource provisioning in Clouds may be performed in compliance with a set of predefined non-functional properties specified and negotiated by means of a Service Level Agreement (SLA) [3]. To facilitate the management of service offerings and the guaranteeing of agreed SLA objectives, advanced SLA enforcement strategies, including appropriate monitoring techniques, are necessary. The heterogeneous nature of individual Cloud platforms makes monitoring to facilitate the management of interoperable or hybrid Clouds challenging. Existing Cloud monitoring tools are mainly designed for specific platforms and have limited support for interoperability. We argue that this issue can be addressed by implementing a robust message bus system to facilitate inter-Cloud management via monitoring.

In this paper, we present a novel integrated approach for achieving interoperability in Clouds and for facilitating the operational management of service deployments across interoperable Clouds. The approach is based on the integration of a holistic message bus system with monitoring techniques. We propose a monitoring framework that gathers data for supervising Cloud service provisioning and for making informed decisions. The message bus system provides a holistic communication mechanism that is capable of supporting messaging at different levels of abstraction within and between Clouds. It realises the basis for communicating information, including monitored data, within and between Clouds in an interoperable manner with the help of open data interchange formats.

The rest of the paper is organised as follows: Section 2 gives some background information and discusses the related work. In Section 3, we present the design of our monitoring and SLA enforcement framework. Section 4 discusses the message bus system, including its architecture and the data interchange format. In Section 5, we present the integrated approach and a use case scenario demonstration while Section 6 concludes the paper and highlights our future work in this direction.

2 Background and Related Work

There are several ongoing Cloud standardisation projects relating to interoperability. NIST[1], OMG[2] and DMTF[3] play an important role in these projects. As part of their efforts, they have defined use cases describing the manner of

[1] National Institute of Standards and Technology.
[2] Object Management Group.
[3] Distributed Management Task Force.

interactions between Cloud providers and consumers. From an interoperability perspective, the relevant use cases can be summarised as follows [9]:

- *User Authentication*: The ability of a user who has established an identity with a Cloud provider to use the same identity to access another provider.
- *Workload Migration*: The act of moving a workload or service that executes in a Cloud to another without major changes.
- *Data Migration*: The ease of exchanging data that resides in a Cloud with others. This can be, for example, monitored data gathered while executing outsourced services.
- *Workload Management*: The development of custom management tools that are capable of managing multiple Cloud resources from different providers.

The work in this paper is focused on addressing interoperability issues regarding workload and data migrations, and the development of custom management tools. The issue of authentication is out of scope and is not further considered.

In the following, we analyse the previous work on achieving interoperability in Clouds. Nguyen *et. al* [11] address interoperability from the perspective of developing interoperable Cloud services that can be simultaneously deployed on multiple IaaS Clouds. Their approach uses a high-level abstraction layer to provide a unified interface to developers for managing the entire service life cycle. However, they do not address means of realising interoperable resource outsourcing. Sotiriadis *et al.* [12] propose a decentralised meta-broker concept for inter-Cloud resource management. In their concept, a broker is responsible for exchanging and monitoring a consumer resource request. On top of these brokers, they place meta-brokers to enable inter-Cloud operation. Their approach does not consider holistic messaging.

Hsieh *et al.* [8] propose a design for a secure interoperable Cloud-based Personal Health Record (PHR) service. To achieve interoperability, they use the Continuity of Care Document (CCD) format for both storing and exchanging individual PHR information. Bahga *et al.* [1] discuss a Cloud-based approach for interoperable electronic health record system named Cloud Health Information System Technology Architecture (CHISTAR) that uses a generic design methodology to achieve semantic interoperability. Both of these approaches are centered on healthcare systems and do not consider compute resource sharing among Clouds.

Similar to our approach, Tovarnak *et al.* [14] discuss requirements for the producer of monitoring information to address issues of representation, processing and distribution. To this end, they propose the use of an extensible data format to structure monitored information to be usable by multiple consumer and thereby achieve interoperability. Their approach is event-based and not general purpose. Williams *et al.* [17] present *Xen-Blanket*, a thin deployable virtualisation layer that can homogenise diverse Cloud infrastructures. But their concept considers only the deployment of VM instances across Clouds.

To the best of our knowledge, none of the existing work considers the integration of monitoring with a holistic message bus system that uses a common data interchange format to realise interoperability and thereby support interoperable Cloud management.

3 Cloud Monitoring Techniques

Monitoring techniques can facilitate the interoperable management of Cloud service provisioning. In this section, we describe a novel resource monitoring and SLA enforcement framework.

3.1 Resource Monitoring and SLA Enforcement Framework

Efficient resource and SLA management in Clouds require appropriate monitoring. Normally, SLA parameters such as *availability, throughput,* and *response time* represent the performance goals of applications. However, in Clouds, applications are provisioned with underlying infrastructure resources, which are characterised by low-level resource metrics such as, *CPU, memory,* and *storage.* Thus, there is a gap between the SLA parameters and the low-level resource metrics. To bridge this gap and guarantee the SLAs of applications, we propose a monitoring framework, which is an extension of the Low-level resource Metrics to High-level SLA (LoM2HiS) monitoring and mapping framework [5]. The framework monitors Cloud infrastructure resource metrics to determine their status while applications are being executed in a Cloud environment. This framework aims to address two issues: (i) monitoring of low-level resource metrics and (ii) mapping of the monitored metrics into SLA parameters so as to monitor the application SLA at runtime.

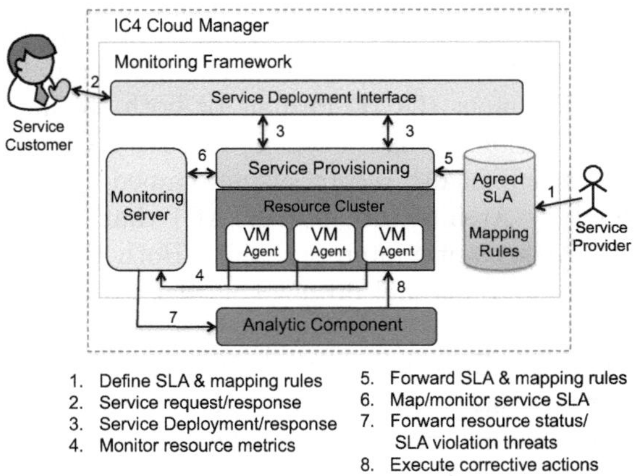

Fig. 1. Monitoring Framework Overview

Figure 1 depicts an overview of the monitoring framework. The provider defines the mapping rules for converting the low-level resource metrics monitored by the embedded agents. The Monitoring Server does the mapping and the evaluation of the application SLAs at runtime. When a violation threat is detected, the analytic component is informed and triggers corrective actions. The LoM2HiS framework has been successfully used for resource monitoring and detecting SLA violations in private Cloud environments and in related areas [6, 7, 13].

3.2 Extensions to the LoM2HiS Framework

The original LoM2HiS framework [5] is designed for monitoring individual Cloud platforms. The monitoring concept uses a centralised approach where the monitoring agents sends the monitored data to a central managing server. Furthermore, the communication of the monitored metrics were limited to one environment due to the communication mechanism being based on the Java Messaging Service (JMS) API and Apache ActiveMQ.

In this redesigned version, we propose a decentralised approach to monitoring where we introduce a hierarchy and divide the resources into clusters with each cluster having its own monitoring server as shown in Figure 1. The monitoring server processes the monitored raw data, applies the mapping rules and evaluate the SLA objectives to detect and inform on SLA violations. In addition, the communication mechanism is now based on a holistic message bus system, which offers us the opportunity to realise inter-Cloud monitoring and messaging. Details of this communication mechanism are presented in the next section.

4 Holistic Message Bus System

The term *holistic* in our context means a complete solution. Thus, we strive to design and implement a unified messaging system usable for communication at the different layers and levels in Clouds. This work should not be confused with the commercial "message bus" platform[4], which provides email services.

4.1 Communication Capability

Cloud computing involves different components and layers of interaction. To enable seamless communication, we aim to realise a mechanism with the following capabilities:

1. *Inter-application communication*: Enables applications executing in a Cloud or in multiple Clouds to interact and exchange information.
2. *Intra-layer communication*: This ability embodies the interaction among resources and their control entities in a Cloud layer.
3. *Cross-layer communication*: Enables the management of layers from the provider perspective. The cross layer communication supports resource allocation, load-balancing virtual machines and application deployment.
4. *Inter-Cloud communication*: Enables the outsourcing of resources or service executions between Clouds. It facilitates federation and Cloud bursting.
5. *Notification/Alerting*: Enables one way communication notifying or alerting users and administrators about the occurrence of particular events.

---

[4] `http://www.messagebus.com/`

From a provider's perspective, these messaging types cover the communication requirements for efficient management of Cloud provisioning. In the next section, we discuss the data interchange format, which is fundamental to our approach for achieving interoperability.

4.2 Data Interchange Format

The data interchange format is a technology-neutral method of organising and transferring data between entities such as applications, devices and organisations. It provides a means of serialising data for transmission over wire level protocols.

There are two widely used groups of data interchange formats (i) self-describing formats like *Extensible Markup Language (XML)*, *JavaScript Object Notation (JSON)*, and (ii) schema-based binary formats like *MessagePack*. The self-descri-bing formats are human readable and easy to understand but are not very compact, hindering efficient transmission. However, schema-based formats allow for efficient transmission but require receivers to be aware of the schema in advance of message delivery and are not human readable.

Thus, in our approach, we are applying a hybrid of self-describing and schema-based formats in order to achieve human readability and compactness for efficient transmission. To this end, we are investigating a means of effectively combining JSON and MessagePack. JSON was chosen over XML because it has been shown to have better performance [16].

To format different applications or data types, we group them into different categories. So, for each category, we define a unique data interchange format for formatting and serialising that category. In our current prototype, we implement two categories (i) infrastructure resource metrics and (ii) application data. The infrastructure resource metric format is used to structure the low-level monitored data from physical/virtual machines and the application data format is used to structure application specific data. The data interchange formats enable the message bus system to perform interoperable communications at different levels in Clouds.

4.3 Design and Implementation

The proposed message bus system is designed to realise the aforementioned communication capabilities. Figure 2 depicts an abstract view of the message bus system.

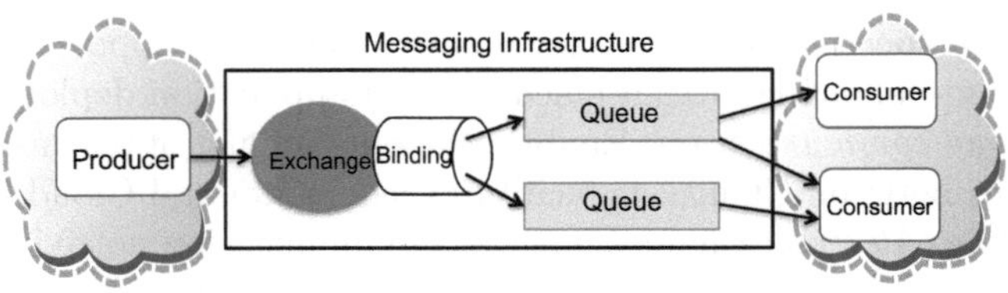

Fig. 2. Cloud Message Bus Overview

As shown in Figure 2, it consist of three components: (i) producer, (ii) messaging infrastructure and (iii) consumer.

Producer
The producer in some cases produces the data/message and in other cases receives the data/message for transmission from a source. It first analyses the data to identify its category in order to apply the correct data interchange format for structuring and serialising the message. The producer has a simple interface for receiving data and this makes it easy to integrate into different levels in Clouds. It is currently written in Java.

Messaging Infrastructure
The messaging infrastructure provides the functions of a message broker. It asynchronously delivers messages from producers to consumers (synchronisation decoupling). The producer does not need to know the nature or location of a consumer. It simply delivers its messages to the broker, which in turn routes them to the appropriate consumer (space decoupling). The broker therefore enables space, time and synchronisation decoupling [15]. This feature facilitates the necessarily loose relationship between a producer and a consumer, which is essential in a distributed system like Clouds.

In our implementation, we use the RabbitMQ broker API[5], which is based on the Advanced Messaging Queue Protocol (AMQP[6]). The broker consist of exchanges, bindings and queues. An exchange is the endpoint of a producer. It receives each message sent and forwards it to the appropriate queue, which is the endpoint of the consumer. The binding connects exchanges and queues, and message forwarding is based on the routing key contained in the message header.

Consumer
The consumer is the receiving end of the communication. It is responsible for receiving and de-serialising the message body. It is implemented in Java and provides a simple interface for easy integration into different Cloud levels.

Our message bus prototype is implemented in Java and uses MessagePack as the data interchange format. In the next section, we discuss a practical integration of the monitoring framework with the message bus system.

5 Integration of Monitoring with Messaging

This integration enables interoperability and facilitates efficient inter-Cloud provisioning management, for example, to enforce agreed SLA objectives in order to avoid violation penalties.

5.1 Use Case Scenario

This use case demonstrates the use of our integrated approach to manage a service outsourcing scenario involving two Clouds. As shown in Figure 3, Cloud A outsources the execution of an application (*A2*) to Cloud B.

[5] `http://www.rabbitmq.com`
[6] `http://www.amqp.org`

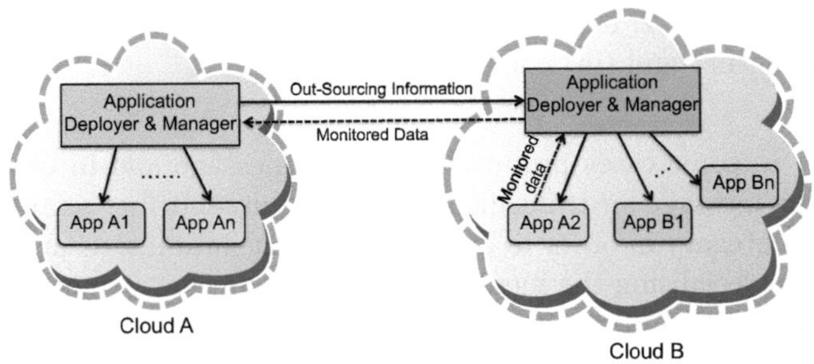

Fig. 3. Service Outsourcing Scenario Overview

In this scenario, the owner of application *A2* establishes an SLA with Cloud A for the execution of this application on his/her infrastructure. Thus, it is his/her responsibility to enforce the agreed SLA. However, if Cloud A does not have the resources to execute this application but Cloud B does, how can the provider transparently leverage the resources of Cloud B for this purpose? And how can the application execution on Cloud B be managed to guarantee the agreed SLA?

The holistic message bus addresses the first question by establishing an inter-Cloud communication channel and uses the application data interchange format to transmit the application for execution on Cloud B. The second question is addressed by the integration of monitoring with the message bus. In this manner, the monitoring framework monitors the resource consumption on Cloud B (as shown in Figure 3) and transmits the monitored data back to Cloud A for processing and enforcement of the agreed SLA terms for the *A2* application.

5.2 Summary

In summary, achieving interoperability among Cloud providers/platforms is essential to realise the full potential of Cloud Computing, especially with the growing market and rapid increase in the number of Cloud providers. Many types of service offering are emerging that can be used in varying constellations. This offers diverse opportunities, for example in cost reduction, by using a composite of low-priced services from different providers instead of subscribing for all the services from a single provider, which can lead to lock in and higher prices. This shows the importance of interoperability in advancing the business aspect of Cloud Computing.

The approach to interoperability proposed in this paper has the potential to shape the future of Cloud service provisioning. It is a practical solution that can unlock and exploit the benefits of Cloud bursting, public and private Cloud inter-operation and Cloud federation. The key advantage of our approach is that it uses emerging techniques, especially the data interchange format and the message bus.

We are currently working on a performance evaluation of the use case scenario described above on a Cloud incubator platform being developed in our research centre. The results of this evaluation will be reported in a follow-up paper.

6 Conclusion and Future Work

In this paper, we proposed an integrated approach to address the issues of interoperability in Clouds. Our goal is not only to achieve platform-neutral inter-Cloud communication but also to extend the capability of Cloud management to enable resource out/insourcing and Cloud bursting.

The proposed monitoring framework provides the ability to measure and determine, in real time, the resource consumption of services/applications executing on Cloud resources. It facilitates efficient management of resources and supports the enforcement of agreed SLA objectives.

The holistic message bus system represents a complete solution for communication in Clouds. It provides intra- and inter-Cloud communication, which can include interactions among applications and across Cloud layers. This is enabled by our prototype data interchange format. The integration of monitoring with this message bus system facilitates interoperability and interoperable Cloud management.

In the future, we will implementing a translation software that mediates between customers with proprietary message types. We are working on defining a mapping interface that would automatically adapt proprietary messages to our defined common data interchange format before transmission, reversing this process when a response is received. Furthermore, we intend to extend the message bus system with fault tolerance strategies to transparently handle error and fault situations.

Acknowledgement. The research work described in this paper was supported by the Irish Centre for Cloud Computing and Commerce, an Irish National Technology Centre funded by Enterprise Ireland and the Irish Industrial Development Authority.

References

1. Bahga, A., Madisetti, V.: A cloud-based approach to interoperable EHRs. IEEE Journal of Biomedical and Health Informatics 17, 894–906 (2013)
2. Bessis, N., Sotiriadis, S., Cristea, V., Pop, F.: Modelling requirements for enabling meta-scheduling in inter-clouds and inter-enterprises. In: 2011 Third International Conference on Intelligent Networking and Collaborative Systems (INCoS), pp. 149–156 (2011)
3. Boniface, M., Phillips, S.C., Sanchez-Macian, A., Surridge, M.: Dynamic service provisioning using GRIA SLAs. In: Di Nitto, E., Ripeanu, M. (eds.) ICSOC 2007. LNCS, vol. 4907, pp. 56–67. Springer, Heidelberg (2009)
4. Buyya, R., Ranjan, R., Calheiros, R.N.: InterCloud: Utility-oriented federation of cloud computing environments for scaling of application services. In: Hsu, C.-H., Yang, L.T., Park, J.H., Yeo, S.-S. (eds.) ICA3PP 2010, Part I. LNCS, vol. 6081, pp. 13–31. Springer, Heidelberg (2010)

5. Emeakaroha, V.C., Brandic, I., Maurer, M., Dustdar, S.: Low level metrics to high level SLAs - LoM2HiS framework: Bridging the gap between monitored metrics and SLAs parameters in cloud environments. In: 2010 International Conference on High Performance Computing and Simulation (HPCS), pp. 48–54 (July 2010)
6. Emeakaroha, V.C., Calheiros, R.N., Netto, M.A.S., Brandic, I., De Rose, C.A.F.: DeSVi: An architecture for detecting SLA violations in cloud computing infrastructures. In: Proceedings of the 2nd International ICST Conference on Cloud Computing, CloudComp 2010 (2010)
7. Emeakaroha, V.C., Netto, M.A.S., Calheiros, R.N., Brandic, I., Buyya, R., De Rose, C.A.F.: Towards autonomic detection of SLA violations in cloud infrastructures. Future Generation Computer Systems 28(7), 1017–1029 (2012)
8. Hsieh, G., Chen, R.J.: Design for a secure interoperable cloud-based personal health record service. In: 2012 IEEE 4th International Conference on Cloud Computing Technology and Science (CloudCom), pp. 472–479 (2012)
9. Lewis, G.: Role of standards in cloud-computing interoperability. In: 2013 46th Hawaii International Conference on System Sciences (HICSS), pp. 1652–1661 (2013)
10. Lewis, G.A., Morris, E., Simanta, S., Wrage, L.: Why standards are not enough to guarantee end-to-end interoperability. In: Proceedings of the Seventh International Conference on Composition-Based Software Systems (ICCBSS 2008), pp. 164–173 (2008)
11. Nguyen, B.M., Tran, V., Hluchy, L.: A novel approach for developing interoperable services in cloud environment. In: 2013 International Conference on Information Networking (ICOIN), pp. 232–237 (2013)
12. Sotiriadis, S., Bessis, N., Antonpoulos, N.: Decentralized meta-brokers for inter-cloud: Modeling brokering coordinators for interoperable resource management. In: 2012 9th International Conference on Fuzzy Systems and Knowledge Discovery (FSKD), pp. 2462–2468 (2012)
13. Stoegerer, C., Brandic, I., Emeakaroha, V.C., Kastner, W., Novak, T.: Applying availability SLAs to traffic management systems. In: Proceedings of the IEEE Intelligent Transportation Systems Conference (ITSC 2011), pp. 1501–1506 (2011)
14. Tovarnak, D., Pitner, T.: Towards multi-tenant and interoperable monitoring of virtual machines in cloud. In: 2012 14th International Symposium on Symbolic and Numeric Algorithms for Scientific Computing (SYNASC), pp. 436–442 (2012)
15. Tran, N.L., Skhiri, S., Zimanyi, E.: Eqs: An elastic and scalable message queue for the cloud. In: 2011 IEEE Third International Conference on Cloud Computing Technology and Science (CloudCom), pp. 391–398 (2011)
16. Wang, P., Wu, X., Yang, H.: Analysis of the efficiency of data transmission format based on Ajax applications. In: 2011 International Conference on Information Technology, Computer Engineering and Management Sciences (ICM), vol. 4, pp. 265–268 (2011)
17. Williams, D., Jamjoom, H., Weatherspoon, H.: The Xen-Blanket: virtualize once, run everywhere. In: Proceedings of the 7th ACM European Conference on Computer Systems, EuroSys 2012, pp. 113–126 (2012)
18. Zhang, Z., Wu, C., Cheung, D.W.: A survey on cloud interoperability: taxonomies, standards, and practice. SIGMETRICS Perform. Eval. Rev. 40(4), 13–22 (2013)

Reducing VM Startup Time and Storage Costs by VM Image Content Consolidation

Kaveh Razavi, Liviu Mihai Razorea, and Thilo Kielmann

Dept. of Computer Science, VU University Amsterdam
{k.razavi,l.m.razorea,thilo.kielmann}@vu.nl
www.conpaas.eu

Abstract. Elastic cloud applications rely on fast virtual machine (VM) startup, e.g. when scaling out for handling increased workload. While there have been recent studies into the VM startup time in clouds, the effects of the VM image (VMI) disk size and its contents are little understood. To fill this gap, we present a detailed study of these factors on Amazon EC2. Based on our findings, we developed a novel approach for consolidating size and contents of VMIs. We then evaluated our approach with the ConPaaS VMI, an open-source Platform-as-a-Service runtime. Compared to an unmodified ConPaaS VMI, our approach results in up to four times reduction of the disk size, three times speedup for the VM startup time, and three times reduction of storage cost.

1 Introduction

Traditionally, program binaries have been the abstraction used for executing code on a certain computing resource. In contrast, to execute an application on an Infrastructure-as-a-Service (IaaS) cloud, the user has to provide a virtual machine image (VMI) that contains all the execution dependencies, typically containing a fully-featured operating system plus application-specific software. One can see the VMI as a new abstraction for executing code on computing resources. The implications of using VMIs should be clearly studied and proper methods be deployed as necessary.

One of these implications is the fact that VMIs are large and abundant, existing on behalf of different users. Thus, it is not feasible to store all of the VMIs on every compute node. In clouds today, a number of storage nodes are dedicated to storing VMIs. Upon user request to create a new VM from a specific VMI, the VMI is transfered from the storage node to a designated compute node either fully and in the beginning, or partially and on demand. In both cases, the virtual disk size and the contents of the VMI become important factors in terms of startup time and the consumption of storage and network resources.

While there have been recent studies into the startup of VMs in clouds [8,12], the effects of the VMI's disk size and contents are hardly understood. To fill this gap, we have studied the impact of these factors on Amazon EC2[1]. We use the

[1] Similar experiments on our own private cloud based on OpenNebula showed results consistent with the ones from EC2. We omit them to comply with space limitations.

D. an Mey et al. (Eds.): Euro-Par 2013 Workshops, LNCS 8374, pp. 75–84, 2014.

results of this study to develop a novel approach for consolidating VMIs. We evaluate our approach with the VMI of ConPaaS [15], an open-source Platform-as-a-Service (PaaS) runtime.

The structure of this paper is as follows: Section 2 studies the effects of disk size and contents on the startup time of VMs. We describe how to consolidate the contents of the ConPaaS service VMI, our primary source of motivation for this work, in Section 3. We evaluate our approach in Section 4. Related work is discussed in Section 5, and Section 6 concludes.

2 Analyzing VM Startup Time in Clouds

In this section, we analyze startup delays on Amazon EC2 while varying the VMI disk size and its contents. We describe the VM startup process on Amazon EC2, before we present the experimental results.

2.1 VM Startup Process on Amazon EC2

Upon a user request to start a VM from a VMI, four steps are executed. **(1)** The EC2 scheduler identifies a suitable physical machine for the VM. Depending on the properties of the requested VM (i.e., instance type), the availability of physical resources, and the number of concurrent requests, this operation can take different amounts of time [8]. As the scheduler delay is beyond the user's control, we can not apply optimizations here. Therefore, we fixed the instance type to *m1.small* for the rest of this paper. However, we do report on the estimated delay of this operation in Section 4.

(2) Next is the transfer of the VMI from the storage node(s) to the designated compute node. Amazon EC2 has two different types of VMIs: instance-store (S3-backed) VMIs, and EBS-backed VMIs. S3-backed VMIs are first transferred from S3 to the compute node before VM startup. With EBS-backed VMIs, the location of the VMI is mounted on the designated compute node, and the VMI is read on-demand by the VM. While EBS-backed VMIs offer slightly faster startup times, each I/O operation from the VM to the VMI will cause a network transfer that costs a small amount of money and a network delay.

(3) In order to save on required storage (costs) and on network transfer from S3 to the EC2 compute node, S3-backed images are stored in a compressed format. This requires a third step, where the S3-backed VMI is decompressed. EBS-backed VMIs are not compressed on storage and do not need this step.

(4) In the final step, the VM starts booting and reads sectors of data from its VMI. The VM booting delay depends on the operating system (e.g. Linux), distribution (e.g. Debian), and on the enabled system services (e.g. a web server). While it is possible to fiddle with the booting process of a specific operating system or distribution, users generally avoid making low-level changes to the operating system stack for reasons of complexity and forward compatibility. There are, however, standardized distribution-specific tools such as [4,19] that can be used to add or remove services from the booting process.

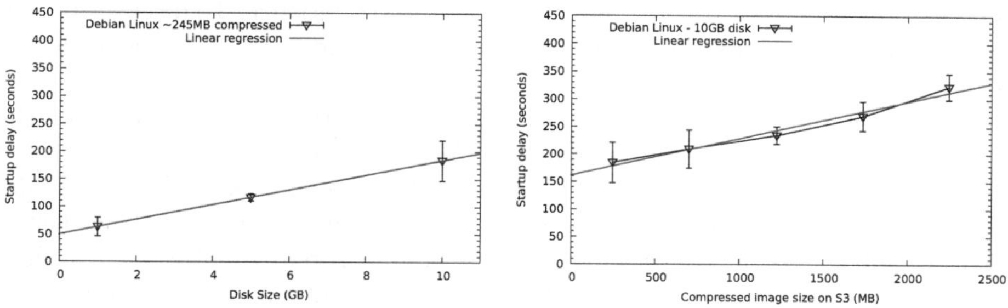

Fig. 1. EC2/S3 startup delay, varying the disk size and contents of the VMI

2.2 Startup Delay While Varying Disk Size and Content

We have used *build-debian-cloud* [2] to build Debian images that can boot on Amazon EC2. The tool takes the desired disk size as a parameter (and fills the image with empty blocks). We start from a Debian distribution and add a file to the image with random ("compression proof") content of a given size to change the compressed size of the image. This way, we can independently study the effects of the uncompressed and compressed image sizes.

Figure 1 shows the result of the experiments while varying the disk size (left) and compressed size (right) with S3-backed images. We have repeated each experiment five times. When varying the disk size, the content size remains the same (except for some negligible file system metadata for the bigger disk size). Thus, the reverse of the regression line's slope estimates the decompression rate (75.9 MB/sec). While varying the compressed size, the disk size remains constant (10 GB) and thus, the the reverse of the regression line's slope gives the S3/EC2 network transfer rate (14.9 MB/sec). These results suggest that, for S3-backed VMIs, it is important to:

a) Reduce the disk content to save on the network transfers for a faster startup. The reduced size of the disk contents also saves required S3 storage space.
b) Reduce the disk size to save on the decompression time for a faster startup.

For the EBS-backed VMIs, regardless of the disk size or content, the startup time remains constant at about 51 seconds. Reduced disk content, and subsequently disk size, however, does save on the EBS storage cost. As mentioned before, the benefit of an S3-backed VMI (vs. EBS-backed) comes from the fact that VM-generated I/O requests to the VMI do not cause network transfers, removing network delays and costs.

3 Consolidating the ConPaaS Services VM Image

Before looking at possible mechanisms to reduce the disk content and size of VMIs, we look at the ConPaaS VMI as a motivating use-case of a typical cloud service VMI. This VMI is scaled out frequently depending on the user's application and workload. Thus, an effective VMI optimization strategy will have a big impact on the perceived performance and/or user experience. To discover prominent optimization strategies, we investigated the process of VMI generation in ConPaaS.

ConPaaS comes with two scripts to generate VMIs that run on either the Xen or KVM virtual machine monitors (VMMs). First, an empty disk with the default size of 3 GB is created and then formatted. Second, using *debootstrap* [5], a minimal Debian system is installed on the disk. Third, a proper Linux kernel is installed and then, the *grub* bootloader is configured. Finally, the required packages for each service are installed and then configured. For example, the MapReduce service installs the packages of *apache-hadoop*.

Looking at these steps, we can make a number of interesting observations. First, there is a large redundancy in the two provided scripts for different VMMs. This means that changing one will most likely result in changing the other. Second, since the required disk size of the VMI is not known in advance, the ConPaaS developers had to add a default value and increase it whenever the free disk space was not sufficient for a new service that brings in new packages. Third, *debootstrap*, while creating a minimal Debian installation, still brings in certain packages such as *man pages* that are not necessary for a production VMI on clouds. Fourth, all the packages of all the services are present in the VMI. This suggests that there is room for image specialization depending on the users' needs of a certain ConPaaS deployment. Based on these observations, we proceed to our three-step approach for consolidating the contents of the ConPaaS service VMI, consisting of (1) specializing to the services needed, (2) pruning the tree of software packages to the bare minimum, and (3) reducing the disk size accordingly.

3.1 VMI Specialization

VMI generation starts from a basic VMI without services, consisting of a minimal Debian installation and the ConPaaS service core. During image specialization, the user specifies which services he wants to add to the image, the type of VMM, as well as the system architecture (e.g., x86/x64). Based on these choices, a customized script is generated automatically, and used to create the VMI.

For ConPaaS, this leads to unifying the two independent scripts (for Xen or KVM) to a single set of scripts as well as the possibility for users to choose various sets of services, depending on their needs.

3.2 Pruning

After creating the image, the next stage uses shell tools to inspect the database of the package management system, in our case apt/dpkg [1,7]. This step automatically analyzes the dependencies between currently installed software packages and decides which of the packages installed by *debootstrap* are not necessary and can safely be removed. Limiting the analysis to the information provided by the package manager reduces the number of opportunities to save disk space, but ensures that the pruning step will not break the package management system.

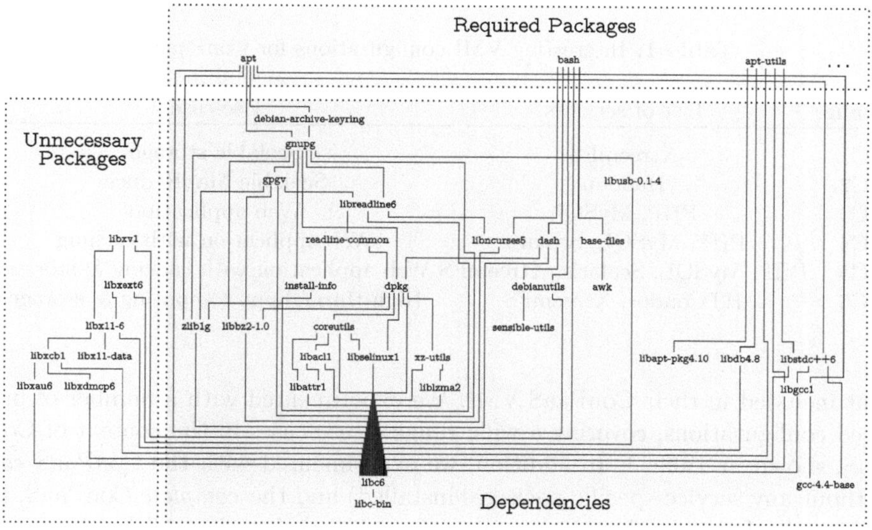

Fig. 2. Example of a partial dependency graph, based on required packages

The pruning algorithm constructs a partial dependency graph by following only dependencies of packages required by the user. Figure 2 shows an example of such a graph. In this diagram, we distinguish packages that are directly *required* by the services the user wants to be hosted on the VMs. Their *dependencies* are determined for inclusion in the VMI. All other packages, that are not part of this hierarchy, are considered *unnecessary*, and will be removed.

3.3 Disk Size Reduction

The previous phase has reduced the contents of the image, but not the image size. The final step calculates the necessary image size, creates a new bootable disk, and copies the contents of the VM to this disk.

Copying the files to a fresh, smaller VMI disk has two benefits. **(1)** For clouds that do not implement compression, the smaller VMI disk results in faster network transfers. **(2)** For clouds that do implement compression, the new VMI disk results in a better compression and thus, faster network transfers. The latter is because most filesystems only remove the i-nodes (vs. the data) when files (from the unnecessary packages) are removed. This means that the corresponding blocks still contain non-zero data that will be included in the compressed image, taking up space needlessly. Starting from a fresh image, with all empty blocks containing zero data, improves the compression rate.

4 Experiments

We tested our VMI consolidation approach with various configurations. With VMI specialization, users now have the option to determine the services they

Table 1. Interesting VMI configurations for ConPaaS

Config.	List of services	Use-case
C1	XtreemFS	Scalable storage
C2	Hadoop	Scalable MapReduce
C3	PHP, MySQL	Web application
C4	PHP, MySQL, Scalaris	Web application with caching
C5	PHP, MySQL, Scalaris, XtreemFS	Web application with caching & storage
C6	HTCondor, XtreemFS	High-throughput computing & storage

want included in their ConPaaS VMI. We experimented with a number of proposed configurations, covering a wide range of use cases in the context of ConPaaS, shown in Table 1. In addition, we experimented with the ConPaaS *core* (without any service-specific packages installed) and the *complete* ConPaaS, including all of the developed services so far; the services from Table 1, as well as a *Selenium* web-application testing service, and a content delivery network service (CDN).

Figure 3 (left) compares the disk size and S3-compressed size of various configurations with the unmodified ConPaaS VMI. The difference between *unmodified* and *complete* is the result of the optimizations from Section 3.2 (reducing the disk contents) and from Section 3.3 (reducing the disk size). The differences between *unmodified* and the configurations described in Table 1, are the result of VMI specialization from Section 3.1, in addition to the other optimizations.

Using the estimated S3/EC2 network performance and decompression rates obtained in Section 2, it is possible to convert the size values in Figure 3 (left) to time estimates. Figure 3 (right) shows the estimated delay in VM startup caused by the network transfer and by decompression. We estimate that pruning and disk resizing together result in an about 40 seconds faster VM startup: 46% faster decompression and 36% faster network transfer. VMI specialization saves from 27 seconds (C6) to 36 seconds (C1): 39% to 53% faster decompressions, and 48% to 65% faster network transfers.

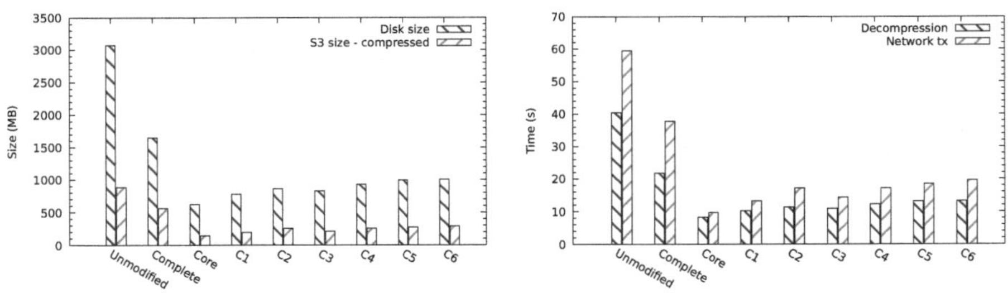

Fig. 3. Left: disk size and contents with service selection and optimizations. Right: the estimated network transfer and disk decompression time on EC2, based on Figure 1.

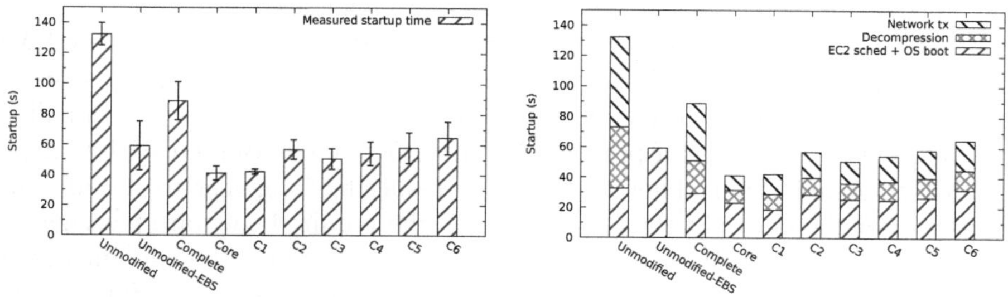

Fig. 4. Left: measured startup time of ConPaaS VMIs with various configurations and optimizations. The unmodified EBS startup time is included as well for comparison. Right: decomposed startup time based on the estimates of Figure 3 (right).

Figure 4 (left) shows the measured startup times of ConPaaS VMIs with various configurations and optimizations. We have repeated each experiment five times. Although variations in startup times are present, they tend to remain comparably small and stable over time as independently shown by [8]. Figure 4 (Right) shows the decomposed startup times into various operations discussed in Section 2.1. Since we have an estimate of network transfer and decompression delay from Figure 3 (right), we can assume the rest of the startup time involves the EC2 resource scheduler and the OS boot time.

In total, depending on service selection, our optimizations result in two to three times faster VM startups for S3-backed VMIs. Figure 4 also includes the startup time of an unmodified, EBS-backed ConPaaS VMI. As expected, due to the on-demand nature of EBS, the startup delay of unmodified ConPaaS (59 seconds), remains close to that of a minimal Debian (53 seconds). While our optimizations do not affect the startup time of EBS-backed AMIs, they do save up to three times in storage cost. Another interesting observation is that, the S3-backed configurations C1-C5 start slightly faster than the EBS image.

In this section, we described the results of our experiments with the proposed approach in generating VMIs. The optimizations mandated by our approach resulted in up to three times faster startup times and up to three times saving on the costs of storing ConPaaS VMI.

5 Related Work

In this section, we discuss related work in three areas: *VM consolidation* generates special-purpose VMIs. *Efficient VMI transfer* deals with the problem of moving VMIs from storage nodes to compute nodes, and *Cloud instance startup time* studies the startup time of VM instances in different clouds.

5.1 VM Consolidation

VMPlant [10] is a service for generating custom VMIs. The user provides VMPlant with 1) machine requirements (e.g. OS, size of memory and disk, etc.), and 2) a set of configuration scripts and their dependencies in the form of a directed acyclic graph (DAG). VMPlant then accordingly generates a new VMI based on previously cached VMIs. In contrast, we generate VMIs from scratch; our optimizations, however, could complement VMPlant's current functionality.

Jebessa et al. [9] argue for purpose-driven VMs to enhance security by means of VMI code reduction. They use a domain-specific language to declare the properties of the desired target VMI such as the required software package set and the target VMM. We use a similar approach to reduce the content of the VMI by looking at the dependency tree of user-selected services. Further, we reduce the necessary disk size of the VMI in the final generation process.

Quinton et al. [16] use package dependency information to install the minimum number of packages for a given virtual appliance. To minimize the disk size, they estimate the installation size of each package. Our final VMI copying step renders such estimations unnecessary.

Charon [6] is a tool that builds on top of NixOS [13]. NixOS has a declarative package management system and Charon uses that to configure virtual machines with the right package set for the provisioned services.

5.2 Efficient VMI Transfer

In our work, we focus on minimizing the size of the VMIs themselves. Complementary, a large body of work is dealing with speeding up the deployment of given VMIs. There are two different scenarios in which efficient VMI transfer becomes a primary concern. In the first scenario, a single VMI needs to be transferred to many physical nodes. Here, peer-to-peer networking is a commonly used technique [3,17,20]. SnowFlock [11] clones VMs from already running ones in less than one second.

In the second scenario, many VMIs need to be transferred to many physical nodes concurrently and start executing on behalf of different users. Schmidt et al. use Unionfs [18], a sophisticated, layered file system along with multicasting to minimize network transfer times of VMIs. VDN [14] is a network hierarchy-aware system for transferring VMIs to compute nodes in units of small chunks that can be retrieved from local neighbors.

All these approaches can be used orthogonally to our VMI content consolidation work. The advantage of our approach is that it does not require any changes to the cloud infrastructure and can hence also be used with commercial IaaS clouds like EC2.

5.3 Cloud Instance Startup Time

Mao et al. [12] study the startup performance of various commercial IaaS clouds by various factors such as OS image size, instance-type and number of instances acquired at the same time. Their experiments only consider the image size, neglecting the effects of the actual disk content. In contrast, we have used a set of experiments that separates the performance implications of disk size and content. Mixing of compression time into network transfer time is apparent in their reported transfer rate of 10.9 MB/s, which is lower than our estimated value of 14.9 MB/s.

Iosup et al. [8] benchmark various aspects of cloud computing. They extensively study resource acquisition delay on Amazon EC2 while comparing different factors such as different instance-types and number of concurrent requests. In this work, we have done a break-down of acquisition delay of Amazon EC2 to find promising areas for optimizing the resource acquisition performance.

6 Conclusions

Fast VM startup times are essential for dynamic scaling of cloud-based services. Both disk size and contents of the user-provided VMIs play an important role in the VM startup time. Furthermore, VMI disk sizes directly translate to monetary costs for storage and network transfer of the VMIs that users have to pay to their cloud providers.

In this paper, we studied the VM startup time as a function of VMI disk size and content. Based on these results, we introduced a novel approach for reducing the disk size and content of VMIs. Using the example of the ConPaaS service VMI, we let users select the desired set of services, based on which the strictly necessary set of software packages is determined and installed on the VMI. A final pass creates a VM disk of the minimal required size. This approach, in general, can be applied to all VM images for which the user can express which top-level software packages are required for its desired functionality.

Our experiments show up to four times reduction in the disk size, and up to three times speedup in the VM startup time for S3-backed VMIs on Amazon EC2. Furthermore, EBS-backed VMIs created with our approach require up to three times less storage costs, compared to an unoptimized VM image.

Acknowledgments. This work is partially funded by the FP7 Programme of the European Commission in the context of the Contrail project under Grant Agreement FP7-ICT-257438, and by the Dutch public-private research community COMMIT/.

References

1. apt-rdepends (June 4 2013), `http://man.devl.cz/man/8/apt-rdepends`
2. Debian bootstrapping script for Amazon machine images and Google Compute Engine images (June 4, 2013), `https://github.com/andsens/build-debian-cloud`
3. Chen, Z., Zhao, Y., Miao, X., Chen, Y., Wang, Q.: Rapid Provisioning of Cloud Infrastructure Leveraging Peer-to-Peer Networks. In: 29th IEEE Int. Conf. on Distributed Computing Systems Workshops, ICDCSW 2009, pp. 324–329 (2009)
4. chkconfig (June 4, 2013), `http://linux.die.net/man/8/chkconfig`
5. debootstrap (June 6, 2013), `http://linux.die.net/man/8/debootstrap`
6. Dolstra, E., Vermaas, R., Levy, S.: Charon: Declarative Provisioning and Deployment. In: 1st International Workshop on Release Engineering, RELENG 2013, pp. 17–20 (2013)

7. dpkg-query (June 4, 2013), `http://man.he.net/man1/dpkg-query`
8. Iosup, A., Ostermann, S., Yigitbasi, N., Prodan, R., Fahringer, T., Epema, D.: Performance Analysis of Cloud Computing Services for Many-Tasks Scientific Computing. IEEE Trans. Parallel Distrib. Syst. 22(6), 931–945 (2011)
9. Jebessa, N.D., van 't Noordende, G., de Laat, C.: Towards Purpose-Driven Virtual Machines. ESSoS Doctoral Symposium 2013 (2013)
10. Krsul, I., Ganguly, A., Zhang, J., Fortes, J.A.B., Figueiredo, R.J.: VMPlants: Providing and Managing Virtual Machine Execution Environments for Grid Computing. In: 2004 ACM/IEEE Conference on Supercomputing, SC 2004 (2004)
11. Lagar-Cavilla, H.A., Whitney, J.A., Scannell, A.M., Patchin, P., Rumble, S.M., de Lara, E., Brudno, M., Satyanarayanan, M.: SnowFlock: rapid virtual machine cloning for cloud computing. In: 4th ACM European Conference on Computer Systems, EuroSys 2009, pp. 1–12 (2009)
12. Mao, M., Humphrey, M.: A Performance Study on the VM Startup Time in the Cloud. In: 5th Int. Conf. on Cloud Computing, CLOUD 2012, pp. 423–430 (2012)
13. NixOS (May 29, 2013), `http://nixos.org/nixos`
14. Peng, C., Kim, M., Zhang, Z., Lei, H.: VDN: Virtual machine image distribution network for cloud data centers. In: The 29th Conference on Computer Communications, INFOCOM 2010, pp. 181–189 (2012)
15. Pierre, G., Stratan, C.: ConPaaS: a Platform for Hosting Elastic Cloud Applications. IEEE Internet Computing 16(5), 88–92 (2012)
16. Quinton, C., Rouvoy, R., Duchien, L.: Leveraging feature models to configure virtual appliances. In: 2nd International Workshop on Cloud Computing Platforms, CloudCP 2012, pp. 2:1–2:6 (2012)
17. Reich, J., Laadan, O., Brosh, E., Sherman, A., Misra, V., Nieh, J., Rubenstein, D.: VMTorrent: scalable P2P virtual machine streaming. In: 8th Int. Conf. on Emerging Networking Experiments and Technologies, CoNEXT 2012, pp. 289–300 (2012)
18. Schmidt, M., Fallenbeck, N., Smith, M., Freisleben, B.: Efficient Distribution of Virtual Machines for Cloud Computing. In: 18th Euromicro Int. Conf. on Parallel, Distributed and Network-Based Processing, PDP 2010, pp. 567–574 (2010)
19. update-rc.d (June 4, 2013), `http://www.tin.org/bin/man.cgi?section=8&topic=update-rc.d`
20. Wartel, R., Cass, T., Moreira, B., Roche, E., Guijarro, M., Goasguen, S., Schwickerath, U.: Image Distribution Mechanisms in Large Scale Cloud Providers. In: 2010 IEEE Second International Conference on Cloud Computing Technology and Science, CloudCom 2010, pp. 112–117 (2010)

Towards Data Interoperability of Cloud Infrastructures Using Cloud Storage Services

Tamas Pflanzner[1] and Attila Kertesz[2,1]

[1] University of Szeged, Department of Software Engineering
H-6720 Szeged, Dugonics ter 13, Hungary
tamas.pflanzner@gmail.com

[2] MTA SZTAKI Computer and Automation Research Institute
H-1518 Budapest, P.O. Box 63, Hungary
kertesz.attila@sztaki.mta.hu

Abstract. Cloud Computing is becoming more and more popular, and various cloud services have appeared to make our lives easier. Mobile devices can also benefit from Cloud services: the huge data users produce with these devices are continuously posted to online services, which may require the modification of these data. Using cloud storage services together with computation-intensive infrastructure services can provide a suitable solution for these needs. In this paper we address the open issue of data interoperability in clouds, and propose an approach to manage and share user data produced by mobile devices in different IaaS clouds. The approach is exemplified with an image generator application, and the performance of the application is evaluated with Android devices and a private IaaS cloud.

1 Introduction

Nowadays, as Cloud Computing is becoming more and more popular, and various cloud services have appeared to make our lives easier. These services are offered at different cloud deployment models ranging from the lowest infrastructure level to the highest software or application level. Within Infrastructure as a Service (IaaS) solutions we can differentiate public, private, hybrid and community clouds according to recent reports of standardization bodies. The previous two types may utilize more than one cloud system, which is also called as a cloud federation [6]. One of the open issues of such federations is the interoperable management of data among the participating systems. Another popular family of cloud services is called cloud storage services. With the help of such solutions, user data can be stored in a remote location – in the cloud. Mobile devices can also benefit from Cloud services: the enormous data users produce with these devices are continuously posted to online services, which may require the modification of these data. Nowadays more mobile devices are sold compared to traditional PCs [7], and Android devices are more and more popular [8]. The aim of our research is to develop a solution that uses cloud storage services together with infrastructure services of cloud federations to enhance the capabilities of mobile devices.

D. an Mey et al. (Eds.): Euro-Par 2013 Workshops, LNCS 8374, pp. 85–94, 2014.

Regarding related works, the need for data interoperability and the extensive use of cloud storage services have been identified by various research and expert groups (eg. [5,3,1]). Managing user data in the cloud also raises privacy issues [9,4] that need to be taken into account during data processing. Nevertheless in this paper we refrain from legal issues and focus on interoperability problems. Dillon et. al [2] gathered several interoperability issues that need to be considered in cloud research, and named a new category called Data Storage as a Service to draw attention to the problem of data management in clouds.

In this paper we address the open issue of data interoperability in clouds, and propose an approach to manage and share user data produced by mobile devices in different IaaS clouds. Therefore the main contributions of this paper are: (i) envisioning a solution for the data interoperability problem of cloud federations, (ii) the development of an image generator application that interconnects mobile devices, IaaS services and cloud storage services, and (iii) the evaluation of our proposed approach using mobile devices and an IaaS Cloud.

The remainder of this paper is as follows: Section 2 presents a classification of cloud storage providers, and describes our approach for data interoperability; Section 3 introduces a scenario for managing user data in a cloud produced by mobile devices. Finally, Section 4 discusses the performed evaluations, and the contributions are summarized in Section 5.

2 An Approach for the Data Interoperability Problem in Cloud Federations

As we have seen in the introduction, retrieving and sharing user data and virtual images among different IaaS Clouds is an open issue. Without concerning data privacy issues, it is also not an easy task to move a user application from one Cloud infrastructure to another. Virtualization techniques and virtual image formats different providers support to run on their Virtual Machines (VMs) are usually incompatible. Retrieving a user's Virtual Appliance (VA, which is a specialized image hosting the user application) from an IaaS Cloud is impossible in most cases, not only in case of commercial providers, but also in academic solutions. Therefore we propose an approach to retrieve and share user application data among different providers with the help of Cloud Storage Services. In this way VAs running at different cloud infrastructures can manage the same data at the same time, and the users can access these data from their own local devices without the need for accessing any IaaS Clouds. This idea is demonstrated in Figure 1. A classification on cloud storage service providers (CSSP) is shown in Table 1. We compared 10 well-known providers focusing on their most important properties. From these providers we have chosen Dropbox [18] as the CSSP to demonstrate our approach, because it has the highest variety of development kits available and its API was the most reliable according to our evaluations. Regarding the IaaS middleware we have chosen OpenNebula.

In the next section we introduce a use case and a sample application that demonstrates the usability of this approach.

Table 1. Classification of Cloud Storage Service Providers

Provider	Initial Storage (GB)	Bonus (GB)	Max. Storage (GB)	Supported OS	Mobile Platforms
Google Drive [14]	5	-	5	Win, Mac	iOS, Android
Amazon CD [15]	5	-	5	Win, Mac	iOS, Android
SkyDrive [16]	7	-	7	Win, Mac, Linux	iOS, Android
SpiderOak [17]	2	1	10	Win, Mac, Linux	iOS, Android
Dropbox [18]	2	0.5	18	Win, Mac, Linux	iOS, Android
IDrive [19]	5	1	50	Win, Mac	iOS, Android
SugarSync [20]	5	0.5	32	Win, Mac	iOS, Android
Glide [21]	30	-	30	Win, Mac, Linux	iOS, Android
CX [22]	10	0.3	16	Win, Mac	iOS, Android, Kindle Fire
Memopal [23]	3	0.5	13	Win, Mac, Linux	iOS, Android, Blackberry

Provider	Version Control	Encryption	Num. of devices	API	SDK
Google Drive [14]	+	-	-	+	Java, Python, PHP, .NET, Ruby
Amazon CD [15]	-	-	8	-	-
SkyDrive [16]	+	-	-	+	Android, .NET, iOS
SpiderOak [17]	+	+	-	+	-
Dropbox [18]	+	+	-	+	iOS, Android, Python, Ruby, Java, OS X
IDrive [19]	+	+	1	+	-
SugarSync [20]	+	+	1	+	-
Glide [21]	+	-	6	-	-
CX [22]	+	+	-	+	-
Memopal [23]	+	+	10	+	-

3 Managing Mobile Data in Clouds

As a use case, we have identified a real world scenario that requires interoperable data management among cloud infrastructures to manage user data produced by mobile devices. Though the computing capacity of mobile devices has rapidly increased recently, there are still numerous applications that cannot be solved with them in reasonable time. Our approach is to utilize cloud infrastructure services to execute such applications on mobile data stored in cloud storages. The basic concept of our solution is the following: services for data management are running in one or more IaaS systems that keep tracking the cloud storage of a user, and execute data manipulation processes when new files appear in the storage (see Figure 2).

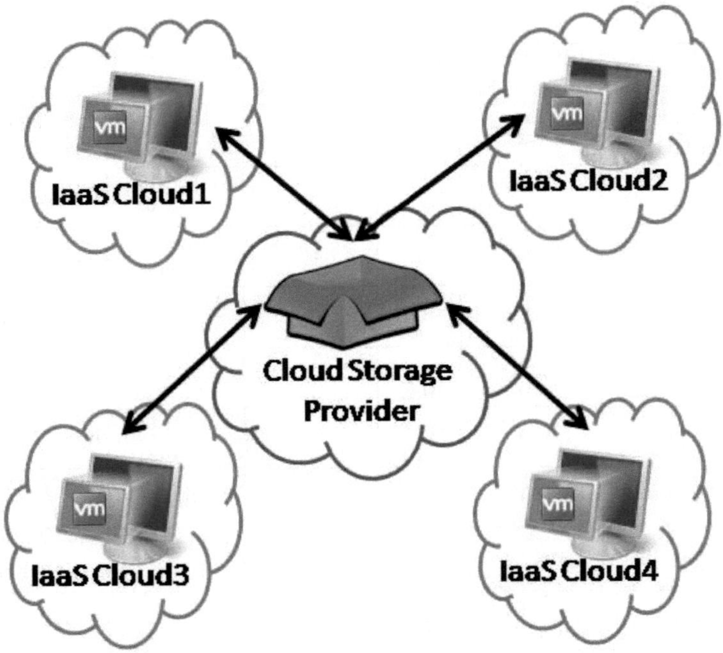

Fig. 1. An envisioned solution for data interoperability in Clouds

The service running in the cloud can download the user data files from the cloud storage, execute the necessary application on these files, and upload the modified data to the storage service. Such files can be for example a photo or video made by the user with his/her mobile phone to be processed by an application unsuitable for mobile devices. In our solution currently developed for Android devices, there is a possibility to configure the processes to be performed on the data with a separate configuration file, which is automatically created and managed by a mobile application running on the users device. This application is also responsible for communicating with the cloud storage, which is Dropbox in our case. The file manipulation applications have been created as a virtual appliance, and have been pre-deployed in our SZTAKI cloud infrastructure based on OpenNebula, to perform our evaluations.

In order to exemplify the usability of this generic approach, we have created a concrete application called *FolderImage*, which can be used to manipulate pictures produced by mobile devices. This program creates thumbnails of each image of the appropriate folder then ensembles them into a single image (called as *folder* image) that represents the folder and gives an overview of its contents to the user. This app can be really useful by providing a glimpse of a directory, when a user has thousands of pictures spread over numerous directories, and she is looking for a specific one.

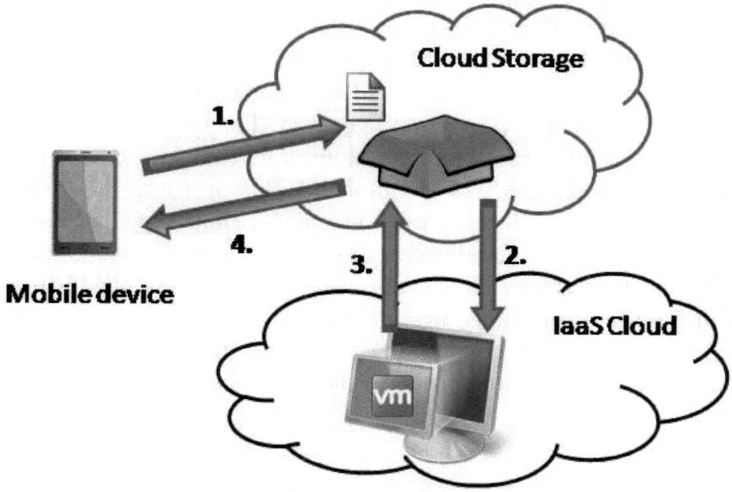

Fig. 2. Enhancing data management of mobile devices

We have developed an Android application that is able to perform this task locally on the user's device, and a Java application performing the same task encapsulated in a VA, deployed in a local cloud. In the following subsections we introduce these applications, then in Section 4 we compare the performance of the two approaches.

3.1 The FolderImage Android Application

In this subsection we introduce in detail how the *FolderImage* Android application has been developed and can be used. This application can be used in two modes: (i) in local operation, when the folder image is generated by using the computing resources of the actual device, and (ii) in cloud operation, when the application communicates directly with Dropbox, in this case the pictures can be uploaded on demand, or synchronized continuously, and the folder image is generated in the cloud, which is downloaded to the device after completion. These modes can be triggered by clicking on the appropriate button in its graphical interface (see Figure 3).

The implementation of the application uses the Android [10] and Dropbox API [11]. It needs to read and write files to the local storage of the device, to access the internet, and to securely communicate with a Dropbox account storage. These capabilities are denoted in its 'AndroidManifest.xml' file. The application itself needs to be registered at the official Dropbox developer website [12]. The 'APP-KEY' retrieved during registration need to be set in the application to allow secure communication and access to the user's storage. If no such key information is given, the application offers the possibility to log in through the device browser to a Dropbox account – in this case the permanently retrieved credentials will be used to access the remote storage.

A screenshot of the graphical user interface (GUI) of the application is shown in Figure 3. After installing and starting the FolderImage application, the user will see a similar look with three buttons. Clicking on the first, top button, it will automatically log in to Dropbox, and after the successful login, the name of the account holder is displayed above the button. The second button can be used to trigger a folder image creation in the cloud, and the third one to perform the folder image generation locally. For simplicity, this prototype uses the 'Photos' directory, and creates a file called 'folder_image_Photos.jpg'. (This prototype can be easily extended to handle any directories on the device storage.) This generated image is also shown in the application GUI, under the buttons. Status messages and updates on image up-, downloads and generation are also shown between the buttons and the folder image. Though this GUI is relatively simple, it is not an easy task to show proper look on devices having different display resolutions.

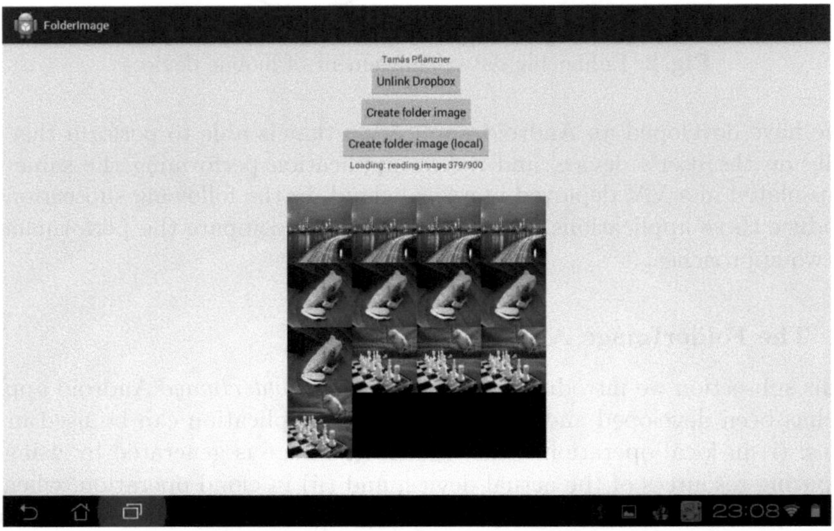

Fig. 3. A screenshot of the FolderImage Android application

As we mentioned, the second and third buttons can be used to generate the folder image. These events trigger the 'createFolderImage' and 'createFolderImageLocal' methods respectively. These methods have five similar steps:

1. list: to generate a list of the images the actual folder contains;
2. download: to access the images of the folder;
3. resize: to generate thumbnails of the images;
4. create: to ensemble the thumbnails;
5. upload: to save the created folder image.

These steps are timestamped, therefore comparison between the local and cloud computation can be easily done. The second step of the local computation (when each image is loaded to the memory) had to be optimized for the local version, because most Android device has a relatively small internal memory for this purpose (eg. 32 MBs). Therefore in this step it is not the transfer time that needs to be considered, but the loading of the pictures to the internal memory one by one to generate separate thumbnails (on the contrary to the cloud version, here the memory is too small to keep all pictures in the memory at the same time). For the cloud version, the images are downloaded from the Dropbox folder to the VA, where the computation is performed. In step 3 thumbnails with 50x50 pixels are generated, then in step 4 they are organized into a matrix that will represent the folder image. Finally, in step 5 the local version only saves the folder image file, while the Java application in the cloud uploads the generated folder image file to the Dropbox storage, which will be retrieved by the device application.

3.2 Image Generation in the Cloud

As we have depicted in Figure 2, the idea of our scenario is to move computation-intensive tasks from a mobile device to the cloud. Therefore we have also created a Java application called *ImageConverter* that is capable of performing the 5 steps discussed in the previous subsection. We have encapsulated this application to a VA, deployed, and started it as a web service running in a local cloud. It also has a direct connection with the user's Dropbox storage. It can continuously synchronize the image directory, and perform the folder image generation once a new image is added to the folder. It can also be set to listen to a specific setup file that instructs it to execute certain methods (eg. performing different kinds of image manipulation processes). Once the 'createFolderImage' method is called from the Android application, the setup file is refreshed, and the web service running in the cloud is notified about this change, which triggers the folder image generating and uploading processes.

If we deployed web services of similar VAs into different IaaS providers, we could execute a set of cloud services that can access the same data storage under a Dropbox account. In this way we could handle and manage data in an interoperable way among different IaaS solutions.

4 Evaluation

As we have already mentioned, we performed our evaluations on a private IaaS Cloud. It has been developed by a national project called SZTAKI Cloud [13], which was initiated to perform research in clouds, and to create an institutional cloud infrastructure for the Computer and Automation Research Institute of the Hungarian Academy of Sciences based on the latest research results to enable a significant improvement of the local IT infrastructure. This new cloud-based infrastructure is more effective and cost efficient than the former physical infrastructure built on traditional concepts and individual specific servers. This improved

Table 2. Capabilities of the used devices in the evaluation

	Samsung Galaxy Mini (phone)	**Asus Slider SL101 (tablet)**	**Cloud VM1**	**Cloud VM2**
OS	Android 2.2	Android 4.0	Ubuntu 12.04 64bit	Ubuntu 12.04 64bit
CPU	600 MHz	1 GHz (dual-core)	1 CPU	4 CPUs
RAM	384 MBs	1 GB	1 GB	4 GBs

institutional infrastructure could even be the first milestone in a global academic paradigm shift, and will serve as a base for further research investigations.

To perform the measurements, we deployed the *ImageConverter* VA to the SZTAKI Cloud. We have deployed them to two different types of virtual images: one having one processor and one GB memory (VM1), and the other 4 processors with 4 GBs of memory (VM2). Meanwhile we have also tested the *FolderImage* application on two different Android devices: on a phone and a tablet. Table 2 summarizes the used resources during the evaluations. Tables 3 and 4 show the evaluation results corresponding to the 5 steps of the executed methods introduced in the previous section. In the first round of measurements we considered a folder containing 450 images, while in the second round we manipulated 900 images.

Table 3. Evaluation results for 450 images

Device	**1. list (ms)**	**2. download (ms)**	**3. resize (ms)**	**4. create (ms)**	**5. upload (ms)**	**Sum (ms)**
Android phone	879	199738	872	10631	1587	213707
Android tablet	304	68334	286	3480	491	72895
Cloud VM1	20	173	135	277	326	931
Cloud VM2	14	189	68	203	181	655

The evaluation results clearly show the differences among the different types of executions. Regarding the Android devices, the tablet performed the generation 3 times faster then the phone in both rounds of experiments. The web service running in VM2 type virtual machine performed two times faster then the other deployment at VM1. The local execution on the Android devices are significantly slower (more then 100 times) then the image generations performed in the cloud. These measurements fulfil our expectations, therefore it is worth both in terms of computation time and energy efficiency to move computation-intensive tasks to clouds from mobile devices.

Nevertheless we have to mention that file transfer times can also affect these execution times. When a significant amount of data should be moved from a mobile device with slow internet connection may result in much worse performance, but if the new images are occasionally uploaded to Dropbox by using high speed wifi connection, still good results can be achieved.

Table 4. Evaluation results for 900 images

Device	1. list (ms)	2. download (ms)	3. resize (ms)	4. create (ms)	5. upload (ms)	Sum (ms)
Android phone	2972	401312	1496	21643	3173	430596
Android tablet	971	133575	509	6957	998	143010
Cloud VM1	44	220	300	575	702	1841
Cloud VM2	24	191	73	541	239	1068

5 Conclusion

In this paper we addressed the open issue of data interoperability in clouds, and proposed an approach to manage and share user data produced by mobile devices in different IaaS clouds. We have introduced a solution for solving the data interoperability problem of cloud federations by using cloud storage services. We have shown how to develop an image generator application that interconnects mobile devices, IaaS services and cloud storage services, and evaluated the prototype application using mobile devices and a private IaaS cloud.

Our future work aims at extending the functionalities of the designed mobile application, and supporting additional IaaS and cloud storage providers, and mobile platforms.

Acknowledgment. The research leading to these results has received funding from the CloudSME FP7 project under grant agreement 608886, and it was supported by the European Union and the State of Hungary, co-financed by the European Social Fund in the framework of TAMOP 4.2.4. A/2-11-1-2012-0001 'National Excellence Program', and by the European Union and the European Social Fund through project FuturICT.hu (TAMOP-4.2.2.C-11/1/KONV-2012-0013).

References

1. Bozman, J.: Cloud Computing: The Need for Portability and Interoperability. IDC Executive Insights (August 2010)
2. Dillon, T., Wu, C., Chang, E.: Cloud Computing: Issues and Challenges. In: Proc. of the 24th IEEE International Conference on Advanced Information Networking and Applications, pp. 27–33 (2010)
3. Fraunhofer Institute for Secure Information Technology. On the Security of Cloud Storage Services, SIT Technical reports (March 2012), `http://www.sit.fraunhofer.de/content/dam/sit/en/documents/Cloud-Storage-Security_a4.pdf`
4. Gagliardi, F., Muscella, S.: Cloud Computing – Data Confidentiality and Interoperability Challenges. In: book: Cloud Computing, Computer Communications and Networks, pp. 257–270. Springer, London (2010)

5. Jeffery, K., Neidecker-Lutz, B.: The Future of Cloud Computing, Opportunities for European Cloud Computing beyond 2010. Expert Group Report (January 2010)
6. Kecskemeti, G., Kertesz, A., Marosi, A., Kacsuk, P.: Interoperable Resource Management for establishing Federated Clouds. In: Achieving Federated and Self-Manageable Cloud Infrastructures: Theory and Practice, pp. 18–35. IGI Global, USA (2012)
7. Mobile and PC shipments (March 2011), http://blog.modernmobileapps.com/post/2011/05/03/Qualcomm-A-Hand-in-Everything.aspx
8. Mobile OS statistics (February 2013), http://www.globalnerdy.com/2013/02/14/idcs-smartphone-stats-for-4q-2012-and-a-review-of-their-mobile-os-share-prediction-for-2015/
9. Varadi, S., Kertesz, A., Parkin, M.: The Necessity of Legally Compliant Data Management in European Cloud Architectures. Computer Law and Security Review (CLSR) 28(5), 577–586 (2012)
10. Android website (April 2013), http://www.android.com/
11. Dropbox API website (April 2013), https://www.dropbox.com/developers/reference/api
12. Dropbox developer website (April 2013), https://www.dropbox.com/developers
13. The SZTAKI Cloud project website (2013), http://cloud.sztaki.hu/en/home
14. Google Drive (May 2013), https://drive.google.com/
15. Amazon Cloud Drive (May 2013), http://www.amazon.com/clouddrive/
16. Microsoft SkyDrive (May 2013), http://windows.microsoft.com/skydrive/
17. SpiderOak (May 2013), https://spideroak.com/
18. Dropbox (May 2013), https://www.dropbox.com/
19. IDrive (May 2013), https://www.idrive.com/
20. SugarSync (May 2013), https://www.sugarsync.com/
21. TransMedia Glide (May 2013), http://www.glideconnect.com/
22. CX (May 2013), https://www.cx.com/
23. Memopal (May 2013), http://www.memopal.com/

Clouds-of-Clouds for Dependability and Security: Geo-replication Meets the Cloud

Miguel Correia

INESC-ID, Instituto Superior Técnico, Universidade de Lisboa, Portugal
miguel.p.correia@ist.utl.pt

Abstract. The complexity of large cloud offerings makes it extremely hard to guarantee their dependability and security. This paper extracts lessons from some years of research on the notion of using several clouds – instead of a single one– with the objective of achieving high dependability and security. We show that using such *clouds-of-clouds* it is possible for services to continue to operate correctly despite dependability and security issues in a subset of the clouds. We show this approach with three cases: clouds-of-clouds for storage with the DepSky system; cloud-of-clouds for data processing with MapReduce; the execution of arbitrary services in clouds-of-clouds with the EBAWA algorithm.

1 Introduction

The complexity of large cloud offerings makes it extremely hard to guarantee their dependability and security. In relation to dependability, that difficulty is clear from the outages suffered by essentially all major offerings in the past few years. Examples are the disruption of an Amazon EC2 region for almost one week in May 2011, and the February 29 2012 disruption of Windows Azure. These two problems alone left the two services much below the often promised availability of five nines. In both cases the problem was a subtle bug that led to a cascade of failures. Security events are less visible than outages, but several studies and news suggest that the problem is equally serious. An alarming case was that of a Google engineer who spied upon user Gmail/Gtalk communication. Other examples are the case of CyberLynk in which an ex-employee deleted a TV series from which there was no other copy (March 2011).

We have been exploring the notion of *clouds-of-clouds* as a solution to this chaos of accidental failures and security events. A cloud-of-clouds is a set of cloud offerings that are used by a consumer to run some service or application. A cloud-of-clouds is a virtual cloud, formed of real, physical, clouds. The notion is strongly related to the term *federated clouds* that also designates virtual clouds formed of real clouds [7]. However, the word "federation" suggests something created by the owners of the clouds, whereas cloud-of-clouds has a weaker semantics, usually associated to something created by cloud consumers: they can create their own cloud-of-clouds for having high security and/or dependability on top of cloud offerings they do not trust enough. Needless to say, the two abstractions

D. an Mey et al. (Eds.): Euro-Par 2013 Workshops, LNCS 8374, pp. 95–104, 2014.

involve solving some of the same problems, such as dealing with heterogeneity of management interfaces and access control mechanisms.

Clouds-of-clouds are an approach for dependability and security because they explore the *redundancy* and *diversity* provided by different cloud offerings, from different companies. The diversity of different clouds can avoid common mode failures, i.e., failures that affect the whole cloud, which was what led to the two above-mentioned disruptions. The bugs that led to the two disruptions did not exist in other clouds (to the best of our knowledge), so a virtual cloud formed of one of those plus other clouds would not fail.

This idea can be better understood by considering some of the dependability and security attributes [4]. A cloud-of-clouds can provide *availability* because most of the clouds will continue to provide their service even if there is a disruption in one (or a few) of them. It can provide *integrity* because most clouds will continue to provide correct data and execution even if one of them does not. A cloud-of-clouds can provide *disaster-tolerance* because clouds can be scattered through the globe, so most clouds will continue to operate even if one is physically destroyed by a natural disaster (earthquake, storm, tsunami, etc.). Finally, a cloud-of-clouds prevents *vendor lock-in* because services must support cloud diversity, although this is not exactly a dependability/security attribute.

We considerer that clouds can fail arbitrarily (Byzantine faults), not only by stopping delivering their service (crash faults). There is considerable evidence of the existence of *accidental Byzantine faults* that can corrupt data and software execution. Two examples: a study in Google datacenters found more than 8% DIMMs affected by errors yearly [18]; a Microsoft study found frequent CPU and core chipset faults in consumer PCs [13]. In relation to *malicious Byzantine faults*, a malicious insider with access to servers' management virtual machines is known to be able to obtain consumer passwords, private RSA keys, and files [16], thus to modify arbitrarily data and software executed in the cloud. The existence of malicious insiders is clear from the mentioned Google and CyberLynk cases.

This paper argues that clouds-of-clouds are a valid mechanism for cloud dependability and security. The argument is supported by three of our recent works[1]. The first – DepSky – exemplifies the use of clouds-of-clouds for *storage* [5]. The second shows the use of a cloud-of-clouds for *data processing* using MapReduce [9]. The third illustrates how clouds-of-clouds can be used to execute *arbitrary services* (e.g., file systems, databases, coordination services) in clouds-of-clouds using state machine replication and the EBAWA algorithm [20].

The three involve *replication* in different clouds. Although clouds-of-clouds might be used differently, this is the generic mechanism we consider in the paper. We use the term *geo-replication* because the individual clouds will be typically scattered geographically, interconnected by the Internet [15].

The paper starts by presenting opportunities and challenges of geo-replication for clouds-of-clouds (Section 2). Then, DepSky, BFT MapReduce, and EBAWA are discussed respectively in Sections 3, 4, and 5. Section 6 summarizes the lessons learned and concludes the paper.

---

[1] Full details about those works can be found on the papers here cited.

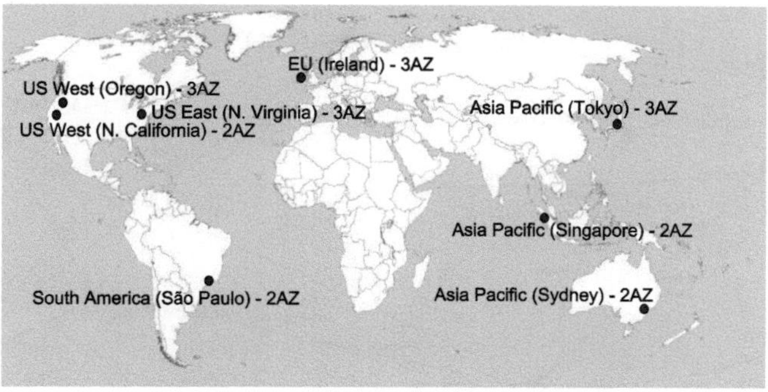

Fig. 1. Geographical redundancy and diversity of Amazon EC2's regions and availability zones

2 Opportunities and Challenges

This section discusses some of the opportunities and challenges of geo-replication for clouds-of-clouds taking Amazon's Elastic Cloud Computing (EC2) service as case of study. A cloud-of-clouds can, and from the dependability point of view should, be based on a set of different offerings from different providers to achieve best diversity. However, it is simpler to consider the case of a single company, which is also adequate as it has a world-wide operation. The discussion that follows is substantiated by a set of experimental data. We run one virtual server (an instance in Amazon's lingo) per Amazon region from August 2–15, 2013 (two weeks). We used Micro instances, i.e., the cheapest. We extracted round-trip times (RTT), throughput values, and information about Internet service providers (ISPs) and Autonomous Systems (ASs) crossed between every pair of nodes[2].

A first opportunity is the existence of *geographical redundancy and diversity*. This becomes clear in Figure 1 that shows Amazon EC2's 8 regions and the number of availability zones (AZs) per region (2 or 3). According to Amazon, "each region is completely independent" (which is coherent with the console that requires accessing one region at a time) and "each availability zone is isolated" [2]. The meaning of "independent" and "isolated" is not entirely clear but from the dependability point of view it suggests a considerable independence between AZs and a higher independence between regions. AZs in a region are connected through low-latency links, but regions are connected by the Internet.

A second opportunity is *network redundancy and diversity*. To understand this aspect, we run *lft* (a variation of *traceroute*) between every pair of instances we placed in EC2 regions and observed the ISPs and ASs crossed. The information about the ISPs for some of the pairs as of August 2nd, 2013, is shown in Figure 2 (we do not show all because they are many). All instances are in ASs from Amazon, which are not displayed, except in the case of the 3 US nodes that

[2] The raw data is available at `http://homepages.gsd.inesc-id.pt/~mpc/paper-data/amazon-ec2-aug2013.rar`

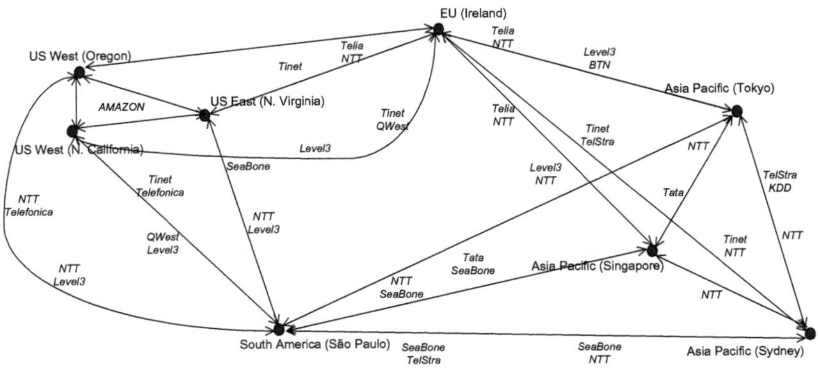

Fig. 2. ISP redundancy and diversity in some of the Amazon EC2 region interconnections in August 2nd, 2013

Table 1. Average and standard deviation of round-trip time (ms) and throughput (Mbps) between some pairs of instances placed in different Amazon EC2 regions

	nv-or	nv-nc	nv-ir	nv-si	nv-to	nv-sy	nv-sp	or-nv	or-nc	or-ir	or-si	or-to	or-sy	or-sp
RTT avg.	83.9	81.2	98.2	261.3	168.9	259.6	148.5	82.1	21.9	178.2	217.1	122.5	197.4	214.8
RTT std. dev.	14.2	13.3	11.3	11.3	12.4	9.2	26.2	5.0	6.6	8.2	12.3	8.5	23.2	9.2
Tput avg.	22.7	23.4	18.9	7.1	10.8	7.1	11.9	21.9	67.5	11.0	8.9	14.5	9.3	7.9
Tput std. dev.	3.0	2.8	3.7	1.2	1.8	0.9	2.8	4.1	20.5	2.5	1.3	2.6	1.7	1.6

are entirely connected by Amazon ASs. Generically it can be observed that several ISPs interconnect the regions, so there is diversity. Moreover, in most cases the ISPs crossed depend on the direction of the communication, indicated in the figure by two sets of ISPs in a link. For instance, when an IP datagram is sent from US West (Oregon) to South America (São Paulo) it crosses NTT and Level3; if sent the other way around it crosses Telefonica and NTT. This suggests the existence of a lot of redundancy. The ASs provide another level of diversity as most ISPs have several. These are not shown in the figure as it would become hard to read.

In relation to challenges, a first one is the *high and variant latencies* between sites. Table 1 shows the RTT between a few pairs of nodes. The regions are represented by the initials of the Country/State (e.g., *or* for Oregon). Even the two closest regions, US West (N. California) and US West (Oregon), show RTTs around 20 ms, which is 100 times more than, say, around 0.2 ms that can be observed in Ethernet LANs. The variation is also considerable.

A second challenge is the *low and variant throughput* between sites, as also observed in Table 1. It is important to note that Amazon provides better throughput to better (more expensive) instances, as shown in [19].

A third challenge is the *economic cost of sending data out of the cloud.* Amazon, as several other offerings, charges nothing for receiving data into its cloud from the Internet, only to send it out. The price for sending data out is zero for the first GB, then starts at 0.12 dollars per GB (up to 10 TB per month) and goes down until 0.05 dollars per GB (for around 500 TB per month) [1]. The cost of sending data out is far from being the only cost of cloud computing: others are for instance the cost of storing data and the cost of running virtual machines (instances).

A fourth challenge is the CAP theorem that states the impossibility of having consistency, availability, and partition-tolerance at the same time [6,11]. The existence of high network diversity suggests that network partitions may not be an issue if best of breed clouds offerings like Amazon AWS are used. Nevertheless, partitions should probably be accounted for and a relaxed consistency may be offered when an partition actually occurs. This is a current topic of research that we, however, do not address more in this paper.

3 Storage – DepSky

DepSky is a software library for implementing storage clouds-of-clouds [5][3]. With DepSky, a consumer can implement a virtual storage cloud. Such a service provides file storage with operations such as create file, read, write, delete file, etc. A DepSky cloud-of-clouds is built on top of a set of legacy, unmodified, storage clouds. Many storage clouds can be used but currently the library has an abstraction layer that supports only four: Amazon S3, Google Storage, Rackspace Files, and Windows Azure Blob Storage. DepSky provides all the properties mentioned in the introduction – availability, integrity, disaster-tolerance, no vendor lock-in – plus confidentiality (file content cannot be disclosed at a cloud).

The core of DepSky are a pair of protocols for reading and writing files in the clouds. These protocols have to tolerate unresponsive clouds, so they have to reason in terms of quorums of clouds, i.e., of subsets of the group of clouds that implements the cloud-of-clouds. Moreover, these protocols have to tolerate Byzantine faults for the reasons mentioned in the introduction. Therefore, DepSky is based on Byzantine quorum (replication) protocols [12]. In the following discussion we consider n clouds at most f of which can fail. DepSky requires $n > 3f$ (e.g., $n = 4$ with $f = 1$).

The key idea of the protocols is simple. To *write a file* in the cloud-of-clouds, the client (i.e., the DepSky library at the user node) first writes the file in (at least) $n - f$ clouds, then writes a file with metadata in the same clouds. The metadata file contains information such as a cryptographic signature and a version. To *read a file*, the client first reads the metadata file from $n - f$ clouds, picks one of the metadata files with the highest version and gets the file from that cloud. If the signature does not correspond to the file retrieved, the file may have been corrupted, so the user retrieves the file from some of the other clouds.

This basic scheme has two limitations: files are stored in clear in all clouds, so confidentiality is worse than if stored in a single cloud; the storage used is n times more than if a single cloud was used, so the cost is on average also n times more. A solution to both problems is for each file: (1) to disperse it in n parts using erasure codes; (2) to generate a random secret key; (3) to encrypt

[3] Online at `https://code.google.com/p/depsky/`

each part of the file with a symmetric encryption algorithm (e.g., AES) and the key; (4) to split the key in n shares using a secret sharing algorithm; and (5) to store one pair {file part, key share} in each cloud. This way individual clouds (more precisely, a collusion of up to f clouds) cannot disclose the key or rebuild the file, so confidentiality is enforced. Moreover, storage space is approximately two times the size of the file.

We did an extensive experimental evaluation of DepSky using four commercial clouds and clients placed around the world in PlanetLab nodes. The more interesting results are the latency, i.e., the time to complete a read or write operation. We compared DepSky's latency with the latencies of the individual commercial clouds. On the negative side, we observed that DepSky's write latency is close to the one of the cloud with worst latency, which was to be expected as DepSky writes in all clouds (or at least $n - f$). DepSky's read latency is close to the latency provided by the cloud with lowest latency, which is good because clouds are often used to distribute content (i.e., more for reading than for writing files).

Our experience with DepSky provides several insights about the design of clouds-of-clouds: (1) The protocols should be based on Byzantine quorum systems to allow reasoning about subsets of clouds and tolerating Byzantine faults. (2) Signed files can be verified so they can be read from a single cloud, possibly the fastest, which typically provides the lowest latency (but not always). (3) Erasure codes are a valuable mechanism to reduce the size of data stored so also the cost involved. (4) Secret sharing can be used to store cryptographic keys in clouds (and avoid a key distribution scheme).

4 Data Processing – BFT MapReduce

Storage is probably the simplest service provided by clouds as it can be abstracted in terms of a simple set of operations: read, write, create, etc. Processing data is arguably more complicated. MapReduce is a programming model and an execution environment for processing large data sets made public by Google in 2004 [10]. *BFT MapReduce* is a modification of Hadoop MapReduce [21] for clouds-of-clouds that aims to provide the attributes mentioned in the introduction: availability, integrity, disaster-tolerance, no vendor lock-in [9]. However, on the contrary to DepSky and EBAWA, it tolerates only accidental Byzantine faults, not malicious Byzantine faults.

Hadoop MapReduce is built to tolerate the most common faults. The job tracker detects and recovers crashed map/reduce tasks and files are stored with checksums to allow detecting their corruption. However, Byzantine faults can corrupt task executions, so these tasks can return wrong outputs. Moreover, if a job is executing in a cloud and there is an outage, the job has to be restarted somewhere else (if the input splits are available somewhere else).

BFT MapReduce uses task replication to solve the first problem and replication in different clouds to solve the second. Consider again n clouds, at most f of which can stop or corrupt tasks (the original scheme is more generic and allows tasks to be corrupted in any cloud but this aspect complicates the presentation so we omit it here). The scheme assumes that the splits are replicated in the n clouds and that $n > 2f$. Every split is processed by a map task in all clouds and all reduces are run in all clouds. The outputs of the replicas are voted and the result of the majority is accepted as correct (which is true due to the assumption of $n > 2f$). Even if a cloud fails the rest continue to execute the job.

This basic scheme has several performance and cost problems so we use three mechanisms to improve it. The first mechanism is to have one job tracker per cloud that controls the execution of tasks in its cloud. This solves the problem of controlling the execution of tasks from another cloud being a bad idea: the associated latency is high; the timeouts to detect if tasks failed have to be considerably higher (to limit wrong detections); the job tracker is a single point of failure.

The second mechanism is deferred execution: only $f + 1$ replicas of each task are executed as long as they all return the same output; when there is disagreement about the output, one or more additional replicas are executed (in other clouds). This reduces the resources needed to execute a job that have to be twice the original resources when there are no faults (if $f = 1$ then $f + 1 = 2$ replicas) or more (if $f > 1$).

The third mechanism is the one with the highest impact on the performance: digest communication. All reduce tasks have to fetch the outputs of all map tasks. When a reduce replica fetches the outputs of $f + 1$ replicas of the same map task it compares them and either accepts that output (if they are equal) or informs the job tracker that more replicas are needed. However, all map and reduce tasks are replicated so the number of outputs to fetch is typically large and fetching outputs through the Internet is slow. Moreover, these outputs can be large, for instance, of the same size of the inputs, therefore not only the delay but also the cost of taking this data out of a cloud will be high. The solution to this problem is to avoid transferring outputs between clouds: reduces only fetch cryptographic hashes (digests) of outputs from other clouds. These hashes are small (e.g., 32 bytes with SHA-256) and the comparison of hashes is equivalent to the comparison of the full outputs as they are collision-resistant [14].

Again our experience with BFT MapReduce provides several insights about the design of clouds-of-clouds: (1) Tasks can be replicated in different clouds to mask faulty executions and cloud failures. (2) Execution of some task replicas can be deferred to spare the resources used in some of the clouds. (3) Control components (the job tracker in this case) should be distributed to avoid control operations and failure detection between clouds and the associated high delays. (4) Whenever possible cryptographic hashes should be sent through the Internet instead of large messages, reducing communication latency and the cost of sending data out of the cloud.

5 Service Replication – EBAWA

Data storage (Section 3) and data processing using MapReduce (Section 4) are important but somewhat specific services for a cloud-of-clouds. *EBAWA* is a

Byzantine fault-tolerant state machine replication (SMR) algorithm for clouds-of-clouds [20][4]. SMR is a classical technique to make arbitrary services dependable (or fault-tolerant) through replication [17]. Example services that can be made dependable using SMR are databases, authentication services, coordination services, and file systems. Storage services and frameworks like MapReduce can also be made dependable this way but less efficiently than using the schemes presented in the previous two sections (e.g., more communication steps, more replicas). Similarly to BFT MapReduce, EBAWA provides availability, integrity, disaster-tolerance, and no vendor lock-in, but it tolerates both accidental and malicious Byzantine faults (as also does DepSky).

The idea of SMR is to replicate a service (a state machine) in n servers in such a way that if f become faulty the service continues operational (availability) and correct (integrity). For that to be possible the service has to be (or made) deterministic. Moreover, all replicas have to start in the same state and have to execute the same operations in the same order. The second aspect requires the use of a total order multicast protocol, which is the core of any SMR algorithm.

The first correct and efficient Byzantine fault-tolerant (BFT) SMR algorithm is known as PBFT [8]. This algorithm, however, was designed with LANs in mind. It has several communication steps (expensive when latency is high) and involves sending many messages. EBAWA is a BFT SMR algorithm like PBFT, but with a set of mechanisms for making it efficient in WANs, which make it adequate for clouds-of-clouds. In EBAWA replicas include a trusted module, the Unique Sequential Identifier Generator service (USIG). This is a local module that has to be implemented in such a way that it can be trusted, e.g., in hardware. The USIG service allows improving several of the characteristics of PBFT because it prevents certain kinds of faulty replica misbehavior: it prevents faulty replicas to send two different messages with the same identifier (an inconsistent fault). This allows to reduce the number of replicas from PBFT's $n > 3f$ to $n > 2f$. It also allows to reduce the number of communication steps by 1.

EBAWA differs from PBFT and similar algorithms by rotating its primary: the primary only orders one batch of requests, then the next replica becomes the primary. This prevents certain performance attacks [3], which are critical in WANs due to the need of using large timeouts (RTTs are much higher than in LANs). It reduces latency as clients can access the replica closest to them. Finally, it provides load balancing because the task of ordering messages is done by all replicas. EBAWA uses a third mechanism for efficiency in WANs: asynchronous views. The idea is that a replica starts an agreement as soon as it receives a client request by sending a prepare message. Replicas without pending client requests skip their turn by sending a special message.

We performed an extensive experimental evaluation of EBAWA in a real WAN (using PlanetLab), in an emulated WAN (Emulab), and in a LAN, showing interesting improvements of performance in comparison to PBFT.

---

[4] In fact EBAWA was designed before the trend on cloud computing so it was focused on the challenge of Byzantine fault-tolerant replication in wide-area networks. This, however, is the main challenge we are interested here in relation to clouds-of-clouds.

EBAWA provides several insights useful for the design of clouds-of-clouds: (1) The USIG service can be used to reduce the number of communication steps and improve the latency of the replicated service (by modifying the system model to include a trusted component). (2) The USIG service can be used to reduce the number of replicas, reducing the number of messages sent and the data sent out of the cloud (reducing the latency and the cost of sending data out). (3) Rotating the primary allows preventing performance attacks, client can access closest replica (reducing the latency), and load balancing. (4) Asynchronous views reduce waiting for the contacted replica to become the primary, so also the latency. (5) Waiting for $n - f$ replicas allows disregarding those with higher RTT, improving the latency.

6 Conclusion

The main argument of the paper is that clouds-of-clouds are a solution for consumers to create dependable and secure clouds on top of cloud offerings they do not trust enough. We have shown this with three cases: storage, data processing, and arbitrary services. A different question is if this solution is usable, due to its time and economic costs. Latency is an issue with clouds-of-clouds but it is also so with normal clouds. We have shown that it is possible to have cloud-of-cloud services with a latency of a few RTTs which is similar to what exists in a normal cloud (think of the delay of a simple HTTP access: 1.5 RTTs for the TCP 3-way handshake plus 0.5 RTTs for the reply, if we consider that the request goes with the last message of the handshake). In terms of costs, they are higher due to the use of more resources, but dependability and security are never free. Clouds-of-clouds seem to be a viable mechanism for dependability and security. If they will be adopted, the future will tell.

Acknowledgments. The three works discussed in this paper was done together with several colleagues and students: Fernando André, Alysson Bessani, Pedro Costa, Lau Cheuk Lung, Marcelo Pasin, Bruno Quaresma, Fernando Ramos, Paulo Sousa, Paulo Veríssimo, Giuliana Santos Veronese. This work was supported by national funds through FCT - Fundação para a Ciência e a Tecnologia, under project PEst-OE/EEI/LA0021/2013 (INESC-ID) and project PTDC/EIA-EIA/115211/2009 (RC-Clouds).

References

1. Amazon EC2 pricing, `http://aws.amazon.com/ec2/pricing/` (accessed August 15, 2013)
2. Amazon EC2 user guide – regions and availability zones, `http://docs.aws.amazon.com/AWSEC2/latest/UserGuide/using-regions-availability-zones.html` (accessed August 15, 2013)
3. Amir, Y., Coan, B., Kirsch, J., Lane, J.: Byzantine replication under attack. In: Proceedings of the IEEE/IFIP 38th International Conference on Dependable Systems and Networks, pp. 197–206 (June 2008)

4. Avizienis, A., Laprie, J.C., Randell, B., Landwehr, C.: Basic concepts and taxonomy of dependable and secure computing. IEEE Transactions on Dependable and Secure Computing 1(1), 11–33 (2004)
5. Bessani, A., Correia, M., Quaresma, B., André, F., Sousa, P.: DepSky: Dependable and secure storage in a cloud-of-clouds. In: Proceedings of the 6th ACM SIGOPS/EuroSys European Systems Conference, pp. 31–46 (April 2011)
6. Brewer, E.: Towards robust distributed systems. In: Proceedings of the 19th ACM Annual Symposium on Principles of Distributed Computing, pp. 7–10 (2000)
7. Cascella, R.G., Blasi, L., Jegou, Y., Coppola, M., Morin, C.: Contrail: Distributed application deployment under SLA in federated heterogeneous clouds. In: Galis, A., Gavras, A. (eds.) FIA 2013. LNCS, vol. 7858, pp. 91–103. Springer, Heidelberg (2013)
8. Castro, M., Liskov, B.: Practical Byzantine fault tolerance. In: Proceedings of the 3rd USENIX Symposium on Operating Systems Design and Implementation, pp. 173–186 (February 1999)
9. Correia, M., Costa, P., Pasin, M., Bessani, A., Ramos, F., Verissimo, P.: On the feasibility of Byzantine fault-tolerant MapReduce in clouds-of-clouds. In: Proceedings of the 1st International Workshop on Dependability Issues in Cloud Computing (October 2012)
10. Dean, J., Ghemawat, S.: MapReduce: simplified data processing on large clusters. In: Proceedings of the 6th USENIX Symposium on Operating Systems Design and Implementation, pp. 137–150 (December 2004)
11. Gilbert, S., Lynch, N.: Brewer's conjecture and the feasibility of consistent, available, partition-tolerant web services. ACM SIGACT News, 51–59 (June 2002)
12. Malkhi, D., Reiter, M.: Byzantine quorum systems. Distributed Computing 11(4), 203–213 (1998)
13. Nightingale, E.B., Douceur, J.R., Orgovan, V.: Cycles, cells and platters: an empirical analysis of hardware failures on a million consumer PCs. In: Proceedings of the 6th ACM SIGOPS/EuroSys European Systems Conference, pp. 343–356 (2011)
14. NIST: FIPS 180-2, Secure Hash Standard (August 2002)
15. Rabinovich, M., Rabinovich, I., Rajaraman, R., Aggarwal, A.: A dynamic object replication and migration protocol for an internet hosting service. In: Proceedings of the 19th IEEE International Conference on Distributed Computing Systems, pp. 101–113 (1999)
16. Rocha, F., Correia, M.: Lucy in the sky without diamonds: Stealing confidential data in the cloud. In: Proceedings of the 1st International Workshop on Dependability of Clouds, Data Centers and Virtual Computing Environments (2011)
17. Schneider, F.B.: Implementing fault-tolerant services using the state machine approach: A tutorial. ACM Computing Surveys 22(4), 299–319 (1990)
18. Schroeder, B., Pinheiro, E., Weber, W.D.: DRAM errors in the wild: a large-scale field study. In: Proceedings of the 11th International Joint Conference on Measurement and Modeling of Computer Systems, pp. 193–204 (2009)
19. Topchiy, S.: Testing Amazon EC2 network speed (March 2013), `http://epamcloud.blogspot.pt/2013/03/testing-amazon-ec2-network-speed.html` (accessed August 15, 2013)
20. Veronese, G.S., Correia, M., Bessani, A.N., Lung, L.C.: EBAWA: Efficient Byzantine agreement for wide-area networks. In: Proceedings of the IEEE 12th International Symposium on High-Assurance Systems Engineering, pp. 10–19 (November 2010)
21. White, T.: Hadoop: The Definitive Guide. O'Reilly (2009)

Towards Standardised SLAs

John Kennedy

Intel, Ireland
John.M.Kennedy@intel.com

Abstract. This paper introduces the concept of standardised Service Level Agreements. It describes the state of the art in four areas that need to be progressed to make standardised SLAs a commercial reality: SLA-aware interfaces, SLA data models, SLA vocabularies and legal frameworks. A summary of SLA-related initiatives within standards development organisations is also presented.

Keywords: Standards, Service Level Agreements, SLAs, Cloud Computing, Interfaces, Data Models, Vocabularies.

1 Introduction

As more and more business moves to the cloud, or has the potential to move to the cloud, the agreements between consumers and providers of cloud-based services become ever more important. These agreements define the service to be consumed, the quality of service to be provided, any restrictions on the usage of the service, and recourse should the agreed terms not be met by either party. Depending on the importance to the consumer of the service being hosted on the cloud, the often innocuous-looking set of terms and conditions can quickly become a Service Level Agreement (SLA) on which the viability of the consumer's business may depend. Similarly, the SLA becomes a significant document for cloud providers, differentiating them from their competition.

Businesses recognising the importance of their SLAs appreciate that they require careful consideration. Depending on the details, the consumers of the cloud may even decide to re-architect their systems to maximise their system availability given the nature of the commitments, and any compensation, the provider offers. From a provider perspective, any personalisation they can offer to accommodate the individual needs of their consumers may give them a competitive advantage. Careful monitoring of actual service performance versus SLA commitments may reveal opportunities to maximise internal efficiencies.

However, the number of clients of a cloud-scale provider typically means that personalised SLAs cannot be offered or accommodated. From a consumer point of view, significant manual effort must be spent reviewing the precise language in each of the SLAs offered by their potential providers. Each potential SLA needs to be reviewed by a person or team of people who can appreciate the legal, business and technical subtleties of the SLA.

D. an Mey et al. (Eds.): Euro-Par 2013 Workshops, LNCS 8374, pp. 105–113, 2014.

The labour-intensive nature of dealing with SLAs prevents providers from offering personalised SLAs, and consumers from easily identifying and comparing the offerings of their potential providers. The lack of standards for SLAs in cloud computing is frustrating adoption of the cloud.

Progress towards standardised SLAs is required to tackle this problem. There are several distinct areas in which progress is required. Interfaces need to be agreed so that SLA-related operations such as discovery, negotiation and agreement can be more automated. The SLAs need to have an agreed structure: an agreed SLA model. The terms inside the SLA need to have a shared understanding: an agreed vocabulary. The legal framework in which the SLA exists must also be robust and unambiguous.

This paper introduces the state of the art in these four areas. Some current and proposed standardisation initiatives related to SLAs are also introduced.

2 What Is an SLA?

The international standard for Information Technology Service Management, ISO/IEC 20000-1:2011 [1], formally defines an SLA to be "a documented agreement between the service provider and customer that identifies services and service targets". It further elaborates that an SLA "can also be established between providers and suppliers etc., can be included in a contract or other form of documented agreement.

Cloud SLAs obviously relate to services provided by a cloud service provider, and in practical terms often include not just definitions of services and service targets, but also details of things such as the recourse in the event of an SLA being broken, the nature of support available for the service, and any requirements that may be imposed on the consumer of the cloud.

In SLAware [2] the author Keven Kearney describes that "SLAs are negotiated agreements between service providers and customers specifying their respective responsibilities and obligations in respect of service delivery and service usage. In addition to providing details of agreement parties, services and SLA duration, SLAs may, among other things, specify prices & costs, quality of service & other performance objectives, help-desk details, schedules for regular maintenance, penalties for SLA violations, exclusion clauses and termination conditions".

The ISO sub-committee responsible for Cloud Computing standards, ISO/IEC JTC 1/SC 38 Distributed application platforms and services (DAPS) [3], is at the time of writing drafting a vocabulary for cloud computing which may include a formalised cloud-specific SLA definition.

In any event, commercial SLAs such as those for Amazon EC2 [4], Windows Azure [5] and Google Apps [6] are today arbitrary in nature. They are typically verbose, complex, static documents – sometimes nested – and of several pages in length. They are published by the cloud provider and describe details of services being offered from the cloud provider point of view.

The development of standards for SLAs has the potential to help automate discovery, negotiation, composition and monitoring of SLAs. The disposition of violations can also be automated. Cloud Consumers can be empowered with the ability to negotiate personalised SLAs tuned to their precise needs – against a selection of providers. Cloud providers can propose flexible offerings and appeal to a wider customer base. Given that various terms in each SLA can be automatically tracked and monitored, providers also have the opportunity to maximise internal efficiencies, safe in the knowledge that their myriad of SLA commitments are being met.

3 SLA-Aware Interfaces

SLAs must be discovered, retrieved, parsed, negotiated, approved, provisioned, monitored and complied with. To reduce or even remove the manual intervention currently required in these various phases of the SLA life-cycle, these various interactions need to be exposed through software interfaces. Whether the interactions are performed by software or by a person using a suitably streamlined user interface, the SLAs need to be exposed and be manipulated by software through an Application Programming Interface – an API.

To avoid unnecessary complication of the standards landscape in Cloud Computing, it is appropriate to consider whether existing standards in Cloud Management can be extended to be made SLA-aware. Two relevant standards currently exist: the Cloud Infrastructure Management Interface (CIMI) [7] published by the Distributed Management Task Force (DMTF) [8], and the Open Cloud Computing Interface (OCCI) [9] published by the Open Grid Forum (OGF) [10].

DMTF is a largely industry-driven organisation developing standards to resolve challenges in the management of distributed computing. CIMI is a relatively new standard designed to enable the management of cloud infrastructure. CIMI is completely focused on Infrastructure as a Service (IaaS) resource management and has IaaS specific semantics: concepts like Machines, Volumes and Networks are all explicitly defined in the formal specification. CIMI is thus designed to accommodate all the typical needs of today's cloud infrastructure stack. Additionally, it can be extended should a provider want to expose additional non-standardised functionality. Although support exists for monitoring, CIMI does not have support for broader SLA concerns at the moment. SLA support would be a valuable addition to the standard should CIMI start to be widely adopted.

OGF, largely an academic and research-institute driven standards organisation, is focused on the needs of the grid computing community. In an attempt to standardise the management of cloud resources, OCCI was first published in 2011, offering a generic RESTful API for managing remote resources. OCCI is a set of three standards (at the time of writing). These define a generic core model, an extension aimed at managing IaaS deployments in particular, and a HTTP rendering. OCCI is designed to be extensible, and so revisions of the formal standard are not required to introduce support for new functionality. There are implementations of OCCI for various cloud management stacks including OpenStack and OpenNebula, and the community is actively working on an XML rendering, a JSON rendering and a monitoring extension. There are tentative plans to extend the API with support for SLAs in 2014. The current intent is to allow SLAs to be defined, negotiated and agreed, and then assigned to particular provisioning requests. It should also be noted that OCCI is used as the core protocol for the CompatibleOne cloud brokering solution [11]. This open-source project has used the extension mechanism to allow SLA terms to be defined and passed between internal components, and brokered systems.

4 SLA Data Models

Whilst an SLA-aware API allows SLAs to be passed between consumers and providers, the internal structure of the SLA itself must also be agreed. There is a need for standardised SLA Data Models.

Numerous projects have begun to tackle this area and the European Commission's "Cloud Computing SLAs – Exploitation of Research Results" report [12] highlights the following research projects which have produced the associated assets that are listed below:

- 4CaaSt: Blueprint Concept
- BREIN: Semantic Annotation in SLA templates
- CloudScale: Scalability Specification
- Cloud-TM: SLA Definition and Enforcement in Transactional Data Stores
- CONTRAIL: SLA Specification and Quality Model
- EGI: Service Catalogue in a Federated Environment
- IRMOS: SLAs at Different Levels
- OPTIMIS: Service Manifest
- Q-ImPrESS: QoS-oriented SLA Specification
- PrestoPRIM : SLA Specification for Preservation Services (risk of data loss)
- SLA@SOI: Service Description
- VISION Cloud: Content-related Terms in SLAs

The SLA@SOI [13] project in particular was explicitly crafted to research, design and demonstrate machine readable SLAs over Service Oriented Infrastructure – now known as cloud computing. As well as constructing an SLA Framework for integration into IaaS offerings, it also tackled the challenge of defining a suitable SLA model.

The resulting model, SLA *, is a generic SLA model designed to accommodate arbitrary SLA terms. It can accommodate both functional and non-functional (e.g. monitoring) parameters, arbitrarily complex expressions, and arbitrary domain-specific vocabularies. It is an abstract model, and so can be rendered in arbitrary formats – BNF, XML, and JSON renderings have all been demonstrated. The most recent version of SLA * is described in the SLA@SOI SLA Management and Foundations deliverable [14]. Software to support the SLA Model has been published open source and is documented on the SLA@SOI SourceForge project wiki [15].

Whilst the SLA* Model focused on syntax, the ongoing FI-WARE [16] project, a European Commission supported Public Private Partnership project, has built on SLA* to develop a model that also comprehends semantics. SLAware is currently a work in progress, but a version has been made publically available [2]. It includes a line-by-line analysis of the Amazon WS SLA, with illustrated examples of how the various terms can be modelled using the SLAware model.

"Region Unavailable" and "Region Unavailability" means that more than one Availability Zone in which you are running an instance, within the same Region, is "Unavailable" to you.

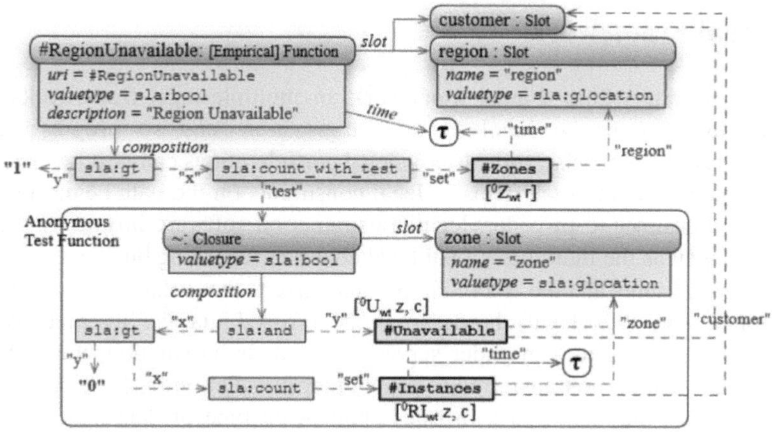

Fig. 1. A clause from the Amazon EC2 SLA, and the clause modelled using SLAware

5 SLA Vocabularies

Whilst an agreed SLA Model allows SLAs to be constructed, it primarily provides a structure and does not necessarily define the individual terms that may be included within. Both parties of an agreement must share an understanding of the terms in the SLA. This can only be achieved by agreeing on a common vocabulary.

There is the potential to agree common terms in a standardised, formal industry wide Cloud vocabulary, perhaps as an evolution to the one currently being developed jointly by ISO SC38 and the ITU-T SG13. However, to accommodate the possibility of arbitrary SLA terms being included in standardised SLAs, additionally flexibility is required. Communities of cloud consumers and providers will need the ability to define and manage their own domain-specific SLA vocabularies. This will allow clusters of cloud providers and consumers in domains such as healthcare, federal government, high-performance grid computing, and small and medium sized business to all maintain their own independent vocabularies, dealing with terms of importance to them, perhaps extending higher level vocabularies that have been agreed across the industry.

The SLA@SOI work previously referred to includes formal definitions of many cloud computing terms. Other related work includes the library of Open Data Center Alliance (ODCA) Usage Models [17] which documents numerous examples of how cloud consumers wish to consume Cloud Computing. The NIST Cloud Computing Technology Roadmap [18] illustrates both Business and Service Level Objectives that SLAs could be required to accommodate. The Intel Cloud Finder [19] is a comprehensive online tool that helps match cloud consumers with cloud providers based on a detailed list of questions which illustrate potential differentiators that should be accommodated in an SLA vocabulary.

6 Legal Framework

Businesses operate within a legal framework, or multiple legal frameworks should numerous jurisdictions be involved in a transaction, and so progress towards standardised SLAs must also address how legal considerations can best be met.

Legal aspects include such items as legal constraints on the data being transferred from cloud consumer to provider, legal constraints on software hosted by the cloud provider, as well as the more traditional legal concerns regarding business contracts.

These issues are all the more important given the relative ease at which international (and thus legal) borders can be crossed via the internet. Whilst a consumer may upload to a provider server within their jurisdiction, the technology exists for their data to be transferred to some other jurisdiction by the cloud provider. Each jurisdiction may have its own rules about what type of data may or may not cross national borders.

An additional level of complication arises in the European Union, where not just national laws apply, but European legislation reducing barriers to business is also relevant.

The European Commissioner for the Digital Agenda, Neelie Kroes, recognises these challenges for business and has acknowledged them in her Davos keynote address in January 2012: "Standards, certification, data protection, interoperability, lock-in, legal certainty and others [...] where these barriers exist, I am determined to overcome them". [20]

The European Commission have since published and launched a European Cloud Computing Strategy to "Unleash the potential of Cloud Computing in Europe" [21]. This strategy includes clarifying the "jungle of standards", and a European Cloud Partnership which will include a pre-commercial procurement consortium on which a commercial cloud ecosystem can be validated. From the legal point of view, the strategy is also specifically developing model safe and fair contract terms for the cloud. This latter initiative is now underway, and is expected to feed into the Cloud for Europe [22] project of the European Cloud Partnership [23] which is due to tender for partners to build its infrastructure during 2014.

7 SLA Standardisation Initiatives

Whilst the preceding discussion has focused mostly on the state of the art towards standardised SLAs, it is the standards development organisations (SDOs) that will ultimately ratify and publish any such standards. Several SDOs recognise this need and have recently become active in the field of standardised SLAs.

7.1 TM Forum

The TM Forum [24] have published numerous SLA-related documents including GB917 SLA Management Handbook, TR178 Enabling End to End Cloud SLA Management and TR197 Multi-Cloud Service Management Pack–SLA Business Blueprint. All are specifically designed to meet the particular SLA needs of the Telecommunications industry.

7.2 NIST

The recently published NIST Cloud Computing Standards Roadmap [25] discusses the potential for standardised SLAs. Version 2.0 of the NIST Cloud Computing Taxonomy, a work in progress, is expected to include a newly defined SLA taxonomy to support US Government procurement of Cloud Computing. Version 1.0 of the NIST Cloud Computing Technology Roadmap [18] includes SLA concept maps.

7.3 EU/ETSI

The European Commission has recently published a report summarising SLA related results from numerous research projects it has funded: Cloud Computing Service Level Agreements - Exploitation of Research Results [12]. It includes recommendations for the Commission's Cloud Select Industry Group on SLAs to consider, for potential rollup to the ETSI Cloud Standards Coordination (CSC) [26] initiative. The report details outputs from more than 21 projects and provides 11 specific recommendations for progressing SLAs. The ETSI CSC is coordinating the European strategy to address cloud standards.

7.4 OGF

The WS Agreement and WS-Agreement Negotiation standards can provide the basis for an SLA negotiation protocol. The OCCI working group [27] is planning to develop SLA extensions to the OCCI standard during 2014.

7.5 ISO

A New Work Item on SLA Framework and Terminology has been proposed. The scope for this work includes an overview of SLAs for Cloud Services, the relationship between a master agreement and SLAs, SLA components, commonly used terms, definitions and contexts. Note that a technically rich standard structure for SLAs is currently not in scope.

8 Conclusion

Progress towards standardised SLAs is required to maximise cost-effectiveness and efficiencies for Cloud Consumers and Providers alike. Ultimately this requires challenges to be addressed in the areas of SLA-aware cloud interfaces, SLA data models, SLA vocabularies, and legal frameworks. Although still in its infancy, progress is being made. Ultimately, significant federal initiatives such as the NIST suite of Cloud Computing initiatives and the European Cloud Computing Strategy may become the key drivers towards the standardisation of SLAs.

References

1. ISO/IEC 20000-1:2011 Information technology – Service management – Part 1: Service management system requirements, http://www.iso.org/iso/catalogue_detail?csnumber=51986
2. Kearney, K.T.: SLAware (January 2012), https://dl.dropbox.com/u/50697125/SLAware%20%28public%20May%202012%29.pdf
3. ISO/IEC JTC 1/SC 38 Distributed application platforms and services (DAPS), http://www.iso.org/iso/home/standards_development/list_of_iso_technical_committees/iso_technical_committee.htm?commid=601355
4. Amazon EC2 SLA, http://aws.amazon.com/ec2-sla/
5. Windows Azure SLA, http://www.windowsazure.com/en-us/support/legal/sla/
6. Google Apps SLA, http://www.google.com/apps/intl/en/terms/sla.html
7. Cloud Infrastructure Management Interface (CIMI) Model and RESTful HTTP-based Protocol, http://dmtf.org/standards/cloud
8. Distributed Management Task Force, Inc., http://dmtf.org
9. Open Cloud Computing Specification, http://occi-wg.org/about/specification/
10. Open Grid Forum, http://www.gridforum.org/
11. CompatibleOne, http://www.compatibleone.org
12. Cloud Computing Service Level Agreements - Exploitation of Research Results, http://ec.europa.eu/digital-agenda/en/news/cloud-computing-service-level-agreements-exploitation-research-results
13. SLA@SOI, http://sla-at-soi.eu/
14. SLA Management & Foundations (including the SLA* model), http://sla-at-soi.eu/results/models/
15. SLA Model Software Resources, http://sourceforge.net/apps/trac/sla-at-soi/wiki/SlaModel
16. FI-WARE, http://www.fi-ware.eu/

17. ODCA Usage Models, http://www.opendatacenteralliance.org/ourwork/usagemodels
18. NIST Cloud Computing Technology Roadmap, http://www.nist.gov/itl/cloud/upload/SP_500_293_volumeI-2.pdf
19. Intel Cloud Finder, http://www.intelcloudfinder.com/
20. Kroes, N.: Davos Switzerland (January 26, 2012), http://europa.eu/rapid/press-release_SPEECH-12-38_en.htm
21. European Cloud Computing Strategy, http://ec.europa.eu/digital-agenda/en/european-cloud-computing-strategy
22. Cloud for Europe, http://www.cloudforeurope.eu/
23. European Cloud Partnership, http://ec.europa.eu/digital-agenda/en/european-cloud-partnership
24. TM Forum, http://www.tmforum.org/
25. NIST Cloud Computing Standards Roadmap, http://www.nist.gov/itl/cloud/upload/NIST_SP-500-291_Jul5A.pdf
26. ETSI Cloud Standards Coordination, http://csc.etsi.org
27. OCCI Working Group, http://occi-wg.org/

First International Workshop on Federative and Interoperable Cloud Infrastructures (FedICI 2013)

Gabor Kecskemeti, Attila Kertesz, Attila Marosi, and Radu Prodan

Program Chairs

Infrastructure as a Service (IaaS) cloud systems allow the dynamic creation, destruction and management of Virtual Machines (VM) on virtualized clusters. IaaS clouds provide a high-level of abstraction to the end user that allows the creation of on-demand services through a pay as you go infrastructure combined with elasticity. As a result, many academic infrastructure service providers have started transitions to add cloud resources to their previously existing campus and shared grid deployments. To complete such solutions, they should also support the unification of multiple cloud and/or cloud and grid solutions in a seamless, preferably interoperable way. Hybrid, community or multi-clouds may utilize more than one cloud system, which are also called as a cloud federations. The management of such federations raise several challenges and open issues that require significant research work to be done in this area.

The 1st Workshop on Federative and Interoperable Cloud Infrastructures (FedICI 2013) aimed at bringing together scientists in the fields of High-Performance Computing and Cloud Computing to provide a dedicated forum for sharing the latest results, exchanging ideas and experiences, presenting new research, development and management of interoperable, federated IaaS cloud systems. The goal of the workshop was to help the community with defining the current state, determining further goals and presenting architectures and service frameworks to achieve highly interoperable federated cloud infrastructures. Priority was given to submissions that focus on presenting solutions to interoperability and efficient management challenges faced by current and future infrastructure clouds.

The Call for Papers for the FedICI workshop was launched early in the year 2013, and at the passing of the submission deadline we had received 10 submissions, which were of good quality and generally relevant to the theme of the workshop. The papers were swiftly and expertly reviewed by the program committee, each of them receiving at least three qualified reviews. The program chair thanks the whole of the program committee and the additional reviewers for the time and expertise they put into the reviewing work, and for getting it all done within the rather strict time limit. Final decision on acceptance was made by the program chair and co-chairs based on the recommendations from the program committee. Being an half-day event, there was room for accepting only 5 of the contributions, resulting in an acceptance ratio of 50%. All the accepted contributions were presented at the workshop yielding an interesting discussion on the role that federated management may play in the broad research field of

D. an Mey et al. (Eds.): Euro-Par 2013 Workshops, LNCS 8374, pp. 114–115, 2014.

Cloud Computing. Presentations were organized in two sessions: in the former two papers discussing live migration and load balancing issues of data centers, and federation capabilities of the BonFIRE testbed were presented, while in the latter three papers describing scientific workflow management in multi-clouds, quality of service guarantees through federation-wide SLAs and work towards an operational setup of the Swiss National Research Infrastructure as a national, heterogeneous federated cloud were presented. This post-workshop proceedings includes the final versions of the presented FedICI papers, taking the feedback from reviewers and workshop audience into account.

The program chairs sincerely thank the Euro-Par organizers for providing the opportunity to arrange the FedICI workshop in conjunction with the 2013 conference. The program chairs also warmly thank MTA SZTAKI and Euro-Par for their financial support making it possible to organize the workshop. Also, the chairs would like to thank the no-cost sponsorship of the Open Grid Forum that brought the workshop great publicity. Finally, the program chairs thank all attendees at the workshop, who contributed to a successful scientific day. Based on the mostly positive feedback, the program chairs and organizers plan to continue the FedICI workshop in conjunction with Euro-Par 2014.

Adaptive Live Migration to Improve Load Balancing in Virtual Machine Environment

Peng Lu, Antonio Barbalace, Roberto Palmieri, and Binoy Ravindran

ECE Department, Virginia Tech, USA
{lvpeng,antoniob,robertop,binoy}@vt.edu

Abstract. Load balancing is one of the main challenges in a Virtual Machine (VM) Environment in order to ensure equal utilization of all the available resources while avoiding overloading a subset of machines. In this paper, we propose an efficient load balancing strategy based on VM live migration. Unlike previous work, our strategy records the history of mappings to inform future placement decisions. We also apply a workload-adaptive live migration algorithm in order to minimize VM downtime and improve the user experience. The evaluation shows that our load balancing technique is faster than previous approaches, thus reducing the decision generating latency by as much as 79%. Furthermore, the results also show that we provide minimal downtime. Compared with competitors, our proposed migration mechanism reduces the downtime by up to 73%.

1 Introduction

Virtual machine (VM) environments, where multiple physical machines and VMs are interconnected via increasingly fast networking technologies, are becoming extremely popular for providing on-demand computational services and high availability. One of the most interesting features is that the pool of available resources (CPU, virtual memory, secondary storage, etc.) can be shared between all the machines through the available interconnections. Several previous works [10,13,17] observed that many resources are actually unused for a considerable amount of the operational time. Therefore, inter-machine load balancing is of great interest in order to avoid situations where some machines are overloaded while others are idle or under-used.

Traditionally, there are several ways to achieve load balancing in networked systems. One straightforward solution is static load balancing, which assigns applications at the beginning. The efficiency of this strategy depends on the accuracy of the prior prediction. A dynamic load balancing strategy can be exploited by migrating processes at run time among different machines in a networked environment, rather than limiting the applications to run on the machine where they are first assigned. To overcome the limitations imposed by process migration, traditionally used in cluster environments, an OS-level methodology that migrates all the running applications together with their hosting OS was presented. This methodology attracted more attention than process migration,

D. an Mey et al. (Eds.): Euro-Par 2013 Workshops, LNCS 8374, pp. 116–125, 2014.

especially through a technique called VM live migration [9]. Live migration is migrating a VM from the source Virtual Machine Monitor (VMM) to the target VMM (usually running on a different host machine) without halting the migrating guest operating system. Most state-of-the-art/practice VMMs (e.g., Xen [7], VMware [22], KVM [1]) provide live migration mechanisms today. Unlike process migration, VM live migration transfers the virtual CPU and emulated devices' state and the guest OS memory data all together. Live migration is the enabling technology behind many beneficial features such as load balancing, transparent mobility, and high availability services. In addition, because it relies on VMM to make a clean separation between hardware and software, live migration also aids in aspects such as fault tolerance, application concurrency, and consolidation management.

VM live migration has several advantages regarding the load balancing problem. A VM hosting several different running applications on a heavily loaded machine can be migrated to another VMM laying idle on another machine in order to exploit the availability of all the resources. Also, adopting live migration instead of a stop and resume migration mechanism natively ensures minimal downtime and it minimally interrupts the VM user's interaction. Here, the downtime is defined as the waiting time between when the VM is unusable by the users (stopped on the source VMM) and when the VM is working again (resumed on the target VMM). We believe a good load balancing strategy should provide minimal downtime for users.

This paper makes the following contributions:

1. We propose a fast and efficient centralized load balancing framework based on history records. The evaluation shows that our load balancing technique is an effective method, while it also reduces the decision generating latency as much as 79% compared with previous approaches.

2. We apply a workload-adaptive approach to provide minimal downtime for different kinds of applications. Results show that our proposed migration mechanism reduces the downtime by up to 73% compared to competitors.

The rest of the paper is organized as follows: Section 2 discusses past and related work. Section 3 presents the design and implementation of our load balancing and live migration mechanism. Section 4 reports our experimental environment, benchmarks used, and evaluation results. We conclude and discuss future work in Section 5.

2 Related Work

The general problem of load balancing in a networked environment has been examined for decades using different strategies [8,11,21]. In user space, Ansel *et. al.* [6] allow dynamic migration of processes by checkpointing and restart. Heo *et. al.* [24] rely on the cooperation between the process and the migration subsystem to achieve its migration. The problem in these user space implementations is that without kernel access, they are unable to migrate processes with location dependent information and interprocess communication.In kernel space, implementations like [14, 23] allow the migration process to be done more quickly and are able to migrate processes with dependencies. Compared with user space process migration, they provide better performance. Although kernel space process migration techniques are more efficient, they require modifications to the operating system kernel.

Some research has been proposed to improve the load balancing performance using VM live migration. Different works [12, 15, 16, 18, 20, 25] use a prediction method to forecast future resource demands based on the current resource utilization. However, in order to get an accurate prediction, these works need to obtain and analyze the system performance continuously, which introduces overhead. Our load balancing strategy doesn't make predictions in advance; instead, we always update and refer to the history record to assist in generating the final decision. Furthermore, previous work didn't consider the migration cost, and the downtime performance is not evaluated in their experimental results. One of our contributions is to design an adaptive VM migration mechanism in order to provide minimal downtime for different kinds of applications. Additionally, we characterize and quantify the downtime, and present the results in Section 4.2.

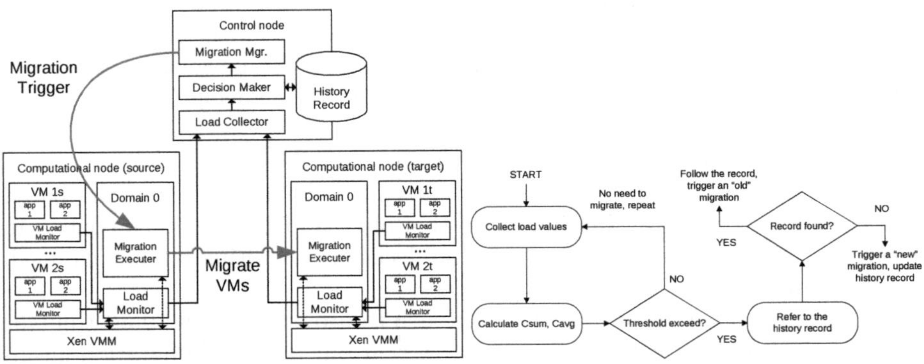

(a) The architecture of DCbalance. (b) Execution flow of DCbalance.

Fig. 1. DCbalance framenwork

3 Design and Implementation

3.1 Load Balancing Algorithm

Our prototype includes several machines which are linked by a network (Figure 1a). We choose one machine as the control node running only the load balancing strategy. The other machines are used as computational nodes with several VMs running on top of them. The load balancing mechanism is centralized: the control node runs the cloud management software that controls all the nodes running VMs.

From a system-level point of view, when a node is heavily-loaded while others are lightly-loaded, the imbalance problem emerges and it's time to generate a load balancing decision. The dynamic load balancing strategy continuously attempts to reduce the differences among all the nodes, by migrating VMs from heavily-loaded to lightly-loaded nodes. Figure 1b breaks down our strategy into steps, which are explained below.

1. **Collect the load values on each computational node.** In this paper we focus on CPU load-balancing and memory load-balancing of different nodes in a VM environment. We model each node as a gray box, which provides different interfaces to live record CPU and memory load information for each node and each running virtual machine.

   We use two methods to measure the load value at user level in Linux: by either using the Linux syscall `sysinfo()`, or reading the information residing in the `proc` file system. For CPU information we check the total `jiffies` that the processor spent executing each VM and the physical machine as well, and compute the utilization percentage for each part. For memory information we record the page operations per second, for example, the number of page faults requiring a page to be loaded into memory from disk.
2. **Determine whether to trigger the live migration or not.** After the control node collects the load values from all computational nodes, the total and average utilizations of all the machines involved in load balancing are computed. We adopt a threshold based strategy for deciding when virtual machines should be migrated between the nodes. The VM live migration will be triggered if C_m, the mean value of the sum of the maximum and minimum distances (respectively $C_{diff_{max}}$ and $C_{diff_{min}}$) from the average utilization (C_{avg}), is greater than a threshold T. C_i is the total CPU utilization of the ith computational node, $i \in 1,..,n$; n is the current number of nodes in the VM environment.

   $$C_{avg} = \frac{1}{n}\sum_{i=1}^{n} C_i$$
   $$C_{diff_i} = C_i - C_{avg}$$
   $$C_{diff_{max}} = \max_{i\in\{1,..,n\}} C_{diff_i}$$
   $$C_{diff_{min}} = \min_{i\in\{1,..,n\}} C_{diff_i}$$
   $$C_m = (C_{diff_{max}} + C_{diff_{min}})/2$$
3. **Schedule the live migration by checking the load balancing history record.** Whenever a migration is triggered, the control node checks the history record for a similar CPUs utilization scenario, i.e. a similar load distribution on the computational nodes. Note that the same C_{avg} doesn't ensure the same CPU utilizations scenario; the mapping is the key. If a previous record exists, we can schedule the VM live migration by choosing the same source and destination nodes. If several similar records exist, we just follow the latest record and schedule the migration. If we can't find such a record, the current situation is totally new and the nodes with C_i value close to $C_{diff_{max}}$ are used as sources, while the nodes with C_i value close to $C_{diff_{min}}$ are used as destinations of the live migration. After the migration, we add such situation (or mapping) as a new entry in the history record.

3.2 Workload Adaptive Live Migration

As opposed to previous works, we aim to provide load balancing with minimal downtime via virtual machine live migration. We focus on effectively balancing the usage of two kinds of resources: the CPU and memory. In our preliminary experiments, however, we found that a general VM live migration mechanism doesn't work well in all cases, such as when dealing with a memory-intensive application. Therefore, we implement a workload-adaptive migration mechanism.

- **Generic application live migration.** By "generic" we mean that there is no memory-intensive workload running in the guest VM, but rather a mixed workload, like Apache [4]. In this case the live migration is implemented by exploiting the pre-copy technique [9,19], however, we compress the dirty memory data before transmitting it. Compressed data takes less time to be transferred through the network. In addition, network traffic due to migration is significantly reduced when less data is transferred between different computational nodes. The technique is summarized in the following.
  1. After the migration is triggered, all the memory pages of the selected VM are transmitted from the source node to the target node while the VM is still running (first migration epoch).
  2. For subsequent migration epochs, the mechanism checks the dirty bitmap to determine which memory pages have been updated during the epoch. Only the newly updated pages are transmitted. The VM continues to run on the source node during these epochs.
  3. Before transmitting in every epoch, the presence of dirty data is checked in an address-indexed cache of previously transmitted pages. If there is a cache hit, the whole page (including this memory block) is XORed with the previous version, and the differences are Run-Length Encoded (RLE). Only the differences (*delta*) from a previous transmission of the same memory data are transmitted.
  4. For the memory data which is not present in the cache we apply a general-purpose quick compression technique implemented in zlib [5].
  5. When this mechanism is no longer beneficial, the VM is stopped on the source node, the remaining data (left pages, CPU registers and device states, etc.) is transmitted to the target node, and the VM is resumed there.
- **Memory-intensive applications live migration.** When dealing with memory-intensive applications in which memory is updated at high frequency, the above presented live migration doesn't work well because it leads to unacceptable overheads. Assume a memory page is frequently updated by a memory-intensive application; its updated copy will be compressed and transferred on each migration epoch. It could be worse considering that a VM can be assigned up to several gigabytes of memory to run the guest OS. Therefore, to load balance workloads characterized by memory-intensive applications, we propose another live migration technique described in the following.

1. After the migration is triggered, all the memory pages of the selected VM are compressed and transmitted from source to the target node while the VM is still active.
2. The VM is then suspended on the source node until a minimal and necessary execution state (or checkpoint) of the VM (including CPU state, registers, and some non-pageable data structures in memory) has been transmitted to the target and resumed there.
3. On the target node, if the resumed VM tries to access a memory page that has not been updated, a page fault will be generated and redirected towards the source. The source node will respond to the fault by fetching the corresponding memory pages, then compressing and transmitting them to the target node (we adopt the same compression method described above).

When the applications running in the VM are mostly memory-intensive, this design ensures that each memory page is compressed and transmitted at maximum twice during a migration. Additionally, if the workload is read-intensive most memory data is only transmitted once.

4 Experimental Evaluation

Our experimental environment includes five machines: one is used as the control node, and the other four (computational nodes) are running the guest VMs. Each computational node is configured with an Intel i5 processor running at 2.3GHz with either 4GB or 6GB of RAM. All machines are connected by a 1Gb Ethernet switch. Our load balancing strategy and migration mechanisms are based on Xen(3.4.0). The operating system (installed on each of the five machines and guest VMs) is Centos 5.2 with the Linux 2.6.18.8 kernel. We refer to our load balancing framework as *DCbalance*. Our competitors include OSVD [16] and DLB [15]. OSVD is also based on VM live migration and integrates performance prediction mechanism. DLB implements a dynamic load balancing algorithm [15] deployed into Xen's original live migration mechanism. We split the performance evaluation in two: a first section about our load balancing strategy and another section about the proposed migration mechanism.

4.1 Load Balancing Strategies Comparison

For this evaluation we run the MPI version of the NPB test suite [2]. We present here the results about the embarrassing parallel (EP) test. EP is a compute-bound benchmark with few network communications [2]. Initially we let each computational node run the same number of VMs. The total workload is divided and assigned to all the VMs on the 4 nodes. We let *node1* execute 50% of the total workload while the remaining 3 nodes execute the rest (16.6% each). Obviously *node1* is overloaded. Each node runs 8 VMs with 256MB assigned as guest memory. Initially the workload assigned to each node is distributed to the VMs

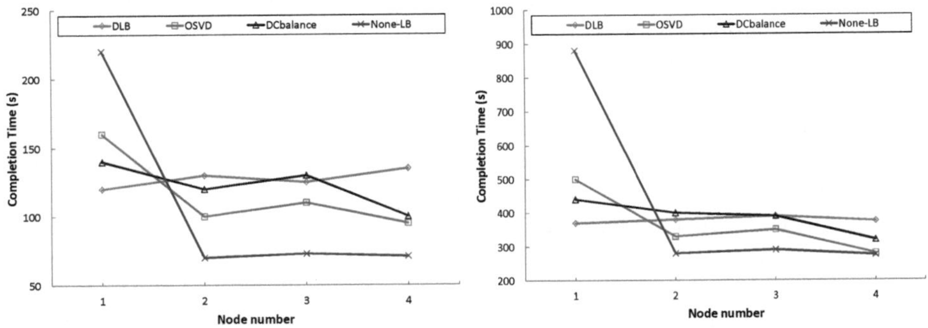

(a) Running NPB-EP.C program (b) Running NPB-EP.D program

Fig. 2. Workload completion time comparison on different problem data sizes

running on the that node. In this experiment we set the threshold T to 0.1 (see Section 3.1).

We first compare the three load balancing strategies with the case that no load balancing strategy is used. Figure 2a shows the completion times when running the class C problem size of the NPB-EP benchmark, "none-LB" is the case in which no load balancing strategy is applied to the workload. The x-axis refers to the node number while the y-axis is the workload completion time in seconds. As mentioned above, initially each node has 8 VMs on average and *node1* is overloaded with half of the total workload. Without any load balancing strategy, *node1* took close to 220 seconds to complete the workload while all other nodes took only about 70 seconds each. When applying any of the three load balancing strategies, however, all the nodes exhibit relatively consistent completion times because the VM(s) on the overloaded node were already migrated to other nodes. We observe that compared with other published load balancing algorithms, DCbalance achieves similar performance. Figure 2b shows the same evaluation but on a larger dataset. Our load balancing strategy can still provide comparable performance when dealing with the larger problem.

Table 1. Workload percentage after migration and triggering latency comparison

LB strategy	#1 Load	#2 Load	#3 Load	#4 Load	Triggering latency
DLB	24%	25%	26%	25%	2.2s
OSVD	27%	35%	17%	21%	3.1s
DCbalance	28%	26%	23%	21%	0.63s
DCbalance-nh	29%	25%	27%	19%	1.09s

We also compare the triggering latency of each load balancing strategy; i.e. the elapsed time between the collection of load information and the time when the decision is generated. We compute the workload percentage as well as the

VMs load values on each node after the migration finish. In this test we used a history record of (the most recent) 20 entries. To evaluate the benefits of the history record, we add another competitor: *DCbalance-nh*, which is our load balancing design without any history record (we set the number of entries to zero). Table 1 shows the results under four load balancing strategies. From the numbers we observe that the DLB algorithm outperforms the others but it needs longer time to generate the decision. The OSVD system incurs even more time due to prediction overhead, and we can also observe that its final decision is not as balanced as DLB. Compared with these two strategies, the main benefit of our strategy is the short time needed for finding the solution, which reduce the triggering latency by as much as 79% compared with the OSVD system. We also observe that it is an efficient method, as the migration decision is comparably fair. From the differences between DCbalance and DCbalance-nh, we conclude that by referring to the history record we gain performance improvements by more quickly generate the migration decision.

4.2 Migration Mechanisms Comparison

We evaluate the performance of migrating VMs running two types of workloads: "generic", by runing the Apache [4] webserver and "memory-intensive", by running Sysbench [3] (e.g., 25% read operations and 75% write operations). We let each node run 4 VMs with the same assigned memory size. We conduct the evaluation while varying the guest memory size from 128MB to 512MB, in order to investigate the impact of memory size on the downtime and other performance characteristics. To verify the effectiveness of our adaptive migration mechanism we again add another competitor, *DCbalance-i*. We refer to our migration design for generic applications as DCbalance, whereas we refer to its improved version which better handles memory-intensive applications as DCbalance-i.

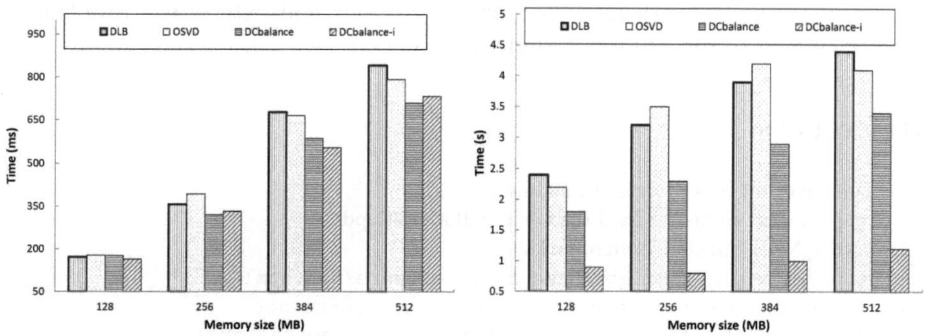

(a) Downtime under Apache (b) Downtime under Sysbench

Fig. 3. Downtime comparison under different workloads

Figure 3a shows the downtime results for the Apache benchmark for four migration mechanisms with three different sizes of assigned guest memory. We observe that all four mechanisms incur minimal downtime (within 1 second). However, because our proposed mechanism further reduces the data to be transmitted by compressing it before migration, it leads to lower downtime numbers. As the assigned guest memory goes up, the gap becomes larger, with a 17% reduction under the 512MB case. Another observation is that there is no obvious difference between the results of DCbalance and DCbalance-i. This is because the DCbalance-i is designed for memory-intensive applications but the Apache benchmark is not memory bounded.

Figure 3b shows the downtime results in the same cases as Figure 3a while running a memory-intensive workload (Sysbench benchmark) which updates the guest memory at high frequency. The findings are clearly different from the previous case. DCbalance still performs better than DLB and OSVD, which incur several seconds each; it reduces the downtime by roughly 35%. However, the DCbalance-i is by far the best mechanism, as it maintains a downtime around 1s in all cases. The downtime is reduced by 73% compared with DLB and OSVD.

5 Conclusion

Our strategy is proven to be fast and efficient as a load balancing approach. Instead of making predictions in advance, we refer to a history record to help schedule the VM migration. Decision generation is up to 79% faster than competitors. Moreover, we apply a workload-adaptive migration mechanism to provide minimal downtime for different kinds of applications, so as to improve the user experience. Results show that our proposed migration mechanism reduces the downtime by up to 73% in comparison to competitors. Future work includes combining the network topology and network communication monitoring with our proposed method in order to make network-aware mapping decisions (and thus reduce the network traffic). Furthermore, we will extend the problem of load balancing to distributed VM environments.

References

1. Kvm: Kernel based virtual machine, `http://www.redhat.com/f/pdf/rhev/DOC-KVM.pdf`
2. NASA NAS Parallel Benchmarks, `http://www.nas.nasa.gov/Resources/Software/npb.html`
3. Sysbench benchmark, `http://sysbench.sourceforge.net`
4. The Apache HTTP Server Project, `http://httpd.apache.org/`
5. Zlib memory compression library, `http://www.zlib.net`
6. Ansel, J., Arya, K., Cooperman, G.: Dmtcp: Transparent checkpointing for cluster computations and the desktop. In: IEEE International Symposium on Parallel Distributed Processing, IPDPS 2009, pp. 1–12 (2009)
7. Barham, P., Dragovic, B., Fraser, K., Hand, S., Harris, T., Ho, A., Neugebauer, R., Pratt, I., Warfield, A.: Xen and the art of virtualization. In: SOSP (2003)

8. Caron, E., Desprez, F., Muresan, A.: Forecasting for grid and cloud computing on-demand resources based on pattern matching. In: 2010 IEEE Second International Conference on Cloud Computing Technology and Science, CloudCom (2010)
9. Clark, C., Fraser, K., Hand, S., Hansen, J.G., Jul, E., Limpach, C., Pratt, I., Warfield, A.: Live migration of virtual machines. In: NSDI (2005)
10. Curino, C., Jones, E.P., Popa, R.A., Malviya, N., Wu, E., Madden, S., Balakrishnan, H., Zeldovich, N.: Relational Cloud: A Database Service for the Cloud. In: 5th Biennial Conference on Innovative Data Systems Research, Asilomar, CA (2011)
11. Curino, C., Jones, E.P., Madden, S., Balakrishnan, H.: Workload-aware database monitoring and consolidation, pp. 313–324 (2011)
12. Heo, J., Zhu, X., Padala, P., Wang, Z.: Memory overbooking and dynamic control of xen virtual machines in consolidated environments. In: Proceedings of the 11th IFIP/IEEE INM, IM 2009, pp. 630–637. IEEE Press, Piscataway (2009)
13. Hui, M., Jiang, D., Li, G., Zhou, Y.: Supporting database applications as a service. In: Proceedings of the 2009 IEEE International Conference on Data Engineering, ICDE 2009, Washington, DC, USA, pp. 832–843 (2009)
14. Hursey, J., Mattox, T.I., Lumsdaine, A.: Interconnect agnostic checkpoint/restart in open mpi. Technical report, New York, NY, USA (2009)
15. Jain, P., Gupta, D.: An algorithm for dynamic load balancing in distributed systems with multiple supporting nodes by exploiting the interrupt service. International Journal of Recent Trends in Engineering 1(1), 232–236 (2009)
16. Li, Z., Luo, W., Lu, X., Yin, J.: A live migration strategy for virtual machine based on performance predicting. In: 2012 International Conference on Computer Science Service System (CSSS), pp. 72–76 (August 2012)
17. Liu, C., Loo, B.T., Mao, Y.: Declarative automated cloud resource orchestration, pp. 26:1–26:8 (2011)
18. Lu, P., Ravindran, B., Kim, C.: Enhancing the performance of high availability lightweight live migration. In: Fernàndez Anta, A., Lipari, G., Roy, M. (eds.) OPODIS 2011. LNCS, vol. 7109, pp. 50–64. Springer, Heidelberg (2011)
19. Nelson, M., Lim, B.H., Hutchins, G.: Fast transparent migration for virtual machines. In: ATEC 2005, Berkeley, CA, USA, p. 25 (2005)
20. Song, Y., Li, Y., Wang, H., Zhang, Y., Feng, B., Zang, H., Sun, Y.: A service-oriented priority-based resource scheduling scheme for virtualized utility computing. In: Sadayappan, P., Parashar, M., Badrinath, R., Prasanna, V.K. (eds.) HiPC 2008. LNCS, vol. 5374, pp. 220–231. Springer, Heidelberg (2008)
21. Subrata, R., Zomaya, A.Y., Landfeldt, B.: Cooperative power-aware scheduling in grid computing environments, Orlando, FL, USA, vol. 70, pp. 84–91. Academic Press, Inc. (February 2010)
22. Waldspurger, C.A.: Memory resource management in vmware esx server. SIGOPS Oper. Syst. Rev. 36, 181–194 (2002)
23. Walters, J., Chaudhary, V.: Replication-based fault tolerance for mpi applications. IEEE Transactions on Parallel and Distributed Systems (2009)
24. Wang, C., Mueller, F., Engelmann, C., Scott, S.L.: Proactive process-level live migration in hpc environments. In: Proceedings of the 2008 ACM/IEEE conference on Supercomputing, SC 2008, Piscataway, NJ, USA, pp. 43:1–43:12 (2008)
25. Xu, J., Zhao, M., Fortes, J., Carpenter, R., Yousif, M.: Autonomic resource management in virtualized data centers using fuzzy logic-based approaches. Cluster Computing 11(3), 213–227 (2008)

Cloud and Network Facilities Federation in BonFIRE

David García-Pérez[1], Juan Ángel Lorenzo del Castillo[2], Yahya Al-Hazmi[3], Josep Martrat[1], Konstantinos Kavoussanakis[4], Alastair C. Hume[4], Celia Velayos López[5], Giada Landi[6], Tim Wauters[7], Michael Gienger[8], and David Margery[9]

[1] Atos Research and Innovation Group, Barcelona, Spain
[2] Hewlett-Packard Laboratories, Bristol, United Kingdom
[3] Chair of Next Generation Networks, Technical University Berlin, Berlin, Germany
[4] EPCC, University of Edinburgh, King's Buildings, Edinburgh, United Kingdom
[5] Distributed Applications and Networks Area, i2CAT Foundation, Barcelona, Spain
[6] Nextworks s.r.l., Pisa, Italy
[7] Department of Information Technology, Ghent University, iMinds, Ghent, Belgium
[8] High Performance Computing Center Stuttgart (HLRS), Stuttgart, Germany
[9] INRIA Rennes - Bretagne Atlantique Research Center, Rennes, France

Abstract. In recent years we have seen how Cloud Computing is changing the way of doing businesses and how services are delivered over the Internet. This disruption is a major challenge for Service Providers and Independent Software Vendors when creating new services and software applications for the Cloud. BonFIRE[1] offers a federated, multi-site cloud testbed to support large-scale testing of applications, services and systems. This is achieved by federating geographically distributed, heterogeneous clouds testbeds where each exposes unique configuration and/or features while giving to the experimenters (users) an homogeneous way to interact with the facility. All those testbeds are controlled by a central set of services commonly denominated "Broker". Additionally, BonFIRE is federated with different network facilities like the Virtual Wall, FEDERICA and AutoBAHN to provide high-level interfaces to network control functionality, in order to simulate diverse network QoS scenarios, enabling vertical federation.

Keywords: Multi-cloud, Federation, Future Internet, Services, Testbed, Bandwidth on Demand, Network QoS.

1 Introduction

Cloud computing is steadily gaining significance not only in the field of IT infrastructure and service hosting and operation, but also in telecommunication services. This encourages cloud providers to develop new technologies to enhance their services in order to increase customer satisfaction on the one hand; and

[1] `http://www.bonfire-project.eu`

D. an Mey et al. (Eds.): Euro-Par 2013 Workshops, LNCS 8374, pp. 126–135, 2014.

to promote strategies to build new business models on the other. In this market, cloud service providers, having different kinds of resources offering different levels of service quality, succeed not only by competition but also by collaboration between each other. There are several advantages of such collaborations for both cloud service suppliers and cloud service customers. Among the advantages for cloud service providers are complementarity of the offered resources to improve resource utilization; and combination of services in order to offer efficient end-to-end solutions. On the other hand, customers have the ability to combine resources and services from different cloud computing providers to create their own environments [1].

Cloud service providers might offer different types of services, with different APIs, various delivery conditions and prices, etc. Therefore, collaboration across cloud infrastructures that interoperate requires mechanisms for resource federation. Federated resources have to be managed at the federation level so as to be offered to users in as uniform a fashion as possible. Several resource management mechanisms are to be specified and standardized at the federation level: resource description, discovery, reservation, provisioning, orchestration, monitoring, and release. Furthermore, mechanisms are required for authentication and authorization, resource control and information exchange across cloud infrastructures.

To this end, cloud federation [2–4] architectures should be designed to include the necessarily mechanisms and fulfill all collaboration requirements. The different Cloud federation architectures proposed in the literature [5] can be classified into three different models as follows:

- **Cloud aggregation:** [6] different partners cooperate to integrate their cloud infrastructures into a unique virtual facility. This architecture usually requires a higher degree of coupling.
- **Cloud bursting or Hybrid Clouds:** [7, 8] combines the existing on premise infrastructure (private cloud) with resources of one or more public clouds.
- **Brokering:** [6] employs a central "broker" component that intermediates between user requests and several Cloud infrastructures.

There are many challenges related to cloud federation that affect interoperability (e.g. different APIs) and portability (e.g. different VM formats) [9].

BonFIRE [10] offers a Future Internet, Federated testbed, that supports large-scale testing of applications, services and systems over multiple, geographically distributed, heterogeneous Cloud and network testbeds. The design of BonFIRE is based in four pillars: Observability, Control, Advanced Features, and Easy of Use. The BonFIRE infrastructure gives the experimenters the ability to control and monitor the execution of their experiments to a degree that is not found in traditional Cloud facilities. The available testbeds allow the evaluation of cross-cutting effects of converged service and network infrastructures. In order to do so, the testbeds expose a set of capabilities beyond those normally provided by production cloud services in a commercial environment, enabling what we define as "Research by Experimentation". In terms of classification, BonFIRE employs a central broker to expose a homogeneous API and interact with the testbeds.

Additionally, BonFIRE includes and federates with private and public clouds and can thus be used to model cloud-bursting scenarios.

The remainder of the paper is structured as follows; Section 2 introduces the different facilities federated and the reason why Brokering was selected as federation solution. Section 3 presents the BonFIRE federation architecture. Section 4 introduces the different tools developed to homogenize access to all Cloud sites. Section 5 introduces the different set of experiments used to validate the platform. Finally, Section 6, presents the conclusions and future work.

2 BonFIRE Federated Clouds and Networks

BonFIRE allows users to execute experiments that use compute, network, storage, site-link and router resources. The experiments are controlled by a set of central services, collectively called the Broker, that interact with the testbeds. In this way, the BonFIRE users can test their applications, services, or systems in different Cloud configurations (e.g. deploy across multiple multi-clouds, or experiment with different Cloud managers available through BonFIRE) using a single, homogeneous interface.

At the core of BonFIRE are seven Cloud testbeds that are located at EPCC (UK), INRIA (France), PSNC (Poland), HLRS (Germany), iMinds (Belgium), Wellness Telecom (Spain) and HP (UK) (fig. 1). All testbeds present different features regarding structure, networking, and resources. Users can also create resources on Amazon EC2 using the BonFIRE interface.

Integration of the BonFIRE Cloud facilities and their interconnection with external facilities is key in BonFIRE. Horizontal (i.e. of similar functionality) integration is achieved through the integration of the different facilities as well as Amazon. Additionally, BonFIRE offers vertical integration of Cloud and network facilities. This enables cross-layer testing to propagate service-level requirements down to the connectivity levels. The iMinds Virtual Wall facility allows experimentation using controlled, emulated networks. BonFIRE is also interconnected with two external facilities to provide vertical integration at the network level. These are the GÉANT AutoBAHN Bandwidth-on-Demand (BoD) system; and the FEDERICA computing network architectures e-infrastructure.

3 BonFIRE Federation Architecture

BonFIRE provides resource level operations through an implementation of the Open Cloud Computing Interface[2] (OCCI) standard. The OCCI was designed for remote management interactions with cloud computing infrastructures. It is an open protocol that is resource-vendor independent, cloud-manager neutral, and can be extended.OCCI acts as the user API for the service lifecycle management of BonFIRE-supported resources. Originally limited to compute, storage,

[2] `http://www.occi-wg.org`

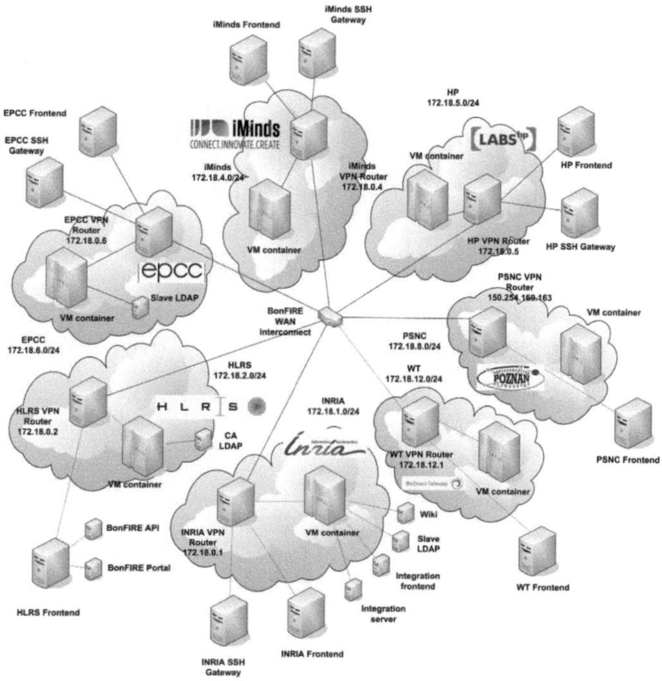

Fig. 1. BonFIRE Cloud Federation Infrastructure

network resources, BonFIRE has extended OCCI to allow operations to site-links and routers, as required by the AutoBAHN and FEDERICA testbeds.

The BonFIRE implementation of OCCI enables defining different kinds of resources with various possible configurations. For instance, a user can create a compute resource and configure it on demand with one of multiple instance types (lite, small, medium, large, or custom), with one or multiple disks (disk image and external storages), with one or more network interfaces, etc. The BonFIRE OCCI supports several management operations and various states of resources. For instance, the possible management operations of a compute resource include: create, stop, resume, shutdown, and delete.

The Resource Manager (RM) (fig. 2) is the lowest layer of the BonFIRE architecture that may be accessed by the end-users, providing the entry point for the users to interact with BonFIRE at resource level. The RM exposes the BonFIRE OCCI interface and maintains the current set of experiments and all the resources associated to them. User operations on non-experiment resources are passed to the Enactor and then on to the appropriate interconnected testbed. User operations on experiment resources are executed at the RM level.

Due to the heterogeneity of BonFIRE Cloud testbeds, the mapping between BonFIRE OCCI and the testbed native interfaces was implemented in different layers. The role of the Enactor is to hide from the RM and from the OCCI the technical details of how to communicate with each specific testbed or external

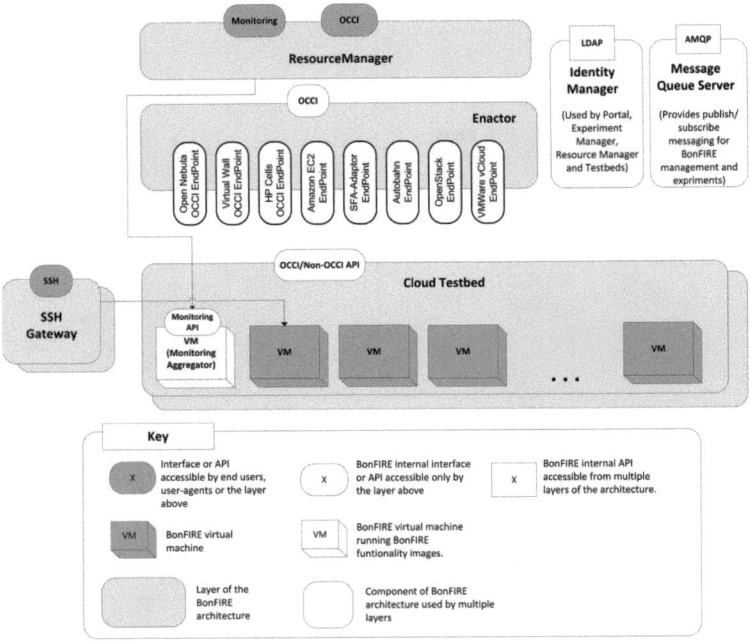

Fig. 2. Lowest level BonFIRE architecture

facility. The Enactor receives OCCI requests from the RM and adapts them to a suitable testbed format. When the Enactor gets the information back from the testbed, it transforms the reply again into BonFIRE OCCI.

Canonical BonFIRE images are generated centrally to provide the Debian squeeze Linux distribution in different sizes for the Xen, KVM and ESX hypervisors. The BonFIRE OCCI supports contextualisation at the time of the creation of the VMs and all images also support this; for instance, software can be installed automatically after booting, and also parameters may be passed directly into the virtual machine on instantiation. As a federated infrastructure, every BonFIRE site receives the same contextualisation information in the VM creation request, but they are free to use it according to each site's own particularities.

BonFIRE offers a private address space for each infrastructure provider, e.g. the whole network subnet 172.18.0.0/16. Due to that, all the created VMs are assigned to a dedicated private network offered by a local provider in its BonFIRE address range. In order to connect the several VM instances at different locations, a BonFIRE-wide VPN was established, which allows communication between separated virtual machines and internal BonFIRE services. For the VPN network installation, the tinc software was used. The tinc service allows the creation of a decentralized network, so there is no single point of failure if one instance loses its connection. Figure 1 gives a brief overview of the whole BonFIRE infrastructure and shows the different IP ranges of the providers.

3.1 User Management

Identity management and authorization is done centrally in BonFIRE. On the one hand, a central LDAP database stores user credentials (username, password and ssh public key) and group membership. On the other, an authorization service stores site access rights as wells as usage limits and peak resource usage for each group. Indeed, groups are a key BonFIRE functionality, that enables efficient collaboration. Group membership is managed by the Principal Investigator of an experiment.

Interactions with BonFIRE services are authenticated against the LDAP database using HTTP basic authentication over ssl. The first service called must authenticate the user, and will carry user information in a dedicated HTTP Header when calling other services. This information is trusted by the service called if and only if the requester can themselves be authenticated using client-side authentication permitted by ssl. In particular, all testbeds in the federation must be configured to authenticate central servers and trust user and group information sent to them using HTTP headers.

The Resource Manager is in charge of doing all authorization by calling the accounting service to check, based on group membership, whether a given user can create or access resources. It will also create temporary credentials and add these, as well as the public keys of all users allowed to access resources, into the context information carried by the OCCI requests. Temporary credentials are used by code running inside the resources that needs to call the BonFIRE API.

Access to resources is secured through SSH. SSH gateways are operated by BonFIRE sites to allow access to the BonFIRE VPN. A classical master-slave configuration is used for LDAP, with slaves on all gateways. This approach avoids a single point of failure, relieves the load on the central database and propagates changes very quickly. VMs are configured with the public keys of users allowed to access them. This allows users to connect to any gateway and, from there, to any VM in the BonFIRE VPN.

3.2 Cloud Testbeds

Depending on Cloud Manager technology, BonFIRE currently offers the following five different types of Cloud testbed:

- **OpenNebula:** The currently operated OpenNebula version 3.6 includes an implementation of an OCCI server based on the OCCI draft 0.8. In order to provide valuable cloud functionality, additional fields of use were added by the BonFIRE developers in order to improve and extend the whole OCCI software stack of OpenNebula.
- **HP Cells**: The OCCI at HP Cells is completely stateless, so there is nothing that can get out of sync with the BonFIRE cental services or with the Cells state. BonFIRE-specific information such as groups, users, etc. are not stored, so the information retrieved on each request from the Enactor is filtered according to the permissions of the requesting user. This OCCI server was implemented specifically to support the BonFIRE project.

- **Virtual Wall:** The Virtual Wall emulation testbed is not a typical cloud environment, as it lacks the ability to dynamically add computes to an already running experiment. However, its functionality offers a first step to bridge the gap between network and cloud experimentation. The Virtual Wall offers the same OCCI resources as the other testbeds in BonFIRE, but their implementation is very different due to its underlying framework, Emulab. For instance, the Virtual Wall maps Compute resources to physical nodes, which prevents virtualisation, but allows the experimenter to take full control of the hardware. In response to the need of experimenters to share larger amounts of storage between different Compute resources, the Virtual Wall implements a notion of shared storage based on the Network File System (NFS).
- **VMWare vCloud:** vCloud does not offer by default an OCCI API. Similar to the case of HP Cells, an OCCI server was developed inside the BonFIRE project that interacts with the VMWare vCloud Director API to support VMWare Cloud facilities. The OCCI server is stateless, all the requests coming from the Enactor are translated and mapped to the proprietary API.
- **Amazon EC2:** The Amazon EC2 endpoint at the Enactor makes use of the API that Amazon provides to connect remotely to their Cloud services. The endpoint only allows to manage two kind of resources: storages and computes that are mapped to their Amazon equivalents, volumes or images and instances. In order to deal with the large volume of information returned, BonFIRE caches some OCCI queries in the Enactor, like listings of EC2's numerous storage resources.

3.3 Network Testbeds

BonFIRE supports experimentation and testing of new scenarios from the services research community, focused on the convergence of services and networks. In order to support network experimentation, BonFIRE is federated with the iMinds Virtual Wall testbed; and is interconnected with two network facilities: FEDERICA and AutoBAHN.

The most distinctive features of the iMinds Virtual Wall are related to its networking capabilities. Whereas the other BonFIRE testbeds only provide a best-effort variant of the Network resource, the Virtual Wall implements three different types of Network resources: Default Networks that provide basic connectivity between two or more Computes; Managed Networks that provide controllable QoS (parameters that can be adjusted are bandwidth, packet loss rate and delay) over the network links; and Active Networks, that, on top of the functionality of Managed Networks, also provide the possibility to control the background traffic (UDP and TCP connections with dynamically adjustable packet size and throughput) on a network link. These networks provided by the Virtual Wall are emulated, using the Emulab software.

FEDERICA is an infrastructure composed of computers, switches and routers connected by Gigabit Ethernet circuits. Through the Slide-based Federation Architecture (SFA) paradigm, FEDERICA offers to BonFIRE experimenters isolated network slices by means of virtualizing routers. This interconnection is aimed to help experimenters to investigate application performance through better control of the underlying network. The following changes were carried out in BonFIRE to incorporate these new network resources: the router resource was added to the BonFIRE OCCI and the network resource was enhanced with two new attributes: network link and vlan. Finally, since FEDERICA offers an SFA interface as federation API, it was necessary to implement an SFA endpoint at Enactor level. The FEDERICA SFA interface expects a unique XML request, where all the slice resources and their configuration are specified. This differs from the BonFIRE architecture, where each resource is requested in a single OCCI call. The main function of the BonFIRE SFA endpoint is to transform BonFIRE's OCCI information model to the SFA information model.

The federation between BonFIRE and the AutoBAHN beta-functionality offered by the GÈANT facility allows the experimenters to request QoS guaranteed network connectivity services between VMs deployed on EPCC and PSNC testbeds. Overcoming the Best Effort limitation of the public Internet, dedicated network services can be established on demand for each experiment, with guarantees in terms of bandwidth, reduced jitter and service reliability. This option is fundamental to offer a controlled connectivity between VMs, so that the experimenters can evaluate the performance of their applications in environments able to emulate a variety of network conditions.

In BonFIRE, a BoD service is represented by a new type of OCCI resource: the site_link. Once the resource is created, it can be used to connect two networks created in the BonFIRE sites at the edge of the site_link: the traffic between the VMs attached to these networks is routed through the dedicated service. The processing of the OCCI requests for site_link resources is managed at the enactor through a dedicated AutoBAHN end-point that is in charge of translating the OCCI specification into the AutoBAHN BoD service format. The Enactor end-point acts as an AutoBAHN client.

4 Practical Experimentation Tools

In response to user-demand, BonFIRE exposes various tools and interfaces to its users. The main API is based on OCCI, an interface familiar to the target users, i.e. Cloud application developers. However, interacting with OCCI may be very cumbersome as the size of the deployments grows, and the format is not easily human-readable.

In order to increase usability, BonFIRE offers other client tools, building on the BonFIRE API. These include: an intuitive web Portal to interact graphically with all components; a BonFIRE Experiment Descriptor written in JSON or OVF; a general-purpose RESTful client that uses the Restfully library to allow interaction via Ruby scripting; and a set of Command Line Interface Tools that can be used interactive or programmatically. Extensive, tutorial-based user documentation accompanies the BonFIRE tools.

The feedback of the experimenters to the diversity of available tools was very positive. They found it very easy to start creating experiments with the web

Portal and progress later to more complex scenarios in which they created their own programs based on the available tools to create and access their experiments. The BonFIRE Portal is key to this progression, as it includes intuitive builders for OCCI and for the experiment descriptor.

5 Validation of the Platform

Validation of the federated cloud and network platform was designed into several phases. In the early stages of the project, three of the core partners of BonFIRE performed Cloud experimentation in several aspects: from application benchmarking in Cloud Computing to study of malicious paterns in applications [11, 12]. In a second phase, we performed two Open Calls, in the first one four independent companies or research groups performed experiments using BonFIRE with topics ranging from service composition, virtual clusters, security, or multimedia [13–15], in the second one, five new experiments ranging from Cloud elasticity, QoS in federated Clouds, testing of commercial home security and management solutions, multimedia interfaces, or orchestration between users and cloud resources[3]. Finally, BonFIRE has just started its Open Access initiative for new users to come and use for free the platform.

6 Conclusions and Future Work

BonFIRE enables Research by Experimentation founded on federation of heterogeneous, cloud and network testbeds and facilities. The BonFIRE Cloud federation model is based on a central broker component that interacts between the user requests, the experimenters, and the different infrastructures. This broker offers to the users an OCCI-based interface that exposes all the Cloud and network features as resources.

The BonFIRE interface exposes to the users an homogeneous view of the heterogeneous testbeds it encompasses. Still, the interface exposes the different characteristics that make each federated site unique. Additionally, user management is centralized; all sites are in one unique WAN network that eases communication between VMs located at different Clouds; and the VMs in all federated Clouds, independently of the employed Cloud Manager, can be contextualized in the same way.

The BonFIRE project is still ongoing. In terms of federation, BonFIRE is working towards a cache facility, which will accelerate resource listings from sites. Unlike other BonFIRE functionalities, this is implemented with tight coupling between sites and central services; the sites are enhance to push events about the state of the resources in the BonFIRE Message Queue. BonFIRE is also investigating OpenStack as a potential target Cloud Manager.

[3] At the time of writting, those experiments were still being executed in the BonFIRE platform, more information about them it is is available in the project webpage: `http://www.bonfire-project.eu`.

BonFIRE is open for free use by organizations and individuals not within the consortium. Over 2013 and 2014 BonFIRE expects to engage an increasing number of experimenters accessing the cloud federated facility.

Acknowledgments. BonFIRE is funded by the EU 7th Framework Programme (FP7/2007-2013) under grant agreement number 257386 and 287938.

References

1. Al-Hazmi, Y., et al.: A Monitoring System for Federated Clouds. In: Proceedings of the 1st IEEE International Conference on Cloud Networking, pp. 68–74 (2012)
2. Keahey, K., et al.: Sky Computing. IEEE Internet Computing 13(5), 43–51 (2012)
3. Rochwerger, B., et al.: Reservoir-When One Cloud is Not Enough. Computer, 44–51 (2011)
4. Vandenberghe, W., et al.: Architecture for the Heterogeneous Federation of Future Internet Experimentation Facilities. Future Network and Mobile Summit (July 2013)
5. Ferrer, A.J., et al.: OPTIMIS: A Holistic Approach to Cloud Service Provisioning. Future-Generation Computer Systems 28, 66–77 (2012)
6. Tordsson, J., et al.: Cloud Brokering Mechanisms for Optimized Placement of Virtual Machines Across Multiple Providers. Future Generation Computer Systems 28(2), 358–367 (2012)
7. Sotomayor, B., et al.: Virtual Infrastructure Management in Private and Hybrid Clouds. IEEE Internet Computing 13(5), 14–22 (2009)
8. Moreno-Vozmediano, R., et al.: Multicloud Deployment of Computing Clusters for Loosely Coupled MTC Applications. IEEE Transactions in Parallel and Distributed Systems 22(6), 924–930 (2011)
9. Petcu, D.: Portability and Interoperability Between Clouds: Challenges and Case Study. In: Abramowicz, W., Llorente, I.M., Surridge, M., Zisman, A., Vayssière, J. (eds.) ServiceWave 2011. LNCS, vol. 6994, pp. 66–74. Springer, Heidelberg (2011)
10. Hume, A.C., Al-Hazmi, Y., Belter, B., Campowsky, K., Carril, L.M., Carrozzo, G., Engen, V., García-Pérez, D., Jofre Ponsatí, J., Kűbert, R., Liang, Y., Rohr, C., Van Seghbroeck, G.: BonFIRE: A Multi-cloud Test Facility for Internet of Services Experimentation. In: Korakis, T., Zink, M., Ott, M. (eds.) TridentCom 2012. LNICST, vol. 44, pp. 81–96. Springer, Heidelberg (2012)
11. Ragusa, C., et al.: A Framework for Modeling and Executing of Infrastructure Contention Experiments. In: 2nd Internation Workshop on Measurement-based Experimental Research, Methodology and Tools, MERMAT, FIA 2013 (2013)
12. Engen, V., Papay, J., Phillips, S.C., Boniface, M.: Predicting Application Performance for Multi-vendor Clouds Using Dwarf Benchmarks. In: Wang, X.S., Cruz, I., Delis, A., Huang, G. (eds.) WISE 2012. LNCS, vol. 7651, pp. 659–665. Springer, Heidelberg (2012)
13. Gomez, A., et al.: Experimenting Virtual Clusters on Distributed Clound environemtns using BonFIRE. In: FIRE Engineering Workshop (2012)
14. Wajid, U., et al.: Testing Optimization in Service EcoSystems (TEOS). In: IEEE International Conference on Web Services (2012)
15. Naqvi, S., et al.: Analysing Impact of Scalability and Heteroneneity on the Performance of Federated Cloud Security. In: 4th IEEE International Workshop on Security in e-Science and e-Research, in conjuction with the 2012 IEEE International Conference on Trust, Security, and Privacy in Computing and Communications (2012)

Execution of Scientific Workflows on Federated Multi-cloud Infrastructures

Daniele Lezzi[1], Francesc Lordan[1], Roger Rafanell[1], and Rosa M. Badia[1,2]

[1] Barcelona Supercomputing Center - Centro Nacional de Supercomputación (BSC-CNS)
{daniele.lezzi,francesc.lordan,roger.rafanell,rosa.m.badia}@bsc.es
[2] Artificial Intelligence Research Institute (IIIA), Spanish Council for Scientific Research (CSIC)

Abstract. Recently cloud services have been evaluated by scientific communities as a viable solution to satisfy their computing needs, reducing the cost of ownership and operation to the minimum. The analysis on the adoption of the cloud computing model for eScience has identified several areas of improvement as federation management and interoperability between providers. Portability between cloud vendors is a widely recognized feature to avoid the risk of lock-in of users in proprietary systems, a stopper to the complete adoption of clouds.

In this paper we present a programming framework that allows the coordination of applications on federated clouds used to provide flexibility to traditional research infrastructures as clusters and grids. This approach allows researchers to program applications abstracting the underlying infrastructure and providing scaling and elasticity features through the dynamic provision of virtualized resources. The adoption of standard interfaces is a basic feature in the development of connectors for different middlewares ensuring the portability of the code between different providers.

Keywords: Programming models, Cloud interoperability, Cloud federation, Standards.

1 Introduction

The revolutionary advent of Cloud computing has changed the way IT services are developed and offered. Enterprises have switched their IT organization moving from on premises owned physical infrastructures to rented on demand services. This new model has implied a shift from capital expense avoiding up-front investments in the procurement of computational infrastructures in favor of a renting model where resources are acquired, by Amazon EC2 [13], Microsoft Azure [7] or Google Apps [6], on a pay per use basis. Similarly, Cloud computing has revealed useful and convenient in many scientific research fields allowing to have access to almost unlimited resources without the need of taking care of the management and deployment of the underlying infrastructure. In the last years, several research projects [12], [10], [4] have analyzed how to face these challenges

D. an Mey et al. (Eds.): Euro-Par 2013 Workshops, LNCS 8374, pp. 136–145, 2014.

exploring the adaptability of virtualization and Cloud computing to research. In particular the European Grid Infrastructure (EGI) [3] has started a specific Federated Cloud Task Force [5] in order to evaluate the adoption of clouds to make the existing infrastructure more flexible and scalable to expand its services to new user communities. An hybrid model for eScience is being gradually adopted with cloud infrastructures, both private and public, offered as complementary solutions to traditional environments as grids and clusters to provide flexibility and cost-effectiveness to the so called long-tail of science. Nevertheless cloud adoption is not so straightforward for non-technical users that have to deal with issues related to the adaptation of their applications to new environments and with the lack of guaranteed portability and interoperability between different providers.

In order to facilitate the execution of applications in the cloud, tools that simplify their development, deployment and transparent execution on federated infrastructures are required. In this paper we present the enhancements to the COMP Superscalar programming framework (COMPSs) [29] to make it interoperable with the EGI Federated Cloud testbed in order to optimize the execution of the related use cases. COMPSs allows the automatic parallelization of sequential applications on top of computational infrastructures as grids and clouds providing elasticity features. In particular, here we focus on the development of a connector for the management of virtual appliances using the Open Cloud Computing Interface (OCCI) [8] specification and on the evaluation of the framework executing a workflow for the biodiversity community in EGI.

The rest of the paper is organized as follows. Section 2 describes the related work and Section 3 introduces COMPSs and how it enables interoperability with several clouds offerings. In particular Section 3.2 presents the main contribution of the paper, the developments to make COMPSs interoperable with the EGI Federated Cloud. Section 4 evaluates the execution of a use case highlighting the benefits of using COMPSs in a federated multi-cloud environment. Section 5 concludes the paper and presents the future work.

2 Related Work

Several frameworks allow the graphical composition of an application workflow and its execution on distributed infrastructures. Taverna [23] is a workflow language and computational model designed to support the automation of complex, service-based and data-intensive processes. A prototype version has been tested on a private cloud testbed deploying Taverna Servers on a set of virtual machines but neither plugins are offered to execute tasks on public clouds nor the possibility exists of elastically modify the pool of resources. In [15] authors evaluate the usage of Pegasus workflow manager on multiple clouds. The setup of the execution is not straightforward because forces the user to manually predeploy several nodes configured as Condor workers, while COMPSs automatically deploys the applications on dynamically created virtual machines. The gUSE framework [18] includes a workflow manager and a distributed computing infrastructure (DCI) bridge that provides standard access, through a Basic Execution Service (BES) [17] compliant interface, to various DCIs including clouds. COMPSs implements a similar approach [20] through a deployment and execution service accessible by compliant clients. In gUSE the support to clouds is delegated to an external service and is still in development phase in the context of the SCI-BUS project [25]. The Contrail project is developing ConPaaS [24], a runtime environment for elastically hosting and deploying applications on federated and multi-clouds following SLA constraints. Applications in ConPaaS are composed of any number of services programmed through a common generic Python interface for the service management and a Javascript part to extend the front-end GUI with service-specific information and control. The main difference with COMPSs is the existence of predefined patterns for the implementation of a service, thus forcing the users to write new code or to adapt the existing one to use the currently provided services. Support to OCCI specification is not available in ConPaaS at writing time.

3 COMPSs Interoperability in the EGI Federated Cloud

3.1 The EGI Federation Model

The federation model of the EGI Cloud Infrastructure Platform provides an abstract cloud management stack to operate an infrastructure integrated with the components of EGI Core Infrastructure Platform. This model defines the required external interfaces and corresponding interaction ports that each resource provider has to support. The former requires the deployment of interoperable standard interfaces for VM management (OCCI), data management (CDMI [22]) and information discovery (GLUE 2). The interaction with the core EGI components includes the integration with the AAI VOMS (Virtual Organization Membership Service) [14] system and with the monitoring and accounting services. An Appliance Repository and a VM Marketplace support the sharing and deployment of appliances across the providers. The EGI Cloud Testbed includes different management middlewares (OpenStack [27], OpenNebula [28], StratusLab, WNoDeS [26] and Synnefo [11]) but the federation model does not impose any specific technology leaving to the providers the responsibility to identify and deploy the solution that fits best their individual needs with the only constraint of providing the appropriate interfaces in order to be interoperable with other implementations.

3.2 COMPSs Integration in the EGI Cloud

COMPSs is a framework, composed of a programming model and a runtime, that aims to ease the development and deployment of distributed applications and web services. The core of the framework is its programming model which allows the programmer to write applications in a sequential way and to execute them on top of heterogeneous infrastructures exploiting the inherent parallelism of the application. The COMPSs programming model is task-based allowing the programmer to select the methods of the sequential application to be executed remotely. This selection is done by means of an annotated interface where all the methods that have to be considered as a task are defined with some annotations describing their data accesses and constraints on the execution resources. At execution time this information is used by the runtime to build a dependency graph and orchestrate the tasks on the available resources. One important feature of the COMPSs runtime is the ability to exploit the cloud elasticity by adjusting the amount of resources to the current workload. When the number of tasks is higher than the available cores, the runtime turns to the cloud looking for the provider that offers the resources that better fit the requirements of the application with a lower economical cost. Symmetrically, when the runtime detects an excess of resources it powers off unused instances in a cost-efficient way. Such decisions are based on information provided by the user who describes the details of the software images and instance templates available for every cloud provider. Since each cloud provider offers its own API, COMPSs defines a generic interface to manage resources and to query details about the execution cost of multiple cloud providers during the same execution. The implementations of this interface, called *connectors*, are in charge of translating the generic requests to the actual provider's API.

In order to support the usage of EGI Federated Cloud IaaS resources, a new connector has been developed to operate with the interfaces and protocols described in subsection 3.1. The support for the VM management is implemented using the rOCCI client [9] that transparently interoperates with the rOCCI servers deployed in the testbed on top of different middlewares as OpenNebula and OpenStack. The connector supports different authentication methods, including X509 type through VOMS proxy certificates. To setup each connector instance, the user indicates which virtual images and instance types are offered by the specific provider; thus, when the runtime asks for the creation of a VM, the connector selects the appropriate image and resource template according to the requirements (in terms of cpu, memory, disk, etc) and invokes the rOCCI client through *Mixins*, extensions of the OCCI Model that allow the instantiation of a VM through templates with additional capabilities (network, storage, etc). For the data management, the support to CDMI protocol is offered through the VENUS-C middleware to store and retrieve input data and final results, as detailed in [17]. The interaction with the deployed resources is done via SSH. To allow the job submission and data transfers between worker VMs, public key exchange is used as authentication method. At boot time, the VM contacts the Perun [19] server to obtain the public key of the user. Once the VM is accessible, the connector contextualizes it configuring the SSH keys and deploying the software packages such as the binaries used by the tasks, the application code and the COMPSs worker application. The connector also implements methods for the computation of the economical and temporal costs on each provider such as the accumulated execution cost, the current cost per hour, the cost per hour for a VM that fulfills certain requirements or the time required to start a new instance.

4 Evaluation

A series of tests has been performed in order to evaluate the performance of COMPSs and the developed connector to run a use case provided by an EGI user community. In the following section we describe the implementation of the application, the deployed testbed, the benchmarks and the results obtained.

4.1 Modeller Service

The *Modeller* Web Service provides a COMPSs implementation of the Extended Open Modeler Web Service (OMWS+) [21] which performs Ecological Niche Modelling (ENM) operations automatically converting multi-stage & multi-parameter experiment requests into a set of single invocations of the openModeller (OM) [16] suite. The Serivce provides operations that execute a COMPSs workflow, whose example dependency graph is depicted in Figure 1, composed of OM operations that *model* a species distribution, *test* it agains an input dataset, *project* the distribution on a geographical map and print it on an image file (*translate*). In the figure the numbers represent the generation order of the tasks by the COMPSs runtime and each type of task is depicted with a color.

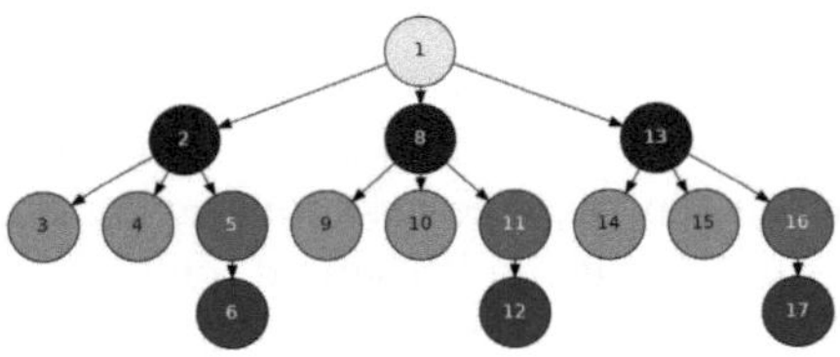

Type	Tasks
Convert	1
Model	2 8 13
Test	3 4 9 10 14 15
Project	5 11 16
Translate	6 12 17

Fig. 1. Dependency graph for an execution of COMPSs workflow with 1 species, 3 modelling algorithms and multiple tests. COMPSs generates three model tasks, two tests operations and three project tasks, one per model.

4.2 Testbed

The Web Service has been deployed on the federated cloud scenario depicted in Figure 2 and composed of the following elements:

- ***Client***: Java application that invokes the Modeller Service.
- ***WS server***: machine running an Apache Tomcat 7.0 [2] WS container hosting the service. It is a Intel Core 2 Quad Q9300 at 2.5 GHz, 4 GB of RAM and 320 GB of disk space. Both, the service main program and the COMPSs runtime execute in this machine located at BSC premises in Barcelona, Spain.

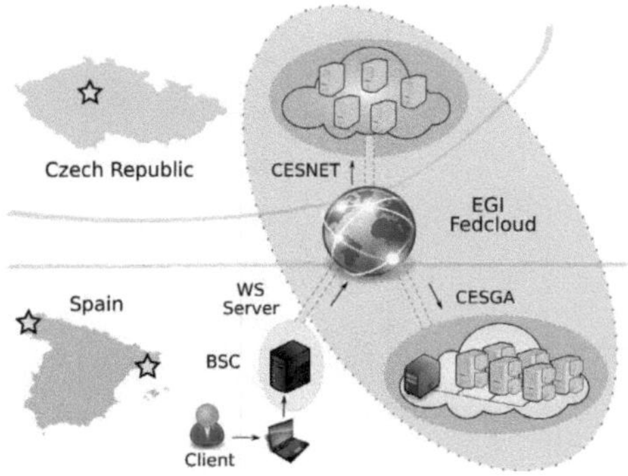

Fig. 2. The testbed comprises two EGI FedCloud providers, CESNET and CESGA, providing VMs to the Modeller Service running at BSC

– ***EGI Federated Cloud***: composed of two providers, CESGA (Spain) and CESNET (Czech Republic) both providing resources through the rOCCI server for OpenNebula cloud middleware. CESGA contributed 33 octo-core servers (256 CPUs) and 14.5 TB of shared NFS/SSH filesystem, CESNET contributed ten 24-core servers, 96 GB of memory and 44 TB of shared filesystem. The providers offered different VM plans; CESGA provided *Large* VMs template consisting of 2 cores and 8 GB of memory. CESNET provided an *XLarge* template which consists of 4 cores and 15 GB of memory. The VMs images, stored in the appliance repository, take up 10 GB and were configured with a Linux distribution, the COMPSs runtime, the Modeller service packages and the OM suite.

4.3 Results

Two different usage modes of the implemented use case are discussed below, representing two ways of usage of the ENM service. In the *Single* test a complex workflow is submitted in a unique request, while in the *Multiple* test, simpler workflows are submitted to the service. When the ENM service starts, it automatically instances one *Large* VM at CESGA and two *XLarge* VMs at CESNET that will be always available throughout different executions. This strategy reduces the initial response time because the first requests can be immediately submitted without waiting for the instantiation of new VMs. The number of pre-deployed instances can be configured in the connector.

Single Request. In order to evaluate the performance of the runtime and how it adapts the VMs pool size to the workload, a single invocation request has been issued. This request includes 6 species and 2 algorithms, thus producing 12 distribution models; each model is then tested and projected generating a total of 36 dependent tasks. This test exploits different VM templates offered by the EGI FedCloud providers by using method constraints defined in the COMPSs

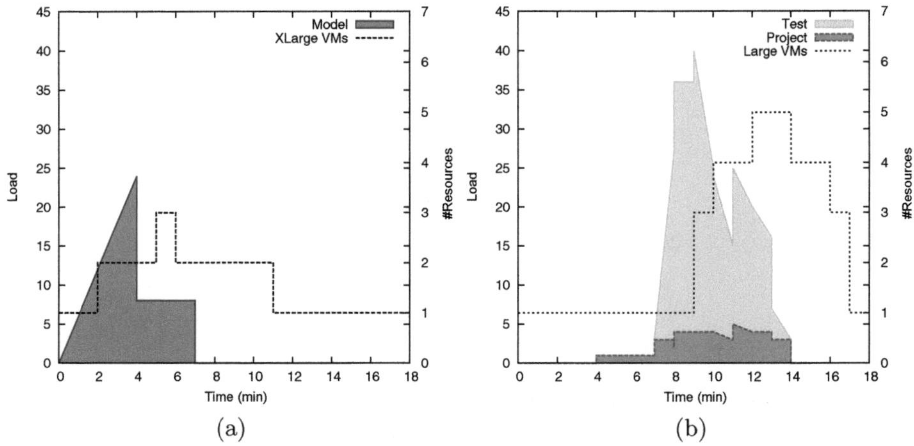

Fig. 3. System load *vs.* available virtual resources during a single request execution. Figure 3(a) and Figure 3(b) represent the *model* and the *test, project* tasks respectively.

application interface. This forces the *model* and *test, project* tasks to be executed on *XLarge* and *Large* VMs respectively. Figure 3 describes the runtime behavior during the execution of a single request; a growth of the number of tasks forces the runtime to acquire new resources while, as the load decreases, virtual resources are progressively released adapting the system needs to the current workload. In the figures, VMs are available after a creation time specific of each provider and released at the end of the tasks currently executed there.

Multiple Requests. This test aims to evaluate the global service performance on a multi-request scenario. In this case, a set of invocations has been issued following a Gaussian random workload pattern, generated by Apache JMeter [1] benchmark suite. The JMeter test plan has been tuned to issue 30 simultaneous

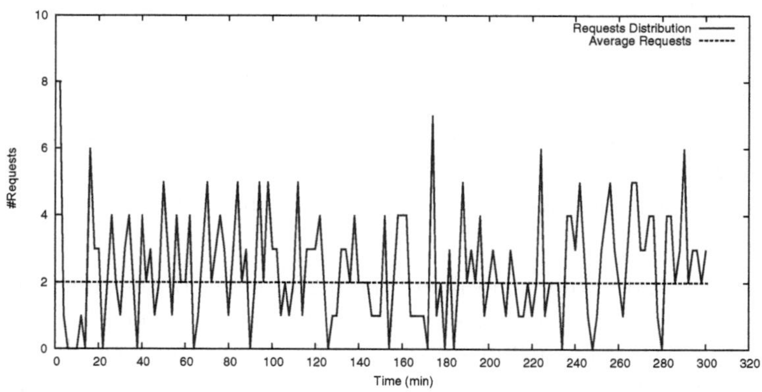

Fig. 4. Requests per minute. The average cadence is set on 2.41 requests/min.

requests in a random time frame of 0/2 minutes during 5 hours as depicted in Figure 4. This suite also permits to obtain and analyze some service Key Performance Indicators (KPI) such as: response time, dynamic resource consumption and throughput. In this experiment, each request requires low computation time, generating a dependency graph composed of three OM tasks (*model*, *test* and *project*) where the last two ones executed in parallel.

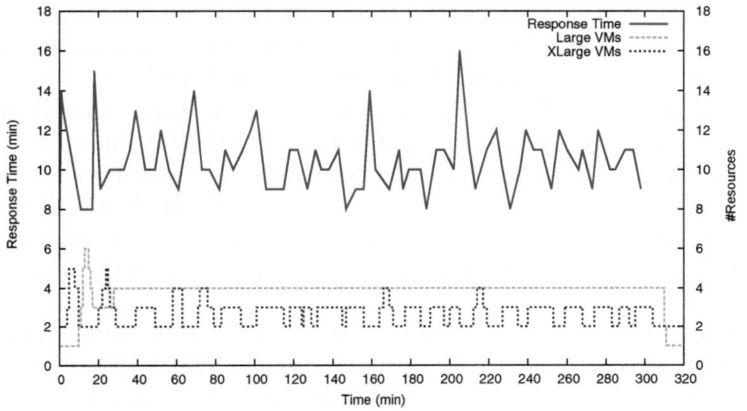

Fig. 5. Response time *vs.* resource consumption

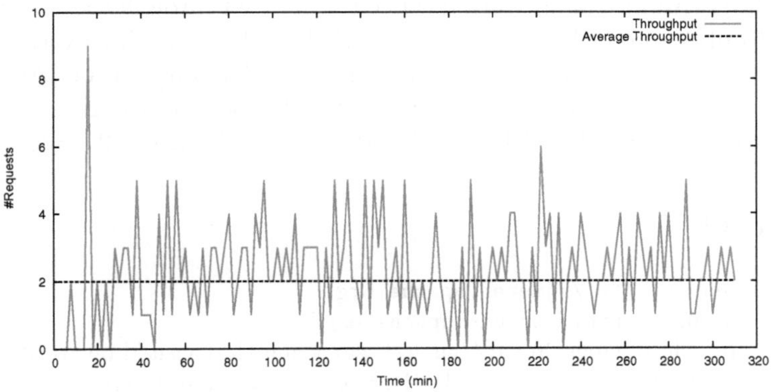

Fig. 6. Responses per minute (throughput). The sustained value is 2.34 responses/min.

The response time is depicted in Figure 5 together with the evolution of the number of virtual resources used in the execution. When multiple requests are issued at the same time (Figure 4) the response time increases and the COMPSs runtime reacts to the rise of the load produced, adapting the number of resources needed to execute every kind of new task, according to the task constraint. As represented in *#Resources* curve, the connector manages *XLarge* type machines at CESNET and *Large* type ones at CESGA.

Another important performance indicator to consider is the global throughput of the service. Figure 6 shows a slightly lower sustained value (2.9%) than the average requests per minute, thanks to the accuracy on the resources management system. This evidences a fast responsiveness of COMPSs framework facing unexpected workload peaks.

5 Conclusions and Future Work

This paper presented the extension of the COMPSs framework to execute applications in the EGI Federated Cloud. The developed OCCI compliant connector allows the orchestration of COMPSs applications on hybrid environments elastically adapting the number of resources to the actual load requirements. The application used in the evaluation, published as virtual appliance in the EGI Marketplace, has been executed in order to evaluate two possible scenarios. The results of the tests demonstrate that the runtime is able to deal with variations of loads of complex workflows by provisioning virtual instances on demand and also to serve multiple independent execution requests properly managing the pool of resources.

The ongoing work includes the improvement of the connector to support contextualization features that will be introduced in the EGI FedCloud in the production phase of the testbed and the enhancement of resource management in order to support the assignment of tasks to multi-core instances.

Acknowledgements. This work has been supported through the grants: SEV-2011-00067 of Severo Ochoa Program, awarded by the Spanish Government and the Spanish Ministry of Science and Innovation under contract TIN2012-34557, the Generalitat de Catalunya (contract 2009-SGR-980) and the European Commission (EUBrazilOpenbio: RI-288754 and EGI-InSPIRE: RI- 261323).

References

1. Apache jmeter, http://jmeter.apache.org
2. Apache Tomcat, http://tomcat.apache.org/
3. Egi-inspire white paper, http://go.egi.eu/pdnon (last visited on April 16, 2013)
4. European Middleware Initiative (EMI), http://www.eu-emi.eu/
5. Federated Clouds Task Force, https://wiki.egi.eu/wiki/Fedcloud-tf:FederatedCloudsTaskForce (last visited on June 4, 2013)
6. Google App Engine, http://code.google.com/appengine
7. Microsoft Azure, http://www.microsoft.com/azure
8. Open Cloud Computing Interface, http://occi-wg.org (last visited on April 16, 2013)
9. The rocci framework, http://dev.opennebula.org/projects/ogf-occi/wiki (last visited on July 17, 2013)
10. Stratuslab, http://stratuslab.eu/
11. Synnefo cloud, http://www.synnefo.org/ (last visited on July 17, 2013)
12. Virtual multidisciplinary ENvironments USing Cloud infrastructures Project, http://www.venus-c.eu

13. Amazon elastic compute cloud, Amazon EC2 (2008)
14. Alfieri, R., Cecchini, R.L., Ciaschini, V., dell'Agnello, L., Frohner, A., Gianoli, A., Lõrentey, K., Spataro, F.: VOMS, an authorization system for virtual organizations. In: Fernández Rivera, F. (ed.) Across Grids 2003. LNCS, vol. 2970, pp. 33–40. Springer, Heidelberg (2004)
15. Berriman, G.B., Deelman, E., Juve, G., Rynge, M., Vöckler, J.-S.: The application of cloud computing to scientific workflows: a study of cost and performance. Physical and Engineering Sciences 371 (1983) (January 1983)
16. de Souza Muñoz, M.E., De Giovanni, R., de Siqueira, M.F., Sutton, T., Brewer, P., Pereira, R.S., Canhos, D.A.L., Canhos, V.P.: openmodeller: a generic approach to species potential distribution modelling. GeoInformatica 15(1), 111–135 (2011)
17. Foster, I.: OGSA Basic Execution Service Version 1.0. Grid Forum Document GFD-RP. 108. (November 13, 2008), http://www.ogf.org/documents/GFD.108.pdf
18. Kacsuk, P., Farkas, Z., Kozlovszky, M., Hermann, G., Balasko, A., Karoczkai, K., Marton, I.: Ws-pgrade/guse generic dci gateway framework for a large variety of user communities. Journal of Grid Computing 10, 601–630 (2012)
19. Krenek, A., Sebestianov, Z.: Perun – fault-tolerant management of grid resources. In: Krakow Grid Workshop 2004, Krakow, pp. 133–140, Academic Computer Centre CYFRONET AGH (2004)
20. Lezzi, D., Memon, S., Rafanell, R., Soncu, H., Riedel, M., Badia, R.M.: Interoperable execution of escience applications on grids & clouds through open standards. In: Proceedings of the Unicore Summit 2012, IAS, Forschungszentrum Jülich GmbH (2012)
21. Lezzi, D., Rafanell, R., Torres, E., De Giovanni, R., Blanquer, I., Badia, R.M.: Programming ecological niche modeling workflows in the cloud. In: The 27th IEEE International Conference on Advanced Information Networking and Applications (AINA 2013), Barcelona, Spain (March 2013)
22. Livenson, I., Laure, E.: Towards transparent integration of heterogeneous cloud storage platforms. In: Proceedings of the Fourth International Workshop on Data-intensive Distributed Computing, DIDC 2011, pp. 27–34. ACM, New York (2011)
23. Missier, P., et al.: Taverna, reloaded. In: Gertz, M., Ludäscher, B. (eds.) SSDBM 2010. LNCS, vol. 6187, pp. 471–481. Springer, Heidelberg (2010), http://www.taverna.org.uk/pages/wp-content/uploads/2010/04/T2Architecture.pdf
24. Pierre, G., Stratan, C.: ConPaaS: a platform for hosting elastic cloud applications. IEEE Internet Computing 16(5), 88–92 (2012)
25. SCI-BUS project: The sci-bus project (2011), http://www.sci-bus.eu/ (last visited on May 31, 2013)
26. Salomoni, D., Italiano, A., Ronchieri, E.: Wnodes, a tool for integrated grid and cloud access and computing farm virtualization. Journal of Physics: Conference Series 331(5), 052017 (2011)
27. Sefraoui, O., Aissaoui, M., Eleuldj, M.: Article: Openstack: Toward an open-source solution for cloud computing. International Journal of Computer Applications 55(3), 38–42 (2012)
28. Sotomayor, B., Montero, R.S., Llorente, I.M., Foster, I.: Virtual infrastructure management in private and hybrid clouds. IEEE Internet Computing 13, 14–22 (2009)
29. Tejedor, E., Badia, R.: Comp superscalar: Bringing grid superscalar and gcm together. In: 8th IEEE International Symposium on Cluster Computing and the Grid, CCGRID 2008, pp. 185–193. IEEE (2008)

Expressing Quality of Service and Protection Using Federation-Level Service Level Agreement

Lorenzo Blasi[1], Jens Jensen[2], and Wolfgang Ziegler[3]

[1] Hewlett-Packard, Italy
[2] STFC, UK
[3] Fraunhofer, Germany

Abstract. Frameworks for service level agreements (SLAs) have been developed to allow services to discover and negotiate SLAs dynamically, without direct human intervention. We give a description of the experiences of two projects which are building on existing work in SLAs: the main advantages being to obtain better overall services (including pricing) for the consumer, and the SLAs are useful as a component of, or extension to, cloud federations. We also argue that the "Quality of Protection" is an important part of SLAs.

1 Background

Traditionally, Service Level Agreements (SLAs) are negotiated between service providers and the customer. The SLA typically describes the terms and nature of the service, as well as specific parameters of the service, perhaps including the cost, target uptime (if it's an online service), level of support, etc. The aim is to have each party agree on the type and level of service provided. Traditionally, SLAs are negotiated between *people* who represent the provider and consumer – in particular, they must have the *authority* to negotiate an agreement.

The availability of online services, and cloud services in particular, changed this scenario. Now the consumer is a person looking for a service, and the provider publishes terms and conditions (T&C), cost, target availability on a web page; and users may need to accept T&C prior to using the service. For a typical cloud service, the customer's needs are small compared to the provider's capacity, and there is no need to enter into negotiations, nor would the provider be interested in negotiating with a large number of small users. When "shopping around" for services, the user can either "take it or leave it'.' For a cloud service, the provider is an automated agent which can deal fully with setting up the new customer. All customers are then treated the same, leading to an economy of scale.

The logical extension is: what if both the customer and the provider are represented by agents? And what if they can not just sign an agreement, but also negotiate terms? In this extended model the human outlines a policy for service delivery by expressing requirements, and leaves it to the agent to look for service providers that match.

The promise of this approach is obvious: now the end user is free to consume services, perhaps simultaneously from multiple providers (assuming of course

D. an Mey et al. (Eds.): Euro-Par 2013 Workshops, LNCS 8374, pp. 146–156, 2014.

they are interchangeable). If a provider drops out, or another becomes cheaper, the agent should negotiate new agreements, and services will eventually move to the new provider.

Moreover, brokering and monitoring services from multiple providers can be a means of obtaining higher Quality of Service (QoS), at least availability and perhaps bandwidth, as in the "InterCloud" vision [5]. This approach could, however, reduce the protection of confidential data, as data may have to be replicated to multiple providers, and an agent may need to have the rights to move it without the owner's intervention. In such a case, a Quality of Protection should be part of the SLA.

The work presented here is the joint experience of two EU-funded projects. Contrail [4] is reusing an SLA framework from a third (earlier) project called SLA@SOI [3]; the OPTIMIS SLA [2] is based on the WSAG4J framework. Contrail is building IaaS federations which can manage cloud resources from multiple providers. OPTIMIS is managing IaaS provider attributes, to orchestrate applications (which may be legacy applications) on the cloud, specifically aiming to manage trust, risk, eco-friendliness, and cost as service parameters.

2 Existing Work

Grid information services are based on LDAP: originally Globus MDS [21], they have evolved into schemata known as GLUE [19] which can be expressed not just in LDAP but also in other formats (e.g., JSON or XML). Grid information services publish the state and availability of the service at some (hopefully recent) point in time, and dynamic data is refreshed regularly; they can be used as non-guaranteed service discovery as well as accounting.

Ruiz-Alvarez and Humphrey [1] developed a framework for describing cloud storage providers: the published information allows a customer to select services based on attributes. Like the grid, it is an instantaneous snapshot of the attributes, valid at the time it is created, and, as cloud service providers do not generally publish this information, requires some other party to update the information from time to time. Formatted in XML, the document includes a description of the providers' interfaces, security, geographic location, as well as samples of past measurements of performance metrics.

Indeed, once we move into negotiated cloud services, a number of requirements and failure modes can be recognised [20], Sec. 3.9, some of which are familiar from distributed computing (transient errors, credential timeouts), some of which could arise in heterogeneous distributed environments (inconsistent naming of capabilities, interoperation problems), and some may be specific to the cloud (the offer will need to be timely and accurate.)

Service discovery and matchmaking are well studied concepts in distributed systems, and a full survey of this work is beyond the scope and the focus of this paper. However, some of the experiences in matchmaking are equally valid for the present work. For example, [9] suggested the need for well-defined semantics, a common possibly extensible framework for agreement/negotiation, the need to accommodate heterogeneity in services, the need for sufficiently expressive queries/matching, and perhaps allowance for a certain "fuzziness" in matching. Like the much earlier [12], the use of semantic web was proposed.

In the Italian Cloud@Home research project [14], the resource is opened not to a specific project but to a possibly unknown customer. More recently, the project looked at the use of SLAs [15]: the QoS for negotiation is based on monitored availability and estimated performance. Potentially, the provider could be an "at home" user (as with BOINC [16]), but the project currently only looks at spare resources in private clouds.

The "InterCloud" project [5] further investigated SLAs for QoS, but mostly aiming for execution time in PaaS [8]. This work relied on an estimation of the execution time of individual "jobs" along with an overall view of the expected number of jobs.

Service Oriented Architecture (SOA) models may look at QoS for web services (e.g., WS-ReliableMessaging) [17], Chap. 13. If we are orchestrating complex services from multiple cloud providers, the lessons of providing QoS with reliable web services becomes relevant. This orchestration of services is, however, at a higher level compared to the approach we take in this paper, and could usefully be the subject of future investigations. More generally, there has been work on federation of clouds, some of which will be touched upon in this paper. NIST is very active in relevant cloud activities [18] and OGF, DMTF, and SNIA are working on standards to enable federations.

3 Use of Standards

WS-Agreement [13] and WS-Agreement Negotiation [11] are open standards from the OGF [10]. To define or contribute to a new standard, projects need to start early, so the work on the standard has a chance of completing during the lifetime of the project. The use of open standards bodies is encouraged so other parties have a chance to contribute, or help test interoperability. While using a standard is no guarantee for interoperability, it reduces the complexity and effort to get two code-independent implementations of, e.g. a SLA negotiation, to successfully cooperate.

4 Federation and SLAs

4.1 Federation Model in Contrail

A Federation in Contrail is a software infrastructure managing a set of independent IaaS providers (but could also encompass storage as a service). Providers are typically competing private organisations, with their services differentiated along the three major axes of price, Quality of Service (QoS) and Quality of Protection (QoP).

Contrail services can be applied also when providers collaborate, such as community clouds, or when several datacentres are connected to the same federation to form a big private cloud. The Contrail federation can thus also be an enabler for Enterprise-level private clouds.

The software infrastructure offered by Contrail is structured into three main levels: *federation*, *provider* and *resource*. Briefly, the resource is the actual IaaS (or other resource), the provider is an abstraction with a common interface which publishes services and serves as an endpoint for SLA negotiations, and the federation provides the overarching control, aiming to realise the "Multi-Cloud" or "Cloud of Clouds" visions [5], [6]. In SLA Management at federation level, user requirements are expressed in a uniform way, independently of the underlying resources, thus enabling scenarios such as Cloud Brokering, Cloud Aggregation and cross-Cloud SLA Enforcement.

Once requirements are defined, the federation looks at available providers and negotiates with them. Actual resources (such as IaaS) are then provided at the resource level (so the provider must know how to authenticate to the resource on behalf of the user), and whenever possible, the provider level monitors the service provided by the resource.

4.2 OVF and SLA for Describing Complex Infrastructures

In Contrail, users can define an "*application*," an infrastructure configuration made up of one or more layers of Virtual Machines (VMs) connected by virtual networks. Applications use OVF, an open standard, to define the resources required for the application. An SLA then refers to a specific OVF descriptor file and expresses guarantees about specific OVF items, such as Virtual Systems. Each OVF VirtualSystem in Contrail specifies a VirtualMachine type (or template) of which multiple instances can be created at provisioning time. The same SLA document can express different guarantees for different items described in the OVF. For example the same SLA can specify that instances of VirtualSystem A must be located in UK and instances of VirtualSystem B must be located in France, thus making it possible to build a disaster recovery system based on two distinct geographical sites.

4.3 Automatic SLA Negotiation and Dynamic Pricing

When the user has described their application using OVF and identified in the SLA proposal all the guarantees which are needed on each element, they can initiate a negotiation via the Contrail Federation. The system will propose a price for each part of the application and will let the user experiment by negotiating different configurations until the right balance between price and QoS is found (Fig. 1).

The provider layer automatically generates an SLA offer complete with a price for the resources described by the OVF and the QoS in the user's SLA proposal. The price for each VirtualSystem defined in the OVF depends not only on the amount of resources (e.g., memory or number of cores), but also on all the guarantees applied to it and identified in the SLA offer (e.g., location or co-location). The price is automatically calculated by the system for the required SLA+OVF configuration on the basis of the standard price list of that provider, but it could also be customised for the specific user by applying personalised marketing techniques. This personalisation helps the provider attract more customers, and weighing price/QoS helps users find the best value for money.

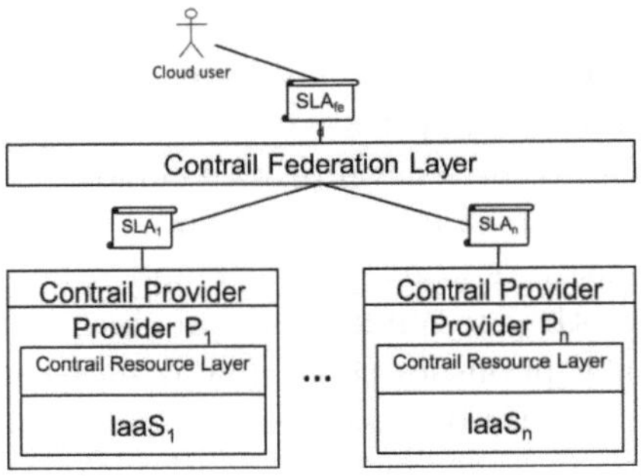

Fig. 1. Multi-level SLA negotiation

When a single provider cannot satisfy all the requirements, the federation can split the application and deploy it as an ensemble of cooperating parts on different providers. Splitting the application will go along with splitting the user's SLA proposal: the federation will negotiate each SLA part with different providers, and at each negotiation round will transparently provide to the user a SLA offer aggregating the best SLA offer for each of the parts. More on SLA splitting can be found in [7]. Further scenarios involving application and SLA splitting include scaling across multiple providers, Cloud bursting, and cross-provider SLA violation enforcement.

4.4 Proposed SLA Terms

Table 1 describes the QoS and QoP terms used (or planned) in Contrail SLAs.

QoS terms for IaaS providers can either express guarantees on the whole infrastructure, such as *availability*, or guarantees on a single resource, such as the *cpu_speed* of a specific VM. Most of the terms supported by Contrail are on single resources. When comparing SLA offers from different providers to find the best one, the value of some terms can be maximised (e.g. *storage_reliability*) or minimised (e.g. *price*), while the value of other terms must match exactly the user request in the SLA proposal. One such term expresses the geographical *location* of computing (VMs) or storage resources: in this case a SLA offer to be selected must match exactly the required countries

The term *Not_co_locate_host*, applied to a single VirtualSystem, specifies that all the VMs created from that VirtualSystem must be scheduled on different hosts, thus paving the way for high availability configurations.

The new *minimum_LoA* is a QoP term that specifies the minimum Level of Assurance (in authentication) that the resource requires, or the user defines for others to access their resource. Sensitive data will require a higher LoA: the federation authentication code sets the user's LoA when they authenticate; the required minimum is set at negotiation time and is also transmitted as an attribute when the authorisation checks run. Access to resources is blocked if *LoA <minimum_LoA*. LoA is discussed further in section 5.1.

Table 1. SLA terms in Contrail

SLA term	Description
vm_cores	number of cores assigned to a VM
memory	RAM size assigned to a VM
cpu_speed	CPU frequency assigned to a VM
cpu_load	average system load of a VM over a 5-minute period
location	country code where the VM is located
availability	% of uptime of the whole provider infrastructure
location	country code where the given shared storage volume is located
storage_reliability	indicates the number of replicas for the given shared storage volume
reserve	number of VMs to be reserved for the given VirtualSystem
co_locate_rack	all the VMs from the given VirtualSystem must be allocated on the same rack
not_co_locate_host	all the VMs from the given VirtualSystem must be allocated on different hosts
minimum_LoA	minimum Level of Assurance that a user wants to be required for accessing her own resources

4.5 Federation Model in Optimis

The OPTIMIS toolkit was developed to support two kinds of providers: the Service Provider (SP) and the Infrastructure Provider (IP). Consequently, the OPTIMIS toolkit supports two different "flavours" of federation:

- a multi-cloud, where the SP uses resources from different cloud providers to deploy a service. This federation is visible to the SP's customer when it selects a service of the SP.
- a cloud federation, which is organised by the IP as part of its internal business processes. Thus, the federation is transparent for the SP and for reasons of data protection SLAs need an explicit term to allow or disallow using IP-federated resources for a concrete service of an SP.

4.6 Role of SLAs in OPTIMIS

SLAs in OPTIMIS are used to describe the SP's requirements on the services offered by an IP [1]. Therefore the SLAs are more technical than those an end-user would see. The SP's requirements are gathered in an XML document, the *Service Manifest*, which is used by the IP to assess whether the requirements can be

[1] The OPTIMIS toolkit is not targeting end-users, thus, and end-user SLAs are not in the scope of OPTIMIS.

fulfilled, have to be negotiated, or cannot be fulfilled at that time. When requirements can be met, the IP converts the Service Manifest into an agreement template for the SP which is then used to create an agreement (possibly after a round of negotiations). The Service Manifest is composed of three parts, the manifest core, which is used for creating the SLA, and the IP and SP extensions. Figure 2 presents the overall structure of the manifest. For a detailed description of the Service Manifest and its API see [22].

If the SP is federating resources, it can negotiate directly with IPs to figure out which are the most suitable Alternatively, the SP can ask a *broker* to organise the federation on its behalf. The broker receives the manifest, selects the suitable IPs, and creates SLAs with all the selected IPs and the SP.

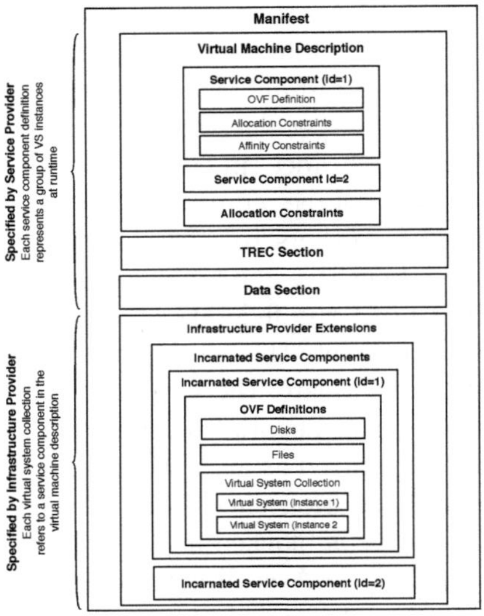

Fig. 2. Example of an infrastructure provider extension in the manifest

4.7 Proposed SLA Terms

The OPTIMIS SLA is based on WSAG4J which in turn is a a reference implementation of WS-Agreement and WS-AgreementNegotiation. Like Contrail, OPTIMIS both reused terms from other projects and developed its own. The latter are describe *trust*, *risk* (of SLA violation), *eco-efficiency* and *cost* (called TREC parameters). Trust is used like Contrail's LoA: An IP starting a federation selects other IPs with a trust level meeting the required trust level specified by the SP. A detailed discussion of the TREC parameters can be found in [23].

The pseudo-XML in Figure 3 shows examples of terms used in Service Manifests, the first showing elasticity, and the second showing eco-efficiency (as usual, '?' denotes that the preceding term is optional, '+' denotes one or more repetitions, and '*' zero or more.)

OPTIMIS also defined QoP terms, specifically data protection and data security, such as geographical locations of the data centres and required level and method for data encryption. Like Contrail, terms for co-location (or non-co-location) are used, which can require same/different rack or same/different datacentre.

5 Comparison and Discussion

The use of automated agents on the service provider side is a classic feature of the cloud (e.g., [18]): the provider does not need to negotiate with each customer individually, so can provide services to a large number of customers, all of whom are treated the same. In turn, the provider saves money by providing the same services to many customers, by the economy of scale, at the cost of having to be elastic: the number of customers is not known beforehand.

The introduction of an automated agent acting on behalf of the users changes the cloud model. Ultimately, with an agent which is capable of discovering, negotiating, selecting, making use of, and combining services makes the consumer/provider relationship more dynamic. There are underlying assumptions: that the providers are interoperable and interchangeable, that they publish their SLA terms consistently and accurately, that they have consistent frameworks for authentication, authorisation, accounting, and monitoring. It may require relocatable services, or even a full federation built on top of the SLA negotiations, to enable users to access multiple providers with a single credential. But the potential gains are important.

```
<opt:ElasticitySection>
  <opt:Rule>
    <opt:Scope>
      opt:ScopeArrayType
    </opt:Scope>
    <opt:KPIName>xs:string</opt:KPIName>
    <opt:Window>xs:duration</opt:Window>
    <opt:Frequency>
      xs:positiveInteger
    </opt:Frequency>
    <opt:Quota>xs:positiveInteger</opt:Quota>
    <opt:Tolerance>
      opt:PositiveDecimal
    </opt:Tolerance>  ?
  </opt:Rule>  +
</opt:ElasticitySection>
<opt:EcoEfficiencySection>
  <opt:Scope>opt:ScopeType</opt:Scope>
  <opt:LEEDCertification>
    opt:LEEDCertificationConstraint
  </opt:LEEDCertification> ?
  <opt:BREEAMCertification>
    opt:BREEAMCertificationConstraint
  </opt:BREEAMCertification> ?
  <opt:EuCoCCompliant>
    xsd:boolean
  </opt:EuCoCCompliant> ?
  <opt:EnergyStarRating>
    opt:EnergyStarRating
  </opt:EnergyStarRating> ?
</opt:EcoEfficiencySection>
```

Fig. 3. Structure of terms used in Service Manifests

Smaller clouds – unlike the traditional cloud scenario, the customer/provider relationship can become more like the grid, where a single customer can use a significant proportion of the provider's capacity (of course, they don't *have* to, it's just that it is possible). The SLA fixes the customer/provider (or IP/SP) relationship and partially removes the need for elasticity, so the usage/capacity ratio does not need to be low. If a provider has an internal capacity of 100PB (say), and the consumer asks for 50PB, it doesn't matter that the consumer cannot double their capacity. In a federation, they can get the remaining capacity from a different provider. The provider knows that the consumer has allocated 50PB and can plan accordingly (for the duration of the agreement).

Potentially cheaper services – the provider can be less elastic than in a traditional cloud, and the planning ahead also means that the pricing of the service can be set lower, at least for long term agreements. Conversely, the customer's agent can look for lower prices from the competitors, and can even monitor the offers for spot pricing.

Better service delivery – as the agent can choose services from multiple providers, it can potentially combine these to obtain better QoS, while carefully tracking the QoP.

The potential gains are interesting, but should also be "reality checked." True mobility can be achieved only if services can be moved from one provider to another. A high level of interoperation is required. The requirements used by the user agents needs to be sufficiently expressive, but must not make it so complex that they won't be able to describe their requirements. Furthermore, the interplay between requirements needs to be better understood. And, above all, the publication of service terms needs to be timely, consistent, and accurate.

5.1 Quality of Protection

We have discussed a Quality of Protection, to be negotiated and agreed alongside the QoS. Unlike bandwidth, terabytes, or CPU hours, the terms in QoP are less well defined, although there are standards which can be built on. The terms of interest to our projects include:

LoA – the Level of Assurance associated with the user's credential. Covering this in depth is beyond the scope of this paper, but it needs to include factors like cryptographic strength, level of trust in identity provider, unique naming, multifactor authentication, usability, *etc.* Although multidimensional, the LoA is usually summarised in a single value. Typically, the *owner* of the resource or service will set the required minimum LoA based on an analysis of risks. Note that the negotiations of the SLAs themselves need a certain LoA, if we are to assert the trustworthiness of the agreement and the non-repudiation of it. With mutual authentication of sufficient LoA, the protection is also mutual: the customer is protected against a rogue provider, and the provider is protected against misuse by the customer because the customer has signed the agreement.

AUP – the Acceptable Use Policy could usefully be tied in with the SLA: by entering into the agreement, the customer asserts that they will comply with the rules and policies set out by the service provider(s). However, the challenge here is to define when it would be acceptable for an automated agent to enter into such an agreement: as before, the user-defined requirements will need to be clear enough that the agent can determine whether the proposed work is in violation of an offered AUP or not, and the offered AUP needs to be machine readable.

Data protection – again, a full discussion of data protection is beyond the scope of this paper, and, perhaps, beyond the capabilities of most non-specialised clouds. For now, the focus is primarily on availability (file is available at any given time) and integrity (it is not lost and not corrupted). Confidentiality is usually covered by encrypting in flight. Protecting personal data adds another level of difficulty: the best we can do in Contrail and OPTIMIS is to use geographic constraints, or have the providers advertise "no personal data."

6 Conclusion

In this paper we described two approaches for SLA-controlled Cloud federation in the two European projects FP7 projects Contrail and OPTIMIS. While the projects evolved independently using different frameworks for SLA creation and negotiation it turned out that the requirements regarding the SLA processing are similar and the underlying standards used are the same. Further work in the context of SLA negotiation will focus on achieving and testing interoperability of the two approaches.

Acknowledgements. This research was carried out as part of the Contrail and OPTIMIS research projects, funded by the European Commission under the 7th Framework Programme, grant agreements no. 257438 (Contrail) and 257115 (OPTIMIS).

References

1. Ruiz-Alvarez, A., Humphrey, M.: An Automated Approach to Cloud Storage Service Selection. In: ScienceCloud 2011, San Jose, California, USA, June 8 (2011)
2. Ferrer, A.J., et al.: OPTIMIS: A holistic approach to cloud service provisioning. Future Generation Computer Systems 28(1), 66–77 (2012)
3. SLA@SOI project homepage. Website, `http://sla-at-soi.eu/` (visited June 2013)
4. Contrail project homepage. Website, `http://contrail-project.eu/` (visited June 2013)
5. Bernstein, D., Ludvigson, E., Sankar, K., Diamond, S.: Blueprint for the Intercloud - Protocols and Formats for Cloud Computing Interoperability. In: Proc. of ICIW 2009, 4th Int'l Conf. Web App. and Services, pp. 328–336 (2009), doi:10.1109/ICIW.2009.55
6. Verissimo, P., Bessani, A., Pasin, M.: The TClouds Architecture: Open and Resilient Cloud-of-Clouds Computing. In: Proc. 2nd Int'l Workshop on Dependability of Clouds (DCDV 2012), together with IEEE/IFIP DSN 2012 (2012)
7. Contrail project, Deliverable D2.2, Architecture Design and QoS constraints matching algorithms in Federations (September 2011), `http://contrail-project.eu/documents/18553/136157/D2.2.pdf` (visited June 2013)
8. Buyya, R., Garg, S.K., Calheiros, R.N.: SLA-Oriented Resource Provisioning for Cloud Computing: Challenges, Architecture, and Solutions, ArXiv 1201.4522 (2012)
9. Pantazoglou, M., Tsalgatidou, A.: A Generic Query Model for the Unified Discovery of Heterogeneous Services. IEEE Transactions on Services Computing 6(2) (2013)
10. Open Grid Forum. Website, `http://www.ogf.org` (visited May 2013)
11. Wäldrich, O., Battre, D., Brazier, F., Clark, K., Oey, M., Papaspyrou, A., Wieder, P., Ziegler, W.: WS-Agreement Negotiation Version 1.0. Technical Report GFD.193 (2011), `http://www.ogf.org/documents/GFD.193.pdf` (visited June 2013)

12. Svirskas, A., Wilson, M., Matthews, B., Arenas, A., Mac Randal, D., Gallop, J., Bicarregui, J., Lambert, S.: Towards an Efficient, Reliable and Collaborative Web: from Distributed Computing to Semantic Description, Composition and Matchmaking of Services, http://epubs.cclrc.ac.uk/bitstream/755/W3C-FSWS-CCLRCPositionPaper-Svirskas_mdw-v3[1].pdf (visited June 2013)
13. Andrieux, A., Czajkowski, K., Dan, A., Keahey, K., Ludwig, H., Nakata, T., Pruyne, J., Rofrano, J., Tuecke, S., Xu, M.: Web Services Agreement Specification (WS-Agreement). Technical Report GFD.192 (October 2011), http://www.ogf.org/documents/GFD.192.pdf (visited June 2013)
14. Distefano, S., Puliafito, A.: Cloud@Home: Toward a Volunteer Cloud
15. Cuomo, A., Di Modica, G., Distefano, S., Puliafito, A., Rak, M., Tomarchio, O., Venticinque, S., Villano, U.: An SLA-based Broker for Cloud Infrastructures. J. Grid Comp. 11(1) (2013)
16. Graham-Rowe, D.: BOINC Puts Idle PCs to Work. New Scientist 180(2426-8) (2003) ISSN 0262-4079
17. Hewitt, E.: Java SOA Cookbook. O'Reilly (2009)
18. NIST Standards Acceleration to Jumpstart Adoption of Cloud Computing, http://www.nist.gov/itl/cloud/sajacc.cfm (visited June 2013)
19. Andreozzi, S., Burke, S., Field, L., Galang, G., Konya, B., Litmaath, M., Millar, P., Navarro, J.P.: GLUE Specification 2.0, Open Grid Forum GFD.147, http://www.ogf.org/documents/GFD.147.pdf (visited June 2013)
20. Badger, L., Bohn, R., Chandramouli, R., Grance, T., Karygiannis, T., Patt-Corner, R., Voas, J.: Cloud Computing Use Cases. NIST ITL Cloud Computing, http://www.nist.gov/itl/cloud/use-cases.cfm (visited June 2013)
21. Czajkowski, K., Fitzgerald, S., Foster, I., Kesselman, C.: Grid Information Services for Distributed Resource Sharing. In: Proc. 10th IEEE Int'l Symp. on High-Performance Distributed Computing, HPDC 2010 (August 2001)
22. OPTIMIS Service Manifest and API, http://www.optimis-project.eu/content/service-manifest-scientific-report (visited May 31, 2013)
23. Lawrence, A., Djemame, K., Wäldrich, O., Ziegler, W., Zsigri, C.: Using service level agreements for optimising cloud infrastructure services. In: Cezon, M., Wolfsthal, Y. (eds.) ServiceWave 2010 Workshops. LNCS, vol. 6569, pp. 38–49. Springer, Heidelberg (2011)
24. Kyriazis, D.: Cloud Computing Service Level Agreements. Technical report, European Commission DG CONNECT, Unit E2 - Software and Services, Cloud (July 2013), http://ec.europa.eu/information_society/newsroom/cf/dae/document.cfm?doc_id=2496 (visited July 15, 2013)
25. cybula - High performance pattern recognition systems. Website, http://www.cybula.com (visited June 30, 2013)
26. CompatibleOne-The Open Source Cloud Broker. Website http://www.compatibleone.org (visited June 30, 2013)

Towards a Swiss National Research Infrastructure

Peter Kunszt[1], Sergio Maffioletti[2] Dean Flanders[3], Markus Eurich[1], Eryk Schiller[8], Thomas Michael Bohnert[4] Andy Edmonds[4], Heinz Stockinger[5], Almerima Jamakovic-Kapic[6], Sigve Haug[6], Placi Flury[7], and Simon Leinen[7]

[1] ETH Zürich, Clausiusstrasse 45, 8092 Zurich, Switzerland
[2] Universität Zürich, Grid Computing Competence Center, Winterthurerstrasse 190, 8057 Zurich, Switzerland
[3] FMI, Maulbeerstrasse 66, 4058 Basel, Switzerland
[4] ZHAW, Obere Kirchgasse 2, 8400 Winterthur, Switzerland
[5] SIB Vital-IT, Quartier Sorge, 1015 Lausanne, Switzerland
[6] University of Bern, 3012 Bern, Switzerland
[7] SWITCH, Werdstrasse 2, 8004 Zurich, Switzerland
[8] University of Neuchâtel, Rue Emile-Argand 11, 2009 Neuchâtel, Switzerland

Abstract. In this position paper, we describe the current status and plans for a Swiss National Research Infrastructure. Swiss academic and research institutions are very autonomous. While being loosely coupled, they do not rely on any centralized management entities. A coordinated national research infrastructure can only be established by federating the local resources of the individual institutions. We discuss current efforts and business models for a federated infrastructure.

Keywords: grid, cloud, distributed computing, federation, funding.

1 Introduction and Overview

Switzerland, as a country, is organized in a very decentralized manner, which has a deep impact on the organization of research and education. At the federal level, there is the national supercomputing center, CSCS in Lugano, the national research network SWITCH and several institutes of research and technology of the ETH Domain. At the cantonal level, there are ten universities, nine universities of applied sciences, and several specialized institutions for research and education. The organizational and funding structures are very heterogeneus. Today, infrastructure provisioning happens exclusively on the institutional level. We believe that the scientific research community, as well as resource providers, may greatly benefit from a coordinated, federated national research infrastructure.

There exist various architectures of federated clouds [1] such as hybrid, broker-based, aggregated, and multi-tiered. The hybrid architecture allows a private cloud to cooperate with a public one by using specific drivers for cloud bursting. For example, OpenNebula [2,3] can cooperate with Amazon (Amazon EC2

D. an Mey et al. (Eds.): Euro-Par 2013 Workshops, LNCS 8374, pp. 157–166, 2014.

driver), and Eucalyptus [4]. StratusLab [5], an OpenNebula-based cloud infrastructure, provides a toolkit to integrate the most recent cloud management technologies. In the broker based model, the broker coordinates the resources of several public clouds. There are a few online broker sites such as BonFire (www.bonfire-project.eu), Open Cirrus (opencirrus.org), and FutureGrid (futuregrid.org).

The Reservoir system [6] provides an infrastructure that may automatically deploy tasks of one organization in the clouds of other partners having spare capacities. A multi-tiered architecture is an interesting option for large companies with geographically distributed resources. Such resources are usually strongly coupled as they serve as sub-services of the same entity. However, we believe that none of these models serve our specific needs adequately for Swiss higher education and research.

There are several examples of past Swiss national initiatives working towards the goal of setting up services to address the needs of several scientific user communities. The Swiss Multi-Science Computing Grid project [7] provided services mainly to the Swiss High Energy Physics community and enabled that community to participate in the European Grid Initiative (EGI). In the life sciences domain, the SyBIT project [8] of the Swiss Initiative for Systems Biology, SystemsX.ch, makes use of the computing and storage infrastructure of all participating institutions. Infrastructure is not organized in a coherent manner, as SyBIT is focusing on bioinformatics support, not infrastructure.

The funding for these efforts is project-based, and is aimed to create infrastructure and services in tight cooperation with a user community. However, it is currently unclear what will happen to the services, infrastructure and all the other additional value created (mostly in the form of specialized know-how) after their funding expires. The user communities still require services beyond their lifetime.

An example of how long-term sustained funding can be set up, is given by the Vital-IT group [9] of the Swiss Institute of Bioinformatics SIB. Vital-IT provides services for bioinformatics in life sciences, coordinating bioinformatics infrastructure and resources for several universities in the Western part of Switzerland. Vital-IT is funded by the participating universities, through federal funds and to a large extent by second and third parties (industrial and academic research grants). Researchers are advised to request these charges as part of their project grant proposals as 'bioinformatics consumables'.

Very recently, the Swiss government has initiated a project to work out a strategy for the development of a sustainable set of services for research, education and digital archiving communities. The individual sustainability models for the services developed are to be established in this project.

In this paper, we describe the current Swiss Academic Compute Cloud project that we use to prototype a federated Swiss infrastructure for research computing. We also summarize our current ideas about necessary policy and accounting models that have to be established to allow for a sustainable distributed Swiss research infrastructure. This should solve the remaining open issue of sustainable operation.

1.1 Cloud Definitions

We believe that it is necessary to specify our own definition of 'cloud' since the term has been used in many, sometimes conflicting contexts.

We expect the following properties from a service with a 'cloud' attribute:

Self serviced. A consumer has immediate access to resources and can unilaterally access computing capabilities, such as server time and network storage.
On-demand. As needed, at the time when needed, with the possibility of automatic provisioning. No need to do the full investment planning upfront.
Cost transparent. Accounting of actual usage is completely transparent to both the user and service provider, which is measured in meaningful terms.
Elastic, scalable. Capabilities can be elastically provisioned and released, in some cases automatically, to scale rapidly up and down, matching demands.
Multi-tenant. The providers computing resources are pooled to serve multiple consumers, with resources dynamically assigned and reassigned according to consumer demands. Ideally, for the customers, other tenants are invisible.
Programmable Services. The services expose a public programmable API that can be used to drive any aspect of the service programmatically.

These properties are technology-agnostic; the way we define cloud services has a consequence on how we expect the services to be exposed to the consumer and what kind of business model and usage policy is in place.

We also use the terms Infrastructure as a Service (IaaS), Platform as a Service (PaaS) and Software as a Service (SaaS) to define different fundamental types of services offered to researchers and educators. All these service types are considered to be part of the cloud ecosystem, they can be built on top of each other or directly on the underlying infrastructure.

2 Ecosystem Architecture

The development of a robust *digital ecosystem* is key to maintain competitiveness of Swiss research. Researchers need easy access to resources for their work and to maintain collaborations across institutional boundaries. We propose the establishment of an open informatics platform, which can be used to create the digital ecosystem by using clouds as an innovation enablement technology for sharing all types of resources.

The architecture of the digital ecosystem is based on cloud services, but at a very high level, it can be divided into the following elements (see Figure 1):

- Identity management (authentication of social and work identities)
- Social platform (information of interest to the researcher)
- Ideation platform (process of developing new services)
- Service Portals (access to resources)

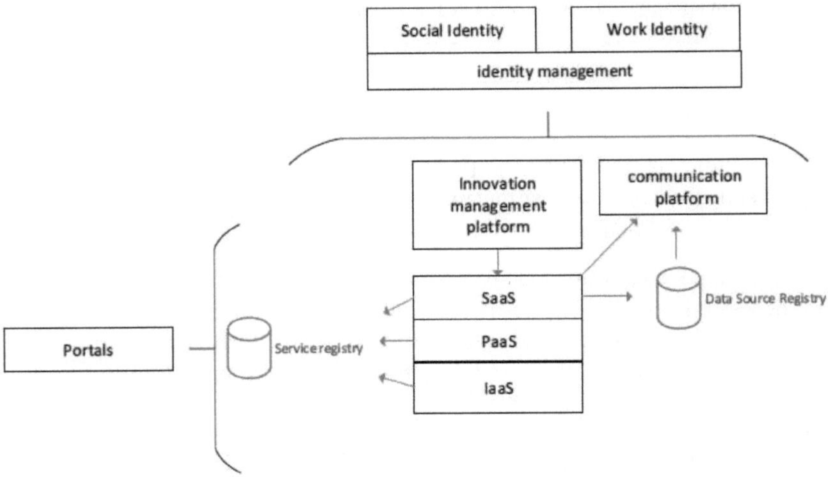

Fig. 1. Architecture of the digital ecosystem

This will provide a platform for researchers, research institutions, societies, and associations to rely on cloud services so that they can focus their energies in areas of value creation. One such example is FASEB [10] (Federation of American Societies in Experimental Biology), which supports individual researchers and societies with tasks common to all of them.

In terms of *identity management*, every member of an institution of higher education in Switzerland has already an identity in a Shibboleth-based federated identity management infrastructure [11]. However, this infrastructure needs to be extended with additional services like inter-institution group management, to meet the needs of the full ecosystem.

Social and *ideation platforms* are instruments aimed to channel researcher requests, needs and ideas into a discussion network, in which problems (expressed in terms of challenges) are evaluated and discussed, and where solutions are agreed, designed, implemented, and then added to the service portals as part of the available service portfolio.

Service portals are a generic model to introduce new technology that can be offered and adapted to meet the needs of a variety of researchers. The services introduced will be based on use-cases delivered by researchers or by the ideation process.

3 The Swiss Academic Compute Cloud Project

The Swiss Academic Compute Cloud Project (SwissACC) has been set up to keep and extend the currently established Swiss-wide computational science platform composed of resources and services of various types (local clusters, grid and cloud infrastructures) as well as the excellent know-how for user and application support. Research communities can profit from this platform either to address their computational needs, or to make use of the platform for collaboration purposes in national and international projects. It provides IaaS, PaaS and SaaS services to communities and helps to build their own service portals or tools.

The project builds upon previous initiatives at the national level such as the Swiss Multi Science Computing Grid (SMSCG) [7], the Academic Compute Cloud Provisioning and Usage [12], VM-MAD [13], GridCertLib [14], RS-NAS [15]; and international projects like EGI [16], Chemomentum [17], and PRACE [18].

The primary goal of SwissACC is to sustain and keep together the research communities that have been brought to distributed infrastructures in the previous Grid and Cloud projects. The secondary goal is to increase the number of supported research communities. A large community can profit from mutual benefits due to economies of scale as they gain more experience and receive more feedback, improving the overall quality of the provided services.

The final goal is to provide a sound basis for decision making on infrastructure models, like in-house vs. outsourcing, and on technologies, like running a cluster, a virtualized infrastructure, or going to a public cloud provider.

The project is composed of infrastructure providers, service providers and user communities that have very close and regular interaction with each other. This allows the project to continuously improve the services and to focus on items that users really need and use. The user support is set up using a collaborative distributed support model, helping scientists in bringing their small and large-scale data analysis pipelines to a flexible cloud-like platform that can easily be shaped to accommodate their needs.

The current infrastructure supports user communities who already solve research problems with help of computational processing. Virtualization techniques from e.g. the VM-MAD [13] and AppPot [19] projects and a powerful toolbox for job management on heterogeneous infrastructures (GC3Pie [20]) allows us to set up a standardized procedure for enabling new research communities. These technologies have allowed us to start supporting new users and communities with relatively little effort. However, it is not enough to just virtualize a certain application; there have to be several middleware layers to assure that this application can scale, e.g. make use of necessary infrastructure services like storage, and is easy to use by the end user.

The SwissACC project currently supports over 20 applications [21] from the domains of life sciences, earth sciences, economics, computer sciences, engineering, cryptography and physics. Table 1 lists the applications supported, which we intend to extend throughout the duration of the project.

3.1 Infrastructure for SwissACC

The SwissACC project has currently access to 5 OpenStack cloud installations at the ETH Zurich, the University of Zurich, SWITCH, the Zurich University of Applied Sciences and the HES-SO site in Geneva. These clouds are relatively small: they range from 100 to 400 CPU cores each, but with relatively good memory and storage.

The project also has access to the Swiss National Grid infrastructure, an aggregation of relatively large clusters, as this is part of the LHC Computing Grid infrastructure.

The OpenStack versions of the various installations are not identical. The coordination does not involve upgrades being rolled out simultaneously across all sites, and we believe it is not necessary to aim for such strong coordination as long as interoperability can be maintained. The OpenStack distributions being used are also not identical. Some are based on Ubuntu, others on Red Hat, Scientific Linux or Fedora.

The choice of OpenStack as a reference cloud software stack has emerged as an evaluation done in a predecessor project, the Academic Cloud Provisioning and Usage project [12]. There, the ETH Zurich and the University of Zurich evaluated the available cloud solutions and set up several pilot cloud installations. OpenStack has been evaluated against other public open cloud stacks (like OpenNebula, Eucalyptus, CloudStack [22]) as well as commercial cloud solutions (Flexiant, StackOps, HP CloudSystem Matrix, etc.).

Table 1. Applications on SwissACC

Institution	Applications	Characteristics	Research Field
IMSB/ETHZ	Rosetta, TPP, HCS pipeline	2-3 users, 152k jobs, 300k walltime hours during last 12 months	life sciences / proteomics
IBF/UZH	gpremium	1 user, 916k jobs, 238k walltime hours, (1.5.2011 – 1.7.2012)	Economics / financial models
GEO/UZH	GEOTop	4-8 users, 37k jobs with 11k walltime hours since June 2012	earth sciences
UniBE/UniNE	A4-Mesh	15 users, real-time data collected since June 2013	environmental research / hydrogeological modeling
Lacal/EPFL	gcrypto	1-4 users, 16k jobs, 32k walltime hours during last 6 months	cryptography
UNIL/Vital-IT	Selectome	1 production user. 71k jobs, 190k walltime hours during last 12 months	Life-sciences/ phylogeny
UniGE	MetaPIGA	execution model still to be defined.	Life-sciences / engineering
LHEP/UniBe	ATLAS	Several (international) users, ca 27k jobs/month with 239k walltime hours	High Energy Physics
WSL/SLF	CATS, Alpine3D, SwissEx	CATS: 1 user, 1month, 2300 jobs, 38k walltime hours SwissEx: cyclic analysis (30' frequency) processing data from 3 IMIS stations	earth sciences/ climate modeling

Commercial cloud solutions are usually very mature, with several layers of well-tested software built into themselves, leveraging these companies' experience in operating large-scale automated infrastructures. These layers make them very complex and not easy to maintain without proper training. Therefore, such systems should be optimally bought directly from the company including expert support, preferably by an on-site full-time specialist.

Lacking the funding for such a system and the expert, we chose OpenStack as the open cloud software stack, since currently it has the largest community and commercial support. However, OpenStack is not yet fully mature as a production system. It is already usable and there are very large installations running it (for example at CERN), but the expectations of what is possible and what the challenges are need to be set correctly, also towards the users. We have exposed a lot of stability and security issues, that are being addressed in newer releases. For example, the accounting and quota management functionality is still largely in development. Our recommendation to our partner resource providers is therefore to slowly ramp-up cloud services offered to the researchers, with proper training and expectation management, initially being mostly for testing and educational purposes. With the right high-level middleware like GC3Pie [20], the free OpenStack solution is already adequate for many use-cases. For more reliable services and more complete installations, a commercial OpenStack-compliant solution might be considered, as offered by Rackspace, Red Hat, etc.

In terms of cloud coordination for technology and adoption, we have initiated a dedicated interest group for cloud computing in the Swiss Informatics Society [23].

4 Cloud Charging Models for Federated Infrastructures

In order to exploit economies of scale, i.e., the consolidation of resources, the institutions need to be able to provide services to each other at a cost. However, there is currently no model and in fact no sufficient legal basis that would allow the institutions to charge each other for their respective incurring service costs. We are therefore proposing several cloud-like business models for the provisioning of services by higher-education centers, allowing for many different charging models for them to choose from, in the hope of starting a process that will eventually allow a much tighter cooperation than is possible today.

Also as part of the Academic Cloud Provisioning and Usage project [12], we tried to gain insights into service consumers' and providers' needs as a basis for a pricing strategy of cloud-based services and for future decision-making. Information was gathered by interviewing research groups currently using central computing services.

The interviews revealed that academic service consumers currently perceive cloud services as a playground for testing, experimenting, and training students. However to date, most academic service consumers do not fully perceive the added value that the cloud computing model can provide. Some groups say they would use cloud services if they were available at a competitive cost. Currently, these cloud-based services are not necessary due to existing private infrastructures or service providers. These service providers do, however, see several advantages that a cloud model could provide in the future, such as flexibility, provisioning of additional services, time to service, self-serving aspects and increased automation, elasticity, and a more balanced workload.

There are three basic pricing schemes that are acceptable for academic consumers of cloud-based services:

'Pay per use' Service consumers are charged a fee according to the time and volume of a computing service that has been consumed.

Subscription The service consumer pays a fee on a regular basis for the usage of a service. Subscriptions allow services to be sold as packages.

'Pay for a share' In this approach service consumers buy a share in order to get a corresponding amount of service.

It is of course possible to offer several of the three models above simultaneously or in a mixed form, for example adjusting the pay-per-use pricing on a pre-subscription volume, as it is already done by Amazon.

The interviews revealed that academic service consumers care little about pricing strategies. They want to focus on science and research. Foremost, they just want services that work. They expect an easy approach and want the university to clear all of the obstacles from their paths. From their perspective, the 'per pay use' and subscription approach can only work if there is a way to get funding for it.

From the service providers' perspective, there is no pricing scheme that outperforms any of the other schemes. Each of the three pricing schemes has certain advantages and disadvantages. The usefulness of one approach can depend on the length of time a given service is needed. Pay per use qualifies best for a short-term service demand that lasts no more than three months or as an addition for peak usage on top of a subscription or share. The subscription scheme might be a good solution for mid- to long-term commitments. The pay for a share approach may be most suitable for long-term commitments, i.e., for more than two years. In our definition of cloud we of course favor the pay-per-use model as it fits the operational-expense-only model best. However, until the funding obstacles for such a model are overcome (both on the provider and the consumer side), we need the other schemes at least during a transition phase, the length of which is to be determined.

Finally, many academic service consumers do not know much about cloud computing and in fact do not care much about what computing resources are used. They just need some powerful computing services in order to do their research. Therefore, the pricing scheme should be simple, yet fair and transparent. In this context, subsidization can play an important role to clear inconveniences out of the service consumers' way. The institutions might set up a subsidization scheme, providing the researchers with free access to resources, or other means for the researchers to pay for cloud-based services.

To the funding agencies, we propose to introduce an 'informatics consumable' concept based on the experience of the Vital-IT competence center. The idea is that projects simply put in a line item called 'informatics consumables', requesting funding to be spent on the available research computing infrastructure to meet their computing and storage needs. Obviously, the evaluation process applied by the funding agencies should take the amount of requested informatics consumables into consideration and the process should check back with the infrastructure providers to find out whether the request is technically sound and whether the requested consumables are adequate. In the Vital-IT model, such consumables also apply to user support services and to standardized data analysis services performed by bioinformaticians at the competence center, providing expertise to projects in this domain that do not have the project partners to perform a standardized analysis of their data.

5 Summary and Outlook

We have presented the current efforts to maintain a federated research computing infrastructure in Switzerland, with details on our thoughts for sustainability and funding models.

We are working towards a sustained national infrastructure model based on federation concepts where researchers can easily gain access to the necessary resources and support persons through local contacts at their individual institutions. Sustainable funding models have been presented but they still need to be refined, accepted and put in place by funding bodies and institutions to have a lasting, sustained effect on the Swiss research landscape.

Given the high expectations that cloud technologies set, there are certain risks that we need to be aware of and address properly. Based on our experience with federation in the context of Grid technologies, we know that it is very important to get actual scientific users on board early, to set expectations correctly and to immediately use new technologies and services.

Our goal is to advance scientific research by lowering the barriers to usage and adoption of information technologies in general. In an ideal scenario, a scientist has the choice to select from a large array of easy to use tools and services to perform his or her research. He or she should also be able to easily publish new scientific services based on their individual research or to contribute to the existing community of tools and services. Such frameworks and services need to be intuitive, resilient to failures, provide meaningful error messages, and integrate with social media to interact with other scientists and service supporters in the right context.

References

1. Moreno-Vozmediano, R., Montero, R.S., Llorente, I.M.: IaaS Cloud Architecture: From Virtualized Datacenters to Federated Cloud Infrastructures. IEEE Computer 45(12), 65–72 (2012)
2. Sotomayor, B., Montero, R.S., Llorente, I.M., Foster, I.: Virtual Infrastructure Management in Private and Hybrid Clouds. IEEE Internet Computing 13(5), 14–22 (2009)

3. Moreno-Vozmediano, R., Montero, R.S., Llorente, I.M.: Multicloud Deployment of Computing Clusters for Loosely Coupled MTC Applications. IEEE Trans. Parallel and Distributed Systems 22(6), 924–930 (2011)
4. Nurmi, D., Wolski, R., Grzegorczyk, C., Obertelli, G., Soman, S., Youseff, L., Zagorodnov, D.: The Eucalyptus Open-Source Cloud-Computing System. In: 9th IEEE/ACM International Symposium on Cluster Computing and the Grid, CC-GRID 2009, May 18-21, pp.124–131 (2009), doi:10.1109/CCGRID.2009.93
5. StratusLab, `http://stratuslab.eu/`
6. Rochwerger, B., Tordsson, J., Ragusa, C., Breitgand, D., Clayman, S., Epstein, A., Hadas, D., Levy, E., Loy, I., Maraschini, A., Massonet, P., Munoz, H., Nagin, K., Toffetti, G., Villari, M.: Reservoir - When One Cloud Is Not Enough. IEEE Computer 44(3), 44–51 (2011)
7. The Swiss Multi-Science Computing Grid project, `http://www.smscg.ch`
8. The Swiss Systems Biology Initiative, `http://www.sybit.net/`
9. Vital-IT: bioinformatics competence center of the SIB Swiss Institute of Bioinformatics, `www.vital-it.ch/`, `www.isb-sib.ch`
10. Federation of American Societies for Experimental Biology, `http://www.faseb.org`
11. Authentication and Authorization Infrastructure (AAI), `http://www.switch.ch/aai/support/presentations/`
12. Kunszt, P., Maffioletti, S., Messina, A., Flanders, D., Mathys, S., Murri, R., et al.: Academic Cloud Provisioning and Usage Project, `https://wiki.systemsx.ch/display/cloudresult`
13. Aleksiev, T., Barkow, S., Kunszt, P., Maffioletti, S., Murri, R., Panse, C.: VM-MAD: a cloud/cluster software for service-oriented academic environments. arXiv:1302.2529 [cs.DC]
14. Murri, R., Maffioletti, S., Kunszt, P., Tschopp, V.: GridCertLib: a Single Sign-on Solution for Grid Web Portals. Journal of Grid Computing 9(4), 441–453 (2011)
15. Gorini, C., Maffioletti, S., Kunszt, P., Tacchella, D., Balazs, C., Briand, C., Murri, R., Messina, A., Corbeil, L.: Remote Scalable Network Attached Storage Project
16. The European Grid Infrastructure, `http://www.egi.eu/`
17. Grid services based environment to enable innovative research, `http://cordis.europa.eu/search/index.cfm?fuseaction=proj.document&PJ_RCN8505182`
18. PRACE Research Infrastructure, `http://www.prace-ri.eu/`
19. Murri, R., Maffioletti, S.: Batch-oriented software appliances. arXiv:1203.1466 [cs.DC]
20. Maffioletti, S., Murri, R., Messina, A.: GC3Pie: a Python toolkit for job management on heterogeneous infrastructures
21. Maffioletti, S., et al.: Applications on the Swiss Multi-Science Computing Grid, `http://www.smscg.ch/WP/applications/`
22. Apache CloudStack project, `http://cloudstack.apache.org/`
23. Swiss Informatics Society, `http://www.s-i.ch/fachgruppen-und-sektionen/cloud-computing/`

11th International Workshop on Algorithms, Models and Tools for Parallel Computing on Heterogeneous Platforms (HeteroPar 2013)

Paolo Bientinesi and Enrique Quintana-Ortí

Program Chairs

HeteroPar 2013 was the eleventh edition of the International Workshop on Algorithms, Models and Tools for Parallel Computing on Heterogeneous Platforms. For the fifth time, the workshop was organized in conjunction with the Euro-Par annual series of international conferences dedicated to the promotion and advancement of all aspects of parallel computing.

Heterogeneity is emerging as one of the most profound and challenging characteristics of today's parallel environments. From the macro level, where networks of distributed computers, composed by diverse node architectures, are interconnected with potentially heterogeneous networks, to the micro level, where deeper memory hierarchies and various accelerator architectures are increasingly common, the impact of heterogeneity on all computing tasks is rapidly growing. Traditional parallel algorithms, programming environments and tools, designed for legacy homogeneous multiprocessors, will at best achieve a small fraction of the efficiency and the potential performance that we should expect from parallel computing in tomorrow's highly diversified and mixed environments. New ideas, innovative algorithms, and specialized programming environments and tools are needed to efficiently use these new and multifarious parallel architectures. The workshop is intended to be a forum for researchers working on algorithms, programming languages, tools, and theoretical models aimed at efficiently solving problems on heterogeneous networks.

The workshop attracted 31 papers; of these, 12 were selected for presentation and are included in these proceedings. Based on both contents and presentation, the article "Scheduling Independent Tasks on Multi-Cores with GPU Accelerators", by Safia Kedad-Sidhoum, Florence Monna, Gregory Mounie and Denis Trystram was chosen as the Best Paper of the workshop.

D. an Mey et al. (Eds.): Euro-Par 2013 Workshops, LNCS 8374, p. 167, 2014.

Data-Management Directory for OpenMP 4.0 and OpenACC

Julien Jaeger, Patrick Carribault, and Marc Pérache

CEA, DAM, DIF, F-91297, Arpajon, France
firstname.lastname@cea.fr

Abstract. Today's trend to use accelerators in heterogeneous systems forces a paradigm shift in programming models. The use of low-level APIs for accelerator programming is tedious and not intuitive for casual programmers. To tackle this problem, recent approaches focused on high-level directive-based models, with a standardization effort made with OpenACC and the directives for accelerator on OpenMP 4.0 release candidate. The pragmas for data management induce some coherence issues in the accelerator memory for code correctnesse. To address this issue, we propose the design for a directory, along with a reduced runtime ABI, to handle correctly data management in these standards. Our design fits a multi-accelerator system. Also, with our directory, we propose a way to handle correctly pragmas on partially overlapping data intervals.

1 Introduction

In the last decade, High Performance Computing moved towards multi-core and many-core architectures. Scientists must not only deal with all the multiple parallelism levels, but also with the programmability difference of available accelerators. While some languages are specific to an accelerator or constructor (e.g., NVIDIA's CUDA), efforts have been made to offer an interface to write codes for CPUs and GPUs in a common way, first with the OpenCL language , and then with the use of directives, allowing the user to add pragmas in their code to work on accelerators.

Several sets of directives for accelerators (CAPS Entreprise's `hmpp`, PGI directives among others) were merged into one set of directives through the OpenACC API and the directives for accelerator in the OpenMP 4.0 release candidate. Usually when programming with accelerators (including GPUs) one has to manage data in memory very carefully. No coherence is implemented between the host and the accelerators, and sometimes also inside an accelerator. This was changed by the use of directives to handle computations on accelerators. Different actions are triggered whether the concerned data are already allocated on the accelerator or not. Hence, there is a need to store the informations about the data transferred to an accelerator.

OpenACC 2.0. The OpenACC API was released in November 2011 with a draft for the second version appearing one year later. In the scope of our work, we will focus on the data management part. The bounds of `data` constructs define *data environments*. A `data` construct includes several clauses to specify if the data need to be transfered from (or back to) the host (*copyin*, *copyout*), is already present (*present*) or need to be

D. an Mey et al. (Eds.): Euro-Par 2013 Workshops, LNCS 8374, pp. 168–177, 2014.

allocated on the accelerator (*create*). More complex clauses are used to allocate and copy the data only if they are not already in the accelerator memory (*pcreate*, *pcopyout*, *pcopyin*). Data specified in clauses are alive only in the scope of their data environment.

OpenMP API 4.0. OpenMP 4.0 specification including directives for accelerators was released in July 2013. One can understand from the document that data management is nearly the same as with OpenACC. The bounds of a *target data* construct defines a *data environment*. A *target data* construct will use the clause *map* with states to specify the data management between the host and the accelerator. The different states (*alloc*, *to*, *from*, *tofrom*) have the same behavior as some clauses in OpenACC (resp. *pcreate*, *pcopyin*, *pcopyout*, *pcopy*).

In the following of this paper, we use OpenACC terms to refer to the two APIs. For example, *pcopy* will refer to *pcopy* in OpenACC and *map(tofrom)* in OpenMP.

In this paper, we propose a directory scheme to handle all the memory management hidden in the directives for accelerators. Our directory is designed to work with several accelerator devices attached to the same host. Moreover, we suggest a simple extension to the two APIs allowing to correctly use data management pragmas on partially overlapping intervals.

The paper is organized as follows: in Section 2, we present three motivating examples to detail the important problems to tackle while managing data with these directives, and to exhibit how should work the use of pragmas on partially overlapping intervals. Section 3 presents the previous work done with directories, and the few efforts already done to propose open implementations of the OpenACC standard. The design of our directory and the different algorithms implemented in the runtime are described in Section 4. Finally, some overhead results of our implementation are shown in Section 5 before concluding in Section 6.

2 Motivating Examples

Our directory is motivated by three major problems. The first one is how to correctly deal with different subparts of the same array spread across nested data environments. The second problem occurs when different pragmas deal with covering subparts of an array accessed through an alias pointer. The last one concerns the use of partially overlapping intervals in nested data environment.

Separate ranges of the same array. When dealing with nested data environments, it is possible that pragmas spread across these data environments handle subparts of the same arrays. Figure 1 shows an example of an OpenACC program with this behavior. The first data environment requests the elements from 0 to 19 of arrays a to be available on the accelerator device, while the second one requests an other subpart of array a. The two subparts of the array are alive, and they are used in the same computation. If the two subparts are allocated in distinct locations of the accelerator memory, the only way to have valid results is to change how we access one of the subparts, using a new pointer. Rewriting the memory accesses can be done on simple codes like the one in Figure 1, but it is impossible to automatically apply it on a more complex code with nested function calls. To have a correct computation, all elements of a should be in the same memory space, with $a[50]$ being fifty elements further than $a[0]$. The pragmas related to the same memory zone have to be matched together inside a common memory area.

```
#pragma acc data
    copyin(b[0:20],a[0:20])
    copyout(a[0:20])
  #pragma acc parallel for
    for (i=0; i<20; i++)
      a[i]+=b[i];
  c=&(a[25]);
  #pragma acc data
    copyin(a[50:20], c[0:20])
    #pragma acc parallel for
      for (i=0; i<20; i++)
        a[i]+=a[i+25]+a[i+50]
```

Fig. 1. OpenACC code using distinct parts of the same array with an alias pointer

Covering ranges and aliasing. Another specific case is when aliasing is use within a computation. This alias pointer can be used in a clause to specify a subpart of a data range already declared in an englobing data environment. The two pragmas should be matched to not reallocate and transfer the data already present on the accelerator. Also, if distinct subparts of an array are merged in the same memory allocation, another problem may appear. In the code example displayed in Figure 1, an alias pointer is used to refer to another subpart of the array a. This new code is valid, since we transfer all the data required by the computations to the accelerator. However, all the data pointers in the different pragmas do not have the same reference address. If intervals are not matched, one might end up with a totally different location for $c[0:20]$ than between $a[0:20]$ and $a[50:20]$, ending with a false code on the accelerator. To link this interval to the other clauses, one first has to fuse the two pragmas on address a, creating a new range from $a[0]$ to $a[70]$, and then find that the intersection with the pragma on address c is not empty. Thus, it is necessary to check the covering range of intervals without the same basic addresses.

Overlapping intervals. In OpenMP 4.0 and OpenACC, using an interval in a data environment which partially overlaps another interval previously defined in an englobing environment is not valid. However, it is possible to handle such cases, considering that the overlapping interval can be divided in multiple pieces: the parts that are already present on the accelerator, and the parts that need to be allocated. Like for the case with separate ranges on the same arrays, a reallocation will be performed on the accelerator to have enough memory to reunite the subparts of the overlapping interval. We suggest two schemes to initialize in this new memory space the data that correspond to parts already present on the accelerator: either use these previous data (as with a `present_or` clause on the subpart), or use the corresponding data from the host memory (as with an update clause on the subpart).

3 Related Work

Directory-based coherency protocols have emerged in the late 70's as a concurrent to *snoopy cache* protocols. Tang *et al.* [16] and Censier *et al.* [4] set the base of the directory-based protocols ([5]). The latest proposed a *Full-map directory*, which stores for each block in global memory its status in every caches. Later approaches aimed to reduce the memory footprint of this full-map directory ([1,6]). The multiplication of cores and caches on the same node brought new interest to directory-based cache coherency. Studies were performed to work on coarse-grain tracking to identify group of blocks which do not require coherence protocol ([3,11,7,18]), allowing some trade-off between performance and accuracy.

Caches protocols were previously used on GPUs for performance issues. A broad range of codes uses a software cache to improve their execution time, from a simple sum-products [15] to cardiac cell modeling [10]. Some of the most known frameworks optimizing and scheduling codes on GPUs use some software cache to have better performance. The frameworks looking for work on all available devices, like XKaapi [8], StarPU [2], FLAME [13] or StarSs [12], often rely on directory schemes to keep the data coherency between the different memories. However, these frameworks check and transfer blocks of data that will be ultimately used by a device. If only a subpart is available in the device memory, the whole block will still be updated, as no scheme allows to maintain the data coherency in a single memory between several transfers on related data. Moreover, the data decomposition is handled by the runtime and the user can not specify a finer granularity.

If the OpenACC standard release was praised, it spawned very few research papers on the subject ([9,17,14]). To the best of our knowledge, the only open implementation for OpenACC that can be found in scientific publications is `accULL`, and neither the `accULL` publications nor the vendor implementation and documentation of OpenACC compilers mentionned how the memory allocations and transfers are handled.

Our work was inspired by the directory-based coherence protocols. If keeping the data location between several devices was already shown useful to improve performence, the idea of some sort of data coherence on a single accelerator memory is rather new and is induced by the directives for data managment on recent APIs. The automatic treatment of the copy clauses needs fundamental ideas of directory-based coherence protocol: which data are on which accelerators, and with which state.

4 Directory Implementation

The purpose of the directory is to store the information of all host data located on accelerators. These data intervals are represented by tuples in our directory. The tuples are the basic block of the directory, embedding all the necessary informations for a given data interval (length, element size, host and accelerator memory pointers, state).

In its design, the directory needs to handle correctly the opening and closure of data environment for all available accelerators. When a new data environment opens, new clauses will be read, and new tuples will be added at the top of the chosen accelerator handler. As we described earlier in Section 2, some fusion between intervals might be necessary before any allocation and copy. All the actions to be performed when entering a new data environment are detailed in Section 4.2. When closing a data environment, all the clauses embedded in the current data environment should be closed and erased. This procedure is described in Section 4.3.

4.1 Directory Design

We designed our directory as a table of stacks, one for each accelerator. The stack allows to represent easily the nesting of data environments, as the newest data environment is always the current one, and we should revert to the enclosing one when the current one is closed. A data environment is represented as a level of the stack, which is composed of two list of tuples. The first list of tuples are the tuples created directly from the incoming clauses of the current data environment. They are called *original tuples*. The second list stores the final tuples after applying the different fusion between the *original tuples* and the already existing tuples. We refer later to these tuples as *artificial tuples*.

In the tuple, the host interval is stored using four values: its basic pointer (a_h), its first element (elt), its length and the size ($size$) of an element. To map it quickly to its accelerator memory, the tulpe also embedded the accelerator address of the first element of the interval (a_{acc}). Hence, when copying the first element of an interval from the host to the device, one has to copy the data from the location $a_h+elt*size$ to the address a_{acc} on the accelerator . Copying the data directly to a_{acc} avoid the unnecessary allocation of element a_h to $a_h + elt * size$ on the accelerator memory. As several reallocations may occur, the memory address on the accelerator is updated after each modifications.

To use this directory, we provide a small ABI, based on the different pragmas, presented in Figure 4. When a data environment is opened, functions *new_dataE()* and *read_pragmas()* create the new stage in the stack and allocate the list for the incoming data. For each clause, a corresponding function exists using the same parameters. Once all the clauses are read, *write_pragmas* applies the fusions then inserts the new tuples in the stack. Finally, when the data environment is closed *end_dataE()* transfers the data and delete the remaining structures.

4.2 Entering a New Data Environment

The insertion of a new tuple in the directory is a critical moment. A lot of informations must be checked (possible fusion, allocation) and updated. The operations to perform at the creation of a new tuple, forming the algorithm in Figure 2, can be decomposed in three main steps: the decoding of data clauses, the fusion of tuples, and the allocation and copy of data intervals.

The first step is the decoding of the clauses in the data environment. Each clause is translated in a tuple, its state being the type of the clause (*copyout,pcopyin...*). The tuple is compared to the other existing *original tuples*. If the interval is completely included in the previous tuples and the clause is a *present_or* clause, then it is deleted, as we will use the existing data and no transfer will occur. If a partial overlap is detected, an error is occured. This is the default behavior according to the APIs. If one wants to handle the case of partial overlap in the runtime, then the interval is decomposed in several subparts, being either totally present in the accelerator memory, or totally absent. Once no other overlap can be found, remaining tuples are inserted in the *original* list at the current level of the stack.

The next step is the fusion of intervals, either due to a common reference address on the host, or due to some covering range between the tuples. We suggest to begin with the fusion of tuples based on their basic virtual address on the host, otherwise some covering range might be missed (as explained in Section 2). The fusion on same basic address is realized between all the tuples in the original list of the current level and the artificial list of the previous one. The resulting fused tuples are inserted in the artificial list of the current level. At this point, a new tuple state is either ALLOC if an allocation is necessary (i.e. the range of the *artificial tuple* is not included in one of its ancestors), or ALIAS otherwise. In Figure 1, the two intervals on a will be fused in a new interval $a[0:70]$, stored in the artificial list of the current level. Since the resulting range is greater than each of its ancestors, the state of this new tuple is ALLOC. An artificial tuple keeps the list of its direct ancestors fused to build it.

```
INPUT: Pl: a list of pragma, D: the stack for the current device.
INPUT: L, the nested level of the current data environment.
for (each pragma p in Pl) do
    new interval i ← read(pragma p)
    if (i is not totally included in data previously transfered) then
        D.L.originalItvList ← i
    else
        if (i is partially included in data previously transfered) then
            Do actions for partially covering intervals
for (each interval tmpi in (D.L.originalItvList ∪ D.(L-1).artificialItvList)) do
    new interval ni ← tmpi
    ni.ancestors ← *tmpi
    D.L.artificialItvList ← D.L.artificialItvList ∪ ni
for (each interval s,t in D.L.artificialItvList such as s≠t) do
    if ((s.addr_host = t.addr_host) or (s.itv ∩ t.itv ≠ ∅)) then
        new interval st ← s ∪ t
        if (st ≠ s and st ≠ t) then
            st.state ← ALLOC
        else
            st.state ← ALIAS
        D.L.artificialItvList ← (D.L.artificialItvList ∪ st) / {s,t}
for (each interval a in D.L.artificialItvList) do
    if (a.state = ALLOC) then
        a.addr_acc = Allocate_acc(a.range)
        for (each interval anc in a.ancestorList) do
            if (anc ⊂ D.L.originalItvList) then
                if (anc.state = COPYIN or anc.state = PCOPYIN) then
                    copy_host→acc(anc.addr_host, a.addr_acc, anc.range)
            else
                copy_acc→acc(anc.addr_acc, a.addr_acc, anc.range)
```

Fig. 2. Algorithm to apply when reading the pragmas of a new data environment

A second fusion based on covering ranges is performed on these new tuples. The memory interval of tuples are compared. If there is an overlap, the two tuples are fused together in a new tuple. Their corresponding list of ancestors are also fused to become the ancestor list of the new tuple. The state of this tuple is ALLOC if its data range is not included in one of the tuples fused to build it, or if at least one of the fused tuples was already in a ALLOC state. Otherwise, the state of this tuple is ALIAS. In Figure 1, array c has a common part with the new artificial interval $a[0:70]$. The result of their fusion has the same range of data. One of its ancestors has a ALLOC state, so the state of the new tuple will also be ALLOC.

The final step consists in the allocation of data on the accelerator according to the list of *artificial tuples* at the current level of the stack, and to perform Actions are performed only for the tuples with a ALLOC state. A memory range corresponding to the data range of the tuple is allocated on the accelerator device. For all the ancestors

```
INPUT: L, the nested level of the current data environment.
INPUT: D, the directory for the current device.
for (each interval t in D.L.artificialItvList)
  if(t.state = ALLOC
    for (each interval a in t.ancestorList)
      if (a ⊂ D.L.originalItvList)
        if (a.state = COPYOUT)
          copy_{ac→h}(t.addr_ac + a.first_h - t.first_h, a.addr_h, a.range)
        D(2×lv) ← D(2×lv) / {a}
      else
        copy_{ac→ac}(t.addr_ac + a.first_h - t.first_h, addr_ac, a.range)
  D.L.artificialItvList ← D.L.artificialItvList / {t}
```

Fig. 3. Algorithm to apply when closing a data environment

of the tuple, a copy takes place, either from host to device if the state of the ancestor is (P)COPYIN, or from another part of the accelerator memory if the state of the ancestor is ALLOC or ALIAS.

4.3 Data Environment Exit

Deleting a stack level in the directory is lighter than the reading of new pragmas. The algorithm for exiting a data environment is shown in Figure 3. When a data environment is closed, the list of *artificial tuples* is unstacked. For each tuple of this list with a ALLOC state, actions will be performed on the different subparts of the interval, depending on its corresponding ancestors state. If the ancestor has a COPYOUT state, it is an *original tuple* requesting to copy the subpart back to the host memory. Data transfer occurs from the accelerator address specified by the ancestor tuple to the host address given by the same ancestor tuple. On the other hand, an ancestor with a ALLOC state means

OpenACC	OpenMP 4.0	ABI
# **pragma** acc data	# **pragma** target data	new_dataE(); read_pragma(); . . . write_pragma();
clauses *pcopy, pcopyin pcopyout, pcreate*	clauses *map(tofrom), map(to) map(from) map(alloc)*	pragma_pcopy(), pragma_pcopyin() pragma_pcopyout(), pragma_pcreate()
clauses *copy, copyin copyout*, textitcreate	no correspondance in OpenMP 4.0	pragma_copy(), pragma_copyin() pragma_copyout(), pragma_create()
# **pragma** acc update	# **pragma** target update	pragma_update()
end of data environment	end of data region	end_dataE();

Fig. 4. ABI for the use of the designed directory scheme

that a previous allocated space exists in a previous data environment. To keep the data coherence between the interleaved data environment, a data copy corresponding to this subpart is necessary between the current memory space and the memory space pointed by the ancestor. Once all the copies are performed, the top stage of the stack is deleted. The new level at the top of the stack contains the two lists for the enclosing (and now current) data environment.

5 Experimental Results

To evaluate our method, we measured the overhead of using our directory through our directory's ABI (shown in Figure 4), compared to using the CUDA API directly. The CUDA kernels are the same, and only the memory transactions (allocations, transfers) with the GPU are handled either using CUDA functions or our ABI. We present the results for two applications on an Intel Xeon Westmere-EP E5620 with a GPU Nvidia Fermi M2090.

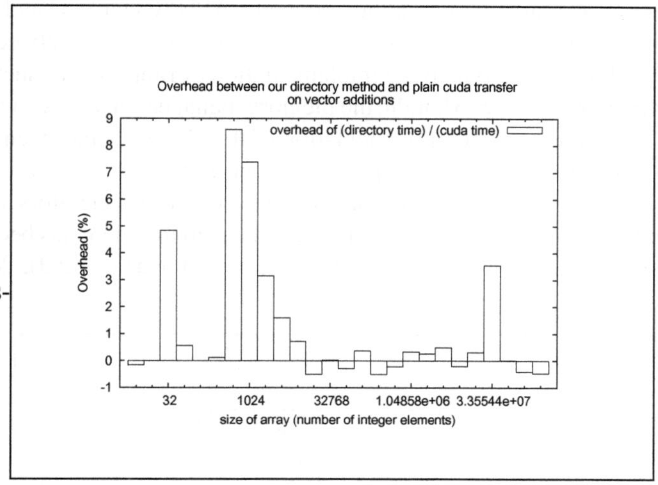

Fig. 5. Overhead between data management with directory compared to plain CUDA allocations and transfers on a succession of vector additions alternating between a CPU and a GPU

The first application is three successive vector additions. The first addition is performed on the GPU, the second one on the CPU and using results from the first addition, and the last one is performed again on the GPU using data produced by the computation on the CPU. The time of the whole routine was measured (allocation and data copy on the GPU before the first addition, the necessary transfers between the different additions, and the copy and deallocation of data after the computation). The results presented in Figure 5 shows that for a small number of data transfers, the overhead is very low (within 10% for small sizes, and less than 5% with meaningful data volume). Here, the overhead is due to the local allocation of tuples in the directory.

Another set of benchmarks was realized on a mono-material hydrodynamic mini-app, GAD. This code solves mono-material Euler equations relying on a Lagragian phase followed by a projection phase. Here, the number of manipulated arrays is larger. Twelve arrays are used on the accelerator, with seven of them requiring to transfer the data between the host and the device before and after the computations. This greater number of arrays used on the GPU results in a similar number of tuples in our directory. When adding a new tuple, there is a greater number of existing tuples to compare to. For every step requiring it, swapping the list of tuples becomes heavy. Here the overhead of the directory can clearly be measured. Looking at the results displayed in Figure 6, one can easily see an overhead of 12 ms, which has a huge impact for small sizes. With a larger size, this fixed overhead becomes negligible compared to the compute time.

6 Conclusion

In this paper, we outline the data management problem that can be brought by directives for accelerators based on the two major APIs (OpenACC and OpenMP). To produce a valid code, some data locality coherency must occur between the different pragmas handling data. To help the implementation of runtimes for such APIs, we developped a directory scheme to handle the memory management between a host and accelerators. A first non-optimized implementation of this directory has been tested, and results about its overhead have been displayed in Section 5.

The two major APIs proposing directives for accelerators are still evolving. In OpenACC 2.0, the concept of non-nested data environment has been introduced through the use of new pragmas (`data begin` and `data end`). While this evolution is not directly compatible with the directory implementation we proposed, since a stack is used to mimic the nested behaviour of data environment, it is rather easy to include this notion in our directory. Since only clauses embedded in the `data begin` can be closed with `data end`, a simple list is enough to store the different intervals handled with these new constructs. In each step of the stack, after the floor for the *artificial tuples* of the current nested data environment, we can add a new floor, where the *artificial intervals* will be fused to the intervals in the new list. That way, when opening or ending a non-nested data environment, only the new separate structures have to be updated, and the original behaviour of our directory will remain unchanged.

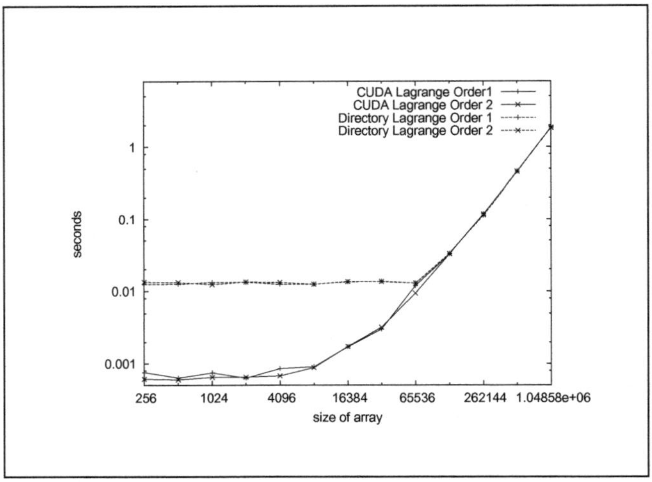

Fig. 6. Time consumption of memory management methods on the GAD code

As an evolution to these APIs, we suggest also to add the support for partially overlapping intervals. In this paper, we explained how it is posssible to handle such cases with this type of directory. New pragmas can be created to this purpose like a `present_and_copyin` (which will use the existing data on parts already present on the accelerator, and copy from the host only the subparts of the interval not present on the accelerator) or `update_and_copy` (which will copy all the interval from the host to the new allocated memory, and updating the parts already present on the accelerator at the clause end).

References

1. Archibald, J., Baer, J.L.: An economical solution to the cache coherence problem. In: 11th ISCA, pp. 355–362. ACM, New York (1984)
2. Augonnet, C., Namyst, R.: A unified runtime system for heterogeneous multi-core architectures. In: César, E., et al. (eds.) 14th Euro-Par Workshops. LNCS, vol. 5415, pp. 174–183. Springer, Heidelberg (2009)
3. Cantin, J.F., Lipasti, M.H., Smith, J.E.: Improving multiprocessor performance with coarse-grain coherence tracking. In: 32nd ISCA, pp. 246–257. IEEE Computer Society, Washington, DC (2005)
4. Censier, L.M., Feautrier, P.: A new solution to coherence problems in multicache systems. IEEE Transactions on Computers C-27(12), 1112–1118 (1978)
5. Chaiken, D., Fields, C., Kurihara, K., Agarwal, A.: Directory-based cache coherence in large-scale multiprocessors. Computer 23(6), 49–58 (1990)
6. Chen, G.: Slid - a cost-effective and scalable limited-directory scheme for cache coherence. In: Reeve, M., Bode, A., Wolf, G. (eds.) PARLE 1993. LNCS, vol. 694, pp. 341–352. Springer, Heidelberg (1993)
7. Cuesta, B., Ros, A., Gomez, M.E., Robles, A., Duato, J.: Increasing the effectiveness of directory caches by deactivating coherence for private memory blocks. In: 38th ISCA, pp. 93–103 (2011)
8. Gautier, T., Lima, J.V.F., Maillard, N., Raffin, B.: Xkaapi: A runtime system for data-flow task programming on heterogeneous architectures. In: 27th IPDPS, pp. 1299–1308. IEEE Computer Society, Washington, DC (2013)
9. Levesque, J.M., Sankaran, R., Grout, R.: Hybridizing s3d into an exascale application using openacc: An approach for moving to multi-petaflops and beyond. In: SuperComputing 2012, pp. 1–11 (2012)
10. Lionetti, F.V., McCulloch, A.D., Baden, S.B.: Source-to-source optimization of cuda c for gpu accelerated cardiac cell modeling. In: D'Ambra, P., Guarracino, M., Talia, D. (eds.) Euro-Par 2010, Part I. LNCS, vol. 6271, pp. 38–49. Springer, Heidelberg (2010)
11. Moshovos, A.: Regionscout: Exploiting coarse grain sharing in snoop-based coherence. In: 32nd ISCA, pp. 234–245. IEEE Computer Society, Washington, DC (2005)
12. Planas, J., Badia, R.M., Ayguadé, E., Labarta, J.: Hierarchical task-based programming with starss. Int. J. High Perform. Comput. Appl. 23(3), 284–299 (2009)
13. Quintana-Ortí, G., Igual, F.D., Quintana-Ortí, E.S., van de Geijn, R.A.: Solving dense linear systems on platforms with multiple hardware accelerators. In: 14th PPoPP, pp. 121–130. ACM, New York (2009)
14. Reyes, R., López-Rodríguez, I., Fumero, J.J., de Sande, F.: `accULL`: An openACC implementation with CUDA and openCL support. In: Kaklamanis, C., Papatheodorou, T., Spirakis, P.G. (eds.) Euro-Par 2012. LNCS, vol. 7484, pp. 871–882. Springer, Heidelberg (2012)
15. Silberstein, M., Schuster, A., Geiger, D., Patney, A., Owens, J.D.: Efficient computation of sum-products on gpus through software-managed cache. In: 22nd ICS, pp. 309–318. ACM, New York (2008)
16. Tang, C.K.: Cache system design in the tightly coupled multiprocessor system. In: Proceedings of National Computer Conference and Exposition 1976, AFIPS 1976, pp. 749–753. ACM, New York (1976)
17. Wienke, S., Springer, P., Terboven, C., an Mey, D.: OpenACC — first experiences with real-world applications. In: Kaklamanis, C., Papatheodorou, T., Spirakis, P.G. (eds.) Euro-Par 2012. LNCS, vol. 7484, pp. 859–870. Springer, Heidelberg (2012)
18. Zhao, H., Shriraman, A., Dwarkadas, S., Srinivasan, V.: Spatl: Honey, i shrunk the coherence directory. In: 20th PACT, pp. 33–44 (2011)

A Source-to-Source OpenACC Compiler for CUDA

Akihiro Tabuchi[1], Masahiro Nakao[2], and Mitsuhisa Sato[1]

[1] Graduate School of Systems and Information Engineering, University of Tsukuba
[2] Center for Computational Sciences, University of Tsukuba

Abstract. OpenACC is a new directive-based programming interface for accelerators such as GPGPU. OpenACC allows the programmer to express the offloading of data and computations to accelerators to simplify the porting process for legacy CPU-based applications. In this paper, we present the design and implementation of an open-source OpenACC compiler that translates C code with OpenACC directives to C code with the CUDA API, which is the most widely used GPU programming environment provided for NVIDIA GPU. We adopt a source-to-source approach using the Omni compiler infrastructure for source code analysis and translations. Our approach leaves detailed machine-specific code optimization to the mature NVIDIA CUDA compiler. An experimental evaluation of the implementation shows that some parallel benchmark codes compiled by our compiler achieve speeds up to 31 times greater than those of CPUs, and that it is competitive with commercial implementations. However, the results also indicate the optimization of OpenACC programs has several problems, such as assigning iterations to GPU threads.

Keywords: OpenACC, GPU, compiler, CUDA.

1 Introduction

An accelerator such as a GPU is a promising device for further increasing computing performance in the field of high-performance computing. Several vendors are providing programming models for accelerators. For example, NVIDIA provides CUDA, which is an extension of C and C++ and provides GPU data and thread management functions, and OpenCL provides a portable programming model for various accelerators. Although CUDA is the most mature and extended approach to GPU programming, achieving a good performance rate usually requires a noticeable coding and optimization effort. To offload a fragment of code to an accelerator using OpenCL or CUDA, programmers need to rewrite a parallel loop to a kernel function executed on each thread of the GPU and to manage data transfers between host and device in an explicit way.

OpenACC [1] is a directive-based programming model that has been proposed as a solution to the complicated programming for offloading codes on accelerators. OpenACC provides a set of OpenMP-like loop directives for the

D. an Mey et al. (Eds.): Euro-Par 2013 Workshops, LNCS 8374, pp. 178–187, 2014.

programming of accelerators in an implicit and portable way. The OpenACC compiler generates codes that transfer data between host and device, and GPU code executed on the device.

In this paper, we present the design and implementation of an open-source OpenACC compiler that translates C code with OpenACC directives to that with CUDA API. This source-to-source approach means detailed machine-specific code optimization is left to the mature CUDA compiler by NVIDIA.

To implement our OpenACC compiler, we use the Omni compiler infrastructure [2] of C and Fortran95 for source code analysis and translations. The public availability of Omni means the research community is able to conduct experiments such as the study of new extensions of OpenACC and program analyses for optimizations. Although CUDA supports only NVIDIA devices, it would be easy to generate codes using the proposed OpenCL as a common programming interface for the heterogeneous devices supported by many manufacturers.

The contributions of this paper are summarized as follows:

- We describe a compiler to translate OpenACC programs into CUDA. The generated CUDA code is compiled by the NVIDIA CUDA compiler.
- Our approach enables the mature CUDA compiler to optimize the GPU code, sometimes better than a commercial compiler that generates the parallel thread execution (PTX) code.
- We present performance measurements to validate our approach by using some parallel benchmark codes.

As related work, efforts have been made to generate CUDA from OpenMP and the directive extension for GPUs. OMPCUDA [5] is the OpenMP compiler that translates to CUDA by using the Omni compiler. OpenMPC [6] also translates OpenMP to CUDA, but it has original directives that can tune performance. Additionally, the block size and other parameters can be tuned by a parameter search. hiCUDA [7] is a directive-based programming model for CUDA. In hiCUDA, the user has to specify the number of blocks and threads explicitly. It is more like CUDA, so it may obtain performance equal to that written by CUDA. OpenHMPP [8] can specify the data transfer between host and GPU and launch GPU kernels by original directives. OpenHMPP can use not only NVIDIA GPU but also AMD GPU by using CUDA and OpenCL as the backend. In addition, accULL [9] is an OpenACC compiler that uses CUDA and OpenCL as the backend. By using OpenCL, accULL can use accelerators supporting OpenCL. This work is similar to ours.

The rest of this paper is organized as follows. In Section 2, we provide an overview of the translation of OpenACC to CUDA with sample code. Section 3 describes the implementation of our OpenACC compiler and the details of code translation. We report our performance evaluation using some benchmark programs in Section 4 and conclude our work in Section 5.

```
1 #define N 1024
2 int main(){
3   int i, a[N], b[N];
4 #pragma acc data copyin(a) copyout(b)
5   {
6 #pragma acc parallel loop
7     for(i = 0; i < N; i++){
8       b[i] = a[i] + 1;
9     }
10  }
11 }
```

Fig. 1. Sample code (sample.c)

2 Translation of OpenACC into CUDA

2.1 OpenACC

OpenACC defines constructs by directives to specify the offloaded region of codes and data in standard C and Fortran programs. The offloaded regions are defined with either parallel or kernel directives, and are executed on an accelerator. Programs with OpenACC directives can be compiled into a hybrid code by OpenACC-compliant compilers.

In the offloaded region, a parallel loop is specified by the loop directive. OpenACC supports three-level parallelism: gang, worker, and vector. The parallel loop is executed in parallel by multiple workers, each of which can also have single instruction, multiple data (SIMD) operations. Similar to the thread blocks in CUDA, a group of workers is managed as a gang in OpenACC.

In the OpenACC model, the host and device memory spaces are independent. Therefore, data referenced in computations in the accelerator need to be transferred between host and device memory. The data transfers are implicitly executed by the compiler, but the programmer can specify them by data directives and reduce unnecessary transfers. The data directive specifies the data environment so that the coherency of the specified data is taken at the region boundary. In addition, the data directive defines data allocated on device memory. The data is copied from host to device at the beginning of the structured block or copied from device to host at the end of the structured block.

Fig. 1 shows the OpenACC sample code. First, line 4 allocates device memory by using the data construct. The values of array a are referenced but not updated in the device, and the values are specified as a *copyin* to transfer them from host memory to device memory at the beginning of the data region. The values of array c are not referenced but updated in the device, so it is specified as a *copyout* to transfer it from device memory to host memory at the end of the data region. Then, line 6 specifies the loop on i as a parallel region with parallelization of the loop by the *parallel loop* directive.

2.2 CUDA

CUDA is the programming environment for NVIDIA GPU, which is the most widely used for GPGPU. In CUDA, a kernel function is written in C and C++.

```
int main(void)
{
  int i; int a[1024]; int b[1024];
  {
    void *_ACC_DEVICE_ADDR_a,*_ACC_HOST_DESC_a,*_ACC_DEVICE_ADDR_b,*_ACC_HOST_DESC_b;
    _ACC_gpu_init_data(&(_ACC_HOST_DESC_a), &(_ACC_DEVICE_ADDR_a), a, ...);
    _ACC_gpu_init_data(&(_ACC_HOST_DESC_b), &(_ACC_DEVICE_ADDR_b), b, ...);
    _ACC_gpu_copy_data(_ACC_HOST_DESC_a, 400);
    {
    _ACC_GPU_FUNC_0(_ACC_DEVICE_ADDR_b, _ACC_DEVICE_ADDR_a);
    }
    _ACC_gpu_copy_data(_ACC_HOST_DESC_b, 401);
    _ACC_gpu_finalize_data(_ACC_HOST_DESC_a);
    _ACC_gpu_finalize_data(_ACC_HOST_DESC_b);
  }
}
```

Fig. 2. Sample code (sample_tmp.c)

A kernel is a function callable from the host and executed on the CUDA device simultaneously by many threads in parallel. A thread is a minimum unit of execution. The threads are organized as a two-level hierarchy: block and grid. A block is a group of threads. A grid is a group of blocks that executes a kernel function. Each thread can be identified by the index of the block to which it belongs and the index of the thread in the block. By using these identifiers, a parallel loop is executed as a kernel function that computes each data.

Device memory is independent of host memory. Device kernels essentially can access only device memory, so device memory allocations and releases and data transfers between host and device are needed for executing kernels. CUDA provides a runtime library for managing device memory, and host programs call them as needed.

2.3 Translation to CUDA

The translation of sample code shown in the previous section is shown in Figs. 2 and 3. The OpenACC code is compiled into two parts. In sample_tmp.c, the data directive is converted to the block to set up the data transfer. The runtime call _ACC_gpu_init_data allocates device memory for arrays *a* and *b*, then the runtime call _ACC_gpu_copy_data transfers *a* from host to device memory at the beginning of the data region. The parallel region is compiled into the separate function _ACC_GPU_FUNC_0 generated by the compiler. _ACC_gpu_copy_data transfers *b* from device to host memory at the end of the data region. Finally, _ACC_gpu_finalize_data frees device memory for *a* and *b*.

The code sample.cu is a CUDA source code that includes a GPU kernel function and a function that launches it. Function _ACC_GPU_FUNC_0 calculates the number of thread blocks and threads from the number of loop iterations and launches the GPU kernel. After that, _ACC_GPU_M_BARRIER_KERNEL waits until the end of GPU kernel execution. Function _ACC_GPU_FUNC_0_DEVICE is a GPU kernel, from which each thread gets an induction variable value *i* from _ACC_gpu_calc_idx and calculates b[i]=a[i]+1.

```
__global__ static
void _ACC_GPU_FUNC_0_DEVICE(int b[1024], int a[1024])
{
  int i, idx, init, cond, step;
  _ACC_gpu_init_block_thread_x_iter(&init,&cond,&step,0,1024,1);

  for(idx=init;idx<cond;idx+=step){
    _ACC_gpu_calc_idx(idx,&i,0,1024,1);
    (b[i])=((a[i])+(1));
  }
}
extern "C"
void _ACC_GPU_FUNC_0(int b[1024],int a[1024])
{
  int _ACC_block_x=(((1023)/(256))+(1)), _ACC_block_y=(1), _ACC_block_z=(1);
  int _ACC_thread_x=(256), _ACC_thread_y=(1), _ACC_thread_z=(1);
  dim3 _ACC_DIM3_block(_ACC_block_x,_ACC_block_y,_ACC_block_z);
  dim3 _ACC_DIM3_thread(_ACC_thread_x,_ACC_thread_y,_ACC_thread_z);

  _ACC_GPU_FUNC_0_DEVICE<<<_ACC_DIM3_block,_ACC_DIM3_thread>>>(b,a);
  _ACC_GPU_M_BARRIER_KERNEL();
}
```

Fig. 3. Sample code (sample.cu)

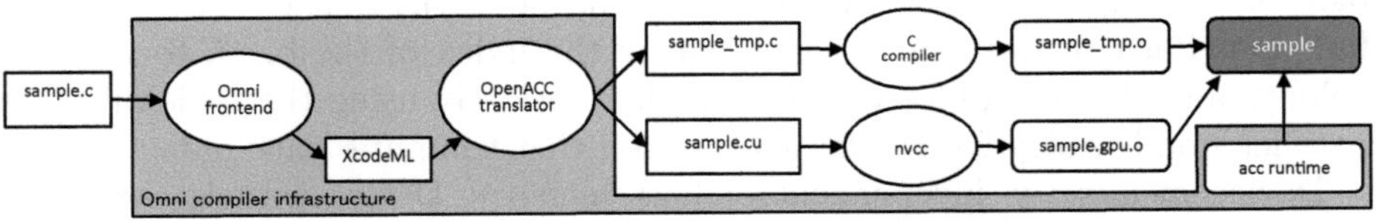

Fig. 4. Flow of compilation

3 Implementation of OpenACC Compiler

3.1 Omni Compiler Infrastructure

Our OpenACC compiler uses the Omni compiler infrastructure, which is a set of programs for a source-to-source compiler with code analysis and transformation. This compiler is also used to implement XcalableMP-dev [4], a GPU extension of XcalableMP [3] that shares a part of code with our OpenACC compiler.

Fig. 4 shows the flow of the compilation. When source code sample.c written in C and OpenACC is compiled, the Omni frontend translates it to an XcodeML file, which is intermediate code written in XML, and the OpenACC translator reads the XcodeML file and generates middle code sample_tmp.c and sample.cu.

Here, sample_tmp.c is host code compiled by the C compiler, and sample.cu is GPU code compiled by the NVIDIA CUDA compiler (NVCC). The compiled object files sample_tmp.o and sample.gpu.o are linked with the OpenACC runtime library. Then, the compiler generates an executable file.

3.2 Compilation of Parallel and Loop Constructs

For each region offloaded by parallel constructs, a function is generated to set up the dimension of thread blocks and to launch the kernel function to a GPU.

```
#pragma acc parallel num_gangs(4) vector_length(128)
{
  /* codes in parallel region */
}
```

(a) ACC parallel

```
__global__ static
void _ACC_GPU_FUNC_0_DEVICE(...)
{
  /* codes in parallel region */
}
extern "C"
void _ACC_GPU_FUNC_0(...)
{
  int _ACC_block_x=(4), _ACC_block_y=(1), _ACC_block_z=(1);
  int _ACC_thread_x=(128), _ACC_thread_y=(1), _ACC_thread_z=(1);
  dim3 _ACC_DIM3_block(_ACC_block_x,_ACC_block_y,_ACC_block_z);
  dim3 _ACC_DIM3_thread(_ACC_thread_x,_ACC_thread_y,_ACC_thread_z);

  _ACC_GPU_FUNC_0_DEVICE<<<_ACC_DIM3_block,_ACC_DIM3_thread>>>(...);
  _ACC_GPU_M_BARRIER_KERNEL();
}
```

(b) translated code

Fig. 5. Code translation of parallel construct

OpenACC supports three-level parallelism: gang, worker, and vector. However, only the block and thread models are provided in CUDA. In our compiler, gang and vector correspond to block and thread, respectively. This means that a gang has a worker, and a worker can use vector operations. The number of blocks and threads can be specified by the *num_gangs* and *vector_length* clauses. If the number of threads is not specified, the number of threads is 256, which is often used for Fermi architecture GPUs, and the number of blocks is determined by the number of loop iterations contained in the region.

When a loop is specified as parallelism by a loop construct, the kernel function executes that loop in parallel. The function executes a part of the loop by _ACC_gpu_init_block_thread_x_iter and calculates the loop index by the inline function _ACC_calc_idx. Additionally, our compiler supports two- or three-dimensional blocking for nested loops. If multiple gang or vector clauses are specified for nested loops, these loops are executed by two- or three-dimensional grids or blocks in CUDA, respectively. This execution may increase data locality in a block and the performance of loop execution may improve. At the moment, our compiler does not allow function calls inside the parallel region except for mathematical functions supported in CUDA.

Fig. 5 shows an example of the parallel construct and the translated code. This parallel construct specifies that the next structured block is executed by 4 gangs and 128 vector operations on the accelerator. In the translated code, the number of blocks and threads are calculated, and the device kernel is launched with the configuration. After that, the host waits for the finish of the device kernel.

Fig. 6 shows an example of the loop construct and the translated code. This loop construct specifies the following loop executed by vector operation. In the translated code, the inline function _ACC_gpu_init_thread_x_iter calculates the range of the loop for the thread. For our loop iteration, the inline function

```
/* inside parallel region */
#pragma acc loop vector
for(i = 0; i < N; i++){
  a[i]++;
}
```

(a) ACC loop

```
/* inside gpu kernel function */
int i, _ACC_idx, _ACC_init, _ACC_cond, _ACC_step;
_ACC_gpu_init_thread_x_iter(&_ACC_init, &_ACC_cond, &_ACC_step,0,N,1);

for(_ACC_idx=_ACC_init;_ACC_idx<_ACC_cond;_ACC_idx+=_ACC_step){
  _ACC_gpu_calc_idx(_ACC_idx,&i,0,N,1);
  a[i]++;
}
```

(b) translated code

Fig. 6. Code translation of loop construct

_ACC_gpu_calc_idx calculates the loop index and executes the increment of the array *a* element.

3.3 Compilation of Data Construct

To translate a region with a data construct, codes for device memory allocations and data transfers from host to device are inserted at the beginning, and codes for device memory releases and data transfers from device to host are inserted at the end. The runtime function _ACC_gpu_init_data allocates device memory for a host variable or an array. The pointer _ACC_DEVICE_ADDR_*name* is the address of device memory for the *name*, and the pointer _ACC_HOST_DESC_*name* is the address of the structure that contains the host address, device address, and size of that variable. Data is transferred between host and device memory by the runtime function _ACC_gpu_copy_data. The direction of transfer is given by the second argument. At the end of the region, device memory is freed by the runtime function _ACC_gpu_finalize_data.

Fig. 7 shows an example of the data construct and the translated code. This data construct specifies that arrays *a* and variable *b* are allocated on the device at the beginning of the region and freed at the end of the region. Array *a* in the copy clause is transferred at the beginning and end of the region, and variable *b* in the copyout clause is transferred at the end of the region.

4 Performance Evaluation

For the performance evaluation, we used the following benchmark programs: Matrix multiplication (MatMul), N-body problem, and CG benchmark in the NAS Parallel Benchmarks (NPB). The Matrix multiplication and the N-body problem are naive implementations. We measured the execution time of each program compiled by our compiler. The execution time includes the time of data movement between the host and GPU and excludes the GPU initialization

```
int a[100], b;
#pragma acc data copy(a) copyout(b)
{
  /* some codes using a and b */
}
```

(a) ACC data

```
int a[100], b;
{
  void *_ACC_DEVICE_ADDR_a,*_ACC_HOST_DESC_a,*_ACC_DEVICE_ADDR_b,*_ACC_HOST_DESC_b;
  _ACC_gpu_init_data(&(_ACC_HOST_DESC_a),&(_ACC_DEVICE_ADDR_a),a,(100)*sizeof(int));
  _ACC_gpu_init_data(&(_ACC_HOST_DESC_b),&(_ACC_DEVICE_ADDR_b),&(b),sizeof(int));
  _ACC_gpu_copy_data(_ACC_HOST_DESC_a, 400); /* 400 means host -> device */
  {
    /* some codes using a and b */
  }
  _ACC_gpu_copy_data(_ACC_HOST_DESC_a, 401); /* 401 means device -> host */
  _ACC_gpu_copy_data(_ACC_HOST_DESC_b, 401);
  _ACC_gpu_finalize_data(_ACC_HOST_DESC_a);
  _ACC_gpu_finalize_data(_ACC_HOST_DESC_b);
}
```

(b) translated code

Fig. 7. Code translation of data construct

time. We ran the codes on one node of a CrayXK6m-200. The CPU of the Cray is AMD Opteron Processor 6272 and its GPU is NVIDIA X2090 (for MatMul and N-body) or NVIDIA K20 (for CG). We used the Cray compiler 8.1.0.143 (for MatMul and N-body) or 8.1.6 (for CG) with the flag *-O3*.

Fig. 8(a) and 8(b) shows the execution time of the Matrix multiplication and the N-body program, respectively. Fig. 8(c) shows the performance of the CG benchmark in Mops/s. In these results, "CPU" indicates the results of the CPU (single core) for code compiled by the Cray compiler, and "GPU (Cray compiler)", "GPU (Our compiler)" and "GPU (Handwritten CUDA)" indicate the results of the Cray OpenACC compiler, our compiler, and the handwritten CUDA code, respectively. Note that handwritten code does not use the shared memory of the GPU. For the Matrix multiplication, the result by 2D blocking of our compiler is also shown.

For the Matrix multiplication, the code by our compiler is 4.6–5.5 times faster than that of the CPU single core, and 1.4–1.5 times faster than that compiled by the Cray compiler. The reason for this difference is the quality of PTX code generated by the Cray compiler, since the Cray compiler generates the PTX code directly, not via CUDA. We found that the PTX code generated by the Cray compiler executes more operations in the innermost loop. Our compiler leaves PTX code generation to NVCC so that we can make use of mature NVIDIA compiler technology for their architecture.

The performance of our compiler using 2D blocking is slightly lower than that of non-2D blocking code because the default 2D block size (16x16 in this case) is not adequate for this program. The handwritten CUDA code also uses a 2D block (16x16). We measured the performance in various 2D block sizes, and the best result was 512x2. In general, it is difficult to know the optimal block size without executing in various block sizes.

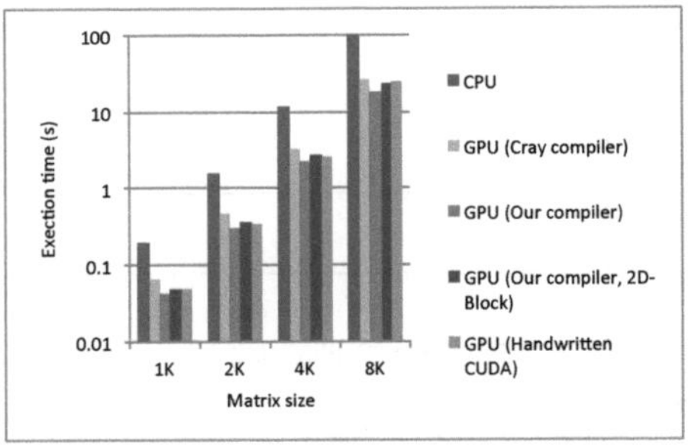

(a) Matrix multiplication

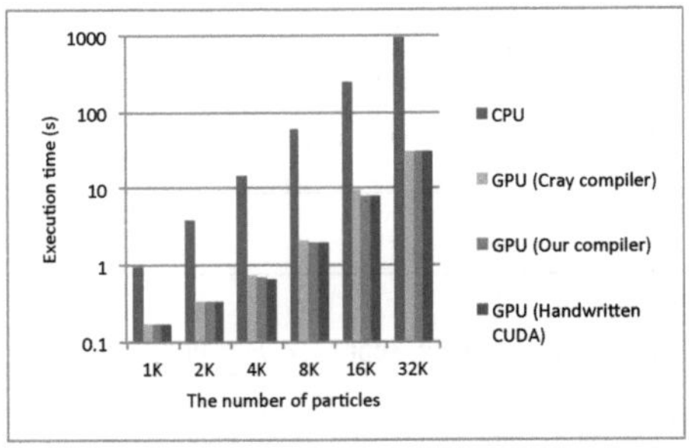

(b) N-body

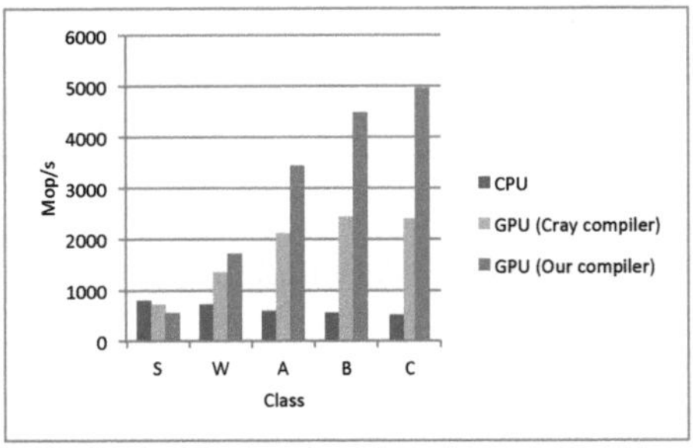

(c) CG benchmark

Fig. 8. Performance comparison using benchmarks

For N-body, our compiler achieves a speedup of 5.4–31 times greater than the CPU single core and 0.95–1.2 times greater than the Cray compiler. The speedup became larger as the problem size increased and the intensity of calculations increased. At the small problem size, the performance of our compiler is lower than that of the Cray compiler because our compiler used fewer Streaming Multiprocessors (SMs). The GPU kernel is executed by the SMs per thread block. If the number of blocks is smaller than that of the SMs, the performance of the GPU kernel becomes low. The default block size of our compiler is 256 threads and that of the Cray compiler is 128 threads. When the problem size is small, the number of launched blocks is too small and fewer SMs are used in comparison with the Cray compiler. Our compiler needs to be improved to determine the block size to avoid choosing too small a number of blocks.

For CG, our compiler achieves a speedup of 0.66–9.7 times over the CPU single core and 0.74–2.1 times over the Cray compiler. For class S in the CG benchmark, the performance of the GPU is lower than that of the CPU because overheads, which include launching kernel functions, synchronization with the device and data transfers, are large compared with the execution time of kernel functions. Additionally, the overhead of reduction in our compiler is large because a reduction kernel uses a temporal array allocated before and freed after the kernel execution. However, the performance of our compiler is higher than that of the Cray compiler in the larger classes, W–C, so the performance of the GPU kernel is better than that of the Cray compiler.

5 Conclusion

In this paper, we presented the design and implementation of a source-to-source OpenACC compiler. The compiler translates C code with OpenACC directives to that with CUDA API. Our compiler implementation uses the Omni compiler infrastructure for analyzing and translating code.

We measured our compiler's performance for Matrix multiplication, N-body, and CG in the NAS parallel benchmarks, and compared the performance with that of a commercial compiler and handwritten CUDA. In most cases, the performance of the GPU program using our compiler is higher than that of the CPU. We observed a speedup of up to 31 times over the CPU single core for the N-body problem. Our compiler makes use of the CUDA backend successfully by the source-to-source approach, and the performance of our compiler is often better than that of the Cray compiler. On the other hand, we found that the grid size and block size are unsuitable for some programs and overheads are larger than that of the Cray compiler.

We are currently working on optimization of the tuning block size at compile time and the reduction of overheads. Our compiler will support the full set of directives for conforming to the OpenACC specification, and we will compare the performance of our compiler against that of PGI and accULL.

References

1. "OpenACC Home", `http://www.openacc-standard.org/`
2. "Omni Compiler Project", `http://www.hpcs.cs.tsukuba.ac.jp/omni-compiler/`
3. "XcalableMP", `http://www.xcalablemp.org`
4. Lee, J., Tran, M.T., Odajima, T., Boku, T., Sato, M.: An Extension of XcalableMP PGAS Lanaguage for Multi-node GPU Clusters. In: Alexander, M., D'Ambra, P., Belloum, A., Bosilca, G., Cannataro, M., Danelutto, M., Di Martino, B., Gerndt, M., Jeannot, E., Namyst, R., Roman, J., Scott, S.L., Traff, J.L., Vallée, G., Weidendorfer, J. (eds.) Euro-Par 2011, Part I. LNCS, vol. 7155, pp. 429–439. Springer, Heidelberg (2012)
5. Ohshima, S., Hirasawa, S., Honda, H.: OMPCUDA: OpenMP Execution Framework for CUDA Based on Omni OpenMP Compiler. In: Sato, M., Hanawa, T., Müller, M.S., Chapman, B.M., de Supinski, B.R. (eds.) IWOMP 2010. LNCS, vol. 6132, pp. 161–173. Springer, Heidelberg (2010)
6. Lee, S., Eigenmann, R.: OpenMPC: Extended OpenMP Programming and Tuning for GPUs. In: Proceedings of the 2010 ACM/IEEE International Conference for High Performance Computing, Networking, Storage and Analysis, SC 2010, pp. 1–11 (2010)
7. Han, T.D., Abdelrahman, T.S.: hiCUDA: a High-level Directive-based Language for GPU Programming. In: Proceedings of 2nd Workshop on General Purpose Processing on Graphics Processing Units (GPGPU-2), pp. 52–61 (2009)
8. "OpenHMPP", `http://www.caps-entreprise.com/openhmpp-directives/`
9. Reyes, R., López-Rodríguez, I., Fumero, J.J., de Sande, F.: accULL: An OpenACC Implementation with CUDA and OpenCL Support. In: Kaklamanis, C., Papatheodorou, T., Spirakis, P.G. (eds.) Euro-Par 2012. LNCS, vol. 7484, pp. 871–882. Springer, Heidelberg (2012)

Compiler-Driven Data Layout Transformation for Heterogeneous Platforms

Deepak Majeti[1], Rajkishore Barik[2], Jisheng Zhao[1], Max Grossman[1], and Vivek Sarkar[1]

[1] Rice University
[2] Intel Labs

Abstract. Modern heterogeneous systems comprise of CPU cores, GPU cores, and in some cases, accelerator cores. Each of these computational cores have very different memory hierarchies, making it challenging to efficiently map the data structures of an application to these memory hierarchies automatically. In this paper, we present a compiler-driven data layout transformation framework for heterogeneous platforms. We integrate our data layout framework with the data parallel construct, *forasync*, of Habanero-C and enable the same source code to be compiled with different data layouts for various architectures. The programmer or an auto-tuner specifies a schema of the data layout. Our compiler infrastructure generates efficient code for different architectures based on the meta information provided in the schema. Our experimental results show significant benefits from the compiler-driven data layout transformation, and demonstrate that the best data layout for a program varies with different heterogenous platforms.

1 Introduction

Recent hardware trends have seen the adoption of heterogeneous systems consisting of standard processor cores, graphics processing cores, and accelerator cores. While the memory hierarchy of standard CPU cores consist of L1, L2 and L3 caches, recent discrete GPU cores have also been embedded with their own L1, and L2 caches. Integrated GPU cores, on the other hand, share the same physical memory with the CPU while using a private L3 cache for the GPU cores. With such differing memory hierarchies within the same system, determining the best data layout can be challenging since the optimal layout for a computational kernel depends on whether the kernel executes on a CPU core, a discrete GPU, or on an integrated GPU (along with other factors). Additionally, the GPU memory performance is impacted by the number of coalesced memory accesses and control-flow divergence, whereas CPU memory performance is impacted by factors such as false sharing, prefetching and data reuse. This implies that the changes in data layout can have major impact on CPU vs. GPU core performance. In general, the programmer has to write different versions of CPU and GPU kernels for different architectures and has to select optimal memory layouts for each data structure. This places a severe constraint on code portability. At the same time, performing these layout transformations automatically for a wide-range of applications including irregular applications is a daunting task.

D. an Mey et al. (Eds.): Euro-Par 2013 Workshops, LNCS 8374, pp. 188–197, 2014.

CUDA and OpenCL are the two primary languages targeting the heterogeneous systems for GPGPU programming. OpenCL can also be used for targeting CPU cores. Many high-level programming models have also evolved in the last few years that deal with heterogeneity [14,21,13,22,6,12]. Choosing a language involves trade-offs between programmer productivity and performance. However, none of these languages provide mechanisms to specify the data layout. Some recent work [20,10,19] provide a library based mechanism, but are limited in scope. For example, Kunkel et.al. [24] emphasize the need for a data layout abstraction. Recently, Wu et al [23] have proved that finding the optimal data layout to maximize the number of coalesced accesses on a GPU is NP-complete. Thus, manually writing high performance portable programs or automatically generating efficient code via optimizing compilers without any domain knowledge is challenging given the proliferation of device technologies on heterogeneous architectures and their differing memory hierarchies. We believe that a compiler-driven data layout transformation framework can help bridge this gap.

In this paper, we present a compiler driven meta-data framework that allows both programmers and tuning experts to specify architecture specific and domain specific information for *parallel-for* loops of a program. A meta-data file is created for an application and is populated with entries on the data layout to be used for a device on the heterogeneous system. The data layout we focus on in this paper include structure-of-array (SOA), array-of-structure (AOS) and intermediate structure-of-array-of-structures (SOAOS). Any high level language which has *parallel-for* loops can be extended to accommodate the meta-data framework. In our work, we target the data-parallel **forasync** construct in Habanero-C [2] and integrate our meta-data framework with the Habanero-C compiler and runtime. Habanero-C compiles the *forasync* construct, to generate OpenCL device and host code for the target heterogenous architecture. The meta-data information is very useful in guiding the compiler optimization passes for the generation of efficient code for a device.

Our paper makes the following contributions:

- A meta-data framework that allows both the programmer and the tuning expert to specify the underlying architecture and domain specific knowledges for parallel-for loops;
- A compiler and runtime framework to automatically generate efficient code based on the meta-data information. We currently focus on AOS, SOA and SOAOS data layouts in our compiler;
- An experimental evaluation of our system using a wide variety of heterogeneous architectures which shows the impact of data layout on 5 distinct applications. On an average, the data layout transformation alone impacted the performance by 7.33× (up to 27.11×) on AMD 4-core A10-5880K CPU, 2.84× (up to 5.57×) on AMD Radeon integrated GPU, 8.32× (up to 29.5×) on NVIDIA Tesla M2050 GPU, 2.19× (up to 5.32×) on Intel 12-core X5660 CPU and 1.9× (up to 3.89×) on Intel integrated i7-3770 GPU.

The rest of this paper is organized as follows. Section 2 presents our meta-data framework. Section 3 discusses the details of our compiler code generation and runtime. Section 4 presents the experimental results on a wide variety of processors. Related work is discussed in Section 5, and finally, Section 6 concludes.

2 Programming Model

Our meta-data framework is built on top of Habanero-C (HC) compiler and runtime infrastructure [9]. The details of the parallel constructs supported by HC can be found at [2]. Our paper focuses on the data parallel *forasync* construct [1]. The syntax of the *forasync* construct is as follows.

```
forasync index(args) size(args) optional<scratchpad(args) seq(args)> {
        // forasync body
}
```

The semantics of the **forasync** construct is similar to a program loop which exhibits *parallel_for* parallelism. The **index** clause is used to specify the loop iterators. The number of variables in the **index** clause gives the dimentionality of the loop. The **size** clause specifies the number of iterations of the loop in each dimension. There are 2 optional clauses, **scratchpad** and **seq** clause. The HC language model takes advantage of the different memory regions available on most GPU hardwares with the help of the **scratchpad** and **seq**.

For each host or the device on a heterogeneous system, it is possible to specify the desired data layout for array-based or structure-based data structures of a given *forasync* loop. The data layouts that we focus on are: (1) AOS: array-of-structure; (2) SOA: structure-of-array and (3) SOAOS: structure-of-array-of-structures. Our compiler (described in Section 3) with the help of the meta-data file is able to transform HC code to one of the SOA, AOS and SOAOS layouts.

The grammar for the meta-data and an example is shown in Figure 1. The

```
arch_name -> Arch name meta_data
meta_data -> (struct_def)* (scratchpad_def)*
struct_def -> Struct name (field_def)*
scratchpad_def -> Scratchpad name
                  (field_def tile_size line_num)*
field_def -> Field type name length
type = fp | dp | ip
length -> (digit)*
tile_size -> (digit)*
line_num -> (digit)*
name = (letter)(letter|digit)*
letter -> _ |A|B|C| . . . |Z|a|b|c| . . . |z|
digit -> 1|2|3|4|5|6|7|8|9|0
```

```
Arch Intel_GPU
 Struct bodypos
   Field fp posx Field fp posy Field fp posz
 Struct bodyacc
   Field fp accx Field fp accy Field fp accz
 Scratchpad local Field fp posx 256 64
 Scratchpad local Field fp posy 256 64
 Scratchpad local Field fp posz 256 64

Arch AMD_GPU
 Struct bodypos
   Field fp posx Field fp posy Field fp posz
   Field fp accx Field fp accy Field fp accz
 Scratchpad local Field fp accx 1024 64
```

Fig. 1. Meta-data Grammar (left) and meta-data file Example (right)

meta-data file consists of a set architecture specific optimization information. The architectural details consist of the data layout information and scratchpad memory allocation information for a given program. Each struct definition has a label *Struct*, a name for the struct and a set of fields. Each field in turn has a label *Field*, the type of the field and the name of the field. The type of fields can be *fp*: a pointer to an array of float values, *dp*: a pointer to an array of double values or *ip*: a pointer to an array of integer values. The scratchpad memory allocation information consists of a set of buffer descriptions. It begins with a label *Scratchpad*, the name of the special memory region, the field, the amount of data which must be cached and the line number of the *forasync*.

[1] Our framework is also applicable to other data-parallel programming languages with a parallel-for like construct.

Restrictions of our meta-data framework
The user cannot alias the fields specified in the meta-data file. We plan to be resolve this issue with the help of an alias analysis. Another limitation in the programming model is that a variable name cannot be repeated in the whole program in different scopes. This limitation can be avoided by a clever variable renaming mechanism. Also, all fields in a struct must be of the same type. We currently do not support more complex data layouts such as AOSOA (Array-of-structure-of-arrays). We leave this for future work.

3 Implementation

Our overall meta-data framework is shown in Figure 2. The application user writes a program in Habanero-C (HC) using the *forasync* construct. Followed by which, either the developer or the tuning expert specifies the meta-data information for the application. We extend the HC compiler infrastructure to perform data layout transformation based on the meta information;. The compiler pass is implemented in the ROSE source-to-source compiler framework [17]. The HC compiler generates OpenCL code from the program with the specified data layout and the corresponding host code.

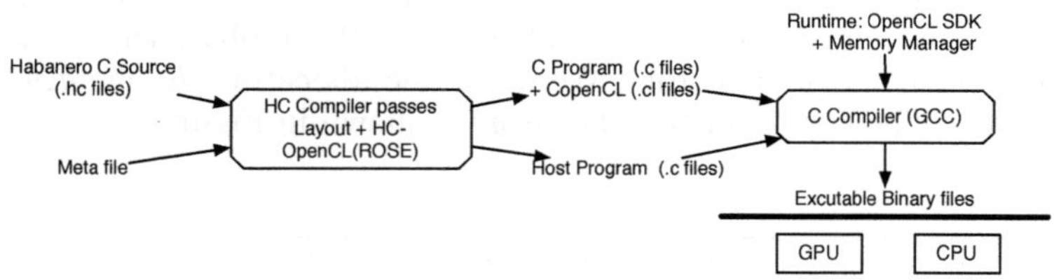

Fig. 2. Compilation Flow

3.1 Data Layout Transformation

The compiler pass first parses the specified meta-data file and it creates a meta-data map for each architecture. The mapping is between the fields and the struct name they belong to. The mapping is done for each such struct meta information. If it finds any scratchpad meta information, it is recorded.

The data layout transformation (DLT) compiler pass generates the code based on the specified data layout in the meta-data file. It generates code which includes new struct definitions and the code that operates on it. Figure 3 shows the algorithm for transforming the program with a given data layout. `DLT` takes the input program and a meta-data file. `createStructDefinitions(M)` adds the struct definitions as specified in the meta-data file to the AST. These structs are defined only once in the global scope. The DLT pass then iterates over all the functions and performs the steps described in lines 4-7.

`tryAddStructInstances(f)` analyzes the function parameters. If any of the parameter names appear in the meta file, an instance of the corresponding struct is declared in the function call. If we abstract the struct as a group of fields names, then one struct instance is declared per group. In next step, `updateInst(I)`

```
function DLT()
  Input  : Meta file M and input program P
  Output: Transformed program P'
  createStructDefinitions(M);
  for each function F in P do
      for each formal f in function parameter list do
          tryAddStructInstances(f);
      for each instruction I in function body do
          updateInst(I);
```

Fig. 3. Data Layout Transformation

checks all pointer or array references in the function body. If any of those reference are via any of the fields in the meta file, then the access is replaced with the corresponding struct instance.

An important factor here is that the type of the function in the original program remains the same. Keeping the function types intact will avoid rewriting the direct and indirect calls to the function from sequential code.

3.2 Memory Management

In the HC programming model, the programmer allocates heap memory to the fields via standard *malloc* and *calloc* calls. We replace these calls with our specialized memory allocators. We name the allocators, *hc_meta_malloc* or *hc_meta_calloc*. The syntax of the allocators is shown in Figure 4.

```
void *hc_meta_malloc(char *fld_name,size_t num_bytes);
void *hc_meta_calloc(char *fld_name,size_t num_elem,size_t size_elem);
```

Fig. 4. Memory Allocators

hc_meta_malloc or *hc_meta_calloc* are wrappers around the standard *malloc* and *calloc* calls. The allocators also pass in the name of the field to the memory allocator. The field name is required by the memory manager and is explained as follows.

The memory manager handles the different layouts and also creates device buffers. The memory manager has two important components, the memory allocator and the layout handler. During the program initialization phase, the layout handler reads the meta file and creates a map of the data layout. The memory manager with the help of the field name, looks into the layout map and allocates the memory.

Figure 5 shows an example code generation of a single kernel with meta data information for an Intel architecture.

4 Evaluation

The goal of the experimental evaluation is to study the performance of different data structure layouts for various programs on multiple architectures.

```
//forasync program
int main(){
   forasync point(i, j) size(M, N) seq(tilesize, tilesize){
               a[i * M + j] = b[i * M + j] + c[ i * M + j];
   }
}
```

```
//meta data
Arch Intel_CPU
  Struct BC
     Field fp b
     Field fp c
```

```
//Compiler generated code
struct BC{float b, float c};
void offload(float * a, struct BC *bc,
       char *kernel_name, char* ocl_kernel)
{
  //OpenCL Host Code
             ..........
}
int main(){
   struct BC *bc = ...........
   offload(a, bc, "kernel_1", Kernel_string);
}
```

```
//OpenCL Kernel Code
Kernel_string="
 struct BC{float b, float c};
 void kernel_1(__global float *a, __global struct BC *bc,
                   int M, int N) {
     i = get_global_id(1);
     j = get_global_id(0);
     a[i * M + j] = bc[i * M + j].b + bc[ i * M + j].c;
  }
";
```

Fig. 5. Example of code generation using a meta-data file

Table 1. Benchmarks

Name	Description	Original Layout	Num of Fields	Input
NBody	N-Body Simulation	SOA	7	32K nodes
Medical	Medical Image Registration	SOA	6	256×256×256
SRAD	Speckle Reducing Anisotropic Diffusion	SOA	4	5020 × 4580
Seismic	Seismic Wave Simulation	SOA	6	4096 × 4096
MRIQ	Matrix Q Computation for 3D Magnetic Resonance Image Reconstruction in Non-Cartesian Space.	SOA	6	64 × 64 × 64

4.1 Experimental Setup

Table 1 describes the benchmarks used in this evaluation.

The N-Body particle simulation benchmark was written from scratch for this work. We focus on the compute intensive kernel which calculates the forces between the bodies.

The Medical Imaging benchmark includes kernels from a medical imaging pipeline used to analyze different types of medical images for defects or abnormalities [15]. This application consists of three main phases: *denoising*, *registration*, and *segmentation*. For our evaluation, we focus on the most computationally significant kernel of the three, *registration*.

The SRAD benchmark from the Rodinia benchmark suite [11] is also used. SRAD is used to "remove locally correlated noise" in "ultrasonic and radar imaging applications based on partial differential equations" [18].

The Seismic benchmark suite was created based on the example included in the Intel TBB benchmark suite [4]. Seismic simulates the propagation of waves during seismic activity.

The MRIQ benchmark from the Parboil benchmark suite [7] computes a Q matrix. The Q matrix represents the scanner configuration used in a 3D magnetic resonance image reconstruction algorithm in non-Cartesian space. The MRIQ code has been converted to SOA layout by hand.

Table 2 shows the different meta-data files used for each benchmark. Since the default layout is SOA, there is no need of a meta file. All OpenCL kernels, glue

Table 2. Application meta-data files

Application	AOS	SOAOS
NBody	**Struct** body **Field fp** posx **Field fp** posy **Field fp** posz **Field fp** accx **Field fp** accy **Field fp** accz	**Struct** pos **Field fp** posx **Field fp** posy **Field fp** posz **Struct** acc **Field fp** accx **Field fp** accy **Field fp** accz
Seismic	**Struct** params **Field fp** S **Field fp** T **Field fp** V **Field fp** D **Field fp** L **Field fp** M	N.A
SRAD	**Struct** direction **Field fp** N **Field fp** S **Field fp** E **Field fp** W	**Struct** direction1 **Field fp** N **Field fp** S **Struct** direction2 **Field fp** E **Field fp** W
Medical	**Struct** disp **Field fp** U1 **Field fp** U2 **Field fp** U3 **Struct** velocity **Field fp** V1 **Field fp** V2 **Field fp** V3	**Struct** disp **Field fp** U1 **Field fp** U2 **Field fp** U3
MRIQ	**Struct** body **Field fp** kx **Field fp** ky **Field fp** kz **Field fp** phiMag	N.A

Table 3. Hardware architectures

Vendor	Type	Model	Freq	Cores	Local Mem	L1$	L2$
Intel	CPU	X5660	2.8GHz	12 (HT)	N.A	192KB	1.5MB
Intel	Integrated GPU	i7-3770U	350MHz-1.15GHz	14	64KB (per half-slice)	N.A	N.A
NVIDIA	Discrete GPU	Tesla M2050	575 MHz	8	8x48KB	16KB	768KB
AMD	CPU	A10-5800K	1.4 GHz	4 (HT)	N.A.	16KB	32MB
AMD	Integrated GPU	Radeon HD 7660	800 MHz	6	6x32KB	N.A	4MB

code, and different layouts for each of these applications were generated from a HC array-based implementation.

Table 3 lists the hardware architectures used in our evaluation. We use a variety of CPU and GPU systems with differing memory hierarchies in order to demonstrate the benefit of our data layout transformation. The compiler used for the sequential versions of each application GCC 4.4.6 (with the flags `-g -O2`). All OpenCL kernels were compiled with their default optimizations enabled. Intel GPU tests were run using the 2013 Release of the Intel OpenCL SDK [3]. Intel CPU tests were performed using 2011 Release of Intel OpenCL SDK, v1.5 [3]. NVIDIA GPU tests were performed using NVIDIA SDK v5.0 [5]. AMD GPU and GPU tests were performed using AMD APP SDK v2.8 [1].

4.2 CPU and GPU Performance

Figure 6 contains results for all the benchmarks. We compare relative execution time for the various data layouts on different CPU and GPU platforms. For a given architecture, we normalize every layout with respect to the fastest executing layout. In this case, **smaller bars imply better performance**. Every column is stacked in 2 levels. The bottom level represents the fraction of total execution time spent in the kernel. This information is retrieved from the OpenCL API. The top stack represents the fraction of total execution time for the remaining execution. This includes communication and OpenCL initialization overheads. The top stack is negligible for Intel GPU. This is because the GPU is integrated one the same die as the CPU and there is no data copying overhead. NVIDIA GPU and AMD architectures show copying overheads. For all the workloads, the AMD CPU/GPU exhibit a large amount of overhead. On further inspection, we discovered that the majority of the overhead was due to significant time difference between OpenCL kernel enqueue and kernel execution. This could be an implementation error in AMD's OpenCL implementation. To analyze the performance differences, we could not find any tools which profile OpenCL code. We make the following analysis based on code and machine characteristics.

For the N-Body benchmark, we see that the SOA and AOS versions perform similarly on the CPU. Since the number of fields are less, all the loads in an iteration fit into the cache and consecutive iterations do not incur any penalty. The array layout performs better on GPUs because SOA layout helps in memory coalescing.

For the Seismic kernel, the SOA layout shows better performance on AMD CPU, whereas the AOS layout is better on Intel CPU. This can be attributed to the difference in cache associativity and sizes between AMD and Intel. On the GPU side, SOA performs well on all 3 GPU hardwares due to coalescing.

The SRAD kernel shows improved performance for the SOAOS layout relative to the SOA and AOS layout for most of the architectures. Surprisingly even on the GPU the AOS and SOAOS layouts performs better than the SOA layout. This is contrary to GPU best practices. The memory access functions in the SRAD kernel are non-affine and irregular. It is difficult for a compiler or programmer to analyze and determine the right layout. Our framework enables rapid prototyping and testing of different layouts for performance on multiple architectures.

MRIQ exhibits little or no variation across layouts. MRIQ is a compute bound kernel and the data structure layout will have little or no effect.

The medical image benchmark shows some interesting properties for different layouts. The AOS layout is better on the CPU whereas the SOA layout is better on the GPU. Medical image kernel is similar to a 3D Jacobi (stencil) computation. The stencil computation is performed separately on three input buffers and the results are written into corresponding output buffers. Keeping the input buffers in a single struct is helpful for the CPU. This is because when you load a point for one of the stencil, you automatically load the points for the other 2 stencils (multiple points fit in a cache line). The array layout would have caused 3 loads for the same point, one in each of the three stencils. On the GPU side, the array layout is better as expected.

Best practices generally dictate the use of array data layouts on GPUs due to improved coalescence of global memory accesses. However, our SRAD and MRIQ results contradict this knowledge. Our metadata framework enables rapid prototyping and optimization of different data layouts, allowing tuning experts to rapidly discover optimal layouts for complex and irregular applications. For the CPU the layout often depends upon the kernel features and memory access patterns. Our programming model can easily port such applications to different architectures.

5 Related Work

Recently, data layouts have been studied in the context of GPUs. DL [20] uses a mapping function and runtime library support to enable architecture specific data layouts. DL does in-place data marshaling on the GPU. Like DL, Dymaxion [10] proposes a set of index mapping functions which are used to optimize memory mappings, with data marshaling done on the CPU side. Sung et. al. [19] used techniques similar to DL to perform data layout transformations for structured grid applications. Their compiler automatically changes the order of n-dimensional array references to maximize memory access coalescing. With the help of micro-benchmarks, low latency strides and an optimal index map are discovered. This technique requires manual host code changes. The main disadvantage of the techniques listed in this paragraph is that the overhead of

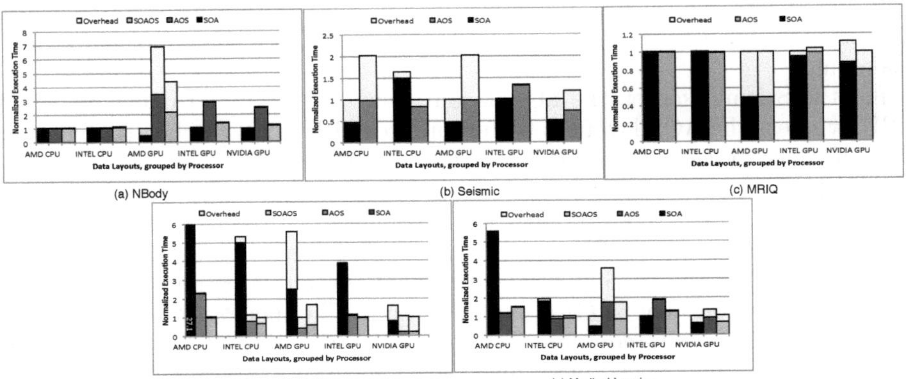

(a) NBody (b) Seismic (c) MRIQ

(d) SRAD (e) Medical Imaging

Fig. 6. GPU, CPU performance relative to the best layout (Lower the better). The darker bars show results for kernel execution time. The light bar shows results for communication and OpenCL initialization overhead.

runtime data marshaling can eliminate or reduce the performance benefits of optimal data layouts. Our compiler based approach does not incur this added overhead. The above runtime-based techniques are also either restricted to a class of applications (such as grid applications) or require manual changes by the programmer. Our compiler-based approach does not require any manual coding.

Ren et. al. [8] introduce an interpreter-based SIMDization mechanism that can parallelize the sequential programs that traverse on irregular data structures (e.g., binary decision tree and regular expression matching). To reduce memory latency, they chose different compacting policies based on layout including depth-first, breadth-first, and level-by-level. These policies improve memory access latencies for the irregular data structures. Compared to their work, our meta-data framework is not tied to any specific applications and that it can be easily extended to support the above data-layouts.

Liu et al [16] describe an automatic layout transformation that first divides arrays into blocks and then maps them to processing units with minimal overlap. Their approach does not perform any AOS to SOA transformation.

6 Conclusions

We present a compiler-driven data layout transformation that is applicable to any data parallel parallel_for programming model. The data layout transformation uses a "meta-file" approach which enables the same source code to be compiled with different layouts without involving the programmer worrying about it. Our experimental results show significant benefits from this approach and demonstrates that the best data layout for a given program can be different for CPU vs. GPU execution. With the growing users of GPUs in mainstream computing, it is important to have a tool like ours to understand the performance debugging. In future, we would like to develop a general heuristic to automatically perform data layout transformation that works across all platforms.

References

1. Amd app sdk v2.8, http://developer.amd.com/tools/heterogeneous-Computing/amd-accelerated-parallel-processing-app-sdk
2. Habanero-c, https://wiki.rice.edu/confluence/display/HABANERO/Habanero-C
3. Intel opencl sdk, http://software.intel.com/en-us/vcsource/tools/opencl-sdk
4. Intel thread building blocks, http://threadingbuildingblocks.org/
5. Nvidia sdk, https://developer.nvidia.com
6. Openacc, http://www.openacc-standard.org
7. Parboil benchmark suite, http://impact.crhc.illinois.edu/parboil.aspx
8. SIMD Parallelization of Applications that Traverse Irregular Data Structures. IEEE Computer Society (2013)
9. Chatterjee, et al.: Integrating asynchronous task parallelism with mpi. In: IPDPS 2013 (2013)
10. Che, et al.: Dymaxion: optimizing memory access patterns for heterogeneous systems. In: SC 2011, pp. 13:1–13:11. ACM, New York (2011)
11. Che, et al.: Rodinia: A benchmark suite for heterogeneous computing. In: ISWC 2009, pp. 44–54 (October 2009)
12. Microsoft Corporation. C++ accelerated massive parallelism specification, http://msdn.microsoft.com/en-us/library/vstudio/hh265136.aspx
13. Cunningham, D., Bordawekar, R., Saraswat, V.: Gpu programming in a high level language: compiling x10 to cuda. In: X10 2011, pp. 8:1–8:10. ACM, New York (2011)
14. Dubach, et al.: Compiling a high-level language for gpus: (via language support for architectures and compilers). In: PLDI 2012, pp. 1–12. ACM, NY (2012)
15. Center for Domain Specific Computing. Cdsc research applications
16. Liu, et al.: Data layout optimization for gpgpu architectures. In: PPoPP 2013, pp. 283–284. ACM, NY (2013)
17. LLNL. Rose compiler infrastructure, http://rosecompiler.org/
18. Rodinia Benchmark Suite. Srad wiki page
19. Sung, et al.: Data layout transformation exploiting memory-level parallelism in structured grid many-core applications. In: PACT 2010, pp. 513–522. ACM, New York (2010)
20. Sung, I.-J., Liu, G.D., Hwu, W.-M.W.: Dl: A data layout transformation system for heterogeneous computing. In: InPar 2012, pp. 1–11 (May 2012)
21. Unat, D., Cai, X., Baden, S.B.: Mint: realizing cuda performance in 3d stencil methods with annotated c. In: ICS 2011, pp. 214–224. ACM, New York (2011)
22. Vincent, C., Jisheng, Z., Jun, S., Vivek, S.: Habanero-java: the new adventures of old x10. In: PPPJ 2011 (2011)
23. Wu, et al.: Complexity analysis and algorithm design for reorganizing data to minimize non-coalesced memory accesses on gpu. In: PPoPP 2013, pp. 57–68. ACM, New York (2013)
24. Zhang, Y., Sinclair II, M., Chien, A.A.: Improving performance portability in openCL programs. In: Kunkel, J.M., Ludwig, T., Meuer, H.W. (eds.) ISC 2013. LNCS, vol. 7905, pp. 136–150. Springer, Heidelberg (2013)

A Hybrid Approach for Solving the 3D Helmholtz Equation on Heterogeneous Platforms

Gloria Ortega[1], Inmaculada García[2], and G. Ester Martín Garzón[1]

[1] Informatics Dpt., Univ. of Almería, Agrifood Campus of Int. Excell., ceiA3, 04120 Almería, Spain
{gloriaortega,gmartin}@ual.es
[2] Dpt. Computer Architecture, University of Málaga, 29080 Málaga, Spain
igarciaf@uma.es

Abstract. We are interested in the resolution of the 3D Helmholtz equation for real applications. Solving this problem numerically is a computational challenge due to the large memory requirements of the matrices and vectors involved. For these cases, the massive parallelism of GPU architectures and the high performance at lower energy of the multicores can be exploited. To do a fair comparison between the benefit of accelerating the three-dimensional Helmholtz equation using GPU architectures and multicore platforms, this paper describes three different parallelization schemes on a multi-GPU cluster and also includes an evaluation of their performance. The three parallel schemes consist of: (1) using the multicore processors (CPU version), (2) using the GPU devices (GPU version); and (3) using a hybrid implementation which combines CPU cores and GPU devices simultaneously (hybrid version). Experimental results show that our hybrid implementation outperforms the other approaches in terms of performance.

Keywords: Helmholtz equation, heterogeneous platforms, MPI, multi-GPUs.

1 Introduction

Modern high performance architectures are characterized by the heterogeneity of their resources. Modern supercomputers are distributed memory platforms based on a network of multicore processors which additionally incorporate accelerator devices such as GPUs [1]. They supply different types of resources to take advantage of the different kinds of parallelism appearing in real world applications (instructions level parallelism, data parallelism, task parallelism and so on). However, the development of software to efficiently exploit the full set of heterogeneous resources of modern computers is still a challenge. Several programming interfaces have to be used to develop software in this context, among them we highlight: MPI to develop applications on distributed platforms [20] and CUDA to accelerate programs through GPUs [13]. It means that programmers must combine several kinds of data structures and programming models to efficiently exploit the resources of the current heterogeneous computers. Development of

D. an Mey et al. (Eds.): Euro-Par 2013 Workshops, LNCS 8374, pp. 198–207, 2014.

software based on several parallel interfaces exhibits additional drawbacks due to its portability can be limited so, parallel implementations have to be tuned for each particular heterogeneous architecture. In this context, the main challenge is to determine an appropriate workload distribution because the computational burden assigned to every processing element should be related to its computational power. Therefore, it is necessary to have a detailed knowledge of both the computing resources and the algorithm [11].

PETSc is a well-known parallel library to solve PDEs, which contains several parallel versions supporting MPI, shared memory pthreads, and NVIDIA GPUs, as well as hybrid parallelism [3]. However, currently the PETSc routines based on CUDA are in progress. There are no benchmarking results published for the multi-GPU implementation using complex numbers.

This paper investigates a parallel approach for the solution of the 3D Helmholtz equation which combines the exploitation of the high regularity of the matrices involved in the numerical methods and the massive parallelism supplied by heterogeneous architecture of modern multi-GPU clusters [1].

In [17] we developed a CUDA version for solving the Helmholtz equation which takes advantage of the regularity of the matrices. It was used to solve Optical Diffraction Tomography (ODT) problems for 2D prototypes. From this experience we realized that the 3D extensions of these models need the support of modern multi-GPU clusters because of their high computational requirements.

The hybrid implementation is based on MPI and CUDA interfaces [7]. Due to the fact that CUDA and MPI produce portable code capable of exploiting both distributed architectures and multicores (if so many MPI processes as cores are launched), none specific interface to exploit the multicore structure has been included in the implementation. Our hybrid version launches MPI processes that exploit the CPU cores or the GPU devices of the multi-GPU cluster.

This way, both types of MPI processes can collaborate exploiting all the resources of the considered heterogeneous architecture. The main advantages of the hybrid implementation are related to two issues. On one hand, a hybrid version is capable of exploiting the different kinds of resources in multi-GPU clusters. This is due to the fact that CPU cores, despite being slower than the GPU devices, will be able to collaborate to the GPU device and accelerate the final computation by the overlapping the computation on CPUs and GPUs. Note that the workload of CPU processes will be significantly less than the workload of the GPU processes. On the other hand, our hybrid approach will overcome the memory limitation of the GPU devices because it can exploit the larger memory resources of multicore nodes. This way, GPUs will accelerate the computation but the size of the GPU workload is limited due to their smaller memories. CPU processes can collaborate with the GPU processes to exploit the large memory of multicore nodes.

The rest of this document is organized as follows. Section 2 describes the Helmholtz Equation. Section 3 is dedicated to explain the characteristics of our hybrid implementation of the 3D Helmholtz equation. Moreover the Biconjugate Gradient Method used as solver of the linear system of equation is shown. Section

4 analyzes the results of our hybrid version. Finally, in Section 5 the main results are outlined and future lines of research are presented.

2 The Problem

The Helmholtz equation can be applied to solve many problems related to steady-state oscillations (acoustical, thermal, electromagnetic, mechanical) [5,8]. The scalar approximation of the Helmholtz equation is defined by the following Partial Differential Equation (PDE):

$$(\nabla^2(\mathbf{r}) + k(\mathbf{r})^2)E(\mathbf{r}) = 0 \tag{1}$$

where ∇^2 is the Laplace operator; E is a complex scalar function defined at a spatial point $r = (x, y, z) \in \mathbb{R}^3$ and $k(\mathbf{r})$ can take real or complex values. This equation naturally appears from general conservation laws of physics and can be interpreted as a wave equation for monochromatic waves (wave equation in the frequency domain) where $k(\mathbf{r})^2$ is related to the wavenumber [19]. This equation can be numerically solved by means of the appropriated transformation based on Green's functions and the spatial discretization [12,19].

The Helmholtz equation is an example of linear elliptic Partial Differential Equation (PDE) which has been extensively studied [19]. Numerical solutions based on Finite Elements Method (FEM) have been developed for the discretization of this kind of differential operator [6]. It is well known that the "pollution effect" limits the reliability of the FEM solution of Helmholtz equation for high wavenumbers [2]. This numerical instability can be avoided only when a very fine mesh is used [4]. So, Helmholtz PDE leads to a very large linear system of equations specially for applications defined in a 3D space. Moreover, the use of FEM makes the matrix system sparse and regular [19,12] (see [19] for more details related to the boundary conditions of FEM).

3 Parallel Implementation of the Iterative Method

For high wave numbers the discretization results in a very large sparse system of linear equations $Ax = b$, where b indicates the independent term, x is the unknown vector and matrix $A \in \mathbb{C}^{N \times N}$. This linear system of equation cannot be solved with direct methods on current computers within reasonable time. The linear system is symmetric but indefinite, non-Hermitian and ill-conditioned which brings difficulties when solving with basic iterative methods [9]. As a result, iterative methods such as the Biconjugate Gradient method (BCG) can be used to effectively solve the Helmholtz Equation [21,10].

The BCG algorithm is an iterative method, which at every iteration includes two Sparse Matrix Vector products (SpMVs) and several dot products and saxpy operations (to analyze BCG in depth read [18,16]).

The SpMV is the operation with the highest computational cost. In [15], a specific storage format (named Regular Format), which takes advantage of the regularity of the sparse matrix of Helmholtz Equation (A), has shown to considerably reduce the memory requirements of the SpMV operation and consequently to improve its performance. The regularities of A can be summarized as follows: A is a symmetric matrix; maximum of seven non-zero elements per row; non-zero elements are located at seven diagonals, where one is the main diagonal, two of them are the first lower and upper diagonals and four of them are located at $\pm D1$-th and $\pm D2$-th diagonals; all the elements of every lateral diagonal are equal (a, b and c); and the main diagonal is defined by a set of complex numbers. Bearing in mind these characteristics, the Regular Format proposed in this work consists of: one array, $A[]$ (complex) of dimension N (where N represents the dimension matrix); three integer values (a, b and c) to store all remaining entries; and two additional integer values ($D1$ and $D2$) which specify the displacements of the lateral diagonals with respect to the main diagonal.

Because of the large dimension of the problems in which the resolution of the Helmholtz equation is required, High Performance Computing is an indispensable tool. This is the reason we have considered the MPI paradigm in this work. MPI provides all the routines that are needed to break the tasks involved in the massive computational process into subtasks that can be distributed to the set of available cores for processing.

As aforementioned, in this work three different strategies for solving the 3D Helmholtz equation are discussed: CPU version to balance the workload among the multiprocessors, GPU version to balance among the GPU devices of the cluster and a heterogeneous implementation which exploits both CPU and GPU processes located into the multi-GPU cluster.

1. CPU version is based on the distribution of the problem among several cores located into different nodes. So, MPI paradigm is used for processing tasks on cores which can belong to nodes with shared or distributed memory. Note that for solving the SpMV operations, we account the regularity of the matrix A for establishing a strategy that allows the reduction of the number and size of the messages among the available processors. So, to compute the SpMV, each MPI process adds redundant elements to the chunk of the vector (at the beginning and at the end). The number of additional elements is fixed ($2 \cdot D2$), hereinafter referred as "halo". These "halos" will be exchanged among the processors for updating the value of the vector before the computation of every SpMV. So, the use of redundant halos reduces the size of the messages and the number of communications among processes to compute the SpMV. This fact allows to exploit the regularity of A by means of the optimization of the communication pattern.
2. GPU version is based on the distribution of the problem among several GPU devices that can be located in the same or in a different node. Then, MPI paradigm is also used. In order to develop cluster applications that take advantage of GPU accelerators, it is necessary to select a GPU programming language and toolkit among the existing. In this work, a high abstraction subroutine library (CUBLAS [14]), which provides commonly used algorithms, has been considered. As it is well known, the key requirement for obtaining

effective acceleration from applications on GPU devices is the minimization of I/O between the host and the GPU. So, CPU-GPU intercommunications are strongly reduced using the strategy based on "halos" also applied in the CPU version.

3. Hybrid version has been designed to exploit all the computing resources of heterogeneous architectures. The idea behind this last implementation is the collaboration among CPU and GPU processes to accelerate the BCG algorithm by the exploitation of the full variety of available resources of multi-GPU clusters using also the "halos" strategy. Here it is important to highlight that a static workload balance scheduling has been considered because the workload of the application is known at compile time and constant during the execution. So, the distribution between the different processes can be done at compile time. This hybrid version presents two main advantages: (1) the parallel computation of GPU and CPU processes, despite CPU is slower than GPU, contributes to accelerate the algorithm execution. We have implemented an efficient collaboration between CPU and GPU by establishing an appropriate balance of the workload assigned to each device; and (2) the hybrid version can exploit the large memory resources of multicore nodes. This way, the memory limitation of the GPUs is overcome by the inclusion of CPU processes in the hybrid strategy.

4 Evaluation

This section shows the experimental results carried out to evaluate the performance of the hybrid version for solving the 3D Helmholtz equation. The hybrid approach is also compared to two different implementations: CPU version and GPU version.

Our experiments were performed on a cluster which is comprised of four compute nodes (Bullx R424-E3. Intel Xeon E5 2650 (16 cores every node) and 64 GB de RAM). Figure 1 depicts the platform. Each node is equipped with two Tesla M2075 GPUs managed by the CUDA driver included in the 5.0 toolkit. Note that each GPU device has 5.24 Gbytes of global memory (total $5.24 \times 8 = 41.92$ Gbytes), and that the size of the memory is one of the main factors which determines to what extend real world problems can be solved when only GPU platforms are used. Figure 1 depicts the structure of the cluster used in our experimental evaluations. Programs were compiled with mpicc and -O2 as optimization option.

The set of test sparse matrices is described in Table 2, where N represents the dimension of the sparse matrix, $D2$ identifies the number of elements of every "halo", and nnz the number of nonzero elements. Note that all the matrices have double-complex datatype and the average number of entries per row is 7 (for more details about the particular structure of the sparse matrix A, related to the discretization of the Helmholtz equation read [15]).

Firstly, a study of the runtime of the CPU and GPU approaches was carried out. Tables 1 and 2 show the experimental results where *Runt* identifies the

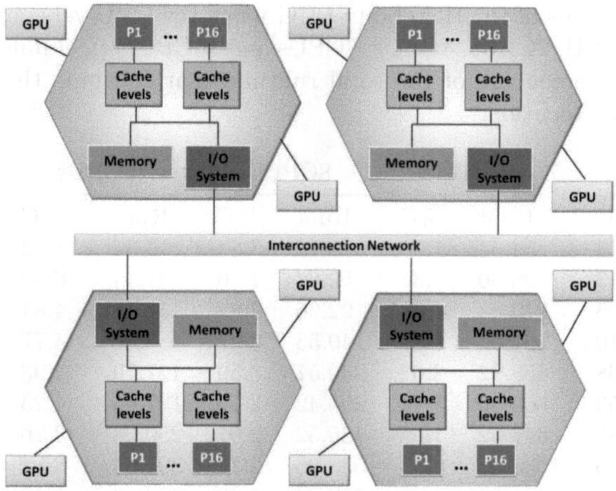

Fig. 1. Structure of the cluster, which is comprised of four compute nodes (16 cores every node) and a total of eight Tesla M2075 GPU devices

Matrix	N	$D2$	nnz
m_160^3	160^3	160^2	2.87E+07
m_200^3	200^3	200^2	5.60E+07
m_240^3	240^3	240^2	9.68E+07
m_280^3	280^3	280^2	1.54E+08
m_320^3	320^3	320^2	2.29E+08
m_360^3	360^3	360^2	3.27E+08
m_400^3	400^3	400^2	4.48E+08
m_440^3	440^3	440^2	5.96E+08
m_480^3	480^3	480^2	7.74E+08
m_520^3	520^3	520^2	9.84E+08

Fig. 2. Set of test matrices

total runtime in seconds of the BCG execution and $\%C$ represents the percentage of the communications penalties with respect to the total runtime (the remaining time is associated to the computation time). Note that CPU and GPU processes have been launched in different nodes since the number of MPI processes has been selected less or equal to the number of available cores on the cluster. To be more specific, the implementation using 2CPUs (2GPUs) has been launched using two nodes of the cluster and the implementations using 4CPUs (4GPUs), 8CPUs (8GPUs) and 16CPUs, using the four nodes of the cluster. Focusing our attention in Table 1, up to 16CPUs have been considered for the parallelization because using more CPU processors (e. g. 32CPUs) the size of the halos are relevant with respect to the local data and consequently the communication penalties deteriorate the performance.

Tables 1 and 2 clearly shown that the runtime ($Runt$) decreases as the number of CPU and GPU processes increases. It is due to the fact that the resolution of the Helmholtz equation using BCG is dominated by the computation. This fact is more evident for the CPU version with the low value of $\%C$ column with values which range from 0.43 to 11.32. In the GPU version, the communication penalties are larger (range from 4.48 to 33.94) and correspond to the additional communication between the CPU and the GPU and to the runtime reduction of the GPU. The value of $\%C$ is directly related to the dimension of the problem to solve, therefore, the bigger is the problem, the less impact of the communication time respect to the total runtime. One issue that can be seen in Table 2 is that the 3D Helmholtz equation could not be solved for the matrices with the largest size due to the limitations related to the global memory resources of the GPUs.

Table 1. Runtimes(s) of 1000 iterations of the Helmholtz BCG using the CPU version with 1, 2, 4, 8 and 16 processors (1CPU, 2CPUs, 4CPUs, 8CPUs and 16CPUs) (Column *Runt*). Column *%C* identifies the percentage of the total runtime that consume the communication processes for every execution.

	1CPU	2CPUs		4CPUs		8CPUs		16CPUs	
	Runt	Runt	%C	Runt	%C	Runt	%C	Runt	%C
m_160^3	214.32	108.12	1.34	54.64	1.95	28.18	3.84	16.34	11.32
m_200^3	377.98	190.80	1.45	98.30	2.31	50.67	4.66	31.44	6.50
m_240^3	719.37	357.22	1.15	179.84	4.08	92.96	2.88	54.38	4.84
m_280^3	1038.38	520.67	1.10	264.55	0.83	140.53	6.22	85.24	4.77
m_320^3	1750.79	920.56	0.68	458.92	2.02	230.57	3.59	127.79	4.93
m_360^3	2217.68	1111.75	1.53	560.56	3.74	295.42	3.70	177.96	4.23
m_400^3	3411.10	1687.70	0.85	847.62	1.69	436.52	2.01	250.03	3.26
m_440^3	4124.25	2095.97	2.56	1035.28	0.43	538.26	2.74	324.65	3.84
m_480^3	5929.36	2963.20	0.49	1489.04	1.20	752.24	1.93	429.89	4.16
m_520^3	-	3410.84	0.61	1743.64	0.81	878.22	2.07	538.24	2.89

Table 2. Runtimes(s) of 1000 iterations of the Helmholtz BCG using the GPU version with 2, 4 and 8 GPU devices (2GPUs, 4GPUs and 8GPUs) (Column *Runt*). Column *%C* identifies the percentage of the total runtime consumed by the communication processes for every execution.

	2GPUs		4GPUs		8GPUs	
	Runt	%C	Runt	%C	Runt	%C
m_160^3	13.89	9.50	7.90	19.40	5.03	33.94
m_200^3	26.60	7.55	14.80	15.84	9.12	30.22
m_240^3	45.73	6.45	24.85	12.28	14.60	25.38
m_280^3	72.49	5.28	38.43	10.44	22.18	22.68
m_320^3	108.15	4.48	55.57	9.32	31.90	19.23
m_360^3	-	-	78.95	8.38	44.22	16.90
m_400^3	-	-	107.42	6.99	58.04	14.85
m_440^3	-	-	-	-	76.73	13.79
m_480^3	-	-	-	-	97.86	11.66
m_520^3	-	-	-	-	-	-

The best results in terms of performance are always obtained by the GPU approach thanks to massive parallelism that GPU devices offer. So, the execution of the resolutions of the 3D Helmholtz Equation based on 1000 iterations of the BCG method using 2, 4 and 8 GPUs are faster than the execution using 2, 4, 8 and 16 CPU processors, with acceleration factors which range from 5.6 to 8.6 when we compare the same number of CPU and GPU processes (2CPUs-2GPUs, 4CPUs-4GPUs and 8CPUs-8GPUs). Moreover, the communications penalties of the GPU version are higher due to the additional communication GPU-CPU and viceversa in the "halos" swap.

In the hybrid version we have considered the executions with 4 and 8 GPU processes as these resources reached the best results in terms of performance for the size of the considered test problems in the evaluation. Table 3 shows the runtime of 1000 iterations of the BCG method based on the 3D Helmholtz Equation using two hybrid configurations: 4GPUs+8CPUs and 8GPUs+8CPUs. The following notation is used, *Runt* identifies the total runtime in seconds of the execution and *GPU*(*s*) and *CPU*(*s*) represent the runtime in seconds of the GPU and CPU processes, respectively. Column *F* identifies the ratio between the workload assigned the CPU and the GPU. The workload assigned to a GPU process is *F* times higher compared to the workload of the CPU process. Different benchmarking processes have been carried out for this cluster and this algorithm to determine the computational burden associated to the hybrid version which provides the best workload balance. The value of *F* has been estimated by a preliminary benchmarking (not automatized) using values which range from 8 to 12 (these values are related to the acceleration factor of solving the same 3D Helmholtz problem in one GPU with respect to one GPU). Column %*I* represents the acceleration factor of the hybrid implementation versus the GPU version with 4 GPUs (for 4GPUs+8CPUs implementation) and 8 GPUs (for 8GPUs+8CPUs implementation). As aforementioned, the workload of the GPU version has to be larger than the workload of the CPU version but taking into account the memory limitation of the GPUs. Therefore, for problems of dimension 440^3, 480^3 and 520^3 with 4GPUs+8CPUs, the memory requirements of the four GPUs are not enough and the value of *F* is less than 8.

Table 3. Profiling of the resolution of the 3D Helmholtz Equation based on 1000 iterations of the BCG method using the hybrid version and two different configurations: 4GPUs+8CPUs and 8GPUs+8CPUs. Column *Runt* identifies the total runtime in seconds of the execution, *GPU*(*s*) and *CPU*(*s*) show the runtime of the GPU and the CPU, respectively, *F* column denotes the factors to balance the workload in the hybrid approach and, finally, %*I* represents the acceleration factor of the hybrid implementation versus the GPU version with 4 GPUs (for 4GPUs+8CPUs implementation) and 8 GPUs (for 8GPUs+8CPUs implementation).

	4GPUs+8CPUs					8GPUs+8CPUs				
	Runt	GPU(s)	CPU(s)	F	%I	Runt	GPU(s)	CPU(s)	F	%I
m_160^3	7.24	5.29	3.31	11	8.45	4.81	3.03	2.48	10	4.24
m_200^3	13.66	10.74	7.49	12	7.73	8.62	5.80	4.22	11	5.45
m_240^3	21.63	17.47	16.17	10	12.96	14.4	9.66	10.09	11	1.40
m_280^3	33.44	27.36	26.75	8	12.98	21.42	15.00	13.67	10	3.43
m_320^3	49.13	41.74	37.95	12	11.58	30.52	22.18	18.58	11	4.35
m_360^3	69.73	60.10	50.61	10	11.67	41.73	29.80	31.36	10	5.61
m_400^3	93.75	83.41	68.05	11	12.73	55.80	43.70	42.81	9	3.87
m_440^3	131.99	101.85	123.08	7	-	73.35	56.62	56.58	11	4.41
m_480^3	329.82	102.76	306.90	3	-	93.38	75.65	73.67	9	4.58
m_520^3	473.82	15.45	459.82	2	-	123.49	97.83	98.14	9	-

As can be observed in Table 3, the runtimes of the CPU and GPU processes are well balanced. Note that in all experiments, 4 GPU or 8 GPU cards are exploited and the runtime decreases as the number of GPU processes increases. It is due to the fact that CPU processes collaborate with the GPU processes to accelerate the computation. Note that the workload balance is not optimal for the matrices m_440^3, m_480^3 and m_520^3 due to the memory limitations of the GPU. So, although the workload of the CPU processes is high, the CPU memory resources allow to extend the dimension of problem with light penalties of performance. For the considered dimension of the problem to solve (from $N = 160^3$ to $N = 520^3$), the approach with 4GPUs+8CPUs reaches the best results in terms of performance compared to the 4GPUs version (acceleration factors range from 8.45 to 12.73). It results evident that this kind of platforms can only be efficiently exploited for very large problems, even larger than the instances considered in this work. It is also clear that the hybrid platform is appropriate to overcome the GPU memory limitations.

5 Conclusions

This paper has described the implementation of a parallel solution for the 3D Helmholtz equation which combines the exploitation of the high regularity of the matrices involved in the numerical methods and the massive parallelism supplied by heterogeneous architecture of modern multi-GPU cluster. Experimental results have shown that this approach outperforms both, the CPU and the GPU approaches when several CPU cores collaborate with the GPU devices. However, we only obtain large acceleration factors using more GPUs when the size of the problem is large enough.

As aforementioned, the difficulty having the workload well-balanced is related to the appropriate distribution of the workload between the CPU and GPU processes, so our current on-going work involves to automatize the benchmarking process to determine the most suitable factor F to exploit the specific architecture considered. Furthermore, another future work will be focused on the development of a hybrid version MPI-OpenMP on the multi-GPU cluster.

Acknowledgments. G. Ortega is a fellow of the Spanish FPU programme. Work partially supported by the Spanish Ministry of Science (TIN2008-01117, TIN2012-37483) and J. Andalucía (P10-TIC-6002, P011-TIC7176), partially financed by the European Reg. Dev. Fund (ERDF).

References

1. Top 500 List (June 2013), `http://www.top500.org/lists/2013/06/`
2. Babuska, I.M., Sauter, S.A.: Is the pollution effect of the FEM Avoidable for the Helmholtz Equation considering high wave numbers? SIAM Rev. 42(3), 451–484 (2000)
3. Balay, S., et al.: PETSc Users Manual. Revision 3.3
4. Bao, G., Wei, G.W., Zhao, S.: Numerical solution of the Helmholtz equation with high wave numbers. Int. J. Numer. Meth. Eng. 59, 389–408 (2004)

5. Dautray, R., Lions, J.L.: Mathematical analysis and numerical methods for science and technology. Springer, Berlin (1990)
6. Ihlenburg, F., Babuska, I.: Solution of Helmholtz problems by knowledge-based FEM. CAMES 4, 397–415 (1997)
7. Jacobsen, D.A., Thibault, J.C., Senocak, I.: An MPI-CUDA Implementation for Massively Parallel Incompressible Flow Computations on Multi-GPU Clusters. In: Proc. of the 48th American Institute of Aeronautics and Astronautics (AIAA) Aerospace Science Meeting, Floria, USA (2010)
8. Junger, M.C., Feit, D.: Sound, Structures, and Their Interaction, 2nd edn. The MIT Press (1986)
9. Knibbe, H., Oosterlee, C.W., Vuik, C.: GPU implementation of a Helmholtz Krylov solver preconditioned by a shifted Laplace multigrid method. J. Comput. Appl. Math. 236(3), 281–293 (2011)
10. Lanczos, C.: An iteration method for the solution of the eigenvalue problem of linear differential and integral operators. J. Res. Nat. Bur. Stand. 45, 255–282 (1950)
11. Lastovetsky, A.L.: Special issue of journal of parallel and distributed computing: Heterogeneity in parallel and distributed computing. J. Parallel Distrib. Comput. 72(10), 1397 (2012)
12. Duraiswami, R., Gumerov, N.A.: Fast Multipole Methods for the Helmholtz Equation in Three Dimensions. Elsevier Science (2004)
13. NVIDIA. CUDA Programming guide. Version 4 (2011)
14. NVIDIA. Du-06702-001_v5.5 CUBLAS user guide. Technical report (July 2013)
15. Ortega, G., Garzón, E.M., Vázquez, F., García, I.: Exploiting the regularity of differential operators to accelerate solutions of PDEs on GPUs. In: Proc. of CMMSE, Benidorm, Spain, June 26-30, pp. 908–917 (2011)
16. Ortega, G., Garzón, E.M., Vázquez, F., García, I.: The BiConjugate gradient method on GPUs. J. Supercomput. 64, 49–58 (2013)
17. Ortega, G., Lobera, J., Arroyo, M.P., García, I., Garzón, E.M.: High Performance Computing for Optical Diffraction Tomography. In: Proc. of HPCS, Madrid, Spain, July 2-6, pp. 195–201 (2012)
18. Saad, Y.: Iterative Methods for Sparse Linear Systems, 2nd edn. SIAM (April 2003)
19. Sadiku, M.N.O.: Numerical Techniques in Electromagnetics, 2nd edn. CRC Press (July 2000)
20. Snir, M., Otto, S., Huss-Lederman, S., Walker, D., Dongarra, J.: MPI-The Complete Reference, 2nd revised edn. The MPI Core, vol.1. MIT Press, Cambridge (1998)
21. Van der Vorst, H.A., Ciarlet, P.G., Iserles, A., Kohn, R.V., Wright, M.H.: Iterative Krylov Methods for Large Linear Systems. Cambridge Univ. Press (2003)

Computation of Mutual Information Metric for Image Registration on Multiple GPUs

Andrew Adinetz[1], Jiri Kraus[2], Markus Axer[3], Marcel Huysegoms[3], Stefan Köhnen[3], and Dirk Pleiter[1]

[1] Jülich Supercomputing Centre, Forschungszentrum Jülich, 52425 Jülich, Germany
[2] NVIDIA GmbH, Germany
[3] Institute of Neuroscience and Medicine (INM-1), Forschungszentrum Jülich, 52425 Jülich, Germany

Abstract. Because of their computational power, GPUs are widely used in the field of image processing. Registration of brain images has already been successfully accelerated with GPUs, but registration of high-resolution human brain images presents new challenges due to large amounts of data and images not fitting in the memory of a single device.

In this paper, we address this issue with two approaches. The first approach replicates image data in system memory of each node and distributes only a part of the data over multiple GPUs. The second approach splits image data between multiple GPUs, and overlaps computation and communication to hide latency. For both approaches, we present a performance analysis and comparison.

1 Introduction

Unraveling the basic organization principles of the human brain represents one of the major challenges in modern neuroscience. The human brain's heterogeneous topology poses a particular challenge to any neuro-imaging technique and prevented the neuroscientists from understanding its complexity so far.

Therefore, the Institute of Neuroscience and Medicine (INM-1) focusses on the assembly of a realistic 3D model of the human brain [1, 2, 3, 4]. This brain model will be referred to as JuBrain [5]. The data set will not only help to reveal the neuro-biological basics of mental capacities, but will also enable characterization of their individual facets and underlying mechanisms. Recent developments in the field of post mortem microscopic neuro-imaging allow researchers to obtain information about the brain that were not available so far, but they also pushed the manageability of data sets to the limits.

The post mortem studies require brains to be cut into thousands of histological sections. Typical section thickness cover the range between 10 microns and 60 microns, which translates into 15.000 and 2.500 sections per human brain that need to be measured one by one. To construct a coherent 3D description (cf. Fig. 1), advanced image registration techniques have to be applied to all sections [6, 7, 8, 9]. However, the assembly of one cellular model of the human brain scanned with the resolution of 1 micron will add up to data sizes of 300 TB per

D. an Mey et al. (Eds.): Euro-Par 2013 Workshops, LNCS 8374, pp. 208–217, 2014.

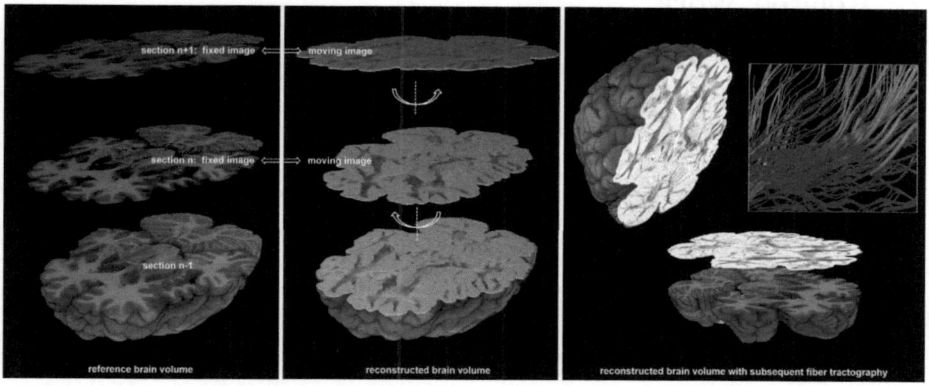

Fig. 1. Schematic of a 3D reconstruction of a human brain: Each registration approach requires a moving image (middle) that is being aligned with a fixed image (left)

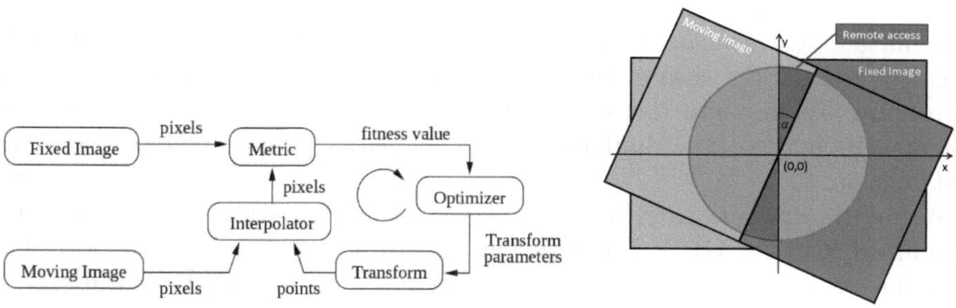

(a) ITK work-flow [10]. (b) Benchmark setup.

Fig. 2. Image registration workflow and benchmark setup

brain considering only the imaging data. The fiber architecture in post mortem brains acquired with polarized light imaging [4] easily reach sizes of 500 GB for a single whole brain section. This means, to deal with the high resolution images and large data sets highly advanced computational concepts are required.

A typical image registration process is shown in Fig. 2a. The process is a feedback loop in which the *Metric* determines the fitness value by comparing the transformed moving image with the fixed image. While iterating the loop, the *Optimizer* selects the transformation parameter. Fig. 2b shows a simple registration problem, where only rotation is used as transformation.

The computationally most demanding step is the metric evaluation, where we use the mutual information metric. In this paper we make several contributions to solve the problem of computing the metric efficiently on multiple GPUs. Firstly, we discuss different strategies for evaluating mutual information metric on GPU clusters for large images. Secondly, we present a performance analysis of prototype implementations for different GPU architectures.

2 Related Work

A major problem of the existing image registration approaches is the time required for the calculations. Since image resolutions and file sizes are continually growing, new approaches to speed up image registration and other image processing algorithms, are needed. Consequently, there is need to take advantage of the high performance provided by modern GPU architectures. Previous studies could already demonstrate that the parallelization of specific registration approaches on the GPU allows fo significant speed ups [11, 12, 13]. Also surveys show that there is still a lot potential to reduce computation time and handle even larger data sets [14, 15].

3 Metric Evaluation

The mutual information metric determines the shared information between two images [6]. Shared information is defined via mutual dependence between the two images. To measure mutual dependence, a joint probability distribution is calculated. In the case of two images, this distribution is defined as a joint histogram. To measure the similarity from the joint histogram, the Shannon entropy [16] is used. The similarity is thus defined as the uncertainty of the joint distribution.

As metric evaluation is the most time-consuming part of the optimization, we offload it to the GPU. For sufficiently small images we can copy both fixed and moving images are copied to the memory of a single GPU at the start of the optimization procedure, and keep them there during the computations. The joint histogram is evaluated on the GPU using atomic operations. It turns out that on Fermi GPUs, atomics are the limiting factor. So we evaluate histogram of individual images from the joint histogram on the host, which reduces the number of atomics by a factor of 3.

We also experimented with the number of pixels processed by each GPU thread. And while for Fermi 1 pixel per thread gives the best results, for Kepler the best single-GPU performance is achieved when each thread processes a grid of 32×32 pixels.

4 Parallelization Strategies

Because high resolution images are too large to fit in device memory of a single GPU, we perform a 2D domain decomposition to use the memory of multiple GPUs. We use block distribution of both fixed and moving image, i.e. we divide both into n equally sized rectangular domains and assign each domain to one GPU. Each GPU is then responsible for calculating the contribution to the joint histogram of the domain it owns. The individual histograms are combined into a single histogram in the second step.

To calculate individual histogram contributions, each GPU reads pixels from the part of the fixed image it owns and applies the given transformation to each of these. This will give coordinates of the moving image pixel for each fixed image pixel. Some of these coordinates fall into the locally stored part of the moving image, and the value of the moving image pixel can then be directly fetched. If the transformed pixel coordinates are stored on a remote GPU, the histogram contribution of that pixel has to be computed differently. We have developed two different approaches for evaluating contributions of remote pixels.

4.1 Replication in System Memory

In this approach we assume the system memory, which compared to the device memory has a much larger capacity, can hold the entire moving image. The device memory holds the fixed image and a local portion of the moving image. If the device needs to access the non-local portion of the image, it has to read from the (pinned) host memory. We call this approach *replication in system memory*, or just *system-memory approach.*

The advantages of this appoach are its simplicity and that it only requires a single kernel launch per GPU for processing. Its disadvantages are that accesses to the non-local parts of the moving image are very slow compared to device memory, and that the interpolation features of the texture unit cannot be used as in the single GPU case. Although the low precision texture interpolation on the moving image data is sufficient to calculate the mutual information metric, we faced accuracy issues when using software interpolation to the non local parts of the moving image and texture interpolation to the local part. We therefore use software interpolation only. Since the kernel is never limited by arithmetic throughput, this has only minor effects on the overall performance.

4.2 List-Update Approach

In another approach we distribute both fixed and moving images. When remote data is required to compute the joint histogram, the local fixed image data as well as the moving image coordinates are sent to the remote node that holds the required moving image data. The computations are performed on the remote node. This reduces communication and synchronization costs, as there is no need for a response message. Since the message size for each pixel is small, many messages are aggregated in a device memory buffer before being sent. Since in this approach for each remote node a list of updates is collected, we call it *list-update approach.*

Since the number of pixels processed inside a single kernel invocation is large, and potentially each pixel can send a message, the number of messages sent during the kernel execution cannot fit into a buffer of reasonable size. Flushing this buffer while the kernel is running to make place for new messages is currently not possible to implement reliably. We therefore decided to split the processed portion of the image into smaller-sized chunks, with one kernel invocation per chunk. As no more than one message is sent per pixel, the size of the chunk can be chosen in such a way that the buffer size is reasonable. Moreover, processing multiple chunks in different streams allows us to overlap computation, i.e. processing pixels and handling list-update messages, with communication to and from GPU as well as between nodes.

We considered two ways of collecting list-update messages within the buffer. One is to allocate a chunk-sized buffer which holds a message for a particular pixel at a predefined position. "compression" kernel then groups messages by the destination node before sending. Alternatively, one can allocate one buffer per destination node and use atomic operations to fill these buffers contiguously. The compression approach has the obvious advantage of using less memory, while the atomic write-out approach does not require any additional passes before sending the buffers.

For both approaches, we apply additional optimizations. For the compression approach, a sent-flag was introduced which indicates whether a message had been sent to avoid unnecessary compressions. For atomic write-out, we exploit synchronous execution of warp threads, which allows doing only one atomic increment per warp per sender, increasing write-out throughput.

Also, for both approaches, AoS (array of structures) or SoA (structure of arrays) message buffer layouts can be used. And while AoS is simpler to implement, SoA can consume less memory per message (9 bytes vs. 12 bytes) since no alignment is required. We also experimented with the number of pixels processed by each thread.

5 Performance Evaluation and Discussion

The benchmark setup employed in our experiments is depicted in Fig. 2b. Both fixed and moving images have the same size. The centers of both are aligned. A circular mask centered at the center of the images is used, and its radius is chosen as 0.9 of the smaller image half-axis. The transformation applied to the moving image is rotation by angle α around the center. This simplified setup has the advantage that we can control the number of remote accesses via angle α.

We start 1 MPI process per GPU and investigate parallelization over up to 4 GPUs. Block distribution of the image among processes is applied, first along x axis, and then along y. The choice of transformation and the mask ensures that for a fixed image pixel inside the mask, the moving image pixel will also fall inside the mask, which reduces load imbalance. The fraction of pixels with remote access is $\beta = \min(\frac{\alpha N}{2\pi}, 1)$, where $N \geq 2$ is the total number of MPI processes. We typically measured the execution times for 101 different values of α with $0° \leq \alpha \leq 180°$ and report average values obtained from 5 measurements.

All experiments presented here were run at Jülich Supercomputing Centre (JSC) using up to 2 nodes of the JUDGE cluster equipped with Fermi GPUs, as well as a Kepler test system. Each node of the JUDGE cluster is equipped with 2 6-core 2-way hyper-threaded Intel X5650 CPUs running at 2.67 GHz, 96 GBytes RAM, and 2 NVIDIA M2070 GPUs with activated ECC and 5.25 GBytes of device memory. The test system comprised 2 8-core, 2-way hyper-threaded Intel E5-2650 CPUs running at 2 GHz, 64 GBytes RAM and 2 NVIDIA K20X GPUs with ECC enabled and 5.6 GBytes of device memory.

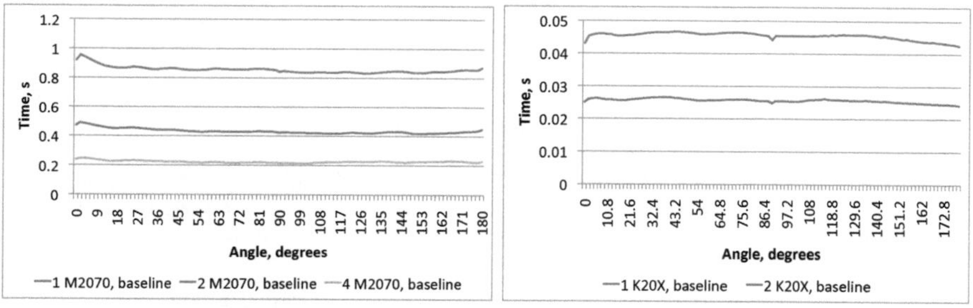

(a) M2070 (b) K20X

Fig. 3. Baseline performance

To obtain baseline performance, we replicated images to all GPUs such that parallel evaluation of the metric requires almost no communications. We used 1 and 32×32 pixels per thread in case of Fermi and Kepler, respectively. The results are presented in Fig. 3. As expected, the scaling is close to ideal, as only the final histogram reduction involves communication. It is also noticeable that due to improved atomics, performance on Kepler GPUs is more than $20\times$ higher than for Fermi.[1].

We then performed experiments with system memory replication approach on different GPUs. We also varied the percentage of GPU memory allocated for storing a moving image halo. The results for different GPU architectures are shown in Fig. 4. As Fermi performance is limited by atomics, a significant fraction of system memory accesses can be tolerated. When the rotation angle α becomes larger, the amount of data being read from system memory increases, and execution times get larger. In Fig. 5 we show both execution time and the number of system memory accesses as a function of α. The number of memory accesses does not only depend on the amount of read data but also on the access pattern. As is shown in Fig. 5b, for small angle α adjacent system memory addresses are read which allows coalesced accesses, i.e. a small amount of data is read efficiently. For $\alpha \simeq 90°$ this is not possible anymore and a result the number of memory accesses increases significantly, i.e. an increased amount of data is fetched in an inefficient way. For $\alpha > 90°$ the amount of data read from system memory increases but now accesses can again be coalesced and thus the number of access reduces.

As Kepler has much higher atomic throughput, the increasing fraction of system memory accesses causes a performance drop also for small angles α. When the coalescing is restored at $\alpha = 180°$, execution time is nevertheless 10-times larger compared to $\alpha = 0$ when all data is read from device memory. Experimentally we found that on Kepler using 4×4 pixels per thread results in best performance. For both GPUs, increasing the halo size provides some performance improvement, but the overall picture remains the same.

[1] Optimization is still on-going so performance improvements are possible for both.

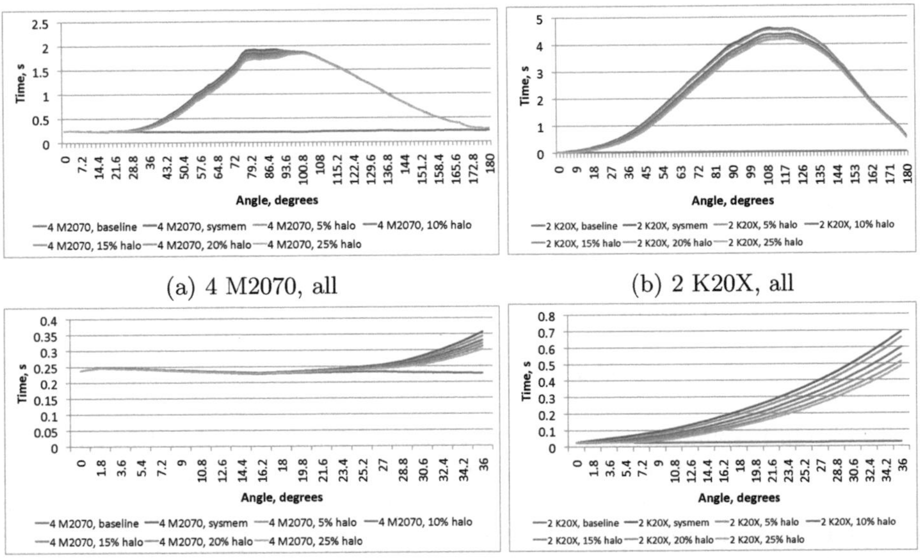

(a) 4 M2070, all

(b) 2 K20X, all

(c) 4 M2070, close-up

(d) 2 K20X, close-up

Fig. 4. System memory replication performance with and without halo

Tests based on the list-update approach were run with 4 streams, a chunk size of 1536×1536, 1 pixel per thread on Fermi and 4×2 for Kepler. We first compared array-of-structures (AoS) and structure-of-arrays (SoA) approaches, and compared atomic and compression write-out. Note that due to the benchmark setup, processing chunks in the same order in all processes will lead to high load imbalance. To lower imbalance, we use a "reflected" order of chunk processing.

Results are presented in Fig. 6. SoA is always better than AoS, since it allows reducing the amount of data transferred. On Kepler message buffer compression results in lower performance, while for Fermi we observe similar performance for either using buffer compression or atomic buffer updates. The latter is consistent with the observation that atomic operations are a bottleneck on Fermi.

We also did performance tracing of our list-update implementation. It turns out that the main limiting factor, at least for Fermi GPUs, is not communication but load imbalance between chunks. It is partially caused by the sequence of atomic operations, making performance data-dependent. Furthermore, the numbers of list-update messages per chunk are different.

5.1 Comparison of Parallelization Approaches

Comparison of performance of both parallelization approaches is presented in Fig. 7. For Fermi GPUs, as using system memory does not compromise performance, system-memory approach is clearly superior for small angle values. As we expect coalescing to be better in real applications, we actually expect the system-memory approach to be better even when the fraction of remote accesses is high.

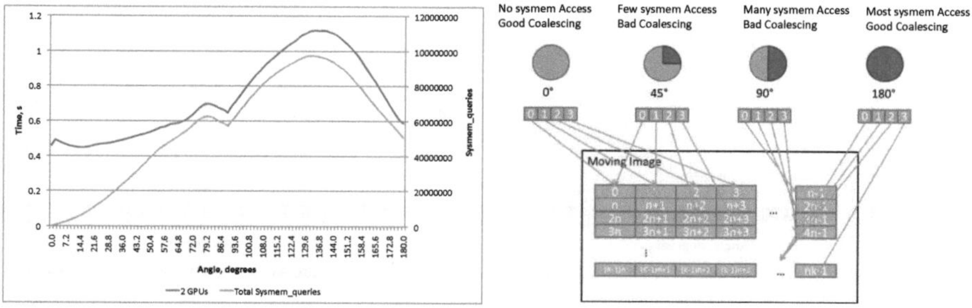

(a) Execution time and number of system memory accesses using 2 M2070 GPUs.
(b) System memory access patterns for different angle α.

Fig. 5. Performance analysis for the system-memory approach

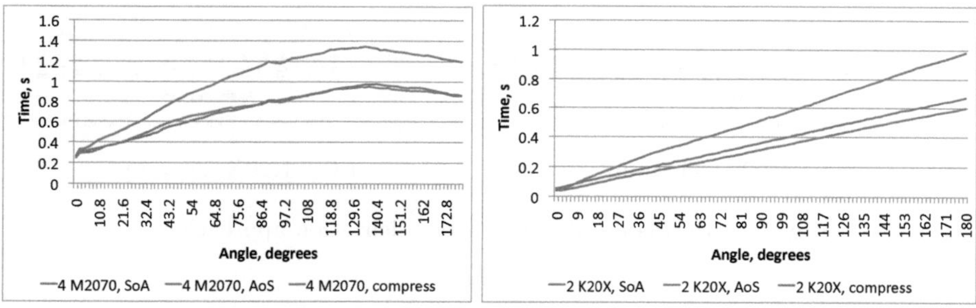

(a) 4 M2070

(b) 2 K20X

Fig. 6. Performance of list-update variants

The situation is quite different for Kepler. System memory accesses are no longer cheap compared to atomics, and the list-update approach provides clearly better execution times, which scale linearly with the fraction of remote accesses, and does not depend on coalescing. And while we expect system-memory approach to do better for real applications, list-update approach will still have higher performance.

There are other concerns in choosing the preferred approach, apart from performance. As we expect major changes of the application to continue, application developer productivity is a major concern. System-memory approach has a clear advantage here, as it required significant less effort to implement (about 50 lines of code, 1 person-day) compared to the list-update approach (about 1000 lines of code, 2 person-weeks).

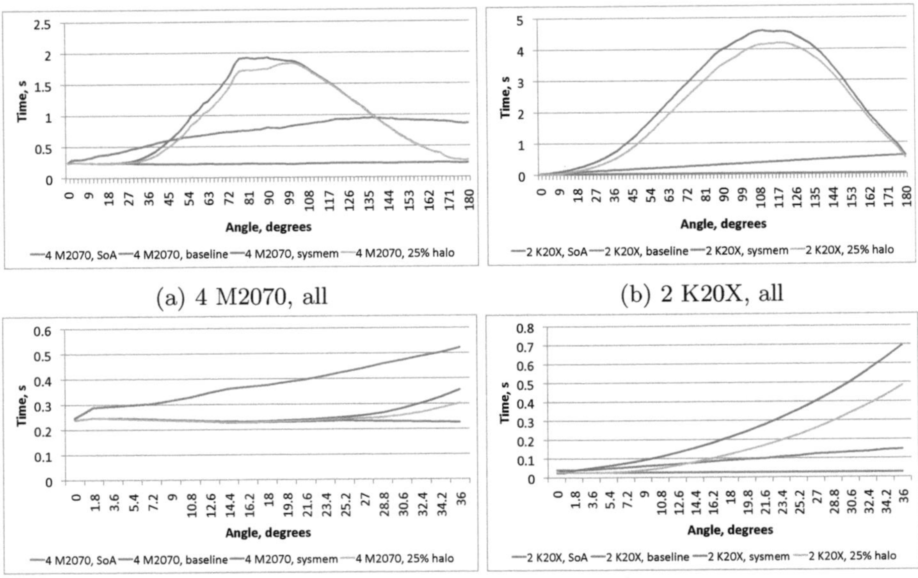

(a) 4 M2070, all

(b) 2 K20X, all

(c) 4 M2070, close-up

(d) 2 K20X, close-up

Fig. 7. Performance of different parallelization approaches

6 Conclusions

In this paper, we presented two approaches to compute the mutual information metric for large images on multiple GPUs. The first approach keeps a full copy of the moving image in system memory, which is much larger than device memory, and only partitions the data hold in device memory. The second approach partitions all image data among multiple GPUs, aggregates remote accesses and overlaps computation and communication to hide latencies. For both approaches, we discussed a number of optimizations and provided a performance analysis.

Surprisingly, it is hard to find a winner. On the one hand, the system-memory approach is clearly superior on Fermi GPUs, but it may suffer from non-coalesced system memory accesses. It does not show load imbalance issues and is clearly simpler in terms of implementation. On the other hand, the list-update approach is better on K20X GPUs but is more complicated. Its performance is mostly independent of the degree of coalescing. In case where more than 2 images needs to be processed, this can also be a better approach.

Acknowledgements. This work was performed in the scope of NVIDIA Application Lab at Jülich which is jointly funded by Forschungszentrum Jülich and NVIDIA.

References

[1] Toga, A.W., Thompson, P.M., Mori, S., Amunts, K., Zilles, K.: Towards multimodal atlases of the human brain. Nature Reviews Neuroscience 7(12), 952–966 (2006)

[2] Zilles, K., Schleicher, A., Palomero-Gallagher, N., Amunts, K.: Quantitative analysis of cyto-and receptor architecture of the human brain. Brain Mapping: The Methods 2, 573–602 (2002)

[3] Zilles, K., Amunts, K.: Segregation and wiring in the brain. Science 335(6076), 1582–1584 (2012)

[4] Axer, M., Amunts, K., Grässel, D., Palm, C., Dammers, J., Axer, H., Pietrzyk, U., Zilles, K.: A novel approach to the human connectome: ultra-high resolution mapping of fiber tracts in the brain. Neuroimage 54(2), 1091–1101 (2011)

[5] `http://www.jubrain.fzjuelich.de`

[6] Modersitzki, J.: Numerical methods for image registration. Oxford University Press, USA (2004)

[7] Studholme, C., Hill, D.L., Hawkes, D.J., et al.: An overlap invariant entropy measure of 3D medical image alignment. Pattern Recognition 32(1), 71–86 (1999)

[8] Palm, C., Axer, M., Gräßel, D., Dammers, J., Lindemeyer, J., Zilles, K., Pietrzyk, U., Amunts, K.: Towards ultra-high resolution fibre tract mapping of the human brain–registration of polarised light images and reorientation of fibre vectors. Frontiers in Human Neuroscience 4 (2010)

[9] Eiben, B., Palm, C., Pietrzyk, U., Davatzikos, C., Amunts, K.: Perspective error correction using registration for blockface volume reconstruction of serial histological sections of the human brain. In: Bildverarbeitung für die Medizin, pp. 301–305 (2010)

[10] Ibanez, L., Schroeder, W., Ng, L., Cates, J.: The ITK Software Guide, 1st edn. Kitware, Inc. (2003), `http://www.itk.org/ItkSoftwareGuide.pdf`, ISBN 1-930934-10-6

[11] Modat, M., Ridgway, G.R., Taylor, Z.A., Lehmann, M., Barnes, J., Hawkes, D.J., Fox, N.C., Ourselin, S.: Fast free-form deformation using graphics processing units. Computer Methods and Programs in Biomedicine 98(3), 278–284 (2010)

[12] Köhn, A., Drexl, J., Ritter, F., König, M., Peitgen, H.O.: GPU accelerated image registration in two and three dimensions. In: Bildverarbeitung für die Medizin 2006, pp. 261–265. Springer (2006)

[13] Köhnen, S., Ehrhardt, J., Schmidt-Richberg, A., Handels, H.: CUDA Optimierung von nicht-linearer oberflächen-und intensitätsbasierter Registrierung. In: Bildverarbeitung für die Medizin 2011, pp. 99–103. Springer (2011)

[14] Shams, R., Sadeghi, P., Kennedy, R., Hartley, R.: A survey of medical image registration on multicore and the GPU. IEEE Signal Processing Magazine 27(2), 50–60 (2010)

[15] Eklund, A., Dufort, P., Forsberg, D., LaConte, S.M.: Medical image processing on the GPU - past, present and future. Medical Image Analysis (2013)

[16] Shannon, C.E.: A mathematical theory of communication. ACM SIGMOBILE Mobile Computing and Communications Review 5(1), 3–55 (2001)

Optimization of a Cloud Resource Management Problem from a Consumer Perspective

Rafaelli de C. Coutinho, Lúcia M.A. Drummond, and Yuri Frota

Institute of Computing – Fluminense Federal University, RJ
{rcoutinho,lucia,yuri}@ic.uff.br

Abstract. Cloud Computing is a distributed computing paradigm in which computing resources are available to users via Internet. Although there are many works on resource management in related literature, few of them tackle the problem from the perspective of commercial cloud consumers. In this paper, the proposed resource management problem selects cloud resources aiming to reduce the payment cost and the execution time of user applications. In order to solve this problem, an integer programming formulation and a heuristic based on Greedy Randomized Adaptive Search Procedure (GRASP) are also introduced. The model and the algorithm were tested over a set of instances constructed from requirements of real applications combined with sets of resources offered by commercial clouds. The obtained results indicate that the presented methods can be an important decision support tool for cloud consumers.

Keywords: Cloud Computing, Resource Management Problem, Optimization.

1 Introduction

Cloud Computing is a distributed computing paradigm in which computing resources are available to consumers via Internet [11]. It delivers infrastructure, platform, and software as services by signing service-level agreements (SLAs) with consumers. In terms of cloud economics, the provider should offer resource-economic services. Novel, power-efficient schemes for caching, query processing, and thermal management are mandatory due to the increasing amount of waste heat that data centers dissipate for application services. Moreover, new pricing models based on the pay-as-you-go policy are necessary to address the highly variable demand for cloud resources. On the other hand, cloud service consumers might have an SLA with a cloud service provider concerning how much bandwidth, CPU, and memory the consumer can use at any given time throughout the day. The cloud consumer has to decide how he or she wants to use cloud services; like whether or not to add in more virtual machines and at what price point that option becomes too expensive to justify the return. In this context, application schedulers have different policies that vary according to the objective function: minimize total execution time, minimize payment cost to execute, minimize the demand for power while maintaining a service-level guarantee for

D. an Mey et al. (Eds.): Euro-Par 2013 Workshops, LNCS 8374, pp. 218–227, 2014.

the consumers, balance the load on resources used while meeting the deadline constraints of the application and so forth. Independently of the objective function, resource allocation problems in clouds are NP-hard problems, so there are no efficient methods to solve them.

As cloud computing becomes more widespread and consequently energy consumption of the network and computing resources grow, more researches have been conducted on energy cost optimization. In [3], the authors analyse the energy consumption in clouds. Some problems that aim to minimize the energy costs can be seen in [7] [13] [14]. A survey about the energy cost for resource allocation and scheduling algorithms based on energy consumption are found in [4] [19]. Concerning the cloud consumer perspective, computing resources can be acquired by reservation or on-demand plans. In [6], it is observed that an interesting reservation plan can be difficult to achieve due to uncertainty of future demands of consumers and resource prices of providers. In this context, the paper proposes an optimal cloud resource provisioning algorithm by formulating a stochastic programming model. Other researches tackle virtualization and the scheduling of virtual resources to physical ones with the objective of minimizing the network costs [20] [22] [2] and the computation costs [22] [18] [28] in clouds or cooperative clouds [21]. In [9], main challenges inherent to the resource allocation problem are highlighted and categorized. An architecture for market-oriented clouds and resource management strategies, as well as an overview of representative clouds platforms, are presented in [5]. Finally, a study that demonstrates the economic feasibility and efficiency of cloud computing for small and medium enterprises is presented in [26]. Most of papers found in the related literature consider the resource allocation problem from the cloud provider view whether in optimization of energy cost or the cost of the services and resources provision. Problems pertinent to cloud consumers, such as optimization of payment costs and execution times to run their applications, are usually neglected in related works.

In this paper, based on the actual way that popular cloud providers, such as *Amazon Elastic Compute Cloud* (EC2) and *Google Cloud Platform* offer resources and services for high performance computing users, a resource management problem that aims to reduce the payment cost and the execution time of the user application is defined. In order to solve it, an integer programming formulation and a heuristic based on Greedy Randomized Adaptive Search Procedure (GRASP) [10] are also introduced. The model and the algorithms were tested over a set of instances constructed from requirements of real applications combined with sets of resources offered by commercial clouds. The obtained results indicate that the presented methods can be an important decision support tool for cloud consumers.

2 Problem Definition and Mathematical Formulation

In literature there are many different definitions of Cloud Computing. According to [27], one reason for the existence of different perceptions is that Cloud

Computing is not a new technology, but a new operational model that brings together a set of existing technologies in a different way. In this work, we consider an Infrastructure-as-a-Service (Iaas) model, i.e., cloud consumers request computing resources as processing power (defined by Gflop[1]), disk storage, memory and architecture type, for a period of time and pays only what he/she uses. For instance, the values charged by a IaaS provider as *Amazon EC2* are mainly based on computer resources allocated for virtual machines (denoted by packages) purchased by the consumer. Cloud providers have a wide variety of package types (e.g. micro, high performance CPU, computers clusters, GPU clusters, high operations I/O, etc.), each one associated with a different cost and configuration, designed to meet different requirements. In this context, consumers have to decide which packages should purchase in order to minimize a specific objective as execution time or payment cost.

To describe this scenario as a mathematical formulation, we set the grounds for all the notation used from here on. Let P be the set of packages types offered by a cloud provider during a set of time periods. We define the set of consumer requirements as the maximum cost C_M, maximum time T_M, disk storage D_S, memory capacity M_C and a processing demand of G_f Gflop. Similarly, each package type $p \in P$ has an associated cost c_p (i.e. the cost of purchasing the package for one period of time) and computing resources as disk storage d_p, memory capacity m_p and a processing power of g_p Gflop per period of time (Gflopt). Moreover, it is common that cloud providers have a maximum limit of N_M purchased packages for each consumer in each period of time. We now define a binary variable x_{pit} for each $p \in P$, $i \in \{1, \ldots, N_M\}$ and $t \in T = \{1, \ldots, T_M\}$, such that $x_{pit} = 1$ if and only if package i of type p is purchased at time t; otherwise $x_{pit} = 0$. Also, define variable t_m as the last time period that a package was purchased by the consumer. The described scenario can be formulated as the following integer programming problem:

$$\text{(CC-IP)} \quad \min(\alpha_1 \sum_{p \in P} \sum_{i=1}^{N_M} \sum_{t \in T} c_p x_{pit} + \alpha_2 t_m) \tag{1}$$

$$\text{subject to} \quad \sum_{p \in P} \sum_{i=1}^{N_M} \sum_{t \in T} c_p x_{pit} \leq C_M \tag{2}$$

$$\sum_{p \in P} \sum_{i=1}^{N_M} d_p \, x_{pit} \geq D_S \, x_{p'i't}, \quad \forall t \in T, \forall p' \in P, \forall i' \in \{1, \ldots, N_M\} \tag{3}$$

$$\sum_{p \in P} \sum_{i=1}^{N_M} m_p \, x_{pit} \geq M_C \, x_{p'i't}, \quad \forall t \in T, \forall p' \in P, \forall i' \in \{1, \ldots, N_M\} \tag{4}$$

[1] flop - floating-point operations.

$$\sum_{p \in P} \sum_{i=1}^{N_M} \sum_{t \in T} g_p x_{pit} \geq G_f \tag{5}$$

$$\sum_{p \in P} \sum_{i=1}^{N_M} x_{pit} \leq N_M, \qquad \forall t \in T \tag{6}$$

$$t_m \geq t \; x_{pit}, \qquad \forall t \in T, \forall p \in P, \forall i \in \{1, \ldots, N_M\} \tag{7}$$

$$x_{pit+1} \leq x_{pit}, \qquad \forall t \in T, \forall p \in P, \forall i \in \{1, \ldots, N_M\} \tag{8}$$

$$x_{pi+1t} \leq x_{pit}, \qquad \forall t \in T, \forall p \in P, \forall i \in \{1, \ldots, N_M - 1\} \tag{9}$$

$$x_{pit} \in \{0, 1\}, \qquad \forall t \in T, \forall p \in P, \forall i \in \{1, \ldots, N_M\} \tag{10}$$

$$t_m \in \mathbb{Z} \tag{11}$$

where $(\alpha_1 + \alpha_2) = 1$.

In the above model, denoted as CC-IP, the objective function 1 seeks both the minimization of costs and total purchased time. The weights α_1 and α_2 define the relevance of each objective established by the consumer. Generally, since these objectives are conflicting, both objectives cannot arrive at optimal levels simultaneously. For example, for values of α_1 close to 1 the formulation prioritizes low-budget solutions with long periods of execution time. Constraint (2) ensures that the paid costs do not exceed the maximum recommended cost. Inequalities (3) and (4) enforce that the storage and memory capacity are, respectively, sufficient large to meet the requirements in each period of time. Similarly, constraint (5) guarantee that the processing power is at least large enough to satisfy the total demand. Inequalities (6) ensures that the number of selected packages does not exceed the cloud providers limit while constraint (7) together with objective function guarantee the correct interpretation of variable t_m. Constraint (8) enforces that there will be no gaps of time in feasible solutions (i.e. if a package is selected at time $t+1$, then it will also be selected at time t). Note that all package permutations yield feasible solutions in CC-IP, thus we add constraints (9) to establish an order between the packages and eliminate symmetry. Constraints (10) and (11) define the binary and integrality requirements on the variables.

3 GRASP for Resource Selection in Cloud Environments

Exact procedures have often proved incapable of finding solutions as they are extremely time-consuming, particularly for real-world problems. Conversely, heuristics and metaheuristics provide sub-optimal solutions in a reasonable time. In this context, we have designed and implemented a Greedy Randomized Adaptive Search Procedure (GRASP) which has been successfully applied in many combinatorial optimization problems [24]. The proposed heuristic *GraspCC* is composed of two phases: a construction phase *coCC* and a local search phase *lsCC*. The construction phase finds an initial solution that may be later improved by the local search phase.

In order to describe this method, we need some additional notation. We define a *solution* $\{(p_1, i_1, t_1), (p_2, i_2, t_2), \ldots\}$ as a set of 3−tuples (p, i, t) representing that package i of type p was purchased on period t. Let $\mathbb{S}$ be the set of all possible solutions. A solution $s \in \mathbb{S}$ is said to be *feasible* if s respects the consumer requirements. We also denote $t_m(s) = \max_{(p,i,t)\in s} t$ as the last period that a package was selected. Moreover, we define below a *cost function* $F : \mathbb{S} \to \mathbb{R}$, which will measure the quality of the solution. Similar to the objective function (1), the function F attempts to minimize costs and time (12) while penalizes the infeasibility regarding maxima time and cost (13). The parameters λ_1 and λ_2 are penalty coefficients associated with the violation of time and cost requirements, respectively.

$$F(s) = (\alpha_1 \sum_{(p,i,t)\in s} c_p + \alpha_2 t_m(s)) \tag{12}$$

$$+ \lambda_1(\max\{0, t_m(s) - T_M\}) + \lambda_2(\max\{0, \sum_{(p,i,t)\in s} c_p - C_M\}) \tag{13}$$

Algorithm 1: *GraspCC*

Input: $P, C_M, T_M, D_S, M_C, G_f, \alpha_1, \alpha_2, \lambda_1, \lambda_2$
Output: solution s^*;
$s^* = \emptyset$; $F(s^*) = \infty$; $i := 0$;
while $i \leqslant iter$
  $s = coCC(P, C_M, T_M, D_S, M_C, G_f, \alpha_1, \alpha_2, \lambda_1, \lambda_2)$;
  $s = lsCC(s, P, C_M, T_M, D_S, M_C, G_f, \alpha_1, \alpha_2, \lambda_1, \lambda_2)$;
  if $(F(s) < F(s^*))$ *and* (s *is feasible*)
    $s^* = s$; $i := 0$;
  end if
end for
return s^*;

We can now state the algorithm *GraspCC* which is shown in Algorithm 1, where the parameter *iter* denotes the maximum number of iterations without improvement in the best solution found. The first task in every iteration of the *GraspCC* is to construct a solution starting from an empty set, in a greedy randomized fashion. This task is performed by algorithm *coCC* which is described in Algorithm 2. In this method, the ordered set L_P is defined, in line 3, as the set of packages $p \in P$ such that its elements appears in descending order of cost and processing power $(\alpha_1 c_p + \alpha_2 g_p)$. At each iteration in lines 4-7 we choose a package $\overline{p}$ among the first β packages to be added to the first period of time. Note that the parameter β defines the degree of randomness the construction phase will have. This process is repeated until the solution satisfies the disk and memory requirements (for $t = 1$), however the maximum time and cost constraints are relaxed in order to achieve diversity in the initial solution. Moreover, in lines (9)-(12) the chosen packages are replicated in future periods until the processing demand is satisfied.

Algorithm 2: *coCC*

1 **Input:** $P, C_M, T_M, D_S, M_C, G_f, \alpha_1, \alpha_2, \lambda_1, \lambda_2$
2 **Output:** solution s;
3 $s = \emptyset$; $L_P = Order(P)$;
4 **while** $(\sum_{p|(p,i,1)\in s} d_p < D_S)$ or $(\sum_{p|(p,i,1)\in s} m_p < M_C)$
5   Choose package $\overline{p}$ (index $\overline{i}$) randomly among the first β elements of L_P
6     $s = s \cup \{(\overline{p}, \overline{i}, 1)\}$;
7 **end while**
8 $\overline{t} = 2$;
9 **while** $(\sum_{p|(p,i,t)\in s} g_p < G_f)$
10     $s = \bigcup_{(p,i,1)\in s} (p, i, \overline{t}) \cup s$;
11     $\overline{t} = \overline{t} + 1$;
12 **end while**
13 **return** s

There is no guarantee that the construction method returns a feasible or a locally optimal solution with respect to some neighborhood. Therefore, the solution s may be improved by a local search procedure denominated $lsCC$ (Algorithm 3). The neighborhood $N_r(s)$ is defined as the family of all solutions obtained by exchanging r tuples in s with another r tuples not in s. The $lsCC$ method starts with the solution provided by the construction phase. It iteratively replaces the current solution by that with minimum cost function F within its neighborhood (lines (3)-(9), where "s improving" means that there is some solution in the neighborhood of the current solution with cost function better than the current s). The local search halts when no better solution is found in the neighborhood of the current solution. In this work we employed a neighborhood with $r \leq 2$, since for values of $r > 2$ it is computationally intensive to perform an exhaustive search.

Algorithm 3: *lsCC*

1 **Input:** $s, P, C_M, T_M, D_S, M_C, G_f, \alpha_1, \alpha_2, \lambda_1, \lambda_2$
2 **Output:** solution s;
3 **while** (s improving)
4   **for all** $\overline{s} \in (N_1(s) \cup N_2(s))$
5   **if** $F(\overline{s}) < F(s)$
6             $s = \overline{s}$
7   **end if**
8   **end for**
9 **end while**

4 Experimental Results and Conclusions

The algorithms described in the previous section were implemented in ANSI C and the CPLEX 12.4 [16] was used to solve the mathematical formulation. All simulated experiments were performed on a computer with processor Intel Core i7 3.4Hz and 12Gb of RAM under Linux (Ubuntu 12.04) operating system. The algorithms were tested over a set of instances constructed from the requirements of RAM memory, disk storage, gflop number, execution time and payment cost of real applications combined with the sets of virtual machine packages available in commercial clouds.

These instances use requirements of five real applications and packages of two commercial clouds. The instances are divided in two groups, one for each cloud. The considered applications are a branch-and-bound algorithm for solving the Quadratic Assignment Problem (QAP) [12], three algorithms that tackle the manipulation of biologic sequence problem (RAXML [25], ModelGenerator [17] and Segemehl [15]) and a typical analysis user job for the CMS experiment [1]. The two commercial clouds are *Amazon EC2* [8] and *Google Cloud Platform* [23]. In *Amazon EC2*, package groups of high performance computing (HPC) clusters were employed, while in *Google Cloud Platform*, it was utilized packages from the *Google Compute Engine*. The instances are described in Table 1, where the columns represent the instance name, the requirements of RAM memory, disk storage, gflop number, the informed maximum time execution and maximum payment cost, respectively.

In order to illustrate the use of the different goals in the proposed cost function, weighted by α_1 and α_2 values, we analyse an instance executed with distinct sets of alpha, representing two extreme cases: (i) the cloud consumer is only concerned with payment cost ($\alpha_1 = 1$ and $\alpha_2 = 0$) and (ii) he/she only prioritizes the execution time ($\alpha_1 = 0$ and $\alpha_2 = 1$). For instance, if for the application nug24-cbb using packages of *Amazon EC2* (nug24-cbb_*am*), the cloud consumer only considers the payment cost, the mathematical formulation gives the following solution: 3 time units for execution time and $46.20 for payment

Table 1. Instance Description

Instance	RAM (GB)	Disk Storage (GB)	GFLOP Number	Time (hours)	Package Number	Cost ($)
nug22-sbb	77	51	5067533	12	20	343
nug24-sbb	154	103	14741914	48	20	998
nug25-sbb	214	142	28792800	60	20	1950
nug28-sbb	528	352	67720666	72	20	4586
nug30-sbb	918	612	120929760	84	20	8190
nug22-cbb	77	51	20270131	12	20	343
nug24-cbb	154	154	88451482	72	20	1498
nug25-cbb	214	214	230342400	120	20	3900
nug28-cbb	528	528	541765325	144	20	9173
nug30-cbb	918	918	967438080	168	20	16380
mod-gen	4	2	3317760	24	20	100
raxml	3	2	3317760	24	20	100
segemehl	64	600	28748390	4	20	192
cms-1000	1500	20	216000000	24	30	1728
cms-1250	1875	25	270000000	24	40	2304
cms-1500	2250	30	324000000	24	45	2592

Table 2. Results of *GraspCC* Metaheuristic and CC-IP Mathematical Formulation using CPLEX with $\alpha_1 = 0.5$ and $\alpha_1 = 0.5$

	GraspCC					CC-IP			
Instances	Function cost	Solution Value Time	Solution Value Payment	Total time	Gap (%)	Function cost	Solution Value Time	Solution Value Payment	Total time
nug22-sbb_*am*	0.0456	1	4.50	0.01	0	0.0456	1	4.50	0.59
nug24-sbb_*am*	0.0130	1	12.10	0.02	0	0.0130	1	12.10	6.79
nug25-sbb_*am*	0.0113	1	17.10	0.05	0	0.0113	1	17.10	10.98
nug28-sbb_*am*	0.0128	1	40.80	0.07	0	0.0128	1	40.80	27.23
nug30-sbb_*am*	0.0344	3	133.50	0.08	0	0.0344	3	133.50	32.42
nug22-cbb_*am*	0.0519	1	11.80	0.03	0	0.0519	1	11.80	0.77
nug24-cbb_*am*	0.0309	2	46.20	0.17	0	0.0309	2	46.20	5.81
nug25-cbb_*am*	0.0458	3	119.70	0.91	0	0.0458	3	119.70	12.01
nug28-cbb_*am*	0.0123	1	36.90	0.07	0	0.0123	1	36.90	21.20
nug30-cbb_*am*	0.2652	23	1034.70	3.63	0	0.2652	23	1034.70	118.42
mod-gen_*am*	0.0217	1	2.10	0.00	0	0.0217	1	2.10	0.50
raxml_*am*	0.0217	1	2.10	0.00	0	0.0217	1	2.10	0.48
segemehl_*am*	0.1688	1	16.80	0.07	0	0.1688	1	16.80	0.26
cms-1000_*am*	0.1630	4	275.20	0.18	0	0.1630	4	275.20	31.82
cms-1250_*am*	0.1572	4	340.20	0.53	0	0.1572	4	340.20	39.50
cms-1500_*am*	0.1625	4	410.40	0.53	0	0.1625	4	410.40	32.83
nug22-sbb_*go*	0.0497	1	4.90	5.36	0.0066	0.0497	1	4.88	77.72
nug24-sbb_*go*	0.0270	1	14.95	20.74	0	0.0270	1	14.95	9194.37
nug25-sbb_*go*	0.0347	3	29.54	38.90	0	0.0347	3	29.54	28081.33
nug28-sbb_*go*	0.0655	6	87.44	133.66	0	0.0655	6	87.44	35278.98
nug30-sbb_*go*	0.1128	11	202.27	42.98	0	0.1128	11	202.27	73656.27
nug22-cbb_*go*	0.1137	2	18.56	17.97	0	0.1137	2	18.56	246.79
nug24-cbb_*go*	0.1173	8	82.91	177.53	0	0.1173	8	82.91	19695.32
nug25-cbb_*go*	0.2417	20	229.00	1186.05	0	0.2417	20	229.00	64758.31
nug28-cbb_*go*	0.0541	5	70.73	60.00	0.0859	* 0.0552	5	70.64	86400.00
nug30-cbb_*go*	0.8502	81	1573.22	2987.79	0	0.8502	81	1573.22	5085.60
mod-gen_*go*	0.0234	1	3.16	2.97	0	0.0234	1	3.16	32.71
raxml_*go*	0.0234	1	3.16	2.91	0	0.0234	1	3.16	29.34
segemehl_*go*	0.5038	3	26.21	52.40	0	0.5038	3	26.21	23.52
cms-1000_*go*	0.4809	13	384.70	27.56	0	0.4809	13	384.70	4458.83
cms-1250_*go*	0.4341	12	449.52	153.13	0	0.4341	12	449.52	34210.73
cms-1500_*go*	0.4796	13	573.46	53.27	0	* 0.4797	13	573.85	86400.00

cost. However, if the cloud consumer only prioritizes the execution time, the mathematical formulation gives the solution: 2 time units for execution time and $84 for payment cost. Thus, note that the proposed objective function that integrates both objectives can guide the consumer's decision. The specification of proper weights (α_1 and $\alpha 2$) to the objectives allows that the cloud consumers take the correct decision in accordance with their needs.

Experiments, reported in Table 2, are a comparison of the *GraspCC* heuristic with the CC-IP mathematical formulation, in terms of solution quality and execution time. The used values were: $\alpha_1 = 0.5$ and $\alpha_2 = 0.5$, $\lambda_1 = 1000$ and $\lambda_2 = 1000$, β equal to the maximum number of packages offered by each cloud provider and $iter = 50$. In this work, both objectives of the cost function were normalized due to their distinct range values. The normalization procedure updates the objective values so that they share the same minimum and maximum values, 0 and 1, respectively. Thus, the payment cost was divided by the most expensive package cost times the maximum time informed by the cloud consumer. Similarly, the execution time component of the objective function was divided by the maximum time informed by the cloud consumer. Each instance is identified by the label n_c, where n is the application name and c is the cloud providers (*am* and *go* identify *Amazon EC2* and *Google Compute Engine*, respectively). The next three columns present the best function cost solution found by *GraspCC* and the costs (not normalized) that compose it: execution time and payment cost, respectively. The fifth column shows the execution time in seconds for *GraspCC* to solve the problem. The next column is the corresponding percentage difference from the optimal solution (named Gap in the table). Analogously, the last four columns present the best feasible solution found by CC-IP, the costs that compose it, the execution time and payment costs, and the time in seconds spent to solve the problem.

For some instances, the CC-IP mathematical formulation took a long time to prove the optimality of the solution, therewith we consider in our experiments an execution time limit of 24 hours. The exact method was not able to find the optimal solution in instances marked with (*) in Table 2 within this time limit. Note that *GraspCC* presented an outstanding improvement of the execution time, in average 99.01% less than the execution time of CC-IP, giving optimal or almost optimal solutions in all tests.

This work was supported of CAPES and FAPERJ (E-26/110.552/2010).

References

1. Adolphi, R., Spanier, S.: The CMS experiment at the CERN LHC, CMS collaboration. Journal of Instrumentation 3(08), S08004 (2008)
2. Alicherry, M., Lakshman, T.: Network aware resource allocation in distributed clouds. In: Proceedings IEEE INFOCOM, pp. 963–971. IEEE (2012)
3. Baliga, J., Ayre, R.W., Hinton, K., Tucker, R.S.: Green cloud computing: Balancing energy in processing, storage, and transport. Proceedings IEEE 99(1), 149–167 (2011)
4. Beloglazov, A., Abawajy, J., Buyya, R.: Energy-aware resource allocation heuristics for efficient management of data centers for cloud computing. Future Generation Computer Systems 28(5), 755–768 (2012)
5. Buyya, R., Yeo, C.S., Venugopal, S., Broberg, J., Brandic, I.: Cloud computing and emerging IT platforms: Vision, hype, and reality for delivering computing as the 5th utility. Future Generation Computer Systems 25(6), 599–616 (2009)
6. Chaisiri, S., Lee, B., Niyato, D.: Optimization of resource provisioning cost in cloud computing. IEEE Transactions on Services Computing 5(2), 164–177 (2012)
7. de Oliveira Jr., F.A., Ledoux, T.: Self-management of applications qos for energy optimization in datacenters. In: Proceedings of the 2nd International Workshop Green Computing Middleware, GCM 2011, pages 3:1–3:6. ACM (2011)
8. Amazon Elastic Compute Cloud (Amazon EC2) (March 16, 2013), `http://aws.amazon.com/pt/ec2/`
9. Endo, P.T., de A. Palhares, A.V., Pereira, N.N., Goncalves, G.E., Sadok, D., Kelner, J., Melander, B., Mangs, J.: Resource allocation for distributed cloud: concepts and research challenges. IEEE Network 25(4), 42–46 (2011)
10. Feo, T.A., Resende, M.G.C.: Resende. Greedy randomized adaptive search procedures. Journal of Global Optimization 6, 109–133 (1995)
11. Foster, I., Zhao, Y., Raicu, I., Lu, S.: Cloud computing and grid computing 360-degree compared. In: Grid Computing Environments Workshop, pp. 1–10. IEEE (2008)

12. Goncalves, A., Drummond, L., Pessoa, A., Hahn, P.: Improving lower bounds for the quadratic assignment problem by applying a distributed dual ascent algorithm. Cornell University Library, Technical Report (2013)
13. Goudarzi, H., Ghasemazar, M., Pedram, M.: Sla-based optimization of power and migration cost in cloud computing. In: 12th IEEE/ACM International Symposium on Cluster, Cloud and Grid Computing, pp. 172–179. IEEE (2012)
14. Goudarzi, H., Pedram, M.: Energy-efficient virtual machine replication and placement in a cloud computing system. In: IEEE 5th International Conference on Cloud Computing, pp. 750–757. IEEE (2012)
15. Hoffmann, S., Otto, C., Kurtz, S., Sharma, C.M., Khaitovich, P., Vogel, J., Stadler, P.F., Hackermüller, J.: Fast mapping of short sequences with mismatches, insertions and deletions using index structures. PLoS Computational Biology 5 (2009)
16. S.A. ILOG. Cplex 11 user's manual (2008)
17. Keane, T., Creevey, C., Pentony, M., Naughton, T., Mclnerney, J.: Assessment of methods for amino acid matrix selection and their use on empirical data shows that ad hoc assumptions for choice of matrix are not justified. BMC Evolutionary Biology 6(1), 29 (2006)
18. Li, Q., Guo, Y.: Optimization of resource scheduling in cloud computing. In: 12th International Symposium on Symbolic and Numeric Algorithms for Scientific Computing, pp. 315–320. IEEE (2010)
19. Luo, L., Wu, W., Di, D., Zhang, F., Yan, Y., Mao, Y.: A resource scheduling algorithm of cloud computing based on energy efficient optimization methods. In: International Green Computing Conference, pp. 1–6. IEEE (2012)
20. Meng, X., Pappas, V., Zhang, L.: Improving the scalability of data center networks with traffic-aware virtual machine placement. In: Proceedings of IEEE INFOCOM, pp. 1–9. IEEE (2010)
21. Niyato, D., Zhu, K., Wang, P.: Cooperative virtual machine management for multi-organization cloud computing environment. In: Proceedings of the 5th International ICST Conference on Performance Evaluation Methodologies and Tools, pp. 528–537, ICST (2011)
22. Pandey, S., Wu, L., Guru, S.M., Buyya, R.: A particle swarm optimization-based heuristic for scheduling workflow applications in cloud computing environments. In: 24th IEEE International Conference on Advanced Information Networking and Applications, pp. 400–407. IEEE (2010)
23. Google Cloud Platform (March 16, 2013), `https://cloud.google.com/products/compute-engine`
24. Resende, M.G.C., Ribeiro, C.C.: GRASP with path-relinking: Recent advances and applications. In: Ibaraki, T., Nonobe, K., Yagiura, M. (eds.) Metaheuristics: Progress as Real Problem Solvers, pp. 29–63. Springer (2005)
25. Stamatakis, A.: Raxml-vi-hpc: maximum likelihood-based phylogenetic analyses with thousands of taxa and mixed models. Bioinformatics 22(21), 2688–2690 (2006)
26. Sultan, N.A.: Reaching for the cloud: How SMEs can manage. International Journal of Information Management 31(3), 272–278 (2011)
27. Zhang, Q., Cheng, L., Boutaba, R.: Cloud computing: state-of-the-art and research challenges. Journal of Internet Services and Applications 1(1), 7–18 (2010)
28. Zhao, J., Zeng, W., Liu, M., Li, G.: Multi-objective optimization model of virtual resources scheduling under cloud computing and it's solution. In: International Conference on Cloud and Service Computing, pp. 185–190 (2011)

Scheduling Independent Tasks on Multi-cores with GPU Accelerators

Safia Kedad-Sidhoum[1], Florence Monna[1,⋆],
Grégory Mounié[2], and Denis Trystram[2,3]

[1] Laboratoire d'Informatique de Paris 6, 4 Place Jussieu, 75005 Paris
[2] Université de Grenoble-Alpes, LIG, 38330 Montbonnot St Martin, France
[3] Institut Universitaire de France

Abstract. More and more computers use hybrid architectures combining multi-core processors and hardware accelerators like GPUs (Graphics Processing Units). We present in this paper a new method for scheduling efficiently parallel applications with m CPUs and k GPUs, where each task of the application can be processed either on a core (CPU) or on a GPU. The objective is to minimize the makespan. The corresponding scheduling problem is NP-hard, we propose an efficient approximation algorithm which achieves an approximation ratio of $\frac{4}{3} + \frac{1}{3k}$. We first detail and analyze the method, based on a dual approximation scheme, that uses a dynamic programming scheme to balance evenly the load between the heterogeneous resources. Finally, we run some simulations based on realistic benchmarks and compare the solution obtained by a relaxed version of this method to the one provided by a classical greedy algorithm and to lower bounds on the value of the optimal makespan.

1 Introduction

Most of the computing systems available today include parallel multi-core chips sharing a large memory with additional hardware accelerators. There is an increasing complexity within the internal nodes of such parallel systems, mainly due to the heterogeneity of the computational resources. In order to take advantage of the benefits offered by these new features, effective and automatic management of the hybrid resources will be more and more important for running applications. These new architectures have given rise to new scheduling problems. The main challenge is to create adequate generic methods and software tools that fulfill the requirements for optimizing the performances.

There exist in the literature a huge number of papers dealing with implementations of specific applications using GPUs or hybrid CPU-GPU architectures. They consist mostly in studying the gains and performances of the parallelisation of some specific numerical kernels [1] or specific applications like multiple alignments of biological sequences,molecular dynamics, etc. Moreover, most of

⋆ This work is supported by a CNRS-Google contract and a french national program GDR-RO.

D. an Mey et al. (Eds.): Euro-Par 2013 Workshops, LNCS 8374, pp. 228–237, 2014.

existing scheduling algorithms and tools are not well-suited for general purpose applications since the architecture of the GPUs differs from CPUs and thus, the GPUs should be considered as a new type of resources to develop efficient approaches. New features have been implemented in some parallel programming environments and runtime systems: they provide hybrid (CPU/GPU) programming operators, automatic scheduling and adequate data movements. For instance, OmpSs [2], StarPU [3] or xKaapi [4] include scheduling policies that are restricted to fast greedy algorithms or work stealing.

Our objective within this work is to propose a new algorithm for a general purpose scheduling for the execution of independent tasks on hybrid CPU-GPU architectures designed for High Performance Computing (HPC). The considered input is a set of independent sequential tasks whose execution times are known. This hypothesis is realistic, since some computing platforms such as StarPU have a module which estimates at compile time the different execution times of the considered tasks. The method that we propose in this work determines the allocation and schedule of the tasks to the computing units, CPUs and GPUs. We analyze in detail this methodology for the case of m cores (CPUs) and k GPUs. This leads to an efficient approximation algorithm which achieves a ratio $\frac{4}{3} + \frac{1}{3k} + \epsilon$ using dual approximation [5] with a dynamic programming scheme. The cost of the algorithm is in $\mathcal{O}\left(n^2k^3m^2\right)$. As this method is costly, we derive a relaxed algorithm and compare it experimentally with one of the most popular algorithm (HEFT [6]).

2 Problem Definition and Related Works

We consider a multi-core parallel platform with m identical CPUs and k identical GPUs. The m CPUs are considered independent from the GPUs that are commanded by some extra driving CPUs, not mentioned here because they do not execute any task. An application is composed of n independent sequential tasks denoted by $T_1, \ldots, T_n$. Each of these tasks has two processing times depending on which type of processor it is allocated to. The processing time of task T_j is denoted by $\overline{p_j}$ if T_j is processed on a CPU and $\underline{p_j}$ if it is processed on a GPU. We assume that both processing times of a task are known in advance (or at least can be estimated at compile time). The makespan is defined as the maximum completion time of the last finishing task. For the problem considered, in the optic of High Performance Computing, the objective is to minimize the makespan of the schedule. The problem will be denoted by $(Pm, Pk) \mid\mid C_{max}$.

Observe that if both processing times are equal ($\overline{p_j} = \underline{p_j}$) for $j = 1, \ldots, n$, $(Pm, P1) \mid\mid C_{max}$ is equivalent to the classical $P \mid\mid C_{max}$ problem, which is NP-hard. Thus, the problem of scheduling with GPUs is also NP-hard and we are looking for efficient approximation algorithms.

$(Pm, Pk) \mid\mid C_{max}$ is a special case of $R \mid\mid C_{max}$. Lenstra et al. [7] propose a PTAS for the problem $R \mid\mid C_{\max}$ with running time bounded by the product of $(n+1)^{m/\epsilon}$ and a polynomial of the input size. Let us notice that if parameter m is not fixed, then the algorithm is not fully polynomial. The authors also prove that unless $P = NP$, there is no polynomial-time approximation algorithm for $R \mid\mid C_{\max}$ with an approximation factor less than 3/2 and present a 2-approximation algorithm. Recently, Shchepin and Vakhania [8] introduce a new rounding technique which yields an improved approximation factor of $2-\frac{1}{m}$. This is so far the best approximation result for $R \mid\mid C_{\max}$. If we look at the more specific problem of scheduling unrelated machines of few different types, Bonifaci and Wiese [9] present a PTAS to solve this problem. However, the time complexity of the polynomial algorithm is not provided so that the algorithm does not seem to be potentially useful from a practical perspective. Finally, it is worth noticing that if all the tasks of the addressed problem have the same acceleration on the GPUs, the problem reduces to a $Q \mid\mid C_{\max}$ problem, with two machines speeds. The first PTAS for $Q \mid\mid C_{\max}$ was given by Hochbaum and Shmoys [10]. The overall running time of the algorithm is $\mathcal{O}((\log m + \log(3/\epsilon))(m/\epsilon)(n/\epsilon)1/\epsilon)$.

Our objective within this work is to build a bridge between purely theoretical algorithms with good performance guarantees and practical low cost heuristics. Thus, we propose a tradeoff solution with a provable performance guarantee and a reasonable time complexity.

3 Theoretical Analysis

3.1 Rationale of the Solving Method

The principle of the algorithm is to use the dual approximation technique [5]. A g-dual approximation algorithm for a generic problem takes a real number λ (guess) as an input and either delivers a schedule of makespan at most $g\lambda$, or answers correctly that there exists no schedule of length at most λ.

We target $g = \frac{4}{3} + \frac{1}{3k}$. Let λ be the current real number input for the dual approximation. In the following, we assert that there exists a schedule of length lower than λ. Then, we have to show how it is possible to build a schedule of length at most $\frac{4\lambda}{3} + \frac{1}{3k}$.

The idea of the algorithm is to partition the set of tasks on the CPUs into two sets, each consisting in two shelves, a first set with a shelf of length λ and the other of length $\frac{\lambda}{3}$, and a second set with two shelves of length $\frac{2\lambda}{3}$. The partition ensures that the makespan on the CPUs is lower than $\frac{4\lambda}{3}$. The same partition can be applied to the set of tasks on the GPUs. Since the tasks are independent, the scheduling strategy is straightforward when the assignment of the tasks has been determined and yields directly a solution of length at most $\frac{4\lambda}{3}$. The main problem is to assign the tasks in each shelf on the CPUs or on the GPUs in order to obtain a feasible solution.

3.2 Structure of an Optimal Schedule

We introduce an allocation function $\pi(j)$ of a task T_j which corresponds to the processor where the task is processed. The set $\mathcal{C}$ (resp. $\mathcal{G}$) is the set of all the CPUs (resp. GPUs). Therefore, if a task T_j is assigned to a CPU, we can write

$\pi(j) \in \mathcal{C}$. We define W_C as being the computational area of the CPUs on the Gantt chart representation of a schedule, i.e. the sum of all the processing times of the tasks allocated to the CPUs: $W_C = \sum_{j \,/\, \pi(j) \in \mathcal{C}} \overline{p_j}$.

To take advantage of the dual approximation paradigm, we have to make explicit the consequences of the assumption that there exists a schedule of length at most λ. We state below some straightforward properties of such a schedule.

Property 1. In an optimal solution, the execution time of each task is at most λ, and the computational area on the CPUs is at most $m\lambda$, and the computational area on the GPUs is at most $k\lambda$.

Property 2. In an optimal solution, if there exist two consecutive tasks on a CPU, if one of these tasks has an execution time greater than $\frac{2\lambda}{3}$, then the other one has an execution time lower than $\frac{\lambda}{3}$. The same can be said of two consecutive tasks on a GPU.

Property 3. Two tasks with processing times on CPU greater than $\frac{\lambda}{3}$ and lower than $\frac{2\lambda}{3}$ can be executed successively on the same CPU within a time at most $\frac{4\lambda}{3}$. This is also valid on a GPU.

The basic idea of the solution that we propose comes from the analysis of the shape of an optimal schedule. From Property 2, the tasks whose execution times on CPU (respectively on GPU) are strictly greater than $\frac{2\lambda}{3}$ do not use more than m CPUs (respectively k GPUs), and hence can be executed concurrently in the first set in a shelf denoted by S_1 (respectively S_5). We denote by μ the number of CPUs and κ the number of GPUs executing these tasks.

The tasks whose execution times are lower than $\frac{2\lambda}{3}$ and strictly greater than $\frac{\lambda}{3}$ on CPU (respectively on GPU) cannot be executed on the μ CPUs occupied by S_1 from Property 1 (respectively the κ GPUs occupied by S_5). Moreover, from Property 3, $2(m-\mu)$ of these tasks on CPU (respectively $2(k-\kappa)$ tasks on GPU) can be executed in time at most $\frac{4\lambda}{3}$ on the remaining $(m-\mu)$ CPUs in the second set and fill two shelves S_3 and S_4 of equal length $\frac{2\lambda}{3}$ (resp. on $(k-\kappa)$ GPUs and fill two similar shelves S_7 and S_8).

The remaining tasks have execution times lower than $\frac{\lambda}{3}$ on CPU (resp. on GPU) and can be executed within a time at most $\frac{\lambda}{3}$ in the first set on the CPUs in another shelf denoted by S_2 (resp. on the GPUs in a shelf S_6).

Thus, we are looking for a schedule on the CPUs in two sets of two shelves: S_1 of length λ, S_2 as well as S_3 and S_4 of length $\frac{2\lambda}{3}$, and a similar schedule on the GPUs, with 4 shelves S_5 to S_8.

Lemma 1. *The length of S_2 is lower than $\frac{\lambda}{3}$.*

Proof. We start by modifying the starting times of the tasks in S_2, in order to have all the tasks justified to the right of the schedule, so that all the processors complete their tasks exactly at time $\frac{4\lambda}{3}$ (like in figure 1). This operation induces on each CPU an idle time interval between the completion of the tasks of S_1

and the starting of the tasks of S_2. We define the load of a CPU as the sum of the execution times of the tasks processed on it. By definition the load is equal to $\frac{4\lambda}{3}$ minus the length of the idle time interval on the CPU. Now consider the following algorithm to schedule the tasks of processing time lower than $\frac{\lambda}{3}$:

Consider the tasks in an arbitrary order $T_1, \ldots, T_f$, f being the total number of tasks remaining to be allocated in S_2; then allocate task T_i to the least loaded processor, at the latest possible date and update its load.

One problem could occur when allocating T_i is that it cannot be completed before the starting time of the tasks of S_2. But at each step, the least loaded processor has a load at most λ; otherwise it would contradict the fact that the total work area of the tasks is bounded by $m\lambda$ (Property 1). Hence, the idle time interval on the least loaded CPU has a length at least $\frac{\lambda}{3}$ and can contain T_i. □

3.3 Partitioning the Tasks into Shelves

In this section, we detail how to fill the shelves (see Figure 1) on the CPUs and on the GPUs by specifying an initial assignment of the tasks to the processors.

In order to obtain a 2-sets and 4-shelves schedule on the CPUs and the same sets on the GPUs, we look for an assignment satisfying the following constraints:

- (C_1) The total computational area W_C on the CPUs is at most $m\lambda$.
- (C_2) The tasks on the CPUs with an execution time strictly greater than $\frac{2\lambda}{3}$ in the allotment, to be scheduled in S_1, use $\mu \leqslant m$ processors. The tasks on the CPUs with an execution time lower than $\frac{2\lambda}{3}$ and strictly greater than $\frac{\lambda}{3}$ in the allotment, to be scheduled in S_3 and S_4, use at most $2(m - \mu)$ processors.
- (C_3) The total computational area on the GPU is at most $k\lambda$.
- (C_4) The tasks on the GPUs with an execution time strictly greater than $\frac{2\lambda}{3}$ in the allotment, to be scheduled in S_5, use $\kappa \leqslant k$ processors. The tasks on the GPUs with an execution time lower than $\frac{2\lambda}{3}$ and strictly greater than $\frac{\lambda}{3}$ in the allotment, to be scheduled in S_7 and S_8, use at most $2(k - \kappa)$ processors.

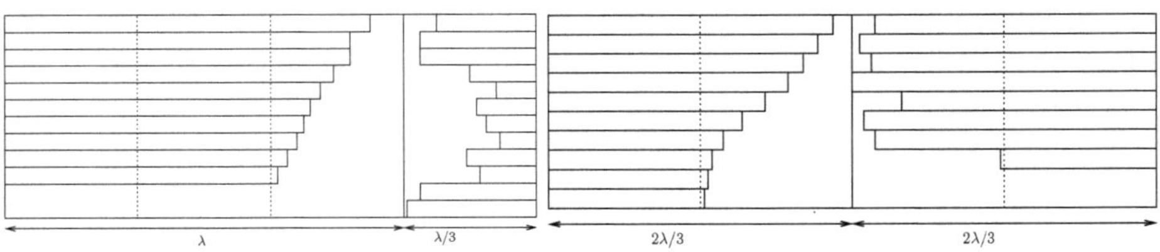

(a) Shelves S_1 and S_2 (b) Shelves S_3 and S_4

Fig. 1. Partitioning the set of tasks into shelves

We define for each task T_j a binary variable x_j such that $x_j = 1$ if T_j is assigned to a CPU or 0 if T_j is assigned to the GPU. Determining if an allotment satisfying (C_1), (C_2), (C_3) and (C_4) exists reduces to solving a three-dimensional knapsack problem that can be formulated as follows:

$$W_C^* = \min \sum_{j=1}^{n} \overline{p_j} x_j \qquad (C_1)$$

$$\text{s.t. } \frac{1}{2} \sum_{2\lambda/3 \geqslant \overline{p_j} > \lambda/3} x_j + \sum_{\overline{p_j} > 2\lambda/3} x_j \leqslant m \qquad (C_2)$$

$$\frac{1}{2} \sum_{2\lambda/3 \geqslant \underline{p_j} > \lambda/3} (1 - x_j) + \sum_{\underline{p_j} > 2\lambda/3} (1 - x_j) \leqslant k \qquad (C_4)$$

$$\sum_{j=1}^{n} \underline{p_j} (1 - x_j) \leqslant k\lambda \qquad (C_3)$$

$$x_j \in \{0, 1\}$$

We propose a dynamic programming algorithm that solves the knapsack problem in $\mathcal{O}\left(n^2 m^2 k^3\right)$. For this purpose, we first have to reduce the states on the GPUs to a smaller number. We use the time intervals of length $\frac{\lambda}{3n}$ and introduce the integer number ν_j of these time intervals required for a task T_j if it is executed on the GPUs: $\nu_j = \left\lfloor \frac{\underline{p_j}}{\lambda/(3n)} \right\rfloor$. $N = \sum_{\pi(j) \in \mathcal{G}} \nu_j$ denotes the total integer number of these intervals on the GPUs. We can define the error on the processing time of each task $\epsilon_j = \underline{p_j} - \nu_j \frac{\lambda}{3n}$ created by this approximation.

This result allows us to consider only N states in the dynamic programming regarding the workload on the GPUs, and the error ϵ_j on each task is at most $\frac{\lambda}{3n}$ so if all the tasks were assigned to one of the GPU, we would have underestimated the processing time on this GPU by at most $n\frac{\lambda}{3n} = \frac{\lambda}{3}$. Then, constraint (C_4) of the linear program becomes

$$N = \sum_{\pi(j) \in \mathcal{G}} \nu_j \leqslant 3kn$$

The truncated computational area of the GPUs is at most $k\lambda$ and thus, the full computational area remains lower than $k\lambda + \frac{\lambda}{3}$. Thus, an upper bound on the length of shelf S_6 can be determined as follows.

Lemma 2. *The length of S_6 is lower than $\frac{\lambda}{3} + \frac{\lambda}{3k}$.*

Proof. The proof is similar to the one of Lemma 1. If all the working processors complete their tasks at $\frac{4\lambda}{3} + \frac{\lambda}{3k}$, with an idle time interval between the end of S_5 and the starting time of S_6, the load of a GPU is equal to $\frac{4\lambda}{3} + \frac{\lambda}{3k}$ minus the length of the idle time interval. If a small task remains to be assigned, the least loaded processor has a load at most $\lambda + \frac{\lambda}{3k}$ since the total work area is bounded by $k\left(\lambda + \frac{\lambda}{3k}\right)$, so the idle time interval on the least loaded GPU has a length of at least $\frac{\lambda}{3}$ and can contain the task to be assigned. □

Once this reduction done, we define $W_C(j, \mu, \mu', \kappa, \kappa', N)$ as the minimum sum of all the processing times of the tasks on the CPUs when the first j tasks are considered, with among the tasks assigned to the CPUs, μ of them having processing times $\overline{p_j}$ greater than $\frac{2\lambda}{3}$ and μ' with $\frac{\lambda}{3} < \overline{p_j} \leqslant \frac{2\lambda}{3}$, respectively κ and κ' of these tasks being assigned to the GPUs such that N time intervals are occupied on the GPUs.

We use a dynamic programming which allows us to compute the value of $W_C(j, \mu, \mu', \kappa, \kappa', N)$ with the values of W_C with $j-1$ tasks considered that were previously computed. If the optimal value of the computational area on the CPUs $W_C^* = W_C(n, \mu, \mu', \kappa, \kappa', N)$, for $1 \leqslant \mu \leqslant m$, $1 \leqslant \mu' \leqslant 2(m-\mu)$, $1 \leqslant \kappa \leqslant k$, $1 \leqslant \kappa' \leqslant 2(k-\kappa)$, $0 \leqslant N \leqslant 3kn$, is greater than $m\lambda$, then there exists no solution with a makespan at most λ, and the algorithm answers "NO" to the dual approximation. Otherwise, we construct a feasible solution with a makespan at most $\frac{4\lambda}{3} + \frac{\lambda}{3k}$, with the corresponding shelves on the CPUs and the corresponding μ, μ',κ, κ' and N values. This constitutes one step of the dual-approximation algorithm, with a fixed guess.

Binary Search. We first take initial lower and upper bounds, B_{min} and B_{max} of our optimal makespan and solve the problem with λ equal to the average of the bounds. Then we adjust the bounds: if the previous algorithm returns "NO", then λ becomes the new lower bound, but if the algorithm returns a schedule of makespan at most $\frac{4\lambda}{3}$, then λ becomes the new upper bound. The number of iterations of this binary search can be bounded by $\log(B_{max} - B_{min})$.

Cost Analysis. Solving the dynamic program for a fixed value of λ requires to consider $\mathcal{O}(n^2m^2k^3)$ states, since $1 \leqslant j \leqslant n$, $1 \leqslant \mu \leqslant m$, $1 \leqslant \mu' \leqslant 2(m-\mu)$, $1 \leqslant \kappa \leqslant k$, $1 \leqslant \kappa' \leqslant 2(k-\kappa)$, and $0 \leqslant N \leqslant 3kn$. Therefore, the time complexity of each step of the binary search is $\mathcal{O}(n^2m^2k^3)$.

4 Experimental Analysis

In order to show the efficiency of our method, we run experiments on random instances and compared them to the classical reference greedy algorithm HEFT used on several actual systems (HEFT stands for Heterogeneous Earliest Finishing Time [6]). For instance, the scheduling decisions in StarPU [3] are based on estimations of the execution times of the tasks on both CPU and GPU resources that are scheduled by HEFT.

4.1 Analysis of HEFT

HEFT proceeds in two phases, starting by a prioritization of the tasks that are sorted by decreasing average execution time and then the processor selection is obtained with the heterogeneous earliest finish time rule.

Lemma 3. *The worst case performance ratio of HEFT is larger than $m/2$.*

Proof. We show on the following instance that the prioritizing phase can provide a schedule whose makespan is far from the optimum. Let us consider an instance with a list of the following tasks: m tasks such that $\overline{p} = 1$ and $\underline{p} = \epsilon$ and for $i = 0, \cdots, m-1$: a single task of type $\mathcal{A}$ such that $\overline{p} = 1 - i/m$ and $\underline{p} = 1 - i/m$; $m - 1$ tasks of type $\mathcal{B}$ such that $\overline{p} = 1 - i/m$ and $\underline{p} = 1/m^2$. These tasks are executed faster on the GPUs.

On this instance, HEFT fills first the m CPUs. Then, it fills alternatively the GPU with one task of type $\mathcal{A}$ and the m CPUs with m tasks of size $\mathcal{B}$. HEFT ends with a makespan equal to $m/2 + 3/2 - 1/m$. It is easy to check that the optimal makespan is equal to $OPT = 1$. □

4.2 Computational Experiments

The HEFT algorithm is an efficient algorithm in practice but it does not provide any performance guarantee. The algorithm we presented in the previous section on the other hand provides a very satisfying performance ratio of $\frac{4}{3} + \frac{1}{3k}$, can be implemented and works in a reasonable amount of time, but its running time may make it a bit slow for users who want an quick response, and do not necessarily need a performance guarantee so precise of $\frac{4}{3} + \frac{1}{3k}$.

The method described before can be modified in order to obtain a performance ratio of 2 in a time $\mathcal{O}(n^2k)$, which would make it comparable to HEFT in terms of running time and still provide a performance guarantee. The idea is based on leaving aside the constraints ordering the tasks into shelves. The only constraint that remains is the one on the computational area on the GPUs being lower than $k\lambda$, λ being the current guess of the dual approximation. With the optimal computational area on the CPUs under this constraint determined by dynamic programming, we can build a schedule with a makespan lower than twice the optimal value.

This algorithm was implemented and compared to HEFT with an experimental analysis based on various classes of instances. All the algorithms are implemented in C++ programming language and run on a 3.4 GHz PC with 15.7 Gb RAM.

We run a series of experiments on random instances of different sizes: 10 to 1000 tasks, with a step of 10 tasks, 2^a CPUs, a varying from 0 to 6, and 2^b GPUs, b varying from 0 to 3. For each combination of these sizes, 30 instances were considered, bringing us to a total of 10500 instances tested in total. The processing times on the CPUs are randomly generated using the uniform distribution U[10,100] so that $\overline{p_j} \in \{1, \ldots, 100\}$ for each task T_j. The distribution of the acceleration factors on the GPUs have been measured in [11] using the classical numerical kernels of Magma [12] in a multi-core multi-GPU machine hosted by the Grid'5000 infrastructure experimental platform [13]. We extracted a distribution of the acceleration factors which reflects the qualitative speed-up on real kernels: we assign to each task an acceleration factor α_j of $1/15$ or $1/35$ with a probability of $1/2$. The resulting processing times on the GPUs are thus $\underline{p_j} = \alpha_j \overline{p_j}$. We calculated the mean, maximal and minimal deviations of the Dynamic Programming (DP) based approximation algorithm and the HEFT algorithm from the optimal values derived from the binary search of our approximation programming.

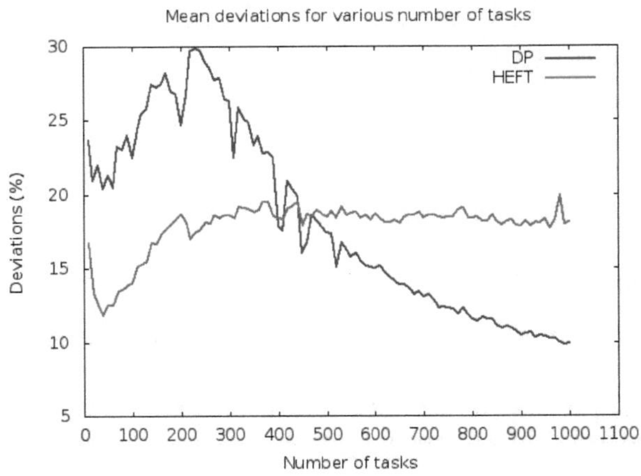

Fig. 2. Mean deviations of DP and HEFT for various n

Table 1. Maximal deviations (%) for DP and HEFT

n	120	160	220	260	280	360	380	660	700	760	780	920	940
DP	76.88	72.73	70.37	70.00	69.14	70.00	70.00	67.42	50.82	42.77	54.47	91.77	63.07
HEFT	123.53	98.44	92.55	94.34	91.90	110.37	91.78	113.48	98.10	98.77	103.15	116.46	96.31

As we can see in Table 1, the maximal deviations of DP are usually below the maximal deviations of HEFT and more importantly these deviations respect the theoretical performance guarantee in the case of DP whereas the maximal deviations of HEFT sometimes go over the 100% barrier corresponding to a performance ratio of 2. We can see in Figure 2 that on average, DP even outperforms HEFT for large numbers of tasks.

5 Concluding Remarks

In this paper, we presented an analysis for scheduling algorithms using a generic methodology (in the opposite of specific *ad hoc* algorithms). We proposed fast algorithms with a constant approximation ratio in the case of independent tasks on a multi-core machines with GPUs. In the case of a single (resp. multiple) GPU(s) a ratio of $\frac{4}{3}+\epsilon$ (resp. $\frac{4}{3}+\frac{1}{3k}+\epsilon$) is achieved. The main idea of the approach is to determine an adequate partition of the set of tasks on the CPUs and the GPUs using a dual approximation scheme. A simulation and experimental analysis have been provided for different kernels to assess the computational efficiency of the proposed methods. We are currently implementing the algorithms presented here in the runtime systems xKaapi and StarPU.

As further investigations of this work, we plan to extend the analysis to more generic problems where the tasks are linked by a precedence relation and to take into account the process of data transfer. We believe that the same algorithmic scheme could be adapted to provide faster scheduling algorithms with a guarantee of 2. For instance, we expect a ratio 2 with a complexity of $(O)(nlog(n))$. These algorithms built using the proposed scheme are good candidates for the integration into runtime systems like StarPU and xKaapi.

References

1. Song, F., Tomov, S., Dongarra, J.: Enabling and scaling matrix computations on heterogeneous multi-core and multi-gpu systems. In: 26th ACM International Conference on Supercomputing (ICS 2012), Venice, Italy. ACM (June 2012)
2. Bueno, J., Planas, J., Duran, A., Badia, R.M., Martorell, X., Ayguadé, E., Labarta, J.: Productive programming of gpu clusters with ompss. In: IPDPS, pp. 557–568. IEEE Computer Society (2012)
3. Augonnet, C., Thibault, S., Namyst, R., Wacrenier, P.-A.: StarPU: A unified platform for task scheduling on heterogeneous multicore architectures. In: Concurrency and Computation: Practice and Experience: Euro-Par 2009, vol. 23, pp. 187–198 (2011)
4. Gautier, T., Ferreira Lima, J.V., Maillard, N., Raffin, B.: XKaapi: A Runtime System for Data-Flow Task Programming on Heterogeneous Architectures. In: Proc. of the 27th IEEE International Parallel and Distributed Processing Symposium (IPDPS), Boston, USA (June 2013)
5. Hochbaum, D.S., Shmoys, D.B.: Using dual approximation algorithms for scheduling problems theoretical and practical results. J. ACM 34(1), 144–162 (1987)
6. Topcuoglu, H., Hariri, S., Wu, M.Y.: Performance-effective and low-complexity task scheduling for heterogeneous computing. IEEE TPDS 13(3), 260–274 (2002)
7. Lenstra, J.K., Shmoys, D.B., Tardos, E.: Approximation algorithms for scheduling unrelated parallel machines. Mathematical Programming 46, 259–271 (1988)
8. Shchepin, E.V., Vakhania, N.: An optimal rounding gives a better approximation for scheduling unrelated machines. Operations Research Letters 33, 127–133 (2004)
9. Bonifaci, V., Wiese, A.: Scheduling unrelated machines of few different types. CoRR abs/1205.0974 (2012)
10. Hochbaum, D.S., Shmoys, D.: A polynomial approximation scheme for scheduling on uniform processors: using the dual approximation approach. SIAM Journal on Computing 17(3), 539–551 (1988)
11. Seifu, S.: Scheduling on heterogeneous cluster environments. Master's thesis, Grenoble university (June 2012)
12. Agullo, E., Demmel, J., Dongarra, J., Hadri, B., Kurzak, J., Langou, J., Ltaief, H., Luszczek, P., Tomov, S.: Numerical linear algebra on emerging architectures: The plasma and magma projects. Journal of Physics: Conference Series 180 (2009)
13. Bolze, R., Cappello, F., Caron, E., Daydé, M.J., Desprez, F., Jeannot, E., Jégou, Y., Lanteri, S., Leduc, J., Melab, N., Mornet, G., Namyst, R., Primet, P., Quétier, B., Richard, O., Talbi, E.G., Touche, I.: Grid'5000: A large scale and highly reconfigurable experimental grid testbed. IJHPCA 20(4), 481–494 (2006)

Towards a Unified Heterogeneous Development Model in Android^{TM}

Alejandro Acosta and Francisco Almeida

La Laguna University, Spain
aacostad@ull.es

Abstract. The advent of emergent SoCs and MPSocs opens a new era on the small mobile devices (Smartphones, Tablets, ...) in terms of computing capabilities and applications to be addressed. The efficient use of such devices, including the parallel power, is still a challenge for general purpose programmers due to the very high learning curve demanding very specific knowledge of the devices. While some efforts are currently being made, mainly in the scientific scope, the scenario is still quite far from being the desirable for non-scientific applications where very few of them take advantage of the parallel capabilities of the devices. We propose Paralldroid (Framework for Parallelism in Android), a parallel development framework oriented to general purpose programmers for standard mobile devices. Paralldroid presents a programming model that unifies the different programming models of Android. The user just implements a Java application and introduces a set of Paralldroid annotations in the sections of code to be optimized. The Paralldroid system automatically generates the native C, OpenCL or Renderscript code for the annotated section. The Paralldroid transformation model involves source-to-source transformations and skeletal programming.

Keywords: Renderscript, source-to-source transformation, Android.

1 Introduction

SoCs (Systems on Chip [1]) have been the enabling technology behind the evolution of many of todays ubiquitous technologies, such as Internet, mobile wireless technology, and high definition television. The information technology age, in turn, has fuelled a global communications revolution. With the rise of communications with mobile devices, more computing power has been put in such systems. The technologies available in desktop computers are now implemented in embedded and mobile devices. We find new processors with multicore architectures and GPUs developed for this market like the Nvidia Tegra [2] and the OMAP^{TM}5 [3] platform that also goes in the same direction.

On the other hand, software frameworks have been developed to support the building of software for such devices. The main actors in this software market have their own platforms: Android [4] from Google, iOS [5] from Apple and Windows phone [6] from Microsoft are contenders in the smartphone market. Other companies like Samsung [7] and Nokia [8] have been developing proprietary frameworks for low profile devices. Coding applications for such devices is

D. an Mey et al. (Eds.): Euro-Par 2013 Workshops, LNCS 8374, pp. 238–248, 2014.

now easier. But the main problem is not creating energy-efficient hardware but creating efficient, maintainable programs to run on them [9].

Conceptually, from the architectural perspective, the model can be viewed as a traditional heterogeneous CPU/GPU with a unified memory architecture, where memory is shared between the CPU and GPU and acts as a high bandwidth communication channel. In the non-unified memory architectures, it was common to have only a subset of the actual memory addressable by the GPU. Technologies like Algorithmic Memory [10], GPUDirect and UVA (Unified Virtual Addressing) [11] and HSA [12] are going in the direction of an unified memory system for CPUs and GPUs in the traditional memory architectures. Memory performance continues to be outpaced by the ever increasing demands of faster processors, multiprocessor cores and parallel architectures.

Under this scenario, we find a strong divorce among traditional mobile software developers and parallel programmers, the first tend to use high level frameworks like Eclipse for the development of Java programs, without any knowledge of parallel programming, and the latter that use to work on Linux, doing their programs directly in OpenCL closer to the metal. The first take the advantage of the high level expressiveness while the latter assume the challenge of high performance programming. The work developed in this paper tries to help bring these to worlds.

We propose the Paralldroid system, a development framework that allows for the automatic development of native, Renderscript and OpenCL applications for mobile devices (Smartphones, Tablets, ...). The developer fills and annotates, using his/her sequential high level language, the sections on a template that will be executed in native, Renderscript and OpenCL language. Paralldroid uses the information provided in these annotations to generate a new program that incorporates the code sections to run over the CPU or GPU. Paralldroid can be seen as a proof of concept where we show the benefits of using generation patterns to abstract the developers from the complexity inherent to parallel programs [13].

The advantages of this approach are well known: Increased use of the parallel devices by non-expert users, rapid inclusion of emerging technology into their systems, delivery of new applications due to the rapid development time and unify the different programming models of Android.

We find the novelty of our proposal in the generation of code for different programming models. The heterogeneity of the Android programming models allows the programmer to obtain the best performance, implementing each section of the application using the programming model that better fits to his/her code. Paralldroid allows to generate code for each programming model, facilitating the development of efficient heterogeneous applications.

The paper is structured as follows, in section 2 we introduce the development model in Android and the different alternatives to exploit the devices, some of the difficulties associated to the development model are shown. In section 3 we present the Paralldroid Framework, the performance of Paralldroid is validated in section 4 using five different applications, transform a image to grayscale, convolve 3x3 and 5x5, levels and a general convolve implementation. Five different versions have been compared, the ad-hoc Java, Native C and Renderscript versions, and the generated Native C and Renderscript versions. The computational results prove the increase of performance provided by Paralldroid at a low cost of development. We finish the paper with some conclusions and future lines of research.

2 The Development Model in Android

Android is a Linux based operating system mainly designed for mobile devices such as mobile phones and tablet computers, although it is also used in embedded devices as smart TVs and media streamers. It is designed as a software stack that includes an operating system, middleware and key applications.

Applications are executed in Android under a Dalvik virtual machine (Dalvik VM). The Dalvik VM executes files in the Dalvik Executable (`.dex`) format which is optimized for minimal memory footprint. The VM is register-based, and runs classes compiled by a Java language compiler that have been transformed into the `.dex` format by the included `dx` tool (see "Compile and Link time" in Figure 1(a)). The Dalvik Executable files with any data and resource files are packaged into the Android Application Package (`.apk`). All the code in a single .apk file is considered to be one application and is the file that Android-powered devices use to install the application. Android relies on Linux for core system services such as security, memory management, process management, network stack, and driver model. The kernel also acts as an abstraction layer between the hardware and the rest of the software stack.

Android applications are written in Java, and the Android Software Development Kit (SDK) provides the API libraries and developer tools necessary to build, test, and debug applications in a Software Development Kit (SDK). The central section of Figure 1(a) shows the compilation and execution model of a Java Android application. The compilation model converts the Java `.java` files to Dalvik-compatible `.dex` (Dalvik Executable) files. The application runs in a Dalvik VM that manages the system resources allocated to this application.

Besides the development of Java applications, Android provides packages of development tools and libraries to develop Native applications, the Native Development Kit (NDK). The NDK enables to implement parts of the application running in the Dalvik VM using native-code languages such as C and C++. This native code is executed using the Java Native Interface (JNI) provided by Java. Using Native code may introduce benefits to certain classes of applications, in the form of reuse of existing code and in some cases increased speed. The section in the right side of Figure 1(a) shows the compilation and execution model of an application where part of the code has been rewritten using the NDK. The compilation process of the Java code is done using the SDK. The Native `.c` is compiled using the GNU compiler (GCC). More recent versions of the NDK allow the use of the Clang compiler to compile Native code, although the default is still to use the GCC [14] compiler. The Dalvik-compatible code of the application is executed in the Dalvik VM. When the Dalvik-compatible code calls a

Native routine, the VM will allocate the resources needed on the system and will allow the Native code to be executed. All the resources used by the native code are controlled by the VM. Note that using native code does not result in an automatic performance increase due to the JNI overload, but always increases the application complexity, its use is recommended in CPU-intensive operations that don't allocate much memory, such as signal processing, physics simulation, and so on. Native code is useful to port an existing native code to Android, not for speeding up parts of an Android application. Some devices support OpenCL for executions on GPU. OpenCL code is implemented on the context of the Native Development Kit (NDK).

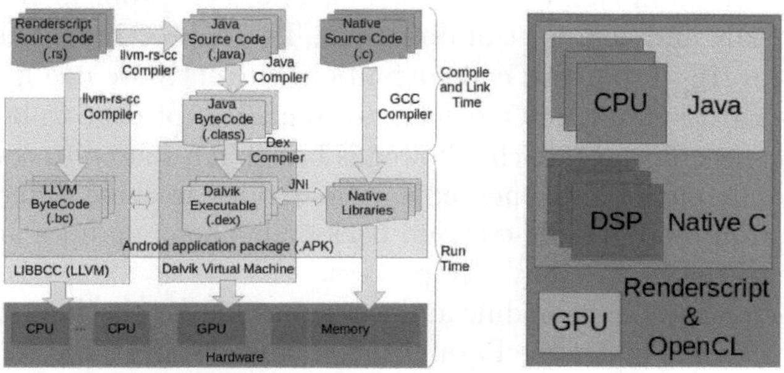

(a) Android compilation and execution model (b) Heterogeneity in android devices

Fig. 1. Compilation and execution model of an application in Android

To exploit the high computational capabilities on current devices, Android provides Renderscript, it is a high performance computation API at the native level (similar to CUDA) and a programming C language (C99 standard). Renderscript allows the execution of parallel applications under several types of processors such as the CPU, GPU or DSP, performing an automatic distribution of the workload across the available processing cores on the device. The section in the left side of Figure 1(a) shows the compilation and execution model used by Renderscript. Renderscript (`.rs` files) codes are compiled using `llvm-rs-cc`, a `Clang` based compiler [15] that produces byteCode (`.bc` files) for a Low-Level Virtual Machine (LLVM), moreover, it generates a set of Java classes wrapper around the Renderscript code. These Java classes, are compiled together with the rest of the Java classes of the application. To execute the Renderscript (`.bc` files) bytecode is used a LLVM (`libbcc`). Again, the use of Renderscript code does not result in an automatic performance increasing. It is useful for applications that do image processing, mathematical modelling, or any operations that require lots of mathematical computation.

As you can see in Figure 1(b) the heterogeneity is inherent to the Android environment. The devices that support Android usually have a heterogeneous architecture composed of CPUs and a GPU and also de development model is heterogeneous. The different programming models in Android allow the programmer to obtain the best performance of each component of these devices, implementing each section of the application using the programming model that better fits to his/her code and using the components that obtain the best performance.

3 Paralldroid

Paralldroid is designed as a framework to ease the development of future parallel applications on Android platforms. We assume that the mobile platforms will be provided with a classical CPU and with some kind of production processor like a GPU that can be exploited thorough OpenCL or Renderscript. In the proposed translation model, the developers define their problem as Java code in the Android SDK and add a set of directives. These directives are an extension of OpenMP 4.0 [16]. From this code definition, currently we can generate automatically the native C, native OpenCL and Renderscript code to be executed in the parallel device. The approach followed is based in a source-to-source translation process. The model implemented can be divided in three different modules (figure 2(a)): front-end, middle-end and back-end. These modules are integrated as a plugin into the Eclipse building process.

The front-end is the first module and is responsible for checking that the code written by the user is under the Paralldroid language syntax and semantics. The syntax and semantic analysis is supported on the library Java Development Tools (JDT) [17] that allows to obtain and manipulate all the elements of a Java class (Annotations, Methods, Fields, ...) easily. The front-end module is launched during the compilation step performed by Eclipse, it invokes the middle-end module when needed and also calls to the back-end module after the generation of the intermediate code. The middle-end takes charge of identifying directives defined by the user and analyze the Java code associated to these directives. All information and elements extracted by this module are stored using an intermediate representation that will be used by the next module. The middle-end is invoked by the front-end module by demand. The back-end takes over the generation of the target code starting from the intermediate representation. The generation is divided in two phases, the generation of the native code and the modification of the original code to allow its access to the native code generated. To access to the native code generated, several modifications in the original code are performed. The entire process is transparent to the user. This module is invoked by the front-end after finishing with the intermediate code generation.

In figure 2(b) you can see as the process of generation is integrated in the Android execution model (figure 1(a)). The Paralldroid generation process is in the top level and analyzes the Java code looking for directives. The files that do not contain directives are compiled directly (central section). If Paralldroid finds a directive for native or OpenCL code generation, this code is generated and the Java code is modified to access to generated native code (right section). The same process is used to generate Renderscript code (left section). The increment of productivity under this approach is clear, moreover when considering that Paralldroid not only generates the OpenCL or Renderscript codes but the

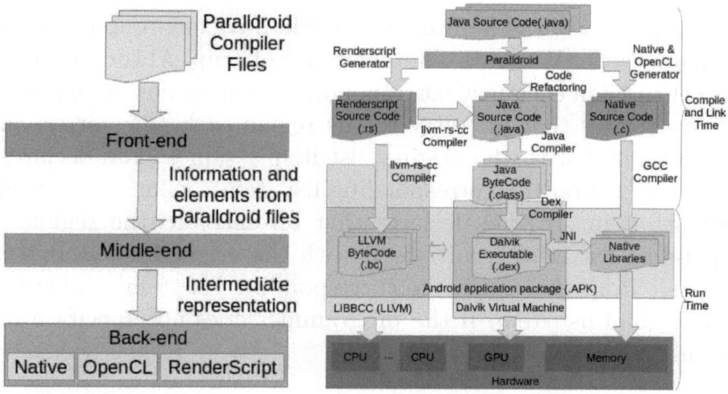

(a) Translation process modules. (b) Paralldroid compilation and execution model

Fig. 2. Translation process and Compilation model in Paralldroid

```
package es.ull.pcg.paralldroid.tests;
public class Grayscale  {
   public void grayscale() {
      int pixel, sum, x;
      int [] scrPxs = new int[width*height];
      int [] outPxs = new int[width*height];
      bitmapIn.getPixels(scrPxs, 0, width, 0, 0, width, height);
      // pragma paralldroid target lang(rs) map(to:scrPxs,width,height) map(from:outPxs)
      // pragma paralldroid parallel for private(x,pixel,sum) rsvector(scrPxs,outPxs)
      for(x = 0; x < width*height; x++) {
         pixel = scrPxs[x];
         sum = (int)(((pixel) & 0xff) * 0.299f);
         sum += (int)(((pixel >> 8 ) & 0xff) * 0.587f);
         sum += (int)(((pixel >> 16) & 0xff) * 0.114f);
         outPxs[x] = (sum) + (sum << 8) + (sum << 16) + (scrPxs[x] & 0xff000000);
      }
      bitmapOut.setPixels(outPxs, 0, width, 0, 0, width, height);
   }
}
```

Fig. 3. GrayScale problem with Paralldroid directives

JNI implementation also. The current version of Paralldroid imposes some constraints that could be overcomed in the future. We only support primitive type variables, the code associated to directives must be Java and C99 compatible.

3.1 Paralldroid Directives

The directives supported by Paralldroid are an extension of OpenMP 4.0, its latest release candidate [18] includes directives for accelerator devices. The set of directives and clauses supported by Paralldroid are:

Target Data Create a device data environment. This directive is responsible for mapping the data to the context of the device. The clauses supported are:

- **Lang** is an extension to the OpenMP standard, we use it to indicate the target language that we want generate: Renderscript, Native or OpenCL.

– `Map` clause maps a variable from the current Java environment to the target data environment. We have different types of map. `Alloc` declares that on entry to the region each new corresponding list item has an undefined initial value. `To` declares that on entry to the region each new corresponding list item is initialized with the original list item's value. `From` declares that on exit from the region the corresponding list item's value is assigned to each original list item. `Tofrom` declares that on entry to the region each new corresponding list item is initialized with the original list item's value and that on exit from the region the corresponding list item's value is assigned to each original list item. If the programmer does not specify a map type, the default map type is `Tofrom`.

Target Create a device data environment and execute the construct on the same device. This directive is responsible for mapping the data and executing the code associated to the directive in the device. The clauses have the same function as in the `Target Data` case.

Parallel for should be used in the context of a `target` directive, this directive is applied to a for loop and is responsible for distributing the load of the for loop between the threads available on the device. The clauses supported are:

– `private` indicates that each thread has a private copy of the variables.
– `firstprivate` is the same that `private` but the variables are initialized.
– `Shared` indicates that all threads share the variables.
– `Colapse` is used for nested loops, the load of all nested loop is distributed between available threads.
– `Rsvector` is an extension to the OpenMP standard. It is used for Renderscript code generation and indicates the input and output vectors used.

Teams should be used in the context of a `target` directive, this directive is responsible for teams or groups of threads. The clauses supported are:

– `Num_teams` indicates the number of teams
– `Num_thread` indicates the number of threads of each team.
– `private` indicates that each team has a private copy of the variables. These variables are shared between all threads in a teams.
– `firstprivate` is the same that `private` but the variables are initialized.
– `Shared` indicates that all teams shared the variables.

Distribute should be used in the context of a `teams` directive, this directive is similar to the `parallel for` directive but in this case distributes the load of the for loop between the teams available on the device. Clauses are similar to the `parallel for` case.

Figure 3 shows a Java implementation for the grayScale problem. This problem has a loop that traverses the pixels array of the image and gets the colour to transform to grayscale. On top of the loop, we add the Paralldroid directives to generate Renderscript code (`target lang(rs)`) and parallelize the loop ((`parallel for`)). As you can see these directives have the OpenMP 4.0 syntax

```
#pragma version(1)
#pragma rs java_package_name(es.ull.pcg.paralldroid.tests)
int width, height;
int *scrPxs, *outPxs;
void root(const int *v_in, int *v_out, uint32_t x_lidrstadkd) {
   int x, sum, pixel;
   x = x_lidrstadkd;
   pixel=scrPxs[x];
   sum=(int)(((pixel) & 0xff) * 0.299f);
   sum+=(int)(((pixel >> 8) & 0xff) * 0.587f);
   sum+=(int)(((pixel >> 16) & 0xff) * 0.114f);
   outPxs[x]=(sum) + (sum << 8)+(sum << 16)+(scrPxs[x] & 0xff000000);
}
```

Fig. 4. Generated Renderscript version of GrayScale problem

with some extension. Figure 4 shows the Renderscript code generated by Paralldroid. The variables mapped by `target` directive (`scrPxs, outPxs, width, height`) are defined in the Renderscript context. The loop is replaced by a root function that will be executed in parallel, private variables of `parallel for` directive are defined inside of root function.

4 Computational Results

To validate the performance of the code generated by our framework, we consider five different applications, four of these applications are based on the Renderscript image-Processing benchmark [19] (transforming a image to grayscale, to convolve 3x3 and 5x5 and levels) and the other one is an additional general convolve implementation developed by ourselves. In all cases, we implemented five versions of code, the ad-hoc version from a Java developer, an ad-hoc native C implementation, ad-hoc Renderscript implementation, and the versions automatically generated by Paralldroid, the generated native C and Renderscript code. We executed these codes over two SoCs devices running Android, a Samsung Galaxy SIII (SGS3) and an Asus Transformer Prime TF201 (ASUS TF201). The Samsung Galaxy SIII is composed of an Exynos 4 (4412) holding a Quad-core ARM Cortex-A9 processor (1400MHz), 1GB of RAM memory and a GPU ARM Mali-400/MP4. The Asus Transformer Prime TF201 is composed of a NVIDIA Tegra 3 holding a Quad-core ARM Cortex-A9 processor (1400MHz, up to 1.5 GHz in single-core mode), 1GB of RAM memory and a GPU NVIDIA ULP GeForce. Both devices run the Android system version 4.1. The GPUs of these devices do not support OpenCL or Renderscript executions, so in this case, the GPUs can not be used as accelerators. In all cases, the Java version will be used as the reference to calculate the speedup. For all the problems we used two images of size 1600×1067 and 800×600.

Figure 5 shows the speedup relative to the ad-hoc java version for the Renderscript benchmark problems using a image of size 1600×1067. In this case the native C versions do not present differences between ad-hoc version and generated version. In all cases, the ad-hoc Renderscript version gets the best results,

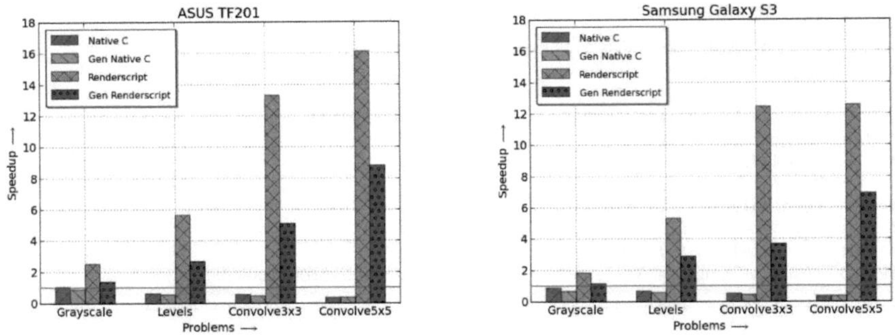

(a) ASUS TF201 (b) Samsung Galaxy SIII

Fig. 5. Speedup for the Renderscript benchmark problems (image 1600×1067)

due to the fact that this version are optimized and use vector operations. Currently Paralldroid does not obtain this level of optimization but it provides a positive speedup at a low development effort. In the Renderscript executions, the computacional load of the instances solved involves an important impact in the performance, problems with more computational load get a better speedup.

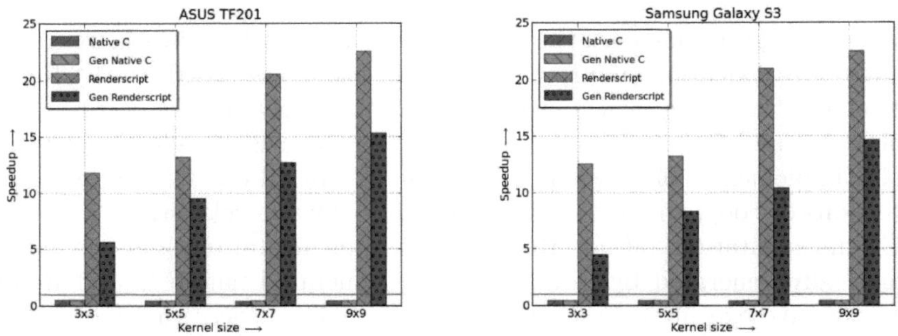

(a) ASUS TF201 (b) Samsung Galaxy SIII

Fig. 6. Speedup for a general convolve implementation (image 1600×1067)

In Figure 6 we show the speedup relative to the ad-hoc Java version for the general convolve implementation using a image of size 1600×1067. In this case we vary the sizes of the convolve kernels in the range 3×3, 5×5, 7×7 and 9×9. As on the previous case, the native C versions provide a similar result. Again, in the generated Renderscript version we get positive speedups in all the cases but the best results are obtained with the ad-hoc Renderscript version.

Figure 6 shows the executions for all the problems using an image of size 800×600. In this case we only show the speedups on the ASUS TF201 device, but we experimentally tested that the running times provided by the Samsung Galaxy SIII device are similar. As on the executions performed with the image

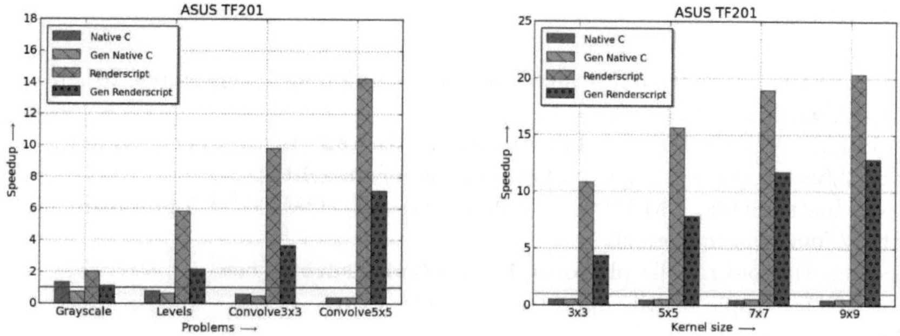

(a) Speedup for the Renderscript benchmark problems

(b) Speedup for a general convolve implementation

Fig. 7. Speedup for 800 × 600 image size in ASUS TF201

of size 1600 × 1067, the ad-hoc Renderscript version gets the best results. The native C versions provide similar results, for the grayscale problems the ad-hoc native version get a better result than the obtained by the generated native version.

In general, the ad-hoc versions get higher performances but their implementations are more complex.

5 Conclusion

We propose Paralldroid, a framework for the automatic generation of native C, Renderscript and OpenCL applications for Android. The Java code annotated by the user is automatically transformed in a native C or Renderscript version. The generation process is automatic and transparent for the Java developer that has no knowledge on parallel programming. Although there is still opportunity for the optimization in terms of the memory transfer among the different devices and in the use of vector operations, the validation tests performed on five different problems prove that the results are quite promising. With a very low development effort the running times are significantly reduced. Paralldroid also contributes to increase the productivity in the parallel developments due to the low effort required. For the near future we plan to introduce further optimizations in the Renderscript generations. We will also consider in our agenda extending the set of annotations supported by Paralldroid to include additional parallel directives as the parallel regions. Another future line of work is the use of Paralldroid to parallelize basic libraries used for the Android programmers so that they could take advantage of the parallel execution.

Acknowledgment. This work has been supported by the EC (FEDER) and the Spanish MEC with the I+D+I contract number: TIN2011-24598.

References

1. SoCC: IEEE International System–on–Chip Conference (September 2012), http://www.ieee-socc.org/
2. NVIDIA: NVIDIA Tegra mobile processors: Tegra2, Tegra 3 and Tegra 4, http://www.nvidia.com/object/tegra-superchip.html
3. Texas Instruments: OMAP™ Mobile Processors : OMAP™ 5 platform, http://www.ti.com/omap5
4. Google: Android mobile platform, http://www.android.com
5. Apple: iOS: Apple mobile operating system, http://www.apple.com/ios
6. Microsoft: Windows Phone: Microsoft mobile operating system, http://www.microsoft.com/windowsphone
7. Samsung: Bada: Samsung mobile operating system, http://developer.bada.com
8. Nokia: Nokia Belle: lastest Nokia symbian platform, http://www.developer.nokia.com/
9. Reid, A.D., Flautner, K., Grimley-Evans, E., Lin, Y.: SoC-C: efficient programming abstractions for heterogeneous multicore systems on chip. In: Altman, E.R. (ed.) Proceedings of the 2008 International Conference on Compilers, Architecture, and Synthesis for Embedded Systems, CASES 2008, Atlanta, GA, USA, pp. 95–104. ACM (October 2008)
10. Memoir Systems: Algorithmic Memory ™ technology, http://www.memoir-systems.com/
11. Nvidia: GPUDirect Technology, http://developer.nvidia.com/gpudirect
12. Anandtech: AMD Outlines HSA Roadmap: Unified Memory for CPU/GPU in 2013, HSA GPUs in 2014, http://www.anandtech.com/show/5493/
13. Peláez, I., Almeida, F., Suárez, F.: DPSKEL: A skeleton based tool for parallel dynamic programming. In: Wyrzykowski, R., Dongarra, J., Karczewski, K., Wasniewski, J. (eds.) PPAM 2007. LNCS, vol. 4967, pp. 1104–1113. Springer, Heidelberg (2008)
14. Android: Native development kit (ndk), http://developer.android.com/tools/sdk/ndk/index.html
15. Clang: a c language family frontend for llvm, http://clang.llvm.org/
16. OpenMP: The openmp api specification for parallel programming, http://openmp.org/wp/openmp-specifications/
17. Eclipse: Eclipse jdt, http://www.eclipse.org/jdt/
18. OpenMP: Openmp application program interface, version 4.0-rc 2, http://www.openmp.org/mp-documents/OpenMP_4.0_RC2.pdf/
19. AOSP: Android open source project, http://source.android.com/

An Automated Approach for Estimating the Memory Footprint of Non-linear Data Objects

Sebastian Dreßler and Thomas Steinke

Zuse Institute Berlin
Takustraße 7
14195 Berlin
{dressler,steinke}@zib.de

Abstract Current programming models for heterogeneous devices with disjoint physical memory spaces require explicit allocation of device memory and explicit data transfers. While it is quite easy to manually implement these operations for linear data objects like arrays, this task becomes more difficult for non-linear objects, e.g. linked lists or multiple inherited classes. The difficulties arise due to dynamic memory requirements at run-time and the dependencies between data structures. In this paper we present a novel method to build a graph-based static data type description which is used to create code for injectable functions that automatically determine the memory footprint of data objects at run-time. Our approach is extensible to implement automatically generated optimized data transfers across physical memory spaces.

1 Introduction

Current programming models for heterogeneous systems with disjoint address spaces require an explicit data transfer. Therefore, data management and migration between devices must be implemented by the programmer. For linear data objects like arrays these tasks are rather simple to implement. Specific programming models, e.g. OpenACC or the Intel Compiler for Intel Xeon Phi, already enable implicit transfers. However, non-linear data objects are not sufficiently supported due to the need for serialization before transfers. This is caused by a lack of sophisticated automatic serialization.

We want to address implicit data movements and propose a three step solution. First, the memory footprint (MF) and transfer direction (intent) of data objects must be determined. Second, an automated serialization and deserialization scheme must be implemented. As third step, code executing the MF determination, serialization and the data transfer must be injected.

In this paper, we focus on the first step. We present an approach that analyzes non-linear data objects and estimates their MF dynamically at run-time alongside with the objects intent. Related methods focus on existing compilers or implement altered programming models. In contrast, our approach utilizes the Low Level Virtual Machine (LLVM) compiler framework. LLVM introduces

D. an Mey et al. (Eds.): Euro-Par 2013 Workshops, LNCS 8374, pp. 249–258, 2014.

an intermediate code representation (IR) where higher level abstractions are disclosed. Thus, information like data types become directly deducible. This enables language independence and removes the need for additional object metadata in our approach.

As we show in the evaluation section, we are able to process a wide range of simple and non-linear data objects, namely scalars, multi-dimensional arrays, and C++ classes with templates, multiple inheritance and iterators with both, static and dynamic allocation. The currently existing limitations concern overlapping pointers, function pointers, and re-allocation. The main contributions of the paper are: i) the design and implementation of two LLVM passes for analyzing data structures and to determine the data-direction of function arguments, and ii) a method for processing simple and non-linear data objects to derive run-time properties (MF) without adding additional metadata.

The paper is structured as follows. Next, we provide an overview on related work. Subsequently, we discuss our implemented analysis process. Then, the handling of different data objects is discussed in detail. That is, we show how they are internally represented and how their MFs are estimated. The evaluation section presents results of several synthetic tests and of real-world applications and discusses the run-time overhead for selected tests. We conclude the paper with a summary and an outlook.

2 Related Work

Determining the MF of data objects relates to type checking compilers. SAFECode [3] for instances provides array bounds checking. The MF of the array must be known to perform this task. Currently, only linear arrays are supported, while our approach also enables analysis of non-linear objects.

HiCUDA [5] targets heterogeneous systems. Allocations and transfers are performed automatically but require *#pragma* directives. Additionally, information regarding the shape of the data must be provided. We want to remove these constraints by performing an automated shape recognition.

Uchiyama et al. [10] propose an automated memory allocation method for OpenMPC [9]. However, for performance reasons CUDA as programming model is often favored. Therefore, the necessity to analyze data objects in existing applications remains. With the use of LLVM, our approach only requires support by a LLVM language frontend, e.g. Clang for C / C++ or DragonEgg for FORTRAN and other languages supported by GCC.

Jablin et al. [7] propose the first fully automatic CPU-GPU communication management. This approach enables the programmer to stay with CUDA. Furthermore, CPU pointers are mapped directly to GPU pointers which means that no serialization before transfers is required. However, once the programmer does not access GPU data in the same way as on the CPU, data must be re-ordered which implies serialization.

In our previous work [4] we focused on simple data objects in C. This paper focuses non-linear data objects with abstractions toward language independence.

3 The Data Type Analysis Process

This section describes the details of the process of analyzing object types and estimating their memory footprint (MF). Fig. 1 shows its general outline and also represents the outline of the discussion.

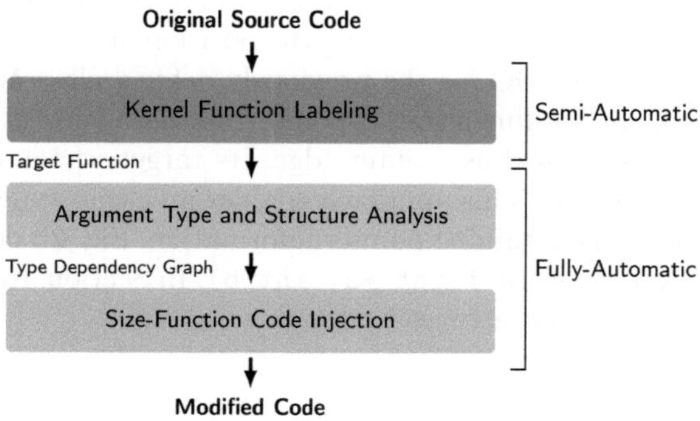

Fig. 1. Representation of the tool flow for automatically estimating the memory footprint of data objects

The analysis process and the subsequent creation of size-functions to estimate the MF both utilize LLVM [8]. In conjunction with LLVM we introduce a graph-based representation of the objects data structure which simplifies the subsequent analysis process.

3.1 Labeling of Kernel Functions

The labeling of a kernel function (KF) marks the function to be analyzed. This is a semi-automatic task since the developer manually chooses the KF. For labeling, source code *#pragma* statements are not an option, since they are not visible in LLVM IR. Instead we use the compiler attribute *annotate*: `__attribute__((annotate("kernel")))` is placed prior the KF. In LLVM IR the attribute is a global variable which we search for during analysis.

3.2 Analysis of the Structure of Function Argument Types

This step reveals the structural type layout of an argument of the selected KF. The goal of the analysis of the type structure is to enable the construction of formulas expressing the MF of instances of data types. For instance, consider the class type definition `class A { int x, y; }`. The MF of an object `A a;` is expressible as $2 \times \text{sizeof}(\mathit{int})$ bytes. Type structure information are directly deduced from LLVM IR during type structure analysis. We store the structural layout in a graph, the *type dependency graph* (TDG), avoiding repetitive analysis.

The TDG is a directed graph. Its vertices represent data types and are labeled with the name of the type and its byte-width, if the data type is a scalar. The TDG may contain cycles to represent recursive type structures. Furthermore, the KF is added as root vertex. This ensures a common known entry point and also makes the TDG unique across different KFs.

If a vertex represents a non-linear data type it contains at least a single outgoing edge. These edges branch the non-linear data type into known subtypes. Edges are labeled with an index containing the position of a subtype in its source type. Fig. 2a depicts the TDG for the previously defined class `A`.

If a variable is a (multi-dimensional) pointer, its base type is extracted. The corresponding edge is labeled as pointer-edge. Its target vertex then represents the type that is pointed to. This approach enables an easier type determination in subsequent steps while retaining pointer information. Fig. 2b depicts the TDG of the function definition `void f(int *a, int b)`. In Section 4 we discuss TDG construction for different data types in detail.

Fig. 2. Example TDGs for two different data type structures. The number at each edge represents the position of the member in the class. Dashed edges represent pointers. a) illustrates the TDG for `class A { int x, y; }`. b) illustrates the TDG for `void f(int *a, int b)`.

3.3 Injection of Size-Functions and Intent Estimation

For each KF argument, we inject an appropriate size-function (SF) and a call to it with LLVM. A SF returns the MF of an argument at run-time. It is generated by traversing the TDG and considering dynamic memory allocations. Section 4 discusses this process in detail.

During run-time all SFs are called and their results are gathered. Their summation occurs in three different sums to distinct between the arguments intent: i) *in*, representing read-only arguments, ii) *out*, representing write-only arguments, and iii) *in-out*, representing read-write arguments.

We used Andersen's algorithm for inter-procedural points-to analysis [1] as basis to determine data directions. In particular, we construct a *data dependency graph* (DDG) containing loads (`LD`) and stores (`ST`) related to the argument.

Kernels with side-effects are considered by tracing function calls and linking correlated arguments. That is, we extend the parent DDG by the one generated from the called function.

For construction, it also is crucial to distinct, whether `LD` and `ST` access an arguments value or only its address. For instance, in LLVM IR, argument addresses are commonly stored at the beginning of a function. These `ST` operations do not belong to the graph, because they do not write a value to the argument.

To determine the data direction, we consider the count of `LD` and `ST` instructions accessing the argument. If only `LD` instructions are recognized, the argument is labeled with *in*. In contrast, it is labeled with *out*, if only `ST` instructions exist. For all other cases, the argument direction is *in-out*.

Once the processing is finished, the altered LLVM IR is compilable to an executable. On execution, SFs are called and their results are gathered as described. The resulting sums can then be further processed, e.g. printed to the console or used for memory allocation.

4 Handling of Data Types

This section discusses how the type dependency graph is constructed for different data types and how a matching SF is derived.

4.1 Scalar Data Types

C / C++ scalar data types, e.g. `int`, utilize a single vertex. The byte-width of the vertex is obtained by calling the LLVM function `getBitWidth` and subsequent division by 8. Alignments are considered if the MF is affected. The SF returns the byte-width of the type.

4.2 Pointers

Pointers are represented by pointer-edges in the TDG. We assume, that the pointed-to value is either a scalar or a pre-allocated (multi-dimensional) array of scalars. The pointer itself does not belong to the MF of the argument. This relies on the assumption, that only the pointed-to object is of interest.

To determine the allocated size, we explicitly search for calls to allocation functions. Currently, only memory allocations by either *malloc* or *new* are supported. A `ST` can be found, if the argument is related to an allocation function. The DDG helps determining this relation. Once a matching allocation call was found, its argument is extracted. At run-time, this argument contains the allocated size in bytes.

If the pointed-to object is a scalar or a one-dimensional array this argument is returned by the SF. However, if a multi-dimensional array was allocated, our tool search for loops surrounding the identified allocation function. We use the LLVM *LoopInfo*[1] pass for this search. Currently, only linear multi-dimensional arrays are fully supported. The SF returns the allocated size in bytes multiplied with the loop count.

4.3 Classes and Structures

In LLVM IR, classes and structures are represented with the LLVM type `struct`, e.g. `class A { int x, y; }` is expressed as `%class.A = { i32, i32 }`. The

[1] `http://llvm.org/docs/doxygen/html/classllvm_1_1LoopInfo.html`

constructed TDG then contains sub-types resembling the structural layout of the class (or struct). Thus, a single vertex is created for the class type and multiple vertices are created for the contained types. Edges between class type and contained types are labeled with indices referring to their location. Fig. 3 provides an example.

```
class Coord {
  int x, y, z;
};

class Value {
  Coord coord;
  double value;
};
```

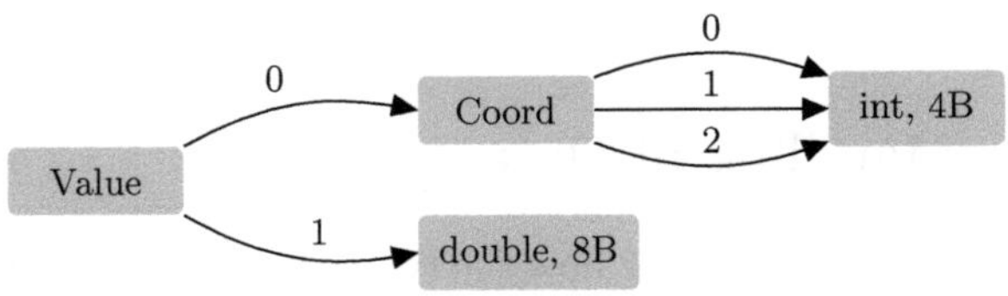

Fig. 3. Example for TDG construction for a small class

The SF of a class gathers the values of the SFs of the contained types. This method is also applicable on hierarchical class structures, classes with inheritance and with templates. These structures are evaluated at compile-time and thus are present in LLVM IR. Inheritance extends the TDG by another class. Types of templates are resolved and placed directly in LLVM IR, thus they are available in the TDG. Structures with recursion, e.g. linked lists, are currently only supported if they are implemented with STL containers. Since the SFs are called at run-time, dynamically typed objects from C++ interfaces are resolved correctly.

4.4 STL Containers

In general, STL containers can be treated like classes. The TDG construction thus follows the rules provided in the previous section. For most cases, type deduction can also be done like described previously. But for e.g. `std::map`, we use the destructor to identify the key / value types since they are obfuscated.

However, SFs use the provided iterators for object traversal. This eases the processing and enables support for the aforementioned recursive structures. The SFs of STL containers call the member `begin` and `end` of an instance and traverses through its elements. For each element, its corresponding size function is called and the returned value is summed. With this technique, element types with likely differing byte-width, e.g. a `vector` of `strings`, are considered. Once all elements were traversed, the SF returns the summed size. In future, our tool will be extended to also support custom iterators.

5 Evaluation

We evaluated our tool-chain with two different test scenarios. Synthetic tests were used to demonstrate the core functionality of the tool-chain. Additionally, we selected real-world applications, each providing different data structures. The automatically estimated MFs and directions were checked against the results of manually inserted computations in our test cases.

Table 1. Abbreviations and KF interfaces for the synthetic test cases (first half) and real-world application test cases (second half)

Name	**Kernel Function Interface**
NEW	`void f(int *a, Y *y)`
STRVEC	`void f(std::vector<std::string> x)`
NESTTPL	`void f(X<std::string> x)`
MAP	`void f(std::map<int, std::string> x)`
TermFrequency	`void tf(int k, std::string *genome, vector<string> *kmer, vector<int> *count)`
Octree	`void OctreeListToMatrixList(OctreeList *l, params *p)`
HPCCG	`int HPCCG(HPC_Sparse_Matrix *A, const double * const b, double * const x, const int max_iter, const double tolerance, int niters, double normr, double *times)`
miniFE	`void driver(const int global_box[][2], int my_box[][2], ComputeNodeType *compute_node, Parameters *params, YAML_Doc *ydoc)`

5.1 Synthetic Test Cases

Table 1 provides an overview on the synthetic test cases. It shows the name and the kernel function interface of every test case. The test cases do not have a function body, i.e. their data-direction is always marked as *in*. We will not discuss these test cases in detail, since their function arguments are self-explanatory. The custom class of the pointer `*y` is defined as `class Y { int x, y; }`. Implementation details on the custom class `X` are provided in Listing 1.1.

5.2 Real-World Application Test Cases

For the following description, we spare a detailed KF interface discussion and solely focus on noticeable data types. Table 1 additionally provides the complete KF interfaces. *TermFrequency* and *Octree* originate from the ENHANCE project [2], while *HPCCG* and *miniFE* were taken from the Mantevo project [6].

TermFrequency computes the amount of short genomic sequences (mers) contained in a genomic string. `mer` is of type `std::vector<std::starting>` and stores the mers. `count` is a `std::vector<int>` and stores the corresponding count of occurrences. This variable is passed as a pointer with data direction *out*.

```
template<class T>    template<class T>    template<class T>
class X {            class Y {            class Z {
public:              public:              public:
  Y<T> y;              std::vector<         std::vector<T> v;
};                       Z<T>             };
                       > z;
                     };
```

Listing 1.1. Class layout definition for the synthetic test NESTED

Octree transposes a list of octrees into a list of matrices. Octrees are commonly used in computer graphics, its vertices always have zero or eight children. The function does not return any data but writes the matrices to disk. `params` is a class containing several values of type `double`. `list` is a custom class that inherits from the type `std::vector<Octree>`. `Octree` in turn contains a vector of child nodes, which again are custom classes containing `double` values. In summary, a nested class structure with inheritance has to be processed.

HPCCG calculates the conjugate gradient of a sparse matrix. The most interesting kernel function argument is the sparse matrix `A`, which is stored in CSR format with several dynamically allocated arrays. Furthermore, member allocation is done inside a separate function. Figure 4a depicts the TDG for `A`.

miniFE performs a FEM calculation. It uses YAML serialization to record performance data. We analyzed the class `YAML_Doc`, since it contains recursive structures. It derives from `YAML_Element` which contains in turn a STL vector recursing again to `YAML_Element`, e.g. `std::vector<YAML_Element*>`. Figure 4b depicts the TDG for `YAML_Doc`.

5.3 Evaluation Results

For each test, the evaluation procedure is as follows. First, we compile the test to LLVM IR. Next, we process and modify it with our tool-chain. Then, we compile the result to an executable binary. During execution, the estimated MFs and data directions are printed to the console alongside with the manually computed values.

The overall result is as follows. Synthetic tests and real-world applications revealed, that our implementation behaves correctly for these particular tests. That is, MFs and data directions were all estimated correctly. Additionally, we measured the run-time overhead for the synthetic test cases with the time measurement and analysis tool *elaps'd*[2]. The results are depicted in Table 2. These measurements revealed the following properties.

The run-time overhead for arrays containing constantly-sized elements is approximately constant (*NEW*). For these data types our tool multiplies the base byte-width of the element with the number of allocated elements.

[2] `http://sdressler.github.io/elapsd`

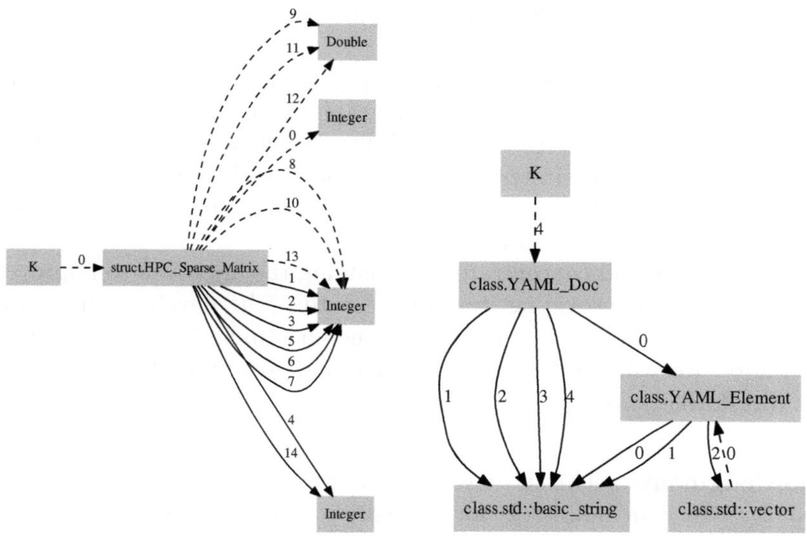

(a) (b)

Fig. 4. (a) depicts the TDG of the sparse matrix utilized in HPCCG. (b) shows the TDG of the class `YAML_Doc` used in miniFE. The vertex K refers to the KF, the index on the outgoing edge represents the position of the argument in the KF.

Table 2. Measured overheads of three selected benchmarks with a linearly increasing number of elements. All measured times are in μs.

#Elements	1000	2000	3000	4000	5000	6000	7000	8000	9000	10000
NEW	0.92	0.86	0.69	0.76	0.54	0.71	0.68	0.78	0.70	0.63
STRVEC	8.14	12.33	22.78	27.76	35.45	38.24	42.12	47.46	53.35	59.23
MAP	5.81	7.47	9.13	13.45	19.53	22.91	27.84	34.17	43.47	52.51

For arrays containing elements with potentially varying sizes (*STRVEC* and *MAP*), the overhead correlates with the number of elements. This is a result from the need to call every size function. If the element itself contains elements with varying sizes, the effect strengthens, i.e. the overhead increases further. In contrast to *STRVEC*, the overhead for *MAP* must not increase linear, since the STL implementation of `std::map` uses a red-black tree. Consequently, its elements may be spread in memory which causes a memory access slowdown. For *STRVEC*, elements are contiguous in memory.

6 Conclusions and Future Work

We presented an automated approach to estimate the memory footprint of non-linear data objects. By using LLVM and a graph-based approach for information deduction, our workflow retains extensibility. To demonstrate its correctness and functionality, synthetic tests and real-world applications were used. Our evaluation showed, that our tool is able to analyze non-linear data structures like deeply nested classes with recursion.

Our future work will concentrate on extending the approach to improve support for objects not providing iterators. For this, the developer may provide additional object information, e.g. which member indicates the end of a list. Furthermore, we will use the presented method to automatically inject data layout transformations.

Acknowledgments. This is developed as part of the ENHANCE project, funded by German ministry for education and science (BMBF), grant No. 01|H11004G. The reference implementation of our tool is available at: `https://github.com/sdressler/objekt`, the terms of the BSD license apply. We would like to thank Florian Schintke for valuable discussions.

References

1. Andersen, L.O.: Program analysis and specialization for the C programming language. PhD thesis, University of Cophenhagen (1994)
2. ENHANCE Consortium. Enhance - enabling heterogeneous hardware acceleration using novel programming and scheduling models (January 2012)
3. Dhurjati, D., Kowshik, S., Adve, V.: SAFECode: enforcing alias analysis for weakly typed languages. ACM SIGPLAN Notices 41, 144–157 (2006)
4. Dreßler, S., Steinke, T.: A Novel Hybrid Approach to Automatically Determine Kernel Interface Data Volumes. Technical report, ZIB (2012)
5. Han, T.D., Abdelrahman, T.S.: hiCUDA: High-level GPGPU programming. IEEE Transactions on Parallel and Distributed Systems 22(1), 78–90 (2011)
6. Heroux, M.A., Doerfler, D.W., Crozier, P.S., Willenbring, J.M., Edwards, H.C., Williams, A., Rajan, M., Keiter, E.R., Thornquist, H.K., Numrich, R.W.: Improving performance via mini-applications. Sandia National Laboratories, Tech. Rep. (2009)
7. Jablin, T.B., Prabhu, P., Jablin, J.A., Johnson, N.P., Beard, S.R., August, D.I.: Automatic cpu-gpu communication management and optimization. ACM SIGPLAN Notices 46, 142–151 (2011)
8. Lattner, C., et al.: The LLVM compiler infrastructure (2010)
9. Lee, S., Eigenmann, R.: OpenMPC: Extended OpenMP programming and tuning for GPUs. In: Proceedings of the 2010 ACM/IEEE International Conference for High Performance Computing, Networking, Storage and Analysis, pp. 1–11. IEEE Computer Society (2010)
10. Uchiyama, H., Tsumura, T., Matsuo, H.: An Automatic Host and Device Memory Allocation Method for OpenMPC (2012)

Communication Models for Resource Constrained Hierarchical Ethernet Networks

Jun Zhu[1], Alexey Lastovetsky[2], Shoukat Ali[3], and Rolf Riesen[3]

[1] Technical University of Eindhoven, Netherlands
[2] University College Dublin, Ireland
[3] Dublin Research Laboratory, IBM, Ireland

Abstract. Communication time prediction is critical for parallel application performance tuning, especially for the rapidly growing field of data-intensive applications. However, making such predictions accurately is non-trivial when contention exists on different components in hierarchical networks. In this paper, we derive an 'asymmetric network property' on TCP layer for concurrent bidirectional communications in a commercial off-the-shelf (COTS) cluster, and develop a communication model as the first effort to characterize the communication times on hierarchical Ethernet networks with contentions on both NIC and backbone cable levels. In particular, we show that if the asymmetric network property was excluded from the model, the communication time predictions will be significantly less accurate than those made by using the asymmetric network property. Furthermore, our observation of the performance degradation caused by the asymmetric network property suggests that some part of the software stack below TCP layer in COTS clusters needs targeted tuning, which has not yet attracted any attention in literature.

1 Introduction

Computing clusters have been the primary commodity platforms for running parallel applications. To build a cost-effective yet powerful cluster environment, high speed networks are widely used to interconnect off-the-shelf computers. For application performance analysis on such clusters, an accurate time prediction for data sets transferred over the communication media is typically required [4]. To that end, several communication models have been proposed, e.g., Hockney [8] and LogP [6]. They have been widely used to analyze the timing behaviors for point-to-point communications on parallel computers. However, these models simply see the network as a black-box, and can capture neither the communication *hierarchy* nor the network *resource sharing* that typically is present in modern large scale systems. Both of these factors, network *hierarchy* and *resource sharing*, make communication time prediction non-trivial and challenging for high performance clusters.

On the other hand, such predictions are needed more now than ever because of the increasing importance of data-intensive applications [7][10] that devote a significant amount of their total execution time in parallel processing to I/O or

D. an Mey et al. (Eds.): Euro-Par 2013 Workshops, LNCS 8374, pp. 259–269, 2014.

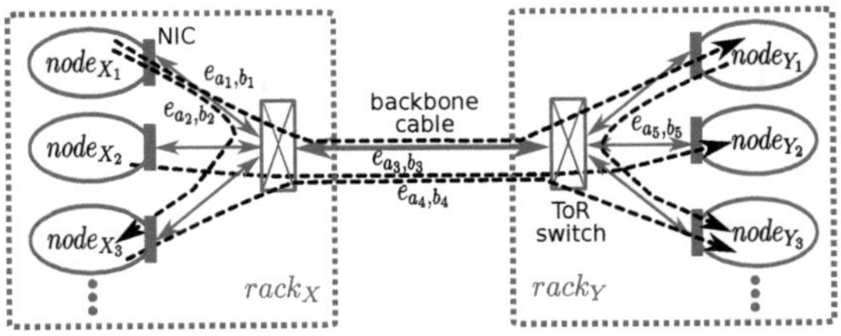

Fig. 1. A tree topology platform: two star-configured racks connected via the backbone cable. The dashed arrows denote one example application with five logical communication links: e_{a_1,b_1}– e_{a_5,b_5}. The processes on each logical link are not explicitly labeled for clarity in the graph.

network communication, instead of computation. A good usable performance analysis of such data-intensive applications requires that the communication model reflect the network properties accurately on state-of-the-art network topologies and technologies.

An example Ethernet cluster, consisting of two racks, is illustrated in Figure 1. It has a scalable tree (star bus) topology, i.e., two star-configured intra-rack segments are connected using a linear backbone cable. The computer nodes in the same rack are connected to a *top-of-rack* (*ToR*) switch via network interface cards (NICs), and each node has a dedicated bandwidth on the intra-rack point-to-point connection. Different ToR switches are connected together to form a hierarchical network. We use this cluster as our testbed system to verify network properties and the proposed communication model. In this testbed, contentions may occur at different levels of the communication infrastructure:

- Network interface cards (*NICs*). In multi-core processors, multi-socket nodes, or a combination thereof, each NIC may be shared by multiple cores concurrently. That is, the number of NICs on each node is generally less than the number of cores and NIC-level sharing exists.
- Backbone cable. Several inter-rack communication operations may be aggregated on the backbone that runs between racks to effectively utilize the high bandwidth available.

For instance, in Figure 1, logical communication links e_{a_1,b_1} and e_{a_2,b_2} share the same NIC on $node_{X_1}$, and e_{a_1,b_1}, e_{a_3,b_3} and e_{a_4,b_4} share the inter-rack backbone instead. When resource contention happens on a *hierarchical* network, it makes communication times prediction more difficult.

Contributions. We derive network properties on parametrized network topology from simultaneous point-to-point MPI operations, and discover the *asymmetric network property* on TCP layer for concurrent bidirectional communications in a COTS Ethernet cluster. To the best of our knowledge, it has not been previously reported in literature, and our work is the first effort to characterize the effect of concurrent communications in *resource-constrained hierarchical* networks. In particular, we show that if the asymmetric network property is excluded from the model, the communication time predictions become significantly less accurate than those made by using the asymmetric network property.

The remainder of this paper is structured as follows. Section 2 discusses some related work. Our MPI micro-benchmark and platform are introduced in Section 3. Section 4 introduces the notations used in this paper. Section 5 introduces some network properties derived from benchmarking. We propose our communication model in Section 6, and present the corresponding experiments in Section 7. Finally, Section 8 concludes the paper.

2 Related Work

Many models have been proposed in the parallel and distributed computing literature to characterize the communication times for parallel computers. In the *Hockney model* [8], the point-to-point communication time to send a message of size m is captured as $\alpha + \beta * m$, where α is the latency for each message and β is the inverse of the network bandwidth. Culler *et al.* [6] describe *LogP* communication model for small messages. The model is aware of the finite network capacity, which is the upper bound on messages in parallel transmission on the network. Hoefler *et al.* [9] further investigate how this model can be modified to capture the timing behaviors for small messages on InfiniBand networks. In [3], *LogGP* is developed, as an extension of the LogP model, to better fit large messages. In [11], a heterogeneous model *LMO* is proposed, which separates the variable contributions of the processors and network in communication timing analysis. However, all of the above work assumes that there is no contention on the network. When multiple communication transactions happen concurrently on the same network resource, the above models assume that the available bandwidth is even shared by all concurrent communications. Let us call this the *symmetric network property*. We will show that this property does not exist for complicated hierarchical networks.

In a recent work [12], a contention-aware communication timing model is proposed for multi-core clusters using an InfiniBand network. This work analyzes the dynamic network contention, and derives the so-called *penalty coefficients* to characterize the bandwidth distribution at the NIC level. This work is similar to ours in the sense that it does not recognize the symmetric network property; instead it explicitly calculates how the total available bandwidth will be divided among the contending communications. This model focuses on a flat star network, in which all computer nodes are connected to a single switch with dedicated bandwidth. However, modern large-scale systems usually have hierarchical network topology. This is the part that had been lacking, and this is what we address in our paper.

3 Micro-benchmark and Platforms

3.1 Micro-benchmark

We designed a point-to-point MPI micro-benchmark to measure concurrent communication times for use in our testbed. In each iteration, a message with a user-specified size is initialized to remove the potential memory or network cache effects. Each time a message is sent from the sender to receiver, a non-blocking receive operation is pre-posted and the receiver records the time spent on message transmission in `tArray` for statistics. For each sender to receiver communication, we repeat the transmission at most `maxIter` times, where `maxIter` is some large number (set to 2000 in our experiments). Specifically, we stop if the width of the 95% confidence interval becomes 2%, or less, of the average measured time. In general, our benchmark can be set up to have any given number of pairs of sender and receiver processes for simultaneous MPI communication operations.

We use OpenMPI 1.5.4 [2] as the MPI implementation. Each MPI process can be bound to any computing resource (core or node) as specified in a given communication pattern, with the support of *processor affinity* in OpenMPI. We only use large message sizes $\geqslant 10MB$ in benchmarking, which suit data-intensive problems. Compared with communication delay, the message latency α (also called propagation delay) is negligible [12].

3.2 Platform Specifications

There are up to 15 nodes settled in each rack of our experimental platform. Each node is a dual-socket six-core (Intel Xeon X5670 6C@2.93GHz) server with an Intel 1Gb NIC card, operated with Red Hat Enterprise Linux 5.5 x86-64. The Ethernet switch is IBM BNT Rack Switch G8264, which supports over 10Gb Ethernet and is interoperable with clients using 1Gb connectivity as well. The theoretical communication bandwidth on different network resources is 1Gbps and 10Gbps for NICs and the optical backbone respectively.

The NIC settings in Linux on each node are tuned to run for Gigabit speed [5]. In our hybrid 1/10 GbE cluster environment, the network round-trip time (RTT) between two nodes on different racks is 450 μs. The socket buffer size is at least RTT * bandwidth. We set the TCP socket buffer size in OpenMPI to 3MB (MCA parameters `btl_tcp_sndbuf` and `btl_tcp_rcvbuf`).

4 Preliminaries

Here, we introduce the notations on application and platform, which will be used to formalize network properties and communication models in the following sections. Let $|\cdot|$ denote the cardinality of a set or vector, and $(\cdot)^{-1}$ the inverse of a value. The index of a vector starts at 0, and the *i-th* element of a vector $\boldsymbol{V}$ is denoted as $\boldsymbol{V}[i]$.

4.1 Application

An application is a collection of concurrent point-to-point MPI operations, denoted as a tuple (P, E). A finite set P contains an even number of processes, which are connected in pairs via a finite set $E \subseteq P^2$ of edges, with $|P| = 2 * |E|$. Each edge $e_{a,b} \in E$ denotes a logical communication link (*dependency*) between a process pair: a sender p_a and a receiver p_b.

4.2 Platform

The network infrastructure of our experimental cluster has a tree topology, as illustrated in Figure 1. In general, the cluster consists of a set R of racks. The set N of computing nodes is the union of all nodes in individual racks. There is one NIC configured for each node and all nodes in the same rack communicate via the ToR switch. A full-duplex communication network is employed in our work. We denote the inverse bandwidth of the NIC, electrical backbone, and optical backbone as β_N, β_E, and β_O, respectively.

4.3 Mapping: Application to Platform

The mapping process binds each process in MPI applications to a computing node in our platform. The binding function is defined as $\mathcal{B}^N : P \to N$, which associates every process $p \in P$ to a *node* $\in N$ to which it is bound. Similarly, how processes are bound to racks is defined $\mathcal{B}^R : P \to R$. For instance, in Figure 1, $\mathcal{B}^N(p_{a_5}) = node_{Y_1}$ and $\mathcal{B}^R(p_{a_5}) = \text{rack}_Y$. In our work, we only map up to one process to each core to eliminate the unnecessary context switching overhead.

4.4 Network Contention

When multiple processes are bound to one (multi-core) node or rack, several simultaneous logical links may share the same NIC or inter-rack backbone. In full-duplex network, we distinguish resource contention on incoming links from that on outgoing links. The set of incoming logical links that are bound to the same resource $x \in N \cup R$, are denoted as $\mathcal{E}^+(x)$. The degree of this set $|\mathcal{E}^+(x)|$ is simply denoted as $\delta^+(x)$, where $\delta^+(\cdot)$ is the indegree function for a resource defined as $\delta^+ : N \cup R \to \mathbb{N}_0$. Similarly, $\mathcal{E}^-(\cdot)$ and $\delta^-(\cdot)$ are defined for outgoing logical links of a resource. For instance, $\mathcal{E}^-(node_{X_3}) = \{e_{a_4,b_4}\}$ and $\delta^-(\text{rack}_X) = 3$ in Figure 1.

For simultaneously bidirectional communication (Section 5.2), we also distinguish logical links with resource sharing at the *same* direction (*with-flow*) to logical links on the *reverse* direction (*contra-flow*).

Congestion Factors. To detect the communication *bottleneck* in a *hierarchical* network, we associate with $e_{a,b}$ a vector $\boldsymbol{S}_{a,b}$ of sets of logical links, defined as follows

$$\boldsymbol{S}_{a,b} = < \mathcal{E}^-(\mathcal{B}^R(a)), \mathcal{E}^-(\mathcal{B}^N(a)), \mathcal{E}^+(\mathcal{B}^N(b)) > \tag{1}$$

where $\boldsymbol{S}_{a,b}$ includes 3 sets of ***with-flow*** logical links of $e_{a,b}$ on the shared resource. For instance, the link e_{a_1,b_1} in Figure 1 has

$$\boldsymbol{S}_{a_1,b_1} =< \{e_{a_1,b_1}, e_{a_3,b_3}, e_{a_4,b_4}\}, \{e_{a_1,b_1}, e_{a_2,b_2}\}, \{e_{a_1,b_1}\} >$$

To detect the congestion bottleneck of a logical link on network resources, a congestion factor $k_{a,b}$ is defined as follows

$$k_{a,b} = \max\{k \mid k = \boldsymbol{\beta}[i] \cdot |\boldsymbol{S}_{a,b}[i]|, \forall i \in [0, |\boldsymbol{S}_{a,b}|)\} \tag{2}$$

where $\boldsymbol{\beta}$ is a vector with platform-dependent inverse bandwidth values, and $\boldsymbol{\beta}[i]$ the *i-th* inverse bandwidth of the network resource on which the set $\boldsymbol{S}_{a,b}[i]$ of logical links are sharing. For instance, when the cluster in Figure 1 has an optical backbone cable, $\boldsymbol{\beta} =< \beta_O, \beta_N, \beta_N >$ and $k_{a_1,b_1} = \max\{3\beta_O, 2\beta_N, \beta_N\}$. That is, the congestion factor is configuration aware in a hybrid network.

Similarly, vector $\bar{\boldsymbol{S}}_{a,b}$ of sets of ***contra-flow*** logical links of $e_{a,b}$ and the *reverse* congestion factor $\bar{k}_{a,b}$ are defined

$$\bar{\boldsymbol{S}}_{a,b} =< \mathcal{E}^+(\mathcal{B}^R(a)), \mathcal{E}^+(\mathcal{B}^N(a)), \mathcal{E}^-(\mathcal{B}^N(b)) > \tag{3}$$

$$\bar{k}_{a,b} = \max\{k \mid k = \boldsymbol{\beta}[i] \cdot |\bar{\boldsymbol{S}}_{a,b}[i]|, \forall i \in [0, |\bar{\boldsymbol{S}}_{a,b}|)\} \tag{4}$$

5 Network Properties

We derive some network properties from MPI benchmarking on a resource constrained network platform. In this section, we characterize the inverse bandwidth $\beta_{a,b}$ of each logical link $e_{a,b}$ in a particular communication pattern, which is time independent. However, when some communication operations finish earlier, the specified communication pattern may vary at different time instance t.

5.1 Unidirectional Communication: Fairness Property

Given an application with a number $|E|$ of point-to-point MPI operations, we design the following unidirectional experiments to inspect the arbitration fairness on different levels of the network hierarchy:

A. **Intra-rack communication** – all sender processes are mapped onto one *node*, while the matching receiver processes are mapped onto another *node* in the same rack.
B. **Inter-rack communication** – all sender processes are mapped onto different *nodes* in rack$_X$, while the matching receiver processes are mapped onto different *nodes* in rack$_Y$.

We observe that when $|E|$ increases, the average bandwidth for logical links on the shared NIC (experiment A) decreases, and that the bandwidth is fairly distributed over all links. The same is for the optical fiber backbone (experiment

B) when $|E| > 10$. When $|E| <= 10$, the 10-Gb optical fiber is not saturated and therefore the average bandwidth is almost constant (940 Mbps), giving a measured maximum aggregate bandwidth $\beta_O^{-1} = 9.4$Gbps. For experiment B using electrical copper backbone, the results are similar to those for a NIC. However, the bandwidth distribution in Experiment B does not really depend on copper versus optical; it is the bandwidth of physical links in the hierarchical network that matters.

Mathematically, the inverse bandwidth $\beta_{a,b}$, based on a *fairness property* of each logical link $e_{a,b}$ can be captured as

$$\beta_{a,b} = \begin{cases} \beta \cdot |E|, \text{ if } \beta = \beta_O \text{ and } |E| > 10 \text{ or } \beta = \beta_E \\ \beta_E, \text{ if } \beta = \beta_O \text{ and } |E| \leqslant 10 \end{cases} \tag{5}$$

where β is the inverse bandwidth of the physical link on which $e_{a,b}$ is located.

5.2 Bidirectional Communication: Asymmetric Property

In a full-duplex network, the network resources might be shared by multiple communication logical links in both directions simultaneously. To study bidirectional communication on shared network resources, we swap the mapping policy for some of the sender and receiver processes in the experiments in Section 5.1. When the number of *incoming* $\delta^+(\cdot)$ and *outgoing* $\delta^-(\cdot)$ logical links vary on the shared node or rack, The inverse bandwidth $\beta_{a,b}$ of each logical link $e_{a,b}$ can be captured

$$\beta_{a,b} = \begin{cases} \beta \cdot \delta_{max}(\cdot), \text{ if } \beta = \beta_O \text{ and } \delta_{max}(\cdot) > 10 \text{ or } \beta = \beta_E \\ \beta_E, \text{ if } \beta = \beta_O \text{ and } \delta_{max}(\cdot) \leqslant 10 \end{cases} \tag{6}$$

where $\delta_{max}(\cdot) = \max\big(\delta^+(\cdot), \delta^-(\cdot)\big)$. The results clearly show that the total duplex bandwidth may not be achieved, when $\delta^+(\cdot)$ and $\delta^-(\cdot)$ do not match (are *asymmetric*) on the shared resource. For instance, when $\delta^+(\cdot) = 12$ and $\delta^-(\cdot) = 1$ in (a), the total bidirectional bandwidth is $\frac{13}{12} \cdot 940$Mbps, instead of $2 \cdot 940$Mbps (according to a fair dynamic bandwidth allocation in full duplex-mode). For instance, when $\delta^+(\cdot) = 2$ and $\delta^-(\cdot) = 1$ in (a), the two incoming and one outgoing logical links all have bandwidth 470Mbps, instead of 470Mbps, 470Mbps, and 940Mbps respectively (according to a fair dynamic bandwidth allocation in full duplex-mode). We have validated this property using a TCP network testing tool Iperf [1] with the same experimental settings on TCP layer. To the best of our knowledge, this bidirectional *asymmetric property* on full-duplex communication network has not been reported in the literature yet.

6 Resource Constrained Communication Model

Here, we present our communication model, in which the inverse bandwidth for logical links can be derived. Let $\bar{E}$ be the set that stores the links for which $\beta_{a,b}$ has been calculated, E the set of links not yet calculated. $PQ(E)$ is a priority queue based on elements $\forall e_{a,b} \in E$, which is ranked by the descending-order of a multi-key

$$\mathcal{K}_{PQ(E)} =< \max(k_{a,b}, \bar{k}_{a,b}),\ k_{a,b},\ \bar{k}_{a,b} > \tag{7}$$

The most congested logical link in a hierarchical network is the one with the highest value of $\mathcal{K}_{PQ(E)}$, which depends both on network capacity and the number of logical links on the sharing network resources.

Algorithm 1: Inverse bandwidth for logical links

```
Output: Inverse bandwidth β_{a,b}, ∀e_{a,b} ∈ E
/* Initialization: set Ē to store calculated links                    */
Ē := ∅
while E ≠ ∅ do
    /* To retrieve the most congested link in PQ(E)                   */
    e_{a,b} := PQ(E).pop()
    β_{a,b} := 0
    if k_{a,b} ⩾ k̄_{a,b} then
        foreach i ∈ [0, |S_{a,b}|] do
            if β[i] · |S_{a,b}[i]| == k_{a,b} then
                β_{a,b} := max(β_{a,b}, inverseBandwidth(i))
    else
        foreach i ∈ [0, |S̄_{a,b}|] do
            if β[i] · |S̄_{a,b}[i]| == k̄_{a,b} then
                E' = S̄_{a,b}[i] ∩ Ē
                /* If contra-flow links saturate the physical link    */
                if ∑{β^{-1}_{x,y} | ∀e_{x,y} ∈ E'} == β^{-1}[i] then
                    β_{a,b} = min{β_{x,y} | ∀e_{x,y} ∈ E'}
                else
                    S̄_{a,b}[i] := ∅
                    PQ(E).insert(e_{a,b})
    /* To update E and Ē, once k_{a,b} is calculated                  */
    if β_{a,b} ≠ 0 then
        E := E \ {e_{a,b}}
        Ē := Ē ∪ {e_{a,b}}
where
Function inverseBandwidth(i)
    E' = S_{a,b}[i] ∩ Ē, E'' = S_{a,b}[i] ∩ E
    β̂ = β[i]
    /* The used bandwidth on the congested physical link              */
    k' = ∑{β̂^{-1}_{x,y} | ∀e_{x,y} ∈ E'}
    /* To calculate link bandwidth based on fairness property         */
    return β_{a,b} := max(β_E, |E''| / (β̂^{-1} − k'))
```

Based on the derived network properties and heuristics from benchmarking, we propose Algorithm 1 to calculate the inverse bandwidth for logical Links with simultaneous MPI communications. The analysis flow works iteratively in a bottleneck driven manner. In each iteration, the most congested logical link in

E is proposed to be analyzed (Line 5), and the bandwidth of this logical link is calculated differently when the network congestion is caused by either with-flow or contra-flow traffic:

- When congestion happens on with-flow traffic (Line 7), the bandwidth is calculated based on the fairness properties on the with-flow bottle network resource (Line 9-10).
- Otherwise (Line 11), the bandwidth is calculated based on the asymmetric properties on the contra-flow bottle network resource (Line 13-17). Heuristically, when contra-flow congestion happens on a non-saturated physical link, the contra-flow congestion on the logical link is disabled and the logical link is sent back to the queue to be re-analyzed (Line 19-20).

While E is not empty, the algorithm explores the links iteratively until all the logical links are analyzed. In the worst case, Algorithm 1 terminates in at most $2 \cdot |E|$ iterations. Furthermore, our communication model could be extended to more complex topologies, such as 2D mesh, in which similar network contention happens in different regions in the network.

7 Experiments and Results

We conducted our experiments on two racks connected via an optical backbone. Each time the same number of nodes are configured in both racks, with a total number of nodes $|N|$ up to 30. To construct one test, we in turn consider each one of the nodes on both racks. For each such node, $node_{\text{src}}$, we randomly select a different node, $node_{\text{dst}}$, from the set N. We then include the directed point to point communication $node_{\text{src}} \rightarrow node_{\text{dst}}$ (as one instance of process pair in our benchmark) in the test with a 50% probability. For each $node_{\text{src}}$, we perform this matching process d times. It ensures that we get random communication patterns in the test, and that our results do not depend on a "lucky" selection of communication patterns. To further ensure that the goodness of our reported results is not a result of biased selection of input, we consider an experiment completed only when enough tests have been performed to give us a certain level of confidence in the average value of ϵ.

We have designed 9 experiments, each with a different set of values for parameters $|N|$ and d, as illustrated in Figure 2. In each experiment, the number of communication links is $N_{\text{trials}} > 500$. A total of 354 randomly generated communication patterns are tested. These communication patterns are non-trivial, with the maximum number of logic links $|E|$ in one pattern up to 57, and the maximum indegree $\delta^+(\cdot)$ or outdegree $\delta^-(\cdot)$ (i.e., the number of concurrent links) on the congested network resource up to 6 for NICs and 10 for the optical backbone.

The distribution of the estimation error ϵ on each cluster of experiments is illustrated in Figure 2. For communication times prediction based on our proposed model (the first row in Figure 2), when d varies from 1 to 3 in experiment settings, there are 83.2%, 77.3%, and 72.1% of communication links respectively, which fall within the margin of error $|\epsilon| \leqslant 10\%$. On the contrary, when the asymmetric property is not considered (the second row in Figure 2), i.e., only with

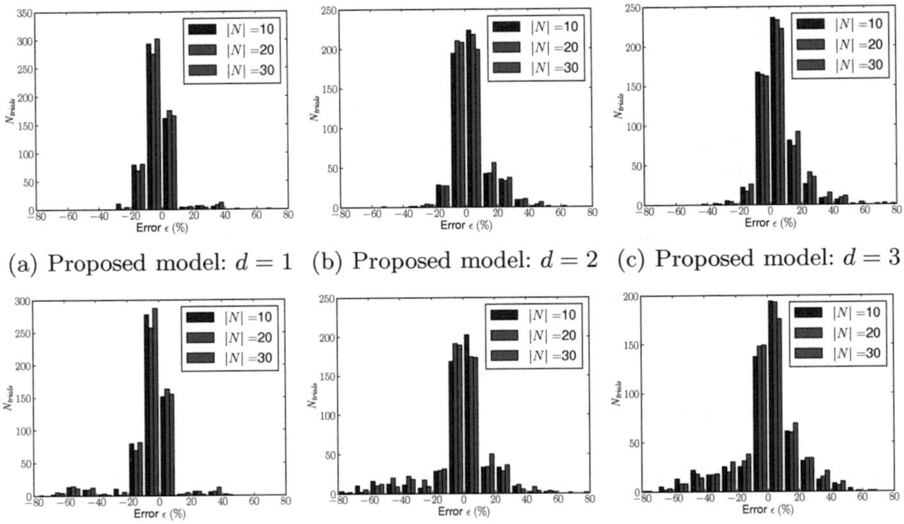

(a) Proposed model: $d = 1$ (b) Proposed model: $d = 2$ (c) Proposed model: $d = 3$

(d) Pure fairness: $d = 1$ (e) Pure fairness: $d = 2$ (f) Pure fairness: $d = 3$

Fig. 2. The histogram of errors on communication times prediction

fairness property, the percentage of these links fall to 66.8%, 58.0%, and 68.8%. The prediction error with pure fairness property can be as worse as −80%, which means the predicted times are 5 times lower than the measured ones. From the experimental results, we see that our model is quite accurate from the averaged value for error $|\epsilon|$. The largest average error occurs for experiment 9, being approximately 9.5% of the measured value with less than 0.2% imprecision.

8 Conclusions and Future Work

In this paper, we derive an 'asymmetric network property' on TCP layer for concurrent bidirectional communications on Ethernet clusters, and develop a communication model to characterize the communication times accordingly. We conduct statistically rigorous experiments to show that our model can be used to predict the communication times for simultaneous MPI operations on resource constrained networks quite effectively. In particular, we show that if the asymmetric network property is excluded from the model, the accuracy of the communication time prediction drops significantly.

As the future work, we plan to generalize our model for more complex network topologies. We would also like to investigate how the asymmetric network property can be tuned below TCP layer in Ethernet networks.

Acknowledgement. The authors would like to thank Kiril Dichev and Dr. Konstantinos Katrinis for useful discussions. The research in this paper was supported by IRCSET(Irish Research Council for Science, Engineering and Technology) and IBM, grant number IRCSET-IBM-2010-06.

References

1. Iperf site, `http://sourceforge.net/projects/iperf/` (retrieved January 24, 2012)
2. OpenMPI site, `http://www.open-mpi.org` (retrieved January 24, 2012)
3. Alexandrov, A., Ionescu, M.F., Schauser, K.E., Scheiman, C.: LogGP: incorporating long messages into the LogP model – one step closer towards a realistic model for parallel computation. In: P. of. the Seventh Annual ACM Symposium on Parallel Algorithms and Architectures, SPAA 1995, pp. 95–105 (1995)
4. Bell, G., Gray, J., Szalay, A.: Petascale computational systems. Computer 39, 110–112 (2006)
5. Leitao, B.H.: Tuning 10Gb network cards on Linux. In: Ottawa Linux Symposium, pp. 169–184 (2009)
6. Culler, D., Karp, R., Patterson, D., Sahay, A., Schauser, K.E., Santos, E., Subramonian, R., von Eicken, T.: LogP: towards a realistic model of parallel computation. SIGPLAN Not. 28, 1–12 (1993)
7. Gokhale, M., Cohen, J., Yoo, A., Miller, W.M., Jacob, A., Ulmer, C., Pearce, R.: Hardware technologies for high-performance data-intensive computing. Computer 41(4), 60–68 (2008)
8. Hockney, R.W.: The communication challenge for MPP: Intel Paragon and Meiko CS-2. Parallel Comput. 20, 389–398 (1994)
9. Hoefler, T., Mehlan, T., Mietke, F., Rehm, W.: LogfP - A Model for small Messages in InfiniBand. In: P. of. the 20th IEEE Int'l Parallel & Distributed Processing Symposium (IPDPS), PMEO-PDS 2006 Workshop (April 2006)
10. Johnston, W.E.: High-speed, wide area, data intensive computing: A ten year retrospective. In: P. of. the 7th IEEE Int'l Symposium on High Performance Distributed Computing, HPDC 1998, pp. 280–291 (1998)
11. Lastovetsky, A., Rychkov, V., O'Flynn, M.: Accurate heterogeneous communication models and a software tool for their efficient estimation. Int'l J. of High Performance Computing Applications 24, 34–48 (2010)
12. Martinasso, M., Méhaut, J.-F.: A contention-aware performance model for HPC-based networks: A case study of the InfiniBand network. In: Jeannot, E., Namyst, R., Roman, J. (eds.) Euro-Par 2011, Part I. LNCS, vol. 6852, pp. 91–102. Springer, Heidelberg (2011)

Non-clairvoyant Reduction Algorithms for Heterogeneous Platforms

Anne Benoit[1], Louis-Claude Canon[2], and Loris Marchal[1]

[1] École Normale Supérieure de Lyon, CNRS & INRIA, France
{anne.benoit,loris.marchal}@ens-lyon.fr
[2] FEMTO-ST, Université de Franche-Comté, Besançon, France
louis-claude.canon@univ-fcomte.fr

Abstract. We revisit the classical problem of the reduction collective operation in a heterogeneous environment. We discuss and evaluate four algorithms that are non-clairvoyant, i.e., they do not know in advance the computation and communication costs. On the one hand, **Binomial-stat** and **Fibonacci-stat** are static algorithms that decide in advance which operations will be reduced, without adapting to the environment; they were originally defined for homogeneous settings. On the other hand, **Tree-dyn** and **Non-Commut-Tree-dyn** are fully dynamic algorithms, for commutative or non-commutative reductions. With identical computation costs, we show that these algorithms are approximation algorithms with constant or asymptotic ratios. When costs are exponentially distributed, we perform an analysis of **Tree-dyn** based on Markov chains. Finally, we assess the relative performance of all four non-clairvoyant algorithms with heterogeneous costs through a set of simulations.

1 Introduction

Reduction is one of the most common collective operations, together with the broadcast operation. Contrarily to a broadcast, it consists in gathering and summarizing information scattered at different locations. A classical example is when one wants to compute the sum of (integer) values distributed over a network: each node owns a single value and can communicate with other nodes and perform additions to compute partial sums. The goal is to compute the sum of all values. Reductions have been used in distributed programs for years, and standards such as MPI usually include a "reduce" function together with other collective communications (see [12,14] for experimental comparisons). Many algorithms have been introduced to optimize this operation on various platforms, with homogeneous [13] or heterogeneous communication costs [10,9]. Recently, this operation has received more attention due to the success of the MapReduce framework [7,15], which has been popularized by Google. The idea of MapReduce is to break large workloads into small tasks that run in parallel on multiple machines, and this framework scales easily to very large clusters of inexpensive commodity computers. We review similar algorithms and use cases in the related work section in the companion research report [1].

D. an Mey et al. (Eds.): Euro-Par 2013 Workshops, LNCS 8374, pp. 270–279, 2014.

Our objective in this paper is to compare the performance of various algorithms for the reduce operations in a non-clairvoyant setting, i.e., when the algorithms are oblivious to the communication and computation costs (the time required to communicate or compute). This models well the fact that communication times cannot usually be perfectly predicted, and may vary significantly over time. We would like to assess how classical static algorithms perform in such settings, and to quantify the advantage of dynamic algorithms (if any). We use various techniques and models, ranging from worst-case analysis to probabilistic methods such as Markov chains.

The design and the analysis of algorithms in a dynamic context has already received some attention. The closest related work is probably [5], in which the authors study the robustness of several task-graph scheduling heuristics for building static schedules. The schedules are built with deterministic costs and the performance is measured using random costs. [2] studies the problem of computing the average performance of a given class of applications (streaming applications) in a probabilistic environment. With dynamic environments comes the need for robustness to guarantee that a given schedule will behave well in a disturbed environment. Among others, [4] studies and compares different robustness metrics for makespan/reliability optimization on task-graph scheduling.

The rest of the paper is organized as follows. Section 2 describes four algorithms and shows that they are approximation algorithms with identical computation costs. In Section 3, we provide more involved probabilistic analysis of their expected performance. Section 4 presents simulated executions of the previous algorithms and compares their respective performance. Finally, we conclude and discuss future research directions in Section 5.

2 Model and Algorithms

We consider a set of n processors (or nodes) $P_0, \ldots, P_{n-1}$. Each processor P_i owns a value v_i. We consider an associative operation $\oplus$. Our goal is to compute the value $v = v_0 \oplus v_1 \oplus \cdots \oplus v_{n-1}$ as fast as possible, i.e., to minimize the total execution time to compute the reduction. We do not enforce a particular location for the result: at the end of the reduction, it may be present on any node.

There are two versions of the problem, depending on whether the $\oplus$ operation is commutative or not. For example, when dealing with numbers, the reduction operation (sum, product, etc.) is usually commutative while some operations on matrices (such as the product) are not. The algorithms proposed and studied below deal with both versions of the problem.

We denote by $d_{i,j}$ the time needed to send one value from processor P_i to processor P_j. A value may be an initial value or a partial result. When a processor P_i receives a value from another processor, it immediately computes the reduction with its current value. We assume that each processor can receive at most one result at a time. The communication costs are heterogeneous, that is we may well have different communication costs depending on the receiver ($d_{i,j} \neq d_{i,j'}$), on the sender ($d_{i,j} \neq d_{i',j}$) and non-symmetric costs ($d_{i,j} \neq d_{j,i}$).

Even though these costs are fixed, we consider non-clairvoyant algorithms that make decisions without any knowledge of these costs.

The computation time of the atomic reduction on processor P_i is denoted by c_i. In the case of a non-commutative operation, we ensure that a processor sends its value only to a processor that is able to perform a reduction with its own value. Formally, assume that at a given time, a processor owns a value that is the reduction of $v_i \oplus \cdots \oplus v_j$, which we denote by $[v_i, v_j]$; the processor may only send this value to a processor owning a value $[v_k, v_{i-1}]$ or $[v_{j+1}, v_k]$, which is called a *neighbor value* in the following.

Reduction Algorithms. During a reduction operation, a processor sends its value at most once, but may receive several values. It computes a partial reduction each time it receives a value. Thus, the communication graph of a reduction is a tree (see Figure 1): the vertices of the tree are the processors and its edges are the communications of values (initial or partially reduced values). In the example, P_0 receives the initial value from P_1, and then a partially reduced value from P_2. In the following, we sometimes identify a reduction algorithm with the tree it produces.

We now present the four algorithms that are studied in this paper. The first two algorithms are static algorithms, i.e., the tree is built before the actual reduction. Thus, they may be applied for commutative or non-commutative reductions. The last two algorithms are dynamic: the tree is built at run-time and depends on the durations of the operations.

The first algorithm, called **Binomial-stat**, is organized with $\lceil \log_2 n \rceil$ rounds. Each round consists in reducing a pair of processors that own a temporary or initial data using a communication and a computation. During round $k = 1, \ldots, \lceil \log_2 n \rceil$, each processor $i2^k + 2^{k-1}$ $(i = 0, \ldots, 2^{\lceil \log_2 n \rceil - k} - 1)$ sends its value to processor $i2^k$, which reduces it with its own value: at most $2^{\lceil \log_2 n \rceil - k + 1}$ processors are involved in round k. Note that rounds are not synchronized throughout the platform: each communication starts as soon as the involved processors are available and have terminated the previous round. We can notice that the communication graph induced by this strategy is a binomial tree [6, Chapter 19], hence the name of the algorithm. This strategy is illustrated on Figure 2(a).

The second algorithm, called **Fibonacci-stat**, is constructed in a way similar to Fibonacci numbers. The schedule constructed for order k, denoted by FS_k

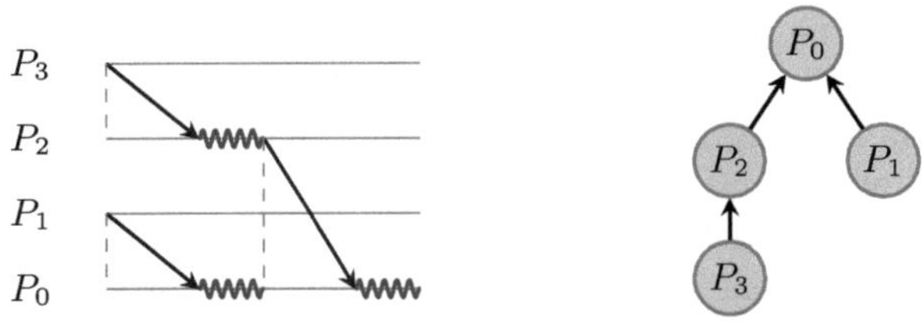

Fig. 1. Schedule and communication graph for reducing four values. Blue arrows represent communications while red springs stand for computations.

($k > 0$) first consists in two smaller order schedules FS_{k-1} and FS_{k-2} put in parallel. Then, during the last computation of FS_{k-1}, the root of FS_{k-2} (that is, the processor that owns its final value) sends its value to the root of FS_{k-1}, which then computes the last reduction. A schedule of order -1 or 0 contains a single processor and no operation. This process is illustrated on Figure 2(b). Obviously, the number of processors involved in such a schedule of order k is F_{k+2}, the $(k+2)$th Fibonacci number. When used with another number n of processors, we compute the smallest order k such that $F_{k+2} \geq n$ and use only the operations corresponding to the first n processors in the schedule of order k.

The previous two schedules were proposed in [3], where their optimality is proved for special homogeneous cases: **Binomial-stat** is optimal both when the computations are negligible in front of communications ($c_i = 0$ and $d_{i,j} = d$) and when the communications are negligible in front of computations ($c_i = c$ and $d_{i,j} = 0$). **Fibonacci-stat** is optimal when computations and communications are equivalent ($c_i = c = d_{i,j} = d$). In the non-commutative case, both algorithms build a tree such that only neighboring partial values are reduced. In the commutative case, any permutation of processors can be chosen.

Then, we move to the design of dynamic reduction algorithms, i.e., algorithms that take communication decisions at runtime. The first dynamic algorithm, called **Tree-dyn**, is a simple greedy algorithm. It keeps a slot (initially empty), and when a processor is idle, it looks into the slot. If the slot is empty, the processor adds its index in the slot, otherwise it empties the slot and starts a reduction with the processor that was in the slot (i.e., it sends its value to the processor that was in the slot, and the latter then computes the reduced value). It means that a reduction is started as soon as two processors are available. Since in the obtained reduction tree, any two processors may be paired by a communication, this can only be applied to commutative reductions.

Finally, **Non-Commut-Tree-dyn**, is an adaptation of the previous dynamic algorithm to non-commutative reductions. In this algorithm, when a processor is idle, it looks for another idle processor with a neighbor value (as described

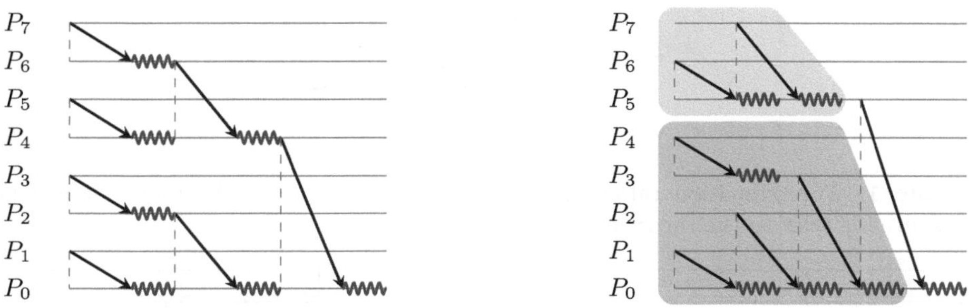

(a) **Binomial-stat** (b) **Fibonacci-stat**

Fig. 2. Schedules for **Binomial-stat** of order 3 and **Fibonacci-stat** of order 4, both using 8 processors. For **Fibonacci-stat**, the two schedules of order 2 and 3 used in the recursive construction are highlighted in green and red.

above). Now, we keep an array of idle processors rather than a single slot. If there is an idle neighbor processor, a communication is started between them, otherwise the processor waits for another processor to become idle.

Worst-Case Analysis. We analyze the commutative algorithms in the worst case, and we provide some approximation ratios, focusing on communication times. A λ-approximation algorithm is a polynomial-time algorithm that returns a solution whose execution time is at most λ times the optimal execution time. We let $\Delta = \frac{D}{d}$, where $d = \min_{i,j} d_{i,j}$ and $D = \max_{i,j} d_{i,j}$. We consider that $c_i = c$, i.e., all computation costs are identical. Results are summarized in Table 1. Due to lack of space, the complete set of theorems and proofs is available in the companion research report [1]. We discuss a subset of the results below.

Theorem 1. *Without computation cost,* **Binomial-stat** *and* **Tree-dyn** *are Δ-approximation algorithms, and this ratio can be achieved.*

The proof is in [1], and we exhibit here an instance on which the ratio is achieved. Let $d_{i,j} = d$ for $1 \leq i < j \leq n$ and $d_{i,j} = D$ for all remaining $1 \leq j < i \leq n$. With both **Binomial-stat** and **Tree-dyn**, we consider that any processor P_i sends its element to a processor P_j such that $i > j$, which takes a time $D\lceil \log_2(n) \rceil$. The optimal solution, however, consists in avoiding any communication of size D (with total time of $d\lceil \log_2(n) \rceil$).

Theorem 2. *Without computation cost,* **Fibonacci-stat** *is a $(\Delta/\log_2\varphi + \Delta/\lceil \log_2 n \rceil)$-approximation algorithm, where $\varphi = \frac{1+\sqrt{5}}{2}$ is the golden ratio ($1/\log_2\varphi \approx 1.44$).*

Proof. Since computation costs are negligible, the makespan of **Fibonacci-stat** schedule in the worst case is kD, with k the order of the Fibonacci schedule [3]. We know that $n > F_{k+1}$ and, by definition of the Fibonacci numbers, we have $F_{k+1} = \frac{1}{\sqrt{5}}(\varphi^{k+1} - (1-\varphi)^{k+1})$. Since $-1 < 1-\varphi < 0$, it follows that $n > F_{k+1} \geq \frac{1}{\sqrt{5}}(\varphi^{k+1} - (1-\varphi)^2)$ (as soon as $k \geq 1$). We therefore have $\varphi^{k+1} \leq \sqrt{5}n + (1-\varphi)^2$, and $(k+1)\log_2\varphi \leq \log_2 n + \log_2\left(\sqrt{5} + \frac{(1-\varphi)^2}{n}\right)$. Thus,

$$k \leq \frac{\log_2 n}{\log_2 \varphi} + \underbrace{\frac{\log_2\left(\sqrt{5} + \frac{(1-\varphi)^2}{n}\right)}{\log_2 \varphi} - 1}_{\leq 1 \text{ when } n \geq 1}$$

Table 1. Approximation ratios for commutative algorithms. Theorem numbers in parenthesis refer to the theorems in [1].

	$c = 0$	any c	$c = d$
Binomial-stat	Δ (Th. 1)	$\Delta + 1$ (Th. 3)	$(\Delta+1)(1+\frac{1}{\log_2 n})\log_2\varphi$ (Th. 4)
Tree-dyn	Δ (Th. 1)	$\Delta + 1$ (Th. 3)	$(\Delta+1)(1+\frac{1}{\log_2 n})\log_2\varphi$ (Th. 4)
Fibonacci-stat	$\frac{\Delta}{\log_2\varphi} + \frac{\Delta}{\lceil \log_2 n \rceil}$ (Th. 2)	$\frac{\Delta}{\log_2\varphi} + \frac{2\Delta}{\lceil \log_2 n \rceil}$ (Th. 5)	Δ (Th. 5)

Thus, $k \leq \frac{\log_2 n}{\log_2 \varphi} + 1 \leq \frac{\lceil \log_2 n \rceil}{\log_2 \varphi} + 1$. Recall that the lower bound is $d\lceil \log_2 n \rceil$, hence the approximation ratio of $\frac{\Delta}{\log_2 \varphi} + \frac{\Delta}{\lceil \log_2 n \rceil}$. □

3 Markov Chain Analysis

In this section, we assume that communication and computation costs are exponentially distributed (i.e., each $d_{i,j}$ for $1 \leq i, j \leq n$ follows an exponential law with rate λ_d and each c_i for $1 \leq i \leq n$ follows an exponential law with rate λ_c).

With this model, both dynamic approaches, **Tree-dyn** and **Non-Commut-Tree-dyn**, may be analysed using memoryless stochastic processes. Intuitively, each state of those processes is characterized by the number of concurrent communications and computations. A state in which there is neither communication nor computation is an absorbing state that corresponds to the termination of a reduction algorithm. In the initial state, there are $\lfloor \frac{n}{2} \rfloor$ concurrent communications (and one idle machine that is ready to send its value if n is odd). The completion time of an algorithm is then the time to reach the final state. To determine this duration, we use the first-step analysis.

Formally, let P be the transition rate matrix of a continuous-time Markov chain and $s \in S$ be each state. Let $\phi(s)$ be a function on S taking real values (it will be the expected duration spent in state s or its variance). Let w_i be the sum of the application of ϕ to each state taken by the process until the final state is reached starting from state s_i. Then, w_i is determined using the first-state analysis:

$$w_i = \begin{cases} \phi(s_i) & \text{if } s_i \text{ is an absorbing state} \\ \phi(s_i) + \sum_{j=1}^{n} p_{i,j} w_j & \text{otherwise} \end{cases}$$

We apply this analysis to determine the expected duration and the variance of **Tree-dyn** with $\lambda_c = 0$. For clarity, n is assumed to be even (the following analysis can be performed to the cases where n is odd by adapting the initial state).

In this case, each state $s_{i,j}$ is characterized by the number of concurrent communications i and whether the slot containing a ready processor is empty ($j = 0$) or not ($j = 1$). The initial state is $s_{\frac{n}{2},0}$ and the final state is $s_{0,1}$.

There are two kinds of transitions: from state $s_{i,0}$ to state $s_{i-1,1}$ (a communication terminates and the intermediate result of the local reduction is ready to be sent to the next available processor) and from state $s_{i,1}$ to state $s_{i,0}$ (a communication terminates and a new one is initiated with the available processor identified by the slot) for $1 \leq i \leq \frac{n}{2}$. In both cases, the rate of the transition is determined by the number of concurrent communications, that is $i\lambda_d$.

In order to determine the expected completion time of **Tree-dyn** (noted $C_{\textbf{Tree-dyn}}$), we define $\phi(s_{i,j})$ as $\frac{1}{i\lambda_d}$, the expected time spent is state $s_{i,j}$ (zero for state $s_{0,1}$). Therefore,

$$C_{\textbf{Tree-dyn}} = w_{\frac{n}{2},0} = \sum_{i=1}^{\frac{n}{2}} \phi(s_{i,0}) + \phi(s_{i-1,1}) = \sum_{i=1}^{\frac{n}{2}} \frac{1}{i\lambda_d} + \sum_{i=1}^{\frac{n}{2}-1} \frac{1}{i\lambda_d} = \frac{1}{\lambda_d}\left(2H\left(\frac{n}{2}-1\right) + \frac{2}{n}\right),$$

where $H(n)$ is the nth harmonic number.

Similarly, we compute the variance of the completion time (noted $V_{\textbf{Tree-dyn}}$) by defining $\phi(s_{i,j})$ as zero for state $s_{0,1}$ and $\frac{1}{i^2\lambda_d^2}$ otherwise:

$$V_{\textbf{Tree-dyn}} = \frac{1}{\lambda_d^2}\left(2\sum_{i=1}^{\frac{n}{2}-1}\frac{1}{i^2}+\frac{4}{n^2}\right).$$

4 Simulation Results

In this section, we consider that the d_{ij} and c_i costs are distributed according to a gamma distribution, which is a generalization of exponential and Erlang distributions. This distribution has been advocated for modeling job runtimes [11,8]. This distribution is positive and it is possible to specify its expected value (μ_d or μ_c) and standard deviation (σ_d or σ_c) by adjusting its parameters. Using two distributions with two parameters each is a good compromise between a simulation design with a reasonable size and a general model. Additionally, further simulations with Bernoulli distributions concurred with the following observations, suggesting that our conclusions are not strongly sensitive to the distribution choice. Each simulation was performed with an ad-hoc simulator on a desktop computer.

Cost Dispersion Effect. In this first simulation, we are interested in characterizing how the dispersion of the communication costs affects the performance of all methods. In order to simplify this study, no computation cost is considered ($\mu_c = 0$). The dispersion is defined through the coefficient of variation (CV), which is defined as the ratio of the standard deviation over the expected value (this latter is set to 1). The number of processors is $n = 64$ and the time taken by each method is measured over 1 000 000 Monte Carlo (MC) simulations (i.e., simulations have been performed with 1 000 000 distinct seeds).

On a global level, Figure 3 shows the expected performance with distinct CVs. When the heterogeneity is noticeable (CV greater than 1), the performance decreases significantly. In those cases, schedules are mostly affected by a few extreme costs whose importance depends on the CV. Additionally, the variability in the schedule durations is also impacted by the CV (i.e., two successive executions with the same settings may lead to radically different performance depending on the schedule).

Several observations can be made relatively to each method. As expected, **Binomial-stat** is similar to **Tree-dyn** for CVs lower than 10%. In this case, the improvement offered by **Tree-dyn** may not outweigh the advantage of following a static plan in terms of synchronization. For CVs greater than 1, both static approaches perform equally with a similar dispersion. For all CVs, **Tree-dyn** has the best expected performance while **Fibonacci-stat** has the worst, and **Non-Commut-Tree-dyn** has the second best expected performance when the CV is greater than 30%. Finally, when the CV is close to 10, all methods are equivalent as a single communication with a large cost may impact the entire schedule duration. In terms of robustness, we can see that **Fibonacci-stat** and

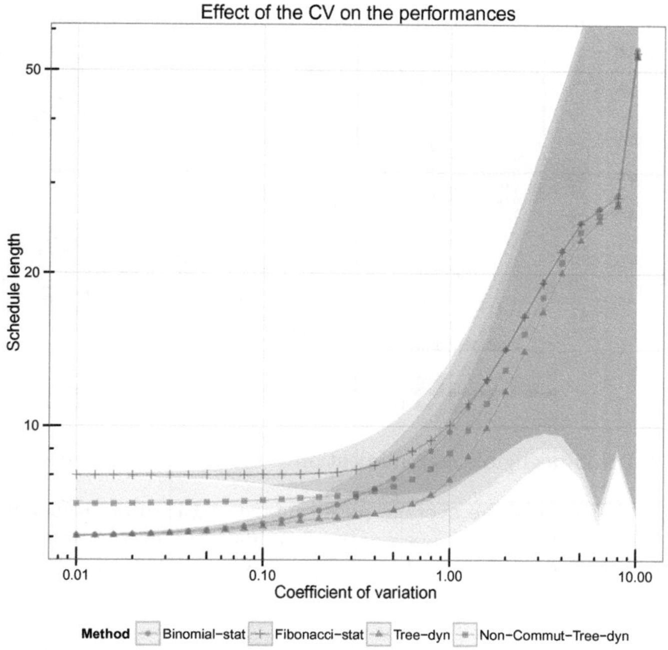

Fig. 3. Average schedule length for each method over 1 000 000 MC simulations with $n = 64$, $\mu_d = 1$, $\mu_c = 0$ and varying coefficients of variation for the communication costs. The lower part of the ribbons corresponds to the 10% quantile while the upper part corresponds to the 90% quantile for each method.

Non-Commut-Tree-dyn are the two best methods for absorbing variations as their expected durations remains stable longer (until the CV reaches 30%). This is due the presence of idleness in their schedules that can be used when required.

Non-Negligible Computation. When considering nonzero computation costs, we reduce the number of parameters by applying the same CV to the computation and to the communication costs (i.e., $\frac{\sigma_c}{\mu_c} = \frac{\sigma_d}{\mu_d}$). As **Fibonacci-stat** is designed for overlapping computations and communications, we characterize the cases when this approach outperforms **Tree-dyn**.

Figure 4(a) shows the improvement of **Tree-dyn** over **Fibonacci-stat** when varying the CV and the ratio $\frac{\mu_c}{\mu_d}$ (the overlapping degree between computations and communications). The contour line with value 1 delimits the area for which **Fibonacci-stat** is better than **Tree-dyn** on average. This occurs when the computation cost is greater than around half the communication cost and when the variability is limited. When the computation costs are low ($\frac{\mu_c}{\mu_d} = 0.1$), the ratio evolution is is consistent with the previous observations.

Figure 4(a) is horizontally symmetrical as any case such that $\frac{\mu_c}{\mu_d} > 1$ is equivalent to the situation where the communication and the computation costs are swapped (and for which $\frac{\mu_c}{\mu_d} < 1$). These costs can be exchanged because a communication is always followed by a reduction operation.

Non-Commutative Operation. Finally, we assess the performance of **Non-Commut-Tree-dyn** by comparing it to all other methods that support a non-commutative operation when varying the dispersion and the overlapping degree as in the previous study.

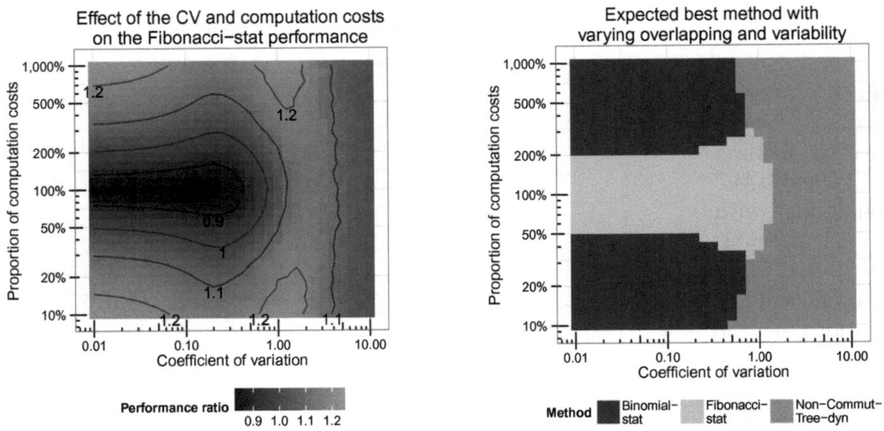

(a) Non-negligible communication (b) Non-commutative operation

Fig. 4. Ratio of the average performance of **Fibonacci-stat** and **Tree-dyn** (a) and method with the best average performance (b) over 1 000 MC simulations for each square with $n = 64$, $\mu_d = 1$, $\frac{\sigma_c}{\mu_c} = \frac{\sigma_d}{\mu_d}$, varying coefficients of variation for the costs and varying $\frac{\mu_c}{\mu_d}$

Figure 4(b) shows the method with the best average performance when varying the CV and the ratio $\frac{\mu_c}{\mu_d}$. We see that **Non-Commut-Tree-dyn** has the best performance when the cost dispersion is large. Additionally, the transition from **Binomial-stat** to **Fibonacci-stat** is when the computation cost reaches half the communication cost (as on Figure 4(a)). With low computation costs ($\frac{\mu_c}{\mu_d} = 0.1$), the results are also consistent with Figure 3.

5 Conclusion

In this paper, we have studied the problem of performing a non-clairvoyant reduction on a distributed heterogeneous platform. Specifically, we have compared the performance of traditional static algorithms, which build an optimized reduction tree beforehand, against dynamic algorithms, which organize the reduction at runtime. Our study includes both commutative and non-commutative reductions. We have first proposed approximation ratios for all commutative algorithms using a worst-case analysis. Then, we have proposed a Markov chain analysis for dynamic algorithms. Finally, we have evaluated all algorithms through extensive simulations to show when dynamic algorithms become more interesting than static ones. We have outlined that dynamic algorithms generally achieve better makespan, except when the heterogeneity is limited and for specific communication costs (no communication cost for **Binomial-stat**, communication costs equivalent to computation costs for **Fibonacci-stat**). The worst-case analysis has also confirmed this last observation.

As future work, we plan to investigate more complex communication models, such as specific network topologies. It would also be interesting to design a better dynamic algorithm for non-commutative reductions, which avoids the situation when many processors are idle but cannot initiate a communication since no neighboring processors are free.

References

1. Benoit, A., Canon, L.-C., Marchal, L.: Non-clairvoyant reduction algorithms for heterogeneous platforms. Research report RR-8315, INRIA (June 2013)
2. Benoit, A., Dufossé, F., Gallet, M., Robert, Y., Gaujal, B.: Computing the throughput of probabilistic and replicated streaming applications. In: Proc. of SPAA, Symp. on Parallelism in Algorithms and Architectures, pp. 166–175 (2010)
3. Canon, L.-C., Antoniu, G.: Scheduling Associative Reductions with Homogeneous Costs when Overlapping Communications and Computations. Rapport de recherche RR-7898, INRIA (March 2012)
4. Canon, L.-C., Jeannot, E.: Evaluation and optimization of the robustness of dag schedules in heterogeneous environments. IEEE Trans. Parallel Distrib. Syst. 21(4), 532–546 (2010)
5. Canon, L.-C., Jeannot, E., Sakellariou, R., Zheng, W.: Comparative Evaluation of the Robustness of DAG Scheduling Heuristics. In: Proceedings of CoreGRID Integration Workshop, Heraklion-Crete, Greece (April 2008)
6. Cormen, T.H., Leiserson, C.E., Rivest, R.L., Stein, C.: Introduction to Algorithms, 3rd edn. The MIT Press (2009)
7. Dean, J., Ghemawat, S.: Mapreduce: Simplified data processing on large clusters. Communications of the ACM 51(1), 107–113 (2008)
8. Feitelson, D.: Workload modeling for computer systems performance evaluation. Book Draft, Version 0.38 (2013)
9. Legrand, A., Marchal, L., Robert, Y.: Optimizing the steady-state throughput of scatter and reduce operations on heterogeneous platforms. Journal of Parallel and Distributed Computing 65(12), 1497–1514 (2005)
10. Liu, P., Kuo, M.-C., Wang, D.-W.: An Approximation Algorithm and Dynamic Programming for Reduction in Heterogeneous Environments. Algorithmica 53(3), 425–453 (2009)
11. Lublin, U., Feitelson, D.G.: The workload on parallel supercomputers: modeling the characteristics of rigid jobs. J. Parallel Distrib. Comp. 63(11), 1105–1122 (2003)
12. Pjesivac-Grbovic, J., Angskun, T., Bosilca, G., Fagg, G., Gabriel, E., Dongarra, J.: Performance analysis of MPI collective operations. In: IEEE International Parallel and Distributed Processing Symposium, IPDPS (April 2005)
13. Rabenseifner, R.: Optimization of Collective Reduction Operations. In: Bubak, M., van Albada, G.D., Sloot, P.M.A., Dongarra, J. (eds.) ICCS 2004. LNCS, vol. 3036, pp. 1–9. Springer, Heidelberg (2004)
14. Thakur, R., Rabenseifner, R., Gropp, W.: Optimization of Collective communication operations in MPICH. International Journal of High Performance Computing Applications 19, 49–66 (2005)
15. Zaharia, M., Konwinski, A., Joseph, A., Katz, R., Stoica, I.: Improving mapreduce performance in heterogeneous environments. In: Proc. of the 8th USENIX Conf. on Operating Systems Design and Implementation, pp. 29–42 (2008)

Managing Heterogeneous Processor Machine Dependencies in Computer Network Applications*

Ralph Duncan, Peder Jungck, Kenneth Ross, Jim Frandeen, and Greg Triplett

CloudShield Technologies, A Science Applications International Corporation (SAIC) Company
212 Gibraltar Drive, Sunnyvale, CA 94089 USA
rduncan@cloudshield.com

Abstract. Executing complex network packet applications typically requires using network processors and parallel processing to handle packet transmission speeds of 1 gigabit per second and beyond. Heterogeneous computing approaches also employ specialized coprocessors, such as associative memory processors for flow matching and regular expression (regex) processors for packet payload searching. Our goals for this kind of heterogeneous processing are to free application developers from hardware-specific details and to develop systems in which we can deploy new hardware and software components in modular, plug-and-play fashion. Our initial contribution to realizing these goals involves (1) expressing classic packet operations in a C dialect as C/C++-style operators; (2) compiling user code into bytecodes for a packet-processing virtual machine that hides machine-specific details; and (3) interpreting the bytecodes with microcoded interpreters that orchestrate an ensemble of heterogeneous processors on the users' behalf.

1 Introduction

As computer networks continue their relentless speed increases the need for increasing packet processing speeds moves in tandem. Since the late 1990s network processing vendors have responded to the need for speed and flexibility by using *network processors* that are optimized for classic packet processing tasks. These processors are often used in conjunction with separate, specialized *coprocessors* [1, 2]. As Douglas Comer observed in a popular textbook [1], designers have generated a variety of architectures that typically use some combination of specialized instructions, parallel processing and pipelining. His 2005 survey of commercial architectures [2] had these categories:

* Intel is a trademark of Intel Corporation in the United States and/or other countries. Broadcom® is a registered trademark of Broadcom Corporation in the United States and/or other countries. Xilinx is a trademark of Xilinx Inc. in the United States and/or other countries. OCTEON® is a registered trademark of Cavium. AMCC is a registered trademark of Applied Micro Circuits Corporation. IDT is a trademark of Integrated Device Technology, Inc. packetC® is a registered trademark of CloudShield Technologies, Inc. in the United States and/or other countries.

D. an Mey et al. (Eds.): Euro-Par 2013 Workshops, LNCS 8374, pp. 280–289, 2014.

- Embedded processors with special instructions for packet processing
- Parallel processors, assisted by specialized coprocessors
- Parallel pipelines of either homogenous processors or heterogeneous ones

Our hardware approach falls into the category for parallel processors, augmented with coprocessors. Our basic building blocks are the following:

- Network processors (*microengines* by Intel) with a reduced instruction set computer (RISC) processor as their host
- Xilinx, Inc.® Virtex® 5 field programmable gate arrays (FPGAs) to perform specialized functions e.g., *ingress processing,* to identify packet *headers*
- Ternary content addressable memory (TCAM) chips (associative memory processors) to match key header fields' contents
- Regular expression *(regex)* processors to match packet *payload* contents to strings specified as regular expressions.

We use the kinds of processors often seen in commercial systems. Thus, our contribution is not a particular ensemble of specialized processors but the use of high-level languages to isolate chip-specifics and interpreters to manage heterogeneity:

- Expressing packet operations with high-level language operators
- Compiling programs into machine-independent bytecodes for packet processinge
- Interpreting bytecode programs via multiple copies of a microcoded interpreter, running in parallel and orchestrating diverse coprocessors' actions

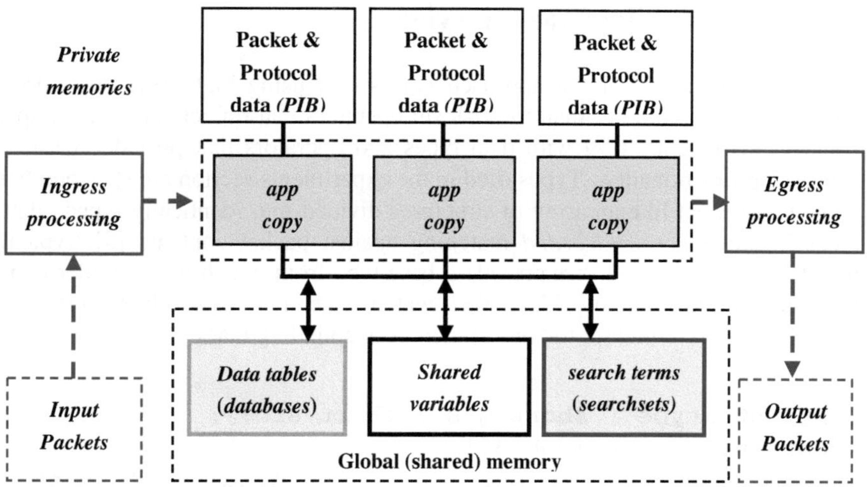

Fig. 1. Parallel packet processing model and language features (in italics). Copyright CloudShield Technologies, 2013.

The paper reviews our programming model, then traces our extended data types and operators from their high-level forms in packetC® [3] through domain-specific bytecodes to their implementation by specialized coprocessors. We present experiments then end by reviewing related work and summarizing.

2 Parallel Processing Model

Our ultimate goal is a flexible system in which we can swap one coprocessor for another or substitute a software component for a coprocessor. To support this, our model of parallel packet processing has the following characteristics.

- It uses coarse-grained parallelism at the packet level to hide machine specifics.
- The host system is expected to provide classic ingress and egress processing (see Fig. 1) but the model does not specify how this to be done.
- Capabilities are specified for matching packet header fields and searching packet payloads but their implementation is not.

Developers express parallelism at a coarse-grained level with a program that completely processes one packet at a time. Thus, we allocate each packet to a specific copy of the application (a *context*) and runs the contexts simultaneously in single program multiple data (SPMD) fashion. Using coarse-grain parallelism frees developers from fine-grain, processor-specific mechanics, like synchronizing low-level tasks.

3 packetC Language Overview

The first component of the approach consists of using high-level operators in the packetC language, rather than lower-level operators that reflect coprocessor specifics. packetC [3] extends C99 with data types and operators that provide classic packet processing functionality. Types used in the experiments section are sketched below.

Databases act like an array of structures divided into identically typed "data" and "mask" halves for *wildcarded* matching against packet contents [5] (typically, to match header fields). Users provide a base type from which the compiler constructs the data and mask halves. Users then match structures against those portions of the data half that have bits set to "on" in their corresponding mask.

```
struct stype { short dest; short src;};
database stype myDB[50];
// myDB element layout is { stype data; stype mask;};
rownum = myDB.match( myStruct ); // do masked search
```

Searchsets are aggregates of strings or regular expressions that are matched against the contents of the packet *payload* via C++-style *methods* [6]. The first of the searchset items to be found is reported in a result structure with position information.

```
searchset pets[3][3] = {"cat", "dog", "owl" };
SearchResult ansStruct;
try {  // match vs. a 3-byte slice of packet
   ansStruct = pets.match( currPkt[64:66] );
}
catch ( ERR_SET_NOMATCH ) {…}
```

4 Translation to Bytecodes

Our approach's second key consists of translating high-level packetC operations into machine-independent *bytecodes* (Fig 2). Just as packetC hides processor specifics from application developers, the bytecodes hide them from the tool-chain and runtime support system to isolate the effects of replacing accelerators with new processors or software equivalents. A single bytecode may express a complex operation that will be implemented by a specialized coprocessor. Due to space constraints we show only a human-readable version of the database match bytecode as a representative example.

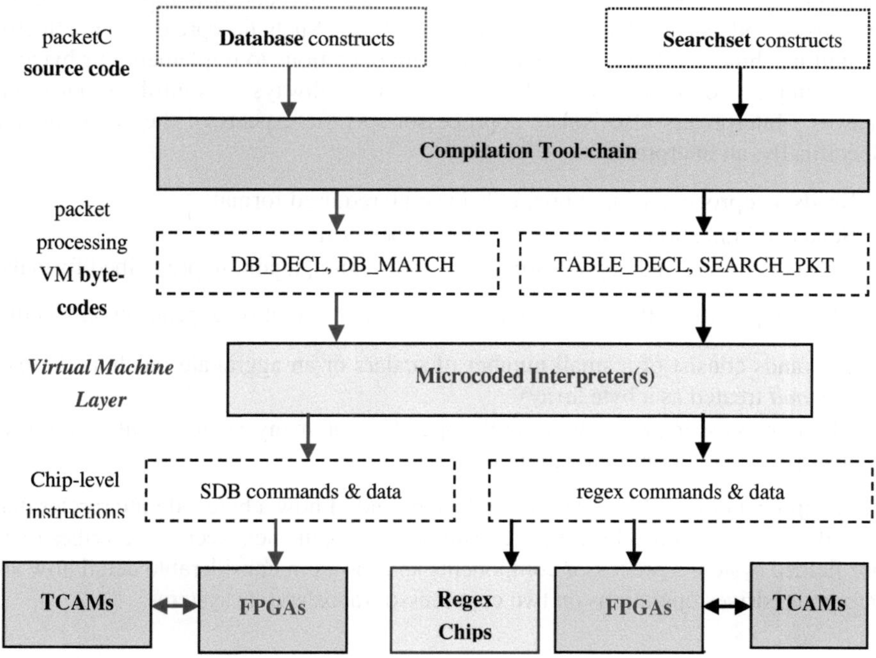

Fig. 2. Example bytecode translation flow for databases and searchsets. Copyright CloudShield Technologies, 2013.

In the example below, a packetC *record* – a structure with data and mask halves – is matched against a database of like elements via a complex DBMATCH bytecode.

```
// packetC code - database match
struct stype { short dest; short src;};
database stype myDB[50];
rownum = myDB.match( myRec ); // match contents of myDB
// Bytecode - database decl, then MATCH operation
DBASE_DECL  myDB [500] 5 // 5 is the ID
DB_MATCH Id, maskKind, inData, inMask, rownum
//    Id: integer indicating with DB to use
//    maskKind: scenario indicator
//    inData: data to match
//    inMask: to combine w/ each element mask
//    rownum: 32bit integer to rec matching DB row #
```

The next section describes how we use interpreters to turn the bytecodes above into coprocessor actions.

5 Interpreter as Heterogeneous Processor Orchestrator

Our approach's third component consists of using microcoded interpreters to execute bytecodes and encapsulate coprocessor specifics. Such interpreters can effectively exploit machine-level resources and fine-grain operations to implement our bytecodes. For example, the interpreters exploit various data pathways to control specialized processors. Interpreters also isolate coprocessor-specific aspects of the communication. Specifically, an interpreter

- Sends a coprocessor input operands in some required format
- Sends an indication of which operation to perform
- Receives results and coprocessor error information, again, in prescribed formats

The complexity of these operations may vary considerably, depending on whether

- Operands consist of a small number of scalars or an aggregate (such as the packet *payload* treated as a byte array)
- The coprocessor performs a single operation or many (which must therefore be distinguished in communications)

An appreciation of how such dependencies and of how a bytecode interpreter manages them is best gained by concrete example. Thus, the next section describes one of our fielded system's processor components and shows in considerable detail how an interpreter drives operations on two coprocessor (accelerator) systems.

6 Implementing Interpreter and Coprocessor Communication

Our products, such as the PN41 [7], use multi-core network processing units (NPUs) optimized for packet operations. The PN41 uses an IXP 2800 with 16 *microengines* as its NPU Although the IXP is often programmed in fine-grain parallel fashion [8], we use the coarse-grained approach described in section 2, with 95 microengine *contexts* running an interpreter and other contexts providing house-keeping functions.

These interpreters interact with multiple kinds of coprocessor to implement operations originally coded as packetC operators, then translated to bytecode form.

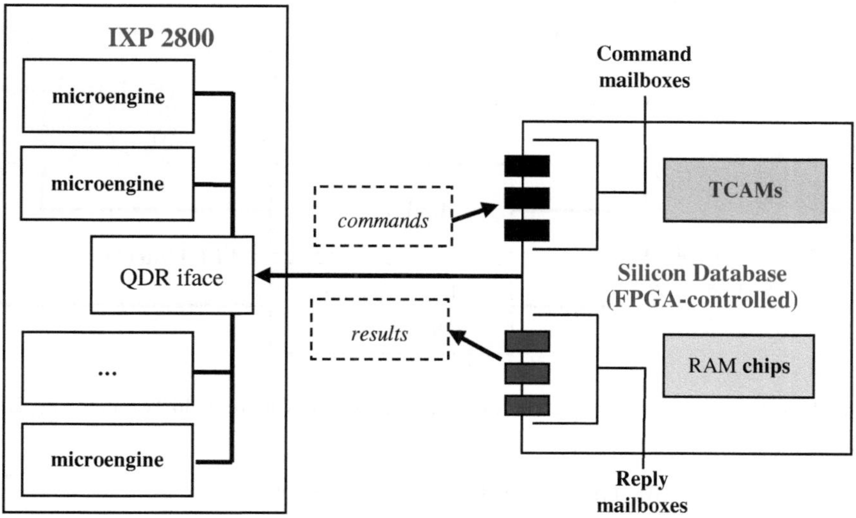

Fig. 3. PN41 Communications between IXP-based interpreters and TCAM chips. Copyright CloudShield Technologies, 2013.

In our first example a Xilinx, Inc.® Virtex® 5 FPGA controls a *silicon database* (SDB) that uses Broadcom NL 5512 TCAM chips to match packetC *databases*. When an interpreter encounters a **match** operation, these actions occur (Fig. 3):

- The interpreter uses a *quad data rate* (QDR) interface to send a match command (in a control language) to a command mailbox associated with the SDB controller.
- The interpreter passes the data to compare and ID of the database to use.
- Depending on the operation, the interpreter may pass a bit mask to use.
- The SDB replies with acknowledgement signals and the results data.

The TCAM performs a given match on all the relevant database entries in parallel, a significant performance benefit. However, moving operands and results back and forth, as well as managing the operation can consume significant time. In practice, optimizing this data movement is an art and science in its own right.

Our second example involves using IDT PAX.port 2500 *content inspection engines* (regex processors) to implement packetC *searchset* **find** operations, typically to search for terms in the packet's *payload* [10]. Such a searchset is an array composed entirely of strings or regular expressions.

Searchset contents are precompiled into a set of regex rules and loaded into a *pattern memory*. As Fig. 4 shows, an interpreter running on a microengine ships command data and the bits within which to search (typically, a slice of the packet payload) to the subsystem via another specialized FPGA. The regex subsystem returns the index of the first searchset element to be found (if any), as well as location data.

The next section presents two experiments that show that this kind of microcoded interpretation with coprocessors achieves high speeds.

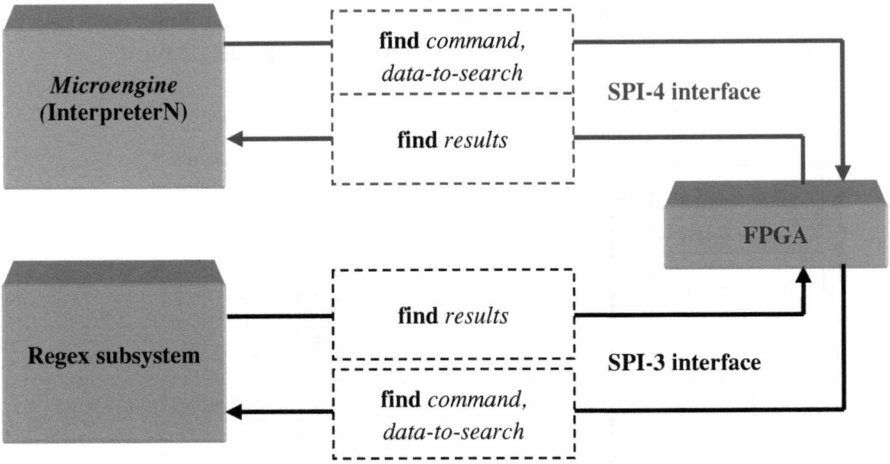

Fig. 4. Searching packet data via a regex system. Copyright CloudShield Technologies, 2013.

7 Experiments Emphasizing Coprocessors

The experiments used a CloudShield PN41 [7] 10 gigabit Ethernet blade to run packetC applications and an IXIA® XM12 traffic generator [11] to produce network traffic at a maximum of 10 gigabits per second (Gbps). Each experiment involved microcode interpreting bytecodes and invoking coprocessors for key operations.

Fig 5(a) shows an experiment that matched a sequence of bytes from a specific packet payload location of each packet against a packetC *database* of 30,000 stored patterns. This database and the high-level **match** operation used the bytecodes and TCAM subsystem shown in sections 4 and 6 above (see also Fig. 3). For this scenario the system produces a maximum output rate of 8.85 Gbps. (See [6] for details).

The experiment shown in Fig 5(b) involved searching each entire packet for the presence of one or more patterns, defined by a packetC *searchset* of 10,000 simple patterns – each containing a wild card substring. This searchset and the high-level **find** operation used the bytecodes and regex subsystem shown in sections 4 and 6 above (see Fig. 4). The maximum speed achieved, 5.9 Gbps, is expected, since the regex subsystem has a maximum speed of roughly 5 Gbps and most of this application's time is spent in the subsystem. For further details, the packetC source constructs and related experiments are described in an analysis of searchsets [6].

A traditional presentation might report comparative metrics for alternative techniques, typically from experimental prototypes. In this paper we report the data points that we have, which are from a commercial product line with more than 10 years in the fields. Our claim is not that techniques we describe are superior in performance to particular alternatives but, instead, that the portability and retargetability benefits of this approach are gained while performing deep packet inspection (DPI) at speeds of two to nine Gbps, which we believe to be state-of-the-practice DPI at this time.

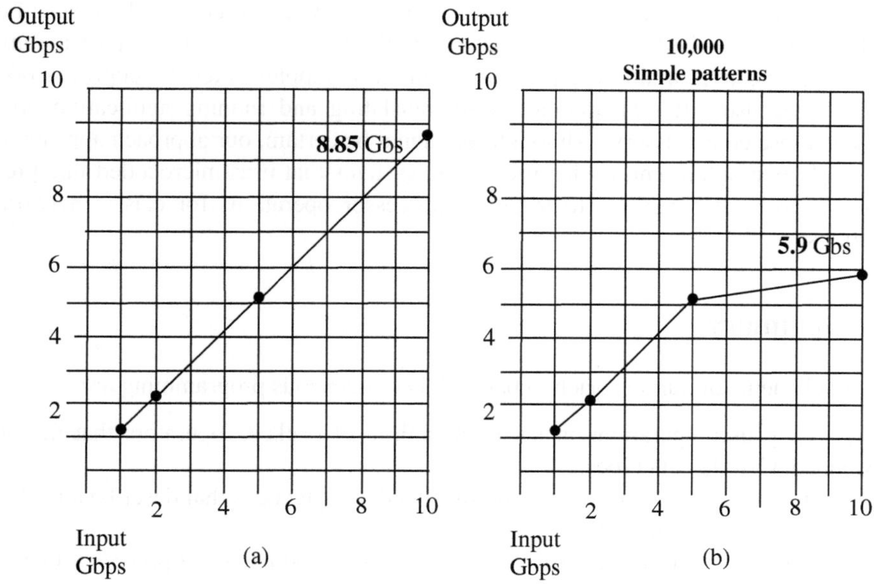

Fig. 5. (a) Using a TCAM coprocessor to match a bit pattern. (b) Using a regex coprocessor to search for string matches. Copyright CloudShield Technologies, 2013.

8 Related Work

Intel Corporation®'s Microengine C [8] is a C dialect targeted to the IXP network processor family. Its processing model involves breaking programs into multiple threads that are partitioned across *microengines*. The user manages communications among threads and swaps out tasks. Microengine C reflects a variety of machine-specific IXP features, such as memory and register classes.

J. Wagner and R. Leupers describe a processor-specific C dialect geared to the Infineon network processor in [12]. Language's extensions let the user map protocol headers to special registers and manipulate those values via operands with arbitrary bit-widths. A collection of compiler *intrinsics* lets users exploit these capabilities.

L. George and M. Blume described the NOVA language for the IXP network processor in [13]. NOVA has features for specifying header representation, including a *layout* construct for packed and unpacked forms and an *overlay* construct for alternative organizations within a layout. Network Protocol Description Language Vin, et al. proposed the Baker programming language [14], a C dialect augmented by data-flow concepts, which emphasized pipelining packet data from function to function.

Cavium Networks, Inc. makes Octeon® networking and communications processor families [15] that use specialized processors for regular expression processing and fast matching. Their software approach appears to use C/C++, augmented by application programming interfaces (APIs) and libraries. AMCC® has also produced network processors (e.g., nP3700) that feature multiple network processing cores and specialized coprocessors, including regex processors [16] and TCAMs [17].

MicroEngineC and C for the Infineon® chip extend C to include machine-specific details, whereas packetC disguises machine particulars. Like AMCC and Cavium, our architecture uses multi-core processing engines, supplemented by coprocessors. However, we use different approaches to translating and running application programs on those coprocessors. Although we cannot be certain, our approach appears to be the only one on current, packet processing systems that uses microcoded interpreters or high-level bytecodes to trigger coprocessor operations for classic network operations.

9 Summary

The key elements of our approach to parallel, heterogeneous programming are

- Expressing user operations in terms of high-level packetC operators that act on extended, C-style data types.
- Compiling user programs to machine-independent bytecodes that describe a packet processing virtual machine.
- Using microcoded interpreters to process bytecodes and trigger coprocessor operations as needed.

packetC high-level operators have proven easy to use and to teach. Both packetC and bytecodes have survived chipset and NPU changes without requiring tool-chain redesign or user code recompilation. The interpreter scheme requires detailed microcode, NPU and coprocessor expertise but only from tool-chain developers, not application code developers. Freed from arcane processor details, users can concentrate on solving problems in terms of high-level networking application domain constructs.

We believe the techniques described above, both individually and in combination, offer significant benefits to other heterogeneous processing practitioners.

Acknowledgements. Mary Pham, Scott Tillman, Greg Triplett, Jim Frandeen and Minh Nguyen made key contributions to coprocessor subsystems, loaders, and the interpreters. The export approval number for the paper is 13-SAIC-0517-1012.

References

1. Comer, D.: Network Systems Design Using Network Processors, Intel 2xxx Version. Prentice Hall, Upper Saddle River (2006)
2. Comer, D.: Network Processors: Programmable Technology for Building Network Systems. The Internet Protocol Journal 7(4) (2004)
3. Jungck, P., Duncan, R., Mulcahy, D.: packetC Programming. Apress, New York (2011)
4. Duncan, R., Jungck, P., Ross, K.: A paradigm for processing network protocols in parallel. In: Hsu, C.-H., Yang, L.T., Park, J.H., Yeo, S.-S. (eds.) ICA3PP 2010, Part I. LNCS, vol. 6082, pp. 52–67. Springer, Heidelberg (2010)
5. Duncan, R., Jungck, P., Ross, K.: packetC language and parallel processing of masked databases. In: Proceedings of the 39th Intl. Conf. on Parallel Processing, San Diego, USA, September 13-16, pp. 472–481. IEEE (2010)

6. Duncan, R., Jungck, P., Ross, K., Tillman, S.: Packet Content matching with packetC Searchsets. In: Proceedings of the 16th Intl. Conf. on Parallel and Distributed Systems, Shanghai, China, December 8-10, pp. 180–188 (2010)
7. International Business Machines Corporation. IBM Blade Center PN41. Product datasheet available from IBM Systems and Technology Group, Route 100, Somers, New York, USA 10589 (2008)
8. Johnson, E.K., Kunze, A.R.: IXP 2400/2800 Programming: The Complete Microengine Coding Guide. Intel Press, Hillsboro (2003)
9. Broadcom Corporation, NL5064, NL5128, NL5256 and NL5512 Proprietary Interface, Knowledge-based Processors, `http://www.broadcom.com/products/Knowledge-Based-Processors/Layers-2-4/NL5000-Family` (retrieved on April 30, 2013)
10. Chao, H.J., Liu, B.: High Performance Switches and Routers, pp. 562–564. John Wiley and Sons, Hoboken (2007)
11. XIA. XM12 High Performance Chassis, `http://www.ixia.com.com/pdfs/datasheets/ch_optixia_xm12.pdf` (retrieved on July 25, 2013)
12. Wagner, J., Leupers, R.: C compiler design for a network processor. IEEE Trans. on CAD 20(11), 1–7 (2001)
13. George, L., Blume, M.: Taming the IXP network processor. In: Proceedings of the ACM SIGPLAN 2003 Conference on Programming Language Design and Implementation, San Diego, California, USA, pp. 26–37. ACM (June 2003)
14. Vin, H.M., Mudigonda, J., Jason, J., Johnson, E.J., Ju, R., Kunze, A., Lian, R.: A Programming Environment for Packet-processing Systems: Design Considerations. In: Network Processor Design: Issues and Practices, vol. 3, pp. 145–173. Morgan Kaufmann (2004)
15. Cavium Networks, Inc. Octeon Multi-Core Processor Family, `http://www.cavium.com/OCTEON_MIPS64.html` (retrieved December 13, 2012)
16. Integrated Device Technology, Inc. IDT Strengthens Collaboration with AMCC by Delivering NSE Development Kit with AMCC Network Processor Evaluation System. News release of (March 1, 2004), `http://ir.idt.com/releasedetail.cfm?ReleaseID=414510` (retrieved December 12, 2012)
17. Melnick, R., Morris, K.: AMCC nPcore NISC Architecture. In: Franklin, M.A., Crowley, P., Hadimioglu, H., Onufryk, P.Z. (eds.) Network Processor Design: Issues and Practices, vol. 2, pp. 327–342. Morgan Kaufmann (2003)

Fourth International Workshop on High-Performance Bioinformatics and Biomedicine (HiBB 2013)

Mario Cannataro

Program Chair

High-throughput technologies (e.g. Next Generation Sequencing, Microarray and Mass Spectrometry) and clinical diagnostic tools (e.g. Magnetic Resonance Imaging) are producing an increasing amount of experimental and clinical data, yielding to the so called age of Big Data in Biosciences. However the storage, preprocessing and analysis of experimental data is becoming the main bottleneck of the biomedical analysis pipeline. Parallel computing and high-performance infrastructures are more and more used in all phases of life sciences research, e.g. for storing and preprocessing large experimental data, for the simulation of biological systems, for data exploration and visualization, for data integration, and for knowledge discovery.

The current bioinformatics scenario is characterized by the application of well established techniques, such as parallel computing on multicore architectures and grid computing, as well as by the application of emerging computational models such as graphics processing and cloud computing. Large scale infrastructures such as grids or clouds are mainly used to store in an efficient manner and to share in an easy way, the huge experimental data produced in life sciences, while parallel computing allows the efficient analysis of huge data. In particular, novel parallel architectures such as GPUs and emerging programming models such as MapReduce, may overcome the limits posed by conventional computers to the analysis of large amounts of data.

The fourth edition of the Workshop on *High-Performance Bioinformatics and Biomedicine* (HiBB) aimed to bring together scientists in the fields of high performance computing and life sciences to discuss the parallel implementation of bioinformatics algorithms, the deployment of biomedical applications on high performance infrastructures, and the organization of large scale databases in biology and medicine. As in the past, also this year the workshop has been organized in conjunction with Euro-Par, the main European (but international) conference on all aspects of parallel processing. The workshop included the invited talk *Epidemic Data Mining: Global Knowledge without Global Communication* that was held by Prof. Giuseppe Di Fatta (University of Reading, UK), and presentations were organized in two sessions, *Large-Scale High-Performance Biomedicine* and *Software Platforms for Bioinformatics and Systems Biology*.

The first session, *Large-Scale High-Performance Biomedicine*, comprised the invited talk and one paper. The invited talk *Epidemic Data Mining: Global Knowledge without Global Communication* discussed the emerging Epidemc Data Mining model, that combines Parallel Data Mining and Epidemic protocols, i.e. a type

D. an Mey et al. (Eds.): Euro-Par 2013 Workshops, LNCS 8374, pp. 290–291, 2014.

of randomised protocols which can provide statistical guarantees of accuracy and consistency of global aggregates in decentralised and asynchronous networks. As a case study, the invited talk presented Epidemic K-Means, that is a distributed and fully-decentralised formulation of K-Means based on Epidemic protocols. In the paper *Heterogeneous Platforms Programming for High Performance Medical Imaging Processing*, Renan Sales Barros et al. evaluated the potential of heterogeneous platforms (e.g. platforms including CPUs, GPUs, and FPGAs) to improve the processing speed of medical imaging applications. In particular, the authors explained the use of a new framework named *FlowCL* that facilitates the development of parallel applications for heterogeneous platforms.

The second session, *Software Platforms for Bioinformatics and Systems Biology*, comprised two papers respectively on genomics data management and on systems biology simulation. In the paper *Transparent Incremental Updates for Genomics Data Analysis Pipelines*, Pedersen et al. proposed a transparent file-based approach, implemented in the *GeStore* system, for adding incremental update capabilities to genomics data analysis tools. The paper showed that using GeStore it is easy to add incremental updates to genomics data processing pipelines, and that incremental updates can reduce the computation time. In the paper *msPar: A Parallel Coalescent Simulator*, Montemuino et al. presented *msPar*, a parallel implementation of the *ms* coalescent simulation program. msPar uses a Master-Worker scheme with on-demand scheduling and MPI to run on an HPC cluster.

The workshop was concluded by a panel on *High Performance Bioinformatics and Biomedicine* chaired by Mario Cannataro. The goal of the panel was to discuss emerging topics and problems regarding the application of High Performance Computing techniques, such as Grid and Cloud Computing, to biomedical, bioinformatics, and systems biology applications. The four panelists, Renan Sales Barros, Giuseppe Di Fatta, Antonio Espinosa, and Edvard Pedersen, discussed the following topics: (i) trends in data mining for e-science; (ii) Apache Hadoop and Google Grid Engine for bioinformatics; (iii) workflow management for bioinformatics.

This post-workshop proceedings includes the final revised versions of the HiBB papers and invited talk, taking the feedback from reviewers and workshop audience into account. The program chair sincerely thanks the Program Committee members and the following additional reviewers: Giuseppe Agapito, Marco Aldinucci, Claudia Misale, and Alessia Sarica, for the time and expertise they put into the reviewing work, the Euro-Par organization, for providing the opportunity to arrange the HiBB workshop in conjunction with the Euro-Par 2013 conference, and all the workshop attendees who contributed to a lively day.

October 2013 Mario Cannataro

Convergence Detection in Epidemic Aggregation

Pasu Poonpakdee[1], Neriman Gamze Orhon[2,⋆], and Giuseppe Di Fatta[1]

[1] The University of Reading, Whiteknights, Reading, Berkshire, RG6 6AY, UK
{p.poonpakdee,g.difatta}@reading.ac.uk
[2] Yaşar University, Üniversite Caddesi, Ağaçli Yol, Bornova, İzmir PK. 35100
gamzeorhon@gmail.com

Abstract. Emerging challenges in ubiquitous networks and computing include the ability to extract useful information from a vast amount of data which are intrinsically distributed. Epidemic protocols are a bio-inspired approach that provide a communication and computation paradigm for large and extreme-scale networked systems. These protocols are based on randomised communication, which provides robustness, scalability and probabilistic guarantees on convergence speed and accuracy. This work investigates the convergence detection problem in epidemic aggregation, which is critical to minimise the execution time for a given approximation error of the estimated aggregate. Global and local convergence criteria are presented and compared. The experimental analysis shows that a local convergence criterion can be adopted to minimise and adapt the number of cycles in epidemic aggregation protocols.

Keywords: epidemic protocols, gossip-based protocols, extreme-scale computing, decentralised algorithms.

In extreme-scale distributed systems, computing and spreading global information is a particularly challenging task. Centralized paradigms are not suitable for this task, as they introduce bottlenecks and failure intolerance; fully decentralised and fault-tolerant approached are needed.

The data aggregation problem refers to the computation of a global aggregation function in a network of nodes, where each node is holding a local value. Examples of global aggregation functions are the sum, the average, the maximum, the minimum, random samples, quantiles, etc. The goal of data aggregation in networks is the determination at each node of the exact value, or of a good approximation, of a global aggregation function over the distributed set of values.

Several distributed aggregation protocols have been proposed. They can be divided into two main classes: tree-based protocols and Epidemic (or Gossip-based) protocols. The former performs a tree-based communication throughout a tree overlay structure (e.g., [1]). Tree-based protocols support a minimum

⋆ This work was carried out while N. G. Orhon was at the University of Reading, UK, for a placement of the Erasmus Training Programme (June-Sept. 2013).

D. an Mey et al. (Eds.): Euro-Par 2013 Workshops, LNCS 8374, pp. 292–300, 2014.

number of communications, but can be affected by single points of failure and require additional communication overhead to manage the overlay structure in dynamic environments. The second class is based on Epidemic protocols, which are robust and scalable, as they use a randomised communication paradigm.

Recently, it has been shown that epidemic protocols can be adopted for the formulation of data mining algorithms [2, 3], even under node churn and network failures [4].

Epidemic protocols have communication costs usually greater than tree-based protocols. In order to achieve a given approximation error, epidemic aggregation protocols have to be run for a sufficient number of rounds and their convergence speed depends on several factors. Limiting the number of protocol rounds is an important aspect for their adoption in practical applications. This work investigates adaptive criteria that detect the convergence to the desired approximation error and minimise the overall duration of the epidemic aggregation.

The rest of the paper is organised as follows. Epidemic protocols are presented in section 1. Section 2 introduces the convergence detection criteria for epidemic aggregation protocols. Section 3 presents the results of simulations and a comparative analysis. Finally, section 4 provides some conclusive remarks.

1 Epidemic Aggregation

Let us consider a networked system where each node i $(1 \leq i \leq N)$ holds some local value x_i and needs to compute a global aggregation function $f(x_1, \ldots, x_N)$. Local approximations of the global aggregate function can be obtained with an epidemic aggregation protocol.

Epidemic protocols are typically described as periodic and synchronous with a cycle length Δ_T and are executed for a number of cycles T_{max}. At all discrete times t $(0 < t \leq T_{max})$, each node independently exchanges information with a peer, which is ideally selected uniformly at random among all nodes in the system. This selection operation is provided by a peer sampling service, the membership protocol, which is also implemented with an epidemic approach. Nodes periodically exchange their local state and the reception of a remote state triggers the update of the local state at a node. The update produces a reduction of the variance in the estimates in the system. The definitions of local state, type of messages and update operation depend on the particular aggregation protocol and the target global function. A good approximation of the global aggregate function can be obtained at every node within a number of protocol cycles.

Membership protocols and aggregation protocols are briefly reviewed in the following sections.

1.1 Membership Protocols

The node sampling service is considered a fundamental abstraction in distributed systems [5]. In large-scale systems nodes cannot build and maintain a complete directory of memberships. A membership protocol builds and maintains a partial view of the system, which is used to provide the random node selection service. The distributed set of views implicitly defines an overlay topology. A membership protocol periodically and randomly changes the local views, thus generating a sequence of random overlay topologies.

The required assumptions are that the physical network topology is a connected graph, a routing protocol is available and an initialisation mechanism for the overlay topology is provided.

Memberships protocols can be seen as a distributed implementation of multiple random walks. After sufficiently many cycles the entries in the local view are uniformly distributed. In regular connected graphs, random walks converge to uniform independent samples of the node set in a polynomial number of steps. In expander graphs, i.e. sparse graphs that are very well connected, random walks converge to the uniform distribution in $O(log(N))$ [6]. For this reason, the initial overlay topology is typically not a concern and simulations, including those presented in this work, often adopt a random graph.

The membership protocol adopted in this work is *CYCLON* [7], which has been chosen for its simplicity, effectiveness and low communication cost. In a preliminary analysis, no significant improvement was found in adopting more accurate and complex approaches (e.g.,[27]).

1.2 Aggregation Protocols

Several epidemic aggregation protocols have been proposed (e.g., [8, 9, 10, 11]). In the Push-Sum Protocol (PSP) [8], the local state of a node i is represented as a pair $\langle s_{i,t}, w_{i,t} \rangle$: the initial value $s_{i,0}$ and weight $w_{i,0}$ depend on the global aggregation function to be computed. For example, for computing the global average, $s_{i,0}$ is initialised with the local value x_i and the weight $w_{i,0}$ with 1.

At each cycle t, each node halves its local value and weight $\langle s_{i,t}, w_{i,t} \rangle = \langle \frac{1}{2} s_{i,t-1}, \frac{1}{2} w_{i,t-1} \rangle$ and sends the other halves to a randomly selected node. In each cycle N messages are sent in total. The global mass of the values $(\sum_{i=1}^{N} s_i)$ and of the weights $(\sum_{i=1}^{N} w_i,)$ is guaranteed to be preserved when a reliable communication protocol is used. This is known as the mass conservation invariant. At any cycle t, the local approximation of the global aggregate is given by the ratio $\frac{s_{i,t}}{w_{i,t}}$, which converges to the true target value under validity of the mass conservation invariant.

The *diffusion speed* is the minimum number of protocol cycles t^* required to achieve a good approximation of the global aggregate function with high probability: $Prob(e_{i,t} < \varepsilon) \geq 1 - \delta, \forall t \geq t^*$, where $e_{i,t}$ the approximation error at node i and ε and δ two arbitrary small positive constants, respectively the maximum approximation error and the maximum probability of greater error than ε. In PSP, the *diffusion speed* t^* has been shown to have a complexity $O(\log(N) + \log(\varepsilon^{-1}) + \log(\delta^{-1}))$ [8].

In [9, 10], two similar algorithms are proposed; they can be both referred to as Push-Pull Gossip protocol (PPG). PPG uses a push-pull scheme that improves the diffusion speed w.r.t. PSP by adopting a symmetric exchange of the local state between communication peers. The node state is represented by a value v_i, which is the local approximation of the global average and is initialised with the local value x_i. At each cycle, a node i randomly chooses a node j to perform a pair-wise averaging operation: the two nodes exchange and update their local values with $\frac{v_i+v_j}{2}$. In PPG, $2 \times N$ messages are sent in total at each cycle.

In several works [12, 13, 11], it has been shown that in asynchronous communication networks PPG violates the mass conservation invariant and does not converge to the correct target value.

The Symmetric Push-Sum Protocol (SPSP) [11] combines the accuracy and simplicity of the push-based approach and the efficiency of the push-pull scheme. SPSP does not require synchronous communication with atomic operations; it achieves a convergence speed similar to the push-pull scheme, while keeping the accuracy of the push scheme. SPSP and the global average as target function have been used in the simulations presented in this work.

2 Convergence Detection

The target value of the aggregation protocol corresponds to the population mean $\mu_x = \frac{1}{N}\sum_{i=1}^{N} x_i$. At each cycle t of the aggregation protocol, a local approximation $v_{i,t}$ of the target value is available. Under validity of the mass conservation invariant ($\sum_{i=1}^{N} v_{i,t} = \sum_{i=1}^{N} x_i, \forall t$), the approximations tend to the target value, i.e. $\lim_{t\to\infty} v_{i,t} = \mu_x, \forall i$. The standard deviation of the approximations in the system is defined as $\sigma_v(t) = \sqrt{\frac{1}{N}\sum_{i=1}^{N}(v_{i,t} - \mu_x)^2}$.

In the simulations, a *global convergence criterion* can be tested by computing the minimum cycle t^* at which the system reaches a small standard deviation: $\sigma_v(t) < \varepsilon, \forall t \geq t^*$ and where ε is a small positive constant.

In practical applications, it is useful to determine a *local convergence criterion*, which can be used to terminate the protocol iterations. The global convergence can be estimated locally by monitoring the approximation error at the node. To this aim, each node can run multiple independent instances of the epidemic aggregation protocol, which are initialised with the same local value x_i. The sample average and the sample standard deviation over the local multiple approximations can be used in place of the population mean and population standard deviation. If m is the number of multiple instances of the protocol at each node, the local approximation at node i and time t is indicated as $v_{i,j,t}$ $(0 < j \leq m)$. The sample mean is given by $\bar{v}_{i,t} = \frac{1}{m}\sum_{j=1}^{m} v_{i,j,t}$ and the corrected sample standard deviation is $s_{i,t} = \sqrt{\frac{1}{m-1}\sum_{j=1}^{m}(v_{i,j,t} - \bar{v}_{i,t})^2}$.

The first local convergence criterion is defined as: $s_{i,t} < \varepsilon$. In the remainder of this work, this local convergence criterion is indicate by $\langle m \rangle M$. For example, $6M$ indicates a local criterion based on six aggregation protocols. In this case, the local convergence criterion is determined at an additional communication cost, which is $(m-1)$ times the cost of a single aggregation protocol.

A second local approach based on a single local protocol can be determined by monitoring the local estimate of the node and the remote estimates of its communication peers over time. A local buffer (FIFO queue) of size h is used to store the local estimate and the remote estimates received with $PUSH$ and $PULL$ messages. At the reception of a message from node j, a node i stores the local estimate v_i and the remote estimate v_j in the local buffer before updating the local estimate. For example, if the buffer has size $h = 4$, at the beginning of the cycle t, it contains a set of estimates $S_i = \{v_{i,t-1}, v_{j,t-1}, v_{i,t-2}, v_{u,t-2}\}$. An average squared error from the target value can be used to determine a local convergence criterion. In this case, the best estimate of the target value is given by the current local estimate $v_{i,t}$.

The second local convergence criterion is defined on the root-mean-square error, $e_{i,t} < \varepsilon$, where $e_{i,t} = \sqrt{\frac{1}{h}\sum_{v \in S_i}(v - v_{i,t})^2}$. This local convergence criterion is indicate by $\langle h \rangle H$. For example, $4H$ indicates a local criterion based on a history buffer of size $h = 4$.

A further and hybrid approach can be defined by combining the previous two local approaches: multiple local protocols are used in combination with a history buffer. This local convergence criterion is indicate by $\langle m \rangle M \langle h \rangle H$. For example, $2M8H$ indicates a local criterion based on a history buffer of size 8 with two local aggregation protocols. In this case, the best estimate of the target value is given by the average of the multiple local approximations, i.e. $\bar{v}_{i,t} = \frac{1}{m}\sum_{j=1}^{m} v_{i,j,t}$. The third local convergence criterion is defined on the root-mean-square error, $e_{i,t} < \varepsilon$, where $e_{i,t} = \sqrt{\frac{1}{h}\sum_{v \in S_i}(v - \bar{v}_{i,t})^2}$.

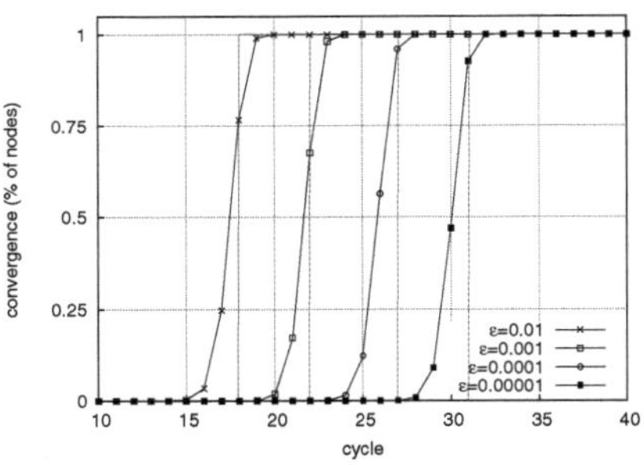

(a) varying ε ($N = 10^4$)

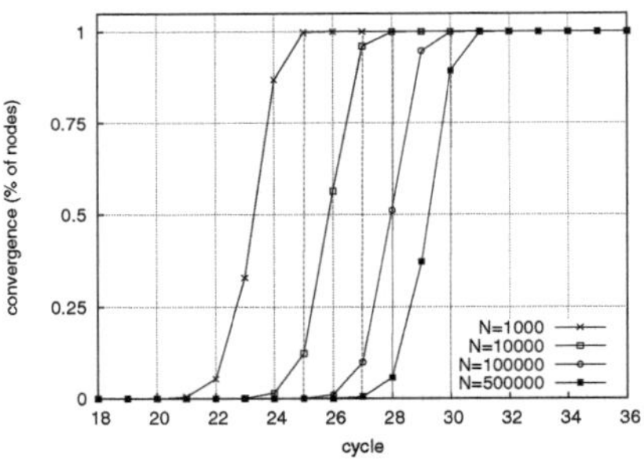

(b) varying N ($\varepsilon = 10^{-4}$)

Fig. 1. Method with multiple protocols ($6M$) for different values of ε and network size N. Corresponding global transitions are shown in dashed lines.

3 Experimental Analysis

We carried out the experimental tests on PeerSim [14], a scalable network simulator based on discrete events. The overlay topology is initialised as a random graph with a constant out degree (30). The simulations are based on the aggregation protocol *SPSP* [11] and the membership protocol *CYCLON* [7] with cache size 30 and shuffle length 15. We have adopted an asynchronous network setting with a uniform distribution of network latencies. The distributed values are initialised with a peak distribution: all nodes have initial value 0, but one that has the peak value N. In all simulations, the target value (average) is 1.0 regardless of the network size.

Figure 1 shows the effect of different values of the threshold ε (figure 1(a)) and of the network size N (figure 1(b)) on the global convergence criterion and the local one based on *six* multiple protocols ($6M$). The charts show the percentage of the nodes that have detected the convergence over time. Each curve shows the results of a single simulation and the global method is represented as a step function (dashed lines) and is used as reference.

In figure 1(a), the global convergence with a maximum error of 10^{-2}, 10^{-3}, 10^{-4} and 10^{-5}, is achieved respectively, at the cycles 18, 22, 27 and 31. The $6M$ curves associated to the different values of ε appear to be equally spaced. This clearly shows the *log* dependency of the diffusion speed on the inverse of the maximum approximation error ε.

In figure 1(b), the global convergence for the network sizes 10^3, 10^4, 10^5 and $5 \cdot 10^5$, is achieved, respectively, at cycles 25, 27, 28, and 30. The $6M$ curves similarly show the dependency of the diffusion speed on the network size.

Figure 2 shows the convergence transition of the different methods with $\varepsilon = 10^{-4}$ and $N = 10^4$. Each curve shows the results of a single simulation and the global method is used as reference.

In figure 2(a), the behavior of the multiple protocols method is shown for different numbers of local protocols (2, 4 and 6). Obviously, the more protocols are used, larger the sample size and a better approximation of the global convergence is achieved. It is observed that the local convergence of most nodes is anticipated with respect to the global convergence.

In figure 2(b), the behavior of the method based on a buffer of historical values is shown for different buffer sizes (2, 4 and 6). It is observed that the local convergence is delayed with respect to the approach $\langle m \rangle M$. This is due to the use of estimates from previous cycles in the $\langle h \rangle H$ convergence detection.

In figure 2(c), the behavior of the hybrid method is shown for a different number of local protocols (2, 4 and 6) and different buffer sizes (8, 16 and 24). The combinations of these two parameters have been chosen to fix the number of historical values from each local protocol to 2 (similarly to $2H$). For example, in $2M8H$ each node has two protocols which contribute with historical values from the past two cycles, for a subtotal of 4 local values. Each node also collects estimates from communication peers of previous cycles for a subtotal of 4 remote values.

Figure 2(d) is used to provide an easy comparison of the different methods. It shows that the hybrid method performs better than the other two methods. The method $2M8H$ has only twice the communication cost of the approach based on a single protocol ($6H$) and is the most similar to the global criterion.

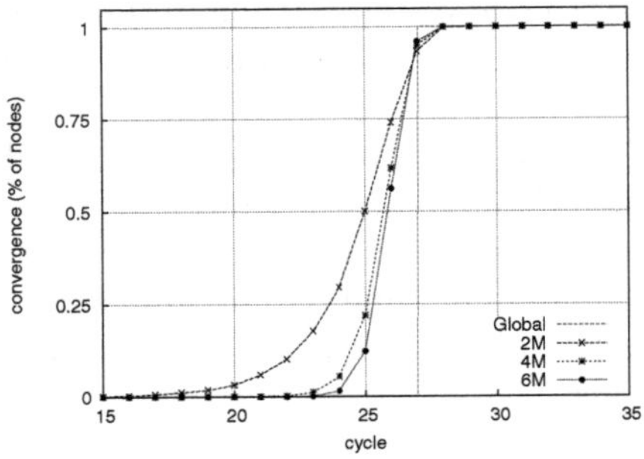

(a) multiple protocols (M)

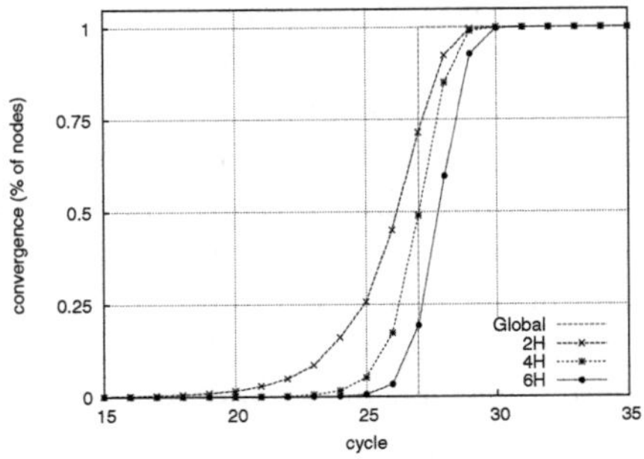

(b) History buffer (H)

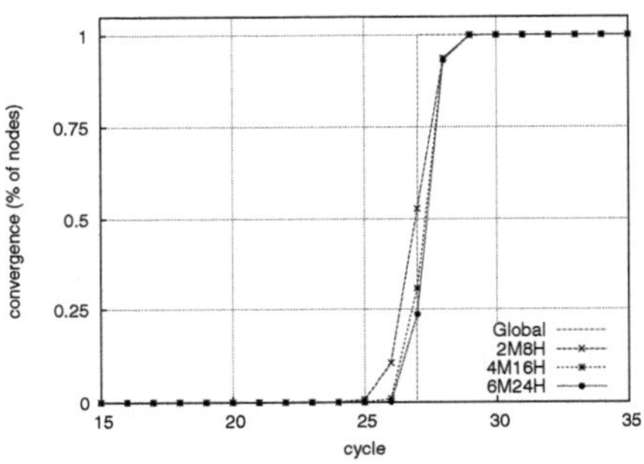

(c) Multiple protocols with buffer (MH)

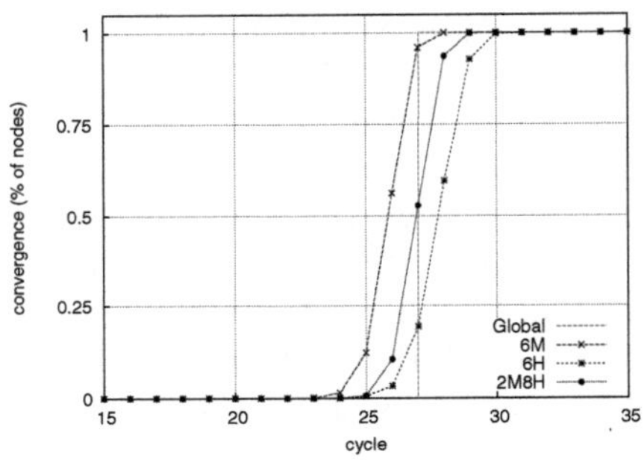

(d) comparison

Fig. 2. Convergence transition of different methods ($\varepsilon = 10^{-4}$ and $N = 10^4$)

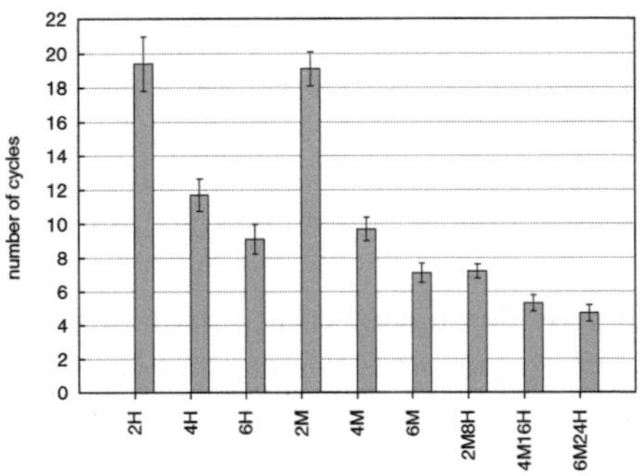

Fig. 3. Average number of cycles in the convergence transition ($\varepsilon = 10^{-4}$ and $N = 10^4$)

In order to validate the qualitative results of figure 2, for each case we have run multiple simulations with 10 different initialisation seeds. For each simulation setting, the number of cycles employed by each method to complete the convergence transition is recorded. The smaller this number, the better the transition approximates the step function of the global method. The average number of cycles and the standard deviation are shown in figure 3. The hybrid method confirms its shorter transition length to achieve a global convergence without a global communication.

4 Conclusions

This work has studied the convergence detection problem in decentralised aggregation based on epidemic protocols. This is important in efficient and practical applications, which require to achieve a given accuracy in the minimum number of cycles. This work has investigated local convergence criteria and has compared them with a global criterion. The experimental analysis has shown that local convergence detection can be employed to minimise and adapt the execution time of an epidemic aggregation protocol. This is an important step towards practical applications of epidemic protocols. Future work will be devoted to study the effect of node churn and network faults on the convergence detection.

References

[1] Dam, M., Stadler, R.: A generic protocol for network state aggregation. In: Proc. Radiovetenskap och Kommunikation (RVK), pp. 14–16 (2005)

[2] Di Fatta, G., Blasa, F., Cafiero, S., Fortino, G.: Epidemic k-means clustering. In: Proc. of the IEEE Int.l Conf. on Data Mining Workshops, pp. 151–158 (2011)

[3] Mashayekhi, H., Habibi, J., Voulgaris, S., van Steen, M.: GoSCAN: Decentralized scalable data clustering. Computing 95(9), 759–784 (2013)

[4] Di Fatta, G., Blasa, F., Cafiero, S., Fortino, G.: Fault tolerant decentralised k-means clustering for asynchronous large-scale networks. Journal of Parallel and Distributed Computing 73(3), 317–329 (2013)

[5] Jelasity, M., Voulgaris, S., Guerraoui, R., Kermarrec, A.M., van Steen, M.: Gossip-based peer sampling. ACM Trans. Comput. Syst. 25(3) (August 2007)

[6] Gillman, D.: A chernoff bound for random walks on expander graphs. SIAM Journal on Computing 27(4), 1203–1220 (1998)

[7] Voulgaris, S., Gavidia, D., Steen, M.: Cyclon: Inexpensive membership management for unstructured p2p overlays. Journal of Network and Systems Management 13(2), 197–217 (2005)

[8] Kempe, D., Dobra, A., Gehrke, J.: Gossip-based computation of aggregate information. In: Proceedings of the 44th Annual IEEE Symposium on Foundations of Computer Science, pp. 482–491 (October 2003)

[9] Jelasity, M., Montresor, A., Babaoglu, O.: Gossip-based aggregation in large dynamic networks. ACM Trans. on Comp. Sys. 23(3), 219–252 (2005)

[10] Boyd, S., Ghosh, A., Prabhakar, B., Shah, D.: Randomized gossip algorithms. IEEE Transactions on Information Theory 52(6), 2508–2530 (2006)

[11] Blasa, F., Cafiero, S., Fortino, G., Di Fatta, G.: Symmetric push-sum protocol for decentralised aggregation. In: Proc. of the Int. l Conf. on Advances in P2P Systems, pp. 27–32 (2011)
[12] Jesus, P., Baquero, C., Almeida, P.: Dependability in aggregation by averaging. In: 1st Symposium on Informatics (INForum 2009), pp. 482–491 (September 2009)
[13] Rao, I., Harwood, A., Karunasekera, S.: Impacts of asynchrony on epidemic-style aggregation protocols. In: Proc. of the IEEE Int.l Conf. on Parallel and Distributed Systems, pp. 601–608 (2010)
[14] Montresor, A., Jelasity, M.: PeerSim: A scalable P2P simulator. In: Proc. of the 9th Int. Conference on Peer-to-Peer (P2P 2009), pp. 99–100 (September 2009)

Heterogeneous Platform Programming for High Performance Medical Imaging Processing

Renan Sales Barros[1], Sytse van Geldermalsen[2], Anna M.M. Boers[1,3,4], Adam S.Z. Belloum[2], Henk A. Marquering[1,3], and Silvia D. Olabarriaga[1]

[1] Biomedical Engineering & Physics, Academic Medical Center, University of Amsterdam, Meibergdreef 9, 1105 AZ, Amsterdam, The Netherlands
[2] Department of Computational Science, University of Amsterdam, Science Park 107, 1098 XG, Amsterdam, The Netherlands
[3] Department of Radiology, Academic Medical Center, University of Amsterdam, Meibergdreef 9, 1105 AZ, Amsterdam, The Netherlands
[4] University of Twente, Postbus 217, 7500 AE, Enschede, The Netherlands

Abstract. Medical imaging processing algorithms can be computationally very demanding. Currently, computers with multiple computing devices, such as multi-core CPUs, GPUs, and FPGAs, have emerged as powerful processing environments. These so called heterogeneous platforms have potential to significantly accelerate medical imaging applications. In this study, we evaluate the potential of heterogeneous platforms to improve the processing speed of medical imaging applications by using a new framework named FlowCL. This framework facilitates the development of parallel applications for heterogeneous platforms. We compared an implementation of region growing based method to automated cerebral infarct volume measurement with a new implementation targeted for heterogeneous platforms. The results of this new implementation agree well with the original implementation and they are obtained with significant speed-up comparing to the sequential implementation.

Keywords: dataflow, framework, heterogeneous computing, heterogeneous platforms, medical imaging processing, OpenCL, parallel programming.

1 Introduction

In medical imaging applications large amounts of data must be processed quickly and accurately, which requires the usage of high performance computing systems. Commodity computer architectures are rapidly developing into systems with multi-core CPUs and with additional accelerated hardware devices such as graphics processing units (GPUs) and field programmable gate arrays (FPGAs). These heterogeneous platforms provide a new alternative to design and implement computationally demanding applications. Consequently, the computation power provided by these heterogeneous platforms should be explored for medical image processing.

D. an Mey et al. (Eds.): Euro-Par 2013 Workshops, LNCS 8374, pp. 301–310, 2014.

Expertise of new programming constructs and concepts is however required for application developers to effectively utilize these platforms. The OpenCL [5] technology was developed with the aim of facilitating heterogeneous platforms usage. OpenCL includes a language for writing functions, called *kernels*, that execute on diverse computing devices. It also includes an application programming interface (API) that is used to control the heterogeneous platforms. A benefit of OpenCL is that the kernels that are coded according to this standard can run on different devices without any modification. This makes it possible to take advantage of computationally powerful devices that are well suited for different tasks. Nevertheless, OpenCL still requires application developers to deal with low level concerns such as the overhead of the code, memory management, and synchronization. In order to evaluate the potential of heterogeneous platforms in medical imaging processing, we needed an easier programming platform. A new framework named FlowCL was developed to provide an intuitive way to create applications utilizing heterogeneous platforms. This framework eliminates the OpenCL API usage, but maintains the OpenCL programming language for writing kernels. A brief description of this framework is presented in Section 2.

We used the FlowCL framework to implement a modified version of a previously developed method of automated measurement of cerebral infarct volume of patients after acute ischemic stroke. This method, which was developed and validated by Boers et al. [3], was modified for heterogeneous platforms. In Section 3, we explain the automated cerebral infarct volume measurement method and the modification implemented in this study. We compared the execution times of the original (sequential) implementation with the new parallel implementation for heterogeneous platforms using FlowCL. We also evaluated the differences between the results of both implementations in Section 4. Finally, the conclusions regarding this work and future improvements are presented in Section 5.

2 FlowCL Framework

During the development of OpenCL applications, programmers have to deal with a low level C library, which requires specialized expertise for effective and efficient code development. There are arious frameworks to mitigate this problem. For example, the Many GPUs Package (MGP) [2] was built on top of the Virtual OpenCL Layer (VCL). VCL is a transparent layer that accesses and manages OpenCL devices in clusters and presents these devices as a single node . MGP is a layer that facilitates the programing using clusters by hiding low level functions. A library named Maestro [10] also tries to reduce the complexity of OpenCL applications development by providing functions for automatic data transfer and task decomposition across OpenCL devices. However, MGP and Maestro do not use extensive optimizations strategies. A more complete framework i is StarPU [1], which is a runtime system capable of scheduling tasks over heterogeneous devices using several optimizations strategies. However, the framework API uses the C programming language and this hampers the usage of high level programming concepts.

FlowCL is a new high level framework that supports rapid prototyping and development with OpenCL, which makes it possible to closely control the execution across all OpenCL devices on one computer system. More details about FlowCL are found in [4]. It hides all low level calls to the OpenCL library API from the application developer. Only the OpenCL kernel code that is designed to run on a selected device must be provided to the framework. Also, FlowCL provides an object-oriented declarative API to easily build applications with the concept of dataflow. The programmer simply declares a set of memory objects and operations. Each operation runs each single kernel function on any available device. This framework automatically applies optimization strategies such as overlapping communication and computation, and asynchronous data transfers and kernel executions.

To use the FlowCL framework, application developers just have to deal with four classes of objects: memory, context, device, and operation. Figure 1 illustrates the relationships between these classes. By having only four classes with limited relationships, FlowCL provides a simpler approach that is easier to understand than OpenCL.

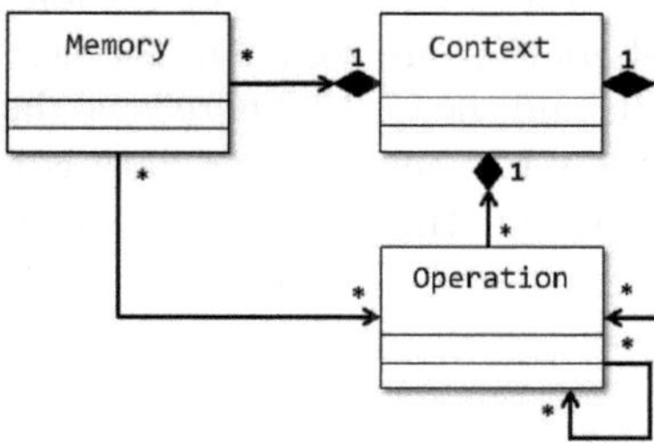

Fig. 1. FlowCL cardinality diagram. A **Context** is instantiated with kernel codes; these codes are usable on all available computing devices. **Memory** objects act as arguments for operations; they are created by a context with a given size and become available to all devices in this context. **Device** represents a computing device. **Operation** runs a specified kernel function on a selected device.

In short, FlowCL framework addresses the following key aspects: it facilitates application development with OpenCL; it provides an object oriented API to build applications with the dataflow concept; it eliminates the OpenCL API, except for kernel code; it automatically manages all devices on heterogeneous platforms; it supports concurrent kernel execution and asynchronous data transfers; and it supports multiple operating systems.

The framework is designed to run in the C++ language and only requires the FlowCL header file inclusion. To illustrate FlowCL usage, the following source code is shown:

```
#include "FlowCL.hpp"
using namespace FlowCL;

int main()
{
    Context con;
    con.CompileFile("source.cl");

    Memory memcpu = con.CreateMemory(1e8*sizeof(int));
    Memory memgpu = con.CreateMemory(1e8*sizeof(int));

    Operation genrand = con.CreateOperation(con.GetCPUDevice(), "GenRand");
    genrand.SetArg(0, memcpu); // CPU already has access to memory
    genrand.SetArg(1, memgpu);
    genrand.SetWorkSize(1e8); // Set finest granularity

    Operation sortcpu = con.CreateOperation(con.GetCPUDevice(), "SortCPU");
    sortcpu.SetArgDependency(genrand, 0, memcpu); // Wait for genrand
    sortcpu.SetWorkSize(1e8);

    Operation sortgpu = con.CreateOperation(con.GetGPUDevice(), "SortGPU");
    sortgpu.SetArgDependency(genrand, 0, memgpu); // Wait for genrand
    sortgpu.SetArgOutput(0, memgpu);
    sortgpu.SetWorkSize(1e8);

    con.Run(); // Blocking run
}
```

This example is visualized in Figure 2. The first operation executes on the CPU and generates random numbers that are sorted in the next two operations that execute in parallel on the GPU and the CPU. There is no data transferred to the sort operation that runs on the CPU because this data is readily available. Once the GPU operation is completed, the data is transferred back and the execution is finished.

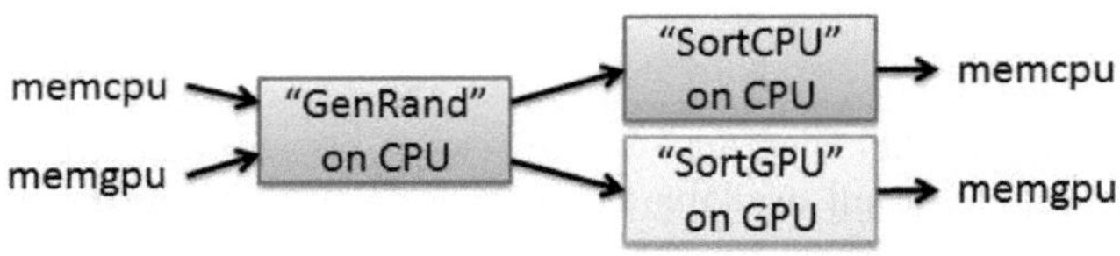

Fig. 2. Sample code visual representation

3 Case Study

In this section we present a case study using heterogeneous computing for measurement of cerebral infarct volume (CIV) of patients with acute ischemic stroke. The CIV has been suggested as an important measure for the effective treatment of these patients [9]. This volume can be manually measured in early follow-up non-contrast CT scans by the delineation of the whole infarct volume. An alternative is to estimate this volume by using the ABC/2 formula, which was originally designed for the estimation of hemorrhage volume [6]. The manual delineation is a tedious and time-intensive task, and the CIV estimation based on the ABC/2 rule only approximates the total CIV. Aiming to address these problems, Boers et al. [3] proposed a method to automatically calculate the CIV in follow-up non-contrast CT scans. This method was validated by comparing it with manual delineations performed by experienced radiologists.

The method proposed by Boers et al. was implemented using MATLAB [7] and took a long time to run (in the order of 10 min). It uses an intensity-based region growing (IRG) algorithm, which is responsible for more than 95% of the total processing time. To evaluate the potential benefit of heterogeneous computing for this application, we replaced this method with a new version of the IRG algorithm developed with the FlowCL framework. The integration of the new IRG algorithm with the previous MATLAB implementation was straightforward because MATLAB allows external code calls.

In short, the objective of this case study is to understand how heterogeneous platforms can be used and what is their potential value for medical imaging applications. To achieve this objective, we run the method for automated CIV calculation with two different implementations of the IRG algorithm, one based on the original MATLAB code and the other using FlowCL. Below we provide an overview of the complete method for automated CIV measurement used in this case study, and then we describe both the sequential and the parallel IRG implementations.

3.1 Automated Cerebral Infarct Volume Measurement

The automated CIV measurement proposed by Boers et al. was designed to process non-contrast CT scans of the whole brain of the patients. The volume measurements are performed for a part of the brain that is segmented from the image using a region growing algorithm (IRG). In this algorithm, a voxel is added to the segmented volume if the difference between its intensity and the average intensity of the segmented volume so far is smaller than a specific threshold. To compute the CIV, this algorithm was repeated for 7 different values of threshold, going from 1.5 until 4.5 with steps of 0.5 Hounsfield units (HU). The algorithm requires a position as starting point (called seed point) in the infarcted lesion. The seed position is set by an experienced radiologist and this assures that the correct infarcted area was selected.

The brain midline is used to prevent the segmented region from leaking to into the contralateral hemisphere, i.e., the region cannot grow into the other side of the brain. This midline is detected based on the geometric center and the most extreme mid-sagittal bone or nasal cartilage structures present on the scan. Also, to avoid leaking into the hypo-attenuated ventricles, the hypo-attenuated region close to the geometric center is segmented and excluded from the segmentation of the infarcted area. All the steps of the segmentation process are illustrated in Figure 3. This process is repeated for 7 thresholds. In the end of this process, the observer must select the best result that most agrees with the scans.

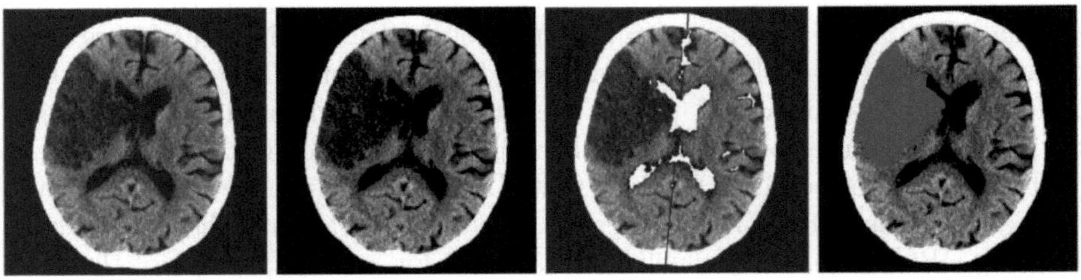

Fig. 3. CIV segmentation steps. From the left to right: a CT scan showing an infarct in the right hemisphere (left of the image); the seed position defined by a radiologist; the determined midline and the ventricles segmentation; and the final segmentation representing the CIV.

3.2 Intensity-Based Region Growing Algorithm

Region growing is a segmentation technique to select an image area that is connected according to a specific condition [8]. In intensity-based region growing (IRG), the intensity of the voxel is used as criterion to include or not a voxel to the region. Starting from a given seed point, the IRG algorithm iteratively adds voxels to the region such that the following condition is satisfied: $|I - A| \leq T$, where I is the intensity of the processed voxel and A is the average intensity of the selected image area. The voxel I must be in the neighborhood of the selected area and it is included in this area when its intensity is smaller than or equal to the threshold T.

Different neighborhood definitions can be applied (e.g., for 3D images it can take 9 or 26 neighbors into account), and the order in which the voxels are considered for inclusion may influence the final result. The IRG is also sensitive to the chosen threshold T; for this reason, 7 different thresholds are used in the CIV method, and the user can pick the best result.

The sequential implementation of IRG in the original CIV measurement method updates the average of the selected image area immediately after the inclusion of each voxel, and the updated average is used in the test to include the next neighboring voxel. In the parallel implementation of IRG, computing devices in the heterogeneous platform simultaneously process the voxels based on the same value of A. The average intensity A is only updated after all the neighbors of a given voxel are considered for inclusion. Therefore the sequential and the parallel algorithms perform inclusion tests based on potentially different values of A, and can deliver different results.

4 Experimental Results and Comparisons

To evaluate the speed-up obtained with the heterogeneous platform, 53 CT scans were processed in two different hardware configurations with the original and the GPU implementations of the automated CIV measurement method. The complete method was executed in both cases, however for timing purposes only

Table 1. Hardware configurations

Hardware Detail	Configuration 1	Configuration 2
CPU Name	Intel Core i7-3930K	Intel Xeon E5-2620
CPU Clock	3.20 GHz	2.00 GHz
GPU Name	NVIDIA GeForce GTX 550 Ti	NVIDIA Quadro K600
GPU Clock	900 MHz	876 MHz
GPU Memory Clock	4104 MHz	1782 MHz
GPU Driver Version	9.18.13.1106	9.18.13.2000

the IRG part was considered. Both hardware configurations have 12 CPU cores and 192 GPU cores, however one is slower than the other – see Table 1.

The CT scans include the entire brain and were performed with thin-section acquisition by using 8 different multi-section CT scanners with at least 16 sections, but mostly with 64 or more sections. The 32-bit MATLAB version 8.0.0.783 (R2012b) was used to run the MATLAB code. Microsoft Visual C++ 2010 was used to compile the region growing algorithm for heterogeneous platforms. These software were executed on 64-bit Microsoft Windows 7 Enterprise operating system on both hardware configurations. Execution times were measure before and after calling the IRG function in the MATLAB code. Note that this time includes overhead of internal function call for the sequential implementation, as well as for the external call of the program for the heterogeneous platform implementation.

All the CT scans were analyzed using exactly the same parameters for 7 threshold values $(1.5, 2.0, 2.5, 3.0, 3.5, 4.0, 4.5)$. Parameters that must be manually configured, such as the region growing seed position, were defined only once and used in all runs of the method. Because different threshold values have a great influence in the size of the segmented volume and, consequently, also in the algorithm execution time, we compare the execution time separately for each threshold value.

Figure 4 shows the speed-up factor for the parallel respectively to the original IRG implementation. As we can see, speed-ups of 36 times were obtained. In general, larger gains are obtained for higher threshold values. Higher thresholds produce bigger segmented volumes, which require more computations and, consequently, result in more expressive speed gains. For lower thresholds, the execution time varies among different scans (larger standard deviation). Small thresholds generate smaller segmented volumes, which are more sensitive to the inclusion of neighboring voxels.

Also note that due to this sensitivity regarding the small volumes, the implementation for heterogeneous platforms can be slower than the original implementation. Note however that only a minor performance reduction is noticed. In most situations the performance of the new implementation is better as presented in figure 5. We must highlight that the automated CIV measurement requires the region growing algorithm to run with 7 different threshold values and, because of this, the performance gains obtained for higher thresholds values

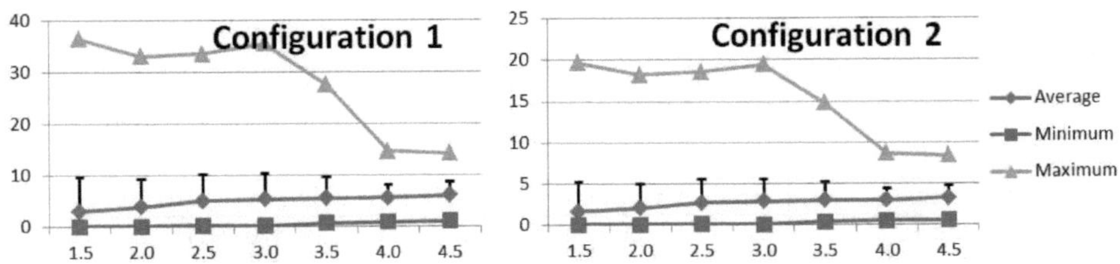

Fig. 4. Speed-up on heterogeneous platforms (vertical axis) for each threshold value (horizontal axis). Bars indicate standard deviation from the mean speed-up calculated for 53 scans.

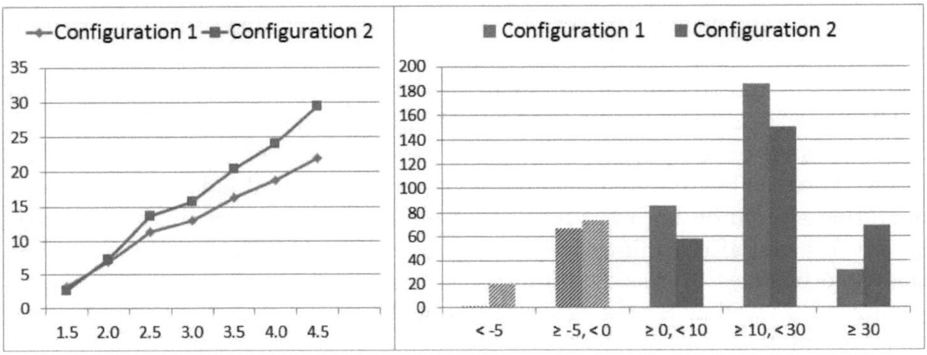

Fig. 5. Differences in execution time between both implementations (new - old). *Left:* Average difference in seconds (vertical axis) for each threshold value (horizontal axis) calculated for 53 scans. *Right:* Histogram of differences in execution times in seconds for all thresholds. The negative ranges indicate the runs where the original implementation was faster than the new implementation.

compensate for the loss for smaller thresholds in the total processing time. In no case the new implementation had a total processing time slower than the original implementation when all 7 thresholds are considered. The new implementation was faster in 82% of the scans using the hardware configuration 1 and in 75% of the scans using the hardware configuration 2.

To evaluate the differences in the quality of results obtained with both implementations we calculate the Dice coefficient for each threshold value individually - see Table 2. Similarly to what we found in the execution time analysis, the greater differences are measured for smaller thresholds. However, this variation in the results does not have a great impact in the method, because the final segmentation must be selected by a human observer which will filter out the segmentations that are not consistent with the images. Moreover, usually the selected segmentation is generated with one of the middle threshold values. The extreme threshold values are used as a safe margin to assure that the most adequate segmentation will be inside this interval.

Table 2. Dice coefficients for each threshold

Threshold Value:	1.5	2.0	2.5	3.0	3.5	4.0	4.5
Maximum:	0.99994	1.00000	1.00000	1.00000	0.99247	0.99141	0.97592
Average:	0.85936	0.89620	0.94856	0.93499	0.91252	0.91199	0.89875
Minimum:	0.34349	0.25384	0.68682	0.84418	0.82026	0.76991	0.75164
Standard Deviation:	0.18170	0.16985	0.07482	0.05082	0.05052	0.06906	0.07345

As shown in Table 2, the Dice coefficients for the threshold between 2.5 and 4 are higher than 0.9. These results indicate good agreement between segmentations when compared to variations found in results obtained with manual segmentation by experts. For example, during the validation of the original method, [3] found that the Dice coefficient for segmentations manually defined by two experienced radiologists were 0.84 ± 0.08 ranged from 0.63 to 0.94 [3].

5 Conclusions and Future Work

In this work we presented how the FlowCL framework, which was developed for intuitive heterogeneous platform programing, was used in a medical imaging application. Part of a previously developed and validated method for automated cerebral infarct volume measurement was adapted for heterogeneous platforms using the FlowCL framework. Only the code related with the intensity-based region growing algorithm was modified. All other pieces of code and software used in the method were not modified. We compared the two implementations of the automated CIV measurement method in order to investigate the potential of heterogeneous platform in medical imaging applications. The results of the implementation for heterogeneous platform were obtained faster and were also consistent with the results of the original implementation. This study shows that heterogeneous platforms can increase performance in medical imaging applications. This indicates that other computationally demanding medical imaging algorithms could also be adapted to run on heterogeneous platforms in a straightforward manner with the FlowCL framework.

In the present study, only GPUs and multicore CPUs were used as computing devices. However, there are other different computing devices, such as FPGAs, that were not included in this study and which can be also used in a more comprehensive future study.

Acknowledgements. Part of this work has been funded by ITEA2 10004: MEDUSA.

References

1. Augonnet, C., Thibault, S., Namyst, R., Wacrenier, P.A.: Starpu: a unified platform for task scheduling on heterogeneous multicore architectures. Concurrency and Computation: Practice and Experience 23(2), 187–198 (2011)

2. Barak, A., Ben-Nun, T., Levy, E., Shiloh, A.: A package for opencl based heterogeneous computing on clusters with many gpu devices. In: 2010 IEEE International Conference on Cluster Computing Workshops and Posters (CLUSTER WORKSHOPS), Heraklion, pp. 1–7 (2010)
3. Boers, A., Marquering, H., Jochem, J., Besselink, N., Berkhemer, O., van der Lugt, A., Beenen, L., Majoi, C.: Automated cerebral infarct volume measurement in follow-up noncontrast ct scans of patients with acute ischemic stroke. American Journal of Neuroradiology (2013)
4. van Geldermalsen, S.: Work In Progress Thesis - FlowCL. Master's thesis, University of Amsterdam (2013)
5. Khronos OpenCL Working Group: The opencl specification (2012)
6. Kothari, R.U., Brott, T., Broderick, J.P., Barsan, W.G., Sauerbeck, L.R., Zuccarello, M., Khoury, J.: The abcs of measuring intracerebral hemorrhage volumes. Stroke 27(8), 1304–1305 (1996)
7. MATLAB: version 8.0.0.783 (R2012b). The MathWorks, Inc., Natick, Massachusetts (2012)
8. Pham, D.L., Xu, C., Prince, J.L.: Current methods in medical image segmentation. Annual Review of Biomedical Engineering 2(1), 315–337 (2000)
9. Saver, J.L., Johnston, K.C., Homer, D., Wityk, R., Koroshetz, W., Truskowski, L.L., Haley, E.C., et al.: Infarct volume as a surrogate or auxiliary outcome measure in ischemic stroke clinical trials. Stroke 30(2), 293–298 (1999)
10. Spafford, K., Meredith, J., Vetter, J.: Maestro: Data orchestration and tuning for opencl devices (2010)

Transparent Incremental Updates for Genomics Data Analysis Pipelines

Edvard Pedersen[1,3], Nils Peder Willassen[2,3], and Lars Ailo Bongo[1,3]

[1] Department of Computer Science, University of Tromsø, Norway
[2] Department of Chemistry, University of Tromsø, Norway
[3] Centre for Bioinformatics, University of Tromsø, Norway
{edvard.pedersen,nils-peder.willassen}@uit.no,
larsab@cs.uit.no

Abstract. A large up-to-date compendium of integrated genomic data is often required for biological data analysis. The compendium can be tens of terabytes in size, and must often be frequently updated with new experimental or meta-data. Manual compendium update is cumbersome, requires a lot of unnecessary computation, and it may result in errors or inconsistencies in the compendium. We propose a transparent file based approach for adding incremental update capabilities to unmodified genomics data analysis tools and pipeline workflow managers. This approach is implemented in the GeStore system. We evaluate GeStore using a real world genomics compendium. Our results show that it is easy to add incremental updates to genomics data processing pipelines, and that incremental updates can reduce the computation time such that it becomes practical to maintain large-scale up-to-date genomics compendia on small clusters.

1 Introduction

Recent advances in scientific instruments, such as next-generation sequencing machines, has the potential of producing data that provide views of biological processes at different resolutions and conditions, opening a new era in molecular biology and molecular medicine [1]. Many of the data analysis techniques developed for analyzing such genomic data integrate data from many experiments with metadata from multiple knowledge bases. The information in the knowledge bases [2] is essential for understanding the biological content of the experiment data. For example, the results of DNA sequencing may not become truly useful before the UniProt [3] knowledge base is used to map sequence bases to genes, the per gene results are compared to results from other experiments, and the significant differences have been mapped to biological functions using the Go [4] knowledge base.

Genomic data integration and analysis is typically implemented as a pipeline with several tools, where the output files of one tool acts as the input files for the next tool. The specific set of tools to use depends on the biological problem that is being investigated. Often large amounts of data must be analyzed, since new sequencing machines produce multiple terabytes of data per experiment [5]. The cost of the analysis can therefore be orders of magnitude larger than the cost of creating the data to be analyzed [6]. Cost efficient data analysis is therefore a key challenge for genomics data analysis.

D. an Mey et al. (Eds.): Euro-Par 2013 Workshops, LNCS 8374, pp. 311–320, 2014.

Integrating new experimental data or updating meta-data may provide novel biological insights. It is therefore important to update a biological compendium when new data becomes available. Meta-data updates are especially important since it represents the state of knowledge in the field [7]. However, current biological analysis tools typically require recalculating the entire compendium for meta-data updates. Such full updates increase the computational time and cost; often to the point where reanalysis is not done.

The cost of reanalysis can be greatly reduced by using incremental updates [8] that limit recomputation to new and updated data. We believe such an approach for incremental updates of genomic data must satisfy the following four requirements. First, most existing analysis tools should be supported without any modifications since it is not practical to maintain modified versions of the many analysis tools used in genomic data analysis pipelines. Transparent incremental updates are therefore needed. Second, the incremental updates should be independent of the job and resource management systems used to run the pipeline tools since genomic analysis pipelines are run on many different platforms. Third, it should be easy to add incremental update support to an existing pipeline. The system should therefore handle update detection, processing of incremental updates, and integration of the incremental update with a previous full update. Fourth, it should scale to large-scale compendium.

To our knowledge, no previous incremental update systems for large-scale data [9–15] satisfy all four requirements. These provide the required functionality and scalability, but do not provide the easy to use transparent incremental updates that are necessary to add incremental updates to existing pipelines. Instead they require either porting applications to a specific framework such as Dryad [16] or MapReduce [17], or writing ad-hoc scripts for input generation and output merging.

We present the GeStore system for incremental update management. GeStore uses a transparent file based approach that satisfies all four requirements. Most pipeline tools take as input one or more files with input and meta-data, and produce output consisting of one or more files. Incremental updates can therefore be implemented by modifying the input or meta-data files such that these only contain the data for an incremental update, and then merging the incremental output with the previous results. Tool code is unmodified, and the only modifications to the pipeline are two GeStore calls for generating input files and merging output files. GeStore provides a plugin framework for implementing parsers, tool-specific incremental file generators, and tool-specific output file mergers. GeStore uses the Hadoop software stack for scalable data processing.

Our contributions are threefold: (i) we propose a promising approach for adding incremental updates to unmodified genomic data analysis pipelines, leading to substantial reduction in time and resources needed to update large biological compendium, (ii) we present the design and implementation of our system, including a framework for implementing plugins that enable transparent incremental updates, and (iii) we present the feasibility of our approach and initial experimental evaluation of our system using a real metagenomics analysis pipeline and real data.

2 GeStore

GeStore is a system for enabling transparent incremental computations for unmodified file-based data analysis pipelines. GeStore consists of a runtime system that provides a plugin framework for incremental input file generation and output file merging, a toolset for parsing and detecting changes in files, and data storage and management (Fig. 1, left). GeStore exports an interface for data feeders, and an interface for workflow managers. Data feeders are typically scripts that periodically download new input data or updated meta-data from remote repositories or local storage systems. All downloaded files are stored in GeStore. Pipeline managers (or pipeline configurations) are modified to call GeStore before running each tool in the pipeline in order to generate the incremental input files used by the tools and to merge the resulting files (Fig. 1, right). GeStore uses HDFS [18] and Hbase [19] to efficiently store incremental files and GeStore meta-data, and Hadoop MapReduce [17] to run scalable change detection jobs. In addition GeStore comprise library functions and tools to add incremental updates to pipeline tools, and client applications to access data stored within GeStore.

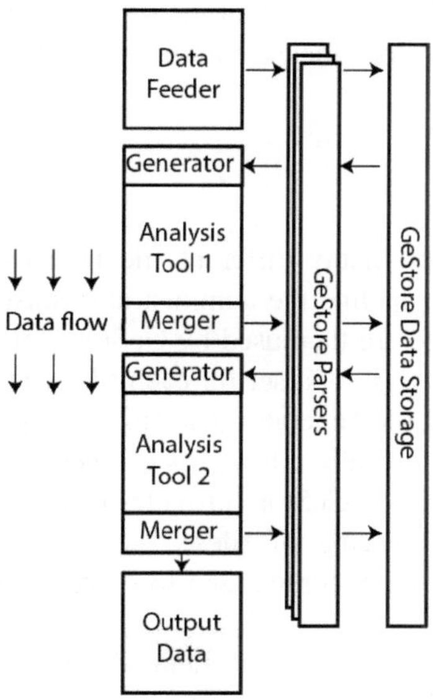

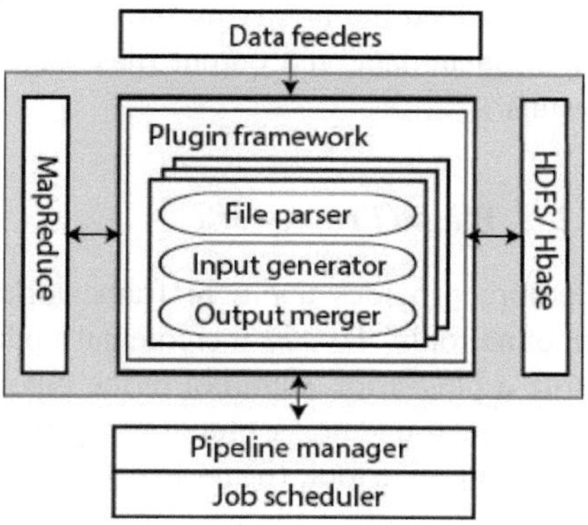

Fig. 1. Incremental pipeline execution (left). GeStore architecture (right).

2.1 File Based Incremental Updates

GeStore uses a transparent file based approach where incremental updates are implemented by modifying the input and meta-data files read by genomics data analysis tools such that these only contain the data for incremental update computations. The tool will then be run as normal, but it will typically produce a partial result. The partial result is merged with previously produced results and stored in GeStore.

We have chosen a file based approach since there are relatively few file formats that are used by many genomics applications. It is therefore feasible to implement parsers that support most file formats and therefore most genomics pipeline tools. In addition, most file formats are simple and structured which makes it easy to write parsers for each format. However, update file generation and output merging is not trivial to implement. It may be necessary to understand the biological content of the data and how the tools read and write the data. For example, for the widely used BLAST [20] tool most changes to the UniProt [3] input data records are for fields that are not used in the computation, and the output data records contains a field (e-value [15]) that is incorrect for incremental updates. Both of these issues can be fixed by writing relatively simple code for ignoring the insignificant fields during change detection and by fixing the e-values in the output data. In addition, the system must provide, low overhead storage for incremental update data, and efficient generation of incremental update files.

GeStore provides an interface that the pipeline system uses to request one or more incremental update input files, and to merge the partial results with previously produced results. These upcalls can be added by adding stages to the pipeline configuration before and after the execute tool step. Alternatively, the GeStore calls can be added by modifying the code in the pipeline manger that manages the lists of input, meta-data, and output files used to setup a tool for execution and to store the results.

2.2 Plugin Framework

GeStore provides a plugin framework to support many different file formats and pipeline tools. To add incremental updates to a pipeline the administrator must first write a plugin for each tool in the pipeline. These are then used by GeStore for each incremental update. A plugin comprise three parts: (i) a parser for each file type used by the pipeline tool, (ii) tool-specific incremental file generator, and (iii) tool-specific incremental output file merger. Each plugin has typically a few tens of lines of code. Many plugins also share parsers and file mergers, and GeStore provides many library functions for parsing, change detection, and merging of files. The plugins are managed by a framework that provides efficient data storage, and low overhead file parsing, generation, and merging.

The file parser must define schemas for the input files and meta files used by a tool, and implement six methods that: (i) provide regular expressions that define the start and end of an entry in the file, (ii) split an entry into columns, (iii) compare two versions of an entry, (iv) check if an entry is well-formed, (v) put the entry into HBase, and (vi) generate output in other formats. The file generator requires implementing one method that specifies the parsers to use for each file format, and the fields to write to the input file. The output merger requires implementing a method to merge the output data with previously produced output data stored in GeStore. This may include minor fixes to output data fields as discussed above.

2.3 Data Storage and Management

GeStore uses the Hadoop software stack for scalable data storage and processing. GeStore maintains: (i) HBase tables and HDFS files with pipeline tool input, output and meta-data file data, (ii) a cache of previously generated incremental update files stored in HDFS, and (iii) HBase tables with per plugin instance state that is used to generate file, merge output files, and provide provenance information.

For file types that have a parser implemented, the data is split into entries and entry fields. These are stored as rows and columns in HBase using a file-format specific schema. The only required column in the schema is a unique ID for each row. The HBase schema can be modified by adding new columns to the table if for example the file format changes or the parser is modified. GeStore use the versioning mechanism in HBase to store only updated fields (i.e. delta compression), and to return the data for a given time period. The timestamp for a version corresponds to either the file generation date, release date, or version.

3 Incremental METApipe

METApipe is used by our biology collaborators to find novel enzymes by analyzing sequence data from marine microbial communities. METApipe is currently run using the GePan pipeline management system (developed by Tim Kahlke at the University of Tromsø). It includes the following tools:

1. Multiple Genome Aligner (MGA): [21] does alignment of closely related DNA sequences. It does not require meta-data from knowledge bases.
2. MGA-exporter: converts the MGA output to the format used by the next stage.
3. FileScheduler: partitions and distributes the input data to the compute nodes.
4. Protein BLAST (BLASTP) [20]: maps sequences to information from the UniProt Swiss-Prot and TrEMBL [3] knowledge bases.
5. HMMer [22]: maps sequences to information from the Pfam-A and Pfam-B [23] protein family databases.
6. Annotator: gathers the results from the preceding tools, and converts the data to a custom format.
7. Annotator-exporter: converts the annotator output to a format that can be used by data visualization and exploration tools.

To add incremental updates to METApipe we had to write parsers for the six file formats used by the pipeline: FASTA, UniprotKB meta-data, Pfam meta-data, BLAST output, HMMer output, and MGA output. We also had to write plugins for the BLAST and HMMer tools. The BLAST plugin corrects incremental e-values as discussed in [15] during merge. The HMMer plugin only generates input files.

The file format plugins were a total of 844 lines of Java code, and the tool plugins were 283 lines of Java code. The results show that file based incremental could be used for all tools in METApipe, and there are relatively few lines of tool specific code.

To integrate GeStore with METApipe, we modified the code that generates the Grid Engine [24] scripts that run the pipeline tool code. GeStore calls were added by changing the file initialization commands to GeStore calls. In total, about 120 lines of code were changed in METApipe. We expect the changes required to other pipeline management systems to be similarly small.

4 Evaluation

Our initial experimental evaluation compares the benefits and overheads of using incremental updates for the METApipe metagenomics analysis pipeline. Our experiments were run on a small cluster with one frontend and eight compute nodes. Each node is equipped with two Intel Xeon E5-1620 CPUs running at 3.6 GHz and 32 gigabytes of RAM. They have a total of 4.5 TB of local HDD. They also have 2.6 TB of NFS storage shared between them. The machines are connected using gigabit Ethernet. We believe such a cluster configuration is realistic for research labs that maintain genomic compendia.

We use a 15 mega base pairs metagenomics dataset from the Yellowstone Park [25] as input data. Processing this small dataset takes 2.5 hours on our small cluster. We incrementally update the dataset on the last day of the month from January 2011 to July 2011. There were 6 updates to Uniprot Swiss-Prot and TrEMBL, and one update to Pfam A and B in that period.

4.1 Update Relationships

To analyze relationships between meta-data changes and input file changes, we averaged all changes in UniProt TrEMBL, UniProt Swiss-Prot, and Pfam-A meta-data collections between January and July in 2011(Table 1). In Swiss-Prot and TrEMBL most changes are to annotation that does not require BLAST recomputation, and hence a significant difference in incremental update execution time. Pfam has a naïve plugin that marks all changes as significant, and has therefore a high rate of significant changes (100%). The Pfam plugin could be improved by doing more precise classifications of non-significant updates. These results demonstrate the benefits of tool specific plugins.

Table 1. Monthly meta-data collection updates between January-July 2011. Averages reported.

	Total entries	Total updates	Significant	New entries
Swiss-Prot	527590	38.76%	0.44%	0.40%
TrEMBL	14738346	32.11%	4.89%	4.88%
Pfam-A	1076	100.00%	100.00%	3.25%

4.2 GeStore Improvements and Overhead

We measured METApipe execution time for full updates and incremental updates with 1, 3, and 6 month periods (Table 2). The analysis time is dominated by BLASTp. Since

BLAST execution time scales linearly with the input size, the smaller incremental input data generated by GeStore significantly reduce BLAST analysis time, and hence total execution time.

Table 2. METApipe execution time split into analysis time and GeStore overhead (all in seconds)

	Analysis	Overhead	Total
Full update (Jan 2011)	9141	0	9141
with GeStore	10718	2562	13280
Incremental (Jan – Feb)	893	755	1647
Incremental (Jan – April)	1736	3497	5233
Incremental (Jan – Juli)	2850	3736	6586

GeStore has an overhead for HMMer of 800 seconds when generating a complete database, and 300 seconds when retrieving a cached database. Generating an incremental update database takes 2800 seconds, this is because the PFam plugin marks all updates as important. BLASTp has an overhead of 1700 seconds for generating a full database. The incremental update time is 300 to 800 seconds depending on the size of the update.

Although GeStore overhead is significant for these experiments it will be much smaller for bigger, more realistic, input dataset sizes since the analysis time depends on input data size, while GeStore overhead depends on meta-data size. In addition, we expect to reduce the Pfam change detection overhead by implementing data aware change detection (as discussed above).

The storage overhead increases sub linearly for UniProt since there are relatively few updates per month (as shown above), the January UniProt database file size is 33 Gb. When stored in HBase it requires 48 Gb of space. However, the total size of the UniProt databases is 252 Gb, but only requires 77 Gb of space in GeStore. For Pfam the storage requirements increase linearly, from to 3.3 Gb to 7.1 Gb and 2.9 Gb and 6.3 Gb respectively for GeStore and total file size. The storage requirements can be significantly reduced by improving the plugin for HMMer.

GeStore achieves similar analysis runtime improvements (90%, for 5% meta-data updates) to incremental BLAST as reported in [15]. Execution time improvements ranging from 20% to 99% are reported in [9–14], but for applications from the data center domain. We have not experimentally compared the execution time improvements and overheads to other large scale incremental update tools since these require modifications to the pipeline tools.

5 Related Work

Systems and frameworks for incremental updates on large scale datasets include Incoop [10], Percolator [11], Nectar [9], DryadInc [12], CBP [13], and HaLoop [14]. In Percolator and CBP the programmer implements a system specific incremental program using respectively event-driven mini transactions and stateful primitives. Incoop, Nectar, DyradInc, and HaLoop use data dependency graphs of Dryad [16] or MapReduce programs to automatically replace the input data for a computation with previously calculated results. GeStore combines these two main approaches; a programmer implements file generators and mergers for unmodified programs. GeStore is independent of the programming model and job management system, so the applications can be executed using Dryad, MapReduce [11], or the Grid Engine [24].

GeStore extends the work in [15] by providing a framework and libraries to implement the necessary pre and post processing of data moved between a data warehouse and genomic analysis tools. This makes it easier to add additional support for additional genomic analysis tools as we have demonstrated by implementing incremental updates for a complete metagenomics analysis pipeline.

Simple change detection is supported by tools such as Unix diff, delta encoding compression systems [26], and version management systems such as CVS [27]. However, the change detection in these do not take into account the complex inter-file relationships found in genomic datasets.

The file tables maintained by GeStore are similar to declarative views maintained by data warehouses [28]. Incremental updates have also been used for non-distributed computation result caching (memoization) as in [8].

Popular approaches for genomics pipeline management are Galaxy [29] and BioConductor [30]. These do not provide incremental computation.

We evaluated GeStore using the locally developed METApipe pipeline. An alternative is the JCVI metagenomics analysis pipeline [31].

6 Conclusions and Future Work

We proposed an approach for adding incremental updates to unmodified genomic data analysis pipelines, leading to substantial reduction in time and resources needed to update large biological compendiums. We presented the design and implementation of the GeStore system, including a framework for implementing plugins that enable transparent incremental updates. We demonstrated the feasibility of our approach and provided an initial experimental evaluation of our system using a real metagenomics analysis pipeline and real data. The cost effective transparent incremental updates provided by GeStore makes it practical to frequently update large genomic compendium with new experimental and meta-data, and thereby enabling novel biological discoveries.

We plan to further evaluate the benefits and overhead of incremental updates for genomics data analysis by applying GeStore to the pipeline producing data for the IMP [32] tool, and to a Galaxy [29] pipeline. Galaxy can also be used to provide a GUI for GeStore configuration and data management.

Acknowledgements. Thanks to Espen Robertsen and Tim Kahlke for help with the GePan pipeline, Jon Ivar Kristiansen for maintaining our cluster, and Martin Erntsen for his comments.

References

[1] Schuster, S.C.: Next-generation sequencing transforms today's biology. Nature Methods 5(1), 16–18 (2008)
[2] Galperin, M.Y., Fernández-Suárez, X.M.: The 2012 Nucleic Acids Research Database Issue and the online Molecular Biology Database Collection. Nucleic Acids Research 40(Database issue), D1–D8 (2012)
[3] Magrane, M., UniProt Consortium: UniProt Knowledgebase: a hub of integrated protein data. Database the Journal of Biological Databases and Curation 2011 (2011)
[4] Ashburner, M., Ball, C.A., Blake, J.A., Botstein, D., Butler, H., Cherry, J.M., Davis, A.P., Dolinski, K., Dwight, S.S., Eppig, J.T., Harris, M.A., Hill, D.P., Issel-Tarver, L., Kasarskis, A., Lewis, S., Matese, J.C., Richardson, J.E., Ringwald, M., Rubin, G.M., Sherlock, G.: Gene Ontology: tool for the unification of biology. Nature Genetics 25(1), 25–29 (2000)
[5] Kahn, S.D.: On the Future of Genomic Data. Science 331(6018), 728–729 (2011)
[6] Wilkening, J., Wilke, A., Desai, N., Meyer, F.: Using clouds for metagenomics: A case study. In: 2009 IEEE International Conference on Cluster Computing and Workshops, pp. 1–6 (2009)
[7] Sandberg, R., Larsson, O.: Improved precision and accuracy for microarrays using updated probe set definitions. BMC Bioinformatics 8(1), 48 (2007)
[8] Liu, Y.A., Stoller, S.D., Teitelbaum, T.: Static caching for incremental computation. ACM Transactions on Programming Languages and Systems 20(3), 546–585 (1998)
[9] Gunda, P.K., Ravindranath, L., Thekkath, C.A., Yu, Y., Zhuang, L.: Nectar: automatic management of data and computation in datacenters. In: Proceedings of the 9th USENIX Conference on Operating Systems Design and Implementation, pp. 1–8 (2010)
[10] Bhatotia, P., Wieder, A., Rodrigues, R., Acar, U.A., Pasquini, R.: Incoop: MapReduce for Incremental Computations. In: Proceedings of the 2nd ACM Symposium on Cloud Computing, p. 7 (2011)
[11] Peng, D., Dabek, F.: Large-scale Incremental Processing Using Distributed Transactions and Notifications. In: Proceedings of the 9th USENIX Conference on Operating Systems Design and Implementation, vol. 2006, pp. 1–15 (2010)
[12] Popa, L., Budiu, M., Yu, Y., Isard, M.: DryadInc: reusing work in large-scale computations. In: Proceedings of the 2009 Conference on Hot Topics in Cloud Computing, p. 21 (June 2009)
[13] Logothetis, D., Olston, C., Reed, B., Webb, K.C., Yocum, K.: Stateful bulk processing for incremental analytics. In: Proceedings of the 1st ACM Symposium on Cloud Computing, SoCC 2010, p. 51 (2010)
[14] Bu, Y., Howe, B., Balazinska, M., Ernst, M.D.: The HaLoop approach to large-scale iterative data analysis. The VLDB Journal 21(2), 169–190 (2012)
[15] Turcu, G., Nestorov, S., Foster, I.: Efficient Incremental Maintenance of Derived Relations and BLAST Computations in Bioinformatics Data Warehouses. In: Song, I.-Y., Eder, J., Nguyen, T.M. (eds.) DaWaK 2008. LNCS, vol. 5182, pp. 135–145. Springer, Heidelberg (2008)
[16] Isard, M., Budiu, M., Yu, Y., Birrell, A., Fetterly, D.: Dryad: distributed data-parallel programs from sequential building blocks. ACM SIGOPS Operating Systems Review 41(3), 59 (2007)

[17] Dean, J., Ghemawat, S.: MapReduce: a flexible data processing tool. Communications of the ACM 53(1), 72 (2010)
[18] Shvachko, K., Kuang, H., Radia, S., Chansler, R.: The Hadoop Distributed File System. In: 2010 IEEE 26th Symposium on Mass Storage Systems and Technologies, MSST, vol. (5), pp. 1–10 (2010)
[19] Apache, "Apache HBase" (2012), `http://hbase.apache.org/` (accessed: April 24, 2012)
[20] Altschul, S.F., Gish, W., Miller, W., Myers, E.W., Lipman, D.J.: Basic local alignment search tool. Journal of Molecular Biology 215(3), 403–410 (1990)
[21] Höhl, M., Kurtz, S., Ohlebusch, E.: Efficient multiple genome alignment. Bioinformatics 18(Suppl. 1), S312–S320 (2002)
[22] Finn, R.D., Clements, J., Eddy, S.R.: HMMER web server: interactive sequence similarity searching. Nucleic Acids Research 39(Web Server issue), W29–W37 (2011)
[23] Finn, R.D., Mistry, J., Tate, J., Coggill, P., Heger, A., Pollington, J.E., Gavin, O.L., Gunasekaran, P., Ceric, G., Forslund, K., Holm, L., Sonnhammer, E.L.L., Eddy, S.R., Bateman, A.: The Pfam protein families database. Nucleic Acids Research 38(Database issue), D211–D222 (2010)
[24] Oracle Grid Engine, http://www.oracle.com/us/products/tools/oracle-grid-engine-075549.html (accessed: May 02, 2012)
[25] Bhaya, D., Grossman, A.R., Steunou, A.-S., Khuri, N., Cohan, F.M., Hamamura, N., Melendrez, M.C., Bateson, M.M., Ward, D.M., Heidelberg, J.F.: Population level functional diversity in a microbial community revealed by comparative genomic and metagenomic analyses. The ISME Journal 1(8), 703–713 (2007)
[26] Douglis, F., Iyengar, A.: Application-specific Delta-encoding via Resemblance Detection. In: Proceedings of the USENIX Annual Technical Conference, pp. 113–126 (2003)
[27] Grune, D.: Concurrent Versions System, A Method for Independent Cooperation, Working paper. IR 113, Vrije Universiteit (1986)
[28] Ceri, S., Widom, J.: Deriving Production Rules for Incremental View Maintenance. In: Proceedings of the 17th International Conference on Very Large Data Bases, pp. 577–589 (September 1991)
[29] Goecks, J., Nekrutenko, A., Taylor, J.: Galaxy: a comprehensive approach for supporting accessible, reproducible, and transparent computational research in the life sciences. Genome Biology 11(8), R86 (2010)
[30] Gentleman, R.C., Carey, V.J., Bates, D.M., Bolstad, B., Dettling, M., Dudoit, S., Ellis, B., Gautier, L., Ge, Y., Gentry, J., Hornik, K., Hothorn, T., Huber, W., Iacus, S., Irizarry, R., Leisch, F., Li, C., Maechler, M., Rossini, A.J., Sawitzki, G., Smith, C., Smyth, G., Tierney, L., Yang, J.Y.H., Zhang, J.: Bioconductor: open software development for computational biology and bioinformatics. Genome Biology 5(10), R80 (2004)
[31] Tanenbaum, D.M., Goll, J., Murphy, S., Kumar, P., Zafar, N., Thiagarajan, M., Madupu, R., Davidsen, T., Kagan, L., Kravitz, S., Rusch, D.B., Yooseph, S.: The JCVI standard operating procedure for annotating prokaryotic metagenomic shotgun sequencing data. Standards in Genomic Sciences 2(2), 229–237 (2010)
[32] Wong, A.K., Park, C.Y., Greene, C.S., Bongo, L.A., Guan, Y., Troyanskaya, O.G.: IMP: a multi-species functional genomics portal for integration, visualization and prediction of protein functions and networks. Nucleic Acids Research 40(Web Server issue), 1–7 (2012)

msPar: A Parallel Coalescent Simulator

Carlos Montemuiño[1], Antonio Espinosa[2], Juan-Carlos Moure[3],
Gonzalo Vera-Rodríguez[4], Sebastián Ramos-Onsins[4], and Porfidio Hernández Budé[3]

[1] Universitat Autònoma de Barcelona, Bellaterra, Spain
cmontemu@acm.org
[2] Universitat Autònoma de Barcelona, Bellaterra, Spain
antonio.espinosa@caos.uab.es
[3] Universitat Autònoma de Barcelona, Bellaterra, Spain
{juancarlos.moure,porfidio.hernandez}@uab.es
[4] Centre de Recerca en Agrigenòmica, Bellaterra, Spain
{gonzalo.vera,sebastian.ramos}@cragenomica.es

Abstract. We implemented a parallel version (hereafter referred as "msPar") of the coalescent simulation program ms, providing the same functionality and output, parallelized using a Master-Worker scheme with on-demand scheduling and MPI to run on an HPC cluster. To our knowledge this is the first time such parallelization has been applied to ms, and shown to be effective in using all computational resources of an HPC cluster, performing up to 42 times faster than original ms when using 72 logical processors. We propose msPar as an alternative to ms and other simulators using approximations to the standard coalescent approach. Source code is available at https://github.com/cmontemuino/mspar

Keywords: HPC, parallel, master-worker, MPI, coalescent.

1 Introduction

Population genetics, a field of biology that studies the molecular diversity within and between species [1], is playing a major role in human genetic research linking hypothesis on sequence variation with empirical observations [2].

As genome-scale data is becoming a common place in genetic research, disagreements between expectation and observation have become clear [3], forcing geneticist to work with more complex evolutionary scenarios [4].

Simulation software is the key tool used in population genetics to generate genetic data. Much effort is continuously put in designing efficient simulation programs that aim to deal both with genome-scale data and complex evolutionary models [2][4].

The more complex the evolutionary model, the less efficient the simulation and vice versa [4]. From the two types of simulation applications, coalescent-based (backward in-time) and forward in-time, the standard coalescent approach shown to be computationally intractable when working at genome scale [4][5][6].

The common approach to overcome this issue is to design new algorithms, compromising the flexibility for the sake of efficiency, but some authors are starting

D. an Mey et al. (Eds.): Euro-Par 2013 Workshops, LNCS 8374, pp. 321–330, 2014.

to make use of new technologies and computer clusters [4][7], as with forward in-time simulators, SimuPop [8], Nemo [9] and Mendel's Accountant [10].

Parallel programming is a promising approach to improve the performance of a broad range of applications, especially bioinformatics applications. In this paper we present an approach to parallelize a coalescent simulator, enabling it to be run in an HPC cluster. We parallelized the Hudson's *ms* coalescent simulator [11], the most classical and widely used coalescent simulator [2][12][13], not only by the community research, but also as a point of comparison when new coalescent simulators are released. We coined this simulator as *msPar*.

We propose to parallelize the coalescent simulator *ms*, without affecting its flexibility when working at genome-scale or to perform analysis requiring high number of iterations, as long as more computational resources are available. We measured execution time of *ms* to generate 528 replicas in an HPC cluster, with a mutation rate of 640 and a recombination rate of 5120 (both scaled to 4N generations), with a sample size of 200 chromosomes and a region of 1e6 bp, resulting in 24 hours. Doubling the recombination rate to 10240 we found *ms* took 7.75 days to complete.

The organization of the article is as follows. In next section we present the background and related work. In section 3, we present the *ms* application and describe its structure. Section 4 describes our proposed solution. We present and discuss the performance results in section 5, and end with some conclusions from this research in section 6.

2 Related Work

Researching in genetics population field was supported by mathematical modeling for over 75 years. Empirical testing of theoretical models is practically impossible for organisms with long generation times. Continuous advances in numerical simulation and wide availability of computational resources allow researchers to use numerical simulation to test mathematical models in virtual populations, and even to analyze genetic data [10][14]. As a direct consequence there is a high number of simulators available, each one tailored to a specific scenario, implying geneticists must decide which simulator to use depending on the research being conducted [12].

From the two approaches to simulation algorithms, forwards in-time (also known as individual based-simulation) and backwards in-time (also known as coalescent simulation), coalescent simulations are most widely used because of its efficiency and flexibility [5][8][12]. Forward in-time simulations have been mostly used for cases where coalescent approach does not suit, as to observe the evolution of allelic spectra from the founder to the current generation [15], when the interest is focused on the evolutionary process itself [2], or teaching purposes [7].

The standard coalescent approach showed to be extremely efficient for short sequences, but becomes computationally demanding and very slow for large genome regions (> 100Mb) with increasing recombination rate. New approaches emerged to overcome this issue, as the sequentially Markov coalescent [4][16][17] and Markov chain Monte Carlo [18]. Among other coalescent simulators developed last years

(GENOME [6], mlcoalsim [19] and MSMS [13]), MaCS [16] and fastsimcoal [17] appeared to be the most efficient ones for large genomic regions and high recombination rates.

3 MS Coalescent Simulator

Hudson's *ms* [11] is a Monte Carlo application widely used by population geneticists and molecular biologists to analyze populations and DNA sequences, and estimate demographic and mutational parameters from a theoretical population evolving under a neutral Wright-Fisher model. Implementing a continuous-time approximation of the coalescent process, *ms* bases its processing in first generating an ARG (Ancestral Recombination Graph) for an initial sample of chromosomes and then placing random mutations over the resulting ARG. The ARG is constructed by stochastically simulating evolutionary events (such as coalescence, migration or recombination) occurring on the ancestral material of sampled alleles backwards in time, until the MRCA (Most Recent Common Ancestor) to all the alleles is found.

We show in Fig. 1 global replica generation process. Starting from bottom, each replica sample is independently and sequentially generated by an orchestration module split up in two independent steps: Genealogy Construction and Mutation Assignment. Genealogy construction is driven by three routines simulating a random set of recombination, migration and coalescence events. The mutation assignment step works over the ARG produce by step 1, generating the different segregation loci in order to produce the final chromosomes. The stochastic feature of the coalescence process is based on an implementation of the Monte Carlo method.

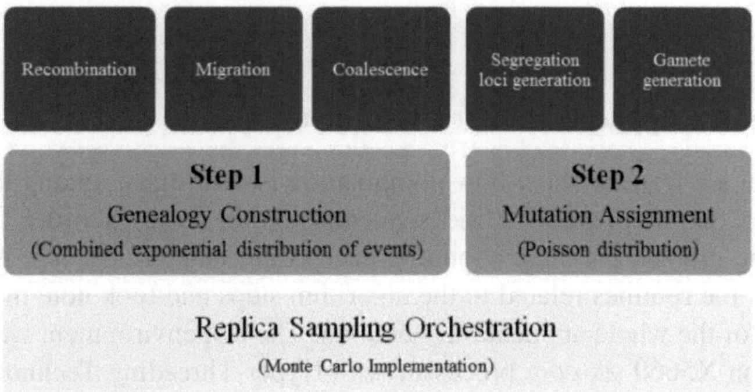

Fig. 1. Schematic representation of the Hudson's ms process to generate a set of replica samples

The first step is to construct the ARG and put it into an array-based data structure. In Fig. 2, we show how the history of each chromosome's segment is represented by the ARG nodes. Each node points to the start segment, the end segment, history is represented by stating the ARG node this node is the parent and the ARG node this node is a child. This structure is shared by the three event routines from step 1 (recombination, migration and coalescence), updating it as soon as one event occurs.

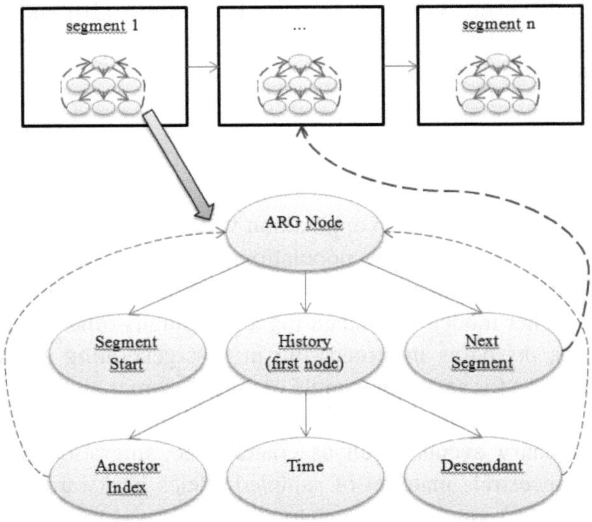

Fig. 2. Data structure of the ARG node. Given n samples, the first n nodes are the tips of the tree. The remaining nodes are the ancestral to the sampled chromosomes.

The complete ARG structure is the input of step 2, where mutations are randomly assigned (following a Poisson distribution) and the replica samples data is finally produced.

The spatial and temporal complexity of *ms* is mainly affected by the population size (n), region (l), and two weighting parameters greater than one, w_1 and w_2, that incorporate the effect of recombination and mutation rates. Temporal complexity is $O(nl + w_1n + w_2l)$ and spatial complexity is $O(nl)$ [20].

3.1 Sequential Application Characterization

In this section we want to show how computation is distributed among the algorithm steps and the output process of the sequential application, in order to determine whether a fine-grained parallelization approach could make sense. We measured the time spent by the routines related to the algorithm steps and took note of the memory consumption of the whole application execution. The test environment was a box with two Intel Xeon X5660 six-core processor with Hyper-Threading Technology running at 2.80 GHz, 12MB L3 cache, and 96 GB of DDR-RAM

In Fig. 3, we show how much time is spent by the algorithm steps and I/O processing. As long as the recombination rate is bigger, it is the percentage of total time needed to construct the ARG due to the occurrence of more events to find the MRCA. The mutation rate is what determines the size of the output, meaning more I/O processing time, but the sum of the mutation assignment step and I/O processing quickly becomes practically negligible when the recombination rate is bigger than 400.

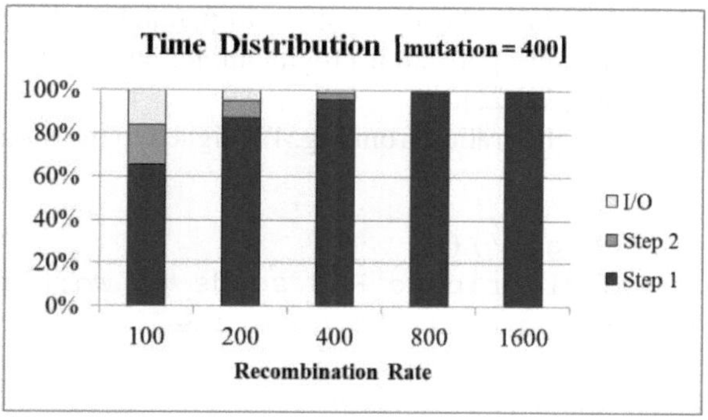

Fig. 3. Time spent by ARG construction step, mutation assignment step, and input/output processing

In Fig. 4, we show how much memory the application uses to generate one single replica as a function of recombination and mutation rates. We observed that mutation rate does not impact memory usage, irrespectively of the recombination rate value. This happens because all data structures are created at genealogy construction step (where recombination events take place), and the mutation rate applies to the mutation assignment step where no new data structures are created.

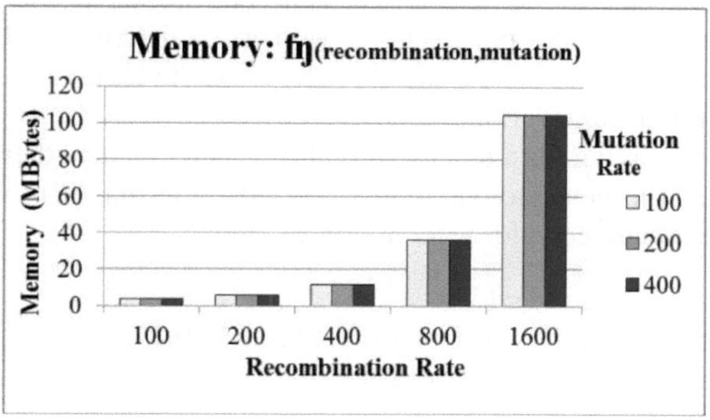

Fig. 4. Maximum resident set size as a function of recombination and mutation parameters

4 Proposal

For analysis requiring millions of population replica samples, each one independently generated, means sequentially running steps 1 and 2 from *ms* millions of times. The result of each of these computations does not depend on the results from any other computation. This is a pleasingly[1] parallel problem [21][22][23].

The high degree of data dependency among routines from step 1 (e.g. shared most variables with global scope), and between steps 1 and 2 prevents the use of a fine-grained parallelization approach without completely refactoring the source code.

[1] Also termed as "embarrassingly".

We propose to apply the Master-Worker pattern to parallelize the *ms* application, a widely used form of parallel application programming, and a natural fit for Monte Carlo applications as well [24][25].

The replica sampling orchestration from Fig. 1 assigned to the master. Its algorithm is as follow:

```
masterProcessingLogic(){
  initialize and distribute RNG seeds to workers
  while there are replicas to generate {
    find an idle worker
    if there is an idle worker {
      assign work to worker
    } else {
      retrieve generated replica from workers
    }
  }
}
```

The master also maintains the idle workers pool. In the beginning, all workers are idle and the pool is full. When one replica is assigned to one idle worker, the worker is removed from the pool. And after one worker has generated its assigned replica, it sends a message to the master and master adds this worker to the pool. When the master reads the generated replica sent by workers, it determines if there are more replicas to be generated and send a signal to the worker to let it know whether to wait for more request or to stop working.

Each worker is waiting for a request of replica generation, and then run both step 1 and 2 (see Fig. 1) to generate one replica and then transmits it back to the master. Following is the pseudo-code for worker's processing:

```
workerProcessingLogic(){
  receive seeds and initialize local RNG
  read experimentation parameters
  while worker is active {
    run step 1
    run step 2
    send replica to master
    receive activation signal
  }
}
```

The inline commands and output is the same as in the original *ms*, but includes additional arguments to setup the parallelization strategy. If the target environment consists of m cores, the parallelization is performed by dividing the N replicas evenly amongst m-1 cores, and remaining core plays the role of the orchestrator.

Master-Worker ecosystem is approached with the MPI model, to spawn worker processes and map them to hardware processors in the system, each one using its own local memory. We specifically use MPI parallel library [26].

Quality of random number streams employed by the master-worker is guaranteed by using the RNG (Random Number Generator) twice. The RNG seeds specified as input parameters are used to initialize the master's RNG. Then the master generates a set of random numbers ultimately used by each worker as seeds to initialize their own RNG.

5 Analysis and Results

In this section we give a description of the experimental setup for gathering and analyzing based on an HPC cluster.

5.1 Experimental Setup

We compare our application with respect to *ms* in terms of execution time performance metric.

Test cases were designed to be simple enough (i.e. without population structure), taking into consideration only recombination, mutation, genetic region and population size, focusing our attention on the performance evolution when the recombination ratio changes. The mutation rate is not the principal factor affecting execution time (see Fig. 3), but as it is still important in the standard coalescent process, we decided to use a scaled[2] mutation rate of 640, that being not too high, it is big enough to let the mutation assignment step to get some computation.

We selected a population size of 200 chromosomes and a region of 1e6 bp (base pairs), considered by geneticists as big for genetic analysis and quite close to what is required in genomic analysis [16].

If evolutionary parameters do not change from one replica to another (as it is in this setup), then differences in the execution time and memory consumption for each replica generation will be negligible. For the recombination rate we decided to start with a scaled value of 2560 because combined with the other parameters makes *ms* consume enough memory (1.3 GB). We doubled it until we reached 10240, which is considered a very big recombination rate.

The number of generated replicas was set in 528 for two reasons: first we wanted ms to execute during enough time (2.75 hours in the minimal setup) for measuring, and second because it allows our Master-Worker to distribute work fairly well in the case of 72 workers.

[2] All neutral parameters are given by per-site rates 4N, where N is the current population size.

5.2 Hardware and Software

We implemented the parallel application in ANSI C, and compiled it using the Linux GNU Compiler 4.4.6. Inter-process communication was implemented using OpenMPI [27] 1.4.3.

We run the binaries on a cluster using up to three nodes each with two Intel Xeon X5660 six-core processor with Hyper-Threading Technology running at 2.80 GHz, 12MB L3 cache, and 96 GB of DDR-RAM. This configuration gives us 12 physical processors per compute node, but due to the Hyper-Threading technology we can get 24 logical processors per node.

5.3 Discussion

As a way to evaluate the *msPar* performance we investigated the speedup and efficiency as a function of increasing numbers of processors. The speedup is defined as $S_p = T_1/T_p$, where p is the number of processors, T_1 is the execution time of the sequential application, and T_p is the execution time of the parallel application with p processors. The efficiency is defined as $E_p = S_p/p$.

We overcommitted the MPI processes per node from 12 to 24. This has a direct impact in the efficiency numbers, as it will be taken into account the 24 logical processors due to the Hyper-Threading technology, instead of the 12 physical processors in each compute node.

In Fig. 5 (a), we show the normalized speedup of *msPar* compared to the sequential version. For the case of maximal recombination we observed a performance degradation. This happened because the node memory was exhausted by the MPI processes. Generating a replica in this scenario means a consumption of ~16 GB, and having 24 MPI processes running with this problem size implies to use more memory (~380 GB) than available physical memory at the node (96 GB), meaning a penalty because the page swapping. In Fig. 5 (b), we show the efficiency we obtained as long as more processes are added for computation. Besides there is a considerable drop-off when the recombination rate is 10240, the efficiency does not significantly change its values in each one of the problem sizes.

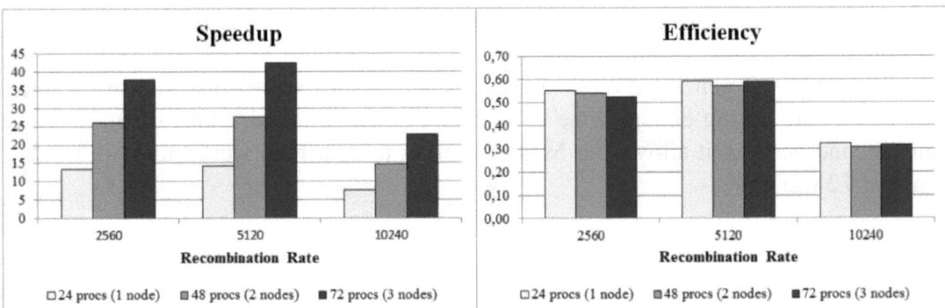

Fig. 5. a) Speedup obtained with 24 processes (1 node), 48 processes (2 nodes) and 72 processes (3 nodes). b) Efficiency showing how well the parallelization goes as long as more processes are added for computation.

The most important contribution for the geneticist is the reduction of the overall running time. Table 1 shows the overall running time *ms* and *mspar* take to complete different problem sizes, demonstrating a significant improvement in the time a researcher should wait to run the experiments.

Table 1. Execution times (in 'd' days, 'h' hours and 'm' minutes) for both ms and msPar

		msPar		
Recombination	ms	72	48	24
2560	2h45m	4m	6m	12m
5120	24h40m	35m	53m	1h44m
10240	7d18h5m	8h11m	12h36m	24h2m

6 Conclusions

Initial results indicate that using the proposed parallel approach we can achieve significant speedup values and much better execution times on an HPC cluster. This can allow population genetic scientists to use *ms* with large genome regions or analysis requiring high number of iterations (e.g. Approximate Bayesian Computation, ABC [28]) otherwise intractable due to time restrictions.

The next step is to refactor the *ms* code in order to remove the data structure dependency and then to apply an hybrid approach (MPI - SMP/GPGPU) depending on the input parameters (genomic region, population size and recombination rate)..

Acknowledgments. This work has been supported by projects number CGL2009-09346 and TIN2011- 28689-C0201-01 of Spanish Ministerio de Ciencia y Tecnologia (MICINN).

References

1. Hudson, R.: Gene genealogies and the coalescent process. Oxford Surveys in Evolutionary Biology 7, 1–44 (1990)
2. Carvajal-Rodríguez, A.: Simulation of Genomes: A Review. Current Genomics 9, 155–159 (2008)
3. Schaffner, S., Foo, C., Gabriel, S., Reich, D., Daly, M., Altshuler, D.: Calibrating a coalescent simulation of human genome sequence variation. Genome Res. 15, 1576–1583 (2005)
4. Carvajal-Rodríguez, A.: Simulation of Genes and Genomes Forward in Time. Current Genomics 11, 58–61 (2010)
5. Kim, Y., Thomas, W.: Simulation of DNA sequence evolution under models of recent directional selection. Brief. Bioinform. 10(1), 84–96 (2009)
6. Liang, L., Zöllner, S., Abecasis, G.: GENOME: a rapid coalescent-based whole genome simulator. Bioinformatics 23(12), 1565–1567 (2007)

7. Peng, B., Chen, H.-S., Mechanic, L., Racine, B., Clarke, J., Clarke, L., Gillanders, E., Feuer, E.: Genetic Simulation Resources: a website for the registration and discovery of genetic data simulators. Bioinformatics, 1–2 (2013)
8. Peng, B., Kimmel, M.: simuPOP: a forward-time population genetics simulation environment. Bioinformatics 21(18), 3686–3687 (2005)
9. Guillaume, F., Rougemont, J.: Nemo: an evolutionary and population genetics programming framework. Bioinformatics 22, 2556–2557 (2006)
10. Sanford, J., Baumgardner, J., Brewer, W., Gibson, P., Remine, W.: Mendel's Accountant: A biologically realistic forward-time population genetics program. SCPE 8(2), 147–165 (2007)
11. Hudson, R.: Generating samples under a Wright-Fisher neutral model of genetic variation. Bioinformatics 18(2), 337–338 (2002)
12. Hoban, S., Bertorelle, G., Gaggiotti, O.: Computer simulations: tools for population and evolutionary genetics. Nature Reviews Genetics 13, 110–122 (2012)
13. Ewing, G., Hermisson, J.: MSMS: a coalescent simulation program including recombination, demographic structure, and selection at a single locus. Bioinformatics 26(16), 2064–2065 (2010)
14. Sanford, J., Nelson, C.: Studies in Population Genetics, pp. 117–135 (August 2012)
15. Peng, B., Kimmel, M.: Simulations Provide Support for the Common Disease–Common Variant Hypothesis. Genetics 175(2), 763–776 (2007)
16. Chen, G., Marjoram, P., Wall, J.: Fast and flexible simulation of DNA sequence data. Genome Res. 19, 136–142 (2009)
17. Excoffier, L., Foll, M.: fastsimcoal: a continuous-time coalescent simulator of genomic diversity under arbitrarily complex evolutionary scenarios. Bioinformatics 27(9), 1332–1334 (2011)
18. Grünwald, N., Goss, E.: Evolution and population genetics of exotic and re-emergin pathogns: novel tools and appoaches. Annual Review of Phytopathol. 49, 249–267 (2011)
19. Ramos-Onsins, S., Mitchell-Olds, T.: Mlcoalsims: multilocus coalescent simulations. Evol. Bioinform. Online 3, 41–44 (2007)
20. Yuan, X., Miller, D., Zhang, J., Hirrington, D., Wang, Y.: An Overview of Population Genetic Data Simulation. J. Comput. Biol. 19(1), 42–54 (2012)
21. Dongarra, J., Foster, I., Fox, G., Gropp, W., Kennedy, K., Torczon, L., White, A.: Source book of parallel computing. Morgan Kaufmann (2003)
22. Breshears, C.: The art of concurrency: a thread monkey's guide to writing parallel applications. O'Reilly Media (2009)
23. Mattson, T., Sanders, B., Massingil, B.: Patterns for parallel programming. Addison-Wesley Professional (2004)
24. Shao, G.: Adaptive scheduling of master/worker applications on distributed computational resources. PhD thesis, University of California at San Diego (2001)
25. Basney, J., Raman, R., Livny, M.: High throughput Monte Carlo. In: Proceedings of the Ninth SIAM Conference on Parallel Processing for Scientific Computing (1999)
26. Pacheco, P.: Parallel programming with MPI. Morgan Kaufmann (1996)
27. Open MPI: open source high performance MPI
28. Beaumont, M., Zhang, W., Balding, D.: Approximate bayesian computation in population genetics. Genetics 162, 2025–2035 (2002)

First Workshop on Large Scale Distributed Virtual Environments on Clouds and P2P (LSDVE 2013)

Laura Ricci, Alexandru Iosup, Andreas Petlund, and Radu Prodan

Program Chairs

Distributed Virtual Environments (DVE) enable geographically distant users to communicate, interact and collaborate within a virtual environment. Collaborative multimedia applications, networked computer games, distributed simulation environments, Collaborative-Supported Cooperative Work (CSCW) are examples of DVEs. In particular, on-line gaming entertainment has acquired lots of popularity in the last years from both industry and research communities.

The market size of on-line gaming has received a 5 billion \$ evaluation in 2010, while the number of total users have reached around 20 million worldwide. With the emergence of readily available cloud platforms, game developers have the opportunity of deploying their networked games in the cloud, or supporting their network solutions with hybrid P2P/Client-Server architectures with dynamically adapting cloud support. This brings possibilities to smaller developers that were reserved for the big studios until recently. Whether the existing cloud architectures are suitable for such high-interactivity loads is not yet properly documented. The main goal of the First Workshop on Large Scale Distributed Virtual Environments on Clouds and P2P, LSDVE 2013, held in Aachen, Germany, on its first edition, has been to encourage research into these basic questions. The workshop has been a venue for researchers both from industry and from academy to present and discuss important aspects of Large Scale Distributed Virtual Environments. The papers presented at the workshop regard both assessment of current state and introduce further research directions.

The paper *Is today's public cloud suited to deploy hardcore real-time services? A CPU perspective* evaluates the actual, practical soft real-time CPU performance of current cloud services, with a special focus on on-line games. To perform this evaluation, a micro-benchmark is repeatedly run at a high frequency giving an overview of available resources over time. The experimental results show that public cloud services deliver performance mostly within the requirements of popular on-line games, where Microsoft Azure Virtual machines give a significantly more stable performance than Amazon EC2.

The paper *Games for Research: A Comparative Study of Open Source Game Projects* detects a set of qualities and features required for a video game to be suitable as a platform for computer science research. The paper analyses four open source games and compares their characteristics with respect to the defined features. The possibilities of enhancing cooperation between the professional and research communities is also discussed.

D. an Mey et al. (Eds.): Euro-Par 2013 Workshops, LNCS 8374, pp. 331–332, 2014.

The paper *Workflow Scheduling in Amazon EC2* points out one of the main challenges in the case of a cloud-based DVE, i.e. the design of algorithms for resource provisioning. In the context of workflow-applications, the answer to the aforementioned issue depends on how the execution of the tasks composing a workflow is scheduled and how the execution of set of tasks is mapped onto a set of resources for makespan minimization. The paper compares two real multi-objective workflow scheduling, MOHEFT and SPEA2*, in the context of Amazon EC2. The carried experiments show that MOHEFT outperforms SPEA2*, and that the analysis of the trade-off solutions can help in selecting good scheduling solutions.

The paper *MeTRO: Low Latency Network Paths with Routers-on-Demand* presents MeTRO, a framework which proposes to dynamically identify and use Internet locations delivering better paths. Metro exploits cloud computer resources to host virtual routers and such routers can be part of a path between two end systems. The paper presents extensive evaluations showing that this method decreases the latency in 58% of the cases studied, albeit increasing the number of hops. The issue of latency reduction is of great importance for the development of large scale virtual environments.

Finally, the paper *Toward Community-driven Interest Management for Distributed Virtual Environment* presents a distributed protocol for Interest Management that integrates two different gossip protocols. The first one is based on a discrete tessellation of the Area of Interest of a peer in order to maximise its coverage by the peer neighbours. The second is based on a distributed algorithm enabling the peers to self-organise themselves in communities.

Additionally to the regular papers, a keynote presentation was given by myself, presenting a general overview of the main challenges in developing a Large Scale Distributed Virtual Environment and of the distributed architectures proposed for these applications.

I wish to thank all who helped to make this first edition of the workshop a success: co-chairs of the workshop, authors submitting papers, colleagues who refereed the submitted papers and attended the sessions, finally the Euro-Par 2013 organizers whose invaluable support greatly helped in the organisation of this first edition of the Workshop.

October 2013 Laura Ricci

MeTRO: Low Latency Network Paths with Routers-on-Demand

Marc X. Makkes[1,2], Ana-Maria Oprescu[1], Rudolf Strijkers[1,2], Cees de Laat[1], and Robert Meijer[1,2]

[1] University of Amsterdam, The Netherlands
[2] TNO Information and Communication Technology, The Netherlands
{marc.makkes,rudolf.strijkers,robert.meijer}@tno.nl, {a.m.oprescu,delaat}@uva.nl

Abstract. The current Internet is a loose federation of independent providers (ISPs) that manually manage inter-domain (ASes) route policies to primarily serve their own interests. The end-user experience may be hindered by two aspects: the ASes only optimize locally, possibly delivering sub-optimal end-to-end connections; the manual management of routing policies for a large amount of prefixes is error-prone. Infrastructure as a Service (IaaS) clouds let users allocate compute resources on demand, at different geographical locations, while Internet connectivity is guaranteed. Therefore, cloud providers represent untapped resources for a better end-user (application) Internet connectivity experience.

In this work we present MeTRO, a framework to construct better than best-effort routed Internet paths. Our method exploits the fact that cloud computer resources may host virtual routers and that one such router can be part of a path between two end systems. We perform an extensive evaluation of our method, by deploying it over 75 NLNOG Ring hosts. We show that our method, practically acting as an overlay network, decreases the latency in 58% of the cases studied, albeit increasing the number of hops. Our framework is specifically useful for monitoring and debugging failures, as well as configuration errors related to Internet reachability.

Keywords: Control framework, cloud computing, programmable networks, virtual routers.

1 Introduction

Route selection in the Internet is a consequence of hand-written policies. These policies are optimized for and reflect local interests of an autonomous system (AS). However, implementation can be erroneous, leading to sub-optimal end-to-end connections [10]. Since there are almost no end-to-end guaranties for Internet, packets may not travel the shortest path to its destination. As a result, routing in the Internet decreases performance of applications.

Applications can influence their own traffic via source routing protocols [8]. However, AS'es usually run protocols like MPLS [18] which work only in a single domain. Recently, several initiatives where created to create programmable

D. an Mey et al. (Eds.): Euro-Par 2013 Workshops, LNCS 8374, pp. 333–342, 2014.

networks [12,19]. Network routers that support OpenFlow [11] technologies can allow computer programs to enforce their own forwarding rules. However, only a few network operators employ such routers, and so the control over the routing decisions remains with the operators. Furthermore, the Internet topology and its qualities at a given moment in time may only be partly known [13], making it difficult to find optimal paths. As a consequence, Internet path control is only possible for a part of a network path.

Here, we turn to cloud technology to gain control packet flows. End-users can allocate virtual resources that can be used as virtual routers. By measuring the quality of the between all virtual routers and end-points, we find the optimal path between two end points. If an path with better characteristics is found over a virtual router, we setup a tunnels and routing to control the traffic.

The automated management of such overlay networks and their respective cloud resources requires dedicated control structures. Once these control structures are designed and implemented, we need to assess to what extent cloud resources deliver significantly better results with respect to the controllability of network properties.

In this paper we introduce MeTRO, a framework of **M**anag**e**ment **T**ools for **R**outers **O**n-demand routers. MeTRO measures and setup routing in a continuous adaptive manner to adjust to change in the Internet. We evaluate our framework in a diverse setup and we find that it can improve on path latency by as much as 95%. MeTRO exhibits such latency improvement behaviour in 58% of the experiments. This reduction means that in a substantial cases that large scale distributed virtual environments [7,16] such as; multiplayer online games, distributed military simulation, and collaborative design, become more responsive.

1.1 Related Work

Savage et al. [14] have shown that even in situations with partial control and knowledge of the Internet topology, alternative paths can be created that have better qualities than those constructed with the current Internet prevailing algorithms. With a technology called Detour, Savage measured the performance of alternative paths that run via intermediate nodes that were coupled to the Internet at various locations. Ly et. al. [9] implemented a similar technology using *traceroute* traces that confirmed the observations of Savage et al. The drawback of both Detour and Ly's approaches is that it requires access to the physical machines representing the intermediate nodes. Our contribution is that we use multiple clouds and an automated framework to find and create better paths in the Internet.

This paper is organized as follows. Section 2 describes our framework for finding optimal paths and identifies three use-cases; we briefly report on related work. Section 3 presents the extensive evaluation setup and discusses the results obtained through a large number of measurements.

2 The MeTRO Framework

Here, we describe the architecture of MeTRO, our control and measurement framework, and its generic approach to cloud-hosted routers. There are currently two strategies to create optimized path in the Internet: 1) let ISPs optimize or 2) use methods such as Detour [14]. Since ISPs have an incentive to optimize themselves based on cost, the only viable option is using methods like Detour. Detour adds a fixed intermediate hop between two hosts, to gain (partial) control over the path that a packet takes in the Internet. However, it requires access to physical machines locate in different administrative domains.

Building on previous work [9,14], we present a framework that takes advantage of clouds to control as well as to optimize traffic latency. Intuitively, MeTRO is a framework that finds the optimal path between two end-points by using virtual machines (VM) residing in the cloud. The main idea it to add one hop (hosted by a VM) between two end-points and learn whether the given intermediate hop leads to a better path between the two end-points. Throughout the paper we use the term "better path" to describe a path between two points which has the lowest latency among the measured paths between these two points.

MeTRO defines two types of *agents*: 1) *agents* which perform measurements and forward the traffic, and 2) a *controller* which collects the measurement results and adjusts the paths between the agents (by setting-up tunnels and routing). An agent typically runs inside a virtual machine, therefore becoming a *virtual router*; the controller may be deployed anywhere.

Figure 1 shows the closed control-loop implemented by our MeTRO framework. The *measurement-collect-adjust* strategy allows our framework to continuously adapt to the dynamic Internet environment. During the **Setup** stage, the end-user chooses the virtual machine types and locations where to deploy each agent. Next, MeTRO will instantiate the corresponding virtual machines and collect their IPs at the controller. During the **Bootstrap** stage, the controller will copy and remotely execute the script that deploys the agent in each virtual machine. These virtual machines will now act as virtual routers. For allocating and bootstrapping the virtual machines we used [15].

Once the virtual routers are running, the MeTRO controller regularly cycles through the following three stages: **Measurement** - executes the latency measurements scripts at every agent; **Collect** - after the measurements are completed, the controller collects all data from every agent, then calculates the fastest paths between the all agents; **Adjust** - if a lower latency path is found, MeTRO will build the corresponding overlay network between the endpoints, and setup routing such that traffic is routed accordingly.

The pseudo-code in Algorithm 1 finds the optimal path between two endpoints $agent_a$ and $agent_b$ by using a RTT table and calculating all the possible paths through h agents. This RTT table is populated by the MeTRO controller via the collected measurements. The algorithm is executed by the controller. The `lat` function calculates the latency of the input path, by using the RTT table and taking into account a constant penalty p for each hop. This penalty represents

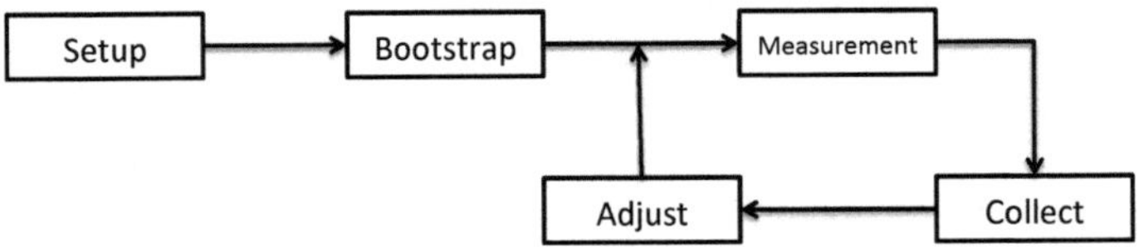

Fig. 1. The closed control-loop implemented by the MeTRO framework

the average time required to forward a packet. The `append` and `remove` functions appends and, respectively, removes the second to last element in the list.

Initially, `lst` set to $agent_a$ and $agent_b$. If multiple better paths are found, the path with the lowest latency is picked for setting up an alternative path between the end-points and dynamically create an overlay network. Currently, we only consider latency for selecting better paths, however, other criteria, such as bandwidth, jitter or a combination of such metrics, can be used to define better paths. The measurements for such network metrics could use tools like Iperf [17] or Nagios [4]. The algorithmic complexity of Algorithm 1 is $\mathcal{O}(n^h)$ where n is the number nodes in the network. While implementing Dijkstra's algorithm is more efficient, we choose this algorithm for more clarity.

Algorithm 1. findLowestPath

Require: $iplst, lst, h, p, agent_a agent_b$
  if h == 0 **then**
    return lst
  else
    fastest = lst
    if lat(fastest,p) > lat(direct,p) **then**
      return $agent_a, agent_b$
    end if
    for ip $\in$ iplst **do**
      if ip $\notin$ lst **then**
        lst.append(ip)
        t = findLowestPath(iplst, lst, h-1, p, $agent_a agent_b$)
        if lat(t) < lat(fastest) **then**
          fastest = t
        end if
        lst.remove(ip)
      end if
    end for
  end if

2.1 Functional Scenarios

Here, we describe three different scenarios where MeTRO can be employed: 1) troubleshooting routing policies 2) reachability monitoring and 3) virtual networks with specific characteristics.

Troubleshooting Routing Policies. Our framework can also be used for finding configuration errors in routing policies. ISPs can determine if their routing policies are optimal by communicating from a given point within their own network to all the measurements nodes. Since clouds offer great flexibility, the ISP can allocate and instantiate multiple VMs around to world by employing our framework. If our measurement framework finds an alternative better path, this means that somewhere in the intermediate network a routing policy is not optimally configured. A simple *traceroute* from all nodes identifies the node where the policy is not optimal.

Clouds provide a flexible alternative to NLNOG Ring, as hosts can be created on-demand for troubleshooting and debugging purposes. In addition, the cost of on-demand virtual machines for collecting views are marginal as opposed to continuously running and maintaining servers. Collecting views using *traceroute* gives insight in how traffic is routed. If a configuration error is made, this will be detectable by comparing multiple views next to each other.

Reachability Monitoring. Our proposed measurement framework can also be used to monitor the reachability of a certain destination throughout the Internet. If a destination is unreachable, it can mean that it is unavailable for every one in the Internet. It can also mean that one of the intermediate ISP "blackholes" the traffic or hijacks the prefix. MeTRO can monitor multiple destinations and check whether specific prefixes are reachable either form inside the network, or outside the network.

Virtual Networks. Another way to use our framework is to create an overlay network using clouds. While overlay networks [6,14] and virtual networks [5] are well studied, our framework can build a virtual network dedicated to optimizing a specific metric, such as latency, bandwidth etc., over multiple ISPs.

Typical beneficiaries of such overlay networks are large scale distributed virtual environments [7,16], like multi-player online games, distributed military simulation, and collaborative design. As measurement nodes are scattered around the network, dynamic tunnels are built between these measurement nodes, and the network changes dynamically on the basis of the underlying characteristics of the ISPs.

3 Experimental Evaluation

Our goal is to assess whether cloud-hosted virtual routers are a viable solution for improving the controllability of network properties. To that end, we compare a physical network of routers to virtual routers deployed in the cloud by analyzing the quality of alternative paths found using our Algorithm 1.

3.1 Experimental Setup

Figure 2 shows an overview of our experimental setup consisting of both physical and virtual resources. The endpoints of each experiment are located in a physical network. We have two types of experiments with respect to the intermediate (used for routing) nodes' location: (a) **physical-physical**, where the intermediate node is also located in the physical network, (b) **physical-virtual**, where the intermediate node is located in a cloud resource. For each type of experiment we also look at each Internet protocol considered: IPv4 and IPv6, where available.

The **physical-physical** experiments represent the baseline performance. Here, we performed measurements from every host to every other host (75 × 74 sets of results). Three round trip time (RTT) measurements where taken every five minutes, over the span of 48 hours, totaling to 129600 measurements from a given node to every other node in the physical network.

For the **physical-virtual** experiments, we selected every possible pair of hosts from the physical network and for each pair we deployed several virtual routers in each cloud zone considered.

To compute the better paths between every two endpoints, we ran our Algorithm 1 with the following parameters: the additional hop penalty $p = 0.3ms$ and the maximum number of hops $h = 8$. The algorithm uses the measurements collected from both the **physical-physical** and **physical-virtual** experiments as input. Hops considered in each experiment are in a single environment, i.e., either NLNOG Ring, BightBox or Amazon EC2.

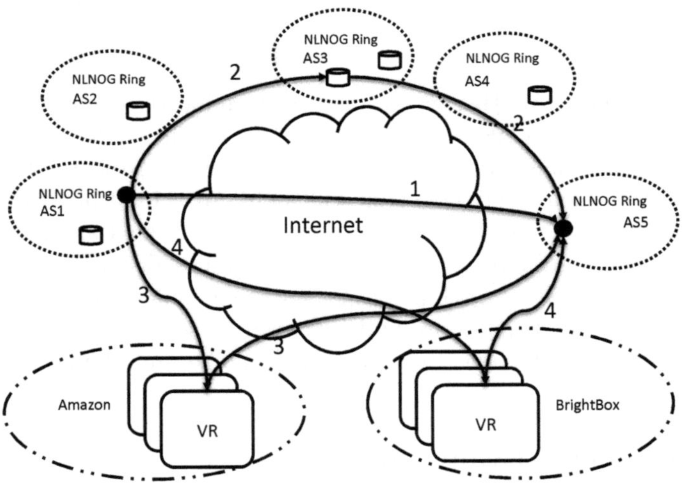

Fig. 2. Overview of our experimental setup using NLNOG Ring, Bright Box and Amazon EC2 resources. 1) a direct path between endpoints located in different ASes 2) A path with an additional hop located in NLNOG Ring 3) and 4) paths using a virtual router (VR).

As a physical network, we used the NLNOG Ring [3], which is an open initiative where network operators donate servers to create network debugging and monitor facilities for their networks. Each participating ISP provides a network measurement node which allows other ISPs to perform measurement and obtain addition information about the Inetnet routing topology At the time of our experiments the NLNOG Ring consist of 75 nodes in 72 different Autonomous Systems. Servers in the ring are located in Europe(68), but also in North America(3), Asia(2), Pacific(1) and Africa(1). All the servers of the NLNOG Ring have IPv4 and IPv6 global reachable addresses.

For our **physical-virtual** experiments we used two different cloud providers: Amazon EC2 [1] and Bright Box [2]. Amazon EC2 has 10 regions, each with several availability zones. The regions are located in North America (4), South America (1), Europe (1), Asia&Pacific (4). Bright Box has one region with 2 availability zones, both being located in Manchester(GB). Amazon EC2 only provides IPv4 connectivity, while Bright Box provides both IPv4 and IPv6 connectivity.

3.2 Results and Discussion

All results are collected in Table 1, Figures 5, 3 and 4. Each of them highlights different aspects of our results and we proceed to discuss each of them in more detail in the following.

Table 1. The total number of "better paths" using a different number of hops located either in the NLNOG Ring (NLNR), BrightBox(BB) or Amazon EC2(AM), for each IP(*v4) and IP(*v6)

#(Number of paths)	NLNRv4	NLNRv6	BBv4	BBv6	AMv4
Direct path Faster	2324	2405	n.a.	n.a.	n.a.
1 hop	1050	1078	515	497	1107
2 hops	1143	696	371	243	2921
3 hops	608	473			9273
4 hops	264	392			23944
5 hops	133	230			
6 hops	24	88			
7 hops	4	38			
8 hops	0	2			

Table 1 shows the number of better paths found for each experiment type and considering $h = 0, 1, \ldots, 8$ hops. We notice that the number of better paths in the NLNOG Ring is inversely proportional to the allowed number of hops (h), while the number of better paths in Amazon is directly proportional to h. This is due to the fact that Amazon has multiple zones located geographically close to each other which results in a factorial explosion of the number of paths per region, while the latency offered by the zones in the same region is quite similar.

Figures 3a and 3b plots in log-normal scale all alternative paths found between every pair of hosts. The x-axis values represent the latency of the direct path between each pair of hosts, while each dot represents the percentage by which the alternative path is faster. Negative percentages represent slower paths.

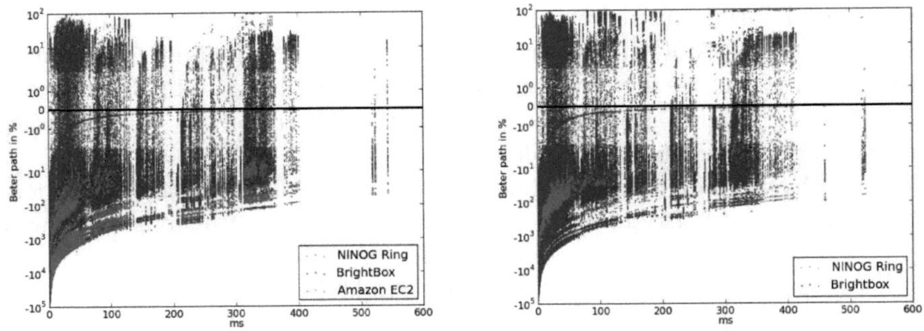

(a) IPv4. (b) IPv6.

Fig. 3. All alternative paths using one hop and different Internet protocols

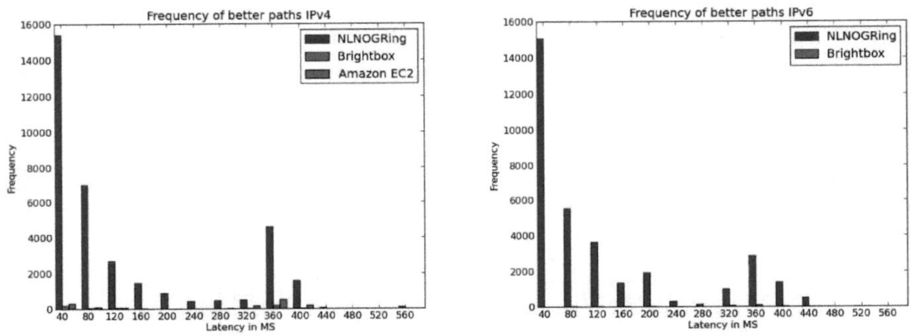

(a) IPv4. (b) IPv6.

Fig. 4. Frequency of "better paths" compared to the direct paths for different Internet protocols

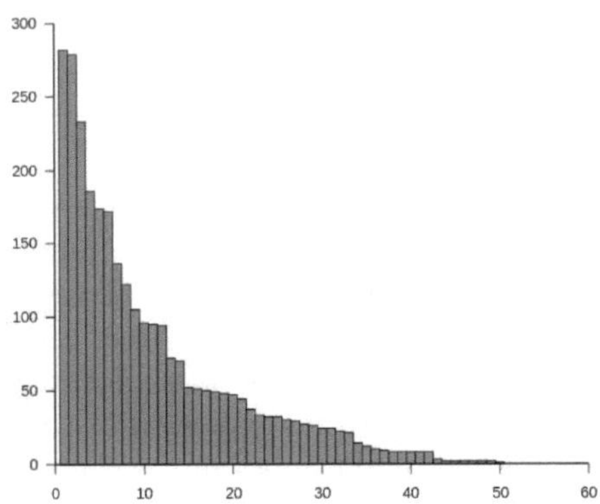

Fig. 5. Some of the NLNOG Ring nodes provide up to 10 times more "better paths" than others

Figures 4a and 4b show how many better paths are available for each latency interval (20ms). By grouping the number of alternative better paths, we can get an indication of where optimizations of paths latency can be performed.

Figure 5 shows the NLNOG Ring nodes that provide better paths. When resolving[1] the IPs of these nodes, we found that the best performing nodes are located physically close to large internet exchanges (e.g. AMS-IX, NYIX, DE-CIS, and LINX).

4 Conclusion

As the Internet optimization domain is partitioned due to the use of BGP, managing static routing policies that are applied to a substantial amount of prefixes in an dynamic environment is left to individual ISP economic priorities and prone to human error. These routing policy errors often leads to bottlenecks, increased latency or traffic can be black holed. To avoid these bottlenecks, users need control and programmability in the network.

In this paper we introduced MeTRO, a framework of tools that uses cloud infrastructure to deploy alternative, virtual routers. Within this framework, we proposed a method to explore alternative paths with specific properties, such as low latency paths. Our results are very encouraging showing that MeTRO decreases the latency in 58% of the cases studied, albeit increasing the number of hops. We showed that our framework can be used to detect unoptimized routing policies in the Internet, monitor the reachability of the Internet and create virtual networks with specific characteristics.

Acknowledgments. This work is supported by Dutch national research program COMMIT. We would like to thank Paola Grosso for reviewing this paper. In addition, we would like to thank Job Snijders and the NLNOG Ring community for providing access and resources to their NLNOG Ring servers and datasets.

References

1. Amazon EC2, http://www.amazon.com/ec2/
2. Brightbox, http://www.brightbox.com
3. The NLNOG RING, http://ring.nlnog.net/
4. Barth, W.: Nagios: System and network monitoring. No Starch Pr. (2008)
5. Chowdhury, N.M.M.K., Boutaba, R.: Network virtualization: state of the art and research challenges. IEEE Communications Magazine 47(7), 20–26 (2009)
6. Duan, Z., Zhang, Z.L., Hou, Y.T.: Service overlay networks: Slas, qos, and bandwidth provisioning. IEEE/ACM Transactions on Networking, TON (2003)
7. Funkhouser, T.A.: Ring: a client-server system for multi-user virtual environments. In: Proceedings of the 1995 Symposium on Interactive 3D Graphics. ACM (1995)

[1] IP resolved using GeoIP http://www.maxmind.com

8. Johnson, D.B., Maltz, D.A.: Dynamic source routing in ad hoc wireless networks. Kluwer International Series in Engineering and Computer Science, pp. 153–179 (1996)
9. Ly, C., Hsu, C.H., Hefeeda, M.: Improving online gaming quality using detour paths. In: Proceedings of the International Conference on Multimedia. ACM (2010)
10. Mahajan, R., Wetherall, D., Anderson, T.: Understanding bgp misconfiguration. ACM SIGCOMM Computer Communication Review 32(4), 3–16 (2002)
11. McKeown, N., Anderson, T., Balakrishnan, H., Parulkar, G., Peterson, L., Rexford, J., Shenker, S., Turner, J.: Openflow: enabling innovation in campus networks. ACM SIGCOMM Computer Communication Review 38(2), 69–74 (2008)
12. Meijer, R., Strijkers, R.J., Gommans, L., De Laat, C.: User programmable virtualized networks. In: Second IEEE International Conference on e-Science and Grid Computing, e-Science 2006, pp. 43–43. IEEE (2006)
13. Nakao, A., Peterson, L., Bavier, A.: Scalable routing overlay networks. ACM SIGOPS Operating Systems Review 40(1), 49–61 (2006)
14. Savage, S., Anderson, T., Aggarwal, A., Becker, D., Cardwell, N., Collins, A., Hoffman, E., Snell, J., Vahdat, A., Voelker, G., et al.: Detour: Informed internet routing and transport. IEEE Micro 19(1), 50–59 (1999)
15. Strijkers, R., Makkes, M.X., de Laat, C., Meijer, R.: Internet factories: Creating application-specific networks on-demand. Computer Networks (to appear, 2014)
16. Ta, D.N.B., Nguyen, T., Zhou, S., Tang, X., Cai, W., Ayani, R.: Interactivity-constrained server provisioning in large-scale distributed virtual environments. IEEE Transactions on Parallel and Distributed Systems 23(2), 304–312 (2012)
17. Tirumala, A., Qin, F., Dugan, J., Ferguson, J., Gibbs, K.: Iperf: The tcp/udp bandwidth measurement tool (2005)
18. Xiao, X., Hannan, A., Bailey, B., Ni, L.: Traffic engineering with mpls in the internet. IEEE Network 14(2), 28–33 (2000)
19. Yemini, Y., Da Silva, S.: Towards programmable networks. In: IFIP/IEEE International Workshop on Distributed Systems: Operations and Management, pp. 1–11. Citeseer (1996)

Is Today's Public Cloud Suited to Deploy Hardcore Realtime Services?
A CPU Perspective

Kjetil Raaen[1,2,3], Andreas Petlund[2,3], and Pål Halvorsen[2,3]

[1] NITH, Norway
[2] Simula Research Laboratory, Norway
[3] Department of Informatics, University of Oslo, Norway

Abstract. "Cloud computing" is a popular way for application providers to obtain a flexible server and network infrastructure. Providers deploying applications with tight response time requirements such as games, are reluctant to use clouds. An important reason is the lack of real-time guarantees. This paper evaluates the actual, practical soft real-time CPU performance of current cloud services, with a special focus on online games. To perform this evaluation, we created a small benchmark and calibrated it to take a few milliseconds to run (often referred to as a *microbenchmrak*). Repeating this benchmark at a high frequency gives an overview of available resources over time. From the experimental results, we find that public cloud services deliver performance mostly within the requirements of popular online games, where Microsoft Azure Virtual machines give a significantly more stable performance than Amazon EC2.

1 Introduction

A game company planning to deploy an online game will traditionally have to face huge costs for data centre space and bandwidth capacity. Because it is hard to predict a game's popularity before it is launched, the game provider is prone to choose over-provisioning in order to meet potential high demands. Over-provisioning boosts the costs of deployment further. "Cloud computing" is a popular way for other application areas to address this problem. Here, the customer is billed based on the resources used, and can scale resources dynamically. Game companies have, however, been reluctant to place their game servers in a virtualized cloud environment. This reluctance is mainly due to the highly time-dependent nature of games. Many studies have reported that the quality of user experience is highly dependent on latency [3] [4]. For example, Chen et al. [3] examine network latency, but it is safe to assume that delays caused by processing will be perceived identically by players. They find that perceived quality of services in games depends strongly on response time, and variations in response time (jitter) from the server are more important than absolute values. The scale of the delays these papers describe as detrimental to the players lays between 50 and 100 ms. Since providers must allow for normal network latencies

D. an Mey et al. (Eds.): Euro-Par 2013 Workshops, LNCS 8374, pp. 343–352, 2014.

in addition to processing time, any significant proportion of this delay incurred by overhead due to the cloud infrastructure should be noted.

The term "Cloud gaming", as currently used, represents "Software as a Service" *(SaaS)* [10], where the software in question is a game. The players will only run a simple thin client, sending player input to the servers, and receiving video and audio from the server. This is the approach followed by OnLive, Gaikai and others. Cloud gaming thus trades the need for local computing power for increased network throughput requirements as well as QoS demands. These services usually use a custom cloud infrastructure optimised for games.

Streaming the game in this way has some disadvantages. First of all, it has significant computing and bandwidth requirements. Many games require the full power of a modern computer to run, and the network traffic is equivalent to video streaming. Using a thin client which simply receives input and outputs video also precludes using any client-side latency-hiding techniques, so games run this way will be more latency sensitive. "Cloud gaming" in this sense is not the topic of this paper.

Conversely, this paper considers using general purpose public clouds to run traditional game servers, serving fully featured game clients. This configuration can be described as online games using cloud infrastructure. Time-dependent applications, like networked games, usually need to be custom-made, and can rarely be built upon typical web- or enterprise frameworks. Hence we need the kind of cloud service known as "Infrastructure as a Service" (IaaS) [10]. This allows the developers to access complete virtual machines, with full access privileges, allowing them to run their fully customised programs in the cloud.

Barker et al.(2010) [2] have investigated many aspects of latency sensitive applications on the Amazon EC2 cloud service. Investigating CPU, disk IO and network performance as well as running an actual game server, they conclude that the variable access to these resources, especially disk and CPU, are enough to degrade performance of latency sensitive applications.

In this paper build on [2] reexamining the CPU stability three years later and add data from one of the competitors that have entered the scene after Amazon: Microsoft Azure. We evaluate the applicability of public infrastructure clouds for use as infrastructure for online games and other highly time-sensitive applications. The work isolates CPU performance, leaving network and other subsystems for further work. We compare response time stability, with respect to processor availability, between cloud services and natively running software, as well as between two different cloud providers. The result is an updated reccommendation for services providers.

Other than [2], work on performance in clouds have so far primarily focused on the typical large, bulk jobs of scientific computing. Schad et al. (2010) [9], Ostermann et al. (2010) [7] and [5] have all worked on long term tasks, most finding relevant variation between runs. For the large workloads investigated in this work, transient performance degradations at a millisecond scale, and even stalls will be averaged out and difficult to detect. These issues are, however, highly relevant for game servers, as well as other soft realtime applications.

2 Experiment Design

To evaluate the virtual machines provided by different cloud services for their suitability in real-time applications, we created a benchmark and calibrated it to take a few milliseconds to run. The absolute average values of the benchmark runtime is not important, as we are only interested in the stability of the result. Neither does the load need to behave like any specific realistic load. This evaluation is only concerned with the actual availability of computing resources on a fine-grained time resolution.

With this in mind, the benchmark was designed as a small loop using array lookups and arithmetic, where the array is sized to be significantly larger than the cache size. This allows us to examine the memory subsystem and the CPU performance in isolation, ignoring external I/O. The tight loop of the benchmark is designed as a "worst case" load scenario for a virtual machine. Each machine was tested with a number of threads equal to the number of cores available to the virtual machine. Note that each instance of the benchmark is single-threaded, and will not show "better" results by increasing the number of cores. For these reasons, the most relevant single metric is the *coefficient of variation*. This value is defined as: $c_v = \frac{\sigma}{\mu}$, where σ is the standard deviation and μ is the mean.

In addition to the benchmark code, the utility "mpstat" was run in the background. Mpstat gives us "% steal", a metric that reports how much of the physical CPU is unavailable to the current OS instance because the hypervisor has assigned it to other instances.

Although the paper's main concern is to investigate the variance in execution time for the benchmark, a by-product is that we get an indication of the processing power provided by the different providers/service levels. This may also be of interest to game providers considering cloud deployment.

The benchmark was run on three different instances in Amazon EC2, in the zone "us-east-1d" (Table 1), as well as three different instances in Windows Azure (Table 2).

Table 1. Technical specifications. from amazon [1].

Micro Instance	613 MiB memory Up to 2 EC2 Compute Units (for short periodic bursts) I/O Performance: Low	USD 0.020 per Hour
Medium Instance	3.75 GiB memory 2 EC2 Compute Unit (1 virtual core with 2 EC2 Compute Unit) I/O Performance: Moderate	USD 0.120 per Hour
High-CPU Medium Instance	1.7 GiB of memory 5 EC2 Compute Units (2 virtual cores with 2.5 EC2 Compute Units each) I/O Performance: Moderate	USD 0.145 per Hour

2.1 Short-Term Runs

To compare the different instances, the benchmarks were run for 18 hours each under the configurations shown in tables 1 and 2. To create a baseline for comparing the cloud services with native dedicated hardware, the same benchmark

Table 2. Technical specifications from Microsoft [6]

Extra small instance	768 MiB memory 1 shared core	USD 0.020 per Hour
Small Instance	1.75 GiB memory 1 CPU Core	USD 0.085 per Hour
Medium Instance	3.5 GiB memory 2 CPU Cores	USD 0.160 per Hour

was run a standalone PC (Intel Core 2 Duo CPU E7500 @ 2.93GHz, 4GB RAM) without any visualization, chosen to be approximately the same class of performance as the cloud computers.

2.2 Time Series

Schad et al. [9] suggest that there might be differences in performance of the cloud systems based on when the benchmark is run, either by time of day or day of week. To investigate this, we ran the benchmark described above for three minutes every half hour for a week (the week of 27th of May, 2013). Between each run, we stopped the instance, and started it again before the next run. According to [9], this should allow us to get a different physical machine every time.

3 Evaluation

3.1 Reference System

The reference system (figure 1) shows the baseline of consistency we can expect from this benchmark while running natively. Deviations from this baseline can be assumed to result from the hypervisor or other aspects of the cloud system. As we can observe, the benchmark here reports extremely consistent results. The c_v is 0.02.

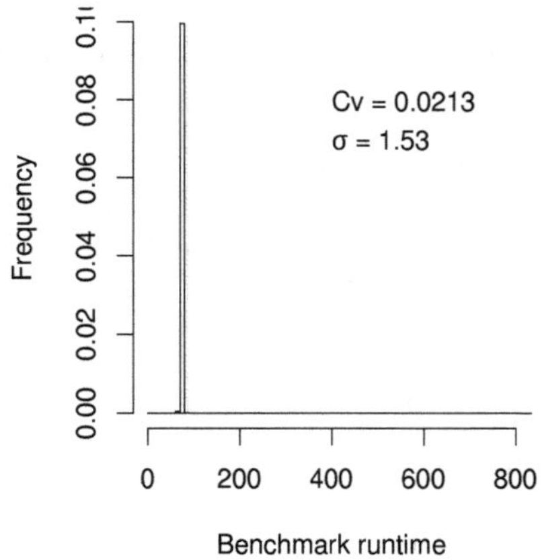

Fig. 1. Benchmark results from reference system

3.2 Amazon EC2

CPU Steal. This metric is only sampled once a second, and so has a low resolution, but with sufficient samples we build up a picture of how much CPU is allocated to each instance, as well as the distribution over time.

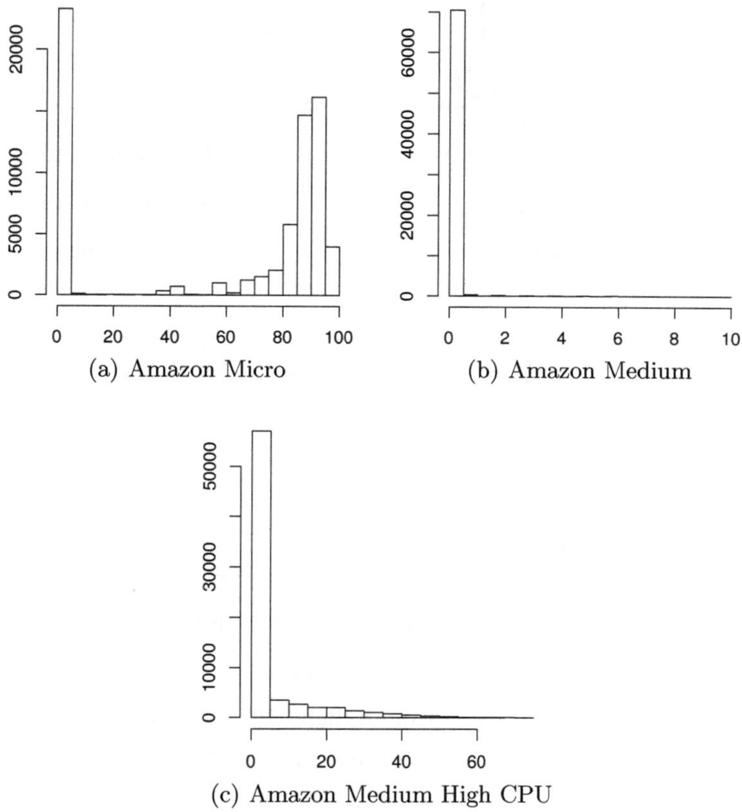

Fig. 2. CPU Steal histograms. Samples every second.

The first thing to note in this data (figure 2) is the fact that all the instance types have a significant number of samples where the current instance has full use of the CPU. These situations will pull the average CPU availability significantly up, allowing the provider to fulfil their obligations despite other samples with much less available resources.

The next point standing out is the "medium" instance. According to the pricing information, the available CPU resources on this instance type equals exactly one core of the current hardware. This seems to create a situation where our instance gets full use of the core most of the time, with very little steal. Increasing the available CPU power to the "high cpu" instance adds another

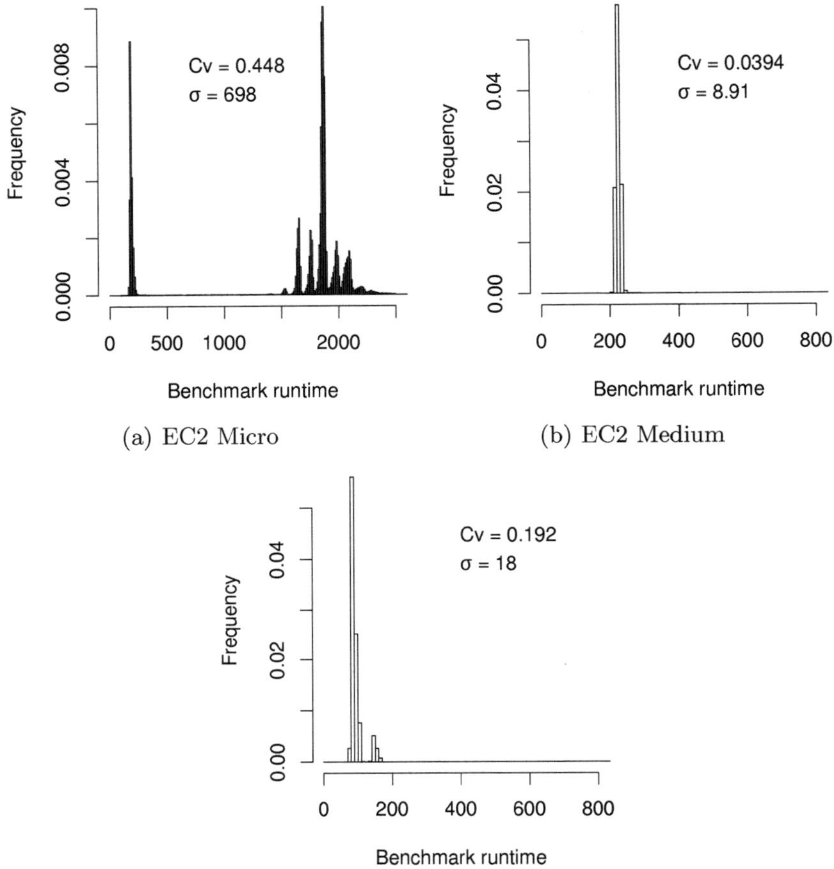

(a) EC2 Micro

(b) EC2 Medium

(c) EC2 Medium High CPU

Fig. 3. Amazon EC2: Histogram of benchmark runtimes. Note different scale on the axis of 3(a).

core, but since the instance on average only has access to part of this core, the cpu steal value increases again.

Benchmark Runtime. These results (figure 3) show several interesting values. First of all, for both the "micro" as well as the "medium, high-CPU" instance, there are two clear peaks. This matches the CPU-steal data, where the low values represent the situations where our instance got full use of the CPU, and the high run-times are the result of periods of higher CPU-steal. Again we see the advantage of the "medium" instance, in that it has a much more stable runtime, with c_v equal to 0.04. This more stable instance type depends on the fact that it allocates exactly one core to the instance. As the processing power granted each instance type is defined by an abstract, hardware independent metric, clients have no guarantee that this situation will continue indefinitely. Rather, when the underlying hardware is upgraded, it is very likely that each core will provide more power, and the currently stable instance type will become unstable.

3.3 Microsoft Azure

CPU Steal. On the "Microsoft Azure Virtual Machine" cloud, the operating system always reports 0 CPU steal, as if it was running on its own dedicated machine. This implies that the hypervisor hides these details from the operating system, or that our instance actually has a dedicated CPU resource.

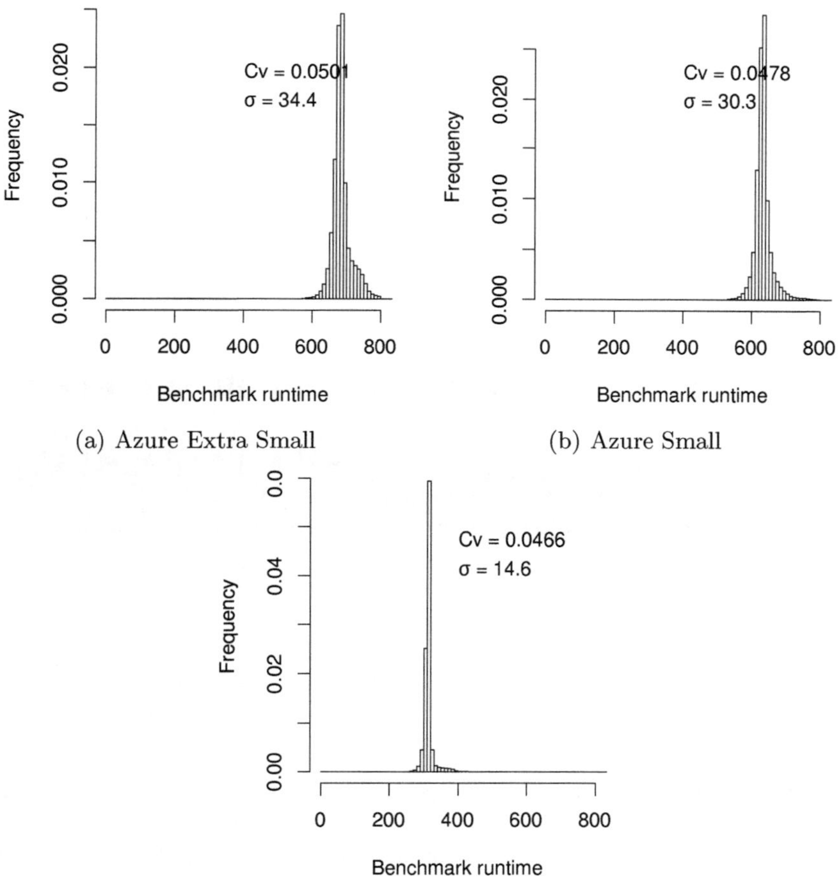

(a) Azure Extra Small

(b) Azure Small

(c) Azure Medium

Fig. 4. Microsoft Azure: Histograms of benchmark runtimes

Benchmark Runtime. Compared to the Amazon case, access to the CPU is significantly more stable in the Azure cloud (figure 4). Regardless of instance type, the runtime of the benchmark is almost completely predictable and stable, c_v is 0.05 for all instance types. The deviation is however twice that of the reference case. Depending on the exact level of time-sensitivity of the load, and its computational cost, this could be acceptable or not. The single-threaded nature of the benchmark explains why the "small" and "medium" show almost identical results.

3.4 Time Series

Figure 5 shows the results of running the benchmark repeatedly over a week on an EC2 Medium Highcpu instance. The two bands of performance are visible throughout the week, and there is no clear difference based on weekday or time of day.

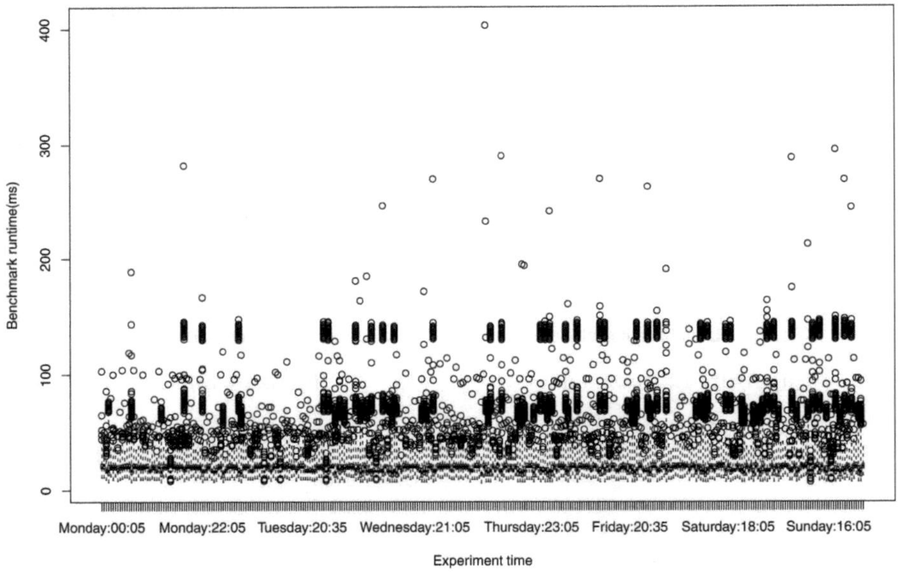

Fig. 5. Time series of Amazon EC2 Medium High CPU

3.5 Overview

Putting it all together (figure 6) we see the quite clear differences between the providers. The low-end instance from Amazon has variations far above the acceptable level for any time-sensitive application. Interestingly the "Amazon EC2 Medium High CPU" is also quite unpredictable, though this configuration is sold as higher performing than the "Medium" type. Among the Amazon offerings examined only the "Medium" instance type is near acceptable. From Microsoft Azure, all instance types are reasonably stable in performance. All show variations above our native machine reference. The significance of these variations depend on the requirements of the application.

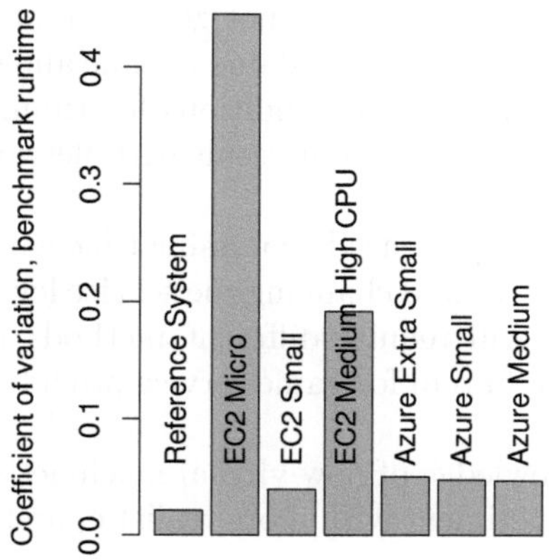

Fig. 6. Summary of benchmarks for the different systems

4 Conclusion

From these simple tests, it seems that the conclusions about CPU usage from [2] still hold for Amazon EC2. For the more time sensitive class of games [4], these delays can add up with network latency to unacceptable levels. Even for less sensitive applications there are some caveats. We do get rare samples where the CPU seems to have stalled for multiple seconds which could discourage users. Microsoft Azure Virtual machines seem to give more stable performance than Amazon EC2, without the extreme latency peaks. Utilizing these results can allow providers of interactive online services to be much more agile and react faster to changes in demand.

For future work on clouds and other virtual machines, we found that the c_v metric of multiple runs of a small, simple benchmark is a good starting point for measuring the consistency of computing resources.

Based on our measurements, access to processors is sufficiently stable on today's IaaS cloud systems to allow for real-time services to be deployed, assuming the servers are run on the right instance types.

Amazon EC2 is better at the higher service levels, although variance at all levels is larger than for Azure. An important element to keep in mind for Amazon EC2 is that migration to a different instance is necessary if a change in service level is needed.

Azure cloud shows less variance in processor availability results than Amazon. Although you get less processor speed for the same price, it is more reliable for planning stability, reducing the need for a specialized service for managing changes between service levels. If a change in service level is needed, though, Azure allows for dynamic changes without the need to migrate the virtual machine.

In this paper we have evaluated Amazon EC2 and Microsoft Azure Cloud. To give wider recommendations we are planning similar experiments using Rackspace and Google Cloud. Google Cloud currently requires the customer to go through an application process for access. We did not get any reply from Google on our request. Rackspace have not been included due to time and space requirements.

To provide a complete view of the conditions for running real-time services on IaaS instances, we need to extend our result with networking measurements, extending [2].

In order to minimize the experienced processing time variance, monitoring the experienced processing time c_v and changing the service level based on the results should be explored. This will require different methods in Amazon EC2 and Azure, but should be a useful tool for game service providers that are concerned about processing jitter.

With more detailed knowledge of how virtual machines in the cloud respond, it would be relevant to experiment with more realistic, preferably highly parallel workloads such as LEARS [8].

References

1. Amazon. Amazon EC2 Instance Types (2013), `http://aws.amazon.com/ec2/instance-types/`
2. Barker, S.K., Shenoy, P.: Empirical evaluation of latency-sensitive application performance in the cloud. In: Proceedings of ACM SIGMM on Multimedia Systems, MMSys 2010, pp. 35–46. ACM, New York (2010)
3. Chen, K.-T., Huang, P., Wang, G.-S., Huang, C.-Y., Lei, C.L.: On the Sensitivity of Online Game Playing Time to Network QoS. In: Proceedings of IEEE INFOCOM 2006(2006)
4. Claypool, M., Claypool, K.: Latency Can Kill: Precision and Deadline in Online Games. In: ACM Multimedia Systems Conference (2010)
5. El-Khamra, Y., Kim, H., Jha, S., Parashar, M.: Exploring the Performance Fluctuations of HPC Workloads on Clouds. In: 2010 IEEE Cloud Computing Technology and Science, pp. 383–387 (November 2010)
6. Microsoft. Microsoft Azure Pricing Details (2013), `http://www.windowsazure.com/en-us/pricing/details/`
7. Ostermann, S., Iosup, A., Yigitbasi, N., Prodan, R., Fahringer, T., Epema, D.: A performance analysis of EC2 cloud computing services for scientific computing. In: Ostermann, S., Iosup, A., Yigitbasi, N., Prodan, R., Fahringer, T., Epema, D. (eds.) Cloud Computing. LNICST, vol. 34, pp. 115–131. Springer, Heidelberg (2010)
8. Raaen, K., Espeland, H.: LEARS: A Lockless, Relaxed-Atomicity State Model for Parallel Execution of a Game Server Partition. In: Parallel Processing ..., pp. 382–389. IEEE (September 2012)
9. Schad, J., Dittrich, J., Quiané-Ruiz, J.: Runtime measurements in the cloud: observing, analyzing, and reducing variance. Proceedings of the VLDB ... 3(1) (2010)
10. Vaquero, L.M., Rodero-merino, L., Caceres, J., Lindner, M.: A Break in the Clouds: Towards a Cloud Definition. Computer Communication Review 39(1), 50–55 (2009)

Games for Research: A Comparative Study of Open Source Game Projects

Stig Magnus Halvorsen[1,2,3] and Kjetil Raaen[1,2,3]

[1] NITH, Norway
[2] Simula Research Laboratory, Norway
[3] Department of Informatics, University of Oslo, Norway

Abstract. Video games have proved to be an interesting platform for computer scientists as games demand the latest technology, fast response times and effective utilization of hardware. Finding the right games to perform experiments are however difficult. Some researchers create their own smaller prototype games to test their ideas, without performing tests in larger scale productions, which decreases the practical applicability of the conclusion. An important reason is the lack of suitable games for research. This paper proposes a list of qualities and features required by researchers for a video game to be suitable for computer science research. Further, it evaluates four games with open source code and discuss their usefulness. We also consider the current state of open source games and possibilities for enhanced cooperation between the professional and research communities.

1 Introduction

Decades have passed by since the first commercially produced and published video game was released, giving birth to the video game industry. Since then, both the popularity and demand for video games has exploded with an insatiable audience demanding more content and more technically advanced features for every major release. This has resulted in one of the world's toughest industries with high development costs and high risks for failure. The industry is thus a technology promoter that keeps pushing hardware and software to the limit in order to satisfy the ever demanding market.

This demand has since the late nineteen-nineties caught the eyes of computer scientists. Computer games have been a tool for research (such as Petlund et al. [11], Raaen et al. [12]), as well a topic of research (such as Claypool & Claypool [3], Eisert [10], Waveren [17]). There are, however, some crucial differences between commercial game developers and researchers. Game developers prioritize rapid creation of content and implementation of a large system, while the computer scientists prioritize investigating and researching individual components of the larger system. Scientists do not have the resources to develop a complete industry standard video game, while game developers rarely publish any results of their research. This indicates that cooperation between the industry and the researchers is beneficial.

Commercial games are rarely available in source code form. New, the code is considered company secret while releasing older code is either ignored or can be too costly. Developers are sometimes willing to co-operate with researchers, but will often limit

D. an Mey et al. (Eds.): Euro-Par 2013 Workshops, LNCS 8374, pp. 353–362, 2014.

how much of the inner workings can be disclosed. This makes the research cumbersome as well as difficult to reproduce, potentially decreasing the quality of the research material.

The current situation makes it hard for computer scientists to get hold of industry standard systems, resulting in researchers creating their own small prototype games specialized for the use of their current research. Examples include White et al. [18] and [12], which both try different concepts in simplified environments. This research should be implemented and tested in complete massive multiplayer games in order to achieve more realistic results.

Other researchers follow the same approach. Ideas need to be embedded in a full scale production in order to get fully realistic results. There is thus a need for a universally available industry standard video game that can be freely used for scientific purposes.

This paper seeks to collect, evaluate and structure scientists' requirements of video games to use in their research. These criteria have been used to evaluate and compare a selection of open source computer games in order to investigate their suitability for scientific work.

2 Method

The primary approach in this work is analyzing gameplay, source code and documentation of open source video games and game engines. Features and qualities found in each game were compared with requirements collected from a online survey.

The authors selected 60 different features both common and uncommon, that were to be evaluated as either *unimportant*, *research requirement*, *engaging requirement*, or *both*. Survey participants were also invited to provide additional requirements. An "engaging requirement", is a feature that is needed for a game to be engaging for potential test subjects. The features were meant to cover most known technical features that are currently realistic to implement in games. Both the basics, such as user input through well-known devices, and less common features, such as voice control are covered.

The survey concerns software, and assumes that the necessary hardware and drivers are in place and working properly for the various features to be fully functional.

The survey was active for approximately a month. We sent invitations to computer scientists that had or were interested in using video games in their research. Most of these researchers were based in Norway among them some scientists from "Simula Research Laboratory" and "SINTEF", but it was also sent to various known researchers abroad. The survey had a total of 22 participants, which is a number that reflects the fact that there were few computer scientists which replied that they felt their experience and work was relevant for the survey.

Participants from the game industry were not invited, because the problem discussed in this paper is unique to academic research.

Games were selected from the list of open source games at Wikipedia [20], from previous research, as well as from the authors' own experience. This approach should give a reasonable overview of which such games are available. Games from Wikipedia's list with updates prior to 2012 are considered inactive and therefore excluded. The games we examined more thoroughly are, *Doom 3 (FPS)*, *OpenArena (FPS)*, *Vega Strike (Action Simulator)* and *PlaneShift (MMO)*.

The first phase of the data gathering process involved installing and playing the respective games. It is a quick and an effective approach to get a great overview of each game, indirectly providing information on various game mechanics, its quality and whether or not it is a stable product. Graphics quality is evaluated visually while playing the game. This gives an immediate indication on the quality of the graphics, and whether more advanced graphical features, such as *shaders*, are supported or not. The approach also reveals implemented user interface mechanisms, such as game menus, buttons, in-game chat and similar.

Some information on embedded physics were retrieved by interacting with the games in ways that might not have been considered by developers. This involves jumping off various ledges, firing weapons at objects not usually considered targets, and experimenting with various game mechanics. Such gameplay reveals much about interaction between objects in the game. Important information is also retrieved by looking at various menus and game settings. Setting up a local server will for instance let you know how many interacting concurrent players the server supports.

The second phase was to retrieve information by collecting data from official websites and documentation available for the games and engines. Primarily to find technical specifications revealing features either implemented in the games, or "hidden" engine features not used by the games. It can alone reveal a significant amount of features and qualities not visible by simply playing the game. It is also more efficient than trying to interpret features hidden within the source code. The amount and quality of the documentation is highly variable. Because open source games require extensive cooperation between geographically distributed developers, much more documentation is available than for commercially developed games.

The final phase is to investigate the undocumented features by studying parts of the source code. This requires obtaining a copy of the source code from the official version control repository or file server, and to open the files in the intended development environment, if any. Some will immediately compile, link and run successfully, while others require the retrieval of game data or additional resources. For games with commercially licensed data, researchers need to purchase or in some way legally obtain these files. These are not needed to analyze the source code, but can make it easier by allowing you to navigate the code through testing and debugging.

The next step is to get an overview of the structure of the code to find out where to look for various potential features. Analyzing the code reveals code standards, features, and the code quality. It can be a time consuming task, we were only interested in examining the code for specific functionality and overall quality, which does not require examining every line of code manually. Once done, a final in-depth search for the unknown features are done, involving basic file search and reading. Some features are easier to determine than others, due to their complexity and nature. Features are marked as they are found or declared missing.

3 Results

The research process of collecting a list the most important features for a computer game resulted in a surprising engagement from some of the researchers invited to participate. A total of 22 researchers participated in the online survey. We received various valuable and interesting feedback on both the contents of the online survey and the research topic itself. The most important was regarding the content of the quantitative survey, which was by some perceived as too limited and that a larger of scale qualitative interviews would have been better.

Table 1. Evaluated features & games

Feature	**Requirement** %	**Unimportant** %	**Doom 3** (idTech 4)	**Open Arena** (ioquake 3)	**Vega Strike** (Vega Strike)	**PlaneShift** (Crystal Space)
Performance	91	5				
Logging system	77	18	✓	~	✓	✓
Latency intolerant	68	18	✓	✓	✗	✓
Simple Physics	68	23	✓	✓	✓	✓
3D Support	68	14	✓	✓	✓	✓
Technical Documentation	68	5				
Simple AI	64	27	✓	✓	✓	✓
2D Support	63	14	✓	✓	✓	✓
Adaptability	59	23				
Scripted AI	59	23	✓	✓	✓	✓
Good Code Quality	59	18	✓	✓	✗	✓
Computational Heavy AI	55	32	✓	✓	✓	✓
Reliability	54	27	✓	✓	✗	✗
Player vs Environment	54	23	✓	✓	✓	✓
Large networked (13-64)	54	36	✗	✗	✗	✓
Packet loss intolerant (TCP)	50	32	✗	✗	✗	✗
Single Player Mode	50	45	✓	✓	✓	✗
Player vs Player (PvP)	50	27	✓	✓	~	✓
Massive networked (65+)	50	41	✗	✗	✗	✓

✓ implemented ~ partially ✗ absent

The remainder of this section contains an in-depth analysis of the selected games, examining them for the quality of the features we found are important in the survey. Results from the survey are presented in table 1, which shows the most requested features. Qualitative features such as performance are not evaluated in the table, but described further in the section for the individual game.

3.1 Doom 3 (IdTech 4)

Doom 3 including the *idTech 4* engine is to the knowledge of the authors the most complex and the most advanced both technically and visually open source game available as of this date. Primary development on the engine was completed before the game's commercial release in 2004 [8]. The source code was published by Timothee Besset (user "TTimo") on *GitHub* in November 2011 [2].

However only the source code has been made freely available, and not the data files. The data files can be obtained by purchasing the game and configuring the compiled game to read these. However, you will not be able to publish new content or updates with the original game data as this is only available under commercial license [1]. This can be used for research, but the complete experimental setup can not be shared.

The engine is mainly written in C++, using OpenGL for 3D graphics, and contains 601032 lines of code [13]. The source code defines various shared libraries as well as an executable.

The source code is of high quality with good naming conventions, some good comments and it is relatively easy to read. It contains clear traces of optimization, which is expected as it is a major production that sold more than 3.5 million copies [15]. This is also an indication of stability, as it has been under industry standard tests and been played by millions. Id Software have also implemented their own memory manager, or *garbage collector*, for faster dynamic memory allocation.

The code contains some less common hacks, where the most notable one overrides all *protected* and *private* keywords setting them to *public*. This is required by their custom run-time type information (RTTI) functionality.

Doom 3 is primarily a single player FPS game, with a online multiplayer mode supporting up to 8[1] players in four different *Deathmatch* modes, allowing free for all fights. However, one of the programmers, John Carmack, has stated that the engine can support more than 4 players but that they decided to restrict it for game design reasons [7]. This can naturally be modified as the source code is freely available. The game is an intense action FPS experience, implying the need for low response times as suggested by [3]. This is reflected in the code with built in latency-hiding mechanisms. Trading reliability for response time, the latency sensitive section of the network code uses the UDP protocol.

A natural part of the single player functionality is the need for "savegames", which is fully supported by the engine. The game was released before the concept of *Cloud storage* went public, so it is not a part of the engine itself but can be obtained by running the game through *Steam*, although not open source.

The original project found on *GitHub* does currently only build on Windows using *Microsoft Visual Studio 2010* or later, and on OSX using *Xcode 3.2* or later. It is using operating system (OS) specific libraries for various low level operations including threading and network. It makes it somewhat cumbersome to port to other platforms, but ports are already available. Some with their own open-source *Git* repositories (Besset [1] and Sanglard [13]). Threads have been utilized for time-critical functions that should not be limited to the frame rate of the game, including sound mixing.

Adapting the engine or game itself to be used for other game types than FPS is possible as it is open source. The engine has, however, primarily been used by FPS games [19], so it is likely that it will require a significant amount of work to modify it into other genres.

---

[1] Original 4 players, the support for 8 players were added in the "Resurrection of Evil" expansion.

There is unfortunately little or no official technical documentation of the engine apart from the source code. An idTech developer published a engine modification guide which is useful, though not totally complete. There is also a very good code/engine review available by Fabien Sanglard [13] but it also lacks some information, including networking. The only thing available close to design documentation is the game manual, but no official documents have been published.

Other available and relatively industry standard engine features are logging, physics, support for scripting, artificial intelligence (AI) and a library for graphical user interface (GUI) components. See table 1 on page 356 for an overview of the most important implemented features.

3.2 OpenArena (Ioquake 3)

OpenArena is a pure first-person shooter developed using *ioquake3*, an open source community developed enhancement of the *idTech 3* engine. idTech 3's source code was released as open source together with the game *Quake III Arena*'s source under the "GNU General Public License" in 2005 [14]. The binary data files generating the content of the game are as with Doom 3 still closed and copyrighted. OpenArena's intention is to provide a free and enhanced alternative to *Quake III Arena*. *Quake III Arena* is, as Doom 3 a commercial computer game, implying a polished and stable game. The *ioquake3* project claims to have fixed many known bugs in the original engine, patched some security issues and that they have enhanced the overall stability of the entire engine and gameplay.

The engine and the game is primarily developed using C, using OpenGL for rendering 3D graphics. The original *idTech 3* engine consists of 367815 lines of source code [13], which is almost half the size of *idTech 4*. The idTech engine and OpenArena are both well recognized and previously used in computer scientific research (such as [17], [10], and Parry [9]). Threads are not utilized to balance the load in *idTech 3* which can create uncommon, yet possible blocking issues in the games. *ioquake3* has fixed this by utilizing threads through the Simple Directmedia Library (SDL) 1.2 (SDL_thread), and by using the platform independent *OpenAL* library for sound. The engine also supports video playback, which is also true for the unmodified version.

OpenArena's gameplay is as its predecessor, Quake III Arena, primarily focused on the online multiplayer experience. It also supports a simple single player game mode, which behaves as a multiplayer game where the opponents' are pre-programmed AIs simulating players and the local machine runs the server. The bots are programmed in C, using a well structured collection of functions for in-game artificial intelligence. OpenArena natively supports up to 12 simultaneous players in one match. Single player progress, achievements and settings are saved on the local hard drive. Multiplayer saves primarily the settings, such as user name and character.

The code quality is in general well structured and documented, through naming conventions, comments and file directory structure. There is a log system available, and an in-game command window with various options. Technical documentation is found on OpenArena's and ioquake3's official websites and *Wikimedia* based encyclopedias.

The game compiles and runs on Windows, OSX and most Linux based platforms and it thus qualifies as easily portable. It is one of the enhancements made by the *ioquake3* project, replacing platform specific libraries with cross-platform supported libraries. Both the idTech 3 and ioquake3 engines are primarily FPS engines, somewhat limiting the adaptability of the engine. It is possible to modify it to support other game genres, but probably not without changing engine specific features.

3.3 PlaneShift (Crystal Space)

PlaneShift is an open source community developed multiplayer online role playing game (RPG) developed using the open source *Crystal Space* engine. All code and the engine is released under the "GNU General Public License" (GPL), while the data content files are copyrighted to "Atomic Blue Non Profit Corporation" and distributed under the "PlaneShift Content License". The license details can be found on their official website [6]. There is only one game mode, multiplayer, where you are able to interact and fight with other players or non-player characters (NPC). Each player needs an individual game account, stored in the game's database, together with character progress and other game data. This gives a "cloud like" storage solution with a globally available database, where you can access your game data from any computer. The official database is however currently only one server, where your data may be erased at any given time. This is because the game is still currently under development, even with most of the key functionality is in place [5]. The game can therefore not be categorized as completely stable, and optimized. Unexpected behavior and bugs do exist as we experienced while playing, but it never crashed. It is however of surprisingly high quality, and will be an interesting candidate when finally released as stable.

Crystal Space, the game's engine, is an highly portable and acknowledged open source software development kit (SDK) for developing 3D applications. It is released under the "GNU Lesser General Public License" and is developed using C++. Various games have been created with the SDK, and it can be classified as highly adaptable. The SDK includes all functionality required by a game, including physics, collision detection, graphics, user input, GUI, and more. It is also possible to find or develop plugins for special needs [16].

The game itself is a more specialized piece of software, serving its purpose as a multiplayer RPG. It is probably easier to adapt than the previous evaluated games, due to the nature of the engine and that the engine provides development tools to make content development easier. PlaneShift has a menu system, a 2D GUI system, some physics and supports joystick as an alternate input device.

3.4 Other

The other games were rejected for various reasons. Most as they are perceived as too old, including graphical rendering techniques which are obsolete for the project to represent a modern, near state of the art video game.

Vega Strike, an Action Spaceship Simulator, was evaluated but rejected as it turned out to be an incomplete game without any official support for online multiplayer gameplay. The game's graphics is also primarily 2D textures with few 3D models, and is thus not considered as a game representative of the industry standards. Other unfinished open source games are *0 A.D.*, *Ancient Beast*, *Chaotic Rage*, *Dungeon Crawl*

Soup, *Flare*, *FreeCol*, *FreeOrion*, *Hedgewars*, *Minetest*, *SpaceZero*, *Teeworlds*, *X-moto*, *SuperTuxKart*, *Sintel The Game*, *Rigs of Rods*, *Unknown Horizons*, and *Unvanquished*.

Other quite popular games such as *BZFlag*([11]) a *Tank FPS*, and *QuakeWorld* (Cordeiro et al. [4]) have been rejected even though they have been previously used for computer science. This is primarily because the games origins back to the late 90ies [20] and are not good enough, even though they are recently updated.

This also includes games as *The Battle for Wesnoth*, *Battle City*, *Flight Gear*, *FreeCiv*, *Open Hexagram*, *PokerTH*, *StepMania*, *Chocolate Doom*, *Tales of Maj'eyal*, *Advanced Strategic Command*, *Angband*, *Biniax*, *OpenRA*, *Zero-K*, *Crossfire*, *M.A.X.R.*, *TripleA*, *UFO: Alien Invasion*, *Widelands*, *C-Dogs*, *Katana Shoujo*, *Mari0*, *CorsixTH*, *Exult*, *Freesynd*, *Gigolomania* and *NX Engine*.

Other games were also rejected as they were too similar, if not on the same engine, as earlier selected and evaluated games. This includes games as *Oolite*, *Red Eclipse*, *Doom 3 BFG Edition*, *Xonotic*, *Cube 2: Sauerbraten*, *Smokin' Guns* and *Warsow*.

4 Discussion

Our results show that no single game is perfect for all scientists. We have evaluated the features of some open source games on a individual project basis. Some projects are so distinctive that their requirements will rarely be similar to the general perception of important features. The feature evaluation scheme can also be used to evaluate the qualities of other computer games for use in research. We find *Doom 3* and *OpenArena* the most useful games for research within the field of computer science. Both are initially made of commercial projects. *PlaneShift* can be used if the experimental state of the game is acceptable.

The quality of the open source games indicates that they are far behind the technology pushing commercially produced industry standard games. This is confirmed by *Doom 3* as it was released in 2004, and is still among the more polished and technically advanced open source games available. Commercial games and engines made open source, like *Doom 3* with the *idTech 4* engine, has poor documentation compared to open source games. Open source games and commercially produced games might be considered as incomparable due to the usual great difference of dedicated resources for the different project types.

Doom 3 reveal some interesting facts regarding the complexity when compared to the older releases. It has a significant amount of more code than the other games, and the project structure is in many ways more cluttered with functionality spread across a heap of files. It is not a surprise as it is a vast game compared to the other, but it makes the code harder to understand and work with. This is probably also true for many new and even larger productions and should be considered when planning a research project.

5 Conclusions

This paper has gathered a list of features and qualities required of a video game suitable for use in computer science research, and has evaluated the suitability of games released with open source code. Our results shows that there are no ideal games that can be used for all research purposes. We have, however, developed a list of features and qualities that are worth considering when looking for attractive games, and found two computer games that are potential candidates.

The two highest rated candidates, *Doom 3* and *Open Arena*, are both made from or based on commercial produced computer games with the source code made publicly available. Among them is *Doom 3* which was released in 2004, the latest, most polished and professional production. It is negative as it is an almost ten year old release, and still one of the best open source alternatives available. This is an indication of the open source game industry's current state, which is way behind the commercial industry. It can be discussed whether or not open source and commercial projects are comparable due to the vast difference in available and dedicated resources.

The rejected games have been flagged as rejected because they are either incomplete and unstable, or no longer can be described as state of the art games; Games that are not comparable to new commercial released games. Some will consider *Doom 3* outdated as well, but it is currently one of the most modern open source alternatives. Eventually this game will also be obsolete. We hope better open source alternatives will emerge.

5.1 Limitations

The informal procedure for gathering the list of candidate games creates a risk that we have missed some potential games. Due to the vast amount of code in each of these projects, we might also have overlooked some undocumented features despite our thorough search.

5.2 Future Research

Our findings should be used to verify previous research using large scale games, where the research have purely been tested with smaller prototypes. The games evaluated as suitable may be used directly to verify the research credibility, and the feature list may be used to evaluate other open source games.

For a more generally useful result, similar work should be performed at a more global level, contacting computer scientists at research institutions all over the world. Further, qualitative work such as interviews with scientists experienced in using games for technical research or as topic for research could give more detailed results regarding requirements. There are other open source games available, and more should be evaluated to obtain a greater list of suitable games. Future reevaluations are also required as games of the current generation games will become outdated and new options will arrive.

Ideally we would like to see more game studios releasing their games as open source. Researchers and industry could achieve mutual benefit from more cooperation on new technologies. Releasing games as open source will require some time and effort from the companies, and is thus usually not perceived as a good investment. Tighter cooperation will alleviate this situation. Researchers could also co-operate with open source projects to achieve a similar goal, but it will likely require more work on the part of the researchers.

References

[1] Besset, T.: Doom 3 repository on github (November 2011), https://github.com/TTimo/doom3.gpl
[2] Besset, T.: Ttimo/doom3.gpl/commit history (November 2011), https://github.com/TTimo/doom3.gpl/commits/master?page=2
[3] Claypool, M., Claypool, K.: Latency Can Kill: Precision and Deadline in Online Games. In: 1st ACM Multimedia Systems Conference (2010)
[4] Cordeiro, D., Goldman, A., da Silva, D.: Load balancing on an interactive multiplayer game server. In: Kermarrec, A.-M., Bougé, L., Priol, T. (eds.) Euro-Par 2007. LNCS, vol. 4641, pp. 184–194. Springer, Heidelberg (2007)
[5] Atomic Blue Corporation. About planeshift (April 2013), http://www.planeshift.it/about.html
[6] Atomic Blue Corporation. Planeshift license (April 2013), http://www.planeshift.it/license.html
[7] GameFront. Game info: Doom 3 | multi player | overview (May 2013), http://doom3.filefront.com/info/Multiplayer
[8] GameSpot. Doom 3 tech info (May 2013), http://www.gamespot.com/doom-3/techinfo/platform/pc/
[9] Parry, L.: L3dgeworld 2.1 input & output specifications. CAIA Technical Report 070808A (August 2007)
[10] Peter Eisert, P.F.: Remote rendering of computer games. In: International Conference on SIGMAP (2007)
[11] Petlund, A., Evensen, K., Griwodz, C., Halvorsen, P.: Tcp enhancements for interactive thin-stream applications. In: 18th International NOSSDAV Workshop, NOSSDAV 2008, pp. 127–128. ACM, New York (2008)
[12] Raaen, K., Espeland, H., Stensland, H.K., Petlund, A., Halvorsen, P., Griwodz, C.: Lears: A lockless, relaxed-atomicity state model for parallel execution of a game server partition. In: 41st ICPPW, ICPPW 2012, pp. 382–389. IEEE Computer Society, Washington, DC (2012)
[13] Sanglard, F.: Doom3 source code review (June 2012)
[14] Shacknews. Quake 3 source code released (August 2005), http://www.shacknews.com/article/38305/quake-3-source-code-released
[15] Shacknews. John carmack and id software's pioneering development work in 3d game engines recognized with two technology emmy awards (July 2008), http://www.shacknews.com/article/38305/quake-3-source-code-released
[16] Crystal Space Team. Crystal space official site (April 2013), http://www.crystalspace3d.org/main/Main_Page
[17] van Waveren, J.: Quake III Arena Bot. PhD thesis, University of Technology Delft (2001)
[18] White, W., Sowell, B., Gehrke, J., Demers, A.: Declarative processing for computer games. In: The 2008 ACM SIGGRAPH Symposium on Video Games, Sandbox 2008, pp. 23–30. ACM, New York (2008)
[19] Wikipedia. Id tech 4 — wikipedia, the free encyclopedia (2013), http://en.wikipedia.org/w/index.php?title=Id_ Tech_4 (Online; accessed April 9, 2013)
[20] Wikipedia. List of open-source video games — wikipedia, the free encyclopedia (2013), http://en.wikipedia.org/w/index.php?title=List_of_open-source_video_games (Online; accessed April 2, 2013)

Toward Community-Driven Interest Management for Distributed Virtual Environment*

Emanuele Carlini[1], Patrizio Dazzi[1], Matteo Mordacchini[2], and Laura Ricci[3]

[1] ISTI – CNR, Pisa, Italy
[2] IIT – CNR, Pisa, Italy
[3] University of Pisa, Italy

Abstract. A fundamental requirement for the discovery and the retrieval of the entities of a distributed virtual environment is the definition of a scalable *Interest Management (IM)* support. This paper presents a distributed protocol for IM that integrates two different gossip protocols. The first one based on a discrete tessellation of the Area of Interest of a peer in order to maximise its coverage by the peer neighbours. The second is based on a distributed algorithm enabling the peers to self-organise themselves in communities. The paper presents a set of experimental results showing the effectiveness of the proposed approach.

1 Introduction

Collaborative Virtual Environments (CVEs) are softwares for supporting the collaboration of many participants located worldwide. Typical examples of CVEs are distributed computer simulations, multi-player on-line games, and collaborative engineering software. The implementation of a CVE exposes a set of entities (which represents the virtual world) and that can be accessed by the participants via network. The virtual representation of a participant in a CVE is called *Avatar*, a virtual alter-ego enabling the interaction with other avatars (participants) and with the passive entities in the CVE. Since the early nineties, a lot of solutions have been proposed to give a distributed organisation to virtual environments. Because of the communication latencies (and the limitations on available network bandwidth, especially in the case of asymmetric network connections, e.g., ADSL), careful attention should be paid for implementing proper data management, consistency and transfer models. To reduce the impact of network related limitations the information about the entities is replicated in several machines. Hence, the general issue is the *discovery* and *retrieval* of the entities in a scalable fashion. This issue is usually referred as Interest Management (IM), and it can be abstracted using a publish-subscribe model [1]. Publishers perform actions (e.g., they move) and subscribers should receive the information about these actions. IM poses well known scalability challenges, in particular when number of participants grows. A large numbers

* This work is funded by the EC under the CONTRAIL (FP7-257438), RECOGNITION (FP7-IST 257756) and EINS (FP7-FIRE 288021) projects.

D. an Mey et al. (Eds.): Euro-Par 2013 Workshops, LNCS 8374, pp. 363–373, 2014.

of approaches have been proposed to efficiently support IM (see [2, 3] for a comprehensive list). One of the main strategies to address IM is to replicate only the entities in the visual/interaction area of players, which is called Area of Interest (AOI) that, typically, consists of a circular area whose centre is the avatar position. In this paper we propose a community based IM in which avatars self-organise themselves in communities by exploiting gossip based protocols. In particular, we limit the IM to the positions of the avatars. Anyhow, we believe that our approach is general enough to be extended and applied to other types of information. Our approach employs an eventually consistent model for the positions of the avatars. According to this model, an avatar changes the value associated to its own position in its local storage contextually with its actual movement. Later, interested peers are informed about the changed avatar position. Gossip protocols are a class of unstructured peer-to-peer communication protocols which involve periodic message exchanges between pairs of peers, eventually resulting in information being spread throughout the system in a way that is pretty similar to human gossiping. The gossip protocols are gaining greater and greater popularity in distributed systems scenarios. Indeed, they demonstrated to be highly efficient solutions for information dissemination and aggregation [4–7]. Moreover, they allow a high degree of scalability and reliability even in constantly changing environments. This is why we decided to adopt them in our proposal for a peer-to-peer IM addressing DVEs. In a previous work of ours [8] we sketched the *Coverage Peer Sampling* protocol: our first attempt regarding the adoption of the gossip protocols to DVEs. The key idea consisted in the tessellation of the AOI of each peer and the organisation of the peer neighbourhood so that the coverage of the peer AOI by its neighbours is maximised. Although such approach showed up encouraging results, it leads peers in adopting a selfish approach in building their neighbourhood. Even if this is not a big issue in several DVE related scenarios, sometimes it may lead to an inefficient percolation of the information flow in the network. In this paper we adjust such approach equipping it with the ability of exploiting network-wide information for organising the peers' neighbourhood that enhance the overall network structure. To this end, we added to each node belonging to the DVE a gossip protocol for network-wide clustering of peers in communities on the basis of their spatial location. The information about the communities are then exploited by the Coverage Peer Sampling protocol to optimise its neighbourhood. This integration is not particularly disruptive since the "stack-ability" property of the gossip protocols, namely the possibility to organise them in stacks that share a common information space but with each layer devoted to a specific goal. This property of Gossip protocols has been exploited in the past for realising quite complex solutions such as ring topologies [9] as well as community building protocols [10, 11]. As community building protocol we chose GROUP [11], a gossip-based approach for distributed community construction that through a voting phase identifies a set of "leaders" which become the representatives of the community. The rest of the paper is organised as follows. In Section 2 we show alternative solutions for IM in DVE and for community recognition in P2P. Section 3 describes the overall architecture of the proposed protocol. A preliminary performance evaluation is presented in Section 4. Finally, in Section 5 we draw our conclusions.

2 Related Work

Discovery and retrieval of resources, entities and/or services is a very broad topic in the P2P literature (e.g. [12–14]). Specifically, IM solutions proposed in the literature for P2P-based DVE can be classified according to the different roles played by the nodes of the infrastructure. Existing solutions span from hierarchical approaches, in which IM is realised through a set of supernodes, to flat approaches in which there is no clear distinction between super and regular nodes. The solutions based on supernodes (e.g., [15, 16]) exploit user-provided resources to realise IM. The virtual environment is partitioned into regions, each one paired with a supernode that periodically informs the peers about their neighbours. In order to cope with the unreliability, these approaches needs to carefully select the supernodes, moreover, failure recovery mechanisms and adaptive mechanisms for region sizing are also needed. For their intrinsic nature, flat approaches pairs with DVEs that are purely P2P. Flat approaches can be either structured or unstructured. Colyseus [17] uses a DHT to store the state of the entities. DHTs offer concrete advantages, e.g., a stable and reliable platform for distributed indexing. However, their latencies may represent an issue. Compared to DHTs, unstructured overlays (such as [15, 18]) give more emphasis to the dynamic grouping of peers. Many of these approaches exploits direct connections among peers that are close one anothers. This strategy pays a reduced network latency, since each recipient is often just one hop away from the source. Other approaches [19, 20] exploit the position of the avatars to define a Voronoi partition of the virtual world to define the overlay connections. As we stated in the introduction, in this paper we combine the Coverage Peer Sampling approach for maximising the AOI coverage with GROUP. GROUP demonstrated to be an efficient solution for community building, anyway in the scientific literature there can be found other approaches. In the following of this section we report two notable solutions that have been proposed in the past. *Ramaswamy et al.* [21] propose CDC, an approach for clustering peers. Like GROUP it assumes that each node only knows its direct neighbours. CDC achieves a network-wide clustering from a set of starting nodes, that behave as aggregators. Each aggregator initiates a stream of votes. The protocol ends up with peers choosing as their own cluster the one associated with the neighbour that received the highest amount of votes. A critical aspect of this solution is that the division of the nodes in clusters is highly dependent on the choice of the aggregators. As a consequence, with this kind of approach it may happen that the initiators nodes are different from the ideal ones to represent the cluster. *Datta et al.* [22] propose LSP2P and USP2P, two approximations of K-Means for P2P environments. LSP2P is based on a gossip protocol to distribute the centroids. The main limitation of this protocol is the assumption that data is uniformly distributed among the peers, i.e., each peer has at least some entry from each cluster. This assumption not necessarily hold in our scenario. The second algorithm, USP2P, uses sampling to give probabilistic guarantees. However, these guarantees are also based on the assumption that data is uniformly distributed among peers. In addition, USP2P requires a set of coordinating peers tath get easily overloaded, since they are responsible for exchanging centroids with a significant number of peers for sampling.

3 Protocol Architecture

Figure 1 shows the stack of gossip-based protocols that every peer in DVE executes. On the bottom we have a random peer sampling (RPS) layer, providing a random view of the system to the other layers. RPS is useful to maintain connectivity, and to prevent the other layers from getting stuck in local solutions. The semantic-driven peer sampling exploits the RPS to build a view of the system which is based on a semantic distance. This is in turn used by the GROUP protocol to elect leaders and build communities. Section 3.2 provides more details about the GROUP protocol. The last component of the architecture is the coverage peer sampling (CPS) layer. The base CPS considers the information coming from the RPS and also executes a gossip protocol to provide the peer with a view of peers that potentially contains relevant entities for its AOI. The enhanced version of the CPS, which we call CPS+, considers also the global information coming from the GROUP layer to compute the view of peers in the DVE. More details on the CPS and CPS are provided in Section 3.3.

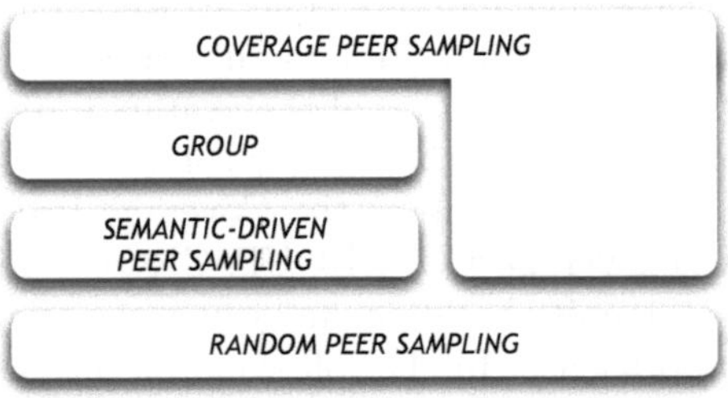

Fig. 1. Gossip Layers

3.1 Gossip Protocols

Gossip protocols are a set of very effective, flexible, yet simple tools for exchanging information and for overlays creation and management purposes. The simplicity of gossip protocols relies on the fact that each node acts on a pure local information basis. The effectiveness of gossip is highlighted by the fact that, using only local interactions, nodes are able to achieve global results, like the maintenance of a connected network. Gossip protocols offer the advantage of reducing the number of messages required to spread information in a P2P network if compared with pure unstructured protocols. Even though their associated communication overhead could be higher than that of structured protocols,

```
while true do
    sleep T seconds;
    q ← selectPeer();
    sendBuffer ← ItemsToSend();
    send sendBuffer to q;
    receive receiveBuffer from q;
    view ← ItemsToKeep();
```

Fig. 2. Active Thread

```
foreach Message m Received do
    extract sender p from m;
    sendBuffer ← ItemsToSend();
    send sendBuffer to p;
    view ← ItemsToKeep();
```

Fig. 3. Passive Thread

gossip-based approaches are more efficient in dealing with networks composed of highly dynamic nodes. When exploiting a gossip-based protocol, each node in a P2P network maintains only a limited, partial, *view* of the network, i.e., a small set of *neighbour* nodes. It periodically exchanges information with another peer properly chosen among its neighbours. This simple, repeated, local data exchange allows the whole network to achieve specific goals and results. Each gossip protocol can be designed using the two skeletons depicted in Figures 2 and 3. Since the functions selectPeer(), ItemsToSend() and ItemsToKeep() determine the peers to communicate with as well as the information exchanged and kept by peers, by changing these methods it is possible to achieve different goals or different overlay organisations. As we already mentioned, the gossip protocols can be composed into layered architectures, in which each layer is devoted to a specific aim. According to this view, each gossip layer has two main duties:

- to maintain and to exchange information regarding the task it is devoted to;
- to feed with proper information the higher gossip levels, if any;

Examples of gossip-based protocols are randomised peer sampling services [23, 24], used to maintain connected networks, even in face of highly dynamic nodes. Another relevant example is given by Vicinity [25], a similarity-based node aggregation protocol, built on top of Cyclon [24].

3.2 GROUP

The local knowledge maintained by each peer typically does not allow a good identification of the features which may characterise communities of peers. In fact, there is not any explicit identification and characterisation of possibly larger groups of peers sharing a certain degree of similarity, such that they can be considered as a community of affined entities. In order to obtain such an explicit community recognition, we want to employ a protocol that exploits the collaboration among peers in order to reach a collaborative definition of the communities and their representation. GROUP is a P2P gossip protocol build on top of a similarity gossip-based set of layers, whose role is to build communities of similar peers and give a way to characterise them. This goal is achieved through the identification of a set of communities representatives that peers select using a P2P voting phase driven by the consensus a peer profile can gather among the other nodes. To this end, each peer gives a bunch of votes to the nodes having a profiles that, at best of its knowledge, are the most similar to its own. The most voted peers are then elected as representatives and, together with the peers that contributed to their election, constitutes a community. A community is simply identified by the profile of its representative peer. The detection of the representative of each community is structured in three following stages: (i) Similar Peers Detection, (ii) Potential Candidates Selection, (iii) Representative Election.

(i) *Similar Peer Detection*: In this phase, the active thread of each peer selects and informs the k most similar peers in its neighbourhood that it is considering them as the most similar ones among its neighbours.

(ii) *Potential Candidates Selection*: The aim of the second phase is to exploit the information coming from the previous one in order to detect the potential community representative of each peer. In this step, each peer selects from its neighbourhood a potential candidate to represent itself, hence to be the representative of its community. Each peer chooses such a potential candidate among the neighbours that have received in the previous phase a number of votes higher than a certain threshold.

(iii) *Representative Election Phase*: In this last phase each peer p chooses as its representative the node R that has collected the highest number of *"potential candidate"* votes. If there are two or more peers that received the same number of votes, p chooses the one with the most similar profile to its own.

It is worth to point out that the members of the communities built by GROUP are not required to keep track of the community structure. No peer is required to have an explicit knowledge about all the other peers in the community. The representative itself is able to recognise (and elect) itself as such by counting the votes it had received, without any other needed interaction and knowledge. Peers label themselves with the community profile in order to recognise themselves as members of the same group.

3.3 Vitruvian

The goal of this layer is to obtain a selection of peers that maximise the retrieval of entities in the virtual environment. In order to better explain this task, let us consider this problem from the point of view of a generic avatar A. At an arbitrary point in time, A has in its local representation of the virtual environment the replicas of the entities that belong to its AOI. When A moves across the virtual environment, its AOI changes accordingly. Hence, to maintain its local representation up-to-date, the peer (P) represented by A must discover the new entities belonging to the new AOI. In order to dynamically acquire these new entities, P must discover the peers that can efficiently provide such information. We call this approach *Coverage Peer Sampling* (CPS). The CPS consists in the implementation of the three functions that characterise any gossip-based sampling protocol (as described in section 3.1), namely $selectPeer()$, $ItemsToSend()$, and $ItemsToKeep()$. In this context, the criterion driving the CPS is the *area coverage*, which is defined as the following. Given a set S of peers and a pivot peer P, the area coverage can be defined as the intersection between the union of the AOIs of the peers in S and the AOI of P. Intuitively, a peer would maintain such a view that maximises the coverage of its own AOI, so to have higher chances to obtain relevant information about entities in its proximity.

selectPeer() This function chooses from the view of P the target peer for the gossip communication, which we refer to as T in the following. If there are peers in the view of P that are contained in its AOI, the algorithm selects the one that maximises the euclidean distance with the current position of P. Conversely, the algorithm selects the peer that minimises the euclidean distance with the current position of P. The rationale behind this behaviour is that, if P has several peers in its AOI, it probably has some knowledge of its immediate proximity. Choosing a peer at the borders of its AOI increases the knowledge of a region that could be explored in the next close future. On the other hand, if no peers are in the AOI of P, a closer peer might have information about a region that P is going to visit soon.

ItemsToSend() Once T has been selected, P has to select the "best" subset of peers in its view to send to T. P ranks the peers in its view by evaluating their AOIs with respect to the AOI of T. To find the optimal subset of peers is a NP-hard problem[1]. Since this function has to be repeated multiple time in a second, the *ItemsToSend()* is implemented as an heuristic, which partitions the AOI's areas into a set of discrete *tiles*. The heuristic takes as input the AOI of T and all the AOI of the peers that compose the view of P, then assigns a score to each tile which is the reciprocal of the number of intersected AOIs. Once the tiles have been assigned with a score, the heuristic computes the score of a peer as the sum of the scores of each intersected tile. Then, the peers are sorted according to their score and inserted in a list L. In this point of the heuristic lies the difference between CPS and CPS+. CPS just returns the first d items of L (where d is the size of the subset to choose). In other words, CPS considers only the area coverage as the criteria for the selection of the peers. Instead, CPS+ also considers the global knowledge of communities, which is provided by the GROUP layer, for the selection of the subset. CPS+ chooses from L the d peers with the highest score that maximises the number of unique communities. This implies that peers with a high score can be discarded in favour of a peer with lower score but with a valuable knowledge about a community.

ItemsTokeep() From a logical point of view, this function shares the same principles of the *ItemsToSend*() one. The only difference is the input: (i) P selects itself as pivot, and (ii) the set of peers to rank includes the peers coming from the random peer sampling layer.

4 Experimental Results

To simulate a region of a VE we consider a squared area of 1200 x 1200 points. The region has 10 circular fixed hotspots, which represents popular places inside the VE. Avatars have an AOI of 50 points, and move on the map according to realistic mobility traces that have been computed according the mobility model

[1] It is easy to demonstrate the equivalence with the *maximum coverage problem*.

presented by Legtchenko et al. [26], which simulates avatars movement in a commercial MMOG[2]. The model works according to the hotspots defined in the region. When an avatar reaches a hotspot, it explores the hotspot for a span of time and eventually it moves to another hotspot. In the simulation all the gossip layers share the same configuration. The cache of the peer is the square root of the total number of peers. The simulation is divided into tick, each tick being 500 milliseconds. The simulations ran on a machine equipped with Java 7, 16GB of RAM, an Intel i5-2550 quad core @3,30 Ghz. To simulate the gossip communications we used Epeerdemics [27]. Figures 4 and 5 show the probability density function (PDF) of the average area coverage of respectively CPS+ and CPS. Note that the CPS+ approach achieves better results. More in detail, it can be observed that the peers reaching an area coverage around 96% in CPS are about 20%, whereas with CPS+ are about the 27%.

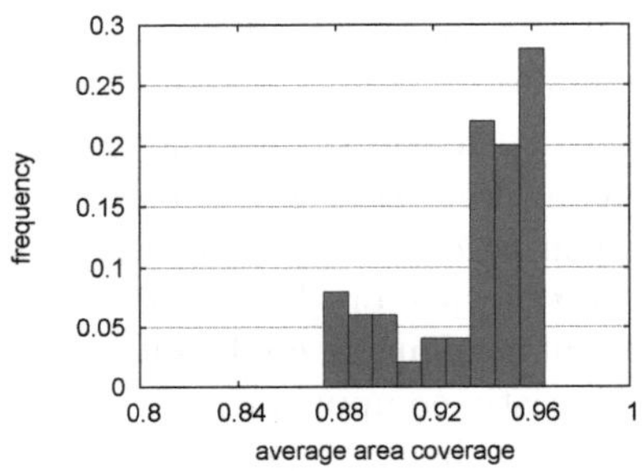

Fig. 4. CPS+

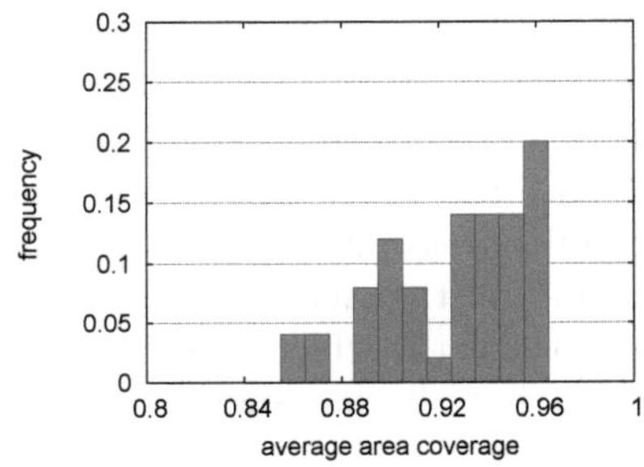

Fig. 5. CPS

More generally, the values of the area coverage are distributed more toward the right side of the spectrum with CPS+ rather than with CPS, highlighting the ability of the proposed system to allow the nodes in the network to achieve a better awareness of their surrounding environment. The second set of experiments compare the CPS and the CPS+ in terms of the overlay they build. We model the overlay as a graph, which is constructed by considering the peers as vertexes and a directed edge between two peers A and B exits if A has B in its view or viceversa. Clearly, a different graph exists for every iteration of the protocol. Our analysis compares the two approaches by analysing the above features in 50 iterations.

Figure 6 shows the average clustering coefficient (CC). Besides an initial startup time, the value of the CC remains stable on the same value in both cases. However, in this case CPS+ shows more variability. It is interesting to notice how the value of CPS+ decreases before the 20th and 40th iterations and then it grows up again. In fact during these iteration, the GROUP protocol elects the new leader. Figure 7 shows the evolution of the diameter of the overlay in the first iteration. After the start-up period, the diameter remains fairly stable after the 10th iteration. In particular CPS has a diameter of 4 while the CPS+ of 3.

[2] Second Life, `http://secondlife.com/`

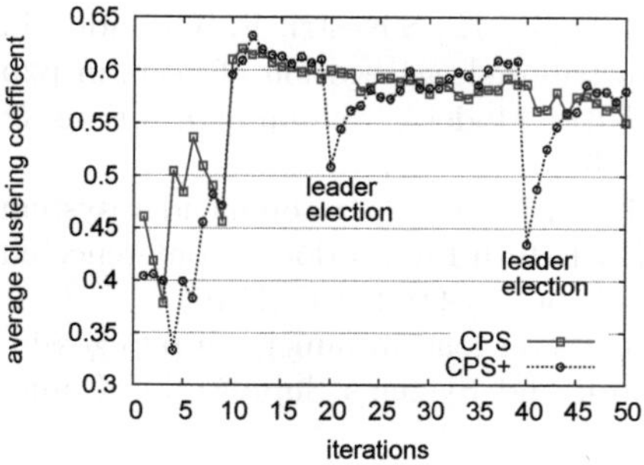

Fig. 6. Clustering coefficent

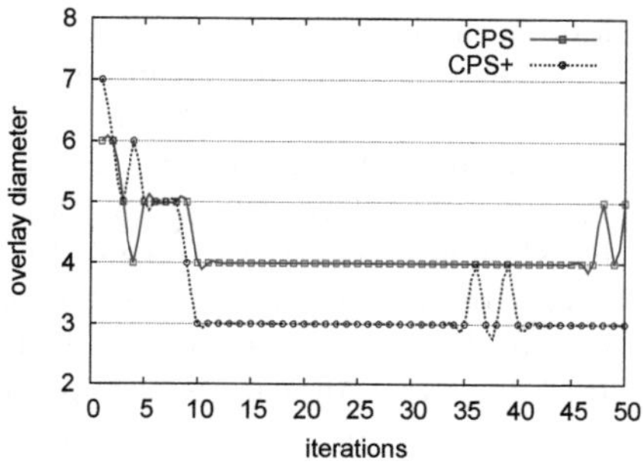

Fig. 7. Diameter

5 Conclusions

In this paper we propose a Interest Management solution for large scale DVEs based on self-emerging communities of avatars. The proposal regard the avatars in a DVE as nodes in a P2P network and exploits a gossip-based interaction among avatars in order to let them self-organise in communities of peers that are exploring nearby locations. Preliminary experimental results show that the proposed approach is able to reduce the diameter of the network graph, improving the results of the previously proposed gossip-based solution that does not create communities. At the same time, it is able to guarantee to each peer a better coverage of the its AoI. Starting from these results, we plan to further analyse this solution by considering larger network sizes. Moreover we plan to study the behaviour of the system in more challenging conditions, like a heavy churning nodes scenario and we are trying to give a formal mathematical definition of the community creation gossip protocol.

References

1. Hu, S.: Spatial publish subscribe. In: Proc. of IEEE Virtual Reality (IEEE VR) Workshop, Massively Multiuser Virtual Environment, MMVE 2009 (2009)
2. Ahmed, D., Shirmohammadi, S.: A dynamic area of interest management and collaboration model for p2p mmogs. In: Proceedings of the 2008 12th IEEE/ACM International Symposium on Distributed Simulation and Real-Time Applications, pp. 27–34. IEEE Computer Society (2008)
3. Boulanger, J., Kienzle, J., Verbrugge, C.: Comparing interest management algorithms for massively multiplayer games. In: Proceedings of 5th ACM SIGCOMM Workshop on Network and System Support for Games, p. 6. ACM (2006)
4. Jelasity, M., Montresor, A., Babaoglu, O.: Gossip-based aggregation in large dynamic networks. ACM Transactions on Computer Systems (TOCS) 23(3), 219–252 (2005)
5. Dazzi, P., Felber, P., Leonini, L., Mordacchini, M., Perego, R., Rajman, M., Rivière, É.: Peer-to-peer clustering of web-browsing users. In: Proc. LSDS-IR, pp. 71–78 (2009)

6. Mordacchini, M., Dazzi, P., Tolomei, G., Baraglia, R., Silvestri, F., Orlando, S.: Challenges in designing an interest-based distributed aggregation of users in p2p systems. In: International Conference on Ultra Modern Telecommunications & Workshops, ICUMT 2009, pp. 1–8. IEEE (2009)
7. Baraglia, R., Mordacchini, M., Dazzi, P., Ricci, L.: A p2p recommender system based on gossip overlays (prego). In: 2010 IEEE 10th International Conference on Computer and Information Technology (CIT), pp. 83–90. IEEE (2010)
8. Carlini, E., Ricci, L., Coppola, M.: Reducing server load in mmog via p2p gossip. In: 2012 11th Annual Workshop on Network and Systems Support for Games (NetGames), pp. 1–2. IEEE (2012)
9. Jelasity, M., Babaoglu, O.: T-man: Gossip-based overlay topology management. In: Brueckner, S.A., Di Marzo Serugendo, G., Hales, D., Zambonelli, F. (eds.) ESOA 2005. LNCS (LNAI), vol. 3910, pp. 1–15. Springer, Heidelberg (2006)
10. Baraglia, R., Dazzi, P., Mordacchini, M., Ricci, L., Alessi, L.: Group: A gossip based building community protocol. Smart Spaces and Next Generation Wired/Wireless Networking, 496–507 (2011)
11. Baraglia, R., Dazzi, P., Mordacchini, M., Laura, R.: A peer-to-peer recommender system for self-emerging user communities based on gossip overlays. Journal of Computer and System Sciences (2012)
12. Carlini, E., Coppola, M., Dazzi, P., Laforenza, D., Martinelli, S., Ricci, L.: Service and resource discovery supports over p2p overlays. In: Proc. of ICUMT 2009, Hersonissos, Crete, Greece, pp. 1–8. IEEE Computer Society (October 2009)
13. Marzolla, M., Mordacchini, M., Orlando, S.: Peer-to-peer systems for discovering resources in a dynamic grid. Parallel Computing 33(4), 339–358 (2007)
14. Marzolla, M., Mordacchini, M., Orlando, S.: A p2p resource discovery system based on a forest of trees. In: Proc. DEXA 2006, pp. 261–265. IEEE (2006)
15. Frey, D., Royan, J., Piegay, R., Kermarrec, A., Anceaume, E., Le Fessant, F.: Solipsis: A decentralized architecture for virtual environments. In: Proceeding of 1st International Workshop on Massively Multiuser Virtual Environments (MMVE 2008), pp. 29–33 (2008)
16. Chen, A., Muntz, R.: Peer clustering: a hybrid approach to distributed virtual environments. In: Proceedings of 5th ACM SIGCOMM Workshop on Network and System Support for Games, p. 11. ACM (2006)
17. Bharambe, A., Pang, J., Seshan, S.: Colyseus: A distributed architecture for online multiplayer games. In: NSDI 2006: 3rd Symposium on Networked Systems Design & Implementation, pp. 155–168 (2006)
18. Hu, S., Chang, S., Jiang, J.: Voronoi state management for peer-to-peer massively multiplayer online games. In: 5th IEEE Consumer Communications and Networking Conference, CCNC 2008, pp. 1134–1138. IEEE (2008)
19. Jiang, J., Huang, Y., Hu, S.: Scalable AOI-cast for peer-to-peer networked virtual environments. Journal of Internet Technology 10(2), 119–126 (2009)
20. Ricci, L., Carlini, E., Genovali, L., Coppola, M.: Aoi-cast by compass routing in delaunay based dve overlays. In: 2011 International Conference on High Performance Computing and Simulation (HPCS), pp. 135–142. IEEE (2011)
21. Ramaswamy, L., Gedik, B., Liu, L.: A distributed approach to node clustering in decentralized peer-to-peer networks. IEEE Transactions on Parallel and Distributed Systems 16, 814–829 (2005)
22. Datta, S., Giannella, C., Kargupta, H.: Approximate distributed k-means clustering over a peer-to-peer network. IEEE Transactions on Knowledge and Data Engineering 21(10), 1372–1388 (2009)

23. Jelasity, M., Voulgaris, S., Guerraoui, R., Kermarrec, A.M., Van Steen, M.: Gossip-based peer sampling. ACM Transactions on Computer Systems (TOCS) 25(3), 8 (2007)
24. Voulgaris, S., Gavidia, D., Van Steen, M.: Cyclon: Inexpensive membership management for unstructured p2p overlays. Journal of Network and Systems Management 13(2), 197–217 (2005)
25. Voulgaris, S., van Steen, M.: Epidemic-style management of semantic overlays for content-based searching. In: Cunha, J.C., Medeiros, P.D. (eds.) Euro-Par 2005. LNCS, vol. 3648, pp. 1143–1152. Springer, Heidelberg (2005)
26. Legtchenko, S.: Blue Banana: resilience to avatar mobility in distributed MMOGs. Networks, 171–180 (2010)
27. Dazzi, P., Carlini, E.: Epeerdemics: A peer-to-peer simulator targeting epidemic-based protocols. ERCIM News 2013 (92) (2013)

Workflow Scheduling in Amazon EC2

Juan J. Durillo[1], Radu Prodan[1], and Weicheng Huang[2]

[1] Institut fur Informatik,University of Innsbruck Austria
{juan,radu}@dps.uibk.ac.at
[2] National Center of High-performance Computing, National Applied Research Laboratories No. 7, Hsinchu, Taiwan
whuang@nchc.narl.org.tw

Abstract. Workflow scheduling has been traditionally targeted to map the execution of set of tasks onto a set of resources for makespan minimization. With the increasing popularity of Cloud computing systems, the financial cost entailed for executing these tasks plays also an important role. Existing works have however combined both, makespan and cost, on a single function and no analysis of the tradeoff between both criteria has been produced. In addition, no work in the context a real commercial cloud system exists. This paper includes a comparison of two real multi-objective workflow scheduling, MOHEFT and SPEA2*, in the context of Amazon EC2. The carried experiments show that MOHEFT outperforms SPEA2*, and that the analysis of the tradeoff solutions can help in selecting good scheduling solutions.

1 Introduction

Scientific workflows are an attractive model for building large scale applications. Typically, a workflow application consists of several (legacy) programs (referred from now on as tasks or activities) in the form of a dependency graph, where the input of some of these programs may depend on the output of the others. The workflow paradigm does not impose any restriction about the activities that compose an application, being possible that they belong to different actors or agents. In such a situation, a Distributed Virtual Environment (DVE) [10] appears as the ideal candidate for the execution of collaborative workflow applications.

Cloud computing is an approach to offer a DVE. Previous work [14] has pointed out, however, that one of the main challenges in the case of a cloud-based DVE solution has to do with the design of algorithms for resource provisioning, i.e., how many resources are required for executing an application. In the context of workflow-applications, the answer to the aforementioned issue depends on how the execution of the tasks composing a workflow is scheduled. Traditionally, that scheduling has been targeted to minimize the time required for executing the workflow, a.k.a makespan.

In a Cloud scenario the *economic cost* plays an important role on the scheduling. Many of commercial Clouds apply a hour-based pricing model, i.e., users are charged per hours of computation. This model introduces a tradeoff between makespan and economic cost. For example, a workflow that can sequentially run

D. an Mey et al. (Eds.): Euro-Par 2013 Workshops, LNCS 8374, pp. 374–383, 2014.

in less than an hour in a single machine may be accelerated by considering a parallel execution on several machines, thus increasing the price but decreasing the utilisation of the rented resources. In addition to this, some commercial clouds offer heterogeneous types of resources at different prices and with different performance. For example, in Amazon EC2 (`http://aws.amazon.com/ec2/pricing/`) a user can choose among different types of instances, where the fastest resource is about eight times more expensive than the slowest one. Under these circumstances, it is clear that workflow scheduling in a Cloud scenario is a multi-objective optimisation problem (MOP) aimed at optimising at least two conflicting criteria: makespan and economic cost. The main characteristic of MOPs is that no single solution exists that is optimal with respect to all objectives, but a set of tradeoff solutions known as *Pareto front*. Solutions within this set cannot be further improved in any of the considered objectives without causing the degradation of at least another objective.

While only a few approaches exist for computing these sets of tradeoff solutions, most of the related works [8,9,2] aggregate the different optimisation criteria in a single analytical function. The main drawback of this approach is that only a single solution, instead of a set, is computed. In addition, approaches computing the whole set of tradeoff solutions have been only applied in the context of utility grids or clusters.

The purpose of this paper is to compare and analyse the solutions computed by two multi-objective workflow scheduling methods on the context of a real commercial Cloud, Amazon EC2. On the one hand, we consider MOHEFT, a multi-objective list-based heuristic which extends the mono-objective workflow scheduing HEFT. Previous work [6] has demonstrated that MOHEFT can compute a high-quality solutions in a set of synthetically defined problems . On the other hand, we consider SPEA2* [17], as an application of evolutionary computation to solve this problem. Both, MOHEFT and SPEA2*, are applied in this work for scheduling two real workflow applications.

The paper is organised as follows. The next section describes the related work. Section 3 includes some definitions for a better understanding of this work. In Section 4, we describe MOHEFT and SPEA2*. We present in Section 5 the experimental setup for evaluating these techniques on Amazon EC2 (Section 6). Finally, we summarise the conclusions and the future work in Section 7.

2 Related Work

Many existing approaches to multi-objective workflow scheduling reduce the problem to mono-objective optimisation and compute only a single solution. There exist two different ways to do so. The first consists in aggregating all the optimisation criteria in a single function by means of using user preferences. Previous work using this approach combine reliability and makespan [2,8,9]. The second line consists in sorting and constraining the different criteria, which are later on optimised in a sequential fashion as much as possible without violating the imposed constraints. An example of work following this approach is [15] where the authors optimise for makespan and economic cost in utility Grids.

Approaches computing the whole Pareto front are also classified on two groups: evolutionary-based methods and list-based heuristic. Examples of evolutionary algorithms applied for multi-objective workflow scheduling are SPEA2*, NSGA-II*, and PAES* [17], a bi-objective genetic algorithm proposed in [12], and R-NSGA-II [7]. Different multi-objective extensions of list-based heuristic are proposed in [4,6] by extending HEFT [16], a popular heuristic aimed at optimising makespan of workflows in heterogeneous systems.

The aforementioned approaches were however always applied in the context of utility Grids. To the best of our knowledge, no application of them in a real commercial Cloud scenario exists. This work differs from related work in this sense. In particular, our target here is the application and comparison of MOHEFT and SPEA2* for workflow scheduling in Amazon EC2.

3 Model

3.1 Workflow Model

We model a *workflow application* as a directed acyclic graph: $W = (A, D)$ consisting of n activities $A = \bigcup_{i=1}^{n} \{A_i\}$, interconnected through control flow and data flow dependencies; $D = \{(A_i, A_j, Data_{ij}) \mid (A_i, A_j) \in A \times A\}$, where $Data_{ij}$ represents the size of the data which needs to be transferred from activity A_i to activity A_j. We use $pred(A_i) = \{A_k \mid (A_k, A_i, Data_{ki}) \in D\}$ to denote the *predecessor* set of activity A_i, (i.e. activities to be completed before starting A_i). We assume that the computational workload of every activity A_i is known and is given by the number of machine instructions required to be executed.

3.2 Resource Model

We assume that our hardware platform consists of a set of m heterogeneous resources $R = \cup_{j=1}^{m} R_j$, which can be of any type as provided by Amazon EC2. In particular, we consider in this paper the five Amazon EC2 resources analysed in [1]. For a given resource R_j of a certain type, we know its average performance measured in GFLOPs and its price per every hour of computation (see [1]). The final price is based not only on the resources' usage, but also in the data stored and transferred among different instances which depends on four components: (1) price per hours of resource's usage PE_{R_i}; (2) price per MB of data storage PS_{R_i}; (3) price per MB of data received PI_{R_i}; (4) price per MB of data sent PO_{R_i}. The prices of these components depend on the Cloud provider.

Amazon EC2 introduces a constraint that must be included in the resource model. While in theory a user can access an infinite pool of resources, in practice most providers restrict this number to a maximum of $N = 20$ instances that can be simultaneously acquired. These N resources can be of any type and do not have to keep invariant during the workflow execution.

3.3 Problem Definition

We use $sched(A_i)$ to denote the resource on which the task A_i is scheduled to be executed. We describe in the following how makespan and cost are computed.

Makespan. For computing the makespan, it is necessary to define the *execution time* $t_{(A_i,R_j)}$ of an activity A_i on a resource $R_j = sched\,(A_i)$ as the sum of the time required for transferring the biggest input data from any $A_p \in pred\,(A_p)$ and the time required to execute A_i in R_j:

$$t_{(A_i,R_j)} = \max_{A_p \in pred(A_i)} \left\{ \frac{Data_{pi}}{b_{pj}} \right\} + \frac{workload\,(A_i)}{s_j}, \tag{1}$$

where $Data_{pi}$ is the size of the data to be transferred between A_p and A_i, b_{pj} is the bandwidth of one TCP stream between the resource where task A_p was executed and the resource R_j, $workload(A_i)$ the length of the task A_i in machine instructions, and s_j the speed of the resource R_j in number of machine instructions per second. Next, we can compute the *completion time* T_{A_i} of activity A_i considering the execution time of itself and its predecessors:

$$T_{A_i} = \begin{cases} t_{(A_i,sched(A_i))}, & pred\,(A_i) = \emptyset; \\ \max\limits_{A_p \in pred(A_i)} \left\{ T_{A_p} + t_{(A_i,sched(A_i))} \right\}, & pred\,(A_i) \neq \emptyset. \end{cases} \tag{2}$$

The workflow makespan is finally defined as the maximum completion time of all the activities in the workflow:

$$T_W = \max_{i \in [1,n]} \left\{ T_{(A_i,sched(A_i))} \right\}. \tag{3}$$

Economic Cost. The economic cost depends on two terms: the computation cost $C^{(comp)}$ and the cost of data transfer and storage $C^{(data)}$.

We define $C^{(data)}_{(A_i,R_j)}$ as the cost of the data transfers $In(A_i)$ and $Out\,(A_i)$ and storage $Data\,(A_i)$ resulting from executing activity A_i on resource R_j:

$$C^{(data)}_{(A_i,R_j)} = Data\,(A_i) \cdot t_{(A_i,R_j)} \cdot PS_{R_i} + In(A_i) \cdot PI_{R_i} + Out\,(A_i) \cdot PO_{R_i}, \tag{4}$$

In defining the cost $C^{(comp)}_{R_j}$ of using a resource R_j, we assume that for each task A_i executed on R_j we record two timestamps: $t^{(start)}_{A_i}$ when the activity starts and $t^{(end)}_{A_i}$ when the activity finishes its execution. We consider without loss of generality that the times for transferring the input $In\,(A_i)$ and the output data $Out\,(A_i)$ are included in the interval between $t^{(start)}_{A_i}$ and $t^{(end)}_{A_i}$.

Let us consider now the set of all p activities scheduled on resource R_j denoted as $\{J_1, \ldots, J_p\}$, where $p < n$ and $sched\,(J_i) = R_j, i \in [1,p]$, sorted based on their start timestamp: $t^{(start)}_{J_1} < \ldots < t^{(start)}_{J_p}$. Based on this ordering, we cluster these activities in $q \leq p$ different *groups* $G^{(j)}_k$, $1 \leq k \leq q$, so that all activities in one group are executed consecutively without releasing the resource. After the activity with the largest start timestamp in the group completes, the resource is released.

We construct the first group $G_1^{(j)} = \{J_1, \ldots, J_r\}, r \leq p$ following three rules:

1. The first activity J_1 belongs to the first group: $J_1 \in G_1^{(j)}$;
2. Every activity $J_i \in G_1^{(j)}, 2 \leq i \leq r$, starts before the current leased hour expires and before the machine is released:

$$t_{J_i}^{(start)} < t_{J_1}^{(start)} + \left\lceil \frac{t_{J_{i-1}}^{(end)} - t_{J_1}^{(start)}}{3600} \right\rceil \cdot 3600. \quad (5)$$

   We divide the total time in seconds of using a resource by 3600 in order to convert it to hours, and use the ceiling operator to round this value to complete hours of computation. This equation guarantees a contiguous resource allocation of activities within one hour slot;
3. The next activity not part of the first group $J_{r+1} \notin G_1^{(j)}, r+1 \leq p$, starts after the last hour of computation elapses and the resource is released:

$$t_{J_1}^{(start)} + \left\lceil \frac{t_{J_r}^{(end)} - t_{J_1}^{(start)}}{3600} \right\rceil \cdot 3600 < t_{J_{r+1}}^{(start)}. \quad (6)$$

Successive groups are built until the last activity J_p has been assigned to one group. The second group $G_2^{(j)}$ is constructed in the same way starting from the task J_{r+1} instead of J_1. The same strategy is used for the rest of the groups. Once all the groups have been created, we define the cost $C_{R_j}^{(comp)}$ of using the resource R_j as the number hours required for executing all groups multiplied by the cost per hour:

$$C_{R_j}^{(comp)} = PE_{R_j} \cdot \sum_{k=1}^{q} \left\lceil \frac{\sum_{A_i \in G_{R_j}^{(k)}} t_{(A_i, R_j)}}{3600} \right\rceil. \quad (7)$$

We compute the economic cost of executing the entire workflow $W = (A, D)$ as the computation cost on all m resources plus the cost for transferring and storing the data:

$$C_W = \sum_{j=1}^{m} C_{R_j}^{(comp)} + \sum_{(A_i, A_j, Data_{ij}) \in D} C_{(A_i, R_j)}^{(data)}. \quad (8)$$

4 Evaluated Techniques

MOHEFT. This method extends HEFT [16] for multi-objective workflow scheduling. MOHEFT [6] requires the number and type of each resource before its execution and the size of the set of tradeoff solutions K. It starts by ranking the tasks in the workflow using the B-rank metric and creating a set S of K empty schedules. Afterwards, MOHEFT iterates over the list of tasks and extends every solution in S by mapping the next task to be executed onto all m possible resources. These new produced schedules are stored in a temporal set S', initially empty. After each iteration, S' replaces S before the next task in the list is considered. Obviously, this strategy results in an exhaustive search if we do not include any restrictions. To avoid it, MOHEFT saves only the best K tradeoffs solutions from the temporary set S' to the set S. These best solutions are selected based on the objective functions and the diversity of the set, i.e., how different are the selected solutions (see [6]). MOHEFT was not originally designed for working with commercial clouds. As a consequence, some modifications are applied in this work to deal with the characteristics of such systems, like the restriction on the maximum number of instances that can be used simultaneously. To deal with this scenario, we extend the algorithm to discard any schedule that use more than N simultaneous resources.

SPEA2*. This algorithm proposed in [17] is a genetic algorithm. It works with a population (set) of solutions which are iteratively recombined with the aim of evolving towards the optima. SPEA2* is initialised with a nearly-optimal solution in terms of makespan (computed using HEFT) and in terms of economic cost (computed with a heuristic aimed at optimising cost). Here, we consider SPEA2* with an population size $K = 10$ and run it for 1000 generations, as performed in [17].

To adapt it for the cloud scenario, we slightly modified SPEA2* in this work. In particular, we enhanced the algorithm with a mechanism for dealing with constrains, similar to the one proposed in [5]. This mechanism always compares first two solutions on the basis of their constraint violation. Solutions which do not violate the constraint are preferred to solutions which violate it (i.e. schedules using 20 or less instances simultaneously are preferred to schedules using more than 20 instances). If both solutions violate the constraint, the one violating it in a lesser extent is preferred (i.e. a solution using 23 machines simultaneously is preferred to a schedule that uses 30). In any other case, solutions are compared considering their makespan and economic cost. By using this mechanism, only the solutions which violate the constraints less survive to the next generation.

It is worth mentioning that SPEA2* is an stochastic algorithm and then it may compute different fronts in different runs of the algorithm. In order to avoid our conclusions be biased by any hazard effect, we run it for five times and always consider the run producing the front with the best values.

5 Experimental Setup

We describe in this section the criteria considered for our comparison, the workflow applications, and the resources infrastructure.

Evaluation Metrics. We consider three criteria for comparing the quality of solutions computed by MOHEFT, and SPEA2*: the shortest makespan of the schedules computed, the cheapest solution reported by each technique. For the sake of comparison we also include HEFT in our graphs describing the results. We also attend to the quality of the computed set of tradeoff solutions. In this last case, we use the hypervolume quality indicator [11]. This indicator assigns a numerical value to each set of tradeoff solutions. The higher this number is, the better the solutions within the set.

We also analyse the computed tradeoff solutions. The idea is to study the balance between makespan and cost, and how much can be gained in one objective by deteriorating the other. For this analysis we rely on a graphical representation of the solutions computed by the two algorithms. The presented graphs start with the most makespan-efficient schedule and continue along the Pareto-front towards the cheapest solution. The two plotted metrics, the cost savings and the makespan deterioration, are presented as percentages relative to the most makespan-efficient solution.

Workflow Applications. We consider in our evaluation two *real-world* workflows coming from our real-world collaborations with domain scientists in the Austrian Grid. These two applications are known as WIEN2k [3] and POV-Ray [13]. The former is a material science workflow for performing structure calculations of solids using density functional theory based on linearized augmented plane-wave; the latter is a free tool for creating three-dimensional graphics. Both workflows contain a high number of independent activities that can be executed in parallel, as well, as sequential parts.

Resource Infrastructure. We consider that the user has access to the default maximum number of $N = 20$ Amazon instances which can be of any of the five types summarised in cite [1]. We assume that no public IP addresses are required for running the experiments on the Amazon EC2 infrastructure. Additionally, the output data transfers from Amazon to the outside Internet are constant, take place only at the end of the workflow execution and thus, do not influence the scheduling results. In this situation, we assume in our experiments that the prices for data sent and received are zero: $PI_{R_i} = 0$ and $PO_{R_i} = 0$.

6 Evaluation

In this section we compare MOHEFT and SPEA2*. For the two considered applications, we have evaluated different workflow instances containing between 100 and 1000 activities.

Wien2k. Fig. 1a shows that MOHEFT always outperformed SPEA2* in terms of the hypervolume. The differences in this metric value are high and tend to increase with the number of workflow activities. An explanation for this behaviour is related to the higher difficulty of solving this workflow application. Our hypothesis is that SPEA2* got stuck in some areas of the search space, thus requiring a prohibitively large number of evaluations for increasing the quality of the computed results. The results for makespan and economic cost displayed

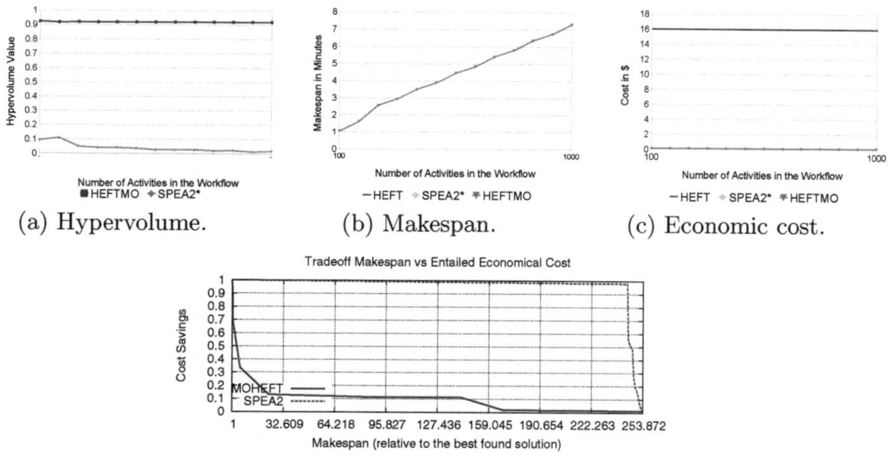

(a) Hypervolume. (b) Makespan. (c) Economic cost.

(d) Tradeoff analysis cost vs makespan.

Fig. 1. Evaluation results for the WIEN2k workflow

in Fig. 1b and 1c. In these criteria, both algorithms performed equally well and computed the solution with the lowest makespan and similar cost.

An example comparing the tradeoff solutions delivered by MOHEFT and SPEA2* is illustrated in Fig. 1d. In this case we can see that huge economic savings can be obtained by MOHEFT with only a small increase in makespan. In this case, SPEA2* requires a huge loss in performance for obtaining similar cost results. For example, MOHEFT computed a solution which halves the price of the schedule with the shortest makespan and experienced only a 5% of time deterioration. Meanwhile, a 1% of cost saving in SPEA2* would have required an increase of 250% in makespan. In 23.3% of the cases, SPEA2* computed schedules requiring more than 20 resources, while all solutions computed by MOHEFT met this constraint.

Pov-Ray. Fig. 2a shows the hypervolume of the sets of tradeoff solutions. Also in this case MOHEFT outperformed SPEA2* for all the evaluated workflow sizes. For this application, the higher the number of tasks in the workflow is, the harder is for MOHEFT to compute a set of tradeoff solutions with high quality. This result can be visualized in the hypervolume that decreases with the number of tasks. This behavior is not that obvious for SPEA2*, however, the quality of the computed fronts are of poorer quality than the ones of MOHEFT, as reflected by the low values of the indicator. As in the previous experiment, all the algorithms computed the same solution with the shortest makespan (see Fig. 2b) and the same cheapest schedule too (see Fig. 2c).

An example of the tradeoff solutions computed by MOHEFT and SPEA2* for this application is shown in Fig. 2d. In this case, while MOHEFT found a solution halving the price for the sake of only 3% increase in makespan, SPEA2* required a 4.7% increase. Nevertheless, the small difference between both techniques has

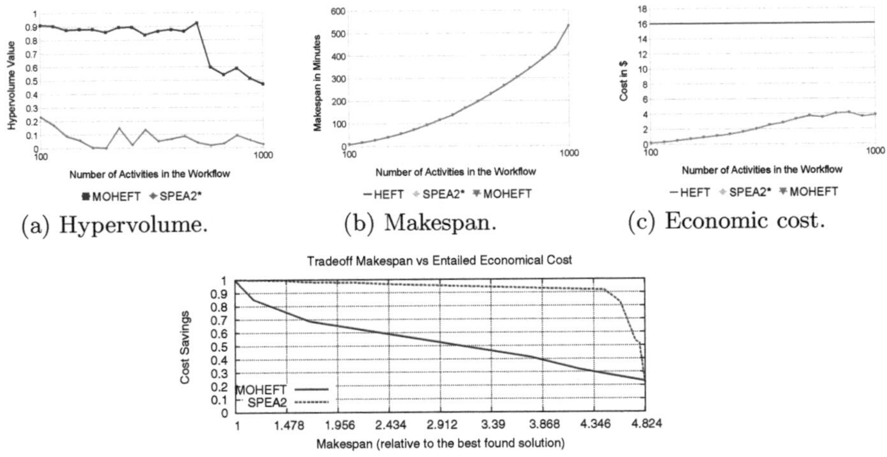

(a) Hypervolume. (b) Makespan. (c) Economic cost.

(d) Tradeoff analysis cost vs makespan.

Fig. 2. Evaluation results for the POV-Ray workflow

to be carefully interpreted, since in 40% of the cases SPEA2* has been unable to produce a workflow schedule using 20 or less resources.

7 Conclusions and Future Work

In this paper we compare the tradeoff solutions computed by two multi-objective workflow scheduler, MOHEFT and SPEA2, in the context of the commercial Clouds Amazon EC2. Both methods are evaluated using real-world applications.

In all experiments, MOHEFT computed schedules with the same makespan as the SPEA2* and similar economic cost; however, MOHEFT outperformed SPEA2* in terms of hypervolume used as an indicator of the quality of the whole set of tradeoff solutions, meaning that for the same cost, MOHEFT computed solutions with shorther makespan. Finally, our experiments revealed that MOHEFT was able to meet the constraints imposed by current commercial Clouds in terms of the maximum amount of instances, while SPEA2* failed on this issue. We also showed the potential of the Pareto front as a tool for decision support in selecting the most appropriate tradeoff solutions. In particular, the visualisation of the Pareto front for some workflow types revealed that one can obtain solutions with a marginal 5% makespan increase by investing half of the money in renting Cloud instances. In future work we intend to evaluate MOHEFT and SPEA2* for other objective functions such as security issues, reliability of spot instances or energy consumption.

Acknowledgements. Juan J. Durillo and Radu Prodan acknowledge Austrian Science Fund project TRP 72-N23 and the Standortagentur Tirol project RainCloud.

References

1. Alexandru, I., Ostermann, S., Yigitbasi, M., Prodan, R., Fahringer, T., Epema, D.: Performance analysis of cloud computing services for many-tasks scientific computing. IEEE Transactions on Parallel and Distr. Systems 1–16 (2010)
2. Assayad, I., Girault, A., Kalla, H.: A bi-criteria scheduling heuristics for distributed embedded systems under reliability and real-time constraints. In: Intern. Conference on Dependable Systems and Networks, DSN 2004. IEEE, Firenze (2003)
3. Blaha, P., Schwarz, K., Madsen, G., Kvasnicka, D., Luitz, J.: Wien2k: An augmented plane wave plus local orbitals program for calculating crystal properties. Tech. rep., Institute of Physical and Theoretical Chemistry, TU Vienna (2001)
4. Canon, L.C.: Emmanuel: Mo-greedy: an extended beam-search approach for solving a multi-criteria scheduling problem on heterogeneous machines. Intern. Heterogeneity in Computing (2011)
5. Deb, K., Pratap, A., Agarwal, S., Meyarivan, T.: A fast elitist multi-objective genetic algorithm: Nsga-ii. IEEE Transactions on Evol. Comp. 6, 182–197 (2000)
6. Durillo, J., Fard, H., Prodan, R.: Moheft: A multi-objective lilst-based method for workflow scheduling. In: 4th IEEE Intern. Conference on Cloud Computing Technology and Science (2012)
7. Garg, R., Singh, A.K.: Reference point based multi-objective optimization to workflow grid scheduling. Int. J. Appl. Evol. Comput. 3(1), 80–99 (2012)
8. Garg, S.K., Buyya, R., Siegel, H.J.: Scheduling parallel applications on utility grids: time and cost trade-off management. In: Proceedings of the Thirty-Second Australasian Conference on Computer Science, ACSC 2009, vol. 91, pp. 151–160. Australian Computer Society, Inc., Darlinghurst (2009)
9. Hakem, M., Butelle, F.: Reliability and scheduling on systems subject to failures. In: Proceedings of the 2007 Intern. Conference on Parallel Processing, ICPP 2007. IEEE Computer Society, Washington, DC (2007)
10. Hu, S.Y., Chen, J.F., Chen, T.H.: VON: a scalable peer-to-peer network for virtual environments. IEEE Network 20(4), 22–31 (2006)
11. Knowles, J., Thiele, L., Zitzler, E.: A Tutorial on the Performance Assessment of Stochastic Multiobjective Optimizers. Tech. Rep. 214, Computer Engineering and Networks Laboratory (TIK), ETH Zurich (2006)
12. Mezmaz, M., Melab, N., Kessaci, Y., Lee, Y., Albi, E.G.T., Zomaya, A.Y., Tuyttens, D.: A parallel bi-objective hybrid metaheuristic for energy-aware s cheduling for cloud computing systems. Journal of Parallel and Distr. Computing (71), 1497–1508 (2011)
13. Plachetka, T.: POVRAY – Persistence of Vision Parallel Raytracer. In: Proceedings of Computer Graphics Intern. 1998, pp. 123–129 (1998)
14. Ricci, L., Carlini, E.: Distributed virtual environments: From client server to cloud and p2p architectures. In: Smari, W., Zeljkovic, V. (eds.) HPCS, pp. 8–17. IEEE (2012)
15. Sakellariou, R., Zhao, H., Tsiakkouri, E., Dikaiakos, M.D.: Scheduling workflows with budget constraints. In: Gorlatch, S., Danelutto, M. (eds.) Integrated Research in Grid Computing. CoreGrid series. Springer (2007)
16. Topcuoglu, H., Hariri, S., Wu, M.Y.: Performance-effective and low-complexity task scheduling for heterogeneous computing. IEEE Transactions on Parallel and Distr. Systems 13(3), 260–274 (2002)
17. Yu, J., Kirley, M., Buyya, R.: Multi-objective planning for workflow execution on grids. In: Proceedings of the 8th IEEE/ACM Intern. Conference on Grid Computing, GRID 2007, pp. 10–17. IEEE Computer Society, Washington, DC (2007)

2013 Workshop on Middleware for HPC and Big Data Systems (MHPC 2013)

Michael Alexander, Gianluigi Zanetti, Anastassios Nanos,
Jie Tao, and Lizhe Wang

Program Chairs

Extremely large, diverse, and complex data sets are generated from scientific applications, the Internet, social media and other applications. Data may be physically distributed and shared by an ever larger community. Collecting, aggregating, storing and analyzing large data volumes presents major challenges. Processing such amounts of data efficiently has been an issue to scientific discovery and technological advancement. In addition, making the data accessible, understandable and interoperable includes unsolved problems. Novel middleware architectures, algorithms, and application development frameworks are required.

This workshop is mainly focused on the intersection of HPC and Big Data with regard to middleware handling and optimizations. The goal of this workshop is to bring together software architects, middleware and framework developers, data-intensive app developers as well as users from the scientific and engineering community to exchange their experience in processing large datasets and to report their scientific achievement and innovative ideas.

The workshop also offers a dedicated forum for these researchers to access the state of the art, to discuss problems and requirements, identify gaps in current and planned designs, and to collaborate in strategies for scalable data-intensive computing.

The workshop featured 3 accepted papers, 2 invited talks and a panel on Heterogenous resource scheduling middleware. Papers of note include Tsoumakos et al. proposing a multi-engine data analytics middleware along with Visegrad et al. presenting an unorthodox yet efficient way to store and retrieve data from distributed storage systems using random network coding. The two invited talks stimulated an interesting conversation between the speakers and the audience, about resource scheduling and off-the-shelf components for Big data systems deployment.

The chairs would like to thank the Euro-Par organizers and the members of the program committee along with the speakers and attendees, whose interaction contributed to a stimulating environment. MHPC is planning to continue the successful co-location with Euro-Par in 2014.

D. an Mey et al. (Eds.): Euro-Par 2013 Workshops, LNCS 8374, p. 384, 2014.

Efficient Random Network Coding for Distributed Storage Systems

Ádám Visegrádi and Péter Kacsuk

Computer and Automation Research Institute,
Hungarian Academy of Sciences, Hungary
{visegradi.adam,kacsuk.peter}@sztaki.mta.hu

Abstract. Making distributed storage systems reliable is an important challenge. Simple replication may cause severe storage overhead when individual components of the system are very unreliable. Using *erasure codes* is a promising solution for this problem, but it presents its own challenges; it makes the design of such a system very complex, and it presents the problem of reparation. *Network coding* has been suggested to be used in the communication in these networks to help reduce overhead.

However, using random network coding *as*—not besides—erasure coding would be an even more promising field to investigate; such a system would have a simple design, need little or no centralization, and reparation of the system could be much simpler than it is in other erasure coding schemes.

The first step on this path is to investigate whether network coding can achieve such a performance that it is a feasible alternative to other erasure codes. This paper presents our experiences about the realization of random network coding based on the discrete logarithm of the finite field. We discuss possible performance optimizations for such a system, and provide performance measurement results focusing on data storage scenarios.

1 Introduction

In the era of Big Data, distributed storage systems are used to deal with the increasing volumes of data. Hadoop[5] and MapReduce[6] have proven that using cheap commodity hardware is a feasible alternative to expensive RAID storages. Even cheaper is to utilise volunteer or community storage, like BOINC[4], where storage space is donated to the system by people interested in it. These approaches use unreliable nodes as a basis for the distributed storage system. This unreliability can be handled by increasing *redundancy* in the system.

Consider the data to be a sequence of k blocks with a uniform size. The basic way to introduce redundancy is to *replicate* the blocks of the data. This approach has its drawbacks. First, the raw storage space required to store some data is the (integer) multiple of the size of the data; and this factor of redundancy has to be very high if the nodes' reliability is too low. Second, as failing nodes remove

D. an Mey et al. (Eds.): Euro-Par 2013 Workshops, LNCS 8374, pp. 385–394, 2014.

replicas of a block of the data from the system, that block may become rare, impairing locality.

Erasure coding (EC) is an alternative to replication, which alleviates both problems of replication, at the cost of CPU time. Erasure coding algorithms—e.g. Reed–Solomon[11] or Fountain codes[10]—create $n > k$ coded blocks from the original data in a way that *any* $k' >= k$ coded blocks will be sufficient for reconstruction. Because *any* k' block is sufficient for reconstruction, much lower factor of redundancy is sufficient than in case of replication[14]. Also, in erasure coding, the factor of redundancy does not have to be an integer. Although this seems to be a trifle, but the difference between a required redundancy of 2.1 and $\lceil 2.1 \rceil = 3$ can be substantial when there are peta-bytes of data.

The problem with erasure coding is the design complexity of the system, and the overhead required for its reparation[12]. In both cases (replication and EC), when blocks go missing, they have to be complemented. In case of replication, only rare blocks have to be further replicated. In case of erasure coding, to complement the missing blocks, the whole data has to be reconstructed, so new coded blocks can be generated from it[12][8]. Dimakis et al. propose regenerating codes[7] to remedy this problem. Regenerating codes use network coding[3] to communicate encoded packets, which enables the reparation of redundancy without reconstructing the original data. However, if the data is very distributed and each node stores only one piece of a data object, this approach may not provide many benefits. This can happen in large volunteer systems, which are of particular interest to us.

A promising approach would be to use *random (linear) network coding*[9] (RNC) to store the data. Linear network coding (LNC) treats the blocks of data as vectors—and the data itself as a matrix—over a finite field $\mathbb{F}(2^w)$ $(w \geq 1)$. Coding is performed by creating linear combinations of the original blocks, while decoding is done by solving the corresponding linear system. LNC has been well studied in the area of networking, as an alternative to routing; and random network coding has been proposed as a simple solution for finding suitable coefficients for linear combinations. RNC can be considered as an erasure coding method, as $n > k$ randomly encoded packets can be generated from the original file, of which any $k' >= k$ will be sufficient for reconstruction. Furthermore, it is stochastically optimal, and it converges to optimal with increasing field size[9].

As an erasure coding, RNC could solve the problems of replication; it would even perform better than traditional erasure coding schemes [2]. Also, the problem of reparation in a RNC system would become quite straight-forward: as stored blocks are random linear combinations (r.l.c.) of the original data blocks, a r.l.c. of the *coded* blocks will *also* be a r.l.c. of the *original* blocks. That is, reparation can be done by randomly selecting existing coded blocks from the system, and creating r.l.c.-s of them—no complete reconstruction is needed, nor the selection and location of specific sets of coded blocks. These properties would make r.l.c. a great candidate for coding data in distributed storage scenarios.

But linear coding is very CPU intensive. Would it be a feasible alternative to other coding schemes? There is little information on the practical implementation of r.l.c. in the literature, and no information on the possible optimizations there are. Also, most simulations and measurments focus only on corroborating the theoretical benefits of r.l.c. (e.g. [2], [7]). In [13], Wang et al. discuss a real implementation of r.l.c.; however, they use only the finite field $\mathbb{F}(2^8)$ and discuss no details on the possible optimizations.

We have implemented r.l.c.[1], and measured the raw coding speed we can achieve with it. In this paper we discuss the practical implementation, possible optimizations, and our performance measurement results of our implementation of network coding, with our conclusion being that, with the right choices, network coding can be a feasible alternative to existing erasure coding methods.

2 Efficient Realization of Network Coding

In this paper we are focusing on Big Data problems; that is, the handling of relatively large files (or data objects in general). In practice, really large files are broken up into smaller *segments*; for simple discussion we will use "file" as a denotation for this unit of storage.

Consider a file to be a sequence of k blocks; each block being $l := \frac{\text{file size}}{k}$ bytes long. Random network coding treats these blocks as vectors over a finite field $\mathbb{F}(2^w)$. For simplicity, we assume the file consists of k *whole* blocks; and for practicality, we assume that the word length, w, is a multiple of 8. Each word is of $u := \frac{w}{8}$ bytes, and each block is a vector of $\frac{l}{u}$ words.

2.1 Discrete Logarithm and Field Size

To study the possibilities of such a system, the first step is to implement finite field operations. Unfortunately, universal finite field implementations impose high overhead on encoding/decoding a file. This is because they rely on an internal representation of polynomials in the finite fields: each word of u bytes of the data—both original *and* coded—has to be converted to the internal representation, which requires extra memory and CPU time. Then, the field operations, whose complexity increases with the size of the field, are performed on these polynomials. And finally, the polynomials have to be converted back to binary words.

In our implementation, we used discrete logarithm tables to perform finite field multiplications. Using pre-calculated logarithm and power tables enables us to perform finite field operations on the words of the data directly. Without conversion, addition and subtraction becomes a simple bit-wise *xor* of the words of the data, while multiplication can be performed in *constant time* regardless of the field size. This approach requires $2(2^w u)$ bytes overhead: a power table and a logarithm table with the same size, each containing 2^w elements, each element being u bytes long. This means that using $\mathbb{F}(2^{16})$ requires only 256kB constant extra memory. Unfortunately, $\mathbb{F}(2^{16})$ is a practical limit, as $\mathbb{F}(2^{24})$ and $\mathbb{F}(2^{32})$ would need 96MB and 32GB respectively.

Using tables instead of generic libraries, the overall performance of encoding/decoding should *increase* with field size. As we are focusing on storage scenarios, we use relatively large blocks: this makes the matrix multiplication the dominant operation (as opposed to matrix inversion, which, in our case, is negligible). Coding—and decoding—is a multiplication of a $k \times k$ matrix (the coefficient matrix) with a $k \times \frac{l}{u}$ one (the file consisting of k blocks). Thus the multiplication is $\Theta(k^2 \frac{l}{u}) = \Theta(k^2 \frac{\text{filesize}/k}{u}) = \Theta(k \frac{\text{filesize}}{u})$ in complexity.

From this, it is clear that the multiplication complexity is inversely proportional to the word length, linearly proportional to the block count k, and linearly proportional to the file size. Practically, if we use constant time field operations like discrete logarithm, this means that using $\mathbb{F}\left(2^{16}\right)$ instead of $\mathbb{F}\left(2^{8}\right)$ should double the speed of the operation. Another consequence of using a larger field is the decreased probability of linearly dependent vectors. This reduces traffic and computation overhead caused by redundant transmission.

2.2 Data Placement

We do not focus on the bottleneck using the disk, network, or any medium creates; we are interested in the bottleneck network coding creates. Therefore, all operations are performed in memory; files are loaded in memory before encoding takes place, and stored to disk after the operation. We measure only the time needed to perform the operation in memory, excluding media overhead.

Even though we exclude the overhead of using a storage or transfer medium, we still face this kind of problem on a smaller scale. In our case, because of large files and blocks, the dominant operation is the matrix multiplication. Because the operation is CPU intensive, it would be optimal to perform it as "close" to the processor as possible; however, these large files will not fit into higher level caches of the CPU. Furthermore, the naïve implementation of the matrix multiplication impedes cache locality. Therefore, we use simple matrix blocking to enhance the performance of multiplication. Also, we learnt that the order of the three nested loops of matrix multiplication is a significant factor in efficiency.

2.3 Details of Implementation

Our implementation is a C/C++ program, highly optimized both by hand and by the compiler (g++). The power and logarithm tables are represented as C arrays, calculated beforehand. Elements of the finite field are represented by raw words of data. This way, addition and subtraction in base-2 finite field can be performed by *xor*-ing the operands. Multiplication and division can be performed in constant time with lookups and integer operations, for example: $a \cdot b = pow\left[(log[a] + log[b]) \bmod (2^n - 1)\right].$

When encoding, a $k \times k$ matrix is generated randomly—using the built-in C `rand()` function—with which the input file is multiplied. If the generated matrix cannot be inverted, it is noted and another matrix is generated; and so on. Please note, that we used the basic Gaussian elimination to invert the matrix. Thus here, "cannot be inverted" does not necessarily mean that the matrix is singular, it can also mean that the rows should have been reordered. However, we will se that in $\mathbb{F}\left(2^{16}\right)$, naïve Gaussian elimination is adequate.

After generating a coding matrix, both the generated matrix and the result of the multiplication is saved to disk. When decoding, the previously generated matrix is inverted, and the result of the previous encoding is multiplied by it.

Manual optimization of the program code was necessary. We have gained marginal but noticeable performance increase with using local constant variables instead of `struct` dereferencing in the loop core. On the other hand, we could almost double the performance of the multiplication by reordering the nested loops.

We implemented both naïve and square-blocked matrix multiplication with adjustable block size to measure the effect of locality. This provided considerable performance gains over simple matrix multiplication.

We also measured the effects of parallelizing the calculations. The matrix is cut into pieces—workunits—that are processed by a thread pool with the specified number of threads. For non-blocked multiplication the workunits correspond to the rows of the matrix, for blocked multiplication, the pieces correspond to blocks.

3 Performance Measurements

Our main interest was the raw performance of network coding, without the overhead of a medium (network, disk, etc.). Therefore, we loaded the (un)coded blocks in memory, measured the time to perform the multiplication, and then save the result back to disk. This way, the only overhead we experienced was that of the CPU–memory bus and cache latency.

We performed the measurements on our test machine, with an Intel i5-2410M dual core, hyperthreaded CPU. We also performed the measurements in our cloud infrastructure. The cloud-based measurements were slower, but they produced similar results, leading to the same conclusions. In this paper, the numbers produced on our test machine are shown.

3.1 Parameters

For a single measurement, the parameters listed in Table 1 can be specified. Some of the measurements were focused only on a subset of the ranges described.

Table 1. Parameters of a single measurement

Field size	q	The size of the field; $q \in \{2^8, 2^{16}\}$.
File size	fs	The size of the input file; $fs \in \left\{64\text{kB} \cdot 2^i \mid i \in [0..13]\right\}$. (That is, 64kB–512MB, exponentially.)
Block count	k	The number of blocks the file is split into; $k \in [2^3..2^7]$.
Mode		Encoding or decoding.
Thread count	$ncpus$	Number of threads to use; $ncpus \in [1..4]$.
Mul. block size	$mulbs$	The size of the square block used in blocked multiplication; $mulbs \in 2^0, \ldots, 2^6$; $mulbs \leq \frac{k}{2}$. If $mulbs = 1$, non-blocked multiplication is performed.

3.2 Results

Field Size. The size of the field is known to affect the reliability of the system, as increasing field size reduces the probability of vectors being linearly dependent[9]. On the other hand, as described in Section 2.1, if field operations take constant time, increasing the field size will increase the performance of the matrix multiplication.

In total, 12,445 matrices were generated during the experiments discussed here. When a matrix is generated, it is checked if it is *acceptable*, that is, if it can be inverted with simple Gaussian elimination; if not, it is thrown away, and a new one is generated. Of all the matrices, 6648 were generated for $\mathbb{F}\left(2^8\right)$ and 5797 for $\mathbb{F}\left(2^{16}\right)$. More matrices were generated for $\mathbb{F}\left(2^8\right)$, as the chance of generating an unacceptable matrix was higher in this case: in $\mathbb{F}\left(2^8\right)$, 1218 matrices were unacceptable, in $\mathbb{F}\left(2^{16}\right)$ only 7. Using the built-in C random generator **81.6787% of the matrices in $\mathbb{F}\left(2^8\right)$ were acceptable, while in $\mathbb{F}\left(2^{16}\right)$, 99.8792%.**

There is also a performance gain when using $\mathbb{F}\left(2^{16}\right)$ (Figure 1). In theory, this gain should be 2, as the operational complexity of the matrix multiplication is inversely proportional to the word size. However, the actual gain was less than this, because the discrete logarithm table is much bigger (256kB versus the 512 bytes for $\mathbb{F}\left(2^8\right)$), which impedes cache locality. The performance gain was usually between 1 and 2, its median varied between 1.467 and 1.221 depending on the number of blocks (k).

Matrix Multiplication. We considered matrix blocking to optimize cache locality. Our Intel CPU has two physical cores, two memory channels and two 32kB L1 caches, one for each core. Theoretically, if we use $\mathbb{F}\left(2^{16}\right)$ and 64×64 blocks, a single iteration would use $64 \times 64 \times 2 \times 3$ bytes $= 24$kB (block size $\times$ element size $\times$ (left-hand, right-hand and result matrices)), which 24kB can fit in the L1 cache, providing superior performance compared to naïve multiplication. In practice, this is close to be true, but results fluctuate marginally, because the logarithm and power tables have to be accessed too.

We experienced that using blocking reduces operation time greatly; however, increasing the block size to from 4 to 64 provides only marginal performance gains (Figure 2).

Another optimization was to reorder nested iterations of matrix multiplication. For the multiplication, we need three indices, i, j and k. These indices iterate over the matrix in the dimensions shown on Figure 3. For matrix multiplication, one can iterate through the target matrix with i and j, and in the innermost loop create scalar products with k. As addition is commutative, the iterations can be reordered. By using nested loops iterating over i, k and then j, we doubled the speed of the multiplication (Fig. 4).

Number of Threads. As matrix multiplication is trivially parallelizable, it was expected, that using multiple physical cores with independent memory channels the speed of the computation can be increased. On the other hand, using

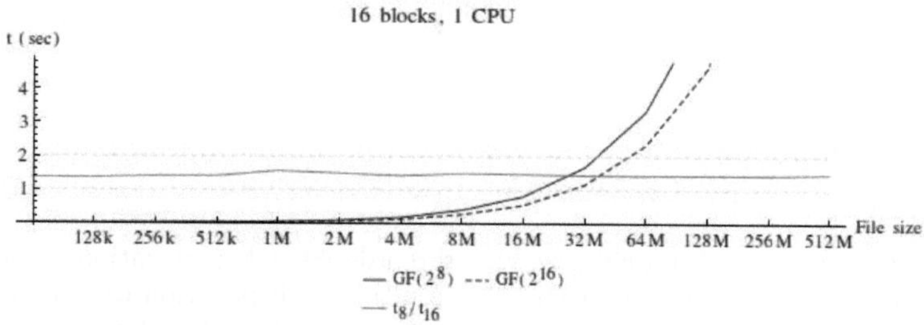

Fig. 1. Performance using $\mathbb{F}\left(2^8\right)$ compared to $\mathbb{F}\left(2^{16}\right)$. The results show that the operational time is linearly proportional to the file size, while in case of $\mathbb{F}\left(2^{16}\right)$, the constant factor is smaller. The ratio of the two results is shown as the grey horizontal graph; the levels of 1 and 2 are shown for reference. The domain spans up to 512M, but the plot is trimmed for visibility.

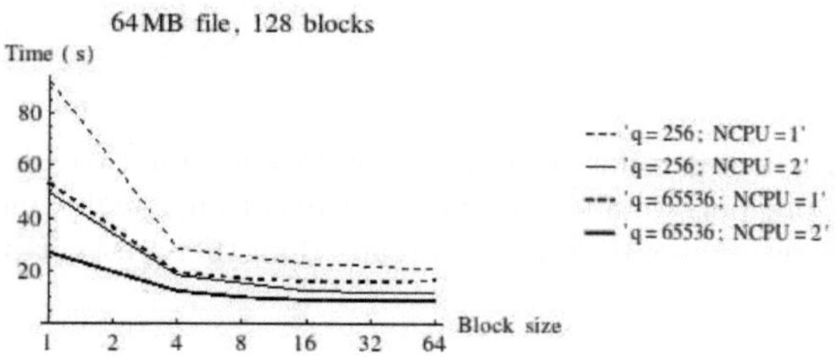

Fig. 2. Performance differences using different block sizes for matrix multiplication. For block size = 1, naïve multiplication was used.

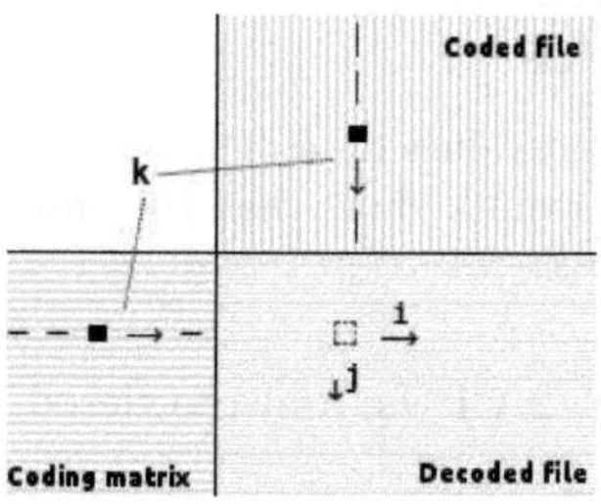


```
1 fill_with_zeroes(decoded_file);
2 for i = 1 to blocklength do
3     for j = 1 to blockcount do
4         for k = 1 to blockcount do
5             decoded_file[i, j]+=coding_matrix[j, k] *
              coded_file[k, i];
6         end
7     end
8 end
```

Fig. 3. Illustration of the indices used for matrix multiplication. The algorithm shown is the "original" algorithm. In the "reordered" algorithm, lines 3 and 4 are exchanged.

more concurrent threads than there were physical cores did not increase the performance. Using two separate cores nearly doubled the performance of the multiplication (Fig. 5).

Overall Performance. Using the best optimization methods we identified, we measured the overall performance of coding for different file sizes and values

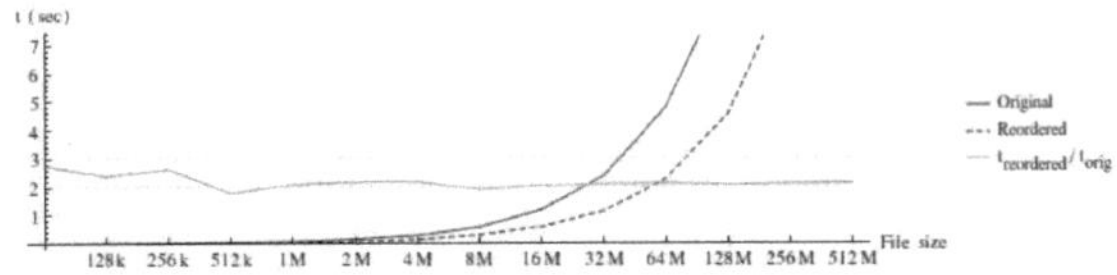

Fig. 4. Performance using original (i, j, k) and reordered (i, k, j) iterations. The results show that using the reordered iteration, the resulting multiplication can be performed at least twice as fast. The domain spans up to 512M, but the plot is trimmed for visibility.

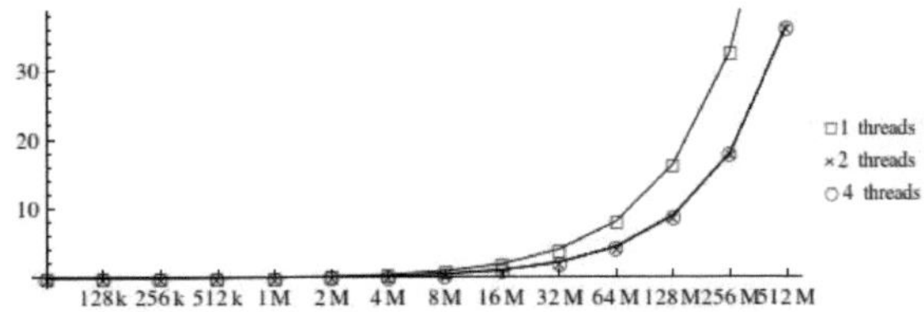

Fig. 5. Performance using different number of threads on two physical cores. The results show that the performance of the multiplication can be increased by using multiple physical cores; while using more threads than there are cores will not increase performance.

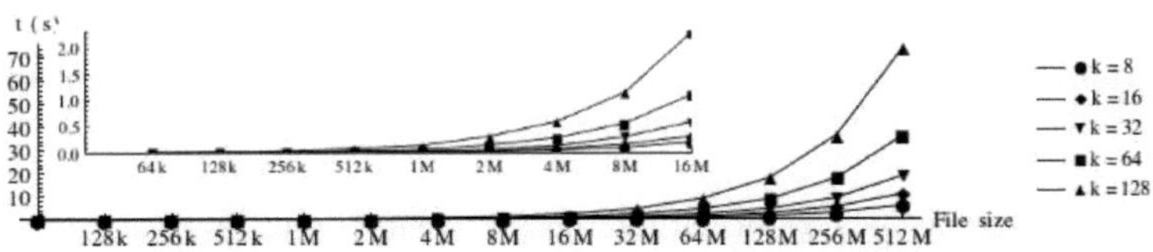

Fig. 6. Performance using files of different sizes, with different values for k. The interval between 64kB and 16MB is magnified for visibility. The results show that the time complexity of the multiplication is linearly proportional to k.

for k. In the following measurements, we used $\mathbb{F}(2^{16})$, 2 CPUs, and reordered, blocked matrix multiplication.

As expected, the time to encode or decode a file takes the same amount of time, as these are practically the same operation with different names for the operands.

Our experiments show that the time needed to perform the multiplication increases linearly with the file size (Fig. 6) and linearly with k (Fig. 7). This accords with our expectations described in Section 2.1. This conclusion holds true regardless of the number of threads we used, or the field size—changing these parameters only changed the resulting numbers, but not the correlations described here.

In terms of *throughput*, as the operation time increases linearly with file size, the throughput will be *constant for a given value of* k, while it will drop linearly as k is increased. Our results are detailed in Table 2.

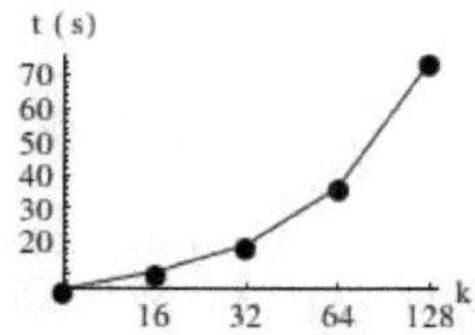

Fig. 7. Performance using different values for k with fixed file size (64MB). The results show that the time complexity of the multiplication is linearly proportional to k.

Table 2. Numerical performance results for each (file size, k) pair. Each value is the time, in *seconds*, a matrix multiplication was performed.

	File size													
k	64kB	128kB	256kB	512kB	1MB	2MB	4MB	8MB	16MB	32MB	64MB	128MB	256MB	512MB
8	0.0009	0.0016	0.0028	0.0076	0.0108	0.0214	0.0490	0.0986	0.1946	0.3780	0.7273	1.4550	2.9411	5.8764
16	0.0016	0.0035	0.0066	0.0107	0.0277	0.0365	0.0811	0.1566	0.3072	0.6480	1.2729	2.5983	5.4194	10.9605
32	0.0023	0.0055	0.0099	0.0256	0.0346	0.0663	0.1304	0.2976	0.5828	1.1390	2.2639	4.5539	9.3095	19.0175
64	0.0043	0.0086	0.0203	0.0439	0.0655	0.1459	0.2780	0.5567	1.1023	2.2089	4.4876	8.8185	18.0695	36.3531
128	0.0134	0.0182	0.0362	0.0810	0.1414	0.3100	0.5904	1.1449	2.2859	4.5113	9.0622	18.1723	36.5472	74.2251

These results show that certain parameter sets can achieve considerable performance, and may be used for suitable data-intensive applications. For example, consider 128MB chunks cut into 16 blocks. Decoding a chunk would take 4.55 seconds. After the initial delay, if the data is processed as a stream, a bandwidth of about 49.3 MB/s can be achieved. As the next chunk can be lodaded from a medium while the previous is being decoded, assuming a medium fast enough, its overhead will only appear in the initial delay, and the decoding bandwidth can be sustained. In the best case above, 87 MB/s of bandwidth could be achieved.

4 Conclusion and Future Work

In this paper we have presented our experiences about the implementation and performance measurements of randomized linear coding. We described several approaches to improve the performance of such a system. From these results, we conclude that, with the right choices, using randomized coding over the finite field $\mathbb{F}\left(2^{16}\right)$ can be a feasible alternative to erasure coding in distributed storage systems.

Learning this, we are now confident that using randomized linear coding instead of classical erasure coding is an area worth investigating. In our future research, we will study the theoretical possibilities of this approach, and will try to further improve the technical methods of realization.

References

[1] Random Network Coding Library, https://github.com/avisegradi/rnc-lib (accessed: October 09, 2013)
[2] Acedanski, S., Deb, S., Médard, M., Koetter, R.: How good is random linear coding based distributed networked storage. In: Workshop on Network Coding, Theory and Applications (2005)
[3] Ahlswede, R., Cai, N., Li, S., Yeung, R.: Network information flow. IEEE Transactions on Information Theory 46(4), 1204–1216 (2000)
[4] Anderson, D.: BOINC: a system for public-resource computing and storage. In: Proceedings of the Fifth IEEE/ACM International Workshop on Grid Computing, pp. 4–10 (November 2004)
[5] Borthakur, D.: The hadoop distributed file system: Architecture and design. Hadoop Project Website 11, 21 (2007)
[6] Dean, J., Ghemawat, S.: MapReduce: simplified data processing on large clusters. Communications of the ACM 51(1), 107–113 (2008)
[7] Dimakis, A., Godfrey, P., Wu, Y., Wainwright, M., Ramchandran, K.: Network coding for distributed storage systems. IEEE Transactions on Information Theory 56(9), 4539–4551 (2010)
[8] Dimakis, A., Ramchandran, K., Wu, Y., Suh, C.: A survey on network codes for distributed storage. Proceedings of the IEEE 99(3), 476–489 (2011)
[9] Ho, T., Médard, M., Koetter, R., Karger, D., Effros, M., Shi, J., Leong, B.: A random linear network coding approach to multicast. IEEE Transactions on Information Theory 52(10), 4413–4430 (2006)
[10] MacKay, D.: Fountain codes. IEE Proceedings-Communications 152, 1062–1068 (2005)
[11] Reed, I., Solomon, G.: Polynomial codes over certain finite fields. Journal of the Society for Industrial & Applied Mathematics 8(2), 300–304 (1960)
[12] Rodrigues, R., Liskov, B.: High availability in DHTs: erasure coding vs. replication. In: Peer-to-Peer Systems IV, pp. 226–239 (2005)
[13] Wang, M., Li, B.: How practical is network coding? In: 14th IEEE International Workshop on Quality of Service, IWQoS 2006, pp. 274–278 (2006)
[14] Weatherspoon, H., Kubiatowicz, J.D.: Erasure coding vs. Replication: A quantitative comparison. In: Druschel, P., Kaashoek, M.F., Rowstron, A. (eds.) IPTPS 2002. LNCS, vol. 2429, pp. 328–337. Springer, Heidelberg (2002)

Hybrid Job Scheduling for Improved Cluster Utilization

Ismail Ari and Ugur Kocak

Computer Engineering Department, Ozyegin University, Istanbul, Turkey

Abstract. In this paper, we investigate the models and issues as well as performance benefits of hybrid job scheduling over shared physical clusters. Clustering technologies that are currently supported include MPI, Hadoop-MapReduce and NoSQL systems. Our proposed scheduling model is above the cluster-specific middleware and OS-level schedulers and it is complementary to them. First, we demonstrate that we can effectively schedule MPI, Hadoop, NoSQL jobs together by profiling them and then co-scheduling. Second, we find that it is better to schedule cluster jobs with different job characteristics together (CPU vs. I/O intensive) rather than two CPU-intensive jobs. Third, we use the learning outcome of this principle to design of a greedy sort-merge scheduler. Up to 37% savings in total job completion times are demonstrated. These savings are directly proportional to the cluster utilization improvements.

1 Introduction

In many universities and research centers scientists depend on shared computing clusters for their computational needs. These scientists are usually from various disciplines such as Physics, Mechanical Engineering, and Computer Science. Some of their jobs are CPU-intensive and some are data-intensive. They also use different distributed processing engines and associated middleware such as MPI [1,2], Hadoop-MapReduce [3], and NoSQL $< key, value >$ engines to execute their jobs. As a worst case scenario (which is common in smaller scientific communities), people email each other to decide who runs a job first, which causes poor cluster utilization, or they all submit their jobs simultaneously leading to clashes and poor performance. Today, there is no easy-to-use, common scheduler to reorder and reprioritize these hybrid jobs to make better execution plans among different clustering technologies. In this paper, we describe the design of a new MPI, Hadoop-MapReduce, and NoSQL hybrid job scheduler that uses jobs′ execution profiles from prior runs and makes global scheduling decisions to improve overall system utilization and job throughput performance.

1.1 Challenges and Potentials in Hybrid Scheduling

In this context, the word *hybrid* can have multiple meanings:

1. First, the interfaces or APIs of distributed processing technologies can be different (*e.g.* MPI vs. MapReduce) and these different middleware will be executed together on one physical platform.

D. an Mey et al. (Eds.): Euro-Par 2013 Workshops, LNCS 8374, pp. 395–405, 2014.

2. Second, the cluster's physical resources can be heterogeneous consisting of relatively powerful and weaker machines.
3. Third, the new overlay hybrid scheduler should know that there are also other underlying cluster-specific job schedulers and operating system (OS)-level process schedulers, which creates a multi-level scheduling scenario.

The ideal hybrid scheduler should have the ability to make a combined scheduling decision considering all of the conditions above. Therefore, it would be fair to state that *hybrid job scheduling is hard.* Yet, we also observe the fact that in scientific communities similar jobs are run repeatedly over the same shared physical clusters as shown in Figure 1. Therefore, there is an opportunity to profile these different jobs in terms of their CPU, memory, disk bandwidth, and network usage and feed this information to a global hybrid scheduler for optimization. The clear benefits of hybrid job scheduling include increased resource utilization, convenience on the user's side, and better job isolation. This paper aims to investigate and highlight some of these potential advantages.

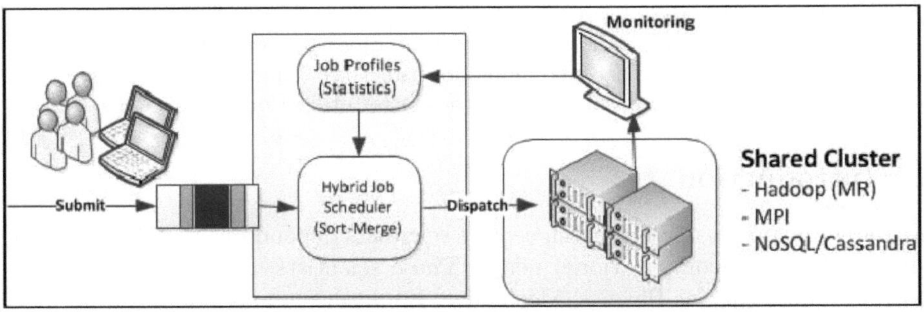

Fig. 1. A hybrid job scheduler for shared physical clusters collects and uses job profiles or statistics from prior runs

In one aspect, the hybrid job scheduler virtualizes the underlying clustering technologies, creating a unified scientific cloud platform service (or PaaS). The underlying cluster infrastructure can be physical or virtual or deployed as a private or public infrastructure cloud service (*i.e.* IaaS). The end users do not have to know these details. In addition, they also would not have to manage the cluster middleware, *i.e.* know whether MPI, Hadoop, NoSQL (HBase[4], Cassandra [5], MongoDB [6]) are installed properly. One scientist running High Performance Computing (HPC) jobs only may not fully utilize all the cluster resources (*e.g.* 100% of the CPU, but no disk bandwidth), but when heterogeneous tasks from different departments are put together better cluster utilization is achievable.

2 Background - Big Data, Hadoop, MPI, NoSQL

The need for clusters have been driven primarily by HPC applications in the past. Today, there is an emergence of High Throughput Computing (HTC) [19,20]

applications that contend for the same cluster resources. Many organizations including universities, telecommunication operators, media & social networks, financial institutions and governments generate Terabytes of data each day and attempt to insert this high "volume" data into databases that already contain Petabytes. Data come from different sources such as sensors, various web/system logs, and mobile phone call detail records (CDR). The mixing of these different data types results in a wide "variety" of data to be processed and stored (*e.g.* unstructured text, semi-structured XML-JSON, structured CSV, or binary audio/video data). The term "Big Data" is used to refer to challenging data management problems that arise due to the high Volume, Velocity, Variety, and Veracity (4Vs) of the data [7]. Relational database management systems cannot cope with 4Vs of data very well, therefore Hadoop and NoSQL systems have quickly penetrated into the scientific and enterprise data infrastructures. Consequently, a variety of the cluster technologies started to get used over the same, shared physical clusters.

2.1 Hadoop

Apache Hadoop is an open-source framework written in Java designed for supporting data-intensive distributed applications. Hadoop framework mainly consists of two components called MapReduce (MR) and Hadoop Distributed File System (HDFS) as shown in Figure 2. The data to be processed is stored in large fixed-sized (64MB) chunks by HDFS for performance and reliability reasons. HDFS consists of a NameNode and DataNodes. MapReduce (MR) is a distributed job execution system consisting of a JobTracker and TaskTrackers. Jobs will be split into many Map and Reduce tasks and sent as JAR files to many machines containing the data in HDFS. Chen, *et al.* [8] give a detailed analysis of MR workloads from two large-scale production Hadoop systems (Yahoo & Facebook) and find great differences between MR use cases. They conclude that "no single benchmark can capture such diverse behavior" [8].

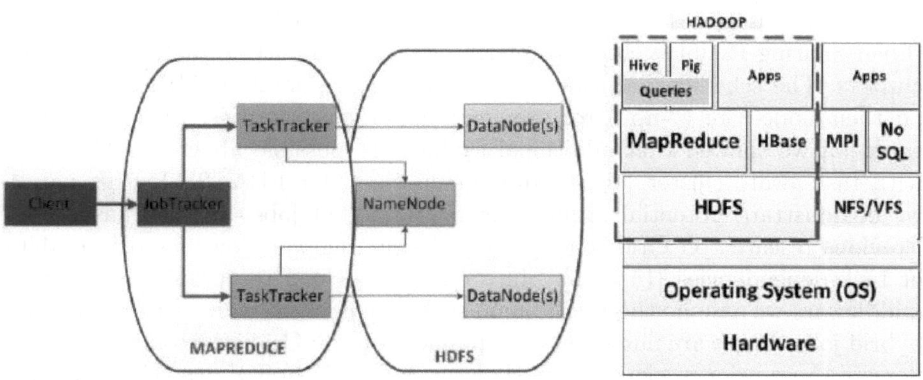

Fig. 2. (Left) Hadoop architecture overview and (right) diagram showing colocation of Hadoop, MPI and NoSQL systems in one machine

2.2 Message Passing Interface (MPI)

MPI is an HPC middleware used for distributed inter-process communication. It is well-standardized and portable. We use the MPICH2 [1] implementation of the standard, but other implementations such as the Open MPI [2] also exist. In our previous HPC-focused work [9], we implemented a cloud computing platform service for Finite Element Analysis (FEA). We found that if the FEA job can be processed effectively on a single multi-core server (*i.e.* with enough CPU cores and RAM), we should use the SMP-style multi-processing. If not, the job will be distributed over multiple servers/processes and MPI will be used for inter-process communication. The scheduler has to make these decisions optimally for hundreds of jobs, simultaneously [9].

2.3 NoSQL - Apache Cassandra

The most commonly used NoSQL systems include HBase [4], Cassandra [5], and MongoDB [6]. We selected Cassandra and continued with it as our NoSQL system. Apache Cassandra [5] is a Java-based NoSQL database initially developed by Facebook. One of its differentiators is that, it has no central servers and uses a pure peer-to-peer approach for scalability. Cassandra does not enforce a schema, thus it is also a $< key, value >$ store like Amazon's Dynamo [10] system. The "table" concept in DBMS is represented by a "column family" in Cassandra. Cassandra opens a thread per worker thread. However, it also uses additional CPU resources for other background jobs, like indexing and flushing, which shows as random spikes in its CPU profile.

3 Related Work - Cluster Job Scheduling

While most state-of-the-art cluster job scheduling tools declare heterogeneous system support, they primarily refer to different hardware capabilities and not middleware interfaces. For HPC jobs, the famous MPI scheduler called LSF (Load Sharing Facility) [11] is primarily used for submitting MPI jobs to MPI clusters. The scheduler adjusts execution order of submitted MPI tasks based on their node-core ("-np") requirements and their priorities. In our previous work [9], we showed that additional savings are possible above the MPI-level with task-aware cluster job scheduling especially for FEA [9]. In this paper, we demonstrate potential savings for hybrid set of jobs, and not just HPC. Previous research on Grid scheduling and scientific workflows focuses on data or task dependencies [14], [15]. Since our jobs belong to completely different middleware we assume there will be no such dependencies and issues among our hybrid jobs. There are numerous past publications on Grid scheduling, but since none of these prior works support Hadoop, MPI and NoSQL we skip a detailed comparison here for brevity. For HTC jobs, there exists two Hadoop schedulers called FIFO and Fair Scheduler [12]. Using these schedulers and careful job pool settings, prioritized co-scheduling of MapReduce jobs is possible. However, these Hadoop schedulers do not accept MPI jobs today.

We are not aware of any system that integrates MPI, Hadoop, and NoSQL systems as we do in this paper. The closest systems to ours include the SLURM Scheduler plugins and HTCondor ClassAds. "SLURM is an open-source resource manager designed for Linux clusters" [24]. It provides a framework for allocating, starting, executing, and monitoring work (typically a parallel job) on a set of allocated nodes for a specified duration. SLURM's modular design accepts plugins inluding scheduler plugins that implement the SLURM scheduler API. To name a few, *builtin scheduler* plugin implements FIFO and *backfill* raises the priority of jobs to start them earlier. "HTCondor's ClassAds are a flexible mechanism for representing the characteristics and constraints of machines and jobs in the HTCondor system" [25]. HTCondor currently has no direct MapReduce support.

One could simply use native or hosted machine virtualization to co-locate different clustering middleware (or platforms) on shared physical cluster infrastructure. In comparsion, our proposed hybrid job scheduling model has one of the simplest forms. In our proposed model, different clusters are placed under the common scheduler, which profiles all the submitted jobs and decides to co-locate (*i.e.* dispatch together) those who use different, heterogeneous types of resources. In this regard, the hybrid job scheduler virtualizes the underlying clustering middleware, creating a unified scientific cloud. There are two other cases called Hadoop over MPI or MPI over Hadoop, where the former refers to converting MapReduce source or binary code using an adapter to MPI code to run over an MPI cluster [21] and the latter refers to the new YARN approach mentioned in Section 2.1. There can also be native and a hosted virtualized models, for mixed Hadoop-MPI virtual clusters. These two virtualization alternatives are quite similar with respect to the higher-layer job scheduling software. However, the natively virtualized clusters provide additional advantages over hosted VMs including dynamic resizing and migration of VMs, and scale easily beyond a single physical machine. As tradeoffs, virtualized clusters have both performance overheads and additional VM management issues [18].

Recent findings [22] also suggests that virtualization may not always be the answer in the HPC world for multiple reasons. First, HPC systems want to squeeze the last bit of performance from the systems whereas virtualization can mean up to 10% of performance hit, since the hypervisor adds yet another layer between the physical resources and the applications. The second reason is HPC systems are already designed for being shared among a community of people in unified scientific communities (*i.e.* with similar HPC jobs) the utilizations can be relatively high [22]. Therefore, the motivations that drive the use of virtualization (*i.e.* increase utilization, save power and same money) are not always there for HPC. Similarly for Hadoop clusters, experts neither recommend virtualization nor RAID, but to save the money and buy more nodes and disk spindles. While the fastest 15K rpm disks are common in HPC, they are not recommended in Hadoop and other HTC clusters, as one can get more parallel I/O bandwidth by buying more 7200 rpm disks. In summary, virtualization is a good choice in dynamic test and development environments where reconfiguration speeds and elasticity are critical. However, HPC and HTC environments run similar and predictable types of workloads and require deterministic performance.

4 Performance Analysis and Results

The experiments for this demo were conducted on a small cluster of two IBM HS22 Blade Servers in an HPC blade chassis with 1Gbps connectivity. Each server has two 2.40GHz Intel Xeon Quad-Core CPUs, 24GB Memory, and two 72 GB 15000rpm disks configured as RAID1. We installed RedHat Linux 5 on these servers. For profiling we used the *sysstat* package [16] and its pidstat command to track CPU, memory and disk read-write bandwidth usage of the processes. All experiments were run 3 times and the results were averaged.

4.1 Workloads

As Hadoop workload we used the classical *terasort* benchmark, which is more IO-intensive than our MPI task. For this experiment, we first created a large (15 GB) file filled with random, unsorted characters using the *teragen* program. Next, we used terasort to read & sort the unsorted data and write back the sorted data. Hadoop version 1.0.2 was used. As MPI workload we used the *dbworld* benchmark, which solves a system of linear equations. The MPI command was executed as follows: <*mpirun -np 8 dbworld_mpi -n 1536 -m 1536*>, where np denotes node-core counts and $n \times m$ are the matrix row-column sizes. We used the MPICH2 implementation [1] of MPI. During Hadoop comparison, matrix size was asjusted to 1348×1348, so that one task does not finish much sooner. This simulates a scenario where the job pipeline is always full.

For Cassandra benchmarking, we wrote a Java program that reads the XML-formatted CDR logs of a real mobile telecom company, indexes and inserts these transformed logs into Cassandra using the Astyanax client (~JDBC) by Netflix. For data distribution we used random sharding technique and no replication. Table 1 shows the average CPU-memory usage %, and read-write bandwidth usage in MB/second for these 3 workloads obtained using the *pidstat* tool. Basically, the MPI and Cassandra benchmark jobs were CPU-intensive (with 99% CPU utilization on average) and the Hadoop terasort job was more IO-intensive than others (10MB/sec reads, 40 MB/sec writes) and had 25% average CPU usage.

Table 1. Resource usage profiles of benchmark cluster workloads

	CPU	Memory	R-W Bandwith
MPI	99%	0.5%	0-0 MB/sec
Cassandra	99%	15%	0-4.3 MB/sec
Hadoop	25%	2.2%	9.8-40.2 MB/sec

Our focus in this paper was to mix and run different types of jobs together for different middleware, therefore we only analyzed interactions among jobs for multiple core count settings and did not vary the system-specific parameters internally. If we vary the size of either one of the benchmarks (MPI problem size, terasort data size, or Cassandra data size), their executions times will be longer, but the learning outcomes will be the same.

4.2 CPU-intensive Jobs and Cluster-Level Job Prioritization

Table 2 shows the results of co-scheduling of two CPU-intensive tasks MPI and Cassandra on a single 8-core (physical) server for different worker (4,8,16) settings. For MPI, the term "worker" refers to the number of cores used (*i.e.* -np) and for Cassandra it refers to the number of loader client threads. "Standalone" refers to non-overlapping, *i.e.* serial and mutually exclusive, execution of these two tasks. With 4 workers the total time to finish both tasks is 20.8 minutes (11.8+9.0). With 8 workers the total time goes down to 15.4 minutes (~26% improvement), but does not improve anymore for 16 workers since hyperthreading does not contribute much for ~100% CPU-intensive tasks. The Cassandra task benefits more from increased core count.

When the two tasks are started simultaneously with the same priorities and they execute in parallel, the OS-level process scheduler shows positive effect. Although both tasks execute longer than their serial execution counterparts (*e.g.* 16.2 mins for MPI and 10.1 mins for Cassandra 4) the system throughput increases from ~6 jobs/hour to ~8 jobs/hour: both tasks have completed at 16.2 minutes for 4 workers, 15.0 minutes for 8, and 13.8 minutes for 16 workers. This shows that 10-20% savings are possible even for CPU-intensive tasks.

Next, we change the priorities of the tasks using the Linux nice command to see if we can control the CPU-shares at the cluster level at run-time. In Cassandra, we change the priority of the server, whereas in MPI the priority of the job is directly changed. -20 and +19 are the highest and lowest priorities, respectively. The results are affirmative in terms of job control. The job with higher priority can perform comparable to its standalone performance, whereas the niced job has to wait (or run slow) until the high-priority job completes. This demonstrates that we can order, prioritize, or re-prioritize jobs belonging to different cluster technologies with respect to each other.

4.3 Hybrid Scheduling of CPU and IO-intensive Jobs

Table 3 shows the serial and hybrid execution of MPI and Hadoop jobs. We used the 15 GB data for the Hadoop terasort benchmark job. The serial execution completed in 1272 seconds total, whereas the hybrid execution completed around 800 seconds. This results in savings of ~37%. The savings are significantly higher compared to co-scheduling of two CPU-intensive jobs, which resulted in 10-20% savings. Note that the execution time of the CPU-intensive MPI job is ~20% higher (800 sec.) in hybrid form (*i.e.* MPI-Hadoop co-scheduled) compared to its serial execution time (671 sec). The Hadoop job also took ~25% longer, but

Table 2. Results of co-scheduling MPI and Cassandra jobs

Worker# Per-Job	Execution	MPI (min)	Cassandra (min)	Total (min)
4	standalone	11.8	9	20.8
	normal - combined	16.2	10.1	16.2
	nice -n -20 for M	14.9	18.4	18.4
	nice -n +19 for M	18.4	10.5	18.4
	nice -n -20 for C	19.9	10.5	19.9
	nice -n +19 for C	13.4	17.7	17.7
8	standalone	9.4	6	15.4
	normal - combined	15	8.6	15
	nice -n -20 for M	11.8	16.3	16.3
	nice -n +19 for M	17.6	7.5	17.6
	nice -n -20 for C	16.8	7.8	16.8
	nice -n +19 for C	10	16.1	16.1
16	standalone	9.5	5.8	15.3
	normal - combined	13.8	10.7	13.8
	nice -n -20 for M	11.3	16	16
	nice -n +19 for M	16.5	6.6	16.5
	nice -n -20 for C	15.6	6.8	15.6
	nice -n +19 for C	10.6	15.4	15.4

Table 3. Results of co-scheduling of MPI and Hadoop jobs

	MPI (sec)	Hadoop (sec)	Tot. Time (sec)
Serial Exec.	671.7	601.0	1272.7
Hybrid Sched.	800.3	769.0	800.3

they both finished at 800.3 seconds. These job latency increases can be attributed to the 20-25% on average CPU usage of the Hadoop job.

5 Generalized Hybrid Scheduler

Now, we briefly describe a greedy sort-merge hybrid job scheduler. First, jobs are profiled based on their resource usage. Job $i(j_i)$ is represented by a triplet $j_i =< c_i, m_i, d_i >$, where c_i, m_i, and d_i represents the average CPU, memory and read+write disk I/O usage of that job, respectively. Clients use our "hsub" command (stands for hybrid submit) and is similar to the LSF qsub-bsub commands. Sample hsub commands are given below:

```
hsub -t mpi -c "mpirun -np 16 ./dbworld params";
hsub -t cassandra -c "java -jar import.jar params";
hsub -t hadoop -c "hadoop jar examples.jar terasort /in /out";
```

where -t denotes the job type (mpi,hadoop,cassandra) and -c parameter gives the command string (parameters are omitted).

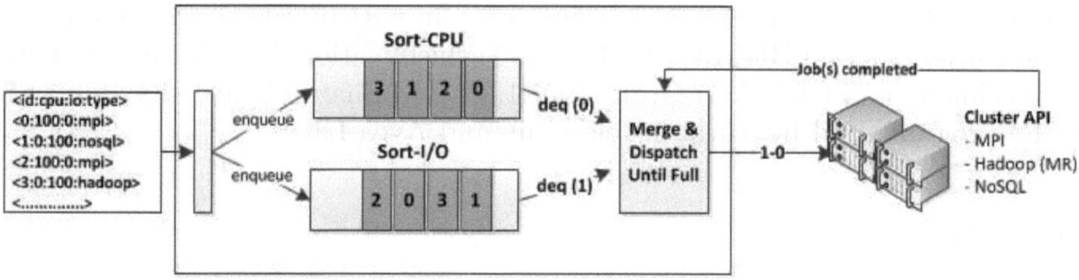

Fig. 3. Greedy sort-merge scheduler

Figure 3 illustrates the operation of this scheduler with a simple example. Jobs belonging to different clusters are submitted to the scheduler by various clients. In this example, a CPU-intensive job will be followed with an IO-intensive job. The scheduler keeps separate lists for each resource (CPU, disk, memory) in the decreasing order of their usage of that particular resource. Jobs are enqueued to all of the lists and then dequeued from the lists in a round-robin fashion. The corresponding capacities are subtracted from the resources, respectively. This way, a CPU-intensive job will first be matched with a disk-intensive job and so on until all jobs are complete. We generated two workloads: first, an HPC-HTC mix (*i.e.* CPU-intensive and IO-intensive mix) and second, a completely random mix on all dimensions (cpu, memory, disk). We compared different job sorting strategies using 1000 simulated jobs. We have written about 500 lines of Java code for the hybrid scheduler simulation. We briefly report the results here. Since the HPC-HTC mix was generated for an ideal case of 100% CPU-intensive ($< 100 : 0 : 0 >$) and 100% IO-intensive ($< 0 : 0 : 100 >$) mix, the greedy scheduler was able to finish 1000 such jobs in 500 epochs. That is 2x performance improvement (50% savings in total time) over a single CPU-based or a single IO-based sorted scheduler. For the random mix, the two schedulers have similar performance around 900 epochs each.

6 Conclusions

In this paper, we analyzed different models for hybrid job scheduling (above middleware and VM-based) over shared physical clusters. Our proposed scheduling layer is above the cluster middleware and OS-level schedulers. We were able to improve cluster utilization and overall throughput (jobs/min) with some increase in per job latency. Our important findings were as follows: (1) We can schedule jobs that belong to different clustering technologies (Hadoop, NoSQL, MPI) together effectively. (2) We found that two CPU-intensive jobs, that can each fully utilize the multi-core and multi-node resources of the cluster can still benefit from co-scheduling, but it is better to schedule I/O and disk-intensive jobs together first. (3) We demonstrated 10-37% decrease in total job processing times. This means that by continuous pipelining of heterogenous job types we can sustain up to 37% improvement in cluster utilization.

Acknowledgment. This work was supported in part by European Union FP7 Marie Curie Program BI4MASSES Grant, Turkish National Institute of Science and Technology (TUBITAK) Grant 190E194, IBM Shared University Research (SUR) program, and by Turkish Telecomm and Avea Labs.

References

1. MPICH project, http://www.mpich.org
2. Open MPI project, http://www.open-mpi.org
3. Apache Hadoop Project, http://hadoop.apache.org/
4. Apache Hbase project, http://hbase.apache.org
5. Apache Cassandra, http://cassandra.apache.org/
6. MongoDB by 10gen, http://www.mongodb.org/
7. What is Big Data? http://www-01.ibm.com/software/data/bigdata/
8. Chen, Y., Ganapathi, A., Griffith, R., Katz, R.: The case for evaluating MapReduce performance using workload suites. In: 2011 IEEE 19th International Symposium on Modeling, Analysis & Simulation of Computer and Telecommunication Systems (MASCOTS), pp. 390–399 (2011)
9. Ari, I., Muhtaroglu, N.: Design and implementation of a cloud computing service for finite element analysis. Advances in Engineering Software 60-61, 122–135 (2013)
10. DeCandia, G., Hastorun, D., Jampani, M., Kakulapati, G., Lakshman, A., Pilchin, A., Sivasubramanian, S., Vosshall, P., Vogels, W.: Dynamo: amazon's highly available key-value store. SOSP 7, 205–220 (2007)
11. Zhou, S., Zheng, X., Wang, J., Delisle, P.: Utopia: a load sharing facility for large, heterogeneous distributed computer systems. Software: Practice and Experience 23(12), 1305–1336 (1993)
12. Hadoop Fair Scheduler, http://hadoop.apache.org/docs/stable/fair_scheduler.html
13. Etsion, Y., Tsafrir, D.: A short survey of cluster batch schedulers, Technical Report, Hebrew University, 2005-13 (May 2005)
14. Deelman, E.: Grids and Clouds: Making workflow applications work in heterogeneous distributed environments. International Journal of High Performance Computing Applications 24(3), 284–298 (2010)
15. Juve, G., Deelman, E.: Resource provisioning options for large-scale scientific workflows. In: Proc. of SWBES Workshop with IEEE E-Science (2008)
16. Sysstat Utils, sebastien.godard.pagesperso-orange.fr/
17. Dhiman, G., Marchetti, G., Rosing, T.: vGreen: a system for energy efficient computing in virtualized environments. In: Proceedings of the 14th ACM/IEEE International Symposium on Low Power Electronics and Design, pp. 243–248. ACM
18. Hu, L., Schwan, K., Gulati, A., Zhang, J., Wang, C.: Net-cohort: Detecting and managing vm ensembles in virtualized data centers. In: Proceedings of the 9th International Conference on Autonomic Computing, pp. 3–12. ACM (2012)
19. Zhan, J., Zhang, L., Sun, N., Wang, L., Jia, Z., Luo, C.: High Volume Throughput Computing: Identifying and Characterizing Throughput Oriented Workloads in Data Centers. In: 2012 IEEE 26th International Parallel and Distributed Processing Symposium (2012)

20. Hwang, K., Fox, G.C., Dongarra, J.J.: Distributed and Cloud Computing, From parallel processing to Internet of things. Morgan Kaufman, Elsevier (2012)
21. Plimpton, S.J., Devine, K.D.: MapReduce in MPI for large-scale graph algorithms. Parallel Computing Journal 37, 610–632 (2011)
22. HPC Virtualization, Virtualization in HPC may not always be the answer as Gillian Law discovers, Scientific Computing World, pp. 21-24 (October/November 2011)
23. Novotny, M.: Job scheduling with the SLURM resource manager, Bachelor Thesis, Masarykova Univerzita
24. SLURM Workload Manager, `http://slurm.schedmd.com/`
25. HTCondor(tm) Version 7.8.8 Manual, `http://research.cs.wisc.edu/htcondor/manual/v7.8/`

The Case for Multi-Engine Data Analytics

Dimitrios Tsoumakos and Christos Mantas

Computing Systems Laboratory
School of Electrical and Computer Engineering
National Technical University of Athens, Greece
{dtsouma,cmantas}@cslab.ece.ntua.gr

Abstract. As big data analytics have become an important driver for ICT development, a large variety of approaches that apply these advanced technologies on a wide spectrum of applications has been introduced. In this paper we argue on the need of a multi-engine environment that will exploit the largely different models, cost and quality of the existing analytics engines. Such an environment further requires an intelligent management system for orchestrating and coordinating complex analytics tasks over the different available engines. After summarizing some of the current approaches in data analytics, we outline the structure of our envisioned *Multi-Engine Management System* and present some of the corresponding research directions in its design and development.

Keywords: Big Data Analytics, Execution Engines, Datastores, Virtualization, Modeling, Architecture, Resource Scheduling.

1 Introduction: Current State of Big Data Analytics Platforms

The field of data analytics includes techniques, algorithms and tools used to inspect collections of data to extract patterns, generalizations and other useful information. Big Data Analytics is – both from the technology point of view and its business repercussions – an important driver for ICT development and for the knowledge-based society itself. While the "data deluge" [1] is an obvious cause for this, it is also the case that businesses are moving away from purely empirical running towards running on factual information. Therefore, the term "Big Data" refers to more than the volume of data, but rather to the combination of data size, heterogeneity and processing complexity [2].

Nowadays, big data analytics is successfully applied in a multitude of diverse areas and disciplines such as risk assessment, pharmaceutics, fraud detection, epidemiology, business process effectiveness, market analysis, anti-terrorism, telecommunications, etc.

Modern datacenters host vast amounts of data that is stored over large numbers of nodes using multiple and possibly heterogeneous storage devices. The corresponding processing requires thousands or even millions of cores. Such data analysis demands a high degree of parallelism, in both storage and computation. Cloud technologies are able to provide the infrastructure to satisfy the immense resource requirements of the data and compute-intensive analytics tasks. Nevertheless, analytics applications must produce near real-time (or interactive) response times to the posed queries. This kind of efficiency is hard to achieve as it directly conflicts with:

D. an Mey et al. (Eds.): Euro-Par 2013 Workshops, LNCS 8374, pp. 406–415, 2014.

1) the size of the data,
2) its structural diversity,
3) data location, and
4) the ad-hoc nature of analytical queries.

The immense rates at which data is produced (point 1) is a fact mainly attributed to the advent of Web 2.0 and social applications, highly increased technology uptake, sensor/satellite networks, scientific advances, etc. Structural data diversity has significantly expanded as an outcome. Besides the well-understood transactional data, information has hence been produced in the form of semi-structured (XML, forms, emails, etc) or purely unstructured (blogs, tweets, multimedia, etc) data, both in already-stored and streaming modes. The combination of points 1 and 2 above justify the reality (and often necessity) of distributed data storage: As voluminous information is collected from different sources, using different schemas and at different rates, it is natural that no single site can store and serve all this diverse data. Last but not least, as the use cases for large-scale analytics increase at high rates, the amount and quality of processing required to achieve the desired output increase in complexity. Processing techniques include (among others) real-time data stream processing, interactive query evaluation (exploratory analysis), predictive analytics, complex Information Retrieval and Machine Learning methods over both text and loosely structured data, data integration, etc.

These issues have given rise to many diverse programming models, execution engines and data stores to assist with large-scale data management. The current architectural "blueprint" for data analytics is depicted in Figure 1: Diverse data sources are managed by specialized technologies that span the areas of data storage and job execution. The semantics and richness of the tasks that can be executed over the data are defined by the system's programming model.

Nowadays, such systems target specific data or process types, outperforming general-purpose solutions (e.g., a relational database) and tightly coupling the three components of Figure 1, namely the models with the execution and datastore engines. The most widespread solution for scaling applications to big data is the Map-Reduce model [3]. Map-Reduce is very effective with computations expressed as data-parallel "mapper" and "reducer" tasks that operate on different data shards and consecutively merge the results. The Map-Reduce model, through a series of open-source and customized implementations (e.g., [4,5,6,7]) is generally acknowledged as the current state-of-the-art in big-data analytics.

Many operations, however, act on irregular data that may be heterogeneous, structured or unstructured, streaming or stored in various formats. Complex analytics applications may also perform computations with dynamic dependencies (e.g., graph traversals or fixpoint computations). Such tasks cannot be easily defined in Map-Reduce, as each phase must store the intermediate graph state and redistribute it across machines before the next phase starts. To alleviate these difficulties, other specialized models and systems have been proposed [8,9,10,11]. While all these systems have had great success, they still showcase their advantages on a limited subset of applications and types of data: For instance, graph-processing engines (e.g. [8]) limit the amount of freedom in the computation at each node (or part of a graph) and fail to fully exploit possible parallelism.

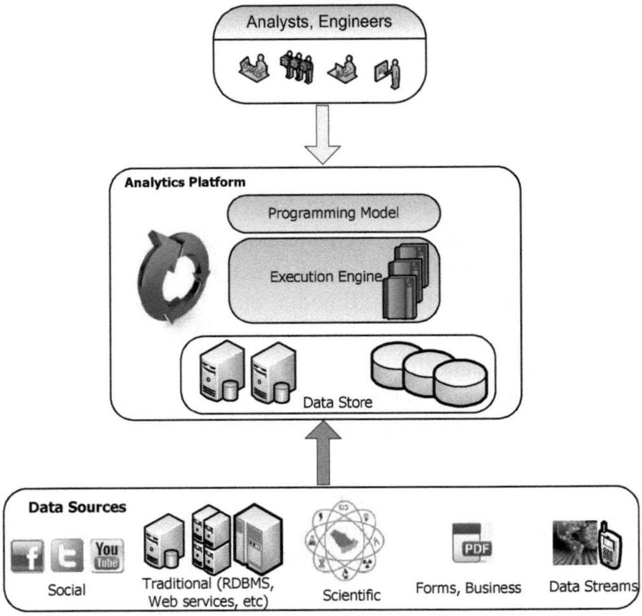

Fig. 1. Standard layering for data analytics processing over big data

Yet, modern data analytics applications are more complex than this. First, dynamic data processing is often very heterogeneous in terms of complexity and time consumption. In graph-structured data, for instance, the amount of stored data and required computation may differ from node to node. Many web-content analytics tasks can be easily parallelized and thus fit the Map-Reduce concept very well. Interactive analytics on semi-structured data requires different execution schemes respectively. It is thus suboptimal for a single model/engine to be used for all different analytics tasks. Different runtimes exhibit different cost and quality performance levels; any modern analytics platform has to be able to *fuse* models and engines of different capabilities in order to adapt to multiple job submissions.

Second, modern datacenters often include many heterogeneous storage formats, each used in multiple contexts and by different applications. This range may include traditional RDBMSs, modern column-stores, unstructured data in raw files, semi-structured data (e.g., XML, RDF), specialized stores (e.g., RDF stores), NoSQL databases, etc. Additionally some or all of the above may use central or distributed storage models. Depending on the data format, the computation of a query may differ in complexity and performance. As it is not always optimal to convert data formats and storage, for legacy or performance optimization reasons, a data analytics framework needs to support and adapt to multiple data storage formats.

Finally, a factor orthogonal to all the aforementioned points is the virtualized environment and its special performance restrictions. Avoiding expensive vendor lock-ins is a priority for many application owners; they would largely prefer being able to utilize both proprietary and popular open-source solutions. Additionally, running resource intensive analytics tasks under heavy load and time constraints require Cloud-enabled strategies to be tightly coupled with the design and deployment of the application.

In this work, we present the case for an adaptive, intelligent analytics platform running over the Cloud. Specifically, we outline a "reference architecture" as well as the derived research directions for a software layer that will perform adaptive resource management among multiple execution engines and datastores. As no single technology has been able to demonstrate optimized performance for different load and data types, we strongly believe that efficient, cost- and quality- based fusion of alternative technologies will achieve what is currently missing, namely: Performance gains, diverse and user-controlled task execution, abstraction, flexibility and robustness. In Section 2 we briefly outline some popular current analytics approaches. In Section 3 we present our vision for a "multi-engine" data analytics platform and conclude our work.

2 Data Analytics Approaches

As the Big Data trend grows stronger in the various industries, data analytics tools evolve in order to handle large scale datasets effectively. Most of the research work is centered on adapting Hadoop [4] to the needs of time-effective data analysis and harvest both the effectiveness and agility of the Map-Reduce programming paradigm and the low query execution time of parallel DBMSs. Pig [12], Hive [13], Sawzall [14], Jaql [15] and Tenzing [16] fall in the category of offering SQL processing on top of Hadoop. Those systems implement SQL or SQL-like functionalities over the Map-Reduce model and are widely used by large enterprises in the industry.

Starfish [17] uses a sampler and a profiler in order to perform dynamic instrumentation of Map-Reduce jobs. This method uses a tracing tool in order to brake down the "data-load", "map" and "reduce" phases of the workload into sub-phases and collect run-time data of the jobs running on Hadoop. This data is used in order to automatically tune a number of configuration parameters affecting Hadoop's performance and achieve optimal execution of the workload, which is not possible to match by invoking the common rules-of-thumb that adept Hadoop users might be familiar with. The authors aim at making Hadoop a *MADDER* tool. MAD stands for Magnetism, Agility and Depth according to [18]. DER sands for Data-lifecycle-awareness, Elasticity and Robustness.

Similarly, Hadoop++ [19] tries to cleanly extend Hadoop by representing its execution pipeline as a physical execution plan and apply relational DB techniques. The first enhancement that Hadoop++ offers is indexing capability. The index, called the *Trojan Index*, is built during the data-load step of map-reduce with no penalty at query time. The second enhancement is a non-invasive join technique, called the *Trojan Join*. This technique exploits the co-partitioning of data in order to make a join of each co-partition at the "map" phase of the execution pipeline. This is far more cost effective than other join or merge operations previously proposed for Hadoop. Again, the aforementioned and other similar approaches choose Hadoop (or its variations) as the single analytics engine to operate upon and try optimize performance based on this specific choice.

Instead of building on Hadoop, ASTERIX [20] takes a different path, together with an emulation layer for existing Hadoop programs. ASTERIX tries to tackle the problem analyzing large scale structured and semi-structured data which processes in parallel, on a shared-nothing infrastructure. The system uses a custom query language called AQL and its own runtime execution layer called Hyracks.

The system proposed in [21], executes workflows based on a generalization of the Map-Reduce programming model and operates on a key/value data store. The data processing is in the form of DAGs and is handled by the Nephele [22] computing engine. Nephele spans the DAG creating the appropriate instances of the user code and executes the workflow.

To overcome Map-Reduce's limitation for interactive data analysis, Google developed Dremel [10] and its public implementation, BigQuery. Dremel is an interactive tool that can produce results within seconds and can be used by non-programmers in order to analyze structured data, possibly in a trial-and-error, interactive, manner. Analysis on unstructured data is limited on regular expression matching. Dremel is based on columnar storage thus being able to achieve high compression rates and high scan throughput without prior indexing. While Dremel is not capable of executing complex data logic, it can act in synergy with the Map-Reduce framework to achieve that kind of functionality.

Commercial solutions for big data analysis mostly involve storage in proprietary parallel DBMSs targeted at OLAP applications. HP's offer is built on top of the IDOL engine [23] and the Vertica parallel analytics database [24]. The latter is a column-oriented DB used for data warehouses that either runs on grids of commodity servers or on the Amazon Elastic Compute Cloud (EC2). IBM also offers a data warehousing and analytics platform [25]. This product runs on custom data warehouse appliances and makes use of hardware data processing on FPGAs, being the building block for some more advanced analytics tools [26]. Very recently, IBM announced their newest "BLU Acceleration" technology for data analytics [27] that includes features such as the ability to skip over data that does not need to be analyzed, the ability to analyze data across different processors and the ability to analyze compressed data. Greenplum provides its own proprietary database [28] which offers a set of parallel functions, but also a custom Hadoop framework [29] and HAWQ [HAWQ], yet another SQL engine on top of Hadoop. Aster Data offers its own analytic management system [30]. A framework that compiles SQL into code that can be run on top of a Map-Reduce infrastructure has also been developed [31]. Microsoft is also involved in this area. It has developed HDInsight [32], a 100% Apache-compatible Hadoop distribution that integrates with its back-end products as well as a cloud-based version of it, that integrates with Azure cloud storage and the Azure SQL Database. Microsoft has also developed the Dryad distributed execution engine [33].

Summarizing this modest list of analytics platforms, we note that current approaches suffer from one or more of the following issues:

- They require or depend on proprietary tools, resulting in expensive vendor lock-ins
- They are optimized for specific data formats or data locations
- They are optimized for specific query/analytics task types

We believe that a modern analytics platform should instead base its operation on intelligent "fusion" of multiple technologies in the areas of data storage and task scheduling/execution. This allows the system to adaptively select between engines of different data models, computation models, costs and performance but also between different technologies and possibly licensing schemes. To achieve this vision, a software platform is required to play the role of the "middleware" layer between the programming model and the low-level data and execution engines. This platform will schedule and manage compute and data tasks among the different technologies in a cloud-friendly mode, i.e., taking virtualization costs and restrictions into account. In the following section we outline a reference architecture for this "Multi-Engine Management System" by describing the major required modules, their functionality and respective research directions.

3 Multi-Engine Management System

Our vision is that analytics platforms should operate on the basis of a unified framework for managing, executing and monitoring multiple, complex jobs. Centrally positioned inside such a system lies the *Multi-Engine Management System* (MEMS). Its goal is to provide adaptive, cost-based and customizable resource management of the diverse resources available in the analytics platform (i.e., storage and run-time engines). The central notion behind MEMS is to utilize detailed models of the costs and performance characteristics of various analytics operations over the multiple engines. These models will then be used to intelligently match user-defined queries (and their policies) with the available engines. This is a challenging area that requires multidisciplinary research and development in Performance Modeling, Decision Systems, Resource Scheduling and Distributed Data Management.

Inside the lifecycle of an analytics job, MEMS will receive job description(s) from Application Management tools along with optimization policies that define the cost and quality constraints set by the user. MEMS will output a thorough execution plan along with its projected cost to the Scheduler whose task is to perform both the initial and continuous resource allocation. A runtime inspector tool will monitor and constantly evaluate/adjust models in order to alter scheduling towards more optimized execution (see Figure 2). In more detail, MEMS functionality will be performed by the following modules:

3.1 Job Parser

The goal of the job parsing tool is to receive input from the Application Management UI (user-defined analytics tasks/queries to be executed) and validate/structure it. In detail, this entails validating and registering the location (both physical and logical) of the required data; identifying the required metrics, dimensions, etc. over the data; identifying execution artifacts such as functions (average, min, max, etc), operators (joins, unions, similarity, clustering) and custom code; and finally, validating the user-defined policy. All this information must be robustly identified, structured as subtasks in a dependency graph and stored in order for the Modeling/Learning Engine module to be able to act upon it.

3.2 Modeling and Learning Engine

In order for the scheduler to choose an optimized execution plan for an analytics task that will span (a) multiple execution engines and (b) multiple data stores, a detailed cost

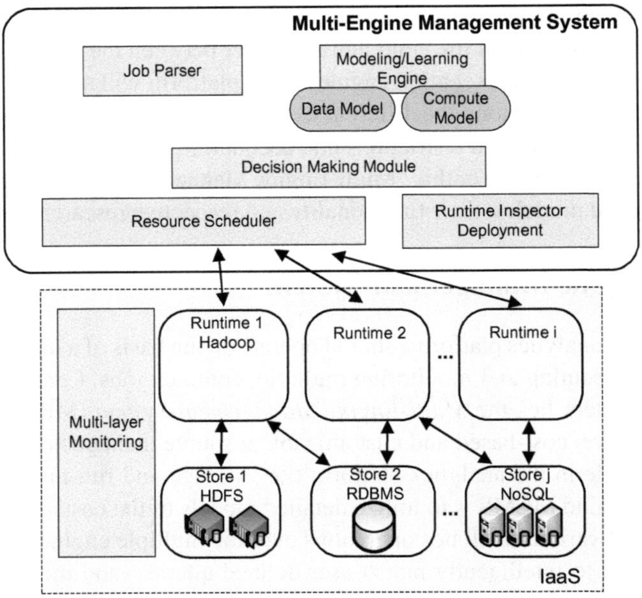

Fig. 2. A conceptual architecture for the MEMS platform

evaluation must be presented. This evaluation must detail what is the projected cost and performance (measured in time, committed resources, I/O operations, etc, but always in relation to the user-defined policies) of the parsed subtasks under variable scenarios (or deployments) of execution. These scenarios assume execution and storage engines to be variables; these variables might also impose extra variables such as the amount of committed resources per execution engine (e.g., number of worker VMs, number of allocated threads), storage size available, storage technologies (e.g., SSDs vs. traditional magnetic disks), etc. In order for such estimates to be feasible and realistic, a fusion of static models with real-time statistics from queries executed over MEMS is required. Static models will be created using detailed benchmarking; learning will be performed in real-time, as new, realistic estimates will enrich the current models both in accuracy and semantic reach. Consequently, work in this area must consider a broad range of methodologies and research activities that include benchmarking, performance modeling and learning. In addition, one must also delve into important characteristics that affect the performance of both data and compute engines such as elasticity requirements (how does altering the amount of resources allotted to a runtime affects its performance [34]) and storage architectures (e.g., shared-nothing vs. Shared-disk architectures, NoSQL databases, columnar stores and their respective advantages and disadvantages).

3.3 Automated Decision Making for Analytics Scheduling

Analytics tasks are often multi-level, resource-demanding jobs that operate on large volumes of diverse data. Their efficient execution is often of the utmost importance.

As MEMS's premise is transparent management of multiple runtimes and storage technologies available to the analytics expert, it is imperative that the assignment of tasks to the different technologies be optimized. This "intelligent" scheduling must be given central stage with a thorough study that will offer both automatic and optimal resource allocation. The problem in hand spawns several directions that must be appropriately studied. Research must consider the most fitting, among various disciplines, method for real-time, robust decision-making. The proposed algorithm must rely on the characteristics of the analytics task in hand and the model produced from the modeling and learning engine in order to schedule and orchestrate the execution of the different parts of the task. This entails deciding where each subtask is to be run, under what amount of resources provisioned, the plan for moving data to/from their current locations and between run-times (if more than one is chosen) and defining the output destinations. Equally important is the operation mode of the decision process: Specifically, the level of aggressiveness of resource commitment, the trade-offs between reactive or proactive invocation and its robustness towards oscillations.

3.4 Scheduling

In this module, methods and tools that translate high level "start runtime R using x amount of resources", "move data from engine Y to Z" commands to a workflow of primitives as understood by the specific runtimes and storage engines must be developed. This requires using standard, open-source or even custom APIs in order to allocate and free virtualized resources and also communicate with the supported platforms (i.e., store and compute engines). An additional challenge here relates to service availability and robustness that must be performed. Mechanisms that restart or reschedule jobs that have failed due to hardware or network errors must be studied. Consequently, work in this area must rely on real-time monitoring and learning mechanisms in order to quickly identify failures and bottlenecks, correlating current running times and results with previous experience and similar workloads. Work in this module must also investigate on the trade-offs of achieving availability and robustness over multiple run-times and storage technologies in a unified manner, keeping these methods transparent and efficient at the same time.

4 Conclusions

In this work, we argued on the necessity of a multi-engine framework to manage and schedule big data analytics tasks. The necessity is dictated by the largely different characteristics, cost and quality of the existing datastore and execution engines. Our vision is the design and consecutive deployment of MEMS, a middleware platform that intelligently coordinates complex jobs over collaborating technologies running on virtualized environments. In addition to the reference architecture and RTD challenges presented for MEMS, it should allow easy integration of multiple runtimes and datastores, be flexible enough to incorporate different programming paradigms and dynamically adjust its behavior relative to user-provided rules on a per-task or per-workflow basis.

References

1. The Economist: The data deluge (2010), http://www.economist.com/node/15579717
2. Ferguson, M.: Architecting a Big Data Platform for Analytics (2012), http://ibmdatamag.com/2012/10/architecting-a-big-data-platform-for-analytics
3. Dean, J., Ghemawat, S.: Mapreduce: simplified data processing on large clusters. CACM 51(1) (2008)
4. The Apache Software Foundation: Apache Hadoop, http://hadoop.apache.org/
5. Liu, H., Orban, D.: Cloud mapreduce: A mapreduce implementation on top of a cloud operating system. In: 2011 11th IEEE/ACM International Symposium on Cluster, Cloud and Grid Computing (CCGrid), pp. 464–474 (2011)
6. Nokia, R.C.: The Disco Project, http://discoproject.org/
7. Amazon Web Services: Amazon Elastic MapReduce, http://aws.amazon.com/elasticmapreduce/
8. Malewicz, G., Austern, M.H., Bik, A.J., Dehnert, J.C., Horn, I., Leiser, N., Czajkowski, G.: Pregel: a system for large-scale graph processing. In: SIGMOD (2010)
9. Seo, S., Yoon, E.J., Kim, J., Jin, S., Kim, J.S., Maeng, S.: Hama: An efficient matrix computation with the mapreduce framework. In: Proceedings of the 2010 IEEE Second International Conference on Cloud Computing Technology and Science, CLOUDCOM 2010 (2010)
10. Melnik, S., Gubarev, A., Long, J.J., Romer, G., Shivakumar, S., Tolton, M., Vassilakis, T.: Dremel: interactive analysis of web-scale datasets. CACM 54(6) (June 2011)
11. Hall, A., Bachmann, O., Büssow, R., Gănceanu, S., Nunkesser, M.: Processing a trillion cells per mouse click. Proc. VLDB Endow. 5(11) (July 2012)
12. Olston, C., Reed, B., Srivastava, U., Kumar, R., Tomkins, A.: Pig latin: a not-so-foreign language for data processing. In: Proceedings of the 2008 ACM SIGMOD International Conference on Management of Data, pp. 1099–1110 (2008)
13. Thusoo, A., Sarma, J.S., Jain, N., Shao, Z., Chakka, P., Zhang, N., Antony, S., Liu, H., Murthy, R.: Hive-a petabyte scale data warehouse using hadoop. In: 2010 IEEE 26th International Conference on Data Engineering (ICDE), pp. 996–1005. IEEE (2010)
14. Pike, R., Dorward, S., Griesemer, R., Quinlan, S.: Interpreting the data: Parallel analysis with sawzall. Sci. Program. 13(4), 277–298 (2005)
15. Beyer, K.S., Ercegovac, V., Gemulla, R., Balmin, A., Eltabakh, M., Kanne, C.C., Ozcan, F., Shekita, E.J.: Jaql: A scripting language for large scale semistructured data analysis. In: Proceedings of VLDB Conference (2011)
16. Chattopadhyay, B., Lin, L., Liu, W., Mittal, S., Aragonda, P., Lychagina, V., Kwon, Y., Wong, M.: Tenzing a sql implementation on the mapreduce framework. In: Proceedings of VLDB, pp. 1318–1327 (2011)
17. Herodotou, H., Lim, H., Luo, G., Borisov, N., Dong, L., Cetin, F.B., Babu, S.: Starfish: A self-tuning system for big data analytics. In: CIDR, pp. 261–272 (2011)
18. Cohen, J., Dolan, B., Dunlap, M., Hellerstein, J.M., Welton, C.: Mad skills: new analysis practices for big data. Proc. VLDB Endow. 2(2), 1481–1492 (2009)
19. Dittrich, J., Quiané-Ruiz, J.A., Jindal, A., Kargin, Y., Setty, V., Schad, J.: Hadoop++: Making a yellow elephant run like a cheetah (without it even noticing). Proceedings of the VLDB Endowment 3(1-2), 515–529 (2010)
20. Behm, A., Borkar, V.R., Carey, M.J., Grover, R., Li, C., Onose, N., Vernica, R., Deutsch, A., Papakonstantinou, Y., Tsotras, V.J.: Asterix: towards a scalable, semistructured data platform for evolving-world models. Distributed and Parallel Databases 29(3), 185–216 (2011)

21. Battré, D., Ewen, S., Hueske, F., Kao, O., Markl, V., Warneke, D.: Nephele/PACTs: a programming model and execution framework for web-scale analytical processing. In: Proceedings of the 1st ACM Symposium on Cloud Computing, pp. 119–130 (2010)
22. Warneke, D., Kao, O.: Nephele: efficient parallel data processing in the cloud. In: Proceedings of the 2nd Workshop on Many-Task Computing on Grids and Supercomputers, pp. 8:1–8:10 (2009)
23. HP Autonomy: IDLE Server, http://www.autonomy.com/content/Products/products-idol-server/index.en.html
24. HP Vertica: Vertica Analytics Platform, http://www.vertica.com/the-analytics-platform/
25. IBM Inc.: IBM Netezza 100, http://www-01.ibm.com/software/data/netezza/100
26. IBM Corp.: IBM PureData System, http://www-01.ibm.com/software/data/puredata/
27. IBM Corp.: IBM Announces New Innovations to Help Organizations Benefit from the Next Natural Resource: Big Data, http://www-03.ibm.com/press/us/en/pressrelease/40768.wss
28. Greenplum, EMC Corp.: Greenplum Database, http://www.greenplum.com/products/greenplum-database
29. Greenplum, EMC Corp.: Greenplum HD, http://www.ndm.net/emcstore/greenplum/greenplum-hd
30. Teradata Corp.: Aster Big Analytics Appliance, http://www.asterdata.com/product/big-analytics-appliance.php
31. Friedman, E., Pawlowski, P., Cieslewicz, J.: Sql/mapreduce: a practical approach to self-describing, polymorphic, and parallelizable user-defined functions. Proc. VLDB Endow. 2(2), 1402–1413 (2009)
32. Microsoft Corp.: Microsoft HDInsight, http://www.windowsazure.com/en-us/manage/services/hdinsight/
33. Isard, M., Budiu, M., Yu, Y., Birrell, A., Fetterly, D.: Dryad: distributed data-parallel programs from sequential building blocks. ACM SIGOPS Operating Systems Review 41(3), 59–72 (2007)
34. Tsoumakos, D., Konstantinou, I., Boumpouka, C., Sioutas, S., Koziris, N.: Automated, Elastic Resource Provisioning for NoSQL Clusters Using TIRAMOLA. In: Proceedings of the the 13th IEEE/ACM International Symposium on Cluster, Cloud and Grid Computing (2013)

Second International Workshop on On-chip Memory Hierarchies and Interconnects: Organization, Management and Implementation (OMHI 2013)

Julio Sahuquillo, Maria Engracia Gómez, and Salvador Petit

Program Chairs

On-chip memory is a major design issue in current chip multiprocessors (CMPs) due to performance and power reasons. Internal memory is typically composed of many structures both private (at least L1 ICache and L1 DCache per core) and shared (e.g. LLC caches) and must be properly organized to mitigate the huge latencies of accessing off-chip DRAM memory. These memory structures must be smartly interconnected to avoid performance penalties. In addition, on-chip memory occupies by two thirds of the processor area, thus performance must be achieved with reasonable power consumption. Moreover most designs must be tailored to meet a given power budget. These design issues become more important with the increasing core counts in future microprocessor generations.

To deal with the mentioned power problem, new memory technologies have emerged. Typically, on-chip memory has been implemented as caches employing Static Random Access Memory (SRAM) technology, which is the fastest existing electronic memory technology. However, as caches occupy more and more of the processor die, this technology presents important design challenges in terms of leakage currents and density. Therefore it is unlikely that future CMPs implement their cache hierarchy completely with this technology. In fact recent processors have already implemented some of their caches with eDRAM technology, which is both less consuming and more dense. As opposite, it is also slower than the SRAM technology.

Once the processor is designed with a given on-chip memory hierarchy, efforts must focus on how to efficiently manage it, specially in the context of multicores where multiple threads compete among them for shared (e.g., memory and NoC) resources. This means that the performance of the system will strongly depend on how interactions among threads are managed. This includes, among others, thread to core allocation polices, cache management strategies, and efficient cache coherence protocols. The goal of the OMHI workshop is to be a forum for engineers and scientists to address the aforementioned challenges, and to present new ideas for future on-chip memory hierarchies and interconnects focusing on organization, management and implementation.

The contributions of this year have addressed most of the main topics covered in the workshop, and the workshop organizers would like to thank all the authors for all their very interesting contributions. In this edition, we were able to accept six submissions that were grouped in two sessions. In addition, the organizers

D. an Mey et al. (Eds.): Euro-Par 2013 Workshops, LNCS 8374, pp. 416–417, 2014.

were proud to present Professor Holger Fröning from University of Heidelberg (Germany) as keynote speaker, who gave a interesting talk focusing on the key topics of the workshop entitled "Data Movement Options for Accelerated Clusters" which jointly with the paper sessions finally resulted in a nice and very exciting one-day program.

The chairs would like to thank the Euro-Par organizers, the members of the program committee for their reviews and feedback, Professor Holger Fröning and the high number of attendees. Based on the positive feedback of all of them, we plan to continue the OMHI workshop in conjunction with Euro-Par 2014.

August 2013

Julio Sahuquilo
María Engracia Gómez
Salvador Petit

Data Movement Options in Accelerated Clusters

Holger Fröning

Institute of Computer Engineering, Ruprecht-Karls University of Heidelberg, Germany
holger.froening@ziti.uni-heidelberg.de

Abstract. The concurrency galore is currently defining computing at all levels. At the high end, it is leading to clusters composed of hundreds or thousands of nodes, each integrating 10-100s of computing cores, and fed with instructions by up to two orders of magnitudes more threads. Technology constraints prohibit a reversal of this trend, and the still unsatisfied need for more computing power has led to a pervasive use of accelerators to speed up computations. Both in terms of energy and time, communication is more expensive than computation. Being amplified by the advent of Big Data, we are observing a fundamental transition to communication-centric systems composed of heterogeneous computing units. This talk will review current techniques for data movements in clusters. This is followed by an introduction to the Global GPU Address Spaces (GGAS) project, which we use to explore data movement optimizations in heterogeneous environments. The talk will conclude with a summary of synergies regarding related research projects.

1 Motivation

We can clearly see that the multi-/many-core trend won't revert. The main reasons include technological constraints, like the end of Dennard scaling, which previously ensured that total chip power stays constant. On the other hand, we can observe a vast increase in technology diversity. For processing tasks, various options exist including x86, ARM, GPUs and MICs. On the storage side, we can choose between spinning disks, SSD-based and PCIe-based FLASH, and DRAM for in-memory computations. While this diversity is a huge research opportunity, the concurrency galore together with the raising interest in heterogeneity will amplify complexity, forming a research challenge. We are facing multiple *Instruction Set Architectures (ISAs)* within one system, different and maybe incompatible task, execution and communication models, and different types of memory and NUMA levels. In addition, energy costs for data movements will dominate the overall energy consumption of future systems, while computations with the help of specialization will only state a tiny fraction in terms of energy [1] [2] [3]. As energy costs for data movements are in first order a constant multiple of the distance, any optimization in energy will require an optimization of locality [3].

In this work we will shortly summarize current trends, observations and insights that lead to another fundamental transition, leading towards communication-centric heterogeneous systems. Data movement optimizations are essential, and we will provide a solution for tailored for GPUs.

D. an Mey et al. (Eds.): Euro-Par 2013 Workshops, LNCS 8374, pp. 418–422, 2014.

2 A Fundamental Transition

Our work to explore data movement optimizations in accelerated clusters is motivated by several observations. The following list summarizes them, before we conclude our key finding.

- **Multi-/Many-core** is already pervasive, and – although highly debated – Big Data is present and won't revert. While memory resources are scarce anyway, the transition to multi-core amplifies the problem in terms of memory capacity per core. DRAM is still the first choice for performance-critical workloads, as can be seen looking at the various in-memory and in-core solutions. Big Data pushes the requirements regarding capacity way beyond what single systems can deliver. However, a possibility to overcome capacity limitations might be sharing at cluster level.
- **Hard power constraints** are the main limitation of computing systems, due to technical, ecological and economic reasons. This applies to devices as small as smartphones or other mobile devices, but also to large-scale facilities like clusters, supercomputers or datacenters. These energy constraints have also led to a huge interest in heterogeneous processing, using accelerators to speed-up certain workloads. This specialization significantly improves energy-efficiency in terms of performance-pre-Watt, however also dramatically increases complexity as different ISAs are employed.
- The **technology diversity** is in-line with this trend towards specialization, and now users have various possibilities to compose a computing system, including processors (CPU, GPU, MIC), memory (DRAM, GDDR, PCM, Hybrid Memory Cube), storage (SSD-based or PCIe-based FLASH, spinning disks), network (multiple Ethernet variants, Infiniband, specialized cluster networks) and even complete systems (Cray, IBM Blue Gene, Seamicro). This diversity can help to maximize the energy efficiency of a system; however certain workload characteristics will likely be favored then. In addition the complexity of a system is increasing.
- **Performance disparities** in terms of throughput are diminishing. For instance, looking at different interconnect technologies we can see that PCIe Gen3 peaks at 16GB/s bandwidth, but cluster interconnects are reaching similar levels: current Infiniband FDR dual-port adapter cards achieve about 12GB/s, the EXTOLL Tourmalet network card will reach about 10GB/s and 100 Gigabit Ethernet is expected to yield similar values. Noteworthy, a single channel DRAM connection translates to about 17GB/s (DDR3-1033). As we can see, the difference in terms of bandwidth between local and remote accesses is diminishing, in particular for accelerators located behind a PCIe interface. This is a huge opportunity to aggregate scarce resources by sharing at cluster level, to overcome capacity constraints and thus to fulfill the demands fed by Big Data [3].

As a result, the multi-/many-core revolution in combination with Big Data, technology diversity, energy constraints, the need for specialization and the diminishing disparities will lead to *a fundamental transition to communication-centric systems composed of heterogeneous computing units.*

3 An Optimized Data Movement Method for GPU Clusters

As it is unfeasible to explore all communication options for heterogeneous systems in a single work, we focus here on data movement optimizations for GPU clusters. GPUs differ significantly in their execution model from CPUs, and experiments have shown that GPUs perform quite poorly when initiating traditional communication methods directly and without any help of the CPUs.

If we shortly review the typical GPU architecture, we can find that it was already described pretty well by Valiant using the *Bulk-Synchronous Parallel (BSP)* model [4]. This model introduces a super-step that is composed of three phases for computation, communication, and synchronization, respectively. GPUs are a prime example for the parallel slackness that is leveraged to schedule and pipeline computation and communication efficiently. GPUs excel in performance if they perform their tasks in such a thread-collaborative way.

If GPUs are employed at cluster level for acceleration purposes, existing communication models do not match this BSP model, resulting in hybrid solutions like MPI+CUDA, MPI+OpenCL or similar. While the increase in complexity is obvious, communication performance can degrade, too. GPUs are not designed to excel in performance when controlling networking hardware, in particular regarding descriptor creation, network device interaction, and synchronization to ensure consistency. The programmer has to use the CPU for these tasks, resulting in highly heterogeneous code and frequent context switches between the GPU and CPU domains.

The GGAS research project [5] uses global address spaces at cluster level to facilitate a communication model that is in-line with the GPU's task model. In particular, GGAS relies on thread-collective communication, minimizes branch divergence, avoids costly context switches to the CPU domain, and allows for zero-copy data movements. Best to our knowledge, GGAS is still the only approach that is in-line with the GPU's thread-collaborative execution model.

Using GGAS, communication is performed by a set of threads collaboratively, by using loads or stores to remote memory. The modern GPUs memory respectively system interface coalesces these fine-grain accesses into bulk transfers. These accesses are intercepted by a network device with appropriate support. Such a support is typically not present in network devices, but only small modifications are required. The network device forwards the request to its destination that is identified based on the used address. From a GPU's point of view, differences between regular host memory accesses and accesses to remote locations are not visible. This maintains the commodity aspect of GPUs, and limits hardware changes to the network interface.

4 Results

We assessed the performance of GGAS using multiple workloads. In [5] we have shown performance results for the Himeno benchmark, which is a stencil code that solves a 3D Poisson equation in generalized coordinates on a structured curvilinear mesh. In [6] we have optimized reduce and allreduce operations for GGAS, also showing performance and energy improvements.

Here, we would like to shortly focus on a workload that puts a very high load on the network interface and the network itself. In the HPCC RandomAccess benchmark [7] a large table is distributed among the different nodes. Each node generates a random stream of XOR updates to be performed on the table. These updates can be coalesced into buckets of up to 1024 entries, each bucket for a certain destination. The updates are then send in a single data movement to the node responsible for the given table partition. This results in many small messages that are exchanged in a push-like manner, making this benchmark highly depending on sustained message rate [8].

While this benchmark is initially developed for CPUs, we re-implemented it for GPUs and used it to analyze performance for different communication models. These include GGAS, a Put/Get model and MPI as the state-of-the-art. We can see that GGAS outperforms MPI by 1.9x in terms of updates-per-second on a 4-node test system. At the same point, GGAS is about 5% faster than a GPU-driven Put/Get communication model.

Noteworthy, the code for GGAS is much simpler compared to MPI and Put/Get. The GGAS model with its thread-collaborative approach for data movement is very easy to understand for an experienced GPU programmer. Furthermore, context switches back to the CPU domain are avoided and control flow can be completely confined to the GPU domain.

5 Conclusion

We can see that performance is at least on-par for most workloads, and often outperforms traditional solutions like MPI+CUDA significantly. At the same time, programming for GPU clusters is dramatically simplified as no hybrid communication model has to be used. The GPU's beauty of simplicity can be maintained at cluster level, avoiding penalties in terms of performance, productivity and usability.

In the future we plan to assess performance with more workloads with varying characteristics like computational intensity, communication patterns and others. In particular we are interested in graph processing, like breadth-first search, strongly-connected-components, or betweenness centrality. We also think that integer workloads like sorts, scans or reductions are becoming increasingly important. We also plan for a GPU-tailored communication library that is based on GGAS, among others.

We plan to embrace future activities in the Alleycat project, which in particular gears to address complexity, usability and productivity while maintaining similar performance levels. Such an approach can be a key to foster the use of heterogeneous processing for other domains besides HPC, including data-warehousing, decision support, data mining, high performance analytics and more.

Acknowledgements. The author would like to thank Sudhakar Yalamanchili and Mark Hummel for the various insightful discussions. Also, Lena Oden and Benjamin Klenk have contributed with discussions to many insights and performed numerous experiments.

We also acknowledge the sponsoring and continuing support by Nvidia, Xilinx and EXTOLL.

References

1. Dally, B.: Gpu computing: To exascale and beyond (keynote). In: International Conference for High Performance Computing, Networking, Storage and Analysis, SC (2013)
2. Shalf, J., Dosanjh, S., Morrison, J.: Exascale computing technology challenges. In: Palma, J.M.L.M., Daydé, M., Marques, O., Lopes, J.C. (eds.) VECPAR 2010. LNCS, vol. 6449, pp. 1–25. Springer, Heidelberg (2011)
3. Yalamanchili, S.: Scaling Resource Compositions in a Flatter World. In: Workshop on Unconventional Cluster Architectures and Applications (UCAA), in conjunction with ICPP 2012, Pittsburgh, US (2012)
4. Valiant, L.G.: A bridging model for parallel computation. Communications of the ACM 33(8), 103–111 (1990)
5. Oden, L., Fröning, H.: GGAS: Global GPU Address Spaces for Efficient Communication in Heterogeneous Clusters. In: IEEE International Conference on Cluster Computing 2013, Indianapolis, US, September 23-27 (2013)
6. Oden, L., Klenk, B., Fröning, H.: On Achieving High Message Rates. In: 14th IEEE/ACM International Symposium on Cluster, Cloud and Grid Computing (CCGrid), Chicago, IL, US, May 26-29 (2014)
7. Aggarwal, V., Sabharwal, Y., Garg, R., Heidelberger, P.: HPCC RandomAccess benchmark for next generation supercomputers. In: IEEE International Symposium on Parallel & Distributed Processing (IPDPS 2009), pp. 1–11. IEEE Computer Society, Washington, DC (2009)
8. Fröning, H., Nüssle, M., Litz, H., Leber, C., Brüning, U.: On Achieving High Message Rates. In: 13th IEEE/ACM International Symposium on Cluster, Cloud and Grid Computing (CCGrid), May 13-16, Delft, The Netherlands (2013)

Impact of the Memory Controller on the Performance of Parallel Workloads

Crispín Gómez Requena

Departamento de Sistemas Informáticos,
Universidad de Castilla–La Mancha, Albacete, Spain

Abstract. Multicore processors have become de facto the typical processors being implemented in almost all microprocessor-based systems ranging from embedded devices to large-scale data centers.

Technology advances allow the integration of a larger amount of cores with each new microprocessor generation. Consequently, the number of memory requests competing for memory rises, so increasing the already huge memory latencies. A straightforward solution to deal with this problem is to increase the number of memory controllers so spreading memory requests among them. However, this solution is not feasible because it would be too costly and it is also limited by technological constraints since core size shrinks at a higher pace than the memory subsystem components.

This paper explores the impact of the number of memory controllers for a medium to large range (manycore) of number of cores with the aim of analyzing the best tradeoff between performance and cost. Results are shown for parallel workloads, which are typically targeted to these processors.

1 Introduction

Chip-multiprocessors (CMPs) have dominated a wide spectrum of the microprocessor market, ranging from embedded to supercomputers, since a few years ago. The on-chip core counts in CMPs have rapidly grown and it is expected to reach several hundreds of cores in the following years [Bell et al.(2008)Bell, Edwards, and Amann, et al]. This trend will even grow in a more significant way in computation-intensive environments like servers, where even we can find current products with tens of cores [Held(2010)]. This means that manycore processors are in the near horizon.

This large number of cores jointly with the tend to implement aggressive out-of-order execution cores contribute to increase contention in the memory subsystem which in turns increases even more the high latency of accessing the main memory. A way to hide this huge memory latencies observed by cores and increase the memory bandwidth is based on using several memory controllers in order to increase the parallelism in the memory access. Having several memory controllers helps to the system performance but at expenses of important energy consumption, which means that the selection of the number of memory controllers in a system must be properly balanced to provide competitive

D. an Mey et al. (Eds.): Euro-Par 2013 Workshops, LNCS 8374, pp. 423–432, 2014.

products in the market achieving the best performance with the least power consumption.

Due to this fact, this paper analyzes the impact of the memory controller design in CMPs. The idea is to provide insights on how many memory controllers are required depending on the core aggressiveness. In particular, as cores are more powerful and a larger number of them are present in the processors, the memory subsystem becomes the main bottleneck, and therefore in this paper we explore the memory subsystem performance, as a measure of the system performance, by analyzing the impact of the number of memory controllers on the latency observed by cores.

In this paper, we assume that a CMP is composed by two main subsystems: core and main memory. Actually, the system performance depends on the interaction among them. On one hand, the cores are the elements that can produce the memory requests and the memory is the one that receives and answers these requests. However, a deep and through study of all the interactions among them is out of the scope of this paper.

From the applications point of view, while it is true that serial workloads still make up a strong segment of the market today, many-core processor designs usually assume parallel workload as recently claimed by James Reinders, Director of Intel Corporation [Jam(2012)]. Thus, in this paper we use parallel workloads to perform this analysis as the workloads that must be considered in highly parallel systems.

Experimental results show that increasing the number of memory controllers in the system helps the machine to reduce the overall memory latency observed by cores which depends on the number of cores and the core aggressiveness and is translated to lower execution times for the benchmarks. Thus, in this paper we claim that a holistic system design must be done considering the features of the different components in order to obtain a balanced system, obtaining the highest benefits of each component.

The remainder of this paper is organized as follows. Section 2 presents the baseline system architecture and discusses pros an cons on the overall performance from the two major subsystems points of view: core and memory. Section 3 highlights the reasons of the the holistic approach by focusing on the benefits of considering interactions among subsystems. Section 4 introduces the experimental framework used in this work. Section 5 presents and analyzes the experimental results. Finally, Section 6 presents some concluding remarks.

2 Major Subsystems: Cores and Main Memory

This section describes the baseline system and discusses the impact of the two major subsystems on performance.

2.1 Baseline Architecture

This paper focuses on high-performance multicore processors. For instance, the Intel SCC prototype consists of 48 cores [Jainschigg(2012)]. This processor consists of 4 memory controllers and 4 memory domains, that is, each MC is used by the closest 12 cores. This scheme, where memory domains are distributed among several MC is the typical expected approach for future systems to reduce memory latency by reducing contention in the MCs (a subset of cores access each MC) and network latency (less hops are required to reach the nearest MCs).

In Figure 1 we show a block diagram of the modeled system. A typical tiled multicore processor is assumed, each core has its private L1 cache and L2 cache, and coherence is supported by using a MOESI-like [et al.(2003)] coherence protocol. Several memory controllers are supported to enhance memory access parallelism, and at the same time, to shorten the average distance from cores to memory controllers.

The design of such a system must address both performance and costs since both are the main concerns. Overall performance depends on the combined performance of the core and memory subsystems. The idea is to achieve a good tradeoff between performance and power.

2.2 Core

System designers have traditionally focused on the processor since it provides the ever increasing demanding computational power of the machine. This computational power increase is being accomplished following three major trends: i) improving the computational power of individual cores, ii) increasing the number or cores, or iii) combining both actions together.

Most processors manufacturers moved to multicore processors with the aim of providing a good tradeoff between performance and power. To this end, first they included several simple (e.g. in-order execution) cores. However, recent

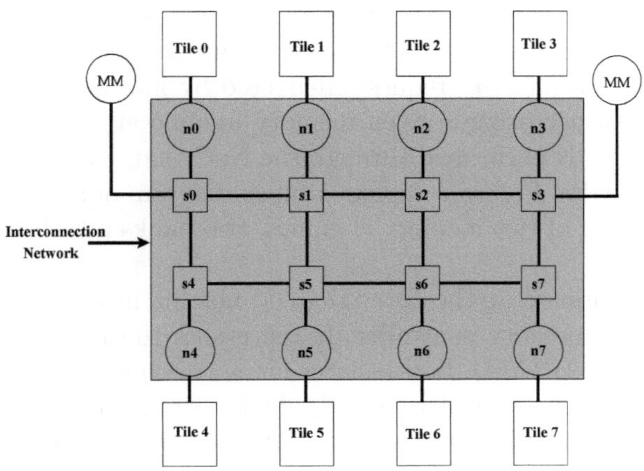

Fig. 1. Baseline processor: cores, on-chip network (NoC) and caches, and MCs. A single memory domain is considererd.

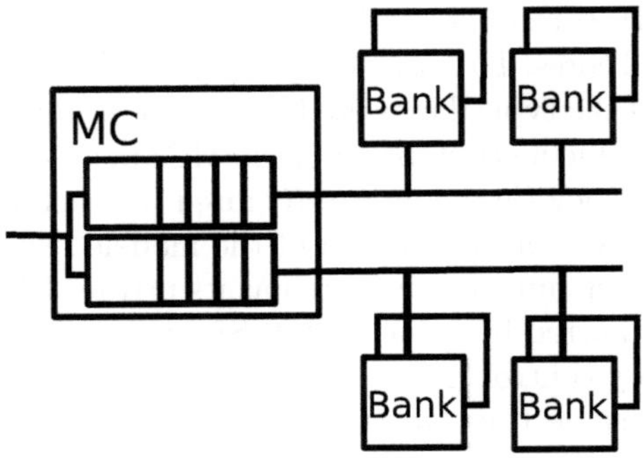

Fig. 2. Scheme of a MC with two memory channels, two banks per channel and two ranks per bank

advances in both technology and microarchitectural techniques, have allowed manufacturers to deploy aggressive out-of-order execution cores in CMPs.

Nowadays even in high performance processors, the power consumption is a concern. So processors are designed both from the power-aware perspective and high-performance point of view. From a high-level point of view, two main features characterize the processor, the number of cores and its aggressiveness. In this work, we explore the impact on performance of both features in a multicore processor as a part within the envisioned baseline system. Different aggressiveness have been explored by varying the decode, issue, and commit width of the computational cores.

2.3 Main Memory

The main memory subsystem has become the major design concern in high-performance processors because it represents a major performance bottleneck, which is even more aggravated with the increasing core counts. This is caused by the large number of memory requests delivered by multiple cores that compete among them for accessing a given memory module attached to a memory controller. This access is performed through the NoC that usually implements a mesh topology in CMPs. Figure 2 depicts a block diagram of a modern memory architecture consisting of two memory channels, two banks per channel and two ranks per bank.

Memory requests issued at the cores that do not hit in the cache hierarchy are enqueued at the memory controller. It represents the interface with main memory modules (e.g. DRAM). It translates memory requests to memory modules commands. Memory controllers usually deploy several queues and handles them according to specific priority policies. The most simple and widely-used is the First Come - First Served (FCFS) in which memory requests are served in arrival order.

Apart from having several memory controllers, with the aim of alleviating the huge memory access latency, the memory is organized in channels, banks and ranks to enhance memory access parallelism. Memory channels are the mean that interconnects the memory controller to the memory chips, that is, a memory controller can issue as many commands concurrently to main memory as number of memory channels. A memory bank holds a set of *rows* also referred to as memory pages, which expand through multiple devices that are accessed at the same time (not shown for clarification purposes).

On the arrival of a command through the channel to the corresponding bank, the bank is accessed and the channel is released until the data is available at the row buffer (bank output). Thus, assuming that a channel transaction lasts one cycle, the memory controller can issue two distinct requests through the same channel in two consecutive bus (channel) cycles if they target different memory banks (i.e. no bank conflict arises). If two requests target the same memory bank, the memory controller will stop the second one until the first one is completed. Finally, banks in a channel can be organized in different ranks. Each rank corresponds to an independent set of devices. Thus banks in different ranks can be accessed in parallel. Thus increasing the number of ranks increases the potential bank level parallelism.

3 Dependencies among the Two Major Subsystems

The system performance and energy consumption depend not only on the individual performance of each subsystem, but on how subsystems interact among them.

The number of cores in each memory domain is, in general, a key design issue, since it affects costs, energy, and performance. Performance of the memory controller can be expressed in terms of latency and throughput. Increasing the number of memory controllers reduces the number of cores in each memory domain, thus the number of access conflicts due to accesses to the same main memory bank is also reduced. In other words, a higher number of memory controllers supports by design a higher level of memory access parallelism. This means that the larger the core counts, the higher the number of memory controllers required for a given memory controller performance. On the other hand, the main memory cost represents an important fraction of the overall system cost [Hennessy and Patterson(2012)].

In order to design a balanced system addressing performance, energy, and cost, a compromise must be met with the number and aggressiveness of cores and the memory subsystem design (number of MCs, number of banks, etc). This work pursues to provide high-performance designers insights on such issues.

4 Experimental Framework

This section presents the simulation environment used for the design exploration study. An extended version of the Multi2sim simulation framework [Ubal et al.(2012)Ubal, Jang, Mistry, Schaa, and Kaeli] has been used to model the devised future manycore embedded system. Contention at the different points of the system has been modeled: link and injection buffer contention at NoC, channel, bank, and queue contention at MC, as well as stalls at the cores due to resource availability and stalls due to memory operations, mispredictions, and so on. Table 1 summarizes the main architectural parameters for the three studied subsystems

As aforementioned, it is expected that manycore processors would be used to executed parallel loads. Therefore, we took some applications from the SPLASH2 benchmark suite [Woo et al.(1995)Woo, Ohara, Torrie, Singh, and Gupta], which characterize the parallel behavior of near future applications. No sampling technique or kernels are used to collect the results, the benchmarks have been executed completely.

5 Experimental Evaluation

Nowadays, as cores are more powerful and more cores are deployed in CMPs, the pressure on the memory memory is greater. This results into memory latency is even more a major design concern since it limits the performance achieved by the CMP. In this section, we explore the system performance depending on the memory subsystem performance as we change the core aggressiveness and the number of memory controllers.

Table 1. Machine parameters

Microprocessor core	
Issue policy	Out of order
Fetch, issue, commit width	2/4/8 instructions/cycle
ROB size (entries)	256
L1 inst. cache	64B-line, 2-way, 32KB, 2-cycle
L1 data cache	64B-line, 2-way, 32KB, 2-cycle
L2 unified cache	128B-line, 16-way, 1MB, 10-cycle
NoC	
Topology	Mesh
Virtual channels	No
Routing algorithm	X-Y
Switch buffer size	2 entries
Memory subsystem	
Memory controller	single queue 64-entry single queue FCFS
Channels	2
Banks / ranks	4 / 1
DRAM access time	300-cycle

5.1 Impact of the Number of Memory Controllers on Performance

Systems with a relatively high number of cores, such as 64-core systems, are heavily constrained by main memory latencies, as depicted in Figure 3. The 64-core system configurations with just a single memory controller show a huge memory latency for all the evaluated benchmarks. Despite the memory access time is 300 cycles, the latency reached by all the benchmarks and configurations increases over 900 cycles, due to the pressure done by the high number cores on the memory subsystem which results in an extreme congestion in the MC and a huge number of bank and channel conflicts.

This congestion turns in unacceptable memory subsystem performance, which will fill the ROB due to pending memory requests and therefore, the processor will be blocked hurting the performance. Considering core aggressiveness, it can be seen that it has a small but increasing influence for FFT and Ocean, but it is markedly stronger in Radix, in which memory latency is increased from 1931 cycles to 2315 cycles when core width goes from 2 to 8 ways. As core width grows, more memory requests can be sent at the same time from the cores to main memory which leads to increase the congestion in the NoC and in the memory itself.

The straightforward solution to alleviate this performance problem is to deploy multiple memory controllers. Nevertheless, the ideal number of memory controllers to achieve a good trade-off between performance and cost is still an open research problem. The aim of this section is to provide insights into this concern. To this end, this section evaluates the impact on performance of adding more memory controllers to a 64-core system. For evaluation purposes, we assume that all the memory controllers are uniformly distributed on the border of the system, except for the 64-memory controller configurations where each core has a MC attached to its switch. We consider the configuration with 64 MCs in spite of being impossible to implement to show an upper bound of the performance that can be obtained by only adding more memory controllers.

Figure 3 shows that, in general, the memory access time linearly decreases with the number of MCs in the system. For instance, in FFT it drops from 2094 cycles with 1 MC to 1788, 1388, 846, and 382 cycles for 2, 8, 16, and 64 memory controllers, respectively. This is the expected outcome, since when deploying more memory controllers the number of bank/channel conflicts is enormously reduced. Furthermore, the NoC utilization is spread all over the different MCs equally distributed along its border which reduces network congestion, and as a side-effect memory access time. As it can be seen, the more MCs that are in the system, the better latency results that are obtained.

However, in order to fully analyze the effect of adding more MCs to the system is not enough to study the memory latency reduction, but its impact on the total execution time of the applications, which is plotted in Figure 4. Having 2 or more MCs clearly has a positive influence on the execution time. Again for FFT and 2 ways, execution time is reduced to 74%, 56%, 42%, and 28% of the execution time with 1 MC. Reductions in execution time from 2 to 64 MCs are linearly consistent in each application, thus again results show that as many MCs there are in the system, the better.

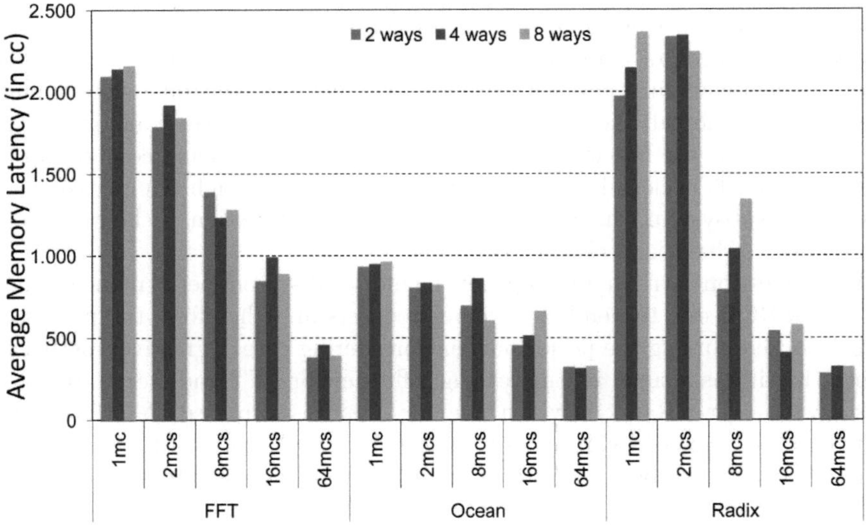

Fig. 3. Average memory latency measured in core cycles for different applications varying the number of MCs and core aggresiveness in 64-core systems

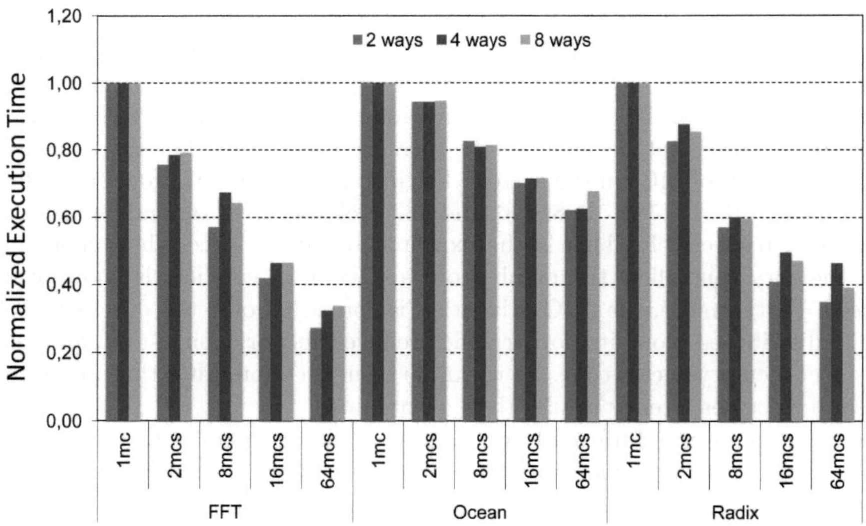

Fig. 4. Normalized execution time for different applications varying the number of MCs and core aggresiveness in 64-core systems

However, cost should also be considered, since in FFT to almost halve execution time from the configurations with 16 MCs to the configuration with 64 MCs, cost is multiplied by 4. So the optimal trade-off between cost and performance lies between 8 MCs and 16 MCs, where performance is increased linearly with the increase in cost of adding more MCs to the system.

6 Conclusions

Multicore/manycore systems have become the fastest growing segment in the microprocessor market. Nowadays power and also as traditionally performance are key design concerns of CMP systems. The two major subsystems that contribute to the system performance are cores and the memory subsystem. In this paper we explore the design space for future high-performance manycore by focusing on the analysis of interactions among the aforementioned two major subsystems. In particular, we explore the memory subsystem performance as a main contributor of the system performance, as a result of the interactions with the other subsystems.

Experimental results show that, increasing the number of memory controllers in the system helps the machine to reduce the overall memory access time and execution time of the applications. A optimum number of cores per MC to achieve a good performance-cost tradeoff is between 8 and 16 cores. Thus, one can conclude that interactions among the two major subsystems should be considered in order to obtain a well balanced global system, and obtaining the most benefits of each component, and therefore obtaining a good performance-cost tradeoff.

Acknowledgments. This work was supported by the Universitat Ppolitècnica de València with tthe grant Primeros Proyectos de Investigacin (PAID-06-10), with reference number 2370, and jointly supported by the Spanish MINECO and European Commission under the project TIN2012-38341-C04-04."

References

[Bell et al.(2008)Bell, Edwards, and Amann, et al] Bell, S., Edwards, B., Amann, J., et al.: TILE64^{TM} processor: A 64-core SoC with mesh interconnect, pp. 88–598

[Held(2010)] Held, J.: "Single-chip cloud computer", an IA tera-scale research processor. In: Guarracino, M.R., Vivien, F., Träff, J.L., Cannatoro, M., Danelutto, M., Hast, A., Perla, F., Knüpfer, A., Di Martino, B., Alexander, M. (eds.) Euro-Par Workshop 2010. LNCS, vol. 6586, pp. 85–85. Springer, Heidelberg (2011)

[Jam(2012)] `http://goparallel.sourceforge.net/ask-james-reinders-multicore-vs-manycore/` (2012)

[Jainschigg(2012)] Jainschigg, J.: (2012), `http://goparallel.sourceforge.net/manycore-mobiles/`

[et al.(2003)] Martin, M.M.K., et al.: Protocol Specifications and Tables for Four Comparable MOESI Coherence Protocols: Token Coherence, Snooping, Directory, and Hammer (2003), `http://www.cs.wisc.edu/`

[Hennessy and Patterson(2012)] Hennessy, J.L., Patterson, D.A.: Computer Architecture: A Quantitative Approach, 5th edn. Morgan Kaufmann Publishers Inc., San Francisco (2012); Appendix E by T. Conte

[Ubal et al.(2012)Ubal, Jang, Mistry, Schaa, and Kaeli] Ubal, R., Jang, B., Mistry, P., Schaa, D., Kaeli, D.: Multi2sim: a simulation framework for cpu-gpu computing. In: Proceedings of the 21st International Conference on Parallel Architectures and Compilation Techniques, PACT 2012, pp. 335–344. ACM, New York (2012)

[Woo et al.(1995)Woo, Ohara, Torrie, Singh, and Gupta] Woo, S.C., Ohara, M., Torrie, E., Singh, J.P., Gupta, A.: The splash-2 programs: characterization and methodological considerations. SIGARCH Comput. Archit. News 23, 24–36 (1995)

[Bailey(1989)] Bailey, D.H.: FFTs in External or Hierarchical Memory. In: Proceedings of the ACM/IEEE Conference on Supercomputing (1989)

Exploiting Parallelization on Address Translation: Shared Page Walk Cache

Albert Esteve, Maria Engracia Gómez, and Antonio Robles

Universitat Politècnica de València,
Camino de Vera, s/n, 46022 Valencia, Spain
alesgar@gap.upv.es, {megomez,arobles}@disca.upv.es
http://www.upv.es/

Abstract. Current processors carry out a Page Table Walk to translate a virtual address into a physical address. This process requires several memory accesses to retrieve the entry from each of the levels of the Page Table Tree. As each main memory access has a large latency, the address translation process may penalize significantly the system performance. Translation Lookaside Buffers (TLBs) avoid completely these accesses by storing the most recent translations. But on a TLB miss a Page Table Walk is required. An effective way to accelerate it is introducing a cache inside/near the MMU to store partial translations.

Recent works have shown the advantages of using a Page Walk Cache on the service of a single core. In this paper we propose a Page Walk Cache shared among the cores of a CMP and analyze its behavior and how it improves performance for parallel applications, comparing it to a private Page Walk Cache scheme. Evaluation results show that shared PTWC increases up to a 19.8% the hit-rate, leading to a TLB miss latency reduction of up to 12.2%, when compared to a private PTWC.

Keywords: virtual memory, page walk, cache organization.

1 Introduction

Virtual Memory is an abstraction that allows multitasking kernels to provide different contiguous virtual address spaces for each task. The operating system manages the assignment of physical space to each different task-specific virtual space, storing the mapping in some hierarchical tables called *Page Tables*.

On a virtual-to-physical address translation process most architectures organize the page table in a multilevel structure containing the mapping for virtual pages. In this scheme a group of small page tables are linked together by a master page table forming a radix tree. Each level of the tree provides a pointer to the next level, but the last one, which provides the final virtual-to-physical translation. Current memory-management units (MMU) use a Translation Lookaside Buffer (TLB) to store the final virtual-to-physical translation, being capable to resolve more than 99% of the address translation requests.

D. an Mey et al. (Eds.): Euro-Par 2013 Workshops, LNCS 8374, pp. 433–443, 2014.

On a TLB miss most of the current processors carry out a Page Table Walk to obtain the virtual-to-physical address translation. This walk usually represents up to two memory accesses in many x86 processors. But, as the virtual space grows also the depth of the multilevel page table structure does. So, for a growing rate of a level per decade, up to four levels are supported by current AMD processors. Notice that the more levels the page table structure has, the larger the impact on performance of TLB misses is, being on a range of 5-14% for non-virtualized environments and up to 48% on a virtualized one [1]. In a virtualized system several virtual machines run concurrently and an extra level of address translation is introduced to translate from guest virtual addresses into host virtual addresses.

To reduce this impact, some recent processors, such as AMD' and Intel' processors, have implemented small MMU caches, private to each core of the CMP, in charge of storing intermediate entries of the page table tree, thus avoiding the latency of the memory accesses due to a page table walk. This caches, also called Page Table Walk Caches (**PTWC**), usually store the highest levels of the Page Table Walk process as they have the most potential for being reused (highest hit rate). In addition, page entries may be initially brought into the L2 cache and treated as data. So, on a PTWC miss, the Page Table entry may be found on the processor's L2 cache. However, this fact may pollute the cache to the detriment of data and instructions.

On the other hand, on a multi-core environment running a parallel application, multiple threads tends to access the same address translation entries, or may potentially share parts (indices) of the virtual address, on what is called *Inter-Core Sharing* patterns [6]. In this context, this paper proposes a PTWC shared by the cores of a CMP. For parallel applications, threads running on different cores share the same virtual space and, therefore, they tend to access the same page entries. On misses from different core TLBs, this will result on a higher hit rate for shared PTWC entries. In particular, results show how our shared PTWC design reduces the misses on the page walk process when compared to the private PTWC approach by up to a 19.8% for the same amount of entries. Consequently, we reduce the latency of a TLB miss for up to more than 12% when using a shared PTWC scheme.

The paper is organized as follows. Section 2 gives some background to the x86 address translation process and some different PTWC organizations. Section 3 describes our Shared PTWC proposal. Section 4 exhibit the tools used to model the system and evaluates how the Shared PTWC performs using some parallel workloads. Finally, in Section 5 some conclusions derived of the previous analysis are given.

2 Background

2.1 Address Translation

In the most recent x86 4-level page tables, the 64-bit virtual address is split into four index fields and a final page offset. The first index is used as an offset

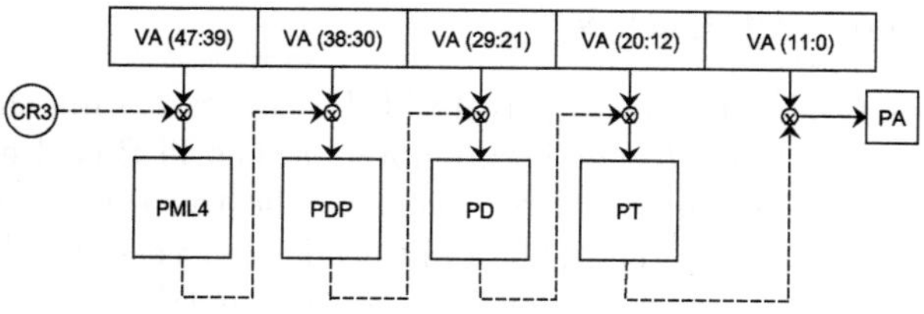

Fig. 1. x86 page walk process to translate a virtual address into a physical address

appended to the address stored in the CR3 register pointing to the root of the page table tree. A page table entry is extracted, which may contain a pointer to the next level of the tree. In that case it is appended to the next virtual address index and another entry is retrieved until the selected entry is either invalid or eventually a pointer (physical address) to the data page, in which case it is stored in the TLB. Notice that one memory access per page table level is required.

Fig. 1 shows how the virtual address is decomposed into four 9-bit indices and one 12-bit offset. The rest of the bits until the 64 bits forming the virtual address are sign extended. Each of the 9-bit indices are used to select an entry in each of the four page table levels, namely: PML4 (Page Map Level 4), PDP (Page Directory Pointer), PD (Page Directory) and PT (Page Table). For the sake of brevity the levels will be refereed to as L_{4-1}, where L_1 is the lower level (PT), and every entry of each page table level will be referred to as *Page Table entry*.

In this scheme L_4 entries maps up to 512GB virtual address range, L_3 maps 1GB, L_2 maps 2MB and, finally, L_1 maps 4KB. Each node at every page table level maps 4KB, as the offset for accessing the entry is the 9-bit index of the virtual address. As the virtual space grows, more page walk levels will be required. It could still grow until six levels, covering the entire 64 bits of the virtual address, thus requiring six memory accesses to complete a translation.

On the other hand, recent architectures such as ARMv7 require up to two stages of memory translation, as it offers hardware support to the memory management virtualization. The first stage translation takes a virtual address as an input and produces an Intermediate Physical Address (IPA). On the second stage the IPA is used as an input to supply the final physical address.

The virtual memory system architecture for ARMv7 defines two alternative translation table formats: short- and long-descriptor page table format. In the later, each of the two possible stages is compound of up to three page table levels. This leads to up to 15 memory accesses required when running virtual machines, as every level of a stage 1 translation from the guest machine will require in turn a complete translation to the host physical address (4 memory accesses per translation level) plus an additional stage 2 translation (3 x 4 + 3).

2.2 Page Table Walk Caches

Page Table Walk Caches are small private MMU caches storing the upper-level page table entries. However, L_1 entries are not stored as TLB is already in charge of doing it. Therefore, in the best case scenario the top three accesses can be resolved by the PTWC, and the MMU only needs to access the slower L2 data cache or main memory to retrieve the L_1 page table entries.

A classification and comparison of different PTWC structures, some of them merely theoretical, are presented on [2]. Page Table Walk Caches can be either tagged using their physical address in memory, as a conventional data cache (VIPT), or using parts (indices) of the virtual address (as a TLB). The former are named Page Table caches whereas the later are named Translation caches. On the one hand, current page table caches basically use the same tagging scheme than a processor' data cache. On the other hand, translation caches store partial translations from the page walk process, allowing the MMU to be able to solve various page table levels by a unique PTWC access. On any of these tagging schemes, elements from different translation levels can be stored on separate caches (split cache) or mixed up into the same cache (unified cache).

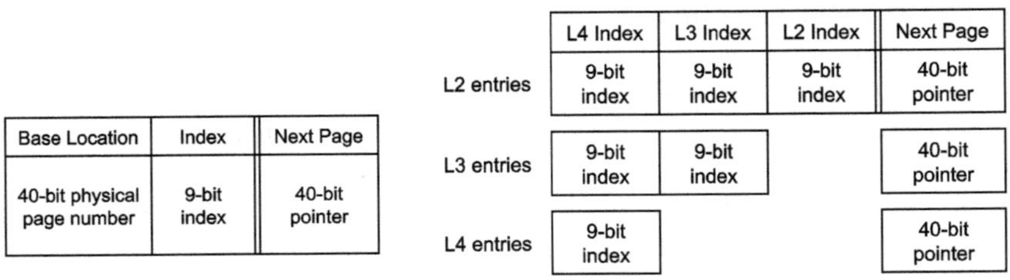

(a) Unified Page Table Cache (b) Split Translation Cache

Fig. 2. Examples of PTWC structures from AMD and Intel processors

The unified page table cache is the design used on modern AMD x86-64 processor (Figure 2(a)), where each entry is tagged with its 40-bit physical page number and the 9-bit index from the virtual address. On the other hand, current Intel x86-64 processors use split translation caches (Figure 2(b)), where the MMU looks up for the entry with the larger amount of matching indices from the virtual address. In both cases a 40-bit physical page number pointing to the next level page table is retrieved.

3 Shared Page Walk Cache

As commented above, on a multi-core environment under a parallel workload, many threads may access the same address space and therefore, hit on the same entries when page walking. In order to take advantage of this we propose a novel Shared Page Walk Cache scheme.

The design of the shared PTWC proposed is based on the Unified Page Table Cache and placed equidistant from all cores in a crossbar-based topology. Page Table design allows the MMU not to be aware whether or not there is a PTWC underneath on the memory hierarchy, as they work as any other processor' cache. On the other hand, the impact of the partitioning scheme (i.e. the caches are unified or split per translation level) depends on the utilization of the address space by the workload involved. Therefore, we chose a unified scheme for the sake of simplicity. The replacement policy is a basic LRU algorithm in a fully-associative organization, so entries with higher hit rate (higher-level entries) are expected to remain more time on the PTWC when competing for slots. Shared PTWC entries format is identical to its private counterpart, including a 40-bit Base Location and a 9-bit Index to retrieve the desired entry and the 40-bit pointer to the next Page Table as the data to be fetched.

The studies presented on Section 4 show how the Shared PTWC behaves varying the size (number of entries) and compare it with a private scheme. Note that in order to truly observe how both designs perform with the same number of entries, in the private PTWC design the number of entries have to be multiplied by the number of cores and use the result as the number of entries of the Shared PTWC design.

Shared PTWC is accessed whenever there is a TLB miss, and as many times per TLB miss as Page Table levels are on the architecture (up to four in the case of an x86-64). The last level entry containing the final virtual-to-physical translation is not stored as in a regular private PTWC design. Furthermore, we assume a separate shared PTWC scheme for data and instructions, as it agrees with the separate private TLB scheme, as shown in Figure 3.

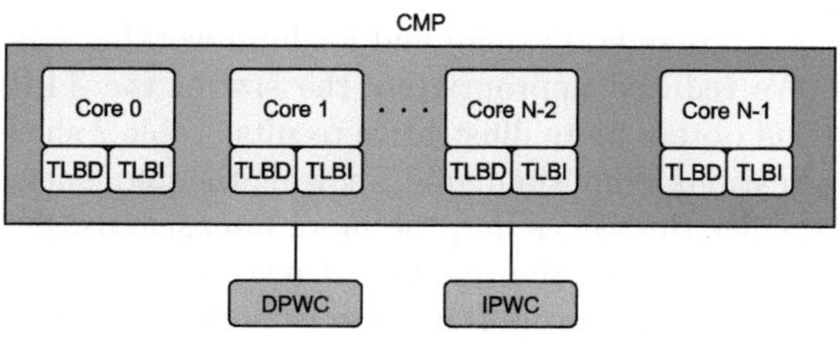

Fig. 3. Basic system structure

The system we consider is a x86-based CMP. The processor' memory hierarchy is compound of separate private L1 caches and a separate shared L2 cache, for data and instructions. Note that our Shared PTWC is placed at the same level as the processor' L2 cache in the memory hierarchy. So we do not use the memory hierarchy to store page walk entries in order to solo evaluate our design.

4 Performance Evaluation

In this section we analyze the performance of the shared PTWC on a multicore environment, showing to what extent the use of a PTWC shared among all the cores of a CMP allows to reduce the overall number of TLB misses ending up in memory accesses, thus reducing their penalty and improving the overall system performance.

4.1 Evaluation Methodology

We evaluate our proposals with full-system simulation using gem5 [3] to simulate an out-of-order multi-core CMP with the characteristics listed on Table 1. We use CACTI 6.0 [4] to compute latency for the PTWC, resulting in an access latency of 1 cycle for 32nm technology.

Table 1. Baseline System Parameters

CPU	One to eight cores, pipelined and out-of-order, x86-64 @1Ghz
L1TLB	Private Split L1 (Data and Instruction) TLB, 8 entries, Fully associative
PTWC	Shared Data and Instruction Caches, up to 128 entries, Fully associative

The proposal is evaluated using several workloads from PARSEC 3.0 [5][7]. Due to time requirements, we are not able to simulate these benchmarks with large working sets. Consequently small and medium working sets has been used to stress TLBs. We reduced appropriately the size of the TLB to match the working set size and obtain more illustrative results. Table 2 shows a characterization of the applications being simulated, showing the frequency of TLB misses. In general, the smaller the values are, the more intensive usage of memory the application does. Particularly, the number of instructions issued and memory accesses between TLB misses varies from various hundreds to tens of thousands. In the case of DRAM accesses it entails a couple of tens as maximum.

All the experimental results are taken on the parallel phase of benchmarks.

4.2 Private vs Shared PTWC Comparison

In this Section, we analyze the behavior of a shared PTWC scheme for an 8-core CMP with respect to a private scheme. The comparison is performed in terms of average hits per TLB miss and memory access speedup regarding using no PTWC. For comparison purposes, we also include results for a single-core PTWC. Different PTWC sizes are analyzed (in a range from 4 up to 128 entries). Note that for the private configuration the total PTWC size will be the number of cores times the individual PTWC size. Figure 4(a) shows the average number

Table 2. Benchmarks and characterization

Workload	Inst/Walk	Mem/Walk	DRAM/Walk
Blackscholes	134006.8	46400.9	17.1
Facesim	8112.7	3382.5	22.3
Fluidanimate	12468.7	3959.0	11.8
Freqmine	1780.0	812.9	1.83
Streamcluster	1008.3	440.0	1.8
Swaptions	398339.9	140618.0	11.8
x264	333.0	121.0	2.0

of hits on PTWC per TLB miss. Notice that, as PTWC store three levels of the page walk process, three hits at most are expected. As can be seen, just eight PTWC entries (twice the TLB size) are enough to achieve an average number of hits per walk equal or greater than 2.9. Further, from 16 entries onward, the PTWC size hardly affects the hit rate. We observe that with lower PTWC sizes the private PTWC scheme outperforms the equally sized shared one. This is due to the fact that on the shared scheme cores are competing for entries on the PTWC, and they are replaced before being reused more frequently than with the private scheme. However, this behavior varies as long as the PTWC size increases. So, above eight entries, shared PTWCs achieve a higher number of hits per walk when compared to the private PTWC. Furthermore, assuming a constant value for the overall storage capacity of the PTWC (i.e. the number of entries of the shared PTWC equals the sum of all private PTWCs), the shared PTWC scheme always provides the highest number of hits per walk, resulting in a reduction of up to 19.8% of misses.

On the other hand, we observe a smaller amount of hits on average when running just one core. This can be explained by the fact that the used workloads maintaining their working set sizes constant for the different analyzed configurations. Therefore, with a single-core, TLBs (and also the PTWC) are stressed to a greater extent.

Figure 4(b) shows the speed-up of the time to resolve TLB misses in terms of the reduction percentage in the number of clock cycles with regard to not using PTWC. The speedup achieved is slightly greater in our shared design for a number of entries superior to eight with respect to private PTWC. However, for a constant overall storage capacity of the PTWC the improvement reaches up to 12.2%. Moreover, if we compare both private and shared PTWC schemes to having no PTWC we observe a maximum speedup of nearly a 75%.

4.3 Shared PTWC Analysis

In this Section we perform a deeper insight into the shared PTWC analysis focusing on the behavior of the entries for the different translation levels. Notice that in a unified PTWC, as assumed, these translation levels compete for the same entries of the PTWC. Hence, we wonder to what extent some translation levels may be favored regarding the other ones.

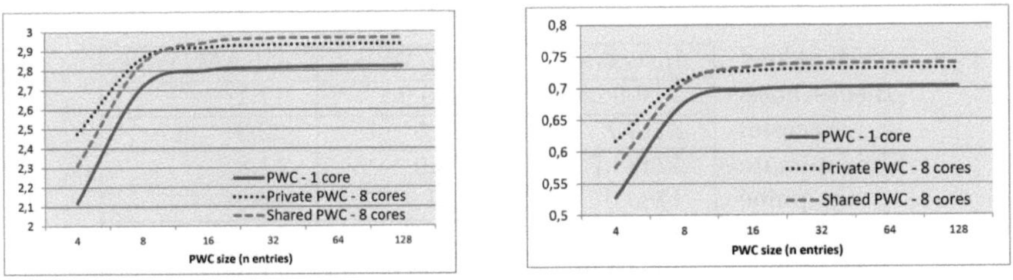

(a) Average hits on PTWC per TLB miss (b) Average percentage of cycles reduction

Fig. 4. Shared PTWC vs Private PTWC

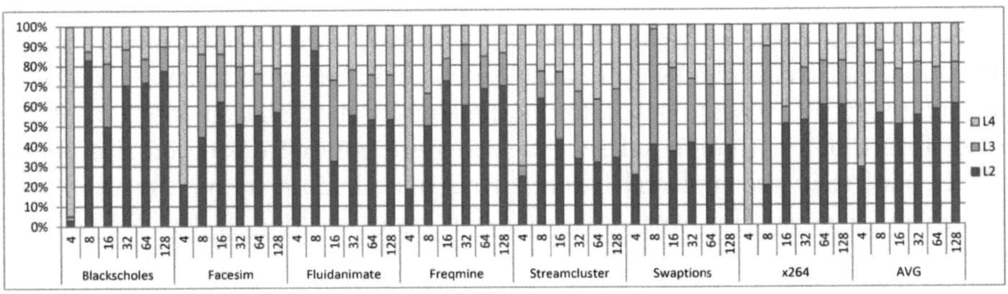

Fig. 5. Contents of the PTWC per translation level

Figure 5 shows the distribution of entries per level on the PTWC. We observe how, in general, the larger the PTWC is, the higher the percentage of entries corresponding to the bottom-most level (L_2). On the contrary, small PTWCs are populated by the highest level entries (L_4). As the higher level entries maps a greater amount of virtual space, there is a greater likelihood of these entries to be reused.

On the other hand, Figure 6 shows the reutilization rate of the entries for each translation level. This metric represents, for each level, the average number of hits achieved by each of the entries of that level during their life-times with regard to the addition of the average values of all the levels. As can be seen, smaller PTWCs evict entries from every level while being less reutilized in proportion. That is the reason why the reutilization rates of the different levels are quite similar, aside those corresponding to L_2 entries, which exhibit the lowest reutilization rate. Further, as the size of the PTWC grows, the L_2 reutilization rate becomes less representative, becoming hardly a 1.3% on average.

Finally, Figure 7 shows the hit-rate of the PTWC (normalized to 3 hits/walk) split into the different translation levels for the analyzed applications. As observed, the hit-rate is evenly distributed among the different translation levels (i.e. 1/3 of hits for each translation level) regardless of the PTWC size. However, the number of entries of the PTWC corresponding to each translation level depends on the level and the PTWC size.

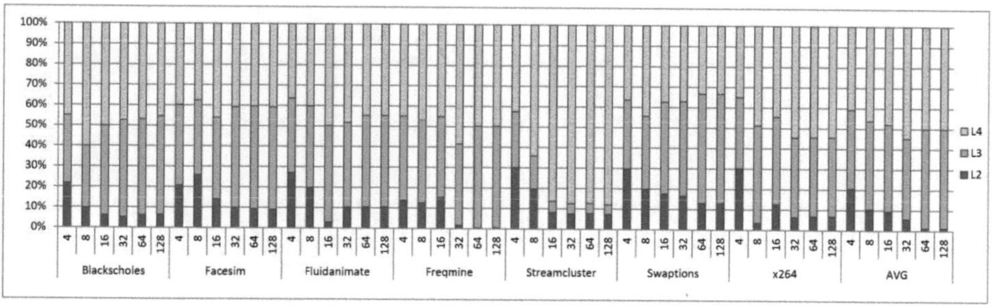

Fig. 6. Reutilization of PTWC entries per translation level

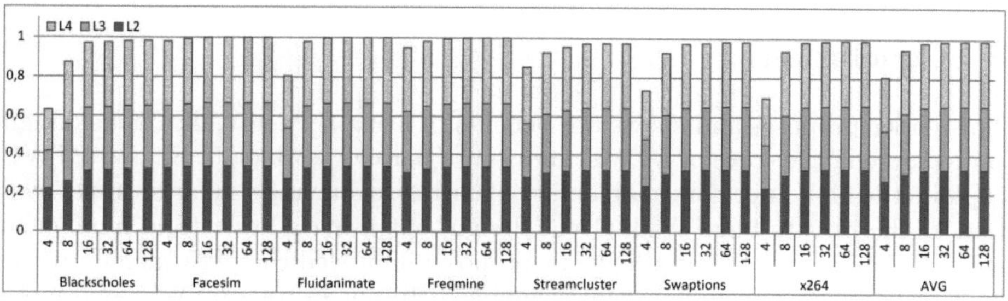

Fig. 7. Hit rate per translation level

According to the previous analysis we can conclude that the hit-rate per translation level is hardly penalized even on small PTWCs. High level entries populate the PTWC in a lower degree, but they are highly reutilized. On the other hand, low level entries extensively populate the PTWC but they are rarely revisited and more frequently evicted. These combination of factors make the hit-rate closely equal for each translation level, as commented above.

4.4 Inter-core Sharing Pattern Analysis

One of the main initial considerations to our Shared PTWC design is to take advantage of the inter-core sharing patterns exhibited by parallel applications to achieve a greater hit-rate even when using smaller cache sizes. In this sense, in order to properly understand the previously showed performance benefits of using a Shared PTWC as alternative to the usual private PTWC, we analyze the proportion of entries of the PTWC being shared by a certain number of cores. We analyze four- (Figure 8(a)) and eight- (Figure 8(b)) core platforms. As observed, in both cases the majority of entries are being shared among all cores. That means that, on average, up to 80% of entries, regardless of the translation level they belong to, are heavily reused among the cores.

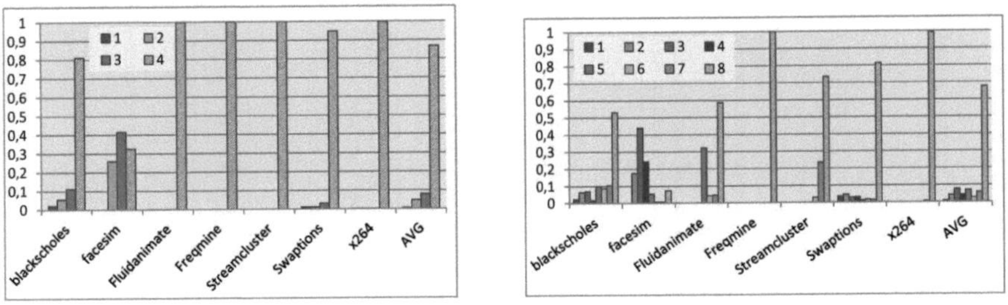

(a) Sharing patterns for 4 cores

(b) Sharing patterns for 8 cores

Fig. 8. Sharing patterns analysis

5 Conclusions

This paper proposes and shows the benefits of using a Page Walk Cache design shared among the cores of a CMP for a set of parallel workloads. Shared PTWC exploits the high inter-core shareability of entries, achieving similar hit rates over that of the private Page Walk Cache design, but using a lower total number of entries. We have also shown how our proposal improved the performance of the page walk process up to 75% when compared to not using a PTWC, and more than 12% when compared to a total equally sized private PTWC scheme.

Shared PTWC is designed as Unified Page Table Cache, being it easy to implement and allowing the MMU to be unaware of the PTWC existence when accessing the main memory to retrieve a page descriptor entry. Moreover, we observed how the Shared PTWC hits on the many translation levels uniformingly, endorsing our design choices.

Acknowledgements. This work was supported by the Spanish Ministerio de Economía y Competitividad (MINECO) and by Plan E funds under Grant TIN2009-14475-C04-01; by the Spanish Ministerio de Economía y Competitividad (MINECO) and by FEDER funds under Grant TIN2012-38341-C04-01 and by the VIRTICAL project (grant agreement n° 288574) which is funded by the European Commission within the Research Programme FP7.

References

1. Bhargara, R., Serebrin, B., Spadini, F., Manne, S.: Accelerating Two-Dimensional Page Walks for Virtualized Systems. In: ASPLOS XIII, pp. 26–35 (2008)
2. Barr, T.W., Cox, A.L., Rixner, S.: Translation Caching: Skip, Don't Walk (the Page Table). In: 37th Int'l Symp. on Computer Architecture, ISCA (June 2010)
3. Binkert, N., Beckmann, B., Black, G., et al.: The gem5 simulator. Computer Architecture News (2011)
4. Muralimanohar, N., Balasubramonian, R., Jouppi, N.P.: CACTI 6.0. Hewlett Packard Labs (2009)

5. Bienia, C., Kumar, S., Singh, J.P., Li, K.: The PARSEC benchmark suite: Characterization and architectural implications. In: 17th Int'l Conference on Parallel Architectures and Compilations Techniques (PACT), pp. 72–81 (2008)
6. Bhattacharjee, A., Lustig, D., Martonosi, M.: Shared last-level TLBs for chip multiprocessors. In: 17th International Conference on High-Performance Computer Architecture, HPCA (February 2011)
7. Gebhart, M., Hestness, J., Fatehi, E., Gratz, P., Keckler, S.W.: Running PARSEC 2.1 on M5. The University of Texas at Austin, Department of Computer Science. Technical Report #TR-09-32 (October 27, 2009)

A Novel Memory Subsystem and Computational Model for Parallel Reconfigurable Architectures

Yamuna Rajasekhar and Ron Sass

Reconfigurable Computing Systems Laboratory
University of North Carolina at Charlotte
{yrajasek,rsass}@uncc.edu

Abstract. While FPGA and other reconfigurable technologies have dramatically increased in size and speed, memory technology has had only modest improvements. Relative to logic speeds, memory latency is virtually flat and physical constraints on external pins limit memory bandwidth. Unfortunately, the traditional cache hierarchy found in fixed-function integrated circuits has evolved to support sequential processors and is ineffective for highly parallel architectures.

This paper proposes a novel memory subsystem and computational model for reconfigurable architectures. It envisions a system where computational cores are oversubscribed with atomic tasks and the memory subsystem enables (1) hiding of latency by enabling the cores to overlap computation and memory transactions and (2) the system to fully utilize the available memory bandwidth. The first step in this grand vision is to change the memory model. Instead of a byte-addressable, global address space, a named segment memory controller is introduced and an FPGA-based implementation presented in this paper.

1 Introduction

Steady increases in the density of Integrated Circuits (IC) has resulted in more transistors per chip and faster transistors. Unfortunately, memory technology has not seen similar improvements. When measured in terms of system clock cycles, memory latency has *grown* dramatically and is expected to approach 1,000 clock cycles to access off-chip DRAM in the next decade [8]. Moreover, it is highly likely that the long-term trend in memory latency, illustrated in Figure 1, will continue for the next decade. While this so called "Memory Wall" was recognized in the mid-1990s [10] chip architects have been able to mitigate the latency issue *for single core microprocessors* through the extensive use of caches and cache hierarchies. But, this approach has come with a high cost. It requires a substantial amount of resources (from 50% to 90% of the transistors on a chip) [6] and it consumes a significant amount of energy to operate [1]. Furthermore, to maximize performance for a specific application (by increasing cache line locality in the hierarchy) requires an enormous effort, to the point that humans typically achieve a tiny fraction of the theoretical performance and instead rely on automated performance tuning [3, 5, 7].

D. an Mey et al. (Eds.): Euro-Par 2013 Workshops, LNCS 8374, pp. 444–453, 2014.

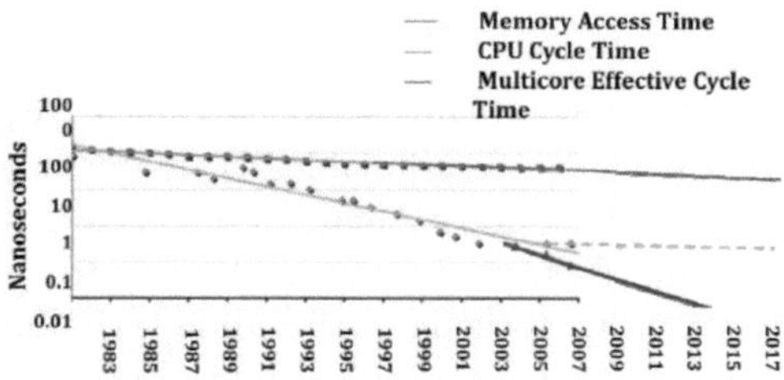

Fig. 1. Memory latency compared to (processor) clock frequency

Further complicating the memory problem facing modern parallel systems is memory bandwidth. First, the traditional cache hierarchy is optimized for single core processor performance. It devalues memory bandwidth in favor of statistically improving the memory latency observed by the processor. From the point of view of a single core microprocessor, every cache hit is a success. However, from the point of view of a memory-bound many core microprocessor, the goal is to fully utilize of the off-chip memory bandwidth. As the cache hit rate increases, it leaves a reactive cache hierarchy guessing how best to use the available bandwidth and, in some cases, doing nothing. Every unused cycle to off-chip memory is lost and cannot be recovered in the future.

This paper introduces a novel memory subsystem that, when combined with an appropriate computational model, is designed to efficiently utilize the available memory bandwidth while hiding memory latency in highly parallel systems. It creates a queue of outstanding memory requests which allows a pro-active memory subsystem to reorder requests to utilize multiple memory channels in the most efficient ways. To accomplish this, we propose an abstraction that separates the computational load from the memory subsystem via multiple banks of scratchpad memories per computational core, an interconnection network, and the proactive memory management subsystem.

This imposes a few constraints on the computational load. First, it assumes that the application has a large degree of parallelism and that many independent tasks are available. For reasons beyond the scope of this paper, we further assume that these are relatively short, atomic sequences; small bits of imperative programs. The reason for multiple banks is so that compute cores can be oversubscribed. By allowing a core to work out of one memory bank allows another bank to be involved in a memory transaction, resulting in the overlap of computation and communication. This is accomplished by multiplexing the banks of memory and the introduction of a scheduler.

Given these assumptions, the system level view becomes a stochastic process with computational cores providing a statistical demand on the memory subsystem that can be represented by a random variable (an arrival rate) and the memory subsystem responding based on a random variable (a service rate). In such a circumstance, the overall goal of the system is to balance computation against the physical limitations of off-chip memory bandwidth to create a queue of enough outstanding requests that the memory subsystem can intelligently order the transactions. From a formal point of view, it is Little's Law [2],

$$N = \lambda \times W$$

where N is the number of outstanding requests, λ is the arrival rate, and W is the wait time. In our case, λ (the computational load) can be manipulated so that N does not exceed the on-chip resources. Hence, we create an artificial stationary process that, as the on-chip resources increase, allows us to approach 100% bandwidth utilization. Combined with the latency-hiding technique introduced in the previous paragraph, this approach has the potential of dramatically improving the overall throughput of highly parallel applications on manycore architectures.

The remainder of this paper describes the first-cut design of the system just outlined. In Section 2, overall (chip level) system is presented along with the details of the proposed memory subsystem. The chip-level design includes a mix of high performance (single thread low latency processor cores) and many high throughput small processor cores. To test the feasibility and practical application of these ideas, a subset of the proposed system has been implemented on an FPGA device. In particular, the ability to connect source and sink of memory segments has been implemented as a B-Tree data structure in hardware. Section 3 describes the physical implementation used to collect the data in the results section, Section 4. A brief summary and description of (the extensive) future work is as described in Section 5.

2 Design

2.1 Abstract Model

An abstract view of a generic system design is illustrated in Figure 2. Here, we assume a system containing several different cores, each with some amount of local memory (or scratchpad). There are two types of cores in the system — Green core and White core. The cores are differentiated based on how they are used. The White core is a modern, highly optimized processor core with a traditional cache hierarchy and intended for sequential parts of the application. The Green cores, which are the cores that use the novel memory subsystem proposed here, provide the parallelism. As such, they are either application-specific accelerators or processor cores that favor small size over speed (to increase the maximum degree of parallelism). In a new programming model and run-time system, described in [4], the White core is responsible for generating a tasks that are sent to the Green cores for computation, assigning more than one task per core. Based on the tasks assigned, a Green core will request the code and data *by name* for all of its tasks simultaneously. Once the memory subsystem has delivered all of the required data for a task to run, the task runs to completion and informs the memory subsystem that a new, named memory segment is available. The central idea is that the memory subsystem can be moving data to the scratchpad memories, and from the scratchpad memories, concurrent with tasks running on the Green cores. When a task completes, the selected scratchpad is changed and the core is reset. Note that under this scheme, there is no global address space, only named memory segments. These memory segments are locally read/write-able in an imperative style but once a task completes and the output is shared with the memory subsystem, it is read-only. Communication and synchronization between the cores is handled by references to named segments. Names are ASCII strings that have been hashed to a fixed-width, binary digest, i.e. SHA-like.

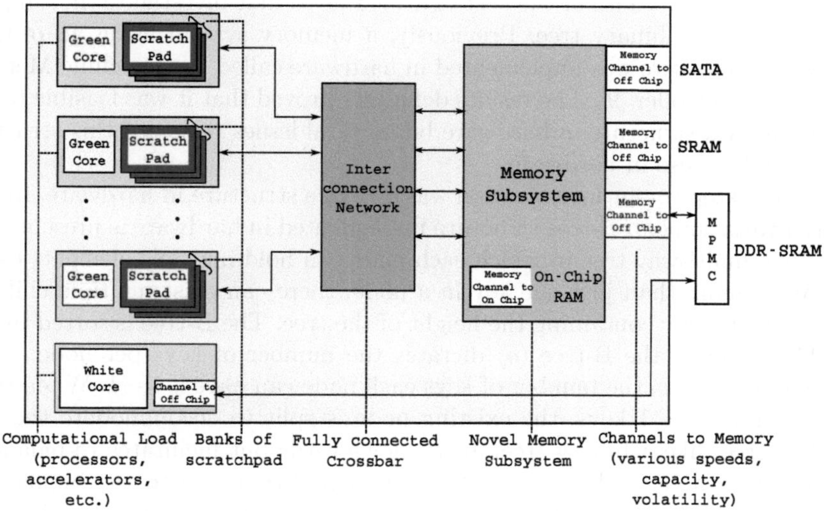

Fig. 2. Many Core Chip Model

This model does not allow for conventional synchronization primitives such as semaphores and it imposes a functional style of programming at the highest level ([4] describes the two-level programming model in detail). However, it does allow for state machines and imperative style programming at the task level and the organization overcomes several very difficult architectural challenges for extreme scale systems; one of which is the Memory Wall. And finally, as the illustration suggests, there could be multiple channels to memory with different speed, capacity, and volatility characteristics. In this paper, we consider one memory channel to a pool of on-chip blocks of RAM. However, we envision a system with multiple channels to RAM that include external SRAM, DRAM, and SATA.

2.2 Theory of Operation

To realize the abstract model of computation presented in this section and utilize the stochastic characteristics, a key operation in the memory subsystem is the ability to dereference memory segment names. This operation takes a name and identifies the location of the memory segment. The segment ideally might exist on chip, in DRAM, or even on a solid state drive.

A factor in large and complex systems is the storage of metadata that has to be accessed often and quickly. This led to the investigation of data structures implemented in hardware to hold system metadata. Several factors have to be taken into consideration while implementing a data structure in hardware. Highly complex data structures that would be ideal in software, may not fare well in hardware because of the cost. This led us to first investigate the simplest data structure, a binary tree. Previously, a memory system using an ordered binary tree structure was implemented in hardware called the Dynamic Memory Allocation Controller [9]. The results definitely proved that it was feasible to implement a data structure in hardware but several issues rendered this structure not optimal for use in hardware.

The next step to our investigation was a B-tree structure in hardware. In this paper, a variation of a B-tree structure implemented in hardware is presented. A B-tree is a multi-way tree in which each node can hold multiple elements called *keys*. With more than just one key in a node, there can exist multiple children (branches) thereby containing the height of the tree. The B-tree is sorted by the *key*. The order of the B-tree (o) dictates the number of keys per node. For a B-tree with order o, the number of keys each node can have is $o-1$. When there are more than $o-1$ keys, the existing node is split to accommodate the new key. A B-tree, like a binary tree, grows downwards but facilitates re-balancing by splitting a node and adding it to its parent. Compared to the binary tree structure, the B-tree has several advantages. It can support more than just two children per node, which leads to reduced access times. Also the possibility of a bad data pattern leading to a linked list is reduced as the B-tree has a way of balancing out the data within a main branch.

3 Implementation

The memory subsystem hardware consists of a master controller, two B-tree modules, and a BRAM pool for data. This hardware serves as an active memory controller, which not only services the requests that are coming in, but can also keep track of pending requests. A unique feature of the memory subsystem is that it can work on variable sized memory chunks. Another feature is that it works on name based memory chunks that make it easy for the processor. For the purpose of this paper, the name is a unique identifier calculated by the master controller. Figure 3 shows a high level block diagram of the memory subsystem.

3.1 B-Tree Module

The B-tree module hardware consists of three main components: a B-tree table (BRAM table), a compare-sort module and a controller. This B-tree structure is used to hold the meta data of the system and is implemented in on-chip memory.

B-Tree Memory Table. The table in the BRAM contains the following fields — key, parent address, left address, right address, node pointer (the base address

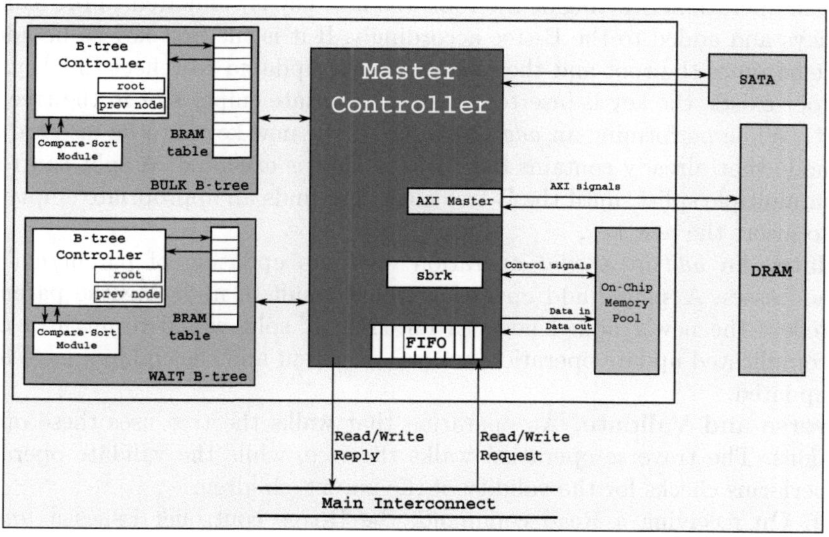

Fig. 3. High level block diagram of the Memory Subsystem

of the data block in memory) and a couple of fields for checking validity and adjacency. Although the B-tree is stored as a table in hardware, in order to achieve the working of a B-tree, it is essential to keep track of the children (branches) and the parent. The size of the *key* is configurable for this data structure. For the purpose of storing the parent and left/right (branches) the BRAM address of the key which is the parent or left/right branch is captured. The node pointer also has some control bits that indicate the memory location (whether on-chip off-chip) of the data block.

B-Tree Controller. The B-tree controller unit is the top-level hardware that performs all the operations and manages the B-tree table. Keeping in mind the working of a B-tree, multiple consequent splits could result in an intermittent change of the root. The B-tree controller comprises of a root register that keeps track of the current root of the B-tree. The B-tree controller also has four *key* registers to hold the four keys of the current node in operation. Additionally, the controller retains the latest node that is fetched in a register on-chip. This results in faster look-ups of any keys near a recently referenced key. Every time a request comes in, this register is checked for a match before proceeding to traverse the B-tree.

As in any conventional cache, the B-tree controller receives *Read* and *Write* commands. These commands are then interpreted by the B-tree controller as B-tree operations and processed accordingly. The B-tree operations include *Add*, *Find*, *Split*, and *Update*. These commands are explained in detail below:

Add. On receiving a Write command, the B-tree controller adds the particular key to the B-tree table. In doing so, the B-tree controller first performs an add operation. Starting at the root, the new key is compared to the existing keys and added to the B-tree accordingly. If it is the first key to be added, it becomes the root and the root register is updated to reflect this key. If a root exists, the key is inserted at an appropriate empty slot in the tree.

Split. While performing an *add* operation, if the new key is to be inserted at a node that already contains four keys, a *split* is executed. A split can result in multiple splits, until the B-tree controller finds an appropriate empty slot to insert the new key.

Update. An *add* or a *spilt* operation warrants updating of parent/children addresses. A simple add operation would result in updating the parent to reflect the newly added node as its child. A split would result in a more complicated update operation, where the parent and the children have to be updated.

Traverse and Validate. An operation that walks the tree uses these operations. The traverse operation walks the tree, while the validate operation performs checks for the validity of the parent/children.

Find. On receiving a Read command, the B-tree controller issues a *find* to retrieve the requested key from the B-tree. This command typically traverses the tree looking for the said key. When the key is found, it retrieves the data packet associated with the key and passes it on the memory subsystem.

Delete. For the purpose of this paper, the delete operation only marks the key corresponding to the memory chunk to be invalid. Once the key has been marked for delete, that key is not considered while traversing the B-tree.

Compare-Sort Module. The keys in each B-Tree node require to be sorted in order to achieve precise placement of the children. The input to this module is a node. This module then uses comparators to compare the keys and returns the node with the keys sorted in ascending order. Several operations of the B-Tree require comparing and sorting the keys. The compare-sort module eases this operation, by making it a two-step, feed-in read-out process.

3.2 BRAM Pool

While the B-tree module is used to store the meta data of the system, there is an additional resource on-chip to store the actual data. As the name suggests, it is a pool of multiple BRAMs that hold the data. The master controller reads from and writes to the BRAM pool. The size of the BRAM pool is decided based on amount of resources available on-chip.

3.3 Master Controller

The master controller is the main pivot that controls the entire system. As shown in Figure 3, the master has control of two B-tree modules — the *BULK* B-tree module and the *WAIT* B-tree module. While the basic hardware of the B-tree modules is the same, the main difference is that the *WAIT* module is used to store any request that comes in which does not have any data associated with it yet. Also, since there will never exist data associated with the requests in the *WAIT* B-tree, this B-tree table does not contain a field to store node pointers. Instead it makes a note of the core that is initiating this request.

For any *write* request that comes in, the master first checks in the *WAIT* tree if there has been a request for this data. If there has been a request, the master first services this request by sending the data associated with the request to the core as stored in the *WAIT* B-tree. Also, in the *WAIT* B-tree, this entry is now marked for delete. Additionally, this data is written into the *BULK* B-tree so any other read requests for this particular data chunk can be serviced accordingly.

The master controller stores the base addresses of the data blocks stored in the BRAMs in the *BULK* tree. Each request has a payload length associated with it. This controller keeps the BRAM pool in check and allocates and frees BRAMs from the BRAM pool. To ensure that the BRAMs are written to properly, the master controller uses a ***sbrk*** register. This register is the hardware equivalent of the *sbrk* memory management system call in Unix. Every time a new data chunk is stored in the BRAM pool, this register increments by the number of bytes equal to the payload length. Thus, this register always points to the latest available location in the BRAM pool. Additionally, there is a FIFO to queue multiple requests that are pending. The AXI master to external DRAM is a part of the master controller but because of the assumption of a single channel to the memory, this is not explained.

4 Results

The design presented has been realized on a Xilinx ML-605 developer board. The Xilinx Embedded development Kit (EDK) version 14.1 was used to develop and synthesize the designs. To test the functionality, a synthetic sequence of message operations (with randomly sized messages) was generated and used to exercise the memory subsystem hardware. The memory subsystem hardware was built as a proof-of-concept system to test the functionality and feasibility of constructing a new approach to memory subsystems using data structures that are implemented in the hardware of the FPGA.

For the initial feasibility test, the size of the key was set to 16 bits. The order of the B-tree is 5 which means there are no more than 4 keys in every node. The size of both the bulk B-tree and the wait B-tree (the BRAM tables) was kept to 1024 nodes. Additionally, size of the BRAM pool was kept to be 4096. The system when synthesized, utilizes 17037 out of the 150720 slices which is about 11%. The structures implemented were kept to a minimum size in order to gauge the resource utilization. On a Virtex 6 FPGA 12 RAMB36E1s are used exclusively for the memory subsystem hardware. This shows that there is a lot of scope to increase the size of the memory subsystem which will in turn help in observing the theoretical results previously stated.

Table 1 shows the time (in clock cycles) for the basic operations. The depth of the tree, *d*, is an important factor to these results. The *Traverse* operation is

Table 1. Clock Cycles for each operation

Operation	Cycles per level
ADD	6
FIND	2
TRAVERSE	$8 \times d$
VALIDATE	$4 + d$

directly proportional to the depth of the tree, specifically, $8 \times d$. The *Validate* operation takes 4 clock cycles and additionally adds one clock cycle per unit increase in depth. This does not apply to the *Add* and *Find* operations as the traversal points the controller to the right place, after which only the new key needs to be added, or in the case of *Find*, returned. The split operation is the most expensive, especially if it results in multiple splits. The time measured for a split is 30 clock cycles. These numbers have been measured in simulation, but the functionality of the memory subsystem has been tested on the FPGA board. In the next version of the system, the idea is to widen the BRAMs to hold an entire node of the B-tree as opposed to just one key. This will help reduce the look up times for the B-tree.

5 Conclusion

The memory subsystem and model proposed attempts to hide memory latency and more efficiently use the bandwidth to external memory. It accomplishes this by proactively managing a large number of outstanding requests in such a way that the channel to external memory is fully utilized. To be successful, it imposes a task-oriented computational model on computational cores and requires them to multi-task in order to generate multiple, overlapping memory requests that can be served by the memory subsystem in any order. Using Little's Law, this paper shows that such an organization creates a stochastic system at the architecture level that hides memory latency, increases the effective bandwidth of an off-chip memory channel, and increases the task completion rate for memory-bound systems. To demonstrate the feasibility of such a memory subsystem, a hardware based B-tree implementation of a proactive cache has been implemented and tested on a Virtex 6 FPGA.

This approach is not appropriate for all settings. In particular, many FPGA-based designs have an enormous degree of parallelism but are not memory bound. It may be the case that there are designs that interface to instruments, sensors and actuators, that provide a continuous source or sink of information. In other cases there are applications that are very computationally intensive and have a relatively small state. Nonetheless, there is a large range of applications in the High-Performance Computing domain (from graph algorithms to iterative algorithms) that fit the proposed model.

In the future, a priority scheme will be implemented to allow the memory subsystem to re-order the tasks to always keep the cores busy with computation. Additionally, this design will be extended to include a Least-Recently Used capability that tracks on-chip blocks in the BRAM pool. This will enable the memory subsystem to handle a wide range of memory technologies that vary in capacity, bandwidth, and latency. For example, it could extend memory subsystem to include non-volatile Flash devices as well as DDR synchronous DRAM, and static RAM.

References

1. Albonesi, D.: Selective cache ways: on-demand cache resource allocation. In: Proceedings of the 32nd Annual International Symposium on Microarchitecture, MICRO-32, pp. 248–259 (1999)
2. Bertsimas, D., Nakazato, D.: The distributional little's law and its applications. Operations Research 43(2), 298–310 (1995)
3. Frigo, M., Johnson, S.: Fftw: an adaptive software architecture for the fft. In: Proceedings of the 1998 IEEE International Conference on Acoustics, Speech and Signal Processing, vol. 3, pp. 1381–1384 (1998)
4. Huang, B., Sass, R., DeBardeleben, N., Blanchard, S.: Pydac: A resilient runtime framework for divide-and-conquer applications on a heterogeneous many-core architecture. In: The 6th Workshop on UnConventional High Performance Computing, UCHPC at Euro-Par 2013 (2013)
5. Johnson, J.R.: Automated performance tuning. In: Proceedings of the 4th International Workshop on Parallel and Symbolic Computation, PASCO 2010, pp. 20–21. ACM, New York (2010), `http://doi.acm.org/10.1145/1837210.1837215`
6. Kozyrakis, C., Patterson, D.: A new direction for computer architecture research. Computer 31(11), 24–32 (1998)
7. Njoroge, N., Casper, J., Wee, S., Teslyar, Y., Ge, D., Kozyrakis, C., Olukotun, K.: Atlas: a chip-multiprocessor with transactional memory support. In: Proceedings of the Conference on Design, Automation and Test in Europe, DATE 2007, pp. 3–8, EDA Consortium, San Jose (2007), `http://dl.acm.org/citation.cfm?id=1266366.1266370`
8. Kogge, P., et al.: Exascale computing study: Technology challenges in achieving exascale systems. Tech. Rep. TR-2008-13, DARPA Information Processing Techniques Office (IPTO) sponsored study (2008), `http://www.cse.nd.edu/Reports/2008TR-2008-13.pdf`
9. Rajasekhar, Y., Sass, R.: A first analysis of a dynamic memory allocation controller (dmac) core. In: Proceedings of the 2011 Symposium on Application Accelerators in High-Performance Computing, SAAHPC 2011, pp. 64–67. IEEE Computer Society, Washington, DC (2011), `http://dx.doi.org/10.1109/SAAHPC.2011.23`
10. Wulf, W.A., McKee, S.A.: Hitting the memory wall: implications of the obvious. SIGARCH Comput. Archit. News 23(1), 20–24 (1995), `http://doi.acm.org/10.1145/216585.216588`

Enhancing Performance and Energy Consumption of HER Caches by Adding Associativity

Vicente Lorente[1], Alejandro Valero[1], and Ramon Canal[2]

[1] Department of Computer Engineering
Universitat Politècnica de València
Valencia, Spain
[2] Departament d'Arquitectura de Computadors
Universitat Politècnica de Catalunya
Barcelona, Spain

Abstract. Unlike other previous techniques, the recently proposed Hard Error Recovery (HER) fault-tolerant cache provides 100% fault-coverage in L1 data caches. This full coverage makes the HER cache appropiate for fault-dominated future technology nodes.

An n-way set-associative HER cache implements one cache way with fast SRAM banks and the remaining ways with eDRAM banks to address power and area. Since the number of eDRAM cache blocks used in a specific HER cache organization depends on the cache associativity (i.e., the implemented number of ways), we expect that the performance and energy consumption provided by a given HER cache design strongly depends on the cache geometry.

In this work we study the behavior of the HER cache design when applied to a highly associative L1 cache like those found in some modern microprocessors. In particular this work explores a 32KB 8-way associative L1 data cache such as the one used in Intel Haswell microarchitecture.

Experimental results show that, at low-power modes compared to a conventional cache with the same storage capacity and number of ways, area, leakage power, and dynamic energy savings of a 4-way HER cache are by 25%, 85%, and 62%, respectively. These percentages are further improved (by 40%, 89%, and 68%, respectively) when the cache associativity is increased to 8 ways, while the performance loss with respect to both an 8-way conventional cache and the 4-way HER cache is minimal.

1 Introduction

As transistor features continue shrinking in future technologies, fabrication process variations make cache memory cells more unreliable at low voltages. If the voltage is lowered beyond a given reliable level, namely Vccmin, the probability of failure increases exponentially due to the higher sensitivity of the cell to parametric variations. The Vccmin of a given cache structure (e.g., L1 or L2 caches) is defined by the highest Vccmin of its memory cells, and it typically determines the Vccmin of the processor as a whole.

On the other hand, current microprocessors support different power modes. High-performance modes focus on speedup the workload, which requires high frequency and voltage levels. On the contrary, low-power modes work at minimum frequency/voltage levels to improve energy savings. However, a high Vccmin limits the ability to support

D. an Mey et al. (Eds.): Euro-Par 2013 Workshops, LNCS 8374, pp. 454–464, 2014.

lower power modes in order to further exploit the trade-off between performance and energy consumption.

Process variation affects in a different way the behavior of the cache memory cell depending on the technology. In fast Static Random-Access Memory (SRAM) cells, it induces Static Noise Margin (SNM) variability which causes errors [1,2,3] in some cells when working below Vccmin. Different approaches have been devised to deal with this problem [4,5,6]. Most existing proposals provide a fault-coverage (percentage of faults that can be detected/corrected) rather low (see Section 2). Since the failure probability increases as the transistors shrink, this coverage is insufficient for future technology nodes [7].

In contrast, in embedded Dynamic RAM (eDRAM) cells, which have been also used in some modern processors [8], errors basically lump into the cell retention time instead of altering the stored value. The worst case of these device variations determines the refresh period for the whole eDRAM array. In other words, eDRAM variation problems can be straightforwardly addressed by increasing the refresh rate. This fact is used in [9] to propose a Hard Error Recover (HER) cache, which combines SRAM and eDRAM technologies to deal with hard-error recovery at low-power mode while sustaining the performance at high-performance mode.

HER caches are implemented with one SRAM fast bank and *n-1* eDRAM banks, corresponding to the *n* ways in *n-way* associative cache. Since the distribution of SRAM and eDRAM cache blocks in a HER cache is defined by the cache associativity, it is expected that HER cache performance and energy consumption will be strongly affected by the specific cache geometry. In this paper, we study the behavior of the HER cache design when applied to a highly associative L1 cache like the one used in Intel Haswell microarchitecture [10].

Experimental results show that an 8-way HER cache saves area, leakage power, and dynamic energy with respect to a 4-way HER cache with the same storage capacity. Compared to a conventional cache, the 4-way cache working at low-power mode reduces area, leakage, and dynamic consumption by 25%, 85%, and 62%, respectively, whereas these percentages are up to 40%, 89%, and 68% for the 8-way HER approach. These benefits are obtained with minimal performance degradation with respect to the conventional scheme.

The rest of this paper is organized as follows. In the next section the most relevant approaches that allow the system to work below Vccmin are summarized. In section 3 a brief review of the HER cache is given. Experimental results, including area, performance and power, are presented in section 4. Finally, the authors give our conclusion in section 5.

2 Related Work

Due to inter and intra-die process parameter variations, memory cells that are marginally functional during manufacturing tests can undergo runtime failures due to voltage-thermal noise, soft errors, or aging effects. Depending on the impact of these effects, different segments of a memory array may move to different reliable design corners that can be determined using post-fabrication characterization. In [11], authors divide the cache in memory blocks and classify them into three types of blocks depending on the threshold voltage variation of their transistors (NMOS and PMOS). Then, different error correcting codes (ECC) are applied to each block according to this classification.

In [12] it is proposed an adaptive cache design that uses up to half the data array to store ECC information at low voltage to reduce energy. In high-performance mode, the whole data array is enabled. They add some hardware structures which are monitored by the operating system to select the desired reliability level. In low-power mode, some physical ways are used to store ECC information. For instance, to support *only* 4-bit error correction for each 64 bits segment at a 520mV supply voltage, the number of ways devoted to ECC can be as high as half the cache ways. In this case, performance degrades by 10% with respect to a defect-free cache.

In [5] it is presented a variation-aware cache architecture, which adaptively resizes the cache to avoid accessing to faulty blocks. When a faulty block is accessed, the bitmap information is used to select a non-faulty block in the same row. The cache implements a self-test circuitry, which tests the entire cache and detects faulty cells. Tests are conducted whenever the operating conditions change. Performance losses are by 1.5% and 5.7% in data and instruction caches, respectively.

In [4] authors propose two architectural techniques that enable microprocessor caches to operate at voltages below Vccmin. These techniques, namely Word-disable and Bit-fix, reduce the effective cache storage capacity by 50% and 25%, respectively. The word-disable scheme combines two consecutive cache lines in low voltage mode to form a single cache line without failing words. The bit-fix scheme uses a quarter of the ways to store positions and fix bits for failing bits in other ways of the set. A test is performed at boot time to identify those segments of the cache that fail at low voltage. The required circuitry increases area by 8% and reduces performance by 10%.

The Reconfigurable Energy-efficient Near Threshold (RENT) cache architecture [13] consists of a near threshold tolerant cache way and several conventional SRAM cache ways. The former way is implemented with large error resilient 8T cells to reduce energy consumption, whereas the remaining cache ways are implemented with conventional 6T SRAM cells to maintain the performance. The near threshold tolerant way is accessed first and, in case of miss, the conventional ways are then accessed. Unlike the above works, bit failures are avoided by choosing an appropriate supply voltage for each way. This scheme reduces energy by 86% at the expense of area due to the use of 8T cells.

Finally, refresh power potentially represents a large fraction of the overall system power, particularly during low-power states when the processor is idle. In [14] the cache refresh power is reduced by increasing the refresh time from 30μs (worst-case) to 440μs. This increase substantially mitigates power but causes errors due to capacitor discharges. This problem can be solved by using costly ECC codes. For instance, for the larger refresh time, authors need to apply the 5EC6ED ECC algorithm, which requires 51 extra bits for each 64B line (10% area overhead). To reduce ECC area overhead, the proposed solution uses a huge 1KB line size for the L3 cache instead of typical 64B lines. This technique reduces power by 93% compared to an eDRAM with no error correction, and by 66% compared to an eDRAM implementing single error correcting codes (SECDEC).

In general, these solutions allow the system to work below Vccmin by disabling those segments of the cache where one or more bits can fail, thus reducing the effective storage capacity. The highest fault coverage is achieved by [11], which can correct up to 6 bit-errors for each 64-bit block. Nevertheless, this is still less than 10% coverage. Providing higher coverages in these proposals could become prohibitive in terms of area, delay, or power.

In short, the presented state-of-the-art proposals will not match the coverage requirements of future technologies. Moreover, in [7], it is further argumented why less than 100% fault-coverage is unsuitable for fault-dominated future technology nodes.

3 HER Caches

The HER cache combines eDRAM and SRAM technologies in order to achieve 100% fault-coverage. For the data array, the HER cache uses k cache banks to implement an n-way set-associative cache, where k/n banks are implemented with SRAM technology and the remaining $k - k/n$ with eDRAM technology.

At high-performance, the HER cache works using the entire storage capacity and architectural decisions are devised to address performance losses. To achieve good performance, in the HER cache the MRU block of each cache set is always stored in an SRAM bank. Moreover, HER caches are designed with no refresh mechanism to reduce energy overhead. Instead, architectural mechanisms are introduced to ensure that no useful data is lost due to capacitor discharges.

At low-power, HER caches provide 100% fault-coverage in set-associative L1 data caches while reducing area and power with respect to a conventional cache. This is achieved by using eDRAM banks to keep copies of SRAM banks data (i.e. replicas). As process variation impacts eDRAM cells retention time but does not change their contents, these replicas enable the processor to recover from any number of SRAM bit failures due to manufacturing imperfections. In consequence, HER caches support 100% fault-coverage of errors due to process variation imperfections, which is a major design concern to be addressed in future technology nodes.

More details about HER caches rationale and implementation can be found in [9].

4 Experimental Results

The HER cache has been modeled on top of the SimpleScalar (with Alpha ISA) simulation framework [15] to obtain the execution time and memory events required for estimating dynamic energy (i.e., cache hits, misses, swaps, writebacks, etc.). All the bank contention induced by these events has also been modeled. The 8-way HER cache has a single cache bank built with SRAM technology, while the remaining banks are implemented with eDRAM. Cache access time, capacitance, area, leakage power, and dynamic energy per access type were estimated with CACTI 5.3 [16] for 45nm. The overall dynamic energy was calculated combining the results of both simulators.

All these results have been obtained for each operation mode, from now on referred to as *hp* (high-performance) and *lp* (low-power) modes, respectively. For the *hp* mode, it has been assumed a voltage/frequency pair of 1.3V/3GHz and no bit failures. Two

Table 1. Architectural machine parameters

Microprocessor core	
Issue policy	Out of order
Branch predictor type	Hybrid gShare/Bimodal: gShare has 14-bit global history plus 16K 2-bit counters Bimodal has 4K 2-bit counters Choice predictor has 4K 2-bit counters
Branch predictor penalty	10 cycles
Fetch, issue, commit width	4 instructions/cycle
ROB size (entries)	256
Memory hierarchy	
L1 data cache	32KB, 4-way and 8-way, 64 byte-line
L1 data cache access time	SRAM: 2-cycle in *hp*, 1-cycle in *lp* eDRAM: 4-cycle in *hp*, 2-cycle in *lp*
L2 data cache	512KB-8way, 64 byte-line, 10-cycle
Main memory access time	100-cycle

different voltage/frequency pairs have been studied in *lp* mode, referred to as *lp1* and *lp2*, respectively. The former assumes 0.7V/1.4GHz and the latter 0.5V/500MHz similar to [12]. The probability of failure for a 45nm node was calculated as 20% and 50% of the SRAM bits, respectively. Although some defective bits can be in the same line, the results presented assume the worst case, that is, all defective bits are located in different cache lines.

For comparison purposes, a conventional SRAM cache has also been modeled. In this scheme, no error failures are assumed regardless of the operation mode. At *hp* mode, the scheme is referenced as Conv cache and at *lp* as ZfConv (zero-failure conventional) cache.

Table 1 summarizes the main architectural parameters. Both integer (Int) and floating-point (FP) SPEC benchmarks [17] were run using the *ref* input sets. After skipping the initial 1B instructions, statistics were collected during 500M instructions.

4.1 Area

This section analyzes the area savings of the HER scheme compared to a conventional SRAM cache of the same storage capacity and number of ways. Table 2 shows the results (in mm^2) for a 45nm technology node, where SRAM and eDRAM cells occupy

Table 2. Tag array and data array areas (in mm^2) of both Conv cache and HER cache schemes

Cache	Tag array (mm^2)		Data array (mm^2)		Data array area	Total area
ways	Conv	HER	Conv	HER	savings (%)	savings (%)
4	0.015	0.030	0.498	0.355	29	25
8	0.015	0.030	0.850	0.490	42	40

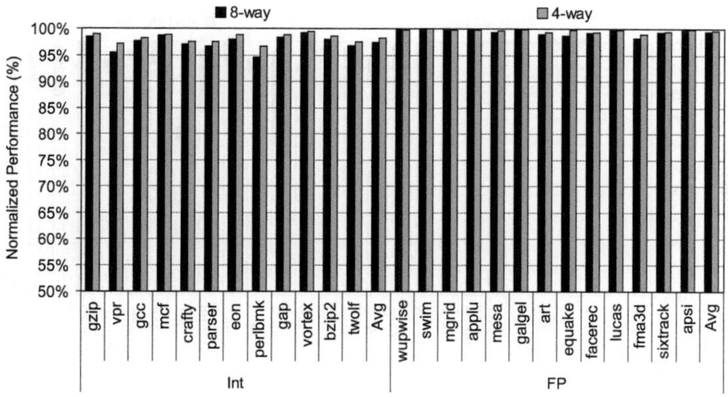

Fig. 1. Normalized performance (%) of the HER caches with respect to the 8-way Conv cache in *hp* mode

an area of $0.296\mu m^2$ and $0.062\mu m^2$, respectively, according to CACTI. The HER cache significantly reduces area thanks to the design is partly implemented with eDRAM technology. As expected, this reduction increases with the cache associativity. Compared to the Conv approach, the area reduction of the data array can be as much as 29% and 42% for 4-way and 8-way HER caches, respectively.

On the other hand, the HER cache uses special error-free SRAM cells to build the tag array, whose size is twice as large as the size of conventional SRAM cells [18]. Even considering both tag and data arrays, area savings are as large as 40% for the 8-way cache.

4.2 Performance Evaluation

Figure 1 shows, for each application, the normalized performance in *hp* mode of HER caches implemented with an *infinite* retention time (i.e. perfect capacitors) with respect to an 8-way conventional cache with the same storage capacity. As observed, the IPC loss is higher in the 8-way HER cache because it stores more blocks in *slow* eDRAM technology. Nevertheless, the performance degradation for Int benchmarks is on average only by 2.63% with respect to the Conv cache; and much lower (by 0.58%) for FP benchmarks. These percentages are by 1.93% and 0.38%, respectively, for the 4-way HER cache.

As real capacitors lose their contents over time, we calculated (as done in [9] for the 4-way HER cache) which is the minimum capacitance to match the performance of HER caches with an infinite retention time. In 8-way HER caches, at least 4fF, 14fF, and 62fF capacitors are required in *hp*, *lp1*, and *lp2* modes, respectively. Unfortunately, current trench capacitors only allow capacitances up to 30fF [19,20]. However, this limitation only affects *lp2* mode, and our experiments show that, compared to an 8-way ZfConv cache, the performance degradation is by 2.69% for Int benchmarks. For the 4-way HER cache, this percentage is by 2.54%.

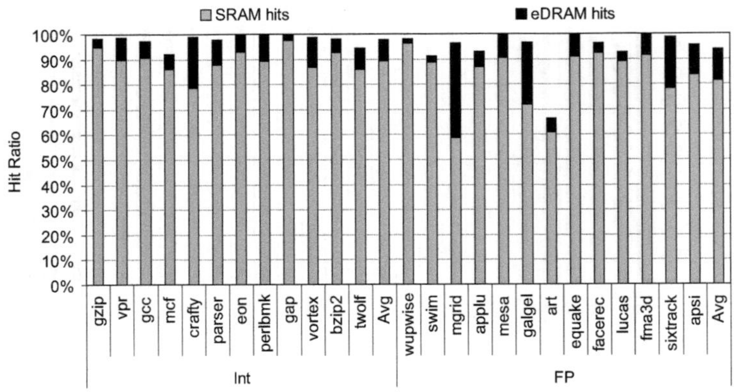

Fig. 2. Hit ratio (%) split into SRAM and eDRAM hits per benchmark for the HER cache in *hp* mode

Table 3. Hit ratio (%) broken down into SRAM, eDRAM, and eDRAM replica hits for the cache schemes across the studied operation modes

Bench. type	Hit ratio (%)	8-way				4-way			
		Conv	HER			Conv	HER		
		hp	*hp*	*lp1*	*lp2*	*hp*	*hp*	*lp1*	*lp2*
Int	SRAM	97.9	89.4	71.6	44.6	97.8	92.6	73.4	42.1
	eDRAM	–	8.5	8.2	8.1	–	5.2	4.7	4.7
	eDRAM replica	–	–	17.9	45.1	–	–	19.3	50.7
	total	97.9	97.9	97.8	97.8	97.8	97.8	97.5	97.5
FP	SRAM	93.7	81.6	66.0	41.2	93.7	86.7	68.8	41.9
	eDRAM	–	12.1	11.9	12.0	–	7.0	6.0	6.0
	eDRAM replica	–	–	15.7	40.4	–	–	17.9	44.8
	total	93.7	93.7	93.6	93.6	93.7	93.7	92.7	92.7

Figure 2 plots the cache hit ratio for each application in *hp* mode for the 8-way HER cache with an infinite retention time. The hit ratio has been split into hits in the SRAM and eDRAM banks. Most cache accesses (by 89% and 82% on average for Int and FP, respectively) are performed in the fast SRAM bank that holds the MRU data, so confirming the effectiveness of the HER cache's swap mechanism even in 8-way set-associative L1 caches.

Table 3 shows the average hit ratio of both cache schemes across the studied operation modes. For *lp* modes, hits in the eDRAM replica are also presented. The eDRAM hit ratio is higher in 8-way caches than in 4-way caches since the former have more eDRAM blocks. In contrast, for *lp* modes, the percentage of hits in the eDRAM replica way is lower in 8-way caches. This is because the data that potentially needs backup (SRAM blocks) are reduced to the half in such caches. For the same reason, the impact on the overall hit ratio of losing an eDRAM way for backups of the SRAM way is less remarkable in 8-way caches.

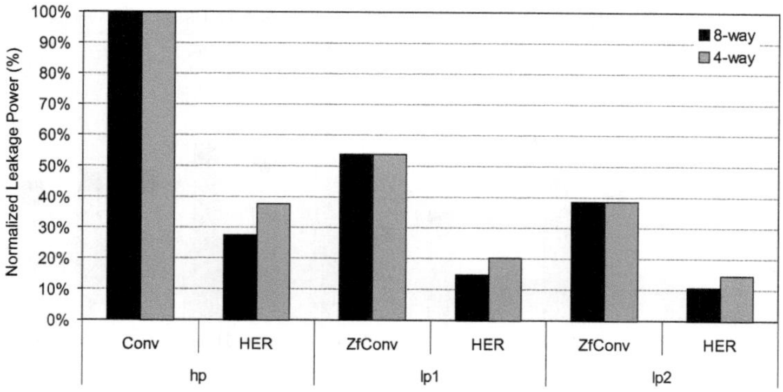

Fig. 3. Normalized leakage power (%) of the studied caches with respect to the Conv cache

4.3 Power and Energy Consumption

Figure 3 illustrates the normalized leakage with respect to the 8-way Conv approach. For HER caches, leakage currents decrease with the number of eDRAM ways since this technology minimizes leakage by design. In contrast, leakage consumption is roughly the same in both 4-way and 8-way conventional (Conv and ZfConv) approaches. This is due to these memories are only SRAM-based and they just reduce leakage because of the lower supply voltage in *lp* modes. Overall, leakage savings provided by the 8-way HER cache are as high as 73% in *hp* mode and 89% in *lp2* mode. These percentages are reduced to 62% and 85%, respectively, in the 4-way cache.

Figure 4(a) and Figure 4(b) plot the dynamic energy for 8-way and 4-way caches, respectively, normalized with respect to a conventional cache with the same storage capacity and number of ways. This consumption has been divided into five categories: SRAM hits, eDRAM hits, eDRAM replica hits, misses, and writebacks. The SRAM hits category includes the access to the eDRAM replica and the access to all the SRAM ways; the eDRAM hits category includes accessing both the SRAM way and the target eDRAM way. In addition, it also considers the energy due to swaps (unidirectional transfers in *lp* mode); the eDRAM replica hits category also takes into account the access to the SRAM faulty lines; the misses category includes not only the access to the SRAM part but also the unidirectional transfers in *hp* mode; and finally, the two latter categories include the energy consumed by both L1 and L2 cache accesses.

As can be seen, for a given operation mode and type of benchmark, the 8-way HER cache reduces the expenses in the SRAM hits category with respect to the 4-way HER cache. This is mainly due to the former accesses to a smaller part of the data array. The results in both eDRAM replica hits and misses category can be similarly reasoned. In addition, the energy due to misses is higher in 4-way caches because the number of such cache events decreases with the associativity. Minor differences can be seen in the writebacks category. In contrast, the consumption related to eDRAM hits increases in 8-way caches. This is due to in such caches more accesses are performed in eDRAM data, which in turn trigger swap operations. Nevertheless, the overall dynamic savings are larger in 8-way caches than in 4-way caches. For integer applications in *hp* mode,

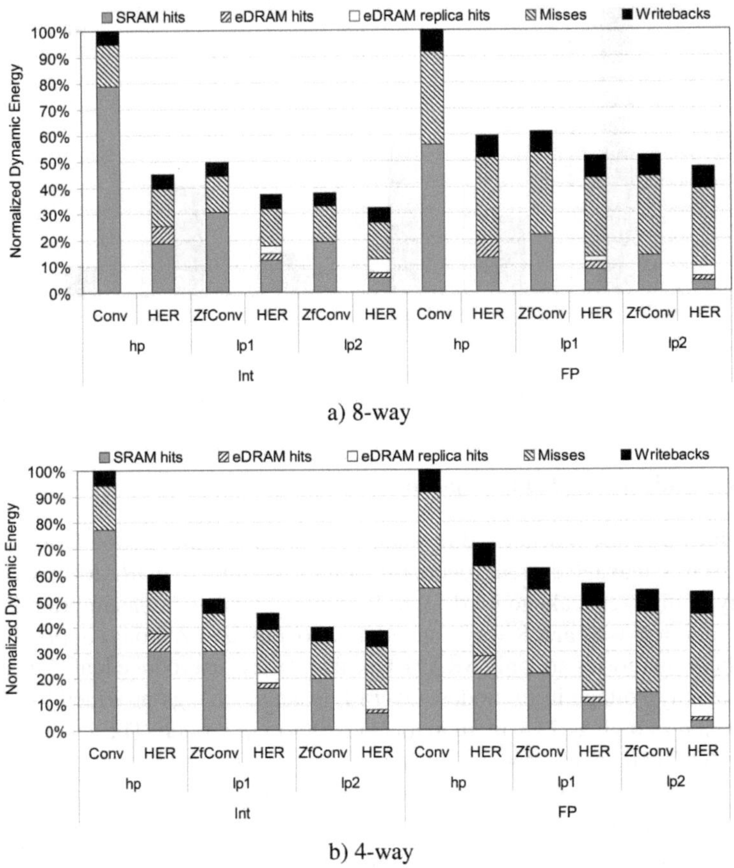

Fig. 4. Normalized dynamic energy (%) *categorized* with respect to the Conv cache

these benefits are by 55% with respect to Conv, while this percentage drops down to 40% for 4-way caches. In *lp2* mode, the dynamic energy reduction is by 66% and 62% in 8-way and 4-way HER caches, respectively.

5 Conclusions

In order to study the impact on performance and power consumption of the cache geometry on HER cache designs, this paper extends the work in [9] by increasing the associativity of the HER cache scheme.

Results show that in low-power mode, when compared to a 32KB-4way HER cache, a 32KB-8way HER cache reduces leakage and dynamic energy by 4.7% and 9.6%, respectively. When compared to a 32KB-4way low-power conventional SRAM cache, these values are by 89% and 68%. These energy savings are mainly due to the higher percentage of eDRAM banks present in the 8-way HER design.

In high-performance mode, when compared to the conventional SRAM cache, the performance losses of an 8-way HER cache are by 2.63% and 0.58%, for integer and floating-point benchmarks, respectively. These results are just a little worse than those of a 4-way HER cache (1.93% and 0.38%).

Finally, this paper also includes an analysis of the area savings provided by the 8-way HER cache. With respect to the conventional SRAM cache, it achieves by 42% data array area savings.

Acknowledgments. This work was supported by Generalitat de Catalunya (2009SGR1250), by FP7 program of the European Commission (TRAMS-248789), by Spanish Ministerio de Economía y Competitividad (MINECO) and by FEDER funds under Grant TIN2012-38341-C04-01 and TIN2010-18368.

References

1. Bhavnagarwala, A.J., et al.: The Impact of Intrinsic Device Fluctuations on CMOS SRAM Cell Stability. IEEE Journal of Solid-State Circuits 36(4), 658–665 (2001)
2. Mukhopadhyay, S., et al.: Modeling of Failure Probability and Statistical Design of SRAM Array for Yield Enhancement in Nanoscaled CMOS. IEEE Transactions on Computer-Aided Design of Integrated Circuits and Systems 24(12), 1859–1880 (2005)
3. Shirvani, P.P., McCluskey, E.J.: PADded Cache: A New Fault-Tolerance Technique for Cache Memories. In: Proceedings of the 17th IEEE VLSI Test Symposium, pp. 440–445 (1999)
4. Wilkerson, C., et al.: Trading off Cache Capacity for Reliability to Enable Low Voltage Operation. In: Proceedings of the 35th Annual International Symposium on Computer Architecture, pp. 203–214 (2008)
5. Agarwal, A., et al.: Process Variation in Embedded Memories: Failure Analysis and Variation Aware Architecture. IEEE Journal of Solid-State Circuits 40(9), 1804–1814 (2005)
6. Ansari, A., et al.: Archipelago: A Polymorphic Cache Design for Enabling Robust Near-Threshold Operation. In: Proceedings of the 17th International Symposium on High Performance Computer Architecture, pp. 539–550 (2011)
7. Nomura, S., et al.: Sampling + DMR: Practical and Low-overhead Permanent Fault Detection. In: Proceedings of the 38th Annual International Symposium on Computer Architecture, pp. 201–212 (2011)
8. Sinharoy, B., et al.: IBM POWER7 multicore server processor. IBM Journal of Research and Development 55(3) (2011)
9. Lorente, V., et al.: Combining RAM technologies for hard-error recovery in L1 data caches working at very-low power modes. In: Proceedings of the Design, Automation, and Test in Europe Conference, pp. 83–88 (2013)
10. Kanter, D.: Intel's Haswell CPU Microarchitecture, "Real World Technologies" (November 13, 2012), `http://www.realworldtech.com/haswell-cpu/`
11. Paul, S., et al.: Reliability-Driven ECC Allocation for Multiple Bit Error Resilience in Processor Cache. IEEE Transactions on Computers 60(1), 20–34 (2011)
12. Alameldeen, A.R., et al.: Adaptive Cache Design to Enable Reliable Low-Voltage Operation. IEEE Transactions on Computers 60, 50–63 (2011)
13. Dreslinski, R.G., et al.: Reconfigurable Energy Efficient Near Threshold Cache Architectures. In: Proceedings of the 41st Annual IEEE/ACM International Symposium on Microarchitecture, pp. 459–470 (2008)

14. Wilkerson, C., et al.: Reducing Cache Power with Low-Cost, Multi-bit Error-Correcting Codes. In: Proceedings of the 37th Annual International Symposium on Computer Architecture, pp. 83–93 (2010)
15. Burger, D., Austin, T.M.: The SimpleScalar Tool Set, Version 2.0. ACM SIGARCH Computer Architecture News 25(3), 13–25 (1997)
16. Thoziyoor, S., et al.: CACTI 5.1. Hewlett-Packard Laboratories, Palo Alto, Technical Report (2008)
17. spec2000: Standard Performance Evaluation Corporation, `http://www.spec.org/cpu2000`
18. Kulkarni, J.P., et al.: A 160 mV, Fully Differential, Robust Schmitt Trigger Based Subthreshold SRAM. In: Proceedings of the ACM/IEEE International Symposium on Low Power Electronics and Design, pp. 171–176 (2007)
19. Keeth, B., et al.: DRAM Circuit Design. Fundamental and High-Speed Topics. John Wiley and Sons, Inc., Hoboken (2008)
20. Mueller, W., et al.: Challenges for the DRAM Cell Scaling to 40nm. In: IEEE International Electron Devices Meeting 4, pp. 336–339 (2005)

Power Saving by NoC Traffic Compression

María Soler and José Flich

Universitat Politècnica de València
{msoler,jflich}@gap.upv.es
http://www.upv.es

Abstract. As technology advances, multiprocessor systems-on-chip (MPSoCs) increase with the number of components, relying on an efficient on-chip network (NoC). As the size of the system increases, NoC performance and power consumption become a central issue.

In this paper we present compression strategies at the NoC level reducing the number of transmitted flits and consequently the energy consumed. The provided mechanism relies on the abundance of memory data blocks filled with zeros in the analysed applications. We provide a hardware implementation for both compression and decompression at a generic network interface (NI). Results show the effectiveness of the compression and decompression mechanisms and the low overhead they introduce. The percentage of traffic reduced by the compression strategy (factor of 3) justifies the added resources.

Keywords: Compression, NoC, Network-on-Chip, Embedded systems.

1 Introduction

Networks-on-Chip (NoCs) [1] have been accepted as the way to efficiently implement communication inside a chip. In the embedded domain, multiprocessor systems-on-chip (MPSoCs) are being implemented, where multiple cores (different IPs) are integrated and interconnected with a specialised NoC.

As system size increases, allowed by technology evolution, the network becomes a principal component, both in terms of performance and power consumption. In this paper we focus on the power consumption of the NoC subsystem.

Traffic compression becomes an interesting approach to save power. Data streams (specially long messages) sent through the NoC can be compressed at injection and decompressed at ejection, saving power and even latency (shorter messages).

We tackle the compression of NoC traffic assuming a coherence protocol running on top of the NoC. This is becoming a general trend since ARM-based systems may accept coherence systems as the baseline design [2]. So, in this paper block memory transfers between the memory controller (MC) and the cache hierarchy have been chosen as the target traffic for compression.

A basic network interface (NI) has been taken as a baseline, only taking into account the existence of a decoupling buffer at the NI for the injection of packets,

D. an Mey et al. (Eds.): Euro-Par 2013 Workshops, LNCS 8374, pp. 465–476, 2014.

and a reception buffer at the NI for the ejection of packets. Communication between the core and the NI is not affected and is completely orthogonal to the solutions provided.

Two different solutions may be applied: parallel and sequential compression. Parallel compression is more resource demanding, but it is also a better informed technique, allowing for a more effective compression. In parallel compression, the end node transfers a whole memory block to the NI (512 bits in our case), with the corresponding buffering overhead. At ejection, however, the NI needs to reconstruct the message and thus, some extra latency is incurred before delivering the complete message to the end node.

The solution we propose is orthogonal to the use of virtual channels. Indeed, an NoC with different virtual channels can be built up by physically replicating one VC-less network. Also, the baseline flit format will be specified and customised to the compression solution provided. Compression information needs to be injected together with the packets so that it can be decompressed at destination. Also, information for the coherence protocol must be included (source node address and memory address). Flit size is assumed to be 32 bits.

With these assumptions, we achieve a high compression rate, thus reducing long-message traffic by a factor of 3, by introducing an overhead of 8.91% in area and 24% in power. However, the large compression factor achieved allows not only to cancel but obtain positive power reductions.

The rest of the paper is organised as follows. In Section 2, the Related Work is summarised. Then, in Section 3, the compression opportunities performed in the frame of the vIrtical project [3] are presented. Subsequently, in Section 4, we introduce the NI taken as a baseline; in Section 5 we present our compression strategy; in section 6 the results obtained are show, followed by a discussion in Section 7 closing by briefly acknowledging our sponsors in Section 8 and giving our final conclusions in Section 8.

2 Related Work

Compression of transmitted information does not seem to be a largely explored field. There are many papers on test data compression for NoCs. Some examples can be found at [4][5] among others. Since compression is performed offline and off the NoC, the strategies explained in these papers are not applicable to our needs. Other papers [6] also deal with compression of the routing table, which again is not what we were looking for. Some papers however study NoC compression strategies, which require special attention. Some examples of these are [7][8][9][10][11][12].

In [7] the USBR, a real time compression technique, removes the most significant bits which do not change, and sends some extra information (which bits change and how long the data block is). This technique is not applicable to the type of data involved in our research.

The authors in [8], integrate compression and decompression with a coherence protocol by adding a protocol processing core. Avoiding unnecessary modification of the existing components prevents us from choosing an option that adds an extra core.

In [9] two compression strategies are presented. The first one, named Cache Compression is not transmission-oriented. The second one is called Compression in the NIs and consists in compressing the information right before injecting. The drawbacks of this second strategy is that it needs to integrate such modules in every NI, when it is not necessary for us, and that it uses a table-based frequent-pattern compression.

Adaptive data compression for on chip network performance optimisation is presented in [10]. It uses a table-based strategy, whilst the nature of the data characteristic to our applications of interest makes using a table redundant.

A similar approach is shown in [11], except that instead of frequent patterns, it is based on frequent values. The authors claim that with a small code-book for end to end communications, that does not need to be the same among different cores, they reduce power consumption in the router up to a 16.7%. This proposal is again not applicable to our needs.

Finally, in [12] an interesting proposal is presented: Another table-based coherence protocol-integrated technique is presented. In this case it allows to completely eliminate some transmissions (in the best case), simplifying and fastening miss handling. Still, tables are redundant to eliminate zero strings.

The particular solution discussed here is not compliant with any of these found in previous literature. It is a new proposal based on the massive appearance of zeros in the applications analysed for the vIrtical project.

3 Compression Opportunities

In the frame of the vIrtical project, representative workloads for the targeted architecture were selected and analysed, concluding that long strings of only zeros are very common in traffic between L2 and the memory controller. Three cases can be distinguished:

- Aligned Consecutively Repeating Patterns (ACRP), consecutive and aligned to byte size.
- non-Aligned Consecutively Repeating Patterns (nACRP), consecutive but not necessarily aligned to byte size.
- non-Aligned non-Consecutively Repeating Patterns (nAnCRP), not necessarily aligned to any data size nor necessarily consecutive.

Table 1 shows the percentage of flits transmitted with the nACRP pattern type, which is the most frequent one. The table shows the results for two encryption applications: sha and aes. The Secure Hash Algorithm (SHA) is a family of cryptographic hash functions. In our case sha1 and sha2 are used as test cases: sha1 is a 160-bit hash function similar to MD5 and sha2 can be further divided into two functions sha256 and sha512 that differ in word size (32-bit and 64-bit respectively). Of the various implementation of the Advanced Encryption Standard (AES) we chose the mode Encryption Code Book (ECB) that encrypts and decrypts each block separately (in our case with two block sizes, 128-bit and 256-bit).

The table shows that 93.45% of the bits transmitted between L2 and the memory controller fall under the nACRP pattern. Due to flit alignment and length restrictions, not all these bits will be eliminated, but over 80% of the transmitted information can in fact be compressed with high resulting benefits.

Table 1. Comparison nACRP zeros

sha			aes-ecb	
1	256	512	128	256
93,45	93,26	93,42	92,83	92,74

4 Baseline Network Interface (NI)

Figure 1 shows the schematic of the NI used as a baseline. It implements two ports connected to the network, one in each direction (for injection and ejection). Injection logic is driven by the node connected to the network (through the NI) and is specific to the protocol used (AMBA, AXI, OCP, ...) Likewise, the NI has an ejection buffer where messages received from the network are temporarily stored and delivered to the node. The logic to read from this buffer is also protocol dependent.

The NI has three other logic blocks, implemented in the solutions provided. The header builder that prepares the header of the flits to be injected. Two logic blocks for the compression/decompression solution. These blocks are intimately linked to the buffers. Finally, both at injection/reception flow control logic is also implemented: the Stop&Go protocol.

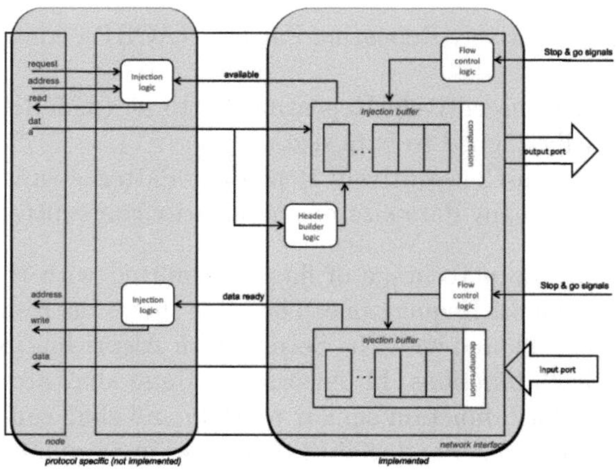

Fig. 1. Baseline NI

The NI evaluated in this work does not support virtual channels. Indeed, injection and ejection buffers consist of a single FIFO queue each. To fully support virtual channels (for correctness) and decouple request and reply messages, both the standard (not implemented) part of the NI and the network are replicated. The results obtained for this paper in terms of area must be multiplied by the number of virtual channels needed. This is partially motivated by the fact that compression logic needs to be applied only to the channel used by long messages carrying memory blocks since the final solution will require separate NIs for the request layer with no compression and the reply layer with built-in compression logic.

5 Parallel Compression Strategy

In this section we develop the compression/decompression strategies. Long packets carry a 64-byte memory block, divided in 20 chunks of 25 bits each plus a remainder (the 12 most significant bits). If all the bits of a chunk are set to zero, the chunk is not transmitted. In order to support chunks and align them to flits, we need to define the packet format for long messages. Since short messages are not compressible, their packet format has been omitted.

In Figure 2 we see the packet format for long messages: FT is a two bit flit-type field in every flit; DST and SRC (7-bit each) are respectively the destination and source of the message; $ADDR_{high}$ is made up of the most significant half of the memory address (16 of 32 bits), while $ADDR_{low}$ corresponds to the least significant half; CM is a command of the coherence protocol; $CHUNK_{ID}$ is the flit-number (2-21) and PAYLOAD is the part of the message the flit carries.

For a memory block of all zeros only flits 0 and 1 will be inject into the network. This is the maximum compression achievable with this strategy. Notice that these two flits carry extra fields (address, source, destination), typically non-zero.

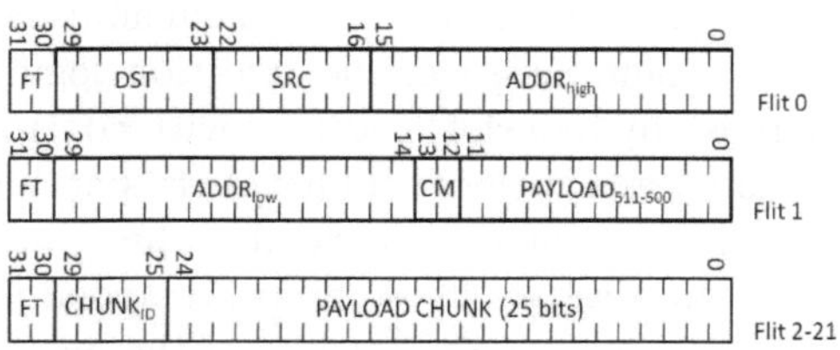

FT	Description
00	Non valid
01	Tail
10	Payload
11	Header

Fig. 2. Long packet format (memory blocks) for parallel compression

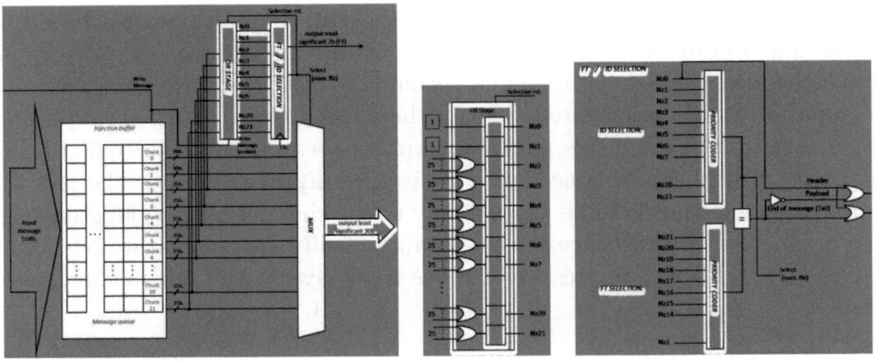

(a) General Picture (b) OR stage (c) FT/ID selection stage

Fig. 3. Injection NI with compression

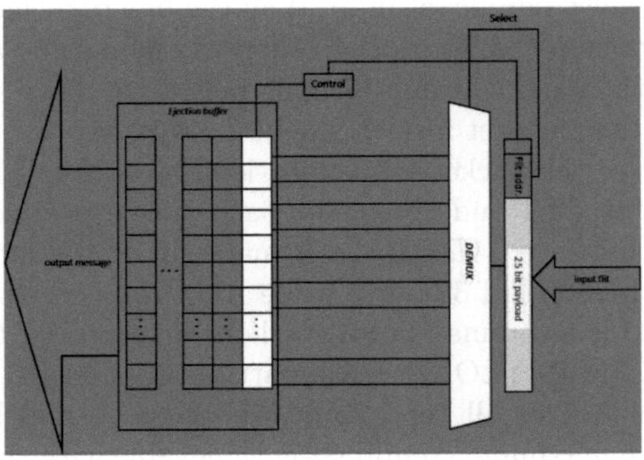

Fig. 4. NI ejection with compression mechanism

5.1 Implementation

Figure 3(a) shows the parallel compression implementation globally. When a node requests to inject a new message, the injection logic copies it into the injection buffer (if there is any free slot) together with control information (destination node, source node, and memory address) thus adding 558 bits in total (packet). The whole packet is treated as payload, although the first 58 bits (the first two flits) are never compressed. Those bits correspond to the source, destination, address, and the 12 most significant bits of the message.

The buffer slot is logically divided in 20 chunks of 25 bits, plus the aforementioned 58 bits (chunks 0 & 1). The chunks are sent to the OR stage (Figure 3(b)) where all-zero strings will be detected. The output, stored in a 22-bit register, Nz, (notice that the first two chunks are not computed with an OR gate but are always set) will be used both to compute the flit type and select the next flit to be injected. This selection drives the multiplexer shown in Figure 3(a). The Nz register is written once per message injected when the message is exposed at the head of the queue (in the first slot), and can be driven by the write signal of the buffer. The Nz register is fed to the FT/ID selection logic (Figure 3(c)) that selects the next flit to inject by means of a priority encoder. The encoder selects the most significant bit set to one. The Select signal is then used to drive the multiplexer at the injection port, as well as to reset the appropriate Nz bit so that, at the next cycle, a different chunk is selected (if any).

In addition, the FT/ID block computes the flit type (see the table in Figure 2) by an additional priority encoder with the Nz bits input in reverse order. This identifies the tail (since the header is self-identified and all other flits are payload).

The decompression strategy, shown back in Figure 4, is much simpler since we do not need to calculate anything. When the first two flit arrive the 30-bit payload are placed at the beginning of the reception buffer and the 25-bit chunks are reset. If the second flit is not the tail, all subsequent flits are placed according to their flit address (bits 29 to 25 of the flit). The tail flit activates the end of message signal.

6 Evaluation Results

We present the results in two separate parts. In the first part, we provide compression effectiveness by analyzing the percentage of traffic being really compressed. For this, we use our simulation platform and inject the application memory access traces obtained in the vIrtical framework. In the second part, we focus our attention on the implementation overheads in area, power and operating frequencies. The discussion section is focused on the combination of both parts.

6.1 Compression Rate Achieved

The compression rate achieved has been analysed by simulation with gMemNoCsim. The scenario modelled is shown in Figure 5(a). Four cores are attached to the same router. The cores are modelled by private L1 caches. Also, an L2 cache is attached to the same router. The memory controller (MC) is attached to a neighbor router.

An invalidation directory-based coherence protocol with MOESI is implemented. Flit size is set to 32 bits, short messages sized to 64 bits (2 flits) and long messages to 512 bits (block size). The size of both injection and ejection buffers will be varied in number of slots (1, 2, 4 & 8) and slot width (32 & 558).

Figure 5(b) shows the traffic between the L2 cache and the memory controller. There is a significant traffic reduction in all the applications analysed. On average, traffic is reduced by a factor of 3.5.

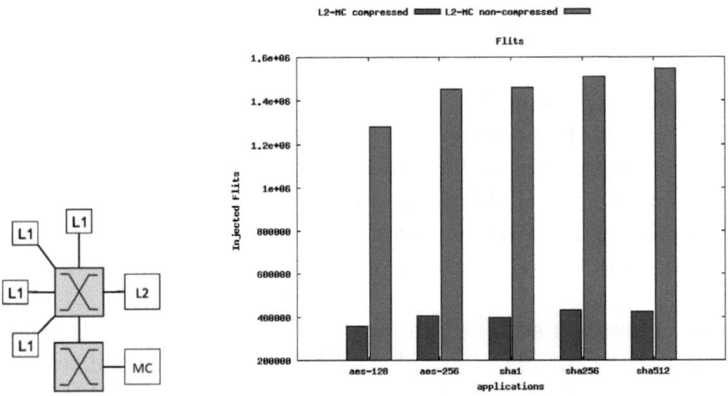

(a) Simulated scenario (b) Number of flits injected into the NoC

Fig. 5. Simulated scenario and result graph

6.2 Implementation Overheads

The compression design has been synthesised using the 45nm technology open source Nangate [45nm. FreePDK] with Synopsys Design Compiler 7 [13]. Table 2 shows the area (in nm^2) for the injection and ejection parts of the NI, both with no compression (baseline) and with built-in compression.

Table 2. Area overheads. Injection. 558-bit slots

	Injection					Ejection				
	No compression		Compression		Overhead	No compression		Compression		Overhead
Slots	Area	/1 slot	Area	/1 slot		Area	/1 slot	Area	/1 slot	
1	6587.09	1	7768.6	1	17.94%	5710.4	1.00	5741.8	1.00	0%
2	12156.7	1.85	13313.9	1.71	9.52%	11168.3	1.95	11788.5	2.05	6%
4	23444.7	3.56	24789.3	3.19	5.74%	22334.2	3.91	25120.6	4.37	12%
8	45839.2	6.96	47911.5	6.17	4.52%	45823.3	8.02	52134.6	9.08	14%

Table 3. Power consumption. Injection & ejection. 558-bit slots

	Injection			Ejection		
Slots	No Compression	Compression	Overhead	No Compression	Compression	Overhead
1	3.104 mW	5.455 mW	75.74%	6.231 mW	6.475 mW	4%
2	7.733 mW	12.62 mW	63.19%	13.32 mW	12.59 mW	-6%
4	16.14 mW	25.72 mW	59.36%	24.93 mW	28.03 mW	12%
8	34.39 mW	50.86 mW	47.89%	56.22 mW	57.07 mW	1%

This trend is different for injection and ejection. For one slot, the compression method takes 18% more area. For the ejection part of the NI the impact is negligible.

Now, let us turn our attention to power consumption. Power has been estimated by using Cadence Encounter 7 [14] both for Place&Route and measurements. Table 3 shows the power consumed by both the injection and ejection part of the NI with and without compression capabilities. As the number of slots increases, percentages of power consumption keep the same. It must be noted that the power consumption achieved by injecting less flits onto the network is not accounted in these tables. In the case of ejection, power consumption overhead is negligible.

In Table 4 we show the minimum periods necessary for each buffer to work properly. These results were obtained by using PrimeTime [15]. As can be seen, a pipelined approach may be required to adjust the design period.

Table 4. Timing overheads. Injection & ejection. 558-bit slots.

	Injection			Ejection		
Slots	No compression	Compression	Overhead	No compression	Compression	Overhead
1	0.63	1.44	128.57%	0.50	0.55	10%
2	0.66	1.74	163.64%	0.65	0.67	3%
4	0.77	2.04	164.94%	0.68	0.78	15%
8	0.92	2.46	167.39%	0.77	0.83	7%

7 Discussion

In this section we compound the results in Section 6 for a possible NI being used by the coherence protocol. Such a NI will be made of different components, servicing different message classes of the coherence protocol (different injector and ejector configurations).

Table 5 shows the area overheads and power consumption of the NI with no compression for 32-bit slots. The numbers in Table 5 are valid for both injection and ejection. These components will be used to handle short control messages of the protocol.

For the number of slots at each component we need to consider slot and flit sizes. Indeed, wide slots will need different network cycles to inject the whole message, while thin slots will need fewer cycles. Therefore, it is reasonable to use fewer slots for long messages than for short messages. We select one slot for large messages and two slots for short messages. With all these considerations, we derive the results by adding the different overheads previously presented. Table 6 shows the results achieved.

To get an idea of the potential benefits of this compression strategy, we have derived the approximate power consumption of the network per flit for both the baseline NI and our compression-enhanced implementation. In the graph in Figure 6, the X-axis corresponds to the compression rate [0:1] and the Y-axis

Table 5. Area and power. Injection & ejection. 32-bit slots.

Slots	Area	Power
1	314.32	0.309 mW
2	655.20	0.826 mW
4	1321.25	1.791 mW
8	2643.48	3.589 mW

Table 6. Overhead of the whole NI

NI component	Area	Overhead	Power	Overhead
Inject long msg. Compression. 1 slot.	7768.6	17.94	5.455	75.74
Eject long msg. Compression. 1 slot.	5741.8	0	6.475	3.91
Inject/Eject short msg. No compression. 2 slots.	655.20	0	0.826	0
Total	14820,8	8.91%	13.582	24%

corresponds to the difference in power consumption between our solution and the baseline (we have taken as a baseline a NI with one injector and one ejector of two 32-bit slots each). We have only taken into account the long message network, since the other network is common to both and would be nullified.

In the graph in Figure 6 we can see that depending on long message injection rate, we can save different amounts of power, but in any case the compression rate needed is 0.3. Since our compression rate is much beyond the needed 30%, it is assured that with data that follows the pattern of the applications studied some power would be saved.

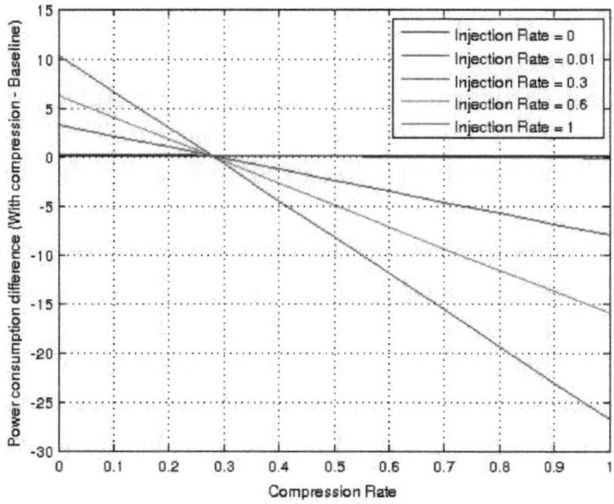

Fig. 6. Difference in power consumption by compression-rate (different injection rates)

8 Conclusions

In this paper we have provided the results obtained in the frame of the vIrtical project. Our goal was to design and analyse compression strategies at the NoC level, saving communication costs, by reducing the number of transmitted flits. The provided mechanism relies on the abundance of memory data blocks filled with zeros, thus easily compressible by using a detection strategy.

Our compression mechanism avoids sending flits without information (i.e. not sending flits that only consist of zeros). This technique is both easily applied and highly efficient. This compression scheme is only applied to long messages (a full memory block, 512 bits), not to short messages (of only 2 flits).

The results displayed in the previous section show the effectiveness of the compression and decompression mechanisms and the low overhead they introduce. The percentage of traffic reduced by the compression strategy (a factor of 3.5) justifies the overheads in resources for compression and decompression. The area overhead for the compression and decompression mechanisms required for a system with coherence support is 8.91% whereas the added power consumption is 24%.

Depending on long message injection rate, we can save different amounts of power, but in any case the compression rate needed is 0.3 (we need to send at least 30% less flits in order to get some power benefit). Since our compression rate is much beyond the needed 30%, it is assured that with data that follows the pattern of the applications studied some power would be saved.

Acknowledgements. This work has been supported by the VIRTICAL project (grant agreement n. 288574) which is funded by the European Commission within the Research Programme FP7.

References

1. Gilabert, F., et al.: Designing network on-chip architectures in the nanoscale era (2010)
2. ARM Limited: AMBA AXI and ACE Protocol Specification (2013)
3. VIRTICAL: sw/hw extensions for heterogenous multicore platforms
4. Froeseand, V., et al.: Reusing noc-infrastructure for test data compression. In: VTS 2010 (2010)
5. Chakiand, S., et al.: Binary difference based test data compression for noc based socs. In: ISVLSI, pp. 114–119. IEEE (2012)
6. Palesiand, M., et al.: A method for router table compression for application specific routing in mesh topology noc architectures. In: SAMOS (2006)
7. Oggand, S., et al.: Improved data compression for serial interconnected network on chip through unused significant bit removal. In: VLSID (2006)
8. Vittanalaand, L., et al.: Integrating memory compression and decompression with coherence protocols in distributed shared memory multiprocessors. In: ICPP 2007 (2007)
9. Dasand, R., et al.: Performance and power optimization through data compression in network-on-chip architectures. In: HPCA (2008)

10. Yuho, J., et al.: Adaptive data compression for high-performance low-power on-chip networks. MICRO 41 (2008)
11. Zhouand, P., et al.: Frequent value compression in packet-based noc architectures (2009)
12. An, B.: Efficient data packet compression for cache coherent multiprocessor systems. In: DCC 2012 (2012)
13. Synopsys, Inc.: Design Compiler User Guide (2011)
14. Cadence Design Systems, Inc.: Encounter User Guide (2011)
15. Synopsys, Inc.: Prime Time User Guide (2011)

A Lightweight Network of IDs to Quickly Deliver Simple Control Messages

Mario Lodde and José Flich

Universitat Politècnica de València, Spain

Abstract. Most of the network traffic in a Chip Multiprocessor (CMP) is due to messages exchanged by the caches according to the cache coherence protocol. Different types of messages have different requirements as far as latency and bandwidth are concerned, so the Network-on-Chip (NoC) should be tailored to fit the needs of each class of messages to maximize overall chip performance.

In this work we extend the Gather Network, a recently proposed dedicated lightweight network which is used for the transmission of many-to-one acknowledgement messages, and adapt it to transmit unicast acknowledgements, obtaining a dedicated network which we call Network of IDs. Evaluation results with Splash-2 and PARSEC applications show that the Network of IDs is able to deliver unicast acknowledgements in a few clock cycles, relieving the NoC from 4.5% of the traffic on average and reducing total energy by 4% on average and up to 8% for some applications.

1 Introduction

Current chip multiprocessors include tens of cores in a single chip, typically organized in a regular structure. A tile-based design is particularly appealing, since design efforts can be focused on a single modular component which is then replicated to build the final system. Figure 1 show the sample system we assume in this work: a 16-core CMP is built replicating a tile which includes a core, a private L1 cache, a bank of L2 cache and a network switch. The Network-on-Chip (NoC) used to connect the tiles is a 4×4 2-D mesh.

Different cores communicate through shared memory, thus the necessity to implement a cache coherence protocol to keep coherent the data stored in the on-chip cache hierarchy. Since most of the traffic in the NoC is due to messages injected by the caches according to the coherence protocols, the NoC and the coherence protocol should be co-designed to achieve the best chip performance, adapting the NoC to meet the requirements of the traffic pattern of coherence messages and tailoring the coherence protocol to efficiently use the resources provided by the NoC.

Various research works have been published in the near past tackling these challenges, which are becoming more and more critical as the number of cores in CMP systems increases. Typically, coherence messages are classified depending on the size: on the one hand there are long data messages, which are sent

D. an Mey et al. (Eds.): Euro-Par 2013 Workshops, LNCS 8374, pp. 477–487, 2014.

answering a block request or when a dirty cache line is replaced in L1; on the other hand there are short control messages, such as block requests, invalidation messages and acknowledgements. If the NoC flit size is set to be equal to the short message size, there are no bandwidth issues as far as short messages are concerned and design efforts can focus on reducing the network latency; data messages however will not fit in a flit and their latency will be higher. If the flit size is as wide as the long message size, data messages will fit in a flit but network resources will be underutilized when a short message is transmitted.

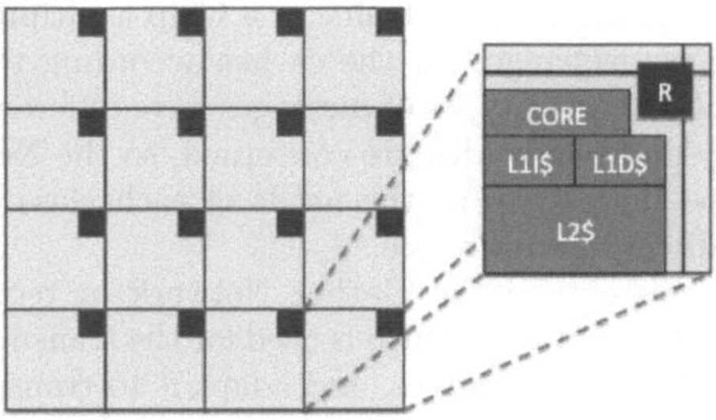

Fig. 1. Tiled CMP system

Another classification can be done depending on whether a coherence message is unicast (e.g. data messages) or it involves collective communication, both one-to-many (e.g. invalidation messages sent to the sharers or broadcast requests used in Dir_0B protocols like Hammer [1]) and many-to-one (e.g. invalidation acknowledgements).

Messages can be classified also depending on the amount of information they deliver: a block request message, for instance, must specify at least the requested block's address, the ID of the requestor and of destination node and the request type (load or store); a data message must specify at least the block address, the destination node's ID, the data type (shared or exclusive) and must contain the data block. All these messages thus need to be mapped to a packet structure which includes proper fields to store that information. Other coherence messages however do not deliver any information at all: if we consider invalidation acknowledgements which are sent by the sharers to the requestor of a block after a write request, the only field which is really needed is the ID of the destination node; if we consider in-order cores, even the block address is redundant since the requestor is blocked waiting for the reception of the acknowledgments. However, these messages are typically transmitted through the NoC using the same short message structure of requests, thus wasting NoC resources and power to transmit a packet in which most of the fields are not used or redundant. Basing on these considerations, we recently proposed a lightweight control network, called the Gather Network [4], used to collect many-to-one acknowledgements in invalidation-based coherence protocols. In this paper we extend the Gather Network and adapt it to transmit unicast acknowledgements (e.g. writeback acknowledgements or directory unblock messages). Evaluation results of our proposal with various applications of the Splash-2 and PARSEC benchmark suites show that unicast acknowledgements are delivered in a few clock cycles (2.5 on average) and the traffic in the regular NoC is reduced by 4.5% on average, leading to an average 4% reduction of total NoC energy.

The rest of this paper is organized as follows: in Section 2 we briefly describe the Gather Network, in Section 3 we extend the Gather Network to allow the transmission of unicast messages, in Section 4 we provide some evaluation results, then Section 5 describes the related work and in Section 6 we draw the conclusions.

2 Gather Network

The Gather Network is a dedicated control network that can transmit, gather and deliver simple control messages. It was specifically designed to manage many-to-one acknowledgements generated by cache coherence protocols in tiled CMP systems. These messages are very simple and the information they include is implicit in the message itself: since the destination node is blocked while it's waiting to receive all the expected acknowledgement messages, the only necessary information these messages need to include is the destination node address. In its first implementation [2], [3] the Gather Network was used to transmit, gather and deliver many-to-one acknowledgements sent by L1 caches in broadcast-based coherence protocols like Hammer when a request is broadcasted by the home L2 bank; since each request is broadcasted to all L1 caches, the block requestor always receives N-1 acknowledgements, where N is the number of cores in the system. This first implementation used a very simple logic providing a very low latency and an extremely low area overhead. The whole Gather Network is composed by a set of subnetworks, each subnetwork being associated to a different tile.

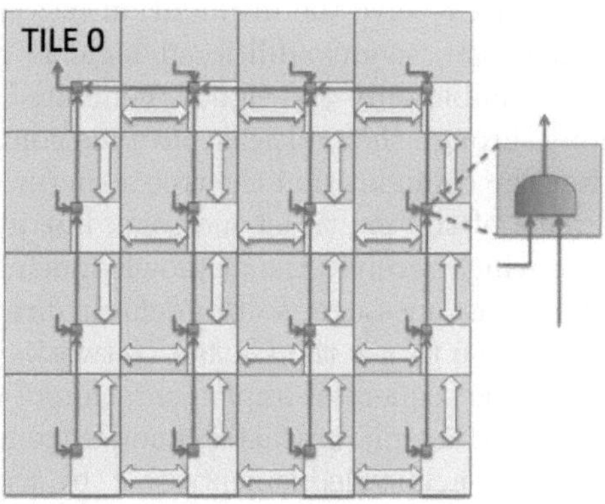

Fig. 2. Logical view of the Gather Network for tile 0

Figure 2 shows the structure of the subnetwork associated to the upper-left tile (Tile 0[1]): it is basically a tree of AND gates, with Tile 0 being the destination at the root of the AND tree and all the other tiles at the leaves. When a tile wants to send an acknowledgement to Tile 0, it just has to set its output of the subnetwork associated to Tile 0; once all the tiles have set their outputs, the output of the AND tree will be set and Tile 0 is notified of the reception of all the acknowledgements. This completely combinational design has been implemented with Synopsis DC and the area overhead of the whole Gather Network resulted to be 2.3% of the area of a single switch, while its critical path resulted to be lower than the slowest module of a switch or lower than twice the latency of the slowest module of a switch depending on the design parameters, meaning that an acknowledgement message can be transmitted in one or two clock cycles respectively between two opposite corners of the CMP.

This simple implementation has some drawbacks:

- since it requires one subnetwork for each tile, its wiring requirements grow with the number of tiles, thus limiting its scalability to a system with tens of tiles (for larger systems the size of the Gather Network would be comparable to the size of the regular NoC).
- this design only allows one pending request for each core; out-of-order cores which can have up tp N outstanding requests would require N subnetwork, thus limiting the scalability.

To address these issues, we implemented the logical behavior of the combinational implementation with sequential logic [4]. This second version of the Gather Network uses sequential modules at each switch, which communicate transmitting the ID of the acknowledgement's destination node, thus improving the scalability since the wiring requirements are reduced to the logarithm in base two of the number of tiles in the CMP.

Both the sequential and the combinational implementations however can be used without coherence protocol modifications only with broadcast-based protocols, since all nodes participate in every acknowledgment phase; this is not true in directory-based coherence protocols: in that case, only the nodes who hold a shared copy of a block receive the invalidation message and answer with the acknowledgement message, so an additional logic is needed to configure the Gather Network and enable only the signals generated by those nodes [3]; the configuration is done through the multicast invalidation message sent by the home L2 bank, and after the configuration the tree structure of the enabled outputs reflect the same path of the multicast message, but in opposite direction. This means that the tile which receives the acknowledgments must be the same tile which issued the multicast message, so the default directory protocol must be slightly modified to be able to use the Gather Network.

In this work we assume the sequential implementation of the Gather Network and adapt the modules to transmit unicast acknowledgements; this allows to use the Gather Network for acknowledgements sent by the home L2 bank as

[1] Tiles are numbered 0 to 16 starting from the upper-left corner of the chip and descending row by row.

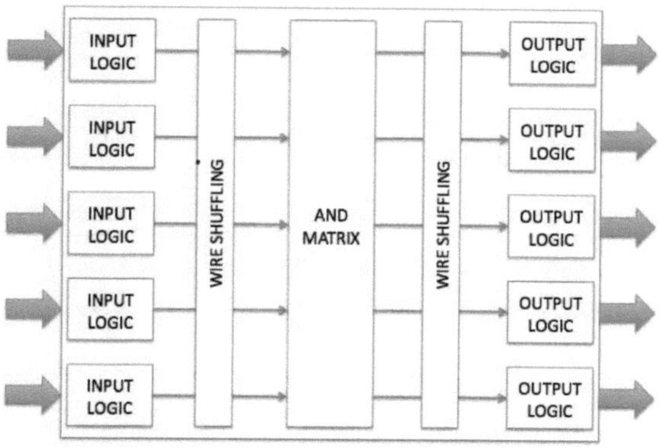

Fig. 3. Network of ID's module at each switch

answer to a writeback message (replacement in the L1 cache) and for invalidation acknowledgements in directory-based coherence protocols without any protocol modification. Since the use of this improved version is not limited to gather operations, we'll call it our Network of IDs.

3 Network of IDs

The Gather Network sequential module can be used to transmit unicast acknowledgements after some simple modification. Figure 3 shows the main structure of this module: the messages coming from neighboring modules or from the local node are processed by an input logic which decodes the destination ID. The decoded signals are grouped by destination node and sent to the AND matrix, where the collective acknowledgement is generated and sent to the proper output port. The structure of the messages exchanged by the Network of ID's modules is shown in Figure 4: for a 4×4 system, four bits are used to codify the destination node's ID and an additional bit indicates whether the message is a unicast acknowledgement or not.

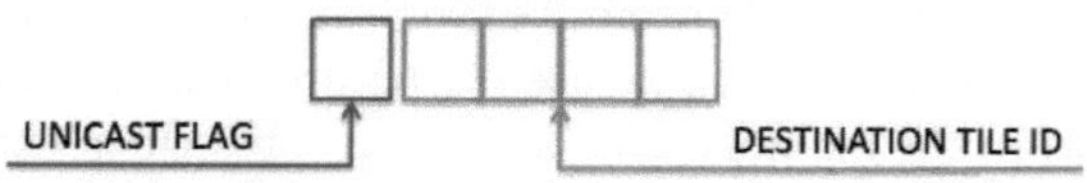

Fig. 4. Network of ID's message structure

Figure 5 shows the main blocks more in detail: at the Input logic the ID is separated from the unicast flag and decoded through a demultiplexer. The AND matrix has an AND gate for each node in the system; signal coming from different ports and destined to the same node are grouped at the same AND gate, then the output of each AND gate is ORed with the unicast flag and the resulting signal is sent to the proper output port, where it is encoded and transmitted to the next hop.

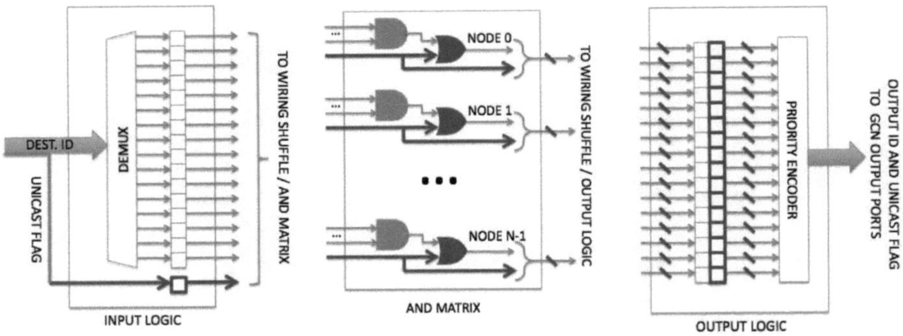

Fig. 5. Input logic, AND matrix and Output logic schemes

The additional logic needed by the network of IDs is marked with thicker lines: at the input logic, the unicast flag is decoupled from the destination node ID and sent to the AND matrix, where it is used to bypass the output signal of the AND gate correspondent to the destination node; at the output ports, an additional bit per destination is added to the registers to mark whether the outbound message must have the unicast flag set or not.

The module has been implemented using the 45nm technology open source Nangate [5] library with Synopsys DC. Cadence Encounter has been used to perform the Place&Route. The additional logic increases the modules area by 47% (the area of the final design is $0.610 \times 10^{-3} mm^2$), which means that each Network of IDs module introduces a 3.38% area overhead compared to the basic NoC switch we assumed in this work.

4 Evaluation

In this Section we provide some evaluation results of the Network of IDs. We implemented the NoC, the Network of IDs and the cache hierarchy of a 4×4 CMP system using our in-house cycle-accurate NoC and cache hierarchy simulator. Since our simulator is trace-driven, we used Graphite [6] and Sniper [7] multi-core simulators to capture the memory accesses of the cores when executing different applications of the Splash-2 and PARSEC benchmark suites. We assumed a MESI directory-based coherence protocol; network and cache parameters are shown in Table 1.

We compared a baseline case in which all messages are sent through the regular NoC and our proposal in which the Network of IDs is used to transmit invalidation and writeback acknowledgements while the NoC is used for all other messages.

Figure 6 shows the load and store latency of our proposal, normalized to the baseline. Load and store latencies are just slightly reduced when the Network of IDs is used, due to two reasons:

Table 1. Network and cache parameters

Routing	XY	Coherence protocol	Directory (MESI)
Flow control	credits	L1 cache size	16 + 16 kB (I + D)
Flit size	8 byte	L1 tag access latency	1 cycle
Switch model	4-stage pipelined	L1 data access latency	2 cycles
Switching	virtual cut-through	L2 bank size	256 kB
Buffer size:	9 flit deep	L2 tag access latency	1 cycle
Virtual channels:	4	L2 data access latency	4 cycles
GCN module delay	1 cycle	Cache block size	64 B

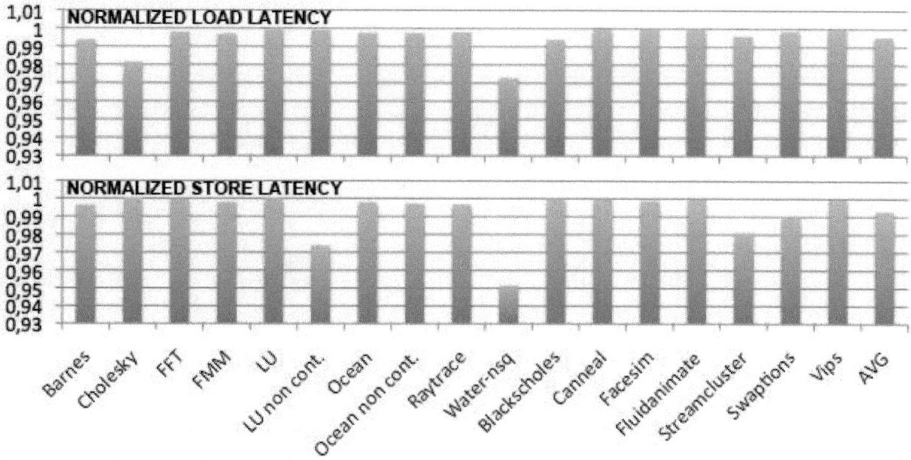

Fig. 6. Normalized load and store latency

- The number of invalidations in the benchmarks we simulated is less than 0.9% of the total number of messages on average, so the impact of optimizing their acknowledgement's transmission on the overall performance is limited.
- The writeback acknowledgments are not on the critical path of load and store requests, so optimizing their transmission only has a marginal impact on load and store latencies.

This implies that the Network of IDs has a negligible impact on execution time for the applications we simulated.

Figure 7 shows the normalized number of messages injected in the NoC. Using the Network of IDs, the NoC is relieved from a percentage of messages which ranges from 17% to 25% depending on the application (21% on average).

However, since the messages transmitted through the Network of IDs are short messages, the NoC traffic reduction in terms of injected flits is lower, as shown in Figure 8: NoC traffic is reduced by a percentage which ranges from 3.5% to 6%, with an average NoC traffic reduction of 4.5%.

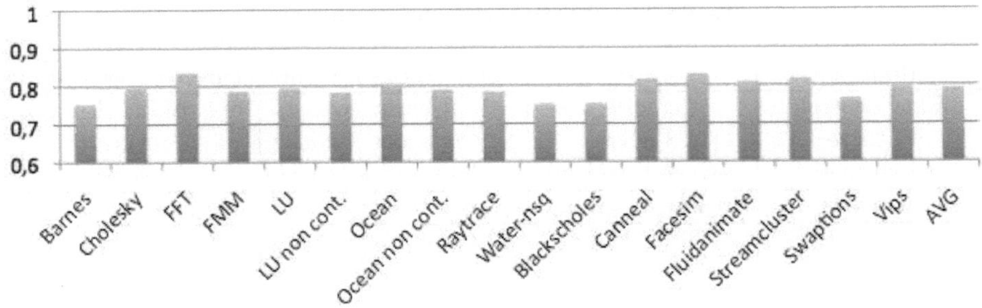

Fig. 7. Normalized number of injected messages

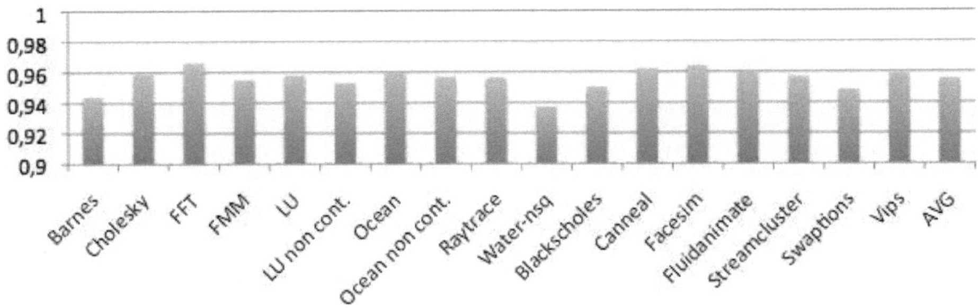

Fig. 8. Normalized number of injected flits

Figure 9 shows the average latency of the messages transmitted through the Network of IDs. On average, the Network of IDs is able to deliver a message in 2.5 clock cycles, and the variability of this value for each application compared to the average is quite low.

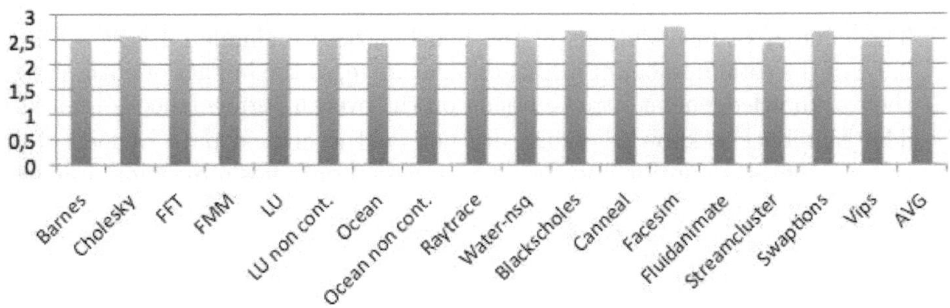

Fig. 9. Average ID network latency

In Figure 10 we show the number of contention events at the output ports of the Network of IDs modules, divided by the total number of messages transmitted through the Network of IDs. We can notice an extremely low contention: on average, one message each 2000 experiences contention at the output port, the worst case being that of LU non contiguous, in which contention is also very low anyway (one message out of 555 experiences contention). Since sending unicast acknowledgements introduce a very low load on the Network of IDs, we believe it can also be used with a broadcast-based coherence protocol, where the total traffic of many-to-one acknowledgements gathering at the Network of IDs modules (behaving as a Gather Network) and unicast acknowledgements would not stress excessively the Network of IDs degrading its performance. We leave this evaluation for future work.

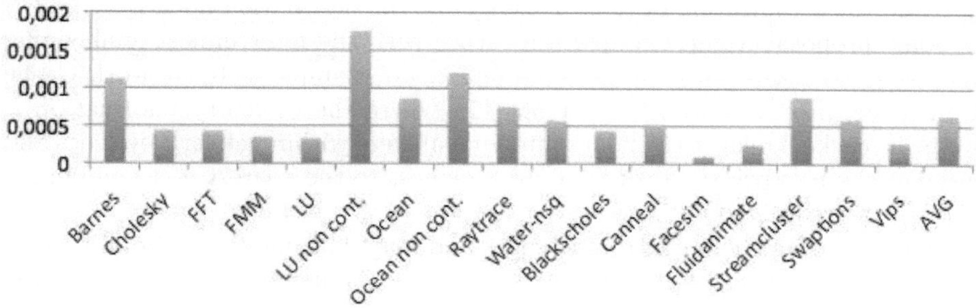

Fig. 10. Number of conflicts per message

Finally, we used Orion 2 [8] to evaluate the NoC energy savings due to the Network of IDs; as shown in Figure 11, the NoC dynamic energy is reduced by 6% on average, which, added to the static energy consumed during the whole application execution, gives a total energy reduction by 4% on average and up to 8%. Energy results include the energy consumption of both the regular NoC and the Network of IDs. The latter has been calculated basing on the power requirements of a single module obtained using Cadence Encounter, and resulted to be less than 0.1% of the total NoC energy for all the applications.

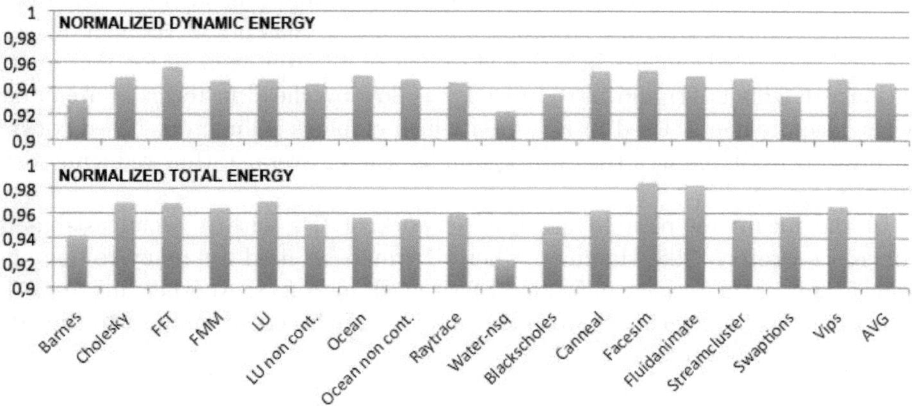

Fig. 11. Normalized energy

5 Related Work

Several works have appeared recently tackling the challenges of optimizing the NoC to meet the demands of the coherence protocol.

Recent proposals to tackle collective communication include hardware NoC mechanisms to optimize multicasts and broadcasts [9] injecting a single message in the NoC and then replicating the message at the switches to reach all the destination nodes, and mechanisms to collect many-to-one messages at the switches to avoid the serialization of those messages at the destination node [10].

Some proposals tightly couple the caches with the interconnect, embedding the cache structure into the network fabric: an example is In-Network Cache Coherence, proposed by Eisley et al. [11], where the directory information is from the cache banks at the nodes into virtual trees within network switches and leave to the network the task to route a request to the nearest nodes holding a copy of the requested data.

Differentiating short control messages and long data messages, Bolotin et al. [12] proposed a priority-based NoC which gives higher priority to short messages in order to reduce cache access latency. Their NoC design also optimizes broadcast short messages and provides support for synchronization.

All these proposals however still use the NoC resources for acknowledgement messages, which actually don't need the information contained in a short message packed besides the destination node's ID. The Network of IDs, explicitly designed for this class of messages, speeds-up the message transmission providing a lightweight structure with minimal resources.

6 Conclusions and Future Work

In this work we proposed the Network of IDs, a lightweight dedicated network added to the regular NoC and used for the transmission of unicast acknowledgement messages. The network has been obtained by adapting the modules of the previously proposed Gather Network. The resulting Network of IDs can deliver unicast acknowledgements in a few clock cycles (2.5 on average for the applications we simulated) and introduces a very low overhead in terms of area and wiring requirements. Used in a system which employs a directory-based coherence protocol, it reduces the NoC traffic by 4% on average, thus reducing also NoC energy by 4%.

In the future we plan to use the Network of IDs with a broadcast-based coherence protocol like Hammer, where it would be used for many-to-one acknowledgement messages and unicast writeback messages. Another future work direction is to employ the Network of IDs to provide hardware support to threads synchronization events.

Acknowledgements. This work has been supported by the VIRTICAL project (grant agreement n 288574) which is funded by the European Commission within the Research Programme FP7.

References

1. Owen, J.M., et al.: United states patent: 7069361 - System and method of maintaining coherency in a distributed communication system (June 2006)
2. Lodde, M., et al.: Heterogeneous NoC design for efficient broadcast-based coherence protocol support. In: NOCS 2012 (2012)
3. Lodde, M., et al.: Heterogeneous network design for effective support of invalidation-based coherency protocols. In: INA-OCMC 2012 (2012)
4. Lodde, M., et al.: Built-in fast gather control network for efficient support of coherence protocols. IET-CDT INA-OCMC 2012 Special Issue (2012)
5. The Nangate Open Cell Library, 45nm FreePDK available online at `https://www.si2.org/openeda.si2.org/projects/nangatelib/`
6. Miller, J.E., et al.: Graphite: A distributed parallel simulator for multicores. In: HPCA 2010 (2010)
7. Carlson, T.E., et al.: Sniper: Exploring the level of abstraction for callable and accurate parallel multi-core simulations. In: SC 2011 (2011)
8. Kahng, A., et al.: Orion 2.0: A power-area simulator for interconnection networks. IEEE Transactions on Very Large Scale Integration (VLSI) Systems 20(1) (2012)
9. Rodrigo, S., et al.: Efficient Unicast and Multicast Support for CMPs. In: MICRO 2008 (2008)
10. Krishna, T., et al.: Towards the ideal on-chip fabric for 1-to-many and many-to-1 communication. In: MICRO 2011 (2011)
11. Eisley, N., et al.: In-Network Cache Coherence MICRO 2006 (2006)
12. Bolotin, E., et al.: The Power of Priority: NoC Based Distributed Cache Coherency. In: NOCS 2007 (2007)

First Workshop on Parallel and Distributed Agent-Based Simulations (PADABS 2013)

Vittorio Scarano, Gennaro Cordasco,
Rosario De Chiara, and Ugo Erra

Program Chairs

Agent-Based Simulations (ABSs) are an increasingly popular tool for research and management in many fields such as ecology, economics, sociology, etc.. In some fields, such as social sciences, these models are seen as a key instrument to the generative approach, essential for understanding complex social phenomena. But also in policy-making, biology, military simulations, control of mobile robots and economics, the relevance and effectiveness of ABSs is recently recognized.

Computer science community has responded to the need for platforms that can help the development and testing of new models in each specific field by providing tools, libraries and frameworks that speed up and make massive simulations. The key objective of this workshop is to bring together the researchers that are interested in getting more performances from their simulations, by using synchronized , many-core simulations (e.g., GPUs), strongly coupled, parallel simulations (e.g. MPI) and loosely coupled, distributed simulations (distributed heterogeneous setting).

Several frameworks have been recently developed and are active in this field. They range from the GPU-Manycore approach, to Parallel, to Distributed simulation environments. In the first category, you can find FLAME GPU, that allows also non GPU specialists to harness the GPUs performance for real time simulation and visualization. For tightly-coupled, large computing clusters and supercomputers a very popular framework is Repast for High Performance Computing (REPAST-HPC), a C++-based modeling system. On the distributed side, recent work on Distributed Mason, allows non specialists to use heterogeneous hardware and software in local area networks for enlarging the size and speeding up the simulation of complex Agent-Based models.

Therefore, our focus and positioning is on the applied side of parallel computing, with a particular emphasis on performances but also on the expressiveness of the frameworks, since the field that is the target of our research is multidisciplinary and does not include only "hard-science" scientists.

Being the first edition, the workshop originated by the team of chair and co-chairs, that have a strong history of cooperation, and that are now in neighbours Universities and Company Research Labs. The idea was, informally, submitted to some important key figures in the field of ABSs, collecting a lot of interest and leading to a numerous and heterogeneous Program Committee. The dissemination

D. an Mey et al. (Eds.): Euro-Par 2013 Workshops, LNCS 8374, pp. 488–489, 2014.

of the CFP brought, over a period of 6 months, more than 800 different users, from over 20 different countries.

In the first session, short tutorials were presented on D-Mason (by Vittorio Scarano, Università di Salerno, Italy), on Rome Optimistic Simulator (by Alessandro Pellegrini, Università "La Sapienza" di Roma, Italy), and about Flame-GPU (by Daniela Romano, University of Sheffield, United Kingdom).

The regular papers presented at PADABS were divided in three main areas, each one with its own session (with some overlapping): Parallel ABSs, Distributed ABSs and Use Cases. The order of the presentation is the same as the order of appearance in the proceedings and follows the same path. Presentations were followed by quick questions/answers but the discussions were lively during the intermissions as well.

Finally, we wish to thank all the authors, the tutorial speakers, the PC Members, the other reviewers, the colleagues that attended the sessions and the EuroPar 2013 organizers for their contribution to the success of the first (and most certainly not the last!) PADABS Workshop.

D-MASON: A Short Tutorial

Vittorio Scarano[1], Gennaro Cordasco[2],
Rosario De Chiara[3], and Luca Vicidomini[1]

[1] ISISLab - Dipartimento di Informatica
Università di Salerno, Italy
vitsca@dia.unisa.it, lvicidomini@unisa.it
[2] Dipartimento di Psicologia
Seconda Università degli Studi di Napoli, Italy
gennaro.cordasco@unina2.it
[3] Centro Ricerca e Sviluppo
Poste Italiane, Italy
dechia24@posteitaliane.it

Abstract. D-MASON framework is a parallel version of the MASON library for writing and running Agent-based simulations. We briefly present MASON architecture, functionalities and some programming examples. Full documentation, additional tutorials and other material can be found at www.dmason.org where the framework can be downloaded.

1 D-MASON: Motivations and Design

Agent-Based simulation Models (ABMs) are an increasingly popular tool for research and management in many, different and diverse fields. In executing such simulations the "speed" is one of the most general and important issues and the traditional answer to this issue is to invest resources in deploying a dedicated installation of dedicated computers, with highly specialized parallel applications, devoted to the purpose of achieving extreme computational performances.

Here we present a framework, D-MASON [3], that is a distributed version of MASON, a well-known and popular library for writing and running Agent-based simulations. D-MASON introduces the parallelization at framework level so that scientists that use the framework (domain expert but with limited knowledge of distributed programming) can be only minimally aware of such distribution.

1.1 MASON

Before presenting the architecture of D-MASON in the next subsections we will, first, introduce MASON toolkit [5,6], a discrete-event simulation core and visualization library written in Java, designed to be used for a wide range of ABMs. The toolkit is written, using the standard Model-View-Controller (MVC) paradigm, in three layers: the *simulation* layer, the *visualization* layer and the *utility* layer. The simulation layer is the core of MASON and is mainly represented by an event scheduler and a variety of fields which hold agents into a given simulation space. MASON is mainly based on

D. an Mey et al. (Eds.): Euro-Par 2013 Workshops, LNCS 8374, pp. 490–500, 2014.

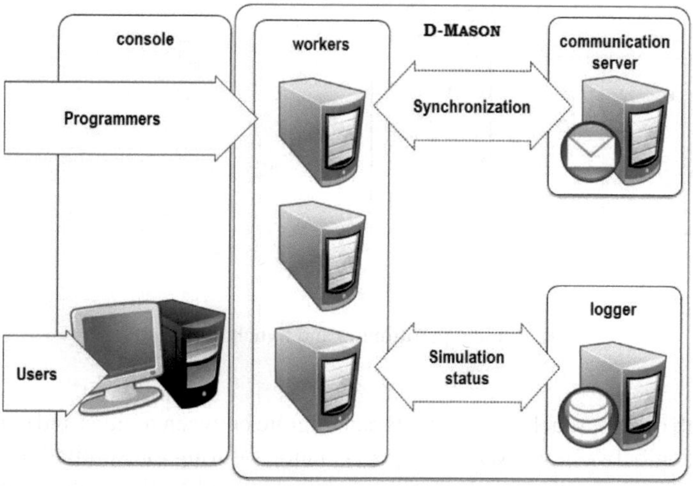

Fig. 1. D-Mason scheme

step-able agent: a computational entity which may be scheduled to perform some action (step), and which can interact (communicate) with other agents. The visualization layer permits both visualization and manipulation of the model. The simulation layer is independent from the visualization layer, which allows us to treat the model as a self-contained entity.

MASON was written with the aim of creating a flexible and efficient ABM framework which assures the complete reproducibility of results across different hardware. This reproducibility feature is considered as a priority for long simulations: for instance it is possible stop a simulation and move it a faster computer once it became available.

1.2 D-MASON

D-MASON is based on a master/workers paradigm (see Figure 1): the master console assigns a portion of the whole computation (i.e., a set of agents) to each worker. Then for each simulation step, each worker simulates the agents assigned and sends back the result of its computation to each interested worker.

D-MASON Features

Field partitioning. By noticing that most ABMs are inspired by natural models, where agents limited visibility allow to bound the range of interaction to a fixed range named agent's *Area of Interest* (AOI), several space partitioning approaches have been proposed [4,7,8] in order to reduce the communication overhead. In D-MASON, the space to be simulated (D-MASON field) is partitioned into regions (see Figure 2 left). Each region, together with the agents contained in it, is assigned to a worker. Since the AOI of an agent is small compared with the size of a region, the communication is limited to local messages (messages between workers, managing neighboring spaces, etc.). The

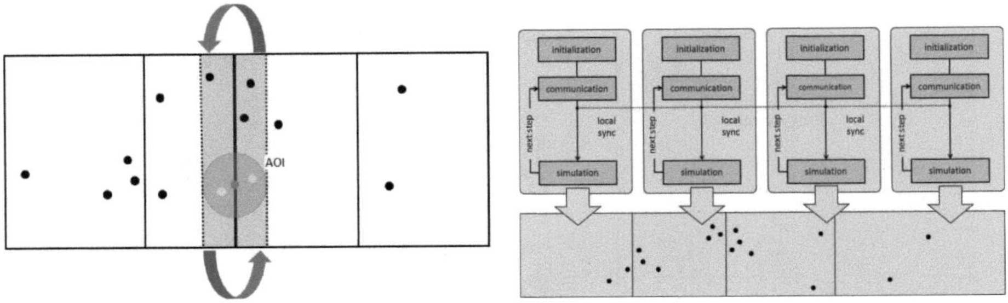

Fig. 2. Field partitioning and Synchronization

problem with this approach is that agents can migrate between regions and consequently the association between workers and agents changes during the simulation. Moreover, load balancing is not guaranteed and need to be addressed by the application.

Synchronization. We view ABMs as step-wise computations; i.e., agents behavior is computed in successive steps named *simulation step*. In order to guarantee the consistency of parallel implementation with respect to the sequential one, each worker needs to collect information about the neighboring regions. Each simulation step is formed by two phases: *communication/synchronization* and *simulation*. First of all, the worker w sends to its neighbors (i.e., the workers responsible for its neighbor regions) the information about:

- the agents that are migrating to them;
- the agents that may fall into the AOI of the agents in neighborhood of w.

This information exchange is locally synchronized in order to let the simulation run consistently (see Figure 2 right). We use a standard approach to achieve a consistent local synchronization of the distributed simulations: each step is associated with a fixed state of the simulation. Regions are simulated step by step. Since the step i of region r is computed by using the states $i-1$ of r's neighborhood, the step i of a region cannot be executed until the states $i-1$ of its neighborhood have been computed and delivered. In other words, each region is synchronized with its neighborhood before each simulation phase.

Communication. D-MASON uses a well-known mechanism, based on the publish–subscribe design pattern, to propagate agents state information: a multicast channel is assigned to each region; workers, then, simply subscribe to the channels associated with the regions which overlap with their AOI to receive relevant message updates. The current version of D-MASON uses Java Message Service (JMS) for communication between workers. We use a communication server, running Apache ActiveMQ Server, that acts as a JMS provider (i.e., it allows to generate and manage multicast channels and route messages accordingly).

Reproducibility. In order to guarantee an easy parallelization and to assure the reproducibility of results, paramount objective of the research areas interested in the ABMs, it is important to design the simulation is such a way that agents evolves simultaneously. Using this approach the simulation become embarrassingly parallelizable (there are no dependencies between agents' state), each simulation step can be executed in parallel overall the agents. Moreover, the order in which agents are scheduled does not affect the reproducibility of results.

Load Balancing. D-MASON uses a simple but efficient technique to cope with heterogeneity. The idea is to clone the software run by high capable workers so that they could serve as multiple workers; i.e., a worker that is x times more powerful than other workers could execute x virtual workers (that is by simulating, concurrently, several regions).

D-MASON Functionalities

D-MASON architecture is divided into four functional blocks: *Management*, *Workers*, *Communication* and *Services* (see Figure 1). The Management layer provides a *master application* which will be used for coordinating the workers, handle the bootstrap and running the simulation. The master is responsible for partitioning the field into regions and assigning them to workers. Currently in D-MASON there are two types of field partitioning: horizontal, where the division is done by splitting the field along one axis and square, where the division is done by using a grid. When all the parameter are set it is possible to start and interact with the entire distributed simulation (e.g. play, pause, stop). The workers are in charge of: simulating the agents that belong to the assigned regions; handling the migration of agents; managing the synchronization between neighboring regions. Workers communicate by using the communication layer based on a publish–subscribe mechanism. Services, logging and visualization (both are optional), interact with the communication server to obtain data for the simulation.

2 Programming with D-MASON

Here is a brief description of the steps one should take to make existing MASON applications run in the D-MASON.

First of all, small changes to the application source code have to be done: the new D-MASON application should extend `DistributedState` instead of `SimState`. The field to be distributed should be the distributed version of the original one. For instance, if the application is based on `SparseGrid2D` its distributed version should use `DSparseGrid2D`. Several additional parameter should be added to the application: type of partitioning (horizontal or square), AOI range and number of regions. Moreover some additional parameters need to be defined to setup the communication layer (for instance, in the current version we are using Apache ActiveMQ, and in this case, the IP address and Port number of the Communication Server should be provided).

In order to instantiate the distributed field, D-MASON provides a specific Factory. For instance, `DSparseGrid2DFactory.createDSparseGrid2D(...)` is used to generate a `DSparseGrid2D` field. This field is the core of the distributed simulation and allows both the simulation and synchronization phases. Each region of the distributed field owns a pseudo-random number generator (i.e., a `MersenneTwisterFast` object).

Another important change that should be made on the distributed application is to change the method used to add agents to the schedule. In MASON applications, agents are usually added to the schedule using the method `scheduleRepeating()`. In D-MASON all the agents are scheduled after each synchronization phase using the method `scheduleOnce()`. Hence `scheduleRepeating()` should never be used in order to avoid scheduling migrated agents.

The method `addToField()` of the abstract class `DistributedState` should be implemented, according to the behavior of the application.

Each agent, used by the application, should extends the abstract class `Remote-Agent` that implements `Steppable`. The method `step()` that defines agent action must take into account that the simulation should evolve simultaneously (see Section 1.2). Hence each agent computes its new state and store it in a temporary buffer. When all the states are computed, all the states are updated atomically. The new location of the agent is set through the method `setDistributedObjectLocation()` which implements the whole logic of agents movements (i.e., it checks whether the agent migrate or not, or whether the agent should be sent to a neighbor because it may fall into one of its agents' AOI.)

We have also implemented three distributed ABMs which are based on existing MASON applications: *DParticle*, *DFlockers* and *DAntsForage* which use DSparseGrid2D, DContinuous2D, DDoubleGrid2D, DIntGrid2D as field.

In the following we intend to provide a clear view of what means for the average MASON user to migrate his/her simulation to D-MASON in order to fully exploit the possibilities of a distributed simulation.

To better clarify we will migrate the `Particle` example which is readily available among the packages of MASON.

3 From Particles to DParticles

the package `Particles` is composed by three classes, as it can be found in the original MASON distribution: `Particle`, it implements the agent that will be simulated by the application; `Particles`, it represents the simulation environment: it allows to run the simulation from the command line without using a GUI; `ParticlesWithUI`, it allows to run simulations with a GUI.

Similarly, in D-MASON, the package `DParticles` containing the following classes: `RemoteParticle`, an abstract class, implementing `RemoteAgent` and containing the remote ID of the agent in the field and its position; `DParticle`, it extends `RemoteParticle` and implements the `distributed` agent that will be simulated by the application; `DParticles`, it represents the `distributed` simulation environment: it allows to run the simulation from the command line without using a GUI; `DParticlesWithUI`, it allows to run simulations with a GUI that is aware of the `distributed` environment.

`RemoteAgent` is parameterized with an `Int2D` object-type because, in this simulation, the field has this specific type to indicate locations, and allows programmers to set, for each agent, an unique identifier and a field position. A `Particle` simply contains two integer parameters, `xdir` and `ydir`, for setting the initial direction that the particle will move along.

`DParticle` has two constructors: the first is empty and it has been introduced for a future implementation of the method `clone()`, and the second one has as parameter, a subclass of the abstract class `DistributedState`.

Listing 1.1. Class Particle

```
...
  public Particle(int xdir, int ydir) {
   public boolean randomize = false;
   this.xdir = xdir;
   this.ydir = ydir;
  }
...
```

Listing 1.2. Class DParticle

```
public class DParticle extends RemoteParticle<Int2D>
{
   public int xdir;  // -1, 0, or 1
   public int ydir;  // -1, 0, or 1

   public DParticle(){ }

   public DParticle(DistributedState state)
   {
     super(state);
   }
```

`Particles` extends the `SimState` class while `DParticles` extends `DistributedState`, parameterized with `Int2D` object-type.

DParticles contains three other variables indicating, respectively, width and height of the field and the way of partitioning the field (that can be one or two dimensions). `Particles` has just one constructor that has as parameter the random generator seed while `DParticles` constructor has as input an objects array, containing several parameters specific for the distributed simulation (e.g. network address, port, etc ...).

In `Particles` there are two fields, the first containing the agents, the second one containing the trails. The creation of the fields and the placement of the agents in them are carried out by a simple loop that instantiates new particles with a random position and direction and place them in the proper field.

In order to add particles to the schedule, it is possible to use `scheduleRepeating()`, that allows to schedule agents repeatedly, and to add particles to the field there is `setObjectLocation()`. In `DParticles` there is the method `createDSparseGrid2D` of the class `DSparseGrid2DFactory` for creating a new distributed field. Note that it is necessary to use a factory to choose the kind of field partition. The agent initial position is computed by the method `setAvailableRandomLocation()` and to add particles in the schedule it is necessary to use the method `scheduleOnce()`, because in the next step a certain agent could not stay in the same part of the field, so using `scheduleRepeating()` will not delete the particle from the schedule. Finally there are other three new methods: a `getter` method for returning the subclass of the `DistributedState`, a method for adding an agent with a given position in the field, a method for attaching a portrayal to an agent.

Listing 1.3. Class Particles

```
public class Particles extends SimState  {
  public DoubleGrid2D trails;
  public SparseGrid2D particles;
  ...
  public Particles(long seed) {
      super(seed);
  }

  public void start() {
   ...
   for(int i=0 ; i<numParticles ; i++) {
     p = new Particle(random.nextInt(3) - 1, random.nextInt
         (3) - 1);  // random direction
     schedule.scheduleRepeating(p);
     ...
     particles.setObjectLocation(p,new Int2D(x,y));  //
         random location
   }
  }

  public static void main(String[] args) {
    doLoop(Particles.class, args);
    System.exit(0);
  }
}
```

Listing 1.4. Class DParticles

```
public class DParticles extends DistributedState<Int2D> {
  static final long serialVersionUID = 9115981605874680023L;
  private static boolean isToroidal = false;
  public DSparseGrid2D particles;
  public DDoubleGrid2D trails;
  public int gridWidth;
  public int gridHeight;
  public int MODE;
  public DParticles(Object[] params) {
    super((Integer)params[2],(Integer)params[3],...);
```

```
            ip = params[0]+"";
            port = params[1]+"";
            this.MODE=(Integer)params[9];
            gridWidth=(Integer)params[5];
            gridHeight=(Integer)params[6];
      }
      public void start() {
         super.start();
         try {
            trails = DDoubleGrid2DFactory.createDDoubleGrid2D(
                gridWidth, gridHeight, this, super.MAX_DISTANCE,
                TYPE.pos_i, TYPE.pos_j,super.NUMPEERS,MODE,0,
                false, "trails");
            particles = DSparseGrid2DFactory.createDSparseGrid2d(
                gridWidth, gridHeight, this, super.MAX_DISTANCE,
                TYPE.pos_i, TYPE.pos_j, super.NUMPEERS, MODE,
                     "particles");
            init_connection();
         } catch (DMasonException e) {
            e.printStackTrace();
         }
         DParticle p = new DParticle(this);
         while (particles.size() != super.NUMAGENTS) {
            particles.setAvailableRandomLocation(p);
            p.xdir = random.nextInt(3)-1;
            p.ydir = random.nextInt(3)-1;
            if (particles.setDistributedObjectLocationForPeer(new
                 Int2D(p.pos.getX(), p.pos.getY()), p, this)) {
              schedule.scheduleOnce(schedule.getTime()+1.0,p);
              if (particles.size() != super.NUMAGENTS)
                p=new DParticle(this);
            }
         }
            ...
    }
```

There are few differences between original `ParticlesWithUI` and the its distributed version, `DParticlesWithUI`. They both extend the class `GUIState`, responsible of instantiating all graphics elements; `DParticlesWithUI` has a constructor which allow to initialize all the parameter fo `DParticles`. The `region` identifier is stored in the variable `name` and is used to show which region is currently visualized.

Listing 1.5. Class ParticlesWithUI

```
public class ParticlesWithUI extends GUIState {
...
public static void main(String[] args) {
ParticlesWithUI t = new ParticlesWithUI();
t.createController();
```

```
}
public ParticlesWithUI() {
super(new Tutorial3(System.currentTimeMillis()));
}
public ParticlesWithUI(SimState state){
super(state);
}
...
}
```

Listing 1.6. Class `DParticlesWithUI`

```
public class DParticlesWithUI extends GUIState {
...
public static String name;
...
public DParticlesWithUI(Object[] args) {
super(new DParticles(args));
name = String.valueOf(
args[7])+""+(String.valueOf(args[8]));
}
public static String getName() { return "Peer: <"+name+">"; }
...
}
```

4 The User'S View: How to Exploit Distributed Simulations

In the process of designing an ABM it greatly helps to use facilities that allow to visualize what is happening and to collect the low level data (e.g. position of agents, values of associated properties etc...) for further analysis. In MASON each simulation is developed together with the visualization, called *portrayal*, that lets the user to understand what is going on. In D-MASON this mechanism is extended to the workers and each worker is able to correctly visualize the region it is in charge of simulating. Of course this is not a suitable solution to be used in any real setting: the scientist should physically move from worker to worker to check what is happening. Furthermore the visualization running on each worker can be considered as a wast of computing power that could be better employed to carry out the simulation.

For the reasons listed above, together with D-MASON, we have implemented a logging facility that is also leveraged to provide a centralized visualization mechanism. The logger (see Figure 1) is in charge of memorize, on each step, the status of the simulation: at the end of a step, each worker sends to it the status of the region it is in charge of. The logger is also used to provide a centralized visualization tool that allows the user to become aware of what is happening. It is possible to use the data collected by the logger to obtain two different centralized visualization (a) a global one which provides a simplified view of the whole field and this allows to just have a simplified

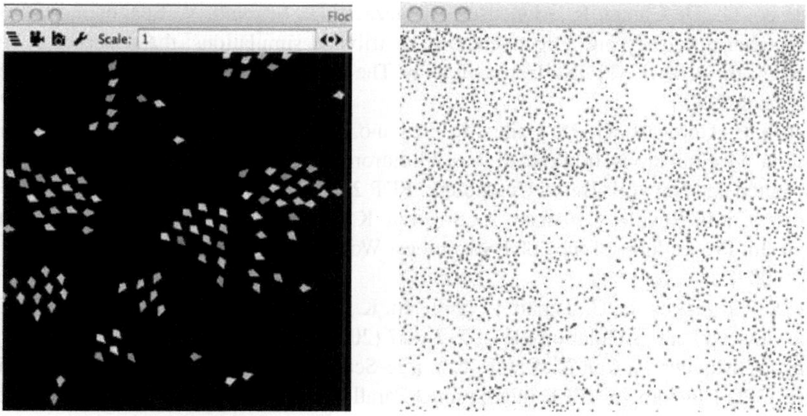

Fig. 3. The two rendering modes: (left) visualization from the portrayal associated to the flocker demo; (right) global visualization showing just the position of the agents

and efficient representation of what is happening (see Figure 3, left); (b) the visualization offered by the portrayal for a specific region of the field (see Figure 3, right). The reason to offer the two modes is that while the (b) is the mode that offers everything is needed to understand the semantic of the simulation, the mode (a) is lighter from the computational point of view so it is more responsive for a rapid look at the simulation. The two visualization modes are implemented within the console application the user can always switch between them.

5 Discussion and Conclusion

This paper reports on an currently undergoing project, D-MASON, that has been developed with the purpose of speeding up the performances of MASON, a very well known and quite widespread framework for ABMs. Several improvements, a better load balancing [1] and a computational steering facility [2], have been introduced to the framework. Further work is already planned to increase the functionality of the system. Finally, the project is available at `www.dmason.org` under a Free and Open Software license.

References

1. Carillo, M., Cordasco, G., De Chiara, R., Raia, F., Scarano, V., Serrapica, F.: Enhancing the Performances of D-MASON - A Motivating Example. In: SIMULTECH, pp. 137–143. SciTePress (2012)
2. Cordasco, G., De Chiara, R., Raia, F., Scarano, V., Spagnuolo, C., Vicidomini, L.: Designing computational steering facilities for distributed agent based simulations. In: Proc. of ACM SIGSIM Conference on Principles of Advanced Discrete Simulation (PADS 2013) (2013)

3. Cordasco, G., De Chiara, R., Mancuso, A., Mazzeo, D., Scarano, V., Spagnuolo, C.: Bringing together efficiency and effectiveness in distributed simulations: the experience with D-MASON. In: SIMULATION: Transactions of The Society for Modeling and Simulation International (2013)
4. Cosenza, B., Cordasco, G., De Chiara, R., Scarano, V.: Distributed load balancing for parallel agent-based simulations. In: Proc. of the 19th Euromicro International Conference on Parallel, Distributed and Network-Based Computing, PDP 2011 (2011)
5. Luke, S., Cioffi-Revilla, C., Panait, L., Sullivan, K.: MASON: A new multi-agent simulation toolkit. In: Proceedings of the 2004 SwarmFest Workshop, Ann Arbor, Michigan, USA, May 9-11 (2004)
6. Luke, S., Cioffi-Revilla, C., Panait, L., Sullivan, K., Balan, G.: MASON: A Multiagent Simulation Environment. Simulation 81(7), 517–527 (2005)
7. Zhang, Y., Mueller, F., Cui, X., Potok, T.: Large-Scale Multi-Dimensional Document Clustering on GPU Clusters. In: IEEE International Parallel and Distributed Processing Symposium (2010)
8. Zhou, B., Zhou, S.: Parallel simulation of group behaviors. In: WSC 2004: Proceedings of the 36th Conference on Winter Simulation, pp. 364–370. Winter Simulation Conference (2004)

The ROme OpTimistic Simulator: A Tutorial

Alessandro Pellegrini and Francesco Quaglia

High Performance and Dependable Computing Systems Research Group
DIAG, Sapienza, University of Rome

Abstract. In this tutorial we present the ROme OpTimistic Simulator (ROOT-Sim), a general-purpose Parallel Discrete Event simulation platform built according to the optimistic synchronization scheme, which allows—via the adoption of a simple/reduced API—to implement simulation models via event handlers relying on standard ANSI-C. We present the set of paradigms which ROOT-Sim is built on, and its internal design, along with the offered facilities. We also explain the simulation-model programming paradigm, and give an example of a basic simulation model, which stands as a building block for more complex ones.

1 Introduction

Simulation is an attractive and well-consolidated methodology to study real-world phenomena. It is continuously exploited in a wide set of fields, including physics, biology and business-oriented processes (such as financial prediction or optimized system-configuration selection). For some application contexts, one relevant aspect relates to the timeliness according to which simulation results are provided to end-users or applications, such as when exploiting simulation as a tool supporting time-critical decision making. Hence, performance aspects while delivering simulation output is a core issue to cope with.

In the context of Discrete Event Simulation (DES), high performance has been targeted via the Parallel-DES (PDES) paradigm [1], which allows exploiting the computing power offered by (high-end) parallel/distributed platforms in order to speedup model execution and to make (very) large and/or accurate models tractable. The basic idea underlying PDES is to partition the simulation model into N distinct simulation objects, which are the core of the simulation process from the model writer's point of view. In fact, each object represents a portion of the real world being simulated. The evolution of simulation objects is described by state transitions, driven by a set of logical/mathematical properties. In order to represent real-world interactions, simulation objects communicate with each other by exchanging pieces of information in the form of events.

From a technical point of view, simulation objects are handled by Logical Processes (LP), which undertake the concurrent execution of simulation events. Traditionally, a PDES run entails a number of concurrent LPs, uniquely identified by a numerical code in the range $[0, N-1]$, and the overall simulation model keeps track of the evolution of the simulated world by relying on a global simulation state S, which is partitioned into various LPs' private and disjoint simulation states S_i, so that $S = S_i \bigcup_{i=0}^{N-1} S_i$ and $S_i \cap S_j = \emptyset, \forall i \neq j$.

D. an Mey et al. (Eds.): Euro-Par 2013 Workshops, LNCS 8374, pp. 501–512, 2014.

In PDES, simulation events are timestamped and their execution is impulsive, meaning that there is no notion of time evolution during an event's processing. The current simulation time at each individual LP is known as Local Virtual Time (LVT), and can be expressed in any measure unit (i.e., one LVT unit can represent seconds, hours, or even years, depending on the actual simulation model). This notion of time is opposed to the Wall-Clock Time (WCT), which is the actual notion of time we are used to. Therefore, in one WCT unit, the LVT advancement can be of one or several units, depending on the actual complexity of the simulation model and on the efficiency of the simulation run.

During the execution of an event, other events can be generated, destined to any simulation object in the system, and are associated with a timestamp value which is greater than or equal to the one of the event currently being executed, i.e. during the execution of the event e_x associated with the timestamp t_x, a new event e_y associated with timestamp t_y can be generated and sent to another simulation object, ensuring that $t_y \geq t_x$. Therefore, event generation evolves according to a causality pattern where the present cannot affect the past.

LPs are in charge of delivering simulation events to the hosted simulation objects, via the invocation of proper event handlers. Simulation-kernel instances take care of dispatching events for processing activities across the various LPs, and of managing inter-LP communication. In particular, they handle the LPs' *event queues*, by reflecting the updates due to incoming messages, and determine the best LP to be dispatched in order to optimize specific execution metrics.

At the same time, when concurrently running the LPs on multiple CPU-cores provided by the underlying parallel/distributed platform, synchronization mechanisms are required in order to ensure that the causality pattern is maintained for both event generation and processing at any LP. Although various definitions of causally consistent execution are devised in literature [2–5], the most widely known and exploited causality criterion expresses that model execution is correct if each LP processes its input events in non-decreasing timestamp order.

To maintain causal consistency two main approaches have been proposed: *conservative* and *optimistic*. The former avoids the possibility of a causal violation at all, relying on block-until-safe policies which suspend event-processing activities at an LP until it is ensured that the execution of its next pending event is coherent with logical-time ordering. The latter—which finds its basis in the Time Warp protocol presented in [6]—aims at full exploitation of the parallelism offered by the underlying computing platform (either local or distributed), which is achieved by avoiding the usage of the aforementioned block-until-safe policies, and by adopting speculative processing. With this approach, causality violations can occur upon the delivery of a so-called *straggler message* to any LP involved in the run, which carries a scheduled event associated with a timestamp t_1 lower than the timestamp t_2 of some already-processed event. In such a case, all the events already processed by the recipient LP, having timestamp t in the interval $t_1 < t \leq t_2$ are no longer causally consistent.

Anytime a causality violation is detected, some rollback recovery mechanism needs to be actuated which involves, at the same time, two orthogonal issues:

1. undoing the effects of inconsistent local processing activities on other LPs;
2. restoring the state of the rolling back LP to a still-consistent past snapshot.

The first task is generally supported via the employment of so-called *anti-messages*, which annihilate events scheduled by the rolling back LP (due to the causal inconsistency). An anti-message is therefore a negative copy of a previously sent message, and is used to signal the destination LP to discard the original message. Clearly, if the event carried by the original message was already processed, we experience a spreading of the rollback occurrence along a chain of LPs, a phenomenon called *cascading rollback*.

On the other hand, the second task poses problems on the side of both performance and application transparency. As for performance, we must consider both CPU usage for supporting checkpoint/restore tasks, and memory usage for keeping recoverability-related data/metadata. On this side, a wide literature exists that has proposed the employment of log/restore techniques (see, e.g., [7–9]), where snapshots of LPs' states are taken according to some (infrequent) policy in order to optimize the tradeoff between log costs and restore latency. Also, these techniques deal either with non-incremental or incremental logging, the latter approach (see, e.g., [10–12]) also trying to reduce the memory usage for log buffers. On the other hand, transparency issues deal with supporting log/restore with no need for state recoverability modules implemented in the application-level code (hence masking the actual synchronization paradigm to the application programmer). This is a non-trivial aspect since it relates to the flexibility according to which the application programmer is allowed to organize the data structures representing the LP state image.

Recently, the memory demand problem associated with logging has been also tackled via *reverse computing* [13], where a state-restore operation is supported via application-level compensation logic that applies backward computation steps until the correct snapshot for resuming the LP is built. For this approach we still find issues in relation to how to generate the reverse code version transparently to the application programmer.

Still in relation to memory usage and recovery, optimistic synchronization is intrinsically linked to the notion of *Global Virtual Time* (GVT). It represents the commit horizon of the optimistic simulation run, i.e. the simulation-time barrier which separates the set of committed events from the still-rollbackable ones. It corresponds to the minimum timestamp of not-yet-processed or in-transit messages/anti-messages. Once the new GVT is available, all the memory buffers keeping events belonging to the committed portion of the simulation (and the related logs) can be released[1]. This procedure is usually termed *fossil collection*. We note that the GVT protocol cannot be executed with unbounded frequency since it imposes some overhead. This leads to further exacerbation of the memory-demand problem, since memory is allocated (and temporarily kept)

[1] For infrequent logging schemes, the only exception is related to the need for keeping data/metadata for at least one logged state image with time t less than GVT, and the events with time in between t and the GVT value, to be able to recover the LP state image to any point in time arbitrarily close, or coinciding with, the GVT value.

to store information related to both speculatively-scheduled events and already committed events.

An additional central point relates to the CPU-scheduling algorithm used to determine which LP, among the ones hosted by a given simulation-kernel instance, must be given control. Several proposals have been made [14–17], but the common choice is the Lowest-Timestamp-First (LTF) algorithm [18], which selects the LP whose next pending event has the minimum timestamp, among all the locally-hosted ones. LTF's advantage is that it does not generate local causality violations. This is because LPs are dispatched similarly to what would happen with a sequential simulator, which imposes a timestamp-ordered sequence of CPU-schedule operations. Hence, rollbacks are generated only due to events scheduled between LPs hosted by different kernel instances.

2 Programming and Object Model in ROOT-Sim

ROOT-Sim [19] is a PDES simulation kernel relying on the optimistic synchronization paradigm. It comes as a static library which can be linked to executables implementing simulation models using the ANSI-C programming standard [20], as if they were completely sequential.

In particular, the user can organize the code in as many functions/files as needed, can perform any I/O operation during the simulation (keeping in mind that I/O operations can degrade performance), can use dynamically-allocated memory to build the simulation state, and so on and so forth. The only exception is that the `volatile` qualifier becomes meaningless (i.e., there is no possibility for a variable to be modified outside the simulation platform). In addition, the model lives in userspace only, so no *NIX system calls should be used. No regular entry point is required for the application-level code (i.e., no `main()` function must be implemented), as entry points for the application code are specified by ad-hoc APIs, which will be discussed in the next section.

The actual simulation is based on events: each LP processes events, and its advancement in the Local Virtual Time (LVT) is connected to their execution, and LPs communicate via messages. ROOT-Sim, as the Time Warp protocol stands, enforces a logical identity between events and messages. This means that a message envelopes an event to be scheduled to some destination LP. Each event (and thus message backing it) is identified by a numerical code, which is defined by the application-level logic. Each type of message is fixed-size. In particular, the application-level code must provide a definition of a `struct` for each event type, where the content of a message (an event) must be specified.

At simulation startup, ROOT-Sim delivers to each LP a special `INIT` event (identified by the reserved code 0) which allows the simulation model to set up its initial configuration. In particular, the model can define its simulation state relying on a sequence of `malloc()` calls, and the initial values can be retrieved by command-line arguments which are delivered as `INIT`-event's payload, resembling the standard ANSI-C `char **argv` vector. During the execution of the `INIT` event, other events can be scheduled at any LP in the system, therefore allowing the actual simulation to start. According to the ROOT-Sim programming model, the first `malloc()` call issued by each LP during the execution of the `INIT` event is considered as the initial part of the LP's simulation state, and will be later passed via a specific pointer to allow the execution of additional events. This can be overridden by a specific API provided by the platform, as it will be discussed later. Nevertheless, this approach allows LPs' states to arbitrarily grow/shrink during the simulation's exection, just relying on additional `malloc()`/`free()` calls. This unique feature means that the user can produce standard code to design the simulation model, with the only requirement that every additional `malloc`'d memory region must be referred via a pointer in the first `malloc`'d structure for the simulation platform to be able to correctly rollback previous simulation states.

2.1 Supported APIs

The core API to allow communication between application-level code and simulation kernel is very simple. It consists of one call function, `ScheduleNewEvent()`, and two callback functions, `ProcessEvent()` and `OnGVT()`. The callbacks must be necessarily implemented in the simulation model to be compliant with the library. Then, the rest of the code can be implemented in any way, albeit respecting the ANSI-C standard. These functions have the following signature/purpose.

`void ProcessEvent(int me, time_type now, int event_type, void *event_content, void *state)` is the callback that supports the actual processing of simulation events, and it is used by the kernel to give control to the application layer. `me` is the ID of the LP being scheduled, `now` is the current value for the local clock, `event_type` is the numerical code for the event to be processed, `event_content` is the information regarding the event itself, and `state` is the current LP's state. Inside of `ProcessEvent()` the execution is fully speculative, i.e. the events that are executed might be eventually undone. The programmer, nevertheless, is completely unaware of this issue, and can simply implement state transitions within this callback. ROOT-Sim will transparently undo (in case of a detected inconsistency) or commit speculative events (whenever a new GVT value is computed and the commitment horizon is moved forward). The only issue concerning `ProcessEvent()` is the execution of non-rollbackable actions. In fact, if the programmer, e.g., prints some text on the screen during the execution of an event that will be eventually rolled back, the output generated will not be reverted. This is a non-trivial problem associated with speculative execution, even more if transparency is enforced and the programmer is given the freedom to implement its model by relying on standard ANSI-C. ROOT-Sim offers a facility which tries to address this issue (at the cost of some delay in the materialization of the actual output), which will be presented in Section 3.

`void ScheduleNewEvent(int receiver, time_type timestamp, int event_type, void *event_content, int event_size)` is a function that allows injecting a new simulation event within the system, to be destined to whichever simulation object. `receiver` denotes the ID of the destination LP, `timestamp` is the LVT associated with the event to be processed, `event_type`, `event_content`, and `event_size` allow the correct identification and delivery of the actual event. For efficiency reasons, events are buffered and asynchronously delivered when the execution of the current one is completed. This allows to pack together more events if the destination LP is the same, and prevents delays in the current event's execution. We note that this asynchronous deliver does not affect the correctness of the execution, as ROOT-Sim will order events in the input queue before scheduling the next event to the destination LP. In case the delay created by this internal buffering generates an out-of-order execution at some LP, then the rollback procedure will restore consistency.

`bool OnGVT(void *snapshot, int gid)` is a callback that gives control to the application layer by also providing a committed snapshot of the simulation object. The execution of `OnGVT()` is therefore not speculative, i.e. any action taken within this function will never be undone. This means that, e.g., any I/O operation within this function is perfectly safe, and therefore it can be used to gather statistics on the ongoing simulation. We note that, since the timestamp associated with `snapshot` refers to the committed portion of the computation, it is forbidden to call `ScheduleNewEvent()` within `OnGVT()`, because this might induce a rollback operation of already committed events. In case the user calls `ScheduleNewEvent()` in this callback, a runtime error will be generated. `OnGVT()` additionally implements a distributed termination control: since `snapshot` is a portion S_i of the Committed and Consistent Global State (CCGS) S, according to [21] a global predicate can be locally evaluated on S_i. If the model determines that the simulation is completed for that particular LP, `OnGVT()` can return the `true` value. ROOT-Sim will collect all return values, and in case all the LPs agree, the simulation will stop.

In addition to the core API, ROOT-Sim has a set of additional facilities. First, `void SetState(void *new_state)` allows the LP to manually specify which is its simulation state. It is not mandatory in a simulation-model's implementation, as explained in Section 2, but gives the programmer more freedom.

ROOT-Sim comes bundled with a fully-featured numerical library, which gives the modeler the possibility to generate random numbers drawn from several distributions. So far, the `Random()`, `Expent()` (exponential), `Normal()`, `Gamma()`, `Poisson()`, and `Zipf()` distributions are implemented. This library is crucial in the development of simulation models (and should be used in place of other libraries) because it adheres to the Piece Wise Deterministic paradigm (see [22]), i.e. the same sequence of numbers will be deterministically produced if a rollback operation is performed. The numerical library maintains one seed per each LP, pseudo-randomly drawn by an initial master seed which can be either randomly computed at simulation startup, or manually specified by the user. This gives full control on the model's execution, giving the possibility to re-study the same configuration (determined by the initial master seed) which will give the same final outcome, independently of the actual events' execution pattern.

3 Internal Features

The simulation platform offers several facilities to support model's simulation in the most effective way, and to control the simulation's execution. Configuration can be specified either at command line, or by relying on an interactive shell which supports execution scripts as well.

The GVT computation interval can be tuned at simulation startup. If the user selects a higher value, the overhead associated with this operation gets reduced, but since the fossil collection operation (see Section 1) is thus executed less often, the overall simulation likely requires more memory to maintain, e.g., older checkpoints. By tweaking this parameter, the user can manually balance the tradeoff between performance and memory consumption.

As mentioned before, at simulation startup ROOT-Sim initializes the internal numerical library starting from a master seed. The user can ask ROOT-Sim to randomly draw this master seed or can specify it manually. In case the seed is randomly chosen, the user can configure ROOT-Sim to store it as the master seed for future runs. In this way, a set of experiments can be conducted on the same events' pattern, therefore comparing the very same model's configuration.

Concerning initialization, ROOT-Sim allows to run the simulation model on a distributed environment, by ultimately relying on MPI for message delivery. Using a description of the machines which can be used to run the simulation (i.e. address for reaching them, and number of CPU-cores), ROOT-Sim transparently sets up the distributed simulation environment. For efficiency reasons, two different mappings between LPs and simulation kernels are available: *block distribution* evenly divides the available LPs across the kernel instances, while *circular* assigns one LP per kernel, in a circular fashion. Depending on the inter-LP interaction, the one that limits at most the number of inter-kernel interactions due to event exchange can be selected, so to reduce the impact on performance.

As for state saving, ROOT-Sim offers a large set of facilities which address both transparency and execution efficiency at the same time. In particular, as mentioned, the simulation state can be scattered across different segments of allocated memory, and log/restore operations can be carried out either in non-incremental [23] or incremental way [24]. Additionally, ROOT-Sim can be configured to switch between these two differentiated modes autonomically and to optimize the checkpointing interval, either by relying on an analytic model [25], or by relying on a genetic algorithm [26].

ROOT-Sim offers the user the possibility to select either the traditional LTF scheduler for event processing selection, or an optimized $O(1)$ variant [27], which selects the next event to be scheduled in a (probabilistic) constant time.

Third-party libraries are almost fully supported. The user is allowed to rely on any third-party library if it is stateless. Support for stateful third-party libraries is currently under development and will be integrated in a future release.

There are several branches of the ROOT-Sim kernel still under development and that will be merged in the main version soon. One relies on multithreading [28] for running in parallel within the same kernel more than one LP and the related housekeeping operations. Another branch supports migration of LPs among different kernel instances depending on the current workload [29], while the orthogonal *load sharing* approach [30] varies the number of CPU-cores assigned to each simulation kernel instance depending on the current workload.

This avoids the costly migration operation, but limits the viability to multi-core machines. Another one allows intersections between LPs' states [31], i.e. global variables can be speculatively accessed and in case of inconsistency they are rolled back as well. Another version supports consistent generation of I/O within the speculative `ProcessEvent()` callback [32], which is done via a proper I/O demon that materializes the output only after discriminating the committed portions and filtering out inconsistent parts of the output stream via optimized stream-management mechanisms.

4 A Code Example

We present here some code snippets implementing a ROOT-Sim application which models a set of N nodes connected as a mesh, sending packets randomly to each other. The first important thing is to define the possible events handled by the model, the content of an event message, and the structure of the state:

```
#include <ROOT-Sim.h>
#define PACKET 1 // Event definition
#define DELAY 120
#define PACKETS 1000000 // Termination condition

typedef struct _event_content_t {
    time_type sent_at;
} event_content_t;
typedef struct _lp_state_t{
    int packet_count;
} lp_state_t;
```

In this model we allow just one application-defined event, `PACKET`, which identifies the transit of a packet in the mesh. Then, we must specify the actual events' logic. `ProcessEvent()` is the only entry point for speculative event processing, so we rely on a `switch` construct to demultiplex them:

```
void ProcessEvent(unsigned int me, time_type now, unsigned int event, event_t *content,\\
                  unsigned int size, lp_state_t *ptr) {
    event_t new_event;
    time_type timestamp;

    switch(event) {

        case INIT: // must be ALWAYS implemented
            state = (lp_state_t *)malloc(sizeof(lp_state_t));
            state->packet_count = 0;
            timestamp = (time_type)(20 * Random());
            ScheduleNewEvent(me, timestamp, PACKET, NULL, 0);
            break;

        case PACKET: {
            pointer->packet_count++;
            new_event_content.sent_at = now;
            int recv = FindReceiver(MESH);
            timestamp = now + Expent(DELAY);
            ScheduleNewEvent(recv, timestamp, PACKET, &new_event, sizeof(new_event));
        }
    }
}
```

```
TOTAL KERNELS............... : 32
TOTAL PROCESSES............. : 1024
TOTAL EVENTS EXECUTED....... : 169923760
TOTAL COMMITTED EVENTS...... : 96932768
TOTAL ROLLBACKS EXECUTED.... : 2357476
TOTAL ANTIMESSAGES.......... : 72208424
AVERAGE ROLLBACK FREQUENCY... : 1.4 %
AVERAGE ROLLBACK LENGTH...... : 30.62 events
EFFICIENCY.................. : 58.11 %
AVERAGE EVENT COST.......... : 11.48 us
AVERAGE CHECKPOINT COST...... : 28.327 us
AVERAGE RECOVERY COST........ : 20.110 us
Simulation started at........ : Thu Mar 21 23:23:07 2013
Simulation finished at....... : Thu Mar 21 23:27:49 2013
Computation time............. : 282 seconds
Last GVT value............... : 50828.568372
Average Committed Event-Rate. : 343733.22 events/second
```

Fig. 1. General Statistics Output File

The code logic is fairly simple: upon `INIT` event, the LP's state is `malloc`'d and initialized, and an initial packet is sent to the LP itself. Whenever a `PACKET` event is received, a local counter is increased, and a packet is sent back to a random LP in the simulation environment. Timestamps are computed according to an exponential distribution, exploiting the internal `Expent()` function.

`OnGVT()` is the second callback to be implemented, which performs a local check on the LP's state. If the number of packets passed through the LP is smaller than `PACKETS`, then the simulation cannot be halted yet:

```
bool OnGVT(lp_state_t *snapshot, int gid) {
    if (snapshot->packet_count < PACKETS)
        return false;
    return true;
}
```

5 Runtime Data

Beyond the statistics that the user can programmatically obtain from the execution of the `OnGVT()` callback, ROOT-Sim has three levels of statistics generation which can be configured at startup. The first (default) level produces a file containing average values for the most common performance metrics on a system-wide scale. An example file is presented in Figure 1. With it, the user can gather information about general execution and overall performance, i.e. the efficiency of the simulation, or the number of events executed.

If the user is interested in the same statistics but at a per-kernel granularity (i.e. not a system-wide average), the second level of statistics generates a text file like the previous one for each kernel instance. This is useful, e.g., to check if the workload of the model is evenly distributed across simulation kernel instances. At the same time, this level produces punctual data during the simulation's execution in the form ⟨GVT phase number, GVT value, committed events in this phase, cumulated committed events⟩ (one tuple per line). This adds some overhead, which is nevertheless minimal because this operation is performed periodically only during the GVT calculation. This is a very useful information to track performance variations during the execution of the simulation model.

The last (more intrusive) level of statistics generation prints on a per-kernel separate file additional information for each GVT phase, in the form ⟨total events, committed events, rollbacks, average event cost, average checkpoint cost⟩.

References

[1] Fujimoto, R.M.: Parallel discrete event simulation. Communications of the ACM 33(10), 30–53 (1990)

[2] Madhava Rao, D., Thondugulam, N., Radhakrishnan, R., Wilsey, P.: Unsynchronized parallel discrete event simulation. In: Winter Simulation Conference Proc., vol. 2, pp. 1563–1570 (December 1998)

[3] Quaglia, F., Baldoni, R.: Exploiting intra-object dependencies in parallel simulation. Inf. Process. Lett. 70(3), 119–125 (1999)

[4] Fujimoto, R.M.: Exploiting temporal uncertainty in parallel and distributed simulation. In: Proc. of the 13th Workshop on Parallel and Distributed Simulation, pp. 46–53. IEEE Comp. Soc. (May 1999)

[5] Cai, W., Turner, S.J., Lee, B.S., Zhou, J.: An alternative time management mechanism for distributed simulations. ACM Transactions on Modeling and Computer Simulation 15(2), 109–137 (2005)

[6] Jefferson, D.R.: Virtual Time. ACM Transactions on Programming Languages and System 7(3), 404–425 (1985)

[7] Bellenot, S.: Global virtual time algorithms. In: Proc. of the SCS Multiconference on Distributed Simulation, pp. 122–127 (January 1990)

[8] Preiss, B.R., Loucks, W.M., MacIntyre, D.: Effects of the checkpoint interval on time and space in Time Warp. ACM Transactions on Modeling and Computer Simulation 4(3), 223–253 (1994)

[9] Palaniswamy, A.C., Wilsey, P.A.: An analytical comparison of periodic checkpointing and incremental state saving. In: Proc. of the 7th Workshop on Parallel and Distributed Simulation, pp. 127–134. ACM (1993)

[10] Rönngren, R., Liljenstam, M., Ayani, R., Montagnat, J.: Transparent incremental state saving in Time Warp parallel discrete event simulation. In: Proc. of the 10th Workshop on Parallel and Distributed Simulation, pp. 70–77. IEEE Comp. Soc. (May 1996)

[11] Santoro, A., Quaglia, F.: Transparent state management for optimistic synchronization in the High Level Architecture. In: Proc. of the 19th Workshop on Principles of Advanced and Distributed Simulation, pp. 171–180. IEEE Comp. Soc. (June 2005)

[12] West, D., Panesar, K.: Automatic incremental state saving. In: Proc. of the 10th Workshop on Parallel and Distributed Simulation, pp. 78–85. IEEE Comp. Soc. (May 1996)

[13] Carothers, C.D., Perumalla, K.S., Fujimoto, R.M.: Efficient optimistic parallel simulations using reverse computation. ACM Transactions on Modeling and Computer Simulation 9(3), 224–253 (1999)

[14] Som, T.K., Sargent, R.G.: A probabilistic event scheduling policy for optimistic parallel discrete event simulation. In: Proc. of the 12th Workshop on Parallel and Distributed Simulation, pp. 56–63. IEEE Comp. Soc. (May 1998)

[15] Quaglia, F., Cortellessa, V.: On the processor scheduling problem in time warp synchronization. ACM Transactions on Modeling and Computer Simulation 12 (July 2002)

[16] Rönngren, R., Ayani, R.: Service oriented scheduling in Time Warp. In: Proc. of 1994 Winter Simulation Conference, pp. 1340–1346. Society for Computer Simulation (December 1994)

[17] Palaniswamy, A.C., Wilsey, P.A.: Scheduling Time Warp processes using adaptive control techniques. In: Proc. of the 1994 Winter Simulation Conference, pp. 731–738. Society for Computer Simulation (December 1994)

[18] Lin, Y.B., Lazowska, E.D.: Processor scheduling for Time Warp parallel simulation. In: Proc. of the 23rd SCS Multiconference on Advances in Parallel and Distributed Simulation, pp. 11–14. IEEE Comp. Soc. (January 1991)

[19] HPDCS Research Group: ROOT-Sim: The ROme OpTimistic Simulator - v 1.0 (October 2012), `http://www.dis.uniroma1.it/~hpdcs/ROOT-Sim/`

[20] Kernighan, B.W., Ritchie, D.M.: The C Programming Language, 2nd edn. Prentice Hall Professional Technical Reference (1988)

[21] Mattern, F.: Efficient algorithms for distributed snapshots and global virtual time approximation. Journal of Parallel Distributed Computing 18(4), 423–434 (1993)

[22] Elnozahy, M., Alvisi, L., Wang, Y.M., Johnson, D.B.: A survey of rollback-recovery protocols in message-passing systems. ACM Computing Surveys 34(3), 375–408 (2002)

[23] Toccaceli, R., Quaglia, F.: DyMeLoR: Dynamic Memory Logger and Restorer library for optimistic simulation objects with generic memory layout. In: Proc. of the 22nd Workshop on Principles of Advanced and Distributed Simulation, pp. 163–172. IEEE Comp. Soc. (2008)

[24] Pellegrini, A., Vitali, R., Quaglia, F.: Di-DyMeLoR: Logging only dirty chunks for efficient management of dynamic memory based optimistic simulation objects. In: Proc. of the 23rd Workshop on Principles of Advanced and Distributed Simulation. IEEE Comp. Soc. (2009)

[25] Vitali, R., Pellegrini, A., Quaglia, F.: Autonomic log/restore for advanced optimistic simulation systems. In: Proc. of the Symposium on Modeling, Analysis, and Simulation of Computer and Telecommunication Systems, pp. 319–327. IEEE Comp. Soc. (2010)

[26] Pellegrini, A., Vitali, R., Quaglia, F.: An evolutionary algorithm to optimize log/restore operations within optimistic simulation platforms. In: Proc. of the 4th International ICST Conference on Simulation Tools and Techniques, SIGSIM (2011)

[27] Santoro, T., Quaglia, F.: A low-overhead constant-time LTF scheduler for optimistic simulation systems. In: Proc. of the IEEE Symposium on Computers and Communications, pp. 948–953 (2010)

[28] Vitali, R., Pellegrini, A., Quaglia, F.: Towards symmetric multi-threaded optimistic simulation kernels. In: Proc. of the 26th International Workshop on Principles of Advanced and Distributed Simulation, PADS, pp. 211–220. IEEE Comp. Soc. (August 2012)

[29] Peluso, S., Didona, D., Quaglia, F.: Application transparent migration of simulation objects with generic memory layout. In: Proc. of the 25th Workshop on Principles of Advanced and Distributed Simulation, pp. 169–177. IEEE Comp. Soc. (June 2011)

[30] Vitali, R., Pellegrini, A., Quaglia, F.: Load sharing for optimistic parallel simulations on multi core machines. SIGMETRICS Performance Evaluation Review 40(3), 2–11 (2012)
[31] Pellegrini, A., Vitali, R., Quaglia, F.: Transparent and efficient shared-state management for optimistic simulations on multi-core machines. In: Proc. 20th International Symposium on Modeling, Analysis and Simulation of Computer and Telecommunication Systems, pp. 134–141. IEEE Comp. Soc. (August 2012)
[32] Antonacci, F., Pellegrini, A., Quaglia, F.: Consistent and efficient output-stream management in optimistic simulation platform. In: Proc. of the 2013 ACM SIGSIM Conference on Principles of Advanced Discrete Simulation, pp. 315–326. ACM (May 2013)

Parallel Hierarchical A* for Multi Agent-Based Simulation on the GPU

Giuseppe Caggianese and Ugo Erra

Università della Basilicata
Dipartimento di Matematica, Informatica ed Economia
{giuseppe.caggianese,ugo.erra}@unibas.it

Abstract. In this work, we describe a Parallel Hierarchical A* (PHA*) for path-finding in real-time using the Graphics Processor Units (GPUs). The technique aims to find potential paths for many hundreds of agents by building an abstraction graph of the input map in an off-line phase and then using this representation to speed up the path-finding during the on-line phase. The approach is appropriate in the case of scenarios based on grid maps and is independent on a specific obstacle configurations. In addition, we propose also a strategy to obtain smooth paths during the search. We show that this approach fits well with the programming model of the GPUs, enabling searching for many hundreds of agents in parallel in real-time applications such as simulations. The paper describes this implementation using the Compute Unified Device Architecture programming environment, and demonstrates its advantages in terms of performance and quality of the paths founded comparing PHA* with a GPUs implementation of Real-Time Adaptive A* and the classic A* algorithm.

Keywords: path-finding, GPUs acceleration, simulation, real-time search.

1 Introduction

Many types of simulations involve agents moving over maps. In particular, in some simulations the agents have different characteristics and behavior and a path planning algorithm is a key task for maintaining as an essential aspect of plausible agent behavior such as collision avoidance and goal satisfaction. Path planning also consumes a great part of the computation time during the simulations, particularly in highly dynamic environments where most of the agents are moving at the same time with varying goals. A fast path planning algorithm is therefore essential for the agents to move smoothly around obstacles and eventually with other moving agents.

Single-agent path planning, where the size of the search space is bounded by the map size, can be tackled with a search algorithm such as A*[5]. Multi-agent path planning is much more challenging than the single agent case in term of CPU resources and memory requirements. Hence, despite its completeness and

D. an Mey et al. (Eds.): Euro-Par 2013 Workshops, LNCS 8374, pp. 513–522, 2014.

solution optimality guarantees, a centralized A* search has little practical value in a multi-agent path planning problem. As the number of agents and the size of the search space increase, searching tends to become computationally burdensome or intractable even for relatively small maps and collections of agents. Trading the method completeness and the solution optimality for improved performance is a typical feature of decentralized approaches, including the method described in this paper.

In the last few years, Graphics Processor Units (GPUs) have increased rapidly in popularity because they offer an opportunity to accelerate many algorithms. In particular, applications that have large numbers of parallel threads that do similar work across many data points with limited synchronization are good candidates with which to exploit GPU acceleration. All of this means that in a multi-agent scenario, we can take into account the idea that exploration of different paths can be performed in parallel with large numbers of threads that explore simultaneous paths. In this way, scalability to larger maps can be achieved with decentralized approaches, which decompose the initial problem into a series of parallel searches. However, a GPU-based path planning must takes into account that it has limited access to the GPU and memory resources, which are allocated with higher priority to other modules such as the graphics engine and more recently to the physics engine.

In this paper, we describe Parallel Hierarchical A*, a path planning system for agents that exploits the GPU to achieve real-time performance. The proposed approach is appropriate in the simulation based on grid maps where a grid cell, called tile, is the smallest unit space that can be occupied by a single agent. Before the beginning of the simulation, the input map is decomposed in blocks. Because these blocks are not guaranteed to be contiguous, they are further divided into regions and each region within a block is represented by single tile. Once the tiles have been established we compute edges between regions. At the end of this process, we obtain an abstract graph which can be used at runtime to find in parallel the potential high-level paths for many hundreds of agents. The entire process from the building of the abstract graph to the planning path of the agents are implemented on the GPU. We show that our Parallel Hierarchical A* fits well with the parallel architecture of the GPU where many threads are necessary to exploit the GPU fully. The method is simple and easy to implement using the programming model of the GPU as for instance the platform chosen in this work NVIDIA's Compute Unified Device Architecture (CUDA). The empirical results demonstrate the performance scale advantage of the GPU for a large number of agents compared to GPU implementations of RTAA* and sub-optimal solutions compared to a CPU implementation of A*, then trading optimality for improved execution performance.

2 Related Works

The first part of this section summarizes hierarchical approaches used for path-finding which are more relevant for this work. The second part reviews related work on path-finding using the GPU in a more general context.

Path-finding approaches based on topological abstraction have been explored in several domains such as computer games and robotics. Hierarchical Path-Finding A* is a hierarchical approach for reducing problem complexity on grid based maps. The works [6][11] are two approaches based on hierarchical representations of a space with the goal of reducing the overall search effort. In [2], Botea et al. presents and Hierarchical Path-Finding A* for reducing problem complexity in path-finding on grid-based maps. The technique abstracts a map into linked local clusters. At the local level, the optimal distances for crossing the cluster are pre-computed and cached. At the global level, an action is to cross a cluster in a single step rather than moving to an adjacent atomic location. In [13], Sturtevant presents an extension of the Botea et al. approach to build automated and minimal-memory state abstractions to speed path-finding. Experimental results show that with 3% more memory, path-finding is up to 100 times faster than A*. We extend significantly this work to massive path-finding scenario and also adapting it to the programming model of the GPU.

Researchers have recently developed parallel-based implementations of path-finding that use the computational power of the GPU. These approaches show that the GPU enables efficient path-finding to support large numbers of agents moving through expansive and increasingly large dynamic environments. In 2008, Bleiweiss [1] implemented the Dijkstra and the A* algorithms using CUDA. In [7], Katz et al. present a cache-efficient GPU implementation of the all-pairs shortest-path problem and demonstrate that it results in a significant improvement in performance. In [12], Stefan et al. obtained speedups for breadth-first search using a bit-vector representation of the search frontier on a GPU. In [8], Kider et al. present a novel implementation of a randomized heuristic search, namely R* search, that scales to higher-dimensional planning problems. They demonstrate how R* can be implemented on a GPU and show that it consistently produces lower-cost solutions, scales better in terms of memory, and runs faster than R* on a Central Processing Unit (CPU). In [3], Erra et al. propose an efficient multi-agent planning approach for GPUs based on an algorithm called RTAA*. The implementation of RTAA* enables the planning of many thousands of agents by using a limited memory footprint per agent.

3 The GPU Programming Model

In the last years, the increasing performance of the GPUs has led researchers to explore mapping general non-graphics computation onto these new parallel architectures. The GPGPU phenomenon has shown some impressive results and the demand to use the GPU as a more general parallel processor motivated NVIDIA to release in 2006 a new generation of graphics cards that significantly extended the GPU beyond graphics through a new unified graphics and computing GPU architecture and the CUDA programming model [9].

From the point of view of hardware model, modern NVIDIA GPUs are fully programmable many-core chips called CUDA cores. In a GPU, the number of streaming multiprocessors (SMXs) ranges from 4 SMX at the low end to 15

SMXs at the high end. For example, the GPU used in our experiments is an economic device of new Kepler generation and it consists of 4 SMXs, each one containing 192 CUDA cores. Each SMX is capable of supporting up to 2,048 threads. Current NVDIA GPUs manage up to 16,384 threads in real-time. All thread management, including creation, scheduling and barrier synchronization is performed entirely in hardware by the SMX with essentially zero overhead.

From the point of view of software model, CUDA is a minimal extension to the C language which permits the writing of a serial program called kernel. A kernel executes in parallel across a set of parallel threads. Following the representation in Figure 1, each thread has a private local memory. The programmer organizes these threads into a hierarchy of thread blocks and grids. A thread block is a set of concurrent threads that can cooperate among themselves through barrier synchronization and have access to the shared memory with latency comparable to registers. The grid is a set of thread blocks that may each be executed independently. All threads have access to the same global, constant or texture memory. These three memory spaces are optimized for different memory usages and thus have different time access. For example, the read-only constant cache and texture cache are shared by all scalar processor cores and this speeds up reads from the texture memory space and constant memory space.

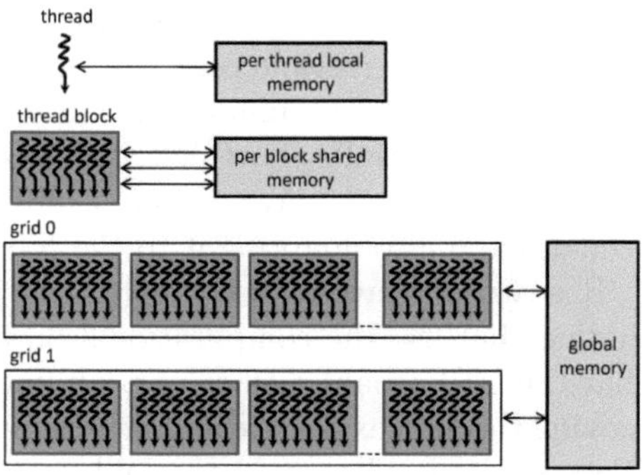

Fig. 1. Levels of parallel granularity and memory sharing on the GPU [10]

4 The Proposed Approach

Our Parallel Hierarchical A* (PHA*) is appropriate for simulation that are based on a grid map. In these simulations, the environment is subdivided into tiles that are the smallest unit space that can be occupied by an agent. Each tile represents a state of the search space and is connected to all nearby tiles. The cost of moving from a tile to each of its neighbors is specified by an integer. This can be used to model terrain elements that are difficult or impossible to pass, for example hills and lakes. A common metric used to measure distance on grid maps, which we adopt for this work, is the Manhattan distance.

In the subsequent sections, we first describe how to build an efficient abstraction graph of the input map by using an off-line phase, and then demonstrate how use this graph during a real-time phase for multi agent path-finding.

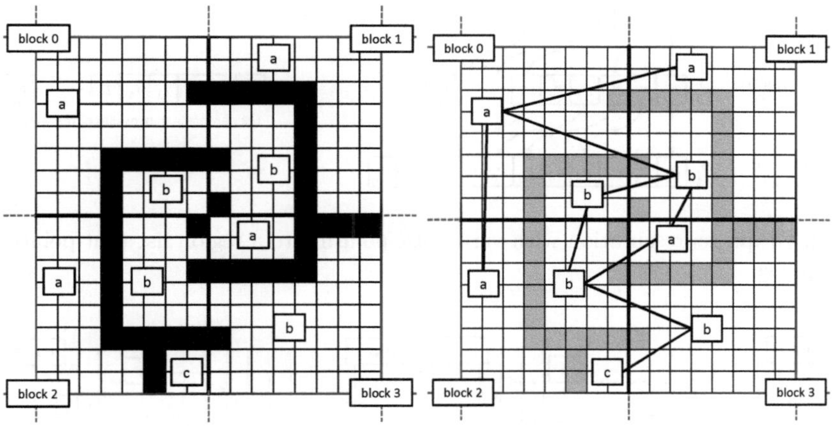

Fig. 2. A subdivision of a grid map in blocks. On the left, the regions identified using a BFS. On the right, the abstract graph.

4.1 Abstract Graph

In this phase, we build a high-level map abstracting away all the details within the tiles of the grid map. The grid map is divided into regular regions called blocks. These blocks are all of the same size and decompose the grid map into non-overlapping search sub-spaces. Because blocks are not guaranteed to be contiguous, we divide the bocks further into connected component called regions. The regions are identified by performing a breadth-first search (BFS) within a block using the GPU as described in Harish et al. [4]. Because there could be more than one region, the BFS is progressively invoked, with different start position, on the same block until all the tiles of the block will be associated with a region. Note that BFS is invoked in parallel over all blocks of the grid map. We illustrate blocks and regions on the left of Figure 2. As for instance, the Block 0 has two regions named 0.a and 0.b.

Each region within a block is represented by a single tile taken at the weighted center of the region. Once these regions have been established, we must compute edges between regions using the following process. For each side of the block, we have a thread that iterates along all the border tiles. The thread compares each border tile of a region with the adjacent border tiles belonging to the nearest region. This process enables to find all connected regions along the borders and hence whenever we find a pair of these regions, we add an edge to the abstract graph. As previously, this step is also performed in parallel and in particular for each block we have four threads one for each cardinal direction. The result of this process is illustrated on the right of Figure 2. As for instance, the region 0.a has three edges to 1.a, 1.b, and 2.a.

In order to use a data structure that fits well to the programming model of the GPU, we represent the graph in compact adjacency list form as illustrated in Figure 3. The array R contains the representative tile of each region. The

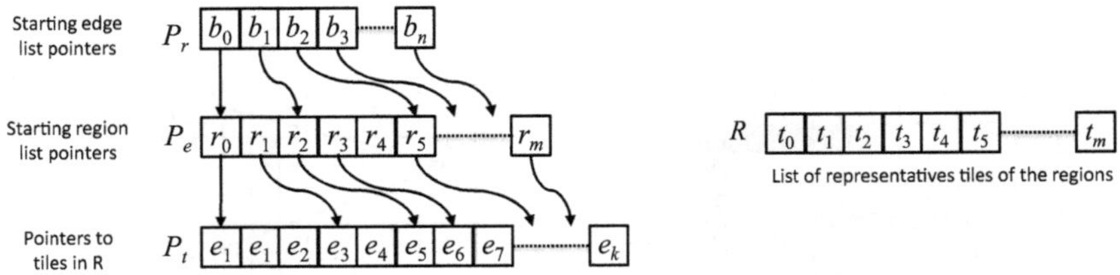

Fig. 3. Graph representation with vertex list pointing to a region list that pointing to an edge list

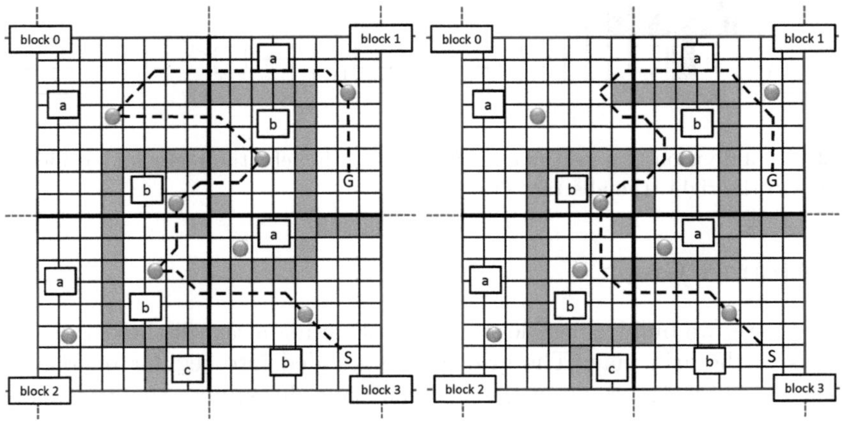

Fig. 4. A path from a start (S) to the goal (G) position. On the left, the path follows the representative tile of each region. On the right, the path enters within the regions and it heads toward the next region.

blocks of the grid map are represented as array P_r. Each entry $P_r[i]$ points to the regions of the block i. These regions are stored as an adjacency list in a large array named P_e from the starting position b_i. By using the index position j of a region in the array P_e we are able to obtain its own representative tile from $R[j]$. The array P_e contains the edges of the graph. Each entry $P_e[k]$ points to the edges of the tile k. These edges are stored as an adjacency list in an array named P_t from the starting positions r_k. Finally, the array P_t contains pointers to the representative tiles in the array R. This graph representation enables to obtain from a given block all the regions and its adjacent regions but also to trace all the adjacency regions from any given region. This feature is an essential requirement for computing paths with Dijkstra in the next phase.

4.2 Path-Finding

Given a set of agents with corresponding start tiles and goal tiles the next step of the path-finding is to find a path in the grid map using the abstract graph. We compute the paths in two steps. In the first step, we use a GPU implementation of Dijkstra[4] to find a path on the abstract graph. In particular, for each agent we

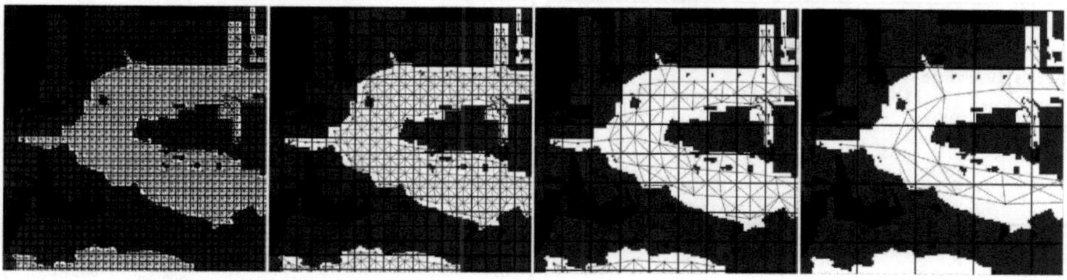

Fig. 5. Detail of the abstract graph for the map den520d

have a thread that computes a complete abstract path. Once a path is found, the second step is to refine this path crossing all the regional tiles using A*[5]. Also in this case, we exploit the GPU for refining the path of each agent allocating a thread per-agent. In both steps, we use the Manhattan distance as heuristic to measure distances on the grid map.

Given a complete abstract path, there are many approach to use this information for computing paths. A simple way to use the abstract path is to follow the representative tile of each region. First search from the starting tile to the first representative tile. Then, search between each region along the abstract path crossing all the representative tile, and finally search between the final region to the goal tile. The main drawback of this approach is that the path computed is much further long as illustrated on the left of Figure 4.

Our solution is to obtain a smoothed path during the searching. The idea is to follow the representative tile of each region but once an agent enters within a region, we force the agent to search immediately for the representative tile of the next region as illustrated on the right of Figure 4. Initially, for each start position we calculate the region where each agent begins to plan the path. Subsequently, the complete path is computed using iteratively search episodes. In each episode, the search is restricted to a small part of the grid map that can be reached from the current tile up to the next region using A*. In particular, each A* search has a representative tile as final position but the stop condition is to reach a new region. Once the agent has stopped within a region, it moves along the resulting trajectory and repeats the search episode process until it reaches the goal tile. This approach is suitable in an environment which tightly limit computational/temporal costs and thus the agents must alternate searching/planning and navigation as for instance in visual simulation.

5 Evaluation and Results

In this section, we show the results of two types of experiments. The first experiment demonstrates the efficiency of our approach. We compare PHA* with RTAA* which are both used to perform searches for many thousands of agents. We chose to compare PHA* with a GPU parallel version of RTAA* because in previous work[3] this implementation was found to be faster than a parallel

Map den520d 256x256				
Agents	Block Size	Execution time PHA* in ms. Off-line Phase	Execution time PHA* in ms. On-line Phase	Execution time RTAA* in ms
512	4	47.72	132.88	4400.75
	8	212.42	86.97	
	16	1269.38	103.91	
	32	9923.20	437.95	
1024	4	42.99	196.57	4699.8
	8	206.63	101.98	
	16	1260.80	121.09	
	32	9750.94	467.12	
2048	4	40.30	321.93	5384.99
	8	192.47	142.96	
	16	1215.06	155.81	
	32	9829.66	550.84	
4096	4	42.54	589.97	6057.33
	8	199.33	225.22	
	16	1212.22	229.37	
	32	9763.42	680.88	

Map tranquilpaths 512x512				
Agents	Block Size	Execution time PHA* in ms Off-line Phase	Execution time PHA* in ms On-line Phase	Execution time RTAA* in ms
512	4	78.15	338.60	6941.13
	8	387.48	168.86	
	16	2489.22	230.54	
	32	20418.30	563.05	
1024	4	68.17	548.14	8057.09
	8	381.87	234.81	
	16	2554.67	283.02	
	32	20508.40	696.79	
2048	4	67.18	980.09	9256.58
	8	389.24	338.69	
	16	2590.20	349.77	
	32	19638.40	800.46	
4096	4	72.42	1866.50	10896.43
	8	419.40	576.60	
	16	2599.50	490.15	
	32	19709.00	1058.40	

Fig. 6. GPU total times: PHA* vs RTAA*

Average Length Path and Percentage Increase									
Map	A*	PHA*							
		block size 4x4		block size 8x8		block size 16x16		block size 32x32	
	length	length	inc. in %	length	inc. in %	length	inc. in %	length	inc. in %
den520d	128.50	164.46	28.23	149.08	15.92	142.56	11.19	137.09	6.67
tranquilpaths	195.75	249.59	27.59	227.13	16.12	216.98	10.98	215.19	10.69

Fig. 7. Quality of the trajectories: PHA* vs A*

CPU implementation of A*. The second experiment is related to the quality of the trajectory found by using the abstract graph and concerns the length of the path obtained from PHA* compared to the A*[5] which is used as optimal path-finding algorithm.

The experiments were performed on two grid maps named den520d and tranquilpaths of sizes 256 × 256 and 512 × 512 respectively, coming from the public repository of Moving AI Lab[1]. An example map with its abstract graph is shown in Figure 5. Start and goal tiles were randomly chosen, and `lookahead`=3 for RTAA*, which is the optimal value for achieving best performance on these two maps. For each grid map, we launched several groups of agents ranging in size from 512 to 4096 with blocks measuring 4 × 4, 8 × 8, 16 × 16, and 32 × 32. Our tests were performed on an Intel Core i7-2600 3.40 GHz, NVIDIA Kepler GTX 650 Ti 1GB, Windows 7. All the kernels were written using CUDA 5.0 and Microsoft's Visual C++ 2010 compiler.

Figure 6 reports GPU total times of the PHA* compared to RTTA*. For the PHA*, we report both times for off-line and on-line phase. Note that off-line times are approximately the same because depends only to the size of the block. The results indicate that our approach is faster than RTAA*. The choice of the block size strongly influences the required time for the off-line phase. In fact

[1] `http://www.movingai.com/benchmarks/`

in this step, the greater effort is required to identify the representative tile of each region (node of the graph) and their connections (edges of the graph). Use smallest blocks mean small regions to explore, most of which corresponding to a single block, contrary biggest blocks lead to big irregular regions requiring more computation time. The same goes for the on-line phase in which the block size determines the behavior of the searches. In this case smallest block corresponds to a higher number of searches between consecutive regions in the abstract path but each region will be quickly explorable. The opposite happens using bigger block because there will be less regions to cross in the abstracted path but more tile to explore in each region. This aspect suggests the versatility of this approach, in the case of empty maps or with scattered obstacles should be useful use biggest blocks while that became absolutely discouraged for map like those used in the experiments. However, in this case our approach shows better results when the block size is 8×8 because this represents the right balance between region dimension and number of sub-paths in the abstract path.

Figure 7 lists the results of the quality test that compare PHA* and A*. This test was executed with 100 searches on both maps using different block size. The results indicate that the length of the paths retrieved with PHA* are worse than the optimal solution. This deficiency caused by the fact that the final path is composed by using the refining of different sub-path but is compensated for in terms of efficiency as shown in performance experiments. However, as illustrate in Figure 7 increasing the size of the blocks involves a path length near the optimal solution because the final path is less affected by the presence of intermediate representative tile and the A* search used for the on-line phase mitigates the result. This different behavior still plays in favor of user that tuning the block size parameter should reach the desired trade-off between speed and better path. For example, in a real-time application, speed is the highest priority and suboptimal paths may be acceptable.

6 Conclusions

In this work, we have demonstrated a parallel implementation of path-finding for agent-based simulation. Through a hierarchical representation of the input map, PHA* offers a simple and powerful way of planning trajectories for many hundreds of agents using a thread to explore each potential path. We propose also a strategy to obtain smooth paths during the search which enables to improve path lengths. Our results show that the GPU implementation enables the real-time use of this technique even in scenarios with a vast number of agents which is common in applications such as simulation. The execution times showed that both phases could be used also in real-time as for instance in scenario with dynamic obstacles that occur in the grid map.

This aspect offers a starting point for interesting future works. Once the system recognizes the presence of dynamic obstacles, our approach should be used to rebuild the entire graph or only the portion of the abstract graph which corresponds to the blocks where changes occurred. Thus, all retrieved paths combining multiple sub-paths should be able to adapt swiftly to changes in the map. For this purpose, we are interested to further enhance the performance of the off-line phase. Finally, we want to improve the quality of the path by exploiting in a better way the knowledge of the map acquired during the off-line phase.

References

1. Bleiweiss, A.: GPU accelerated pathfinding. In: Proceedings of the 23rd ACM SIGGRAPH/EUROGRAPHICS Symposium on Graphics Hardware, GH 2008, Aire-la-Ville, Switzerland, pp. 65–74. Eurographics Association (2008)
2. Botea, A., Müller, M., Schaeffer, J.: Near Optimal Hierarchical Path-Finding. Journal of Game Development 1(1), 7–28 (2004)
3. Erra, U., Caggianese, G.: Real-time Adaptive GPU multi-agent path planning, vol. 2, ch. 22, pp. 295–308. Morgan Kaufmann Publishers Inc. Computing Gems Jade Edition edition (2011)
4. Harish, P., Narayanan, P.J.: Accelerating large graph algorithms on the GPU using CUDA. In: Aluru, S., Parashar, M., Badrinath, R., Prasanna, V.K. (eds.) HiPC 2007. LNCS, vol. 4873, pp. 197–208. Springer, Heidelberg (2007)
5. Hart, P., Nilsson, N., Raphael, B.: A formal basis for the heuristic determination of minimum cost paths. IEEE Transactions on Systems Science and Cybernetics 4(2), 100–107 (1968)
6. Holte, R.C., Perez, M.B., Zimmer, R.M., MacDonald, A.J.: Hierarchical A*: searching abstraction hierarchies efficiently. In: Proceedings of the Thirteenth National Conference on Artificial Intelligence, AAAI 1996, vol. 1, pp. 530–535. AAAI Press (1996)
7. Katz, G.J., Kider Jr., J.T.: All-pairs shortest-paths for large graphs on the GPU. In: Proceedings of the 23rd ACM SIGGRAPH/EUROGRAPHICS Symposium on Graphics Hardware, GH 2008, Aire-la-Ville, Switzerland, pp. 47–55. Eurographics Association (2008)
8. Kider, J., Henderson, M., Likhachev, M., Safonova, A.: High-dimensional planning on the GPU. In: 2010 IEEE International Conference on Robotics and Automation (ICRA), pp. 2515–2522 (May 2010)
9. Kirk, D.B., Hwu, W.-M.W.: Programming Massively Parallel Processors: A Hands-on Approach, 1st edn. Morgan Kaufmann Publishers Inc., San Francisco (2010)
10. Nickolls, J., Buck, I., Garland, M., Skadron, K.: Scalable parallel programming with CUDA. Queue 6(2), 40–53 (2008)
11. Shekhar, S., Fetterer, A., Goyal, B.: Materialization trade-offs in hierarchical shortest path algorithms. In: Scholl, M.O., Voisard, A. (eds.) SSD 1997. LNCS, vol. 1262, pp. 94–111. Springer, Heidelberg (1997)
12. Stefan, E., Damian, S.: Parallel state space search on the GPU. In: International Symposium on Combinatorial Search, SoCS (2009)
13. Sturtevant, N.R.: Memory-efficient abstractions for pathfinding. In: Proceedings of the Third Artificial Intelligence and Interactive Digital Entertainment Conference, Stanford, California, USA, June 6-8, pp. 31–36. The AAAI Press (2007)

Agent Migration in HPC Systems Using FLAME*

Claudio Márquez, Eduardo César, and Joan Sorribes

Computer Architecture and Operating Systems Department (CAOS),
Universitat Autònoma de Barcelona, 08193 Bellaterra, Spain
claudio.marquez@caos.uab.es, {eduardo.cesar,joan.sorribes}@uab.cat
http://caos.uab.es/

Abstract. In HPC agent based applications, the complex interaction rules would likely cause workload imbalances that negatively affect the simulation time. In addition, the imbalance problem may vary during the application execution in accordance to the behavior of the agents. Consequently, a solution to this problem should be able to dynamically balance the load. A dynamic load balancing scheme could be based on migrating agents between processing units. In this paper, we propose a modification of the agent-based simulation framework FLAME that provides the automatic generation of the routines needed to dynamically migrate agents among different computational units. However, most agent-based simulation frameworks do not include routines for migrating agents. Moreover, we demonstrate their use in a simple load balancing scheme on a specific application.

Keywords: Agent-based Simulation, FLAME, Migration Agents, SPMD, Load Balancing, Application Tuning.

1 Introduction

Agent-Based Modelling (ABM) is a popular technique for simulating complex systems in several domains such as economical, medical, biological and social science. Basically, Agent-Based Modelling and Simulation (ABMS) describe the system's behavior through the interactions of a set of autonomous entities in the environment.

Large ABMS applications facilitate the study of complex problems. In this case, they should be deployed in a High Performance Computing (HPC) environment to provide sufficient resources and be executed in a reasonable amount of time because in most cases ABMS are CPU intensive and require large amounts of memory [1].

Moreover, agent based applications show significant variations in the amount of computing and communication time. These variations are given by the large amount of interactions among agents, and the different rules of behavior exhibited by most of these models. Moreover, the evolution of the simulation may

* This work was funded by MICINN Spain, under the project TIN2011-28689-C02-01.

D. an Mey et al. (Eds.): Euro-Par 2013 Workshops, LNCS 8374, pp. 523–532, 2014.

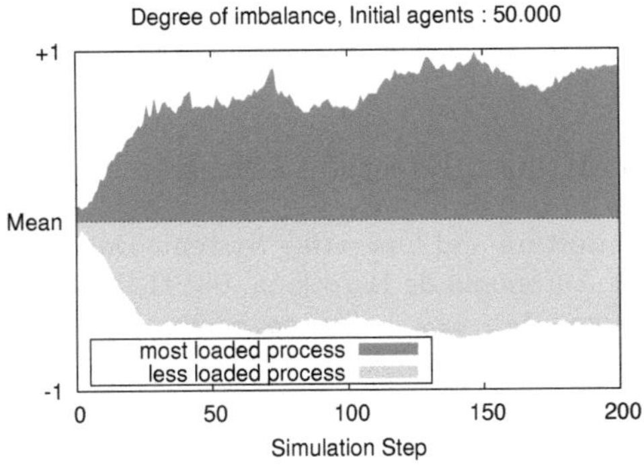

Fig. 1. Degree of computing imbalance during the simulation of the SIR model

produce dynamic changes in the workload. Therefore, during the execution of the simulation, load imbalances are likely to appear. Figure 1 shows the degree of imbalance of a simulation of 50.000 agents in a cluster of 128 processes.

In order to solve such problems, schemas for dynamically adjusting the load should be used. However, it would be very helpful for such dynamic schemas that the parallel simulation environments include mechanisms that allow the migration of agents between different computational units.

Currently, a few ABMS parallel applications oriented to HPC environments can be found. Ecolab [2] is an object-oriented environment written in C++ and MPI. Repast HPC [3] was recently released in 2012, and written in C++ using MPI for parallel operations. Contrary to Ecolab, Repast HPC was created from the beginning for large-scale distributed computing platforms. Although both Ecolab and Repast HPC are based on a Single Program Multiple Data (SPMD) paradigm, they do not include generic migration routines, so the developer should deploy the whole migration code. Moreover, D-Mason [4] is a framework written in Java, based on a master/worker paradigm. D-Mason is focused on using the idle desktop workstations and subdividing the workload among these heterogeneous machines. In addition, recent improvements [5] of D-Mason provide load balancing schema. Finally, FLAME [6] framework allows the production of automatic parallelizable code to run on a large HPC infrastructure. This framework is based on a SPMD paradigm, it has been continuously developed since 2006, and it used for economic modelling in the EURACE [7] project. FLAME is written in C using MPI, and is aimed principally at the economical, medical, biological and social science domains.

Current implementations of dynamic load balancing strategies are often developed using centralized or hierarchical approaches. On one hand, centralized approaches commonly report a high computational cost and scalability problems. In the other hand, decentralized approaches can present problems regarding the quality of the balance because the neighboring processes exchange incomplete information. In [8] a centralized load balancing based on space repartitioning is proposed. In [9] a hierarchical multi-level load balancing strategy is presented, and centralized and hierarchical schemas are compared. In [10] a decentralized algorithm based on moving the boundary between the neighbor region is defined. In [11] three algorithms using recursive domain decomposition in a binary tree structure are compared using balance speed and communication costs. In [12] a complex partitioning approach based on irregular spatial decompositions is presented. In [13] distributed cluster-based partitioning and load balancing schema for problems of flocking behaviors are defined. In its current version, the code generated by FLAME lacks the necessary routines to allow the migration of agents; therefore, all migration routines should be implemented directly on the generated code.

This paper describes a modification of the FLAME framework for automatically generating, from the agents's specification, the routines necessary for migrating agents between different computational units. The approach aims to implement dynamic policies for deterministic agent-based simulations, which define the agents as state machines.

The rest of this document is organized into five sections. First, Section 2 briefly describes FLAME. Next, the migration routines are presented (3). The results section shows how these routines have been used for implementing a simple load balancing schema for a SIR ABMS application (4). The final section includes the conclusions and the future work(5).

2 FLAME

In contrast to common ABMS environments, FLAME is a tool that enables the necessary source code to be generated for the simulation; hence, it is not a simulator in itself. FLAME automatically generates the simulation code in C through a template engine. In the same way, FLAME provides a set of template files that the template engine uses to generate the simulation code getting information from the model definition. The model definition consists of X-Machine Markup Language (XMML) files, which is a dialect of XML and the implementation of the agent functions contained in C files. The migration routines are automatically generated from a set of extra template files as shown in figure 2(b). Figure 2(a) shows the files required by the FLAME framework to create the simulation code, and figure 2(b) shows the FLAME diagram including the proposed improvement.

2.1 Functional Description

The deployment of agents is based on finite state machines called X-machines, which consist of a finite set of states, transitions between the states and actions. To perform the simulation, FLAME keeps each agent as an X-machine data structure, whose state is changed via a set of transition functions. Furthermore, the transition functions perform message exchanges between agents if necessary. Then, the simulation environment is composed mainly by a set of X-machines defined by their state transitions, internal memory, and agent messages.

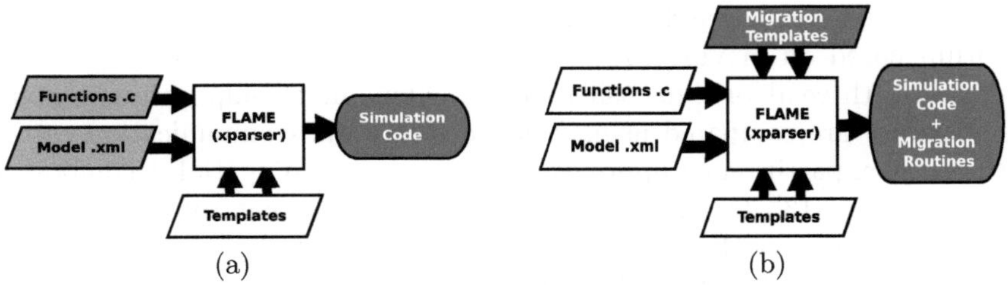

Fig. 2. Base-diagram of the FLAME framework and diagram with the improvement

The X-machines are kept in linked lists, one for each state of a specific agent. When the simulation starts, the X-machines are inserted into the list related to the initial state. Then the corresponding transition function is applied to each X-machine. Once this has been done, these X-machines are inserted into the list related to the next state. This process is repeated until the last state, which determines the end of the iteration is reached.

2.2 Parallelization

In HPC environments, FLAME communications are managed by the Message Board Library *libmboard*, which uses *MPI* to communicate between processes. *Libmboard* handles the messages of the agents through message managing mechanisms and filtering before sending messages to local agents and agents belonging to external processes. FLAME handles deadlocks through synchronization points, which ensure that all the data is coordinated among agents using an SPMD pattern.

Figure 3(a) shows the communication pattern between local agents and external agents using *libmboard* library. This library sends all messages to the agents through a coordinated communication between different *MPI* processes.

The parallel distribution of the agents in FLAME is based on two static partitioning methods: geometric partitioning and round-robin partitioning. Currently, FLAME does not have mechanisms to enable the movement of agents between processes. Thus, the workload in each parallel process will rely on the initial population of agents.

Consequently, evolution of the simulation may produce computation imbalance causing overhead, and also may produce excessive external communications due to the interaction among agents (as shown in figure 3(b)). Therefore, the time required to complete the simulation will be negatively affected.

3 Migration of Agents

An agent migration mechanism is necessary to implement policies in order to solve load/communication imbalance problems. However, developing this mechanism can be a time consuming task because, among other reasons, the programmer must understand the code generated by the framework for each specific

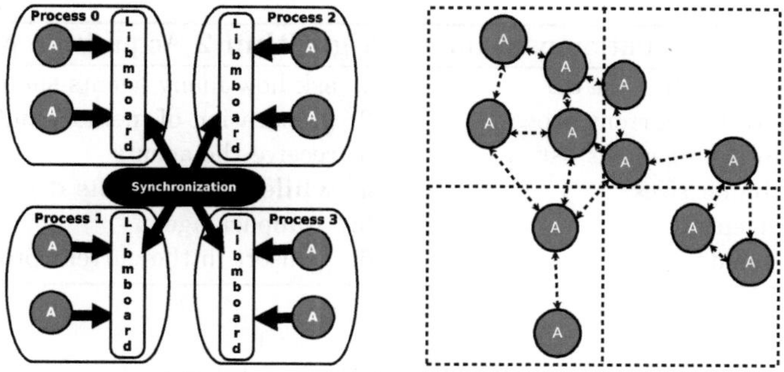

Fig. 3. *(a)* Parallel communication and synchronization via libmboard. *(b)* Workload problems associated with the distribution of agents.

simulation code. Consequently, enhancing the tool for automatically generating efficient routines for migration agents could be very helpful.

In order to achieve this new feature, the developer should only add three new templates for generating the migration routines. Then, the template engine processes these templates to obtain the information about the agent model from the definition file. This information includes issues such as: agent types, the variables (properties) of the agents and the size of each agent's variable.

Internally, the template engine interprets the template's information using the information about the agent model, and generates migration routines with the simulation code (as shown in figure 2(b)). Once the simulation code has been created, the migration routines can be used for automatically adding and removing agents from any process. The migration process can be subdivided into two procedures: *contribution* and *acquisition*.

On one hand, **contribution procedure** consist of removing, packing and sending the selected agents in the sender processes. In this procedure, the agents to be migrated are held in a set of *linked lists* identified by the *id* of the target process. Later, the agents are stored in a set of contiguous memory buffers to be packed. At this point, the buffer sizes have been automatically calculated and created by the routines. Finally, the sender processes will have a collection of buffers to be sent as agent packages (one for each recipient process).

On the other hand, the **acquisition procedure** consists of receiving, unpacking and adding the agents in the recipient processes. The packages of agents are stored in buffers to be unpacked. Once the agents have been unpacked, they are inserted with the other agents in the recipient process. Algorithms 1 and 2 show the procedures involved during the migration of agents.

In order to send the agents to a recipient process in a single communication, the agents need to be stored in contiguous memory before being sent. This migration is accomplished by packing and unpacking data using *MPI* functions. Before being used, these *MPI* functions require memory buffers whose sizes depend on the type and amount of agents. Additionally, the sending and receiving

Algorithm 1 Contribution procedure

```
while agents to be sent do
    remove of the current process
    insert in the recipient list
calculate buffer sizes
pack the agents
send the agents
```

Algorithm 2 Acquisition procedure

```
ask how many agents should receive
preparation of memory buffers
receive the agents
while packed agents do
    unpack agent
    insert in the current process
```

of the agents has been deployed using *MPI* asynchronous functions to overlap the costs of communication and computation.

Before performing the migration process, a criterion must be established to decide which agents should be sent. Then the migration process starts through the migration routines mentioned in section 3.1. The migration process should also be required to decide when it should be performed. Nevertheless, this partially depends on the criterion by which the agents were selected. Below, the main migration features incorporated into FLAME are described.

3.1 Migration Routines

The migration routines are specifically generated for each type of agent in the model, so it is possible to perform migrations after any transition. The following list introduces the main migration routines. The prefix NAME indicates the name of a specific type of agent.

- *Init_migration*: Initializes global variables and data structures involved in the migration.
- *Pop_NAME*: Moves agents to a specific *linked list* and removes them from the current process.
- *Pack_NAME*: Packs all agents kept in the *linked lists* in contiguous memory buffers, one for each recipient.
- *send_NAME/recv_NAME*: These routines are prototypes to define how to send and receive agents.
- *Unpack_NAME*: Unpacks the packed agents received. Then, inserts the received agents to the X-machine list of the current process.
- *Push_NAME*: Add an agent to the current process.

With these functions inserted into FLAME, it is possible to incorporate a load balancing schema based on the migration of agents between processes.

4 Experimental Results

The main objective of this section is to demonstrate that, using the migration routines, it is possible to migrate agents and correct imbalance problems in ABMS applications. For testing purposes only, the SIR epidemic model described below is used [14]. The simulation workload changes dynamically due to the random distribution of death and birth rates. In this experiment, the initial distribution of agents is based on a round-robin distribution and performed during 200 simulation steps.

The SIR model describes the spread of an epidemic within a population on a 2D toroidal space. The population is divided into three groups: the Susceptible (S), the Infectious (I), and the Recovered (R). For this reason, this model is called SIR. In summary, the susceptible are those individuals who are not infected and not immune, the infectious are those who are infected and can transmit the disease, and the recovered are those who have been infected and are immune. Additionally, natural births and deaths during the epidemic are included in this SIR model, so individuals could die from the disease or by natural death due to aging. Consequently, births and deaths represent a dynamic creation and elimination of agents; therefore, the workload can change as the simulation proceeds.

In this example, generated functions are tagged as `Person` because agents are defined as `Person` in the model specification. First, the function call *Init_migration()* is inserted before the configuration section of the *libmboard* access mode. Then, all configuration sections of the *libmboard* access mode are set up in *MB_MODE_READWRITE* mode.

Algorithm 3. Overview of the load balancing schema described in [15]

collect all computing times for each process
$tolerance \leftarrow threshold * avg\_time$
if $\forall i \in procs, \exists\ proc_i / |imbalance(proc_i)| \geqslant tolerance$ **then**
    sort computing times in descending order
    $i, j \leftarrow$ index of the first and last process in the *sorted list*, respectively
while $|imbalance(proc_i \wedge proc_j)| \geqslant tolerance$ **do**
    $contribution\_range_i \leftarrow exceeded\_time_i \pm tolerance$
    $j \leftarrow$ index of the last process in the *sorted list*
    while $|imbalance(proc_i \wedge proc_j)| \geqslant tolerance$ **do**
        $acquisition\_range_j \leftarrow required\_time_j \pm tolerance$
        calculate expected migration for $proc_i | proc_j$
        sort underloaded computing times
        if $|imbalance(proc_i)| \leqslant tolerance$ **then** break
        $j--$
    sort overloaded computing times
    $i \leftarrow$ index of the first process in the *sorted list*
    if $|imbalance(proc_i)| \leqslant tolerance$ **then** break
Execute the asynchronous exchanges

For the **load balancing schema**, we used a schema for SPMD applications described in [15]. This schema dynamically decides the global reconfiguration of the workload using an imbalance threshold, a computing time, and the number of agents. The computing times and the number of agents are monitored in each iteration during the simulation. This approach is executed by all the processes without a central unit of decision. Therefore, each process knows the global load situation and executes the algorithm with the same input. Consequently, all processes calculate the same reconfiguration of the workload. The schema is triggered when an imbalance factor is detected outside the tolerance range. This factor indicates the percentage of imbalance in respect to the mean, and the tolerance range defines the permissible degree of imbalance (see algorithm 3).

During the experiments, the load balancing schema is activated after the fifth simulation step. After each load balancing activation, the schema is disabled during one simulation step because the computing measurements vary when the migration process has been launched. The migration routines were tested using FLAME 0.16.2, libmboard 0.2.1 and OpenMPI 1.4.1. The experiments were executed on an IBM Cluster with the following features: 32 IBM x3550 Nodes, 2xDual-Core Intel(R) Xeon(R) CPU 5160 @ 3.00GHz 4MB L2 (2x2), 12 GB Fully Buffered DIMM 667 MHz, Hot-swap SAS Controller 160GB SATA Disk and Integrated dual Gigabit Ethernet. Tests consists of a case without load balancing schema, and three imbalance tolerances: 0.3(30%), 0.15(15%) and 0.05(5%).

The simulations were started with an initial population of 50.000 and 100000 agents (scenarios A and B, respectively), carrying capacity of 50.000 and 100.000, and 10 of space dimensions of 1.000x1.000 and 900x900, respectively. The environmental configuration of the simulations for both scenarios were set up as infected = 10, lifespan = 100, average offspring = 4, infectiousness = 65, chance recovery = 50, and disease duration = 20. Moreover, for both scenarios, 16, 32, 64 and 128 cores were used.

Given that the agents were distributed through a round-robin distribution, depending on the number of processes and the initial agents, the initial number of agents per process can be equal or similar. Figures 4(a) and 4(b) compare the execution time with a varying number of processes by comparing different values of tolerance with the original simulation without the load balancing schema.

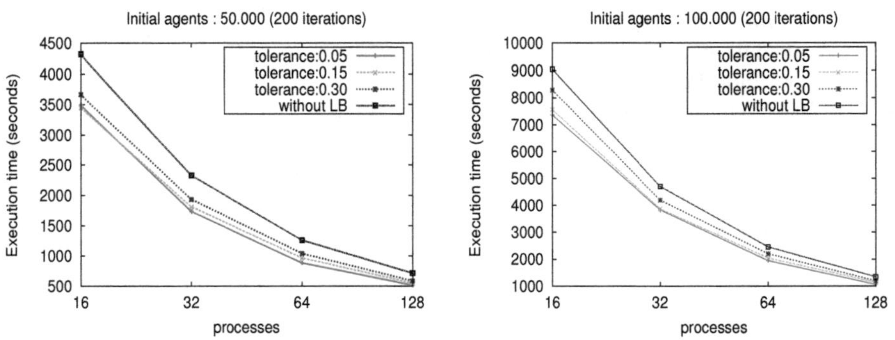

(a) (b)

Fig. 4. Executions times in both scenarios

Table 1. Summarize of the execution of scenario B, 100.000 agents for 128 processes

tolerance	pack	unpack	agents-sent	kbytes-sent	exchanges	exec-time(sec)	gain(%)
-	-	-	-	-	-	2462,49	-
0,30	0,007	0,005	19985	937,38	119	2206,21	10,4
0,15	0,008	0,006	24080	1129,97	249	2048,76	18,8
0,05	0,010	0,007	37283	1751,89	870	1953,43	24,8

Here, both scenarios have better results using the load balancing schema. Moreover, in most cases, if the imbalance tolerance is reduced the improvement is better.

In Table 1, a reduced value of imbalance tolerance results in a better execution time. By contrast, achieving a better balance involves a larger amount of agents migrated and a larger amount of exchanges between processes. For this reason, a load balancing schema should consider the communication overhead caused by the amount of exchanges during the migration process.

5 Conclusion and Future Work

ABMS applications may present computational and communicational imbalances during the simulation process. Therefore, the simulation environment should be equipped with migration mechanisms to make modifications in the workload of the overloaded and underloaded processes.

In this paper, a modification of the FLAME framework for automatically generating agent migration functions is presented. Using the same FLAME code generation methodology, the migration routines are automatically generated from templates. Therefore, this improvement will allow the inclusion of load balancing strategies. In this manner, the workload among the different processes can be dynamically adjusted during the simulation.

It is planned to generalize a load balancing strategy and research on balancing communication times.

References

1. Allan, R.: Survey of agent based modelling and simulation tools. Engineering 501, 57–72 (2009)
2. Standish, R.K., Leow, R.: Ecolab: Agent based modeling for C++ programmers. CoRR cs.MA/0401026 (2004)
3. Collier, N., North, M.: Repast SC++: A platform for large-scale agent-based modeling. Large-Scale Computing Techniques for Complex System Simulations (2011)
4. Cordasco, G., De Chiara, R., Mancuso, A., Mazzeo, D., Scarano, V., Spagnuolo, C.: A framework for distributing agent-based simulations. In: Alexander, M., et al. (eds.) Euro-Par 2011, Part I. LNCS, vol. 7155, pp. 460–470. Springer, Heidelberg (2012)

5. Carillo, M., Cordasco, G., Chiara, R.D., Raia, F., Scarano, V., Serrapica, F.: Enhancing the performances of D-MASON—a motivating example. In: Pina, N., Kacprzyk, J., Obaidat, M.S. (eds.) SIMULTECH, pp. 137–143. SciTePress (2012)
6. Kiran, M., Richmond, P., Holcombe, M., Chin, L.S., Worth, D., Greenough, C.: FLAME: simulating large populations of agents on parallel hardware architectures. In: AAMAS, pp. 1633–1636 (2010)
7. Deissenberg, C., Vanderhoog, S., Dawid, H.: EURACE: A massively parallel agent-based model of the european economy. Applied Mathematics and Computation 204(2), 541–552 (2008)
8. Zhou, B., Zhou, S.: Parallel simulation of group behaviors. In: Proceedings of the 36th Conference on Winter Simulation, WSC 2004. Winter Simulation Conference, pp. 364–370 (2004)
9. Zheng, G., Meneses, E., Bhatele, A., Kale, L.V.: Hierarchical load balancing for Charm++ applications on large supercomputers. In: Proceedings of the 2010 39th International Conference on Parallel Processing Workshops, ICPPW 2010, pp. 436–444. IEEE Computer Society, Washington, DC (2010)
10. Cosenza, B., Cordasco, G., De Chiara, R., Scarano, V.: Distributed load balancing for parallel agent-based simulations. In: Proceedings of the 2011 19th International Euromicro Conference on Parallel, Distributed and Network-Based Processing, PDP 2011, pp. 62–69. IEEE Computer Society, Washington, DC (2011)
11. Zhang, D., Jiang, C., Li, S.: A fast adaptive load balancing method for parallel particle-based simulations. Simulation Modelling Practice and Theory 17(6), 1032–1042 (2009)
12. Vigueras, G., Lozano, M., Orduña, J.M.: Workload balancing in distributed crowd simulations: the partitioning method. J. Supercomput. 58(2), 261–269 (2011)
13. Solar, R., Suppi, R., Luque, E.: Proximity load balancing for distributed cluster-based individual-oriented fish school simulations. Procedia Computer Science 9, 328–337 (2012); Proceedings of the International Conference on Computational Science, ICCS 2012
14. Worth, D., Chin, S., Greenough, C.: FLAME tutorial examples: a simple SIR infection model. Technical Report RAL-TR-2012-017, Rutherford Appleton Laboratory (November 2012)
15. Márquez, C., César, E., Sorribes, J.: A load balancing schema for agent-based SPMD applications. In: PDPTA (2013)

Communication Strategies in Distributed Agent-Based Simulations: The Experience with D-MASON

Gennaro Cordasco[1], Ada Mancuso[2], Francesco Milone[2], and Carmine Spagnuolo[2]

[1] Dipartimento di Psicologia, Seconda Università degli Studi di Napoli, Italy
gennaro.cordasco@unina2.it
[2] Dipartimento di Informatica, Università degli Studi di Salerno, Italy
{mancuso.ada,milone.francesco1988,spagnuolocarmine}@gmail.com

Abstract. Agent-Based simulation Models (ABMs) are a very powerful experimental tool of analysis, used in many scientific and technological communities of researchers, to assess and predict the dynamic unfolding of a series of events or processes, according to the imposition of certain conditions, given by the analyst. The computing power usually represents a limit for such simulations and the traditional answer to the need for computing power is to invest in computer resources. D-MASON is a framework for parallelizing simulations developed on top of MASON toolkit. The goal of D-MASON is to exploit wasted computing power in a network of computers, eventually heterogeneous, as a research lab or a cluster of workstation.

In this paper we present a novel communication strategy using *Publish/Subscribe* paradigm through a layer based on the MPI Standard.

Keywords: Publish/Subscribe, MPI, Agent-based simulation models, MASON, D-MASON, Parallel Computing, Distributed Systems, High Performance Computing.

1 Introduction

Fast computers have stimulated the rapid growth of a new way of doing science. The two broad classical branches of theoretical science and experimental science have been joined by computational science. Computational scientists simulate on computers phenomena too complex to be reliably predicted by theory and too dangerous or expensive to be reproduced in the laboratory. Successes in computational sciences over the past ten years have caused demand for supercomputing resources, to improve the performance of the system and to allow the growth of the models, in terms of number of agents and complexity of interactions. From a computer scientist's perspective it is natural to think to distribute the execution of the simulations among multiple machines: it is well known that the speed of single-processor computers is reaching some physical limits. For these reasons parallel computing has become the dominant paradigm for computational scientists who need the latest development on computing resources in order to solve their problems [7].

D-MASON [5] is a tool that allows the execution of simulations written for MASON [3, 10, 11] in a network of computers, dealing effectively with several challenging

D. an Mey et al. (Eds.): Euro-Par 2013 Workshops, LNCS 8374, pp. 533–543, 2014.

problems in designing a tool for distributed simulations like communication strategies, synchronization algorithms and usability requirements.

D-MASON guarantees *effectiveness*, because with D-MASON *you can do more* than what you can do with MASON and *efficiency*, because the porting of MASON applications in D-MASON requires only some modifications without the need for redesigning them [6]. An important quality of D-MASON is its high modularity. As an example, in D-MASON the communication is based on a *Publish/Subscribe* interface, but the developer is free to implement this interface in different ways. Currently D-MASON implements Publish/Subscribe communication paradigm exploiting *Apache ActiveMQ/Java Message Service* (JMS). Previous versions of D-MASON implemented the Publish/Subscribe paradigm using different approaches (i.e., TCP Sockets and Java RMI [13]).

In this paper we present a communication strategy, based on the Publish/Subscribe paradigm, that uses the MPI Standard [18] as an example of centralized communication. We show that our MPI based Publish/Subscribe mechanism reaches performance comparable to D-MASON and in some configurations it gets some small improvements. It is worth to mention that the MPI based approach provides some byproduct: (i) the MPI approach allows to avoid the communication server that can represent a bottleneck for the whole system; (ii) the synchronization between processors is easier, because MPI collective communication primitives are blocking.

2 D-MASON

D-MASON is a discrete-event simulation system based on a master/workers paradigm: the master assigns a portion of the whole computation to each worker. It is possible to list three kinds of simulation system: *continuous system*, where the state changes continuously with respect to time, *discrete system*, where the state is modified only at specific points in time, and *hybrid system*, which comprises both continuous and discrete elements [9]. In such simulations time leaps through distinct points in time, named *simulation steps*, in which agents behavior is computed. The field is partitioned into cells that are assigned to the workers and agents migrate from a worker to another, according to their own behavior. For each simulation step a worker simulates the agents in its own field and sends back the result of the computation to the interested workers.

D-MASON faces the following problems:

Field Partitioning. In D-MASON the space of the simulation can be divided into horizontal or square cells. Each worker is assigned one cell and its agents. An agent has a limited visibility of the simulation space called *Area of Interest (AOI)*. Since the AOI radius of an agent is small compared with the size of a cell, the communication is limited to local messages between neighboring cells.

Synchronization. In a discrete-event simulation, events need to be processed in a non-decreasing timestamp order, because an event with a smaller timestamp can potentially modify the state of the system and thereby affect events that happen later. We call this phenomenon *causality constraint*. In literature two major parallel simulation methods are defined based on how *causality constraint* is enforced. *Conservative parallel simulation* eliminates the possibility of any causality errors, that is each simulation step represent a barrier and events are always executed in the right order. *Optimistic parallel simulation* allows steps to be processed out of order. Once a causality error is detected the offending worker/cell has to rollback and recover from such an error. This kind of systems requires state saving and recovery mechanisms [9]. D-MASON adopts a conservative approach: a simulation step is divided in two phases: *communication/synchronization* and *simulation*. Each cell sends to its neighbors the information about the agents that are migrating to them or may fall into the AOI of their agents. Each step is associated with a fixed state of the simulation. Cells are simulated step by step: the step i of a cell c is computed using the states $i-1$ of c's neighbors, so the step i of a cell cannot be executed until the states $i-1$ of its neighbors have been computed and delivered.

Communication. D-MASON uses the Publish/Subscribe paradigm: a multicast channel is assigned to each cell and cells simply subscribe to the channels associated with the cells which overlap with their AOI to receive the needed updates. D-MASON exploits Java interfaces' mechanism to define the operations of the communication layer in order to simplify changes to the implementation of the Publish/Subscribe without affect the whole system. In the remaining part of this paper we provide a comparison between the *JMS Strategy* and the *MPI Strategy*.

The architecture of D-MASON is divided into four functional blocks. The *System Management* provides a master application for coordinating the workers, handling the bootstrap and running the simulation. The *Workers* are in charge of simulating the agents that belongs to the assigned regions, handling the migration and managing the synchronization between neighboring regions. The *Communication Layer* provides a simple interface defining the operations of the Publish/Subscribe paradigm. The *Global Viewer* is a tool that visualizes the whole simulation. D-MASON is available at [17].

3 MPI Strategy

The main goal of our paper is to check whether the communication in D-MASON architecture can be improved using the MPI layer. Obviously MPI does not allow directly Publish/Subscribe functionalists so we had to manage them in a different layer according to the Communication interface of D-MASON which exposes some routines to publish and receive messages on specific topics.

We define *synchronization time* as the time required to exchange all messages at the end of a simulation step. We assign to each MPI Process a D-MASON worker and use *communication groups* to describe the communication among cells. The *synchronization time* is partitioned in communication rounds, each of which contains a group communication.

3.1 MPI

MPI is a library specification for message-passing, designed for high performance on both massively parallel machines and on workstation clusters. MPI has emerged as one of the primary programming paradigms for writing efficient parallel applications, it provides point-to-point and collective communications and guarantees portability with all platforms compliant with the MPI Standard. MPI provides several collective operations which are very important because they sustain very high parallel speed-ups for parallel applications [18]. We considered two solutions for using MPI in D-MASON: a Java implementation of MPI or a Java binding of MPI.

The Need for Thread Safety. Since the architecture of D-MASON uses a thread for each operation (send or receive) on the same cell, during the choice of the MPI implementation, it is important to consider thread safety implementations.

We aim for a programming model that is a mixture of message passing and multithreading, that is an MPI process including multiple threads making MPI calls. An MPI process together with its threads is uniquely identified by the MPI layer, so when an MPI process, handling one or more threads, receives a message, this one will be received by all the threads of that process.

In the literature we found several Java implementations of the MPI standard [2,8,20]. MPJ Express is an open-source library for message passing compliant with MPI-1.1, offering the same thread-safety guarantees of MPI-2. The comparison between MPJ Express and other MPI implementations is reported in [16]. Open MPI Project [19] is an open source MPI-2 Standard implementation that is developed and maintained by a consortium of academic, research and industry partners. Combining the expertise, technologies, resources from all across the *HPC* community it offers the best MPI library available. The *prerelease 1.9a1r27886* of Open MPI and the current *trunk* on Open MPI'SVN [19] offers *mpiJava*, a Java binding of MPI-1.1 Standard [1,4].

We chose, for its performance, *mpiJava* as MPI implementation, even though it offers no guarantee of thread safety.

Group Communication. The communication model in D-MASON is potentially $n - to - n$, that means that each node of the network may need to communicate with all others. We chose the Publish/Subscribe paradigm to meet the requirements of flexibility and scalability of the system.

The collective communications offered by MPI allows to make a series of point-to-point communications in one single call. MPI processes can be grouped and managed by an object called *Communicator* [14].

The group communication routines we used are:

- `MPI_Bcast`: sends the same data to all processes in a communicator;
- `MPI_Gather`: collects data from many processes to one single process, the root process, allowing a group to get all needed information in a single step.

Significant research has been carried out in the past for improving collective communication using parallel algorithms based on the message size and optimized for the specific platform. As an example, the function `MPI_Bcast` for small messages uses binomial tree algorithms, for shared memory systems employs pipelining to improve buffer utilization [12].

3.2 Architecture

The Communication Layer of D-MASON exploits the flexibility of the Publish/Subscribe paradigm to virtualize groups of communication between the agents. In the distributed simulation these groups communicate at the end of each simulation step.

We can detect two states of the computation in which all the processes are performing the same action: the connection with the Publish/Subscribe server, because after this phase all workers are connected in the network and the master can see them and spread the computation; the end of each simulation step because at this point of the simulation, each cell has to receive and send updates to start the next step. The purpose of our strategy is to create an MPI infrastructure that abstracts the Publish/Subscribe pattern used in D-MASON, ensuring the decoupling between topics and MPI processes and the scalability of the number of topics by exploiting the collective communication primitives offered by the MPI Standard.

We designed the communication layer using MPI under the following set of assumptions:

1. each cell creates its own topic to publish its updates;
2. each cell subscribes to at least one topic; a cell can not start a new simulation step until it receives updates from all the topics it is subscribed to;
3. subscription is static: each cell executes the subscription routines only before starting the simulation;
4. the simulation and communication/synchronization phase do not interleave. The publish is invoked only at the end of the simulation step when all the updates for each field are available.

In our strategy each cell is an MPI process and a topic is represented with an MPI Group. So in order to create a topic, an MPI process creates an MPI Group and a subscription corresponds to a MPI Group join.

Using the JMS Strategy the initialization of the communication can happen before the creation and subscription of topics, on the other hand, using the MPI approach, the creation and subscription of topics has to be performed before any communication. We exploit the assumptions 2 and 3 in order to perform a global communication phase to exchange information of topics among the MPI processes. This phase is divided in n rounds: in the round i-th round the process with *rank* i sends information about the topic created and the topic which it is subscribed to. The other processes receive this information and update their local list of topics. At the end of this phase each cell of the simulation knows, for each topic, who are the publishers and the subscribers.

Summarizing, using the JMS Strategy the communication phases are: connection to the server Publish/Subscribe, creation and subscription to topics, simulation step and synchronization. In the MPI strategy the communication phases are: creation and addition to MPI Groups, that represent D-MASON topics, creation of MPI Communicators, simulation step and synchronization.

Another key difference between JMS Strategy and MPI Strategy is that, in the JMS Strategy, the communication is asynchronous: At the end of a simulation step each cell publishes to its topics and creates some message listeners. Each message listener is executed on a separate thread, to receive the updates from the topics to which it is subscribed. In the MPI Strategy, on the contrary, we put in a sequence the access to the MPI layer, forcing the process in a scheduled synchronous communication.

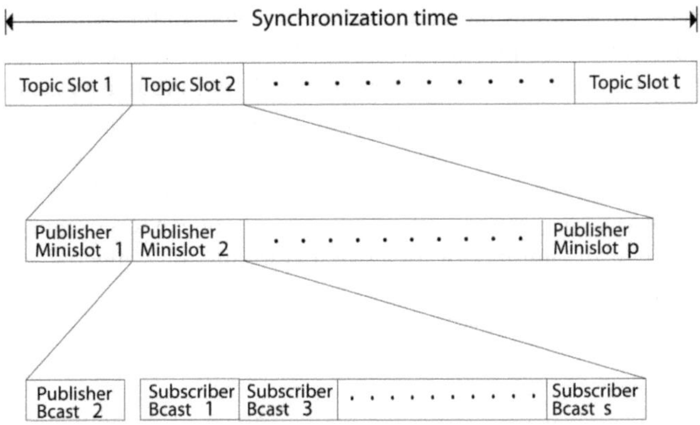

Fig. 1. `MPI_Bcast` approach

3.3 Proposed Implementations

Our implementations are based on the assumptions 2 and 4 listed in the subsection 3.2, which allow to detect when the synchronization phase must be performed. According to the assumptions 2 and 4, at the end of a simulation step, each cell publishes on its topics; when the last publish routine is invoked it is possible to start the synchronization phase. Since we use the same communication schedule on each cell, we avoid communication deadlocks due to multiple concurrent accesses to the MPI layer.

MPI_Bcast. The first proposed solution uses as collective communication primitive the `MPI_Bcast` function. In this model time is divided in t time-slots, each slot is associated to a D-MASON topic, as in Figure 1. The i-th slot is in turn divided in p minislot, each of which represents the *publication turn* of the process publisher of the topic i. In the minislot j the process owner of the minislot invokes `MPI_Bcast` to send updates to subscribers, while the other processes subscribed to topic i invoke `MPI_Bcast` to receive updates from the topic i.

MPI_Gather. By observing that, during each simulation step, each cell needs to collect information from its neighborhood, we decided to use the `MPI_Gather` function to gather all the message needed in a single step. This allows to decrease the number of communication phases while increasing the messages size. In this solution a communication phase is divided into n time-slots, where n is the number of MPI processes (cf. Figure 2). During each phase i the process i invokes `MPI_Gather` to receive updates from all the neighborhood.
We define:

Union Group i: which contains all MPI processes present in the MPI Group of the topics to which the region i is subscribed;

Communicator Group i: as the Communicator of the Union Group i.

During the phase i:

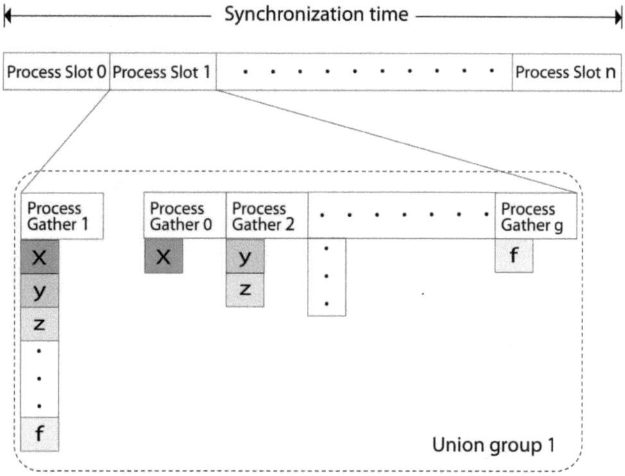

Fig. 2. `MPI_Gather` approach

- The MPI process i executes an `MPI_Gather` in reception.
- All the MPI processes $j \neq i$ in the Union Group of i: create a message for i containing all messages from the topics for which j is the publisher and to which i is subscribed, and invoke an `MPI_Gather` in sending.

Parallel. Inspecting the source code of the version of *mpiJava* used, available at [19], we observed that in the implementation of `MPI_Bcast` and `MPI_Gather` there is a type check on the data: when it detects that the data to send or receive is an *Object* type it invokes a sequence of `MPI_Send` or `MPI_Receive` to the members of the MPI Group. We then found out that in the MPI Strategy, when a cell invokes a routine for collective communication it executes `MPI_Send` and `MPI_Receive` sequentially to or from all the members of the group. Since the performance of the communication with MPI depends strongly on the collective communication routines, we developed a specific strategy, named *parallel*, to increase the degree of parallelism during the communication. At the end of each step we have n invocations to execute sequentially. We recall that a process can invoke a function at a time, so while it is receiving it can not send anything. We create C communication pairs $\langle$sender, receiver$\rangle$ considering all the communications that happens during the synchronization phase. The synchronization phase is divided, as shown in Figure 3, in Γ rounds where the round γ contains c disjoint pairs, that can communicate at the same time (that is, each process appears only once as a sender or a receiver).

Clearly we would like to minimize the size of Γ. This problem is a well-known NP-Hard problem: *Edge coloring* [15]. An edge coloring of a graph is a minimum assignment of colors to the edges of the graph so that no adjacent edges have the same color. Clearly the number of colors needed to edge color a simple graph is at least Δ where Δ is the maximum degree of the graph. In our problem we identify processes with vertices, communication pairs with edges and rounds with colors. Edge coloring has applications in scheduling problems and in frequency assignment for fiber optic networks. In the literature there are several greedy strategies that construct coloring that

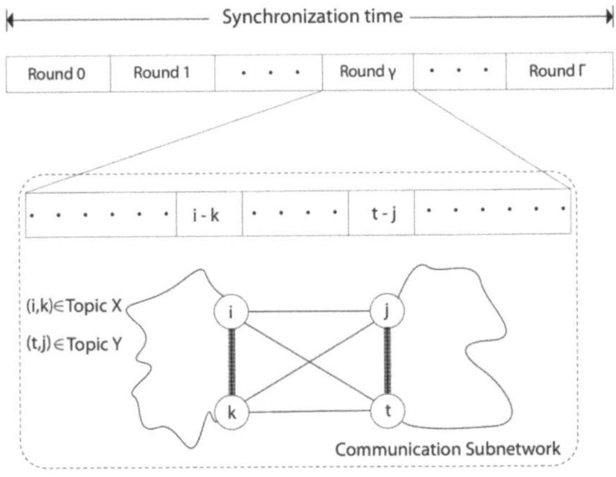

Fig. 3. `Parallel` approach

use at most $\Delta + 1$ colors. We propose the following simple randomized strategy. Let E be the edges set and Γ be the set of colors (rounds). We consider a random permutation of the edges in E. For each uncolored edge $e \in E$, we check whether there is a color in Γ which, once assigned to e, avoids conflicts. If no colors are available we generate a new color for e, and we add it to Γ. The algorithm runs, in the worst case, in $\mathcal{O}(|E|^2)$, and uses, $\Delta + 1$ colors on average.

4 Strategies Comparison

We compared the different strategies running two simulations: *Flockers* and *Ant foraging*. *Flockers* is a model stated in 1986 by Craig Reynolds that simulates the behaviour of a flock. In this model *"flockers"* moves according to three simple rules: *separation*, they steer to avoid crowding local flockers, *alignment*, they steer toward the average heading of local flockers, *cohesion*, they steer to move toward the average position (center of mass) of local flockers.

Ant Foraging simulates the foraging process of ant colonies. At the start of the simulation ants are in the nest and no ant knows where the food source is. The food discovery happens through an adaptive and iterative process: ants forager random walk on several paths, lying pheromone traces along the visited path, that is used by future ants to evaluate the quality of the path, and once they find the food source they come back to the nest reinforcing the good path with pheromone traces in a stigmatic fashion. This kind of simulation is characterized for an high load imbalance: when the ants find the food source, then they will move only on the shortest path between the nest and the food source.

We ran both the simulations using 4 workers, for 100 simulation steps (Flockers) and until the first ant reaches the food (Ants). Several configurations where considered where the parameter AOI (that influence the amount of communications) ranges from

10 to 50, and the number of agents range from $500,000$ to $5,000,000$. The size of the simulation field has been changed in a way that keeps constant the field's density (according to the original density of the sequential version of the simulations available in MASON). For instance on *Flockers* we start using a 2D field of dimension $7,500 \times 7,500$ with $500,000$ agents up to a 2D field of dimension $23,800 \times 23,800$ with $5,000,000$ agents. The tests have been performed on 4 machines configured ad follow: CPU Intel Core i7 $2.53Ghz$, Memory $8GB$, Operating System Ubuntu 11.04, Oracle JDK 1.6.35, ActiveMQ $5.51v$, OpenMPI $1.9a1r27886$ nightly snapshot of $01/21/2013$.

We have tested the following strategies: JMS and MPI (Bcast, Gather, Parallel). Figure 4 depicts the comparison between the four strategies, JMS, Bcast, Gather and Parallel, on *Flockers* with $AOI = 10$. The JMS performance are placed on the X axis as a benchmarks for the other strategies. In general we discovered that MPI strategies tend to be better on massive simulations up to a certain value where the MPI Strategies show an additional load due to the Garbage Collection and an heavy disk I/O burst, which will be the subject of our future studies.

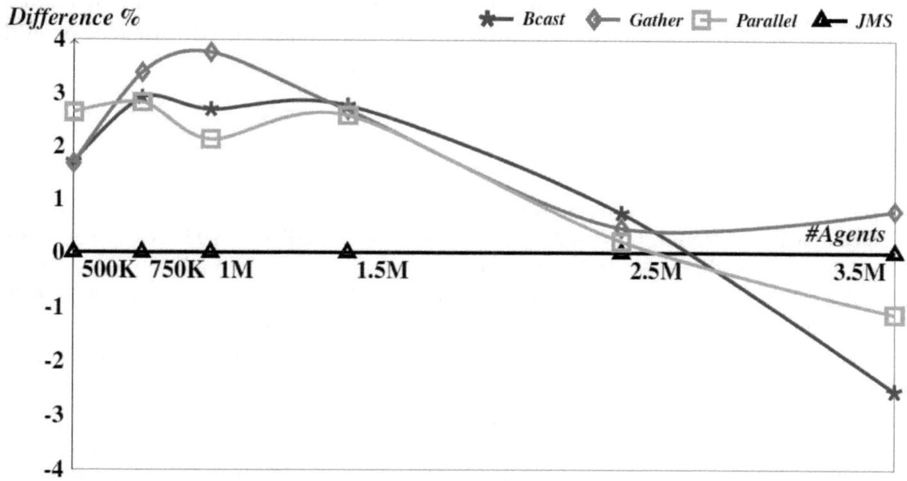

Fig. 4. Performance comparison among JMS Strategy, Bcast, Gather, Parallel. The X axis represents the number of agents while the y axis represents the time difference expressed in percentage compared to the JMS Strategy (lower is better).

It is worth to mention that in our small test scenario, with only 4 workers, the benefit of the Parallel solution with respect to the other solutions do not appear yet. On the other hand in bigger simulations, with a high number of cells (at least 16) we expect significant enhancements of the performance. Indeed using n MPI processes with degree Δ our algorithm uses at most $\Delta + 1$ communications rounds. In a 2×2 grid in which each cell has 8 neighbours (topic subscriptions), we have 8×4 communication rounds using the Bcast and at most $(8 + 1) \cdot 2$ communication rounds (we multiply by 2 because each edge of the communication graph is bidirectional) using the Parallel: we gain in percentage less than the 50% of rounds. In a 4×4 grid in which each cell has

8 neighbors, we have $8 \cdot 16 = 128$ communication rounds using the Bcast and again at most $(8 + 1) \cdot 2$ communication rounds using the Parallel, so we gain in percentage more than the 85% of rounds.

5 Conclusions and Future Research

The performance results described in the previous version shows that the improvement of the D-MASON communication layer is not an easy shot. Although the MPI approach allows to avoid the communication server and favors the synchronization among workers, the performance of the two approaches (MPI based and JMS) are comparable at least for medium size simulations. On the other hand we discovered that on massive simulations the MPI approach suffers an additional load due to the an heavy disk I/O burst, which requires further investigations.

The strategies used show improvement highly related to the implementation of the Java Virtual Machine and the version of mpiJava, we find out that from the JDK 1.4 three new functions has been introduced to allow JNI code to create, examine, and manipulate direct buffers. The actual version of mpiJava does not use this new feature of the JDK, we think that this new function are able to increase the performance of MPI strategy and will also be the subject of future research.

References

1. Baker, M., Carpenter, B., Fox, G., Ko, S.H., Lim, S.: mpijava: An object-oriented java interface to MPI. In: Rolim, J.D.P. (ed.) IPPS-WS 1999 and SPDP-WS 1999. LNCS, vol. 1586, pp. 748–762. Springer, Heidelberg (1999)
2. Baker, M., Carpenter, B., Shafi, A.: Mpj express: towards thread safe java hpc. In: 2006 IEEE International Conference on Cluster Computing, pp. 1–10. IEEE (2006)
3. Balan, G.C., Cioffi-Revilla, C., Luke, S., Panait, L., Paus, S.: MASON: A Java Multi-Agent Simulation Library. In: Proceedings of the Agent 2003 Conference (2003)
4. Carpenter, B., Fox, G.C., Ko, S.-H., Lim, S.: mpijava 1.2: Api specification (1999)
5. Cordasco, G., De Chiara, R., Mancuso, A., Mazzeo, D., Scarano, V., Spagnuolo, C.: A framework for distributing agent-based simulations. In: Alexander, M., et al. (eds.) Euro-Par 2011 Workshops, Part I. LNCS, vol. 7155, pp. 460–470. Springer, Heidelberg (2012)
6. Cordasco, G., De Chiara, R., Mancuso, A., Mazzeo, D., Scarano, V., Spagnuolo, C.: Bringing together efficiency and effectiveness in distributed simulations: the experience with D-MASON. In: SIMULATION: Transactions of The Society for Modeling and Simulation International (2013)
7. Gropp, W., Lusk, E., Skjellum, A.: Using MPI: portable parallel programming with the message-passing interface, 2nd edn. MIT Press, Cambridge (1999)
8. Hafeez, M., Asghar, S., Malik, U.A., ur Rehman, A., Riaz, N.: Survey of MPI implementations. In: Cherifi, H., Zain, J.M., El-Qawasmeh, E. (eds.) DICTAP 2011, Part II. CCIS, vol. 167, pp. 206–220. Springer, Heidelberg (2011)
9. Liu, J.: Parallel discrete-event simulation (2009)
10. Luke, S., Cioffi-revilla, C., Panait, L., Sullivan, K.: Mason: A new multi-agent simulation toolkit. University of Michigan (2004)
11. Luke, S., Cioffi-Revilla, C., Panait, L., Sullivan, K., Balan, G.: Mason: A multiagent simulation environment. Simulation 81(7), 517–527 (2005)

12. Mamidala, A.R., Kumar, R., De, D., Panda, D.K.: Mpi collectives on modern multicore clusters: Performance optimizations and communication characteristics
13. Mancuso, A.: Un framework per simulazione massiva distribuita basata su agenti D-MASON: Comunicazione e system management, B. Sc. Computer Science's Thesis (2011)
14. Message. MPI-2: Extensions to the Message-Passing Interface. Technical report, University of Tennessee, Knoxville, TN, USA (July 1997)
15. Misra, J., Gries, D.: A constructive proof of vizing's theorem. Inf. Process. Lett. 41(3), 131–133 (1992)
16. `http://mpj-express.org/performance.html` (accessed: April 25, 2013)
17. `http://www.isislab.it/projects/dmason/`. D-MASON Official Website (accessed May 2013)
18. `http://www.mcs.anl.gov/research/projects/mpi/index.htm` MPI Standard Official Website (accessed: April 25, 2013)
19. `http://www.open-mpi.org/`. Open MPI Official Website (accessed: April 25, 2013)
20. WeiQin, T., Hua, Y., WenSheng, Y.: Pjmpi: pure java implementation of mpi. In: Proceedings of the Fourth International Conference/Exhibition on High Performance Computing in the Asia-Pacific Region, vol. 1, pp. 533–535. IEEE (2000)

MCMAS: A Toolkit to Benefit from Many-Core Architecure in Agent-Based Simulation

Guillaume Laville[1], Kamel Mazouzi[2], Christophe Lang[1], Nicolas Marilleau[3], Bénédicte Herrmann[1], and Laurent Philippe[1]

[1] FEMTO-ST Institute,
CNRS / Université de Franche-Comté, France
[2] Mésocentre de calcul de Franche-Comté,
Université de Franche-Comté, France
[3] UMI 209 - UMMISCO,
Institut de Recherche pour le Développement (IRD),
UPMC, France

Abstract. Multi-agent models and simulations are used to describe complex systems in domains such as biological, geographical or ecological sciences. The increasing model complexity results in a growing need for computing resources and motivates the use of new architectures such as multi-cores and many-cores. Using them efficiently however remains a challenge in many models as it requires adaptations tailored to each program, using low-level code and libraries. In this paper we present MCMAS a generic toolkit allowing an efficient use of many-core architectures through already defined data structures and kernels. This toolkit promotes few famous algorithms (diffusion, path-finding, population dynamics) which are ready to be used in an Agent Based Model. For other needs, MCMAS is based on a flexible architecture and can easily be enriched by new algorithms thanks to development features. The use of the library is illustrated with two models and their performance analysis.

Keywords: Multi-Agent Systems, Parallel Computing, GPGPU.

1 Introduction

Multi-agent systems (MAS) are often used to describe large complex systems as biological, geographical or ecological ones. Increasing the size or precision of agent based simulations is a common way to obtain more accurate results, but it also results in increased computation costs. Since the raise of CPU computation power is not sufficient to absorb these expanding modeling needs, parallel architectures are now becoming a required mean to gain performance. However, their use requires fundamental improvement in model runtimes provided by platforms such as NetLogo [1] or GAMA [2]. Several projects as D-MASON [3] or Repast-HPC [4] have introduced distributed computing techniques into MAS in order to make use of parallel CPU architectures. The goal of these works is to accelerate or enlarge the simulations.

D. an Mey et al. (Eds.): Euro-Par 2013 Workshops, LNCS 8374, pp. 544–554, 2014.

Last years have seen the emergence of GPU or many-core cards based on massively parallel SIMD (Single Instruction Multiple Data) architectures. GPGPU computing is already used in various domains as linear solvers, video streaming or image processing. Most of these applications are based on matrix data structures well-adapted to parallel processing. Since most of personal computers are equipped with a GPU card, taking advantage of these GPU and many-core architectures has become one way of speeding up Agent Based Simulations. MAS are however often characterized by less-regular data accesses and unpredictable behaviors due to algorithms offering multiple execution branches or random aspects. They thus do not fit the single instruction flow model and adaptations in their execution workflow are thus required to allow agents to run concurrently.

Some works have already demonstrated the gain of using GPU to run MAS in various domains as cellular automaton [5], mobile agent path finding [6], genetic processes [7] or life science [8]. These works present specific adaptations of existing MAS to GPU. In these models individual behaviors driven by mathematical laws (path finding) or equations (cellular automatons) can be considered as the application of the same process on each individual (Single Program, Multiple Data or SPMD execution). This approach does not however work for the majority of MAS, and algorithmic adaptations are often required. Note that the full-GPU approach sometime limits the possible use in MAS and that an hybrid approach, based on CPU plus GPU, may fit a larger number of MAS.

The FLAME-GPU [9] platform proposes an all-in-one solution to run MAS on GPU. The framework relies on a detailed XML description of the agents and on C-like code fragments to support several target architectures. This approach implies that the MAS is developed for the framework and thus cannot (re)use an existing model nor interface with other MAS runtimes.

The contribution of the paper is a toolkit, called MCMAS (Many Core MAS), that provides functions to facilitate the implementation of MAS simulations on many-cores architectures and better exploit their computing power. The library can be interfaced with existing agent platforms to acts as a wrapper for GPU code that allows integration of optimized model parts within other simulators. We present in section 2 the MCMAS library. Its interface and extension facilities are illustrated on two use cases: the collembola model and the mior model. The model performance results are detailed in section 3. We then conclude on the possibilities of the MCMAS platform and its possible application to other models or use cases in section 4.

2 MCMAS

Porting a MAS on GPU requires a model adaptation to benefit from this architecture. We developed the MCMAS library to facilitate the implementation of models on GPU and many-core architectures. To achieve this MCMAS proposes a set of commonly used functions and data structures that simplify the implementation of new models and allows the integration of new functionalities in the shape of plugins. Note that MSMAS has yet only be tested on GPU and on few

CPU cores but it should also match many-core architectures as Intel Xeon Phi as it is based on a SIMD execution model.

2.1 Basic MCMAS

Choosing a programming language is the first step to adapt an agent model to a GPU platform. On the one hand the Java programming language is often used for the implementation of MAS due to its large availability and its high-level object-oriented programming. On the other hand GPU platforms only offer dedicated languages, CUDA or OpenCL, so that a model implementation requires some part of GPU-specific development or the use of GPU enabled libraries. MCMAS offers a higher level Java interface linked with OpenCL GPU-code through the JOCL library [10] (see figure 1). We decided to retain OpenCL for its portability and the possibility to run programs on both CPU and non-GPU many-core architectures such as the Xeon Phi.

OpenCL provides access to CPU or GPU threads using an asynchronous interface. This library is based around three main concepts. The *kernel* represents a program to be executed on the GPU. The *work-item* is analogous to the concept of thread on CPU. The *work-group* is a set of work-items that share memory. An OpenCL execution consists in running the same kernel on numerous work-items. Synchronization operations, as barriers, can only be used across the same work-group. Data used by the work-items can be stored in local (high speed) or global (low speed) GPU memory. Since the size of this local memory is often limited to a few hundred of kilobytes, choosing this number often implies a compromise between the model synchronization or data requirements and the available resources. In the case of agent based simulations, each agent can thus naturally be mapped to a work-item. Work-groups can then be used to represent groups of agents or simulations sharing common data (as the environment) or algorithms (as the background evolution process). This process is described in more details in the case of the MIOR model[11].

Similar data structures are used by whole classes of MAS. One such example is the grid, which can be either integrated in the algorithm, as in SugarScape [5] where each cell represents the fundamental unit of modeling, or used to discretize a continuous environment as path-finding simulations [12]. These grids can be considered as 2d or 3d matrices representing agents' data or their environment. Another data representation often encountered in MAS is the usage of coordinate systems to position agents in the simulation space [13].

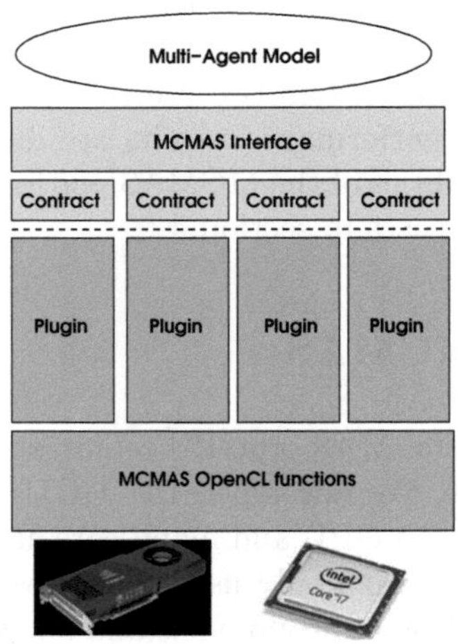

Fig. 1. MCMAS general architecture

These common structures lead to the usage of similar algorithms in many simulations, such as distance computation in 2d or 3d space, diffusion processes, reduction operations, SIMD transformations applied to each cell of the model. These kinds of processing can be parallelized and executed on the GPU, leading to possible performance gains, without heavy modifications to the model scheme.

To facilitate the addition of new functions, MCMAS is based on a dynamic architecture allowing the registration of new plugins at runtime. This allows two usage approaches: (i) the adaptation of the whole MAS model on GPU by writing a new implementation of the algorithm, a **model parallelization**, or (ii) the usage of many-core optimized primitives in an existing MAS model, a **process parallelization**. This dual extensible architecture allows the designer to either use already developed plugins or to roll its own solutions, based on the parallelized operations required by its model.

The MCMAS interface is based on the `MCMASContext` object. This context contains all the data (for instance device context and execution queue) required to run any MCMAS low-level operation and plugins. The context can be created using a wide variety of constructors, to allow the customization of the environment depending of the available execution resources and the functionalities needed: profiling, debugging... This MCMAS context can then be either used to initialize MCMAS plugins using the `newInstance()` method, or to directly call low-level OpenCL operations, using the accessors provided for the underlying OpenCL objects.

MCMAS provides a standard set of data structures (grids, vectors, structures) as a mean to pass data to plugin methods. Methods are provided to facilitate the translation of existing Java data structures to these formats. Each plugin is also free to define its own data structures, either for its own usage or for general use. A springy data architecture has been designed to expand the existing MCMAS collection.

2.2 Process Parallelization Use Case

The Collembola model is an agent based model focusing on landscape biodiversity. It reproduces the diffusion of arthropodes life forms (collembola) across plots of an identified territory of the Morvan. This environment is constituted of forested, cultivated and artificial areas. The model goal is to study the impact of modifications of this environment on biodiversity. The model subdivides each plot in surface units and follows the evolution of the number of individuals in time. This evolution can be decomposed into four steps: (i) *arrival* of new individuals, (ii) *reproduction* of each parcel population, (iii) *diffusion* between cells, and (iv) *selection* of surviving individuals. The algorithm contains two costly operations which can be parallelized: diffusion, reduction of cell properties to obtain global data. The **reproduction** process represents an update of each plot population to take into account the new individuals. It consists of a walk-through on all the cells to update their population and is implemented using the reduction plugin of MCMAS. The **diffusion** process represents the collembola propagation on new plots. For each cell the population is computed taking into account the immigration flow from its eight neighbors. The process is implemented using the diffusion plugin. The two costly operations use already existing MCMAS plugins to speed up their computations, with few changes in the simulation and without advanced parallelization expertise, as illustrated on figure 2.

```
public void run() {
    MCMASContext context = new MCMASContext();
    ReductionPlugin reduce = ReductionPlugin.newInstance(context);
    DiffusionPlugin diffuse = DiffusionPlugin.newInstance(context);
    doNewArrivals();  // Simulate new individuals' arrival on CPU
    reduce.taggedIntReduce(...); // Launch reproduction on GPU
    diffuse.diffuse8(...); // Launch diffusion on GPU
    doDeath(); // Kill individuals on a not favorable terrain on CPU
}
```

Fig. 2. Usage of MCMAS in the Collembola model

In both cases the GPU is used as a specialized co-processor for the existing simulation. This permits a progressive adaptation of the existing Java model to benefit from many-core architectures.

2.3 Developing a New MCMAS Plugin

A MCMAS plugin is a Java class who implements the `MCMASPlugin` interface. This interface allows plugins to be instantiated from a MCMAS context. This context will then be used by the plugin to allocate new data structures, launch operations or adapt its execution.

Beyond the basic methods required by the interface, each plugin can provide its own free-form set of operations. New MCMAS plugins and structures are packaged as Java libraries. By convention all classes belonging to the same plugin lives in a `mcmas.plugins.<plugin name>` package to maintain code isolation and facilitate the discovery of new plugins.

Most plugin-provided operations are organized around the standard GPU execution workflow: (1) OpenCL source code retrieval and compilation, (2) copy of Java data into input data structures, (3) execution of one or more kernel, (4) retrieval of output data and translation into Java data structures, and (5) resource cleanup and return from the primitive call. Memory allocations in each plugin can be managed at two levels. At instance level the memory is used for the lifetime of the plugin. At method level the memory is used for temporary copies of input and output parameters and to manage the execution progress.

2.4 Model Parallelization Use Case

The MIOR (MIcro-ORganism) [14] model simulates local interactions in a soil between microbial colonies and organic matters. The MIOR model can be used in multi-scale MAS, such as Sworm [15]. Since the evolution takes place at a microscopic scale each unit of soil corresponds to many such simulations that justify the computing cost of this process.

```
// Create a new MIOR model template
MiorWorld model = new MiorModel();
model.nbOM = 310; model.nbMM = 38; model.size = 200;
MCMASContext context = new MCMASContext(MCMASContext.GPU);
MiorPlugin plugin = MiorPlugin.newInstance(context);
// Execute 100 instances simulating 1000 steps each time.
int [][] CO2Values = new int[100][1000];
plugin.runNSimulations(model, 100, CO2Values, 1000);
```

Fig. 3. Usage of the MIOR plugin from Java code

The MIOR model is based on two types of agents: (i) the Meta-Mior (MM), microbial colonies consuming carbon and (ii) the Organic Matter (OM), carbon deposits occurring in soil. Each Meta-Mior agents exhibits two distinct behaviors. By *breathing* it converts mineral carbon from the soil to carbon dioxide CO_2, released in the soil. By *Growing* it fixes the carbon present in the environment to reproduce itself (augments its size). This last action is only possible if the colony breathing needs are covered, i.e. if enough mineral carbon is available. The model is implemented as an MCMAS plugin as described on Figure 4, to allow an easy use in a Java program (Figure 3).

```
public class MiorPlugin extends MCMASPlugin<MiorPlugin> {
  // Static method implemented by all MCMAS plugins (factory)
  public static MiorPlugin getInstance(MCMASContext context) {
    new MiorPlugin(context.getContext(), context.getQueue();
  }
  private MiorPlugin(Context context, CommandQueue queue) {
  }
  public void runNSimulations(...) {
  }
}
```

Fig. 4. Implementation of the MIOR plugin

2.5 Using MCMAS from Existing MAS Frameworks

The MCMAS library can also be used to delegate computations in existing MAS frameworks. An intermediary agent is required to translate the existing models requests into calls to MCMAS plugins, and to manage the interactions with the MCMAS platform as shown on figure 5. This translation layer between MCMAS and the MAS framework allows a transparent use of the

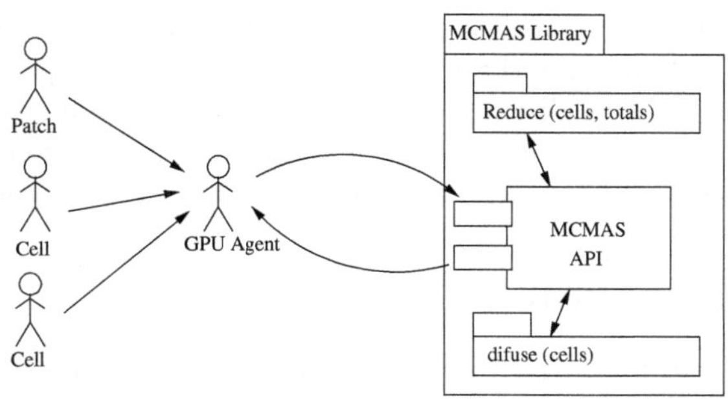

Fig. 5. MCMAS integration in MAS framework

library without disturbing the existing model architecture. For instance, in the case of GAMA, this integration can be realized by extending the agent description language with MCMAS related functions. For that, an eclipse plugin associated with GAMA and XText should be developed. In the case of the Madkit framework [16], a threaded agent should be implemented. The latter may ordered by other simulation agents through a dedicated agent communication language.

3 Experiments

The performance of the use case models is presented in this section to show the gain that can be obtained by delegating some functions or by implementing a plugin that use the MCMAS library. Note that the GPU runs are compared to the Java implementation of the model instead of their initial Netlogo implementation as it would not be fair to compare programs to interpreted code (Netlogo implementations are much more slower).

3.1 Collembola Model Results

In this part we present the performance of the Collembola model with the MCMAS library on CPU and GPU execution platforms. Due to the cost of data transfers between CPU and GPU, performance gains depend on the size of the model. Therefore we have run the simulations with different scaling factors for the agent population size. The reference execution is a sequential execution of the simulation on a standard processor, an Intel Core i7 2600K running at 3.4GHz. Since MCMAS also target multi-core platforms, using CPU-based OpenCL implementations, we execute the simulations in parallel on the same processor to point out the gain of what can be expected from CPU parallelism. Then to illustrate the performance on GPU hardware we have run the simulations on two mainstream GPU platforms: a Radeon HD 6870 and a GeForce 560Ti.

Figure 6 shows the results obtained when running the simulations. As expected the use of the MCMAS library increases the performance of the simulation. The best obtained speedup is factor of 4 between the sequential run and the GeForce run. The Radeon curve is limited to a scaling factor of 20 due to buffer size limitations imposed by the AMD-provided OpenCL runtime.

Note that the curves exhibit a odd-even pattern. Since this phenomenon is visible on distinct hardware, drivers and OpenCL implementations, it is likely due to the model decomposition process based on warp of fixed power-of-two sizes. The results show that the gain closely depends on the hardware platform.

3.2 MIOR Results

Two platforms are used to assess the performance of the complete GPU implementation of the MIOR model as a MCMAS plugin. The first one is representative of hardware available in HPC clusters: a cluster node dedicated to GPU computations with two quad-cores Intel X5550 processors running at 2.67GHz

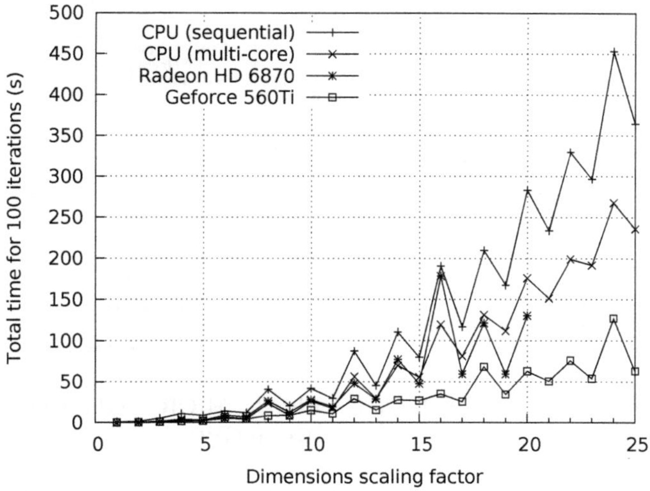

Fig. 6. Performance of the Collembola model

and a Tesla C1060 GPU device running at 1.3GHz and composed of 240 cores. The second platform is a personal computer based on an Intel Q9300 CPU, running at 2.5GHz, and a Geforce 8800GT GPU card, composed of 112 cores and running at 1.5GHz. The purpose of these two platforms is to assess the benefit that could be obtained either when a MAS modeler has access to specialized hardware as a cluster or tries to take benefit from its own personal computer.

The MIOR experiments illustrate the effect of increasing the level of adaptation of the algorithm to GPU hardware. The **GPU (naive)** implementation is a direct implementation of the existing algorithm and its data structures. The **GPU (optimized)** implementation uses compact representations of the topology and the low level MCMAS interface.

We measure the execution duration for 50 simulations on the two hardware platforms. A size factor is applied to the problem: at scale 1, the model contains 38 MM and 310 OM, while at the scale 6 these numbers are multiplied by six. The size of the environment is modified accordingly to maintain the same average agent density in the model. This scaling factor displays the impact of the size of the simulation on performance.

Figures 7 and 8 gives the performance of the simulation runs on the two platforms (the CPU curves give the performance of the local CPU). We can note that for small problems execution time for all implementations are very close. This is because the GPU implementation does not have enough threads (representing agents) for an optimal usage of GPU resources. This trend changes after scale 5 where the optimized GPU version begins to take advantage of the naive GPU and CPU implementations. This advantage continues to grow with the scaling factor and reaches a speedup of 10 at the scale 10 between the fastest single-simulation GPU implementation and the naive one.

Multiple trends can be observed on both figures. First the optimizations for the GPU hardware show a big, positive impact on performance, illustrating

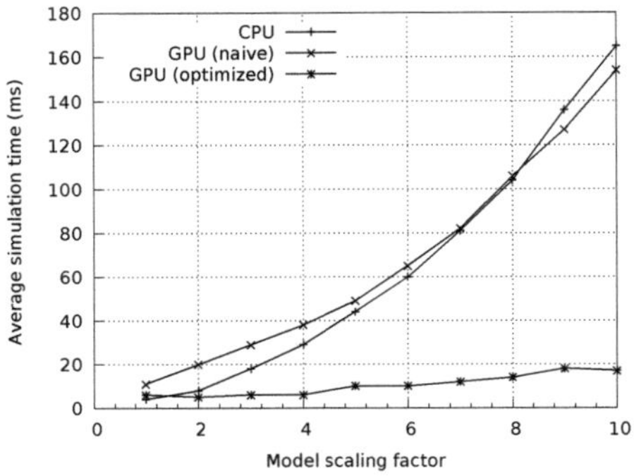

Fig. 7. MIOR performance on Tesla

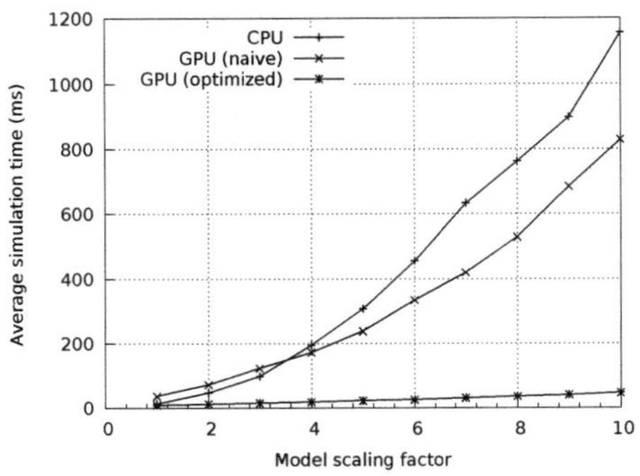

Fig. 8. MIOR performance on mainstream GPU

the strong requirements on the algorithm properties to ensure the execution efficiency. These charts also show that despite the vast difference in number of cores between the two GPU platforms the same trends can be observed in both cases. We can therefore expect similar results on other GPU cards, without the need for more adaptations.

4 Conclusion

In this article we present MCMAS, a solution to facilitate the use of many-core architectures and allow the integration of optimized model parts within agent based simulators. To achieve this, two possible approaches are supported by our toolkit: (i) use MCMAS as an optimized algorithm library; or (ii) use MCMAS as many-core runtime to develop specific algorithms or MAS. The usage can be mixed by the model designer, depending on the its model needs and of the amount of development required.

The first approach is to use the interfaces and plugins already provided by MCMAS. These plugins cover classic problems in MAS simulations as path-finding, diffusion or population dynamics. These predefined algorithms are ready to be used to accelerate one or more aspects of an existing CPU simulation, without huge changes in the existing implementation.

The second approach is to develop new plugins for MCMAS to enable the implementation of more specialized or performance-critical algorithms directly on the underlying many-cores platform. This approach implies the development of OpenCL kernels, called from MCMAS, to execute portions of the computations. Once written, these kernels can be used both on CPU, GPU or any other OpenCL supported platform: this allows the reuse of the same program on a wide range of architectures, ranging from personal computers to computing clusters, or dedicated GPU nodes, without modification or manual re-compilation.

Our main goal is now to enrich the MCMAS platform to support more MAS problems and to refine the support of new data structures to generalize the possible applications of this platform.

Acknowledgement. Computations presented in this article were realized on the supercomputing facilities provided by the **Mésocentre de calcul de Franche-Comté**.

References

1. Sklar, E.: Netlogo, a multi-agent simulation environment. Artificial Life 13(3), 303–311 (2011)
2. Taillandier, P., Vo, D.-A., Amouroux, E., Drogoul, A.: GAMA: A simulation platform that integrates geographical information data, agent-based modeling and multi-scale control. In: Desai, N., Liu, A., Winikoff, M. (eds.) PRIMA 2010. LNCS, vol. 7057, pp. 242–258. Springer, Heidelberg (2012)
3. Carillo, M., Cordasco, G., De Chiara, R., Raia, F., Scarano, V., Serrapica, F.: Enhancing the performances of D-MASON - a motivating example. In: SIMULTECH, pp. 137–143 (2012)
4. Collier, N., North, M.: Parallel agent-based simulation with REPAST for high performance computing. In: SIMULATION (2012)
5. D'souza, R.M., Lysenko, M., Rahmani, K.: Sugarscape on steroids: Simulating over a million agents at interactive rates. In: Proceedings of the Agent 2007 Conference (2007)
6. Silveira, R., Fischer, L., Ferreira, J.A.S., Prestes, E., Nedel, L.: Path-planning for RTS games based on potential fields. In: Boulic, R., Chrysanthou, Y., Komura, T. (eds.) MIG 2010. LNCS, vol. 6459, pp. 410–421. Springer, Heidelberg (2010)
7. Maitre, O., Lachiche, N., Clauss, P., Baumes, L., Corma, A., Collet, P.: Efficient parallel implementation of evolutionary algorithms on GPGPU cards. In: Sips, H., Epema, D., Lin, H.-X. (eds.) Euro-Par 2009. LNCS, vol. 5704, pp. 974–985. Springer, Heidelberg (2009)
8. Laville, G., Marilleau, N., Lang, C., Mazouzi, K., Philippe, L.: Using GPU for multi-agent soil simulation. In: PDP 2013, Belfast, Ireland, pp. 392–399. IEEE Computer Society Press (February 2013)
9. Richmond, P.: FLAME GPU Technical Report and User Guide (CS-11-03). Technical report, Department of Computer Science, University of Sheffield (2011)
10. JOCL: Java bindings for OpenCL, `http://www.jocl.org/` (June 07, 2013)
11. Laville, G., Mazouzi, K., Lang, C., Marilleau, N., Philippe, L.: Using GPU for multi-agent multi-scale simulations. In: Omatu, S., Paz Santana, J.F., González, S.R., Molina, J.M., Bernardos, A.M., Rodríguez, J.M.C. (eds.) Distributed Computing and Artificial Intelligence. AISC, vol. 151, pp. 197–204. Springer, Heidelberg (2012)
12. Fischer, L., Silveira, R., Nedel, L.: GPU accelerated path-planning for multi-agents in virtual environments. In: Proceedings of the 2009 VIII Brazilian Symposium on Games and Digital Entertainment, SBGAMES 2009, pp. 101–110. IEEE Computer Society, Washington, DC (2009)

13. Erra, U., Frola, B., Scarano, V., Couzin, I.: An efficient GPU implementation for large scale individual-based simulation of collective behavior. In: Proceedings of the 2009 Int. Workshop on High Performance Computational Systems Biology, HIBI 2009, pp. 51–58. IEEE Computer Society, Washington, DC (2009)
14. Bousso, M., Cambier, C., Masse, D., Perrier, E.: An offer versus demand modelling approach to assess the impact of micro-organisms spatio-temporal dynamics on soil organic matter decomposition rates. In: Ecological Modelling, pp. 301–313 (2007)
15. Blanchart, E., Marilleau, N., Drogoul, A., Perrier, E., Chotte, J.L., Cambier, C.: Sworm: an agent-based model to simulate the effect of earthworms on soil structure. EJSS. European Journal of Soil Science 60, 13–21 (2009)
16. Gutknecht, O., Ferber, J.: Madkit: a generic multi-agent platform. In: Proceedings of the Fourth International Conference on Autonomous Agents, AGENTS 2000, pp. 78–79. ACM, New York (2000)

Supporting the Exploratory Nature of Simulations in D-MASON

Gennaro Cordasco[1], Rosario De Chiara[2],
Fabio Fulgido[3], and Mario Fiore Vitale[3]

[1] Dipartimento di Psicologia
Seconda Università degli Studi di Napoli, Italy
gennaro.cordasco@unina2.it
[2] Centro Ricerca e Sviluppo
Poste Italiane, Italy
dechia24@posteitaliane.it
[3] ISISLab - Dipartimento di Informatica
Università di Salerno, Italy
{f.fulgido,mvitale86}@gmail.com

Abstract. Agent-Based Models (ABM) are a class of models which, by simulating the behaviors of multiple agents (i.e., independent actions, interactions and adaptation), aims to emulate and/or predict complex phenomena. The "emergence" of such complex phenomena is often computation intensive and requires tools, libraries and frameworks, capable of speeding up and facilitate the design of complex simulations.

In this paper we present new developments on D-MASON, that is a distributed version of MASON, a well-known and popular library for writing and running Agent-based Simulations.

The new developments are: a) a tool that allows the parallel exploration of the behavior parameter space; b) an infrastructure that improves the management of distributed simulations in terms of easy deployment of new simulations, automatic update, versioning control and distributed logging.

Keywords: Agent-Based Simulation, Distributed Systems, System Management.

1 Introduction

Agent-based modeling is a style of modeling in which multiple agents and their interactions with each other and their environment are explicitly represented in a program with the aims of understanding and generating complex phenomena. An agent-based model (ABM) consists of: a set of agents, a set of agent relationships and an environment to host the agents and where they take action. ABMs have become very popular in various research fields, such as biology[25], ecology, economics[1], political science, social science[15] etc.. A fundamental benefit of ABMs is the discovery and explanation of emergent behavior. Emergent behaviors of complex systems are patterns that do not depend on individual components of a system but are generated by their interaction to one another. For instance, emergent behavior is ubiquitous in biological systems (chemical

D. an Mey et al. (Eds.): Euro-Par 2013 Workshops, LNCS 8374, pp. 555–564, 2014.

interactions among cells) and in groups of animals (flocking of birds and schooling of fish).

In [12] the very nature of simulations implemented by a computer program is described, such programs are involved in an exploratory process where the model is iteratively refined, as the problem it is meant to be simulated is better understood. For this reason the framework which is used must provide facilities to debug the model, support the re-runs of experiments and to the collection of the generated data.

A common approach for improving the efficiency of ABM is to distribute the overall computation on a number of *Logical Processors* (LPs). Parallelization and distribution of the computational load has two important motivations in the Agent-Based Modeling field:

- the *speed* running a model faster allows, in the same time, to make more thorough exploration of the (possible) complex behavior. An efficient simulator should allow to run experiments long enough to make emergent behaviours evident;
- the *size* of the models can be crucial to ensure that the emerging behavior is indeed shown and made evident; when models are too small, some of the effects might be hidden, not evident and/or emerge very late.

Several parallel implementation of ABMs frameworks have been proposed [5,6,8,19].

A good parallel implementation should face several conflicting issues: (a) balance the overall load distribution among the LPs; (b) minimize the communication overhead due to the interdependencies existing between the tasks executed on the LPs; (c) synchronize the evolution of the simulation among the LPs that provide the computing power.

The general behaviors of a simulation associated to an ABM can be quite complex and therefore it is not possible to apply analytical methods to understand what is happening. This is particularly true when one looks at the parameters' space of an ABM: a common approach is to sample the parameter space in order to figure out the behavior of the model over a wide range of different conditions.

Speeding up such exploration is important for the researcher because the emergence of some phenomena might be evident just for some specific subsets of the parameters: small changes made to a single parameter may lead to a radical modification of the dynamics of the whole system.

In this paper we present a tool that increases the support for the exploratory nature of simulations by implementing a parallel behavioral parameter space exploration. Indeed a parallel architecture can be easily exploited by letting multiple simulations run at once with different parameters distribution on multiple machines [3].

An alternative to parallel behavioral parameter space exploration is proposed by the authors in [11]. They run a simulation and store information about its states and transitions between them. Under the assumption that multiple runs are often similar, they try to save computing time by reusing event computations done during the first simulation. This approach requires to build an *updateable* model for the simulation, along with a comparison predicate in order to evaluate if two states of a simulation are similar (i.e. applying the same transition to both leads to the same destination state, and therefore the previously computed destination state can be reused) or different (a new destination state have to be computed and the simulation needs to be *updated*). This kind of framework seems to be effective for computing-intensive simulations but less adaptable to agent-based massive simulations, due to the difficulty to build a comparison predicate and to the large memory footprint needed to store the state of such massive simulation.

2 Distributed Simulation and D-MASON

Some aspects of ABMs implementation, like the parameter space exploration, can be effectively parallelizable. Other aspects, like running massive simulation (i.e., simulating a large number of agents) and/or simulations which deal with complex agents, that is, computationally intensive agents, are more difficult to be parallelizable. A common approach to the parallelization of massive simulations is just an instance of a more general problem of parallelizing a sequential computation by dividing it into smaller computations (subtasks) and assigning them to different processes for parallel executions. This two phases represent two key steps in the design of parallel algorithms [16]. The communication and the synchronization between the different subtasks are typically some of the greatest obstacles in getting good performances.

As an example a simple way to partition the whole computation into subtasks is to assign a fixed number of agents to each available LP. This approach named *agents partitioning* enables a balanced workload distribution but usually introduces a significant communication overhead (all–to–all communications are required to synchronize the simulation).

Other strategies which partition the work in a smarter way [7] have been proposed in order to reduce the time due to the communication and synchronization between processes.

Agent-Based Simulations are designed accordingly to a discrete-event paradigm where the simulation time is split in steps named *simulation steps*, often but not necessarily, of the same duration. So, as the simulation advances, the step number increases.

We used D-MASON [6] a general purpose framework for discrete-event ABMs. D-MASON enlists the aid of two or more LPs to carry out the simulation: each of the LPs is derived from MASON and is in charge of a portion of the set of the agents.

MASON [17,18] toolkit is a discrete-event simulation core and visualization library written in Java, designed to be used for a wide range of ABMs. The toolkit is composed of two independent layers: the *simulation* layer and the *visualization* layer. The main reasons that suggested the development of a distributed version of MASON are:

- MASON is one of the most expressive and efficient library for ABMs (as reported by many reviews [2,20,22]);
- MASON architecture, that clearly separates visualization by simulation, greatly helped during the process of development of a distributed version of the library[17,18];
- the significant amount of research and simulations already present in MASON, which can be easily ported to D-MASON, makes it particularly cost effective for the scientists.

Considering that most ABMs are inspired by natural models where agents are placed in a bi-dimensional (or tri-dimensional) space (some examples are [10,13,14,21,24])

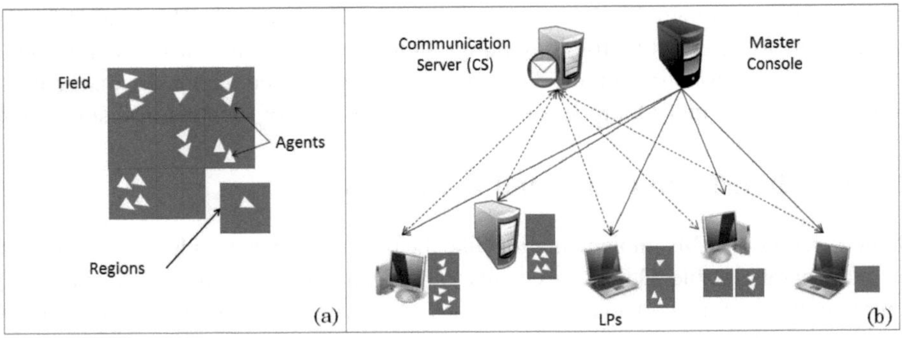

Fig. 1. The Architecture of D-MASON

and agents' communications/interactions are limited to a delimited area of interest (AOI), D-MASON exploits a space partitioning approach: the space to be simulated (the field) is partitioned into regions (see Fig. 1.(a)). Each region, together with the agents it contains, is assigned to a LP; each LP is in charge of: simulating the agents that belong to the assigned region, handling the migration of agents between regions and managing the synchronization between neighboring regions (see Fig. 1.(b)).

Since the AOI extension of an agent is small compared with the size of a region it belongs to, the communication is often limited to local messages within the same LP. LPs in charge of the simulation of neighboring regions, are locally synchronized in order to let the simulation run consistently. LPs communicate by using a publish–subscribe mechanism design pattern: a multicast channel is assigned to each region.

D-MASON is released under a Free and Open Software license and is available at [9].

3 D-MASON Enhancements

In this section we describe the extensions of the D-MASON system management. These extensions add new features to D-MASON aimed at improving the usability of the environment for the researcher who is designing a simulation. We extended D-MASON by adding two facilities: a tool for the parallel exploration of the behavior parameter space and an infrastructure that improves the management of distributed simulations.

3.1 Exploring Parameter Space

As observed in Section 1, the exploration of the parameters' space requires the execution of a large number of simulations with different parameters distributions [3,23]. These executions are independent therefore can be safely carried out in parallel.

In the following we present a semi-automatic tool that supports such exploration. The tool performs three functionalities: selection of parameters, management of parameters and execution.

Selection of parameter. D-MASON allows the programmer to select, via Java *annotations*, which parameter of the simulation can be explored. The programmer can also annotate, for each parameter, its domain and/or its suggested value. A portion of an annotated source Java file is in Figure 2. In this specific case, both the parameters `width`, `height` and `numFlockers` are annotated using the keyword `@batch`. Moreover for the parameter `height` the programmer has also defined the domain (100 – 300) and the suggested value (250).

```
public class DFlockers extends DistributedState<Double2D>
{
    private static final long serialVersionUID = 1L;
    public DContinuous2D flockers;
    private static boolean isToroidal=true;
    @batch
    public double width = 150;
    @batch(
        domain = "100–300",
        suggestedValue = "250"
    )
    public double height = 150;
    @batch
    public int numFlockers = 20;
   ...
}
```

Fig. 2. A portion of a source file with annotations

Management of parameters. D-MASON includes a tool, named *Batch Wizard*, which takes in input the `.jar` file of a specific D-MASON simulation and extracts the list of annotated parameters. Then, by using the application depicted in Figure 3, the user is able to define for each parameter the set of values to be analyzed (to explore the parameter space) and the number of runs to be executed for each fixed set of parameter (to evaluate the stability of the model). Each parameter can be explored in four different ways:

Fixed: the parameter has a single fixed value, which can be the one suggested by the programmer by annotations or another value chosen by the user.

By values: the user provides a set of values to be evaluated.

Range: the user defines a range of values by providing a lower endpoint, an increment and the upper endpoint.

Distribution: the values of the parameter are picked from a probability distribution. In this case the number of runs is used to pick different values. Three probability distributions are currently available: *uniform, normal* and *exponential*. For each probability distributions, its parameters (for instance, mean and standard deviation for the normal distribution) can also be selected by the user.

The last two options (Range and Distribution) are available only for numeric parameters. During the setup phase of the simulation the tool provides to the user the number of tests necessary, for the exploration of the parameters, in the current configuration.

Other options are the number of LPs n_{LP} for each run and the possibility of enabling or not the load balancing functionality, see [4]. The output of the Batch Wizard is an XML file similar to the one in Figure 4.

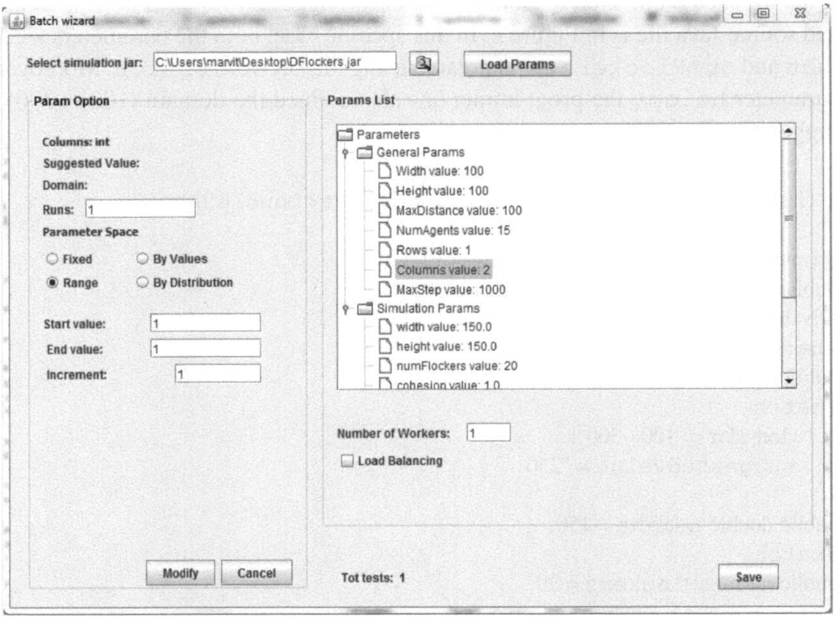

Fig. 3. The management of parameters via the Batch Wizard

```
<?xml version="1.0" encoding="UTF−8" ?>
<Batch>
  <simulationName>vampires.jar</simulationName>
  <neededWorkers>10</neededWorkers>
  <isBalanced>false</isBalanced>
  <simulationParams>
    <paramFixed name = "numRoosts" type = "int" runs = "10" mode = "fixed">
      <value>10</value>
    </paramFixed>
      <paramList name = "numBats" type = "int" runs = "5" mode = "list">
      <item>200</item>
      <item>2000</item>
    </paramList>
  ...
</Batch>
```

Fig. 4. An example of XML file generated by the Batch Wizard

Execution. At the execution time the XML file described above is read and validated and the system prepares the sets of simulations to run. The system builds two sets: a *test list* which is the list of all the configurations to be executed, and a *LPs list* which is a partition of available LPs, such that each set in the list contains at least n_{LP} LPs. The user can choose whether the execution must be sequential or parallel. During a parallel batch execution each set of LPs, in the LPs list, executes at the same time a different test. However, different runs will use, concurrently, a single communication server (CS).

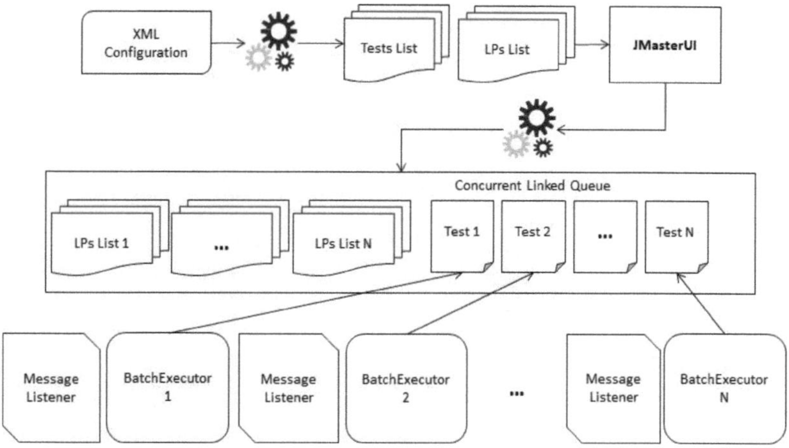

Fig. 5. Batch execution

The execution of a batch is performed by several *Batch Executors* (on sequential batch executions a single Batch Executor is used). A Batch Executor is in charge of starting and stopping a single run of a simulation. Briefly, a batch executor manages a set of LPs and as soon as the execution of the simulation terminates, it picks another test from the test list and starts its execution (see Figure 5).

3.2 A Novel Management Infrastructure

We present now a novel infrastructure that improves the management of distributed simulations in terms of easy deployment of new simulations, automatic update, versioning control and distributed logging. The novel architecture is depicted in Figure 6. An FTP Server has been added to the system with the goal of enabling the exchange of files between the console (master) and the LPs. The use of the FTP server is explained in the following.

Deploy of New Simulations and LP Software Update. First of all the FTP server is exploited for the deployment of new simulations. In the previous version of D-MASON (v. 2.0) , simulations were encoded within the D-MASON package, and consequently the development of a new simulation required to rebuild the entire package and restarting the entire system (i.e. Console, LPs and CS). In this enhanced version of D-MASON(v. 2.1), new simulations are compiled separately in a `.jar` file and are added to the system via the Console application (see Figure 7). The `.jar` file and a corresponding digest file are store into a specific directory of the FTP Server. Then the Console application sends, via the CS, a message to the LPs, containing the name of the simulation file, the address and the port of the FTP server. Each LP then check checks whether it already has that specific simulation and, if so, it checks, using the digest file, if it has the correct version. If the LP does not have the simulation file, or if the digest files do not match (that is, the new simulation file is an update of a previous version), then the LP download the simulation file from the FTP server and, in the case of update, it replaces the previous file.

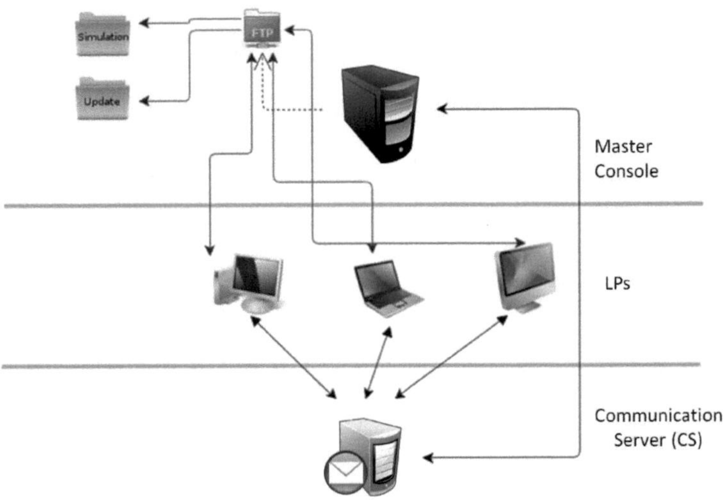

Fig. 6. The novel infrastructure

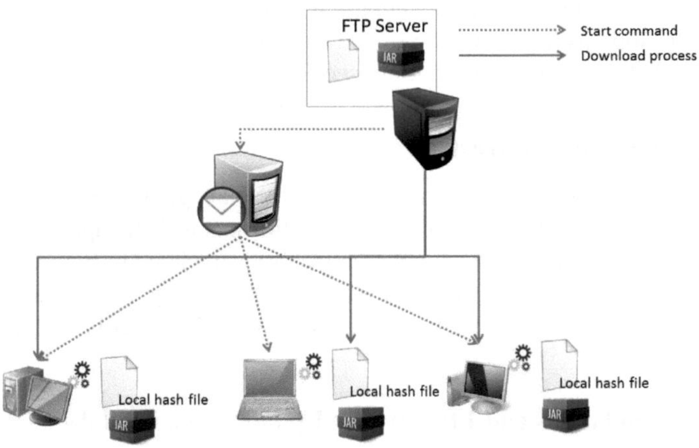

Fig. 7. Deploy of a new simulation

A similar approach is used to update the software running on each LP. Since the upgrade processes affects only the LPs connected to the system, we have also developed a mechanism that allows each LP, during the connection to the system, to check whether there have been updates or new simulation files have been deployed. Moreover, before starting a new simulation the console checks that all the LPs are aligned to the same software version and the same simulation file.

Distributed Logging. The novel management infrastructure is also exploited to collect and aggregate the log files generated by each LP. When a simulation is completed, the Console sends a *gather* command to the LPs. When the LPs receive this command, they upload the log files on the FTP server, so that they can be aggregated into a single file that can be used for subsequent analysis.

4 Discussion and Conclusion

This paper reports on an currently undergoing project, D-MASON, that has been developed with the purpose of speeding up the performances of MASON, a very well known and quite widespread framework for ABMs.

This work has been motivated by the the need for a system management facility that is extremely important for the deployment, the tuning and the analysis of complex simulations on multiple machines.

We have shown a) a tool that allows the parallel exploration of the behavior parameter space, and b) a simple architecture that speeds the deployment and the analysis of distributed simulations.

References

1. Agents of Change. The economist, July 22 (2010)
2. Berryman, M.: Review of Software Platforms for Agent Based Models. Technical Report DSTO-GD-0532, Australian Government, Department of Defence (2008)
3. Calvez, B., Hutzler, G.: Parameter space exploration of agent-based models. In: Khosla, R., Howlett, R.J., Jain, L.C. (eds.) KES 2005. LNCS (LNAI), vol. 3684, pp. 633–639. Springer, Heidelberg (2005)
4. Carillo, M., Cordasco, G., De Chiara, R., Raia, F., Scarano, V., Serrapica, F.: Enhancing the Performances of D-MASON - A Motivating Example. In: SIMULTECH, pp. 137–143. SciTePress (2012)
5. Collier, N., North, M.: Parallel agent-based simulation with Repast for High Performance Computing. In: SIMULATION: Transactions of the Society for Modeling and Simulation International (2012)
6. Cordasco, G., De Chiara, R., Mancuso, A., Mazzeo, D., Scarano, V., Spagnuolo, C.: Bringing together efficiency and effectiveness in distributed simulations: the experience with D-MASON. In: SIMULATION: Transactions of The Society for Modeling and Simulation International (2013)
7. Cosenza, B., Cordasco, G., De Chiara, R., Scarano, V.: Distributed Load Balancing for Parallel Agent-based Simulations. In: Proc. of the 19th Euromicro International Conference on Parallel, Distributed and Network-Based Computing, PDP 2011 (2011)
8. Deissenberg, C., van der Hoog, S., Dawid, H.: Eurace: A massively parallel agent-based model of the european economy. Applied Mathematics and Computation 204, 541–552 (2008)
9. Distributed-Mason Project (2011), `http://www.isislab.it/projects/dmason/`
10. Dykstra, P., Elsenbroich, C., Jager, W., de Lavalette, G.R., Verbrugge, R.: Put your money where your mouth is: Dial, a dialogical model for opinion dynamics. Journal of Artificial Societies and Social Simulation 16(3), 4 (2013)
11. Ferenci, S.L., Fujimoto, R.M., Ammar, M.H., Perumalla, K., Riley, G.F.: Updateable simulation of communication networks. In: Proceedings of the Sixteenth Workshop on Parallel and Distributed Simulation, PADS 2002, pp. 107–114. IEEE Computer Society, Washington, DC (2002)

12. Gilbert, N., Troitzsch, K.G.: Simulation for the Social Scientist. Open University Press (2005)
13. Hartshorn, M., Kaznatcheev, A., Shultz, T.: The evolutionary dominance of ethnocentric cooperation. Journal of Artificial Societies and Social Simulation 16(3), 7 (2013)
14. Hatna, E., Benenson, I.: The schelling model of ethnic residential dynamics: Beyond the integrated - segregated dichotomy of patterns. Journal of Artificial Societies and Social Simulation 15(1), 6 (2012)
15. Levin, S.A., Strogatz, S.H. (series eds.), Epstein, J.M. (ed.): In: (ed.) Generative Social Science: Studies in Agent-Based Computational Modeling. Princeton University Press (2007)
16. Xu, Z., Hwang, K.: Scalable parallel computing: technology, architecture, programming. WCBMcGraw-Hill (1998)
17. Luke, S., Cioffi-Revilla, C., Panait, L., Sullivan, K.: MASON: A new multi-agent simulation toolkit. In: Proceedings of the SwarmFest Workshop, May 9-11, Ann Arbor, Michigan, USA (2004)
18. Luke, S., Cioffi-Revilla, C., Panait, L., Sullivan, K., Balan, G.: MASON: A Multiagent Simulation Environment. Simulation 81(7), 517–527 (2005)
19. Lysenko, M., D'Souza, R.M.: A framework for megascale agent based model simulations on graphics processing units. Journal of Artificial Societies and Social Simulation 11(4) (2008)
20. Najlis, R., Janssen, M.A., Parkerx, D.C.: Software tools and communication issues. In: Proc. Agent-Based Models of Land-Use and Land-Cover Change Workshop, pp. 17–30 (2001)
21. Patel, A., Crooks, A., Koizumi, N.: Slumulation: An agent-based modeling approach to slum formations. Journal of Artificial Societies and Social Simulation 15(4), 2 (2012)
22. Railsback, S.F., Lytinen, S.L., Jackson, S.K.: Agent-based simulation platforms: Review and development recommendations. Simulation 82, 609–623 (2006)
23. Szabó, A., Bocsi, R., Ferschl, G., Bálint, B., Gulyás, L.: Experiments with complex agent-based systems using the meme tool: A case study. In: ASME (2009)
24. White, A.: An abstract model showing that the spatial structure of social networks affects the outcomes of cultural transmission processes. Journal of Artificial Societies and Social Simulation 16(3), 9 (2013)
25. Wimsatt, W.C.: False models as means to truer theories, pp. 23–55. Oxford University Press, London (1987)

Parallel ABM for Electricity Distribution Grids: A Case Study

Fanny Boulaire, Mark Utting, and Robin Drogemuller

Queensland University of Technology,
2 George Street,
Brisbane, Queensland 4000
{Fanny.Boulaire,Mark.Utting,Robin.Drogemuller}@qut.edu.au

Abstract. This paper introduces a parallel implementation of an agent-based model applied to electricity distribution grids. A fine-grained shared memory parallel implementation is presented, detailing the way the agents are grouped and executed on a multi-threaded machine, as well as the way the model is built (in a composable manner) which is an aid to the parallelisation. Current results show a medium level speedup of 2.6, but improvements are expected by incorporating newer distributed or parallel ABM schedulers into this implementation. While domain-specific, this parallel algorithm can be applied to similarly structured ABMs (directed acyclic graphs).

Keywords: electricity distribution grid, network, composable ABM.

1 Introduction

Agent-based models (ABMs) have been used for diverse applications in many domains for their ability to capture the actions and interactions of the agents composing a complex system so that the overall behaviour of the system can be assessed [1]. This paper describes an ABM applied to the electricity domain. The aim of the project this work belongs to is to develop a planning tool for optimal investment strategy of electricity distribution networks over large areas and long planning horizons. A mix of renewable energy, energy storage and other new technologies are compared with traditional practices to assess their impact on the operation of the distribution network.

Traditionally, electricity has been generated at large centralised power stations and then distributed to consumers over a wired network. The introduction of renewable energy systems at various levels within the transmission/distribution system adds complexity to the system due to injection of electrical power in locations that were not initially designed to receive power, mismatches between time of availability and time of demand and reduced control over the phase of generated power. Ergon Energy [2], the industry partner in this project, provides electrical power to approximately 700,000 customers over an area exceeding 1,000,000 km^2. The Ergon network consists of approximately 150,000 km of power lines and 1,000,000 power poles, together with associated substations and transformers, and has a total asset value of

D. an Mey et al. (Eds.): Euro-Par 2013 Workshops, LNCS 8374, pp. 565–574, 2014.

AU$10.6B. Ergon are using the software presented in this paper to support network infrastructure investment decisions, looking for the most appropriate combination of technologies and practices to reduce overall costs.

An Ergon user interacts with the software by selecting nodes within the network structure to be analysed against various scenarios, observing the impact these changes within the network might have on the overall system. A user may analyse a single network topology against a range of user demand predictions or, inversely model user demand predictions against a range of potential network configurations. Initially the system represented the infrastructure of the distribution grid, the attachment points to the transmission grid, solar and wind renewable energy sources as well as emergency diesel generation and the different types of consumers. During development it was recognised that battery storage and the demands of electric vehicles will be needed.

This tool is therefore being built to answer a wide range of questions, which can arise as time passes, taking into account both the technical and economic constraints of the system, and doing so in an integrated manner. Consequently, the tool was built in a composable manner to ensure its flexibility and extensibility. The wide range of physical asset types within the system, the wide range of potential configurations within each asset type, the need for communication of deep, complex issues between the software engineers and domain experts and a desire for flexibility into the future all indicated that an ABM approach had desirable characteristics. ABM was chosen as the modelling technique mainly because the evolution of the electricity grid is unknown due to the many new technologies being employed; in this case the past is no predictor of the future. Also, the ability to describe the agents at various scales, both over space and time, was important to capture the different system characteristics accurately and dynamically.

As the model grew, adding more agents of varied types, the simulation slowed down, leading to the need for parallelization. A parallel implementation of the agent scheduling was done to speed up the execution time and because the structure of the model could be broken down into independent tasks with known common patterns. This paper presents this parallel implementation using a fine-grained shared memory parallelism performed on a multi-core computer, detailing the technical implementation dependent on the overall tool architecture.

The first part of this paper describes the overall architecture of the tool, built in a composable manner, which defines the requirements of the implementation. Then, the description of the parallel implementation within that software framework is given and performances of the parallel implementation are discussed.

2 ABM Planning Tool Architecture

This section briefly describes the overall architecture of the ABM planning tool to provide an understanding of the constraints on the agent-based model, which in turn influences the parallel execution of the agents.

2.1 Composition of the Model Using Plugins

Because the tool was built with the need for evolution in mind, so that many questions could be answered and these in an integrated way, a composable approach was taken. For this, OSGI (formerly Open Services Gateway Initiative) [3], a specification that enables writing modular software, was chosen as the underlying technology for the software. As described by its community of users, it "*reduces complexity by providing a modular architecture for today's large-scale distributed systems as well as small, embedded applications*". This specification has been used by the Eclipse Community, whose plugins are OSGI bundles [4]. The tool presented in this paper is built using Eclipse plugins which are our unit of modularity.

The breakdown of the software in plugins is done over different layers. First, one main plugin is defined, called MODAM (MODular Agent Model), which can be seen as the core of the whole framework. It contains the schemas that define the different extensions, which are used by the different plugins to support interconnection [5]. It also contains the schedulers (sequential and parallel), and ensures the automatic creation of the objects and agents from the plugins using factories.

The different plugins contributing to the creation of the ABM are defined according to their logical meaning. A plugin can be defined for a given analysis type, for example the amount of electricity a solar panel can produce. Within each of these logical units further breakdowns can be performed, to contain different logical or functional units. So far, 3 types of functional units have been distinguished within a logical one. These can be seen through the different extensions that are defined in the MODAM plugin: asset factory, agent factory and data provider. Details about the software architecture can be found in [6]. Using solar panels as an example, the asset factory creates the solar panel assets with their physical characteristics (capacity, derate factor…), the agent factory the behaviour of the solar panel according to a photovoltaic (PV) output model dependent on the weather conditions, and the data provider reading the weather information at the location of the solar panel, being an input to the PV model.

A distinction has been made between assets and agents; this is further explained below.

2.2 Integration of Assets and Agents Over Separate Layers

When looking at an implementation of an agent in an ABM, it is normally mainly defined through its behaviour in relation to its environment and other agents, using only the characteristics that are required to determine the agent's action. That is, the object's characteristics and behaviours are combined in one single class and only the necessary attributes are modelled. Also, the agents are often instantiated in a central class where the relationships amongst given agents are set, as well as their scheduling for the simulation. Such an approach can be sufficient when building a model that has well-defined boundaries. However, when planning on extending the functionality of a model, such an approach can be restraining, as reuse is limited because of this tight coupling and access to the code is required to extend the model.

For our ABM implementation, a distinction has been made between the characteristics and the actions of our agents. Fig. 1 shows a schematic representation of the two distinct layers that compose our model implementation: the asset and the agent layer. In the context of this paper, an 'asset' is the object that contains the physical aspects, and an 'agent' holds only the behaviour. The two are however linked, and the behaviours can be informed using the asset's characteristics.

Fig. 1 shows that the different elements composing the simulation are coming from different factories that are in separate plugins. Often there is a one-to-one relationship between an asset and an agent, but it is not required. Indeed, as shown on the figure, an agent representing the behaviour of a single asset can be built combining multiple behaviours – this is the case for a premise agent, which is the combination of electricity consumption and demand-side management behaviours which can come from two distinct plugins and modified as more information becomes available to define the behaviour. It is not necessary to load both behaviours for all scenarios. This architecture also supports the loading of alternative behaviours, for example consumption, against a single implementation of demand-side management. Conversely, a single behaviour can be assigned to a group of assets, which is the case when doing a load flow analysis for example.

Finally, it can be seen that while many plugins have been used to implement the model, only one integrated network graph has been created and it runs as one single agent-based model – the one on the Agent Layer.

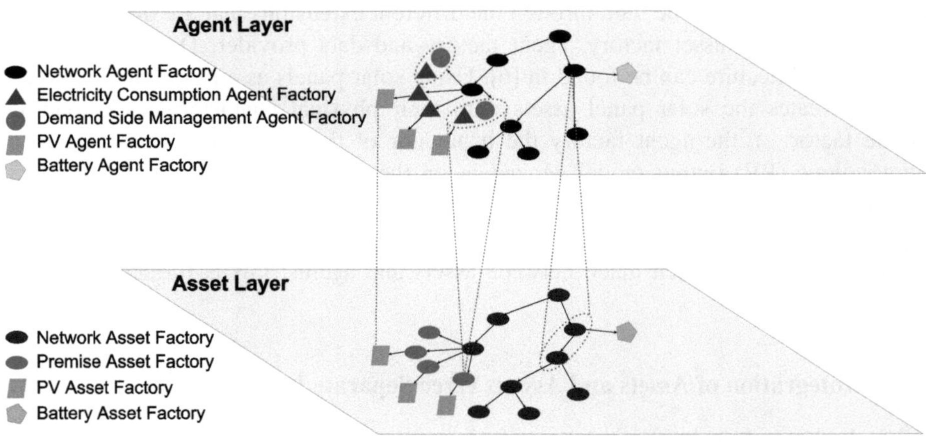

Fig. 1. Schematic representation of the ABM architecture

3 Parallel ABM for the Electricity Distribution Grid

Having defined the structure of the agent-based model implementation, this section describes its parallel implementation, which is a fine-grained parallelism on a single shared memory computer. The following sections describe the different aspects relating to the parallelization of the agent-based model execution:

- Ordering of the agents at simulation setup
- Parallel execution of the agents at runtime

It should be noted that the application presented in this paper is not a generic solution for parallel ABM; it is related to the specific case study presented here. However, because the nature of the problem is a graph structure, whose execution benefits from parallelisation, it can be applied to other applications of similar nature. Also, a distributed ABM could be built on top of this implementation, but this is outside of the scope of this paper.

3.1 Ordering of the Agents at Simulation Setup

Because of the dependence of some agents on other agents that define their relationships and interactions, the ordering of the agents' execution is extremely important. Due to the way the agent-based model is built, this ordering needs to follow the architecture constraints. This means that two types of ordering needed to be considered: ordering within the same plugin, and ordering across plugins.

Because plugins can be used independently of one other, it was necessary to have agents ordered within the plugin in which they are defined. This ordering is handled within the code where the developer has access to the agents themselves through their relationships to one another. Because it is a graph structure, this was handled using '*Before*' and '*After*' attributes, to define a strict *partial order* over the agents. A partial order is a transitive relation that is irreflexive and antisymmetric, i.e. corresponds to a directed acyclic graph which is what is represented in our system.

The second type of ordering regards those agents that are dependent on other agents defined in another plugin. This cannot be defined in advance in either plugin, since it is possible for the plugins to be developed independently so neither one knows about the other. This type of ordering is a bit more sophisticated as it requires ordering agents from at least 2 sets, where within each of these sets, agents are also ordered. For this, partial ordering of the agents is again used. An example of this is given in Fig. 2. It shows 3 plugins, 2 of which can be run in parallel (Plugin A and B) with the third one requiring having its agents called after both of them. In each of them we have 3 agents; plugin A and C have their agents ordered sequentially, and plugin B has 2 agents that are ordered sequentially (b_1 and b_2) and one that can be called anytime (b_3). The ordering between plugin B and plugin C means that all agents in plugin B must finish their step methods before any agents in plugin C can start.

The ordering of the agents is set through an argument in the command line, using "-order" and a combination of the plugins. In the example given in Fig. 2, the ordering argument looks like:

-order = (*td*(PluginA) || *bu*(PluginB)); PluginC

Where *bu* stands for bottom up, and *td* for top down ordering; || shows that PluginA and PluginB are to be ordered in parallel, and the semi-colon (;) is to show sequential ordering.

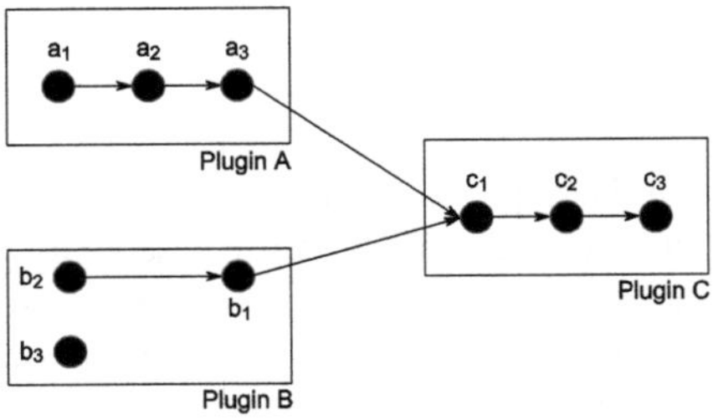

Fig. 2. Example of ordering of agents within plugins and amongst plugins

3.2 Parallel Execution of the Agents at Runtime

Given the nature of the problem, each agent in the graph has to wait for one or more agents to be executed before it can proceed with its own action. A barrier to efficient and speedy processing is therefore a blocking condition where an agent is waiting on others' execution. Indeed, early versions of our parallel ABM treated each agent as a separate task, but profiling showed that this resulted in too much overhead synchronising between hundreds of thousands of small tasks.

So, in order to speed up the execution of the ABM, the partial order from the previous section is broken down into many small independent groups on which the calculations are performed. The size of these groups can be varied by the user using the parameter *–ThreadGroupSize* on the command line. Then these groups of agents can be executed in parallel on *n* threads, specified by the Java command line argument –*Threads*. Details of these two phases are as follows:

1. **Setting up of the queue** - Grouping is done at the beginning of a simulation, and whenever new agents are created, by traversing the partial order, using a depth-first search. These groups are defined and queued in a linear order, with each group recording any previous groups that it depends upon. Mathematically, the groups form equivalence classes over the agents and the partial order over the groups is derived from, or is an abstraction of, the partial order over the agents. These group sizes are less than or equal to the number specified by *ThreadGroupSize*, depending on the configuration of the graph – e.g. when an agent has multiple parents.
2. **Execution of the agents –** Execution is done repeatedly for each time step. Within each time step, it is also repeated until the whole graph has been executed.
   (a) Depending on the number of threads (*n*), the *n* first available groups of agents, or task, in the pool are executed in parallel. The calculations are performed within each of these groups and assigned to the top node that can be used in the next task.
   (b) As soon as a thread becomes free, it accesses the next available task in the pool and checks its dependencies to see if they have finished processing. If they have, the step method of the group of agents is executed.

Fig. 3 illustrates this algorithm using a small extract of a network with two main branches – one starting with a feeder line L1 and another one with the feeder line L2, that then join at a bus B4. Under that bus, 5 houses are represented, some of which have solar panels installed.

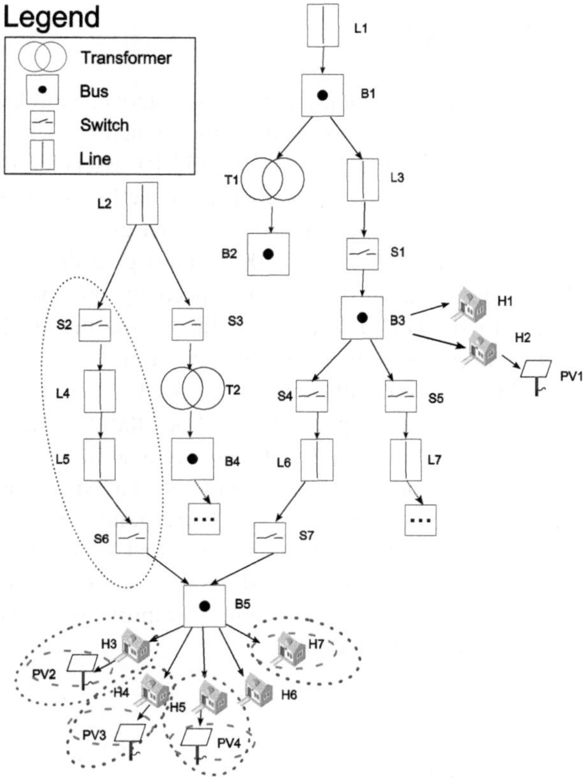

Fig. 3. Small extract of a distribution network, implemented with a parallel ABM

Following the description above, each agent would have been ordered during the simulation setup in the module manager, indicating the order in which the agents need to be run. This ordering can be either top-down or bottom-up depending on the user's instructions.

From this ordering, the pool would have been created, first placing the agents at the leaves of the branches, i.e. those that do not have any dependency on other agents. From the example given in Fig. 3, with a *ThreadGroupSize* of 1, agents PV1, PV2, PV3, PV4, H1, H6 and H7 would be at the beginning of the queue followed by H2, H3, H4, H5, and so on. With a *ThreadGroupSize* of 4, we would have at the top of the pool, [PV2, H3], [PV3, H4], [PV4, H5], H6 and H7, followed by B5, and then [S6, L5, L4, S2] and [S7, L6, S4]. These groups contain fewer agents than 4 because they all impact on B5 which has multiple parents.

Following this, depending on the number of threads (n), the n agents are taken from the queue and their step method executed. As the agents' execution is finished, the thread is freed and the following task within the pool is then executed.

4 Results and Discussion

Following the parallelised implementation described above, simulations were performed on an i7-2600 CPU (4 cores + hyper threading) machine. The test case was for a medium-size town in Queensland, containing 75,910 assets of different natures (premises, lines, transformers…), and each asset had exactly one agent in this example. Parameter sweeps were performed and showed that using *n+1* threads (where *n* is number of cores) and *ThreadGroupSize*=1000 would give the fastest runs. Using group sizes of 1000, Fig. 4 shows the relative speed up obtained for numbers of threads varying from 1 to 10. The *ideal* (dashed) line shows the ideal performance if each of the available processors were fully utilised; from 4 to 8 cores, the slope is lower because hyper-threading typically gives less speedup than real hardware cores [7]. It can be seen here that a speed up of 2.6 could be attained when using 8 threads (green line). It can be noted on this graph that there are 3 additional series titled *start*, *step* and *stop*. These correspond to the three phases that have been distinguished within a step method of an agent execution; *step* corresponds to the calculations that are performed after obtaining the information (*start*) that is required to perform its decision and before it is sent (*stop*) to the next agent or stored in memory when requested by an agent. The *step* series shows the most improvement, which is the most important as it requires the most computing.

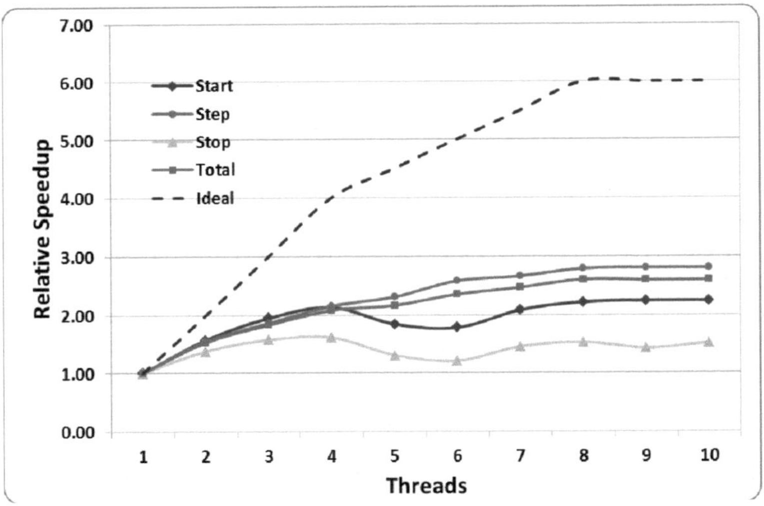

Fig. 4. Relative speedup of the parallel implementation of ABM model for the electricity grid

The speedup obtained here is application-specific, as it depends on the relations between the agents and the granularity of their step methods. Our current scheduling algorithm, which is an NP-hard scheduling problem, gives medium speedup levels. It is however an improvement from other tested algorithms. There is on-going research to further improve the speedup.

An important point is the deterministic execution of the code. The outputs of the simulation are identical whether the simulation is run in parallel or sequentially which is an important feature. In some other implementations of parallel ABMs, determinism is not required, and even sometimes not desirable. In this case determinism is essential because of the impact of order of agent execution, which can be defined as a directed acyclic graph.

The i7-2600 CPU with 4 cores and hyper threading is being used to test the parallel algorithms due to the ability to constrain the entire execution environment. The full system is run on an SGI Altix XE Cluster with 128 nodes and 1924 x 64bit Intel Xeon Cores with a maximum 101.8 TeraFlops using single precision mode and 15,264 GigaBytes (GB) of main memory. Unfortunately, exclusive access to the cluster for experimentation purposes is not possible.

5 Related Work

Many applications are available to support the development of agent-based models ([8]; [9]). More recently, some of them have been further developed to support parallel and distributed ABMs, as the need for faster execution times and support of larger and larger models has arisen. This is the case for D-MASON [10], which is the parallel and distributed version of MASON, or Repast-HPC (High Performance Computing) [11] for Repast Simphony. Other platforms such as JADE [12] which is a middleware for distributed multi-agent application based on peer-to-peer communication architecture are also available. Most research on parallelizing ABMs has focussed on distributed computers, but there has been some research on multicore implementations, such as the study of spatial interactions by Gong et al. [13]. They achieve high speedups from 1-32 cores, but do not ensure determinism, so all their agents can be executed in parallel (with a small amount of locking required to ensure data integrity), which is essentially an embarrassingly parallel scenario. In contrast, we preserve determinism and our applications typically have complex and deep dependency graphs between agents that constrain the possible parallelism.

MASON was initially selected as the ABM engine for our software platform for its ease in separating the engine (which we were interested in) from the rest of the platform as well as for its execution speed. However, it was later replaced by our own implementation of a scheduler in Java. At the time the tool was being developed, D-MASON was not available and its availability has only recently come to the knowledge of the authors of this paper. Consequently, the work presented here has not been tried using D-MASON. D-MASON implements distributed ABMs rather than the shared memory parallelism discussed herein. This fine-grained parallelism is designed to speed up the simulation of networks of closely connected agents with frequent communication, while distributed ABM approaches are more suited for loosely connected sets of agents with less communication. Distributed ABM is complementary to the methods presented here. A combined approach will be tested in the future.

6 Conclusion

A parallel implementation of an agent-based model for planning the electricity grid has been presented. This implementation, which is application-specific, was based on the structure of the agent-based model, reduced to a directed acyclic graph. Agents were ordered, and then grouped respecting the ordering, to be executed in parallel over different threads. Results showed a relative speedup of 2.6, using an i7-2600 CPU (4 cores + hyper threading) machine, which further research will aim at improving. While this fine-grained shared memory parallelism is specific to the structure of this ABM, it can be applied to other ABMs with similar agent structures.

This application was built using the MODAM framework [6] which aims to answer diverse questions applied to the electricity grid. This software framework, which supports flexible and extensible models, was presented to provide an understanding of the structure of the model. This framework has two schedulers (sequential and parallel) which have been implemented in-house. The use of other schedulers from distributed and parallel ABM tools, such as D-MASON and Repast-HPC, will be investigated in future research to see if the speed of the simulations can be further improved.

References

1. North, M.J., Macal, C.M.: Managing Business Complexity. Oxford University Press (2007)
2. `http://www.ergon.com.au/about-us/company-information/corporate-profile` (accessed on June 02, 2013)
3. `http://www.osgi.org/Main/HomePage` (accessed on February 01, 2013)
4. `http://www.vogella.com/articles/OSGi/article.html` (accessed on September 09, 2012)
5. EclipseZone, `http://www.eclipsezone.com/eclipse/forums/t97608.rhtml` (accessed on February 13, 2013)
6. Boulaire, F.A., Utting, M., Drogemuller, R.: MODAM: A MODular Agent-based Modelling Framework. In: International Conference on Software Engineering (ICSE), San Fransisco, CA, USA (2013)
7. Intel Corporation, `http://software.intel.com/en-us/articles/how-to-determine-the-effectiveness-of-hyper-threading-technology-with-an-application/` (accessed on July 26, 2013)
8. Berryman, M.: Review of Software Platforms for Agent Based Models. Department of Defense, D.S.T.O. (ed.) (2008)
9. Jackson, S.K., Railsback, S.F., Lytinen, S.L.: Agent-based Simulation Platforms: Review and Development Recommendations. Simulation 82, 609–623 (2006)
10. Cordasco, G., Chiara, R.D., Raia, F., Scarano, V., Spagnuolo, C., Vicidomini, L.: Designing computational steering facilities for distributed agent based simulations. In: Proceedings of the 2013 ACM SIGSIM Conference on Principles of Advanced Discrete Simulation, pp. 385–390. ACM, Montreal (2013)
11. Collier, N.: Repast HPC Manual (2012)
12. Bellifemine, F., Caire, G., Poggi, A., Rimassa, G.: JADE - A White Paper. Exp in Search of Innovation 3 (2003)
13. Gong, Z.Y., Tang, W.W., Bennett, D.A., Thill, J.C.: Parallel agent-based simulation of individual-level spatial interactions within a multicore computing environment. International Journal of Geographical Information Science 27, 1152–1170 (2013)

A Distributed Simulation of Roost-Based Selection for Altruistic Behavior in Vampire Bats

Mario Paolucci[1] and Luca Vicidomini[2]

[1] Laboratory of Agent Based Social Simulation
ISTC-CNR Rome, Italy
mario.paolucci@istc.cnr.it
[2] Dipartimento di Informatica
Università di Salerno, Italy
lvicidomini@unisa.it

Abstract. Vampire bats exhibit a unique behavior: they help unlucky conspecifics by sharing part of their meal. This altruistic act seems to happen in their group of reference even between individuals not genetically related. Inspired by this biological example, we have developed a simulation that reproduces its essential traits, where group selection counteracts selective pressure towards cheating: the roosting effect.

Previous work on the same theme has shown how the roosting effect can cope with sensible mutation levels. Here, leveraging the features of D-Mason that allows to run massive simulations on a distributed environment, as well as performing a batch scheduling of the experiments, we derive a relationship between mutation rate and roost size.

Keywords: Agent-Based Simulation, Distributed Systems, Parallel Batch Execution, Vampire bats, Group selection.

1 Introduction

Vampire bats (Desmodus Rotundus) are a fascinating species, exhibiting a unique helping behavior that has been studied extensively, prominently by G. Wilkinson [2,17]. These little guys help unlucky conspecifics (that is, those who did not find enough blood to drink in their nightly hunt) by regurgitating in their mouth part of their semi-digested meal. This altruistic act seems to happen in their group of reference, the *roost*, even between individuals not genetically related. If confirmed, as it seems to be the case, this would rule out kin-based explanations of this behavior [2]. The alternative explanation normally proposed is that of reciprocal altruism, although group selection has been also proposed [6,13].

The case of vampires is especially interesting because there are a few characteristics of this kind of help as it happen in nature that set it apart as a special one. In the wild, vampire bats have a random chance to find food which is about 93%, and their metabolism is so fast that need to feed at least once in two days. Unlucky individuals can be saved by fellow help - unless these happen to be non-altruists, who deny help, potentially causing death by starvation. These harsh conditions are ideal to rule out direct reciprocation strategies.

D. an Mey et al. (Eds.): Euro-Par 2013 Workshops, LNCS 8374, pp. 575–584, 2014.

Inspired by this biological example, we have developed a simulation (see below "the model") that reproduces the essential traits of the target phenomenon. We only assume the existence of roosts as a limitation to interaction - everything in a simulated bat lifecycle happens inside roosts. Thus, the only force to balance the evolutionary pressure for non-altruism is group selection; groups with too many non-altruists are ineffective for helping, and, finally, condemn their members to an early death.

Everything here is included as mechanism: algorithms explicitly dictate when an agent reproduces, thrives or dies; there is no explicit target or utility function. Instead, we enforce competition by limiting the maximum number of agents that the (eco)system can support. This, besides stopping an expansion that would prevent calculation, has the effect of increasing competition - an effective roost will split faster, occupying precious space in the limited niche.

Group Selection is an evolutionary theory with an interesting story of misunderstandings, masterfully told in Sober and Wilson's book [15]. Due to an early formulation that presented serious shortcomings, the theory suffered a long lapse of obscurity before returning to reclaim a place in the evolutionary biologist's toolbox [8,15,18]; in the meantime, only its alternatives, including kin selection [9], reciprocal altruism [16], and the selfish gene theory [5] have received attention.

Previous work on the same theme [12] has shown how the roosting effect can cope with sensible mutation levels, pointing out how the most robust size of roosts was comparable with the size actually found in nature. However, there was no attempt to derive a relationship between mutation rate and roost size, that we explore in the present work.

2 Mason and D-Mason

Previous implementation of the model was build in NetLogo, a multi-agent programmable modeling environment. Two of the biggest drawbacks of NetLogo are [1] its slowness and its oversimplified language. NetLogo is a widely spread platform for ABMs due its language's expressive power that allows a scientist to create prototypes or full models after few hours of learning. However, its single-thread execution model and its high-level, interpreted language makes NetLogo one of the slowest platforms [14] limiting its usage to models with few hundred agents. Moreover, NetLogo, being not a true object-oriented language, makes it difficult to structure a complex model; for example, it is unclear in the code how methods are associated to agents.

On the contrary, Mason is designed with the goal of maximizing execution speed even on computationally demanding models with thousand agents [10]. Mason allows a developer to take advantage of Java's Object-Oriented programming paradigm and clean syntax, enabling him/her to build complex and structured models promoting the use of Model-View-Controller (MVC) software design pattern. Although its focus on performance, Mason is still designed as a single-threaded application.

A distributed version of Mason, called D-Mason has been introduced in [3,4]. D-Mason is able to run models featuring millions of agents and shows increased performance over the single-threaded version. Unlike many PDES platforms, where each agent is an independent entity that must synchronize with other agents, a different strategy is used to distribute a MASON simulation in D-MASON called *space partitioning.* Considering that most ABMs are inspired by natural models where agents are placed in a bi-dimensional or tri-dimensional space and agents communicate and interacts with neighbors within a limited range called area of interest (AOI), D-MASON partitions the space to be simulated (called *field*) into *regions.* Each region, together with the agents it contains, is assigned to a Logical Process (LP); then each LP is in charge of: simulating the agents that belong to the assigned region; handling the migration of the agents; managing the synchronization between neighboring regions.

Since the AOI extension of an agent is small compared with the size of a region it belongs to, the communication is often limited to local messages within the same LP. LPs in charge of the simulation of neighboring regions, are locally synchronized in order to let the simulation run consistently. LPs communicate by using a publish-subscribe mechanism design pattern: a multicast channel is assigned to each region. Each region publishes its updates on its channel and subscribes the channels of its neighbors. D-MASON is released under a Free and Open Software license and is available at [7].

3 The Model

Each step of the simulation represents a day in the life of the bats.

A day includes two stages: during the night stage, bats hunt. About 93% of the population finds foods to survive until the next hunt, while the remaining 7% begin to starve. Since vampires do not accumulate resources and each good hunt gives them no more than 60 hours autonomy, two failures in a row are fatal. In the simulation, each bat performs about 1.65 episodes of double unsuccessful hunt per year. The only way to prevent starvation and death is receiving help from fellows.

During the daily stage, bats perform social activities. Each day, random couples are formed by vampires within the same roost in order to perform *grooming.* In our simulation, grooming plays the only role of allowing for help requests. If a vampire (the requestor) is starving, that is, went through two consecutive hunting failures, it will request help to the current grooming partner. In normal conditions, the potential donor will honor the request when possible, that is, if returning from a successful hunt. Some agents, the cheaters, will always refuse help.

After the grooming phase, bats reproduce increasing the size of the roost. In this simulation, individuals are sexless and they reproduce by cloning every ten months, starting from the twentieth, in order to model the juvenile phase. To obtain a reasonable rate of reproduction, at each occurrence each agent has 50% probability to clone. The *mutation rate* defines the probability that a clone will change behaviour - from altruistic to cheater and vice versa.

When the number of living bats in a single roost exceeds a threshold called *launch size*, the roost splits in two roosts, each with half of the bats of the original roost. The launch size is a property defined per-roost; furthermore, when a "mother" roost splits in two, the newly created roosts' launch size is set to their mother's launch size varied by a random quantity between −20% and +20% of the mother's launch size.

3.1 The Mason Implementation

Since interactions among vampires are limited to individuals belonging to the same roost, we decided to model the roosts as agents, instead of the bats. This allows us to save memory and to easily reproduce 24 hours of real time as one simulation step. At every simulation step, each agent (that is, each roost) executes its `step()` routine that simulates a day in the life of the bats in that roost.

Each roost has a list of its in-roost so, at each step, the roost-agent scans his list and simulates the night stage of the day, where vampires hunt. After the hunt, random couples of in-roosts are formed, allowing vampires ask for help if one of the bats in the couple is starving, which will result in a donation or a refusal from the daily grooming partner.

Then the roost removes from the simulation the bats dead by starvation or age and allows the survived bats for reproduction. If, following the reproduction phase, the number of in-roosts reaches the roost's launch size, the roost splits in two (remaining in the same location) and its vampires are equally divided among the newly created roosts.

3.2 Distributing the Simulation in D-Mason

In order to port the Vampires simulation from Mason to D-Mason, few changes are necessary. D-Mason does require agents to have spatial coordinate so it can perform the space partition distribution strategy, as already stated in Section 2. In our model, agents do not have the notion of space (a kind of model often referred to as "soup" model or aspatial [11]) so we scattered the roosts randomly through the field. Since agents do not communicate with each other in any circumstance, we reduced the AOI to zero, thus reducing the communication among regions and achieving maximum possible speed in the simulation.

Exploiting D-Mason synchronization mechanism through agents' positions, we investigated a custom balance technique to be sure that the total number of agents is equally divided among the regions forming the field. Just before every simulation step, the simulation collects the number of agents in every region of field (that is, in every LP). A simple balancing mechanism consist in migrating part of the agents in the region on the left, if that region has significantly less agents (i.e. 10% of the total number of living agents). In our test runs, we noticed that roost splits were almost equally distributed among the LPs so the balancing mechanism rarely become operational and was later abandoned.

4 Research Question

The purpose of the simulation is to give a characterization of the relationship between roost size and mutation rate in simulated vampire bats that evolve an altruistic behavior thanks to group selection, in contrast with a non-altruistic (cheating) behavior that is advantageous for the individual but lethal for the roost.

From this point of view, a simulated bat world is thus characterized by a single exogenous variable, the mutation rate that is kept constant between agents and through a simulation run, and by an endogenously varying group size that is expressed by two correlated quantities: the launch size, that is, the maximum roost size, that triggers fission when reached, and the actual roost population. Being there at any time in the simulation an abundance of roosts, both quantities should be considered random variable in themselves.

Other, possibly confounding, exogenous variables are the maximum number of agents in the world (carrying capacity), that puts a cap on the expansion of the bats population, and the initial values of roost size, launch size, and population. In the next section, we set up these variables and show how we prepared the model for batch processing.

5 Setting-up the Model for Batch Processing

The batch scheduler of D-MASON requires a compatible simulation and an XML file containing data for batch execution and parameter space. D-MASON comes with its own Batch Wizard that takes in input a compatible simulation and allows a scientist to generate the batch XML description file.

In order to have a batch-compatible simulation, we need to mark up the parameters that will vary through the different runs. Marking the parameters will allow D-MASON to inspect a simulation in order to extract name, type, suggested value and domain for the parameters.

Parameters are marked using Java annotations, a standard mechanism that allows to attach metadata to Java code, available from JDK version 1.5. D-MASON defines a `batch` annotation contained in the package `dmason.annotation`:

```
@Retention(RetentionPolicy.RUNTIME)
public @interface batch {
    String domain() default "";
    String suggestedValue() default "";
}
```

For each *batch parameter* we can also specify two options:

- *domain* is a tool-tip string that the D-MASON's Batch Wizard will display to the user;
- *suggestedValue* is a value that the D-MASON's Batch Wizard will propose as default. The model should suggest a good "default" value that will allow to run the model with a "standard" behavior.

In our simulation we will vary the following parameters:

- *carrying capacity*: is the maximum number of bats allowed to live at each step;
- *initial population*: is the initial number of living bats;
- *initial launch size*: is the initial threshold over which a roost will split;
- *mutation rate*: the percentage of newborn bats that will invert their parent's altruistic/cheater trait.

For instance, we show how we annotated the *carrying capacity* parameter:

```
@batch(suggestedValue = "5000")
private int carryingCapacity = 5000;
public int getCarryingCapacity() {
    return carryingCapacity; }
public void setCarryingCapacity(int carryingCapacity) {
    this.carryingCapacity = carryingCapacity; }
```

After all of the batch parameters are annotated, we need to export the simulation package as a JAR archive that will contain the Java classes that are part of our model. The JAR archive is necessary to build the batch XML file descriptor using the D-MASON's Batch Wizard (Figure 1).

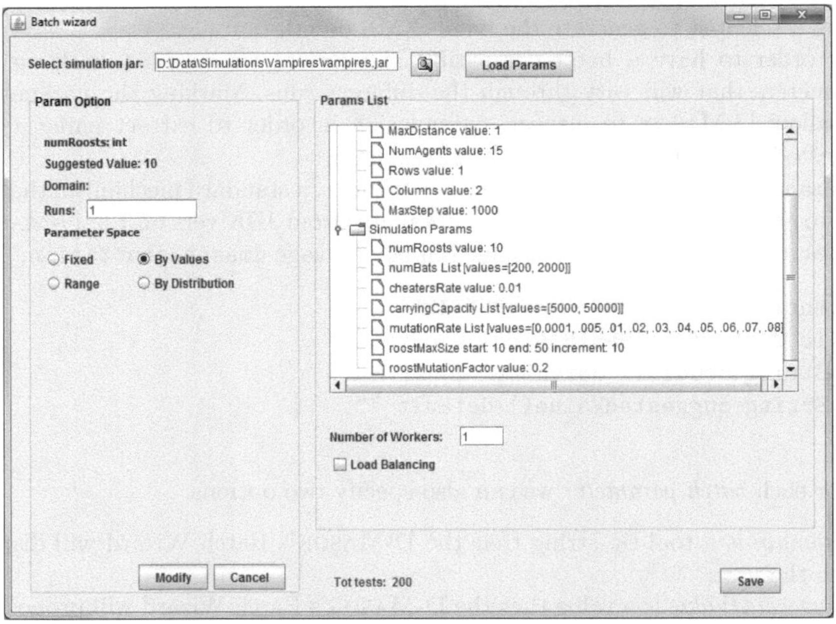

Fig. 1. Batch wizard

For each parameter we can specify a fixed value, a list or a range of values, or define a probability distribution that will generate the values. The parameter space we decided to explore is shown in Table 1, consisting in 132 cases.

Table 1. The first set of experiments

Initial population	List: 200, 2 000
Carrying capacity	List: 5 000, 50 000
Mutation rate	List: 0.0001, 0.001, 0.005, 0.01, 0.02, 0.03, 0.04, 0.05, 0.06, 0.07, 0.08
Initial launch size	Range: from 10 to 50, step 20
Number of steps	Fixed: 1 000 000

During the preliminary phase we ran a small set of experiments in order to determine the best way to distribute the simulation. We observed that a single experiment required approximately 7 hours to complete on a single LP, due the very high scalability of the model (our agents do not move nor communicate with others) the simulation time decreases almost linearly with the number of LPs.

Our final set-up consisted in three PC with the following configuration:

- CPU Intel Core i7 2600 @ 3.40 GHz
- RAM 8 GB
- Operative System: Windows 7 Professional 64 bit
- Java Virtual Machine 1.7.0

Each PC ran 4 LPs configured with the maximum limit of 2 GB of memory space available, for a total of 12 LPs available. The whole set of experiments took 3 days and 5 hours to complete.

After the first analysis of the resulting data, we designed a new set of experiments, shown in Table 2. This second set of experiments consisted in 36 cases and was run using the same configuration above, for a total running time of 2 days and an half.

Table 2. The second set of experiments

Initial population	Fixed: 2 000
Carrying capacity	Fixed: 50 000
Mutation rate	List: 0.0001, 0.001, 0.005, 0.01, 0.02, 0.03, 0.04, 0.05, 0.06
Initial launch size	Range: from 20 to 50, step 10
Number of steps	Fixed: 3 000 000

6 Results

Let us first examine the quantities of interest in a specific time. With the chosen parameters, we show the final distribution of values for roost size and launch size in Figure 2. As it can be seen, the distribution of both roost composition and launch size is skewed (as it can be expected for a distribution of integer values limited by zero), with what looks like a few outliers to the right. The shape justifies the use a summary value as the mean to represent both roost population and launch size.

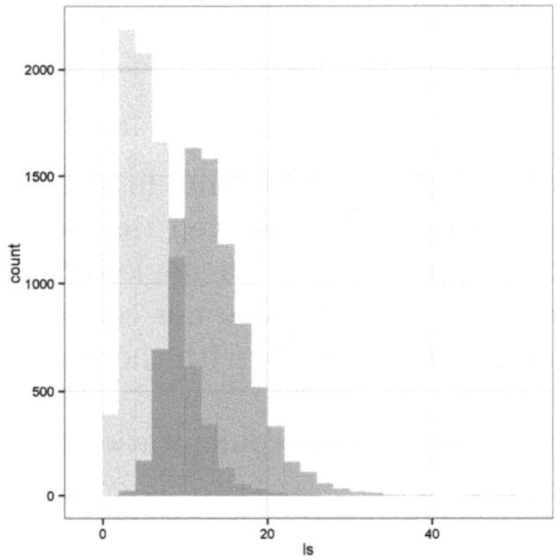

Fig. 2. Distribution of values for ls and roost population at the end of a simulation (mr:0.06, ils:50, ip:2000, cc:50000). The shape on the left (green) is roost population, the one on the right launch size.

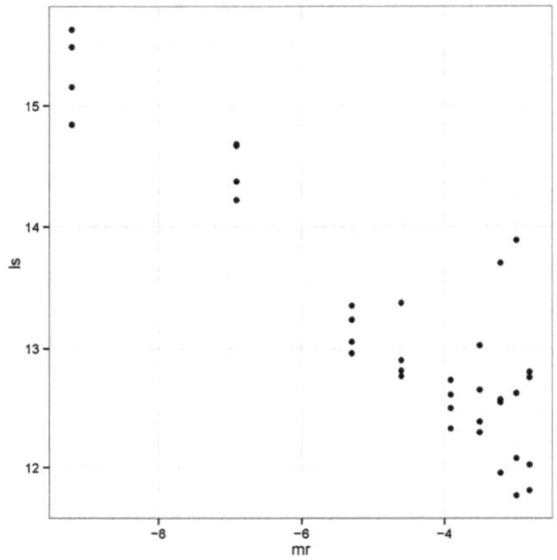

Fig. 3. Launch size against mutation rate in semi-log scale

Thus, we can present the mean values for our observed quantities, in relation to the mutation rate and to the potential confounding factors. The results are summarized in Table 3. As the table shows, the mean for the launch size is found to have an inverse dependence on mutation rate. While for very small values of mutation rate the launch size does not depend on its initial value, we also observe a positive correlation of initial launch size with the launch size at the end of the simulation. Thus, at least for high mutation rates, the system still exhibits memory of its initial state after 3 million steps.

In order to make sense of the relationship between mutation rate and launch size, we plot them in a semi-logarithmic scale in Figure 3. The figure suggests a linear relation, thus hinting to a relation of the shape $ls = h + k\ e^{-\alpha\ mr}$.

Table 3. Mean values of launch size per mutation rate and initial value

mutation rate	initial launch size 20	30	40	50
0.0001	15.16	15.49	14.84	15.63
0.001	14.68	14.22	14.67	14.37
0.005	12.96	13.24	13.35	13.06
0.01	12.91	13.37	12.82	12.77
0.02	12.74	12.62	12.34	12.51
0.03	12.39	12.30	12.66	13.03
0.04	11.96	12.58	12.56	13.70
0.05	11.77	12.08	12.63	13.89
0.06	11.81	12.02	12.81	12.76

If we assume an inverse exponential relation between ls and mr, we can fit it to get approximate values for the parameters. In Figure 4, we show the goodness of fit for the calculated function:

$$ls = 12.591 + 2.692\ e^{-298.038\ mr}$$

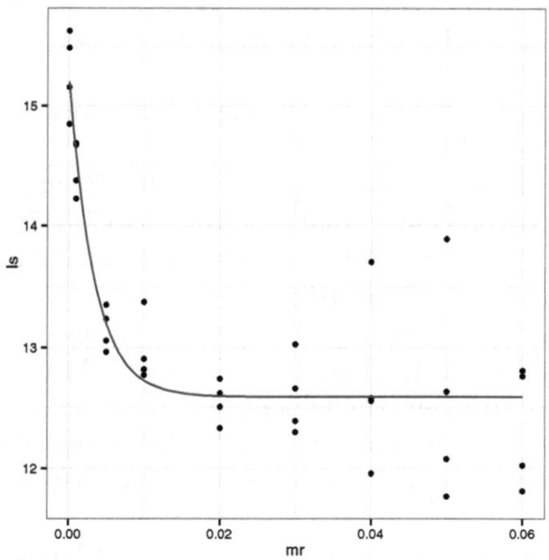

Fig. 4. Launch size against mutation rate with fitting function

7 Conclusions

In this paper we have shown how an evolutionary simulation of a mechanism-based model of the evolution of altruism through group selection could be carried thanks to a distributed platform. Without D-MASON, we could not have ran the simulations long enough to see the emergence of this effect, neither we could have sketched the empirical law that connects mutation rate and launch size. A future research question is that of investigating theoretical reasons underlying that relation.

References

1. Berryman, M.: Review of Software Platforms for Agent Based Models. Technical Report DSTO-GD-0532, Australian Government, Department of Defence (2008)
2. Carter, G.G., Wilkinson, G.S.: Food sharing in vampire bats: reciprocal help predicts donations more than relatedness or harassment. Proceedings of the Royal Society B: Biological Sciences 280(1753) (2013)
3. Cordasco, G., De Chiara, R., Mancuso, A., Mazzeo, D., Scarano, V., Spagnuolo, C.: A framework for distributing agent-based simulations. In: Alexander, M., et al. (eds.) Euro-Par 2011 Workshops, Part I. LNCS, vol. 7155, pp. 460–470. Springer, Heidelberg (2012)
4. Cordasco, G., De Chiara, R., Mancuso, A., Mazzeo, D., Scarano, V., Spagnuolo, C.: Bringing together efficiency and effectiveness in distributed simulations: the experience with D-MASON. In: SIMULATION: Transactions of The Society for Modeling and Simulation International (2013)
5. Dawkins, R.: The Selfish Gene, 30th anniversary edition. Oxford University Press, USA (2006)
6. Di Tosto, G., Paolucci, M., Conte, R.: Altruism Among Simple and Smart Vampires. International Journal of Cooperative Information Systems 16(1), 51–66 (2007)
7. Distributed-Mason Project (2011), `http://www.isislab.it/projects/dmason/`
8. Field, A.J.: Why multilevel selection matters. Journal of Bioeconomics 10(3), 203–238 (2008)
9. Hamilton, W.D.: The evolution of altruistic behavior. The American Naturalist 97(896), 354–356 (1963)
10. Luke, S., Cioffi-Revilla, C., Panait, L., Sullivan, K., Balan, G.: MASON: A Multiagent Simulation Environment. Simulation 81(7), 517–527 (2005)
11. Macal, C.M., North, M.J.: Tutorial on agent-based modelling and simulation. Journal of Simulation 4(3), 151–162 (2010)
12. Paolucci, M., Conte, R.: Roost Size for Multilevel Selection of Altruism Among Vampire Bats. In: Antunes, L., Takadama, K. (eds.) MABS 2006. LNCS (LNAI), vol. 4442, pp. 69–79. Springer, Heidelberg (2007)
13. Paolucci, M., Conte, R., Di Tosto, G.: A Model of Social Organization and the Evolution of Food Sharing in Vampire Bats. Adaptive Behavior 14(3), 223–238 (2006)
14. Railsback, S.F., Lytinen, S.L., Jackson, S.K.: Agent-based simulation platforms: Review and development recommendations. Simulation 82(9), 609–623 (2006)
15. Sober, E., Wilson, D.S.: Unto Others: The Evolution and Psychology of Unselfish Behavior. Harvard University Press (October 1999)
16. Trivers, R.L.: The Evolution of Reciprocal Altruism. The Quarterly Review of Biology 46(1), 35–57 (1971)
17. Wilkinson, G.S.: Reciprocal food sharing in the vampire bat. Nature 308(5955), 181–184 (1984)
18. Wilson, D.S., Wilson, E.O.: Evolution "for the Good of the Group". American Scientist 96(5), 380+ (2008)

A Study on the Parallelization of Terrain-Covering Ant Robots Simulations

Alessandro Pellegrini and Francesco Quaglia

DIAG, Sapienza, University of Rome

Abstract. Agent-based simulation is used as a tool for supporting (time-critical) decision making in differentiated contexts. Hence, techniques for speeding up the execution of agent-based models, such as Parallel Discrete Event Simulation (PDES), are of great relevance/benefit. On the other hand, parallelism entails that the final output provided by the simulator should closely match the one provided by a traditional sequential run. This is not obvious given that, for performance and efficiency reasons, parallel simulation engines do not allow the evaluation of global predicates on the simulation model evolution with arbitrary time-granularity along the simulation time-axis. In this article we present a study on the effects of parallelization of agent-based simulations, focusing on complementary aspects such as performance and reliability of the provided simulation output. We target Terrain Covering Ant Robots (TCAR) simulations, which are useful in rescue scenarios to determine how many agents (i.e., robots) should be used to completely explore a certain terrain for possible victims within a given time.

1 Introduction

Thanks to the expressive power intrinsically exhibited by agent-based models, agent-based simulation constitutes a proven solution to study complex real-world scenarios. In these models, agents exhibit individual or collective interactions, which have been shown to reliably express interactions between different objects/entities in real world phenomena such as disaster rescue [1], computational sociology [2], logistics [3], biomedical applications [4], and economic analysis [5].

On the other hand, for several application domains, one core aspect to cope with is the timeliness according to which the simulation system is able to deliver its outputs. One example is related to supporting (time-critical) decision making [6] via, e.g., what-if analysis carried out through agent-based simulation models, such as when employing agent-based models in disaster-rescue contexts. To achieve timeliness in the delivery of simulation outputs, parallelization techniques have been adopted with success in several fields (see, e.g., [7]).

Nevertheless, one peculiar aspect of agent-based simulation models is that they are employed not only to study steady state or equilibrium properties of a system, rather to determine the exact simulated-time when a given predicate becomes true. High precision in the determination of such a time instant would require frequent inspection of the state of the simulation model (ideally at

D. an Mey et al. (Eds.): Euro-Par 2013 Workshops, LNCS 8374, pp. 585–594, 2014.

each state transition, namely after the execution of each simulation event). This may result feasible in traditional sequential simulation, where the unique running thread may quickly retrieve the information for predicate evaluation from the data structures (representing the simulation model state) within its address space. On the other hand, when employing parallel/distributed simulation techniques, such a fine grain inspection along the simulation-time axis may result inviable due to the overhead for process coordination, which may hamper the achievable speedup. Also, for high performance optimistic parallel simulation, where the computation performed might be subject to rollback due to violations of event-causality caused by speculative processing, the inspection on the simulation model trajectory may be explicitly delayed to the time instant when a given portion of the computation becomes committed (namely no rollback can even occur in that portion of simulated-time while further executing the simulation model). As a consequence, a shift may appear between the simulated time when the parallel run detects that the predicate holds, and the corresponding simulated time when the sequential run tracks the holding of the same predicate.

In in this article we present a study on the tradeoff between performance and reliability of the simulation outputs when exploiting optimistic PDES techniques, particularly the ROOT-Sim PDES platform [8,9], for the case of simulations of Terrain-Covering Ant Robots (TCAR). More in detail, we study how the frequency of inspection on committed portions of the parallel simulation run impacts both the achievable speedup and the distribution of the estimated simulated-time for fully exploring a target spatial region. This has been done while varying the population of robots (which determines the simulation model complexity), and by relying on parallel runs carried out on a 32-core HP ProLiant machine equipped with 64 GB of RAM, which is representative of current off-the-shelf commodity facilities for scientific computing. Beyond providing results for this specific application context, to the best of our knowledge, this is the first study along the direction of evaluating the reliability of asynchronous (non-time stepped) parallel simulation outputs for the assessment of non-steady state properties of the real-world phenomenon targeted by agent-based simulation.

The remainder of this paper is structured as follows. In Section 2, related work is discussed. The target TCAR model is depicted in Section 3. The parallelization approach for TCAR simulations via ROOT-Sim is presented in Section 4. Experimental data are reported in Section 5.

2 Related Work

In literature, several special-purpose simulation environments to support agent-based simulations have been presented. In the MASON framework [10] special attention was paid to performance, trying to address computing-intensive models (i.e., large scenarios with many agents), and to portability, ensuring reproducibility of results across different hardware architectures. Interfaces can be connected to simulation models, and the simulations can be paused and moved to different computers (which is regarded as a benefit in case of long simulations). A distributed version is also presented [11], which relies on time-stepped synchronization and on the master/slave paradigm. Compared to this work, we focus on performance/reliability tradeoffs for the case of asynchronous (non-time stepped) PDES, which is recognized as a more scalable paradigm for generic simulation-object interaction patterns.

Pandora [12] is a C++-based simulation framework enabling executions in parallel/distributed environments. It features several AI algorithms for supporting agents' decision making, provides python binding (which is a benefit for inexperienced programmers), and is complemented by Cassandra, a visualization tool created to detect spatial-temporal patterns generated by the simulation for post-analysis. On the other hand, we use ROOT-Sim [8,9], a general-purpose PDES simulation framework, to support agent-based simulation. We do not rely on specific agent-based facilities, rather the simulation model is written in plain ANSI-C, giving the modeler the freedom to implement the logic using general-purpose libraries. This lead us to develop a highly efficient C-based simulation model for TCAR, which represents a stress case for parallel runs due to very reduced event granularity (about 0.7 microseconds on the used architecture).

The work in [12] has studied the efficiency and scalability of agent-based models in the Cloud. The authors analyze how the simulation performance changes when moving the simulation framework and the model from a cluster to the Cloud. We target a different aspect, because we only focus on optimistic simulation on clusters in order to show what is the price (in terms of results accuracy) to be paid for having a considerable performance gain.

The work in [13] recognizes the importance (in terms of performance) of relying on the PDES paradigm to carry on complex and resource-intensive simulations. Differently from our goal, the authors concentrate on the difficulty which might arise when mapping any agent-based model onto the PDES paradigm, and propose a middleware which can easily help in this task.

In [14], the performance of one particular simulation model run on top of GPUs is presented, showing that relying on graphic cards to carry on agent-based simulations can provide a considerable speedup with respect to sequential simulations—passing from hours to seconds. In this work, we address CPU simulation, where general models with any kind of intra-agent synchronization and any change in the size of the simulation state is allowed during the evolution of the model, thus allowing to implement complex scenarios much more easily.

The work in [15] tries to bridge the gap between the results in [13] and [14], proposing a simulation environment which can benefit from the PDES paradigm (run on CPUs) and the availability of a large number of cores in GPUs. In particular, within the PDES event handlers, the simulation-model writer can specify which code blocks can be run on top of GPUs, and then the simulation platform offloads that computation to the graphic cards. In our proposal, we target transparency, i.e. the simulation model writer simply writes the model's logic, and then the simulation framework efficiently runs it in parallel.

Another proposal related to the present study can be found in [7]. It addresses the tradeoff between reliability of the simulation output and simulation speed when running large-scale numerical simulations (such as molecular dynamics simulations) on GPU architectures. The focus of [7] is on the effects of data representation, namely single vs double precision floating point representation, on the speed of GPU based runs. This is orthogonal to the tradeoff we target in our study, namely the one between the overhead for global predicates' evaluation in parallel runs vs the precision in the detection of the simulated-time when the predicate is verified.

Finally, the work in [16] addresses the issue of parallelizing multi-agent path planning via parallelization of a forward search algorithm on GPUs, where the parallelization approach tries to cope with the exponential growth of the search space vs the number of agents. Conversely, our simulation model is targeted at executions on CPUs, and implements a map coverage scenario based on a unique dynamic robot-move plan evolving according to probabilistic rules.

3 Reference Simulation Model

The agent-based simulation model which we have targeted for our experimental study is a variant of the Terrain-Covering Ant Robots (TCAR) model presented in [17]. This type of simulation model is particularly interesting for the assessment of rescue scenarios. In particular, if some kind of accident occurs in a region which is either unknown by the rescuers or altered by the accident itself, the first action in order to actually rescue the victims is to explore the whole region.

The terrain is modeled as an undirected graph, therefore an agent (i.e., an ant robot) is able to move from one space region to another in both directions. This mapping is created by imposing a specific grid on the space region. The agents are then required to visit the entire space (i.e., cover the whole graph) by visiting each cell (i.e., graph node) once or multiple times. In our implementation, the model is able to simulate a square region (12 Km^2) divided into 4900 hexagonal cells (rather than square cells, as in the original model). This allows for a better representation of the agents' mobility in the real world, as real ant robots (as physically realized in [18]) have the ability to steer to any direction during the exploration. Robots start from specific border-cells in the terrain, and from each cell a given number of robots starts moving around (mimicking the fact that rescue teams start from specific positions, and unleash robots for discovery).

The model relies on a node-couting algorithm, where each cell is assigned a counter which gets incremented whenever any robot visits it, i.e. tracks the number of *pheromones* left by ants, to notify other ones of their transit. Whenever an agent (i.e., an ant robot) reaches a cell, it increments the counter and determines its new destination. Choosing a destination is a very important factor to efficiently cover the whole region, and to support this the trail counter is used. In particular, the ant robots adopt a greedy approach, so that when a robot is in a particular cell, it targets the neighbor with the minimum trail count. A random choice takes place if multiple cells have the same (minimum) trail count.

Although this greedy approach might not be optimal, it allows for a complete coverage of the region taking into account the simplicity of the agents, which may have a very limited and noisy sensing capability [18]. In the original model, whenever an agent is in a given cell, it accesses the information stored in the neighbor cells (i.e., trail counters) to make its decision. This is a *pull* approach, which, as we will discuss in Section 4, might entail a non-negligible performance drop when running parallel/distributed simulations.

According to the original specification of the model [17], each ant robot moves from one cell to another in a time interval of variable length (provided that the destination is reachable, i.e. no obstacle is in between the current and the destination cell). In our configuration of the model, we have made two important choices: i) there are no obstacles in the terrain; ii) time interval is drawn according to an exponential distribution with mean value 100 sec (corresponding to the typical speed of an ant robot of 50 cm per sec), which models the set of variables that can potentially impact the robot move. As for choice i), this allows us to study a *lower bound* of complete region-coverage time. In fact, inserting any obstacle will prevent agents to freely move around, not allowing certain actions, and increasing the exploration time. Choice ii), instead, allows us to study how much time is required by a group of agents to explore a small area with a very high detail, due to the intrinsic speed limitations (one meter per second [18]).

4 Parallelization

We have implemented the model[1] described in Section 3 in order to be run on top of the ROme OpTimistic Simulator (ROOT-Sim) [8,19]. This is an open source C/MPI-based simulation platform targeted at POSIX systems, which implements a general-purpose parallel/distributed simulation environment relying on the optimistic (i.e., rollback-based) synchronization paradigm. It offers a very simple programming model relying on the classical notion of simulation-event handlers, both for processing events and for accessing a committed and globally consistent state image upon Global Virtual Time (GVT) calculation. The GVT value corresponds to the (periodically) reevaluated commitment horizon of the optimistic (speculative) simulation run. No causality violation, hence no rollback, can even occur for processed simulation events whose timestamp falls before the current GVT value. GVT updates typically trigger memory recovery procedures, e.g., of obsolete state logs.

As in typical PDES engines, in ROOT-Sim the simulation model can be partitioned into N simulation objects, each one modeling a subportion of the whole environment. Each simulation object $i \in [0, N-1]$ is associated with a private simulation state S_i, so that the global simulation state is $S = \bigcup_{i=0}^{N-1} S_i$ and $S_i \cap S_j = \emptyset \; \forall i, j \; i \neq j$. Any simulation objects is handled by a Logical Process (LP), which takes care of executing the events which are passed by the simulation framework to the application layer. Any LP implements a *process-event* callback (to be invoked by the platform), which is in charge of updating the data structures representing the current state of the simulation object. Each event passed

[1] The source code of our implementation is available at
`http://www.dis.uniroma1.it/$\sim{}$hpdcs/ROOT-Sim/tcar.tbz.`

in input to the callback is associated with a Local Virtual Time (LVT), which describes the (simulated) time advancement of the currently scheduled LP.

Events can be scheduled across simulation objects via a *schedule-event* API supported by ROOT-Sim, which maps onto application transparent message-interactions within the parallel platform. Also, log/restore of the LP state for correctly recovering causality errors within the optimistic processing scheme (caused by out of timestamp-order speculation) is fully transparent to the application programmer and autonomically optimized (e.g in terms of the selection of the frequency of log operations as a function of the rollback probability of any individual LP) [20]. Hence, the programmer can use any kind of (dynamic) data structure to implement the simulation object within the application code (which allows the LP callback function to be implemented according to the ANSI-C standard), and is provided with the illusion of a sequential discrete-event run, while the LPs are actually executed in parallel across different processes.

ROOT-Sim also supports a very peculiar service that, once a new GVT value is available, transparently rebuilds a Committed and Consistent Global Snapshot (CCGS), formed by a collection of individual LPs' states [21]. This occurs via update operations applied to local committed checkpoints of individual LPs so to eliminate mutual dependencies among the final-achieved state values. Once the CCGS is built, each LP gains control via an additional callback within the API, referred to as *OnGVT*, by also having access to the copy of its state image belonging to the CCGS. Such a service can support, e.g., termination detection schemes based on global stable predicates evaluated on a committed and consistent global snapshot. This is a relevant alternative to typical optimistic PDES engines where the run is assumed to be completed only when overstepping a given GVT value. However, the evaluation of the global predicate on the CCGS has a frequency which is bounded by the frequency of GVT calculation, thus a temporal shift can occur before the simulation application layered on top of the ROOT-Sim platform can track the holding of a global predicate while simulation time advances. This is the core point we address in our study, which is targeted at evaluating the effects of variations of the frequency of GVT calculation (which may impact the speedup of the parallel run, given that it contributes to the overhead for distributed coordination) on the estimation of the final time for area-coverage within the TCAR model.

The TCAR model depicted in Section 3 has been implemented on top of ROOT-Sim by having each LP modeling an individual hexagonal cell within the target coverag area, while robots trajectories are simulated via proper mobility events across the LPs. As mentioned, the original TCAR model adopts a *pull* approach for gathering trail counters from adjacent cells. Considering our programming model, where LPs communicate by means of (transparently handled) message passing (i.e, LPs' simulation states are disjoint), a large number of events should be exchanged to proceed in the simulation, whenever an agent must change its position. Given that the optimistic synchronization protocol [22] shows higher efficiency when the number of exchanged messages is reduced, we have rather adopted a *push* approach, relying on a notification message which is used to inform all neighbors of the newly updated trail counter whenever an agent enters a cell. Then, each LP stores in its own simulation state the neighbors' trail-counters values. In this way, agents are able to make their decisions locally. The set of events which are generated/executed by the simulation model and handled by ROOT-Sim callback operations are the following:

- **REGION_IN**: an ant robot enters a given cell. When this event is executed, the trail counter is incremented. Then, an `UPDATE_NEIGHBORS` event is scheduled at all adjacent cells, with an associated timestamp which is equal to the `REGION_IN`'s one. This means that every neighbor is immediately notified of the presence of a new ant robot in this cell at a given simulation time.
- **UPDATE_NEIGHBORS**: upon receiving this event, the LP taking care of its execution finds in the local simulation state the entry describing the trail counter for the sender of this event. Its value is updated with the one piggybacked by this event. This allows any ant robot in the cell to have (locally) a global view of the state of the neighbors.
- **REGION_OUT**: this event is associated with an ant robot leaving a cell. The logic associated with this event entails finding which is the neighbor to be reached (by consulting the locally stored information on neighbors' trail counters) and therefore scheduling a `REGION_IN` event to the destination cell. We note that, since the time spent by an agent in the cell is modeled by the difference between the timestamps associated with a `REGION_IN` event and its subsequent `REGION_OUT` event, and given that a `REGION_IN` event in any neighbor cell entails the immediate (i.e., at the same timestamp) update of all trail counters in the neighbors, upon the execution of a `REGION_OUT` event the ant robot can safely consult the locally-stored neighbors' trail counters, being sure that they contain the most up-to-date information, obtained using the aforementioned *push* approach.

ROOT-Sim natively schedules an `INIT` event at the beginning of the simulation at every LP in the system, so to allow them to initialize their private simulation states. At simulation startup, every LP determines what is its position in the square region (in terms of hexagonal coordinates) and checks whether it is a boundary cell or not. In the positive case, the LP stores this information in order to prevent ant robots to leave the terrain. The cells which (at configuration time) are selected as sources for unleashing the ant robots (e.g., the cells associated with the position of rescue teams on the terrain) detect this, and schedule at themselves an initial `REGION_IN` event, at simulation time 0.

5 Experimental Results

We have run experiments on a 32-core HP ProLiant server equipped with 64GB of RAM and running Debian 6 on top of the 2.6.32-5-amd64 Linux kernel. We have used 32 instances of the ROOT-Sim kernel (i.e., every instance takes care of about 154 cells, namely LPs) giving each instance one available CPU-core. The simulation model has been run until reaching 100% coverage of the whole region,

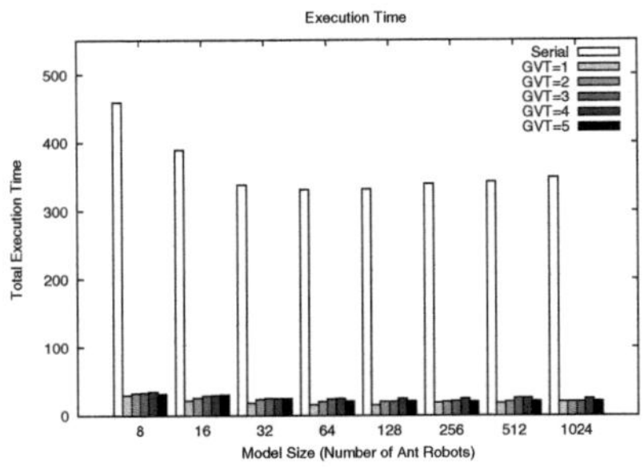

Fig. 1. Global Execution Times

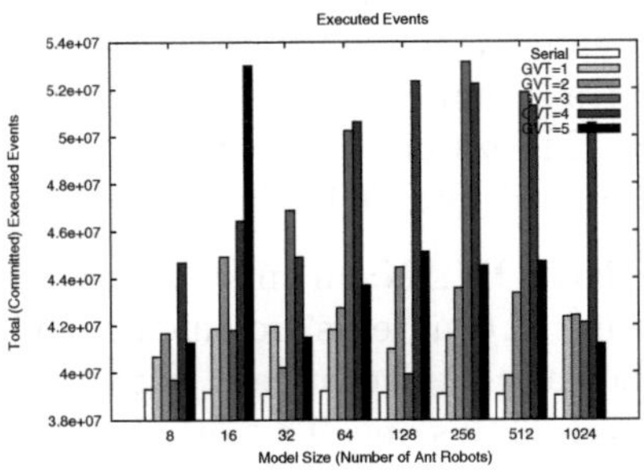

Fig. 2. Committed Events

with a visit factor of 20 (i.e., every cell must be visited at least 20 times before the simulation can complete). This has been done in order to avoid interference in the performance data due to the initial I/O (to access configuration files) and setup operations executed in the early phase of the simulation run. We have set ingress cells for robot unleash to 4, mimicking a situation where the rescue terrain is accessed by a limited number of rescue teams. Each rescue team is able to unleash a variable number of ant robots, in the range [4, 32], thus having a number of agents in the simulation in between 8 and 1024.

We have compared the optimistic parallel results with sequential ones, i.e. where events are executed sequentially relying on a competitive scheduler based on Calendar Queues [23]. The GVT computation period in ROOT-Sim has been varied in between 1 and 5 sec (in wall-clock-time) to check how the confidence interval in the simulation results changes. Each plot is averaged over 20 different runs, both in the parallel and in the sequential case. The initial random seed has been varied across the different runs, in order to account for variations in the execution dynamics, but the set of seeds in the sequential and parallel executions is the same, to really compare similar execution patterns.

In Figure 1 we present the global execution times for both the sequential and the parallel execution (on top of ROOT-Sim) of the TCAR simulation model. By the results, we see that the parallel execution provides a speedup in between 15 and 22. Different settings for the GVT computation interval provide a different completion time. In particular, the higher the GVT, the higher the simulation wall-clock-time. This is not related to a loss of precision in the simulation, it is rather due to the way the simulation termination condition is evaluated. As mentioned, the GVT reduction protocol is a periodic computation. If the termination condition is verified immediately after the GVT reduction, then a non-negligible amount of wall-clock time will pass before it will be checked again (leading simulation time to advance). On the other hand, for significantly increased values of the GVT period, the opposite behavior is noted, since the delayed GVT computation allows to catch the termination condition right after it holds. This situation can be seen as well in Figure 2, where the total number of (committed) events executed by the simulation are reported. As it can be clearly seen, the parallel runs commit a higher number of events than the sequential one. Also,

Table 1. Mean Completion Simulation Time (in Simulated Hours)

Configuration		Sequential	GVT=1	GVT=2	GVT=3	GVT=4	GVT=5
16 Robots	Mean	211.86	216.31	218.27	218.69	234.99	221.81
	Std. Dev.	1,56	15.11	13.28	11.07	12.46	15.64
128 Robots	Mean	26.56	27.37	28.41	28.29	32.61	29.24
	Std. Dev.	0.16	1,08	1,37	3,25	1.83	1.01

the peak values for the parallel runs are not alway noted for larger GVT period, just for the reasons explained above.

In order to assess the results' reliability, in Table 1 we present the LVT values at which two intermediate configurations of the simulation were stopped. These are the ones with 16 and 128 robots. The reported information is useful to model writers, as it is part of the outcome of the simulation itself. In particular, this tells how much time (in simulated hours) the ant robots would need to cover the entire region. From the data (presented in form of mean time and standard deviation), it can be clearly seen that the sequential simulations offer the most stable result. Interestingly, the parallel executions show a completion simulated time which is always higher than the sequential one. This is related, again, to the way the termination condition is checked upon GVT reduction. This aspect is very relevant, showing that the outcome of parallel (optimistic) simulation does not give the most precise result, rather it places a (correct) upper bound on it. Of course, it is up to the simulation model writer to decide how much this divergence from the precise simulation results can affect her simulation, and how much benefit she can gain from the increased performance.

References

1. Takahashi, T., Tadokoro, S., Ohta, M., Ito, N.: Agent based approach in disaster rescue simulation - from test-bed of multiagent system to practical application. In: Birk, A., Coradeschi, S., Tadokoro, S. (eds.) RoboCup 2001. LNCS (LNAI), vol. 2377, pp. 102–111. Springer, Heidelberg (2002)
2. Macy, M.W., Willer, R.: From factors to actors: Computational sociology and agent-based modeling. Annual Review of Sociology 28(1), 143–166 (2002)
3. Junli, L.: Agent-based logistics simulation system design and implementation. In: Proceedings of the 2nd IEEE International Conference on Computer Science and Information Technology, ICCSIT, pp. 602–606. IEEE Computer Society (2009)
4. Macal, C., North, M.: Tutorial on agent-based modeling and simulation part 2: How to model with agents. In: Proceedings of the 2006 Winter Simulation Conference, pp. 73–83. Society for Computer Simulation (2006)
5. Page, S.E.: Agent-based models. In: Durlauf, S.N., Blume, L.E. (eds.) The New Palgrave Dictionary of Economics. Palgrave Macmillan (2008)
6. Karmakharm, T., Richmond, P.: Large scale pedestrian multi-simulation for a decision support tool. In: TPCG, pp. 41–44 (2012)
7. Taufer, M., Padron, O., Saponaro, P., Patel, S.: Improving numerical reproducibility and stability in large-scale numerical simulations on GPUs. In: IPDPS, pp. 1–9 (2010)

8. The High Performance and Dependable Computing Systems Research Group (HPDCS), Sapienza, University of Rome: ROOT-Sim: The ROme OpTimistic Simulator - v 1.0 (October 2012), `http://www.dis.uniroma1.it/~hpdcs/ROOT-Sim/`
9. Pellegrini, A., Vitali, R., Quaglia, F.: An evolutionary algorithm to optimize log/restore operations within optimistic simulation platforms. In: Proceedings of the 4th International ICST Conference on Simulation Tools and Techniques, SIMUTools, SIGSIM (2011)
10. Luke, S., Cioffi-Revilla, C., Panait, L., Sullivan, K., Balan, G.: Mason: A multiagent simulation environment. Simulation 81(7), 517–527 (2005)
11. Cordasco, G., De Chiara, R., Mancuso, A., Mazzeo, D., Scarano, V., Spagnuolo, C.: A framework for distributing agent-based simulations. In: Alexander, M., et al. (eds.) Euro-Par 2011 Workshops , Part I. LNCS, vol. 7155, pp. 460–470. Springer, Heidelberg (2012)
12. Wittek, P., Rubio-Campillo, X.: Scalable agent-based modelling with cloud hpc resources for social simulations. In: Proceedings of the 4th International Conference on Cloud Computing Technology and Science, CloudCom, pp. 355–362. IEEE Computer Society (2012)
13. Hybinette, M., Kraemer, E., Xiong, Y., Matthews, G., Ahmed, J.: Sassy: A design for a scalable agent-based simulation system using a distributed discrete event infrastructure. In: Proceedings of the 2006 Winter Simulation Conference, WSC, pp. 926–933. Society for Computer Simulation (2006)
14. Richmond, P., Walker, D.C., Coakley, S., Romano, D.M.: High performance cellular level agent-based simulation with FLAME for the GPU. Briefings in Bioinformatics 11(3), 334–347 (2010)
15. Marurngsith, W., Mongkolsin, Y.: Creating GPU-enabled agent-based simulations using a PDES tool. In: Omatu, S., Neves, J., Rodriguez, J.M.C., Paz Santana, J.F., Gonzalez, S.R. (eds.) Distrib. Computing & Artificial Intelligence. AISC, vol. 217, pp. 227–234. Springer, Heidelberg (2013)
16. Caggianese, G., Erra, U.: Exploiting gpus for multi-agent path planning on grid maps. In: HPCS, pp. 482–488 (2012)
17. Koenig, S., Liu, Y.: Terrain coverage with ant robots: a simulation study. In: Proceedings of the Fifth International Conference on Autonomous Agents, AGENTS, pp. 600–607. ACM (2001)
18. Svennebring, J., Koenig, S.: Building terrain-covering ant robots: A feasibility study. Autonomous Robots 16(3), 313–332 (2004)
19. Pellegrini, A., Vitali, R., Quaglia, F.: The ROme OpTimistic Simulator: Core internals and programming model. In: Proceedings of the 4th International ICST Conference on Simulation Tools and Techniques, SIMUTools, ICST (2011)
20. Vitali, R., Pellegrini, A., Quaglia, F.: Autonomic log/restore for advanced optimistic simulation systems. In: Proceedings of the Symposium on Modeling, Analysis, and Simulation of Computer and Telecommunication Systems, MASCOTS, pp. 319–327. IEEE Computer Society (2010)
21. Cucuzzo, D., D'Alessio, S., Quaglia, F., Romano, P.: A lightweight heuristic-based mechanism for collecting committed consistent global states in optimistic simulation. In: DS-RT, pp. 227–234 (2007)
22. Jefferson, D.R.: Virtual Time. ACM Transactions on Programming Languages and System 7(3), 404–425 (1985)
23. Brown, R.: Calendar queues: a fast O(1) priority queue implementation for the simulation event set problem. Communications of the ACM 31, 1220–1227 (1988)

Sociality, Sanctions, Damaging Behaviors: A Distributed Implementation of an Agent-Based Social Simulation Model

Michele Carillo[1], Nicola Lettieri[2], Domenico Parisi[3], Francesco Raia[1], Flavio Serrapica[1], and Luca Vicidomini[1]

[1] Dipartimento di Informatica, Università degli Studi di Salerno
84084 Fisciano (SA), Italy
{michele.carillo,francesco.raia,flavio.serrapica}@gmail.com,
lvicidomini@unisa.it

[2] Dipartimento di Diritto, Economia Management e Metodi Quantitativi,
Università degli Studi del Sannio, 82100 Benevento (BN), Italy
nlettieri@unisannio.it

[3] Istituto di Scienze e Tecnologie della Cognizione - Consiglio Nazionale delle Ricerche
Roma (RM), Italy
domenico.parisi@istc.cnr.it

Abstract. The explanatory and predictive power of social simulations is more and more connected with the development of models accounting for the complexity of real (inter-individual and intra-individual) social dynamics. From this perspective, a promising research path is complementing very simple models, more suitable to illuminate core dynamics of social phenomena, with increasingly more complex and empirically grounded simulations (big data-driven models, higher number of agents, more detailed and realistic description of cognitive and communication mechanisms underlying individual and group behaviors). The choice has two strictly intertwined effects: not only a different modeling approach, but also the need for more powerful tools.

The paper presents a distributed implementation of an agent-based model exploring the interplay between damaging behaviors, sanctions and social mechanisms of learning and imitation, a topic investigated in many areas of social science from economics to legal science. Taking cue from a previous work based on a simple NetLogo simulation, the work shows how distributed solutions can help in developing more complex, wide and semantically rich models.

Keywords: Agent-based simulation models, Parallel Computing, Distributed Systems, High Performance Computing, Socially Behaviours.

1 Introduction

The explanatory and predictive power of social simulations is more and more connected with the development of models accounting for the complexity of real (inter-individual and intra-individual) social dynamics. From this perspective, a promising research path is complementing very simple models, particularly suitable to illuminate core dynamics of social phenomena with increasingly more complex and empirically grounded

D. an Mey et al. (Eds.): Euro-Par 2013 Workshops, LNCS 8374, pp. 595–604, 2014.

simulations (big data-driven models, higher number of agents, more detailed and realistic description of cognitive and communication mechanisms underlying individual and group behaviors).

The choice has two strictly intertwined effects: not only a different approach to modeling, but also the need for more powerful simulation tools. While particularly suitable for people without programming background, simulation environments commonly used by social scientist show limits in supporting the development and the execution of complex and massive models. Distributed computing solutions appear to be, in the light of this, an important and powerful ally.

The paper presents a distributed implementation of an agent-based model exploring the interplay between damaging behaviors, sanctions and social mechanisms of learning and imitation, a topic investigated in many areas of social science from economics to legal science. Taking cue from a NetLogo simulation we have modified adding new details and features, the paper shows how distributed solutions can help in developing more semantically rich models with a higher level of complexity and a higher number of agents.

The work is structured as follows: we first present the model on which this case study is based describing the set of changes in the model that pushed us to explore the use of D-MASON framework [8], a parallel version of MASON [12,13], a library for writing and running agent-based simulations developed by George Mason University's Evolutionary Computation Laboratory and the GMU Center for Social Complexity. We then discuss implementation issues.

2 Case Study

Our work takes the cue from a research [11] aiming at using social simulations to explore the dynamics involved in the containment of a wide class of human behaviors: damaging behaviors. For many different and complex reasons (from economic needs to culture etc), human beings often exhibit behaviors that damage others and societies try to find ways to contain them. If left unchecked, damaging behaviors can become so frequent and diffused that the advantages of living together may be exceeded by the disadvantages of being damaged by others, and this may put the very existence of the society into question. Therefore, for any minimally complex human society it is necessary to include mechanisms that induce its members to refrain from exhibiting behaviors that damage others. This set of mechanisms encompasses different phenomena spanning from social norms to reputational sanctions, from law enforcement to religion itself.

The research by which the case study here presented has been inspired tried to tackle the issue of damaging behaviors containment by developing a simple evolutionary agent-based model of the mechanism of sanction usually implemented by legal systems (for further details see [11]). More specifically, we have developed a model aiming to explore how the effect of punishment is affected by other factors like the opportunity to increase one's well-being without the risk of sanctions, by the mechanisms of imitation driven by social relations and, more in general, by the adaptive capabilities that push human beings to maximize their well-being.

The extreme abstraction of the simulations presented in our previous work with respect to the factors playing a role in the phenomenon under investigation, raised new research questions and a strong interest towards the opportunity to realize more realistic models.

A gradually more detailed description of cognitive dynamics involved by sanctions and damaging behaviors appears to be helpful in deepening our understanding. Memory, just to give an example, is an relevant factor in this vein. When acting, human beings are very often conditioned by previous experiences. Modeling agents that remember and consider what happened to them and around them when deciding how to behave is therefore an interesting step forward (see, for instance, the role assigned to memory in the study of the emergence of social norms by Andrighetto et al. [1], Conte et al. [6], Campennì et al.[3]).

A similar point can be made about other features of the model (number of the agents, communications, movement) that adding details to the description of the target phenomenon allows to make more meaningful analysis.

ABM environment like Netlogo have shown to suffer serious limitations in speed while simulating a high number of agents especially when agents are endowed with memory capabilities. Drawing inspiration from the consideration of these limits, before dealing with the development of a new version of the previous model we have decided to explore the use different tools to realize variants of the original model adding different features. Here below, in a nutshell, a schematic description of the realized using MASON/D-MASON.

(a) The model is a replica of the model presented in our previous work: the spread of behaviors (both damaging and honest) evolves according to a genetic algorithm that selects for reproduction agents with a high level of fitness simulating dynamics of cultural transmission. Agents do not move and choose randomly the agents to be damaged.
(b) The content of the model is the same of the previous experiment. The payoff of damaging actions is however proportional (10%) to the level of fitness of damaged agent. Agents to be damaged are chosen between the neighbors randomly.
(c) Agents move randomly and damage neighbors with a higher level of fitness.
(d) Agents move toward similar (characterized by a similar level of honesty/dishonesty) and tend to form clusters. Agents have an adaptive field of vision (an area of interest inspired by the model of thoughtless conformity to social norms proposed by Epstein [10]) which becomes larger when the behaviors exhibited by the neighbors are very homogeneous.
(e) Besides moving in order to get close to others and having an adaptive field of view, agents have a memory which allows them to keep track of the likelihood of the sanctions applied around them (ratio between the number of damaging actions done in their neighborhood and the number of sanctions applied in the last 10 steps of the simulation). The level of certainty of sanctions affects agents propensity to perform damaging (a high level of certainty of punishment reduces the chances in the agent to perform damaging actions).

3 MASON and D-MASON

In the following section, we describe the tools used during the design and development phases.

3.1 MASON

MASON toolkit is a discrete-event simulation core and visualization library written in Java, designed to be used for a wide range of ABMs. The toolkit is composed of two independent layers: the **simulation** layer and the **visualization** layer. The simulation layer is the core of MASON and is mainly represented by an event scheduler and a variety of fields which hold agents into a given simulation space. MASON is mainly based on step-able agent: a computational entity which may be scheduled to perform some action (step), and which can interact (communicate) with other agents. The visualization layer permits both visualization and manipulation of the model. The simulation layer is independent from the visualization layer, which allows us to treat the model as a self-contained entity. MASON was written with the aim of creating a flexible and efficient ABM which assures the complete reproducibility of results across different hardware. This reproducibility feature is considered as a priority for long simulations because it allows to stop a simulation and move it among computers. For more details see [13,12,2]. A development tutorial of MASON can be found at [14].

3.2 D-MASON

D-MASON adds a new layer named D-simulation which extends the MASON simulation layer. The new layer adds some features that allows the distribution of the simulation work on multiple, even heterogeneous, machines (workers). The new layer does not alter in any way the existing layers. Moreover, it has been designed so as to enable the porting of existing applications on distributed platforms in a transparent and easy way. From a functional point of view D-MASON architecture is divided into three functional blocks: **Management**, **Workers** and **Communication**. The Management layer provides a master application which will be used for coordinating the workers, handle the bootstrap and running the simulation. D-MASON is based on a master/workers paradigm which exploits a space partitioning approach: the master partitions the space to be simulated (the field) into regions. Each region, together with the agents contained in it, is assigned to a worker; then each worker is in charge of: simulating the agents that belong to the assigned region; handling the migration of agents; managing the synchronization between neighboring regions (this information exchange is required in order to let the simulation run consistently).

Workers communicate by using a publish-subscribe mechanism. D-MASON uses a standard approach to achieve a consistent local synchronization of the distributed simulations: each step is associated with a fixed state of the simulation. Regions are simulated step by step. Since the step i of region r is computed by using the states i-1 of r's neighborhood, the step i of a region cannot be executed until the states i-1 of its neighborhood have been computed and delivered. In other words, each region is synchronized with its neighborhood before each simulation step.

This mechanism has been strengthened in [9]. In order to use global parameters we need data to be gathered, reduced and scattered to each region before each simulation step. The reduction task comprises two phases. First each worker sends its data to a GLOBAL_DATA topic, whose only subscriber is a specific machine named *Collector*. Once all data for a given step is received, the Collector calculates the aggregated data and publishes it to a GLOBAL_REDUCED topic, whose subscribers are all the workers. Using this two phase approach the number of messages needed for the synchronization grows linearly in the number of workers.

4 Model Implementation

We present two versions of the Sociality, Sanctions, Damaging Behaviors (SDB) model implemented respectively in MASON and D-MASON.

4.1 MASON

We implemented the SDB model into MASON by creating the following classes:

- **Human**, implements *Steppable*. This class defines the Artificial Intelligence (AI) of the simulation.
- **Behaviour**, abstract class. This class exposes the actions that the AI can do.
- **(Dis)honest**, extends *Behaviour*. These classes define the type of action that the agent does (honest or dishonest).
- **NewGenAgent**, implements *Steppable*. This class handles the genetic algorithm.
- **SociallyDamagingBehavior**, extends *SimState*. This class initializes the simulation.

An interesting aspect of the SDB model is the **genetic algorithm**, described in [11]. This algorithm requires global variables [9]. The class *NewGenAgent* is an AI that at each **epoch** executes the genetic algorithm. At the end of each epoch (e.i. after a predefined number of simulation steps), all agents are sorted according to the fitness value and only the best 50% of these one will evolve (evolving agents). During the evolution each evolving agent generates two new agents that inherit its DNA, perturbed with a value in a range from -0.05 to 0.05. Then all the old agents will die, so at every new epoch the number of agents remains unchanged. If the number of agents is odd, a single evolving agent will transmit its DNA at three new agents.

4.2 D-MASON

The porting of a simulation from MASON to D-MASON is extremely easy [4,8]. It involves only some methods (of MASON implementation) that cannot be invoked in the distributed environment, so they will be replaced with those one provided by D-MASON. A version of the SDB model into D-MASON has been developed by creating the following classes that represents the distributed version of the classes defined above:

- **RemoteHuman⟨E⟩**, extends ***OvalPortrayal2D*** and implements *Serializable, RemoteAgent⟨E⟩*. This class describes the agent subject to migration
- **DHuman**, extends *RemoteHuman⟨**Double2D**⟩* and implements *Steppable*, ***Orientable2D***.
- **DBehaviour**, abstract class that implements *Serializable*.
- **DSociallyDamagingBehavior**, extends *DistributedState⟨**Double2D**⟩*.

5 Enhancement in D-Mason

In this section, we will describe some new features introduced in D-MASON in order to deal with the new requirements provided by the SDB.

5.1 Global Parameters in the Distributed SDB Model

An implementation of the detailed mechanism for the use of global parameters in D-MASON is described in [9]. Once identified the parameters that must be global, the simulation must expose the follow methods for any global parameter:

- getGlobalVarname
- setGlobalVarname
- globalVarname(){return true;}
- reducerGlobalVarname(Object[] params)

where *Varname* is the name of the global parameter. In addition to this, there is a thread called **Reducer**, which runs only when there are global parameters. Its purpose is to invoke the *reducer* method present in the class DSociallyDamagingBehavior. The *reducer* method must contain all the necessary information for the calculation of the global parameter. After invoking the *reducer* method, the **Reducer** takes the result and updates the specific parameter with *setGlobalVarname* method. The **Reducer** was developed in such a way to be executed at any simulation step. Unfortunately, the SDB model requires this functionality only once per epoch so a mechanism that allows to invoke the **Reducer** in a specific simulation step is required.

5.2 Global Parameters: *A New Implementation*

We implemented a support class for counting the global parameters at a determinate step of the simulation, named *UpdateGlobalVarAtStep*. For conformity, we use the same notation of methods regarding the global parameters, but to distinguish a global parameter that must be refreshed at any step, from another one that must be refreshed in a specific step, we define three kinds of parameters:

1. **global**: it is updated at any steps
2. **globalEvery**: it is updated in a specific step
3. **globalReinitialize**: it is updated in a specific step and reset some specific parameters of the simulation

As specified, a parameter **globalEvery** is a type of parameter that must be update after a certain number of steps, (for instance when we want know how many honest actions in average, have been performed during the last 50 steps). The third, is a kind of parameter more sensible, because has the same properties of **globalEvery** parameter, but is used to execute more complex operations, like the genetic algorithm of the SDB model.

In the following we present an example that allows the management of global parameters: we want to track the number of honest actions in the simulation every 10 steps. Like in the case of global parameters , first we enable the **globalEvery** parameter:

```
public boolean globalEveryHonestActions(){ return true; }
```

In order to avoid ambiguity, the simulation has to track two values for each global parameter: a global (simulationwide) value obtained before each simulation step and a local (regionwide) value updated during a simulation step and sent at the end of each step. So we need to add getter and setter methods for these values:

```
public int getLocalHonestActions(){
    return localHonestActions;
}
public void setLocalHonestActions(int count){
    localHonestActions = count;
}
public int getGlobalEveryHonestActions(){
    return globalEveryHonestActions;
}
public void setGlobalEveryHonestActions(int count){
    globalEveryHonestActions = count;
}
```

To know the interval between two calls of the reducer method, we declare the following method:

```
public long getEveryHonestActionValueOf(){ return 10; }
```

As above mentioned, the **Reducer** will call the method reduceEveryHonestActions to obtain the global value, this value will be scattered to each workers.

```
public int reduceEveryHonestAction(Object[] data){
    int sum = 0;
    for (int i = 0; i < data.length; i++)
        sum += ((Integer)d).intValue();
    return sum;
}
```

To use the **globalReinitialize** parameter we perform the same declaration of the globalEvery parameters, but the *reducer* method will contain code that will reset some specific parameters of the simulation. To guarantee the effectiveness of the update of **globalReinitialize** parameters, we changed the class **GlobalParametersHelper**, which is a class that manage all global parameters, in particular we changed the method **receiveAndUpdate**. This method should be called by a field after the call of the *sendGlobalParameters* (method of the same class) and before the simulation phase of the current step begins. By invoking the method *receiveAndUpdate*, first the global and globalEvery (if available) parameters will be updated, subsequently the globalReinitialize parameters (if avaiable) will be updated, because the simulation will be reinitialized with the correct parameters. In fact, a globalReinitialize reducer method performs operations that may include other global parameters, which has to be already updated.

We describe now the class *UpdateGlobalVarAtStep* situated in the **dmason.sim.globals.util** package. With the addition of these new global parameters, we want to get at any step of the simulation the global parameters updated. For this purpose, the class UpdateGlobalVarAtStep contains a method named *getAllGlobalVarForStep* that get all global parameters to be updated at a specific step. This method takes in input a *long* which specify a step and returns a list of all global parameters that need to be updated at that specific step. This class maintains separated data structures to store global parameters and globalEvery parameters (or globalReinitialize). Using this class, in particular the method *getAllGlobalVarForStep*, it is possible to avoid the transfer of empty messages by fields and by the **Reducer**. In fact, it checks the number of global parameters existing in the simulation, and only where this number is greater than zero, the update messages are exchanged.

5.3 Other Changes in D-Mason

In this subsection, we describe a new panel of the *Master* application, developed to set the simulation parameters, and the addition of a new method in the field, useful for the *genetic algorithm*.

Parameters setting. In D-Mason, the Master application allows the setting of the parameters relative to the environment of the simulation (width and height of the fields, number of agents, . . .), but it doesn't allows the setting of the model parameters (AOI of an agent, probability values, . . .). We then added a new panel to the Master, that allows the setting of these parameters. This panel is called **ModelPanel** and is situated in the package **dmason.util.SystemManagement**. To see the simulation parameters, the simulation class must expose the getter and setter methods for the parameters to show in the panel. Since the textfield used for editing the parameters returns a string and has not knowledge of the type of the parameters, the class exposes a method for the type checking of the parameters: e.g. if we have an integer parameter named numAgent and we set it as a string type from the panel, the **checkParameters** method will notify with an error the wrong setting. Figure 1 depicts the new panel.

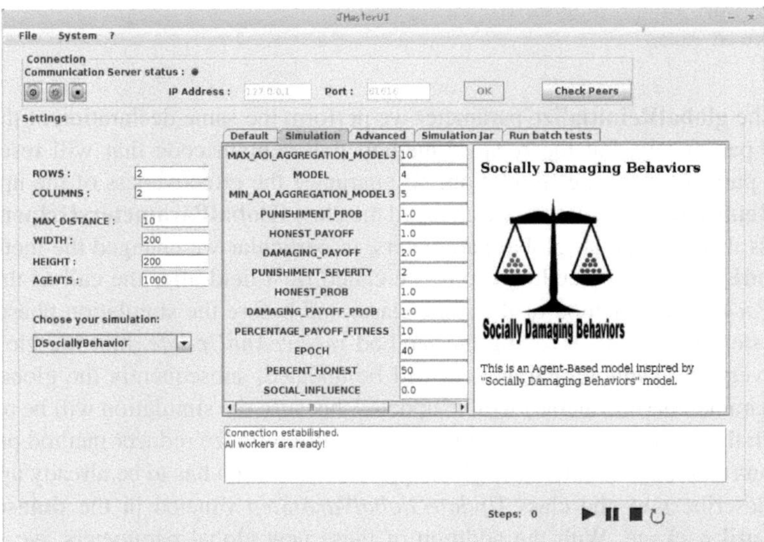

Fig. 1. The setting parameters panel

Fields: new methods. The genetic algorithm is applied to all the agents of the simulation. Each Region in order to apply the genetic algorithm, needs to know the set of agents that belongs to the region. On the other hand, in order to manage the migration of agents, the data structure, available on each region, might contain also agents that do not belongs to the region (because they migrated or they are needed during the simulation step), so the data structure available is not suitable and we decided to add the following methods:

- *getAllVisibleAgent*
- *resetAddAll*

The first method skims from the data structure the agents outside the region. The second method, instead, is used for adding agents generated by the genetic algorithm in the correct position of the region data structure.

Genetic algorithm. The development of the genetic algorithm in MASON is straightforward. On the other hand in D-MASON, the management of global parameters implies more attentions by the developer. First, a local variable, which is a list of all agents of the field, has to be declared and initialized invoking the method *getAllVisibleAgent*, previously mentioned. Subsequently, a global variable relative to the local variable, previously mentioned, has to be introduced. Then the setter method and the respective method *reducerReinitialize* must be exposed for both variables. The reducer method sorts the list of all agents in descending fitness value (ties are broken using agent identifiers). Once the list is sorted, only the 50% of the agents survives, and the element at the end of this new list is returned. When this median element is received, the method *setGlobalReinitialize* is invoked, which inspects all its agents and compare them with the median agent received. This method performs the genetic algorithm: if an agent has a fitness value less than that of the median agent, it dies; instead if it has a fitness value greater than the median agent value, it reproduces.

6 Efficiency of Distributed Model

We tested the difference of performance between the model on MASON and the one on D-MASON. Specifically we evaluate the performances of the model with the highest computational load (point (e) of Section 2). The simulation comprises 200, 000 agents. We selected the parameters of the simulation in such a way the simulation converges after 12 epochs, each one of 100 simulation steps. The test was performed on a cluster of workstation with 14 CPU Intel (R) Xeon (TM) 2.80GHz, 3GB RAM, Gigabit Ethernet and Debian 6 as the operating system. We performed the first test on MASONexploiting a single machine on the cluster, and we repeated the same test in D-MASON distributing the simulation on 9 machines on the cluster. The execution of the model on MASON took about 46 minutes to reach the 1, 200 simulation steps due to the high computational load concentrated on a single machine. Using D-MASON the same result takes about 10 minutes, getting a speedup of 4.6.

7 Conclusions

Even if still in progress, the experience gained during the case study/experiment has hinted the role that more powerful Agent based model environments could play in deepening the understanding of social dynamics. The possibility of designing more complex and gradually more realistic models will probably affect in the next future (together with big data [7]) the way social phenomena are studied. The computational power of tools, clearly, is not sufficient by itself. The availability of new and more powerful research tool calls also for a change in social sciences.

References

1. Andrighetto, G., Campenni, M., Conte, R., Paolucci, M.: On the immergence of norms: a normative agent architecture. In: Proceedings of AAAI Symposium, Social and Organizational Aspects of Intelligence (2007)
2. Balan, G.C., Cioffi-Revilla, C., Luke, S., Panait, L., Paus, S.: MASON: A Java Multi-Agent Simulation Library. In: Proceedings of the Agent 2003 Conference (2003)
3. Campenni, M., Andrighetto, G., Cecconi, F., Conte, R.: Normal= normative? The role of intelligent agents in norm innovation. Mind & Society 8, 153 (2009)
4. Carillo, M., Cordasco, G., De Chiara, R., Raia, F., Scarano, V., Serrapica, F.: Enhancing the performances of d-mason - a motivating example. In: Pina, N., Kacprzyk, J., Obaidat, M.S. (eds.) SIMULTECH, pp. 137–143. SciTePress (2012)
5. Cioffi-Revilla, C.: Simplicity and reality in computational modeling of politics. Computational and Mathematical Organization Theory 15, 26 (2009)
6. Conte, R., Andrighetto, G., Campenni, M., Paolucci, M.: Emergent and immergent effects in complex social systems. In: Proceedings of AAAI Symposium, Social and Organizational Aspects of Intelligence (2007)
7. Conte, R., Gilbert, N., Bonelli, G., Cioffi-Revilla, C., Deffuant, G., Kertesz, J., Loreto, V., Moat, S., Nadal, J.-P., Sanchez, A., et al.: Manifesto of computational social science. The European Physical Journal Special Topics 214(1), 325–346 (2012)
8. Cordasco, G., De Chiara, R., Mancuso, A., Mazzeo, D., Scarano, V., Spagnuolo, C.: Bringing together efficiency and effectiveness in distributed simulations: the experience with d-mason. In: SIMULATION: Transactions of The Society for Modeling and Simulation International (2013)
9. Cordasco, G., De Chiara, R., Raia, F., Scarano, V., Spagnuolo, C., Vicidomini, L.: Designing computational steering facilities for distributed agent based simulations. In: Proceedings of the 2013 ACM SIGSIM Conference on Principles of Advanced Discrete Simulation, SIGSIM-PADS 2013, pp. 385–390. ACM, New York (2013)
10. Epstein, J.M.: Learning to be thoughtless: Social norms and individual computation. Comput. Econ. 18(1), 9–24 (2001)
11. Lettieri, N., Parisi, D.: An evolutionary agent-based model of the interplay between punishment and damaging behaviors. Artificial Intelligence and Law (June 2013)
12. Luke, S., Cioffi-revilla, C., Panait, L., Sullivan, K.: Mason: A new multi-agent simulation toolkit. University of Michigan (2004)
13. Luke, S., Cioffi-Revilla, C., Panait, L., Sullivan, K., Mason, G.B.: Mason: A multiagent simulation environment. Simulation 81(7), 517–527 (2005)
14. Mason Tutorial (2013), `http://cs.gmu.edu/ eclab/projects/mason/docs/tutorial0/`
15. Neumann, M.: A classification of normative architectures. In: Simulating Interacting Agents and Social Phenomena: The Second World Congress (2010)

Sixth Workshop on Productivity and Performance (PROPER 2013)*

Martin Schulz

Program Chair

Driven by current trends in microprocessor design, the number of processor cores and hardware threads available on modern supercomputers grows rapidly from generation to generation while the amount of memory per core will be decreasing. To keep pace, applications need to harness much higher degrees of parallelism while ensuring efficient use of the underlying computing resources, which can be highly concurrent many core systems or heterogeneous accelerator architectures (or a combination of both). Additionally, applications must adhere to additional constraints, in particular with respect to power consumption (both peak and average power) and resilience.

Writing codes that run correctly and efficiently on such complex systems is extraordinarily challenging. At the same time, applications themselves are becoming more complex as well, which can be seen in emerging scale-bridging applications, the integration of Uncertainty Quantification (UQ), or advances in algorithms. Combined, these trends place higher and higher demands on the application development process and thus require adequate tool support for debugging and performance analysis. The PROPER workshop series serves as a forum to present novel work on scalable methods and tools for high-performance computing. The workshop covers parallel program development and analysis, debugging, correctness checking, and performance measurement and evaluation. Further topics include the integration of tools with compilers and the overall development environment, as well as success stories reporting application performance, scalability, reliability, power and energy optimization, or productivity improvements that have been achieved using tools. The workshop is supported by the Virtual Institute - High Productivity Supercomputing (VI-HPS), an initiative to promote the development and integration of HPC programming tools. Workshop topics include:

- Tools and tool approaches for parallel program development and analysis
- Infrastructure for building parallel program development and analysis tools
- Correctness checking and program verification
- Performance measurement and evaluation
- Success stories about optimization or parallel scalability achieved using tools

* This work was in part performed under the auspices of the U.S. Department of Energy by Lawrence Livermore National Laboratory under Contract DE-AC52-07NA27344. (LLNL-CONF-644154)

D. an Mey et al. (Eds.): Euro-Par 2013 Workshops, LNCS 8374, pp. 605–606, 2014.

This year's instance of the PROPER workshop started with a keynote by Victor Lee from Intel on "Performance productivity challenges and researches for the future of computing" providing a comprehensive overview covering the core topics of this workshop. The keynote was followed by two sessions with a total of six presentations of contributed papers. These papers were selected from 16 submissions after a comprehensive and rigorous review process. Each paper received three written reviews by a diverse program committee, which was then followed by an online discussion to determine the accepted papers.

The first session focused on runtime measurements and analysis and contained papers by Josef Weidendorfer on a tool set to determine data transfer requirements of applications ("Data Transfer Requirement Analysis with Bandwidth Curves"), by Philip Roth on an approach to track the impact of individual values in computations ("Tracking a Value's Influence on Later Computation"), and by Ilya Zhukov et al. covering the new measurement system for the Scalasca tool set ("Assessing measurement and analysis performance and scalability of Scalasca").

The second session focused on program analysis as well as algorithms and contained papers by Olivier Aumage et al. focusing on static analysis for SIMD optimizations ("Detecting SIMDization Opportunities through Static/Dynamic Dependence Analysis"), by Herbert Jordan et al. on a framework for the implementation of compiler transformations ("A High-Level IR Transformation System"), and by Guillaume Aupy et al. on a highly parallel algorithm for QR factorization ("Implementing a systolic algorithm for QR factorization on multicore clusters with PaRSEC").

Overall, PROPER 2013 was very successful. This would not have been possible without the help from a large group of people: I would like to thank the EuroPar team, in particular Felix Wolf the general chair, Dieter an Mey, the workshop chair, and Bernd Mohr the proceedings chair. Further, I would like to thank the program committee for their comprehensive and timely reviews, as well the presenters of the six papers. Last, but certainly not least, I would like thank the authors of all submitted papers for considering PROPER 2013, as well as the audience for their stimulating discussions in the Q&A sessions. I hope this workshop can be repeated next year and I am looking forward to PROPER 2014 in Porto.

Data Transfer Requirement Analysis with Bandwidth Curves

Josef Weidendorfer

Technische Universität München
Munich, Germany
weidendo@in.tum.de

Abstract. The amount of data transfer required by (parallel) applications can be of significant importance for performance due to bandwidth limitations in real systems. For intra-node, data transfer refers to memory accesses, and usually, cache miss counts are used for performance analysis. However, they cannot explicitly show utilization of links and buses in the memory hierarchy. In this paper, we propose an explicit visualization of the bandwidth requirements of applications within memory hierarchies. This is based on a machine model without bandwidth limits. We show its usefulness within the context of a simple 2D stencil iterative solver, with and without cache optimization applied.

1 Introduction

A lot of applications are bound not by compute capability, but by limited bandwidth available in a system. It is predicted that for future architectures, the energy required to transfer a byte will go down much slower due to technology advances than the energy required for a calculation [2]. Thus, bandwidth requirements will play an even more important role for the performance achievable by an application. As the distance of a data transfer is significant for cost regarding both energy and time, the exploitation of a memory hierarchy using caches is essential for good performance. Further, with multi-core architectures, contention on shared links can be a major obstacle for performance. For applications with low computational intensity, cache optimization may not be important because it makes the sequential code run faster, but much more so because it reduces contention and allows scaling with the number of used cores.

Detection of whether a given bandwidth restriction is actually the bottleneck is astonishingly tricky. The reason is that achievable bandwidth depends on whether prefetchers are active, whether the accesses are sequential, strided or random. Slowdown due to memory accesses may appear on the connection to the memory module, between chips, or within the cache hierarchy on-chip. Using hardware performance counters to understand these issues is difficult. Miss counts often are almost useless, and prefetcher behavior and bus utilization can not easily be attributed to source.

In this paper, we propose an analysis method for the bandwidth requirements of applications which decouples bandwidth analysis from other effects.

D. an Mey et al. (Eds.): Euro-Par 2013 Workshops, LNCS 8374, pp. 607–616, 2014.

This is done using a machine model whose performance is purely bound by only one resource limit, such as peak instruction throughput or peak computational performance. The model assumes that there are no stall cycles due to data dependencies or other latency, and that any peaks in bandwidth requirements are smoothed out by corresponding hardware or compiler techniques such as instruction reordering or prefetching for best utilization. This way, the analysis is able to show steady bandwidth requirements of hot code paths. As visualization, we propose *bandwidth curves*, which show how much of the runtime a given bandwidth is exceeded by application demands. They make it is easy to see the slowdown induced by a bandwidth limitation, and provide an upper bound for the performance achievable. For our proposed analysis method, we developed a corresponding tool. It uses runtime instrumentation (via Intel's Pin tool [7]) to work with compiled binaries. Execution is simulated within the assumed model, and bandwidth curves are generated. To show the usefulness of our approach, we present a case study in which cache optimization is applied to a memory bound iterative solver. The positive effect of the optimization is easily visible in the curves.

2 Related Work

Most performance analysis tools today use hardware performance counters to show behavior regarding the memory system [1,6]. Typically, hit and miss counts are provided, as well as utilization of the memory bus (percentage of cycles the bus is busy). On newer processors, it is possible to get a statistical distribution of memory access latency (e.g. the data load latency analysis on Intel processors). However, contention detection can be difficult by using such measurements.

Cache optimization tries to increase the locality of memory accesses, as caches help most if memory accesses are "local", either in a spatial or temporal way. Spatial locality can be interpreted as how many bytes of a cache line are used before being evicted [10]. For temporal locality, the stack reuse distance metric is valuable [4]. It shows how large a fully associative cache needs to be to cover a given percentage of memory accesses. A lot of research exists to calculate this metric in a reasonable fast way [3,5,8], and extend it to multi-core [9]. However, stack reuse does not provide any information about bandwidth requirements. The roof-line model [11] is a 2D visualization showing the inherent performance limits of a machine for single kernels, taking the computational intensity into account. While this is very intuitive, it cannot provide contention analysis at various points of the memory hierarchy, and does not apply to complex applications. To the best of the author's knowledge, there are no tools concentrating on bandwidth requirement visualizations similar to the one proposed in this paper.

3 Performance and Machine Model

A real machine has a lot of different resources, such as core pipeline with computational units, the memory system with cache hierarchies, buses, and I/O.

Each of them has its own capacity limits, and for different phases of an application, different resource limitations may be relevant for the observed performance. However, it is often difficult to understand whether a given resource really is the dominant bottleneck, as the difference between theoretical peak performance and real exploitable performance is often influenced by micro-architectural effects.

To overcome these obstacles for performance analysis, we propose an abstract machine model which allows us to focus on application requirements regarding bandwidth demands. We assume that the performance of the application is fully determined just by the restrictions of one resource. For numerical applications, a good choice for the latter is the achievable computational capacity of a machine in GFlops per second. This way, the bandwidth requirements of the application can be expressed in the amount of bytes moved per floating point operation executed, which is known in literature as *computational intensity* of a given program phase. Another choice to determine the base performance of the application may be the assumption that the machine can execute a given number of instructions per clock cycle, and is therefore restricted by the throughput of the instruction decoder. Thus, we assume that the application always runs at some constant peak performance, and we observe the resulting bandwidth requirements. A comparison with real bandwidth limitations allows us to check whether this limitation is a real bottleneck.

Our tool simulates the execution of a binary on a machine model. It observes how much data is moved over specific connections in the system (e.g. from core to L1) in a given time unit, which is determined by the execution of one instruction or one floating point operation. Thus, if T is the number of time units for the complete program, for $t \in \{1, \ldots, T\}$, r_t may be the number of bytes read at time t by a core from its L1 cache. Then $R = \sum_{t=1}^{T} r_t$ is the total amount of bytes read at this point in the system. If we strictly use this model, we will observe a number of bytes moved in some cycles, and nothing in others. However, real systems will smooth out such peak requirements by starting transfers early, or reordering instructions while waiting for data to arrive. Thus, a real system will exploit the available bandwidth capacities, and not stop using the bandwidth only because the application does not execute a move instruction in a given clock cycle. It is important to model this behavior. To this end, we average the bandwidth requirement using a sliding window of a given time length W. The average number of bytes moved at time t is

$$\bar{r}_t = \frac{1}{W} \sum_{w=0}^{W-1} r_{t-w}$$

(with $r_t = 0$ for $t < 0$). A good value for W may be in the order of the latency of a memory access (a few hundred cycles), as such latency is covered by hardware prefetchers. Also with average bandwidths, we easily can calculate the total amount of data transferred at a given point (with $r_t = 0$ for $t > T$):

$$R = \sum_{t=1}^{T+W} \bar{r}_t = \sum_{t=1}^{T} r_t \, .$$

Thus, if we draw $\bar{r}_t$, the area under the curve is the amount of data transferred.

To understand bandwidth requirements of multi-threaded code, it is useful to assume that every thread is bound to run on a dedicated core, and there is no over-subscription. This will show a worst-case scenario regarding contention, which should help the analysis to find bottlenecks. In addition, it makes our model independent from scheduling and migration decisions in the operating system, and thus makes the analysis more general. The model should approximate multi-core systems. Here, we assume a single memory module shared by all cores. For the shared connection to the memory, we just sum up the bandwidth requirements of all cores, within each time unit of our simulation. This strategy may not match reality, as code executed on different cores on real hardware may be slowed down by various effects which depend on the actually executed code. However, for HPC code, it is quite likely that code with similar behavior is executed (e.g. the same loop body when using OpenMP parallel for).

The model works fine with simulating arbitrary caches in the data paths. Caches exploit locality properties of memory access patterns, and thus work as a kind of filter for bandwidth requirement analysis. They potentially reduce the requirements. But caches also play another role in multi-core chips: they allow for fast communication among cores by keeping the data to be communicated on-chip. By simulating a cache coherence protocol (MSI), we capture bandwidth requirements between cores. Fig. 1 shows the configuration of a typical multi-core chip with a separate cache for each core, and a shared cache for all cores. Bandwidth figures are useful for each of the data paths denoted by arrows, as each of them could become a bottleneck. The arrows between the private caches denote communication among cores where the data needs to be fetched from the other core. For this, available bandwidth typically is lower than coming from the shared cache, as coherence actions are involved. Our model captures bandwidth requirements of data paths in one multi-core chip. However, it easily can be extended to match multi-socket systems with a single memory module. Extending the model further for systems with multiple memory modules is straight-forward, but needs the simulation of allocation strategies for memory pages. This is future work. Similarly, extending the analysis to systems with different memory name spaces (such as clusters) is possible.

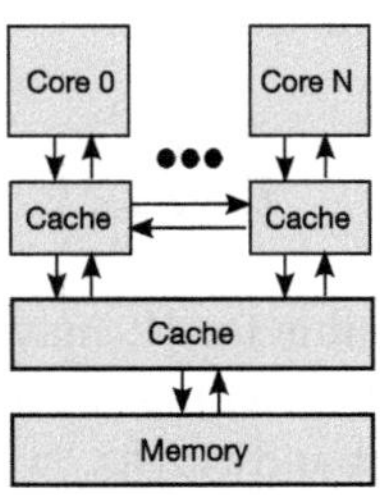

Fig. 1. A multi-core system with connections interesting for bandwidth analysis

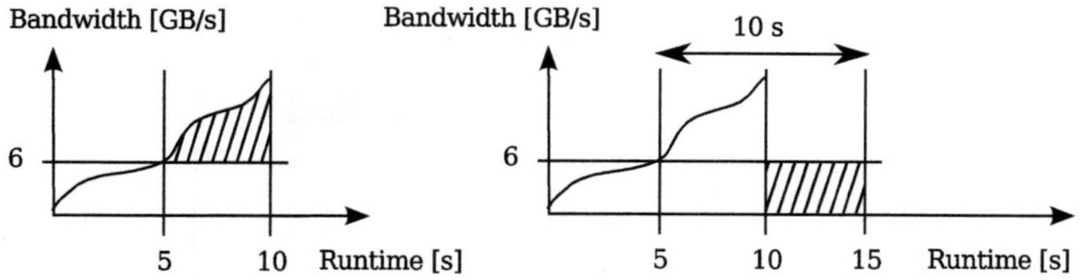

Fig. 2. Slowdown effect of limited bandwidth shown by a Bandwidth Curve

4 Bandwidth Curves

To understand whether a given bandwidth requirement actually constitutes a bottleneck on an approximated real system, a comparison with bandwidth restrictions of the system must be done. Up to now, we assume the bandwidth requirement analysis to be a trace over the program run for every interesting point in some data path, showing the (smoothed) bandwidth requirement for each point in time of the program execution. As the collected amount of data easily gets prohibitive, we need to aggregate data online. Thus, instead of drawing a figure for $\bar{r}_t$ for $t \in \{1, \ldots, T\}$, we reorder the time steps by permutation $o : \{1, \ldots, T\} \to \{1, \ldots, T\}$ such that $\bar{r}_{o(t)} \leq \bar{r}_{o(t+1)}$. The resulting monotonic increasing curve will show how long/often the bandwidth requirement (in bytes per time unit) exceeds at a given limitation.

In the example of Fig. 2 (left), the curve exceeds 6 GB/s during half the runtime of the program corresponding to our machine model. On a real system, the connection cannot transfer at higher bandwidth. The hatched area will result in an observed slowdown. As shown on the right, by filling a rectangle of the same area, we can calculate the slowdown exactly in absolute time. Even more, as half the runtime within our machine model is also limited by the bandwidth, these 5 seconds add up to the absolute time estimation due to the limitation (this is in contrast to the first part, which is only limited by the single resource restriction in the machine model). Thus, in the example, at least 10 seconds are definitely needed due to the bandwidth limitation of 6 GB/s on the real system.

5 Prototype Implementation

Our prototype tool uses Pin [7] on Linux. In contrast to Valgrind (an open-source framework very similar to Pin), it can run multiple guest threads (the program to be observed) in parallel on a multi-core host system[1]. We model a 2-level inclusive cache hierarchy as shown in Fig. 1. Replacement policy is LRU with write-back for L1 and L2. A MSI cache coherence protocol between private L1 caches is implemented, with invalidations done implicitly by incrementing an epoch counter on write for each line in L2. Gnuplot-compatible files for the bandwidth

[1] There is work going on to allow for this feature in future Valgrind versions.

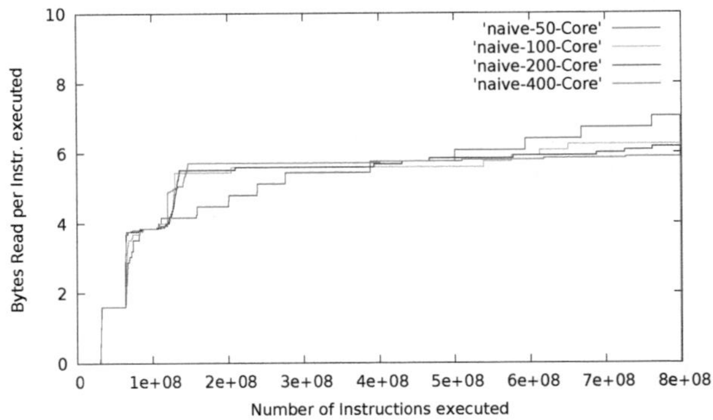

Fig. 3. Influence of smoothing parameter W (50, 100, 200, 400), naive version

curves of each interesting data path are generated at program termination. The current version is not optimized and has a slowdown factor of around 100. We expect that we can improve on that significantly by doing the sliding window smoothing in batches. We will make the tool publicly available as open source.

6 Case Study

For the following examples of the bandwidth curves, we analyzed an iterative Jacobi solver over a quadratic domain $N \times N$ with fixed boundary condition, using the following update rule:

$$v_{x,y}^{t+1} := \frac{1}{4}(v_{x-1,y}^{t} + v_{x,y-1}^{t} + v_{x+1,y}^{t} + v_{x,y+1}^{t})$$

With $N = 2500$, the alternately used two matrices need 100 MB of memory with every value stored in double precision. The naive version, which sweeps over the matrices for one domain update, needs to load 16 bytes and write 8 bytes per update from memory (2 rows fit into on-chip cache, half of read bytes due to read-for-ownership before write). After some initialization, we run 24 iterations. Intel compiler 13.0 is used with OpenMP enabled.

6.1 Influence of Smoothing Window Length

Fig. 3 shows the effects of changing the parameter W for smoothing the bandwidth requirements. The 24 iterations need around 800 million instructions, and the average number of bytes read is around 6 bytes per instruction (the actual number depends on the code produced by the compiler) most of the time. The lower numbers (around 150 million instr.) come from start-up and initialization. As the solver code in the naive versions consists of a tight inner loop with equal memory access requirements, we would expect just a simple line over the program run. However, for $W = 50$, this is not true. Checking the assembler code,

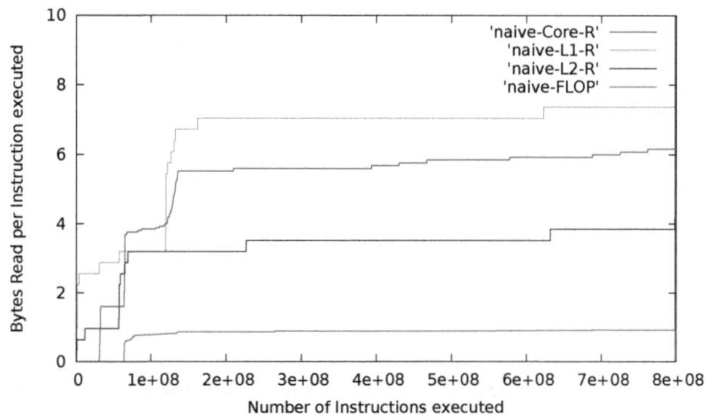

Fig. 4. Bytes read into Core, L1, shared L2, and FLOPs, naive version

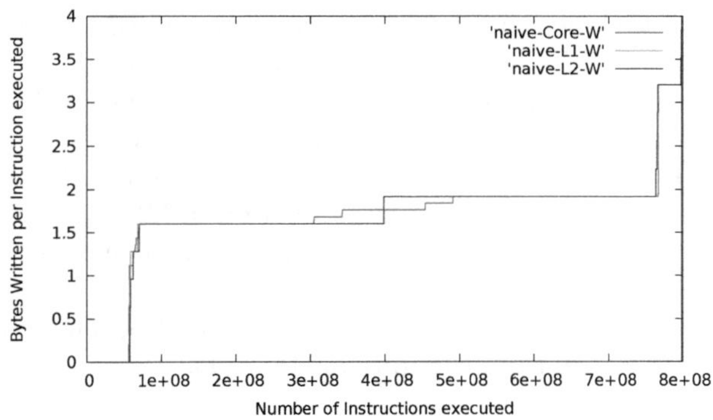

Fig. 5. Bytes written from Core, L1, shared L2, naive version

the compiler did some unrolling, and 50 instructions are not enough to get the steady behavior for the inner loop. However, the curves for $W = 100$, 200 and 400 are almost the same.

6.2 Effects of Caches

In the following, we use $W = 200$ as smoothing window, and the cache hierarchy of Fig. 1. Each core has a private 32 kB L1 data cache, and there is a shared 3 MB L2 cache. As most HPC codes do fit into L1 instruction cache, we ignore loads into the memory hierarchy due to code fetched by the cores.

As in the previous figure, for Fig. 4 we use the number of instructions executed as time unit. For bytes read, the curves show different data paths: bytes read by Core (as in Fig. 3), bytes read from shared L2 into L1, and bytes read from main memory. This figure shows that the bandwidth requirement by L1 may be higher than by the core. With $N = 2500$, the L1 is not large enough to hold even one line of each matrix, and thus each time data has to be reloaded. This in

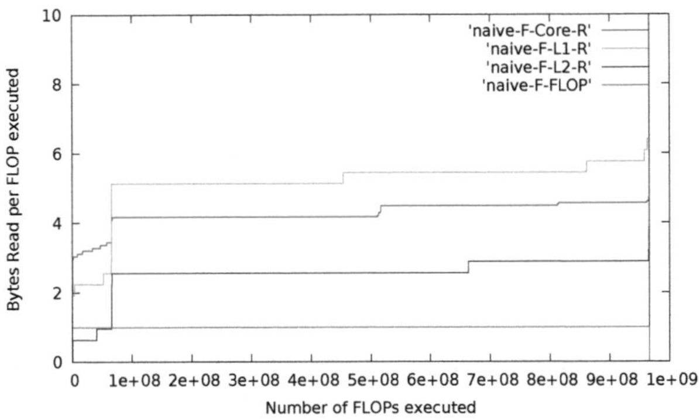

Fig. 6. Bytes read into Core, L1, shared L2, naive version

itself just means the same requirements by the core and L1. However, each write to a newly allocated cache also line triggers a previous read (RFO), explaining the larger figures by L1. We also can measure the number of FLOPs executed per instruction, in the same way as bytes transferred. As can be seen, the code does around 1 FLOP per instruction (this comes from the fact that the compiler mostly produces SSE instructions), and in relation to L2 requirements, there are 4 bytes loaded from memory per FLOP executed. Fig. 5 gives the same for bytes written. For the writes, the caches can not help at all. The average number of bytes written per instruction executed is around 1.8. The peak on the left (around 3.5 bytes) comes from the initialization phase.

6.3 Normalization to FLOPs Executed

Up to now, we used as time unit the instructions executed. Fig. 6 shows the same Fig. 4 (bytes read), but related to FLOPs executed. First, one can see that the FLOP count, normalized to FLOP count, is a straight line at 1, as expected. There are almost one billion FLOPs executed, and there is a strange peak at the very end: as start-up does not do any FLOPs, there is a huge number of bytes read for the first FLOP executed in the program (which is ordered to the left).

6.4 Visualization of Cache Optimization

For cache optimization, the domain is recursively split into blocks fitting into L1. However, within one iteration, there is no reuse of data. Thus, we do multiple iteration updates per block. Because of missing dependencies on block boundaries, the second iteration on a block must not update a boundary of depth 1, the third not a boundary of depth 2 and so on. When two neighboring blocks are done, the missing borders in-between are updated. As block splitting is done recursively by bisection (depending on block dimension either horizontally or vertically), doing the border updates after coming back from the bisection is

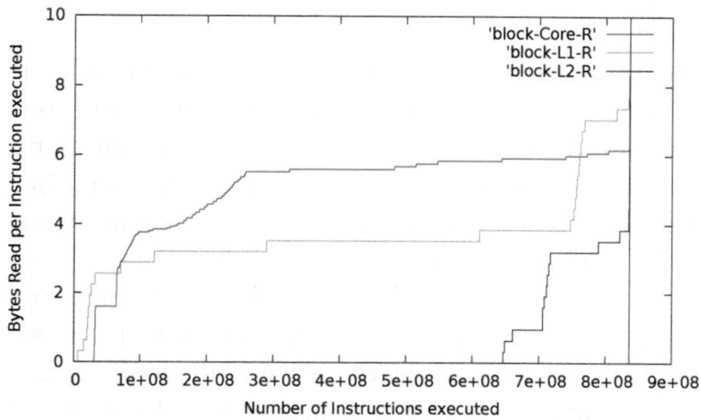

Fig. 7. Bytes read into Core, L1, shared L2, blocking version

straight-forward. The resulting optimization takes the number of iterations to block as variable parameter.

We show the results corresponding to the naive version (Fig. 4) in Fig. 7. We use an iteration blocking of 12. With blocking, the number of instruction executed is increased to around 840 million. The curve showing reads from the core did not change much though, in contrast to the figures for bytes read by L1 and by L2. L1 bandwidth requirements is much reduced. Typically for blocking, only for a small part of the time there is the original requirement. Similar for L2, however, most of the time, there is nothing read from memory at all. This shows the effectiveness of the optimization.

6.5 Multi-threaded Code

The OpenMP version of the 2D iterative solver splits the matrices into slices of equal size. As each thread executes the same code, the curves are the same for the privately used data paths, and are scaled by the number of threads for the shared connection to memory.

Table 1 shows user runtime numbers (threads summed up) for the example code measured on a quad-core Ivy Bridge (2.7 GHz), and the time predicted by our model to be spent at least due to a 15 GB/s read limit from memory. As expected, in contrast to the blocked version, the memory limitation plays an important role for the naive version, and becomes more significant in relation to measured runtime for a larger number of threads.

Table 1. Runtimes of iterative solver and estimations due to memory limitation

[s]	runtimes				due to limitation			
threads	1	2	3	4	1	2	3	4
naive	0.23	0.38	0.57	0.76	0.13	0.28	0.43	0.59
blocked	0.13	0.16	0.20	0.26	0.02	0.04	0.06	0.08

7 Conclusion

In this paper, we propose a way to analyze the data transfer requirements of applications independent from other effects. For an example code, the resulting visualizations are quite insightful. The assumed peak resource restriction in the machine model may be too optimistic for good estimations in the absence of bandwidth bottlenecks. But even in this case, our method at least assures that memory bandwidth is not an issue.

An analysis tool must provide a relation to source lines/data structures. We plan to use a sampling approach. At random points in time, we store instruction pointer and data structures referenced for all accesses in the smoothing window. Thus, each sample gives us a combination of accesses which make up a given bandwidth. Further, bandwidth requirement analysis can be combined with spatial locality analysis to show how much of the transferred data is actually used by cores. The combination will tell whether data layout changes are useful to achieve better bandwidth behavior.

Acknowledgment. Thanks to C. Trinitis for fruitful discussions and proofreading, and to the anonymous reviewers whose critics resulted in a much better paper.

References

1. Intel VTune Amplifier, `http://software.intel.com/en-us/intel-vtune-amplifier-xe`
2. International Technology Roadmap for Seminconductors (2012), `http://www.itrs.net/Links/2012ITRS/2012Chapters/2012Overview.pdf`
3. Almási, G., Caşcaval, C., Padua, D.A.: Calculating stack distances efficiently. In: Proceedings of the 2002 Workshop on Memory System Performance, MSP 2002, pp. 37–43. ACM, New York (2002)
4. Bennett, B.T., Kruskal, V.J.: LRU stack processing. IBM Journal of Research and Development 19, 353–357 (1975)
5. Berg, E., Hagersten, E.: Statcache: A probabilistic approach to efficient and accurate data locality analysis. In: Proc. of the Int. Symposium on Performance Analysis of Systems and Software (2004)
6. de Melo, A.C.: Performance Counters on Linux. Presentation at the Linux Plumbers Conference (September 2009)
7. Luk, C., Cohn, R., Muth, R., Patil, H., Klauser, A., Lowney, G., Wallace, S., Reddi, V.J., Hazelwood, K.: Pin: building customized program analysis tools with dynamic instrumentation. In: Proc. of PLDI 2005. ACM, New York (2005)
8. Niu, Q., Dinan, J., Lu, Q., Sadayappan, P.: PARDA: A fast parallel reuse distance analysis algorithm. In: Int. Parallel and Distributed Processing Symposium (2012)
9. Schuff, D.L., Kulkarni, M., Pai, V.S.: Accelerating multicore reuse distance analysis with sampling and parallelization. In: Proc. of the 19th Int. Conf. on Parallel Architectures and Compilation Techniques. ACM, New York (2010)
10. Weidendorfer, J., Trinitis, C.: Collecting and exploiting cache-reuse metrics. In: Sunderam, V.S., van Albada, G.D., Sloot, P.M.A., Dongarra, J. (eds.) ICCS 2005. LNCS, vol. 3515, pp. 191–198. Springer, Heidelberg (2005)
11. Williams, S., Waterman, A., Patterson, D.: Roofline: an insightful visual performance model for multicore architectures. Comm. ACM 52(4) (April 2009)

Tracking a Value's Influence on Later Computation*

Philip C. Roth

Oak Ridge National Laboratory, Oak Ridge, TN, 37831 USA

Abstract. Understanding how a program behaves is important for effective program development, debugging, and optimization, but obtaining the necessary level of understanding is usually a challenging problem. One facet of this problem is to understand how a *value* (the content of a variable at a particular moment in time) *influences* other values as the program runs. To help developers understand value influence for their programs, we are developing a tool that allows a user to tag a value as being of interest, and then track the influence of that value as it, or values that were derived from it, are used in later computation, communication, and I/O. We believe that understanding how a value's influence propagates will enable algorithm designers to more easily identify optimizations such as the removal of unnecessary computation and communication. In this paper, we describe our value influence tracking approach and our tool's design and implementation status.

1 Introduction

Understanding how a program behaves is necessary for effective program development, debugging, optimization, and fault tolerance. One facet of this problem is the challenge of understanding how a program's *values* are propagated through time and space as the program runs. For instance, one of a program's input values may contribute to nearly all of a program's output values, whereas another may contribute to very few (or none). We call this contribution the value's *influence* on other values. Knowing the degree of a value's influence can provide insight into how to optimize a program. For example, N-body algorithms often include the notion of a *cut-off distance*. If two entities are further apart than the cut-off distance, the algorithm does not consider the effects of either entity on the other, reducing the total amount of computation and computation required by an implementation of the algorithm. The results of a value influence analysis can

* Support for this work was provided through the Scientific Discovery through Advanced Computing (SciDAC) program funded by U.S. Department of Energy, Office of Science, Advanced Scientific Computing Research. The work was performed at the Oak Ridge National Laboratory, which is managed by UT-Battelle, LLC under Contract No. DE-AC05-00OR22725 to the U.S. Government. Accordingly, the U.S. Government retains a non-exclusive, royalty-free license to publish or reproduce the published form of this contribution, or allow others to do so, for U.S. Government purposes.

D. an Mey et al. (Eds.): Euro-Par 2013 Workshops, LNCS 8374, pp. 617–626, 2014.

identify not only that this type of optimization is feasible, but can also suggest what a good cut-off distance should be by indicating when the value's influence becomes small enough that it can be ignored in the computation without causing too great of an error in the algorithm's result. In general, value influence analysis can help a developer determine how much detail needs to be included in a model to balance its fidelity with the cost of computing the model. We hypothesize that many developers of scientific aplications do not know with certainty the best level of detail to include in their model, and thus we expect there are often opportunities for optimizations that give results that are still "good enough." In addition to performance optimization, a value influence analysis may also inform decisions about fault tolerance by allowing a developer to know how *unintended* changes to a value can impact the program's results. If a value's influence over later computation is large, the developer may wish to protect the value with a strong resilience strategy.

To facilitate the understanding of value influence propagation, we are developing an empirical approach for tracking value influence as a program executes, and developing a prototype tool that implements this approach. In this approach, a value may be tagged at some point during the program's execution as being a value of interest. After a value is tagged, the approach tracks how the tagged value is used in later computations and how it propagates to other program address spaces. When a tagged value is used in a computation, its influence data is combined with that of other inputs to the computation and the resulting influence value is associated with the computation's output value. For instance, when the statement $c = a + b$ executes, if the influence associated with variables a and b are 0.5 and 0.2, respectively, then the influence associated with the output value c would be 0.35 assuming the value influence analysis uses the "average" function to combine influences. Although this example is presented at the statement level, we track value influence at the machine instruction level to reflect the computation that is actually executed on the system and to avoid the complexities of a source code-level analysis. Our initial work on value influence tracking targets scientific and engineering applications, and our approach supports applications that use the Message Passing Interface [2,3] (MPI) for communication and synchronization, and multithreading technologies like OpenMP [8].

2 Value Influence

In this section, we detail the concept of value influence and discuss the challenges in propagating value influence as a program executes.

2.1 Assigning and Combining Value Influences

To track value influence, we maintain a set of pairs (L, I), where I is the influence associated with the current value held at location L, where L can represent either a location in memory or a register. Whenever the value held at a location L_k is used in an operation, its associated influence I_k is combined with the influence values of the other operation inputs, and the resulting influence I_{output} is associated with the value at the output location L_{output} in our set of location-influence pairs. Influence values I are real-numbered values in the interval $[0, 1]$. When a value is tagged as being of interest, it is assigned an influence of 1. To control the storage requirements for our approach, if a location is not included in our set the influence of its current value is assumed to be zero.

When a value is used as an input to an operation, its influence must be combined with that of the other inputs and associated to the output value using some combining function, F. The simplest way to combine influences is to use a logical OR operation, such that the influence associated with the output value is 1 if any of the input values have a non-zero influence. With this combining function, the value influence analysis indicates which values depend (directly or indirectly) on the value(s) initially tagged as being of interest, but cannot tell how much the initial value contributed to later values. Combining functions that take into account the operation being performed provide a more nuanced view of value influence propagation. For instance, for a **sum** instruction the combining function may average the influences of the input values. In contrast, for a **max** instruction (available in some instruction set architectures such as Intel's Streaming Single Instruction Multiple Data Extensions), the combining function may use the influence associated with the maximum value as the influence of the output. As an example, if a program adds two variables u and v, u's value has an associated influence of 0.3 and v's value has an influence of 0.5, the value produced as the output of the instruction and stored in a destination *dest* is assigned an influence of 0.4, the average of the influences of u and v. A very sophisticated combining function might take into account not only the type of operation but also the input values themselves. For instance, if the two input values for a **sum** instruction are 1×10^9 and 0.5, the combining function may give the first value's influence much more weight than the second's influence.

2.2 Variable Lifetime

Our value influence tracking approach associates an influence with a memory location or register. Because the number of registers is limited, and because frames are added and removed dynamically from the stack as a thread runs, it is common that two or more variables share the same memory location or register at different moments during a program's execution. Compilers use the concept of *variable lifetime*—the execution interval during which its value is still needed for some future operation—to determine whether two variables can share the same register or memory location. When two variables share the same register or memory location, and the influence of at least one of them is being tracked, our approach takes variable lifetime into account so that it does not mistakenly use a dead variable's influence data instead of that of the live variable that shares its register or memory location. Information about variable lifetime is not explicitly present in the code generated by most compilers, but our approach correctly determines when to "forget" the influence data of a dead variable for most code, because the influence data associated with the dead variable's value is replaced when live value is initialized. If the value used to initialize the live variable has no associated influence data, the influence data associated with the now-live variable is deleted. The only situation where our value influence tracking approach does not handle influence propagation correctly as a natural by-product of the code's initialization of live registers is when the code uses a register or memory location without initializing it.

2.3 Tracking Influences for Multiple Initial Values

Tracking the influence of multiple values within the same run of the program can be accomplished with minor additions to the approach as presented so far. We differentiate between two multiple-value scenarios: one where the program's run is separated into a sequence of phases, and another where the influences of multiple values are tracked simultaneously.

We support value influence tracking for one value per program phase by providing mechanisms (such as application programming interface [API] calls) that allow access to the current value influence data and that can reset the value influence data in preparation for the next phase.

To support tracking the influence of multiple values simultaneously, a "color" is associated with each influence value. The influence data associated with a location is now a set of $(color, influence)$ pairs. When a value is first tagged as being of interest, its initial influence is assigned a color that is unique within the current phase. Then, when an operation uses input variables to produce an output variable, the combining function combines the influences for each color individually to produce the influence data vector associated with the output value. For instance, if the influences associated with the values of variables u and v are $\{(0, 0.2), (1, 0.4), (2, 0.7)\}$ and $\{(0, 0.4), (1, 0.5)\}$, respectively, the influence associated with the output value when u and v are summed is $\{(0, 0.3), (1, 0.45), (2, 0.35)\}$ (assuming the influence combining operator is the "average" function). If the input does not have an associated influence for a given color (e.g., v does not have a color 2 influence), it is assumed to be zero. Thus, in the example, the color 2 influences of 0.7 and 0 are averaged to give 0.35, and this is assigned as the color 2 influence on the result.

Because of the need to store multiple influences per location, and the need for the combining function to combine influences for each color independently, tracking the influences of multiple values per phase can add a significant overhead in both space and time to the basic value influence tracking approach. The actual time and space requirements depend on the number of initial values being tracked and the number of times those values, and values derived from them, are used in operations during the computation.

2.4 Multithreaded Programs

Multithreaded programs present an interesting set of challenges when tracking variable influence. In a multithreaded program, a value in a memory locations is shared among all of the program's threads. Any thread may read or write that value whenever the thread is executing on a processor core. To avoid race conditions in accessing this influence data, we use a mutual exclusion lock (also known as a mutex) to protect the internal data structure that maintains influence variables for values in memory. For values in registers, we use thread-local storage so that we are sure to use the correct influence data for a register as threads are switched onto and off of processor cores.

2.5 MPI Programs

We aim to support value influence tracking not only for multithreaded programs involving a single address space, but also for MPI programs involving multiple MPI processes each with its own address space. Such programs use MPI API functions to transfer data from one address space to another and to synchronize the program's processes. Our approach to support MPI programs require the ability to detect when the program transfers data, and the ability to modify the behavior of that transfer. The MPI standard defines a *profiling API* that provides both of these features. This interface allows link-time interposition of a function between the caller of an MPI function like `MPI_Send` and the library's implementation of that function. By defining a collection of interposition functions corresponding to MPI's data transfer functions, we can detect when the application is sending data from one address space to another using MPI those functions. Our interposed versions of the MPI data transfer functions use the underlying MPI data transfer functions to transfer both the application-level data and any influence values associated with that data. Two-sided and collective operations use the same two-sided and collective operations, respectively, to transfer the influence data as the application data. One-sided MPI operations require the use of a separate "value influence service thread" (VISTs) to run in each MPI process for maintaining and serving the value influence data, plus an out-of-band channel for transferring influence data between interposed MPI one-sided functions like `MPI_Put` and these VISTs.

3 Implementation

We are implementing the value influence tracking approach described in Sect. 2 in a tool called *VIT*. In this section, we discuss some of the *VIT* implementation details.

When tracking value influence, we associate influence data with a memory address (for values in memory) or a register ID (for values in registers). This approach gives us a concise way to represent locations, but because memory addresses and register IDs are from distinct name spaces, this approach requires us to keep separate collections of location-influence pairs for memory locations and registers. In our current *VIT* implementation, we use the C++ standard template library's `map` class to hold location-influence pairs. Because a given CPU core's registers are accessible only to the thread executing on that core, we use thread local storage when associating a register-influence map with each thread.

VIT is built on the Intel Pin instrumentation meta-tool [7]. Pin allows developers to create tools (commonly called *Pintools*) that analyze and instrument the machine code of an x86 or x86_64 executable program. Pin uses *dynamic instrumentation*—the instrumentation code is added while the program is executing. The instrumentation code is Pintool-specific. For instance, the instrumentation for an instruction mix tool would analyze each instruction as it was executed and count the number of instructions of each type. In contrast, the instrumentation for a simple performance tool may count the number of times each function is called and to measure how long it takes to execute each function.

VIT uses Pin's trace instrumentation mode to insert the bulk of its instrumentation code. When Pin gives control to *VIT*'s trace-level instrumentation because a new trace of instructions is about to be executed, *VIT*'s trace-level instrumentation examines each instruction in the trace to determine whether the instruction writes a value to a destination location (a memory location or register). If so, the *trace-level* instrumentation code inserts *instruction-level* instrumentation for that instruction. This instruction-level instrumentation computes the value's new influence as described in Sect. 2.1 and associates the new influence data with the destination location in the appropriate location-influence map.

A user must specify to *VIT* which values are of interest for tracking their influence, and when to output the *VIT* influence data. *VIT* provides a simple C-based Application Programming Interface (API) for user control. The user can specify a value of interest using the API function `VIT_Track` by inserting a call to this function into the application's source code such that it will be executed when the user wants to start tracking the influence of that variable's value. For instance, to start tracking the influence of a variable's value in the tenth iteration of the application's main loop, the user might insert a call to `VIT_Track` as the body of an if-then statement whose condition is that the iteration number is 9 assuming iteration numbers start from zero. This approach to specifying for which values to track influence, and when to start tracking, provides flexible control over when to start tracking but requires the user to insert calls to `VIT_Track` in their application.

In our prototype implementation, *VIT* outputs the value influence data to standard output when the program completes. *VIT* also provides API functions `VIT_Report` and `VIT_Reset` for outputting the value influence data at other times and for resetting the data, e.g., to restrict value tracking to a certain phase or particular iteration of a loop.

4 Status

We have implemented the basic intra-process *VIT* functionality and are currently implementing inter-process influence tracking functionality for two-sided and some collective MPI data transfers. For our prototype implementation, we are using the *average* operation when combining influences, regardless of the instruction's operation.

To demonstrate *VIT*'s current functionality, we applied it to a self-written application that solves the two-dimensional heat equation $\partial T/\partial t = \alpha\nabla^2 T$ (where T is the temperature of the material and α is its thermal diffusivity) using an explicit discretization and forward time-centered space (FCTS) method [10] with a five point stencil. The program keeps the problem state in two 2-dimensional arrays of double precision values where each value represents a discretization point of the problem domain. One array holds the current state and its values are used to compute the updated state in the other array. This implementation is single threaded. We tracked the influence of one of the problem domain boundary values as the program executed its time step loop. Because the program uses a five-point stencil, the value's influence "diffuses" through the problem state array by advancing one row and column per time step similar to the way that heat diffuses throughout the problem domain as the simulation proceeds.

The bulk of *VIT*'s output is a sequence of $(address, influence)$ pairs for memory locations with non-zero influence values. If the program contains a symbol table, each address can then be translated to a symbolic name of a corresponding program variable using software like the GNU Binary File Descriptor (BFD) library or SymtabAPI [9]. (Our prototype implementation does not perform this translation, nor does it report influence values associated with registers.) Figure 1 shows visualizations of this *VIT* output for select time steps produced as influence was propagated through the application's state arrays. In the figure, each cell represents a memory location in the array. Each cell is colored according to the influence value associated with the cell's associated memory location. We wrote a simple utility to convert from the addresses in *VIT* output to the indices of cells within a two dimensional array. The influence values quickly decrease from the initial value of 1, so the visualizations use a log scale to retain contrast between the cells representing memory locations with non-zero influence and those with zero influence. Because the heat transfer application uses a double buffering approach, the value influence "wavefront" alternates between the two problem state arrays. Thus, for the figure we display value influence data for one array after even numbers of time steps and the other after odd numbers of time steps. As expected, the program took 62 time steps for the influence data to propagate across the 64-element-wide problem state array. (The array boundaries are one element wide and immutable). Note that this influence propagation pattern is independent of the heat transfer problem being solved.

Applying *VIT* to our example heat transfer application exposed three problems with the prototype implementation's intra-process value influence tracking. First, the influence values drop rapidly as the computation proceeds. We determined that our prototype implementation does not handle register-based addressing modes in the expected way, treating them as uses of a register in the computation of the instruction's result. Although this interpretation is technically correct, we are modifying *VIT* to distinguish between registers used for addressing and registers providing source values for the computation. Second, *VIT* does not currently support Single Instruction Multiple Data (SIMD) instructions that operate on multiple values. However, because the SIMD arithmetic units

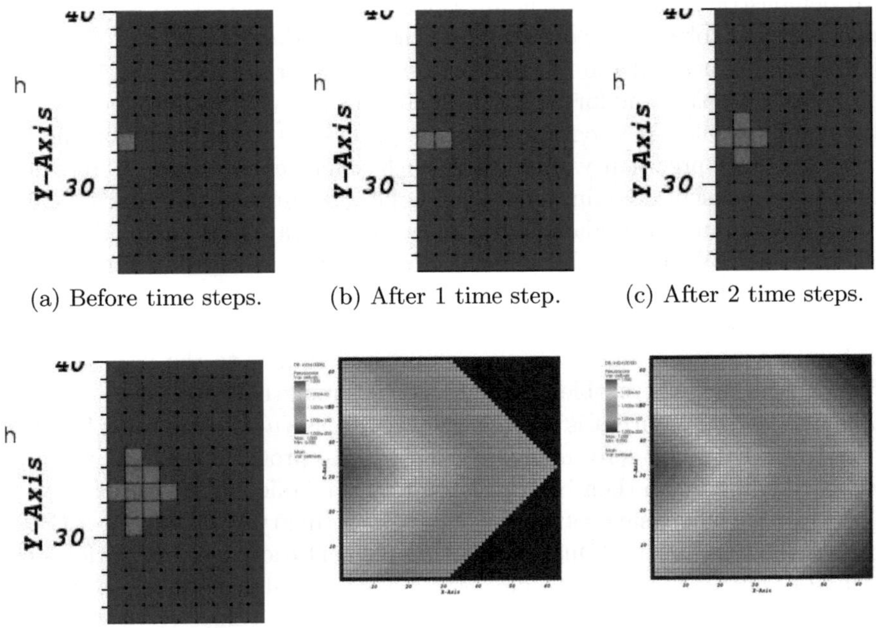

(a) Before time steps. (b) After 1 time step. (c) After 2 time steps.

(d) After 3 time steps. (e) After 62 time steps. (f) After 100 time steps.

Fig. 1. Value influence propagation for two-dimensional heat transfer application, starting with a single value on the boundary of the problem state array

tend to be faster than traditional x87 floating point hardware, modern compilers often generate code for the SIMD units even when operating on single values. The executable code produced by GCC for our example application uses this approach, and our prototype *VIT* implementation handles it correctly. Finally, our prototype *VIT* implementation does not correctly propagate influence data for instruction sequences that use the traditional x87 floating point hardware. Although we have not yet identified the root cause of this problem, doing so is a low priority in light of the common use of SIMD hardware by modern compilers.

5 Related Work

Program slicing [12,13,6,14] is a technique for determining which statements were used to produce the value of a given variable at a point in the program's execution (backward slicing) or for determining the statements that will directly or indirectly use the value of a given variable at some future point in the program's execution (forward slicing). Our value influence tracking approach is similar to forward program slicing in that it focuses on the value of a variable at a specific point in the program's execution, and that both are concerned with how that value is used in the future computation. Unlike traditional forward program slicing that is concerned with determining which future statements use the value (a code-centric view), our value influence tracking approach takes a data-centric perspective by determining which other values the initial value influences. Also, unlike the traditional analysis, our approach is concerned not only with *whether* a value had influence on future values, but also *how much* influence it had. Weiser's original program slicing approach [13] uses a static analysis of the program's source code that produces a conservative result containing all statements that *might* be executed for a given variable, regardless of the program's inputs. Dynamic slicing approaches [6] limit the output to only those statements that are actually executed for specific inputs. In that respect, our empirical value influence tracking approach is more similar to the dynamic program slicing approaches than the traditional static slicing approach. A forward program slicing approach could be used by a value influence tracking tool like *VIT* to limit the time required to perform the value influence analysis, since executing the program slice would not execute statements (and any associated *VIT* instrumentation) that could not possibly transfer influence.

Chopping [4,11] is the technique derived from slicing that is closely related to our value influence tracking approach and *VIT* tool. For a given set of source variables and a set of sink variables, chopping is concerned with determining the set of statements that use the values of the source variables to produce the values of the sink variables. In our value influence tracking approach, we do not restrict the influence tracking to a particular set of sink variables. Also, the original chopping approach [4] supported only source and sink variables within the same function. This restriction was overcome by Reps et al [11]. Like Reps' work, our approach is able to track value influence across function boundaries.

Taint Analysis [5,1] is a computer security technique for tracking data that is "tainted" as it propagates through a computation, similar to the way we track a value's influence. When a tainted value is used to produce another value the resulting value is also considered tainted, so that taint is propagated through the computation as it progresses. Kang et al [5] present a *Dynamic Taint Analyis* technique that tracks taint using an infrastructure similar to Pin, and Ganai et al [1] track taint for multi-threaded programs. These approaches are similar to our value influence tracking approach in the way that they propagate taint information, but differ from our approach in that the taint analyses consider taint as a boolean characteristic: either a value is tainted, or it is not. In our case, we quantify the amount of influence that is transferred when values of interest are used to compute a new value. Also, this existing work does not consider analyses for programs running on distributed memory systems such as the compute nodes of an HPC system.

6 Summary

In this paper, we presented the concept of value influence tracking and the design of a tool, *VIT*, that implements that concept. We described the challenges and an approach for tracking value influence in multi-threaded programs, and in MPI-based parallel programs. We described our prototype *VIT* implementation that supports value influence tracking and demonstrated it with a simple scientific application.

Once we complete *VIT*'s basic intra- and inter-process functionality, we plan to evaluate the trade-offs of using more sophisticated influence combining operations such as those described in 2.1. We will also add the support for more MPI collectives, and support for MPI one-sided data transfers. We also plan to evaluate whether and how well this general influence tracking approach applies to other parallel programming models than MPI, and whether and how it can be applied to programs that use accelerators like graphics processing units (GPUs).

References

1. Ganai, M., Lee, D., Gupta, A.: DTAM: dynamic taint analysis of multi-threaded programs for relevancy. In: Proceedings of the ACM SIGSOFT 20th International Symposium on the Foundations of Software Engineering, FSE 2012, pp. 46:1–46:11. ACM, New York (2012)
2. Gropp, W., Lusk, E., Skjellum, A.: Using MPI: portable parallel programming with the message-passing interface. Scientific and engineering computation, 2nd edn. MIT Press, Cambridge (1999)
3. Gropp, W., Thakur, R., Lusk, E.: Using MPI-2: Advanced Features of the Message Passing Interface. MIT Press, Cambridge (1999)
4. Jackson, D., Rollins, E.J.: Chopping: A generalization of slicing. Tech. rep., Pittsburgh, PA, USA (1994)
5. Kang, M.G., McCamant, S., Poosankam, P., Song, D.: DTA++: Dynamic taint analysis with targeted control-flow propagation. In: NDSS. The Internet Society (2011)
6. Korel, B., Laski, J.: Dynamic slicing of computer programs. J. Syst. Softw. 13(3), 187–195 (1990)
7. Luk, C.K., Cohn, R., Muth, R., Patil, H., Klauser, A., Lowney, G., Wallace, S., Reddi, V.J., Hazelwood, K.: Pin: building customized program analysis tools with dynamic instrumentation. SIGPLAN Not. 40(6), 190–200 (2005)
8. OpenMP Architecture Review Board: OpenMP application program interface, version 3.1. OpenMP Architecture Review Board (July 2011)
9. Paradyn/Dyninst Groups, University of Wisconsin-Madison and University of Maryland: SymtabAPI programmer's guide, 8.1 release (March 2013)
10. Press, W.H., Teukolsky, S.A., Vetterling, W.T., Flannery, B.P.: Numerical Recipes, 3rd edn. The Art of Scientific Computing. Cambridge University Press, New York (2007)
11. Reps, T., Rosay, G.: Precise interprocedural chopping. SIGSOFT Softw. Eng. Notes 20(4), 41–52 (1995)
12. Weiser, M.: Program slicing. In: Proceedings of the 5th International Conference on Software Engineering, ICSE 1981, pp. 439–449. IEEE Press, Piscataway (1981)
13. Weiser, M.: Program slicing. IEEE Transactions on Software Engineering SE-10(4), 352–357 (1984)
14. Xu, B., Qian, J., Zhang, X., Wu, Z., Chen, L.: A brief survey of program slicing. SIGSOFT Softw. Eng. Notes 30(2), 1–36 (2005)

Assessing Measurement and Analysis Performance and Scalability of Scalasca 2.0

Ilya Zhukov and Brian J.N. Wylie

Jülich Supercomputing Centre, Forschungszentrum Jülich, 52425 Jülich, Germany

Abstract. The Scalasca toolset was developed to provide highly scalable performance measurement and analysis of scientific applications on current HPC platforms, including leadership systems such as IBM BlueGene/Q and more traditional Linux clusters. Its primary focus is support for C/C++/Fortran applications using MPI and OpenMP, and mixed-mode combinations thereof, offering detailed call-path profiles for each process and thread produced by runtime summarization or augmented with wait-state analysis of event traces. A new generation of Scalasca (2.0) uses the community-developed infrastructure comprising of Score-P and associated components, while continuing to provide the previous functionality. By comparing the new version of Scalasca with its predecessor, using the applications from the NPB3.3-MZ-MPI benchmark suite, we validate core functionality and assess overheads and scalability. Although adequate for general use, various aspects are identified for further improvement, particularly for larger scales.

Keywords: parallel performance measurement/analysis, scalability, MPI+OpenMP.

1 Introduction

Various studies have compared the usability and overheads of different performance tools for MPI applications on IBM BlueGene systems [1,7] and Linux clusters [5], however, we are particularly interested in comparing two generations of the Scalasca toolset [3] and its implementations on these two quite different classes of HPC computer system. We also focus on measuring and analysing the performance of combined OpenMP with MPI in recognition of the current predominance of this parallelization paradigm in the most scalable applications.

2 Scalasca and Score-P

Scalasca analyses of the execution performance of parallel applications consist of detailed call-path profiles for each process and thread which allow both quantification and localization of performance issues. Metric severity differences between processes and threads, which may indicate imbalance, and the program call-paths where these occur, can be readily identified and compared, or refined via

D. an Mey et al. (Eds.): Euro-Par 2013 Workshops, LNCS 8374, pp. 627–636, 2014.

hierarchical exploration. A wide range of valuable metrics can be determined independently for each process and thread during measurement via runtime summarization. Additional metrics indicating more specific parallel execution inefficiencies, requiring correlation of events on different processes that is prohibitive during measurement, can be determined via a parallel replay analysis of event traces. Locations of particularly severe instances of such issues found in the event traces can also be used to direct interactive trace visualization tools such as Vampir [4] to present them for detailed investigation.

While this usage has been supported for some years by Scalasca, community-developed software components promise closer integration with other tools and a larger basis for extending and improving functionality. For this purpose a number of Scalasca components have been re-developed with and for the community (the OPARI source instrumenter and CUBE analysis report utilities and GUI), along with a new OTF2 event trace format, however, the main new development is the Score-P instrumentation and measurement infrastructure [6]. The latter provides a functional replacement for Scalasca's original infrastructure (known as EPIK), generating summary analysis reports in CUBE format and/or event traces in OTF2 format for Scalasca's parallel trace analyzer (SCOUT).

Existing users of the Scalasca toolset are therefore able to continue to use the familiar commands to instrument their parallel application programs (SKIN), launch the instrumented executables under the control of the measurement configuration and analysis nexus (SCAN), and post-process and examine the resulting summary and trace analysis reports (SQUARE).

The new Scalasca instrumenter essentially only offers limited backwards compatability, since the Score-P instrumenter itself provides all of the functionality and can be used directly. Each instrumenter operates in the same fashion, using OPARI and other source instrumenters as appropriate, though command-line switches and manual instrumentation API have incompatible syntax.

The Scalasca measurement execution configuration and analysis nexus should also appear familiar in its operation. As before it verifies and sets the execution configuration for a measurement experiment, validates the resulting measurement artifacts and where appropriate automatically initiates parallel trace analysis using the same configuration of compute nodes, processes and threads. The most visible difference is that experiment archive directories are distinguished with the `scorep_` prefix (rather than `epik_`). While command-line configuration options are essentially unchanged for basic operation, Score-P environment variables must be used for detailed configuration and although many are similar to those for EPIK measurements there are also notable differences. For example, whereas EPIK uses separate memory buffers for call-path profile and event trace data on each thread along with per-process definition buffers, Score-P uses a memory buffer pool on each process for all of its internal measurement management and collection. As well as being more convenient, the latter pool can also be more memory efficient. Similarly, a file with a list of routines to filter during measurement can be specified in the same way on the SCAN command-line (and also for testing with SQUARE), however, its Score-P syntax is different.

For tracing experiments, event trace files with associated definition files are written directly into the archive directory as before, but the OTF2 library is used by the Score-P measurement libraries to write the files and by the SCOUT analyzer to read them. SIONlib [2] is employed to optimize parallel file I/O and avoid excessive numbers of files. The parallel replay analysis of the traces then follows, and an augmented analysis report is collated and written using the new version of CUBE.

Finally, the new Scalasca analysis report examiner, using the latest version of the CUBE utilities and GUI, is only superficially distinguished by the new report format (with a different file extension). Old and new analysis reports have very similar hierarchical structures of metrics, regions/call-paths and nodes/processes/threads, however, for reading and writing efficiency a binary file format is used for metric severity values rather than the previous XML. The new format also provides greater flexibility and functionality, e.g., for storing either inclusive or exclusive metric severity values. Notably, the Score-P measurement system does not yet provide any topological information for processes and threads nor compute nodes and processors, either in its own summary analysis reports or as part of the trace metadata definitions.

The first release of the new generation of Scalasca — version 2.0 — supports Score-P 1.2 and was co-released in August 2013. Measurements from this are refered to as Scalasca2 (S2) in comparison to the latest first generation Scalasca 1.4.3 release (S1) of March 2013.

3 Experimental Setup

3.1 Machines

It is of interest to compare these Scalasca generations on the two production HPC resources at Jülich Supercomputing Centre[1], since they offer quite different execution environments.

Juropa[2] is a high-performance cluster of 3288 compute nodes each with 24 GB of memory and dual quad-core Intel X5570 (Nehalem-EP) processors supporting 2-way hardware threading, connected via a non-blocking fat-tree Infiniband QDR network. The operating environment provides Intel compilers and ParaStation MPI running under SuSE Linux with Lustre filesystems.

Juqueen[3] is a highly scalable IBM BlueGene/Q system consisting of 28 racks each with 1024 PowerPC A2 processors with 16 GB of memory and 16 cores supporting 4-way hardware threading, and a custom 5D torus interconnect. Applications running under Linux microkernels on compute nodes use IBM XL compilers and proprietary MPI library with GPFS filesystems.

To effectively utilise the available hardware resources, a maximum of 16 OpenMP threads is appropriate for Juropa compute nodes, whereas 64 OpenMP threads is more suitable for Juqueen compute nodes.

[1] `http://www.fz-juelich.de/ias/jsc/EN/`

[2] `.../Expertise/Supercomputers/JUROPA/JUROPA_node.html`

[3] `.../Expertise/Supercomputers/JUQUEEN/JUQUEEN_node.html`

3.2 Applications

Many HPC applications now use combined MPI and OpenMP parallelization, therefore the multi-zone versions of the NAS Parallel Benchmarks (NPB3.3-MZ-MPI) [8] which run on a wide range of computer systems were chosen as the basis for the comparison. There are three separate pseudo-application benchmark codes — BT-MZ (block tri-diagonal solver), SP-MZ (scalar penta-diagonal solver) & LU-MZ (lower-upper Gauss-Seidel solver) — written in Fortran77 to solve various sizes of computational fluid dynamics problems (refered to as 'classes') at varying scales. Larger problem classes take longer to execute and require more memory.

Notably, while an arbitrary number of OpenMP threads can be used when executing, LU-MZ has a fixed number of even-sized zones and can therefore only be configured with a maximum of 16 MPI processes, whereas BT-MZ and SP-MZ can be configured with up to 16384 MPI processes (for the largest problem class 'F'). SP-MZ has equally-sized zones, but BT-MZ's zones have unequal sizes and correspondingly varying amounts of computation.

BT-MZ incorporates a static load balancing capability, varying the number of OpenMP threads for each process, however, this is ineffective when the threads are confined to the same processor on BlueGene systems (or same compute node on Juropa), and to avoid detrimental over-subscription such load balancing must be disabled. BT-MZ class F runs on Juqueen with the maximum 16384 MPI processes, though execution efficiency drops substantially with more than 4096 processes (each with 64 OpenMP threads). Analysis of the performance of BT-MZ execution with Scalasca has shown that at larger scale computational imbalance deteriorates particularly severely in the `z_solve` routine [9].

There is insufficient memory available on Juqueen compute nodes to run SP-MZ class F, however, SP-MZ class E runs and scales well with up to 4096 MPI processes (each with 64 OpenMP threads). With a maximum of only 16 MPI processes, LU-MZ is hardly suitable for systems like BG/Q where the smallest allocatable partition comprises 32 processors. Nevertheless, 16-process versions of all three benchmarks were configured for class D and run successfully on Juqueen as well as a Juropa partition of 16 compute nodes.

For reference we take the (wallclock) execution time reported for each benchmark kernel, which is relatively stable and not subject to variations in starting and initializing processes and their final completion. As well as uninstrumented optimized executables, additional executables for measurement were also prepared using the instrumenters from Scalasca 1 & 2. In each case, the instrumenter directed the respective compiler to insert instrumentation calls at every source routine entry and exit, as well as using OPARI2 for source-code instrumentation of OpenMP directives and linking the MPI+OpenMP measurement libraries. (In the course of subsequent measurement iterations, measurement control commands were incorporated in LU-MZ sources and measurement filter files generated for BT-MZ.)

To avoid performance variations that may arise from hardware partitions and sets of compute nodes, each experiment consisted of a series of measurements as well as reference executions in the same batch job using the same allocated compute resources. Parallel filesystems ($WORK) are required for efficient file I/O for tracing experiments, however, they are non-dedicated resources such that variability in performance is unavoidable.

4 Results

Apart from functionality known not to be available yet from Score-P, initial comparison of analysis reports produced by Scalasca 1 & 2 verified their correctness and completeness (with only minor issues). Separate series of experiments were undertaken to compare measurement and analysis overheads and scalability of the two versions.

4.1 Measurement Overhead

For each of the three benchmarks, Class D versions for 16 MPI processes were prepared on both Juropa and Juqueen, and these fully-optimised, uninstrumented executables run to have reference execution times, reported in Tab. 1.

Compilation and linking times of approximately 39–43 seconds on Juqueen increase to 45–47 seconds when instrumenting with both versions of Scalasca. On Juropa, compilation and linking times of 14–16 seconds increase to 37–43 seconds with Scalasca1, and 31–35 seconds with Scalasca2. Both versions of Scalasca use OPARI2 to process source files containing OpenMP, direct the compilers to insert routine entry and exit instrumentation calls, and additionally link the measurement libraries. Since shared libraries are available with Scalasca2 on Juropa, dynamic linking is faster than static linking done by Scalasca1. Although recompilation of the application is required, the additional time is moderate and the instrumented executables can be configured for different measurements.

An initial set of summary measurements were taken and scored by Scalasca to determine whether adjustments would be desirable or required, e.g., to specify buffer sizes for tracing measurements. Tab. 1 includes the maximum trace buffer capacity requirements (max_tbc) per-thread for Scalasca1 and per-process for Scalasca2. While there are no serious issues for SP-MZ, the score reports identify that traces produced by BT-MZ and LU-MZ would be too large to fit in available memory during measurement. The BT-MZ measurements also had kernel execution times much larger than the reference executions, by 1–2x for Scalasca1 and 2–4x for Scalasca2, indicating significant measurement dilation.

The BT-MZ score reports identified several user-level source routines that were executed very frequently and consequently would be responsible for the vast majority of the trace buffer capacity requirements (as well as ultimate trace size). These routines are short-running and tend to have disproportionately large measurement dilation, while not contributing to analysis of MPI or OpenMP parallel efficiency issues. Although the Intel compiler on Juropa appended an extra underscore character to the routine names, the exact same set of routines and scoring assessment applied for the IBM XL compiler on Juqueen. Measurement

Table 1. Reference execution times for NPB3.3-MZ-MPI benchmark kernels (class D, 16 processes) and characteristics of default and revised Scalasca 1&2 measurements on Juropa and Juqueen. Revised configurations using a measurement filter file for BT-MZ and explicitly instrumented measurement pause after 20 timesteps for LU-MZ.

	Juropa			Juqueen		
	16x16 BT-MZ	16x16 LU-MZ	16x16 SP-MZ	16x64 BT-MZ	16x64 LU-MZ	16x64 SP-MZ
Reference execution time [sec]	177.11	280.29	153.49	315.46	321.83	319.18
S1 default measurement time [sec]	378.20	258.05	151.39	907.63	333.24	408.32
S1 revised measurement time [sec]	184.41	272.79		375.72	333.29	
S2 default measurement time [sec]	581.10	265.08	153.57	1619.38	335.27	304.27
S2 revised measurement time [sec]	181.57	300.01		348.00	335.17	
S1 default measurement dilation [%]	114	7.9	1.4	188	3.5	27.9
S1 revised measurement dilation [%]	4.1	2.7		19.1	3.6	
S2 default measurement dilation [%]	228	5.4	0.1	413	4.2	4.7
S2 revised measurement dilation [%]	2.5	7.0		10.3	4.1	
S1 default thread max_tbc [MB]	13,488	6,396	74	6,438	1,603	119
S1 revised thread max_tbc [MB]	31	602		31	86	
S2 default process max_tbc [MB]	181,174	21,230	2,321	182,249	21,692	4,991
S2 revised process max_tbc [MB]	365	3,120		1,441	1,988	

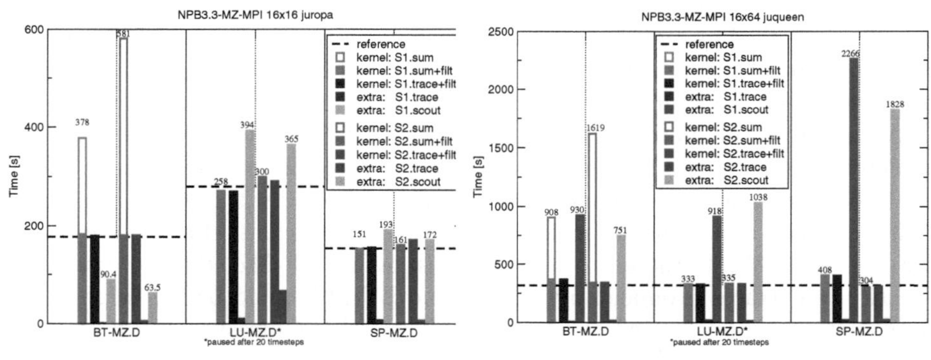

Fig. 1. NPB3.3-MZ-MPI benchmark class D experiments on Juropa (*left*) and Juqueen (*right*) comparing measurement dilation of execution kernels and additional time associated with trace collection and SCOUT trace analysis: for each benchmark, Scalasca1 left of dotted line and Scalasca2 on right. Black dashed lines show the uninstrumented reference kernel execution time, the first bar in each set is the kernel execution time for summary measurement (with and without filter for BT-MZ), with the following three bars separating kernel execution time for trace measurement, generation and analysis times.

filter files listing the names of these routines were therefore prepared and applied for subsequent summary and tracing measurements.

In comparison, while LU-MZ measurements showed acceptable dilation of up to 8% on Juropa and less than 5% on Juqueen, the LU-MZ score reports identified an OpenMP flush directive in the `sync_left` routine (`syncs.f:27`) that would be responsible for prohibitive trace buffer capacity requirements. Although it is possible to direct the Scalasca instrumenter not to instrument OpenMP flush directives, that would then compromise the subsequent analysis since OpenMP flush time would not be distinguished from computation time. With over 15% of total execution attributed to OpenMP flush time (and almost entirely from this particular one of the 5 flush directive use locations), it is desirable to retain this key part of the execution performance analysis. In this case, it is preferable to only measure a subset of the 300 LU-MZ.D timesteps, by explicitly inserting a conditional pause region in the source code of the timestep loop using the provided measurement control APIs. For LU-MZ.D, additional instrumented executables were prepared where measurement was paused after 20 timesteps, and corresponding trace buffer capacity requirements thereby reduced substantially.

Measurement dilation and execution overheads for experiments with Scalasca 1 & 2 are shown in Fig. 1. Although unfiltered BT-MZ measurements suffer significant dilation, the filters employed to reduce traces to managable sizes are also effective in bringing dilations down to acceptable levels (below 20% on juqueen and only 7% on juropa). As well as dilated execution time of the measured application, trace generation and subsequent analysis with the SCOUT analyzer require compute nodes to be allocated for additional time. (Time for collating and writing summary measurements is negligible and not shown.) At this scale, trace generation times are small (even for the larger LU-MZ trace files), however, the trace analysis times are found to be highly dependent on the application and computer system (though Scalasca2 analysis is generally slightly faster than Scalasca1). If memory was available to trace the full 300 LU-MZ.D timesteps, rather than only 20, times for trace generation and analysis would be more than ten times longer.

4.2 Scalability

Execution times of the three benchmarks (classes C, D, E & F) with different numbers of MPI processes (one per processor) on Juqueen are shown in Fig. 2(a). In comparison to their execution times on 128 processors, with 4096 processors (i.e., 32 times as many) SP-MZ.E demonstrates an excellent speed-up of 29 whereas BT-MZ.E has a speed-up of only 8.4.

While the excellent speed-up characteristics of SP-MZ.E on Juqueen make its execution performance analysis less important for tuning, the absence of scaling artifacts also suggests it to be preferable when examining and comparing the scaling efficiencies of performance analysis tools.

Fig. 2(b) shows the SP-MZ.E kernel execution times for summary and tracing measurements with Scalasca1 and Scalasca2 (blue and orange lines,

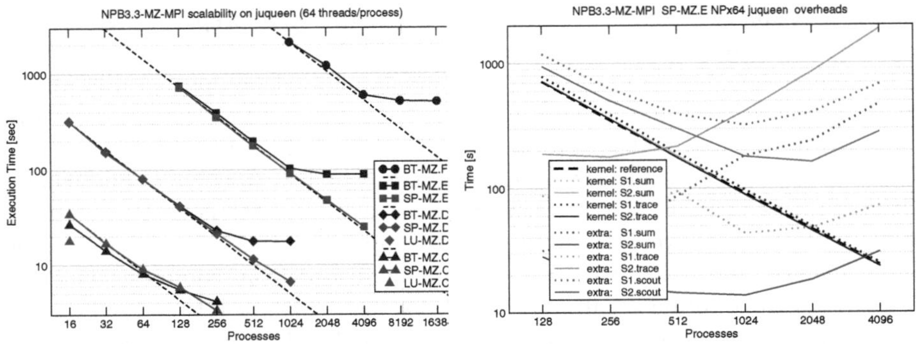

(a) Kernel execution times (b) SP-MZ.E measurement experiments

Fig. 2. Executions times on Juqueen BG/Q with 64 OpenMP threads per MPI process. (a) NPB3.3-MZ-MPI kernel execution times for the benchmark classes C (*triangle*), D (*diamond*), E (*rectangle*) & F (*circle*). (b) SP-MZ.E measurement dilation and execution overheads with Scalasca1 (*dotted lines*) & Scalasca2 (*solid lines*).

indistinguishable for different experiment types) and extra time associated with measurement and analysis. From comparison with the uninstrumented reference SP-MZ.E kernel execution times (black dashed line), measurement dilation was a maximum of 11% with Scalasca1 and 7% with Scalasca2 (compared with 28% and 5%, respectively, for SP-MZ.D_16x64 in Tab. 1). The larger dilation from Scalasca1 may be attributed to additional callpath consistency checking and metrics calculated.

Summary measurement finalization times (red lines in Fig. 2(b)) increase roughly linearly with the number of processes for which measurements are written to the analysis report. These are notably larger for Scalasca1 due to the extra metrics, along with the additional metadata describing the hardware and application topologies (not yet provided by Scalasca2), and report collation and writing time becomes significant at scale.

Trace generation times (green lines in Fig. 2(b)) similarly increase with the number of processes for which event data is written. Since Scalasca2 doesn't yet use the much more efficient SIONlib, creation and writing of trace files is currently considerably slower and less scalable than Scalasca1, and prohibitive for thousands of processes. Whereas Scalasca2 creates two files for every thread, Scalasca1 uses SIONlib to create only one file per I/O bridge on BG/Q and write thread data aligned to filesystem blocks as sections within these multifiles. As a result Scalasca2/OTF2 traces on disk only grow slowly from 246 GB for 128 processes to 292 GB with 4096 processes, whereas Scalasca1/SIONlib traces which are initially 25% smaller grow to be about four times larger than their counterparts (shown in red in Fig. 3(b)).

Trace analysis times (magenta in Fig. 2(b)) follow the same trend for both versions of Scalasca's automated trace analyzer SCOUT: good scalability for up to 512 processes (matching that of SP-MZ.E) is reversed for larger configurations. The time breakdown in Fig. 3(a) shows that for Scalasca1 this is primarily

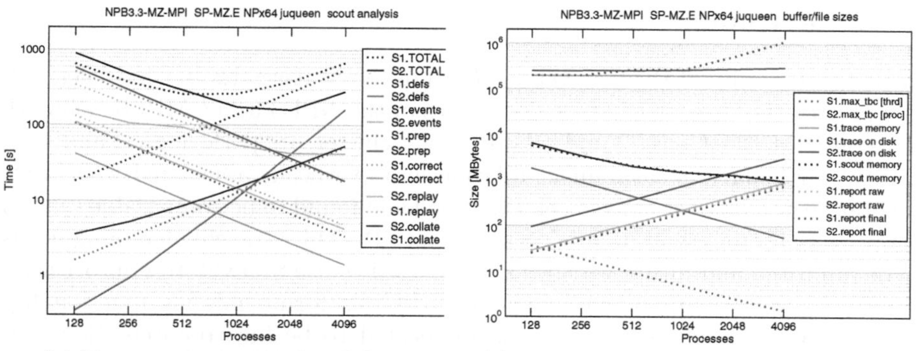

(a) Trace analysis time breakdown (b) File sizes and memory requirement

Fig. 3. Scaling of SP-MZ.E tracing experiments on Juqueen with Scalasca1 (*dotted lines*) & Scalasca2 (*solid lines*). (a) Breakdown of time in stages of SCOUT automated trace analysis. (b) Trace buffer content and file size on disk, trace analyzer memory requirement, and analysis report size.

explained by the time to collate and write the linearly growing analysis report sizes, whereas for Scalasca2 it is reading the trace metadata definitions that dominates at scale. At smaller scales, Scalasca2 is dominated by time to preprocess the already loaded trace data. Scalasca2 trace replay analysis is found to be consistently faster than its predecessor.

While Fig. 3(b) shows that the size of the largest trace buffers decreases linearly, the total amount of trace event data in memory buffers is largely independent of the number of processes (approx. 190 GB) and disk space for the resulting trace files is somewhat larger. Also both versions of the Scalasca trace analyzer require similar amounts of memory and produce raw trace analysis reports of comparable size.

To be efficient and flexible, analysis reports written directly by the Scalasca measurement libraries and parallel trace analyzers contain a minimal set of unstructured metrics. These intermediate Scalasca2 reports in CUBE4 format are 4–8% larger than Scalasca1 reports in CUBE3 format. Additional metrics are derived and a hierarchy of metrics created during subsequent offline post-processing. The final analysis reports are four times larger with Scalasca2, but processed 4–5 times faster by the scoring utility, since they store inclusive metric values for more efficient reading rather than the exclusive values supported by Scalasca1. Analysis report sizes and post-processing times are proportional to the complexity of the raw reports, determined by the number and type of callpaths but also by the number of processes (and threads per process). Whereas the Scalasca1 metric remapper utility uses hard-coded metric derivations and mappings, the Scalasca2 version is configurable via specification files. Remapping the SP-MZ.E trace analysis reports for 4096 processes takes just over 10 minutes with Scalasca1, but roughly 20 times longer with Scalasca2.

5 Conclusion

Basic functionality of the new version (2.0) of the Scalasca toolset has been validated with the three MPI+OpenMP codes of the NPB3.3-MZ-MPI benchmark suite on IBM BlueGene/Q and a large Linux cluster. Its performance and scalability, particularly measurement dilation and overheads associated with trace generation and analysis, have been examined and found to be comparable (and in many cases better) than its predecessor. Score-P/OTF2 tracefile handling needs to be improved and future versions are expected to use SIONlib to improve scalability. As well as supporting additional HPC platforms, missing functionality such as topology descriptions are also expected to be incorporated. However, currently the most critical limitation of Scalasca2 is the very slow and inefficient analysis report post-processing (remapper), which is inconvenient both for experiments with complex call-trees or large numbers of processes/threads.

References

1. Chung, I., Walkup, R., Wen, H., Yu, H.: MPI performance analysis tools on BlueGene/L. In: Proc. ACM/IEEE SC 2006 Conference on High Performance Networking and Computing, Tampa, FL, USA. ACM Press (November 2006)
2. Frings, W., Wolf, F., Petkov, V.: Scalable massively parallel I/O to task-local files. In: Proc. ACM/IEEE SC 2009 Conference Portland, OR, USA (November 2009), `http://www.fz-juelich.de/jsc/sionlib/`
3. Geimer, M., Wolf, F., Wylie, B.J.N., Ábrahám, E., Becker, D., Mohr, B.: The *Scalasca* performance toolset architecture. Concurrency and Computation: Practice and Experience 22(6), 702–719 (2010), `http://www.scalasca.org/`
4. GWT-TUD GmbH: VAMPIR. Technische Universität Dresden, Dresden, Germany, `http://www.vampir.eu/`
5. Iwainsky, C.: an Mey, D.: Comparing the usability of performance analysis tools. In: César, E., Alexander, M., Streit, A., Träff, J.L., Cérin, C., Knüpfer, A., Kranzlmüller, D., Jha, S. (eds.) Euro-Par 2008 Workshops. LNCS, vol. 5415, pp. 315–325. Springer, Heidelberg (2009)
6. Knüpfer, A., Rössel, C., an Mey, D., Biersdorff, S., Diethelm, K., Eschweiler, D., Geimer, M., Gerndt, M., Lorenz, D., Malony, A.D., Nagel, W.E., Oleynik, Y., Philippen, P., Saviankou, P., Schmidl, D., Shende, S.S., Tschüter, R., Wagner, M., Wesarg, B., Wolf, F.: Score-P – A joint performance measurement run-time infrastructure for Periscope, Scalasca, TAU, and Vampir. In: Proc. 5th Parallel Tools Workshop, Dresden, Germany, pp. 79–91. Springer (2012), `http://dx.doi.org/10.1007/978-3-642-31476-6_7`, `http://www.score-p.org/`
7. Mohr, B., Wylie, B.J.N., Wolf, F.: Performance measurement and analysis tools for extremely scalable systems. Concurrency and Computation: Practice and Experience 22(16), 2212–2229 (2010)
8. Van der Wijngaart, R.F., Jin, H.: NAS Parallel Benchmarks, Multi-Zone versions. Tech. Rep. NAS-03-010, NASA Ames Research Center, Moffett Field, CA, USA (July 2003), `http://www.nas.nasa.gov/Software/NPB/`
9. Wylie, B.J.N.: Parallel performance measurement & analysis scaling lessons. In: Proc. SC 2012 Workshop on Extreme-Scale Performance Tools, Salt Lake City, UT, USA (November 2012), `http://juser.fz-juelich.de/record/128166`

Detecting SIMDization Opportunities through Static/Dynamic Dependence Analysis

Olivier Aumage, Denis Barthou, Christopher Haine, and Tamara Meunier

Inria – University of Bordeaux, France

Abstract. Using SIMD instructions is essential in modern processor architecture for high performance computing. Compilers automatic vectorization shows limited efficiency in general, due to conservative dependence analysis, complex control flow or indexing. This paper presents a technique to detect SIMDization opportunities, complementing in a more detailed way compiler optimization reports. The method is based on static and dynamic dependence analysis, able to analyze codes not vectorized by a compiler. This method generates user-hints to help vectorize applications. We show on TSVC benchmark the benefits of this approach.

Keywords: SIMDization, performance tuning, dependence analysis.

1 Introduction

For modern multi-core architectures, the Single Instruction, Multiple Data (SIMD) instructions are essential in order to reach high levels of performance. With the increase of vector width – up to 16 floats for Intel Xeon Phi SIMD vectors for instance – SIMD instructions are real performance multipliers. Several options are given to the application developer in order to vectorize a code: explicit vectorization through assembly instructions, intrinsics, GCC vector extensions or other language extensions (such as Intel SPMD Program compiler for instance [20]) or implicit vectorization through the automatic vectorizer of the compiler.

Explicit vectorization, however, is complex and time consuming, assembly and intrinsics-based approaches also are not portable and GCC extensions only offer a limited subset of arithmetic operations. Consequently, the vectorization effort for most applications is delegated to the compiler, which may not entirely succeed or even completely fail to meet the programmer expectations, depending on the code structure and complexity. Indeed, an over-conservative dependence analysis, an incomplete static information concerning the control-flow or a strided data layout are among the main reasons why the compiler may not generate vector code, even though the code actually is vectorizable. Therefore, determining whether the code is vectorizable, independently of any compiler limitations, as well as pinpointing the issues that may hinder vectorization and the transformations required to enable it are critical capabilities for the developer.

This paper proposes a new approach for detecting vectorization opportunities for application innermost loops. This approach is based on a twofold static

D. an Mey et al. (Eds.): Euro-Par 2013 Workshops, LNCS 8374, pp. 637–646, 2014.

and dynamic dependence analysis of the binary code, and generates vectorization hints for the user. By combining a static and dynamic dependence analysis, our method identifies the limiting factors for vectorization, such as misaligned data, non contiguous data together with opportunities to vectorize, obtained through rescheduling, loop transformations, reduction rewriting and vectorizable idiom rewriting. The runtime analysis is essential in capturing dependences in presence of complex control flow or structure indexing. Our technique provides feed-back to the user, pinpointing at the origin line in the source (using debugging DWARF information). This approach is complementary to what compiler optimization reports can provide, bringing a more detailed analysis of vectorization opportunities, in particular of the opportunities missed by the compiler. We show the benefits of the hints generated through a study of the extended TSVC benchmarks[14] (Note: The extended TSVC suite of 151 loops is itself based on the original TSVC suite [3] of 135 loops). While our method primarily targets SIMDization efforts, it would be applicable to more general vector computing hardware.

Section 2 first presents the implementation background we use, Section 3 describes the hybrid dependence analysis, using both static and dynamic analysis. Section 4 uses this analysis to perform SIMDization analysis and generate hints. Finally, we show in Section 5 the results obtained on TSVC benchmarks.

2 MAQAO Background

The analyses proposed in this paper are implemented within MAQAO and use the compression scheme in MAQAO for memory traces. We briefly recall their features used in the following.

MAQAO is a performance tuning tool [2], that analyzes the binary code of applications, written in C/C++ or Fortran. MAQAO builds the control flow graph and the call graph of the code. It proposes an API to instrument statically a binary code and generate a new binary. This instrumentation is able to capture any value in the code, and in particular can be used to trace memory accesses, count loop iterations, capture function parameters. Compared to PIN [12], a tool with similar functionalities, MAQAO performs only static analysis of binaries and static rewriting (from binary to binary). PIN, on the contrary, dynamically rewrites binary codes while they execute, and performs analysis on the fly. As the static analysis of MAQAO is offline, as well the instrumentation process, the overall cost for analyzing a binary with MAQAO is much smaller than with PIN.

MAQAO captures memory streams by instrumenting all instructions that access memory. For each instruction instrumented, the flow of addresses captured is compressed on-the-fly using a lossless algorithm, NLR, designed by Ketterlin and Clauss[8]: The successive values captured by the instrumentation are represented by a program with loops and expressions. The expressions describe memory addresses and depend on the surrounding loop counters. Figure 1 shows an example of traces for a simple code, assuming elements of the arrays 4-byte long floats. Expressions can only depend linearly on the loop counters, and loop bounds only depend linearly on surrounding loop counters. The memory addresses described form union of polytopes. Hence the method not only captures the memory workingset, it also captures a schedule for the accesses.

```
for(i=1; i<100; i++)
  C[i] = C[i - 1] + B[2 * i];
```

(a) Code example

```
for i0 = 0 to 98
   write 0x2ba1a3bd442c + 4 * i0
```

(b) Compressed trace for `C[i]`

```
for i0 = 0 to 98
   read 0x2ba1a3bd4428 + 4 * i0
```

(c) Compressed trace for `C[i-1]`

```
for i0 = 0 to 98
   read 0x2ba1a4000000 + 8 * i0
```

(d) Compressed trace for `B[2 * i]`

Fig. 1. Example of trace compression using NLR. For the code in (a), one compressed trace per memory access is produced, (b), (c) and (d).

Three important features for these traces are used in this paper: (i) Regular strides are captured. This is important for SIMD optimization, since this will decide whether data layout restructuration is needed or not. In Figure 1.(b), the stride is 4, meaning data of array C is contiguously accessed in this write. For the array B, the stride of 8 shows that one float out of 2 is read, data is not contiguously accessed. (ii) Regular streams are fully traced, in a compact form. This enables the computation of dependence distances. (iii) For multi-dimensional data, memory expressions provide spatial locality information through the ordering of the strides. This can be used in order to propose loop restructuring hints.

For irregular patterns, new loops are created, possibly leading to a trace with no compression if no regularity is found.

3 Hybrid Static/Dynamic Dependence Graph

The dependence analysis we propose is a combination of a static dependence analysis, for registers, and dynamic dependence analysis for memory dependences. The static dependence analysis on registers is already implemented in MAQAO and corresponds to an SSA analysis. Memory dependences are obtained by tracing with MAQAO all memory accesses within the innermost loops, and then computing dependence distances.

Static, Register-Based Dependence Graph. The dependence graph on registers is resulting from an SSA (static single assignment form[4]) analysis, proposed by MAQAO. In addition to the existing analysis, we tag all dependences where a register is read for an address computation. The graph is then partitioned according to these edges (cutting the graph through these edges), usually in two parts: Instructions preceding these edges are address computation instructions (such as index computation, update of address registers), while instructions after these edges are actual computation (memory accesses, floating point operations,

...) for which SIMDization may be applied. When an indirection occurs, the dependence graph has a path with two tagged edges and can therefore be partitioned into three or more subgraphs. The partition of instructions following all tagged edges is said to be the *computational part of the graph*, while the other instructions are part of the *address computation part* of the graph. In the rare cases where it is not possible to cut the graph following tagged edges, we assume there is no computational part.

Dynamic Dependence Graph. Dynamic dependences are essential to capture what the compiler may have missed, concerning the control flow or the way data structures are indexed. The dynamic dependence graph is built from the memory trace for each read and write instructions in innermost loops.

Algorithm 1 describes how dependence distances are computed. $w.trace$ denotes the trace captured for an instruction w. For each couple of read and write accesses in a loop, we first perform an interval test, based on their trace (line 2), and then compute a *dependence distance*. The dependence distance is defined as the number of loop iterations between two instructions accessing the same memory location. When two traces have the same loop structure, the substraction between the traces (line 4) substracts the expressions that are at the same position in the trace. If the result is not the same constant value for all substractions, then $*$ is returned, otherwise the constant value is returned. The special $*$ dependence distance notation between two instructions denotes the fact that their dependence distance is not constant during the execution of the program. Note that only uniform dependences are captured this way but as far as SIMDization is concerned, this captures all vectorization opportunities that do not require non-local code transformation.

Algorithm 1. Dynamic Dependence computation for an innermost loop L

```
1  for w, a write and r, a read in L do
2      if w.trace ∩ r.trace ≠ ∅ then
3          if loops of w.trace = loops of r.trace then
4              return r.trace − w.trace;
5          else
6              return ∗;
7          end
8      else
9          return 0 ;
10     end
11 end
```

For the example in Figure 1.b and 1.c, both traces have the same structure, the same strides, and the difference between the read and the write addresses is an offset of -4. Then we evaluate how this difference can be compensated by a variation in the loop indices (here $i0$). We find a unique solution within the loop bounds, 1 and this shows that the dependence distance between the write and the read is 1. In general, finding the vector of iteration counters that compensate for the offset between the read and the write leads to a multi-dimensional dependence vector. Only read after write dependences are evaluated, and the sequential order of the assembly code is used to compare relative positions for reads and writes. Note that all distances for register dependences correspond

```
for (int i = 1; i < LEN2; i++) {
  for (int j = 1; j < LEN2; j++) {
   bb[j][i] = bb[j][i-1] + cc[j][i];
}
```

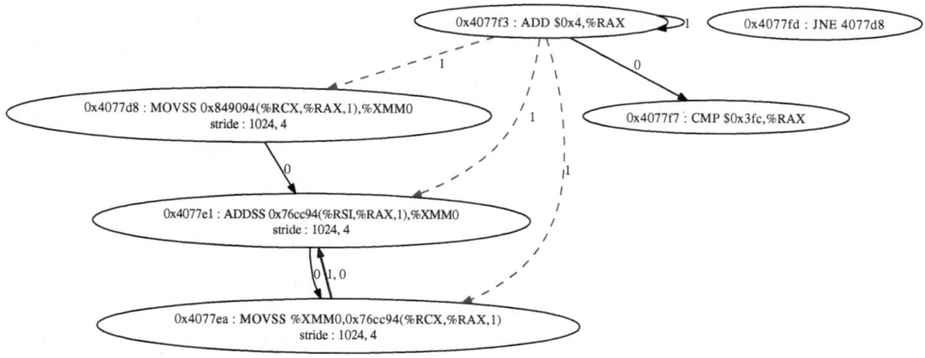

Fig. 2. Code and dependence graph for one loop of function s2233 in TSVC benchmark

in this case to innermost loop carried dependences. Figure 2 presents the s2233 function from TSVC and its dependence graph, combining both the static and dynamic graphs. The nodes each represent an assembly instruction, along with its strides when it is a memory access. The dashed edges in red represent dependences for registers used in address computation. Cutting the graph along these edges separates the computational part (left nodes) from the address computation and control part. The bold blue edge, labelled with 1, 0 represents the memory dependence corresponding to `bb`, directly computed from the trace. The strides denoted on the edges have two values: 1024 and 4. The first one corresponds to the stride for the innermost loop, j, and the second to the i loop. This shows that here, none of the accesses have good spatial locality.

4 SIMDization Analysis

The SIMDization analysis is in two steps: First, we determine whether the code has a parallelism compatible with a SIMDization, independently of any data layout or control limitations (such as large stride). Then, we refine the analysis to detect special cases and accordingly guide the programmer towards enabling and improving the vectorizability of the code.

Vectorizable Dependence Graph. The dependence graph (static and dynamic) is first partitioned according to address computation edges as described previously. The graph is said vectorizable if one of the three conditions applies to the computational part of the graph: 1) There is no cycle. 2) There is a cycle, with a cumulative weight greater than the width of SIMD vectors. 3) There is a cycle, with a cumulative weight smaller than the width of SIMD vectors, and the instructions of the cycle all are of one of the following types: `add`, `mul`, `max`, `min`.

The cycle corresponds to a reduction. A code with a vectorizable dependence graph may require transformations in order to be SIMDizable. This is detailed in the following section.

Code Transformation Hints. We propose to identify a number of transformations required for the SIMDization of the code, depending on the dependence graph, on the stride expressions, and on the control flow graph.

Data alignment: When the graph is vectorizable without cycle, misaligned data is detected by comparing the starting address of all memory streams with the width of SIMD vectors. In the simpler case, the user can either change memory allocation of heap-allocated data structures, or use pragmas for aligning stack-allocated data. When for instance $A[i]$ and $A[i+1]$ occur in the same code, one of the two accesses is misaligned. This would require shuffle instructions, or unaligned loads/stores whenever they exist.

Rescheduling: When the graph is vectorizable without cycle, there may still exist some dependences with non-null distance. Due to the fact that the analysis is performed on assembly code, this may require some modifications at the source code such as some rescheduling of loads/stores and computations, splitting some larger instructions. A template of the vector code is generated by our tool (an example is given in the following section), giving a correct instruction schedule after SIMDization.

Loop transformations: Loop interchange is proposed when all accesses within the loop have a large innermost loop stride, and another loop counter in the expression corresponding to the same outer loop has a stride 4 (for floats and ints). Interchanging these two loops would result in better locality and enable SIMDization.

Loop reversal: Traces with negative stride expressions lead to this hint. Note that if other reads for instance have a positive stride, the reversal is not beneficial any more.

Data reshaping required: This is a fallback hint for large innermost loop strides, and for codes with indirection (detected on the static dependence graph). On the Sandybridge and Xeon Phi architectures, instructions for loading or storing non-consecutive elements into/from SIMD vector have been added to the ISA (GATHER on Xeon Phi and Sandybridge and SCATTER on Xeon Phi). Use of these instructions, through assembly code or intrinsics, is an alternative to data reshaping.

Versioning required: The static analysis on the code may lead to a conclusion different from the trace analysis. For instance, the trace may find a regular stride for a memory stream whereas statically, this stream results from an indirection, or depends on a parameter. Similarly, the dynamic control flow (the real path taken) may be a subset of a more complex static control flow. In these cases, the trace may have captured only one behavior of the code, for a particular input. The vectorization may only be possible in this case through the versioning of the loop, depending on the values of the array, of a parameter.

Table 1. MAQAO vs GCC and Intel ICC compilers

Tool	Maqao	GCC	ICC
Detected vectorizable cases	123	46	104
Corresponding MAQAO hint			
- Reduction	30	15	24
- Idiom	8	3	7
- Data alignment issue	11	4	4
- Code restructuration	53	6	39
- Loop interchange or data tranpose	9	4	7
- Rescheduling	9	1	1
- Control	23	0	17

Idiom Recognition: When the code is vectorizable, with 0 dependence distances or with reductions, the dependence graph can match a predefined dependence graph representing a well known computation. The shape of the dependence graph and the instructions themselves are matched with the predefined graphs. In this case, the user can call a library function instead of trying to vectorize the actual code.

The predefined functions considered are so far: dot product, daxpy, copy, sparse copy (copy with an indirection either in the load or in the store), but more complex functions can be added with ease.

5 Tests on TSVC Benchmark

The TSVC benchmark has 151 codes with small loops, illustrating different vectorization difficulties. We first present the output generated by our method on one example and then show aggregated results for all TSVC benchmarks.

Figure 3 presents a code with an alias between two arrays. This kind of alias can hinder automatic vectorization and only dynamic dependence analysis or possibly interprocedural alias and points-to analysis are able to cope with such situation. Here, the dynamic dependence shows that the dependence distance between the write of `x[i+1]` and the read of `array[i]` is 64 iterations. Thus vectorization is possible as long as vector width is < 64. The source line and name of the file are provided by MAQAO and extracted from debug information. User-friendly names are associated for most frequent instructions found in the computational part of TSVC. The dependence between the store and load is represented by the dependence vector on the indices.

Table 1 presents the overall hints generated by the analysis on all TSVC benchmarks. Out of the 151 functions to analyze, 123 are detected as SIMDizable, with 0, 1 or more hints provided by MAQAO. If we focus on the codes that are said vectorizable and are not vectorized by GCC, for 23 of them, speed ups greater than 2 are obtained through hand vectorization, compared to GCC generated codes.

```
for (int i = 0; i < LEN - 1; i++)
  xx[i+1] = array[i] + a[i];
```

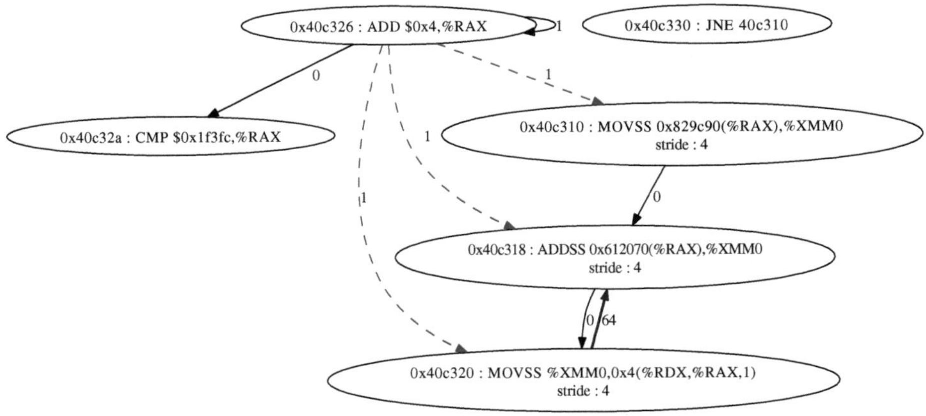

Fig. 3. Code and dependence graph for the loop in function s424 of TSVC benchmark. `array` is aliased with `xx` with an offset of 63 floats.

6 Related Works

With the advent of short vector SIMD instructions in modern processors, SIMDizability and automated SIMDization have been the topic of several research efforts. Indeed, making use of these SIMD units has early been recognized as key for performance [11]. Compilers such as from Intel, IBM or PGI, as well as GNU GCC [18,17,16,22] have received much auto-vectorization effort to enable and extend their capabilities [9,9,5,1]. Scout [10] has been designed to vectorize at a higher level, by translating scalar statements to vectorized statements using SIMD intrinsics. However, Malecki *et al.* showed in their SIMDization tests [14] on the TSVC suite that many potentially vectorizable constructs are left unaddressed by state of the art compilers, either because some known theoretical techniques have not yet been implemented, because no known theoretical techniques exist for codes with complex structure, or because the compiler must act conservatively as a consequence to a lack of available information at compile-time [19].

The purpose of tools based on dynamic dependency graph analysis [13] such as our MAQAO approach is therefore to explore SIMDizability from an entirely different point of view. As such, MAQAO is a complementary analyser with respect to vectorizing compilers, for application programmers to investigate where and how their code could be restructured to enable or improve vectorization by the compiler. Holewinski *et al.* propose a similar approach [7], which is the closest from our own work, to the best of our knowledge so far. However, their implementation does not preserve structural information about the application such as iterated memory references inside loop nests. This limits the amount of details that can be reported to the programmer, and this also limits the richness of the information that could be injected back inside a vectorizing compiler to improve its output. Our approach instead preserves such key information, which distinguishes from prior efforts. An hybrid compile-time/run-time approach is proposed by Nuzman *et al.* [15] using a two-step vectorization scheme. The compile-time step performs expensive analysis operations. The run-time, specialization step is performed by an embedded just-in-time compiler. This approach enables some degree of adaptiveness to the hardware at run-time. However, the run-time step does not alter the vectorizability status using dynamic dependency information. Adaptiveness is also explored by Park *et al.* [6] by guiding the application of optimizations in a predictive manner through a machine-learning approach, and by Tournavitis *et al.* [21] in a technique associating profile-driven auto-parallelization together with machine-learning.

7 Conclusion and Future Work

We have presented in this paper a new method to help users vectorize their code. The approach generates hints identifying what are the vectorization opportunities, and what are the bottlenecks in the code preventing SIMDization. The technique we propose is unique with respect to other efforts on the topic in that it uses a static dependence analysis on the binary code, at the register level, enriched with a dynamic dependence analysis for memory accesses. The combination of both provides a detailed picture of vectorization and possible transformations necessary for SIMDization. We have shown on TSVC benchmark the accuracy of our analysis.

As future work we plan to expand the range and quality of our analysis by detecting other loop transformations automatically (such as loop distribution or reroll) for SIMDization, and also to test this approach to larger, varied application codes.

References

1. Allen, R., Kennedy, K.: Optimizing Compilers for Modern Architectures: A Dependence-Based Approach. Morgan Kaufmann (2002)
2. Barthou, D., Rubial, A.C., Jalby, W., Koliai, S., Valensi, C.: Performance tuning of x86 OpenMP codes with MAQAO. In: Tools for High Performance Computing, Springer, Heidelberg (2010)
3. Callahan, D., Dongarra, J., Levine, D.: Vectorizing compilers: a test suite and results. In: Conference on Supercomputing (1988)
4. Cytron, R., Ferrante, J., Rosen, B.K., Wegman, M.N., Zadeck, F.K.: Efficiently computing static single assignment form and the control dependence graph. ACM Transactions on Programming Languages and Systems (1991)
5. Eichenberger, A.E., Wu, P., O'Brien, K.: Vectorization for SIMD architectures with alignment constraints. In: ACM SIGPLAN Conf. on Programming Language Design and Implementation (2004)
6. Park, E., Pouchet, L.-N., Cavazos, J., Cohen, A., Sadayappan, P.: Predictive modeling in a polyhedral optimization space. In: ACM/IEEE Intl. Conf. on Code Generation and Optimization (2011)

7. Holewinski, J., Ramamurthi, R., Ravishankar, M., Fauzia, N., Pouchet, L.N., Rountev, A., Sadayappan, P.: Dynamic trace-based analysis of vectorization potential of applications. In: ACM SIGPLAN Conf. on Programming Language Design and Implementation (2012)
8. Ketterlin, A., Clauss, P.: Prediction and trace compression of data access addresses through nested loop recognition. In: ACM/IEEE Intl. Conf. on Code Generation and Optimization, pp. 94–103. ACM, New York (2008)
9. Kong, M., Veras, R., Stock, K., Franchetti, F., Pouchet, L.N., Sadayappan, P.: When polyhedral transformations meet SIMD code generation. In: ACM SIGPLAN Conf. on Programming Language Design and Implementation (2013)
10. Krzikalla, O., Feldhoff, K., Müller-Pfefferkorn, R., Nagel, W.E.: Scout: A source-to-source transformator for SIMD-optimizations. In: Alexander, M., D'Ambra, P., Belloum, A., Bosilca, G., Cannataro, M., Danelutto, M., Di Martino, B., Gerndt, M., Jeannot, E., Namyst, R., Roman, J., Scott, S.L., Traff, J.L., Vallée, G., Weidendorfer, J. (eds.) Euro-Par 2011, Part II. LNCS, vol. 7156, pp. 137–145. Springer, Heidelberg (2012)
11. Larsen, S., Amarasinghe, S.: Exploiting superword level parallelism with multimedia instruction sets. In: ACM SIGPLAN Conf. on Programming Language Design and Implementation (2000)
12. Luk, C.K., Cohn, R., Muth, R., Patil, H., Klauser, A., Lowney, G., Wallace, S., Reddi, V.J., Hazelwood, K.: Pin: building customized program analysis tools with dynamic instrumentation. In: ACM SIGPLAN Conf. on Programming Language Design and Implementation (2005)
13. Mak, J., Mycroft, A.: Limits of parallelism using dynamic dependency graphs. In: International Workshop on Dynamic Analysis (2009)
14. Maleki, S., Gao, Y., Garzarán, M.J., Wong, T., Padua, D.A.: An evaluation of vectorization compilers. In: International Conference on Parallel Architectures and Compilation Techniques, PACT (2011)
15. Nuzman, D., Dyshel, S., Rohou, E., Rosen, I., Williams, K., Yuste, D., Cohen, A., Zaks, A.: Vapor SIMD: Auto-vectorize once, run everywhere. In: ACM/IEEE Intl. Conf. on Code Generation and Optimization (2011)
16. Nuzman, D., Henderson, R.: Multi-platform auto-vectorization. In: ACM/IEEE Intl. Conf. on Code Generation and Optimization (2006)
17. Nuzman, D., Rosen, I., Zaks, A.: Auto-vectorization of interleaved data for SIMD. In: ACM SIGPLAN Conf. on Programming Language Design and Implementation (2006)
18. Nuzman, D., Zaks, A.: Autovectorization in GCC-two years later. In: Proceedings of the GCC Developers Summit (2006)
19. Petersen, P.M., Padua, D.A.: Static and dynamic evaluation of data dependence analysis. In: International Conference on Supercomputing (1993)
20. Pharr, M., Mark, W.R.: ispc: A SPMD compiler for high performance CPU programming. In: Conf. InPar (2012)
21. Tournavitis, G., Wang, Z., Franke, B., O'Boyle, M.F.: Towards a holistic approach to auto-parallelization: integrating profile-driven parallelism detection and machine-learning based mapping. In: ACM SIGPLAN Conf. on Programming Language Design and Implementation (2009)
22. Trifunovic, K., Nuzman, D., Cohen, A., Zaks, A., Rosen, I.: Polyhedral-model guided loop-nest auto-vectorization. In: International Conference on Parallel Architectures and Compilation Techniques (2009)

A High-Level IR Transformation System

Herbert Jordan, Peter Thoman, and Thomas Fahringer

University of Innsbruck, Institute of Computer Science
Technikerstrasse 21a, 6020 Innsbruck, Austria
{herbert,petert,tf}@dps.uibk.ac.at

Abstract. The development and implementation of source-to-source code transformations based on high-level intermediate representations (IRs) is a labor-intensive, error-prone task. It tends to result in large code bases which are hard to read and maintain. Although not encountered within widely used source-to-source compiler infrastructures, transformation systems tackle this issue by utilizing declarative descriptions of unification-based term rewriting rules. However, unification lacks the ability of (arbitrarily) deep term inspection and is limited to tree nodes exhibiting a fixed arity – a property not generally satisfied by high-level IRs or programming languages.

In this paper we present a declarative tree transformation system which exceeds the expressiveness of conventional unification based systems by operating on arbitrary tree structures. We define its formal foundation, describe its implementation within the Insieme compiler project and provide real-world code examples. The latter demonstrate the expressive power, usability and intuitiveness of our solution.

Keywords: Compiler, Program Transformation, Term Rewriting, Pattern Matching, Regular Expressions.

1 Introduction

Within contemporary compiler infrastructures, source-to-source transformations are typically implemented by a (long) hand-coded sequence of operations inspecting and manipulating some AST-like internal representation (IR). This approach is not only labor-intensive and error-prone, thus limiting productivity, but even more crucially it also reduces maintainability due to its tendency to result in obscure code [10].

Although rarely encountered within widely utilized compiler infrastructures, transformation systems tackle this issue by offering a declarative, rule based interface for the definition of transformations [2, 8, 11]. Fundamentally, each rule consists of a pattern and a replacement template. Any term matching the pattern is replaced by an instantiation of the template. In general, the pattern matching is based on unification, resulting in two restrictions. On the one hand, unification can only impose limited constraints on the matched term. For instance, it can not check whether within an arbitrary nesting level of a matched term a given subterm occurs. On the other hand, unification builds upon an algebraic structure,

D. an Mey et al. (Eds.): Euro-Par 2013 Workshops, LNCS 8374, pp. 647–656, 2014.

hence tree nodes are restricted to a fixed arity [2, 11]. Yet, within AST-like IRs, constructs which do not naturally exhibit a fixed arity (e.g. compound statements or argument lists) are omnipresent. Frequently this issue is circumvented by representing variable-sized lists using artificial function symbols (or grammar rules) linking individual elements to recursively composed lists. However, not only does this approach conceal the structure of the internal representation, it also increases the complexity of defining patterns and rewrite rules.

Within this paper we present a novel combination of unification-based term rewriting rules and regular expressions allowing the declarative description of complex transformations for arbitrary tree structures – in particular high-level compiler IRs.

2 Design Goals

This section provides an informal overview of the intended capabilities of our pattern matching and rewriting system by discussing a list of example use cases. A simple case, which is already not directly supported by unification based approaches, is to check whether a given variable $v1$ is present within some code fragment. We would like to write something similar to

$$aT(v1) \tag{1}$$

where the construct aT denotes *"anywhere in the tree"*. A more extended case would be the requirement to check whether the expression $exp1$ is present as a full expression within a given compound statement. In this case we would like to write something similar to

$$\{\_^*, exp1, \_^*\} \tag{2}$$

where $\_$ denotes a wildcard and * the Kleene operator (any number of repetitions, including none).

In many cases patterns will be defined not only to constrain the structure of some input but also to extract information. For instance, it might be necessary to obtain the variable being declared by some declaration statement. In this case we would like to use a pattern involving a variable similar to

$$decl(\$x) \tag{3}$$

to obtain the requested information. Matched against the input declaration

$$int\ a\ =\ 5 \tag{4}$$

pattern (3) should yield the variable mapping $\{x \mapsto a\}$. Furthermore, in a case where all variables declared within a compound statement should be obtained, the pattern

$$\{(\neg decl(\_))^*, (decl(\$x), (\neg decl(\_))^*)^*\} \tag{5}$$

matched against

$$\{int\ a\ =\ 5;\ f(a);\ bool\ b\ =\ true;\ int\ c\ =\ 7;\} \tag{6}$$

should yield $\{x \mapsto [a, b, c]\}$. It should also be possible to constrain the values pattern variables are bound to. For instance, if the selection should be limited to declarations of integer variables we would like to use a pattern similar to

$$\{(\neg decl(var(int, \_))^*, (decl(\$x : var(int, \_)), (\neg decl(var(int, \_))^*)^*\} \quad (7)$$

Here, $var(t, n)$ is a pattern construct matching an IR variable n of type t and the construct $\$x : y$ defines a pattern variable x matching every structure satisfying the pattern y. Applying this pattern to fragment (6) should result in $\{x \mapsto [a, c]\}$.

In some cases we want more. For instance, we might need a pattern identifying variables being declared but never used. This should be covered by

$$\{decl(\$x), (\neg aT(\$x))^*\} \quad (8)$$

Hence, a declaration of some IR variable captured by the pattern variable $\$x$ followed by a sequence of statements not including this particular variable. Note the difference to the previous examples. In pattern (5) the pattern variable $\$x$ is bound to a list of sub-trees, once for each declaration in the list, while in the current example $\$x$ should be bound only once to the variable being declared at the beginning of the compound statement. In the subsequent repetition $(\neg aT(\$x))^*$ the variable is supposed to be the fixed to the value previously bound to $\$x$.

From this observation we derived the following desirable rule for variable bindings: within every iteration of a repeating sub-pattern p, variables may be re-bound to new values, unless already bound before entering p the first time. If they were already bound, then, within all repetitions, previously bound variables remain bound to the value determined before entering p.

Of coarse, pattern (8) is limited to situations where the unused variable is declared by the first statement in a compound. This restriction is lifted by using

$$aT(decl(\$x)) \wedge \{(\neg aT(\neg decl(\$x) \wedge \_(\_^*, \$x, \_^*)))^*\} \quad (9)$$

where $\wedge$ is the conjunction of patterns and $\_(\_^*, p, \_^*)$ matches any node with a child matching the pattern p. The pattern searches for any sub-tree declaring a variable $\$x$ which is never referenced outside the declaration.

As a final challenge for the pattern syntax we would like to define a pattern capable of listing all *for* loops within a perfectly nested loop nest. The problem here is that the loop nest might be arbitrarily deep. The Kleene operator is limited to horizontal matching, along the list of children of a single node. For this class of use cases an operator defining a recursively nested tree structure is required. We define an additional primitive $rT.x(p)$ which is equivalent to p with the additional effect of binding the pattern p to the recursive variable x. Within p the term $rec.x$ can be used as a placeholder for the full pattern p. Based on this operators we can define a pattern for a for-loop nest using

$$rT.x(\$l : forStmt(\neg forStmt(\_) \vee rec.x)) \quad (10)$$

where $forStmt(b)$ matches any for-loop with a body matching the pattern b. The variable $\$l$ will be bound to a list of all loops of the matched loop nest.

Finally, patterns should provide a means to match the input for transformation rules. For instance, the rule

$$\{\$xs, \{\}, \$ys\} \rightarrow \{\$xs, \$ys\} \quad (11)$$

is designed to match any compound statement which includes an empty compound statement and to eliminate this inner statement. On the right hand side of the rule the replacement is specified by a template utilizing the variables of the left hand side. Also, unlike all previous examples, in this case the pattern variables $\$xs$ and $\$ys$ match lists of trees instead of individual trees.

3 Method

Our approach is divided into two layers – the *core primitives*, defining its expressive power and a variety of *derived constructs* created by composing core primitives to provide more user-friendly, domain-specific connectors. This separation enables essential algorithms including the pattern matching to focus on a minimal set of constructs while the developers utilizing our system can define patterns and rules using constructs customized for their specific domain, e.g. an IR. Furthermore, potential modifications on the target structure during the course of its development can be reflected within the layer of derived constructs, thereby effectively adjusting all patterns built on top of those.

Within this sections the formal foundation and the core primitives of our patterns and replacements are specified while derived constructs are covered within the following two sections.

3.1 Tree Structure

Before defining a grammar for patterns and replacements a definition of the structures to be operated on has to be provided.

Let $\mathbb{A}$ be a set of atomic values (e.g. the union of integers, names and booleans) and $\mathbb{K}$ be a set of the node types to be distinguished. Any tree generated by the production

$$T ::= a \mid k(T^*)$$

where $a \in \mathbb{A}$ and $k \in \mathbb{K}$ is a valid input for our infrastructure.

This definition is generic enough to cover arbitrary trees. In particular it does not depend on a fixed arity for any node type $k \in \mathbb{K}$. For the remainder of this paper, let $\mathbb{T}$ be the set of all trees generated by the production rule given above for suitable sets $\mathbb{A}$ and $\mathbb{K}$.

3.2 Patterns

Within our framework we distinguish two kinds of patterns – tree and list patterns. While tree patterns describe the structure of individual trees, list patterns cover the composition of lists of trees (=forests).

Let $\mathbb{V}$ be a set of variable identifiers. Tree patterns ϕ and list patterns ψ are generated by the following pair of mutually recursive production rules

$$\phi ::= \_ \mid t \mid \neg\phi \mid \phi \wedge \phi \mid \phi \vee \phi \mid \_(\psi) \mid k(\psi) \mid x : \phi \mid aT(\phi) \mid rT.x(\phi) \mid rec.x$$

$$\psi ::= \epsilon \mid \phi \mid \psi, \psi \mid \psi \vee \psi \mid x : \psi \mid \psi^*$$

where $t \in \mathbb{T}$, $k \in \mathbb{K}$, $x \in \mathbb{V}$ and ϵ is the empty list. Furthermore, let Φ be the set of all possible tree patterns and Ψ be the set of all list patterns.

Semantics. We define the semantics of patterns by defining the sets $T_\phi \subseteq \mathbb{T}$ and $T_\psi \subseteq \mathbb{T}^*$, matched by a tree pattern ϕ and a list pattern ψ respectively.

Let $t, m, n, r \vdash \phi$ denote the fact that the tree $t \in \mathbb{T}$ matches the tree pattern ϕ, and $s, m, n, r \vdash \psi$ denote the fact that the sequence $s \in \mathbb{T}^*$ matches the list pattern ψ, based on the tree variable mapping $m : \mathbb{V} \to \mathbb{T}$, the list variable mapping $n : \mathbb{V} \to \mathbb{T}^*$, and the recursive context map $r : \mathbb{V} \to \Phi \times (\mathbb{V} \to \mathbb{T}) \times (\mathbb{V} \to \mathbb{T}^*)$. The following rules provide a inductive definition of the relation $\vdash$ based on the structure of a tree pattern ϕ

$$
\begin{array}{lll}
t,m,n,r \vdash \_ & \text{iff } \mathit{true} & \text{(wildcard)}\\
t,m,n,r \vdash t & \text{iff } t = t & \text{(constant)}\\
t,m,n,r \vdash \neg\phi & \text{iff not } t,m',n',r \vdash \phi \text{ and } m \subseteq m' \text{ and } n \subseteq n' & \text{(negation)}\\
t,m,n,r \vdash \phi_1 \wedge \phi_2 & \text{iff } t,m',n',r \vdash \phi_1 \text{ and } t,m,n,r \vdash \phi_2 & \\
 & \quad \text{and } m' \subseteq m \text{ and } n' \subseteq n & \text{(and)}\\
t,m,n,r \vdash \phi_1 \vee \phi_2 & \text{iff } t,m,n,r \vdash \phi_1 \text{ or } t,m,n,r \vdash \phi_2 & \text{(or)}\\
t,m,n,r \vdash \_(\psi) & \text{iff } t = k(t_1,\ldots,t_l) \text{ and } [t_1,\ldots,t_l],m,n,r \vdash \psi & \text{(any node)}\\
t,m,n,r \vdash k(\psi) & \text{iff } t = k(t_1,\ldots,t_l) \text{ and } [t_1,\ldots,t_l],m,n,r \vdash \psi & \text{(node)}\\
t,m,n,r \vdash x : \phi & \text{iff } t, m \setminus \{x\}, n, r \vdash \phi \text{ and } (x \mapsto t) \in m & \text{(var)}\\
t,m,n,r \vdash aT(\phi) & \text{iff } t' \text{ subtree of } t \text{ and } t',m,n,r \vdash \phi & \text{(any tree)}\\
t,m,n,r \vdash rT.x(\phi) & \text{iff } t,m,n,\{x \mapsto (\phi,m,n)\} \oplus r \vdash \phi & \text{(recursion)}\\
t,m,n,r \vdash rec.x & \text{iff } x \mapsto (\phi,m',n') \in r \text{ and } t,m',n',r \vdash \phi & \text{(rec. end)}
\end{array}
$$

and a list pattern ψ

$$
\begin{array}{lll}
s,m,n,r \vdash \epsilon & \text{iff } s = \epsilon & \text{(empty)}\\
s,m,n,r \vdash \phi & \text{iff } s = [t] \text{ and } t,m,n,r \vdash \phi & \text{(single)}\\
s,m,n,r \vdash \psi_1,\psi_2 & \text{iff } s = s_1,s_2 \text{ and} & \\
 & \quad s_1,m,n,r \vdash \psi_1 \text{ and } s_2,m,n,r \vdash \psi_2 & \text{(sequence)}\\
s,m,n,r \vdash \psi_1 \vee \psi_2 & \text{iff } s,m,n,r \vdash \psi_1 \text{ or } s,m,n,r \vdash \psi_2 & \text{(or)}\\
s,m,n,r \vdash x : \psi & \text{iff } s,m,n \setminus \{x\}, r \vdash \psi \text{ and } (x \mapsto s) \in n & \text{(var)}\\
s,m,n,r \vdash \psi^* & \text{iff } s = \epsilon \text{ or} & \\
 & \quad s = s_1,s_2 \text{ and } s_1,m_1,n_1,r \vdash \psi \text{ and} & \\
 & \quad s_2,m_2,n_2,r \vdash \psi* \text{ and } m \subseteq m_1 \text{ and} & \text{(repetition)}\\
 & \quad m \subseteq m_2 \text{ and } n \subseteq n_1 \text{ and } n \subseteq n_2 &
\end{array}
$$

where all free variables are existentially quantified, s_1, s_2 denotes the concatenation of two sequences s_1 and s_2, and $A \oplus B$ denotes the mapping obtained by overriding and extending B by the relations in A. A tree $t \in \mathbb{T}$ is an element of T_ϕ if there are mappings m and n such that $t, m, n, \emptyset \vdash \phi$ holds. Correspondingly, a sequence $s \in \mathbb{T}^*$ is an element of T_ψ if there are mappings m and n such that $s, m, n, \emptyset \vdash \psi$ holds.

3.3 Matches

Let $\mathbb{U}_0 = \mathbb{T} \uplus \{\bot\}$ where $\bot$ is the value assigned to unbound variables. Let $\mathbb{U}_{n+1} = \mathbb{U}_n^*$ for all $n \in \mathbb{N}$. The set $\mathbb{U}$ of potential values assigned to variables is given by

$$\mathbb{U} = \bigcup_{0 \leq i} \mathbb{U}_i$$

Furthermore, let $d_\phi : \mathbb{V} \to \mathbb{N}_0$ be the function assigning every variable $x \in \mathbb{V}$ the repetition-depth of its leftmost, outermost occurrence within a pattern ϕ. Hence, whenever encountering a repetition (ψ^*) or a recursion ($rT.x(\phi)$) along the path from the root of the parse tree of pattern ϕ to the first occurrence of x, the depth is increased by one.

A valid variable match $m : \mathbb{V} \to \mathbb{U}$ of a pattern ϕ assigns each variable $x \in \mathbb{V}$ within ϕ an element of $\mathbb{U}_{d_\phi(x)}$ if x is a tree variable and an element of $\mathbb{U}_{d_\phi(x)+1}$ if x is a list or recursion variable. Let $\mathbb{M}$ denote the set of all variable matches. A matching algorithm needs to verify whether a given tree t matches a pattern ϕ and compute a variable match $m \in \mathbb{M}$ recording the necessary instantiations of the involved variables.

3.4 Replacements

The replacement expression is a representation of a script turning a matched tree $t_m \in \mathbb{T}$ and a match result $m \in \mathbb{M}$ into a new tree substituting t_m. For the definition of replacement expressions we distinguish three types of generator expressions: expressions computing results of type $\mathbb{T}$ (tree generators, τ), results of type $\mathbb{T}^*$ (list generators, σ), and results of type $\mathbb{U}$ (value generators, υ). Their structure is defined by the three production rules

$$\begin{aligned}
\tau &::= \upsilon \mid k\,(\sigma) \mid \tau\,[\tau/\tau] \\
\sigma &::= \upsilon \mid \epsilon \mid [\tau] \mid \sigma, \sigma \\
\upsilon &::= \lambda_c \mid \lambda_t\,(\upsilon) \mid \tau \mid \sigma \mid let\ x = \upsilon\ in\ \upsilon \mid \forall x \in \upsilon\ .\ \upsilon
\end{aligned}$$

where $k \in \mathbb{K}$ is a node type, $\lambda_c : \mathbb{T} \times \mathbb{M} \to \mathbb{U}$ is a function creating values, $\lambda_t : \mathbb{U} \to \mathbb{U}$ is a function transforming values and $x \in \mathbb{V}$ is a variable. Let Δ, Σ and Υ denote the set of expressions being generated by τ, σ and υ respectively.

The semantics of our generator expressions are given by the functions $\Gamma_\Delta : \mathbb{T} \times \mathbb{M} \times \Delta \to \mathbb{T}$, $\Gamma_\Sigma : \mathbb{T} \times \mathbb{M} \times \Sigma \to \mathbb{T}^*$ and $\Gamma_\Upsilon : \mathbb{T} \times \mathbb{M} \times \Upsilon \to \mathbb{U}$ defined by

$$\Gamma_\Delta\,(t, m, \tau) = \begin{cases}
\Gamma_\Upsilon(t, m, \upsilon) & \text{if } \tau \text{ is } \upsilon \text{ and } \Gamma_\Upsilon(t, m, \upsilon) \in \mathbb{T} \quad (expr) \\
k\,(\Gamma_\Sigma(t, m, \sigma)) & \text{if } \tau \text{ is } k\,(\sigma) \quad (node) \\
let\ t_1 = \Gamma_\Delta\,(t, m, \tau_1)\ in & \\
let\ t_2 = \Gamma_\Delta\,(t, m, \tau_2)\ in & \\
let\ t_3 = \Gamma_\Delta\,(t, m, \tau_3)\ in & \\
t_1[t_2/t_3] & \text{if } \tau \text{ is } \tau_1\,[\tau_2/\tau_3] \quad (substitution)
\end{cases}$$

$$\Gamma_\Sigma\,(t, m, \sigma) = \begin{cases}
\Gamma_\Upsilon(t, m, \upsilon) & \text{if } \sigma \text{ is } \upsilon \text{ and } \Gamma_\Upsilon(t, m, \upsilon) \in \mathbb{T}^* \quad (expr) \\
\epsilon & \text{if } \sigma \text{ is } \epsilon \quad (empty) \\
[\Gamma_\Delta\,(t, m, \tau)] & \text{if } \sigma \text{ is } [\tau] \quad (single) \\
\Gamma_\Sigma\,(t, m, \sigma_1), \Gamma_\Sigma\,(t, m, \sigma_2) & \text{if } \sigma \text{ is } \sigma_1, \sigma_2 \quad (sequence)
\end{cases}$$

$$\Gamma_\Upsilon\,(t, m, \upsilon) = \begin{cases}
\lambda_c\,(t, m) & \text{if } \upsilon \text{ is } \lambda_c \quad (ctor) \\
\lambda_t\,(\Gamma_\Upsilon(t, m, \upsilon')) & \text{if } \upsilon \text{ is } \lambda_t\,(\upsilon') \quad (transform) \\
\Gamma_\Delta\,(t, m, \tau) & \text{if } \upsilon \text{ is } \tau \quad (tree) \\
\Gamma_\Sigma\,(t, m, \sigma) & \text{if } \upsilon \text{ is } \sigma \quad (list) \\
\Gamma_\Upsilon\,(t, \{x \mapsto \Gamma_\Upsilon(t, m, \upsilon_1)\} \oplus m, \upsilon_2) & \text{if } \upsilon \text{ is } let\ x = \upsilon_1\ in\ \upsilon_2 \quad (let) \\
let\ [u_1, \ldots, u_n] = \Gamma_\Upsilon\,(t, m, \upsilon_1)\ in & \\
let\ f = \lambda y.\Gamma_\Upsilon\,(t, \{x \mapsto y\} \oplus m, \upsilon_2) & \\
in\ [f\,(u_1), \ldots, f\,(u_n)] & \text{if } \upsilon \text{ is } \forall x \in \upsilon_1\ .\ \upsilon_2 \quad (foreach)
\end{cases}$$

where $t_1[t_2/t_3] \in \mathbb{T}$ denotes the tree obtained by replacing all occurrences of $t_3 \in \mathbb{T}$ within $t_1 \in \mathbb{T}$ by $t_2 \in \mathbb{T}$.

3.5 Bringing it All Together: Rules

Finally, a *rule* is defined by a pair $\phi \to \tau$ where $\phi \in \Phi$ is a tree pattern and $\tau \in \Delta$ is a tree generator expression as defined above. When applying a rule on a tree $t \in \mathbb{T}$ it is determined whether there are mappings m and n such that $t, m, n, \emptyset \vdash \phi$. If so, the match result $m' \in \mathbb{M}$ is computed and utilized to generate the replacement $\Gamma_\Delta(t, m', \tau) \in \mathbb{T}$.

4 Implementation

Our approach has been implemented in the Insieme compiler and runtime project [3]. The Insieme project aims to establish a unified platform for conducting research and developing tools in the field of parallel programming languages. It supports OpenMP, OpenCL, MPI and Cilk as well as extensions and hybrids of those. The foundation of the compiler component is laid by a unified, high-level intermediate representation exhibiting unique properties [4]. Crucially, its structure is constrained to be a tree, not including any back or cross edges. This trait turns the Insieme IR into a convenient domain for our system. Yet, our pattern concept is independent of the actual tree structure. Adapters for handling alternative IRs including GCC's GENERIC [5] as well as the Clang [1] or the Rose AST [7] may be implemented.

Our implementation is based on C++11, and represents patterns and replacements as objects, with common connectors mapped to overloaded C++ operators. This approach has multiple advantages: *composability* (simple pattern composition using variables, operators and functions), *extensibility* (new user-defined constructs may be added), *reliability* (pattern fragments can be tested independently using common unit testing frameworks, and their types and arities are checked at compile time), and *productivity* (all integrated development environment features including code completion apply to patterns, and users are not required to learn a new language syntax). The examples in Section 5 illustrate some of these advantages.

Due to overloading, multiple variations of the same pattern construct can be offered, which is particularly useful when defining derived constructs dealing with IR primitives. For instance, there might be two overloaded functions

```
TreePattern forStmt() { ... /* some k(..) primitive */ ... }
TreePattern forStmt(const TreePattern& body) { ... }
```

where the first creates a pattern matching any for loop while the latter allows the user to constrain the body of any matched loop. Based on those, the statements

```
auto noFor = !forStmt();
auto p = forStmt(noFor) | forStmt(forStmt(noFor));
```

create a pattern p matching a single for loop or two perfectly nested loops.

The Matching Algorithm. The centerpiece of our system is the pattern matching algorithm. In our implementation it is based on a back-tracking approach following the rules presented in Section 3.2. While for most primitives the check whether a given tree matches the corresponding pattern is straightforward (e.g. the constant t, wildcards, negations and conjunctions) the processing of a few primitives requires more sophisticated steps. For instance, to determine whether a forest s satisfies a pattern ψ_1, ψ_2 the sequence s needs to be split up into two sub-sequences s_1 and s_2. However, the splitting point can only be guessed at this point – and in case it was wrong altered in a back-tracking step.

To increase the probability of guessing right as soon as possible we employ several pruning heuristics. For instance, if a sequence pattern of the shape $\psi_1, \psi_2, \ldots, \psi_n$ contains constant tree patterns ($\psi_i = t$) or patterns demanding a fixed node type (e.g. $\psi_i = k(\ldots)$) these elements are identified within a potential candidate list $t_1, \ldots, t_m$ before the remaining, potentially more complex patterns are matched against the interjacent sub-sequences. Also, memoization is utilized to avoid resolving identical sub-problems multiple times.

Nevertheless, the worst case complexity of our matching algorithm is exponential. However, so far, for real-world patterns encountered within our daily interaction with the system the search space pruning heuristics are effective enough to not impose a substantial performance issue. Also, the system benefits from the limited average length of sequences encountered within ASTs.

5 Examples

In general, when defining sophisticated patterns the definition of auxiliary connectors is beneficial. Therefore, in addition to the constants any (_), anyList (_*), the primitive connector node(...) matching any node with a given child list and the derived connector step(a), which is equivalent to node(*any << a << *any) where the << operator is the sequence connector of list patterns, we have defined the following constructs

```
inline TreePattern all(const TreePattern& a) {
    return rT((a & node(*rec)) | (!a & node(*rec)));
}
inline TreePattern outermost(const TreePattern& a) {
    return rT(a | (!a & node(*rec)));
}
inline TreePattern innermost(const TreePattern& a) {
    return rT((!step(aT(a)) & a) | node(*rec));
}
```

The derived constructs all, outermost and innermost collect all / the outermost / the innermost sub-trees matching a given input pattern. Based on those, patterns locating loops at corresponding code positions can be constructed by

```
auto a = all(var("x", forStmt()));
auto b = outermost(var("x", forStmt()));
auto c = innermost(var("x", forStmt()));
```

Also, a pattern identifying a used variable and all its accesses is created by

```
auto x = var("x");
auto use = !declStmt() & step(x);
auto p = aT(declStmt(x)) & aT(use) & all(var("y",use));
```

The resulting pattern p checks for the presence of a declaration defining a utilized variable x and collects all its uses within the pattern variable y.

A Real-World Transformation. To demonstrate the applicability of our system to more complex tasks we present a transformation designed to eliminate redundant sync calls within Cilk applications, which was used in a recent publication [9]. A sync is deemed redundant if there has not been any spawn invocation since the last sync.

Let spawn and sync be constants representing patterns matching applications of the corresponding operators. In a first step we define the pattern

```
auto unsynced = rT(spawn | node(*any << aT(rec) << *!sync));
```

matching code fragments potentially resulting in an unsynchronized state. This is the case for a plain spawn statement or whenever an arbitrarily nested spawn is not followed by a sync on the same or an enclosing scope. In the next step the predicate unsynced is utilized to define the predicate synced as well as the desired pattern p identifying redundant sync statements:

```
auto synced = !unsynced;
auto p = compound(
    opt(*any << sync) << *synced << var("x", sync) << *any
);
```

The pattern p searches code fragments in which an optional (opt (..)) safe sequence of explicitly (on the same scope) or implicitly (nested) synchronized statements is followed by a sync call, which gets bound to variable x. The replacement expression

```
auto r = substitute(root, var("x"), noop);
```

can be utilized to generate a proper substitute for any matched statement. Here root is the root of the matched sub-tree, var("x") extracts the value bound to variable x and noop is a constant representing an expression conducting no operation. It replaces the identified redundant sync call x by a noop. Finally, the following code fragment combines p and r into a (transformation) rule and applies it to a target-code fragment in:

```
Rule syncElimination = Rule(p,r);
auto out = syncElimination(in);
```

The application of the rule includes the computation of a match result for pattern p and forwards it to the replacement expression r to produce the desired result.

6 Related Work

To the best of our knowledge there is no comparable transformation support for high-level source-to-source manipulation frameworks for the IRs of GCC [5],

Clang [1] and Rose [7]. In those popular systems, transformations have to be encoded based on basic IR manipulation utilities. However, some IRs rely on the unification based pattern matching capabilities of their implementation language, including CIL [6] which has been implemented using OCaml. For others, several independent transformation systems are available [8]. Examples include Stratego [11] and TXL (the Tree Transformation Language) [2]. Both are based on unification based term rewriting approaches. The main focus of those transformation systems is on steering the application of rules by fixing *strategies* for applying them, which is beyond the scope of our system.

7 Conclusion

Within this paper we present a novel approach for implementing code transformations within source-to-source compilers. By combining concepts of conventional term rewriting solutions and regular expressions our approach is capable of handling arbitrary tree structures. The expressiveness of our patterns is further extended by the introduction of the aT (any tree) and rT (recursive tree) constructs. We have formalized our approach and provided a list of examples, including a real-world transformation. The latter demonstrated the intuitive, declarative characteristic and practical applicability of our solution.

References

[1] clang: a C language family frontend for LLVM (2012), `http://clang.llvm.org/` (Online May 30, 2013)

[2] Cordy, J.R.: The TXL source transformation language. Science of Computer Programming 61(3), 190–210 (2006)

[3] Insieme Compiler and Runtime Infrastructure. University of Innsbruck, `http://insieme-compiler.org`

[4] Jordan, H., et al.: INSPIRE: The Insieme Parallel Intermediate Representation. In: PACT. ACM (2013) (to be published)

[5] Merrill, J.: Generic and gimple: A new tree representation for entire functions. In: GCC Developers Summit, pp. 171–179 (2003)

[6] Necula, G.C., McPeak, S., Rahul, S.P., Weimer, W.: CIL: Intermediate language and tools for analysis and transformation of C programs. In: Nigel Horspool, R. (ed.) CC 2002. LNCS, vol. 2304, pp. 213–228. Springer, Heidelberg (2002)

[7] Quinlan, D.: ROSE: Compiler support for object-oriented frameworks. Parallel Processing Letters 10(02-03), 215–226 (2000)

[8] The Program Transformation Wiki (2013), `http://program-transformation.org/` (May 30, 2013)

[9] Thoman, P., Jordan, H., Fahringer, T.: Adaptive Granularity Control in Task Parallel Programs Using Multiversioning. In: Wolf, F., Mohr, B., an Mey, D. (eds.) Euro-Par 2013. LNCS, vol. 8097, pp. 164–177. Springer, Heidelberg (2013)

[10] Visser, E.: A survey of rewriting strategies in program transformation systems. ENTCS 57, 109–143 (2001)

[11] Visser, E.: Program transformation with stratego/XT. In: Lengauer, C., Batory, D., Blum, A., Odersky, M. (eds.) Domain-Specific Program Generation. LNCS, vol. 3016, pp. 216–238. Springer, Heidelberg (2004)

Implementing a Systolic Algorithm for QR Factorization on Multicore Clusters with PaRSEC

Guillaume Aupy[1], Mathieu Faverge[2], Yves Robert[1,3], Jakub Kurzak[3], Piotr Luszczek[3], and Jack Dongarra[3]

[1] LIP laboratory - École Normale Supérieure de Lyon, CNRS, INRIA, UCBL, and Université de Lyon, France
[2] Laboratoire LaBRI, IPB ENSEIRB-MatMeca, Bordeaux, France
[3] University of Tennessee Knoxville, USA

Abstract. This article introduces a new systolic algorithm for QR factorization, and its implementation on a supercomputing cluster of multicore nodes. The algorithm targets a virtual 3D-array and requires only local communications. The implementation of the algorithm uses threads at the node level, and MPI for inter-node communications. The complexity of the implementation is addressed with the PaRSEC software, which takes as input a parametrized dependence graph, which is derived from the algorithm, and only requires the user to decide, at the high-level, the allocation of tasks to nodes. We show that the new algorithm exhibits competitive performance with state-of-the-art QR routines on a supercomputer called Kraken, which shows that high-level programming environments, such as PaRSEC, provide a viable alternative to enhance the production of quality software on complex and hierarchical architectures.

1 Introduction

Future exascale machines are projected be massively parallel architectures, with 10^5 to 10^6 nodes, each node itself being equipped with 10^3 to 10^4 cores. At the node level, the architecture is a shared-memory machine, running many parallel threads on the cores. At the machine level, the architecture is a distributed-memory machine. This additional level of hierarchy dramatically complicates the design of new versions of the standard factorization algorithms, that are central to many scientific applications. In particular, the performance of numerical linear algebra kernels are at the heart of many grand challenge applications, and it is of key importance to provide highly efficient implementations of these kernels to leverage the potential of exascale platforms.

This article introduces a new systolic algorithm for QR factorization on clusters of multicore nodes. The main motivation is to enhance the state-of-the-art algorithms, that use tile kernels and several elimination domains per panel, that enforce the inter-node communication between neighbors only. The systolic algorithm targets a 3D torus, which is the underlying interconnection topology of the contemporary and up-coming HPC systems. For instance, Blue Gene/L is a 3D torus of size $64 \times 32 \times 32$ [1], Kraken, a Cray XT 5, is a 3D torus of size $25 \times 16 \times 24$ [2]. In addition, the Cray XT3 and XT4 also are architectures based on a 3D torus [3]. Our systolic algorithm uses a two-level

D. an Mey et al. (Eds.): Euro-Par 2013 Workshops, LNCS 8374, pp. 657–667, 2014.

allocation of tile rows to the faces of the torus cube, in order to restrict the reduction tree for each panel to only local communication.

Implementing such a complex algorithm with low-level primitives would require non-trivial and error-prone programming effort. However, using the PaRSEC software [4] has enabled us to implement, validate, and evaluate the algorithm on Kraken, within a few weeks of development. Although we use a high-level environment, we report competitive performance results with state-of-the-art QR routines, thereby showing that PaRSEC provides a viable alternative to enhance the production of quality software prototypes on complex hierarchical architectures.

The rest of the paper is organized as follows. Section 2 provides background information on QR factorization algorithms, and surveys state-of-the-art algorithms in the literature. Section 4 presents the new systolic algorithm, while Section 5 provides additional details of its implementation using the PaRSEC software. Section 6 presents experimental results obtained on the Kraken supercomputer. Finally, we close with concluding remarks in Section 7.

2 Background

2.1 Tiled-QR Factorization

The general shape of a tiled QR algorithm for a tiled matrix of $m \times n$ tiles, whose rows and columns are indexed from 0, is given in Algorithm 1. Here i and k are tile indices, and operate on square $b \times b$ tiles, where b is the block size. Thus, the actual size of the matrix is $M \times N$, with $M \equiv m \times b$ and $N \equiv n \times b$. The first loop index, k, is the panel index, and $elim(i,\mathbf{CurPiv}(i,k),k)$ is an orthogonal transformation that combines rows i and $\mathbf{CurPiv}(i,k)$ to zero out the tile in position (i,k). Each elimination $elim(i,\mathbf{CurPiv}(i,k),k)$ consists of two sub-steps: (i) first in column k, tile (i,k) is zeroed out (or eliminated) by tile $(\mathbf{CurPiv}(i,k),k)$, which is called the pivot; and (ii) in each subsequent column $j > k$, tiles (i,j) and $(\mathbf{CurPiv}(i,k),j)$ are updated; all these updates are independent and can be triggered as soon as the elimination is completed. The algorithm is entirely characterized by its *elimination list*, which is the ordered list of all the eliminations $elim(i,\mathbf{CurPiv}(i,k),k)$ that are executed.

Algorithm 1. Generic QR algorithm

```
begin
  for k = 0 to min(m,n) − 1 do
    for i = k+1 to m − 1 do
      elim(i, CurPiv(i,k), k)
```

Algorithm 2. Elimination $elim(i,\mathbf{CurPiv}(i,k),k)$

```
begin
  (a) With TS (Triangle on top of square) kernels
  GEQRT(CurPiv(i,k), k)
  TSQRT(i, CurPiv(i,k), k)
  for j = k+1 to n − 1 do
    UNMQR(CurPiv(i,k), k, j)
    TSMQR(i, CurPiv(i,k), k, j)

  (b) With TT (Triangle on top of triangle) kernels
  GEQRT(CurPiv(i,k), k)
  GEQRT(i, k)
  for j = k+1 to n − 1 do
    UNMQR(CurPiv(i,k), k, j)
    UNMQR(i, k, j)
  TTQRT(i, CurPiv(i,k), k)
  for j = k+1 to n − 1 do
    TTMQR(i, CurPiv(i,k), k, j)
```

To implement an orthogonal transformation $elim(i,\mathbf{CurPiv}(i,k),k)$, we can use either *TT* kernels or *TS* kernels, as shown in Algorithm 2. *TT* kernels are needed to allow for several eliminator tiles in a given column, but are less efficient than *TS* kernels. More detailed information on the various kernels is provided elsewhere [5]. In a nutshell, a tile can have three states: square, triangle, and zero. Transitions between these states occur through the following kernels:

- *GEQRT* is the transformation of one square tile to a triangle tile,
- *TSQRT*$(i,\mathbf{CurPiv}(i,k),k)$ is the transformation of a square tile (tile i) into a zero tile, using a triangle tile (tile $\mathbf{CurPiv}(i,k)$) at step k,
- *TTQRT*$(i,\mathbf{CurPiv}(i,k),k)$ is the transformation of a triangle tile (tile i) into a zero tile using a triangle tile (tile $\mathbf{CurPiv}(i,k)$) at step k.

3 Related Work

While the advent of multi-core machines is somewhat recent, there is a long line of papers related to tiled QR factorization. Tiled QR algorithms have first been introduced in Buttari et al. [6,7] and Quintana-Ortí et al. [8] for shared-memory (multi-core) environments, with an initial focus on square matrices. The sequence of eliminations presented in these papers is analogous to the prior work [9], and corresponds to reducing each matrix panel with a flat tree: in each column, there is a unique eliminator, namely the diagonal tile.

The introduction of several eliminators in a given column has a long history [9,10,11,12,13,14]. For shared-memory (multi-core) environments, recent work advocates the use of domain trees [15] to expose more parallelism with several eliminators while enforcing some locality within domains. A recent paper [16] introduces tiled versions of the Greedy algorithm [17] and the Fibonacci scheme [10], it shows that these algorithms are asymptotically optimal.

There are recent efforts for distributed-memory environments. The algorithm of [18] uses a hierarchical approach: for each matrix panel, it combines two levels of reduction trees. First, several local binary trees are applied in parallel, one within each node, and then a global binary tree is applied for the final reduction across nodes. Yet another implementation [19] also uses a hierarchical approach, and it also uses a 1D block distribution. The main difference is that the first level of reduction is performed with a flat tree within each node. Note that the hierarchical algorithm (HQR) used previously [5] can be parametrized to implement this original algorithm [19] as well as a more efficient variant with cyclic layout. The HQR algorithm [5] is the reference algorithm for multi-level clusters: it provides a flexible approach, and allows one to use various elimination trees (Flat, Binary, Fibonacci or Greedy) at each level.

4 The SYSTOLIC-3D Algorithm

Platform and data layout – We first detail the 3D torus architecture. Within a $p \times q \times r$ 3D torus, processor $P_{a,b,c}$ has a direct communication link with processors $P_{a-1 \bmod p,b,c}$, $P_{a+1 \bmod p,b,c}$, with processors $P_{a,b-1 \bmod q,c}$, $P_{a,b+1 \bmod q,c}$, and with processors $P_{a,b,c-1 \bmod r}$, $P_{a,b,c+1 \bmod r}$. We have a $m \times n$ tile matrix. Tiles are mapped as follows: we use a two-level cyclic distribution for the rows (directions a and b in the torus) and a cyclic distribution for the columns (direction c in the torus). The mapping is defined formally as follows: proc P_{abc} is assigned all tiles $T_{t,s}$ such that $t \equiv b \mod q$, $\frac{t-b}{q} \equiv a \mod p$ and $s \equiv c \mod r$. We give an example of the two-level cyclic distribution for the rows in Figure 1a, for a matrix with 27 rows mapped onto a $3 \times 3 \times r$ torus.

General description – As stated in Section 2.1, a tiled-QR algorithm is entirely defined by the ordered list of eliminations. The algorithm eliminates the tiles using a hierarchical approach, using the 3D torus to minimize inter-processor communication contention. In order to do this, pivots should be propagated across physical links in the torus, and only to neighbor nodes, before each elimination. Figure 1 describes the elimination of the first column of the matrix.

Consider a given step k of the factorization. The k-th tile column is distributed across a face of the cube, i.e. a square of $p \times q$ processors (those whose third index is $c_0 \equiv k \mod r$). Let dimension a be "horizontal" and dimension b be "vertical". There are three levels of elimination in the algorithm:

1. The first level of elimination corresponds to local tiles and uses *TS* kernels. There are pq pivots in this step, one for each processor in the square, and they correspond to rows numbered $k, k+1, \cdots, k+pq-1$. These pivots are used to eliminate all local tiles within each processor, hence they do not require any communication across the square. We use a flat tree reduction for this step, but other elimination trees could be chosen freely. This first elimination level is illustrated in Figure 1a when $k = 0$.
2. The second level of elimination consists of concurrent flat trees along the vertical dimension, and uses *TT* kernels (see Figure 1b). There are p pivots for this level, namely the kth elements of rows $k, k+q, \cdots, k+q(q-1)$. Each of these pivots will sequentially eliminate the $q-1$ subsequent tiles, which are located in the corresponding grid column.
3. The third level of the elimination consists of a single flat tree along the horizontal dimension (see Figure 1c). There remains a single pivot, in row k, that sequentially eliminates with *TT* kernels the $q-1$ remaining tiles.

At the end of step k, row number k will have been routed through at most $p+q-2$ physical communication links. The communication pattern is the same for the other faces of the cube. The whole algorithm is summarized in Algorithm 3.

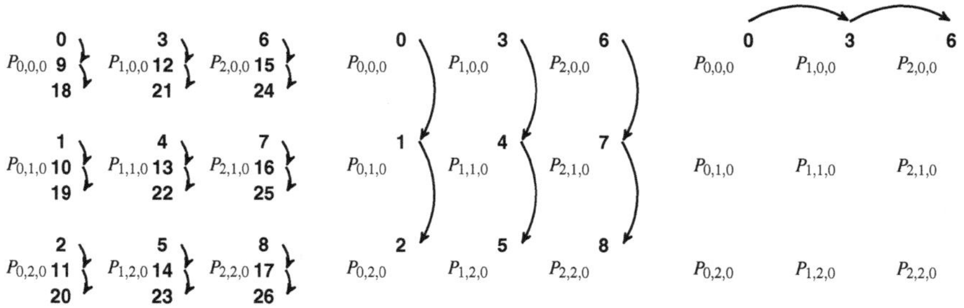

(a) 1st elimination level (b) 2nd elimination level (c) 3rd elimination level

Fig. 1. Elimination in the first panel (panel 0) of all tiles below the diagonal (rows 1 to 27) on a 3×3 processor square (face 0 of the 3*D*-torus)

Algorithm 3. The SYSTOLIC-3D algorithm

```
begin
  for k = 0 to min(m,n) − 1 do
    define i2 ← k mod d ;
    /* Local FlatTree */
    for l = k to k+d^2 − 1 do
      GEQRT(l,k);
      for x = l+d^2 to m − 1 by d^2 do
        TSQRT(x,l,k);
        for j = k+1 to n − 1 do
          UNMQR(l,k,j);
          TSMQR(x,l,k,j);
    // Note that from now on, we
       do not need to use GEQRT
       anymore, all the
       remaining tiles are
       triangles.
    /* Vertical FlatTree */
    for l2 = i2 + 1 to d − 1 do
      TTQRT_V(k+(l2 − i2),k,k);
      for j = k+1 to n − 1 do
        TTMQR_V(k+(l2 −
        i2),k,k,j);
    for l2 = 0 to i2 − 1 do
      TTQRT_V(k+d^2 +(l2 − i2),k,k);
      for j = k+1 to n − 1 do
        TTMQR_V(k+d^2 +(l2 −
        i2),k,k,j);
    for l = k+d to k+d^2 − 1 by d do
      for x = l+1 to (l − i2)+d − 1 do
        TTQRT_V(x,l,k);
        for j = k+1 to n − 1 do
          TTMQR_V(x,l,k,j);
      for x = l − i2 to l − 1 do
        TTQRT_V(x,l,k);
        for j = k+1 to n − 1 do
          TTMQR_V(x,l,k,j);
    /* Horizontal FlatTree */
    for x = k+d to k+d^2 − 1 by d do
      TTQRT_H(x,k,k);
      for j = k+1 to n − 1 do
        TTMQR_H(x,k,k,j);
```

5 Implementation with PaRSEC

This section details the implementation of the SYSTOLIC-3D algorithm using PaRSEC. With an infinite number of resources, the scheduling could follow a greedy heuristic: the execution would progress as fast as possible.

The elimination list of the algorithm is the composition of the reduction trees at all of the different levels. All eliminators are known before the execution. Each component of an elimination is triggered as soon as possible, i.e., as soon as all dependencies are satisfied: first we have the elimination of the tile, and then the updates in the trailing panels. Note that the overall elimination scheme is complex, and mixes the elimination of tiles at all levels. However, with a fixed number of resources, it is necessary to decide an order of execution of the tasks, hence to schedule them: this is achieved through the PaRSEC environment.

5.1 Introduction to PaRSEC

PaRSEC is a high-performance fully-distributed scheduling environment for systems of micro-tasks. It takes as input a problem-size-independent, symbolic representation of a Direct Acyclic Graph (DAG) of tasks, and schedules them at runtime on a distributed parallel machine of multi-cores. Data movements are expressed implicitly by the data flow between the tasks in the DAG representation. The runtime engine is then responsible for actually moving the data from one machine (node) to another, using an underlying communication mechanism such as MPI. A full description of PaRSEC, and the implementation of classical linear algebra factorizations in this environment, is provided elsewhere [20,21].

To implement any QR algorithm in PaRSEC, it is sufficient to give an abstract representation of all the tasks (eliminations and updates) that constitute the QR factorization, and how data flows from one task to the other. Since a tiled QR algorithm is fully determined by its elimination list, it suffices to provide a function, that the runtime engine is capable of evaluating, and that computes this elimination list. The PaRSEC object obtained in this way is generic: when instantiating a PaRSEC QR factorization, the user simply gives the size of the platform ($p \times q \times r$), defining a new DAG at each instantiation. Note that this DAG is not fully generated: PaRSEC keeps only a parametric representation of the DAG in memory, and interprets symbolic expressions at runtime to explicitly represent only the ready tasks at any given time. This technique is similar to the Parametrized Tasks Graphs [20], and to HQR [5].

At runtime, task executions trigger data movements, and create new ready tasks, following the dependencies defined by the elimination list. Tasks that are ready to compute are scheduled according to a data-reuse heuristic: each core will try to execute close successors of the last task it ran under the assumption, that these tasks require data that was recently touched by the completed task. This policy is tuned by the user through a priority function: among the ready tasks for a given core, the choice is done by following a hint from this function. To balance the load between cores, tasks on the same node in the algorithm (residing on the same shared memory machine) are shared between the computing cores, and a NUMA-aware job stealing policy is implemented. The user is responsible for defining the affinity between data and tasks, and to distribute the data between the computing nodes. Thus, he defines which tasks should execute on which node, and he is responsible for this level of load balancing. In our case, the data distribution is the data layout given in Section 4. Since all kernel operations modify a single tile (or a tile and its reflectors, which are distributed in the same way), we chose the strategy "owner computes" for the tasks: tasks' affinity is set to the node that owns the data that is going to be modified, and the input data might need to be transferred from other nodes.

5.2 Implementation Details

The implementation of SYSTOLIC-3D in PaRSEC involves limited effort compared with other software strategies, that we are aware of. We only implemented a few functions that are used by PaRSEC to generate the dependency graph. They depend on the current elimination step k as follows:

1. **CurPiv**(i,k), returns the pivot to use for the row i at step k;
2. **NextPiv**(pivot, k, start), returns the next row which will use the row "pivot" as a pivot in step k after it has been used by row "start";
3. **PrevPiv**(pivot, k, start), returns the previous row which used the row "pivot" as a pivot in step k before it has been used by row "start";

We have decomposed each one of these functions in two sub-functions: (i) a low-level function, which takes all the *TS* operations into account, and which calls the *local FlatTree* because operations are local to each node; and (ii) a high-level function, which takes all the *TT* operations into account, and where the pivot will "move" across the architecture. Using these functions, PaRSEC is able to construct a dependency graph between the different tiles in order to run the algorithm as efficiently as possible.

6 Experimental Evaluation

In this section, we report experimental results obtained on Kraken. We compare the SYSTOLIC-3D algorithm with a number of competing implementations such as vendor library routines and recent algorithms from literature.

6.1 Experimental Setup

All runs were done on the Kraken supercomputer at the National Institute for Computational Science [2]. The Kraken machine is a Cray XT5 system operated by the University of Tennessee and located in Oak Ridge, Tennessee, U.S.A. The entire system consists of 9048 computing nodes. The experiments presented here used up to 1989 nodes, which is about one fifth of the machine. Each node contains two 2.6 GHz six-core AMD Opteron (Istanbul) processors, 16 GB of memory and the Cray SeaStar2+ interconnect.

We have compared SYSTOLIC-3D with several state-of-the-art algorithms, using three matrix sizes: (i) small matrices, of size $M = N = 10,368$; (ii) medium matrices, of size $M = N = 20,736$; and large matrices, of size $M = N = 41,472$. Here is the list of the algorithms used for comparison:

- SYSTOLIC-3D is the algorithm described in this paper. Table 1 shows the 3D grid configuration (p,q,r) used for each matrix size ($M = N$) and for each total number of nodes T, where $T = p \times q \times r$. Note, that there is no guarantee, that the nodes assigned to the experiment will indeed form the desired 3D torus. They can be scattered across the machine. To the best of our knowledge, the only way to guarantee that assigned nodes indeed form a 3D torus would be to reserve the entire Kraken machine: something beyond our capabilities.
- HQR is the hierarchical QR factorization algorithm [5], which was also implemented using the PaRSEC software. We compare several variants of HQR, which all use the same FLAT-TREE low-level reduction tree, but which use different high level (or distributed) reduction trees [5]:
  1. HQR-FLAT uses the FLATTREE reduction;
  2. HQR-FIBO uses the FIBONACCI reduction;
  3. HQR-BINARY uses the BINARYTREE reduction;
  4. HQR-GREEDY uses the GREEDY reduction.

  Because HQR uses a 2D-processor grid, we use T nodes configured as a $(pq) \times r$ 2D grid.
- SYSTOLIC-2D is a variant of SYSTOLIC-3D where q is set to 1 and then runs on a 2D grid of size $(pq) \times r$. We introduced it for the sake of comparison with the HQR variants – SYSTOLIC-2D can be viewed as yet another HQR variant with a new high-level reduction tree.

We compare all the previous algorithms that were implemented with PaRSEC with the following algorithms from the literature [22] on the very same hardware:

- SYSTOLIC-1D is the virtual systolic array decomposition [22]. As its name indicates, it targets a 1D-linear array of processors. Note that SYSTOLIC-1D has been implemented using a hand-written communication engine over MPI – not PaRSEC.

Table 1. Partition of the nodes into a 3D torus for each matrix size and each total number of nodes T

$M=N=10,368$				$M=N=20,736$				$M=N=41,472$			
T	$p\times q\times r$	T	$p\times q\times r$	T	$p\times q\times r$	T	$p\times q\times r$	T	$p\times q\times r$	T	$p\times q\times r$
4	$2\times2\times1$	52	$6\times3\times3$	16	$4\times2\times2$	210	$6\times5\times7$	64	$4\times4\times4$	840	$10\times6\times14$
12	$3\times2\times2$	80	$5\times4\times4$	48	$4\times4\times3$	320	$8\times5\times8$	192	$8\times4\times6$	1232	$11\times7\times16$
18	$3\times3\times2$	96	$6\times4\times4$	80	$5\times4\times4$	405	$9\times5\times9$	336	$7\times6\times8$	1632	$12\times8\times17$
28	$5\times2\times3$	128	$8\times4\times4$	112	$6\times4\times5$	486	$9\times6\times9$	480	$8\times6\times10$	1989	$13\times9\times17$
42	$7\times2\times3$			168	$7\times4\times6$			648	$9\times6\times12$		

- HPL 4/3 N^3 is the virtual performance of the High Performance Linpack LU factorization using the flops count of QR: $O(\frac{4}{3}N^3)$.
- LibSci QR is the QR factorization from ScaLAPACK used in the Cray Scientific Library.
- HPL 2/3 N^3 is the High Performance Linpack LU factorization with the actual flops count of LU: $O(\frac{2}{3}N^3)$.

For each set of results, we ran the different algorithms ten times, and we take the average performance over all these executions.

Our decision to include performance numbers for HPL's LU factorization might seem controversial due to the fundamental differences between the LU and QR factorization algorithms including their numerical properties, operation-count, and the runtime behavior. However, from the end-user perspective, both LU and QR solve a system of linear equations, both are backward stable, and only an explicitly stated rule [23] prohibits QR from scoring the entrants to the TOP500 ranking. With this in mind, we include results for the LU factorization, and include the case when we pretend that LU performs as many Flops as QR: $O(\frac{4}{3}N^3)$ (this may be simply treated as time-to-run comparison) as well as the case where we report the actual performance rate based on the actual amount of floating point operations LU: $O(\frac{2}{3}N^3)$.

6.2 Performance Results

The first observation is that PaRSEC-based algorithms (Systolic-3D, Systolic-2D and all HQR variants) always perform better than LibSci QR and HPL 4/3 N^3, the QR factorization algorithms from Kraken's standard software stack. This observation holds for all matrix sizes, and this makes our main point: owing to the PaRSEC system, we have been able to experiment with a variety of complex, hierarchical algorithms, without paying the price of lengthy development effort.

Note, how Systolic-3D , HQR variants, and Systolic-1D compare with each other. Systolic-3D has approximatively the same efficiency as HQR-Binary and HQR-Greedy on all matrix sizes. For matrices of size $M=N=10,368$, HQR-Flat is 54% more efficient on 1536 cores ($\approx$ 1700 GFlops compared to $\approx$ 1100 GFlops), and Systolic-1D ($\approx$ 1900) GFlops is 73% more efficient. This difference increases with the size of the matrix: for $M=N=41,472$, HQR-Flat reaches $\approx$ 16000 GFlops, and Systolic-1D reaches $\approx$ 21000 GFlops on 23868 cores, where Systolic-3D

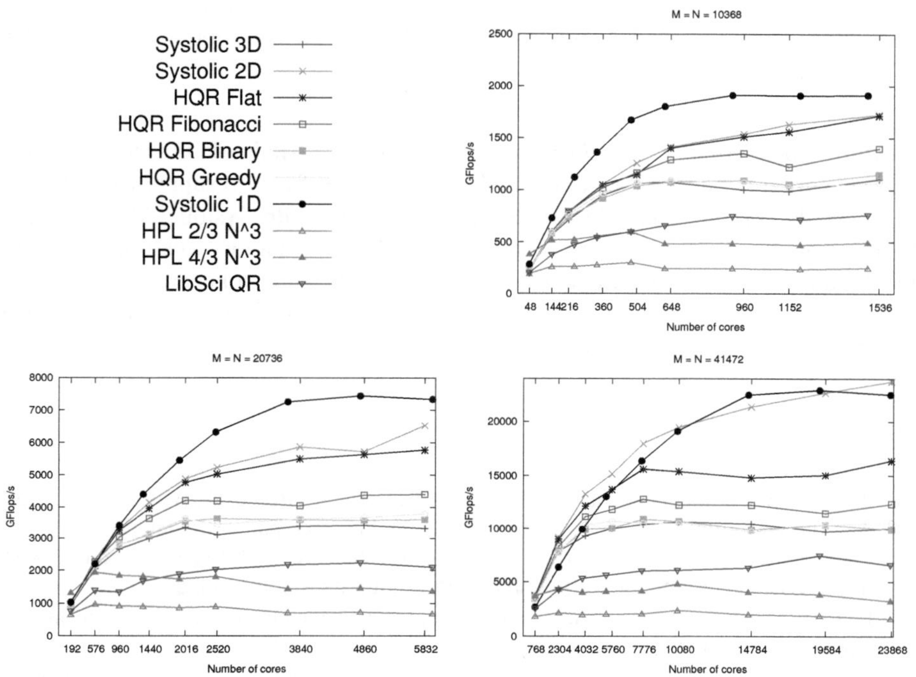

Fig. 2. Performance of the various algorithms for different problem sizes

is bound by $\approx$ 10600 GFlops (half the performance of SYSTOLIC-1D). However, for $M = N = 41,472$, and with a small number of cores, SYSTOLIC-3D performs better than SYSTOLIC-1D.

As mentioned earlier, it is infeasible to guarantee, that the assignment of Kraken nodes from our batch queue submissions form a true 3D torus. We expected the constraints to be less stringent when using a 2D torus, and this turns out quite true: SYSTOLIC-2D, the implementation of SYSTOLIC-3D on a 2D torus, performs very well for all matrix sizes, and is the best algorithm for larger matrices of size $M = N = 41,472$.

7 Conclusion

In this article, we have presented a systolic QR factorization algorithm, SYSTOLIC-3D, which aims to minimize the amount of communication in the reduction trees. We have shown that mapping this systolic algorithm onto a 3D torus leads to a competitive factorization kernel with strong scaling capabilities. As of today, the main limitation to fully validate the experiments is the lack of possibility to reserve an actual 3D torus architecture on the Kraken supercomputer. Still, the performance of the new algorithm, together with its 2D counterpart are very encouraging. Both versions dramatically outperform LIBSCI QR and HPL 4/3 N^3, the vendor QR factorization implementations on Kraken, and also HPL 2/3 N^3, the widely-used LU factorization routine (despite its favorable flop count). This last observation fully demonstrates the usefulness of the

PaRSEC system, which has enabled us to experiment with complex, hierarchical QR algorithms, without paying the price of lengthy and complex development effort of distributed memory software engineering.

Acknowledgements. Yves Robert is with Institut Universitaire de France. This work was supported in part by the ANR *RESCUE* project. It was also supported in part by grant #SHF-1117062: "Parallel Unified Linear algebra with Systolic ARrays (PULSAR)" from the *National Science Foundation* (NSF). The authors would like to thank the *National Institute for Computational Sciences* (NICS) for a generous time allocation on the Kraken supercomputer. Finally, the authors would also like to thank Thomas Hérault for his help with PaRSEC.

References

1. Adiga, N.R., Almási, G., Almasi, G.S., Aridor, Y., Barik, R., Beece, D., Bellofatto, R., et al.: An overview of the BlueGene/L supercomputer. In: Supercomputing Conference (2002)
2. The National Institute for Computational Sciences: Kraken machine size, http://www.nics.tennessee.edu/computing-resources/machine_size
3. Bhatele, A., Kale, L.V.: Application-specific topology-aware mapping for three dimensional topologies. In: IPDPS (2008)
4. Bosilca, G., Bouteiller, A., Danalis, A., Herault, T., Lemarinier, P., Dongarra, J.: DAGuE: A generic distributed DAG engine for high performance computing. Parallel Computing 38(1), 37–51 (2012)
5. Dongarra, J., Faverge, M., Herault, T., Jacquelin, M., Langou, J., Robert, Y.: Hierarchical QR factorization algorithms for multi-core clusters. Parallel Computing (2013)
6. Buttari, A., Langou, J., Kurzak, J., Dongarra, J.: Parallel tiled QR factorization for multicore architectures. Concurrency: Practice and Experience 20(13), 1573–1590 (2008)
7. Buttari, A., Langou, J., Kurzak, J., Dongarra, J.: A class of parallel tiled linear algebra algorithms for multicore architectures. Parallel Computing 35, 38–53 (2009)
8. Quintana-Ortí, G., Quintana-Ortí, E.S., van de Geijn, R.A., Zee, F.G.V., Chan, E.: Programming matrix algorithms-by-blocks for thread-level parallelism. ACM Transactions on Mathematical Software 36(3) (2009)
9. Sameh, A., Kuck, D.: On stable parallel linear systems solvers. J. ACM 25, 81–91 (1978)
10. Modi, J., Clarke, M.: An alternative Givens ordering. Numerische Mathematik 43, 83–90 (1984)
11. Pothen, A., Raghavan, P.: Distributed orthogonal factorization: Givens and Householder algorithms. SIAM J. Scientific Computing 10(16), 1113–1134 (1989)
12. da Cunha, R.D., Becker, D., Patterson, J.C.: New parallel (rank-revealing) *QR* factorization algorithms. In: Monien, B., Feldmann, R.L. (eds.) Euro-Par 2002. LNCS, vol. 2400, pp. 677–686. Springer, Heidelberg (2002)
13. Demmel, J.W., Grigori, L., Hoemmen, M., Langou, J.: Communication-avoiding parallel and sequential QR and LU factorizations: theory and practice. Technical Report 204, LAPACK Working Note (2008)
14. Langou, J.: Computing the R of the QR factorization of tall and skinny matrices using MPI_Reduce. Technical Report 1002.4250, arXiv (2010)
15. Hadri, B., Ltaief, H., Agullo, E., Dongarra, J.: Tile QR factorization with parallel panel processing for multicore architectures. In: IPDPS (2010)

16. Bouwmeester, H., Jacquelin, M., Langou, J., Robert, Y.: Tiled QR factorization algorithms. In: SC. ACM/ IEEE Computer Society Press (2011)
17. Cosnard, M., Robert, Y.: Complexity of parallel QR factorization. Journal of the A.C.M. 33(4), 712–723 (1986)
18. Agullo, E., Coti, C., Dongarra, J., Herault, T., Langou, J.: QR factorization of tall and skinny matrices in a grid computing environment. In: IPDPS (2010)
19. Song, F., Ltaief, H., Hadri, B., Dongarra, J.: Scalable tile communication-avoiding QR factorization on multicore cluster systems. In: SC. ACM/IEEE Computer Society Press (2010)
20. Bosilca, G., Bouteiller, A., Danalis, A., Herault, T., Lemarinier, P., Dongarra, J.: DAGuE: A generic distributed DAG engine for high performance computing. In: HIPS (2011)
21. Bosilca, G., Bouteiller, A., Danalis, A., Faverge, M., Haidar, A., Herault, T., Kurzak, J., Langou, J., Lemarinier, P., Ltaief, H., et al.: Flexible development of dense linear algebra algorithms on massively parallel architectures with DPLASMA. In: PDSEC (2011)
22. Kurzak, J., Luszczek, P., Gates, M., Yamazaki, I., Dongarra, J.: Virtual systolic array for QR decomposition. In: IPDPS. IEEE Computer Society Press (2013)
23. Dongarra, J.J., Luszczek, P., Petitet, A.: The LINPACK benchmark: Past, present, and future. Concurrency and Computation: Practice and Experience 15, 1–18 (2003)

Sixth Workshop on Resiliency in High Performance Computing in Clusters, Clouds, and Grids (Resilience 2013)*

Stephen L. Scott and Chokchai (Box) Leangsuksun

General Co-Chairs

Clusters, Clouds, and Grids are three different computational paradigms with the intent or potential to support High Performance Computing (HPC). Currently, they consist of hardware, management, and usage models particular to different computational regimes, e.g., high performance cluster systems designed to support tightly coupled scientific simulation codes typically utilize high-speed interconnects and commercial cloud systems designed to support software as a service (SAS) do not. However, in order to support HPC, all must at least utilize large numbers of resources and hence effective HPC in any of these paradigms must address the issue of resiliency at large-scale.

Recent trends in HPC systems have clearly indicated that future increases in performance, in excess of those resulting from improvements in single- processor performance, will be achieved through corresponding increases in system scale, i.e., using a significantly larger component count. As the raw computational performance of these HPC systems increases from today's many-petascale to tomorrow's exascale capability, their number of computational, networking, and storage components will grow from the several hundred thousand computation cores in today's systems to one million or more in the foreseeable future. This substantial growth in system scale, and the resulting component count, poses a challenge for HPC system and application software with respect to fault tolerance and resilience.

Furthermore, recent experiences on extreme-scale HPC systems with non-recoverable soft errors, i.e., bit flips in memory, cache, registers, and logic added another major source of concern. The probability of such errors not only grows with system size, but also with increasing architectural vulnerability caused by employing accelerators, such as FPGAs and GPUs, and by shrinking nanometer technology. Reactive fault tolerance technologies, such as checkpoint/restart, are unable to handle high failure rates due to associated overheads, while proactive resiliency technologies, such as migration, simply fail as random soft errors can't be predicted. Moreover, soft errors may even remain undetected resulting in silent data corruption.

The goal of this workshop is to bring together experts in the area of fault tolerance and resilience for HPC to present the latest achievements and to discuss the challenges ahead. We would like to thank our program co-chairs, Christian Engelmann and Patrick Bridges, along with our program committee, for putting together such a strong program of 7 high-quality papers for publication.

* The rights of this work are transferred to the extent transferable according to title 17 U.S.C. 105.

D. an Mey et al. (Eds.): Euro-Par 2013 Workshops, LNCS 8374, pp. 668–669, 2014.

Resilience Workshop History and Websites

Resilience 2013 held in conjunction with EuroPar 2013 in Aachen - Germany, is the follow-on workshop to the successful *Resilience 2012* held in conjunction with EuroPar 2012 in Rhodes Island Greece, *Resilience 2011* held in conjunction with EuroPar 2011 in Bordeaux - France, *Resilience 2010* held with GGCRID 2010 in Melbourne - Australia, *Resilience 2009* in Munich - Germany, and the earlier *Resilience 2008* held in conjunction with CCGrid in Leon - France. Other past events associated with the *Resilience 2013* workshop include the: *High Availability and Performance Computing Workshop (HAPCW)* series in 2003-2006, 2008; and *HPC Resiliency Summit: Workshop on Resiliency for Petascale HPC* in 2008-2010 in Santa Fe, New Mexico. Also, there is the *International Conference on Availability, Reliability and Security (ARES)* from 2006-2008.

Links to workshop sites:
(Replacing YEAR with numeric value.)

- Resilience 2011-2013: xcr.cenit.latech.edu/resilienceYEAR
- HAPCW 2003-2006, 2008: xcr.cenit.latech.edu/hapcwYEAR
- Resiliency Summit: www.csm.ornl.gov/srt/conferences/index.html
- Resiliency Workshop 2008-2010: xcr.cenit.latech.edu/resilienceYEAR

Program

The Resilience 2013 workshop program included presentations of contributed peer-reviewed papers, opening and closing remarks, as well as an open discussion session at the workshop closing.

- Opening Remarks, Stephen L. Scott - Workshop Co-Chair
- *"Evaluate the Viability of Application-Driven Cooperative CPU/GPU Fault Detection,"* Dong Li, Seyong Lee and Jeffrey Vetter
- *"GPU Behavior on a Large HPC Cluster,"* Nathan Debardeleben, Sean Blanchard, Laura Monroe, Phil Romero, Daryl Grunau, Craig Idler and Cornell Wright
- *"A Case for Adaptive Redundancy for HPC Resilience,"* Saurabh Hukerikar, Pedro C. Diniz and Robert F. Lucas
- *"Reliable Service Allocation in Clouds with Memory and Capacity Constraints,"* Olivier Beaumont, Lionel Eyraud-Dubois, Pierre Pesneau and Paul Renaud-Goud
- *"Model-Driven Resilience Assessment of Modifications to HPC Infrastructures,"* Christian Straube and Dieter Kranzlmüller
- *"Asking the right questions: benchmarking fault-tolerant extreme-scale systems,"* Patrick Widener, Kurt Ferreira, Scott Levy, Patrick Bridges, Dorian Arnold and Ron Brightwell
- *"Using Performance Tools to Support Experiments in HPC Resilience,"* Thomas Naughton, Swen Böhm, Christian Engelmann and Geoffroy Vallée
- Discussion & Closing Remarks, Stephen L. Scott - Workshop Co-Chair

Evaluating the Viability of Application-Driven Cooperative CPU/GPU Fault Detection

Dong Li, Seyong Lee, and Jeffrey S. Vetter

Oak Ridge National Laboratory, Oak Ridge, TN
{lid1,lees2,vetter}@ornl.gov

Abstract. Trends in high performance computing are bringing increased heterogeneity among the computational resources within a single machine. The heterogeneous CPU/GPU platforms, however, exacerbate resilience problems faced by current large-scale systems. How to design efficient resilience strategies is critical for the wider adoption of heterogeneous platforms for future exascale systems. The conventional resilience strategy for GPU brings significant performance and power overhead, because they employ a one-size-fits-all approach to enforce uniform data protection. In addition, the isolation between CPU and GPU protection loses potential optimization opportunities provided by the heterogeneous CPU/GPU platforms. In this paper, we explore the viability of using an application-driven CPU/GPU cooperative method to detect faults occurred on GPU global memory. By selectively protecting application-critical data and leveraging time and space redundancy in CPU to detect faults, we bring only 2.2% performance overhead while capturing more than 90% errors that cause incorrect application results.

Keywords: fault detection, heterogeneous computing.

1 Introduction

Trends in high performance computing are bringing increased heterogeneity among the computational resources within a single machine. For example, the GPU accelerator, a major source of heterogeneity today, is already adopted in HPC systems. With appropriate mapping between workloads and heterogeneous resources, the heterogeneous platforms can accelerate performance and/or improve energy efficiency for applications with varying performance characteristics. However, the heterogeneous platforms exacerbate resilience problems faced by current large-scale systems. First, the GPU-like accelerator brings higher processor density and memory bandwidth consumption, which tends to cause higher error rates. Second, the diversity of devices demands various fault protection mechanisms, and these mechanisms must be customized to the needs of architecture and system software. How to design efficient resilience strategies for heterogeneous platforms is an open question. The answer to this question is critical for the wider adoption of heterogeneous platforms for future exascale systems.

The conventional resilience mechanism usually employs a one-size-fits-all approach: a uniform protection is enforced, regardless of application semantics.

D. an Mey et al. (Eds.): Euro-Par 2013 Workshops, LNCS 8374, pp. 670–679, 2014.

As a result, a number of resilience mechanisms (e.g., hardware ECC, process replication, and system-level checkpoint/restart) come with large performance and power overhead. However, our recent work [1] reveals that the application data structures can display diverse vulnerability because of variant application behavior and memory access patterns. It is possible to use an application-driven approach to selectively protect data, such that we can reduce fault tolerance overhead.

Furthermore, the conventional resilience strategy enforces isolated protection in most cases. For example, on high-end computing systems, the main memory on the CPU side can be protected by heavyweight Chipkill ECC, while the global memory on the GPU side has no protection or has protection with lightweight SECDED ECC. There is no cooperation for data protection between CPU and GPU, and also the resilience mechanisms are separated from each other. However, heterogeneity provides new opportunities to improve resilience. In particular, each computing unit (e.g., CPU or GPU) can provide space and time redundancy to another. Hence, it is possible to implement a cooperative resilience mechanism by shifting some protection responsibility for one computing unit to another. This cooperative methodology can potentially reduce overhead accompanied with resilience mechanisms.

In this work, we rethink the traditional resilience strategy on a heterogeneous CPU/GPU platform, and explore the viability of using an application-driven CPU/GPU cooperative method to detect faults occurred on GPU global memory. In particular, we investigate a software-based fault detection mechanism on GPU. This resilience mechanism provides protection to data based on application knowledge and data vulnerability analysis, and greatly reduces fault detection overhead. We reveal that this resilience mechanism, however, is not suitable to be completely implemented on GPU, because it has abundant control flow and limited parallelism. This results in low occupancy and poor power efficiency on GPU. In addition, completely implementing the fault detection on GPU may increase memory footprint, which prohibits us from using GPU computing with larger input problems. To solve the above problems, we shift parts of GPU fault detection logic to CPU and embrace a cooperative fault detection. Our method brings only 2.2% performance overhead while capturing more than 90% errors that cause incorrect application results.

2 Related Work

The GPU was originally designed for applications that are intrinsically fault tolerant (e.g., image rendering). Hence it did not have any resilience mechanism. However, the wide adoption of GPU for scientific applications makes GPU reliability become a concern. In fact, recent work has shown that the error rate on some GPUs can be as high as four failures per week [4].

Hardware-Based Resilience on GPU: Fermi is the first GPU that supports hardware ECC. Fermi's register files, shared memory, L1 and L2 caches and DRAM memory are SECDED ECC protected [9]. With hardware ECC, the application can suffer from large performance loss. For example, LAMMPS suffers from 30% performance loss [5], FFT, S3D and SCAN suffer from 21%, 20% and 28% respectively based on our own experience. Jeon and Annavaram propose a hardware-based approach to opportunistically detect GPU computation errors [6]. They exploit idle resource (idle cores from underutilized warps or idle execution unit) to implement dual modular redundancy. Similarly, Tan and Fu [7] leverage the idle time in GPU streaming processors during branch divergence and pipeline stalls to implement computation redundancy to detect errors. Sheaffer et al. [8] introduce a series of architecture modification to implement hardware redundancy (e.g., redundant ALU).

In general, hardware-based resilience demands architectural support and lacks flexibility. It is difficult to inform hardware of the application semantics for error detection, and hence the hardware-based approach cannot provide flexibility required by adaptive low-overhead protection.

Software-Based Resilience on GPU: Yim et al. [10] introduce a guardian process to intercept crash events and restart the GPU kernel using checkpoints. They also instrument the source code, duplicate non-loop code, and insert range checking code for loops. Dimitrov et al. [11] investigate three software redundant execution approaches. In the first approach, they simply duplicate memory copy and kernel executions; in the second approach, they selectively duplicate instructions to interleave redundant execution with the original code; in the third approach, they leverage thread-level parallelism by assigning redundant computation to redundant thread blocks.

The above software-based approaches can introduce significant performance overhead (15%-100%), because they are ignorant of data vulnerability difference and enforce a uniform protection. Our work is different from them by selectively protecting data. Also, we partition the fault detection functionality between CPU and GPU, and leverage time and space redundancy provided by the heterogeneous platform to reduce protection overhead.

3 Approach

We aim to implement a software-based fault detection (SBFD) mechanism for GPU. Compared with hardware-based mechanisms, the SBFD provides great flexibility to control how to enforce protection. SBFD allows programmers to implement tunable protection according to application-specific vulnerability without introducing hardware overhead. Our study focuses on fault detection on GPU main memory. We assume that data resident on other architectural subsystems (e.g., register file and data bus) is well protected by hardware ECC or MCA [3]. In addition, we limit our study to the silent soft error because of its concealing nature to applications and programmers. Any soft error that causes bit flips on memory cells should be captured by our method.

To evaluate the viability of our approach, we select the benchmark k-means from Rodinia benchmark suite [12], since k-means is extensively used for many data intensive scientific applications, including geo-statistics, astronomy, and

```
do{
  delta = 0.0F;

  /*The clustering loop offloaded to GPU*/
  for(tid=0; tid<nthreads; tid++)
  {
    for (ii=0; ii<_UNROLLFAC_; ii++) {
      i = tid + ii*nthreads;
      max_dist = FLT_MAX;

      /* find the cluster center id with min distance to pt */
      ...

        /* if membership changes, increase delta by 1 */
        if (membership[i] != index) delta += 1.0F;

     /* assign the membership to object i */
     membership[i] = index;

     /* update new cluster centers */
     partial_new_centers_len[tid][index]++;
     for (j=0; j<nfeatures; j++)
       partial_new_centers[tid][index][j] += feature[i][j];
    }
  }

  /*Array reduction performed on CPU*/
  for (i=0; i<nclusters; i++) {
    for (j=0; j<nthreads; j++) {
      new_centers_len[i] += partial_new_centers_len[j][i];
      partial_new_centers_len[j][i] = 0;
      for (k=0; k<nfeatures; k++) {
        new_centers[i][k] += partial_new_centers[j][i][k];
        partial_new_centers[j][i][k] = 0.0F;
      }
    }
  }

  /* replace old cluster centers with new_centers on CPU*/
  for (i=0; i<nclusters; i++) {
    for (j=0; j<nfeatures; j++) {
      if (new_centers_len[i] > 0)
        clusters[i][j] = new_centers[i][j] / new_centers_len[i];
      new_centers[i][j] = 0.0F;
    }
    new_centers_len[i] = 0;
  }
} while (delta > threshold && loop++ < 500)
```

Listing 1.1. The major computation loop of k-means

computer vision. The pseudo-code for the major computation loop of k-means is shown in List 1.1. In general, k-means divides a set of data objects into clusters (represented by the array *membership*) according to object features (the array *feature*). Each cluster is represented by the mean value or centroid (the array *new_centers*). The number of data objects in each cluster is represented by the array *new_centers_len*. The algorithm iteratively associates each data object with its nearest centroid based on some chosen distance metric. Within each iteration, the new centroid is re-calculated by averaging the features of all data objects within each cluster. The benchmark offloads the data intensive clustering workload into GPU, while updating centroid happens on CPU. The arrays *partial_new_centers* and *partial_new_centers_len* save temporal data where the GPU clustering produces and consumes. These two arrays are iteratively offloaded to CPU, and CPU performs reduction operations on them to update centroids.

In this section, we will first present our vulnerability study for five data structures (i.e., *clusters, feature, membership, partial_new_centers* and *partial_new_centers_len*) in the k-means GPU kernel in Section 3.1. These data structures take close to 100% of global memory footprint of the GPU kernel.

There are other thread-private data (e.g., *tid, nclusters*, and *nthreads*). These data are used within control flows and array indices, and hence they are critical to the application resilience. However, these data structures are small in terms of size. They can be protected by heavyweight hardware ECC (e.g., double-chipkill) without causing noticeable performance and energy overhead; hence they are not the focus of our study. Based on the vulnerability study in Section 3.1, we discuss our selective data protection method and present how it is implemented with a cooperative CPU/GPU approach in Section 3.2.

3.1 Fault Injection

We develop a user-level fault injection framework to emulate single-bit and multi-bit transient faults by flipping bits in specific program variables (e.g., a data array). The framework consists of a set of C library functions to inject faults and an enhanced GPU CUDA compiler. To inject faults, the user needs to decide the fault injection target (i.e., which program variable), the condition to inject faults (e.g., the fault should occur after a specific program statement or occur at a specific iteration), and the specific faulty position within the target variable. The compiler then inserts the fault injection function calls into the GPU kernel based on user decisions. At runtime, a GPU thread will trigger bit flips based on those function calls.

To study vulnerability of data structures, we fully emulate the randomness of fault occurrences. In particular, we emulate both temporal and spatial randomness. The temporal randomness means that the fault occurs randomly during the GPU kernel execution; the spatial randomness means that the fault occurs randomly in any position with the target variable. To minimize computation and memory overhead for emulating the random fault injection on GPU, we use a CPU/GPU cooperative approach. In particular, CPU generates necessary random numbers and passes them to GPU either through GPU kernel parameters or through GPU global memory, and then GPU performs actual fault injections using those random numbers.

Figure 1 shows the fault injection results. We perform fault injection tests for each data structure for 200 times. In each test, we use a randomly selected GPU thread to randomly inject one fault (either single-bit, 2 bits, or 4 bits) into the target data. The figure indicates that *membership* is the most resilient to errors; this is due to two factors: *self error containment* and *self error correction.* As shown in List 1.1, the corruption in *membership* may change the value of *delta* (line 15 in List 1.1), which in turn may increase the number of invocations of the enclosing *do-loop* (line 48 in List 1.1). However, the error is not propagated to any other code section (i.e., the self error containment), and a correct value will be re-assigned to the *membership* in the next iteration of the do-loop (line 18 in Listing 1.1) (i.e., the self error correction).

In fact, *partial_new_centers* and *partial_new_centers_len* data structures also have the similar self-error-correction property; even though corruptions in these data may be propagated to CPU regions, CPU will reset these data at each iteration of the do-loop (line 31 and 34 in List 1.1). However, Figure 1 reveals that these two data structures display very diverse vulnerability; *partial_new_centers_len* is very vulnerable, while *partial_new_centers* is not. This divergent error behavior is mainly due to the accuracy difference between integer operations and floating point operations on GPU. The integer addition, which is the main operation performed on *partial_new_centers_len*, does not lose accuracy as long as there is no overflow. Therefore, most of the faults in *partial_new_centers_len* can affect the application output data, *clusters*. On the other hand, the floating point addition, which is the main operation for *partial_new_centers*, may lose accuracy due to truncation and roundoff errors inherited in floating point operations. This fundamental inaccuracy loss sometimes works as a filter to remove errors. For example, if a fault accidentally happens to the exponent portion of an array element in *partial_new_centers*, the addition operation may truncate out the faulty element during internal normalization when the corrupted value is much smaller than the original value. In this case, if the original value was zero or already much smaller than the other operand , this truncation will not affect the output. Therefore, not all faults injected to *partial_new_centers* are propagated to the output data *clusters*. Moreover, propagation of errors in *partial_new_centers* to the output data is dependent on other data, *new_centers_len* (line 42 in List 1.1); if *new_enters_len* has a zero value, the corresponding element of the output data will not be updated. In this case, the errors in *partial_new_centers* will not be propagated to that element of the output data.

We also found that the output data *clusters* is less susceptible to fault injection than other data structures. This is because k-means has an inherent fault-tolerant property. The main do-loop repeats computations until the output data meet certain conditions. If a fault is injected to *clusters*, it is likely that the corruption changes the output data in a way not to meet the termination condition. Therefore, errors in the output data may increase the number of iterations of the do-loop, but the increased iterations may self-correct the output data.

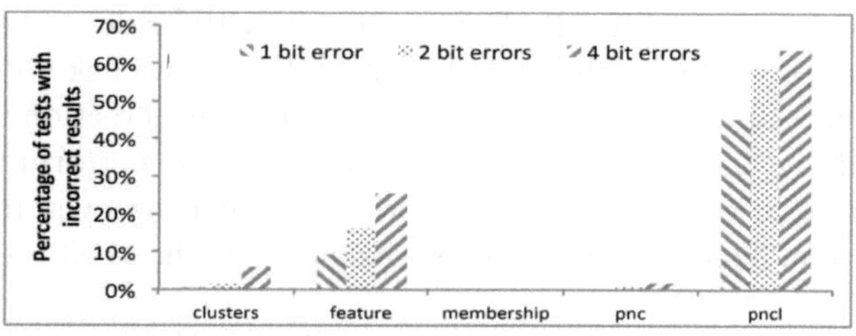

Fig. 1. Fault injection results. pnc=partial_new_center, pncl=partial_new_center_len.

3.2 Cooperative CPU/GPU Fault Detection

Based on the fault injection and application knowledge, we conclude the data structures *feature* and *partial_new_center_len* are the most vulnerable. Assuming that bit errors are uniformly distributed across time and memory space and independent of each other, only capturing the errors in these two data structures will capture 99% (1 bit error), 97%(2 bits error) and 92% (4 bits error) errors in global memory that cause incorrect application results. Moreover, only protecting these two data structures instead of all application data can reduce fault detection overhead.

We explore efficient protection for the two data structures at the software level. The array *feature*[NOBJS][NFEATURES] ($NOBJS$ is the number of data objects, and $NFEATURES$ is the number of features) is a read-only two dimensional array in the GPU kernel. A specific element *feature*[x][y] specifies the *yth* feature value for the *xth* data object. In general cases, the number of data objects is much larger than the total number of GPU threads, and each thread is in charge of $\_UNROLLFAC\_$ data objects ($\_UNROLLFAC\_ = 100$); also the number of features is much less than the total number of GPU threads. To protect *feature*, we add a checksum value for each data object. The checksum i is the summation of all feature values for the data object i. The baseline checksums are calculated before the do-loop, and saved for checksum verification. At the end of the GPU kernel, the checksums are re-calculated and verified with the baseline. If there is any difference, the fault is detected at the *feature* array.

With the above checksum-based fault detection, each thread is involved in a limited number of floating-point addition operations (i.e., $O(NFEATURES)$), and the load is well balanced between threads. However, to completely implement the above algorithm, we must transfer the baseline checksums to the GPU global memory before each kernel invocation. The size of the baseline checksums is in proportion to $NOBJS$. Furthermore, uploading the baseline checksums to GPU exposes them to the same memory architecture as other GPU data, and hence they suffer the similar error rate and there is no sufficient protection for the baseline checksums.

To solve the above problem, we leverage memory space redundancy on the CPU side to save the baseline checksums. On the CPU side, the main memory is usually better protected with hardware ECC. Hence, we ask CPU to keep the baseline checksums. Furthermore, we decouple the fault detection into checksum calculation and checksum verification, and ask CPU to perform the checksum verification. In addition, the checksum verification can be overlapped with the GPU computation, hence removing the verification overhead off the computation critical path.

The data structure *partial_new_center_len*[NTHREADS][NCLUSTERS] ($NTHREADS$ is the total number of GPU threads, and $NCLUSTERS$ is the number of clusters) is an array with both read and write accesses. Because it is not read-only, the above checksum-based approach cannot work. To detect faults, we leverage an implicit invariance existing in $partial\_new\_centers\_len$. In particular, each element $partial\_new\_centers\_len[x][y]$ is reset as zero before the GPU kernel invocation, and then adds by at most 1 at each iteration of the inner loop (the line 21 in List 1.1). Hence, after the GPU kernel is finished, we can bound the value of each element in *partial_new_centers_len* by $[0, \_UNROLLFAC\_]$. We check the validness of each element with CPU after the kernel is finished. This fault detection method does not add any extra computing on GPU. The element value validation occurred on CPU can also be overlapped with the GPU kernel execution, hence minimizing the fault detection overhead.

Discussion: We do not claim the full fault coverage with the above fault detection algorithms. For *feature*, like other checksum-based fault tolerance algorithms [13] [14], the checksum can result in false negative tests when the error effects from multiple array elements are nullified when calculating checksum. However, this kind of scenario is extremely uncommon, given the rareness of soft errors. In addition, the error in *partial_new_center_len* can still make the element value fall within the bound, hence resulting in false negative tests. However, this kind of scenario is much less common than the other scenarios detectable by our algorithm, assuming that the error has an even chance to occur on every data bit. Hence, the invariance-based algorithm can still capture most of errors.

4 Evaluation

We evaluate our approaches in this section. Figures 2 and 3 compare data transfer size and performance for three fault detection scenarios, including *no resilience* (i.e., the original code), *GPU-only* (i.e., fault detection implemented on GPU only), and *GPU+CPU* (i.e., cooperative fault detection)

Figure 3 shows that *GPU-only* brings 11.1% performance loss, comparing with *no resilience* scenario. The performance loss is due to two reasons: first, the extra data transfer from CPU to GPU (shown in Figure 2) occurs to fetch the reference *feature* checksum data to GPU; second, the extra fault detection logic is added into the application critical path on GPU. *GPU+CPU* significantly reduces the data transfer from CPU to GPU by 23%, because data verification logic is offloaded to CPU, and the reference checksum data does not have to be uploaded to GPU. However, the data transfer from GPU to CPU increases, because GPU has to offload updated checksums to CPU for verification at each iteration. As a result, the total data transfer size between GPU and CPU for the *GPU+CPU* is the same as that for GPU-only. However, the performance of *GPU+CPU* is improved by 8.1%, comparing with that of *GPU-only*. Considering the same data transfer size for the two scenarios, the performance improvement must come from the overlapping of CPU and GPU work. Note that we have to synchronize CPU and GPU when overlapping CPU and GPU work. However, even with the synchronization overhead, we still get performance improvement. In general, the optimized cooperative CPU/GPU fault detection brings only 2.2% performance loss, comparing with *no resilience* scenario.

Furthermore, considering the fact that the data verification logic with *GPU+CPU* is implemented with only one single CPU thread, while with *GPU-only* the logic is implemented with massive parallelism with low GPU occupancy, we derive that the *GPU-only* implementation is not as power efficient as

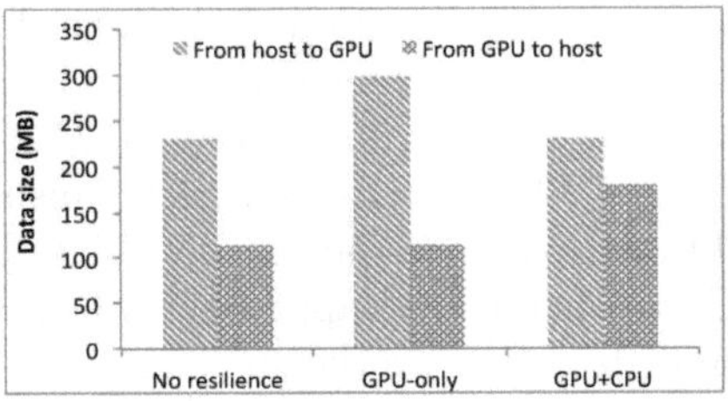

Fig. 2. Compare data transfer size between various resilience scenarios

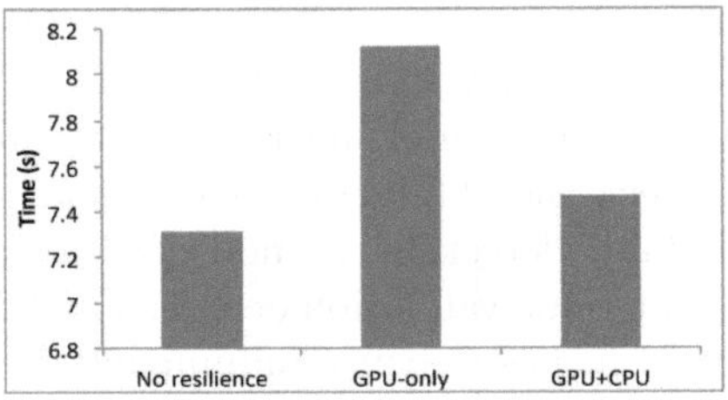

Fig. 3. Compare performance between various resilience scenarios

GPU+CPU, because CPU can power down the idle cores (CPU only uses one thread) while GPU cannot. Also, the thermal-design power (TDP) of the main stream GPU is comparable or even much larger than CPU. Hence, using CPU to implement data verification is more power-efficient.

Figure 4 displays the fault injection results with our fault detection mechanism. There are four groups of bars within the figure. The first two groups of bars (i.e., *feature* and *r_feature*) are for the results when injecting faults into *feature*, while the last two groups of bars (i.e., *pncl* and *r_pncl*) is for *partial_new_centers_len*. The first and the third groups of bars represent the percentage of fault injection tests that causes incorrect application results. These bars are already shown in Figure 1, but we list here again to show if our fault detection mechanisms have captured them. The second and the fourth groups of bars represents the percentage of faulty tests captured by our mechanism. We perform 200 fault inject tests for each test. The y axis represents the percentage of tests that have incorrect application results (i.e., visible errors) for the first and the third groups of bars, or the percentage of tests that have errors detected by our mechanism for the third and the fourth groups of bars.

The figure shows that for *feature* and *pncl* our mechanism captures all of errors that cause incorrect application results. However, our mechanism reports more errors than necessary (i.e., having false positive cases). Those cases do not cause incorrect application results because of statistical nature in k-means. However,

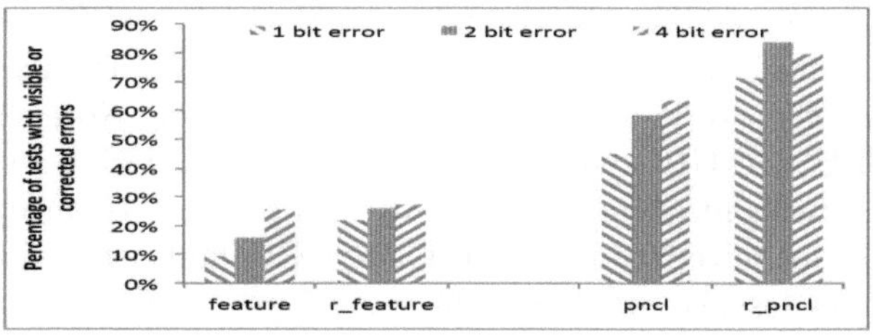

Fig. 4. Fault injection results with cooperative fault detection. pnc=partial_new_center, pncl=partial_new_center_len; r_* refers to the cases with fault detection enforced.

our mechanism only focuses on data structures themselves without application algorithm knowledge, hence resulting in false positive fault detection.

5 Conclusions

In this paper, we target on reducing fault detection overhead on a heterogeneous CPU/GPU platform. Based on the fault injection tests and application knowledge, we selectively protect data according to data-structure-specific vulnerabilities, instead of using a one-size-fit-all approach to protect data. This application-driven approach can capture most of errors that cause incorrect application results, while resulting in reduction in resilience overhead. Furthermore, by dismantling the fault detection mechanism and offloading part of it to CPU, we can further reduce the detection overhead.

References

1. Li, D., Vetter, S.J., Yu, W.: Classifying Soft Error Vulnerabilities in Extreme-Scale Scientific Applications Using a Binary Instrumentation Tool. In: SC 2012 (2012)
2. Honarkhah, M., Caers, J.: Stochastic Simulation of Patterns Using Distance-Based Pattern Modeling. Mathematical Geosciences (2010)
3. Iyer, R., Nakka, N., Kalbarczyk, Z., Myra, S.: Recent Advances and New Avenues in Hardware-Level Reliability Support. IEEE Micro (2005)
4. Haque, I.S., Pande, V.S.: Hard Data on Soft Errors: A Large-Scale Assessment of Real-World Error Rates in GPGPU. In: CCGRID 2010 (2010)
5. Brown, W.M.: GPU Acceleration in LAMMPS. In: LAMMPS User's Workshop and Symposium (2011)
6. Jeon, H., Annavaram, M.: Warped-DMR: Light-Weight Error Detection for GPGPU. IEEE Micro (2012)
7. Tan, J., Fu, X.: RISE: Improving the Streaming Processors Reliability Against Soft Errors in GPGPUs. In: PACT 2012 (2012)
8. Sheaffer, J., Luebke, D., Skadron, K.: A Hardware Redundancy and Recovery Mechanism for Reliable Scientific Computation on Graphics Processors. In: Proceedings of Graphic Hardware (2007)
9. ECC and Keeneland GPUs, `http://keeneland.gatech.edu/`
10. Yim, K.S., Pham, C., Saleheen, M., Kalbarczyk, Z., Iyer, R.K.: Hauberk: Lightweight Silient Data Corruption Error Detector for GPGPU. In: IPDPS 2011 (2011)
11. Dimitrov, M., Mantor, M., Zhou, H.: Understanding Software Approaches for GPGPU Reliability. In: GPGPU 2009 (2009)
12. Che, S., Boyer, M., Meng, J., Tarjan, D., Sheaffer, J.W., Lee, S.-H., Skadron, K.: Rodinia: A Benchmark Suite for Heterogeneous Computing. In: IISWC 2009 (2009)
13. Wu, P., Ding, C., Chen, L., Gao, F., Davies, T., Karlsslon, C., Chen, Z.: Fault Tolerant Matrix-Matrix Multiplication: Correcting Soft Errors On-Line. In: Workshop on Latest Advances in Scalable Algorithm for Large-Scale Systems (2011)
14. Huang, K.-H., Abraham, J.A.: Algorithm-Based Fault Tolerance for Matrix Operations. IEEE Transactions on Computers C-33(6), 518–528 (1984)

GPU Behavior on a Large HPC Cluster

Nathan DeBardeleben, Sean Blanchard, Laura Monroe, Phil Romero, Daryl Grunau, Craig Idler, and Cornell Wright

Los Alamos National Laboratory,
High Performance Computing Division*, Los Alamos NM 87544, USA
{ndebard,seanb,lmonroe,prr,dwg,cwi,cornell}@lanl.gov

Abstract. We discuss observed characteristics of GPUs deployed as accelerators in an HPC cluster at Los Alamos National Laboratory. GPUs have a very good theoretical FLOPS rate, and are reasonably inexpensive and available, but they are relatively new to HPC, which demands both consistently high performance across nodes and consistently low error rate.

We modified a standard acceptance procedure to test GPU performance, error rate and reliability characteristics, and ran the test suite on a Fermi HPC cluster at LANL. We discuss here our methodology for this testing, and present results relevant to the deployment of GPUs in an HPC environment.

In this paper we show performance variability, power usage variability (possibly related), and some reliability concerns on the GPUs tested. We argue for rigorous testing of these devices in deployment as a way of characterizing their behavior.

Keywords: graphics processing units, high performance computing, reliability, acceptance testing, fault-tolerance, resilience, error correction.

1 Introduction

Graphics Processing Units (GPUs) are a promising technology in the field of high-performance computing (HPC). GPUs are highly parallel co-processors, providing FLOPS at low power consumption. They were developed as co-processors for the graphics and gaming industry and were co-designed to fit the needs of these real-time applications, using the fast SIMD parallel pipeline that addressed graphics needs. This SIMD parallel architecture is also suited to many scientific problems, so research and development on the use of GPUs for scientific simulation and HPC intensified in the 2000s.

GPUs are a fairly new technology in HPC, so many interactions of GPUs with HPC systems are not yet fully characterized. These include such questions as the

* A portion of this work was performed at the Ultrascale Systems Research Center (USRC) at Los Alamos National Laboratory, supported by the U.S. Department of Energy contract DE-FC02-06ER25750. The publication has been assigned the LANL identifier LA-UR-13-24171.

D. an Mey et al. (Eds.): Euro-Par 2013 Workshops, LNCS 8374, pp. 680–689, 2014.

reliability of the GPU, the patterns of errors that do occur and the performance of GPUs as an ensemble within an HPC system. These questions are especially important in a highly coupled high-performance computing system, in which performance or reliability problems on a single GPU might affect the entire calculation.

In this paper, we investigate these questions on two large-scale Fermi systems sited at Los Alamos National Laboratory (LANL), and describe our observations testing real systems in the field. We also investigate the error-correction capabilities of the GPU. This is especially interesting in that main-memory DRAM uses chipkill-correct ECC, whereas GPUs use only Single-Error Correct Double-Error Detect (SECDED). SECDED provides a lesser amount of protection against memory errors, so it is of interest to understand how the reliability of GPU SDRAM compares to that of main memory DRAM.

2 High Performance Computing

HPC combines multiple computers together via a high-performance interconnect to work in parallel on problems that are too large to be solved by individual computers. Such HPC clusters are built from thousands to tens of thousands of individual nodes that communicate with one another via a high-speed interconnect. Current top HPC clusters have as many as 1.5 million processors and up to 1.5 Petabytes of memory. These numbers have increased significantly in recent years; further significant increase is expected in the future as HPC systems evolve to handle ever larger problems.

2.1 Node Performance and Reliability Effects on HPC Calculations

The applications running on many HPC systems, such as those at LANL, are tightly coupled simulations of physical phenomena. As the simulation evolves, nodes communicate with each other to propagate information representing the physical phenomena that affect adjacent regions such as temperature, pressure, electrical charge, particle migration and so forth. The simulation progresses in small increments of simulated time, known as time-steps. Information from adjacent regions is required for each time-step, so high-speed, low latency communication between nodes is required for efficient use of the HPC system's processors.

Importantly, delays in the completion of a time-step on one processor will often mean that the other nodes which need adjacent region information to proceed will also be delayed. This can cause a cluster to run overall at the speed of its slowest node.

The sheer quantity of hardware in an HPC system magnifies the effects of the failure rate of its individual components. A cluster with 10,000 nodes, with a mean time between failure (MTBF) for each node of 10 years, would have an MTBF of under 9 hours, when considered as a cluster. Other non-node-based failure modes would drive the real-world MTBF even lower.

3 GPUs in HPC

With the co-development of general programming languages and GPU hardware in the late 2000s, the GPU pipeline became much more accessible for general scientific programming, and the GPU became attractive as an accelerator in HPC architectures. The first GPU-based heterogeneous cluster to make the Top 500 list [12] was Tokyo Tech's TSUBAME in November 2008. The November 2012 list contains 53 GPU-based computers, including the number 1 entry, Titan.

The GPU is a massively parallel SIMD architecture; each GPU has many streaming multi-processors (SMs), each having many cores. The GPU has a hierarchical memory structure. There is a small amount of SRAM shared memory per SM that can be accessed across all cores in the SM. Part of this shared memory can be used as cache, as on CPUs. There is a larger amount of GDDR5 global memory available to all SMs on the GPU. Finally, main memory on the node can be accessed through the limited bandwidth of a PCIe bus between the GPU and the motherboard.

3.1 GPU Memory and Error Protection

The Fermi generation GPU tested here is the first to support Error Correcting Code (ECC) memory protection [8]. Each M2090 has 6GB of GDDR5 memory. GDDR5 memory is based on DDR3 technology but uses synchronous DRAM (SDRAM).

While the Fermi's Single-Error Correct Double-Error Detect (SECDED) error protection is certainly a major improvement over uncorrected errors for HPC loads, this error protection is not as effective as the standard on non-GPU HPC systems. Most of these systems depend on main-memory DRAM equipped with chipkill-correct ECC [4]. A recent study of the Jaguar supercomputer at Oak Ridge National Laboratory (ORNL) showed that chipkill-correct ECC reduces the detectable uncorrectable error rate of memory by 42X compared to SECDED [11]. Because of this, we believe that a greater understanding of the reliability of GPU memory is needed for their effective use in the HPC environment.

3.2 GPU Strengths and Weaknesses

GPUs are very attractive for HPC for several reasons. They provide high FLOPS, as well as a good FLOPS/watt ratio. GPUs are readily available and reasonably inexpensive, in terms of the compute power they provide. They are expected to be available and supported for some time to come. This future support is important, since code developed for these clusters may be in use for decades, and the clusters themselves may be in use for five or more years.

However, GPUs have some drawbacks. The memory hierarchy can make it difficult to get optimized results, and sometimes presents a bottleneck that cannot be avoided. GPUs do require an in-depth understanding of the hardware to get the best results. The uncertainty around reliability should be investigated further in view of the difference between the error-correction used on the GPU and that used on main memory. Finally, the technology is under rapid development and so needs testing with each hardware and software change, as different releases can lead to quite different performance and reliability results.

4 Testing Methodology

All LANL HPC systems undergo a lengthy test and verification process before hand-over to the target user community. The goal is to provide a reliable, high performing, well prescribed system to the users in as timely a manner as possible after the system has been constructed at the vendor's site.

At LANL, testing is conducted under the Gazebo[6] framework which submits jobs to keep the system busy to a desired level. Gazebo can identify system utilization and node coverage, provide test pass/fail summaries, and basic job results analytics. For the new GPU-based systems, we extended our testing framework to examine GPU performance and reliability, in addition to the standard CPU tests performed on every new system.

Tests used for this paper included Oak Ridge National Laboratory's Scalable HeterOgeneous Computing (SHOC) Benchmark Suite [2], NVIDIA's High-Performance Linpack (HPL) [5], NBody [10], and GPU Bandwidth tests, and Laboratoire d'Informatique de Robotique et de Microelectronique de Montpellier's GPUburn [3]. All low-level hardware (level 0) SHOC tests were run to identify low-level/hardware performance variations across nodes. Most of the results presented in Section 5 are from single-node experiments performed on these systems. This was because these experiments were scavenging free nodes of the system in production while regular users were utilizing the rest of the cluster.

We tested a large-scale cluster, Moonlight, whose nodes were equipped with PCI-attached NVIDIA Fermi GPU accelerators, which were top-of-the-line in their generation of GPUs. Moonlight is a 308-node, dual-socket, 8-core Intel Sandy Bridge cluster that has 32GB main memory and two NVIDIA Tesla M2090 GPGPUs [9] per node. It is interconnected with a QLogic Infiniband fabric operating at 40 Gbit/sec (4x QDR). While the cluster is equipped with PCIe-3.0, the M2090 GPU is PCI2-e.

While Kepler, the next generation of NVIDIA's GPU, is out, LANL does not yet have access to large-scale Kepler clusters for testing. Furthermore, we wanted to test hardware in production use by scientists, and there is a latency between the time systems are procured and the time they are brought into production.

5 Results

For our experiments, we tested using all of the software packages mentioned in Section 4. We focus in this section on issues that surfaced during the SHOC and HPL runs. In particular, we saw unexpected variation in GPU-to-CPU transfer rate on the SHOC tests, which might lead to lowered performance across the cluster on our highly coupled simulations. We noticed an unusual distribution of the GPU-only HPL performance results, which could indicate unusual performance distributions on our simulations. We also saw low power draws on one of the GPUs that led to low performance and which relate somewhat to the odd distribution of the GPU-only HPL performance results. Finally, we saw an inordinate number of high residuals on HPL, which might indicate susceptibility to silent data corruption (SDC) during actual production use of the machine. In the following sections we detail these experiments.

The performance tests in Section 5.1 and 5.2 were run on a system in production usage at LANL running CUDA 4.1. Later, CUDA was upgraded to 5.0, and some of these problems improved. The reliability tests in Section 5.3 were run on the same system after the upgrade to CUDA 5.0.

5.1 GPU-to-CPU Data Transfer Variation

We used the SHOC BandwidthTest to conduct tests on data transfer rates from the CPU to the GPU and vice versa. We performed 200 tests at transfer sizes from 1KB up to 512MB. These tests were done for transfers from CPU to GPU and from GPU to CPU.

There were no significant variations in CPU-to-GPU transfers found. However, for GPU-to-CPU transfers, we saw major slowdowns in the transfer rates for some data of size greater that 4 MB. Figure 1 shows how the transfer rate of data from the GPU to CPU varies as the size of the transfer increases. Notice the transfer rate generally increases as the transfer size increases.

However, for some sets of the largest data, we saw data transfer rates around 13x slower than more typical transfers of the same data size. These fluctuations can be seen in the bottom right of Figure 1. This kind of fluctuation could have very negative effects on tightly coupled scientific applications that perform at the speed of the slowest component.

This strange behavior disappeared once we upgraded from CUDA 4.1 to CUDA 5.0. Driver problems are not uncommon on cutting-edge systems such as these, however, this demonstrates the need for rigorous testing on future versions of CUDA to ensure that this kind of anomalous behavior doesn't occur in different releases. It is encouraging that our cycle-scavenging and acceptance testing framework was able to find this problem so that it could be addressed.

5.2 HPL Performance Variation across Nodes

High Performance Linpack was used to characterize performance with and without the GPUs. An HPL test that used only the CPUs on a single node was run hundreds of times across all nodes (for coverage) and was found to produce a near normal performance distribution as can be seen in Figure 2. The CPU-only HPL runs show little change in performance from run to run and is consistent with our previous experiences running this benchmark.

This was not true when the HPL test utilized both the GPUs and CPUs on a single node, as shown in Figure 3. The combined GPU and CPU test shows very wide variation from run to run with distinct peaks at a variety of performance

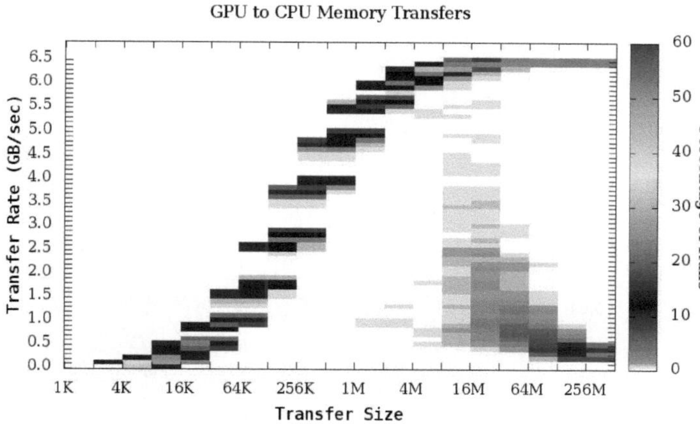

Fig. 1. The distribution of data transfer rates from GPU to CPU colored by percentage of runs of a given size at a given rate. The fluctuations in transfer rate can be seen in the data at the lower right of the graph. We saw a significant fraction of these larger datasets being transferred at rates less than 1 GB/sec, much slower than the usual rate of 6+ GB/sec shown in the upper right of the graph. This effect disappeared after upgrading to Cuda 5.0, underscoring the requirement for rigorous testing.

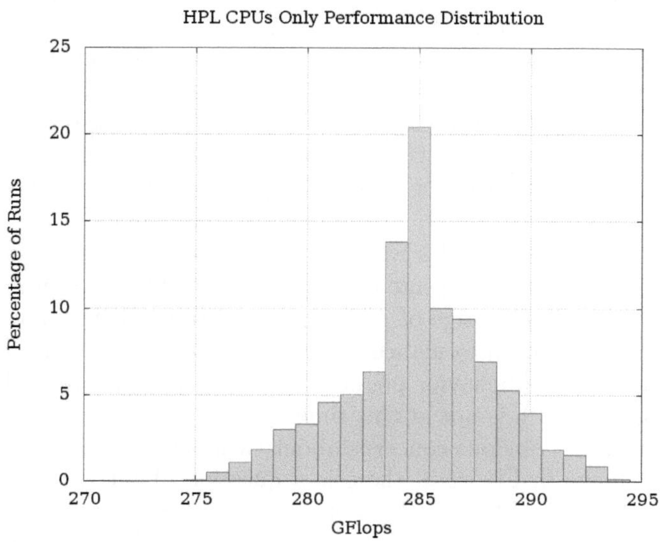

Fig. 2. CPU-only HPL performance shows a reasonable fit to a normal distribution with a standard deviation of only 3.2 GFlops

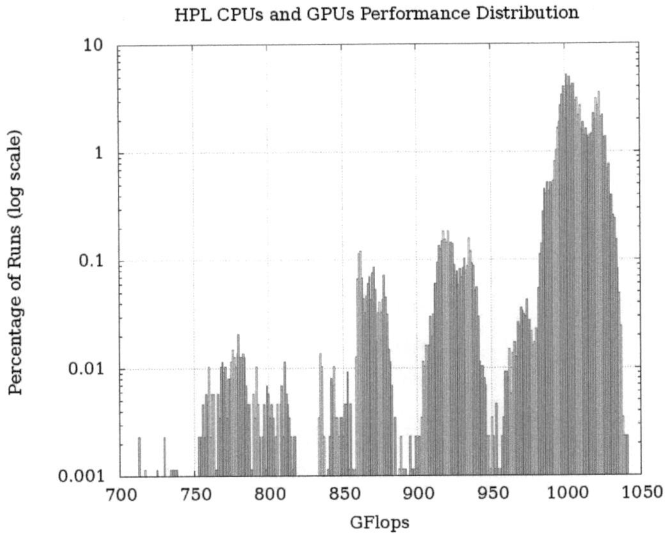

Fig. 3. GPU/CPU HPL performance has a distribution that is definitely not normal and has a standard deviation of 28.2 GFlops. In particular, this distribution shows two distinct peaks, and a long tail to the left with two small peaks visible representing low-performing tests. Please note the log scale.

levels. Inconsistencies in performance of this nature are of particular concern to the HPC community as tightly coupled applications tend to run at the speed of the slowest processing unit.

In an effort to explain the variations observed in the combined GPU-CPU HPL test, we looked at the power used by the GPUs under load. HPL was run more than 134,000 times and the maximum power usage was recorded for each run. The results of these runs appear in Figure 4 where each data point represents the HPL performance and the associated power usage of each GPU on that node.

One would expect the GPUs working in tandem would have similar power usage and this would be represented as a circle in the plot. However, GPU0 was observed to draw a wide range of power over the runs. GPU1 shows much less variability. Lower HPL performance correlates with those runs in which GPU0 draws low power. This behavior possibly indicates a hardware problem on the Moonlight nodes, which is not at this time resolved.

In addition to the obvious concerns about variable performance and variable power usage shown in Figure 4, there is a question about the total power usage of each GPU. The PCI specification is for 225 Watts, and it is evident the GPU counters are reporting a power draw above this value. We do not have a feeling for sensor accuracy and it is possible that these counters may be inaccurate. However, it is well understood that hardware running at the extremes (both upper and lower) of specification can incur reliability and dependability problems. There is also an interesting anomaly in GPU1 power draw (which becomes bi-modal) when GPU0 draws around 240W. The cause of this is still undetermined at this time.

These tests consumed a great many system and analyst cycles and, after upgrading to CUDA 5.0, we were unable to revisit them as the NVIDIA monitoring library (nvml) is broken. The tool does not return information about the power usage of the second GPU and, consequently, it fails to provide the information necessary to run the power experiment.

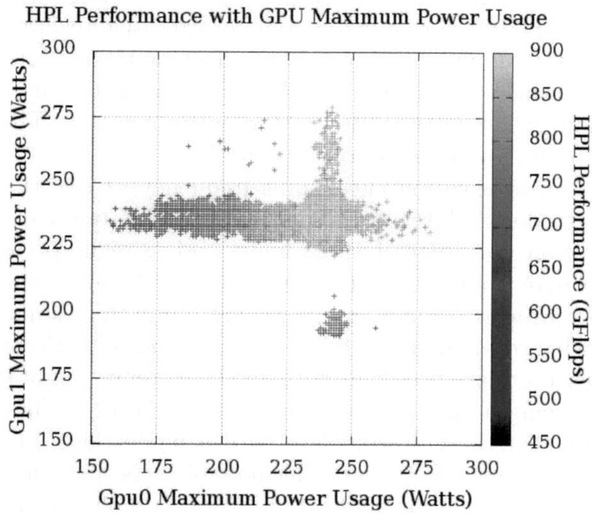

Fig. 4. GPU-only performance colored by HPL performance. The points in this graph represent (GPU0, GPU1) power draws, and do not represent the number of nodes showing each power draw pair. The great majority of the nodes show both GPUs falling into the 225-250 watt range. As might be expected, low power draw on either GPU is associated with low performance. GPU0 shows greater variability in power usage than GPU1, and all of the lowest-performing runs are associated with low power usage on GPU0. GPU0 power use variability is an unresolved question on this machine.

5.3 Residuals and Double Bit Errors

To look for potential reliability problems we examined a single month of HPL output after upgrading to CUDA 5.0. HPL computes $Ax - b = 0$ and calculates *residual errors*. Residuals are places where the calculation is not zero due to rounding. Small rounding errors are common across platforms. However, the residuals should be small when compared to the numerical accuracy of any particular platform. As seen in Table 1, the results from a single month of HPL testing contained many excessively large residuals.

Table 1. Results of HPL runs including excessive residuals found and double bit errors that occurred during HPL runs

Total Runs	Total Hours	Bad Residuals	DBEs
40,171	16,738	1624	27

Approximately 4% of our HPL runs resulted in errors. Of the 1,624 excessive residuals, 27 of them corresponded with logged reports of at least one double-bit error (DBE) occurring on one of the GPUs being used. These measured events lead to fault rates of 0.097 per hour per node for excessive residuals and 0.00161 per hour per node for double bit errors. On a machine the size of the Moonlight cluster, 308 nodes, this would result in 30 bad residuals per hour and 0.5 double-bit errors per hour when extrapolated to the entire machine. These rates seem inordinately high and are of great concern.

This suggests an application checkpoint frequency of less than an hour as a way to mitigate double-bit errors alone. Checkpoint frequencies on current HPC systems are on the order of 16-24 hours and exascale predictions are for frequencies anywhere from tens of minutes to several hours [7,1].

There are several worrisome points here. We found approximately 1,600 instances of excessive residuals that did not correspond with logged DBEs. It is not clear whether there are problems with the DBE reporting of these GPUs or whether we are seeing a large number of multi-bit errors (MBEs). This makes us wonder if SECDED ECC is sufficient or if a higher level of memory error protection is needed on the GPU. Another possibility is that there is something else going on that we do not yet understand that is unrelated to memory.

6 Conclusions

We have presented a study of a large number of tests performed on a GPU cluster are Los Alamos National Laboratory. For some of the tests we found no problems, but for certain applications we found some problematic results. It is not uncommon in HPC systems to have problems exposed only by tests that exercise the system in a particular manner.

The types of problems we discovered required a large commitment of resources and were found on the cluster when in production. The system had already passed standup and acceptance testing and was in use by scientific teams. We posit that these problems were obscure and unlikely to have been found on small systems and stand-alone machines but clearly have performance and reliability impacts. While some of these problems went away after upgrading driver versions, it is important to recognize that software upgrades are often held off until fully evaluated for performance, correctness, and security testing. As such, a driver upgrade may not be a simple undertaking on a production system.

The addition of memory error protection on the GPUs is a welcome and clearly required addition in the HPC arena. However, there appear to be problems associated with high error rates and/or error reporting. Additionally we found performance variability that seems to be associated with power usage variability on systems at LANL. Whether this is also the cause of the reliability problems has not been determined.

GPUs are a relatively new addition to the HPC market and were not created initially with scientific computing in mind. For these reasons, we think it prudent to scrutinize all aspects of the technology. We have shown the importance of rigorous (and ongoing) testing and examination of logs, application results, and internal counters on the GPUs, and have shown the importance of maintaining current versions of device driver hardware where possible. In the future, we hope to explore whether these effects persist into later generations of NVIDIA GPUs.

References

1. Cappello, F., Geist, A., Gropp, B., Kale, L., Kramer, B., Snir, M.: Toward exascale resilience. International Journal of High Performance Computing Applications 23, 374–388 (2009)
2. Danalis, A., et al.: The scalable heterogeneous computing (shoc) benchmark suite. In: Proceedings of the 3rd Workshop on General-Purpose Computation on Graphics Processing Units, GPGPU 2010, pp. 63–74. ACM, New York (2010), http://doi.acm.org/10.1145/1735688.1735702
3. Defour, D., Petit, E.: Gpuburn: A system to test and mitigate gpu hardware failures. In: Proceedings of the International Conference on Embedded Computer Systems: Architectures, Modeling and Simulation (May 2013)
4. Dell, T.J.: A white paper on the benefits of chipkill-correct ecc for pc server main memory (1997)
5. Fatica, M.: Accelerating linpack with cuda on heterogenous clusters. In: Proceedings of 2nd Workshop on General Purpose Processing on Graphics Processing Units, GPGPU-2, pp. 46–51. ACM, New York (2009), http://doi.acm.org/10.1145/1513895.1513901
6. Idler, C.: Gazeo (2013), http://www.github.com/losalamos/Gazebo
7. Kogge, P., et al.: Exascale computing study: Technology challenges in achieving exascale systems (2008)
8. NVIDIA: NVIDIA's Next Generation CUDA Compute Architecture: Fermi (2009), http://tinyurl.com/ykawxw9
9. NVIDIA: Tesla m2090 dual-slot computing processor module (June 2011), http://tinyurl.com/3wbxd46
10. Nyland, L., Harris, M.: 31 Fast n-body simulation with cuda, ch. 31
11. Sridharan, V., Liberty, D.: A study of dram failures in the field. In: Proceedings of the International Conference on High Performance Computing, Networking, Storage and Analysis, SC 2012, pp. 76:1–76:11. IEEE Computer Society Press, Los Alamitos (2012), http://dl.acm.org/citation.cfm?id=2388996.2389100
12. top500: Top500 supercomputer sites (November 2012), http://www.top500.org/lists/2012/11/

A Case for Adaptive Redundancy for HPC Resilience*

Saurabh Hukerikar, Pedro C. Diniz, and Robert F. Lucas

Information Sciences Institute,
University of Southern California,
Marina del Rey, CA 90292, USA
{saurabh,pedro,rflucas}@isi.edu

Abstract. Redundancy both in space and time has been widely used to detect and in some cases correct errors in High Performance Computing (HPC) systems. With the HPC community seeking exascale class supercomputers by the end of the decade, unrealistic expectations for correct system behavior will result in exorbitant costs in terms of performance lost and energy expended. Resilience strategies will need to find balance between fault coverage and the overheads incurred. In this work, we propose an adaptive approach that factors in application level knowledge together with runtime inference about the fault tolerance state of the system to dynamically enable redundant multithreading (RMT). Our approach is based on simple programming language extensions, tightly integrated with a compiler infrastructure and a runtime framework that enables managing the performance overheads of redundant computation.

1 Introduction

In the era of exascale supercomputers, systems will frequently encounter faults that lead to system errors and failures. With smaller transistor feature sizes and lower supply voltages in each new process generation, chips are projected to become increasingly vulnerable to errors [1]. Single Event Upsets (SEUs) that cause soft errors are an important class of errors and with shrinking transistor geometries, the likelihood that these result in multi-cell upsets (MCU) will also increase. Error correcting codes (ECC) in memory and parity in latches and registers have been used for detection and in some cases correction so that the errors remain transparent to the application and system software. Exascale High Performance Computing (HPC) systems are projected to deploy millions of processor cores and memory chips organized in complex hierarchies [2]. Even if individual component reliabilities were to remain the same as they are today,

* This research has been supported by the Scientific Discovery through Advanced Computing (SciDAC) program funded by the U.S. Department of Energy, Office of Science, Advanced Scientific Computing Research (Award Number DE-SC0006844). Partial support for this work was also provided through a contract from Sandia National Laboratories (Award Number 1315083).

D. an Mey et al. (Eds.): Euro-Par 2013 Workshops, LNCS 8374, pp. 690–697, 2014.

the sheer scale of these systems would make the Mean Time to Interrupt (MTTI) so small that a significant fraction of the applications' execution times would be spent on failure recovery actions.

Redundancy, either in space or in time, has been widely used for error detection and recovery. An N-modular redundancy approach entails creating as many replicas of the computation whose results are compared to verify correctness and errors are masked through majority voting. In HPC systems, software managed system level approaches that use complete replication at the process level have been shown to reduce the number of interrupts that an application experiences [3]. Redundant multithreading (RMT) involves running identical copies of the same program as independent threads. When there is an output mismatch, the checker flags an error and initiates a recovery sequence. Redundant computation constitutes a preemptive approach to fault tolerance and there is a significant performance degradation associated with using it for entire programs. In future exascale class supercomputing systems, there will be billions of processes and threads, and applying redundancy systemwide for error detection and masking will result in massive penalties to application performance and energy.

We believe that redundancy should be judiciously applied, factoring in the requirements of the application as well as the fault tolerance state of the system. In this paper, we propose an approach that allows the selective use of multithreaded redundancy based on the programmer's insight. The approach is based on modest programming model extensions that allows programmers to specify what regions of the application code require robust computation. Additionally, whether to enable the redundant multithreading is based on monitoring and inference of fault events by a runtime system. This selective and adaptive use of redundancy seeks to minimize the large performance overheads associated with complete replication. We present an initial framework and preliminary results, and discuss future research directions for future exascale systems.

The rest of the paper is organized as follows: Section 2 looks at various redundancy based fault tolerance approaches in hardware and software and makes the case for adaptive redundancy. Section 3 explains the programming construct, its syntax and semantics. Section 4 describes the role of the runtime, and Section 5 presents the experimental evaluation and some initial results while Section 6 describes the ongoing and future work.

2 Background

In HPC systems, studies have argued for multi-modular redundancy in compute nodes and have shown to accommodate a reduction in individual component reliability by a factor of 100-100,000 to justify the 2x or 3x increase in cost and energy [4]. Ferreira *et. al* [5] evaluate the costs and benefits of using MPI process replication as an alternative to the widely used checkpoint restart protocols, while Stearley *et. al* [6] observe that partial process replication helps increase the Job Mean Time to Interrupt (JMTTI) of tasks, but that there is no alternative to full process replication for highly resilient operation. However, given the scale of future exascale systems in terms of number components and the complexity of applications, complete node-level or process-level multi-modular redundancy would incur exorbitant overhead to costs, performance and energy.

Hardware solutions that employ redundancy are transparent to the supervisor software and application programmer, but require specialized hardware. In the domain of commercial transaction processing, fault tolerant servers such as the Tandem Non-Stop [7] and later the HP NonStop [8] used two redundant processors running in locked step. Later the IBM G5 [9] employed two fully duplicated lock-step pipelines to enable low-latency detection and rapid recovery. The overheads of energy and cost to widely employ such hardware techniques for exascale HPC systems however, would be extremely high. Approaches that leverage multiple contexts in Simultaneous Multithreaded (SMT) processors have also been studied. Such RMT approaches show slightly lower power and performance overheads in comparison to redundant locked-step processor based systems [10] [11].

Software-based redundant multithreading approaches tend to offer more flexibility and are less expensive in terms of silicon area as well as chip development and verification costs. SWIFT [12] is a compiler-based transformation which duplicates all program instructions and inserts comparison instructions during code generation and the duplicated instructions fill the scheduling slack. The DAFT [13] approach uses a compiler transformation that duplicates the entire program in a redundant thread that trails the main thread and inserts instructions for error checking.

The primary limitation of complete replication approaches is that they indulge in preemptive robustness and therefore they account for neither the type of faults, their location and frequency, nor the requirements of the application code and any algorithm specific fault tolerance features of the application.

3 Programming Language Extensions

Many classes of algorithms used in scientific applications selectively require robust computation. However, there are no convenient mechanisms for the programmer to partition the application code into such regions and for the system to utilize such knowledge. For example the Fault Tolerant Generalized Minimal Residual (FTGMRES) algorithm [14] can be partitioned into reliable and unreliable phases. Robust computation is required of only the reliable phases for eventual convergence to the right solution. Several iterative linear solvers [15] and multigrid solvers [16] contain phases that tend to show different fault resilience features. Rather than complete program level redundancy, only the code contained within these programmer defined regions can be executed by multiple redundant threads.

We present a programming model extension that is based on a preprocessor pragma directive that enables delineating code into regions that require robust computation. The compiler inserts the code that enables such regions to be run by multiple independent threads and to compare their respective outputs. The syntax is depicted below:

```
#pragma robust shared<variable list ...>
{
  /*
   code
   ...   */
}
```

The language extension provides OpenMP style data scoping clauses: *shared* to specify the global variables that the code section may consume as input or output; and a *private* clause (not shown above) to list variables whose scope is limited to the section. The compiler used in this work is based on the ROSE [17] source-to-source compiler infrastructure. We use source outlining to extract the code section encompassed by the `#pragma robust` directive to create an outlined function whose pointer can be passed to a threading library. We also extend the application code through source level transformations that insert instructions that compare the values of the sentinel value generated by the redundant threads and informs the runtime system in case of a mismatch in values. In this initial implementation, we also create a duplicate copy of the global data that the section modifies to avoid data races and synchronization issues between the redundant threads.

4 Runtime System

4.1 Runtime Adaptation

While the programmer driven partitioning described in Section 3 seeks to manage the application performance overhead to some extent, most redundancy approaches also do not take into account the fault tolerance state of the system which may alter due to external environmental factors as well as operational features of the system. Soft errors are random external events attributed to alpha particles that originate from within the chip packages and high-energy neutrons from cosmic radiation. Power management techniques that dynamically scale the voltage and frequency also impact the reliability of circuits [18]. Faults attributed to silicon aging that emerge due to temperature induced stresses and other ambient conditions tend to manifest themselves gradually. The occurrence of such faults may be distributed in bursts or as random individual events and therefore the robustness offered by redundant execution would be best served when the system state is vulnerable.

Our runtime system *adapts* to the changing fault tolerance state of the underlying system by enabling RMT execution when the fault tolerance state degrades, for example, if the system experiences too many ECC errors in the caches, or if an application level algorithm based fault tolerance (ABFT) method detects errors once too often. The runtime is implemented as an independent light-weight process that monitors the state of the application and interfaces with the operating system through an interrupt handler mechanism. The runtime maintains a log of fault events in the system. It also maintains a Dynamic Resilience Map

(DRM) [19] which contains the mapping of program-level data structures, functions and code segments, their program-level address offsets, and the corresponding mapping in physical memory, so that it can reason about the significance of the location of the error in the context of the application's logical address space.

For this initial implementation of the runtime system, the notion of a fault event is generalized and may represent a corrected ECC error in the memory, a processor exception or even an error detected by an application level algorithmic fault tolerance method. Also, the current implementation uses a threshold value of event count when deciding whether to initiate the redundant multithreading. The development of better heuristics that base the decision of whether to enable and subsequently disable redundant multithreading on the type and location of the fault, whether the event occurred as an isolated event, or shows a pattern over a period of time, is the subject of ongoing work.

4.2 Core Mapping Policies

The runtime system also makes possible spatial redundancy such that it can leverage multiple processor cores in the context of shared memory multiprocessor (SMP) by assigning the redundant threads to separate processor cores. We explore two policies:

- Adaptive RMT - Trailing Thread: This policy executes the duplicate thread on the same processor core so that the input data variables can be shared by both threads and therefore has some data locality advantages.
- Adaptive RMT - Core Mapping: This policy maps the RMT threads on a separate core in a SMP. This provides more complete fault coverage since the redundant threads are executed on separate hardware, but needs the input data to be replicated and communicated to the private cache of the core that runs the duplicate redundant thread.

The runtime can therefore make a reasoned trade-off between the fault coverage requirement and performance overhead. For this implementation the policy for core affinity of the redundant threads is configured at initialization and we are currently exploring heuristics that can dynamically select between the two policies based on type and frequency of fault events.

5 Experimental Evaluation

5.1 Methodology

We analyze the impact of adaptive redundant multithreading approach with DGEMM, a double-precision matrix-matrix multiplication kernel that is a basic building block for dense matrix linear algebra. We utilize the partitioning based on the `#pragma robust` directive described in Section 3 on the inner product of DGEMM. We evaluate application performance to understand the benefits achieved from the programmer guided selective redundancy and the runtime based adaptive enabling of RMT for the following cases:

- Baseline: Process level redundancy where the program is executed by independent operating system created processes.
- Complete RMT - Trailing Thread : The runtime is configured so that redundant multithreading is enabled throughout the application run but only the `#pragma robust` annotated sections are executed by a redundant thread that trails the main thread on the same processor core.
- Complete RMT - Core Mapped Thread : A redundant thread is also created for all annotated sections, but the runtime maps the redundant threads to different cores.
- Adaptive RMT - Trailing Thread: The redundant multithreading is enabled dynamically by the runtime upon occurrence of fault events and all subsequent `#pragma robust` annotated sections are executed by a trailing thread on the same processor core.
- Adaptive RMT - Core Mapping: RMT is also enabled based on runtime inference but the redundant threads are mapped to separate processor cores.

The objective of the complete RMT experiments is to evaluate the performance benefit of selective application of redundancy to only the inner product of the DGEMM rather than the complete program. The adaptive RMT configurations evaluate performance benefit of turning on robustness only when the system experiences fault events. Our fault injection framework allows injection of faults at any point in the application execution and these are logged by the runtime. We generate a single fault event per application run and the instant of event generation is randomized across experiment runs and we perform 10000 runs per matrix problem size. For these experiments, the runtime system is configured such that the threshold for switching the application into redundant multithreading mode is a single error event. The evaluation platform is an Intel ^{TM}Xeon 8-core 2.4 GHz compute node running the Linux operating system.

5.2 Results

The figure 1 shows the average execution time for each configuration. The baseline is the performance of process level redundancy where the entire program is executed twice and the final results compared. When redundancy is applied to only programmer annotated regions, but *all* sections in the DGEMM are redundantly executed, the average execution time (of all problem sizes) is 85% of the baseline time for the trailing thread configuration. Further benefit is realized when the redundant thread is assigned to a separate processor core and the average execution time is 25% lower than the baseline and shows much as 42% lower execution time for the largest matrix problem size. For the runtime adaptation, the performance results reflect the average execution time across the 10000 experimental runs. For these runs redundant multithreading is enabled only upon detecting a fault event by the runtime system and the average execution time for all problem sizes is 65% of the baseline execution time with trailing redundant threads. When the dynamically enabled redundant threads are mapped to separate cores, the average execution time is 41% faster than baseline and as much as 52% faster than baseline for the largest problem size.

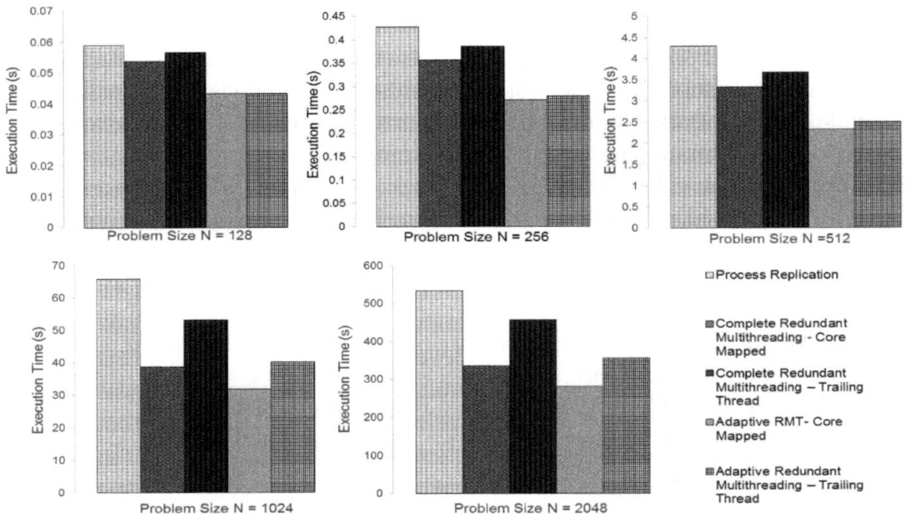

Fig. 1. Results: Performance Comparison of Adaptive Redundant Multithreading

6 Conclusion and Future Work

Redundancy is an effective strategy in the detection and in some cases correction of errors but incurs extremely high overheads. In this paper we presented a software based adaptive application of redundant multithreading that allows for a balanced and reasoned trade-off between application resiliency and performance overheads incurred. Redundancy is enabled based on runtime inference of the system's fault tolerance state and through a simple language extension the programmer's requirements for robustness are incorporated. The initial results suggest that the approach holds promise in managing the trade-off between performance and fault coverage, but much work remains to be done. We are currently broadening the definition of events to include more fault models and fault distribution patterns that are relevant to future exascale systems. This will allow design of effective runtime heuristics that will intelligently enable and eventually disable RMT as well as guide core assignment of redundant threads.

References

1. Shivakumar, P., Kistler, M., Keckler, S., Burger, D., Alvisi, L.: Modeling the effect of technology trends on the soft error rate of combinational logic. In: International Conference on Dependable Systems and Networks, pp. 389–398 (2002)
2. Kogge, P., Bergman, K., Borkar, S., et al.: Exascale Computing Study: Technology Challenges in Achieving Exascale systems. Technical report, DARPA (September 2008)

3. Riesen, R., Ferreira, K., Stearley, J., et al.: Redundant computing for exascale systems. Technical report, Sandia National Laboratories (December 2010)
4. Engelmann, C., Ong, H.H., Scott, S.L.: The Case for Modular Redundancy in Large-scale High Performance Computing Systems. In: International Conference on Parallel and Distributed Computing and Networks, pp. 189–194 (February 2009)
5. Ferreira, K., Stearley, J., Laros III, J.H.: et al.: Evaluating the viability of process replication reliability for exascale systems. In: Proceedings of 2011 International Conference for High Performance Computing, Networking, Storage and Analysis, pp. 1–12 (2011)
6. Stearley, J., Ferreira, K., Robinson, D., et al.: Does Partial Replication Pay off? In: IEEE/IFIP 42nd International Conference on Dependable Systems and Networks Workshops, DSN-W (2012)
7. McEvoy, D.: The architecture of tandem's nonstop system. In: Proceedings of the ACM 1981 Conference. ACM, New York (1981)
8. Bernick, D., Bruckert, B., Vigna, P., Garcia, D., Jardine, R., Klecka, J., Smullen, J.: NonStop Advanced Architecture. In: International Conference on Dependable Systems and Networks, pp. 12–21 (2005)
9. Slegel, T., Averill III, R.M., Check, M., et al.: IBM's S/390 G5 Microprocessor Design. Micro, pp. 12–23. IEEE (1999)
10. Reinhardt, S.K., Mukherjee, S.S.: Transient fault detection via simultaneous multithreading. SIGARCH Computer Architecture News, 25–36 (May 2000)
11. Vijaykumar, T., Pomeranz, I., Cheng, K.: Transient-Fault Recovery using Simultaneous Multithreading. In: 29th Annual International Symposium on Computer Architecture, pp. 87–98 (2002)
12. Reis, G., Chang, J., Vachharajani, N., Rangan, R., August, D.: SWIFT: Software Implemented Fault Tolerance. In: International Symposium on Code Generation and Optimization, pp. 243–254 (2005)
13. Zhang, Y., Lee, J.W., Johnson, N.P., August, D.I.: DAFT: Decoupled Acyclic Fault Tolerance. In: Proceedings of the 19th International Conference on Parallel Architectures and Compilation Techniques, PACT 2010, pp. 87–98 (2010)
14. Bridges, P.G., Ferreira, K.B., Heroux, M.A., Hoemmen, M.: Fault-tolerant linear solvers via selective reliability. CoRR (2012)
15. Bronevetsky, G., de Supinski, B.: Soft Error Vulnerability of Iterative Linear Algebra Methods. In: Proceedings of the 22nd Annual International Conference on Supercomputing, ICS 2008, New York, NY, USA, pp. 155–164 (2008)
16. Casas, M., de Supinski, B.R., Bronevetsky, G., Schulz, M.: Fault resilience of the algebraic multi-grid solver. In: Proceedings of the 26th ACM International Conference on Supercomputing, ICS 2012, New York, NY, USA, pp. 91–100 (2012)
17. Rose Compiler, `http://www.rosecompiler.org`
18. Melhem, R., Mosse, D., Elnozahy, E.: The interplay of power management and fault recovery in real-time systems. IEEE Transactions on Computers 217–231
19. Hukerikar, S., Diniz, P.C., Lucas, R.F.: A Programming Model for Resilience in Extreme Scale Computing. In: IEEE/IFIP 42nd International Conference on Dependable Systems and Networks Workshops, DSN-W (2012)

Reliable Service Allocation in Clouds with Memory and Capacity Constraints

Olivier Beaumont[1], Lionel Eyraud-Dubois[1],
Pierre Pesneau[2], and Paul Renaud-Goud[1]

[1] Inria & University of Bordeaux, Bordeaux, France
{olivier.beaumont,lionel.eyraud-dubois,
paul.renaud-goud}@inria.fr
[2] University of Bordeaux & Inria, Bordeaux, France
pierre.pesneau@inria.fr

Abstract. We consider allocation problems that arise in the context of service allocation in Clouds. More specifically, on the one part we assume that each Physical Machine (denoted as PM) is offering resources (memory, CPU, disk, network). On the other part, we assume that each application in the IaaS Cloud comes as a set of services running as Virtual Machines (VMs) on top of the set of PMs. In turn, each service requires a given quantity of each resource on each machine where it runs (memory footprint, CPU, disk, network). Moreover, there exists a Service Level Agreement (SLA) between the Cloud provider and the client that can be expressed as follows: the client requires a minimal number of service instances which must be alive at the end of a time period, with a given reliability (that can be converted into penalties paid by the provider). In this context, the goal for the Cloud provider is to find an allocation of VMs onto PMs so as to satisfy, at minimal cost, both capacity and reliability constraints for each service. In this paper, we propose a simple model for reliability constraints and we prove that it is possible to derive efficient heuristics.

Keywords: Cloud, reliability, resilience, linear programming, VM allocation, multidimensional bin packing.

1 Introduction

1.1 Reliability and Energy Savings in Cloud Computing

In this paper, we consider reliability issues in the context of Cloud Computing platforms, when allocating a set of independent services running as Virtual Machines (VMs) onto Physical Machines (PMs) in a Cloud Computing platform. Cloud Computing [19,1] is a well-suited paradigm for service providing over the Internet. Using virtualization, it is possible to run several Virtual Machines on top of a given Physical Machine. Since each VM hosts its complete software stack (Operating System, Middleware, Application), it is moreover possible to migrate VMs from a PM to another in order to dynamically balance the load.

Even in the static case, mapping VMs with heterogeneous computing demands onto PMs with capacities is amenable to a multi-dimensional bin-packing problem. Indeed,

D. an Mey et al. (Eds.): Euro-Par 2013 Workshops, LNCS 8374, pp. 698–706, 2014.

in this context, each physical machine comes with its computing capacity (*i.e.* the number of flops it can process during one time-unit), its disk capacity (*i.e.* the number of bytes it can read/write during one time-unit), its network capacity (*i.e.* the number of bytes it can send/receive during one time-unit), its memory capacity (given that each VM comes with its complete software stack) and its failure rate (*i.e.* the probability that the machine will fail during the next time period).

On the other hand, each service comes with its requirement along the same dimensions (memory, CPU, disk and network footprints) and a reliability demand that has been negociated through the SLA [9]. In order to deal with capacity constraints in resource allocation problems, several sophisticated techniques have been developed in order to optimally allocate VMs onto PMs, either to achieve good load balancing [18,3] or to minimize energy consumption [5,4]. Most of the works in this domain have therefore concentrated on designing offline [12] and online [13] Packing variants.

In this paper, we propose to use a new set of variables in order to deal with this multi-dimensional bin-packing problem. More specifically, we use the specific structure of the problem, and in particular the fact that the number of VMs a given PM can host is very small in practice, since each VM comes with its complete software stack. Therefore, our approach consists in enumerating all possible configurations (a configuration being defined by the set of services running on a machine) and using them as variables in the optimization problems. Indeed, if the number of different services a PM can simultaneously host is bounded, then the number of possible configurations has polynomial size.

Reliability constraints have received much less attention in the context of Cloud computing, as underlined by Cirne *et al.* [9]. Nevertheless, related questions have been addressed in the context of more distributed and less reliable systems such as Peer-to-Peer networks. In such systems, efficient data sharing is complicated by erratic node failure, unreliable network connectivity and limited bandwidth. Thus, data replication can be used to improve both availability and response time and the question is to determine where to replicate data in order to meet performance and availability requirements in large-scale systems [15,17,16]. Reliability issues have also been addressed by High Performance Computing community. Indeed, recently, a lot of effort has been done to build systems capable of reaching the Exaflop performance [10] and such exascale systems are expected to gather billions of processing units, thus increasing the importance of fault tolerance issues [8]. Solutions for fault tolerance in Exascale systems are based on replication strategies [11] and rollback recovery relying on checkpointing protocols [6].

This work is a follow-up of [2], where the question of how to evaluate the reliability of an allocation has been addressed and a set of deterministic and randomized heuristics have been proposed in the context of a single type of constraint related to CPU usage. Moreover, in [2], in order to avoid difficulties related to the bin packing problem, we assumed that the overall CPU demand of a service could be split arbitrarily on an arbitrary number of machines. Under this assumption, the packing problem was equivalent to a mono-dimensional splittable item bin packing problem, that can be solved in polynomial time without cardinality constraints.

In this paper, we therefore consider a more general model and we rely on the additional assumption on the number of VMs running on a PM in order to obtain tractable formulations of the optimization problem, that consist, from the provider point of view, in obtaining an allocation of services to physical machines so as to satisfy both capacity and reliability constraints.

1.2 Model and Notations

In this section, we introduce the notations that will be used throughout the paper. Our target cloud platform is made of m physical machines $\mathcal{M}_1, \mathcal{M}_2, \ldots, \mathcal{M}_m$. We consider the behavior of this platform over the course of one given time period (for example over one day), and we assume that during that time period, it is not practical to reallocate instances of services to physical machines. The goal of our allocation procedure is thus to provision extra instances (replicas) for the services, which will actually be used if some machines fail during the time period. The success of the allocation is determined at the end of the time period: a service is successful if enough instances are still running at the end of the time period.

As already noted, machine $\mathcal{M}_j$ is characterized by its capacity along several dimensions, *i.e.* memory, CPU, disk, network,... Since memory plays a specific role in our model, we consider it separately, and we note K the number of other resources. For the sake of simplicity, we assume that machines are homogeneous (extending this work to a constant number of machine classes is possible) and we will denote by MEMCAPA the memory capacity of the machines, and by CAPA_k, $1 \leq k \leq K$ the capacities of the machines along other dimensions. Moreover, we consider a given failure probability FAIL, that represents the probability of failure of any given machine during the time period.

On this Cloud platform, we have to run n services $\mathcal{S}_1, \mathcal{S}_2, \ldots, \mathcal{S}_n$. DEM_i identical and independent instances of service $\mathcal{S}_i$ are required, and the instances of the different services run as Virtual Machines. In turn, service $\mathcal{S}_i$ is characterized by its capacity along several dimensions, *i.e.* memory, CPU, disk, network,... We will denote by MEMPRINT_i the memory footprint of service $\mathcal{S}_i$ and by $\text{PRINT}_{k,i}$, $1 \leq k \leq K$ the footprints of service $\mathcal{S}_i$ along the other dimensions. Several instances of the same service can be run concurrently and independently on the same physical machine and we will denote by $\mathcal{A}_{i,j}$ the number of instances of $\mathcal{S}_i$ running on $\mathcal{M}_j$.

Therefore, $\sum_i \mathcal{A}_{i,j}\text{MEMPRINT}_i$ represents the overall memory footprint of the services running on $\mathcal{M}_j$ and therefore, it has to be smaller than MEMCAPA, $\forall j$. The same applies for the other resources and in general $\forall j, k$, $\sum_i \mathcal{A}_{i,j}\text{PRINT}_{k,i} \leq \text{CAPA}_k$.

On the other hand, $\sum_j \mathcal{A}_{i,j}$ represents the overall number of running instances of $\mathcal{S}_i$. In general, $\sum_j \mathcal{A}_{i,j}$ is larger than DEM_i since we use replication (*i.e.* over-provisioning) of services in order to enforce the reliability requirements. We will denote by ALIVE the set of machines which are still running at the end of the time period. In our model, at the end of the time period, the machines are either up or completely down, so that the number of instances of Service $\mathcal{S}_i$ running on $\mathcal{M}_j$ is $\mathcal{A}_{i,j}$ if $\mathcal{M}_j \in \text{ALIVE}$ and 0 otherwise. Therefore, $\text{ALIVEINST}_i = \sum_{j, \mathcal{M}_j \in \text{ALIVE}} \mathcal{A}_{i,j}$ denotes the overall number of running instances of $\mathcal{S}_i$ at the end of the time period and $\mathcal{S}_i$ is running properly at the end of the time period if and only if $\sum_{j, \mathcal{M}_j \in \text{ALIVE}} \mathcal{A}_{i,j} \geq \text{DEM}_i$.

Of course, our goal is not to guarantee that all services should run properly at the end of the time period with probability 1. Indeed, such a reliability cannot be achieved in practice since the probability that all machines fail is clearly larger than 0 in our model. In general, as noted in a recent paper of the NY Times [14], Data Centers usually over-provision resources (at the price of high energy consumption) in order to (quasi-)avoid failures. In our model, we assume a more sustainable model, where the SLA defines the reliability requirement REL_i for Service $\mathcal{S}_i$ (together with the penalty paid by the Cloud Provider if $\mathcal{S}_i$ does not run with at least DEM_i instances at the end of the period). Therefore, the Cloud provider faces the following optimization problem:

ValidAllocation$(m, n, \text{DEM}, \text{REL})$: Find an allocation $\mathcal{A}$ of the instances of services $\mathcal{S}_1, \mathcal{S}_2, \ldots, \mathcal{S}_n$ to machines $\mathcal{M}_1, \mathcal{M}_2, \ldots \mathcal{M}_m$ such that

- **Packing:** $\begin{cases} \forall j, \sum_i \mathcal{A}_{i,j}\text{MEMPRINT}_i \leq \text{MEMCAPA} \quad \text{and} \\ \forall j, k\ , \sum_i \mathcal{A}_{i,j}\text{PRINT}_{k,i} \leq \text{CAPA}_k. \end{cases}$
- **Reliability:** $\forall i,\ \mathcal{P}(\text{ALIVEINST}_i \geq \text{DEM}_i) \geq \text{REL}_i$, *i.e.* the probability that at least DEM_i instances of $\mathcal{S}_i$ are running on alive machines after the time period is larger than the reliability requirement REL_i.

1.3 Outline of the Paper

As we have noticed it, **ValidAllocation** is in general a difficult problem. First, it has been proved in [2] that given an allocation $\mathcal{A}$, determining if reliability constraints are enforced is in general #P-Complete. Moreover, in its general form, the Packing problem is a multi-dimensional bin packing problem that is NP-Complete and hard to approximate. Therefore, in Section 2, we propose a different model that takes into account the specific characteristics of the solution in order to obtain a formulation of the optimization problem, that can be given to an optimization solver, and produce a solution in a small amount of time. The results obtained on a characteristic set of instances are given in Section 3 and the conclusions and perspectives in Section 4.

2 Reformulation of the Optimization Problem

In this section, we propose a different formulation of the optimization problem **ValidAllocation**. In Section 2.1, we formulate the optimization problem for a single service as a non-linear optimization problem that can be solved efficiently under the assumption that we restrict the search to almost homogeneous allocations. Then, in Section 2.2, we rely on the fact that in practice, the number of services that can be run simultaneously on a given PM is usually very small, so that it is possible to enumerate all possible valid allocation schemes for a machine. Moreover, we will assume that the demand DEM_i of the different services is large, so that we can accurately approximate a binomial distribution by a normal distribution when estimating the number of alive instances of a service at the end of the time period.

2.1 Case of a Single Service

ValidAllocation is in general difficult to solve for two different reasons, *i.e.* (i) estimating the reliability of a single heterogeneous allocation is in general #P-Complete and

(ii) with several services, it is equivalent to a multi-dimensional bin packing problem. The question related to bin packing will be addressed in Section 2.2 and we concentrate in this section on the case of a single service.

Without reliability constraints, the minimal number of resources in order to run service $\mathcal{S}_i$ whose demand is DEM_i, whose footprint along dimension k is $\text{PRINT}_{k,i}$ and whose memory footprint is MEMPRINT_i can be found with:

$$\text{Minimize} \sum_j \mathcal{A}_{i,j} \text{ such that } \begin{cases} \forall j, & \mathcal{A}_{i,j}\text{MEMPRINT}_i \leq \text{MEMCAPA} \\ \forall j,k, & \mathcal{A}_{i,j}\text{PRINT}_{k,i} \leq \text{CAPA}_k \\ \forall j, & \mathcal{A}_{i,j} \geq 0 \end{cases}$$

where equivalently, if $A_{\max,i} = \min(\min_k(\frac{\text{CAPA}_k}{\text{PRINT}_{k,i}}), \frac{\text{MEMCAPA}}{\text{MEMPRINT}_i})$, all capacity constraints can be written as $\forall j, 0 \leq \mathcal{A}_{i,j} \leq A_{\max,i}$. Recall that as a number of instances of a service, all $\mathcal{A}_{i,j}$ is an integer.

In order to incorporate the set of constraints related to reliability in the above IP (Integer Program), we rely on the approximation of the binomial distribution $\mathcal{B}(N,p)$ by the normal distribution $\mathcal{N}(Np, Np(1-p))$ that is valid as soon as N is large [7] (typically, the approximation is considered as valid as soon as both Np and $N(1-p)$ are larger than 5, what is easily satisfied in our setting).

For $l < A_{\max,i}$, let us denote by n_l^i the number of machines where exactly l instances of service $\mathcal{S}_i$ are allocated. By the assumption of our model, the number of alive machines among those n_l^i machines follows a binomial distribution: $\mathcal{B}(n_l^i, p)$ where $p = 1 - \text{FAIL}$. By approximating this with a normal distribution, we get that the number of alive services on those machines is distributed as $l \times \mathcal{N}(pn_l^i, p(1-p)n_l^i) = \mathcal{N}(pln_l^i, p(1-p)l^2n_l^i)$, because of normal law properties. Summing over l, we obtain the distribution of the number of alive instances: $\text{ALIVEINST}_i \sim \mathcal{N}(p\sum_l ln_l^i, p(1-p)\sum_l l^2 n_l^i)$. Then, let us denote by z_{REL_i} the value (that depends on REL_i only, and can be obtained in a normal distribution table) such that $\mathcal{P}(\text{ALIVEINST}_i \geq \text{DEM}_i) \geq \text{REL}_i$ as soon as $p\sum_l ln_l^i - z_{\text{REL}_i}\sqrt{p(1-p)\sum_l l^2 n_l^i} \geq \text{DEM}_i$. Therefore, the following optimization problem provides a valid allocation that minimizes the number of replicas used for Service i:

$$\text{Minimize} \sum_j \mathcal{A}_{i,j} \text{ s. t. } \begin{cases} p\sum_j \mathcal{A}_{i,j} - z_{\text{REL}_i}\sqrt{p(1-p)}\sqrt{\sum_j \mathcal{A}_{i,j}^2} \geq \text{DEM}_i \\ \forall j,\ 0 \leq \mathcal{A}_{i,j} \leq A_{\max,i} \\ \forall j,\ \mathcal{A}_{i,j} \geq 0 \end{cases}$$

The constraint $p\sum_j \mathcal{A}_{i,j} - z_{\text{REL}_i}\sqrt{p(1-p)}\sqrt{\sum_j \mathcal{A}_{i,j}^2} \geq \text{DEM}_i$ states both that enough resources should be allocated to $\mathcal{S}_i$ and that the dispersion of these resources over PMs should be small. This corresponds well to what we observed in [2] (in the case without memory constraints), where homogeneous allocations were considered. Therefore, we will restrict the search to quasi-homogeneous allocations, where the number of instances $\mathcal{A}_{i,j}$ on machine j can be either $\mathcal{A}_i$ or $\mathcal{A}_i + 1$ for some value of $\mathcal{A}_i < A_{\max,i}$.

In order to determine the best (in terms of number of required resources) quasi-homogeneous allocation, the first step is to determine $\mathcal{A}_i$. $\mathcal{A}_i$ should be such that allocating $\mathcal{A}_i$ instances to all m machines should not be enough to enforce reliability constraint, but that allocating $\mathcal{A}_i + 1$ resources to all m machines should be enough, *i.e.* $\mathcal{A}_i = \left\lfloor \frac{\text{DEM}_i}{pm - z_{\text{REL}_i}\sqrt{p(1-p)}\sqrt{m}} \right\rfloor$.

Then, it is easy to see that the number m_i of machines that receive $\mathcal{A}_i + 1$ instances (the other $m - m_i$ machines being allocated $\mathcal{A}_i$ instances) needs to be at least $\lceil x \rceil$, where x satisfies the equation

$$pm\mathcal{A}_i + px - z_{\text{REL}_i}\sqrt{p(1-p)}\sqrt{px(\mathcal{A}_i+1)^2 + p(m-x)(\mathcal{A}_i)^2} = \text{DEM}_i,$$

which is equivalent to the following second order equation:

$$(pm\mathcal{A}_i - \text{DEM}_i - px)^2 - z^2_{\text{REL}_i}p(1-p)\left(px(2\mathcal{A}_i+1) + pm{\mathcal{A}_i}^2\right) = 0.$$

2.2 Enumerating the Set of Valid Allocations

As already noted in the introduction, **ValidAllocation** is in general difficult since even in absence of failures, it is equivalent to a general multi-dimensional bin packing problem, that is known to be hard to solve and to approximate. On the other hand, the dimension that corresponds to the memory constraints has several characteristics that make it suitable for optimization. Indeed, since each VM comes with its full software stack (say, a few Gigabytes), the number of VMs that can be handled simultaneously on a given PM is relatively low. Therefore, one can assume that no PM will be able to run more than $n_{\max}$ services and we will treat $n_{\max}$ as a constant (the reader should have in mind that a typical value for $n_{\max}$ is 3 or 4).

Let us denote as a configuration $\mathcal{C}_c$ a set of $n_{\max}$ services $\mathcal{S}_{c_1}, \mathcal{S}_{c_2}, \ldots, \mathcal{S}_{c_{n_{\max}}}$. We assume that each machine runs exactly $n_{\max}$ services without loss of generality, by adding a fictitious service whose footprint in any direction is 0. To be valid, configuration $\mathcal{C}_c$ must satisfy $\sum_{i=1}^{n_{\max}} \text{MEMPRINT}_{c_i} \leq \text{MEMCAPA}$ and $\forall j,k$, $\sum_{i=1}^{n_{\max}} \text{PRINT}_{k,c_i} \leq \text{CAPA}_k$. Let us now denote by $\mathcal{S}$ the set of possible valid configurations. There are at most a polynomial size number $n^{n_{\max}}$ of such configurations and the validity of each configuration can be verified in constant time. Using $\mathcal{S}$, it is possible to write a linear program (LP) that finds a valid allocation that makes use of a minimal number of machines. In the following LP, λ_c denotes the number of machines that follow configuration $\mathcal{C}_c$.

$$\text{Minimize} \sum_c \lambda_c \text{ such that } \begin{cases} \forall i, & \displaystyle\sum_{c,\ \#\{\mathcal{S}_i \in \mathcal{C}_c\} = \mathcal{A}_i+1} \lambda_c = m_i \\ \forall i, & \displaystyle\sum_{c,\ \#\{\mathcal{S}_i \in \mathcal{C}_c\} = \mathcal{A}_i} \lambda_c = m - m_i \\ \forall c, & \lambda_c \geq 0 \end{cases}$$

3 Numerical Results

In this section, we describe an experimental analysis of the homogeneous heuristic, obtained from randomly generated scenarios.

3.1 Experimental Setting

We consider an experimental setting with two dimensions of resource which represent memory and CPU usage. The memory footprints of all services are assumed to be approximately the same, and we consider that the available memory at each machine is enough to run 4 service instances. On the other hand, the CPU usage of each service is generated uniformly at random between 1% and MAXCPU % of the CPU capacity of the machines. For the parameter MAXCPU, we use three different values: 100%, 50%, and 25%, which implies that the CPU capacity of each machine is enough to run (on average) 2, 4, and 8 service instances. This allows us to consider a wide range of scenarios: when MAXCPU is 100%, the most constrained resource is CPU, whereas when MAXCPU is 25%, the most constrained resource is memory. For the intermediate case where MAXCPU is 50%, both resources have the same importance. The failure probability of each machine is set to 0.01, and the reliability requirements of each service is randomly generated in the following way: a random number is picked uniformly between 4 and 16, and the reliability requirement is set to $1 - 10^{-x/2}$ (hence reliability requirements lie between 0.99 and 0.99999999).

We generate small scenarios with $n = 20$ services, and large scenarios with $n = 50$ services. For each value of the parameters n and MAXCPU, we generate 100 scenarios. For each scenario, we compute, as a lower bound, the number of bins necessary to provide enough capacity to hold all services, without any packing constraint. We also run the homogeneous heuristic by solving the integer version of the linear program with

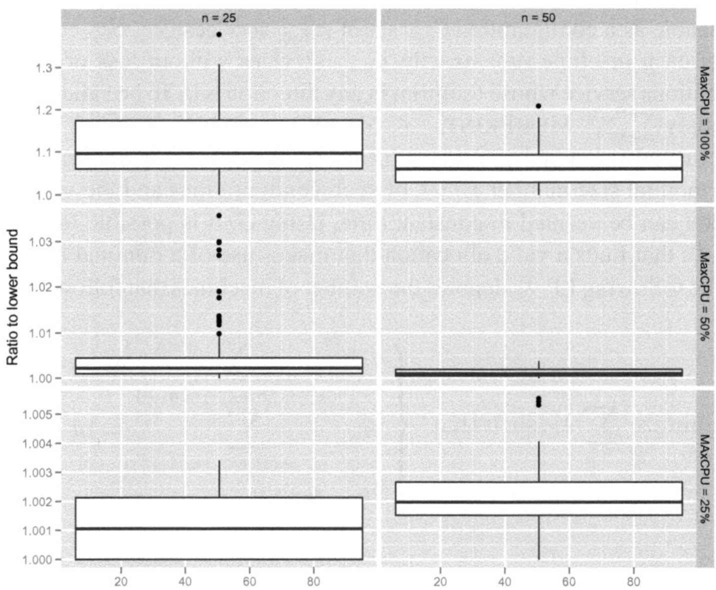

Fig. 1. Experimental results with $n = 20$ and $n = 50$ services

CPLEX with a 10 second time limit. In most cases, CPLEX was able to find an optimal integral solution, and for the largest scenarios the best solution found in 10 seconds was used.

3.2 Results

Experimental results are shown on Figure 1, where we give boxplots for the ratio of the number of bins used by the homogeneous heuristic to the lower bound.

We can see that our heuristic gives very efficient solutions, especially in the cases where memory is the strongest constraint (MAXCPU $= 25\%$). When MAXCPU $= 100\%$, it is more difficult to use all of the CPU capacity of the machines, and the performance of the homogeneous heuristic is not as close to the lower bound. But even in that case, it uses on average 10% more bins than the lower bound, and most of the time only 20% more. This shows that it is possible to provide efficient packing solutions that exhibit good reliability guarantees.

4 Conclusion

We have considered the difficulty introduced by reliability constraints when considering service allocation in Clouds in presence of failures. In this context, replication (or equivalently over-subscription) is used in order to enforce reliability demand. We have proposed a new formulation of the optimization based on a relaxation of an approximation of probability distributions that enables the design of a sophisticated heuristic, that turns out to be very efficient in a large number of scenarios.

References

1. Armbrust, M., Fox, A., Griffith, R., Joseph, A., Katz, R., Konwinski, A., Lee, G., Patterson, D., Rabkin, A., Stoica, I., et al.: Above the clouds: A berkeley view of cloud computing. EECS Department, University of California, Berkeley, Tech. Rep. UCB/EECS-2009-28 (2009)
2. Beaumont, O., Eyraud-Dubois, L., Larchevêque, H.: Reliable Service Allocation in Clouds. In: IPDPS 2013 - 27th IEEE International Parallel & Distributed Processing Symposium, Boston, États-Unis (2013), http://hal.inria.fr/hal-00743524
3. Beaumont, O., Eyraud-Dubois, L., Rejeb, H., Thraves, C.: Heterogeneous Resource Allocation under Degree Constraints. IEEE Transactions on Parallel and Distributed Systems (2012)
4. Beloglazov, A., Buyya, R.: Energy efficient allocation of virtual machines in cloud data centers. In: 2010 10th IEEE/ACM International Conference on Cluster, Cloud and Grid Computing, pp. 577–578. IEEE (2010)
5. Berl, A., Gelenbe, E., Di Girolamo, M., Giuliani, G., De Meer, H., Dang, M., Pentikousis, K.: Energy-efficient cloud computing. The Computer Journal 53(7), 1045 (2010)
6. Bougeret, M., Casanova, H., Rabie, M., Robert, Y., Vivien, F.: Checkpointing strategies for parallel jobs. In: 2011 International Conference for High Performance Computing, Networking, Storage and Analysis (SC), pp. 1–11. IEEE (2011)

7. Box, G.E., Hunter, W.G., Hunter, J.S.: Statistics for experimenters: an introduction to design, data analysis, and model building. Wiley Series in Probability and Mathematical Statistics (1978)
8. Cappello, F.: Fault tolerance in petascale/exascale systems: Current knowledge, challenges and research opportunities. International Journal of High Performance Computing Applications 23(3), 212–226 (2009)
9. Cirne, W., Frachtenberg, E.: Web-scale job scheduling. In: Cirne, W., Desai, N., Frachtenberg, E., Schwiegelshohn, U. (eds.) JSSPP 2012. LNCS, vol. 7698, pp. 1–15. Springer, Heidelberg (2013)
10. Dongarra, J., Beckman, P., Aerts, P., Cappello, F., Lippert, T., Matsuoka, S., Messina, P., Moore, T., Stevens, R., Trefethen, A., et al.: The international exascale software project: a call to cooperative action by the global high-performance community. International Journal of High Performance Computing Applications 23(4), 309–322 (2009)
11. Ferreira, K., Stearley, J., Laros III, J., Oldfield, R., Pedretti, K., Brightwell, R., Riesen, R., Bridges, P.G., Arnold, D.: Evaluating the viability of process replication reliability for exascale systems. In: Proceedings of 2011 International Conference for High Performance Computing, Networking, Storage and Analysis, p. 44. ACM (2011)
12. Garey, M.R., Johnson, D.S.: Computers and Intractability, a Guide to the Theory of NP-Completeness. W.H. Freeman and Company (1979)
13. Hochbaum, D.: Approximation Algorithms for NP-hard Problems. PWS Publishing Company (1997)
14. Data centers waste vast amounts of energy belying industry image, `http://www.nytimes.com/2012/09/23/technology/data-centers-waste-vast-amounts-of-energy-belying-industry-image.html`
15. Ranganathan, K., Iamnitchi, A., Foster, I.: Improving data availability through dynamic model-driven replication in large peer-to-peer communities. In: 2nd IEEE/ACM International Symposium on Cluster Computing and the Grid, p. 376 (May 2002)
16. Santos-Neto, E., Cirne, W., Brasileiro, F., Lima, A.: Exploiting replication and data reuse to efficiently schedule data-intensive applications on grids. In: Feitelson, D., Rudolph, L., Schwiegelshohn, U. (eds.) JSSPP 2004. LNCS, vol. 3277, pp. 210–232. Springer, Heidelberg (2005)
17. da Silva, D.P., Cirne, W., Brasileiro, F.: Trading cycles for information: Using replication to schedule bag-of-tasks applications on computational grids. In: Kosch, H., Böszörményi, L., Hellwagner, H. (eds.) Euro-Par 2003. LNCS, vol. 2790, pp. 169–180. Springer, Heidelberg (2003)
18. Van, H., Tran, F., Menaud, J.: SLA-aware virtual resource management for cloud infrastructures. In: IEEE Ninth International Conference on Computer and Information Technology, pp. 357–362. IEEE (2009)
19. Zhang, Q., Cheng, L., Boutaba, R.: Cloud computing: state-of-the-art and research challenges. Journal of Internet Services and Applications 1(1), 7–18 (2010)

Model-Driven Resilience Assessment of Modifications to HPC Infrastructures

Christian Straube and Dieter Kranzlmüller

Munich Network Management (MNM) Team,
Ludwig-Maximilians-Universität München, Germany,
Leibniz Supercomputing Center (LRZ), Munich, Germany
straube@nm.ifi.lmu.de

Abstract. The increasing influence of surrounding factors on HPC infrastructure operations, e.g., increasing cost pressure or evolving power consumption, requires an analysis of the indented effects of modifications in the context of the entire HPC infrastructure and its capabilities, before this modification is further (costly) explored or executed actually. Therefore, a meta model is provided that enables a domain-spanning capability effect analysis, which respects the complex component interplay of contemporary HPC infrastructures. The meta model in turn is used as basis for the model-driven development of tooling support.

Keywords: Infrastructure, Availability, Reliability, Modeling, Optimization.

1 Introduction

Conventional *cause-effect–analysis* (CEA) is a distinguished tool to analyze the (theoretical) technical effects of a modification in a well-defined specific area, e.g., the impact of using symmetric active/active redundancy (*cause*) on reliability (*effect*). The findings are used to alter the modification or to support the decision-making about its execution. Nevertheless, development in the *surroundings* and in the *layout* of contemporary HPC infrastructures require an extension of modification planning and evaluation: before it is investigated *how* a particular effect in a specific area can be achieved, it must be decided whether *this intended effect and its consequences are reasonable at all* in the context of the entire HPC infrastructure. Especially from an operations point of view, this decision is made upon the expected effects to the HPC infrastructure's *capabilities*, e.g., the "capability to consume less energy", and consequently, we call the analyzed effects *capability effects.* The resulting **capability effect analysis** is based upon two pillars: a complex multi-domain optimization problem and the HPC infrastructure components interaction.

The optimization problem is defined by the evolution in several surrounding factors of HPC infrastructures, like increasing cost pressure (*cost*), evolving power consumption (*energy*) or ever more demanding scientific calculations

D. an Mey et al. (Eds.): Euro-Par 2013 Workshops, LNCS 8374, pp. 707–716, 2014.

(*performance*). For instance, increasing redundancy to address short-time breakdown (*reliability*) [1], simultaneously increases energy consumption and degrades performance due to redundancy overhead, leading to an optimization problem between the dimensions *reliability*, *energy*, and *performance* [2]. Consequently, **capability effect analysis must be domain-spanning**, to weigh out trade-offs in the context of the entire HPC infrastructure as basis for the decision-making about the modification's investigation and execution.

Considering component interactions is important since HPC infrastructures provide their functionality by a qualitative and quantitative complex component interplay, which hardens separating the specific contribution of a particular component. Additionally, most characteristics are combined and influenced by different aspects, even within a single domain, e.g., system performance includes computing cores as well as communication, interconnect, and I/O performance [3,4]. Hence, effects induced by local modifications on a single component can quickly cascade and affect the HPC infrastructure partly or completely in an unpredictable way. Consequently, **capability effect analysis must cover effect cascading within the entire HPC infrastructure**, and not only a particular component or a (small) subset.

Capability effect analysis applies the generic CEA concept with different input causes, as depicted in Figure 1: on the left, conventional CEA investigates the correlation of a planned modification (*cause*: PM_i) and its (theoretical) technical effect within a single dimension (*effect*: TE_i). In contrast, the capability effect analysis on the right, uses the *intended effects* (IE_j) of the planned modifications from all considered dimensions and the component interaction as causes to calculate a capability effect (CE_z) vector that is used to weigh out trade-offs and to decide, whether a modification is further explored or executed actually (dashed arrow).

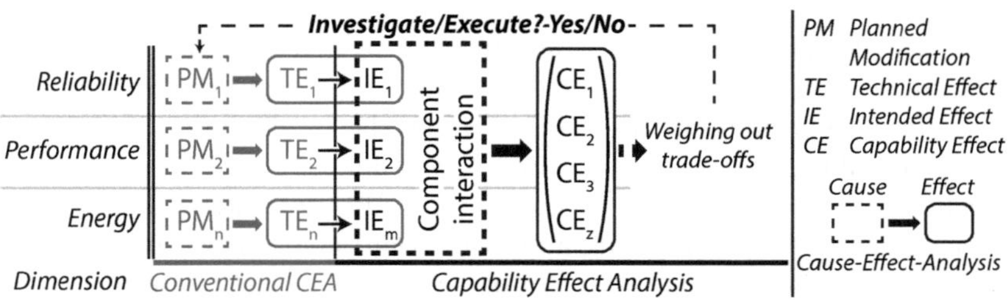

Fig. 1. Difference of conventional cause-effect–analysis and capability effect analysis

In summary, decision-making about a planned modification's execution should be built upon systematic planning and analysis of its expected or intended capability effects [5,6]: the modification is only executed if its intended capability effects will lead to an improvement for the aforementioned optimization problem. *How* the modification is executed is neglected in this consideration and passed over, e.g., to conventional CEA approaches. Applying this to the example above, redundancy should be increased (*modified*) only if it actually improves reliability (*effect*) and the increasing energy consumption and performance losses do not outweigh the benefits (*effect optimization problem*). How redundancy is concretely implemented is examined by one of the plenty existing approaches.

Although there are a lot of distinguished and mature approaches to conduct conventional CEA for resilience aspects, none of them can be used for capability effect analysis as explained in Section 2. In [7,8] a meta model is presented, which is dedicated to provide capability effect analysis functionality in the above described manner, but lacking resilience aspects. The objective of this paper is to extend the meta model by resilience aspects in three steps: 1) Section 3.1 provides a condensed overview of relevant quantification and modeling methodologies, 2) Section 3.2 extracts their commonalities, and 3) Section 4 derives a generic and flexible model extension based on the extracted elements. The paper focuses on the capabilities *availability* and *reliability*, because of their important role for most of resilience aspects, e.g., the enhanced capability *dependability*, especially in the area of upcoming exascale systems and the increasing number of components [9]. Related domains, like performance or energy efficiency, are under investigation at the moment to prepare them for application in capability effect analysis.

2 Related Work

This section investigates suitability of related work to model *capability effect characteristics and their interplay* to facilitate capability effect analysis. Related work is split in two groups, one focusing on resilience related aspects, and one on modeling HPC infrastructures in general. For each group, the general investigation is illustrated by representative examples.

The first group contains a lot of mature approaches that address certain detailed aspects of resilience very well. Nevertheless, all of them have at least one of the following drawbacks: 1) focusing on technical details and not on capability effects (*wrong input*), or 2) covering only (a few) resilience aspects and omitting other dimensions (*not domain-spanning*). Hence, neither the tool nor its underlying model can be used. An example for the first drawback is [10] that analyzes the impact of sub-optimal checkpointing (*modification*) on application efficiency (*capability*). An example for the second drawback is [11], developing a method to automatically select the best-fitting model to describe resource availability (*capability*), but without considering the interplay with other resilience capabilities or with capabilities of other dimensions.

The second group contains models to describe a network, computer system or a distributed system in general. The main drawback of this group is that it mainly models technical details and not capability effects and their interplay, especially not resilience capabilities. A representative example is the *Common Information Model* (CIM) [12]. Even if some capabilities are described, e.g., the attribute `NetworkAdapter.MaxSpeed`, to our knowledge there are no resilience capabilities and most attributes describe technical aspects that are relevant only for modifications, e.g., the attribute `MediaAccessDevice.MaxBlockSize`.

3 Measurement and Modeling Methodology Overview

This section forms a theoretical basis for the model extension development by considering the relevant measurement and methodologies in a condensed overview (Figure 2, based on [13,14]). The commonalities of the considered elements, the model is required to cover in order to facilitate capability effect analysis, are extracted, as well. Commonality extraction focuses on the *calculation results* of the considered methodologies, because they express the intended effects (cf. Figure 1). To the contrary, details about modifications, e.g., the distinction of failures according to their causes, their severity, or their impact area [13,14], are neglected, since they do not alter the measurement or calculation methodology, but only the used input, as further examples in this section illustrate.

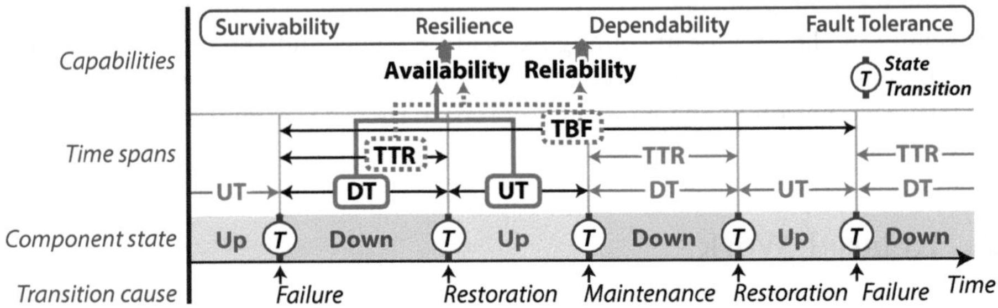

Fig. 2. Correlation of component states, state transitions, and quantification to derive availability and reliability figures

3.1 Elementary Concepts

A component is in the ***up state*** whenever it delivers a *correct service* or a *system function* as it is described by the functional specification [14]. A ***failure*** is a temporary or permanent termination of this ability and it causes a transition from correct to incorrect service or to ***down state*** [14]. A ***restoration*** (also called *replacement* or *repair*) causes a transition from *down* to *up state* [15,16]. The time period a component is in the up state or down state is described by the ***Uptime (UT)*** or ***Downtime (DT)***, respectively. The time it takes to conduct a restoration is measured by the ***Time to Repair/Restore (TTR)***. The time span between the occurrence of two consecutive failures is described by the ***Time between Failures (TBF)*** [13]. For all itemized measurements there are mean values labeled with a prefix ***M***, which are used to describe or calculate a component's availability and reliability among other capabilities. Especially the *MTBF* plays a central role, because of its strong correlation to failure interpretation, .e.g, it describes the frequency of (hardware) failures [15,17]. An example of the aforementioned neglected details is the equality of $DT = TTR$ and $UT = TBF$ dependent on the consideration of scheduled maintenance [13,15], which does not influence the calculation methodology, but only the input values that are used to calculate availability and reliability.

3.2 Availability and Reliability

Component ***availability*** describes the delivery of being in the up state, component ***reliability*** describes the continuousness of being in the up state under stated conditions over a specified period of time [2,14]. There are many ways to structure and refine the two capabilities and their calculation rules, e.g., by distinguishing mission availability and work mission availability [18], or by describing different calculation rules for *Total Availability*, *Scheduled System Availability*, and *Mean Time between Job Interrupts* [19]. Since a modification's intended effects are expressed by calculation and measurement results (cf. Section 3) – e.g., reliability is calculated or expressed by *MTBF* –, we introduce a structuring that distinguishes capabilities and their calculation by the format of these calculation results. The structuring is depicted in Figure 3, showing the three result formats *binary* (yes/no), *fraction* ($\mathbb{R}$), and *probability* (%), and the two influencing dimensions, which are described subsequently.

The first dimension is the *line of sight* (x-axis in Figure 3), describing whether the past or the future is analyzed: A ***retrospective view*** analyses existing data or empirical observations, which can be obtained in many ways, e.g., gathering field data or processing log files [20]. The main challenge about a retrospective view is the underlying data, as it is of varying quality or very rare, since it is collected by observing parts failing while operating, a seldom event for well designed components [2]. In contrast, a ***prospective view*** creates predictions of future events by applying different probability distributions, like Weibull, Pareto or hyperexponential distributions. Depending on the objective, the existing empirical observation, and the considered component type, each distribution has specific advantages, e.g., Pareto is often advocated for lifetime estimation, whereby Weibull is more suitable for various resource availability data [21,11].

The second dimension is the *considered time* (y-axis in Figure 3), describing whether only a certain ***point in time*** is analyzed or an ***interval between two points in time***, whereby the interval can be finite or infinite. Since reliability describes the continuousness, it is always calculated for a period of time, whereby availability can also be calculated for a point in time, as depicted in Figure 3 by the thick lines at the top and at the right hand side of the possible formats.

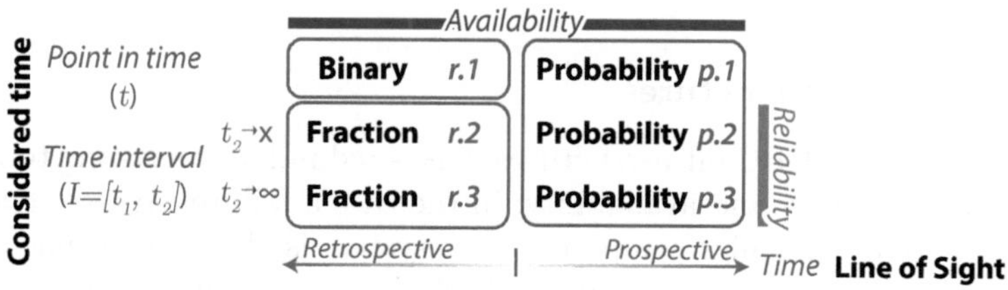

Fig. 3. Result types of availability and reliability calculation rules

Subsequently, a non-exhaustive list of examples is provided to further explain the differences, using the referencing labels (r.1)–(p.3) as depicted in Figure 3.

The *binary* result (r.1) states whether a component was available at a certain point in time in the past. An example for (r.3) is the *steady-state availability*

A_s describing the equilibrium behavior of a component. It is calculated by $A_s = \frac{MTBF}{MTBF+MTTR}$ [22], using existing data for $MTBF$ and $MTTR$. An example for (p.1) is the *instantaneous availability* or *point availability* $A(t)$, which is defined as the probability of finding a component in the up state at time t [22]. It is calculated by an integral as described in [18,22]. Another example for (p.1) is the "bathtub curve", describing the failure rate development over time dependent on the component's age describing parameter t [15]. An example for (p.2) is the *interval availability*, which describes the expected fraction of time the component is up in a given interval I and is calculated by an integral. Reliability values in (p.2) and (p.3) are calculated by integrals and probability distributions as described by [2].

In summary, every way to calculate availability or reliability generates a result having one of the three described formats.

3.3 Composite Values

As explained in Section 1, HPC infrastructures provide functionality by combining (several) components. Since the above investigated calculation rules mostly cover only one particular component, they have to be combined to results for combined components or sub systems, as well, leading to *composite values*. For instance, the composite availability value of a compute node is built up of the availability values of the contained components, like CPUs, internal bus, local memory, and network card. The composite availability value of the compute area in turn is build up of all compute node (composite) availability values.

Basically, composite values can be calculated by basic mathematical functions, like product, sum or mean. For instance, composite steady state availability can be calculated by multiplying the values of $\frac{fR_i}{fR_i+rR_i}$, whereby, fR_i describes the failure rate, and rR_i the repair rate of component i [2]. It assumes that a combined component or sub system is available if and only if all of the contained components are available, or in other words, if one of the product operands is 0 (the component is not available), the overall result is also 0. An example to calculate the composite reliability R_c of a compound component is *Part Count Analysis (PCA)* that uses the sum operator as described by [23].

3.4 Redundancy Structures

Compound nature of HPC infrastructures makes redundancy a strong tool to improve system reliability and availability: in the case a failure causes a transition to *down state* of a particular component, the system is able to continue to operate using a redundant component instead [9]. A system's redundancy structure can be described by ***boolean functions*** that use variables c_i to describe that "component c_i is available". For instance, the boolean function $\varphi = (c_1 \vee c_2) \wedge c_3$ expresses that a system consisting of two redundant compute nodes c_1, c_2 and a network c_3 is available if the network and at least one of the two compute nodes is available [2]. A ***fault tree*** is a graphical representation of a redundancy structure, whereby the leaves represent availability (boolean variables), and inner nodes contain functions to calculate the overall system availability by processing the leave values up to the root.

4 An Integrated Model

This section extends the meta model described in [7,8] in two consecutive steps: 1) derive a set of criteria from the extracted commonalities (cf. Section 3); 2) extend the model guided by the derived criteria set.

4.1 Model Extension Criteria

The development of the extended meta model was guided by a set of criteria. To apply the same development methodology as for the existing meta model, in this first step, a set of criteria is derived that guides the model extension. The criteria are labeled as *C.R[1-6]* to emphasize the commonality to [7] (expressed by *C*–riterion), but at the same time, to show the focus on resilience (expressed by *R*–esilience).

C.R1 – Different Calculation Rules and Result Types. There are several ways to calculate availability and reliability values, whose result is of one of the types *binary*, *fraction*, and *probability* (cf. Section 3.2). The neta model has to cover the result types and their manifold calculation rules on a component level. Additionally, it has to respect that every calculation rule has a different set of parameters,e.g., standard deviation, shape parameter, or a point in time.

C.R2 – Composite Values. Respecting the composite nature of HPC infrastructures requires the meta model to support the different ways of calculating *composite values* (cf. Section 3.3). To cover real world elements sufficiently accurate, calculation rules must be definable on a component level.

C.R3 – Redundancy Handling. Sufficient coverage of redundancy aspects requires the meta model to describe fault trees. To foster time and cost saving, analysis should be able to start with the most critical components [2] and hence, covering component criticality is required.

C.R4 – Decision-Making. To support (manual) decision-making and foster automatic problem solving, for every capability an improvement direction is necessary. For instance, an increase of *MTBF* is an improvement, whereby a decrease of *MTTR* is an improvement.

C.R5 – Multiple Data Sources. To address the varying quality, uncertainty, incompleteness, and rareness of data used by retrospective and prospective analysis (cf. Section 3.2), the meta model has to support different data sources on component level. For instance, there are reliable vendor specifications for a CPU, but only incomplete empirical observations for the local memory.

C.R6 – Inherited Criteria. The extended meta model's criteria are *C1–Real World Element Selection*, *C2–Multiple Levels of Model Granularity*, *C3–Openness and Flexibility*, and *C4–Simplicity* [7]. To ensure that the resulting meta model fulfills these origin criteria, the extension must fulfill them as well.

4.2 Extending the Meta Model by Resilience Aspects

The meta model extension, whose result is depicted in Figure 4 as UML class diagram, is subsequently described, guided by the criteria *C.R1–C.R6*.

Fulfillment of C.R1 – The result types *binary*, *fraction*, and *probability*, are represented by interfaces in the `value` package. The `ProbabilityValue` is sub classed to emphasize different probability distributions like Weibull or Pareto, and to ensure by type safety that only results of the same distribution are processed together. Different parameter sets per calculation are handled by the key-value map parameter each interface method uses.

Fulfillment of C.R2 – The interfaces in the package `compositeValue` express the different ways to calculate composite values, whereby some simple operations are indicated. The interfaces are implemented by the `Composite` class that represents a (sub tree) root in the HPC infrastructure modeling tree [7,8].

Fulfillment of C.R3 – The `Component` class is extended by an attribute `criticalityLevel`, whose value can be set by applying existing approaches like fault injection [24] or CIM database analysis. To foster reusability of boolean functions, they can be prepared by the class `RedundancyFunction` and used by different `Component` objects.

Fulfillment of C.R4 – A `Capability`'s improvement direction is described by an enumeration attribute `improvementDirection`, which is a sufficient data structure, since there can only be one improvement direction at the same time.

Fulfillment of C.R5 – To respect different data situations per component, every `Component` is associated with a `AnalysisRuntimeCapabilityValue` that implements one of the different capability value types. These values can be

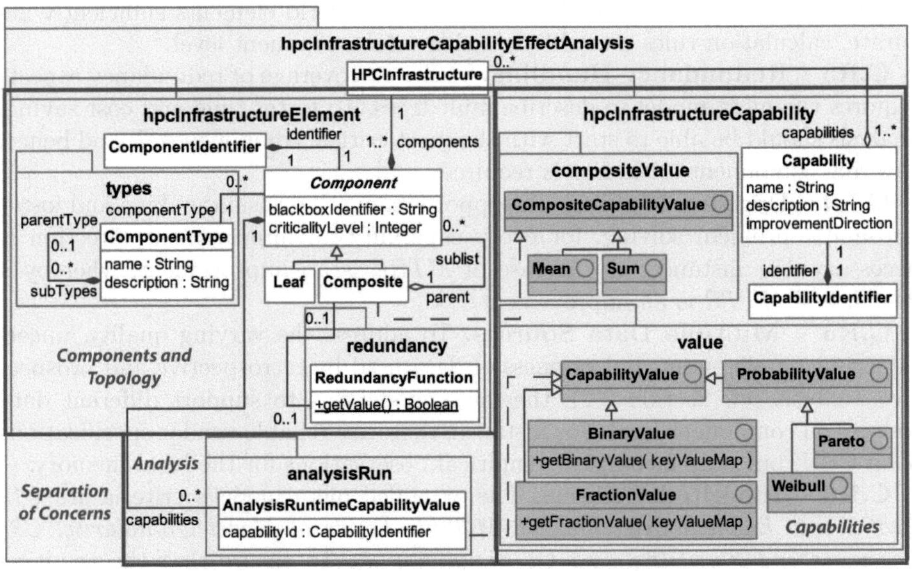

Fig. 4. UML class diagram of the capability model

provided by different calculation rules, e.g., the availability of a storage `Component` can be "calculated" as fixed value provided by a vendor's specification, whereby the availability of a CPU `Component` can be calculated by a bathtub curve.

Fulfillment of C.R6 – The meta model extension fulfills the four origin criteria, because 1) it focuses on capability effects and hence, results in a *valid model* (*C1*), 2) it does not hamper the black box approach (*C2*), 3) it follows the *Separation of Concerns* (SoC) of the meta model, marked by the three rectangles in Figure 4, since the interfaces are only loosely coupled, and the set of prepared interfaces can flexibly enhanced by individual ones (*C3*), and 4) it supports the tree based modeling of an HPC infrastructure (*C4*).

5 Conclusion and Future Work

Capability effect analysis examines the domain-spanning cascading of a modification's intended effect within an entire HPC infrastructure to support the decision about the investigation and execution of a modification: only if the modification's intended effects produce an improvement as intended of the entire HPC infrastructure, the modification is executed. In [7,8] a meta model is presented, dedicated to support capability effect analysis, but lacking resilience consideration. This paper extends the meta model by resilience aspects in three steps: 1) give a condensed overview of relevant methodologies, 2) extracts their commonalities, and 3) derive a generic and flexible meta model extension based on the extracted elements. A *Model Driven Development* (MDD) process uses the developed meta model to generate a graphical editor that supports modeling (complex) HPC infrastructures and handling resilience aspects for capability effect analysis. The created HPC infrastructure model in turn serves as input for generating optimization code to address the optimization problem noted in Section 1. This process is currently applied to analyze the *SuperMUC* at the LRZ, a three PetaFlop/s HPC system.

References

1. Elliott, J., et al.: Combining Partial Redundancy and Checkpointing for HPC. In: Proc. of the 32th Intl. IEEE Conf. on Distributed Computing Systems, ICDCS (2012)
2. Eusgeld, I., Fechner, B., Salfner, F., Walter, M., Limbourg, P., Zhang, L.: Hardware Reliability. In: Eusgeld, I., Freiling, F.C., Reussner, R. (eds.) Dependability Metrics. LNCS, vol. 4909, pp. 59–103. Springer, Heidelberg (2008)
3. Chen, D., et al.: Looking Under the Hood of the IBM Blue Gene/Q Network. In: Proc. of the Intl. ACM/IEEE Conf. on High Performance Computing, Networking, Storage and Analysis, SC 2012 (2012)
4. Meswani, M., et al.: Modeling and Predicting Disk I/O Time of HPC Applications. In: Proc. of the High Performance Computing Modernization Program Users Group Conf., HPCMP-UGC (2010)
5. Broadbent, M., Weill, P.: Management by Maxim: How Business and IT Managers Can Create IT Infrastructures. Sloan Management Review 38(3), 77–92 (1997)

6. Song, H., et al.: Availability Modeling and Evaluation on High Performance Cluster Computing Systems. Journal of Research and Practice in Information Technology 38(4), 317–335 (2006)
7. Straube, C., Kranzlmüller, D.: A Meta Model for the Analysis of Modification Effects onto HPDC Infrastructures. Submitted to 27th Intl. Conf. on Architecture of Computing Systems, ARCS 2014 (2014)
8. Straube, C., Kranzlmüller, D.: An IT-Infrastructure Capability Model. In: Proc. of the 10th ACM Conf. on Computing Frontiers, CF 2013 (2013)
9. Jones, W., et al.: Application Monitoring and Checkpointing in HPC: Looking Towards Exascale Systems. In: Proc. of the 50th Annual Southeast Regional Conf. (2012)
10. Jones, W., et al.: Impact of Sub-Optimal Checkpoint Intervals on Application Efficiency in Computational Clusters. In: Proc. of the 19th Intl. ACM Symposium on High Performance Distributed Computing, HPDC 2010 (2010)
11. Nurmi, D., Brevik, J., Wolski, R.: Modeling Machine Availability in Enterprise and Wide-Area Distributed Computing Environments. In: Cunha, J.C., Medeiros, P.D. (eds.) Euro-Par 2005. LNCS, vol. 3648, pp. 432–441. Springer, Heidelberg (2005)
12. DMTF: Common Information Model (CIM) Metamodel (Specification). Technical Report DSP0004, Distributed Management Task Force, DMTF (2012)
13. Lu, C.: Failure Data Analysis of HPC Systems. CoRR abs/1302.4779 (2013)
14. Avizienis, A., et al.: Fundamental Concepts of Dependability. Technical report, University of California, Los Angeles, UCLA (2010)
15. Verbrugge, S., et al.: General Availability Model for Multilayer Transport Networks. In: Proc. of the 5th Intl. Workshop on Design of Reliable Communication Networks, DRCN 2005 (2005)
16. Pedicini, G., Green, J.: SPOTlight on Testing: Stability, Performance and Operational Testing of LANL HPC Clusters. In: Proc. of the Intl. ACM/IEEE Conf. for High Performance Computing, Networking, Storage and Analysis, SC 2011 (2011)
17. Boukerche, A., et al.: Towards Building a Highly-Available Cluster Based Model for High Performance Computing. In: Proc. of the 20th Intl. Parallel and Distributed Processing Symposium, IPDPS 2006 (2006)
18. Birolini, A.: Reliability Engineering: Theory and Practice. Springer (2007)
19. Stearley, J.: Defining and Measuring Supercomputer Reliability, Availability, and Serviceability (RAS). In: Proc. of the Linux Clusters Institute Conf. (2005)
20. Chandler, C., et al.: Towards Resilient High Performance Applications Through Real Time Reliability Metric Generation and Autonomous Failure Correction. In: Proc. of the Workshop on Resiliency in High Performance (2009)
21. Xu, J., et al.: Networked Windows NT system field failure data analysis. In: Proc. of the Intl. Pacific Rim Symposium on Dependable Computing (1999)
22. Trivedi, K.: Probability and Statistics with Reliability Queuing and Computer Science Applications. John Wiley & Sons, Inc. (2001)
23. Military Handbook: Reliability Prediction of Electronic Equipment. Technical Report MIL-HDBK-217F, Department of Defense (1991)
24. Bagchi, S., et al.: Dependency Analysis in Distributed Systems using Fault Injection: Application to Problem Determination in an e-commerce Environment. In: Proc. of the 12th Intl. Workshop on Distributed Systems, DSOM 2001 (2001)

Asking the Right Questions: Benchmarking Fault-Tolerant Extreme-Scale Systems

Patrick M. Widener[1], Kurt B. Ferreira[1], Scott Levy[2], Patrick G. Bridges[2], Dorian Arnold[2], and Ron Brightwell[1]

[1] Sandia National Laboratories*, Albuquerque, NM
{patrick.widener,kbferre,rbbrigh}@sandia.gov
[2] University of New Mexico, Albuquerque, NM, USA
{slevy,bridges,darnold}@cs.unm.edu

Abstract. Much recent research has explored fault-tolerance mechanisms intended for current and future extreme-scale systems. Evaluations of the suitability of checkpoint-based solutions have typically been carried out using relatively uncomplicated computational kernels designed to measure floating point performance. More recent investigations have added scaled-down "proxy" applications to more closely match the composition and behavior of deployed ones. However, the information obtained from these studies (whether floating point performance or application runtime) is not necessarily of the most value in evaluating resilience strategies. We observe that even when using a more sophisticated metric, the information available from evaluating uncoordinated checkpointing using both microbenchmarks and proxy applications does not agree. This implies that not only might researchers be asking the wrong questions, but that the answers to the right ones might be unexpected and potentially misleading. We seek to open a discussion on whether benchmarks designed to provide predictable performance evaluations of HPC hardware and toolchains are providing the right feedback for the evaluation of fault-tolerance in these applications, and more generally on how benchmarking of resilience mechanisms ought to be approached in the exascale design space.

1 Introduction

Issues surrounding reliability in extreme-scale systems are now attracting substantial research attention. Increasing size, component counts, and complexity of modern and projected systems are presenting unpalatable reliability implications for applications. Some estimates point to exascale systems suffering multiple failures per hour, seriously hindering application throughput and thereby squandering considerable hardware and software investment.

The HPC community has arrived at this untenable position largely due to a strong emphasis on peak CPU performance as an indicator of design and deployment success.

---

* Sandia National Laboratories is a multi-program laboratory managed and operated by Sandia Corporation, a wholly-owned subsidiary of Lockheed Martin Corporation, for the U.S. Department of Energy's National Nuclear Security Administration under contract DE-AC04-94AL85000.

D. an Mey et al. (Eds.): Euro-Par 2013 Workshops, LNCS 8374, pp. 717–726, 2014.

The growth in popularity of the Top 500 list, for example, has been extremely valuable as a means of increasing the visibility of issues in early extreme-scale system design. While understandable and even beneficial, this emphasis on floating point performance provides little information on how to design applications and system software to deal with the fast-approaching reliability crunch. The disconnect is underscored by the common practice of generating results for the Top 500 list using application runs that avoid the defensive resilience measures (i.e. checkpointing) that are pervasive in front-line HPC applications.

This reliability information deficit will greatly hinder the designers of HPC systems and applications. Similarly to how power and heat constraints are shaping design decisions for exascale systems, sustainable HPC design will need to accommodate fault-tolerance as a first-class objective. Evaluation of systems and their applications must become more sophisticated in order to properly inform the design process. Current evaluations of both systems and software rely strongly on CPU performance-oriented benchmarks such as the NAS Parallel Benchmarks suite. Conceived in an HPC environment with infrequent failures, such benchmarks will have decreasing utility. Another consideration is that such benchmarks do not reflect the behavior of front-line HPC applications. Several well-known applications consist of compositions of computational kernels designed to solve different stages of large problems, and their approaches to resiliency are driven by the nature of those compositions. Their checkpointing strategies change based on application state volatility in each stage of the problem (i.e. the behavior of the computational kernel in question).

Standardized, repeatable benchmarks and problem sets that reflect deployed application behavior and yield a more appropriate metric could alleviate these problems. Recent studies of resilience issues have investigated *efficiency*, defined as the proportion of application runtime spent on the problem rather than on fault-tolerance activities such as checkpoint/restart, as a more informative metric. Efficiency becomes increasingly appropriate as "effective" performance measurements are reduced by increasing system fault rates.

With this paper, we hope to encourage a discussion on useful methods of obtaining information on the application efficiency made possible by architecture, system software, and fault-tolerance design choices. We observe that correlations in efficiency that might be expected between computational kernels from the NAS benchmarks set, "mini-apps" from the Sandia Mantevo project, and front-line scientific codes are not strongly apparent. We believe this is an appropriate departure point on how benchmarking should be considered in a new HPC regime where resilience concerns trump CPU performance. A more complete evaluation of benchmarking in a comprehensive set of fault-tolerance scenarios as well as proposals for evolving existing benchmark sets into a standard fault-tolerance benchmarking suite remain for future work. Our preliminary study indicates, however, that a discussion among the HPC resilience community on how to properly consider the behavior of current and proposed extreme-scale systems and applications is both appropriate and timely.

2 Related Work

This section briefly discusses the context of our work in checkpointing and benchmarking research.

2.1 Checkpointing

The most prevalent method of defensive fault-tolerance mitigation in modern applications, coordinated checkpointing periodically writes global application or system state to stable storage [1]. Consistent application state snapshots are enforced through global barrier synchronization. When a process fails, all application processes can then be restarted from a known-good, globally consistent state. Algorithmic approaches borrowed from the distributed computing domain [1] allow applications to generate consistent checkpoints without using barriers, avoiding increasingly expensive global synchronization.

Other techniques from distributed computing have given rise to uncoordinated or asynchronous checkpointing [2,3,4,5,6,7,8,9]. In these systems, nodes do not synchronize when they checkpoint, but they also keep a log of their sent messages on stable storage. Nodes restoring from local asynchronous checkpoints can then reconstruct a local state consistent with the application global state by replaying inbound messages from other nodes (using their logs).

We are not strictly concerned here with contributing to the active research comparing and contrasting these two approaches. However, we note that an informed choice between them requires knowledge of the application: how much state is maintained locally, shared with other cooperating nodes, or is easily reconstructed and therefore a candidate for leaving out of a checkpoint. A benchmarking suite that allows such choices by more closely reflecting the composition and behavior of complex applications is more likely to provide guidance on which checkpointing method is appropriate.

2.2 Benchmarks for HPC

Several benchmarking suites are widely used in the high-performance computing community. The Top500 list, itself an evolution of the Mannheim Supercomputer Statistics lists of the late 1980s, introduced the use of the LINPACK [10] linear equation solver as a standard, repeatable benchmark tool. The growing popularity of the Top500 list arguably also led to a reductive emphasis on floating point performance as a design goal, although at the time the available headroom in HPC performance was so great as to make this reasonable.

Finding LINPACK an unsuitable representative for their applications, the designers of the NAS Parallel Benchmarks [11] created first a set of specifications and later a set of reference implementations of a group of small benchmark kernels. Although providing a more nuanced view of supercomputing performance through the aggregation of several types of computational problems, the emphasis on floating point performance persisted.

More recent efforts have addressed the need to represent computational tasks from deployed applications through the creation of proxy applications. Comprising simplified versions of those applications able to execute scaled-down problem instances, benchmark collections from various organizations such as NERSC [12], Sandia [13] and Argonne [14] have refined performance evaluation still further. As these approximations of deployed application behavior become more popular, realistic evaluations of resilience strategies and effects are being pursued through both direct experimentation and simulation [15]. We submit that an emphasis on more sophisticated metrics such as efficiency as well as a more comprehensive consideration of resilience approaches are logical next steps in this evolution.

3 Comparing Benchmarks to Applications

In this section we investigate the correlation between efficiency profiles of a mixed set of microbenchmark/proxy application/full application combinations using uncoordinated asynchronous checkpointing. We made these choices because: 1) in a coordinated scheme, since checkpoint durations and intervals are fixed, the behavior of benchmarks and applications would be similar; 2) alternatives to coordinated checkpointing are necessary for exascale systems; and 3) it seems necessary to examine alternatives to benchmarks (such as NAS) that were designed years ago for coordinated checkpointing environments.

We used a modified message trace-driven simulator [16] to measure application efficiency (a discussion of our modifications and validation of this simulation framework can be found in [15]). Using this framework we found that, using uncoordinated checkpointing, the choice of benchmark can be significant, as codes computing essentially the same problem produced varying performance results. We argue that these results do not necessarily imply the superiority of any particular benchmark; rather, they illustrate that, as different checkpointing approaches are dictated by increasing application/system scale and the associated reliability concerns, evaluating application efficiency may not be as straightforward as evaluating floating point performance.

3.1 Simulation Results and Discussion

Figures 1 through 3 show the uncoordinated checkpoint performance of a number of common HPC microbenchmark applications using the simulator described previously [15]. In each of these figures we assume a two minute checkpoint interval and a one second checkpoint commit time (time to write a checkpoint). For simplicity we assume there are no failures in the each of these runs, but note that failures should not change the shapes of the curves shown. Additionally, we assume a message logging protocol to keep all checkpoints consistent but attribute no runtime overhead to this logging protocol. We believe this is a reasonable assumption for send-deterministic applications given recent work on optimizing message log sizes [17,18,19,20]. The "D" size class of NAS benchmarks were used, and other problem instances were sized accordingly.

Figure 1 illustrates the efficiency of two popular conjugate gradient solvers, NAS-CG and the mini-application HPCCG [21]. From this figure, we see that the overhead of uncoordinated checkpointing varies greatly between these two workloads even though they are solving similar problems. Most importantly, given that node counts are expected to increase significantly in future systems, the trends suggest that the difference

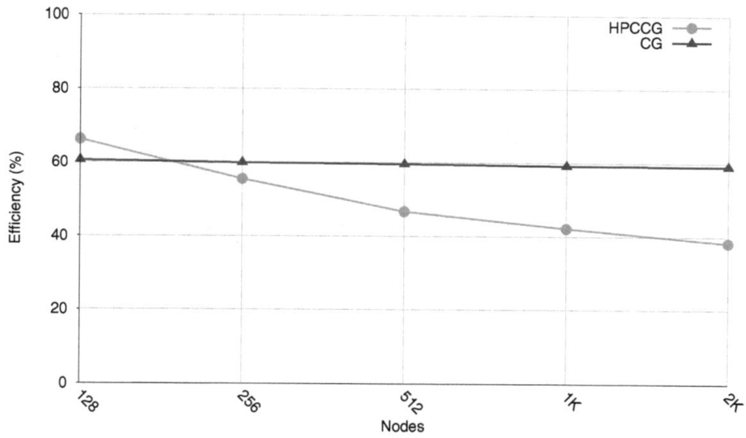

Fig. 1. Application Efficiency of NAS-CG and HPCCG with uncoordinated checkpointing

in performance between these two workloads increases with node count. In addition to the efficiency differences, the floating point performance of these two workloads also varies greatly. Using the same compiler, optimization flags, platform, and physical application layout, HPCCG executes 100x more flops/second than does CG.

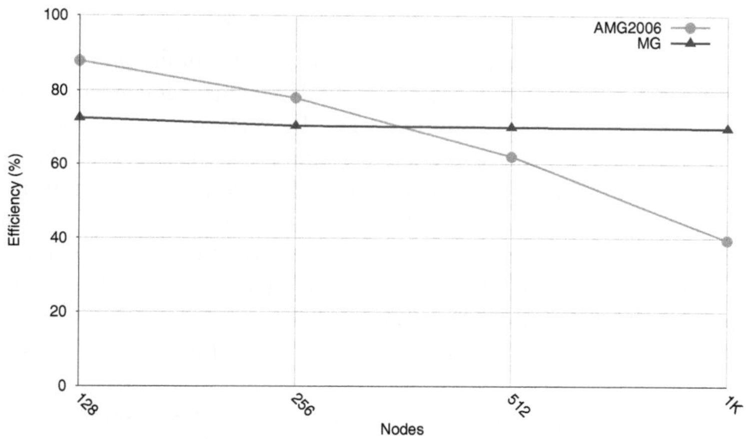

Fig. 2. Application Efficiency of the NAS-MG and AMG with uncoordinated checkpointing

Similarly, Figure 2 shows the efficiency of NAS-MG and AMG from the ASC Sequoia Benchmark suite [22], two popular multi-grid linear system solvers used in many DOE simulation workloads. Again, we see each of these workloads behave very differently while solving a similar problem. Also, again the difference in performance increases dramatically as node count increases.

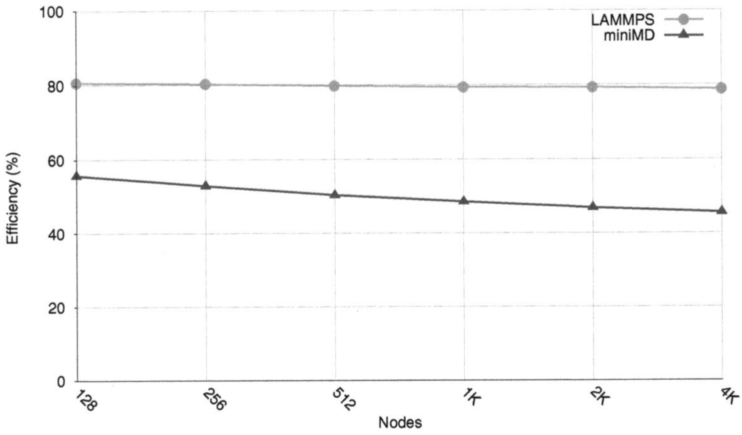

Fig. 3. Application Efficiency of miniMD and LAMMPS with uncoordinated checkpointing

Finally, Figure 3 contains the efficiency results for the application LAMMPS [23,24] and the Mantevo mini-application molecular dynamics code miniMD [21]. Of the comparisons shown in this paper, miniMD and LAMMPS behave most similarly with uncoordinated checkpointing. This fact is not a surprise given these two workloads share a significant amount of source code and an overlap in the development teams. However, even with these workloads sharing considerable portions of source code, there exists a significant difference in performance with uncoordinated checkpointing.

As we see from this section, applications computing very similar problems and even using very similar algorithms can respond to a resilience mechanism (in this case uncoordinated checkpointing) in very different ways. In an effort to better understand the differences, we next examine each application's communication pattern. In Figure 4 we show a comparison of the most frequently called MPI functions for each of the workloads. In this figure, we only include MPI functions which contribute to a significant portion of the total function count. From the figure we see that, as could be expected, for NAS-CG and HPCCG as well NAS-MG and AMG these benchmarks compute their respective problems in a very different manner, leading to their respective differences in efficiency. In contrast, the miniMD and LAMMPS MPI function profiles look very similar.

We believe these results point to two important issues when evaluating resilience for extreme-scale systems. First, as opposed to coordinated checkpointing in which checkpoints can be taken at known quiesced synchronization points, under uncoordinated checkpointing application communication patterns can significantly affect application efficiency. Second, understanding how communication patterns and other non-local operations impact performance is important in designing algorithms for faulty environments. These results point to a need to consider resilience a first-class concern in designing algorithms for future systems where failures will be common, as opposed to the resilience-as-an-afterthought approach that has been used successfully in the past with coordinated checkpointing.

NAS-CG		HPCCG	
MPI_Send()	33.33%	MPI_Send()	19.97%
MPI_Irecv()	33.33%	MPI_Irecv()	19.97%
MPI_Wait()	33.33%	MPI_Wait()	19.97%
		MPI_Allreduce()	19.97%

(a) NAS-CG and HPCCG

AMG		NAS-MG	
MPI_Iprobe()	49.63%	MPI_Irecv()	33.33%
MPI_Testall()	49.63%	MPI_Wait()	33.33%
MPI_Wait()	0.36%	MPI_Send()	32.88%

(b) AMG and NAS-MG

miniMD		LAMMPS	
MPI_Send()	33.81%	MPI_Wait()	30.56%
MPI_Irecv()	32.23%	MPI_Send()	30.56%
MPI_Wait()	32.23%	MPI_Irecv()	30.56%

(c) miniMD and LAMMPS

Fig. 4. Pairwise comparison of the most frequently-called MPI routines in each pair of programs as percentages of the total number of MPI calls

4 Application vs. System Resilience

The choice between application-directed and system-directed resilience action has been explored in some detail. Our results in the previous section imply that appropriate resilience strategy choices are likely to be highly application dependent upon information not sufficiently exposed by microbenchmarks. Similarly, delegating responsibility for resilience to the operating system also disregards knowledge and context and can greatly affect performance measurements. This can take several forms:

- System-directed checkpointing ignores significant work that real applications do for their own resilience. Furthermore, system checkpoints are typically larger and (since they are conducted without input from the application) may contain redundant or stale data.
- Real applications have evolved downstream ecosystems based on consumption of checkpoint products such as telemetry, analysis/visualization and steering processes. System-directed checkpointing that assumes complete control of resilience policy decisions can interfere with these downstream processes and reduce their utility.

Ideally, the distinction between application- and system-provided resilience would become much less stark. System resilience utilities, as opposed to exercising complete control over policy decisions, should instead act more as resource monitors (as other operating system constructs such as schedulers and memory managers do). In such an arrangement, system checkpointing libraries would expose hardware resilience information and allow collaboration between applications and the system. This would allow applications to continue to satisfy downstream consumers of resilience data as well as provide a measure of fine-grain control to future benchmark suites.

5 Concluding Remarks

This work was motivated by our growing awareness of a disconnect between the increasing emphasis on resilience issues in exascale systems research and the nature of the tools being used to evaluate the responses to those issues. Classical benchmarking tools, while entirely appropriate for the era in which they were designed, will be of decreasing utility in the face of current exascale design trends. As we have discussed, several "next-generation" benchmarking approaches are under development which promise a more nuanced picture of the performance of real applications under the new constraints implied by those trends. We believe, however, that resilience will be a fundamental issue for exascale, and that a community-wide discussion of what kinds of benchmarks and metrics are most valuable is both necessary and timely.

The establishment and popularity of the Top500 list clearly had beneficial results, driving advances in hardware, system software and application design and implementation which in turn have had numerous trickle-down effects for HPC research. Other "500" lists have emerged, each lending visibility to specific areas: energy consumption and sustainability are highlighted by the Green500 (`www.green500.org`), and the different HPC design decisions necessary to support efficient graph-based analytics algorithms by the Graph500 (`www.graph500.org`). Resilience is becoming widely accepted as a core design goal for HPC systems, roughly paralleling the path that energy efficiency concerns followed to prominence. While it may strike some as facetious, a "Resilient500" list could have similar beneficial effects: addressing a core emerging design concern (as does the Green500) by spurring an interested community to establish commonly accepted information-rich metrics and benchmarks (as the Graph500 organizers are doing).

We also note that important vehicles for this type of discussion are already underway. The DOE ASCR Co-Design Centers [25] (ExaCT [26], ExMatEx [27], CESAR [28]) are each charged with an application area important for the future of exascale system design. In particular, these efforts will focus on the fusion of scientific problem requirements (which we have shown can have notable impact in performance evaluation) with architectural and system software concerns (providing visibility to hardware resilience issues as well as propagation of resilience information throughout the software stack). Their unique charter makes the Co-Design Centers an ideal venue for efforts to further develop and standardize resilience-aware benchmarking.

References

1. Chandy, K.M., Lamport, L.: Distributed snapshots: determining global states of distributed systems. ACM Trans. Comput. Syst. 3(1), 63–75 (1985)
2. Ahn, J.: 2-step algorithm for enhancing effectiveness of sender-based message logging. In: SpringSim 2007: Proceedings of the 2007 Spring Simulation Multiconference, pp. 429–434 (2007)
3. Jiang, Q., Manivannan, D.: An optimistic checkpointing and selective message logging approach for consistent global checkpoint collection in distributed systems. In: Proceedings of the 2007 IEEE International Parallel and Distributed Processing Symposium (March 2007)

4. Johnson, D.B., Zwaenepoel, W.: Recovery in distributed systems using asynchronous message logging and checkpointing. In: Proceedings of the Seventh Annual ACM Symposium on Principles of Distributed Computing, pp. 171–181 (1988)
5. Alvisi, L., Marzullo, K.: Message logging: Pessimistic, optimistic, causal, and optimal. IEEE Trans. Softw. Eng. 24(2), 149–159 (1998)
6. (Mootaz) Elnozahy, E.N., Alvisi, L., Wang, Y.-M., Johnson, D.B.: A survey of rollback-recovery protocols in message-passing systems. ACM Comput. Surv. 34(3), 375–408 (2002)
7. Bosilca, G., Bouteiller, A., Cappello, F., Djilali, S., Fedak, G., Germain, C., Herault, T., Lemarinier, P., Lodygensky, O., Magniette, F., Neri, V., Selikhov, A.: MPICH-V: Toward a scalable fault tolerant mpi for volatile nodes. In: Conference on High Performance Networking and Computing (SC 2002), Baltimore, MD, pp. 1–18 (November 2002)
8. Lemarinier, P., Bouteiller, A., Herault, T., Krawezik, G., Cappello, F.: Improved message logging versus improved coordinated checkpointing for fault tolerant MPI. In: IEEE International Conference on Cluster Computing, pp. 115–124 (2004)
9. Saito, Y., Shapiro, M.: Optimistic replication. ACM Comput. Surv. 37(1), 42–81 (2005)
10. Dongarra, J.J., Luszczek, P., Petitet, A.: The linpack benchmark: past, present and future. Concurrency and Computation: practice and experience 15(9), 803–820 (2003)
11. Van der Wijngaart, R.F., Wong, P.: NAS parallel benchmarks version 2.4. Technical report, NAS technical report, NAS-02-007 (2002)
12. Antypas, K., Shalf, J., Wasserman, H.: NERSC-6 workload analysis and benchmark selection process. Technical Report LBLNL-1014E, Lawrence Berkeley National Laboratories (2000)
13. Sandia National Laboratories. Mantevo, `http://software.sandia.gov/mantevo`
14. CESAR, Argonne National Laboratory. The CESAR Proxy-apps, `https://cesar.mcs.anl.gov/content/software` (retrieved June 10, 2013)
15. Ferreira, K.B., Levy, S., Bridges, P.G.: A simulation infrastructure for examining the performance of resilience strategies at scale. Technical Report SAND 2013-3180, Sandia National Laboratories (April 2013)
16. Hoefler, T., Schneider, T., Lumsdaine, A.: Loggopsim: simulating large-scale applications in the LogGOPS model. In: Proceedings of the 19th ACM International Symposium on High Performance Distributed Computing, pp. 597–604. ACM (2010)
17. Riesen, R., Ferreira, K., Da Silva, D., Lemarinier, P., Arnold, D., Bridges, P.G.: Alleviating scalability issues of checkpointing protocols. In: Proceedings of the International Conference on High Performance Computing, Networking, Storage and Analysis, SC 2012, Los Alamitos, CA, USA, pp. 18:1–18:11. IEEE Computer Society Press (2012)
18. Guermouche, A., Ropars, T., Snir, M., HydEE, F.C.: Failure containment without event logging for large scale send-deterministic MPI applications. In: IPDPS, pp. 1216–1227. IEEE Computer Society (2012)
19. Ropars, T., Guermouche, A., Uçar, B., Meneses, E., Kalé, L.V., Cappello, F.: On the Use of Cluster-Based Partial Message Logging to Improve Fault Tolerance for MPI HPC Applications. In: Jeannot, E., Namyst, R., Roman, J. (eds.) Euro-Par 2011, Part I. LNCS, vol. 6852, pp. 567–578. Springer, Heidelberg (2011)
20. Guermouche, A., Ropars, T., Brunet, E., Snir, M., Cappello, F.: Uncoordinated checkpointing without domino effect for send-deterministic MPI applications. In: International Parallel Distributed Processing Symposium (IPDPS), pp. 989–1000 (May 2011)
21. Sandia National Laboratory. Mantevo project home page, `https://software.sandia.gov/mantevo` (April 10, 2010)
22. Lawrence Livermore National Laboratory. Asc sequoia benchmark codes, `https://asc.llnl.gov/sequoia/benchmarks/#amg` (April 6, 2013)
23. Plimpton, S.J.: Fast parallel algorithms for short-range molecular dynamics. Journal Computation Physics 117, 1–19 (1995)

24. Sandia National Laboratory. LAMMPS molecular dynamics simulator, http://lammps.sandia.gov (April 10, 2010)
25. Advanced Scientific Computing Research program, Office of Science, US Department of Energy. SciDAC Co-Design, http://science.energy.gov/ascr/research/scidac/co-design/ (retrieved June 10, 2013)
26. Center for Exascale Simulation of Combustion in Turbulence (ExaCT), http://exactcodesign.org/ (retrieved June 10, 2013)
27. Exascale Co-Design Center for Materials in Extreme Environments (ExMatEx), http://exmatex.lanl.gov/ (retrieved June 10, 2013)
28. Center for Exascale Simulation of Advanced Reactors (CESAR), https://cesar.mcs.anl.gov/ (retrieved June 10, 2013)

Using Performance Tools to Support Experiments in HPC Resilience*

Thomas Naughton[1,2], Swen Böhm[1], Christian Engelmann[1], and Geoffroy Vallée[1,]

[1] Computer Science and Mathematics Division,
Oak Ridge National Laboratory, Oak Ridge, TN, USA
{naughtont, bohms, engelmannc, valleegr}@ornl.gov
[2] School of Systems Engineering,
The University of Reading, Reading, UK

Abstract. The high performance computing (HPC) community is working to address fault tolerance and resilience concerns for current and future large scale computing platforms. This is driving enhancements in the programming environments, specifically research on enhancing message passing libraries to support fault tolerant computing capabilities. The community has also recognized that tools for resilience experimentation are greatly lacking. However, we argue that there are several parallels between "performance tools" and "resilience tools". As such, we believe the rich set of HPC performance-focused tools can be extended (*repurposed*) to benefit the resilience community.

In this paper, we describe the initial motivation to leverage standard HPC performance analysis techniques to aid in developing diagnostic tools to assist fault tolerance experiments for HPC applications. These *diagnosis* procedures help to provide context for the system when the errors (failures) occurred. We describe our initial work in leveraging an MPI performance trace tool to assist in providing global context during fault injection experiments. Such tools will assist the HPC resilience community as they extend existing and new application codes to support fault tolerance.

1 Introduction

As large-scale systems increase in size and complexity the high performance computing (HPC) community is exploring ways to cope with the emerging and projected dependability challenges. This is driving research in the area of fault tolerance (FT) and resilience for HPC. The efforts range from algorithmic approaches that seek to make applications failure-oblivious or naturally fault tolerant down to system level changes that offer modular redundancy and differentiated resource allocations based on resilience requirements. These advances have been highlighted in recent whitepapers and workshop reports [4,6,11,5].

The dominant programming model for current HPC systems is based on the message passing interface (MPI). Therefore it is understandable that a number of efforts have focused on enhancing MPI to support fault tolerant computing. The resilience community

* The rights of this work are transferred to the extent transferable according to title 17 U.S.C. 105.

D. an Mey et al. (Eds.): Euro-Par 2013 Workshops, LNCS 8374, pp. 727–736, 2014.

has also recognized that there is a significant need for tools to assist in resilience experimentation. Unfortunately, there exist very few resilience tools. Most existing tools provide monitoring capabilities to gather metrics about the health of a system, but there is a significant lack of tools to analyze and interpret this data in order to create a global view of the system status and resiliency. Furthermore, users, researchers and system administrators have very different views of the resiliency of the system and existing tools are not appropriate for capturing meaningful resilience data for users and researchers (including data mining tools).

Performance tools on the other hand have been widely studied, deployed and used in the context of HPC. We believe that reusing and possibly extending these "performance tools" can assist the HPC resilience community as it begins to develop "resilience tools". Then the rich set of HPC tools for MPI applications can be extended or *repurposed* to benefit the resilience community. For instance, much of the focus on resilience for MPI is limited to fail-stop errors [2] but tools are lacking to capture the local & global state of the job in the event of a failure. We believe it is possible to use performance tools for MPI on HPC systems to obtain data that can be useful in this resilience oriented context and expose valuable information about the job state in the context of failures. In addition, fault injection (FI) is a standard approach to controllably introduce synthetic errors into a target to aid in the study of the system's fault tolerance properties. These FI tools are beginning to emerge in the context of HPC to assist in the study of application resilience. These tools provide the basis for experimental studies and must be adapted to work in a large-scale computing context. Beyond the basic mechanisms, these tools should also provide support for understanding the state of the system under test to aid in the analysis phase of the experiments. These *diagnosis* procedures help to provide context for the system when the errors (failures) occurred.

In this paper, we describe the motivation to leverage an existing HPC technique to help develop a diagnostic tool that can benefit users and developer experimenting with MPI FT. We describe our initial work in leveraging an MPI performance trace tool to assist in providing global context during resilience experiments, e.g., fault-injection studies. The following sections are organized as follows: in Section 2 we provide background on resilience and performance tools. In Section 3 we outline the scope and discuss our initial approach for realizing a diagnostics tool for MPI resilience to assist with application fault tolerance experiments. Then in Section 4 we experiment with the approach using the MPI Fault Tolerance Working Groups (MPI-FTWG)'s reference prototype. Section 5 mentions some related work that has leveraged performance oriented tools for resilience experimentation. Finally, in Section 6 we discuss plans for future work and conclusions for this paper.

2 Background

It is common for HPC software developers to employ tools to aid with the analysis of their parallel applications. Performance tools enable the user to obtain supplementary information to better understand the execution behavior of the parallel applications running on the machine. There are different approaches and methods to obtaining this performance data. A common approach is to trace the execution, recording the time for each event under observation. These traces can then be used in postmortem analysis to identify functions or regions of the execution where performance degraded.

In this section, we present an overview of HPC performance tools, their benefits, how they could be used in the context of system resiliency, as well as the associated challenges. We more precisely focus on tracing tools for MPI applications and their usage for postmortem analysis to gather data about system and application resilience, as well as the impact of failures on application performance (including the impact on fault-tolerant or failure-aware applications). The MPI trace file provides useful data for establishing local and global context for the tasks in the parallel job. This can include very simple information like which rank(s) failed? Which ranks were communicating when failure was detected? How long did collectives delay when failure occurred? What functions had the failed rank(s) executed before the failure? Some of these questions can be aided by the fact that it is possible to get traces for "golden" and "failed" runs of the application and do postmortem comparisons. This includes looking at the performance/resilience trade-offs for the application. This can help to answer questions like what MPI functions did the application spend the most time in: (i) during non-error cases?, and (ii) during error cases?

2.1 Benefits of Performance Tools in the Context of Resilience

As previously said, performance tools typically provide the capability of producing an execution trace associated with timing details. From this data, it is possible to extract both the *dependencies* between parts of the parallel applications (between ranks in the context of MPI), as well as *timing* details for the entire parallel application by combining timing data from all the nodes involved in the computation. This data is useful for creating diagnostic data, especially when applications incorporate API's for managing errors: this trace data can be used to explain where additional time is being spent for fault-tolerance and possibly to understand the propagation of errors throughout the parallel application. Therefore, these "performance tools" may provide the basis to gather data to assist in developing HPC "resilience tools".

For instance, in the context of MPI, trace files provide several useful pieces of data in the form of a log of events from the execution of a parallel job. These are time stamped event logs that may include all or a subset of the MPI functions that the application has executed. The logs provide the ordering of functions on a per rank basis within the overall job. Depending on the tool used, the traces may also contain the arguments/parameters and return values for the functions. In the case of MPI, this can include the communicator identifier that is in use. The function entry and exit time are also included, which is typically used to establish performance bottlenecks and attribute portions of the overall wall-clock and CPU time to sections of the execution.

In fault injection experiments, establishing the context for the target is crucial to understanding how failures propagate. The distributed nature of MPI applications adds to the complexity of the problem because the dependencies are not just in a single location, but potentially distributed across multiple processes in the parallel job. Therefore, establishing the context at both the local and global levels is beneficial. What functions are executing at the target rank and at other ranks is useful information.

2.2 Challenges Created by the Use of Performance Tools

One challenge of tracing that must be controlled for when using these tools in a resilience context is file generation. In some instances, if a rank fails, the trace file might not be generated. Also, the file may only contain a partial trace for the failed rank(s) due to buffering. Again, this requires that the methods used to introduce synthetic errors (failures) for resilience testing may have to modify the tracing system to flush logs before injecting the failure. This idealized failure to aid experiments/data gathering is typical for FI tools to provide controlled behavior under failure. The point being that care must be taken to avoid losing or corrupting traces during resilience experiments.

2.3 MPI-FT API

The MPI Fault Tolerance Working Group (MPI-FTWG) has developed additions for the standard that are to be reviewed for inclusion by the MPI Forum. The extensions for MPI are defined in the *User Level Failure Mitigation (ULFM)* proposal, which is described in [2]. These ULFM extensions provide support for detection and notification of process failures for communicating MPI processes. These changes are to provide a basis for building applications that can be extended to be failure-aware, i.e., applications can be notified of rank failures during their execution. The following provides a very brief summary of the ULFM extensions.

The proposed specification [2] adds two new MPI error types: `MPI_ERR_REVOKED` and `MPI_ERR_PROC_FAILED`. Failure notification is done through communicator error handlers. An application can change the default handler (`MPI_ERRORS_ARE_FATAL`) to `MPI_ERRORS_RETURN` and when an error occurs the associated error handler will be called to allow the application to cope with the issue. The ULFM API provides a function, `MPI_Comm_agree()`, to establish consensus over a group of processes in a communicator. When an application is notified of failed ranks, it can revoke (`MPI_Comm_revoke()`) the communicator to force other members of the group to recognize the failure as well. Once revoked, the failed ranks can be removed from a communicator by calling `MPI_Comm_shrink()`, which reduces the size of the associated group. This function is similar to `MPI_Comm_split(comm, newcomm)` with the live ranks of `comm` forming the group returned in `newcomm`. There are functions to locally acknowledge failures on the communicator (`MPI_Comm_failure_ack()`), which quells future notifications about that rank's failure. Additionally, a user can query for failures that have been locally acknowledged via `MPI_Comm_failure_get_acked()`. The MPI-FTWG's reference prototype is implemented in Open-MPI.

3 Requirements and Approach

This investigation is interested in adding assistance for applications taking advantage of the fault-tolerance mechanisms that are being introduced for MPI. We are focused on two classes of users: application developers and fault-tolerance implementers. We will limit the error model to fail-stop, where a fault in a MPI process results in a detectable error that causes the process to fail and stop executing. This is the error model that is being focused upon by the MPI Forum's Fault Tolerance Working Group (MPI-FTWG). The model assumes that failure detection occurs when communication takes place with the failed process(es), e.g., point-to-point, collectives, etc. (Note, the proposed MPI-FTWG extensions also provide a method for forcing the propagation of errors to other members of a group, e.g., `MPI_Comm_revoke()`.)

It can be very difficult to have a global view of the execution state for a parallel job. A MPI tracing tool provides details about what actions have been performed by each process (rank) in the parallel job. The results of these traces can provide details on application characteristics without doing detailed source code analysis as the actual functions and the communication patterns among the ranks are available for postmortem analysis. The trace files provide empirical data that can be used to establish dependencies. The dependencies can then be used to focus further resilience experiments, e.g., fault-injection campaigns. They can also be used to reason about the state of the application upon failure and the propagation of the failure throughout the application.

We assume the testing environment can be managed to avoid trace data corruption and/or loss. This includes controlling the I/O buffering within the trace to ensure we get output from the ranks even if a failure occurs in the job. This likely requires some additional considerations when introducing the errors, e.g., ensuring that failing ranks call `exit()` before terminating. These are part of the controlled environment that should be provided to support fault-injection experiments.

Our approach is to instrument each rank of the MPI job to generate trace files. These files capture all MPI functions at a given rank and the arguments passed to the functions. The application should not need to be modified for the purpose of gathering the data, with the exception of possibly adding support to control failure behavior to ensure traces are generated (i.e., process signal handlers for controlled exit, etc.). The FT-enabled applications will run in both a standard (failure-free) and failure mode.

To evaluate this approach we have prototyped the idea using existing performance tools. We used the DUMPI MPI tracing library that was developed by Sandia as part of their SST/macro project [8]. The traces are recorded in a binary format with utilities to convert the results to plain text. The library records both the input arguments and return values[1] for the MPI functions. The library can also support tracing individual functions, and can be configured to record performance counter data using PAPI [8]. There are utilities for converting DUMPI trace files to Open Trace Format (OTF) files, which could be used with existing performance visualization tools like Vampir.

The DUMPI library was extended to support the MPI-FTWG's proposed ULFM extensions [2]. This allows us to gather trace data for the existing MPI-1 and MPI-2 functions supported by DUMPI, as well as the ULFM functions while experimenting with applications that have been enhanced to take advantage of the FT extensions.

4 Experimentation

We performed a set of experiments on a single desktop and a small Linux testbed to investigate our approach with trace data for example codes. The tests used a basic

[1] The documentation states the return codes are tracked but the version we used only tracked `MPI_Init()`.

molecular dynamics code (*simpleMD*) that performs a Lennarad-Jones simulation. The application is written in C and accepts an input files for parameters (e.g., number of time steps, report frequency, etc.). At set intervals the rank-0 of the application prints computed properties (e.g., temperature, kinetic, potential and total energies) and writes to a checkpoint file. The application support restart from the checkpoint file using a command-line option on the `mpirun` command line.

The existing MPI application was enhanced to use the MPI-FTWG's ULFM API. The changes added additional error checking to the MPI calls and forced roll-back to a previous time step if an error occurred during the simulation. This roll-back does not require a full restart of the application but does use the checkpoint data from previous successful steps. The application uses a single communicator, but to accommodate ULFM's shrink functionality, we duplicate `MPI_COMM_WORLD` to have a consistent handle (`smd_comm`) that can be used throughout the application. Lastly, to simulate failures, we modified the `simpleMD` application to force a rank to terminate if the environment variable `ULFM_TEST_FAIL` was enabled. In summary, the steps to add ULFM support to the simpleMD application where:

Step-1: Change all instances of `MPI_COMM_WORLD` to use "smd_comm" handle
Step-2: Change error handlers to `MPI_ERRORS_RETURN`
Step-3: Modify main simulation loop to recognize process failures (`MPI_ERR_REVOKED` and `MPI_ERR_PROC_FAILED`)
Step-4: On error, all call `MPI_Comm_revoke()` and `MPI_Comm_shrink()`
Step-5: Replace "smd_comm" handle with newcomm obtained from shrink
Step-6: Roll back to previous iteration and continue from previous checkpoint

4.1 Performance+Resilience

We ran the `simpleMD` application on our test cluster to gather non-failure and induced-failure trace data. The non-failure traces showed that the application was entirely symmetric and used a large number of explicit synchronizations (`MPI_Barrier()`. This is understandable because this is a demonstration application and not necessarily intended to scale to large process counts. We confirmed that none of the ULFM functions were used during the non-failure runs. We also noticed that during our induced-failure tests we called the revoke function twice when only one should be necessary. The tests used 32 nodes of the cluster with 1 rank per node. We could see from the test runs that the wall-time for the shrink was small (less than a half second) but the time spent in the two revokes was between 2-5 seconds (approx. $1-2\%$ of job wall-time) for the job with 1 of the ranks in the forced failure.

As highlighted in Section 3, the trace data provides useful diagnostic information to help explain where additional time is being spent for fault-tolerance and to help understand error propagation through the parallel application. The experiments are performed with specific care to ensure the DUMPI trace files are generated when the failures are introduced into the ULFM enabled application.

4.2 Global Context for Fault Injection

The application was run under normal circumstances to generate a failure-free trace. As a way to evaluate the benefits for fault-injection experiments (Section 3), we use the trace results to identify instances where the communication log could be used to gain insights into the behavior of the application when performing fault-injection experiments. Here we discuss two instances where the trace data was useful for gathering global context during two tests. Note, these tests used the `simpleMD` application with 1000 time steps and status reported every 10 steps.

The trace data in the failure test case can also provide diagnostic information for instances where the target application hangs and global-context can be useful to determine what the overall job is doing e.g., which ranks are waiting. This can be an indicator for portions of the application that are not receiving the notification about rank failures, i.e., problems with detection. This trace data provided diagnostic information that was useful when investigating hangs and other unexpected behavior.

During experiments with the ULFM enhanced application we ran a basic test that caused a specific rank to fail to trigger the ULFM detection and force a rollback to previous checkpoint. The steps for the test were as follows:

1. Set an environment variable to signal a failure at runtime.
2. Start 3 ranks with executable linked to trace library ('md-dumpi'). The application runs for 1000 time steps.
3. At hard-coded time step 500, and victim-rank set to rank 1, we simulate a failure by calling `exit()`.
4. Ranks 0 and 2 detect this process failure via ULFM based on return codes from MPI calls (`MPI_ERR_PROC_FAILED` or `MPI_ERR_REVOKED`). They call revoke and then shrink to get a new communicator (`smd_comm`). They fall back to earlier phase and re-initialize data and restart from a saved checkpoint.
5. The program finishes and you see the same result for the last time step as in the non-failure case.

After running this test we discovered unexpected results in the trace files. The root rank (rank 0) finished properly and the trace ended with a call to `MPI_Finalize()`. The forced-fail rank (rank 1) had a shorter trace that ended in calls to get rank, which was expected for the error reporting function that prints the rank. However, the other rank (rank 2) also had a shorter trace with more time steps than rank 1, but fewer than rank 0 and the final lines were not `MPI_Finalize()` but instead resembled that of rank 1. The final result output from the application matched the results from previous runs so the application exited properly and the fault-tolerance mechanisms worked. After closer review of output logs we also noticed that the application only reported the execution time of one rank. This combined with the unexpected results in the trace files made us review the ULFM enhancements to the application. We then recognized a flaw in the fault-injection logic as outlined in the steps above. The ULFM shrink routine reduces the size of the communicator. During the re-initialization the ranks update their rankID for the restored communicator. The hard-coded selection of rank 1 for the simulated failure was repeated on the "new" rank 1 (which was originally rank 2). After adjusting our victim rank selection method, we achieved the expected results and had both ranks complete properly. The revised steps are as follows (*italics indicate the updated parts*:

1. Set an environment variable to signal a failure at runtime.
2. Start 3 ranks with executable linked to trace library ('md-dumpi'). The application runs for 1000 time steps.
3. At hard-coded time step 500, *and victim-rank is set to original `MPI_COMM_WORLD` size minus 1* (`mcw_size - 1`), we simulate a failure by calling `exit()`.
4. *Ranks 0 and 1* detect this process failure via ULFM based on return codes from MPI calls (`MPI_ERR_PROC_FAILED` or `MPI_ERR_REVOKED`). They call revoke and then shrink to get a new communicator (`smd_comm`). They fall back to earlier phase and re-initialize data and restart from a saved checkpoint.
5. The program finishes and you see the same result for the last time step as in the non-failure case.

This error in the fault-injection logic was simple but illustrates the sort of problems that occur without having some global context. The trace files were a clear indication that the application completed properly but the global job (all ranks) did not operate as we expected/intended. The fault-tolerance methods were operating properly so we achieved the correct results and if not for the additional review from the unexpected trace output we likely would have missed this FI logic error until much later in the testing process.

The previous tests were performed on a single machine. When we moved the same tests over to the Linux cluster we encountered unexpected hangs when we forced a failure. We could tell from the console logs that the rank terminated. We then forced all the stalled ranks to terminate and write their trace files to disk using a signal handler to force them to call `exit()`. When looking at the traces from all the ranks we could see two useful pieces of information. First, all of the ranks were a few steps beyond the failed rank (based on trace file time steps) and all live ranks were at the same time step in a blocking collective. Second, we could see that none of the expected ULFM routines for communicator revocation or shrinking had occurred. This helped to explain why they were all stalled in the collective, because the failure had not been propagated to the different ranks in the job. To remedy this issue we changed our synthetic failure function to use `MPI_Abort(MPI_COMM_SELF,-1)` instead of `exit(1)`. This allowed the failure information to be propagated by the MPI runtime system and allowed the test to run as expected. This is either a configuration problem for the ULFM prototype or possibly a bug/limitation of the current prototype code.

5 Related Work

Recently, research on hardware performance characterization has extended preexisting tools to aid in resilience studies for soft errors in HPC applications. In [10], a fault injection tool was developed that leveraged the binary instrumentation tool *PIN*. Their tool, *BIFIT*, was used to introduce errors into specific symbols/data-structures of three real-world HPC applications to study the effect of simulated "soft errors". They used the instrumentation tool to inject bit-flips into application-specific regions of global, heap and stack data objects. They also leveraged the memory profiling support of their performance tools to identify candidate injection sites. In contrast to this work, we use performance traces to gather context about the application to identify errors during fault-injection experiments and to provide global context about the application. The trace data could also provide candidate ranks for injecting process failures based on the communication patterns.

The following research has also leveraged HPC performance tools to develop resilience and diagnostic tools. The Extreme-scale Simulator (xSim) is a performance investigation toolkit for running MPI applications at extreme scale by running on existing machines in a heavily oversubscribed mode [3]. The Sandia SST/Macro [8] project has similar goals but employs a different approach. Both of these performance tools employ parallel discrete simulation to study the effects of different hardware characteristics on application performance as the systems scale up in size. The xSim project is currently working to extend the performance toolkit to provide support for resilience investigations. Another related area is that of large-scale debugging and diagnosis for parallel HPC applications [1,7]. The challenges are similar in that you must be able to gather data about the distributed application and provide details for diagnosis to identify the cause of the error. The AutomaDeD [9] project combined sampling and classification/clustering methods to help identify abnormalities that can provide signatures for software faults (bugs) to aid in debugging while maintaining reasonable performance.

6 Conclusion

There are many well established tools and techniques for performance evaluation and experimentation with HPC applications. This pre-existing infrastructure can provide useful data for resilience experiments. We have briefly discussed some initial efforts to extend an existing MPI tracing package to support the MPI FTWG's proposed ULFM specification. The data obtained from these traces can assist application developers and FT implementers for diagnosing problems and help with postmortem analysis.

To investigate the usefulness of the trace tools we extended a simple molecular dynamics application to use the ULFM enhancements to MPI. Our initial experiments used the trace files from the tests to help gain insights into the context of the job during resilience experiments. The traces helped to highlight two problems we encountered during fault injection experiments: i) a fault-injection logic error that resulted in correct results (application output), but more ranks than anticipated being killed; ii) an issue in failure detection/propagation with the ULFM prototype that was effected by the method used to simulate the rank failure. The trace files can also help to explain changes to overall performance when MPI fault tolerance mechanisms are employed.

In future work, we plan to continue our initial efforts to use the MPI tracing library for other work in resilience tools. The next steps will be to add support for generating these traces to the Extreme-scale Simulator (xSim). The xSim performance analysis toolkit was recently extended to support capabilities to assist in resilience studies, e.g., process and job fault-injection. Using the simulator will improve control for several items (e.g., time skew, IO buffer flushing, failure scheduling). Another potential benefit of traces is that they can provide a "replay" log for communication when combined with simulation tools. This could allow for reviewing complex interleaving of events when working on adding fault tolerance to existing codes.

Acknowledgement. The rights of this work are transferred to the extent transferable according to title 17 U.S.C. 105. This manuscript has been authored by UT-Battelle, LLC, under Contract No. DE-AC05-00OR22725 with the U.S. Department of Energy. The United States Government retains and the publisher, by accepting the article for publication, acknowledges that the United States Government retains a non-exclusive, paid-up, irrevocable, world-wide license to publish or reproduce the published form of this manuscript, or allow others to do so, for United States Government purposes.

References

1. Ahn, D.H., de Supinski, B.R., Laguna, I., Lee, G.L., Liblit, B., Miller, B.P., Schulz, M.: Scalable temporal order analysis for large scale debugging. In: Proceedings of the ACM/IEEE Conference on High Performance Computing (SC). ACM (2009)
2. Bland, W., Bouteiller, A., Herault, T., Hursey, J., Bosilca, G., Dongarra, J.J.: An evaluation of user-level failure mitigation support in MPI. In: Träff, J.L., Benkner, S., Dongarra, J.J. (eds.) EuroMPI 2012. LNCS, vol. 7490, pp. 193–203. Springer, Heidelberg (2012)
3. Böhm, S., Engelmann, C.: xSim: The extreme-scale simulator. In: Proceedings of the International Conference on High Performance Computing and Simulation (HPCS), Istanbul, Turkey, July 4-8, pp. 280–286. IEEE Computer Society, Los Alamitos (2011)
4. Daly, J., Harrod, B., Hoang, T., Nowell, L., Adolf, B., Borkar, S., DeBardeleben, N., Elnozahy, M., Heroux, M., Rogers, D., Ross, R., Sarkar, V., Schulz, M., Snir, M., Woodward, P., Aulwes, R., Bancroft, M., Bronevetsky, G., Carlson, B., Geist, A., Hall, M., Hollingsworth, J., Lucas, B., Lumsdaine, A., Macaluso, T., Quinlan, D., Sachs, S., Shalf, J., Smith, T., Stearley, J., Still, B., Wu, J.: Inter-Agency Workshop on HPC Resilience at Extreme Scale (February 2012)
5. DeBardeleben, N., Laros, J., Daly, J.T., Scott, S.L., Engelmann, C., Harrod, B.: High-end computing resilience: Analysis of issues facing the HEC community and path-forward for research and development. Whitepaper (December 2009)
6. Dongarra, J., Beckman, P., et al.: The international exascale software roadmap. International Journal of High Performance Computer Applications 25(1) (2011)
7. Hursey, J., January, C., O'Connor, M., Hargrove, P.H., Lecomber, D., Squyres, J.M., Lumsdaine, A.: Checkpoint/Restart-enabled parallel debugging. In: Keller, R., Gabriel, E., Resch, M., Dongarra, J. (eds.) EuroMPI 2010. LNCS, vol. 6305, pp. 219–228. Springer, Heidelberg (2010)
8. Janssen, C.L., Adalsteinsson, H., Cranford, S., Kenny, J.P., Pinar, A., Evensky, D.A., Mayo, J.: A simulator for large-scale parallel computer architectures. International Journal of Parallel and Distributed System Technology 1(2), 57–73 (2010)
9. Laguna, I., Gamblin, T., de Supinski, B.R., Bagchi, S., Bronevetsky, G., Anh, D.H., Schulz, M., Rountree, B.: Large scale debugging of parallel tasks with automaded. In: Proceedings of 2011 International Conference for High Performance Computing, Networking, Storage and Analysis, pp. 50:1–50:10. ACM, New York (2011)
10. Li, D., Vetter, J.S., Yu, W.: Classifying soft error vulnerabilities in extreme-scale scientific applications using a binary instrumentation tool. In: International Conference for High Performance Computing, Networking, Storage and Analysis (SC). ACM (November 2012)
11. Snir, M., Wisniewski, R.W., Abraham, J.A., Adve, S.V., Bagchi, S., Balaji, P., Belak, J., Bose, P., Cappello, F., Carlson, B., Chien, A.A., Coteus, P., DeBardeleben, N.A., Diniz, P., Engelmann, C., Erez, M., Fazzari, S., Geist, A., Gupta, R., Johnson, F., Krishnamoorthy, S., Leyffer, S., Liberty, D., Mitra, S., Munson, T., Schreiber, R., Stearley, J., Hensbergen, E.V.: Workshop report: Addressing failures in exascale computing (April 2013)

First Workshop on Runtime and Operating Systems for the Many-Core Era (ROME 2013)

Carsten Clauss and Stefan Lankes

Program Chairs

Since the beginning of the multicore era, parallel processing has become prevalent across the board. However, in order to continue a performance increase according to Moore's Law, a next step needs to be taken: away from common multicores towards innovative many-core architectures. Such systems, equipped with a significant higher amount of cores per chip than multicores, pose challenges in both hardware and software design. On the hardware side, complex on-chip networks, scratchpads and memory interfaces as well as cache-hierarchies, cache-coherence strategies and the building of coherency domains have to be taken into account.

However, the ROME workshop focuses on the software side because without complying system software, runtime and operating system support, all these new hardware facilities cannot be exploited. Hence, the new challenges in hardware/software co-design are to step beyond traditional approaches and to wage new programming models and OS designs in order to exploit the theoretically available performance as effectively as possible.

The focus of the this year's ROME workshop stood in the tradition of a successful series of events hosted by the Many-core Applications Research Community (MARC). Although the ROME workshop was not considered as a self-contained MARC symposium, the organizers and several members of the program committee are part of the MARC community. Both organizers have also served as hosts and symposium chairs at the recent MARC Symposium 2012 in Aachen, Germany. Prior MARC Symposia took place at ONERA research center in Toulouse, France and at the Hasso Plattner Institute in Potsdam, Germany.

In the call for papers of the 1st ROME workshop, researchers from different fields were invited to present their work on many-core related software research regarding operating systems, runtime environments and programming models, and the resulting research questions for the upcoming generation of heterogeneous and/or massive parallel systems. While the Intel Single-chip Cloud Computer (SCC) served as common research platform for most MARC members, other interesting research on next generation many-core platforms were also relevant for this event.

Upon the call for papers, the program committee received 14 contributions from 9 countries. Each submitted paper was assigned to at least three PC members for review and reviewers were encouraged to give a very detailed review in order to justify their votes. Finally, 10 contributions have been accepted for presentation, resulting in a pleasant acceptance rate of 71%, and all accepted papers were successfully presented during the full-day ROME workshop at the Euro-Par Conference 2013 in Aachen, Germany.

D. an Mey et al. (Eds.): Euro-Par 2013 Workshops, LNCS 8374, pp. 737–738, 2014.

The organizers were very happy that Tim Mattson from Intel Corporation volunteered to give an invited keynote with the title "Predicting the Future in a Rapidly Changing Many-core World" for the ROME workshop: "The talk discussed how software changes in response to transitions in hardware and described the structure of how changes occur by analogy with biological evolution. In particular, the talk described *punctuated equilibrium theory* and how we can apply that perspective to the interaction between academic research and industrial R&D. The result is we can look at what is happening in academia now and the inflection points in hardware from industry to make solid predictions on where software needs to go over the next decade."

Just like for the last MARC events, Intel Corporation sponsored an award for the best paper presented at the ROME workshop. According to the average review scores, the award was handed over at the end of the last session to Ramon Nou, representative also for his co-autors Jacobo Giralt and Toni Cortes, for their paper "DYON – Managing a New Scheduling Class to Improve System Performance in Multicore Systems".

The organizers would like to take the opportunity and give thanks to all authors and contributors of the ROME workshop. Special thanks go to the program committee and all sub-reviewers, to Intel Corporation for sponsoring the best paper award, and to the whole Euro-Par conference committee for making this event possible and successful. Thank you all very much!

October 2013 Stefan Lankes and Carsten Clauss

Evaluation Methodology for Data Communication-Aware Application Partitioning

Imran Ashraf, S. Arash Ostadzadeh, Roel Meeuws, and Koen Bertels

Computer Science and Engineering Group,
Department of Software and Computer Technology,
Delft University of Technology, Delft, The Netherlands
{I.Ashraf,S.A.Ostadzadeh,R.J.Meeuws,K.L.M.Bertels}@TUDelft.nl

Abstract. Heterogeneous multicore architectures appear to be a promising solution to the ever-increasing computational demands of applications in embedded as well as high-performance computing domains. Nevertheless, inefficient application partitioning for such systems may result in a considerable reduction in the anticipated performance improvement. Consequently, proper mechanisms are required to evaluate quality of different partitions in an early phase of application mapping. This evaluation is especially important in the case of reconfigurable accelerators, as the synthesis phase of their hardware blocks is quite time-consuming. Hence, an early evaluation of application partitioning mechanisms for such architectures can reduce time-to-market.

In this paper, we propose a data communication-aware methodology for evaluating the quality of application partitions as well as partitioning algorithms. We also present an open source tool which implements the proposed methodology. Moreover, we evaluate several heuristic algorithms to further substantiate the applicability of the proposed methodology and the utilization of the developed tool. The applications are used as test inputs for the sake of comparisons in terms of relative and absolute quality measurements of the partitioning solutions.

Keywords: Application partitioning, Performance evaluation, Heuristic algorithms, Data communication analysis.

1 Introduction

Heterogeneous multicore architectures are gaining popularity in embedded devices as well as high-performance computers [1]. This new trend poses specific challenges regarding the programmability of these architectures. One such challenge is application partitioning, in which an application is divided into smaller parts to be mapped onto various Processing Elements (PEs). This is a critical task because inefficient partitioning may reduce the anticipated performance improvement. It has also been discussed that the communication among various parts of an application entails a major design challenge [2,3].

The criteria that drive application partitioning include, among others, the nature of computations, execution times on PEs, memory requirements, area

D. an Mey et al. (Eds.): Euro-Par 2013 Workshops, LNCS 8374, pp. 739–748, 2014.

avaialble on PEs, etc. Due to the huge size of the search space, finding an optimal *partition* is an NP-hard problem [4]. Therefore, heuristic algorithms are commonly utilized to find solutions in short time. Nevertheless, the *partition* found by a heuristic may or may not be close to the optimal solution. Hence, it is very important to be able to evaluate the quality of the solution(s) found by a heuristic method and to make a robust comparison with the solutions found by other existing or future partitioning algorithms.

Due to a large variety of architectures and the lack of proper benchmarks, it is hard to reproduce experimental results, for fair comparison, on the target platforms [5]. Moreover, the complexity furthers in case of reconfigurable architectures as the application development process involves building and synthesizing hardware blocks. Hence, a proper methodology is required to quickly evaluate the quality of the partitioning algorithms.

An interesting observation is that only a small number of functions primarily contribute to the overall application execution time. Similarly, a limited number of functions are responsible for the main inter-task data communication. By considering these two observations, we can potentially reduce the huge design space exploration effort. Thus, the comparison with optimal partitions found by an exhaustive search becomes feasible, in spite of the general intractability of the application partitioning problem.

In this work, we propose a methodology for evaluating partitions found by various application partitioning algorithms. Furthermore, we compare the outcome of several partitioning algorithms based on the quality of the found solutions. We define cost metrics based on the execution contribution of the functions and the data communication. The execution contribution and data communication information are obtained by profiling the application [6][7]. Our main contributions are summarized as follows:

- formulation of the proposed data communication-aware application partitioning evaluation methodology;
- design and implementation of an open source tool that implements this methodology;
- evaluation of a multi-objective partitioning algorithm as a case study for synthetic applications and real benchmarks.

The rest of the paper is structured as follows. Section 2 overviews the related research work. Section 3 presents the proposed evaluation methodology. Section 4 describes the modular design of the *partition* evaluation tool. Subsequently, Section 5 provides a detailed case study describing the evaluation of a multi-objective partitioning algorithm to illustrate the methodology. Section 6 details the experimental results. Finally, Section 7 provides the conclusions and future research directions.

2 Related Work

Efficient application partitioning for multicore platforms has been an active field of research in the last decade. The problem has been approached in diverse

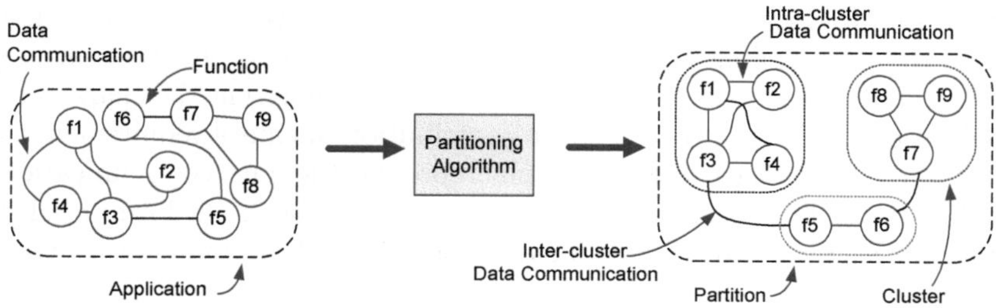

Fig. 1. A partitioning algorithm takes an application as input and produces a *partition* at the output. The depicted *partition* is composed of three clusters.

ways and at various granularity levels, ranging from fine-grained (basic blocks or loops) to coarse-grained (functions), heuristic and evolutionary approaches, as reviewed in [7]. The work presented in [6] utilizes a data communication graph, annotated with area estimates to do partitioning in a semi-automatic way. A generalized framework for automatic code partitioning is discussed in [8]. Some works regarding code partitioning for platforms containing reconfigurable accelerators are reviewed in [7].

An empirical evaluation is provided in [9], where graphs are compared using Chaco framework [10]. Communication costs among vertices in these graphs are based on cut edges. The quality of a *partition* is found by the application execution time on the target platform. However, finding the quality of *partitions* by executing the application on reconfigurable platforms, if possible in all cases, is a tedious and time-consuming task, as it involves synthesizing hardware blocks for reconfigurable units. Our methodology is able to perform an early evaluation without the need to run on the target platform.

Another evaluation is provided in [5], which presents a comparison of four partitioning approaches. The authors associate cost metrics with *partitions* and provide a comparison of these approaches. However, their focus is on the hardware/software partitioning, which is a subset of the generalized partitioning problem. Our work provides a generic evaluation methodology for any number of parts in a partition.

3 Evaluation Methodology

Figure 1 depicts the application partitioning process and the terminology used in the proposed evaluation methodology, which is a 4-step process described below.
Step 1: Formulation of the cost function. Partitions can be evaluated by calculating their costs using a cost function. A cost function takes a *partition* as input and assesses its quality. Various factors can contribute to the quality of a *partition*, for instance, how well the clusters are balanced, inter-cluster data communication, etc. In this step, the factors of interest are determined to formulate the cost function.
Step 2: Implementation of the partitioning algorithm. The partitioning algorithm to be evaluated is implemented in this step. The algorithm takes the application as input and outputs a *partition* of the application.

Step 3: Specification of the input set. In this step, the applications that are input to the partitioning algorithm are specified. These applications are represented as graphs, where the values of graph vertices represent the characteristics of applications, for instance, execution contribution, memory requirements, area estimates, etc. The edges in these graphs represent the data communication between functions. The specification of an input application boils down to selecting numbers for vertices and edges, which can be obtained randomly or by profiling real applications.
Step 4: Evaluation and comparison. In this step, the cost of the *partition* found by the *partitioning algorithm* is evaluated by the cost function. The evaluated cost can be used to perform comparisons and to rank the *partition* based upon its quality. This ranking can be:

Absolute — where the comparison is performed with the optimal *partition* found by an exact solution or an exhaustive search (only for applications with small number of functions).

Relative — when optimal *partitions* cannot be found, thus the cost is compared in relation to the costs of *partitions* found by other algorithms. In the next section, we present the details of the tool that implements the proposed methodology.

4 PET Implementation

We developed the Partition Evaluation Tool (PET[1]), to evaluate the quality of partitions and compare various partitioning algorithms. This tool is implemented in C++ in a flexible way to allow the partitioning strategies to be evaluated easily. We define the relevant concepts used in the PET discussion as follows.

Application class models the concept of the application which needs to be partitioned by the partitioning algorithm. An application has two important members, namely functions and edges.
Function represents the subroutine in an application, which performs a certain task of the application. Each function has an execution contribution depending upon the task assigned to it.
Edge is a directed link denoting the communication between a pair of functions in an application. The amount of data that is communicated is represented by the weight of the edge.
Cluster represents the collection of functions which can be mapped onto a single core/PE of the target platform. The number of functions in a cluster is controlled by the capacity of that cluster. As an example, in reconfigurable systems, this capacity may represent the maximum number of slices reserved for a single PE. When a cluster is full, its status is changed from *UnFinished* to *Finished*.
Partition refers to the union of clusters, where each cluster contains various functions. A viable partition holds the semantics of the application with the combination of functions in clusters that can be mapped onto various cores/PEs

[1] Sources available at `http://imranashraf.github.com/PET`

in a multicore platform. The cost of a *partition* can be evaluated by a call to the *Cost()* method of this class.
PartitioningAlgorithm is an abstract class that can be used to implement the algorithm(s) used to perform partitioning. This can be achieved by implementing the *Apply()* virtual function of the *PartitioningAlgorithm* class for some algorithm of interest.

5 Case Study

In this section, we present the evaluation of a multi-objective task clustering algorithm [7], to illustrate our partition evaluation methodology and the utilization of PET in this regard. This algorithm initiates task clustering at the function-level based on dynamic profiling information. This includes the data communication among functions and the information about their execution time. The overall goal of the heuristic algorithm is to get a well-balanced cluster containing tightly inter-connected functions. The steps of the evaluation methodology are described below:
Step 1: Formulation of the Cost Function. We assume an application containing n functions to be partitioned into k clusters. These functions can be specified as vertices $v_i, 1 \leq i \leq n$ in a graph. The execution cost EC_{v_i} of a vertex v_i, is the cost of executing this function on a PE when it is mapped as a part of a cluster. The execution cost of a cluster C_i is defined as: $EC_{C_i} = \sum_{v_j \in C_i} EC_{v_j}, 1 \leq i \leq k, 1 \leq j \leq n$.

Vertices v_i and v_j have an edge e_{ij} connecting them, with the weight w_{ij} representing the amount of the data that is communicated. The set of all the edges in a graph makes an edge set E of the graph. The set of edges which cross the boundary of a cluster C_i form the set of external edges $Eext_{C_i}$ of this cluster with respect to the rest of the partition. This edge set represents the communication cost of the cluster C_i with respect to the other clusters. Furthermore, the set of edges internal to a cluster C_i form the internal edge set $Eint_{C_i}$, as it represents the communication among functions inside C_i. For this case study, we consider the following two metrics to formulate the total cost of a *partition*:

1. **Balancing Penalty (BP)** accounts for the load balancing among clusters in a partition. It basically depends upon the distance between the execution cost EC_{C_i} of cluster C_i and the average execution cost of all the clusters in a partition $BP_{C_i} = \left| \frac{\sum_{j=1}^{k} EC_{C_j}}{k} - EC_{C_i} \right|, 1 \leq i \leq k$. Balancing penalty BP_P of a partition P is defined as $BP_P = \sum_{i=1}^{k} BP_{C_i}$.
2. **Communication Cost (CC)** is the cost associated with external communication of a cluster with respect to the other clusters in the partition. Communication cost CC_{C_i} of a cluster C_i is $CC_{C_i} = \sum_{e_{ij} \in Eext_{C_i}} w_{ij}$. The communication cost CC_P of a partition P is defined as $CC_P = \sum_{i=1}^{k} CC_{C_i}$.

The total cost TC_P of a partition P is then defined as:

$$TC = \alpha BP_P + \beta CC_P;\ 0 \leq \alpha \leq 1, 0 \leq \beta \leq 1\ and\ \alpha + \beta = 1, \quad (1)$$

where α and β are relative weights associated with BP and CC metrics, respectively. These weights can be selected by the designer based on the platform at hand, to stress one metric relative to the other. For instance, if workload balancing is important then, one can select a higher value of α than β. On the other hand,when communication is expensive, β can get a higher value than α.

It is worth mentioning here that this is just one way of specifying the cost function as the weighted sum of the objectives of interest. Our approach is similar to the one discussed in [11], where the difference of values of each objective is explained in detail. On the same lines, we have assigned the values to each objective as their percentage contribution in the total execution and communication cost for BP and CC, respectively, instead of using their actual values.

Step 2: Implementation of the Partitioning Algorithm. We implemented the clustering algorithm as a derived class of the abstract *PartitioningAlgorithm* class of PET. The *Apply()* function implements the functionality of this heuristic algorithm on an input application. The result is a partition of the input application containing the clusters with various functions.

Step 3: Specification of the Input Set. We generated a number of synthetic application graphs to be used as test inputs. Due to space limitation, we will only discuss the real applications. We used applications from Standford Parallel Applications for Shared Memory Architectures (SPLASH-2) Benchmark Suite [12]. We used the MAIP and QUAD tools from Q^2 profiling toolset [6] to extract the percentage contribution of functions and to get the communication graphs. It should be noted that getting the profiling data by using any other profilers will not change the methodology or the evaluation process.

Step 4: Evaluation and Comparison. We performed the absolute ranking by finding the optimal *partition* determined by the exhaustive search. We compared the cost of *partition* found by the heuristic algorithm against the best possible partition, using *bruteforce()* class to generate all the possible partitions for the generated applications. The cost of each *partition* is evaluated by the *Cost()* method of the *Partition* class. Apart from the absolute ranking, we also performed relative ranking of the *partitioning algorithm* against the best solutions found by simulated annealing, evolutionary and tabu search. The detailed results of these evaluations and comparisons are provided in the following section.

6 Experimental Results

In this section, we provide the results of the experiments performed to evaluate the cost of heuristic algorithm and the cost of *partitions* found by the exhaustive search. We performed these experiments on a 2.66 *GHz Intel(R) Core(TM)2 Quad* CPU, with 4 *GB* RAM. We used the value of 0.5 for α and β to give equal weights to both cost metrics. Values given to these relative weights should be based on the target platform and care must be taken while revising them.

In order to present the evaluation for real benchmark applications, we selected three applications from SPLASH-2 benchmark suite, namely *Barnes*, *Fmm* and *Raytrace*. We also selected *Clustalw* [13] sequence alignment application and *KLT* [14] feature tracking application for the evaluation. Figure 2 presents the comparison of the cost of the partition found by Heuristic Search (HS) with the costs of the solutions found by Simulated Annealing (SA), Tabu Search (TS) and Evolutionary Search (ES). It can be seen that HS performs close to other algorithms. For *Barnes* and *Fmm*, which are relatively smaller applications, SA performs better, but for the remaining three bigger applications, TS outperforms all the other algorithms.

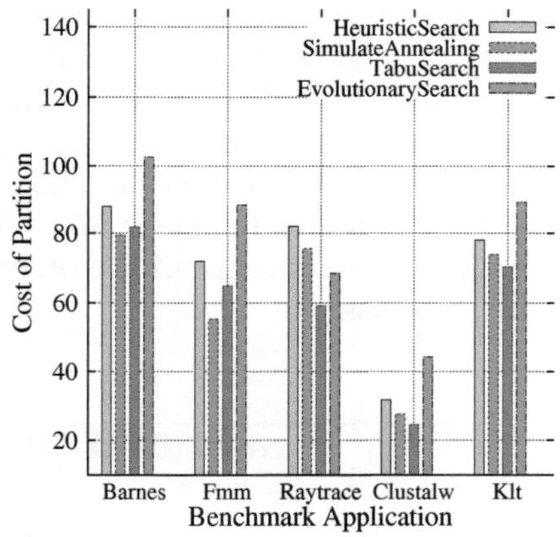

Fig. 2. Comparison of cost of partition found by HS against the cost of partition found by SA, TS and ES for the real applications

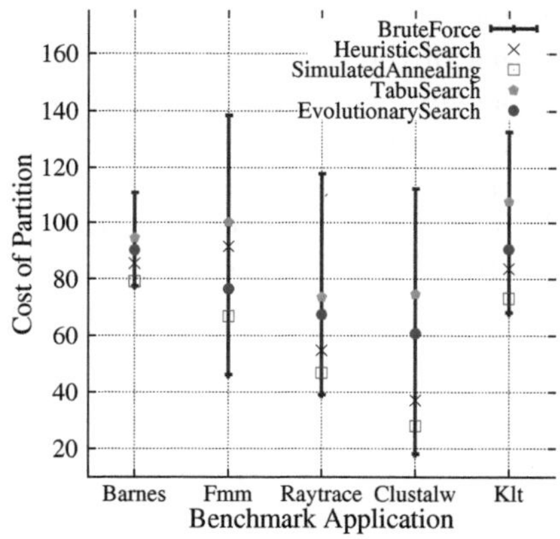

Fig. 3. Absolute ranking of the cost of the partition found by HS, SA, TS and ES from the real applications

An important point worth mentioning is that HS performs comparable to SA, TS and ES in terms of cost.However, HS takes very less time to find the solution compared to other algorithms. To give an idea, for the *KLT* application, HS took $815\mu s$ to find the solution, whereas, TS took $18m$.

In the above experiments, we performed evaluations relative to other algorithms. Absolute ranking can also be performed by comparing the costs against the cost of the optimal solution found by Brute Force (BF). Performing this exhaustive search to find the optimal *partition* of four clusters will require about 8 years on the computer used in these experiments for an application with 25 functions. The considered applications contain 38 to 103 functions, hence, performing the exhaustive search for the optimal *partition* is not practical. Thus, we limited the number of functions to a threshold value of 18, picking the top functions according to the execution time and data communication contribution. This feature is also supported by the tool, where we can specify this threshold value in terms of the number of functions for execution contribution and communication

Table 1. Specifications of the Real Benchmark Applications used in the Evaluation

#	Applic.	No. of Functions	% Exec. Covered	% Comm. Covered
1	Barnes	38	99.19	99.45
2	Fmm	70	91.86	84.12
3	Raytrace	85	75.32	77.55
4	Clustalw	89	96.06	86.17
5	KLT	103	99.85	98.73

weights for filtering the top kernel functions in the application. Table 1 provides detailed specifications of the five applications. Column 3 provides the number of functions in each application. As it can be seen in Column 4 and 5, considering a subset of the top contributing functions covers most of the heavily executing and heavily communicating functions in these applications. The results of the absolute ranking are provided in Figure 3. The vertical lines show the range of the cost of solutions found by BF for each application. It can be seen that HS is able to find close-to-optimal solutions. The costs of solutions found by SA, TS and ES are also marked for comparison. Overall, SA outperforms all the other algorithms, as it is able to find close to optimal solutions.

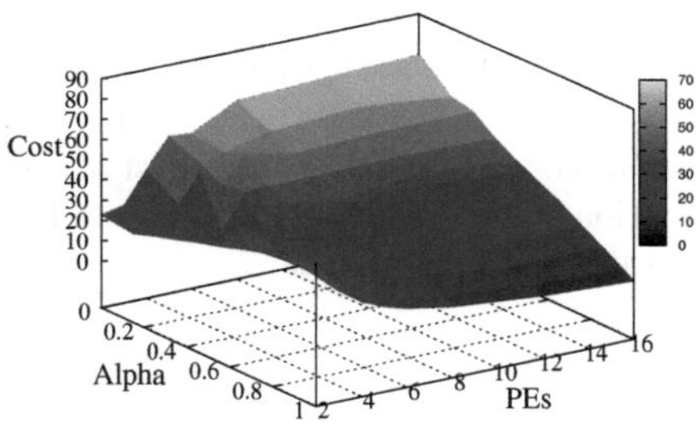

Fig. 4. Effect of variation of α and No. of PEs on cost of the partitions found by tabu search for the *Raytrace* application from SPLASH-2 benchmark suite.

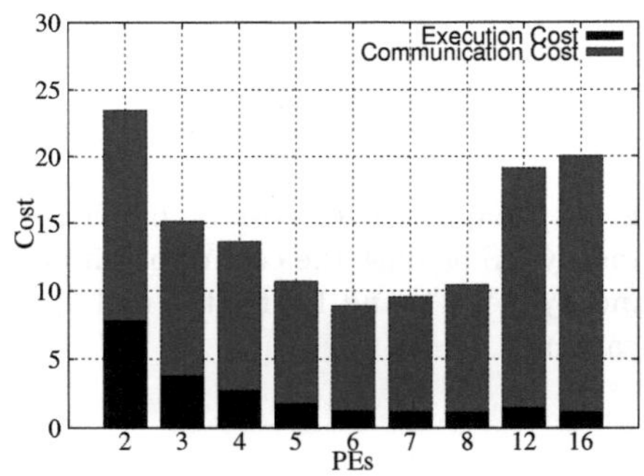

Fig. 5. Variation of execution and communication cost of Clustalw application. Minimum cost values correspond to the optimal number of PEs (at $PEs = 6$) for the given α and β.

In the above experiments, we have kept α and β fixed. Figure 4 presents the variation of the costs of partitions found by Tabu Search algorithm for *Raytrace* application from SPLASH-2 benchmark suite. It can be seen in this figure that for lower values of α (higher values of β) increasing more PEs, increases cost because of the increased communication among PEs. Higher values of α (lower values of β) implies that the communication is not expensive on the platform at hand and adding more PEs will decrease the total cost of partition. Similar analysis can also be performed for various values of α and β and the number of PEs for other applications.

Another important result which can be obtained from this evaluation is the optimal number of PEs required for a given application for a given platform (values of α and β). Adding more PEs may reduce the execution time of an application by performing the job in parallel, however, the disadvantage is the increase in data communication among the PEs, which may kill the anticipated speedup. This analysis can especially be important for platforms where number of PEs can be reconfigured. For instance, in Molen architecture [15], the number of cores can vary from 2-5 with an upper limit imposed by the resources on FPGA. Even for non-reconfigurable platforms, where number of cores cannot be altered, the additional PEs can be switched-off to save the energy consumption.

In order to perform the analysis for optimal number of PEs, we have modified the equation to calculate the total cost of the *partition* to consider the effect of the addition of PEs as follows:

$$TC = \alpha(EC_s + EC_p/N) + \beta CC \; ; \; 0 \leq \alpha \leq 1, 0 \leq \beta \leq 1 \; and \; \alpha + \beta = 1, \quad (2)$$

where EC_s is the execution cost of the serial region of the application, EC_p is the execution cost of the parallel region of the application and N is the number of PEs. In this simple equation, we have assumed that the cost of the parallel region of the application scales with the number of the available PEs. Furthermore, we did not consider the overhead of parallelization, etc, in this analysis, as the main objective here is to show the effect of increasing the number of PEs on the execution and the communication costs of a *partition* for an application for certain values of α and β. Figure 5 provides a plot of the execution and the communication cost of the *Clustalw* application for a number of values of PEs. For this graph, we have given equal weights to α and β. It can be observed from this plot that increasing the number of PEs reduces the execution cost, but the interaction among PEs in the form of data communication increases resulting in an increase in the communication cost. The optimal number of PEs corresponds to the minimal cost values, which in this case happens when the number of PEs is equal to 6.

7 Conclusions

A key factor that substantially affects the performance of heterogeneous multicore architectures is the scheme used to partition an application. Hence, a proper mechanism to evaluate various partitioning schemes is important. In this work, we presented a methodology to evaluate application *partitions* for multicore architectures. Functions are assumed as vertices in a graph and the communication among functions is represented by the weights of the edges connecting them. We presented PET— a flexible and modular partition evaluation tool— implementing the proposed methodology.

We provided the detailed relative and absolute evaluations of a heuristic task clustering algorithm, as a case study to prove the effectiveness of our methodology. From the evaluation, it was concluded that the heuristic algorithm is able to find close to optimal solutions in very short time compared to other algorithms selected in this comparison. In our future work, we plan to add the profiles of applications from various domains in our tool. Furthermore, benchmark suites can be added to broaden the choices for input set specifications. Utilization of Pareto based multi-objective application partitioning evaluation can also be investigated to provide the whole Pareto-front.

Acknowledgements. This research is partially supported by the Artemisia iFEST project (grant 100203), the Artemisia SMECY project (grant 100230), the FP7 Reflect project (grant 248976) and the Higher Education Commission (HEC) Pakistan.

References

1. Buchty, R., et al.: A survey on hardware-aware and heterogeneous computing on multicore processors and accelerators. Concurrency and Computation: Practice and Experience 24(7), 663–675 (2012)
2. Martin, G.: Overview of the mpsoc design challenge. In: DAC, pp. 274–279 (2006)
3. Haritan, E., et al.: Multicore design is the challenge! what is the solution? In: DAC, pp. 128–130 (June 2008)
4. Tahaee, S.A., et al.: A polynomial algorithm for partitioning problems. ACM Trans. Embed.Comput. Syst. 9(4), 34:1–34:38 (2010)
5. López-Vallejo, M., et al.: On the hardware-software partitioning problem: System modeling and partitioning techniques. ACM Trans. Des. Autom. Electron. Syst. 8(3), 269–297 (2003), `http://doi.acm.org/10.1145/785411.785412`
6. Ostadzadeh, S.A., Meeuws, R., Ashraf, I., Galuzzi, C., Bertels, K.: The Q^2 Profiling Framework: Driving Application Mapping for Heterogeneous Reconfigurable Platforms. In: Choy, O.C.S., Cheung, R.C.C., Athanas, P., Sano, K. (eds.) ARC 2012. LNCS, vol. 7199, pp. 76–88. Springer, Heidelberg (2012)
7. Ostadzadeh, S.: Quantitative Application Data Flow Characterization for Heterogeneous Multicore Architectures. Ph.D. thesis, TU Delft, Netherlands (December 2012)
8. Sairaman, V.: A generalized framework for automatic code partitioning and generation in distributed systems. Graduate School Theses (June 2010)
9. Leland, R., et al.: An empirical study of static load balancing algorithms. In: Proceedings of the Scalable High-Performance Computing Conference, pp. 682–685 (May 1994)
10. The chaco user's guide, version 1.0. Tech. rep. (October 1993), `http://www.cs.sandia.gov/~bahendr/chaco.html`
11. Schloegel, K., et al.: A new algorithm for multi-objective graph partitioning. In: Proceedings of Europar, pp. 322–331. Springer (1999)
12. Singh, J.P., et al.: Splash: Stanford parallel applications for shared-memory. SIGARCH Comput. Archit. News 20(1), 5–44 (1992)
13. Thompson, J.D., et al.: CLUSTAL W: improving the sensitivity of progressive multiple sequence alignment through sequence weighting, position-specific gap penalties and weight matrix choice. Nucleic Acids Research (1994)
14. Lucas, B.D., et al.: An Iterative Image Registration Technique with an Application to Stereo Vision, pp. 674–679 (1981)
15. Vassiliadis, S., et al.: The MOLEN Polymorphic Processor. IEEE Transactions on Computers 53(11), 1363–1375 (2004)

Elastic Manycores*
How to Bring the OS Back into the Scheduling Game?

Marcus Völp and Michael Roitzsch

Technische Universität Dresden, Germany
{voelp,mroi}@os.inf.tu-dresden.de

Abstract. By introducing asynchronous lambdas, many programming languages have leaped ahead in the race for programmable manycore systems, leaving the operating system and its scheduler behind. Instead of hiding application-inherent parallelism behind pools of threads with opaque behavior, asynchronous lambdas allow programmers to explicitly state which parts of a program can be executed in parallel and when this form of parallelism is available. Introducing stretch as a universal performance metric and externalizing part of the lambda-provided knowledge not only to the runtime but also to the operating system scheduler, this paper tries to lay the foundation for OS scheduling to catch up on the road towards heterogeneous *elastic manycore systems.*

1 Introduction

With the gear shift of Moore's Law from frequency scaling to expanding concurrency, we have seen programmability and coordination to become increasingly challenging: To draw optimal performance and energy efficiency out of the given transistor budget, we can no longer rely on homogeneous manycore systems, where all cores are clones of a single kind. Instead, we find our common application mixes much better supported by increasingly heterogeneous systems [17,18]. Starting with instruction extensions, which are no longer available on all cores, we find systems today, where the resources for these extensions are shared, where multiple types of cores co-exist simultaneously and where special purpose and general purpose accelerators (such as H.264 [19] and AES accelerators or GPGPUs) reside next to large and small general purpose cores.

Applications that want to exploit these systems must provide binary code for the best suited cores or accelerators and be able to extract the parallelism that is available in their algorithms. At the same time, the code must have alternative implementations ready to adjust to inferior cores and to run at reduced parallelism if the premium resources are currently required for more urgent needs.

Languages and runtimes such as X10 [7], OpenCL [14], Grand Central Dispatch (GCD) [1], C++ [12], Lithe [20] and the Parallel Pattern Library [13] have

* This work is in part funded by the DFG through the cluster of excellence "Center for Advancing Electronics Dresden" and by the EU and the state of Saxony through the ESF young researcher group IMData.

D. an Mey et al. (Eds.): Euro-Par 2013 Workshops, LNCS 8374, pp. 749–758, 2014.

already made important steps in this direction: To extract the available parallelism, they encourage a programming concept we call *asynchronous lambdas.* Programmers encapsulate independent work into lambda functions and submit them to queues for asynchronous execution. OpenCL already provides limited support for generating alternative binaries for different instruction sets from the same source code. Finally, static and dynamic analysis of the source code allows us to associate lambdas with meta data such as a lambda dependency graph, heuristics on the use of FPU or accelerator instructions, or information on how lambdas access the data they process. However, to be useful for short term scheduling decisions we need to find a compact representation for all the above information.

This paper investigates elasticity and stretch as guiding metrics, which we believe can serve as such a compact representation. Rather than describing each lambda individually, we summarize alternatives and homogeneously parallel lambdas to a single elastic lambda and stretch this lambda both in time and in the number of cores when we schedule it in our heterogeneous system.

After taking a closer look at asynchronous lambdas in Section 2, we shall see in Section 3 how stretch characterizes the above choices. As guiding examples, we shall use a JPEG blur filter and a database join operator, which we introduce in the following section.

2 Asynchronous Lambdas

The programming paradigm of asynchronous lambdas relieves the developer from explicitly managing parallelism with threads. Instead, the code expresses latent parallelism: The developer states explicitly which code pieces can potentially run in parallel. The runtime layer can decide dynamically, which pieces do run concurrently. It thus translates the latent parallelism to actual parallelism.

Asynchronous lambdas combine a programming pattern based on asynchronous invocation and a lambda programming language feature to deliver unique properties.

Asynchronous invocation originates from event-based programming [16]. High-throughput network servers experience scalability bottlenecks when assigning each incoming request to a dedicated thread. Performance improves when organizing the server such that queues collect pieces of work and execute them asynchronously [22]. Queuing work instead of explicitly spawning a thread allows the runtime layer to control the number of threads [6], employing strategies like thread pooling.

Lambdas automatically transfer state by capturing variables from the enclosing lexical scope. This relieves the programmer from manually collecting contextual data. Lambdas also preserve the logical locality of the code, because they appear inline and not as separate functions. The code looks like a serial flow of instructions and is easier to read than code written for threaded or callback parallelism.

We call the combination of both concepts asynchronous lambdas, but different terms have been coined within different language communities. Table 1 presents a selection of popular implementations. Our ideas are most closely related to GCD.

Table 1. Complete or Partial Implementations of Asynchronous Lambdas

Implementation	Term
Apple Grand Central Dispatch (GCD)	Block
Microsoft Parallel Patterns Library	Lambda
Intel Threading Building Blocks	Task
C++11	Lambda
Google Go	Goroutine
X10	Activity
Lithe	Block

2.1 Dispatch Queues

Dispatch queues allow the programmer to express parallelism by submitting lambdas for asynchronous execution. Such queues come in two flavors: serial and parallel queues. Lambdas submitted to a serial queue execute one after the other, never running two of them at the same time. This guarantee not only implies protection for critical sections [3], it also allows developers to reason about the order of lambda execution.

Lambdas on a parallel queue execute concurrently and may complete in any order. Parallel queues also support barrier lambdas, which represent serial islands within otherwise parallel work. Barrier lambdas always execute exclusively on their queue and do not start until all previously submitted lambdas have completed.

Because execution on queues occurs asynchronously, lambdas are submitted to the queues by the program before they are executed. Dispatch queues therefore *expose dynamic program structure* to the runtime library but not yet to the OS scheduler. Instead, implementations like GCD inspect the queues and decide how many threads to employ. In fact, GCD on OS X actually interacts with the kernel in a scheduler activation [2] style.

But we think there is a lot more information to harvest. The queues essentially provide a limited look into the future execution of the application. Serial queues and barriers express dependencies between the lambdas, which allows to derive a job graph for the scheduler. Although no asynchronous lambda runtime implements this today, we even imagine alternative binary versions of the same source-level lambda to exploit specialized units of heterogeneous manycores. An example will illustrate:

2.2 Example 1: Blurring a JPEG Image

Imagine a little app that applies a blur filter to a compressed JPEG image. The user selects the file to manipulate and the program filters it in the background to keep the app responsive. The code looks like this (in GCD's block syntax):

```
dispatch_barrier_async(queue, ^{
    jpeg_decode(file, image);
});
size_t pixels = image->w * image->h;
dispatch_apply(pixels, queue, ^(size_t i){
    blur_kernel(image, i);
});
dispatch_barrier_async(queue, ^{
    jpeg_encode(image, file);
});
```

Fig. 1. Dispatch Code of Blur Filter

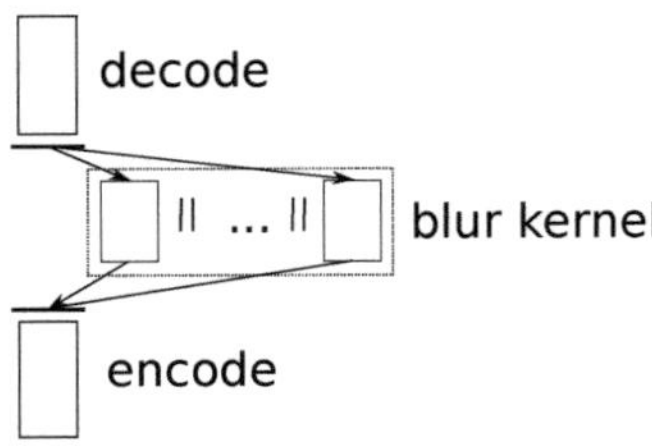

Fig. 2. Dispatched Lambdas and the Resulting Dependencies

First, the JPEG file is decoded asynchronously. The barrier prevents the subsequent filtering to start before decoding is complete. Then, the blur compute kernel is dispatched once for every pixel of the image. A final barrier lambda encodes the in-memory image to a JPEG representation again. This code runs without performing any work synchronously. All lambdas execute in the background. Therefore, the dispatch queue exposes a complete picture of the pending work to the runtime, including the dependency fan-out from the decode step and the dependency fan-in on the encode step. Fig. 2 shows these dependencies. Lambdas are denoted as blocks, barriers as horizontal bars. A number of execution options arise:

- The blur kernel can execute in parallel, because it must run for every pixel. The runtime may decide to exploit all, some, or none of this parallelism, taking the cost of data transfer between cores into account.
- Even if available cores share the same ISA, there may be variations between them. Imagine a mixture between complex out-of-order cores and smaller in-order cores. JPEG decoding and encoding may run faster on an out-of-order core, because the single-threaded JPEG code benefits from hidden memory latencies. But those complex cores may be scarce and could be occupied by other applications.
- Within a heterogeneous manycore, some of the cores may support special instructions like a fused multiply-add, which the blur kernel can exploit. This requires alternative binaries for the blur kernel so that the runtime can pick the one that best matches the available instructions. Such alternative binaries may even be generated at runtime [9].

– Offloading massively parallel work to a GPU can also be beneficial [21]. But in addition to a different ISA and programming environment, we also have to orchestrate explicit data transfer to and from such accelerators and account for its costs.

2.3 Example 2: Database Join Operation

Similar decisions come up when executing a large-scale database join, an operation that processes two data sets and outputs all pairs that match a given predicate. The placement of execution relative to data influences processing times considerably. Additionally, data transfer characteristics may change depending on the form of the data. For sorted data or when sorting is cheap, a parallel merge join algorithm [5] can be employed. Otherwise, a partitioned hash join [15] is called for, which pre-selects data into cache-friendly partitions to accelerate the core's evaluation of the join predicate on all possible pairs. This inter-core data transfer adds to the execution cost, so the physical core layout should match the transfer pathways to reduce traffic.

We believe decisions as outlined in the two examples must be made by an operating system scheduler. Only the scheduler can aggregate knowledge from multiple applications and mediate between their competing needs. But currently, much of the knowledge needed to make those decisions is buried within applications. We want to analyze the program structure available in the dispatch queues and export a suitable compact representation to the scheduling layer. The next section describes this representation.

3 Elasticity and Stretch

Clearly, exporting all dispatched lambdas together with their dependencies and metadata gives the operating system an accurate and detailed view on application needs. However, at the same time, pushing all this information down to the operating-system scheduler would increase scheduling complexity beyond acceptable bounds. Our approach to counteract this complexity is to aggregate groups of similar lambdas into a single elastic job and to stretch this job both vertically along the timeline and horizontally in terms of number and types of used cores.

In addition to the scheduling options, execution constraints are passed to the scheduler as deadlines, so it can separate desirable from unwanted schedules. Timing constraints, e.g., in the form of application-provided end-to-end deadlines, also allow the scheduler to explore non-work-conserving scheduling opportunities. The real-time community is also beginning to explore runtimes for task models with intra-task parallelism [10].

In the following, we detail the aggregation of lambdas that encapsulate alternative implementations of the same functionality. We also discuss homogeneously parallel lambdas and the factors that influence their stretch.

3.1 Alternatives

Fig. 3 shows the time required to execute three alternative implementations of the blur filter from Example 1 on different CPUs. We assume that the small in-order core and the two types of large out-of-order cores share the same ISA. Executing the general purpose CPU alternative (white) on any of the out-of-order cores may improve performance due to the large cores' better latency hiding abilities. However, due to their size and power hunger, we have to expect only few large cores in future manycore systems. By emulating the fused multiply-add instruction, we may also execute the second alternative (checkered) on all cores. However, its performance improvement is likely lost in the emulation overheads. As usual for this type of code, we expect the highest performance improvements from running the GPU kernel of the blur filter (black). However, keep in mind that we need to transfer the data to and from this accelerator. We shall return to this point in Section 3.3.

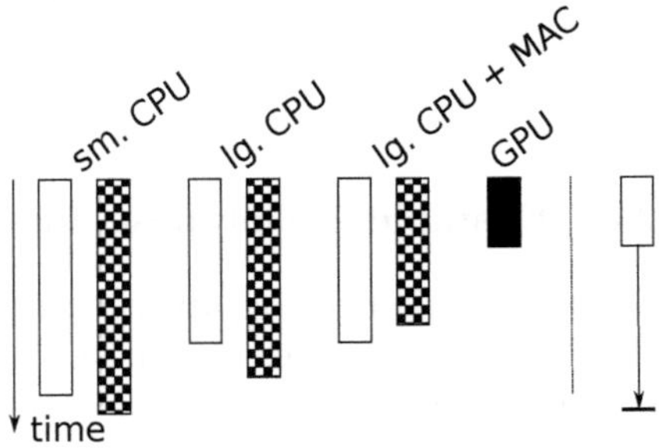

Fig. 3. Aggregation of Lambdas, which Encapsulate Alternative Implementations

How long does it take to blur a single pixel in the worst or in the best case, or with a given probability p? Clearly, giving answers to such questions requires knowledge about the minimum, maximum or p-percentile of the execution time distribution. However, if we assume to know these values for all alternatives and types of CPUs, we can aggregate this information in a type-agnostic way by taking the smallest of these values as the base (worst/best/p-percentile) execution time c of the lambda and by taking the distance to the largest of these values as a metric for how far this elastic lambda can be stretched. More precisely, we consider both constant influences b (such as just-in-time compilation of the code for a respective target) and influences that grow linearly with the base execution time. That is, the stretch s of a lambda is given by:

$$s = ac + b \tag{1}$$

where a is a linear factor. The execution time of the lambda may therefore vary between c and $c + s = (a + 1)c + b$. It is easy to see that minimizing this lambda's stretch minimizes its execution time. However, it remains to be seen whether we can extend this desired property also to the entire application, to parts of the system or even to the elastic manycore as a whole. What we do get however, is a guideline on how much effort we have to spend on finding the optimal placement for this application. As long as the application meets its deadlines while all of its lambdas are maximally stretched, we are free to allocate the lambdas to arbitrary types of cores. Vice versa, losing the freedom to stretch a lambda beyond a certain point means we can only run the lambda on cores where the corresponding alternative is able to complete in time.

Our second example not only entails alternative implementations of the same algorithm but also implementations of alternative algorithms providing the same functionality. For example, Graefe et al. [11] make the point that database management systems (DBMS) should support both hash- and sort-based join operators. In our setting, both variants appear as alternatives. More precisely we see the DBMS guided dispatch of a number of lambdas to sort the data in parallel followed by a similar block of parallel activity for merging the results according to the join criterion. For the alternative, similar blocks of independent lambdas are dispatched for the data partitioning and pre-selection step and for the actual join within these partitions.

3.2 Homogeneous Parallelism

The second, horizontal dimension along which we stretch elastic jobs spans spatially across the cores of the system. This time however, all aggregated lambdas must be executed to complete the encapsulated functionality. To simplify the discussion, we focus on homogeneous parallelism. That is, we are going to aggregate lambdas with negligible variations in their individual execution times and with approximately equal data transfer times.

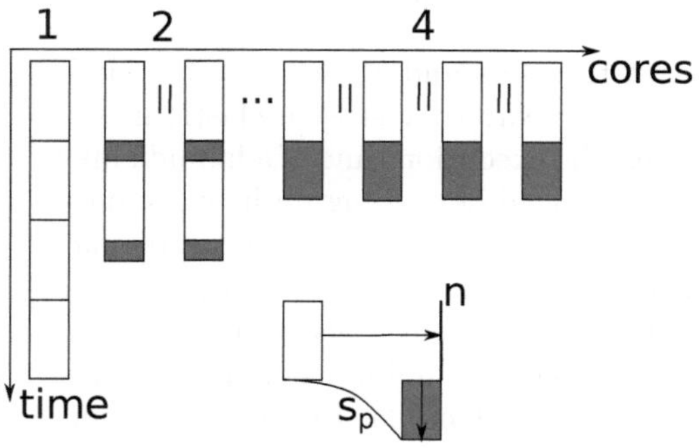

Fig. 4. Aggregation of Homogeneous Parallelism

Fig. 4 illustrates our approach. Parallel loop constructs such as the `dispatch_apply` function in Fig. 1 Line 5, dispatch a number of independent lambdas with the options to execute them sequentially, in parallel, or as parallel groups of sequentially executed lambdas. Synchronization,[1] cache traffic when accessing shared objects and the overhead of the parallelization constructs may prolong the individual lambdas although the loop in its entirety is likely to complete faster if we spread it over additional cores. We record this vertical stretch of the lambda execution times in the function s_p, which maps the assigned cores to the parallelization overhead. For the horizontal stretch it is more convenient to regard sequential execution as maximally stretched and the complete parallel case as the base. This way we preserve the property that losing the possibility to stretch lambdas beyond a certain point limits our freedom to allocate lambdas flexibly on fewer cores.

[1] Although locks may still be used inside lambdas, programming concepts such as GCD discourage their use. Instead, critical sections should be dispatched as separate lambdas. We will look at synchronization overhead to accommodate for these legacy uses and to extend our approach to more advanced synchronization patterns such as transactional memory.

Unlike Collette et al. [8], we do not extend our elastic jobs to also cover the vertical stretch caused by executing lambdas sequentially. If we need the execution time for the construct for k cores, we can simply obtain it as

$$\left\lceil \frac{n}{k} \right\rceil (c + s_p(k)) \tag{2}$$

where c is the base execution time of the elastic job. We believe we can build on the additional flexibility of our model by allowing the number of allocated cores to change over time. Assume the lambda is executed on k_0 cores for $c + s_p(k_0)$ and on k_1 cores for $c + s_p(k_1)$. Then $n' = n - k_0 - k_1$ lambdas remain and Equation 2 gives us the required execution time if we replace n by n'.

3.3 Data Transfers

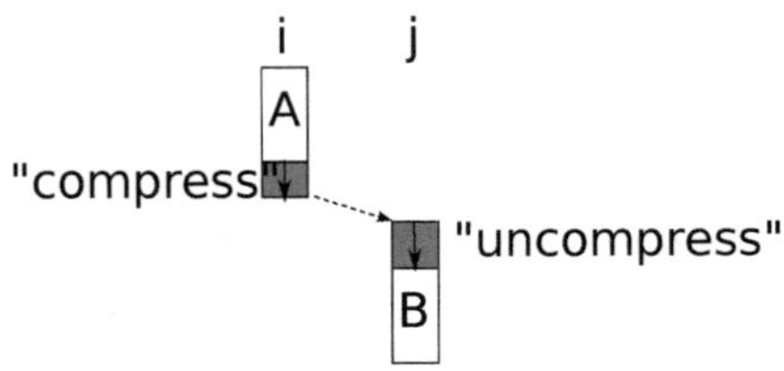

Fig. 5. Stretch due to Data Transfers

Data transfers and alternatives are similar in the way they stretch elastic many-cores: the execution time of a lambda may be prolonged depending on how the data is transferred to its core. Overheads may arise from implicit transfers, for example in the form of cache access latencies [4] that cannot be hidden behind the execution of the lambda. However, transfers may also involve explicit data preparation steps. The fundamental differences are that at least two lambdas are involved in determining the stretch and both are affected by its consequences. Fig. 5 illustrates this point. Lambda A executing on core i produces some data that is later on required by lambda B on core j. Data may be transferred in uncompressed form. However, one option to speed up this transfer is by compressing the data on core i thereby stretching A's execution time and decompressing it after the transfer on core j with a similar influence on B. In a sense, the JPEG en-/decode step of Example 1 can be seen as such a compression/decompression step. In our second example, data partitioning and pre-selection are essential steps for the performance of the partitioned hash join operator.

In Section 3.1, we have distinguished a base execution time and a stretch of this base execution time. This is not possible for data transfers because more than one lambda is involved in the transfer. A minimal stretch of A (e.g., when snooping the data out of core i's private caches) may well impose a significant overhead on B whereas other transfer methods may result in a reduced effort for B at the cost of prolonging A's execution time. For this reason, we attribute data transfers completely as stretch to the lambdas which access this data during their computation.

Given the placement of the data sources, we determine the source and destination stretch by taking into account the minimum and maximum execution times and influences of the available transfer methods and by aggregating these results for all possible destination cores. Again, the more stretch we are able to tolerate on the source cores, the more destination cores and transfer methods remain at the destination side. At the same time, these remaining transfer methods determine the minimum stretch that we have to tolerate at the destination side. The more of this stretch the destination side can accept, the more freedom we have in choosing the destination core and transfer method.

4 Conclusions

Catching up with recent improvements in programming languages, this paper argues for elasticity and stretch as guiding principles for scheduling in heterogeneous manycore systems. Although stretch-based scheduling is still in its infancy, we have seen that elastic asynchronous lambdas, which we spread horizontally over available cores and vertically on the timeline, are a suitable representation of application-internal knowledge. Latent parallelism and implementations for alternative instruction sets can be communicated to the scheduler. Together with deadlines as execution constraints, this knowledge strengthens the position of the operating system and allows it to schedule work on the complex hardware of the future.

References

1. Introducing blocks and grand central dispatch. In: Mac Developer Library. Apple Inc. (August 2010), `https://developer.apple.com/library/mac/#featuredarticles/BlocksGCD/`
2. Anderson, T.E., Bershad, B.N., Lazowska, E.D., Levy, H.M.: Scheduler activations: Effective kernel support for the user-level management of parallelism. ACM Transactions on Computer Systems 10(1), 53–79 (1992)
3. Best, M., Mottishaw, S., Mustard, C., Roth, M., Fedorova, A., Brownsword, A.: Synchronization via scheduling — techniques for efficiently managing shared state. In: Programming Language Design and Implementation (2011)
4. Blagodurov, S., Zhuravlev, S., Dashti, M., Fedorova, A.: A case for numa-aware contention management on multicore systems. In: Proceedings of the 2011 USENIX Annual Technical Conference, USENIX ATC, USENIX, pp. 1–16 (June 2011)
5. Blasgen, M.W., Eswaran, K.P.: Storage and access in relational data bases. IBM Systems Journal 16(4), 362–377 (1977)
6. Blumofe, R.D., Joerg, C.F., Kuszmaul, B.C., Leiserson, C.E., Randall, K.H., Zhou, Y.: Cilk: An efficient multithreaded runtime system. In: Proceedings of the 5th ACM SIGPLAN Symposium on Principles and Practice of Parallel Programming, pp. 207–216. ACM, New York (July 1995)
7. Charles, P., Grothoff, C., Saraswat, V., Donawa, C., Kielstra, A., Ebcioglu, K., von Praun, C., Sarkar, V.: X10: An object-oriented approach to non-uniform cluster computing. In: Proceedings of the 20th Conference on Object-Oriented Programming, Systems, Languages, and Applications, OOPSLA, pp. 519–538. ACM, New York (2005)
8. Collette, S., Cucu, L., Goossens, J.: Integrating job parallelism in real-time scheduling theory. Information Processing Letters 106(5), 180–187 (2008)

9. DeVuyst, M., Venkat, A., Tullsen, D.M.: Execution migration in a heterogeneous-isa chip multiprocessor. In: Proceedings of the 17th International Conference on Architectural Support for Programming Languages and Operating Systems, ASPLOS, pp. 261–272. ACM, New York (March 2012)
10. Ferry, D., Li, J., Mahadevan, M., Agrawal, K., Gill, C., Lu, C.: A real-time scheduling service for parallel tasks. In: Proceedings of the 19th IEEE Real-Time and Embedded Technology and Applications Symposium. RTAS, IEEE, Los Alamitos (April 2013)
11. Graefe, G., Linville, A., Shapiro, L.D.: Sort versus hash revisited. IEEE Trans. Knowl. Data Eng. 6(6), 934–944 (1994)
12. ISO/IEC, I.S.O.: 14882:2011: Programming Languages C++, 3rd edn. (September 2011)
13. Kerr, K.: Visual C++ 2010 and the parallel patterns library. MSDN Magazine (February 2009)
14. Khronos OpenCL Working Group: The OpenCL Specification, 1.2 edn. (November 2012)
15. Kim, C., Sedlar, E., Chhugani, J., Kaldewey, T., Nguyen, A.D., Blas, A.D., Lee, V.W., Satish, N., Dubey, P.: Sort vs. hash revisited: Fast join implementation on modern multicore cpus. In: Int. Conference on Very Large Data Bases (VLDB), Lyon, France (August 2009)
16. Krohn, M., Kohler, E., Kaashoek, M.F.: Events can make sense. In: Proceedings of the 2007 USENIX Annual Technical Conference. USENIX ATC, USENIX (June 2007)
17. Kumar, R., Farkas, K.I., Jouppi, N.P., Ranganathan, P.R., Tullsen, D.M.: Single-ISA heterogeneous multi-core architectures: The potential for processor power reduction. In: Proceedings of the 36th Annual IEEE/ACM International Symposium on Microarchitecture MICRO, vol. 36, p. 81. IEEE Computer Society, Washington, DC (2003)
18. Kumar, R., Tullsen, D.M., Ranganathan, P., Jouppi, N.P., Farkas, K.I.: Single-ISA heterogeneous multi-core architectures for multithreaded workload performance. In: Proceedings of the 31st Annual International Symposium on Computer Architecture, ISCA 2004. IEEE Computer Society, Washington, DC (2004)
19. Kun, Y., Chun, Z., Guoze, D., Jiangxiang, X., Zhihua, W.: A hardware-software co-design for h.264/avg decoder. In: Solid-State Circuits Conference, ASSCC 2006, pp. 119–122. IEEE Asian (November 2006)
20. Pan, H., Hindman, B., Asanovic, K.: Lithe: Enabling efficient composition of parallel libraries. In: HotPar (August 2009)
21. Rossbach, C.J., Currey, J., Silberstein, M., Ray, B., Witchel, E.: Ptask: Operating system abstractions to manage gpus as compute devices. In: Proceedings of the 23rd ACM Symposium on Operating Systems Principles, SOSP. ACM, New York (October 2011)
22. Welsh, M., Culler, D., Brewer, E.: Seda: An architecture for well-conditioned, scalable internet services. In: Proceedings of the 18th ACM Symposium on Operating Systems Principles, SOSP, pp. 230–243. ACM, New York (2001)

DYON: Managing a New Scheduling Class to Improve System Performance in Multicore Systems*

Ramon Nou[1], Jacobo Giralt[1], and Toni Cortes[1,2]

[1] Barcelona Supercomputing Center (BSC), Spain
name.surname@bsc.es
[2] Technical University of Catalonia (UPC), Spain

Abstract. Due to the increase in the number of available cores in current systems, plenty of system software starts to use some of these cores to perform tasks that will help optimize the application behaviour. Unfortunately, current Onload mechanisms are too limited. On the one hand, there is no dynamic way to decide the number of cores that is taken from applications and given to these system helpers. And, on the other hand, the onload mechanisms do not offer enough control over when and where onloading tasks should to be executed. In this paper we propose a new Onload Framework that addresses these issues.

First, we propose DYON, a dynamic and adaptive method to control the amount of extra CPUs offered to the Onload Framework to generate benefits for the whole system.

And second, we propose a submission mechanism that given a task, executes it if there are idle resources or rejects it otherwise. This feature is useful to move the execution of small pieces of code out of the critical path (allowing parallel execution) when this is possible, or discard them and execute a code that will not rely on them.

1 Introduction

Currently, processors have an increasing number of cores used for CPU intensive workloads, but these cores are not exploited when they are idle. This extra capacity can be used, for instance, to reduce a kernel critical path by executing code in parallel, or to run additional services that provide additional benefits. Consider an I/O analyser as IOAnalyzer [2] (to improve the I/O scheduler) as an example of service (we will henceforth call them *Onloaded Services* in general).

* This work was partially supported by the EU IST program as part of the IOLanes project (contract FP7-248615), by the Marie Curie Initial Training Network grant"SCALing by means of Ubiquitous Storage (SCALUS)", by the Spanish Ministry of Economy and Competitiveness under the TIN2012-34557 grant, and by the Catalan Government under the 2009-SGR-980 grant. We would also like to thank Neurocom for letting us use their TariffAdvisor application and Alberto Miranda for his help. Source available for kernel 2.6.32 under request at the IOLanes project [1].

D. an Mey et al. (Eds.): Euro-Par 2013 Workshops, LNCS 8374, pp. 759–768, 2014.

This service can reduce the I/O time of a job with some I/O phases up to 5 times [2] if the disk scheduler becomes optimal. This benefit affects the rest of the system, which can increase its performance or go to an IDLE state faster.

If the code is not executed (idle resources are unavailable) the system will continue working, but could we get extra benefits with additional resources to those services? Yes, however the additional resources should be controlled dynamically. For example, an HPC job with a processing stage and an I/O stage will rarely obtain benefits if we change the I/O Scheduler. We can apply a dynamic CPU partition method modifying the two stages behaviour forcing non-idle resources to be offered only in the I/O stage. The proposed mechanism is called **DYON**.

An example of dynamic partition is the memory utilization between the page cache [3,4] and normal memory. The key is that the page cache reduces a possible access to disk and thus, having more page cache should be beneficial in most cases. Additionally, the kernel knows when the page cache size should be modified via *malloc* calls. The CPU has a different behaviour: we can not assign percentages of CPU directly (kernel divides cores using masks), and we neither know in advance CPU requirements nor the maximum amount that we have to offer to produce benefits to the system.

Onloaded Services need additional ways to be executed not found in current Linux systems: for example, parallelized critical path code needs to know immediately if it is going to be executed (using only idle resources), or processes doing I/O analysis should be executed using a low priority and stopped immediately if the resources are going to be used. In this paper we propose the **Onload Framework** that allows to execute those tasks and services only if there are idle resources. With our proposal, we immediately know if the onload code is being executed so we can then continue with a parallel workflow or move to a normal workflow if the execution is not possible. The Onloaded Framework also allows us to control the tasks priorities providing the needed tools to manage DYON.

Summarizing, the contributions of this article are the next ones:

1. An **Onload Framework** enhancing Linux *workqueues* with new capabilities, along with a new scheduling class (SCHED_ONLOAD).
2. **DYON**, a dynamic CPU distribution method that maximizes the system performance (CPU Cycles per I/O) modifying previous services priority.

2 Existing Mechanisms Overview

One of the current ways to execute code is the *workqueues* [5] mechanism, used by some components in the Linux kernel to defer tasks. The *workqueues* are implemented with a shared queue, being rarely used due the variability in workloads. Recently they has been extended with the inclusion of Concurrency Managed Work Queues [6], moving to a single pool of threads that serves all queues. A single thread pool implementation avoids contention among threads from each pool, but traditionally it has been difficult to find a solution for all components. For example, some modules have built mechanisms on top of work queues to handle ordering restrictions [7] and others simply use their own *workqueues* since it is the easiest way to defer work inside the kernel.

The execution under the *workqueues* mechanism does not allow a conditional execution of a parallel or sequential workflow depending on whether the task will start executing or not (taking into account that these onloaded tasks will only use idle resources).

Another mechanism is the SCHED_IDLE scheduling class, the processes of such class are also enqueued and we do not know when they will be executed. Those mechanism defer tasks, but deferring is in some scenarios undesired as the execution can delay indefinitely not allowing a conditional execution of the code.

3 Onload Framework Mechanism

Our framework complements the *workqueues*, with a potential to parallelize tasks and workflows and with a narrower target.

3.1 Design

The framework is designed for short kernel tasks and short/long off-kernel/user tasks. The former, requested by the kernel, lack the issues (deadlocks, delays [8]) that are problematic for the *workqueues* management. Off-kernel tasks, requested by a user level application, have similar requirements but they are preemptable because they can not be trusted (as may block the framework). The common and default behaviour of the framework is that it cannot preempt, so either it accepts a task to be run immediately or it rejects it. Conceptually this means either taking advantage of additional resources if they are present or doing it as it was planned if they are not. We are going to enumerate the different features and design principles:

Notifications - Tasks are executed asynchronously from the requester, so there must be a callback mechanism to notify the end of a task. This callback can be as simple as unlocking a semaphore. It is an optional feature, the tasks can implement a different mechanism in their code.

Parallelism - Some of the operations we plan to onload might take advantage of parallelism, and this means our framework needs to provide a way to express it. For that matter, a range of CPUs[1] can be requested at once. Using a range increases the possibility of success of the request, which is obviously critical since otherwise the user would have to poll downwards from its maximum degree of parallelism until the system can satisfy its requirements. At any moment, tasks can retrieve the value of a private sequential id for this parallel operation and the total number of threads collaborating.

Offloading - The framework also works in specialized resources (GPGPUs, SPUs, etc.) seen by the framework user as an extended CPU mask with both CPUs and these specialized cores. The user changes the target processor to execute the requested task only by modifying this mask.

Deadlines - A task can be queued for a short time (*deadline*) while there are not idle resources. The task will not use more than those idle resources on the

[1] We use CPU as simplification, referring to the smallest processing unit that can run a task.

machine, which will not happen using *workqueues*. This was implemented for tasks like deduplication: setting up a deadline can be seen as a way to express that the block to be deduplicated is not needed after the deadline.

NUMA selection - If we specify a memory address, the mechanism will try to use an idle core near the memory address automatically.

Interface - The interface to onload tasks is similar to that of *workqueues* but semantically richer and designed for parallel operations. Work requests are defined with the following list of parameters: *Function to onload, argument to pass to the function, callback, CPU mask, minimum and maximum number of resources requested, buffer address and a deadline value.*

3.2 Implementation

The Onload Framework is implemented as a pool of threads in the kernel, each bound to a core, from which only a subset will be available at a given moment depending on the system load. If one thread is ready, it means its associated CPU is idle so a task can be onloaded.

Internally, threads can be on two main states: ready and running. Availability of a thread/CPU is expressed through a bitmap that is updated atomically on every context switch. Checking whether there are idle resources to onload a task is a fast operation. Apart from request time, a task (using the deadline feature) can also be scheduled on two other points. Each time a CPU is about to idle, the queue is checked, then one of the pending tasks could be selected. Similarly, after an onloading task is finished, if its associated CPU run queue is still empty, another of the pending tasks can be dequeued to be run immediately.

Whenever a new work request arrives at the framework, first its number of CPU threads requirement (for example, use only core #4) is checked. If there are idle cores to onload, the framework moves their associated threads to the running list and then they wake up with a description of the task to perform. This is a pointer to a function with three parameters: a void pointer and an id plus the number of threads allocated for the task. While this task is running, others can be accepted as long as there are resources to fulfill them all. Scheduling decisions are simple at this point, but could be more elaborated if the optional deadline functionality becomes more important in the future.

Once a task is finished, its associated callback is invoked and then the current CPU load is checked. If its runqueue is still empty, the framework inspects if there is another onload task waiting (to maximize CPU utilization). If it is not, the thread is put back to the pool and the CPU marked as unavailable.

The scheduling is handled through a new scheduling policy which is set with the POSIX function *sched_ setscheduler()*. Current Linux versions implement five different policies: FIFO, round robin, other (standard), batch and idle. Our framework adds an extra one, SCHED_ONLOAD, whose effect is those processes will only be scheduled whenever there are idle cores (similar to SCHED_IDLE but with lower priority and different preemption scheme). For our IOAnalyzer example means that the processing and analysis threads are of the SCHED_ONLOAD class so their execution is subject to the existence of idle cores.

4 DYON - Dynamic Mechanism

As we have explained in Section 1, for certain types of services it is appropriate to offer additional resources to increase the system performance. For example, if we offer some extra CPU to IOAnalyzer we can get an extra gain surpassing the loss of performance. With the default policy, we will not get this extra gain resulting in a slower working system. Summarizing, **DYON** offers more or less performance to some threads that are aiding the system to improve the overall system performance.

4.1 Selection Mechanism

This dynamic system does not have a monotonic relationship between the CPU partition (Onloaded Services and the rest of the system) and the performance obtained. Therefore, we do not know if increasing or decreasing the processing power offered is going to affect the performance. For this reason, we need to test all the possibilities.

The method used to select the most beneficial partition is iterative and guided by past performance. This method is based on the Armed Bandit [9], which chooses the next partition based on the near-past observed performance. As it is probability based, sometimes non-favourable partitions will be used. Those non-favourable partitions may become favourable at any time, recalibrating the system.

To summarize, the global workflow is the next one: each t seconds we obtain P(performance) for the current partition n_i. The new performance is merged with previous performance values for the same partition. Once we have the system values stored, we update the different probabilities (gradually) to favor the best partition and select, using the afore-mentioned probabilities, the new partition that will be used. We do not do any filtering as noise is considered to be inside the system to optimize.

To get a finite number of partitions, we divide the CPUs in a number, n, of parts. For example, 5 parts will divide the system processing power in : 0%, 25%, 50%, 75% and 100%. A 25% means that a 25% of the CPUs will be dedicated to Onloaded Services. Furthermore, 0% will select the default SCHED_ONLOAD policy, meaning that only idle resources will be used.

4.2 Metrics Chosen to Improve

To guide our dynamic system, we are going to use an I/O oriented metric extended to cover CPU Only scenarios. The metric, CPIO [10] (Cycles per I/O, lower is better), is defined as the next formula:

$$\frac{(user\ cycles + system\ cycles) * CPUFreq * \#Cores}{system\ I/O\ blocks\ read + written}$$

We change it with $(user\ cycles + system\ cycles)^{-1}$ (lower is better) to cover applications without I/O. Thanks to CPIO we can compare two system snapshots

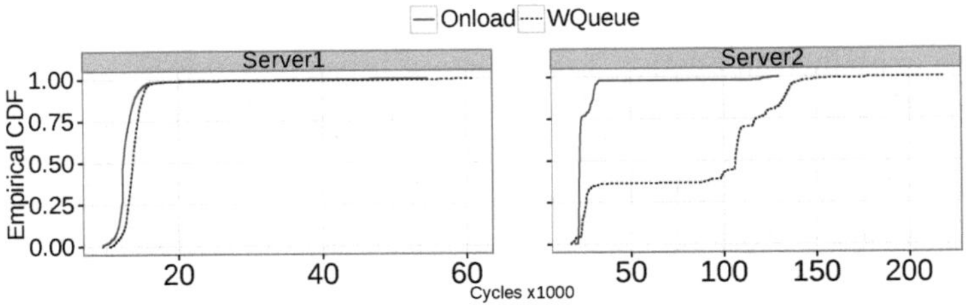

Fig. 1. ECDF for CPU Cycles to create-execute-finish a task on different servers

and decide if an action produces a better working global system without the need of application metrics that are not always available.

5 Evaluation

We will evaluate the two components presented, i) the Onload Framework with the Workqueues in a common scenario (creation-execution-finish of a task) and ii) DYON using IOAnalyzer as Onload Service.

5.1 Onload Framework - Task Creation-Execution-Finish Comparison

If we exclude checking the CPU availability, onloading a task could be similar to queueing the task to be run by the global workqueue. The workqueue needs to be empty and restricted to schedule on a different CPU than the requester. We use 2 servers: Server 1 has 4 cores and Server 2 has 8 cores. Figure 1 shows the range of # of CPU cycles to create, execute and finish a task (1000 runs). Our proposal is more stable(less variation) when we have a longer number of cores as the restriction of running the task on a different core results on high variability for the workqueue mechanism, evidencing it is not the appropriate way to onload a task in the Linux kernel given a processor restriction. This comes from the fact that they do not take processor availability into account. Other features of the Onload Framework are not directly comparable.

5.2 DYON

The system under test is an Intel Core 2 Quad CPU Q9300 @ 2.50GHz with 4Gb of RAM with a ST31500341AS HDD (Server 1 in previous experiment). The onloaded service selected for the evaluation is an I/O workflow analyzer to select the I/O scheduler (IOAnalyzer [2]) for the current workload automatically. As the service is highly optimized, we modified it in order to increase its CPU consumption. We will use the following applications and benchmarks to build the evaluation scenario creating a 3-phases workload, composed as explained in Table 1, generating an heterogeneous workload. Each application has its own performance metric that will be used to evaluate the system.

TariffAdvisor (TA) is a real parallel application [11], it uses CPU to make fast rating for Telecom operators and does intensive writes to store the results. The metric studied is the *reports per second* obtained (higher better).

Flexible I/O (FIO) [12] is a benchmark doing sequential I/O to 10 files in parallel. The performance metric is the *runtime* (lower better).

CPU is a basic CPU consumer, it tries to use a 100% of each CPU for the time specified. The metric to improve is the number of operations (higher better). Offering CPU power to the Onload Framework, reduces its performance.

Table 1. Workload phases description

Phases composition	**Description**
TA + CPU	An equilibrated value is the best as we are running one CPU intensive parallel process and one I/O intensive process.
TA + FIO + CPU	We have 2 I/O processes and 1 CPU consumer. The best global performance will be obtained improving the I/O.
CPUc	In this phase CPU is a direct target to optimize. Hence, the best option is to reduce the CPU devoted to onload services to 0% to lower the CPIO metric.

We will evaluate three scenarios using the IOAnalyzer service to optimize the I/O Scheduler of the TA and FIO (able to offer a 50% of improvement for each application): i) The static partition of CPUs, ii) The dynamic partition using CPIO metric or application metrics and iii) the selection mechanism reactivity.

i. Static Partition. For this experiment, we partition the CPU from 0% to 100% in 10% steps, so 90% means that 90% of extra non-idle resources are available to IOAnalyzer. For each of the partitions we are running the 3-phases workload defined in Table 1 obtaining a normalized mean performance value for the entire workload.

On Figure 2 (left side) we show each static partition performance as a boxplot. We can observe how with a 50% static partition the median performance (box horizontal line) is higher than any other partition. On the other side, a 80% static partition is a 10% less efficient than the optimal. The default partition (0%) which only offers idle resources to IOAnalyzer, also obtains less performance than the optimal.

If we analyse each workload phase, the optimal partition changes (50% for TA+CPU, 70% for TA+FIO+CPU and 0% for CPU) as the effect of IOAnalyzer over the applications depends on the level of I/O (1, 2 or 0 applications generating I/O respectively). This produces an heterogeneous workload, being a perfect target for a dynamic method as **DYON**.

ii. Dynamic Partition. Using the previous Fig.2 (right side), we show the performance obtained running DYON guided by CPIO metric (CPIO, blue) and Application metrics (App, red).

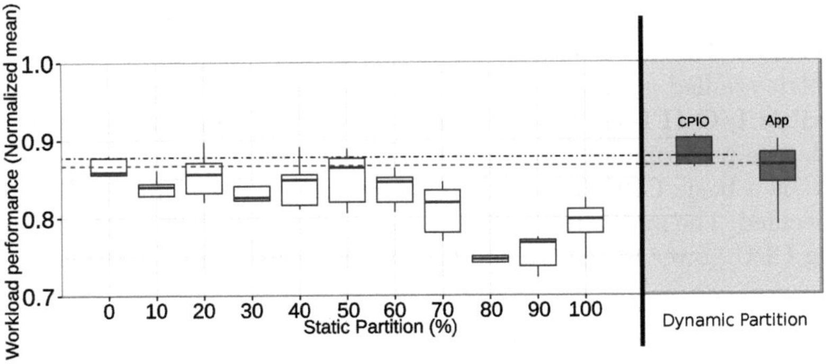

Fig. 2. Static partition (left side) showing the mean application performance on Y-Axis of the three phases described on Table 1. Results with DYON using CPIO or application metrics are on the right side.

With any of the two metrics, we are able to obtain more performance than the optimal static partition (50%) as we are on an heterogeneous workload. In the case of CPIO we obtain clearly a 1.5% more, but the benefits with Application metrics are lower.

This may be surprising at first: On the one hand, CPIO optimizes the global system behaviour but it does not know anything about the jobs performance. On the other hand, application metrics potentially can offer better results as the output is more direct if they are of enough quality. Precisely, quality is the problem on our scenario: for example, TA application metrics only report how many records per second we have in the last period: It does not include any relation with the CPU used for that processing, i.e., effectiveness reducing the information offered to **DYON** in comparison with CPIO.

If we analyse each of the phases separately (not shown), we obtain more performance with **DYON** than any static partition in the (TA+FIO+CPU) phase because it is heterogeneous. However, CPUc phase obtains 10% less performance than the maximum attainable: As this workload does not benefit from IOAnalyzer, any resource taken from it will decrease its performance. As **DYON** needs to try different partitions to find the best one, these tries give resources to IOAnalyzer, but result in no benefit to the CPU application.

iii. Selection Mechanism and System Reactivity. There are two considerations in order to have a working selection mechanism as the one we are proposing:

Number of partitions. Having a lot of partitions reduces the capacity of the algorithm to react. For example, with 10 partitions and only 1 of them optimal (not a very common scenario) we need in median 17 tries or iterations to find and select the optimal value in a stable way (two consecutive tries) as we can see on Fig. 3a. On the same scenario, we have more than a 75% of the selections going to the optimal partition (Fig. 3b). The other 25% will be devoted to near optimal partitions and occasionally testing other ones. However, as the performance of the other partitions is bad the maximum performance will be 75% of the optimal.

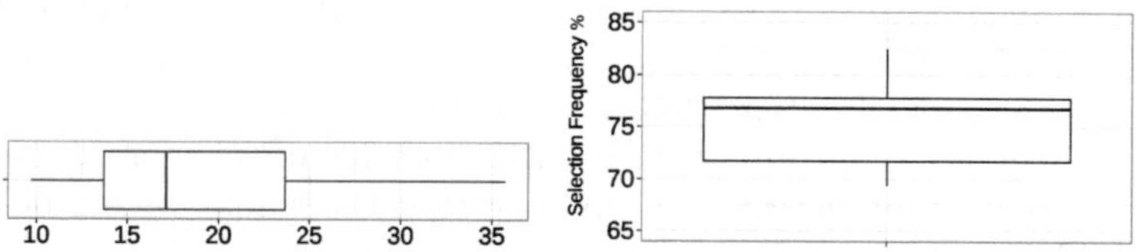

(a) Iterations to Optimal (b) Optimal value frequency

Fig. 3. Selection mechanism and System Reactivity

Time between checks. Between each partition change, the selection mechanism waits t seconds. For the previous experiments we selected a high t value (15 seconds) to accentuate bad selections. However, when we were designing the experiment, we found that the test time must be selected accordingly: with a short test time (to be able to run more repetitions, in a reasonable time) the dynamic mechanism will not be able to detect/learn about how the system behaves. Additionally, changes below t inside a workload will not be detected directly.

Reducing test time below that value will produce unexpected results (mainly not being able to find the optimal value). To show this described effect, we repeated **TA+CPU** phase using an 8 times shorter workload than in the evaluation increasing the variability and reducing the performance obtained (Figure 4, compares the each static partition performance for the phase, as 11 vertical bars, with the performance obtained with **DYON** as a blue boxplot). This is produced because all the partitions and its associated performance has not been explored.

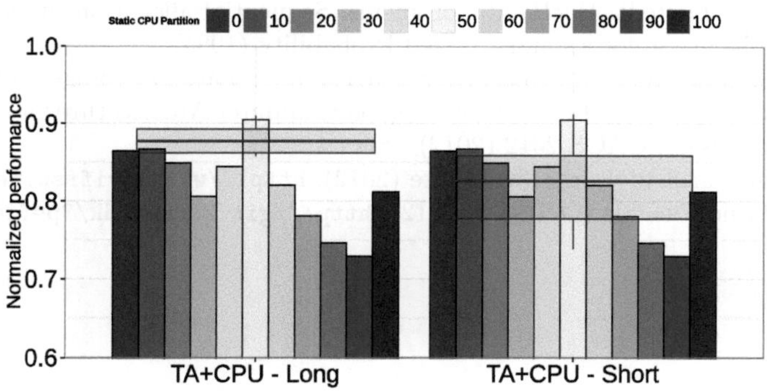

Fig. 4. Effect of the test length on the dynamic mechanism

6 Conclusions

The Onload Framework complements Linux *workqueues* to support our Onloaded Services, background-like services and tasks aiding the system, and offer new workflow capabilities to parallelize code based on the resources available.

We show that if we allow to use more CPU to those Onloaded Services we can obtain extra benefits. To control the quantity of CPU offered to those services dynamically we created **DYON**, a dynamic CPUs partition system. **DYON** is guided by CPIO metric, providing a way to compare two system snapshots and decide if the the new CPU partition is providing more or less performance.

We have seen on the evaluation as CPIO metrics offers more performance than direct application metrics as CPIO captures the whole system behaviour. With **DYON** we obtain more performance than any static selection.

References

1. FORTH, UPM, BSC, IBM, INTEL, NEUROCOM: IOLanes - Advancing the Scalability and Performance of I/O Subsystems in Multicore Platforms (2010), `http://www.iolanes.eu`
2. Nou, R., Giralt, J., Cortes, T.: Automatic i/o scheduler selection through online workload analysis. In: Apduhan, B.O., Hsu, C.H., Dohi, T., Ishida, K., Yang, L.T., Ma, J. (eds.) UIC/ATC, pp. 431–438. IEEE Computer Society (2012)
3. Bovet, D.P., Cesati, M.: Understanding the linux kernel. O'Reilly (2003)
4. Love, R.: Linux System Programming: Talking Directly to the Kernel and C Library. O'Reilly Media, Inc. (2007)
5. Molnar, I.: Inclusion of Work Queues on Linux (2012), `http://lwn.net/Articles/11247/`
6. Heo, T.: RFC of Concurrency Managed Workqueues patch (2012), `http://lwn.net/Articles/355347/`
7. Klassert, S.: RFC of padata patch (2012), `http://www.mail-archive.com/linux-cryptovger.kernel.org/msg03329.html`
8. Heo, T.: RFC of Concurrency Managed Workqueues patch take 2 (2012), `http://lwn.net/Articles/367289/`
9. Berry, D.A., Fristedt, B.: Bandit problems: Sequential allocation of experiments. Monographs on Statistics and Applied Probability (1985)
10. Akram, S., Marazakis, M., Bilas, A.: NUMA Implications for Storage I/O Throughput in Modern Servers. In: 3rd Workshop on Computer Architecture and Operating System co-design, CAOS 2012 (2012)
11. Neurocom: TariffAdvisor / TariffSuite (2012), `http://www.tariffsuite.com`
12. Axboe, J.: fio Flexible IO Tester (2012), `http://git.kernel.dk/?p=fio.git`

Energy-Efficient and Fault-Tolerant Taskgraph Scheduling for Manycores and Grids

Patrick Eitschberger and Jörg Keller

FernUniversität in Hagen,
Faculty of Mathematics and Computer Science,
58084 Hagen, Germany
{patrick.eitschberger,joerg.keller}@fernuni-hagen.de
www.fernuni-hagen.de/pv/

Abstract. Taskgraphs model a broad range of parallel applications. Despite static scheduling, processor failures can be overcome with the help of task duplication, which we explored in a previous proposal. With the advent of processor frequency scaling, energy can be saved by the runtime system as it is informed about gaps in the schedule and task dependencies, and thus can slow down processors as long as dependencies do not lead to a makespan increase. In the case of a fault, a makespan increase can be traded for additional energy investment by accelerating the task duplicates that run tasks from the crashed core. We evaluate our proposal with a large benchmark suite of taskgraphs with different sizes for a generic manycore architecture.

Keywords: taskgraph scheduling, task duplication, fault tolerance, frequency scaling, energy efficiency, power-aware computing, manycore computing, grid computing.

1 Introduction

Many parallel applications can be decomposed into a set of tasks prior to execution. Thus they can be modeled by static taskgraphs, where each node is a task with a given runtime, and arcs (u, v) represent dependabilities, where a task u produces output of a known size upon completion, which must be transferred to task v that can only start if that input is available. For a given machine (we assume p identical processing units), a taskgraph must be scheduled, i.e. each task must be assigned to a processor with a given start time, when it is executed without interruption until it completes. For a valid schedule, at most one task may be active at any time, and the start times must represent the dependabilities between tasks, taking into account the communcation time if dependent tasks are mapped to different processing units. Typically, the goal of the scheduler is to minimize the makespan, i.e. the time when the last processing unit completes processing its assigned tasks.

At any time, a processing unit may fail, either because it is shutdown by its owner (a frequent situation in grids with contributed resources) or because of a

D. an Mey et al. (Eds.): Euro-Par 2013 Workshops, LNCS 8374, pp. 769–778, 2014.

software fault (application or system hangs, a not too infrequent case in many-cores with new architecture and thus new operating systems and compilers), or because of a hardware or network fault. In that case, redundancy must be available to continue processing of the taskgraph. As an alternative to temporal redundancy in the form of dynamic re-scheduling, which often leads to notably increased makespan, use of structural redundancy in the form of task duplication has emerged as a static technique to cope with failures. While it is clear that placements of tasks and duplicates on different processing units will ensure tolerance of one processor failure, the question of overhead in the fault-free case arises. While we developed techniques to avoid overhead by placing duplicates appropriately [4,3], the additional processing of duplicates still increases the energy consumption of the taskgraph computation, which emerges as a new measure besides — and sometimes more important as — the makespan.

On the other hand, processor frequency scaling opens the dual possibility to save energy by slowing down tasks, thus filling gaps in the schedule without increasing makespan, and accelerating duplicates in case of a failure, to trade makespan increase against additional energy investment in this case. While frequency scaling typically is handled by the operating system according to usage rate, this is not appropriate for taskgraph computations as the local operating system has no information about the dependencies between tasks on processors belonging to different operating system instances. This information is available in the runtime system for the taskgraph computation, and manycores like Intel SCC delegate frequency scaling to user level and thus enable a reduction of energy consumption for our application scenario. Thus, the placement of tasks enables trading energy savings in the fault-free case against overhead in the fault case, and trading overhead in the fault case against additional energy investment. In contrast to other works, that optimize makespan for a given energy budget, our problem is to optimize energy consumption given a target makespan and the user preferences above.

Energy-efficiency in taskgraph scheduling has been considered in previous works. Kianzad et al. [7] consider frequency scaling in taskgraph scheduling, however they focus on integration of the scheduling and scaling steps. In contrast, we start with an existing schedule, insert duplicates for fault-tolerance and perform frequency scaling. Cong et al. [2] consider energy savings by exploiting input-dependent variations of task runtimes, i.e. they focus on dynamic frequency scaling, while we compute frequencies statically. Pruhs et al. [8] consider the situation where a certain energy budget is available for the taskgraph computation, and statically compute schedules with optimal makespan for that budget by scaling processor frequencies accordingly. Yet, none of those works considers fault-tolerance. In contrast, works that use task duplication for fault-tolerance, such as [5], do not consider energy consumption. While Unsal et al. [9] investigate energy aspects of fault-tolerance in real-time systems, they use application-level fault-tolerance techniques instead of task duplication. Thus, the combination of the three aspects is, to our knowledge, not known from the literature.

We compare several placement strategies for duplicates with the help of a simulator for a taskgraph runtime system [3] that we adapt to take frequency scaling into account and enable a forecast of energy consumption. The simulator assumes a generic manycore architecture with a standard model for dynamic power consumption, i.e. at frequency f, a core consumes power proportional to f^α, where $2 \leq \alpha \leq 3$, cf. e.g. [8]. We use $\alpha = 3$ based on previous experiments on the Intel SCC [1], but leave out constant factors and low-order terms for simplicity. As the frequency and thus the power consumption is fixed during execution of a task, the energy spent for that task is the product of power and task runtime.

As inputs, we take the taskgraphs from a benchmark suite of synthetic taskgraphs [6] that is organized according to several structural criteria, and thus allows to categorize results for certain types of taskgraphs. Our results indicate that the average energy improvement is between 30% and 80%, where 20% to 65% results from scaling down the frequency for idle times and up to 20% results from slow down tasks and thus scaling down the frequency for tasks.

The remainder of this paper is structured as follows. In Section 2 we present the extended scheduling algorithm. Section 3 presents and analyzes the simulation results. In Section 4, we conclude and give an outlook on open problems and future work.

2 Efficient Fault-Tolerant Scheduling

We start by reviewing the ideas from [4], and briefly introduce two extensions [3]. We concentrate on improving the energy efficiency of taskgraph schedules by scaling the frequencies of cores down, where tasks can be prolonged without any increase of the makespan. Furthermore we also improve the performance of the schedules in case of a fault, where the execution of the duplicates leads to an overhead and thus to a higher makespan. In these cases the duplicates can be accelerated by scaling up the frequency of the corresponding cores to reduce or completely undo the overhead.

2.1 Previous Approach

The approach of Fechner et al. [4] provides fault-tolerance to taskgraph schedules by task duplication. It starts with an already existing schedule (and taskgraph) and extends the schedule by including a duplicate task for each original task. The scheduling is done prior to execution, thus it is done statically. A duplicate (D) has to be placed on another Processing Unit (PU) than its corresponding original task, so that in case of a PU failure the schedule execution can be continued. We assume a fail-stop model, where the failure might be induced by a hardware, software, or network fault.

If the original task has finished its work it sends a commit message to the corresponding D, so that the D can abort its execution. Thus in every case either only the original task or only the D is finished and has to send its results to the successor tasks. Because of the communication overhead, a D starts with a little delay called *slack*.

Mostly there are gaps in the schedule because of dependencies between the tasks. Especially those gaps can be used for an efficient placement of the Ds. In some cases the gaps might be too small to place a D. So the placement could lead to a shift of all successor tasks and thus to an overhead in the fault-free case. To avoid such an overhead and also to minimize the overhead in case of a fault, three different strategies for the placement are presented in [4].

In the first strategy only so called dummy duplicates (DD) are used. A DD is a placeholder for a D. It is placed with runtime 0 and only in case of a fault it is extended to a full duplicate task. Such a DD can be placed in gaps or between succeeding tasks. In this way, overhead in the fault free case can be avoided in general, but this strategy does not take much advantage of the gaps. In Fig. 1b an example placement of the DDs is illustrated. The corresponding taskgraph and input schedule are shown in Fig. 1a. For a better understanding the slack and the communication costs are disregarded.

The second strategy uses the schedules from the first strategy and converts DDs to Ds if there is a gap before the DDs. Only those DDs are converted that are placed at the end time of the corresponding original tasks. The size of the converted Ds is bounded by the length of the gap before the Ds. Thus in case of a fault a fraction of the D is already executed so that it only has to be extended for the remaining part of the original task. The modified schedule is illustrated in Fig. 1c. The second strategy uses the gaps more efficiently in comparison with the first strategy.

In the third strategy some of the gaps in the input schedule are partly extended to fill that gaps more efficiently with Ds. In this strategy a small overhead is allowed in the fault free case for a better overhead in case of a fault. Fig. 1d illustrates the modified schedule.

In [3] we firstly include the consideration of the communication times between the tasks, because those communication times influence the placement of the Ds and DDs. For that we assume to have a homogeneous network. The different communication times in the taskgraphs represent the different amounts of information that has to be transferred to the corresponding successor tasks. For example one task only needs an integer value, another task needs an array of floats, etc. A second extension in [3] is that we also consider task slowdowns as a special kind of fault. When the performance of a task decreases (because the PU is used for other duties, e.g. in grids with contributed resources), the corresponding D or DD is used instead if it can be finished earlier.

2.2 Energy Efficiency Improvements

In our previous work our goal was to guarantee no overhead in a fault free case and to have only a minimal overhead in case of a fault. But today and also in the future energy consumption might be more important to minimize. Usually the operating system offers some energy functions and automatically scales the processor frequency with respect to the usage rate. Especially for taskgraph

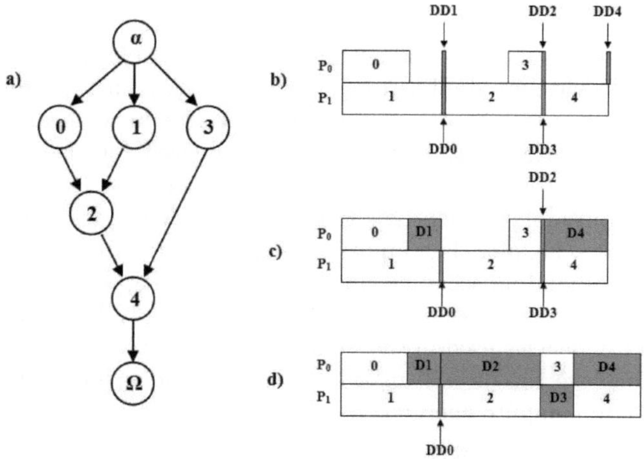

Fig. 1. An example taskgraph and three strategies in comparison

scheduling such automatic energy functions cannot be used because the operating system has no information about the schedule and task dependencies and thus cannot decide if it can slowdown a task and scale down the core frequency without increasing the makespan of the whole schedule. In such a case only the scheduler resp. the underlying runtime system has the information about the taskgraphs and schedules. Thus the energy management has to be done there.

In our approach we implemented a simulator for a taskgraph runtime system that supports energy management functions. One example platform where one can use such a runtime system is the Single-Chip Cloud Computer (SCC), which is a research processor from Intel. The SCC consists of 24 dual-core tiles, i.e. 48 cores. With this platform, the user can scale the frequency and voltage of cores during the runtime of a program. The frequency scaling can be done for each tile, the voltage scaling only for groups of 8 cores. To calculate for each task the lowest possible frequency one has to check if a task could be extended or slowed down without increasing the makespan. It is important to note that the prolongation of a task could lead to a shift of the start time for some other tasks. But as long as these shifts do not have any influence on the makespan the extension does not have to be reduced. In the fault free case (where it is only senseful to extend or slowdown the tasks) only original tasks and their corresponding duplicates have to be considered. Because DDs are only placeholders for a duplicate, they are placed with runtime 0, and thus do not have to be extended. Duplicates on the other hand could also be slowed down or only be shifted, if the corresponding original task is slowed down too. But in case of only a shift the energy consumption would be higher than if the duplicate is also be slowed down. Thus, a slowdown of the duplicate in this case would be preferable to get the highest energy improvement. In the following the implementation of the simulator is described before we also present techniques that use frequency scaling to improve the makespan and thus also the overhead in case of a fault.

2.3 Implementation

Our implementation generates and evaluates three schedules for each taskgraph: a basic schedule without duplicates and without frequency scaling, a schedule extended by duplicates, and a schedule where frequency scaling is applied to tasks and duplicates. The latter two are evaluated for the fault-free case (see below), and for the case of a fault (see next subsection).

As plenty of optimal and heuristic taskgraph schedulers are available, we did not integrate the scheduler, but input a taskgraph (in standard taskgraph format) and a corresponding schedule (in the corresponding schedule format). For this schedule, each task is assigned frequency $f_{normal} = 1$. This is a relative frequency, as all frequencies used in the sequel, to be multiplied with the frequency necessary to achieve the desired makespan (in wall-clock time). As we use the frequency only to compute energy consumption and relate different energy consumptions by percentages, using a relative frequency simplifies matters without any disadvantage. In each gap (between executing two tasks or after finishing the last task till the makespan), we assume a core to run at a frequency f_{idle}. For schedules without frequency scaling, we both consider $f_{idle} = f_{normal}$ and $f_{idle} \ll f_{normal}$.

The second schedule is generated by placing duplicates as explained in the previous subsection. The duplicates also are assigned frequency $f_{normal} = 1$.

A third schedule is generated by scaling all tasks and their duplicates, i.e. by assigning task frequencies f_a possibly smaller than f_{normal}, that still allow to finish the schedule by the makespan. As frequency scaling is a computational expensive non-linear optimization problem, we apply a greedy heuristic, to be explained below.

The energy consumption for each schedule is then computed for the fault-free case. For each task (and duplicate) T_a, its runtime t_a and frequency f_a are used to compute the task energy consumption $t_a \cdot f_a^3$ as the product of time and power consumption. For each gap, the energy consumption is computed similarly by using the length of the gap and the idle frequency f_{idle}. The total energy consumption is obtained by summing the energy consumption over all tasks, duplicates, and gaps.

The frequency scaling heuristic basically tries to scale down the frequency of a task followed by a gap of length x to $f_a < f_{normal}$ such that the task runtime t_a is increased by a so-called *buffer* $x' \leq x$, i.e. by a factor $f_{normal}/f_a = (t_a + x')/t_a$ such that the gap is filled as far as possible but timing constraints from dependencies are not violated. Consider first an example without duplicates depicted in Fig. 2. Task T1 with runtime 4 is followed by a gap of length 2, yet can only be extended by 1 time unit ($f_1 = 4/(4+1) = 0.8$ because of the communication to task T3 that needs 3 time units and must be completed by the start time 8 of task T3. Task T2 cannot be extended although it is followed by a gap, because the communication time to task T4 leaves no room. Task T3 can be scaled down to $f_3 = 0.5$ because the gap to the makespan has length 2. Task T4 cannot be scaled down as there is no gap afterwards.

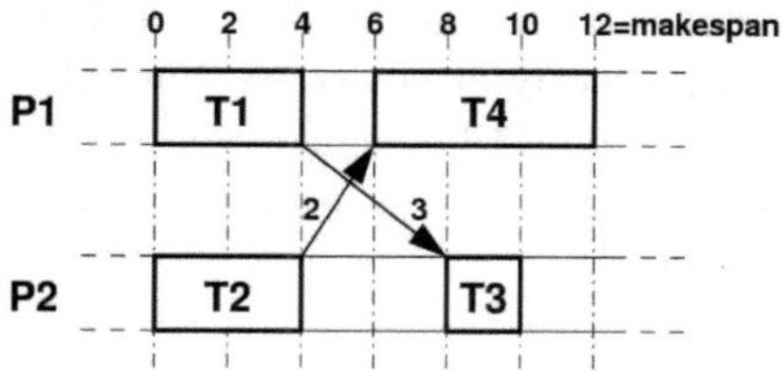

Fig. 2. Example schedule to illustrate the frequency scaling heuristic

If the resulting task frequency is lower than f_{idle}, then it is set to f_{idle}. The tasks are considered one by one in the order given in the schedule.

A duplicate is treated like a task for computing the buffer. To avoid the situation that a task finishes later than its duplicate after frequency scaling, each task and its duplicate are scaled down to the same frequency, by using the minimum of the two buffers. Furthermore, if a task is followed by a gap and a duplicate, then the task can take over the duplicate task's buffer if it can use it without violating other constraints. This means that the duplicate must also be followed by a gap and its start time is increased accordingly, i.e. the gap is moved before the duplicate. Note that a dummy duplicate is treated like a duplicate with runtime 0.

2.4 Performance Improvements in Case of a Fault

Until now we have only considered energy efficiency in the fault-free case. However, in case of a fault, avoiding a reduction of performance might be more important than the energy efficiency. We can use frequency scaling as well to improve the performance in such a case. When a PU crashes, it cannot be restarted as we use the fail-stop-model as explained above. Thus all following tasks on that PU will not be executed and the corresponding duplicates and dummy duplicates on the other PUs have to be extended and used to complete the schedule. Because of the extensions there might be an overhead that could result in a longer makespan. To minimize or totally undo this overhead one might also use some energy management functions.

If a D or DD has to be extended, the runtime system can save the current frequency (of that PU) and calculate the frequency that is needed to undo the overhead. This frequency is higher than f_{normal}, and thus leads to increased energy consumption. If the calculated frequency is higher than the supported maximum frequency of that PU, the frequency is set to the maximum frequency. Thus, the ability to undo the overhead largely depends on the frequencies that are supported by the PUs. After the execution of the corresponding extended D or DD the frequency can be scaled down to the previous frequency if the next task is an original task or a D that does not have to be extended. If the next task is a D or DD that has to be extended, the frequency can be scaled directly to the new calculated frequency. If there is a DD that does not have to be extended and that is placed at the finish time of the prior task without a gap, the next task is considered. If the next task starts at the same time where the DD is placed (in this case there is no gap between the tasks) and if the next task has to be extended, the frequency can directly be scaled to that calculated frequency. Only in case of a gap the frequency could be scaled down to the previous frequency. To avoid some of the high frequencies in case of a fault one could use the buffers from the previous subsection.

3 Experimental Results

We evaluate the energy-efficiency of our proposal with a benchmark suite of synthetic taskgraphs [6] comprising 72,000 optimal schedules that differ in the number of PUs (2, 4, 8, 16 and 32), the number of tasks (7 - 12, 13 - 18 and 19 - 24), edge density, the edge length and the node and edge weights. Furthermore we also used a simple list scheduler, that maps the tasks on that PU where they can start their execution first. For 36,000 taskgraphs, the number of tasks is as above, to see how energy consumption for non-optimal schedules with larger gaps can be improved. For 36,000 tasks graphs, the number of tasks is up to 250 to see how our proposal works for larger schedules.

There are totally three different variants for each strategy that result from the consideration of the communicaton times in our previous work [3]. Variant a) is the placement like explained above. In variant b) we use so called waitdummies to reduce the overhead in a fault free case and in variant c) we consider some of the communication times only in a fault case so that we can already quarantee no overhead in a fault free case. In Fig. 3 the improvements for the different strategies and variants and also for the original schedules without any fault-tolerant aspects (strategy 0) are presented for the different test benchmarks (TB). In these experiments we used the value 0.1 for f_{idle}.

Each bar in Fig. 3 is divided into two parts. The dark part represents the improvements of scaling down the frequency to $f_{idle} = 0.1$ in gaps, the light part represents the improvements of using the buffers to slowdown the tasks by scaling down their frequencies. In total the average energy improvements for the different testsets vary from around 30% for the testset TB-Optimal up to around 75% for the testset with the large testcases generated with the simple list scheduler. As expected most of the improvements result from the idle times (between 20% and 65%). The results reflect also that the schedules of the "TB-Optimal" testset are highly optimized and have only a few resp. short gaps in comparison to the other testsets. With using also the buffers, the energy improvements can be increased up to additional 20%. The highest improvements are for strategy 1 in all variants (abc). This results from only using DDs in the first strategy that do not need additional space and usually can be shifted without increasing the makespan. For the strategies 2 and 3 (abc) the improvements are lower, because in these cases there are a lot of Ds and thus fewer or smaller gaps.

In Fig. 4 the overhead improvements in case of a fault are presented for the test benchmarks with small schedules, averaged over all schedules and all possible fault positions, cf. [3]. As settings we used $f_{idle} = 0.1$ and 2.0 as maximum possible frequency. The overhead can be reduced by 27% to 38%. The highest

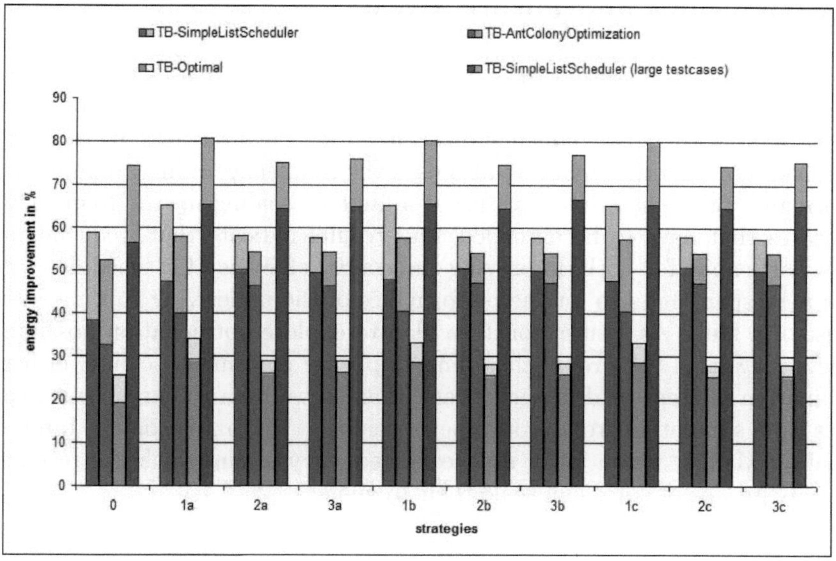

Fig. 3. Average Energy improvement

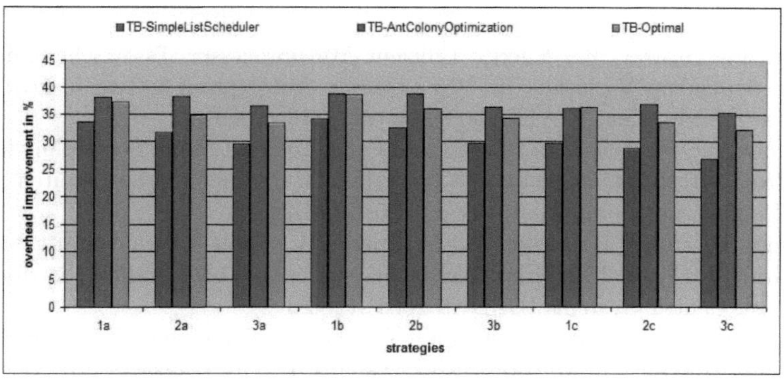

Fig. 4. Overhead improvement in the fault case

improvements show in strategy 1 because the DDs have not been slowed down in the fault free case and thus most of the DDs can still be extended without increasing the makespan. In strategies 2 and 3 the overhead improvement is smaller for a better energy efficiency in the fault free case, but the improvement is still high as only the duplicates are speeded up that have to be extended in case of a fault. We could also see that using only part of the buffer for energy reduction in the fault-free case leads to a reduced overhead in the fault case, however we cannot detail this for lack of space.

4 Conclusions and Future Work

We have presented a static task scheduling algorithm that uses task dupliction to handle processor failures and also increases the energy efficiency in a fault free case by scaling the core frequency down for some tasks without increasing the makespan. On the other hand we also used the frequency scaling to improve the performance of the schedules in case of a fault by scaling up the frequency for duplicates that have to be extended. Our results indicate that frequency scaling is worthwhile for both, improving the energy efficiency for schedules with a given makespan and also for the performance of the underlying runtime system in case of a fault. As future work, we plan to explore optimization possibilities by deviating from the order scheduling–duplicate placement–scaling, either by combination of steps or different orders. Finally, we plan to extend our experiments from simulations to a prototype system that we can use on the Intel SCC or Kalray MPPA, which allow user-level frequency scaling with the restriction that only groups of cores can scale their frequencies.

References

1. Cichowski, P., Keller, J., Kessler, C.: Modelling Power Consumption of the Intel SCC. In: Proc. 6th MARC Symposium, pp. 46–51 (2012)
2. Cong, J., Gururay, K.: Energy Efficient Multiprocessor Task Scheduling under Input-dependent Variation. In: Proc. Design, Automation & Test in Europe Conference & Exhibition (DATE 2009), pp. 411–416 (2009)
3. Eitschberger, P., Keller, J.: Effcient and Fault-Tolerant Static Scheduling for Grids. In: Proc. 14th IEEE International Workshop on Parallel and Distributed Scientific and Engineering Computing, PDSEC 2013 (2013)
4. Fechner, B., Hönig, U., Keller, J., Schiffmann, W.: Fault-Tolerant Static Scheduling for Grids. In: Proc. 13th IEEE Workshop on Dependable Parallel, Distributed and Network-Centric Systems (DPDNS 2008) (2008)
5. Hashimoto, K., Tsuchiya, T., Kikuno, T.: Effective Scheduling of Duplicated Tasks for Fault Tolerance in Multiprocessor Systems. IEICE Transaction on Information and Systems E85-D(3), 525–534 (2002)
6. Hönig, U., Schiffmann, W.: A comprehensive test bench for the evaluation of scheduling heuristics. In: Proc. 16th IASTED International Conference on Parallel and Distributed Computing and Systems (PDCS 2004), pp. 437–442 (2004)
7. Kianzad, V., Bhattacharyya, S., Ou, G.: CASPER: An Integrated Energy-Driven Approach for Task Graph Scheduling on Distributed Embedded Systems. In: Proc. 16th IEEE International Conference on Application-specific Systems, Architectures and Processors, ASAP 2005 (July 2005)
8. Pruhs, K., van Stee, R., Uthaisombut, P.: Speed Scaling of Tasks with Precedence Constraints. Theory of Computing Systems 43(1), 67–80 (2008)
9. Unsal, O., Koren, I., Krishna, C.M.: Towards Energy-Aware Software-Based Fault Tolerance in Real-Time Systems. In: Proc. International Symposium on Low Power Electronics and Design (ISLPED 2002), pp. 124–129 (2002)

Designing Applications with Predictable Runtime Characteristics for the Baremetal Intel SCC

Devendra Rai, Lars Schor, Nikolay Stoimenov,
Iuliana Bacivarov, and Lothar Thiele

Computer Engineering and Networks Laboratory,
ETH Zurich, 8092 Zurich, Switzerland
firstname.lastname@tik.ee.ethz.ch

Abstract. Thus far, most of the research into many- core computation has focussed on improving the average performance of an application, such as the average throughput. However, applications such as medical ultrasound not only require high throughput, but also require *predictable* performance characteristics, and are generally implemented on platforms explicitly designed for real-time computing. This paper proposes design strategies which enable high performance multiprocessing applications to achieve predictable communication latencies, computation times and *reaction latencies* over on-chip many-core platforms, such as the Intel SCC. The strategies presented in this paper can be incorporated into existing many core application design frameworks, wherein the responsibility of achieving predictable timing performance can be relegated to the framework itself. Experiments using two representative applications validate our strategies and show that it is indeed possible to use on-chip many core platforms for real time multiprocessing.

Keywords: Multi-Processor System, On-Chip Many-Core System, Real Time, Single-chip Cloud Computer.

1 Introduction

Research in high performance computing has focussed primarily on improving the average performance (e.g., throughput, latency) of large applications. However, soft real time applications, such as the diagnostic medical ultrasound not only require high throughput, but also require that the application's run-time characteristics are consistent and predictable. Systems like the Intel SCC are viewed primarily as high performance computing platforms, rather than as platforms capable of providing predictable runtime environment. We believe that on-chip many-core platforms such as the Intel SCC will become mainstream in the near future. Other examples of such platforms are the Tilera and Kalray MPPA many core processors, see [1,2]. Therefore, it is interesting to ask whether it is possible to architect many-core applications which can execute with predictable performance characteristics on the Intel SCC, making such platforms

D. an Mey et al. (Eds.): Euro-Par 2013 Workshops, LNCS 8374, pp. 779–789, 2014.

attractive for implementing soft real time high throughput applications. Moreover, it may be required that a given multiprocessing application react to events (e.g., control messages) in a bounded time. With this motivation, this paper proposes software design architecture with the following objectives:

1. Enable an application to execute with a predictable timing performance;
2. Enable an application to react to control messages in a predictable timeframe (henceforth, *bounded reaction latency*).

Our approach does not assume any special operating system features or services, and is therefore portable across platforms. We assume a general data-flow process network model of computation, which is extensively used to design and implement streaming applications(e.g., medical ultrasound). All results are validated on the baremetal SCC, and we emphasize that merely using the baremetal approach does not *automatically* lead to predicable performance characteristics.

2 Related Work

Although it is possible to port one of several multiprocessor real-time operating systems (RTOS) to the Intel SCC, an RTOS may consume a significant portion of the available computing resources on the chip, thus motivating the need for a baremetal solution, see [12]. As a result, C-language based programming frameworks such as BareMetalC [7] and BareMichael [11] are now available which allow the applications to run directly on the SCC cores, without the need of an operating system. In addition, baremetal-compatible communication libraries such as RCCE [9], iRCCE [3] provide intra- and inter core communication. Puffitsch *et. al.* use the baremetal approach to execute task-sets in real time on the SCC, but their approach is restricted to periodic tasks with no pre-emption, and the tasks are not required to respond to events within a bounded latency, see [8]. In contrast, this paper assumes general data-flow process networks, which can react to (also, pre-empted by) events within a statically bounded time.

3 Background

3.1 The Intel SCC Processor

The SCC processor [4] is a 48-core experimental processor from Intel, featuring 24 organized into a 4×6 grid and linked by a 2D mesh on-chip network. A tile contains a pair of P54C processor cores, a router, and a 16 KB block of SRAM, which is used for message passing. Each core has L1 instruction and data caches (16KB each) and a unified level 2 (L2) cache (256KB).

3.2 Data Flow Process Network Model of Computation

We assume of a set of concurrently executing deterministic processes, communicating with each other in a *point-to-point* manner, via bounded FIFOs.

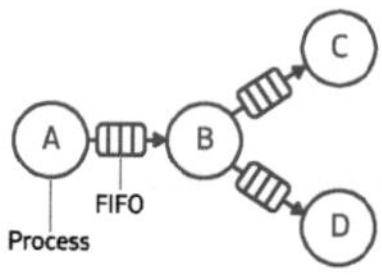

Fig. 1. A Data flow Process Network

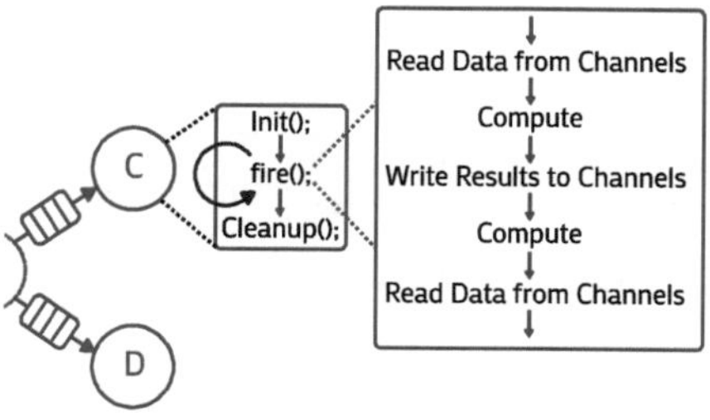

Fig. 2. Structure of a Process

A process attempting to read (write) an empty (full) FIFO blocks (or stalls) till the read (write) operation can be successfully completed A process can only execute (*fire*) when it has acquired sufficient data to proceed with its computation. Process networks have natural support for parallelism making them an attractive model for describing multiprocessing systems, specially digital signal processing systems.

Structure of the Process. The functionality of each process in a network is split into three parts: *initialization*, *execution* and *cleanup*, with each part executed by a call to a pre-defined function, see Figure 2. The initialization function (`init`) prepares a process for execution, by initializing variables, and allocating memory, if necessary. The main functionality of the process is encapsulated in the `fire` function, and runs as long as necessary, continuously reading data from input channels, computing, and writing results to one or more output channels. The `fire` function therefore, consists of *compute* segments, surrounded by channel read and/or channel write segments. The compute segments involve purely processing of already acquired data, and the time to execute each of these segments depends on the nature of acquired data. The segment with the longest computing time is called the *dominating segment.* The `cleanup` function is called once the process terminates its core functionality, and is used for returning resources to the system, or gathering performance statistics.

The *Master* Process and the Modified Process Structure. Controlling the behaviour of the application at runtime is achieved via a special process, called the *master process*, which can send appropriate control messages to the application at runtime. For brevity, we only discuss the `stop` control message, which is used to indicate to a process that it must exit its `fire` function and proceed to execute the `cleanup` function. Its structure follows the layout of the process in Figure 2.

Further, in order that a process can react to control messages, its structure has been modified as shown in Figure 4. After every call to `Read` (or `Write`) function, the process checks for the control message (for example, `stop`), and takes appropriate action. Inserting a check for control message after every call to `Read` or `Write` is automatically done at the pre-compilation stage. In the

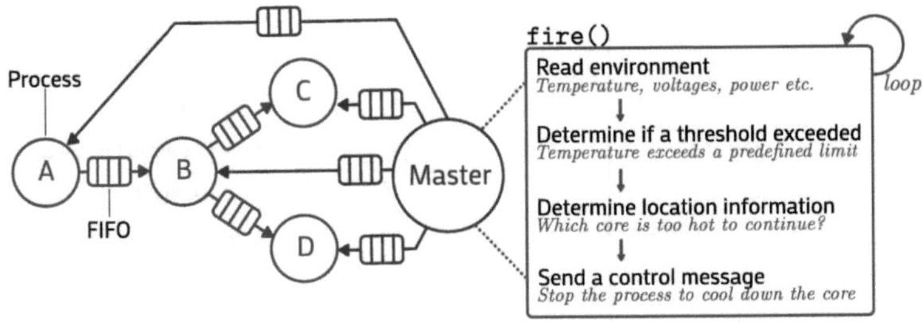

Fig. 3. An example of the *master process*. Additional control channels are also shown

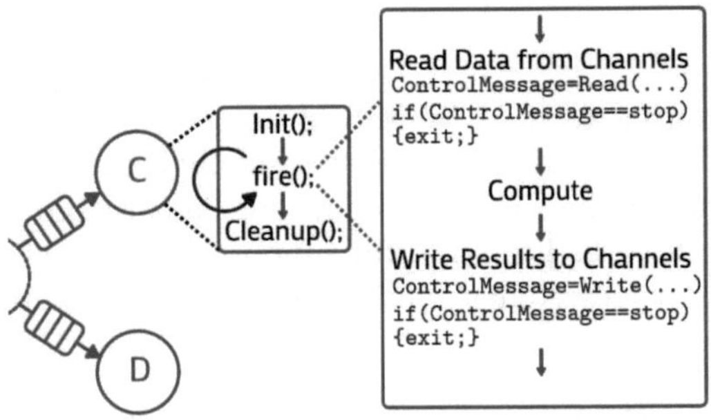

Fig. 4. Modified process structure

rest of this paper, the process from the original network is denoted simply as a *process* in order to distinguish it from the *master process*.

4 Achieving Predictable Timing Characteristics

4.1 Definitions

For the purpose of this paper, *predictable timing characteristics* consists of three parts: (a) Observed time to execute any given compute segment is within a known bound; (b) Observed time to send a fixed size message is within a known bound; and (c) Observed time for an application to react to a control message is within a known bound.

We define reaction time of a process as:

$$R_p = t_{p,C^*} - t_{m,C^*} \tag{1}$$

where R_p is the reaction time of a process p, t_{p,C^*} is the time when a process receives the control message, and t_{m,C^*} is the time when the master queues a control message for transmission (i.e., when a call to `iRCCE/RCCE_send` is placed).

4.2 Proposed Solution

The proposed solution has been divided into the following sections:

1. A new communication interface such that for any process, the delay in receiving a control message is independent of the size of data messages being exchanged between processes, thus ensuring bounded reaction times;
2. Mapping between processes and cores which reduces uncertainties in communication times between processes;
3. Eliminating factors that may lead to unpredictable compute segment times.

4.3 A New Communication Interface

We do not place any limit on the length of data messages exchanged between processes. However, arbitrarily long messages lead to arbitrarily long communication times, leading to unpredictable delays in reading a control message from the master. Clearly, in order to ensure bounded reaction times, the control message communication must be decoupled from the normal data communication. In addition, as per the assumed model of computation, it must be ensured that a process attempting to read a channel with insufficient data must not proceed further as long as all data has not been acquired. Therefore, we propose a `Read`[1] function, which is called by the process to acquire data, and is implemented on top the iRCCE library:

```
ControlMessage = Read (ID, *buffer, size, source);
```

The function returns `ControlMessage`, holding the value of any control message, if received, and all other symbols have usual meanings. In order to decouple data messages from control messages, the `Read` function:

1. Receives an arbitrary sized message in chunks not exceeding a fixed size;
2. Intersperses checking for a control message from the master with reading data messages;

As indicated earlier, if a process receives a control message (e.g. `stop`), the process exits its `fire` function and proceeds to `cleanup`, see Figure 4. In order to ensure that the MPB has guaranteed space for holding control messages, we require that:

$$\texttt{CHUNK\_SIZE} + |C^*| \leq |MPB| \tag{2}$$

Where $|C^*|$ is the maximum size of the control message, and $|MPB|$ is the size of the MPB on each tile of the Intel SCC. Very small values of chunk size results in a large number of calls to the communication library, leading to inefficiency, but also decrease the latency with which a process checks for a control message. Thus, the choice chunk size reflects a tradeoff made by the designer at compile time. It is clear that the sender process must co-operate with the receiver process, and therefore, it must split a large message in small chunks, each not exceeding `CHUNK_SIZE` in size. The above discussion is summarized in Figure 5. Referring to Figure 5, the receiver process expects `n` bytes from the sender, and therefore calls its `Read` function. The communication interface reads the message in chunks, interleaving with reading (if any) control message from

[1] The discussion for the corresponding `Write` function is analogous.

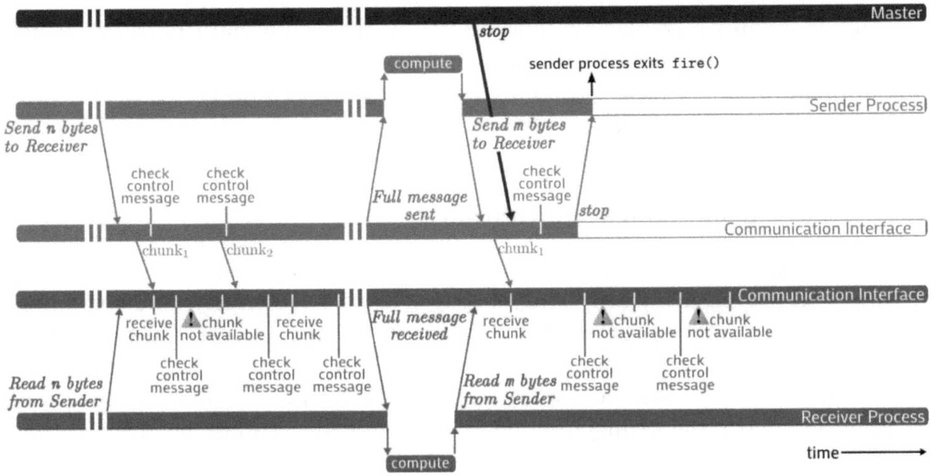

Fig. 5. Timeline of two communicating processes along with a master

the master. Notice that all processes (including the master) are asynchronous, and there may be instants when the receiver expects to receive a data chunk from the sender, but is not successful. In such situations, the communication interface must not block, and must proceed to checking for the control messages from the master. In order to ensure that the communication interface does not return to the caller without having acquired sufficient data, the communication interface keeps a running count of total message size received with each new chunk. Such non-blocking receive for data messages justifies the use of non-blocking communication library, such as the iRCCE.

Timing Bounds The worst case reaction time of a process is defined as follows:

$$R_p^* = t_{read|write}^* + S_p^* + t_{m,C^*}^* \tag{3}$$

where R_p^* is the worst case reaction time of process p, $t_{read|write}^*$ is the maximum time to completely receive (or send) one CHUNK_SIZE of message, S_p^* is the length of dominating segment of process p, and t_{m,C^*}^* is the maximum time to transport the control message from the master to process p.

4.4 Process-to-Core Mapping

The mapping of processes to cores impacts timing properties of an application due to at least two factors:

Process Interference : Unless carefully scheduled, two or more processes sharing the same core lead to non-deterministic demands on the available computing resources (such as MPB, tile router), thereby causing non-real time behaviour. The timing performance of the application is improved by mapping only one process to a tile (and switching off the unused core).

Communication Traffic Interference : If message streams between more than one pair of sender-receiver processes contend at an intermediate router, then, timing disturbance due to such cross traffic may be observed at both pairs of processes. Therefore, processes must be mapped in a manner that minimizes cross traffic at all active routers on the chip, see [10].

4.5 Eliminating Other Interferences

Timing predictability of an application is further improved by disabling all interrupts and L2-caches, which is a common practice in the design of real time systems.

5 Experiments and Results[2]

5.1 Methodology

Since reaction time (see (3)) is influenced by dominating segments as well as communication, the overall objective of this section is to show that R^* computed using (3) upper bounds all values of reaction times observed when running real applications. In order to determine representative values for $t^*_{read|write}$, S^*_p and t^*_{m,C^*}, a series of calibration experiments are performed on the Intel SCC:

Message Read-Write Timings. A simple producer process was mapped to core 0 and a simple consumer process was mapped at hop distances of 1,2,3 and 4 from the producer. The message size transmitted by the producer ranged from 32 bytes to 3KB. Timings were recorded under ideal and noisy conditions, and were measured with reference to the core's local time-stamp counter (TSC). In order to ensure that the reported timings are correct, the sender and receiver clocks were first synchronized using a barrier, and then, the sender transmitted its local time stamp to the receiver. The receiver computed the message travel time by referencing the received time-stamp with its own on-core time stamp counter, and thereby avoiding costly accesses to the global time-stamp counter. In the first set of experiments, only the producer-consumer pair was active on the chip, and the observed timing model is summarized in (4). The reported model matches well with the timings reported in [6].

$$t_{p \to p'}(\text{clock cycles}) = 5.289|P| + 57.53|H| + 894.4 \quad (4)$$

Where $t^*_{p \to p'}$ is the worst-case time in delivery a given message, $|P|$ is the packet size of the message in bytes, and $|H|$ is the *hop-distance* between the sender and the receiver (measured along the message transport route). Next, one traffic generator process was mapped onto one core in each tile of the SCC, with the objective of creating heavy traffic at each router of the SCC. The producer and consumer processes did not shared any core with the traffic generators. The corresponding worst case time is presented in (5).

[2] Experiments were performed on a remote baremetal SCC.

$$t^*_{p \to p'}(\text{clock cycles}) = 4.908|P| + 9921 \tag{5}$$

Notice that the worst case time is independent of the hop distance between cores. Each model was derived out of a total of 800 observations. Note that the reported times include *both* the message transmission time, *and* the time to read the full message by the consumer.

Dominating Segments. Dominating segments were evaluated by carefully isolating computing segments from communicating segments in each process of the selected application. Next, the application was run with an input known to lead to high compute times. For signal processing application, these inputs are known in advance. For instance, for Demosaicing, a RAW image with lot of high-frequency components will lead to high compute times. From the calibration runs, the dominating segment of each process is calculated.

Once all calibration runs are complete, the upper bound on reaction times (R^*) is calculated using (3).

5.2 Results

For experiments, two large applications, the *Demosaicing* [5], and the *motion-JPEG* (MJPEG) decoder are selected. The SCC was booted with the following parameters: tile clock: 533MHz, router: 800MHz, DDR3: 800MHz, with L2-caches disabled. The size of control messages was set to 32 bytes, and CHUNK_SIZE was set to 3KB. Both applications are compute and communication intensive.

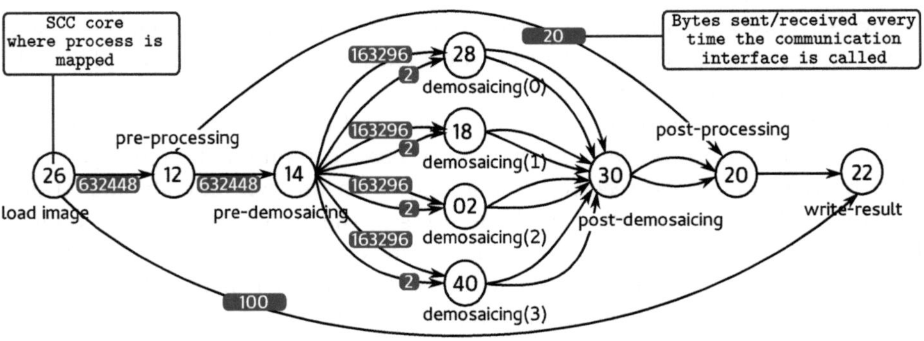

Fig. 6. The Demosaicing application with the mapping details. Size of data messages exchanged between processes is also shown. Master process was mapped to core 24.

Reaction Times for the Demosaicing Application. The Demosaicing process network is shown in Figure 6. Notice that the process-to-core mapping ensures that one tile does not host more than one process, and the cross traffic at routers is minimised. Reaction times for each process in the Demosaicing application are shown in Figure 8, with lines representing observed values from experiments, while the bars represent the bounds computed during calibration runs. Notice that the bounds are tight.

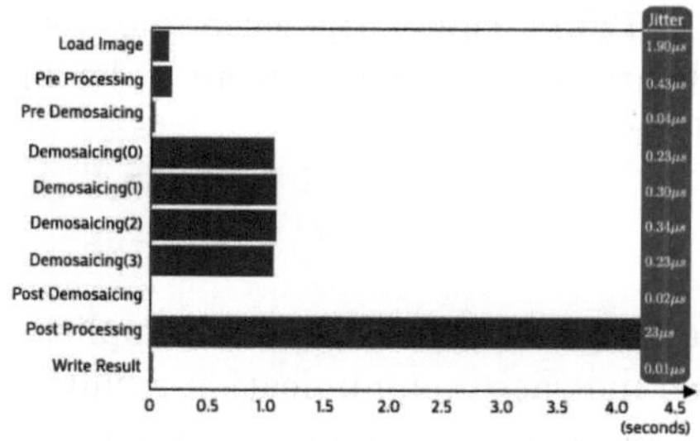

Fig. 7. Lengths of dominating segments for each process in the Demosaicing application

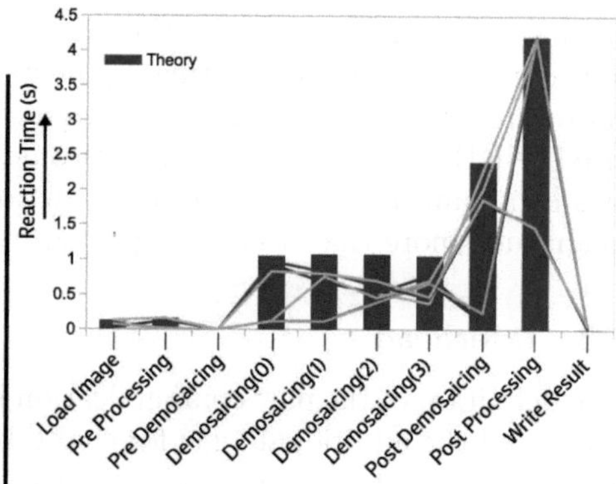

Fig. 8. Reaction Times for the Demosaicing application for 10 observations. Lines show observed timings during experiments.

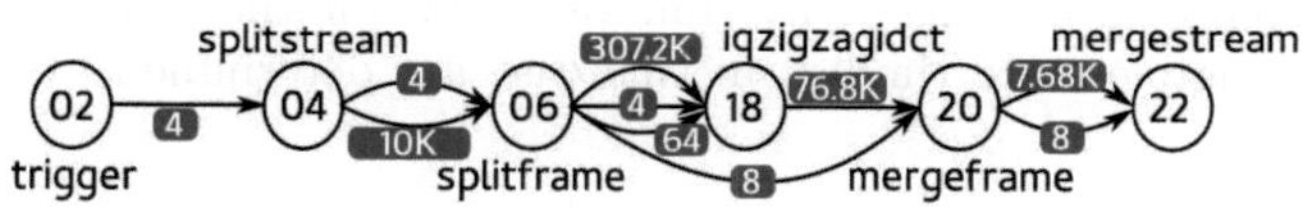

Fig. 9. The Motion JPEG decoder. Master process was mapped to core 16.

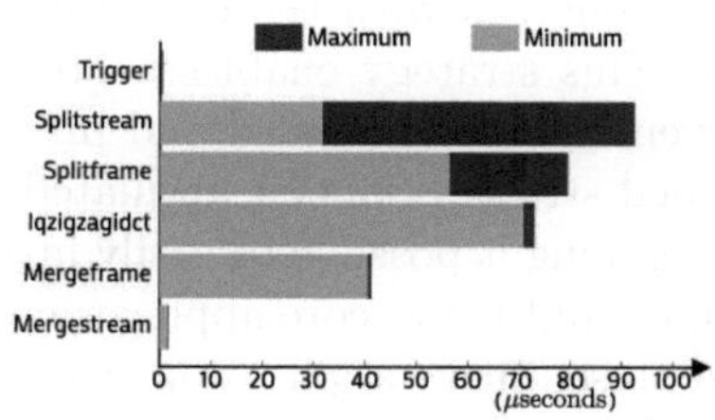

Fig. 10. Size of dominating segments for the MJPEG decoder

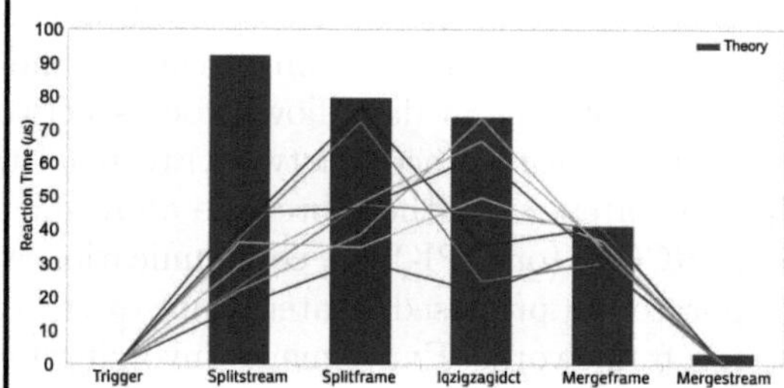

Fig. 11. Reaction Times for the MJPEG decoder for 10 observations

Reaction Times for the Motion-JPEG Decoder. The MJPEG decoder process network is shown in Figure 9. The splitstream and splitframe processes search for certain markers in the encoded image. The amount of time spent in searching for the marker depends on the frame itself, and hence, the dominating segments in these processes show large variations. Consequently, for calculating worst case reaction time R_p^*, the maximum size of corresponding dominating segments is used. Figure 10 shows the lengths of dominating segments for the MJPEG application, while Figure 11 compares the predicted value of reaction times to those observed over 10 experiments involving 30 frames each. Notice that unlike the

Demosaicing application, reaction times in MJPEG application are not determined solely by the dominating segments, but are also influenced by communication times. Also notice that the *iqzigzagidct* process communicates messages of size 76.8KB, which according to (5) would take $725\mu s$. Unless the entire message was communicated in chunks, the reaction times would have been an order of magnitude more than what is reported in Figure 11.

5.3 Overhead

The definition of the new communication interface was common to both applications, and the additional logic for chunk-based message communication resulted in a mere 528 byte overhead. The chunk-based message communication *improved* the timing efficiency of message communication, leading to a 4.7% improvement in per-frame timing for MJPEG decoder. This is because chunk-based communication mitigated the number of times shared memory was accessed during message passing, which more than compensated for larger number rounds required to send the complete message. Any time overhead for the Demosaicing application was negligible since timings in this case are determined by dominating segments.

6 Summary

We demonstrated that it is indeed possible to achieve predictable runtime performance, and bounded reaction time of applications on the Intel SCC processor. To this end, we proposed a non-blocking communication strategy which interleaves data and control communication, and also complies with the execution semantics of general data flow process networks. This strategy enables a process (or an entire process network) to react to events with a bounded and predictable latency. Furthermore, the above-mentioned strategy was encapsulated in an RCCE- (or MPI-) like communication API, making it possible to easily incorporate the proposed strategy into existing multi- and many-core application design frameworks. Experiments involving two representative applications validate our technique and show that predictable performance, including bounded reaction latencies can be achieved easily on baremetal SCC, and indeed on any many-core processor.

Acknowledgements. This work was supported by EU FP7 project EURETILE, under grant numbers 247846. Lars Schor was also partially supported by an Intel PhD Fellowship.

References

1. http://www.kalray.eu/
2. http://www.tilera.com/products/processors
3. Clauss, C., et al.: Evaluation and Improvements of Programming Models for the Intel SCC Many-Core Processor. In: Proc. HPCS, pp. 525–532 (2011)

4. Howard, J., et al.: A 48-Core IA-32 Message-Passing Processor with DVFS in 45nm CMOS. In: Proc. ISSCC, pp. 108–109 (2010)
5. Li, X.: Demosaicing by successive approximation. IEEE Transactions on Image Processing 14(3), 370–379 (2005)
6. Mattson, T.G.: Using Intel's Single-Chip Cloud Computer (SCC), `http://communities.intel.com/docs/DOC-19269` (online February 2012)
7. Mattson, T.G., et al.: The 48-core SCC Processor: The Programmer's View. In: Proc. SC, pp. 1–11 (2010)
8. Puffitsch, W., Noulard, E., Pagetti, C.: Mapping a multi-rate synchronous language to a many-core processor. In: 2013 IEEE 19th Real-Time and Embedded Technology and Applications Symposium (RTAS), pp. 293–302 (2013)
9. van der Wijngaart, R.F., et al.: Light-weight Communications on Intel's Single-chip Cloud Computer Processor. SIGOPS Oper. Syst. Rev. 45(1), 73–83 (2011)
10. Zimmer, C., Mueller, F.: Low contention mapping of real-time tasks onto tilepro 64 core processors. In: 2012 IEEE 18th Real-Time and Embedded Technology and Applications Symposium (RTAS), pp. 131–140 (2012)
11. Ziwisky, M., et al.: BareMichael: A Minimalistic Bare-Metal Framework for the Intel SCC. In: Proc. MARC, pp. 66–71 (2012)
12. Åkerholm, M., Samuelsson, T.: Design and Benchmarking of Real-Time Multiprocessor Operating System Kernels. Master's thesis, Mälardalen University (2002)

Reliable and Efficient Execution of Multiple Streaming Applications on Intel's SCC Processor

Lars Schor, Devendra Rai, Hoeseok Yang, Iuliana Bacivarov, and Lothar Thiele

Computer Engineering and Networks Laboratory,
ETH Zurich, 8092 Zurich, Switzerland
firstname.lastname@tik.ee.ethz.ch

Abstract. Intel's Single-chip Cloud Computer (SCC) is a prototype architecture for on-chip many-core systems. By incorporating 48 cores into a single die, it provides unique opportunities to gain insights into many-core software development. Earlier results have shown that programming efficient and reliable software for many-core processors is difficult due to a lack of appropriate programming tools. In this paper, we present a programming framework to execute multiple applications specified as Kahn process networks on the SCC. These applications might be started or stopped at runtime based on requests of the user. The proposed application programming interface (API) abstracts low-level implementation details from the application designer enabling high-level performance analysis and automated mapping optimization. To efficiently execute workload specified by the proposed API, a lightweight runtime-system and an automated program synthesis backend are presented. Extensive experiments are carried out to characterize the performance of the proposed framework.

Keywords: Many-Core Programming, Single-chip Cloud Computer, SCC, Runtime-System, Mapping, Distributed Application Layer, DAL.

1 Introduction

The demand for high computing power of novel real-time multimedia applications coupled with a single core's inability to support such high demands forces hardware designer to choose architectures with a high degree of parallelism. Intel's Single-chip Cloud Computer (SCC) [5] is a prototype of such architectures. By incorporating 24 tiles, each composed of two cores and local memory, into a single die, the SCC provides software developers early insights in developing software for highly parallel and distributed architectures.

The performance of such systems will critically depend on the efficient execution of applications on multiple cores. However, programming parallel applications for distributed systems, and Intel's SCC processer in particular, is difficult due to several reasons. The programmer has to handle the data transfer between cores using low-level message passing libraries and the distribution of the workload across the cores. For instance, unequally distributed workload results

D. an Mey et al. (Eds.): Euro-Par 2013 Workshops, LNCS 8374, pp. 790–800, 2014.

in low throughput or high latencies. Thus, traditional (low-level) methods to design and program parallel applications are not anymore appropriate to many-core systems that are architecturally more complex. Consequently, the goal is to provide an application programming interface (API) and design-flow that abstracts low-level implementation details from the application designer enabling high-level performance analysis and automated mapping optimization.

Programming in a high-level language has typically various advantages including being less error-prone and having various design optimization steps automated. A promising paradigm to program distributed systems is to use process networks as model of computation (MoC). Process networks have the advantage that they explicitly express the parallelism of an application and separate computation from communication. Such separation of concerns enables the parallelization of computation and communication allowing process networks to fully exploit the available resources. At the same time, using a process network as MoC allows the designer to rapidly evaluate the performance of different design candidates and hardware/software partitioning options. The distributed application layer (DAL) [11], for instance, uses the Kahn process network (KPN) [6] MoC to specify applications. Due to the well-defined semantics of the KPN model, data races, non-determinism, or the need for strict synchronization are avoided. In addition, the DAL MoC uses a finite state machine (FSM) to represent interactions between applications. Each state represents an execution scenario, i.e., a certain set of applications running in parallel. At runtime, the user can switch between the execution scenarios by starting or stopping applications.

Analyzing the performance, providing quality-of-service guarantees, and optimizing the process-to-core mapping of workload specified by the DAL MoC has been described in [7, 11]. This paper reports our work to execute workload specified by the DAL MoC onto the SCC. This includes the definition of a high-level API for programming parallel applications specified as KPNs that abstracts low-level architectural details from the application designer enabling high-level performance analysis, process clustering, or mapping optimization. The runtime-system comes with the capability to start and stop processes, and to create and destroy FIFO channels at runtime leading to low memory footprint. Great emphasis is placed on minimizing the communication overhead by using a highly optimized inter-process communication protocol. In particular, the RCKMPI library [2] is used as middleware layer for communication between cores. Finally, extensive experiments are carried out on Intel's SCC processor to characterize the performance of the proposed framework and runtime-system.

The Eclipse SDK has been extended with an editor for the DAL MoC, a high-level mapping optimization framework, and the program synthesis backend proposed in this paper. The plugin is available for download under `http://www.tik.ee.ethz.ch/~euretile/dalipse`.

The remainder of the paper is structured as follows: The SCC is revised in Section 2. In Section 3, the DAL MoC is presented. In Sections 4 and 5, the runtime-system and program synthesis backend are described. Section 6 presents experimental results and related work is reviewed in Section 7.

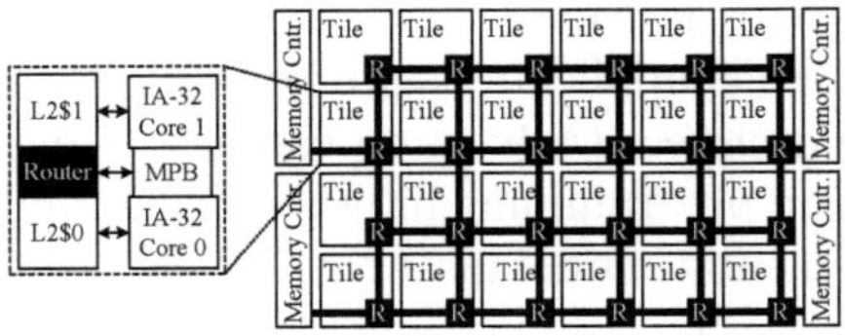

Fig. 1. Schematic outline of Intel's SCC processor

2 Single-Chip Cloud Computer

The SCC processor [5], schematically outlined in Fig. 1, is a 48-core experimental processor from Intel. It consists of 24 tiles that are organized into a 4×6 grid and linked by a 2D mesh on-chip network. A tile contains a pair of P54C cores, a router, and a 16 KB block of SRAM. Each core has an independent L1 and L2 cache. The on-tile SRAM block is also called "message passing buffer" (MPB) as it enables the exchange of information between cores.

The most commonly used software platform for Intel's SCC is to run a Linux kernel on each core. For communication purpose, various message passing libraries have been developed including RCCE [14], iRCCE [1], and RCKMPI [2]. Instead of implementing our own software platform, we run our runtime-system on top of the Linux kernel. This enables us to use the basic multi-threading mechanisms provided by the Linux kernel.

3 DAL Model of Computation

The dynamic behavior of the workload is captured by a set of execution scenarios that form a finite state machine (FSM). Each state represents a set of concurrently running applications and each state transition corresponds to an application start or stop request. An example of a FSM is outlined in Fig. 2.

Applications are specified as KPNs [6]. More precisely, an application consists of autonomous processes that can only communicate through unbounded point-to-point FIFO channels, see Fig. 3 for an example. However, as channels with unbounded capacity cannot be realized in real implementations, we use a KPN semantics-preserving implementation with finite buffers that are accessed using blocking read and write functions [4]. Blocking means that a process stalls if it attempts to read data from an empty channel or write to a full channel.

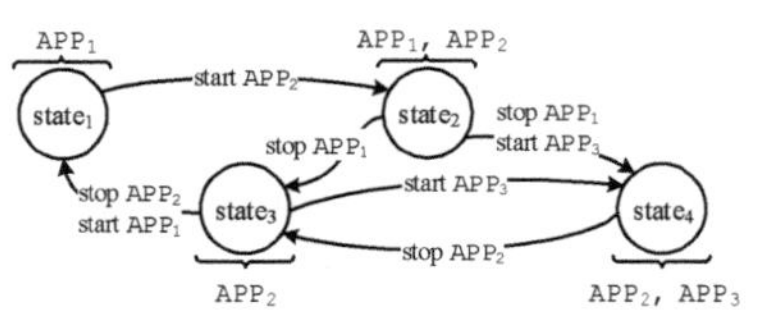

Fig. 2. Example of a FSM specifying the dynamic behavior of the workload

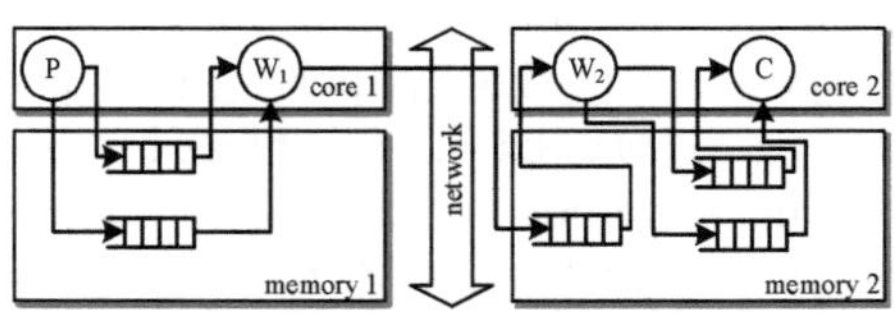

Fig. 3. Application specified by the KPN MoC together with its mapping

Listing 1. Specification of a KPN with two processes

```
<processnetwork>
  <process name="prod">
    <port type="output" name="out"/>
    <src type="c" location="prod.c"/>
  </process>
  <process name="cons">
    <port type="input" name="in"/>
    <src type="c" location="cons.c"/>
  </process>
  <channel cap="8" name="channel">
    <send process="prod" port="out"/>
    <rec process="cons" port="in"/>
  </channel>
</processnetwork>
```

Listing 2. Implementation of a KPN process using the proposed API

```
procedure INIT(ProcessData *p)
  initialize();
end procedure

procedure FIRE(ProcessData *p)
  fifo->READ(buf, size);
  manipulate();
  fifo->WRITE(buf, size);
end procedure

procedure FINISH(ProcessData *p)
  cleanup();
end procedure
```

The proposed API for KPNs is outlined in Listings 1 and 2. The topology, i.e., the connections between processes by FIFOs, is specified in an XML format. The functionality of the individual processes is specified in C/C++ and is composed of three procedures. The INIT procedure is executed once at startup of the application. Afterwards, the execution of a process is split into individual executions of the FIRE procedure, which is repeatedly invoked by the system scheduler. Finally, the FINISH procedure is called before an application is stopped. Each process can read from its input and write to its output channels by calling the high-level READ and WRITE procedures.

4 Runtime-System

Executing a workload specified according to the DAL MoC on Intel's SCC processor requires a runtime-system and a program synthesis backend. The task of the runtime-system is thereby to provide an implementation of the API, i.e., services for inter-process communication, a mechanism to iteratively execute processes by calling their FIRE procedure, and services to manage processes and channels at runtime.

Inter-Process Communication. To be efficient, the runtime-system has to differ between communication over shared and distributed memory, see Fig. 4. While ring buffers in private memory are used for intra-core communication, an advanced architecture-dependent FIFO implementation is required for efficient inter-core communication.

In general, the FIFO channel might be implemented in private memory of the sender or receiver, or in shared memory. We implemented the FIFO channels in the private memory of the receiver and used the RCKMPI library [2] for inter-core communication. The RCKMPI library automatically takes the memory organization of the SCC into account and uses the MPB, if appropriate. As no DMA controller is available on the SCC for inter-core communication, we launch a LISTENER thread on each core. The LISTENER thread is responsible for

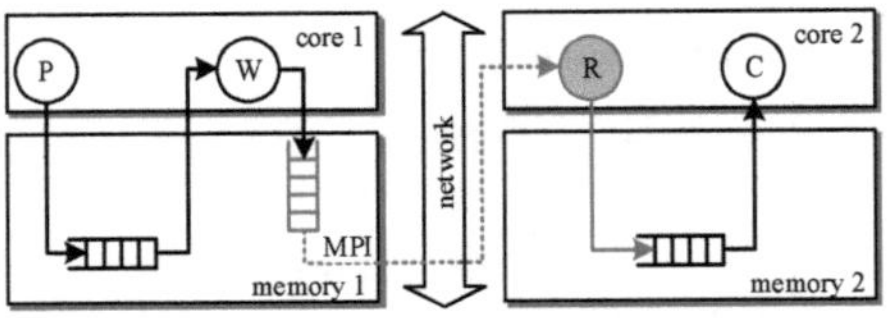

Fig. 4. Example of intra- and inter-core communication. Virtual FIFO and LISTENER thread are illustrated in grey.

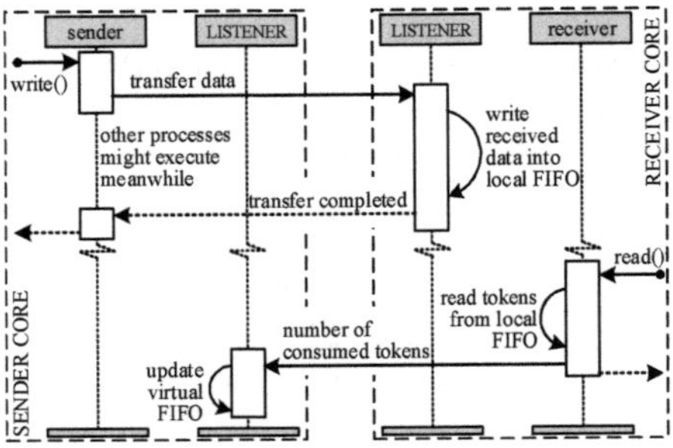

Fig. 5. Inter-process communication protocol between processes located on different cores

handling all incoming traffic and writing the data to the correct FIFO channel. To keep the LISTENER thread lightweight, it uses the memory of the local FIFO channel as receive buffer for the data transfer, thereby avoiding expensive allocation and copy operations.

To avoid deadlocks, the LISTENER thread must not be blocked at any time, i.e., we have to ensure that a data transfer is only initialized if the receiver has enough available space to store the data. This is ensured by a virtual FIFO at the sender. The virtual FIFO has the same metadata (amount of free space) as the actual FIFO, but if a process attempts to write, the data is either directly transferred or the calling process is blocked as long as the receiver has not enough space to store the data. The disadvantage of this approach is that the virtual FIFO has to know when the receiver process has consumed data, which is ensured by a signal. The inter-process communication protocol is sketched in Fig. 5.

Multi-processing. As our runtime-system runs on top of a Linux kernel, we use the multi-processing features provided by the operating system (OS) to run multiple processes in a quasi-parallel fashion on a single core. In particular, processes are mapped onto POSIX threads and scheduled by the OS' scheduler. When a process is blocked due to empty input or full output channels, the scheduler automatically selects a different process to execute.

Process and Channel Management. The FSM enables the programmer to start and stop applications at runtime. We will show in the next section that this dynamism is handled by a runtime-manager in the form of an additional process network. The runtime-system has therefore to provide services to install, uninstall, start, and stop processes, and to create and destroy FIFO channels.

The memory footprint of the system is reduced by storing the individual processes as dynamic libraries that are loaded when the application is started. Thus, installing a process involves loading and dynamically linking the corresponding library, and then executing its INIT procedure. Similarly, uninstalling a process involves executing the FINISH procedure and unloading the dynamic library. The procedure to create a channel depends on the mapping of the sender and receiver. If both processes are mapped onto the same core, a local FIFO channel

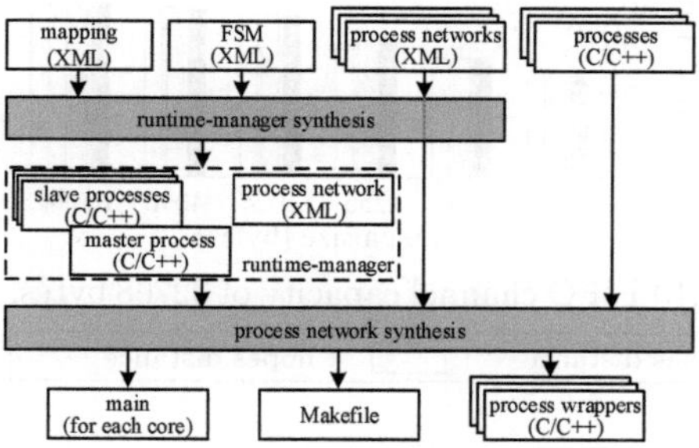

Fig. 6. Program synthesis flow generating the source code of the runtime-manager and the process wrappers

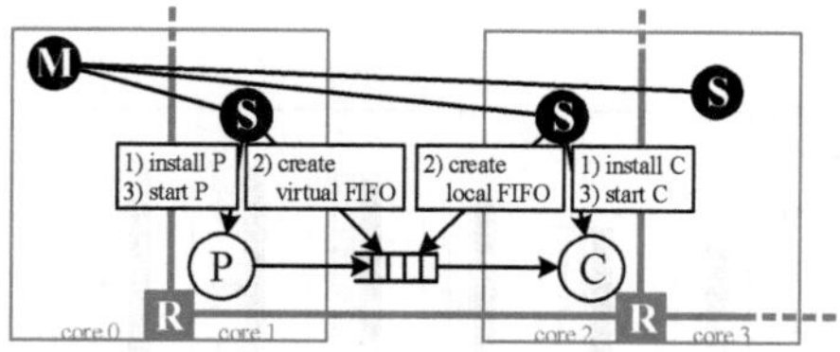

(a) Process network setup.

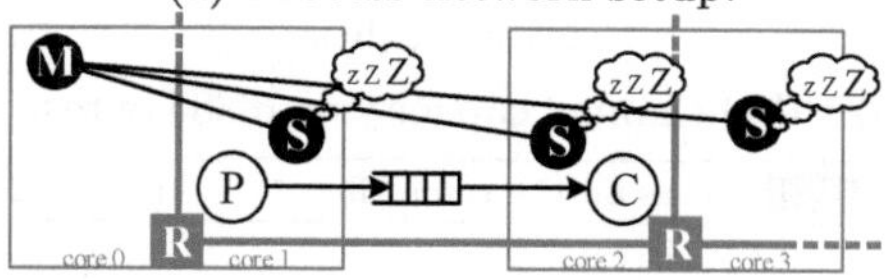

(b) Process network execution.

Fig. 7. Structure of the proposed runtime-manager. "M" and "S" represent master and slave processes, respective.

is instantiated. Otherwise, a virtual FIFO channel is instantiated at the sender and a local FIFO channel at the receiver. Afterwards, virtual and local FIFO channels are registered at the corresponding LISTENER thread. A FIFO channel is destroyed by deregistering it at the LISTENER thread and freeing the memory buffer. Finally, a process is started by registering the thread at the scheduler, and stopped by aborting the FIRE procedure and deregistering it from the scheduler.

5 Program Synthesis Backend

A program synthesis backend is the second component required to execute a workload specified by the DAL MoC. It basically consists of creating the runtime-manager, embedding each process into a POSIX thread, and creating a MAIN function for each core, see Fig. 6.

Runtime-Manager Synthesis. The task of the runtime-manager synthesis is to automatically construct a runtime-manager that satisfies the given system specification. The result of this step is a process network with one master process and one slave process per core that uses the additional services provided by the runtime-system to manage the processes and channels, see Fig. 7. The runtime-manager monitors the system, starts and stops individual process networks depending on the requests of the user. The master process thereby manages the dynamic execution of the system and the slave processes are responsible for the management of the processes and FIFO channels. Thus, the master process distributes the actual computation to the slave processes. Once the slave processes performed their work, they go to sleep until the master process sends them a new job making the proposed runtime-manager very lightweight in the sense that it does not affect the execution of the process network.

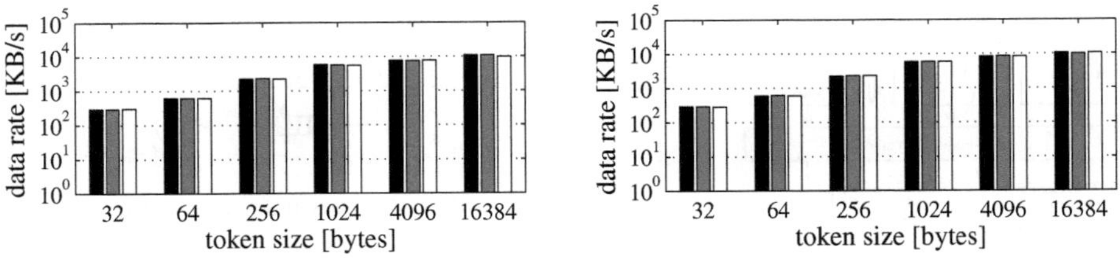

(a) FIFO channel capacity of 16384 bytes. (b) FIFO channel capacity of 32768 bytes.

cores on the same tile | 2 hopes distance | 4 hopes distance

Fig. 8. Data transfer rate between two cores for three different hop distances

Process Network Synthesis. Finally, the process network synthesis step embeds each process into a POSIX thread and creates a MAIN function for each core. Embedding each process into a POSIX thread is achieved by a process wrapper that repeatedly calls the FIRE procedure of the process. The process definition is then stored together with the process wrapper as a dynamic library in the file system so that it can be loaded on request of a slave process. The MAIN function has two tasks. First, it starts the LISTENER thread. Then, it initializes the processes and channels of the runtime-manager and turns the control of the system over to the master.

6 Experimental Results

In this section, we provide experimental results characterizing the framework.

Experimental Setup. An Intel SCC processor running at 533 MHz for the cores and 800 MHz for the routers and DDR3 RAM has been used for the experiments. A Linux image with kernel 2.6.32 has been loaded on each core. RCKMPI has been configured to use the default channel, i.e., the SCCMPB channel. The ICC-8.1 compiler with optimization level -O2 is used for all experiments.

Data Transfer Rate. A synthetic application consisting of two processes and one FIFO channel has been designed to measure the data transfer rate between two cores. The application executes 100000 iterations and in one iteration, the source process writes one token to the FIFO channel and the sink process reads the token from the FIFO channel. No other processes except the runtime-manager are running on the SCC. Figure 8 shows the data transfer rate between two cores whereby the token size is varied between 32 bytes and 16384 bytes. The experiment has been repeated for two capacities of the FIFO channel and three hop distances between the cores. The observed peak data rate is 11 Mbytes/s. While hop distance and capacity have small influence on the data transfer rate, the rate significantly increases with the size of a single token.

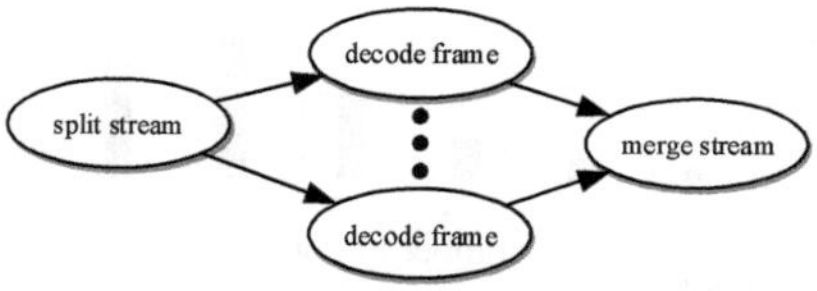

Fig. 9. KPN of the distributed MJPEG decoder

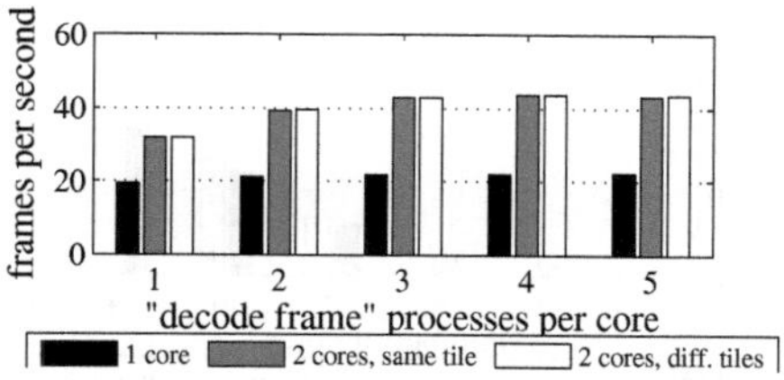

Fig. 10. Decoded frames per second using the MJPEG decoder

Runtime-System Overhead. As the runtime-manager sleeps after performed work, the overhead of the runtime-system can mainly be assigned to the LISTENER thread. To measure this overhead, we use a sequential implementation of a motion JPEG (MJPEG) decoder. Decoding 5000 frames takes thereby about 162.0 s if the MJPEG decoder is executed in parallel to the LISTENER thread and 158.9 s if it is executed as an individual application. Thus, the measured overhead is less than two percent.

Context Switching Overhead. To characterize the effect of multi-processing on a single core, we consider a distributed implementation of the MJPEG decoder, see Fig. 9 for the process network. The network has multiple "decode frame" processes decoding a complete frame in a single iteration. In Fig. 10, the decoded frames per second using the MJPEG algorithm are compared for implementations mapping a different number of "decode frame" processes onto one core. Furthermore, the graph differs between three configurations. First, only one core, then both cores of a tile, and finally two cores of different tiles are used to execute the "decode frame" process. It shows that the frame rate increases significantly if two processes are mapped onto a single core as communication and computation can partially overlap. Furthermore, the frame rate does not decrease even if five processes are mapped onto each core indicating a low multi-processing overhead.

Speed-Up Due to Parallelism. Finally, we evaluate the speed-up due to available number of cores for four different applications. Besides the MJPEG decoder, a MPEG-2 decoder, a ray-tracing, and a quicksort algorithm are studied. The ray-tracing algorithm generates an image of 100×100 pixels and can concurrently analyze multiple rays. We map either one or two such processes onto one core. The quicksort algorithm sorts an array with 5000 elements and can have multiple instances of a "sort" process to concurrently sort multiple sub-arrays. Two configurations with either four or eight "sort" processes are considered. The MPEG-2 decoder concurrently decodes multiple macroblocks. We again map either one or two such processes onto one core

In Fig. 11, the speed-up is compared for implementations running on a different number of cores. The speed-up is calculated with respect to an implementation running on a single core. The maximum speed-up that can be achieved is 20.7 for the MJPEG decoder application. As MJPEG is an intraframe-only

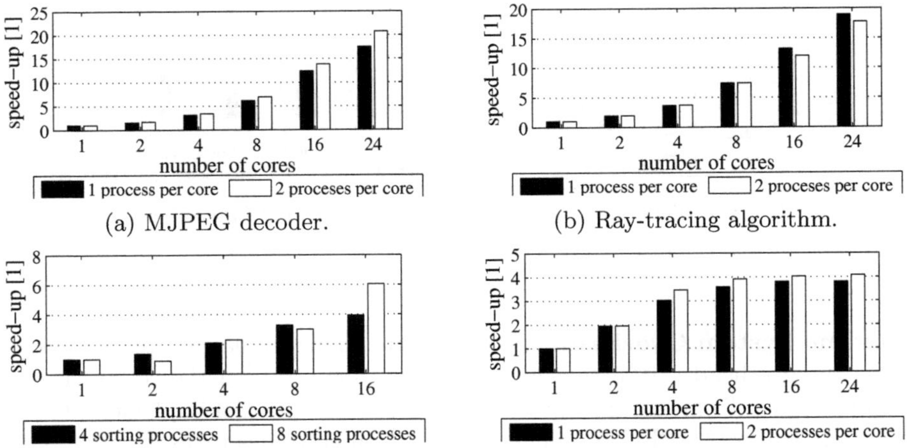

(a) MJPEG decoder.

(b) Ray-tracing algorithm.

(c) Quicksort algorithm.

(d) MPEG-2 decoder.

Fig. 11. Speed-ups of four benchmarks for a varying number of cores

compression scheme, the frames can be decoded in parallel on different cores. The ray-tracing algorithm achieves a speed-up of almost 20 on 24 cores. As each ray can individually be analyzed, the ray-tracing algorithm is well-suited for parallelization. The speed-ups achieved with the quicksort algorithm are much smaller than with the previous applications. This might be because additional time is required to partition the input array into sub-arrays and then to collect the intermediate results. A maximum speed-up of 6.0 on 16 cores is achieved when eight "sort" processes are running in parallel. Finally, due to data-dependencies between the frames, the MPEG-2 application only achieves a speed-up of about 4.1. The speed-up increases linearly for a small number of cores before collecting and distributing frames become the bottleneck for higher parallelization.

7 Related Work

To abstract low-level implementation details from the application designer, various high-level programming environments have been developed for Intel's SCC processor. For instance, a distributed Java virtual machine for Intel's SCC processor is proposed in [10]. In [9], Barrelfish OS is presented that provides the user a single OS instance to manage the complete set of available computing cores. The closest related work is presented in [13] by mapping distributed S-Net streaming networks onto Intel's SCC processor. Similar to our work, functions are written in a standard programming language and then mapped onto stream-processing components (so-called boxes). In contrast, our framework permits stateful processes and interactions between applications. Furthermore, the formal design approach enables high-level performance analysis and mapping optimization at design-time so that quality-of-service constraints can be provided.

The KPN [6] model of computation has been the basis for many frameworks to design multi/many-core systems including Daedalus [8], DOL [12], and SHIM [3]. Most of these frameworks support a wide-variety of target platforms and have recently been extended to dynamic workload. Our approach, in contrast, uses a formal specification of the dynamic behavior in the form of a FSM, which enables an efficient analysis and execution of multiple dynamic KPN applications.

8 Conclusion

In this paper, we have presented a high-level programming framework that allows to execute multiple applications specified as Kahn process networks on Intel's SCC processor. To abstract low-level implementation details from the application designer, a high-level API has been proposed. The API does not only specify the individual applications but also their interactions enabling dynamic behavior in the sense that applications can start and stop at runtime. To efficiently execute workload specified by the proposed API on the SCC, we presented a lightweight runtime-system and an automated program synthesis backend. In particular, efficiency is obtained by a distributed runtime-manager that loads processes and instantiates channels only when the application is actually started. The paper has shown that the proposed program synthesis backend can be extended to integrate high-level performance analysis and process-level mapping optimization enabling quality of service guarantees. Finally, we applied the approach to various streaming applications demonstrating the advantages of programming applications with the proposed framework.

Acknowledgments. This work was supported by EU FP7 project EURETILE. Lars Schor was also partially supported by an Intel PhD Fellowship.

References

1. Clauss, C., et al.: Evaluation and Improvements of Programming Models for the Intel SCC Many-Core Processor. In: Proc. HPCS, pp. 525–532 (2011)
2. Comprés Ureña, I.A., Riepen, M., Konow, M.: RCKMPI – Lightweight MPI Implementation for Intel's Single-chip Cloud Computer (SCC). In: Cotronis, Y., Danalis, A., Nikolopoulos, D.S., Dongarra, J. (eds.) EuroMPI 2011. LNCS, vol. 6960, pp. 208–217. Springer, Heidelberg (2011)
3. Edwards, S.A., Tardieu, O.: SHIM: A Determinstic Model for Heterogeneous Embedded Systems. IEEE Trans. VLSI Syst. 14(8), 854–867 (2006)
4. Geilen, M., Basten, T.: Requirements on the Execution of Kahn Process Networks. In: Degano, P. (ed.) ESOP 2003. LNCS, vol. 2618, pp. 319–334. Springer, Heidelberg (2003)
5. Howard, J., et al.: A 48-Core IA-32 Message-Passing Processor with DVFS in 45nm CMOS. In: Proc. ISSCC, pp. 108–109 (2010)
6. Kahn, G.: The Semantics of a Simple Language for Parallel Programming. In: Proc. of the IFIP Congress, vol. 74, pp. 471–475 (1974)

7. Kang, S.H., et al.: Multi-Objective Mapping Optimization via Problem Decomposition for Many-Core Systems. In: Proc. ESTIMedia, pp. 28–37 (2012)
8. Nikolov, H., et al.: Systematic and Automated Multiprocessor System Design, Programming, and Implementation. IEEE T. Comput. Aid. D. 27(3), 542–555 (2008)
9. Peter, S., et al.: Early Experience with the Barrelfish OS and the Single-chip Cloud Computer. In: Proc. MARC, pp. 35–39 (2011)
10. Saballus, B., et al.: A Scalable and Robust Runtime Environment for SCC Clusters. In: Proc. MARC, pp. 71–74 (2011)
11. Schor, L., et al.: Scenario-Based Design Flow for Mapping Streaming Applications onto On-Chip Many-Core Systems. In: Proc. CASES, pp. 71–80 (2012)
12. Thiele, L., et al.: Mapping Applications to Tiled Multiprocessor Embedded Systems. In: Proc. ACSD, pp. 29–40 (2007)
13. Verstraaten, M., et al.: On Mapping Distributed S-Net to the 48-core Intel SCC Processor. In: Proc. MARC, pp. 41–46 (2011)
14. van der Wijngaart, R.F., et al.: Light-weight Communications on Intel's Single-chip Cloud Computer Processor. SIGOPS Oper. Syst. Rev. 45(1), 73–83 (2011)

A Formally Verified Static Hypervisor with Hardware Support for a Many-Core Chip

Geoffrey Plouviez[1], Emmanuelle Encrenaz[2], and Franck Wajsbürt[2]

[1] ANSSI, Paris, France
geoffrey.plouviez@ssi.gouv.fr
[2] UPMC Sorbonne Université, Paris, France
{emmanuelle.encrenaz,franck.wajsburt}@lip6.fr

Abstract. This work presents a co-hosting approach of multiple software stacks within a many-core system-on-chip.

We present a many-core virtual machine monitor executing software stacks in virtual machines.We confine the virtual machines from each others to prevent a malicious virtual machine user to compromise an other virtual machine or the virtual machine monitor (or hypervisor). We have made a formally verified many-core hypervisor that relies on our own hardware protection mechanism.

Keywords: Hypervisor, many-core, formal verification, B method.

1 Introduction

For decades, the frequency rising was bringing the computing capability up, but nowadays this is achieved through the increase of the number of cores [16]. This computation capability development allows the execution of multiple virtual machines (abbreviated VM) on the same physical machine. Virtualization maximizes the usage of available hardware resources in order to reduce the cost and improve the flexibility. But, in a world where the information's sensitivity and interconnection handled by computer is continuously increasing, we have to guarantee the respect of isolation properties between VMs. Conjointly to those evolutions, some mathematical tools give us the opportunity to prove formal properties on increasingly bigger software [2].

Designing secure hypervisor and operating system is still an open issue and we think that the security properties should be enforced by formal methods. Our proposal is a formally verified software hypervisor running on top of hardware isolation mechanisms.

The rest of this paper is organized as follow : Section 2 gives an overview of the underlying many-core hardware architecture. Section 3 presents the hardware isolation mechanisms. Section 4 presents the formally verified software hypervisor that initializes the isolation hardware. Section 5 is a cycle accurate performance evaluation and the section 6 presents related work.

D. an Mey et al. (Eds.): Euro-Par 2013 Workshops, LNCS 8374, pp. 801–811, 2014.

2 Hardware Overview

The hypervisor is built on the top of the TSAR architecture[1] [14]. To our knowledge, TSAR is the only open many-core shared memory chip with both systemC and VHDL models available. A 512 MIPS32 CPU core systemC model is available. At VHDL level, a 12 MIPS32 prototype runs on FPGA. Eventually, the TSAR project aims for reaching thousands cores per chip. *This work is not part of the TSAR project, we use the TSAR systemC model because it is the only open-source available many-core chip.* Despite this choice, this approach should be valid on any many-core architecture which is shared memory based with a deterministic network-on-chip routing algorithm.

2.1 TSAR Architecture

The TSAR architecture backbone is a mesh with a two levels interconnection network. The global level is a network-on-chip handling global communication between clusters. Each cluster has its own local interconnect and owns an address space segment which is defined by the address most significant bits. Each cluster includes 4 MIPS32 CPU with a 32 Kilo-bytes L1 cache with MMU for each CPU, a RAM, an interrupts concentrator (ICU), a gateway to the global interconnect, a 256 Kilo-bytes L2 cache and the local memory. Each MIP32 CPU boots from its local memory. User cluster internal architecture can be seen in the figure 1 on the facing page.

These clusters are interconnected through a 2 dimensions mesh global network. Clusters are labelled according to their position in the mesh which defines a mapping of the overall address space (see 2 on the next page). *All this work was already done when we began and we haven't had have any influence on it.*

3 Hardware Virtualization Support

Due to the high number of low performance CPU cores inside a TSAR chip, we partitioned the clusters between VMs and the hypervisor. With this design a CPU core can only belong to a unique VM or to the hypervisor. In order to prevent any timing channel related to the global network, a VM will spread out on a contiguous set of clusters. The physical hard drives (abbreviated HD) will be set up in the hypervisor partition. An example of hypervisor partition (the vertical box) set-up with three VMs (the horizontals boxes) can be seen in figure 2 on the facing page.

3.1 Virtual Machines Isolation

The VM isolation mechanism is based on hardware barriers implemented through doors. These doors have to be deployed on every connection between two global

[1] Tera-Scale ARchitecture is a MEDEA+ European funded project, grant 2A718.

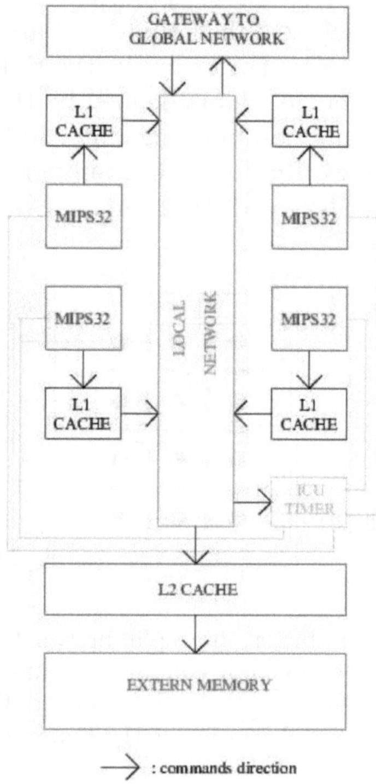

Fig. 1. Inside a user cluster

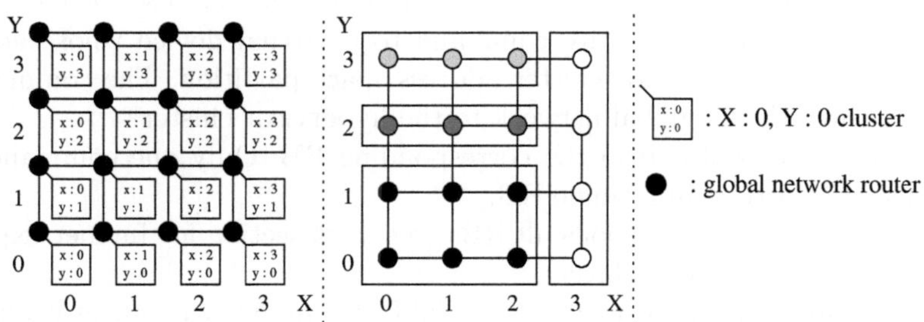

Fig. 2. The Left figure shows the global network and address space, each cluster owns a specific memory segment. **The Right figure** is an address space partitioning example: the horizontal boxes are the VMs partitions and the vertical box is the hypervisor partition.

network routers. A door can be open, and everything is allowed to go through, or closed and nothing can pass. These doors materialize the VM border and are controlled by the hypervisor. When the doors are closed, the VM cannot send a command to another VM. For example, the right part of figure 3 shows two confined VMs by the blocking doors defined by the central line. The other doors, inside the VMs, are in a non-blocking state. In this approach, a VM is a contiguous set of cluster rows. By doing this, only one VM will get CPU with ID 0, only one VM will get CPU with ID 1, etc.

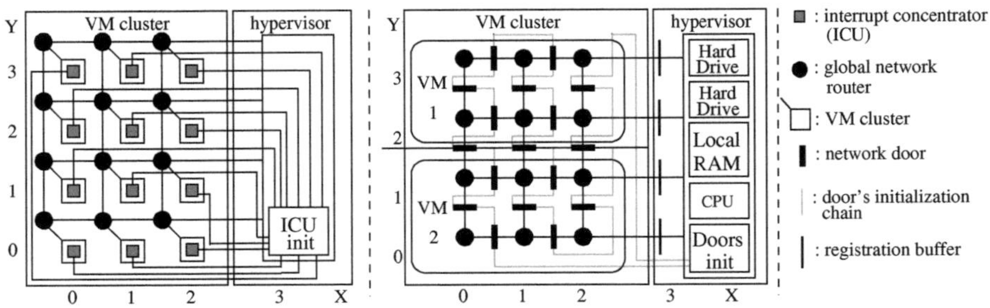

Fig. 3. This is a complete 12 cluster chip split in two figures. **Left figure:** interrupt support, each user cluster interrupt concentrator has a dedicated interrupt line connected to a component inside the hypervisor cluster. **Right figure:** two virtual machines are setup with two hard drives inside the hypervisor cluster.

3.2 Hypervisor Isolation

We have a strict isolation between VMs, but they need to access the HD through the hypervisor which is the only one accessing them. To achieve this goal, we designed another hardware component, the *registration buffer* (abbreviated RB) (see right figure 3). The RBs and hypervisor interactions are described as follow:

- A VM sends a read or write command to a virtual device whose address belongs to the hypervisor cluster address space partition. The command is routed through the global network to the hypervisor cluster.
- The command is stored in the corresponding RB. Only one command can be stored at a time in a single RB.
- The software hypervisor polls all RBs (see next section for further explanations about the software layer).
- The software hypervisor loads an available command, virtualizes it and initializes the corresponding HD.
- At the HD request completion, the software hypervisor reads the device status and writes the command answer to the command source RB.

With this approach, a VM cannot directly access a HD but has the ability to interact with the hypervisor. Each RB is addressable by a single VM only, the VM corresponding to its cluster row: this takes advantage of the fact that a virtual machine is a contiguous set of clusters rows. Those RBs only buffer commands for the communication from the VM clusters to the hypervisor cluster. In the opposite way, from the hypervisor cluster (HD, hypervisor CPU e.g.) to a VM cluster, there is a direct access without control in order to reach full speed for HD DMA transfers. When a RB is overloaded by I/O access from a VM, the RB FIFO is permanently filled by a command packet. The overloading will then be retro-propagated to the global network routers the command were routed through. This means that the VM will overload its own router but it won't affect another virtual machine global network routers or HD access priority.

Interrupts. The hypervisor has to forward the HD hardware interrupts to the VM. Sending the interrupts through the global network is dangerous: the hypervisor would depend of the network availability. So, we designed a component physically wired to each cluster interrupt concentrator and which control registers are located in the hypervisor cluster (see left part of figure 3 on the previous page). For each cluster, there is a dedicated wire connecting the interrupt concentrator to the interrupt initiator located inside the hypervisor cluster. An issue is the need to share an interrupt line between different devices. If a VM owns three clusters, it has access to three interrupt lines. So, if this machine has four HD, one line has to be shared between two HD. With shared interrupt line the guest kernel has to poll the two devices to identify the interrupt initiator.

Limitations. All cores start on the chip power-up. The VM creation and instantiation happen at this time. It is not possible to dynamically create or destroy virtual machines, it is static. This limitation is based on the fact we are unable to stop a running virtual machine. A specific hardware support or a dedicated software hypervisor instance running on each core would handle this. Despite this limitation the software layer was designed to support dynamic VM management.

4 Software Overview

4.1 Services Provided by the Hypervisor

The hypervisor handles the administrator commands like creating a VM or a virtual HD at the chip power-up. The hypervisor also virtualizes the VM I/O access : the read/write commands from a VM to a virtual HD virtual register and the way-back : the hypervisor reads the status device register of each physical HD and propagate the request completion information to the VM.

From the hypervisor's point of view, virtual resources are contiguous sets of physical resources: a VM is a contiguous cluster set and a virtual HD is a contiguous physical sector set on a single physical HD. We do not want to have overlapping VMs or overlapping virtual HDs.

From the VMs point of view, a virtual HD is a set of memory mapped registers which are located in the hypervisor address space partition. When a VM reads from or writes to these registers, the command is sent to the corresponding cluster where the virtual registers belong : the hypervisor cluster. The command is then stored in a RB.

4.2 Structure of the Hypervisor

The hypervisor itself is an infinite loop that reads commands from three sources at each iteration : the administrator's command list, all RBs and all devices status register. Because it is not possible to dynamically instantiate virtual machines at the moment, the administrator's command list is stored inside the hypervisor binary. It means that each change to the list implies to compile the hypervisor again. A *create VM* command means that the hypervisor has to initialize the global network doors like explained in the hardware overview section. For HD, the hypervisor validates that the VM does not try to escape from its virtual HD or its memory partition by a DMA access. It means the hypervisor checks the target DMA address, target sector and buffer size sent to the physical HD. The hypervisor is the only software component directly accessing the physical devices.

Polling physical HD prevents interrupt storms attacks and it deterministically handles hardware events. Interruptions imply non-determinism and with the B method the non-determinism is a source of a huge proving effort. One could argue that polling is a waste of computing power because the CPU could be used for something else. In this situation this is wrong : when this software hypervisor is polling it has nothing else to do. The issues implied by polling are an increased worst case latency to handle hardware events and an increased electric consumption.

4.3 Formal Design of the Hypervisor

We designed the hypervisor with the B-Method [1]. With this tool we can start from an abstract machine and we go down to an implementation machine, then translated to compilable C code that has been formally demonstrated conform to the original formal specification. Everything is statically allocated, this is why the hypervisor metadata is always allocated to the worst case. The B Method does not handle dynamic memory allocation. The static memory allocation is the reason why virtual HD are contiguous set of sectors: filesystems with fragmentation support have a very high worst case price to pay in metadata size. About the tool itself, the AtelierB[4] from Clearsy is freely available for non-commercial use and has been successfully used in the industry [2].

Properties. With the help of the AtelierB, we proved that the generated C code respects the following properties :

1. A command to a HD references the requesting VM virtual HD only.
2. A command to a HD addresses the requesting VM memory only, not the hypervisor nor an other VM memory.
3. The hypervisor checks the target physical device status and only accepts the command from a VM if the physical device is ready. If the device is not ready, the command stays stored in the RB. We do not want the hypervisor to get stuck by a busy physical device.
4. The absence of buffer overflows, integer overflows, divide by zero.

5. The impossibility to reach inconsistent states like detaching a virtual HD from a running VM.
6. Loops termination.

Properties 1,2 and 3 are verified with the help of preconditions enforcement, while properties 4 and 5 need the adjunction of invariants and 6 the exhibition of a variant.

At the non-verified low level glue code we implemented a denial of service protection: before reading a command from a RB, the hypervisor checks if a full command is waiting to be processed and that the RB is free to receive the answer: we do not want the hypervisor to get stuck by a denial of service on the answer transmission. The hypervisor is made of 3080 B lines generating 2114 proof obligations. 308 proof obligations have been manually discharged, all the others were automatically discharged. The generated C code represents 3256 lines headers included.

Remarks about Determinism. We manually checked the absence of break or syscall assembly instruction in the hypervisor executable code. The hypervisor code and data fit entirely into the CPU memory cache. We are relying on polling and the hypervisor CPU L1 cache does not have any MMU (it doesn't need one, unlike the VM cluster), the physical HD are accessed without cachability and the I/O programming access are synchronous. This induces that the hypervisor has a deterministic execution flow. The HD virtualization algorithm is constant in time as it will be shown in the performance section. This constant time makes denial of service or covert channel attacks more difficult. All the metadata are statically allocated so an attacker cannot rely on a metadata exhaustion based denial of service.

5 Performances

The hypervisor runs on a simulated MIPS32 based many-core chip. Because there are many differences between our simulated hardware architecture and a standard hardware Intel architecture, we cannot analyze the performance differences with a VMWare, Xen or a Hyper-V hypervisor. Such an analysis does not seem pertinent to us. Instead we made a cycle accurate measure of our hypervisor performance needs.

5.1 Timing Analysis

To analyze these results, we estimated the physical HD access rate per second on standard computers. We extract statistics, from Linux based computers, for three machine profiles and we summarized the results in the following table.

Machine profile	HD operation count per second	Physical HD average processing time in milliseconds
Desktop machine	**3.88**	45
Computing server	**10.54**	43
File server	**378**	78

We consider the average physical HD process time to be 50 milliseconds which is 5 000 000 cycles at 100 MHZ. We didn't measure the HD processing time of the TSAR platform because it is a simulated SystemC IDE HD with unrealistic latency. We also didn't measure the time needed to create a VM because it can be used only once : at chip power-up.

The time used by a I/O access can be decomposed in five terms:

1. The time a command **is buffered in a RB (WC)**
2. The time the hypervisor needs to **virtualize a command (VC)**
3. The time for the **device to process the command (P)**
4. The time the **device answer is buffered before being** read by the hypervisor **(AW)**
5. The time to **virtualize the response** by the hypervisor **(VA)**

The command buffered time (WC) in the RB depends on the hypervisor load : before processing a specific command, the hypervisor may have to virtualize some other commands and some physical HD events. The WC worst case is: $(registration\ buffer\ count - 1) * VC + (physical\ HD\ count * VA)$. This is the same concept for the response virtualization time so the worst device answer waiting time (AW) case is: $(registration\ buffer\ count) * VC + (physical\ HD\ count - 1) * VA$. In order to evaluate WC and AW, we have to evaluate the VC and VA first.

To measure the hypervisor performances, we wrote some scenarios. We want to measure the impact of :

- the number of VMs running at the same time and their size
- the number of physical and virtual HDs
- the number of accessed sector per request
- VMs sharing same physical HDs through their virtual HDs

Results. We measured the VC by reading the hypervisor CPU cycle count at the time the hypervisor reads the command from the RB and then we read the hypervisor CPU cycle count when the hypervisor is about to initialize the physical HD. The VC is the subtraction between those two CPU cycle counts. We followed the same methodology for the VA evaluation. After measurement, the VC is 16 912 cycles and the VA is 101 cycles for each scenarios. These constant times is explained by the constant time algorithm we chose and the determinist execution flow. The worst WC is $3 * 16\,912 + 4 * 101 = 51\,140$ cycles on the platform. The worst AW is $4 * 16\,912 + 3 * 101 = 67\,951$ cycles. The worst virtualization latency for a I/O access from a VM is $51\,140 + 67\,951 + 16\,912 + 101 = 136\,104$ cycles which is 2.7% of the device process time (5 000 000 cycles), in the worst case. Those results are summarized in the table below.

Terms	worst WC	VC	P	worst AW	VA
Cycles	51150	16912	5000000	67951	101

Extending those results to the different machines profile HD usage above:

- On a **desktop computer**, the hypervisor spend $3.88 * 16912 + 3.88 * 101 =$ 66 010 cycles in the VC/VA per second. This is 0.06% of the CPU frequency.

- On a **computing server**, the hypervisor spend $10.54*16912+10.54*101 =$ 179 317 cycles in the VC/VA per second. This is 0.17% of the CPU frequency.
- On a **file server**, the hypervisor spend $378*16912+378*101 = 6\,430\,914$ cycles in the VC/VA per second. This is 6.43% of the CPU frequency.

5.2 Surface Analysis

Because we stopped at the SystemC model, the surface analysis relies on an estimation based on the memorising elements. The non-virtualized TSAR platform is built on twelve clusters of four 32 kilobytes L1 caches and one L2 256 kilobytes cache. The sum of all memory caches is then $12*4*32+12*256 = 4608$ kilobytes = 36 864 kilobits. Each door embeds 81 memory bits. There are 12 clusters and each clusters have 4 network connection to neighbors cluster, this is why all the memory doors sum is : $12*4*81 = 3\,888$ bits. The door's initialization component use 51 memory bits. Each RB takes 1 268 memory bits, so for the whole platform the RB total cost is $4*1\,268 = 5\,072$ memory bits. The hypervisor CPU cache size is 32 kilobytes like the hypervisor's cluster RAM. The cache and the RAM represent 64 kilobytes which is equivalent to 512 kilobits. The doors, RBs and initialization component surface is 8.8 kilobits. The whole virtualization solution represent $8.8+512 = 520.8$ kilobits which is *1.41*% of the whole platform without virtualization support.

6 Related Work

Direct assignment of physical cores to VMs or hypervisor is not something new but neither **SplitX** [11] (2011) nor **NoHype** [9] (2010) were engineered with formal methods. Also, **NoHype** must be used with virtualization I/O ready devices, we do not have such a constraint. **HyperSafe** [18] (2010) is a hardened hypervisor with implementation error security mechanisms like W $\oplus$ X, CFI, etc. Formal verification protects us against some programming errors so we may not need these protections, but people could argue that these hardening are complementary to formal verification, this is the defense in depth approach. **VaxVMM** [8] (1990) was undergoing a formal verification of its formal specification against a policy at the project cancellation and **SeL4** [10] is still the only micro-kernel with a fully verified C code. **SeL4** is a micro-kernel, it needs external non-verified drivers to run. It is not self-sufficient. **Qubes** [7] (2010) and **Nizza** [6] (2005) are operating systems based on the micro-kernel concept : the drivers are running as userland threads in separated address spaces. These projects aim to minimize the trusted computing base size. Formal verification and the micro-kernel concept are two different solutions that could be complementary. **Hyper-V** [12] (2009) is a multi-cores hypervisor which is being formally verified. The authors have built a x64 multi-processor formal model in order to reason on Hyper-V. We lack information on Hyper-V to make a deeper analysis. **Secvisor** [15] (2007) and **Terra** [5] (2003) authenticate guest kernel code before running it. These projects solve the trusted boot problem but not the runtime security weaknesses. A Secvisor analysis with the murφ model checker discovered two flaws. Model checking relies on an abstract model so it cannot detect implementation mistakes like a buffer overflow. **Xom** [13] (2003) and **Overshadow** [3] (2008) encrypt and sign memory to protect from illegal memory access. Memory encryption and signature protect against illegal memory access but it won't protect against a buffer overflow in the TCP/IP stack for example. Xom was analyzed with the murφ model checker and one security flaw was found. **XMHF** [17] (2013) runs a single guest with directly assigned I/O devices. The C code was analyzed with the CBMC model checker to enforce the integrity property. Delegating all I/O device driver to an untrusted guest is not secure to us : these are part of the trusted computing base.

7 Conclusion

We presented a hypervisor relying on a hardware and a software layer. The hardware layer simple approach and the proven properties on the software layer made us trust the control flow integrity and the DMA control. The full isolation aspect of the virtualization made us confident for covert channel concerning VM cluster: the absence of hardware sharing suppresses many covert channels. About availability, the bounded time and space and the full isolation aspect of the hypervisor make us confident in the hypervisor's ability to handle a denial of service attack.

References

1. Abrial, J.-R.: The B-Book: Assigning Programs to Meanings. Cambridge University Press (1996)
2. Behm, P., Desforges, P., Meynadier, J.-M.: MÉTÉOR: An industrial success in formal development. In: Bert, D. (ed.) B 1998. LNCS, vol. 1393, p. 26. Springer, Heidelberg (1998)
3. Chen, X., Garfinkel, T., Lewis, E.C., Subrahmanyam, P., Waldspurger, C.A., Boneh, D., Dwoskin, J., Ports, D.R.: Overshadow: a virtualization-based approach to retrofitting protection in commodity operating systems. SIGOPS Oper. Syst. Rev. 42(2), 2–13 (2008)
4. Clearsy. AtelierB homepage, `http://www.atelierb.eu`
5. Garfinkel, T., Pfaff, B., Chow, J., Rosenblum, M., Boneh, D.: Terra: a virtual machine-based platform for trusted computing. In: Proceedings of the Nineteenth ACM Symposium on Operating Systems Principles, SOSP 2003, pp. 193–206. ACM, New York (2003)
6. Härtig, H., Hohmuth, M., Feske, N., Helmuth, C., Lackorzynski, A., Mehnert, F., Peter, M.: The nizza secure-system architecture. In: IEEE CollaborateCom 2005 (2005)
7. Rutkowska, J., Wojtczuk, R.: Qubes os. Technical report, Invisible Thing Lab (January 2010)
8. Karger, P.A., Zurko, M.E., Bonin, D.W., Mason, A.H., Kahn, C.E.: A retrospective on the vax vmm security kernel. IEEE Trans. Softw. Eng. 17(11), 1147–1165 (1991)
9. Keller, E., Szefer, J., Rexford, J., Lee, R.B.: Nohype: virtualized cloud infrastructure without the virtualization. In: Proceedings of the 37th Annual International Symposium on Computer Architecture, ISCA 2010, pp. 350–361. ACM, New York (2010)

10. Klein, G., Elphinstone, K., Heiser, G., Andronick, J., Cock, D., Derrin, P., Elkaduwe, D., Engelhardt, K., Kolanski, R., Norrish, M., Sewell, T., Tuch, H., Winwood, S.: sel4: formal verification of an os kernel. In: SOSP 2009: Proceedings of the ACM SIGOPS 22nd Symposium on Operating Systems Principles, pp. 207–220. ACM, New York (2009)
11. Landau, A., Ben-Yehuda, M., Gordon, A.: Splitx: split guest/hypervisor execution on multi-core. In: Proceedings of the 3rd Conference on I/O Virtualization, WIOV 2011, p. 1. USENIX Association, Berkeley (2011)
12. Leinenbach, D., Santen, T.: Verifying the microsoft hyper-V hypervisor with VCC. In: Cavalcanti, A., Dams, D.R. (eds.) FM 2009. LNCS, vol. 5850, pp. 806–809. Springer, Heidelberg (2009)
13. Lie, D., Thekkath, C.A., Horowitz, M.: Implementing an untrusted operating system on trusted hardware. SIGOPS Oper. Syst. Rev. 37, 178–192 (2003)
14. LIP6. Tsar project homepage, `https://www-soc.lip6.fr/trac/tsar`
15. Seshadri, A., Luk, M., Qu, N., Perrig, A.: Secvisor: a tiny hypervisor to provide lifetime kernel code integrity for commodity OSes. In: SOSP 2007: Proceedings of Twenty-first ACM SIGOPS Symposium on Operating Systems Principles, pp. 335–350. ACM, New York (2007)
16. N. Y. Times: Intel halts development of 2 new microprocessors
17. Vasudevan, A., Chaki, S., Jia, L., McCune, J., Newsome, J., Datta, A.: Design, implementation and verification of an extensible and modular hypervisor framework. In: IEEE Symposium on Security and Privacy (2013)
18. Wang, Z., Jiang, X.: Hypersafe: A lightweight approach to provide lifetime hypervisor control-flow integrity. In: Proceedings of the 2010 IEEE Symposium on Security and Privacy, SP 2010, pp. 380–395. IEEE Computer Society, Washington, DC (2010)

Toward a Self-aware System for Exascale Architectures

Aaron Landwehr, Stéphane Zuckerman, and Guang R. Gao

Department of Electrical and Computer Engineering
University of Delaware, United States
aron@udel.edu, {szuckerm,ggao}@capsl.udel.edu

Abstract. High-performance systems are evolving to a point where performance is no longer the sole relevant criterion. The current execution and resource management paradigms are no longer sufficient to ensure correctness and performance. Power requirements are presently driving the co-design of HPC systems, which in turn sets the course for a radical change in how to express the need for scarcer and scarcer resources, as well as how to manage them. It is our opinion that systems will need to become more introspective and self-aware with respect to performance, energy, and resiliency. In this *position paper*, we explore the major hardware requirements we believe are central to enabling introspection and self-awareness, as well as the types of interfaces and information that will be needed for such runtime systems. We also discuss a research path toward a self-aware system for exascale architectures.

1 Introduction

As we move toward an exascale future with ever expanding capacities in terms of both cores and resources, we have reached a point in computing where current execution paradigms no-longer suffice. High performance computing systems have begun to approach a point where the ever growing multiplicity of transistor counts and components is not sustainable in terms of energy consumption. It has been said that at the current rates, extrapolated into the future, an exascale computer system would consume over 1.5 GW of power [18]. These ever expanding power requirements necessarily result in the need for a fundamental and radical shift in terms of programmability and adaptation. We believe that systems will need to become hierarchically introspective and self-aware to be able to adapt to steep performance and energy requirements.

Problem Statement. There are number of key facets that need to be addressed to enable a truly introspective and self-aware system capable of performing well and efficiently. The first is that a form of co-design needs to occur in terms of hardware and software. Exascale hardware needs to support a number of integral features to enable controlling system software to monitor and adapt to the current system state and any requirements passed to it in the form of power or performance. In broad terms, there will need to be some form of an

D. an Mey et al. (Eds.): Euro-Par 2013 Workshops, LNCS 8374, pp. 812–822, 2014.

observe-decide-act (ODA) loop to monitor, make decisions, and to control both the hardware and software aspects of a system [7]. The second is that the system needs to be capable of adapting for power and performance while at the same time maintaining correct and reliable operation. It is key to recognize that these conflicting goals form a basis for a multi-variable problem which will be further complicated by the need to run multiple programs on a system with thousands of components. There is an open question on how to self-adjust and to meet these goals.

This *position paper* proposes the following contributions: (1) we evaluate and motivate the important hardware requirements for a truly self-aware and introspective system (using a specific target architecture), and (2) we provide a vision and discuss important research venues for self-aware exascale systems.

This paper is organized as follows: Section 2 discusses our target exascale architecture; Section 3 evaluates the hardware requirements essential for an introspective system software; Section 4 provides research venues for self-adaptation at the exascale level; Section 5 discusses the related work; and we conclude in Section 6.

2 Background

Target Exascale Architecture and Associated Toolchain. For the purpose of this discussion, we introduce our target exascale architecture (TEA) which is similar to the one described by Knauerhase et al. [11]. At the lowest level, the TEA is organized into blocks consisting of a Control Engine (CE), several eXecution Engines (XEs), and a block shared memory. An XE's fundamental usage is to execute arbitrary code without interruption. The CE on the other hand is designed to control and schedule work to a number of local XEs within a given block. A detailed description of the TEA is provided in Figure 1(a). Both XE and CE cores contain a set of identical components: some local memory (for data and code), ALUs, a clock/power gate control unit, and some network functionality. In addition, XEs also feature a floating-point unit, as well as a performance monitoring unit (PMU). The XEs, being designed solely for execution, do not have logic to directly handle interrupts or traps and instead any interrupts are offloaded to the CE within the block. The architecture itself is designed to operate at close to threshold voltages, as well as to control the power and clocks of functional units (FUs) within the system in order to minimize energy usage. A detailed description of the TEA toolchain is shown in Figure 1(b).

Codelet Program Execution Model and System Software Model. The TEA will be hierarchical in nature with numerous components. Coarse grain or monolithic approaches to adaptation do not befit this type of architecture. We strongly believe that these types of program execution models (PXMs) will be incapable of effective self-adaptation. Instead we believe that the focus should be on using and incorporating fine-grained PXMs within a self-adaptation framework. There have been number of discussions to decide which program execution model should

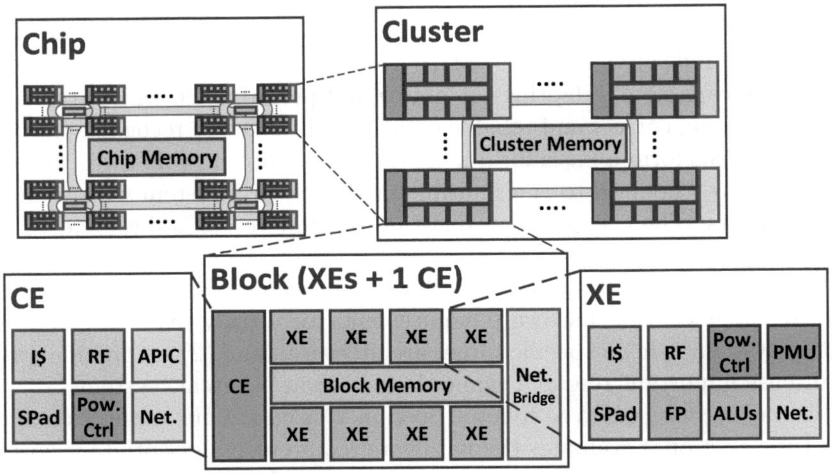

(a) Our Target Exascale Architecture consists of heterogeneous cores in a hierarchical configuration with network interconnects at each level, organized into blocks, clusters, and chips. The exact number of cores and levels is not important for our discussion.

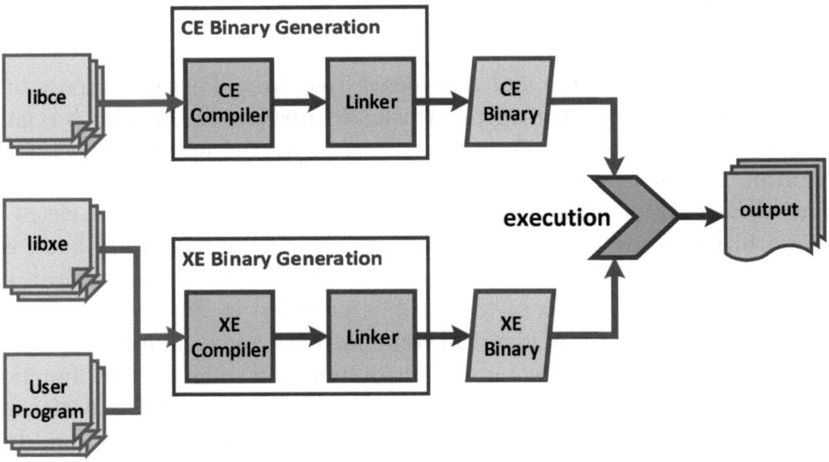

(b) Target Exascale Architecture Toolchain: XEs and CEs are specialized and may have a distinct instruction set architecture. As a result, a special compiler and linker may need to be used to produce the binaries for each. Each has a library providing a basic runtime system. In the case of an XE, the library is linked with the user program.

Fig. 1. Our Target Exascale Architecture and associated toolchain

be used for exascale systems. One such PXM is the codelet model [24], which has already been implemented in various ways [13,21]. It features an abstract machine model that fits very well with our TEA.

3 Requirements for Self-adaptation

In this section, we discuss the underlying hardware requirements in order to implement a self-adaptive, self-aware system. Many of these will be integral for enabling a self-adaptive system software and others will simply improve or make its job easier in adapting. Primarily, this section serves as a "wish" list of features that we believe are important for adaptation in any exascale architecture. We target three main objectives for self-aware systems: energy/power efficiency, performance, and resiliency. However, the benefits of a tailored performance monitoring unit are discussed first.

Role of the PMU in Exascale Systems. Before moving on to the detailed requirements in the subsequent subsections, we discuss the PMU as an important mechanism toward enabling adaptation. From an energy perspective, the counters can be combined with instruction energy cost metrics in order to indirectly monitor energy. From the perspective of performance monitoring, the PMU can directly give many different instruction count metrics that are useful in characterizing performance. From a resiliency perspective, counts of correctable errors can be used to aid proactive monitoring for potential issues and as a mechanism to determine whether the system software should be cautious with the work it is scheduling. Being given a plethora of counters and the ability to run them concurrently will greatly aid in information gathering for a self-adaptive system. As such, it is our belief that the PMU will serve as the primary means of information gathering for both performance and energy adaptation, and will be one of the most important mechanisms of a self-adaptive system.

Energy. For any large-scale computer system (including current petascale systems), the primary goal in self-adaptation is to minimize energy consumption. As discussed previously, the PMU will be integral in this goal. At the most basic level, the PMU provides various performance related metrics. This includes counts of various different instruction types such as local/remote reads, writes, ALU operations, FPU operations, DMA operations, etc. These counts are useful directly for determining the workload characteristics and optimality of running tasks (and of higher level components in the system). For example, if the runtime system is able to determine that a task is spending the majority of its time idling while waiting for remote memory through the usage of some combination of remote read and DMA operations, it could clock gate the processor running the task while the data of the task is moved to a more localized memory. For another example, through the count of FPU operations, the runtime system could determine that only integer calculations are performed on a given XE, and thus decide to power gate its FPU.

The PMU can also be used indirectly to estimate energy usage. This is possible if the energy cost of various instructions and components in the system are known or estimable, and an energy model is developed. Essentially, the costs of instructions could be combined with the counts read from the PMU to form a picture about the overall energy usage. This information would then be used in conjunction with specified power budgets to determine if actions need to be taken in order to meet goals.

Our TEA is expected to be capable of adjusting the state of FUs, at least at a functional unit block (FUB) granularity – which is at a finer granularity than FUs. To motivate this, consider task kernel hinting. Given a compiler with the capability to identify the types of instructions used by a task kernel and given mechanism for the runtime to hook into this information, it could identify explicitly which units would not be used by a given task and simply power gate them. Furthermore, the same strategy could be applied at an even finer-granularity to turn off individual pipelines within FUs.

Performance. We expect the TEA's system software to be responsible for task scheduling and resource allocation. Thus, it needs to be able to monitor performance in order to achieve adaptation. There are various types of performance metrics that will be important. These can range from different types of resource utilization (network, CPU, memory, etc.) to workload distribution, etc. Characterizing sections of the system will require monitoring to be relatively fine-grained. We believe that the ideal granularity is at the codelet level.

Using the PMU events described, performance within the runtime can be evaluated. For example, by knowing the frequency and types of memory counts, the system software can determine network utilization and whether the communication is relatively localized. This information is useful for determining how optimal the current task scheduling is in terms of performance and energy efficiency. If for instance, the system software can determine that groups of tasks are communicating frequently but are not localized to the same block, it could migrate the tasks to one block in order to localize the network traffic.

Resiliency. Fault tolerance is one of the most important aspects of a self-adaptive system. Without proper hardware support, the software will be unable to cope with failures or to meet goals in exascale systems. Furthermore, the system software would necessarily be burdened with the detection and prevention of faults through costly primitive means. This could potentially entail such things as duplicating tasks and verifying the results of all task computations within the system. In short, lack of proper hardware support for resiliency will significantly affect other aspects of self-adaptation.

It is our belief that the hardware must be able to detect faults within the components of the system. The primary motivation for this is to minimize runtime scope and energy costs. A system software burdened with the aforementioned details will be extensive and inefficient. This leads not only to a high cost in software support, but also a reduction in energy efficiency and performance. For example, task duplication could force the same task to be re-run three times simply to determine which set of components is faulty.

The hardware needs not only to detect and/or correct faults but also a means to deliver information about the failure to the system software. It is absolutely essential for an introspective system software to know which FUs have failed in order to reschedule any tasks that require or depend on the failed hardware resources.

4 Research Venues

In this section, we discuss our vision of exascale self-adaptation. At a high level, the runtime system of exascale architectures will need to make intelligent decisions to control various hardware features to reduce power consumption, as well as to schedule tasks and move data. First, we start with a discussion of adaptation at a fine-grained level and from there move toward a discussion of adaptation at a more coarse-grained level.

Fine-grained Adaptation An exascale architecture must include power management at a fine-grained level. We foresee adaptation occurring through an ODA mechanism as shown in Figure 2. A CE will implement an ODA loop for self-adaptation. Information will come from various hardware and software mechanisms within the system, and goals will come from the user or program. Finally, various actions will occur in the form of adjustments to hardware state or some type of software change.

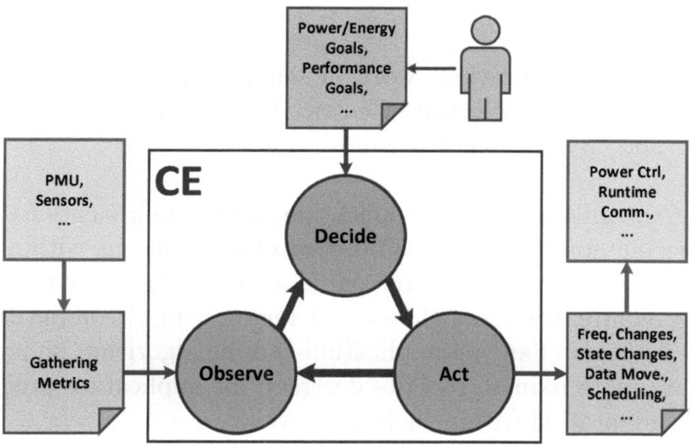

Fig. 2. Mapping our target exascale architecture to an observe-decide-act mechanism

Some of the decisions that we foresee are whether to clock gate or power gate components, as well as whether to adjust the frequency of components. For a small example of adaptation within our TEA, consider Figure 3. The right side shows a block's state at various stages during execution. The left side shows three distinct decisions occurring between those stages. In the example, all blocks are initially enabled. However, the CE observes that only two scheduled tasks are currently running and from there decides to disable the unused XEs. This decision is then translated into an action of writing to each XE's Clock Control to put them into a clock gated state. Next, the CE observes that there are many remote DMA operations occurring and decides to lower the frequency of the block to conserve energy. This decision is then translated into an action of writing to the Block Frequency Control. Finally, the CE observes that there are no floating point operations occurring within the second XE and decides to power gate the FP functional unit. This decision is then translated into an action of writing to the XE Power Control.

Coarse-Grain Adaptation. At a coarse-grain level, a form of hierarchical management will need to occur. For this, there will need to be a communication subsystem between CEs in order to communicate system state. In terms of energy and performance, it will be important to be able to generalize localized information about specific sections of the system and to communicate that information without transferring large amounts of data. In short, CEs will need to aggregate their local information and to package it into condensed form for usage by nodes higher up in the hierarchy. This aggregated information would include the health and resource allocations in subsections of the system. The higher-level nodes would be tasked with making decisions based upon this information, for example, whether to allocate data or schedule a task to a particular section of the system.

5 Related Work

Below we discuss other previous work in self-adaptation. The approaches fall into three categories: "Application-Centric Adaptation," "Component-Centric Adaptation," and "System-Centric Adaptation."

Application-Centric Adaptation. Application-centric approaches focus on adaptation for specific applications or a subclass of applications within a given domain. Quality of service (QoS) is one large area of active research [1,9] due to the real time requirements and the ever-changing field of computing resources. Other works focus on changing application specific algorithm policy [22]. Some approaches are more akin to toolkits designed for application programmers to use to enable adaptation within their software [6].

Component-Centric Adaptation. Component-centric approaches are a form of adaptation that focuses on monitoring and adapting a particular component or resource of a system. For example, there has been research in adapting cache policies [10], dynamic reconfiguration of memory hierarchies [3], and self-optimizing memory controllers [8].

System-Centric Adaptation. System-centric approaches focus on adaptation at the system level. Historically the role of resource management has been given to the operating system (OS). In the case of highly parallel systems, we can divide these approaches into several categories: full OSes, lightweight kernels, micro kernels, and high-level runtime systems. Full OSes adapted to cluster-like

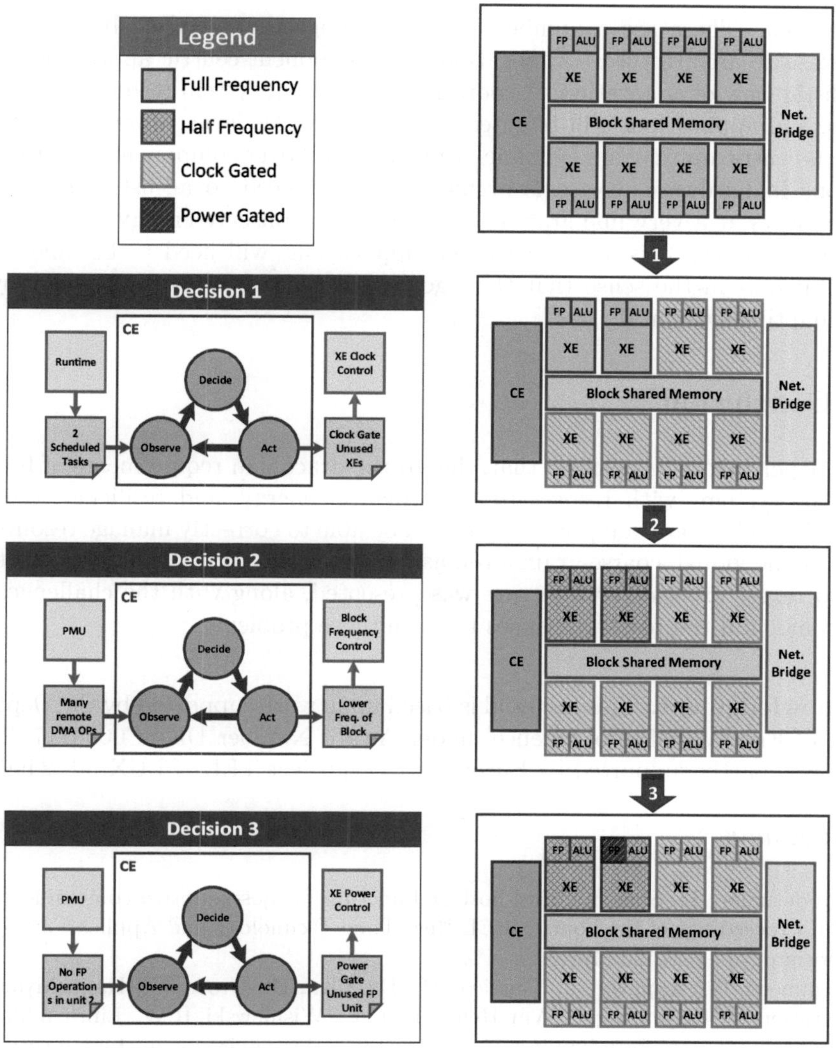

Fig. 3. Target exascale architecture adaptation example

environments [20] are mainstream OSes customized for high-performance needs. Lightweight kernels [4,5] implement a reduced set of features directly accessible to the application programmer and forward calls for missing features to a "fuller" OS. Micro kernels [12,15,17] implement basic OS services (memory addressing, process management, inter-process communications) as privileged code and implement every other service as some form of unprivileged library [2]. Finally, high-level runtime systems implement some form of resource management on top of the host OS [14,19,23] or expose some form of languages (or frameworks) that provide mechanisms for an application to adapt [7,16].

Discussion. There are a number of shortcomings that need to be addressed for exascale architectures. Application and component-centric approaches lack a holistic view of adaptation. A coordination between system resources, components, and applications will be integral at the exascale level. Moreover, current system-centric approaches lack fine-grained control over components due to limitations in hardware. Exascale architectures will need to adjust the state of components at a very fine granularity in order to conserve energy and to meet power envelopes. This also means that applications will need to become first-class citizens in the sense that their goals will need to be accounted for by a self-adapting system.

6 Conclusion

This paper takes the position that, due to the draconian requirements of future exascale systems with respect to performance, energy, and resiliency, only a proactive, self-aware, adaptive system will be able to correctly manage resources, both at the global, coarse-grain level, as well as at the finest-grain level. To this end, a target exascale architecture was presented, along with the challenges to overcome, and the research venues to solve those problems.

Acknowledgment. This material is based upon work supported by the Department of Energy [Office of Science] under Award Number DE-SC0008717. This work was partly supported by European FP7 project TERAFLUX, id. 249013.

References

1. Abdelzaher, T., Shin, K.: End-host architecture for qos-adaptive communication. In: Proceedings of the Fourth IEEE Real-Time Technology and Applications Symposium, pp. 121–130 (1998)
2. Ammons, G., Appavoo, J., Butrico, M., Da Silva, D., Grove, D., Kawachiya, K., Krieger, O., Rosenburg, B., Van Hensbergen, E., Wisniewski, R.W.: Libra: a library operating system for a jvm in a virtualized execution environment. In: Proceedings of the 3rd International Conference on Virtual Execution Environments, VEE 2007, pp. 44–54. ACM, New York (2007)
3. Balasubramonian, R., Albonesi, D., Buyuktosunoglu, A., Dwarkadas, S.: Memory hierarchy reconfiguration for energy and performance in general-purpose processor architectures. In: Proceedings of the 33rd Annual ACM/IEEE International Symposium on Microarchitecture, MICRO 33, pp. 245–257. ACM, New York (2000)
4. Ballesteros, F.J., Evans, N., Forsyth, C., Guardiola, G., McKie, J., Minnich, R., Soriano-Salvador, E.: Nix: A case for a manycore system for cloud computing. Bell Labs Technical Journal 17(2), 41–54 (2012)
5. Giampapa, M., Gooding, T., Inglett, T., Wisniewski, R.: Experiences with a lightweight supercomputer kernel: Lessons learned from blue gene's cnk. In: 2010 International Conference for High Performance Computing, Networking, Storage and Analysis (SC), pp. 1–10 (2010)

6. Goel, A., Steere, D., Pu, C., Walpole, J.: Swift: A feedback control and dynamic reconfiguration toolkit. Technical report, Oregon Graduate Institute (1998)
7. Hoffmann, H.: SEEC: A Framework for Self-Aware Management of Goals and Constraints in Computing Systems. PhD thesis, Massachusetts Institute of Technology (February 2013)
8. Ipek, E., Mutlu, O., Martínez, J.F., Caruana, R.: Self-optimizing memory controllers: A reinforcement learning approach. SIGARCH Comput. Archit. News 36(3), 39–50 (2008)
9. Ivanovic, D., Carro, M., Hermenegildo, M.: Towards data-aware qos-driven adaptation for service orchestrations. In: 2010 IEEE International Conference on Web Services (ICWS), pp. 107–114 (2010)
10. Kim, C., Burger, D., Keckler, S.W.: An adaptive, non-uniform cache structure for wire-delay dominated on-chip caches. SIGOPS Oper. Syst. Rev. 36(5), 211–222 (2002)
11. Knauerhase, R., Cledat, R., Teller, J.: For extreme parallelism, your os is sooooo last-millennium. In: Proceedings of the 4th USENIX Conference on Hot Topics in Parallelism, HotPar, vol. 12, p. 3 (2012)
12. Krieger, O., Auslander, M., Rosenburg, B., Wisniewski, R.W., Xenidis, J., Da Silva, D., Ostrowski, M., Appavoo, J., Butrico, M., Mergen, M., Waterland, A., Uhlig, V.: K42: building a complete operating system. In: Proceedings of the 1st ACM SIGOPS/EuroSys European Conference on Computer Systems 2006, EuroSys 2006, pp. 133–145. ACM, New York (2006)
13. Lauderdale, C., Khan, R.: Towards a codelet-based runtime for exascale computing: position paper. In: Proceedings of the 2nd International Workshop on Adaptive Self-Tuning Computing Systems for the Exaflop Era, pp. 21–26. ACM (2012)
14. Li, B., Nahrstedt, K.: A control-based middleware framework for quality-of-service adaptations. IEEE J. Sel. A. Commun. 17(9), 1632–1650 (2006)
15. Nightingale, E.B., Hodson, O., McIlroy, R., Hawblitzel, C., Hunt, G.: Helios: heterogeneous multiprocessing with satellite kernels. In: Proceedings of the ACM SIGOPS 22nd Symposium on Operating Systems Principles, SOSP 2009, pp. 221–234. ACM, New York (2009)
16. Ribler, R., Vetter, J., Simitci, H., Reed, D.: Autopilot: adaptive control of distributed applications. In: Proceedings of the Seventh International Symposium on High Performance Distributed Computing, pp. 172–179 (1998)
17. Sacha, J., Napper, J., Mullender, S., McKie, J.: Osprey: Operating system for predictable clouds. In: 2012 IEEE/IFIP 42nd International Conference on Dependable Systems and Networks Workshops (DSN-W), pp. 1–6 (2012)
18. Scogland, T., Subramaniam, B., Chun Feng, W.: Emerging trends on the evolving green500: Year three. In: 2011 IEEE International Symposium on Parallel and Distributed Processing Workshops and Phd Forum (IPDPSW), pp. 822–828 (2011)
19. Sharifi, A., Srikantaiah, S., Mishra, A.K., Kandemir, M., Das, C.R.: Mete: meeting end-to-end qos in multicores through system-wide resource management. SIGMETRICS Perform. Eval. Rev. 39(1), 13–24 (2011)
20. Sterling, T.L., Savarese, D., Becker, D.J., Dorband, J.E., Ranawake, U.A., Packer, C.V.: Beowulf: A parallel workstation for scientific computation. In: ICPP (1), pp. 11–14 (1995)
21. Suettlerlein, J., Zuckerman, S., Gao, G.R.: An Implementation of the Codelet Model. In: Wolf, F., Mohr, B., an Mey, D. (eds.) Euro-Par 2013. LNCS, vol. 8097, pp. 633–644. Springer, Heidelberg (2013)

22. Thomas, N., Tanase, G., Tkachyshyn, O., Perdue, J., Amato, N.M., Rauchwerger, L.: A framework for adaptive algorithm selection in stapl. In: Proceedings of the Tenth ACM SIGPLAN Symposium on Principles and Practice of Parallel Programming, PPoPP 2005, pp. 277–288. ACM, New York (2005)
23. Zhang, R., Lu, C., Abdelzaher, T., Stankovic, J.: Controlware: a middleware architecture for feedback control of software performance. In: Proceedings of 22nd International Conference on Distributed Computing Systems, pp. 301–310 (2002)
24. Zuckerman, S., Suetterlein, J., Knauerhase, R., Gao, G.R.: Using a codelet program execution model for exascale machines: position paper. In: Proceedings of the 1st International Workshop on Adaptive Self-Tuning Computing Systems for the Exaflop Era, pp. 64–69. ACM (2011)

A Scalability-Aware Kernel Executive for Many-Core Operating Systems*

Gabor Drescher, Timo Hönig, Sebastian Maier,
Benjamin Oechslein, and Wolfgang Schröder-Preikschat

Friedrich-Alexander University Erlangen-Nuremberg
{drescher,thoenig,sebastian.maier,oechslein,wosch}@cs.fau.de

Abstract. Number, variety, and organization of the on-chip processing elements of many-core processors demand a radical rethink in operating systems design. One may come from a multitude of allocatable units that bestows every execution thread its own core: single-threaded cores will be usual, multi-threaded cores will be unusual. The paper presents a scalability-aware kernel executive, SAKE, that is currently designed against such background targeting at large-scale heterogeneous many-core systems. Benchmarks on a 48-core machine motivate custom system software and special purpose systems for such modern machines.

1 Introduction

Multi-core architectures with a fistful (2–8) of processing elements are actually yesterday's news in the parallel systems community, many-core architectures with 10^3 and more processors on a chip arise on the horizon. Based on [10] an annual increase of 40% for the number of cores per processor has been projected [5] that would bring chips of about 5×10^3 cores by the year 2020. Given the full configuration of Kepler GK110 (i.e., 15 SMX units of 192 cores each [15]), the promise of this projection, namely to have processors with up to 480 cores in 2013, has been already overachieved fivefold at the time being. However, it appears that assembly and operation of several thousands of cores on a single chip must be differentiated. Because of power constraints, the number of per-chip transistors that can switch at full frequency drops exponentially (*utilization wall*): large portions of chip area have to be left passive (*dark silicon*) in order to stay within the power budget of the chip [20]. Nevertheless, compared to the current state, the number of cores being plugged into future (general purpose) processors will increase significantly.

These sorts of parallel processors will be *heterogeneous* in terms of on-chip processing elements, communication facilities, and memory organization. But heterogeneity will also concern non-functional features such as (clock) speed and energy (demand), to enable overall system operation in ecological means. Shared

* This work was supported by the German Research Foundation (DFG), partly under grant no. SCHR 603/8-1 and by the Transregional Collaborative Research Centre "Invasive Computing" (SFB/TR 89).

D. an Mey et al. (Eds.): Euro-Par 2013 Workshops, LNCS 8374, pp. 823–832, 2014.

and distributed memory will coexist on a single chip. Analog with Intel's single-chip cloud computer (SCC [9]), at a certain level, cache coherence is no longer implemented in hardware. Despite dark silicon, with future many-core systems there will be so many cores available on a chip that every single thread will be able to run on its own private core. Single-threaded cores will be the common case, multi-threaded ones the exceptional case. All this calls for a radical change in the way operating systems manage processors; it also calls for programming and system paradigms suited for very fine-grained parallelism [18,11].

The most important aspect is to tackle *scalability* issues in particular by, but not limited to, the operating systems for these machines. In addition to analytical approaches, constructive methods are much-needed that decrease number and length of sequential program sections—ideally to zero. In particular, this means the continuous/exclusive use of *non-blocking synchronization* to prevent race conditions in cases where critical sections cannot be removed constructional by a clever arrangement of kernel-level data structures and program sections [14]. In addition to this fundamental design decision, a further measure is to rely on application-level control of sharing kernel-level data structures amongst concurrent processes [3]. Another option is to treat, at some higher level of abstraction, a many-core processor as a network of independent processing elements, assuming no inter-core sharing of in-memory data structures at the lowest level but rather bank on message passing for communicating processes even in case of an underlying shared-memory system [1]. Notwithstanding these commendable examples (Synthesis, Corey, Multikernel), they actually break new ground only rudimentary as the traditional view of processor multiplexing is still the dominating aspect when operating a single processing element (i.e., core)—and this is the primary challenge our approach tackles.

Scalable operating systems for many-core processors have to focus on *absolute parallelism* as a mandatory feature and consider pseudo-parallelism as an optional feature that might come into play for other reasons. The former is given only by means of real (i.e., physical) processing elements, whereas the latter implies their virtualization (e.g., in terms of a conventional threading concept). With this view, however, conventional threads do not constitute the adequate minimal subset of operating-system functions to implement concurrency. Rather, an *event-based approach* that especially suggests a single-stack kernel as basis for the many execution "threads" promises a much more efficiently operating parallel-computing platform [11].

Operating systems may employ cores in a *functionally dedicated* manner to hide latencies, reduce background noise, speed up system operations, but also for energy savings and heat abstraction. This encompasses system-call dispatching to idle or derated cores [21], offloading of interrupt and event handling, asynchronous I/O completion, or messaging assist [6], or even the serialized execution of critical sections in case of high contention [17,12]. Such a use of cores may be organized statically or dynamically in analogy to remote execution facilities developed for distributed systems in order to temporarily confiscate idle workstations [19].

This present paper is on a *Scalability-Aware Kernel Executive* (SAKE) for many-core processors that has an *interrupt model* at the basis of the design and ends in an event-based, single-stack implementation. In this model, which organizes related designs into members of an operating-system family, kernel functions (released due to system calls or traps) always run to completion, but may be overlapped by concurrent activities of the same core (due to interrupt requests) or caused by other cores. The run-to-completion principle particularly implies non-blocking synchronization of concurrent processes competing for (write access to) shared data structures, which happens *lock-free* [14, p. 2–3] in the present implementation variant of SAKE. The single-stack concept provides the basis for strong process locality while executing within the kernel and, thus, prevents stressing of the caches.

The remainder of this paper is structured as follows. Section 2 motivates the need for scalability-aware operating systems to meet the requirements for (future) heterogeneous many-core processors. This motivation is based on measurements of SAKE prototypes taken on a 48-core machine and their comparison to Linux. Section 3 presents our approach building on these prototypes. First, we describe how to statically analyze hot spots in the prospected energy demand of non-sequential programs in order to emit thread migration hints and recommendations for energy saving and heat abstraction purposes. In a second step we show how to exploit this information at run-time. For this we present the concepts and preliminary design of a scalable application run-time executive in terms of energy and heat demands. Finally, Section 3 draws some conclusions and briefly refers to future work.

2 Know Where the Shoe Pinches

A key issue of parallel programs destined for many-core processors is *scalability*. This is particularly true for operating systems. Utilizing today's parallel processing power is one of the recent challenges in computer science worldwide and the impact of the underlying operating system became increasingly apparent. Experiments with Linux 2.6 on a 16-core processor revealed a tremendous decline in performance by a factor of 40 once a second core was in charge of application processing [3]. Even worse, absolutely no performance increase was encountered when the number of cores increased gradually up to 16.

In order to support the SAKE approach we prototyped LAOS[1] to evaluate new system designs regarding performance and scalability on many-core machines. Our primary focus is on thread scheduling and synchronization on modern x86-64 machines. Two different operating-system kernels were implemented as members of the LAOS family. Both provide basic services such as dynamic creation of threads, thread scheduling and common synchronization primitives like semaphores, mutexes, condition variables and barriers. The members mainly differ in architectural matters: *LAKE* represents a novel multi-core event-based design [7] in terms of a *latency-aware kernel executive* and *MAOS* follows a rather

[1] `https://www4.cs.fau.de/Research/LAOS/`

conventional process-based design [13] of a *many-core operating system kernel.* To provide the operating system services in an inherently parallel environment, all kernel-internal synchronization is performed in a non-blocking fashion by employing atomic instructions of the processor such as compare-and-swap and atomic arithmetic instructions. No spinlocks or similar blocking primitives were used for intra-kernel synchronization. In a similar way deferred interrupt handling is established without blocking synchronization.

Both LAKE and MAOS implement the same core functionality. Hence, from a user's point of view, there are no functional differences observable at the system call layer. The strong argument for such an implementation kicks in with the non-functional property of parallel scalability. Performance measurements revealed a huge benefit in performance when compared to recent Linux/Glibc versions. Parallel application benchmarks were carried out, comparing LAKE, MAOS and Linux on the same machine executing an identical program. In the following, three benchmarks are described as well as the hard- and software environment.

All benchmarks were carried out on a 48-core system with AMD 6180SE processors that run at 2.6 GHz. The system comprises eight cache-coherent NUMA nodes and has an overall amount of 64 GB of RAM. The benchmarks for Linux were taken using kernel version 3.8.0 and the GNU C library 2.17. All benchmark programs were compiled with GCC 4.7.3, as were our two custom kernels.

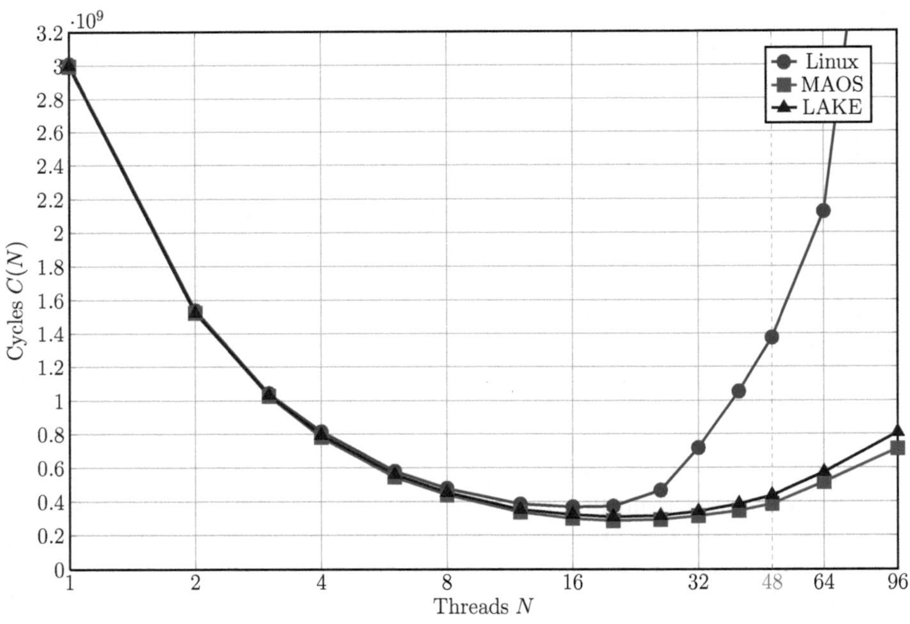

Fig. 1. Parallel iterative Jacobi benchmark, CPU cycles vs. number of threads

The *Jacobi* test uses the correspondent iterative method to solve a boundary value problem in parallel. The problem domain is geometrically split up into

Table 1. Maximum speedup in benchmarks

	Linux	MAOS	LAKE
Jacobi	8.18	10.52	9.75
Dijkstra	5.16	6.88	6.27
ServerClient	12.42	33.69	15.39

Table 2. Number of cores where performance saturates

	Linux	MAOS	LAKE
Jacobi	16	20	20
Dijkstra	12	16	20
ServerClient	16	40	48

stripes. Threads work in parallel on these stripes and blocking synchronization is used to communicate whether common values between neighboring threads and stripes are ready for access. In the *Dijkstra* benchmark the shortest paths between nodes in a weighted graph are computed. Each iteration of the algorithm is carried out in parallel and a synchronization barrier is needed to separate the iteration rounds. Performance in high contention scenarios on synchronization primitives is measured in the *ServerClient* test. Threads contend on mutex and semaphore operations that guard access to shared buffers. The number of buffers, number of threads, and ratio of producers and consumers is adjustable. Here, four producers and one consumer are created per CPU core and two global buffers are accessed by turns. All problem sizes are chosen to fit in the processor caches to eliminate main memory bottlenecks. Clearly, the benchmarks could be made more efficient with regards to synchronization, but our main focus here is on kernel level scalability. The results are comparable, since exactly the same benchmarks were performed on all systems.

All benchmarks show similar results and scaling behavior as observable in Table 1 and 2. Therefore, we only discuss the Jacobi benchmark in greater detail. In Figure 1 two observations can be made: First, the amount of system time with up to eight threads is negligible compared to the computation carried out by the user threads, regardless whether a fully featured Linux system or one of our systems is used. Second, increasing the number of threads reveals the scaling characteristics of the OS kernels themselves and the overall performance of the system is affected. The thread management overhead in Linux quickly leads to a performance drop, In contrast to this, both our kernels are able to push the maximum speedup of the algorithms forward and show a much slower performance degradation when the management overhead becomes prevalent (see Table 1 and Table 2).

These advantages support the aim to design and implement custom system software, or even special purpose systems, where exceptional performance or other superior non-functional properties are crucial. Such scalable kernels can serve as a basis for our application run-time executive as described in Section 3.2. This executive then provides an execution model for applications that in turn can be tuned towards optimizing for non-function properties like energy consumption by employing techniques covered in Section 3.1.

3 The SAKE Approach

In the following we describe the SAKE approach and its benefits for future operating system design. We outline the advantages of our approach over traditional commodity operating system designs, especially for special purpose operation scenarios in which parallel computing tasks are performed on many-core platforms featuring heterogeneous computing cores.

The SAKE architecture consists of two main components: A static code analysis component which exploits symbolic execution to determine prospective run-time behavior of program code and a scalability-aware run-time execution component that efficiently executes these program code snippets by evaluating the run-time hints previously deposited by the static code analysis component. At the example of the ARM big.LITTLE [4] platform we demonstrate how to exploit unique characteristics of upcoming many-core processors most efficiently.

3.1 Proactive Hot-Spot Analysis of Energy Needs

Modern processors designs provide novel features to decrease the energy consumption most effectively. The introduction of new energy saving features has a significant impact on system software as they demand for sophisticated control mechanisms. This task is implemented at operating system level. Software-driven hardware features which are essential to increase energy-efficiency are lying fallow without such low-level support of the system software.

However, semiconductor companies choose different approaches to turn this endeavor into reality. Intel, for example, introduces new sleep states (C-states C6 and C7) for their latest generation of x86 processors (codename Haswell) which allows to reduce the energy consumption during idle periods to a tenth compared to the previous generation of Intel chips. In contrast to this, ARM currently works on multi-core chip designs (ARM big.LITTLE [4]) which feature heterogeneous processing cores that vary significantly with regards to their computing speed and energy demand. Compared to other multi- or many-core processors which have heterogeneous computing cores, the ARM big.LITTLE features heterogeneous computing cores that share the same architecture (ARMv7) but differ in various other aspects. The chip offers powerful Cortex-A15 cores (pipeline with 15 to 24 stages, out-of-order execution) as well as energy-efficient low-performance Cortex-A7 cores (pipeline with 8 to 10 stages, in-order execution). As the Cortex-A7 cores operate 2.3x to 3.8x more energy-efficient than the Cortex-A15 cores, operating systems need to ensure tasks are assigned properly depending on their performance requirements.

To support the operating system at correctly assigning tasks to CPU cores, we are analyzing program code proactively ahead of run-time to determine performance- and energy-hotspots of program code. For this procedure we use the SEEP framework [8] which exploits symbolic execution techniques in order to automatically extract possible program paths and their expected run-time behavior. During this code analysis we extract both, performance and energy requirements of program code at function level. To determine energy estimates for program code, platform-specific energy profiles are being used. These energy profiles allow offline analysis (no manual energy measurements are required) which makes it possible to automate the energy analysis process. In parallel to the energy estimation analysis we are recording performance counter events to extract run-time characteristics. This information reveals the resource and performance demand of each individual code snippet.

The results of the analysis are deposited by means of run-time hints that are later on used by the run-time executive to assign tasks to the most suitable CPU core. Further, the task scheduler can merge these hints with run-time information to improve the task migration strategies during execution.

3.2 Concepts of a Scalability-Aware Run-Time Executive

The application-level execution model of SAKE running on top of the low-level OS-kernel is derived from OctoPOS [16]. It focuses on leveraging micro-parallelism in applications, hence, the run-time system has to deal with a potentially large number of possibly short execution snippets that in principal can be executed in parallel. This leads to the following requirements:

To cope with the large amount of entities, the representation of the individual pieces of a program has to be slim and efficient to both keep the size of the individual item in memory and its initialization time low. As execution snippets can be short, the overhead for switching from one snippet to the next also has to be kept low. Otherwise it would not pay off to split the application into small snippets, as switching overhead would start to dominate the overall run-time of the application program.

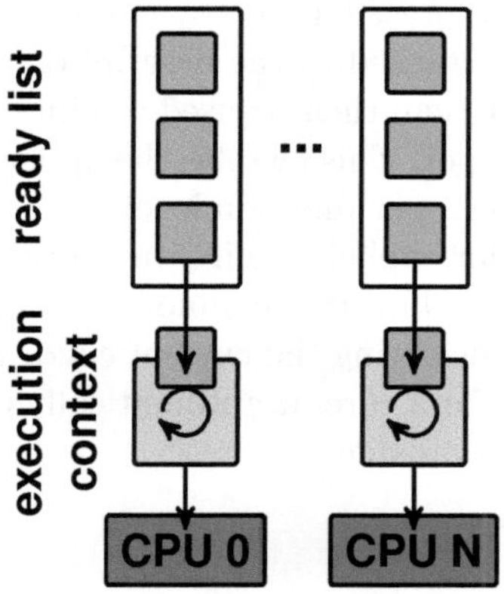

Fig. 2. Normal execution

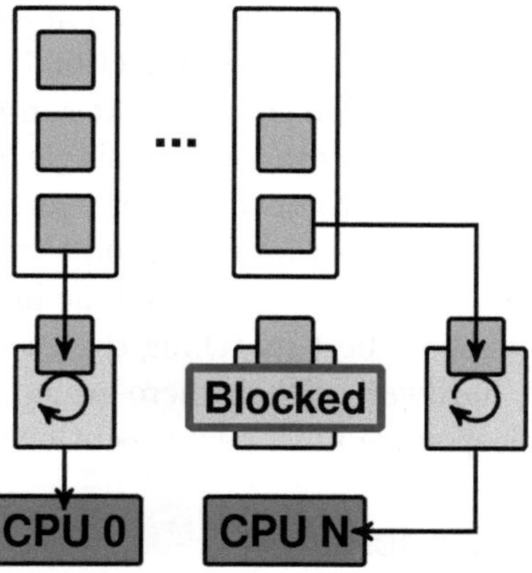

Fig. 3. Handling of blocking operations

Therefore, execution snippets are represented as function pointers with an associated data pointer used to store the arguments. In contrast to traditional threads, however, snippets should have run-to-completion semantics. This enables an implementation where there is no run-time state in form of a stack associated with each snippet. Instead, as can be seen in Fig. 2, execution snippets one after another can be executed atop of execution contexts. Once a snippet finishes, which means its function returns, no state is left within the execution context. So the next item can be executed on the same context just by calling its function pointer without involving a rather costly context switch.

This scheme somewhat resembles Cilk [2] whose execution model enforces strict run-to-completion semantics for its procedures. It works fine as long as execution snippets have run-to-completion semantics and the application programmer takes care of ensuring this property. However, to ease programmability and to provide support for typical parallel design patterns like fork-join execution models, SAKE's run-time executive, however, allows blocking operations. As can be seen in Fig. 3 in the case an execution snippet performs a blocking call, for example to wait for other snippets to complete their execution, the associated execution stack cannot be used to execute the following snippet, as the execution state is still needed on resumption. In this case the executive provides a new stack to execute the following snippets and saves the context of the blocking snippet to the stack of the old context. Consequently, the cost for context switching only has to be paid when the application program really needs it.

The whole model can be implemented in a cooperative fashion, as all participants are entities of the same application. Hence, timing isolation between single execution snippets by employing techniques like time slicing is not necessary. This further contributes to an efficient implementation.

The granularity of execution snippets is application defined and generally provides more control to the programmer than a traditional threaded approach. Apart from exploiting micro-parallelism by massive parallelization, this also can be used to optimize for other, non-functional properties like energy awareness. To leverage the energy efficiency benefits provided by the big.LITTLE hardware platform energy properties for execution snippets can be precalculated by employing the techniques described in Section 3.1. and then attached to the description of the single execution snippets. At run-time, this data can then be used as hints to select a proper core for each single execution snippet. This enables the application programmer to optimize for energy efficiency on a per-function level.

During program execution there is no need for explicitly migrating a program to another core, as this is done implicitly by distributing the annotated snippets to the core best matching the energy profile considering the current condition of the hardware. When there are no snippets left for a core, it automatically enters a sleep state until new execution snippets are available.

4 Conclusion

With future many-core systems, single-threaded cores will be the rule and multi-threaded ones the exception. This calls for a radical change in the way operating systems manage processors respectively processor cores. A key issue of parallel programs destined for many-core processors is *scalability*, and this is particularly true for operating systems. Constructive methods are much-needed that decrease the portion of sequential program sections ideally down to zero.

The SAKE approach presented in the paper has its focus on constructive measures that mainly concern architectural features of operating-system kernels designated to run (massively-parallel) many-core processors. Confirmed by experiments on a 48-core machine with prototyped event-based and process-based operating-system kernels, specialization is the preferred way to go in order to best exploit hardware features in favor of excellent application performance. Linux, by way of example of a prominent representative of an operating system that transforms a many-core processor into a general-purpose (abstract) machine, easily becomes second quality as far as scalability is concerned.

We aim at improving performance of operating-system kernels in strictly application-oriented manner. Particularly this includes measures for energy-efficient execution of software to enable overall system operation in ecological means. SAKE bases on static program analysis to automatically extract run-time hints for energy-aware parallel processing by the kernel. In addition, the kernel complements this with a straw-weight processing model of run-to-completion execution snippets of blocking capabilities to efficiently support fork-join patterns of standard parallel programs—"SAKE wa hyaku-yaku no chō."

References

1. Baumann, A., Barham, P., Dagand, P.-E., Harris, T., Isaacs, R., Peter, S., Roscoe, T., Schüpbach, A., Singhania, A.: The Multikernel: A new OS architecture for scalable multicore systems. In: Matthews, J.N., Anderson, T.E. (eds.) Proceedings of the 22nd ACM Symposium on Operating System Principles (SOSP 2009), pp. 29–44. ACM, New York (2009)
2. Blumofe, R.D., Joerg, C.F., Kuszmaul, B.C., Leiserson, C.E., Randall, K.H., Zhou, Y.: Cilk: An efficient multithreaded runtime system. In: Ferrante, J., Padua, D., Wexelblat, R.L. (eds.) Proceedings of the Fifth ACM SIGPLAN Symposium on Principles and Practice of Parallel Programming (PPoPP 1995), pp. 207–216. ACM, New York (1995)
3. Boyd-Wickizier, S., Chen, H., Chen, R., Mao, Y., Kaashoek, M.F., Morris, R., Pesterev, A., Stein, L., Wu, M., Dai, Y., Zhang, Y., Zhang, Z.: Corey: An operating system for many cores. In: Draves, R., van Renesse, R. (eds.) Proceedings of the 8th USENIX Symposium on Operating Systems Design and Implementation (OSDI 2008), pp. 43–57. USENIX Association, Berkeley (2008)
4. Brian, J. Advances in big.LITTLE technology for power and energy savings. Tech. rep., ARM Ltd. (2012)
5. Brorsson, M.: Scalability and programmability in the manycore era. Draft Synopsis for an EU FP7 STREP Proposal (January 2009)
6. Brüning, U., Giloi, W.K., Schröder-Preikschat, W.: Latency hiding in message-passing architectures. In: Siegel, H.J. (ed.) Proceedings of the 8th International Symposium on Parallel Processing (IPPS 1994), pp. 704–709. IEEE Computer Society, Washington, DC (1994)
7. Drescher, G. Applying eventbbased design principles to a many-core OS kernel. Master's thesis, University of Erlangen-Nuremberg (2012)
8. Hönig, T., Eibel, C., Kapitza, R., Schröder-Preikschat, W.: SEEP: Exploiting symbolic execution for energy-aware programming. In: Proceedings of the Fourth Workshop on Power-Aware Computing and Systems (HotPower 2011), pp. 17–22. ACM, New York (2011)

9. Intel Labs. The SCC platform overview. Rev. 0.80, Intel Corporation (January 2012)
10. IRTS. International technology roadmap for semiconductors (2007), `http://www.itrs.net/Links/2007ITRS/Home2007.htm`
11. Knauerhase, R., Cledat, R., Teller, J.: For extreme parallelism, your OS is sooooo last-millennium. In: Proceedings of the 4th USENIX Workshop of Hot Topics in Parallelism (HotPar 2012). USENIX Association, Berkeley (2012)
12. Lozi, J.-P., David, F., Thomas, G., Lawall, J., Muller, G.: Remote core locking: Migrating critical-section execution to improve the performance of multithreaded applications. In: Heiser, G., Hsieh, W. (eds.) Proceedings of the 2012 USENIX Annual Technical Conference (USENIX ATC 2012), pp. 65–76. USENIX Association, Berkeley (2012)
13. Maier, S.: Leveraging non-blocking synchronization in a process-based many-core OS kernel. Master's thesis, University of Erlangen-Nuremberg (2013)
14. Massalin, H., Pu, C.: A lock-free multiprocessor OS kernel. Tech. Rep. CUCS-005-91, Department of Computer Science, Columbia University, New York, NY 10027, USA (June 1991)
15. NVIDIA Corp. NVIDIA's next generation CUDA compute architecture: Kepler GK110. Whitepaper V1.0 (2012)
16. Oechslein, B., Schedel, J., Kleinöder, J., Bauer, L., Henkel, J., Schröder-Preikschat, W.: OctoPOS: A parallel operating system for invasive computing. In: McIlroy, R., Sventek, J., Harris, T., Roscoe, T. (eds.) Proceedings of the International Workshop on Systems for Future Multi-Core Architectures (SFMA 2011), USB Proceedings of Sixth ACM European Conference on Computer Systems (EuroSys 2011), pp. 9–14 (2011)
17. Suleman, M.A., Mutlu, O., Qureshi, M.K., Patt, Y.N.: Accelerating critical section execution with asymmetric multi-core architectures. In: Soffa, M.L., Irwin, M.J. (eds.) Proceedings of the 14th International Conference on Architectural Support for Programming Languages and Operating Systems (ASPLOS-XIV), pp. 253–264. ACM (2009)
18. Teich, J., Henkel, J., Herkersdorf, A., Schmitt-Landsiedel, D., Schröder-Preikschat, W., Snelting, G.: Invasive computing: An overview. In: Hübner, M., Becker, J. (eds.) Multiprocessor System-on-Chip: Hardware Design and Tool Integration, ch. 11, pp. 241–268. Springer Science+Business Media, Springer, New York (2011)
19. Theimer, M., Lantz, K.A., Cheriton, D.R.: Preemptable remote execution facility for the V-System. In: Baskett, F., Birrell, A., Cheriton, D.R. (eds.) Proceedings of the Tenth ACM Symposium on Operating System Principles (SOSP 1985), pp. 2–12. ACM, New York (1985)
20. Venkatesh, G., Sampson, J., Goulding, N., Garcia, S., Bryksin, V., Lugo-Martinez, J., Swanson, S., Taylor, M.B.: Conservation cores: Reducing the energy of mature computations. In: Hoe, J.C., Adve, V.S. (eds.) Proceedings of the 15th International Conference on Architectural Support for Programming Languages and Operating Systems (ASPLOS-XV), pp. 205–218. ACM (2010)
21. Wentzlaff, D., Agarwal, A.: Factored operating systems (fos): The case for a scalable operating system for multicores. ACM SIGOPS Operating Systems Review 43(2), 76–85 (2009)

Towards Predictability of Operating System Supported Communication for PCIe Based Clusters

Pablo Reble and Georg Wassen

Chair for Operating Systems, RWTH Aachen University, Germany
{reble,wassen}@lfbs.rwth-aachen.de

Abstract. In unconventional clusters, the operating system can provide helper tasks to work around missing hardware features or to improve the performance. We present in this paper a concept of operating system supported data transfer via remote memory access through PCI Express. The performance of such many-core clusters is very sensitive to interferences. We analyze the predictability of on-chip and inter-device data transfers. Using the example of two tightly coupled Intel SCCs, we evaluate our approach with methods of real-time research.

1 Introduction

Using graphics cards for general purpose computing tasks introduced the use of PCI Express (PCIe) coupled processing devices for high performance computing (HPC). The Intel Xeon Phi is a recent example that this trend continues. Today, available coprocessor cards based on the Intel Many Integrated Core (MIC) architecture have about 60 cores with 4-way hyper-threading running an embedded Linux and can by default not be used as a standalone system. Resulting unconventional clusters possess a certain heterogeneity and can consist of multiple coherency islands with small to large processor cores. Unconventional means in this context that systems contain components that are not conventionally used today in HPC and have not been developed or were not primarily intended for this use.

Programming models and effective communication are open issues for such systems. Available devices are massively parallel and able to execute hundreds of threads in parallel. But, for instance limited single thread performance of a small core can become a bottleneck for communication, which can degrade the overall system performance. Regarding such a scenario, remote memory access of a small core can be accelerated by invocation of a large core. A further use case for Operating System (OS) supported communication is the emulation of missing hardware support on device side.

The Intel Single-chip Cloud Computer (SCC) is a 48 core research processor and realized as a PCI Express device. In its nature as a research processor, it provides flexibility for the realization of a virtual on-chip network extension, as demonstated by building a Cluster of two SCCs [1].

D. an Mey et al. (Eds.): Euro-Par 2013 Workshops, LNCS 8374, pp. 833–842, 2014.

In this setup, a proxy task is running on the front-end of the PCI Express device. This task being part of the operating system driver serves communication requests of the SCC cores and thereby transparently extends its functionality. The contribution of the paper is the analysis of the predictability in such a communication scenario and optimizations to the communication task. Due to hardware limitations, the emulation of a Cluster-of-Clusters consisting of multiple SCC systems requires a proxy on host side and therefore builds an excellent base for this analysis.

The next section covers related work for the approach to address on-chip non-coherent shared memory through memory-mapped network interconnects. The remainder of this paper is structured as follows: In Section 3, we describe basics of the Intel SCC research platform, including on-chip and inter-device communication through Remote Memory Access (RMA). In Section 4, we analyze the timing behavior of on-chip and inter-device communication for non-coherent memory-coupled cores regarding different load situations. Section 5 summarizes this paper and gives an outlook for future work.

2 Previous Work

The Single-chip Cloud Computer (SCC) experimental processor [2] is a *concept vehicle* created by Intel Labs as a platform for many-core software research. This so called Cluster-on-Chip architecture waives cache coherency and provides hardware support for message passing. The combination of this experimental processor architecture and RCCE [3], a simple message-passing environment, builds a platform for many-core software research.

A simple and pessimistic approach to overcome the missing cache-coherency is to enable caches only for private memory regions and disable caches for shared memory regions. Obviously, the latter will lead to a performance drawback. Moreover, weaker memory models can be managed in software without major changes to the application software [4]. RCCE targets a one-sided communication system, consisting of software controlled on-chip memory which is used for classic two sided message-passing communication. Nevertheless, one sided communication and synchronization can be more effectively implemented if the underlying hardware architecture is taken into account [5]. For busy wait synchronization schemes, we figured out that a quantified back-off is very useful to avoid a highly contended on-chip mesh interconnect, which can lead to a starvation of cores with a high communication distance. Furthermore, hierarchical synchronization algorithms can be used to avoid situations with a high concurrency [6,7].

The idea of a virtual expansion of an on-die network across systems to emulate a CPU with up to hundreds of cores has been introduced by Gries et al. [8] using high-speed serial I/O connectors on the board. Extending the functionality of the host driver to act as a proxy follows the identical approach and has the advantage that the SCC hardware systems including its FPGA remain unchanged. However, this pure software solution leads to a communication latency which is about one magnitude higher than on-chip access and introduces a certain jitter because of the invocation of a proxy task in the host's operating system. Nevertheless, the presented prototype [1] has been realized and enables a virtual expansion of the on-die network across SCC systems.

The effect of execution time jitter onto large parallel applications has been identified and understood long ago [9]. Most analyses come to the conclusion that the operating system is a major source of *system noise* and show ways to circumvent it mostly by reducing interrupts [10] either via modification of a common operating system or by running specialized, reduced kernels.

3 Intel Single-Chip Cloud Computer

The SCC is a recent example for a Cluster-on-Chip architecture with 48 general purpose processing units on a single die, arranged in 24 tiles on a two dimensional mesh. This experimental many-core architecture provides message-passing support with software controlled on-chip SRAM. Due to the intended use is as a communication buffer for implicit message passing, this memory is called Message Passing Buffer (MPB).

To control shared access to non-coherently cached memory such as the MPB, a special instructions to selectively invalidate tagged data has been added to the instruction set. As a result, private memory regions of a certain core can be excluded from being invalidated. Except the first level cache, this tagged data bypasses the caches. Because of the applied write through policy for tagged data, a write combining buffer is used for this tagged data to accelerate continuing write accesses that hit the same cache-line and transfer those data as a burst.

3.1 SCC System

The SCC system has been implemented as a PCI Express device instead of a standalone system, i. e. a coprocessor. Because of its hardware dimensions, an expansion card has to be used to connect the external SCC case to a host PC, called Management Console PC (MCPC).

The SCC processor cores are not able to directly send a data packet to another PCI Express device without host invocation. Routing of the on-chip network is pre-computed and highly optimized because of its major impact to the overall system performance. As a result, the proprietary network packet format prevents a possible encoding of a remote destination other than the host via the PCI Express interconnect. Another limitation represents the SCC cores being based on the classic 32 bit in-order Pentium architecture (P54C) with only one outstanding memory request. This implicates a translation of physical core (32 bit) to system addresses (46 bit). To perform this translation, a configurable Lookup Table (LUT) with 256 entries is used.

For the realization of a transparent interconnect, Lookup Table entries have been used to map off-device memory. As a result, a proxy task on the host can generate remote requests, that address a specific page frame. Multiple devices transparently map the on-chip communication buffer of a remote device, which enables the use of the native programming interface RCCE. However, the default communication scheme heavily using remote read access for communication must be changed to achieve a good performance based on a strictly transparent memory-mapped interconnect [1].

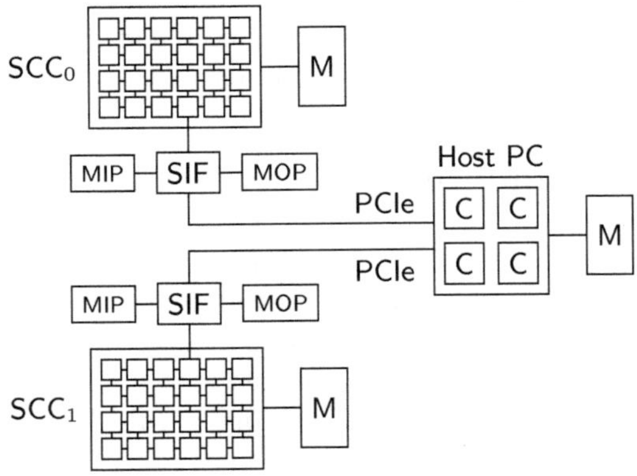

Fig. 1. Inter-Device Communication concept

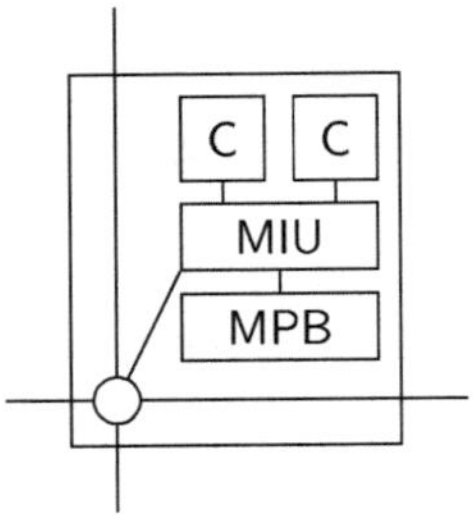

Fig. 2. Tile block diagram

Figure 1 shows the resulting setup of the multi coprocessor prototype which are connected through PCI Express to a shared host PC (MCPC). The off-chip System Interface (SIF), which is implemented in an FPGA, handles the communication between the SCC processor and the host. The option to generate automatic write acknowledges significantly decreases the latency for a remote write access. Unlike reading, write accesses to a remote SCC can be interleaved, which makes the remote write operation preferable for the communication of multiple SCCs.

RCCE [3] has the option to be used without operating system support. Various bare-metal projects use RCCE variants for communication. As a light-weight communication library, RCCE uses the MPB buffers for data transfer. The default communication protocol is based on a *local-put remote get* communication scheme. A blocking communication with `RCCE_send()` and `RCCE_recv()` works as follows: First, the sender puts the message to its local communication buffer. Second, for the indication of this event, the sender toggles a flag at the receiver's side. Finally, the sender waits for the indication that the receiver has copied the message to its private memory. This basic communication scheme has the advantage that each core exclusively writes to its local communication buffer, which simplifies the synchronization model.

3.2 Communication

Traditionally, a Remote Memory Access (RMA) is non-uniform in a cluster environment regarding the latencies of read and write operations. Obviously, for a Cluster-on-Chip architecture, access costs to non-coherent but shared memory regions can also differ for orders of magnitude, dependent on their physical location (on-chip SRAM, off-chip DRAM, or inter-device e. g. via PCI Express).

On-chip. Cluster-on-chip architectures with software controlled on-chip memory can be interpreted as a basic one-sided communication system. Remote Memory Access represents a method to further expand this model to memory-mapped interconnects as a transparent communication path. Regarding the implementation of a Coprocessor as a PCI Express device, the memory-mapped interconnect is already built-in and provides a low-latency access in the sub-microseconds range.

A virtual expansion of the on-die network has to use the proprietary packet format of the SCC platform on host as well as on device side that uses high-speed serial I/O or PCI Express as the base data transfer layer. Focusing the realization through a proxy task, a memory access of the processor cores is translated and routed in hardware through the on-die interconnect the same way as a remote access which is routed in software.

Inter-device. A disadvantage especially for a multi-device cluster is the default use of *remote get* for the realization of two sided communication in RCCE. In a multi-device environment, Remote Memory Access can be used to map remote communication buffers in a transparent way. However, a further increasing communication distance in such an environment makes *remote put* the preferable method to transfer data. An analysis of a *remote put* communication scheme has shown [1], that a simple proxy task which virtually extends the on-chip network by just forwarding network packets, needs a change of the communication scheme to obtain acceptable performance.

3.3 Operating System Supported Communication

Each SCC has its own proxy task which handles network packets that target another device. The tasks can send to both SCCs, to answer requests and forward packets. They are started as kernel threads and use Direct Memory Access (DMA) for communication to the SCC device. The original driver uses interrupts to signal completion of DMA transfers. In this mode, the advantage is that the load on the host CPU is fairly low. Disadvantage is a higher communication latency, as the analysis shows, which is presented in the next section. For the intended use of the communication task, this behavior is acceptable. For instance, load an operating system to the memory of the SCC device, change its configuration and debugging.

Now, extending the functionality of the communication task to a proxy which is used to connect multiple SCC devices, changes the requirements. A low and predictable latency becomes more important. Therefore, we implemented an optimized mode, which uses active polling while waiting for events to avoid context switches and keep the latency as low as possible. Additionally, receiving network packets from the SCC is done by polling the SIF for incoming messages. On notification, the data is read from the MOP (cf. Fig. 1) to a local buffer and processed. To send network packets from the host to an SCC, the proxy task waits for the disposition of the MIP and copies its data to the SIF that will forward it to the target.

4 Evaluation

The evaluation is split into a theoretical examination of the timing and benchmarks to provide appropriate values.

4.1 Timing Analysis

The timing of the communication within the exemplary non-coherent system (on-chip and on-device) as well as between two such systems coupled via a proxy task on the host PC (inter-device) is not only dependent on the jitter originating from system software such as interrupts, but also depends on hardware effects, for example caches and contended shared data paths.

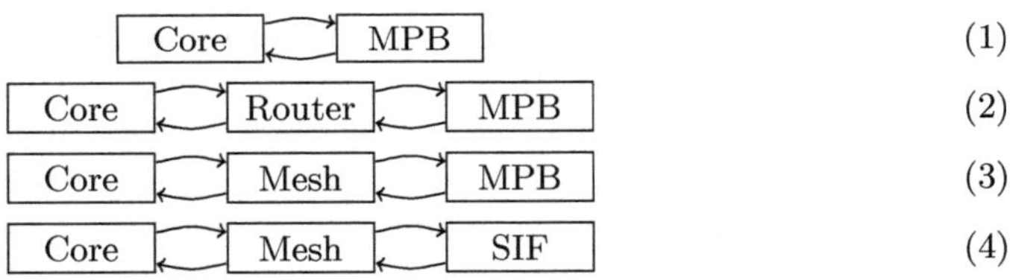

Fig. 3. On- and off-chip communication schemes: (1) local MPB (bypass), (2) local MPB (no bypass), (3) remote MPB, (4) SIF registers (off-chip)

The on-device communication (on- and off-chip) can be divided into four cases (Fig. 3). Case (1) is the access to the local Message-Passing Buffer (MPB). The core uses load and store instructions to access a physical address that is located directly at the same tile. While this access would not expect any jitter, a hardware bug prevents its usage [11, p. 8]. Any access to the local MPB must cross the router (2) where it is potentially influenced from traffic on the mesh network. The MIU accesses the router (Fig. 2) with a request-grant protocol [2] so that the timing of an access back to the local MPB has an upper bound. Reading a value over the mesh network is implemented with request and answer packets. Writing transfers the value and waits for an acknowledge. Thus, the access to a remote MPB (i. e. on a different tile) requires two network packets on the mesh (3) that certainly are affected by other transfers. Finally, the off-chip (but still on-device) access to registers located in the SIF (4) may additionally be obstructed by the logic implemented in an FPGA.

The inter-device communication (Fig. 4) can access memory of the host PC (5) and the Message-Passing Buffers of another SCC (6, 7). The elementary transfers

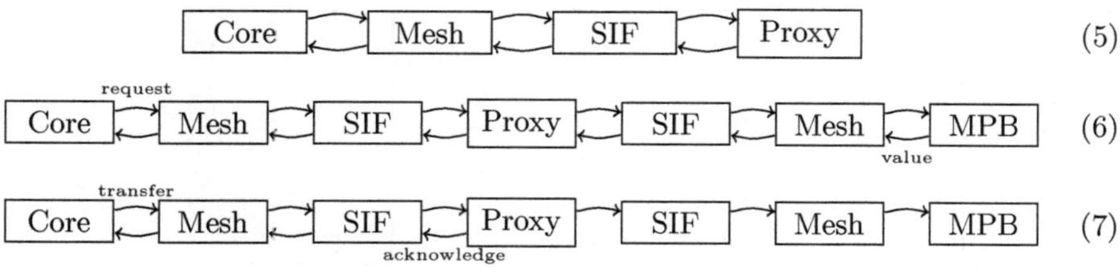

Fig. 4. Inter-device communication schemes: (5) host PC (memory or virtual register), (6) inter-device MPB read (*remote get*), (7) inter-device MPB write (*remote put*)

to and from the SIF are subject to the same jitter as on-device communication. Between the SIF and the proxy task is a PCI Express connection with a latency above 2 000 ticks (aprox. 4 μs). The anticipated source of the largest jitter is the proxy task on the host PC itself. During processing, the polling for following messages is delayed. Further, the proxy task can be interrupted or blocked by the scheduler. As writing to a different device (*remote put*) is acknowledged by the proxy task (7), not only the average latency is better, but also the additional jitter of the rest of the transfer is cut off.

Generally, hardware jitter is difficult to avoid. Some influence can be reduced by carefully placing the tasks considering data streams. Gaps in the execution with a factor even in the range of 10 to 100 impose very little overhead to the overall execution time of a single core if they occur very seldom. But as shown by Tsafrir et al., the occasional interrupt of one of a large number of tightly synchronized processes has a larger impact on the parallel application [9].

4.2 Benchmarks

To support the previous theoretical analyses and to understand the dimensions, components, and sources of jitter, the following low-level benchmarks are executed in a strictly controlled environment. All cores[1] have booted a Linux instance and RCCE processes are started on all of them. All processes block interrupts during the benchmark by clearing the interrupt flag. For our benchmark process, this mimics bare-metal execution. In the idle scenarios, other processes spin locally on their time-stamp counter to avoid side-effects. Load is generated by spinning on a register located at the tile containing cores 6 and 7 where the SIF is connected to generate mesh transfers without loading the internal SIF logic. All times were taken with the low-overhead RDTSC instruction and presented in CPU cycles (ticks).

The on-device latencies of an idle SCC are presented in Table 1. The small jitter (difference between maximum and minimum) of the SCC hardware makes execution predictable, even for on-chip accesses to remote MPBs. Each network hop adds approximately 8 ticks to the latency. Repeating the test from Core 0[2]

[1] Running with (core/mesh/memory) frequencies in MHz: (533/800/800).
[2] Located at the tile in bottom left corner of the 6x4 2D mesh.

Destination	Network hops	latency (ticks) min.	max.
local MPB	0	75	77
remote MPB	3	127	134
SIF	1	188	197
SIF	2	194	204
SIF	3	202	209
SIF	4	205	215
SIF	7	223	230

Table 1. On-device latencies on idle system

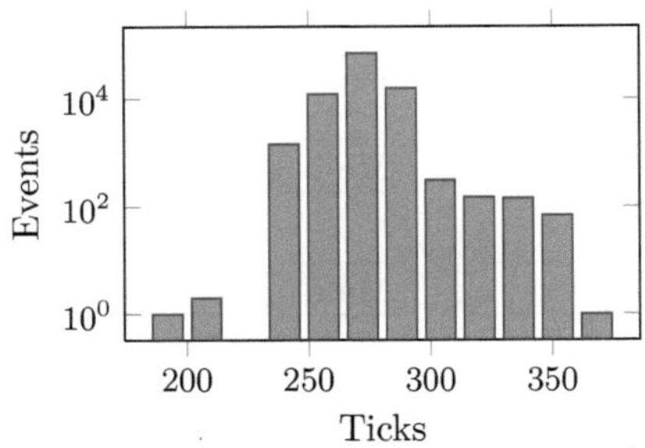

Fig. 5. Latency distribution of Core 0 access to the SIF under max. mesh load.

to the remote MPB over 3 network hops with varying load results in latencies of 175–298 ticks. The load was generated by mesh transfers from a different number of other cores to a register on the same tile where the MPB used for the test is located. This stresses the router and the MIU, but not the target MPB.

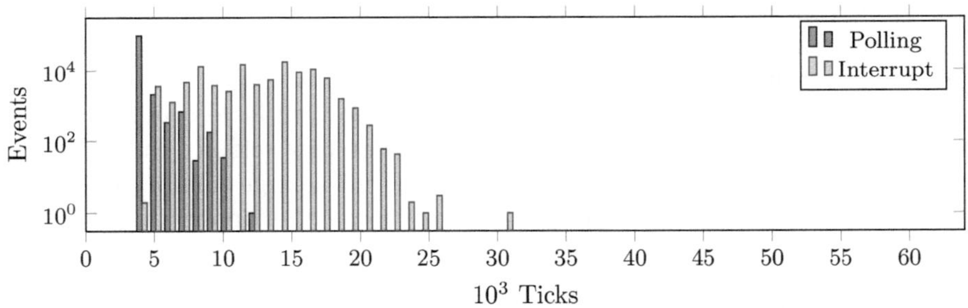

Fig. 6. Latency distribution of Core 0 accessing the proxy task (MCPC idle)

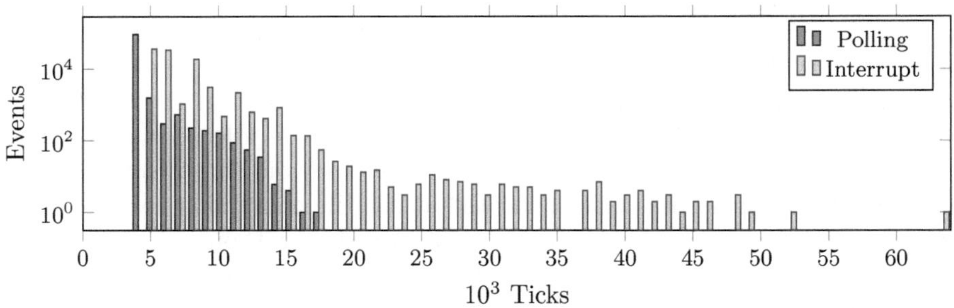

Fig. 7. Latency distribution of Core 0 accessing the proxy task (MCPC load)

The access to the SIF[3] from Core 0 under maximum mesh load is subject to greater but still manageable jitter (Fig. 5). The average access time becomes

[3] Located at bottom (connected to the third rightmost tile) on the 6x4 2D mesh.

slower than on an idle chip depending on the mesh load as well as the location of the memory access.

A core accessing memory locations served by the proxy task (inter-device) is subject to even more jitter. These tests were executed on an idle SCC (Fig. 6) and with heavy load (i. e. compiling the Linux kernel on all CPUs) on the MCPC (Fig. 7) where the jitter is caused by the SIF itself and the proxy task. As shown in Table 1, the jitter of the path up to the SIF is very low (205–215 ticks). Thus, the variation in latencies above 5 000 ticks can only originate from the overhead of the PCI Express transfers and the execution time of the proxy task itself on the host CPU. The larger events above 20 000 ticks are interrupts and scheduling effects on the loaded host system. In the default Interrupt mode (▯▯), the proxy task is subject to a larger distribution of latencies and a higher influence on system load. In the optimized Polling mode (▮▮), the proxy task uses 100 % CPU time which is less efficient for other programs on the MCPC but reduces the inter-device communication latency and the impact of load. This difference is significant for real-time applications as well as beneficial for massively parallel applications. This shows that optimizing the proxy task to use polling instead of interrupts and reserving dedicated CPUs of the MCPC helps improving the inter-device communication.

5 Conclusion and Outlook

The analysis of low-level timing details has shown a good timely predictability of a tiled Network-on-Chip based architecture using in-order processor cores, exemplarily for the Intel SCC which can even be rated suitable for soft real-time applications. The predictability holds true for constraining the access to local resources and reducing access to remote MPBs and memory. Every real-time task needs at least some input or output to work on (either data or access to sensors/actors). These transfers need to be analyzed with regard to concurrent transfers on the mesh network to finally assess real-time suitability.

The inter-device communication either with the host PC or in Cluster-of-Clusters settings is subject to larger jitter requiring a very pessimistic estimation of the worst-case execution times. The proxy task is part of the operating system driver of the PCI Express device and currently running in a kernel thread with standard priority. This can be improved in the future by applying isolation methods [12,13] to the host operating system to reduce the disruption of the proxy task as far as possible. Besides increasing the scheduling priority, a promising enhancement is the isolation of the kernel thread. That means pinning it to a dedicated core, moving all other processes away and configuring hardware interrupts to be served on different cores. Further reducing the remaining interrupts (timer, inter-processor) would require the modification of the host PC's Linux kernel.

Acknowledgment. Pablo Reble was supported by an Intel PhD fellowship.

References

1. Reble, P., Clauss, C., Riepen, M., Lankes, S., Bemmerl, T.: Connecting the Cloud: Transparent and Flexible Communication for a Cluster of Intel SCCs. In: Proceedings of the Many-core Applications Research Community (MARC) Symposium at RWTH, Aachen, Germany, RWTH Aachen University (November 2012)
2. Intel Corporation: SCC External Architecture Specification (EAS), Revision 1.1 (November 2010)
3. Mattson, T., van der Wijngaart, R.: RCCE: a Small Library for Many-Core Communication. Intel Corporation. Software 2.0-release (January 2011)
4. Lankes, S., Reble, P., Clauss, C., Sinnen, O.: Revisiting Shared Virtual Memory Systems for Non-Coherent Memory-Coupled Cores. In: Proceedings of the 2012 International Workshop on Programming Models and Applications for Multicores and Manycores (PMAM 2012) in Conjunction with the 17th ACM SIGPLAN Symposium on Principles and Practice of Parallel Programming (PPoPP 2012), New Orleans, LA, USA (February 2012)
5. Reble, P., Clauss, C., Lankes, S.: One-sided Communication and Synchronization for Non-Coherent Memory-Coupled Cores. In: Proceedings of the 2013 International Conference on High Performance Computing and Simulation (HPCS 2013), Helsinki, Finland (July 2013)
6. Reble, P., Lankes, S., Clauss, C., Bemmerl, T.: A Fast Inter-Kernel Communication and Synchronization Layer for MetalSVM. In: Proceedings of the 3rd MARC Symposium. KIT Scientific Publishing, Ettlingen (2011)
7. Reble, P., Lankes, S., Zeitz, F., Bemmerl, T.: Evaluation of Hardware Synchronization Support of the SCC Many-Core Processor (poster paper). In: 4th USENIX Workshop on Hot Topics in Parallelism (HotPar 2012), Berkeley, CA, USA (June 2012)
8. Gries, M., Hoffmann, U., Konow, M., Riepen, M.: SCC: A Flexible Architecture for Many-Core Platform Research. Computing in Science & Engineering 13(6), 79–83 (2011)
9. Tsafrir, D., Etsion, Y., Feitelson, D.G., Kirkpatrick, S.: System Noise, OS Clock Ticks, and Fine-Grained Parallel Applications. In: Proceedings of the 19th Annual International Conference on Supercomputing, ICS 2005, pp. 303–312. ACM, New York (2005)
10. Morari, A., Gioiosa, R., Wisniewski, R., Cazorla, F., Valero, M.: A Quantitative Analysis of OS Noise. In: 2011 IEEE International Parallel Distributed Processing Symposium (IPDPS), pp. 852–863 (2011)
11. Intel Corporation: The SCC Programmer's Guide, Revision 1.0 (January 2012)
12. Wassen, G., Lankes, S., Bemmerl, T.: Real-Time on Many-Core Systems – Where real-time and high-performance can benefit from each other (poster abstract). In: Proceedings of the Many-core Applications Research Community (MARC) Symposium at RWTH, Aachen, Germany, RWTH Aachen University (November 2012)
13. Wassen, G., Lankes, S., Bemmerl, T.: Harte Echtzeit für Anwendungsprozesse in Standard-Betriebssystemen auf Mehrkernprozessoren. In: Herausforderungen durch Echtzeitbetrieb - Echtzeit 2011, Boppard, Germany, pp. 39–48. Springer (2012)

Sixth Workshop on UnConventional High Performance Computing (UCHPC 2013)

Jens Breitbart, Anders Hast, and Josef Weidendorfer

Program Chairs

Recent issues with the power consumption of conventional HPC hardware resulted in new interest in both accelerator hardware and low-power mass-market hardware. The most prominent examples are GPUs, yet FPGAs, DSPs and other embedded designs may also provide higher power efficiency for HPC applications, as they are used in energy-restricted environments, such as smartphones or tablets. The so-called "dark silicon" forecast, i.e. not all transistors can be active at the same time, may lead to even more specialized hardware in future mass-market products. Exploiting this hardware for HPC can be a worthwhile challenge. As the word "UnConventional" in the title suggests, the workshop focuses on usage of hardware or platforms for HPC, which are not (yet) conventionally used today, and may not be designed for HPC in the first place. Reasons for its use can be raw computing power, good performance per watt, or low cost. To address this unconventional hardware, often, new programming approaches and paradigms are required to make best use of it. A second focus of the workshop is on innovative, (yet) unconventional new programming models. To this end, UCHPC tries to capture solutions for HPC which are unconventional today, but could become conventional and significant tomorrow, and thus provide a glimpse into the future of HPC.

This year was the 6th time the UCHPC workshop took place, and it is the 4th time in a row it is co-located with Euro-Par (each year since 2010). Before that, it was held in conjunction with the *International Conference on Computational Science and Its Applications 2008* and with the *ACM International Conference on Computing Frontiers 2009*. However, UCHPC is a perfect addition to the scientific fields of Euro-Par, and this is confirmed by the continuous interest we see among Euro-Par attendees for this workshop. While the general focus of the workshop is fixed, the topic actually is a moving target. For example, GPUs were quite unconventional for HPC a few years ago, but today a notable portion of the machines in the Top500 list are making use of them. Currently, the exploitation of mobile processors for HPC – including on-chip GPU and DSPs – are a hot topic, and we originally planned for an fitting invited talk on the EU Mont-Blanc project. Also, FPGAs slowly get more interesting for HPC due to increased productivity – the topic of our 2nd invited talk this year.

Regarding scientific research papers, we got fourteen submissions this year. Out of them, five papers were accepted by our rigorous program committee. Further, we invited Oliver Pell from Maxeler Technologies to give a talk about FPGA usage for HPC, and a spontaneously organized panel about "How to solve the power issue for future HPC systems?". This replaced the talk about the EU Mont-Blanc project due to an unforeseen unavailability of Daniele Tafani

D. an Mey et al. (Eds.): Euro-Par 2013 Workshops, LNCS 8374, pp. 843–844, 2014.

(Leibniz Supercomputing Centre). The reason for the lively discussion in the panel, and the positive feedback we got from the audience surely was due to the high-profile panelists who agreed to join in the last minute: Satoshi Matsuoka (Tokyo Institute of Technology), Tim Mattson (Intel), Oliver Pell (Maxeler Technologies), Martin Schulz (Lawrence Livermore National Laboratory), and Carsten Trinitis (Technische Universität München and University of Bedfordshire). For the first time, we arranged for a best paper award. The winning paper is "PyDac: A Resilient Run-time Framework for Divide-and-Conquer Applications on a Heterogeneous Many-core Architecture" by B. Huang, R. Sass, N. Debardeleben, and S. Blanchard. Congratulations! In addition to a handcrafted trophy (special thanks go out to our good guys from the workshop of the computer architecture chair at TUM), there was a special reward: a laptop with an AMD APU processor, sponsored by AMD (thanks to Ren Wu from our steering committee for this arrangement).

These post-workshop proceedings include the final versions of the papers presented at UCHPC and accepted for publication. They take the feedback from reviewers and workshop audience into account. The organizers want to thank the authors of the papers. Without them, the workshop would not exist. We sincerely thank the Euro-Par 2013 team for providing the opportunity to arrange the workshop in conjunction with the conference, and would like to thank them for a very nice environment and the perfect organization. Further, we appreciate the hard work of the members of our International Program Committee. They again did a perfect job at reviewing the submissions. Last but not least, we thank the — again — large number of attendees this year. They contributed to a lively day. Based on the positive feedback, the organizers and the steering committee plan to continue the UCHPC workshop in conjunction with Euro-Par 2014.

September 2013

Jens Breitbart
Anders Hast
Josef Weidendorfer

PyDac: A Resilient Run-Time Framework for Divide-and-Conquer Applications on a Heterogeneous Many-Core Architecture

Bin Huang[1], Ron Sass[1], Nathan DeBardeleben[2,*], and Sean Blanchard[2,*]

[1] Reconfigurable Computing Systems Lab
University of North Carolina at Charlotte
{bhuang2,rsass}@uncc.edu
[2] Ultrascale Systems Research Center
Los Alamos National Laboratory,
High Performance Computing Division, Los Alamos NM 87544, USA
{ndebard,seanb}@lanl.gov

Abstract. Heterogeneous many-core architectures that consist of big cores and small cores promise a good balance between single-thread performance and multi-thread throughput. Such systems impose challenges on the runtime system design. One such challenge is the reliability of the hardware and it is likely that the runtime system will need to contain faults and reduce the chance of a fault from propagating.

We propose a Python-based run-time framework called *PyDac*. PyDac supports a two-level programming model based on the divide-and-conquer strategy. This framework isolates all of data that a small core is working on. Therefore, a faulty small core can be reset independently and the task restarted. To test this run-time, an unconventional heterogeneous architecture consisting of PowerPC and ARM cores was emulated on an FPGA. We demonstrate feasibility of this runtime design with Strassen's algorithm.

Keywords: Heterogeneous Many-core Architecture, FPGA, Runtime System, Resilience.

1 Introduction

Power constraints have led to technologies such as aggressive supply voltage scaling [15] and asymmetric many-core architecture [6,13]. Since some of these techniques will make the devices more susceptible to faults, additional attention to system resilience is required. Presently, two trends have emerged to address this concern. First, is the increased reliance on checkpoint/restart. As the number of cores increase (both cores per chip and cores per system) and the rate of errors

* A portion of this work was performed at the Ultrascale Systems Research Center (USRC) at Los Alamos National Laboratory, supported by the U.S. Department of Energy contract DE-FC02-06ER25750. The publication has been assigned the LANL identifier LA-UR-13-24170.

D. an Mey et al. (Eds.): Euro-Par 2013 Workshops, LNCS 8374, pp. 845–854, 2014.

increases, the frequency and volume of the system state that needs to be stored to non-volatile memory becomes intractable [7]. Second, the use of higher levels of abstraction (by adding layers to the software stack) increases system brittleness because it continues to assume that routine failures are handled below it rather than above it. Unfortunately, neither of these trends are sustainable.

Moreover, the sheer number of parallel cores in future chips will continue to overwhelm current memory hierarchies, creating a situation where the memory subsystem limits the rate of computation, not the availability of parallelism or clock rate. To address this, some have suggested software controlled data movement (rather than hardware controlled) in the memory hierarchy. A recent development has suggested message passing through non-cache-coherent shared memory as programming model [16]. Others have proposed radically new memory hierarchies. For example, in the Fresh Breeze project, Dennis *et al.* propose a view of main memory as a collection of write-once memory chunks [9]. The write-once principle frees programmers from maintaining the consistency of shared objects and leads to a functional view of memory because one parallel task will not overwrite the internal memory of another task.

In this paper, we assume a view of main memory that is similar to Fresh Breeze. Specifically, we assume a flatter memory hierarchy that consists of a set of simple processor cores. Each core has multiple independent scratch-pad memories (locally byte-addressable blocks of memory) that are actively managed. In contrast, the conventional memory subsystem consists of a hierarchy of reactive caches. This arrangement is interesting to us because if the cores are oversubscribed with tasks, it allows the memory subsystem to transfer data to one scratch-pad while another task is executing on another. This allows for better utilization of the off-chip memory bandwidth and helps hide latency.

In addition to these simple cores that are intended to provide increased throughput to the system (tasks completed per second), the chip architecture includes some very fast, complex cores. The latter are present to reduce single task latency and might be hardened to protect against faults. To distinguish between the two, the small, simple cores are called *green cores* and the large, fast ones are called *white cores.* An on-chip network connects the green cores to the novel memory subsystem described earlier while the white cores have a conventional memory hierarchy. The two memory subsystems share the (off-chip) DRAM memory resources through a multi-ported memory controller.

Given this unconventional architecture, one of the fundamental questions for a runtime system is how to contain faults to a single core and reduce the chance of a fault propagating from the current task to a future task. To address this issue, we propose a Python-based runtime framework called *PyDac.* The distributed design allows every green core to operate independently allowing a faulty green core to be reset individually and the lost task is restarted with its original input.

In order for this to work, the programming model must be able to create a large number of small, independent tasks. PyDac accomplishes this with a two-level programming model. At the top, programs use a divide-and-conquer strategy to decompose the problem into smaller subproblems and then it recursively calls itself on the subproblems. The recursion continues until the problem is small enough that a direct solution on a green core is possible. (This direct solution is called the base case in divide-and-conquer.) In this model, the recursion follows a functional style of programming that fits the write-once memory model, identifies the parallelism, and decomposes the data. At the low level, the base problem can be solved using an imperative style which is strongly embraced by the computational science community. Thus, the programming model follows a historically successful approach of using productivity-enhancing techniques (such as object-oriented programming with C++/Java and communicating sequential processing with MPI) at the high-level coupled with imperative-style programming at the low-level.

The PyDac runtime supports this programming model by starting the application on a Python virtual machine running on a white core with a modern, full-featured operating system. When the base case is invoked, a thread is created, the bytecodes, and inputs are assigned to a green core. Running on the green core is a Python virtual machine. The green core's virtual machine was originally designed for embedded systems and does not require an operating system. Once the memory transfer is complete, the virtual machine executes the byte codes and the return value of the function becomes a new (read-only) memory segment.

To understand the viability of the proposed runtime, the *green-white* architecture has been implemented on an FPGA using PowerPC processor for a white core and ARM processors for multiple green cores. This hardware was intended to represent a mix of energy-efficient, simple cores and fast, conventional processor cores. The rest of the paper is organized as follows. Section 2 details the design and implementation of PyDac. Strassen's Algorithm is a well-known divide-and-conquer algorithm and section 3 uses it to evaluate PyDac. Section 4 discusses the related works. Section 5 concludes the paper and discusses future directions we are taking this research.

2 Design and Implementation

2.1 Runtime Design

Based on the assumption of architectural changes, we designed the PyDac runtime system so that it is capable of enforcing resilient execution and running on heterogeneous hardware. Fig. 1 presents a very high-level view of this design. The *green-white* architecture combines cores with different characteristics. Running on each of these cores are one or more tasks that are independent and parallel.

We presume tasks running on green cores are lightweight and stateless and that the runtime system isolates all of the data that the tasks are working on. Therefore, fault confinement and recovery of green cores is local. For example, recovery of green cores can be done by a software reset as well as a task re-assignment. A replicated process running on another green core can detect or

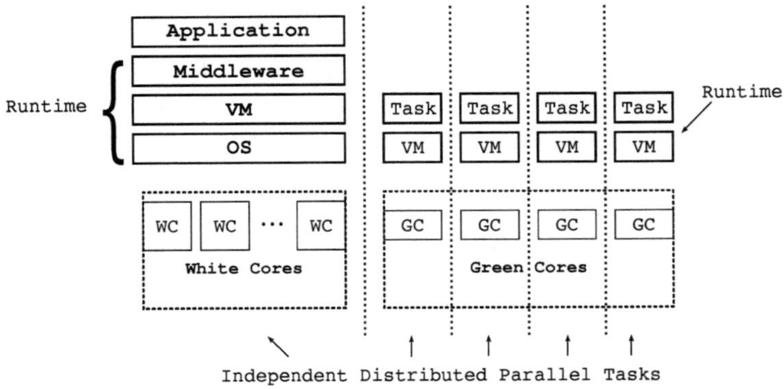

Fig. 1. Proposed resilient runtime system on *green-white* architecture

prevent a fault from further propagation by voting. Once local recovery is performed, the runtime system restores the parent-child link for a recovered task and reuses the orphan task [20]. On the other hand, white cores are designed with less aggressive voltage scaling. They are also built on more reliable, tested hardware and have a non-trivial amount of die space dedicated to fault detection and recovery. We expect faults on white cores and interconnect to be rare events. Heavy-weight tasks running on them will be backed by remote storage (either remote memory or non-volatile storage).

Heterogeneous hardware that is either an application-specific instruction processor (ASIP) or programmable hardware can result in better performance and power efficiency than conventional, general-purpose hardware[8]. However, adoption of heterogeneous hardware normally increases programming effort in three aspects: a) explicit memory management, b) programming for separate instruction set architectures (ISAs), and c) programming with cumbersome languages (e.g. hardware description language for programmable logic). To tackle this problem, our runtime system treats heterogeneous hardware as functional blocks which solely consume input and produce output. We expect these functional blocks are programmed by performance tuning experts. It is the responsibility of the runtime system to manage data movement between these functional blocks. Also, in our runtime system, we use virtual machine bytecode as an abstraction layer for separate ISAs.

2.2 PyDac Implementation

Based on the design goals, PyDac has been implemented with a number of key features:

- Runtime system is distributed as multiple virtual machines (VMs)
- Operating system (OS) layer is removed from the software stack on green cores
- A user-level thread library provides programming model support

– It reuses Python modules popular in computational science community such as Numpy [18]

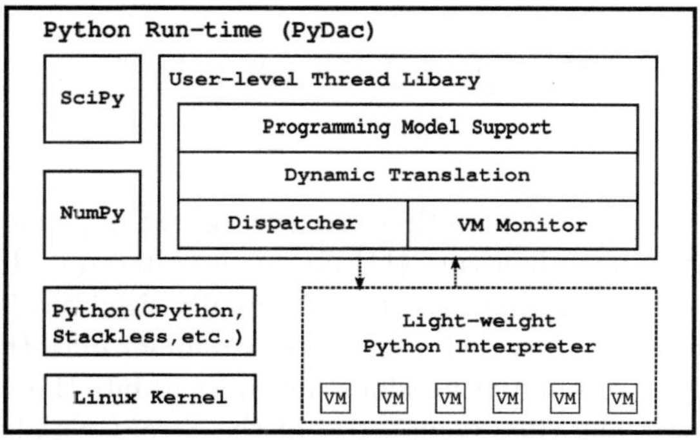

Fig. 2. High-level block diagram of PyDac runtime framework

As illustrated in Fig. 2, PyDac consists of three modules: a full-featured Python interpreter which supports many standard libraries, a lightweight Python interpreter (code-named *PyMite* [2]) designed for micro-controllers, and a user-level thread library. PyDac provides support for the *divide-and-conquer* programming paradigm.

The lightweight Python interpreter was chosen for the current implementation for two reasons. Firstly, its memory footprint is very small, which easily fits into an on-chip scratch-pad memory. Therefore, it does not generate memory requests to the off-chip memory. Secondly, it is built on the same set of bytecodes as the official Python interpreter (version 2.6), where a task represented by a same set of virtual machine bytecodes can be migrated between distributed VMs.

The glue layer between the full-featured Python interpreter and the lightweight interpreter is a dynamic translation layer. In the divide-and-conquer programming paradigm, programmers specify a function name and input data for a compute kernel which solves a base problem. The dynamic translation layer converts the function object (which is treated as a first-class object in Python) and input data into two C language byte arrays. The lightweight interpreter treats a function/data pair as an independent parallel task. A function byte array can be distributed to multiple VM instances in single program multiple data (SPMD) fashion. As soon as the base problem is solved, the dynamic translation layer re-constructs the computation results into objects recognizable to full-fledged Python.

In the PyDac runtime framework, resilient execution mainly comes from isolation of function objects and data objects. These objects are scheduled to run on green cores. If a process running on a green core is hit by a fault, it can be restarted by the dispatcher. Because the OS has been removed from the software stack on green cores, restarting a green core does not affect the OS running on the white core.

Segregation of input parameters for parallel base case tasks enables a functional view of scratch-pad memory, where input parameters of one task cannot be modified by other tasks. Also, internal memory of one task is hidden and no part of a task depends on values outside internal memory or input memory of the task. Therefore, the resulting tasks are completely independent.

3 Experimental Setup and Results

3.1 Scalability

In order to test the proposed runtime framework, we implemented a synthetic benchmark of Strassen's algorithm [11] on our architecture. The Strassen's algorithm partitions a square matrix into four equally sized block matrices. These block matrices are further divided in a recursive manner until they become small enough such that the sub-matrix and local variables fit into the scratch-pad memory of a green core. The time complexity of the Strassen's algorithm is better than conventional triple-loop matrix multiplication for large matrices; however, it is the large degree of parallelism that makes this operation attractive.

In order to test the proposed runtime system, we emulated the *green-white* architecture on a Xilinx Virtex5 Field-Programmable Gate Array (FPGA) device. Table 1 shows details of our configuration. Seven ARMv2a soft processors called *Amber* [1] were emulated. The number of green cores is mainly bounded by the available on-chip memory resource on the FPGA. Each green core is equipped with 144KB local scratch-pad memory (for both VM executable and input/output parameters). The VM executable occupies 128KB out of 144KB. As the size of local scratch-pad memory continues to increase as technology advances, the percentage of VM executable in scratch-pad memory will be less significant. Moreover, scratch-pad memories are single-cycle latency on-chip memories. Our current experimental system does not have a direct memory access (DMA) unit. Therefore, it is the responsibility of the PowerPC 440 to move data to scratch-pad memory in and out through the system bus. We expect DMA units would be present on final implementations of green cores.

Table 1. Summary of the experimental platform

FPGA Board	Xilinx ML510
White Core	1 PowerPC440 at 500 MHz
Green Cores	7 ARM (v2a) cores at 50 MHz
Python	CPython 2.6.4 (on PowerPC440) Pymite 0.9 (on ARM)

Fig. 3 shows scalability on the *green-white* from two different perspectives. In the first sub-figure, the sub-matrix size increases while problem size is fixed at 16×16. Performance of one green core is the base line. It shows that sub-matrix size in 8×8 achieves best performance in current system while the problem size is fixed. 8×8 sub-matrix fully utilizes the scratch-pad memory of each green core. In the second sub-figure, we hold sub-matrix at 8×8 and scale the problem size.

The largest matrix size (64×64) is bounded by system constraints. Performance of three green cores is the base line. In both cases, ideal speed-up is not achieved because the current *green-white* implementation does not have DMA support.

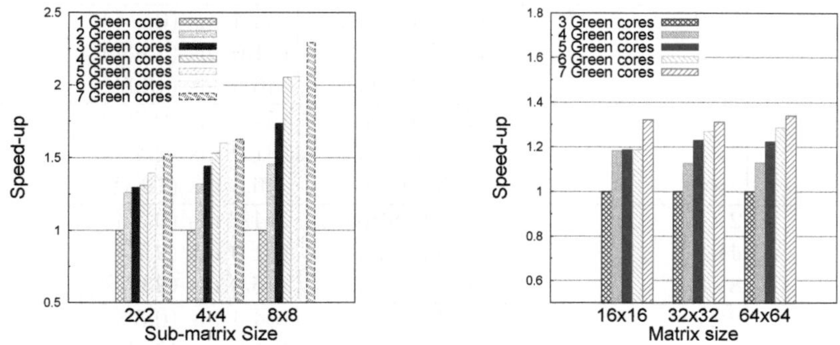

Fig. 3. Speed-up on *green-white* architecture

3.2 Local Recovery of Sub-matrix Computation

We measured the execution time of performing a local recovery on green cores. We are particularly interested in recovery from soft errors induced by aggressive voltage scaling. In order to understand how well PyDac performs when the system is hit by faults, we study a scenario where a fault is detected during a sub-problem computation and the dispatcher needs to immediately restart the green core and re-assign the compute task and data.

Table 2 presents mean-time-to-recompute on a green core under different workloads and its percentage in total runtime. The mean-time-to-recompute is counted as the time from re-dispatching objects (immediately after fault is detected) to when a new result is produced. We assume the mean-time-to-recompute a specific sized sub-matrix is the same. Therefore, the mean-time-to-recompute for a single sub-matrix was collected from running all tasks on one green core.

The percentage numbers in Table 2 vary according to the matrix size and sub-matrix size. When the sub-matrix size is too small (e.g. 2×2), the total runtime is dominated by the overhead of processes but recomputation time takes up a very small amount of the total runtime. When the sub-matrix size is relatively large (e.g. 8×8), the overall runtime is the best but compute time (and, subsequently, the recomputation time) for a single sub-matrix increases.

One can see that, for the system tested, there are some clear tradeoffs between overall performance and the time required to recover from a failure. For systems with relatively low failure rates one might choose to run with larger sub-matrix sizes. However, for systems that have traded reliability for increases in performance and/or power efficiency one might choose to run with smaller sub-matrices. This tradeoff is particularly interesting in FPGA systems where there is the possibility to manage this tradeoff somewhat dynamically. This leads us to believe that it is worth continuing to explore our approach.

Table 2. Mean-Time-to-Recompute

# of Utilized *Green* Cores	Sub-matrix Size for problem size (16×16)	Total Runtime	Mean-Time-To-Recompute a sub-matrix (percentage)
1	2×2	60754.5 ms	154.4 ms (0.3%)
	4×4	9787.4 ms	181.0 ms (1.8%)
	8×8	2558.9 ms	346.0 ms (13.5%)
2	2×2	46223.3 ms	154.4 ms (0.3%)
	4×4	7426.9 ms	181.0 ms (2.4%)
	8×8	1757.0 ms	346.0 ms (19.7%)
3	2×2	46903.8 ms	154.4 ms (0.3%)
	4×4	6785.8 ms	181.0 ms (2.7%)
	8×8	1475.0 ms	346.0 ms (23.5%)
4	2×2	46387.6 ms	154.4 ms (0.3%)
	4×4	6392.2 ms	181.0 ms (2.8%)
	8×8	1246.4 ms	346.0 ms (27.8%)
5	2×2	43543.7 ms	154.4 ms (0.4%)
	4×4	6122.1 ms	181.0 ms (3.0%)
	8×8	1243.8 ms	346.0 ms (27.8%)
6	2×2	41342.7 ms	154.4 ms (0.4%)
	4×4	6062.0 ms	181.0 ms (3.0%)
	8×8	1241.7 ms	346.0 ms (27.9%)
7	2×2	39876.1 ms	154.4 ms (0.4%)
	4×4	6015.7 ms	181.0 ms (3.0%)
	8×8	1116.7 ms	346.0 ms (31.0%)

4 Related Work

It has been shown that for many workloads heterogeneous hardware achieves better performance and power efficiency than conventional, general-purpose hardware [8]. The Cell processor [14] combines processors optimized for performance per transistor on compute intensive applications, with processors with a more conventional architecture. The Cell processor also introduces software-controlled memory to allow overlapping computation with memory transfer. The SARC architecture [19] reuses Cell Synergistic Processing Elements but adds application-specific instructions. Moreover, ARM's big.LITTLE™architecture [12] focuses on mobile applications (multi-threaded but not highly parallel). The *green-white* architecture targets scientific computing which features massive parallelism. In our system, sequential tasks are performed by the *white* cores and the parallel tasks run on the *green* cores. Akin to the Cell processor, the *green-white* architecture adopts software-controlled memory.

A few runtime systems have been specifically designed for the divide-and-conquer scheme. Cilk [4] is a C-based runtime system implemented with a work-stealing scheduler. It was designed to run on shared-memory systems and Cilk-NOW [5] extends Cilk to run on a network of UNIX workstations.

Atlas [3] is a Java-based runtime system that adapts the Cilk programming model, extends work-stealing of Cilk scheduler with a hierarchy, and borrows fault tolerance mechanism from Cilk-NOW. Satin [17] is also a Java-based runtime system that extends work-stealing with a cluster-aware capability. Sequoia [10] abstracts a memory hierarchy as a tree of distributed memory modules and constrains the compute kernels to operate on leaf nodes. PyDac attempts to address recovery from faults at the core-level.

5 Conclusions and Future Work

Heterogeneous architectures are promising for building future HPC systems. In order to utilize new architectures, we proposed a runtime framework, PyDac, to bridge the envisioned computation model and assumed chip architecture. PyDac is built upon distributed virtual machines and has a unique mechanism that isolates all the data that a small/simple core is working on. Because of this, PyDac can recover a faulty small/simple core locally. To test this idea, we emulated a heterogeneous many-core system with one hard PowerPC 440 core and seven soft ARM cores on an FPGA device. Our synthetic benchmark of Strassen's algorithm shows the feasibility of PyDac for supporting a computational model based on the divide-and-conquer strategy. Our results show that it costs little overhead for the runtime system to locally recover from a failure on a small/simple core. This is an encouraging step toward a runtime system that is capable of keeping the application mean time to interrupt high.

In the future, we plan to switch to more mature processors than ARMv2a. We are currently designing hardware that reduces the number of green cores to free resources for achieving a larger size of scratch-pad memories. Also, with future chips that promise larger on-chip memory, we will be able to increase sub-matrix size and to conduct larger-scale tests.

References

1. Amber: ARM-compatible core, `http://opencores.org/project,amber`
2. Python on a chip, `http://code.google.com/p/python-on-a-chip/`
3. Baldeschwieler, J.E., Blumofe, R.D., Brewer, E.A.: ATLAS: an infrastructure for global computing. In: Proceedings of the 7th Workshop on ACM SIGOPS European Workshop: Systems Support for Worldwide Applications, pp. 165–172. ACM (1996)
4. Blumofe, R.D., Joerg, C., Kuszmaul, B., Leiserson, C., Randall, K., Zhou, Y.: Cilk: An efficient multithreaded runtime system, vol. 30. ACM (1995)
5. Blumofe, R.D., Lisiecki, P.A., et al.: Adaptive and reliable parallel computing on networks of workstations. In: USENIX 1997 Annual Technical Conference on UNIX and Advanced Computing Systems, pp. 133–147 (1997)
6. Borkar, S.: The exascale challenge (2010)
7. Cappello, F., Geist, A., Gropp, B., Kale, L., Kramer, B., Snir, M.: Toward exascale resilience. International Journal of High Performance Computing Applications 23(4), 374–388 (2009)

8. Chung, E.S., Milder, P.A., Hoe, J.C., Mai, K.: Single-chip heterogeneous computing: Does the future include custom logic, FPGAs, and GPGPUs? In: Proceedings of the 2010 43rd Annual IEEE/ACM International Symposium on Microarchitecture, pp. 225–236. IEEE Computer Society (2010)
9. Dennis, J., Gao, G., Meng, X.: Experiments with the Fresh Breeze tree-based memory model. Computer Science - Research and Development 26, 325–337 (2011), http://dx.doi.org/10.1007/s00450-011-0165-1, doi:10.1007/s00450-011-0165-1
10. Fatahalian, K., Horn, D.R., Knight, T.J., Leem, L., Houston, M., Park, J.Y., Erez, M., Ren, M., Aiken, A., Dally, W.J., et al.: Sequoia: programming the memory hierarchy. In: Proceedings of the 2006 ACM/IEEE Conference on Supercomputing, p. 83. ACM (2006)
11. Golub, G.H., Van Loan, C.F.: Matrix Computations, 3rd edn. JHUP (1996)
12. Greenhalgh, P.: Big.little processing with ARM Cortex-A15 & Cortex-A7. White Paper (2011)
13. Hill, M.D., Marty, M.R.: Amdahl's law in the multicore era. Computer 41(7), 33–38 (2008)
14. Hofstee, H.P.: Power efficient processor architecture and the cell processor. In: 11th International Symposium on High-Performance Computer Architecture, HPCA-11, pp. 258–262. IEEE (2005)
15. Kaul, H., Anders, M., Hsu, S., Agarwal, A., Krishnamurthy, R., Borkar, S.: Near-threshold voltage (NTV) design: opportunities and challenges. In: Proceedings of the 49th Annual Design Automation Conference, DAC 2012, pp. 1153–1158. ACM, New York (2012)
16. Mattson, T., Riepen, M., Lehnig, T., Brett, P., Haas, W., Kennedy, P., Howard, J., Vangal, S., Borkar, N., Ruhl, G., et al.: The 48-core SCC processor: the programmer's view. In: Proceedings of the 2010 ACM/IEEE International Conference for High Performance Computing, Networking, Storage and Analysis, pp. 1–11. IEEE Computer Society (2010)
17. van Nieuwpoort, R., Maassen, J., Kielmann, T., Bal, H.E.: Satin: Simple and efficient Java-based grid programming. Scalable Computing: Practice and Experience 6(3) (2001)
18. Oliphant, T.: A Guide to NumPy, vol. 1. Trelgol Publishing, USA (2006)
19. Ramirez, A., Cabarcas, F., Juurlink, B., Alvarez Mesa, M., Sanchez, F., Azevedo, A., Meenderinck, C., Ciobanu, C., Isaza, S., Gaydadjiev, G.: The SARC architecture. IEEE Micro 30(5), 16–29 (2010)
20. Wrzesinska, G., van Nieuwpoort, R., Maassen, J., Bal, H.E.: Fault-tolerance, malleability and migration for divide-and-conquer applications on the grid. In: Proc. of 19th IPDPS, vol. 56. Citeseer (2005)

Investigating the Integration of Supercomputers and Data-Warehouse Appliances*

Ron A. Oldfield, George Davidson, Craig Ulmer, and Andrew Wilson

Sandia National Laboratories**
{raoldfi,gsdavid,cdulmer,atwilso}@sandia.gov

Abstract. Two decades of experience with massively parallel supercomputing has given insight into the problem domains where these architectures are cost effective. Likewise experience with database machines and more recently massively parallel database appliances has shown where these architectures are valuable. Combining both architectures to simultaneously solve problems has received much less attention. In this paper, we describe a motivating application for economic modeling that requires both HPC and database capabilities. Then we discuss hardware and software integration issues related to a direct integration of a Cray XT supercomputer and a Netezza database appliance.

1 Introduction

High-performance computing (HPC) systems, particularly large-scale parallel supercomputers, have traditionally been exclusively used to solve complex scientific problems; however, recent interest in data-analytic problems in the areas of cyber security, social networking, economic modeling, and others, along with the exponential growth of data required for these applications, is motivating the use of HPC systems to solve these problems as well.

Some analytics applications are particularly well suited for HPC computing because of their numerical requirements. For example, applications that use latent semantic analysis (LSA) [7] and eigen-value decomposition could make use of highly-tuned numerical algorithms such as those in Sandia's Trilinos numerical solvers [14]. Other applications could exploit the tremendous in-core memory of HPC systems. While cluster solutions require substantial culling of the data before analysis, a supercomputer could analyze much larger data sets, perhaps identifying global relationships among the data that could not be found at a smaller scale.

Although HPC platforms provide effective capability to address numerical-computing requirements of analytics codes, they are missing other key features. For example, a common objective is to find relationships between elements in a large data-warehouse

** Sandia National Laboratories is a multi-program laboratory managed and operated by Sandia Corporation, a wholly owned subsidiary of Lockheed Martin Corporation, for the U.S. Department of Energy's National Nuclear Security Administration under contract DE-AC04-94AL85000.

D. an Mey et al. (Eds.): Euro-Par 2013 Workshops, LNCS 8374, pp. 855–864, 2014.

appliances (DWA) such as a Netezza, XtremeData, LexisNexis, and others. Social networking and document clustering both fit into this category. Other applications, like Sandia's N-ABLE code [10], generate data that has to be "ingested" into a DWA for post analysis. While HPC systems provide access to large parallel file systems, there is often no support for database access. In addition, HPC systems are designed for fast access through proprietary networks to internal resources, but are not designed for efficient access to remote resources. Thus, providing network access from an HPC system to a remote DWA creates severe bottlenecks.

The increasing desire to support a dual-use for HPC platforms that includes traditional physics-driven science codes and data-driven analytics is creating serious concerns for system architects. One approach is to design a system capable of efficiently handling both workloads, but the characteristics of science-based and analytics-based applications differ enough that this approach may not be practical or cost-effective. An alternative is to find ways to tightly couple HPC systems and data-warehouse appliances to exploit each systems special hardware and software features. In this paper, we explore the second option.

This paper describes an effort at Sandia to couple a Cray XT4 and a small Netezza DWA. We describe a motivating use case based on economic modeling, describe the necessary software and hardware modifications to support such an integration, and perform three different experiments to evaluate our approach.

2 Motivating Use Case: Analysis of Complex Economic Systems

A number of interesting use cases exist to motivate the integration of HPC and DWA systems, but there is one particular Sandia application we targeted for this work, economic modeling. The National Infrastructure Simulation and Analysis Center (NISAC) is a center at Sandia National Laboratories that analyzes economic impacts and interdependencies of disruptions in our national infrastructure. Disruptions include, for example, changes in U.S. border security technologies, terrorist acts on commodity futures markets, disruptions in food supply chains, and power and rail disruptions.

The tool used for economic modeling is the NISAC Agent-Based Laboratory for Economics (N-ABLE) [10]. N-ABLE is an agent-based microsimulation tool with the goal of modeling complex economic systems through the interactions of massive numbers of individual entities. N-ABLE agents employ simple market-based rules for production and consumption that, when considered economy-wide, lead to "emergent" behavior that would be hard to predict in a purely mathematical model.

N-ABLE agents are simple pieces of C++ code that model economic activity of entities such as banking firms, power companies, telecommunication firms, and others. On HPC systems, a simulation consists of tens of thousands of agents that communicate events using the Message Passing Interface (MPI).

Agent simulations produce "snapshots" at periodic intervals that represent the set of transactions executed by representative agents since the last snapshot. Data from the simulation needs to be ingested into a database for interactive exploratory analysis; however, constraints in I/O performance and functionality make this process cumbersome and slow. The standard approach is to stage this data to files. An out-of-band, sequential, process then merges and ingests that data into the database.

The primary goal of the N-ABLE simulation is to rapidly identify key economic impacts of changes to our national infrastructure. To address those concerns in a timely manner it is critical to minimize the total time to solution for the entire workflow, which includes the HPC simulation, ingest of results into a database, and analysis of the simulation results by analysts. In the current implementation, the most significant time constraint is the time to ingest simulation data into the database.

N-ABLE is a great candidate for an integrated HPC/DWA system. The snapshot operation could avoid the off-line staging process by ingesting data directly into the database, and a tight coupling of a DWA and HPC could reduce ingest time, addressing the network bottleneck between the HPC system and the database host.

3 Architectural Differences between HPC and DWA

Many years of research have gone into hardware and software design for HPC and DWA systems. In both cases, systems are designed to support a relatively small set of applications. While HPC systems are generally designed for problems in *computational science* [21], DWAs are primarily designed for analytics applications in business intelligence [17] or cyber intelligence [25]. As we discuss in the next few paragraphs, the hardware and software needed to support these applications do not always overlap.

3.1 HPC Systems

Computational science applications typically model some physical phenomena such as predicting climate changes, simulating nuclear fusion, or simulating the interactions between molecules. To model this behavior, scientists rely on approximations that use parallel numerical methods to solve partial differential equations. The finite-element and finite-difference methods used to solve these equations have distinct phases of computation, communication, and I/O; and require effective load balancing to maximize resource utilization [4]. These requirements motivated supercomputing vendors to build large-scale distributed-memory systems with high-speed, low latency networks and powerful parallel file systems. Software and allocation strategies are designed to be predictable and simple, using a space-sharing as opposed to time sharing for node allocation, explicit message passing, and user control of memory management.

Figure 1a illustrates the partitioned architecture typically used for parallel supercomputers. This is the model used by the Cray XT, XE, and XMT series and the IBM BlueGene series of supercomputers. A partitioned architecture system [13] is comprised of compute nodes that use a lightweight kernel [16,24] operating system and service nodes running a full-fledged operating system, typically some variant of Linux. By design, lightweight kernels provide a very limited set of functionality to the application. In the case of Catamount [15] and Compute Node Kernel [24], the operating systems used by Cray XT and IBM, there is no support for demand paged virtual memory, no support for local disk, and little or no support for multi-threading. Cray Linux Environment [27], the operating system used by compute nodes of the more modern multi-core systems such as the Cray XT and XE sysetms, provides some of these services, but is still somewhat restricted when compared to full Linux distributions.

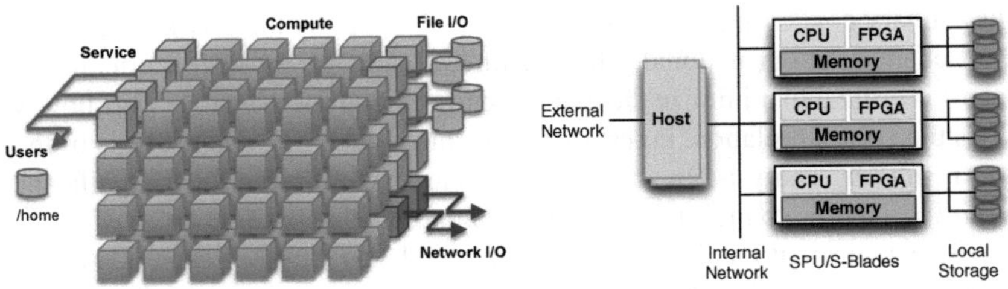

(a) HPC System Architecture. **(b)** Netezza System Architecture.

Fig. 1. Architecture of a traditional supercomputer and Netezza DWA [11]

In addition to the specialized operating systems, high-end parallel supercomputers typically use proprietary networks with specialized protocols. For example, the Cray XT3 and XT4 use the SeaStar network interface [2] that provides extremely high bandwidth, but is only accessible through the Portals programming interface [3]. Cray XE systems use the Gemini interconnect capable of millions of MPI messages per second [1], but it also uses the proprietary uGNI API for access. These systems have limited support for TCP on the compute nodes, and no support for ODBC, the standard API used to access remote SQL databases.

3.2 Data Warehouse Appliances

Data warehouse appliances (DWA) are systems with special hardware to process relational queries (e.g., SQL) on massive datasets. The history of special database architectures for SQL processing goes back many decades to the use of data base computers (DBC) [8]. Commercial uses for database processing became the driver for more advanced capabilities later used for scientific computing. For example, the Teradata DBC/1012 [23] developed in the early 1980s was one the first to demonstrate commercially viable use case for massively parallel processing (MPPs).

The Netezza [11], formed in 2000 and acquired by IBM in 2010, was one of the first companies to treat the database machine as a true appliance [6], exposing the machine through a query interface, but providing powerful storage and processing capabilities internally. While there are now a number of companies offering hardware and software support for SQL-based data-warehouse appliances such as XtremeData, Oracle, Teradata, and Greenplum, we focus our discussion on the Netezza architecture.

In the same way Teradata demonstrated commercial uses for MPP, the Netezza system was the first to demonstrate a commercially-viable use case for active storage [22]. The Netezza system, illustrated in Figure 1b, leverages key concepts of the active-storage research to construct an MPP SQL-processing system that performs most of the processing at or near the stored data. They even employ field-programmable gate arrays (FPGAs) to filter data before it even hits the processor memory. For example, Netezza uses FPGAs to restrict selections in queries and compress and decompress data at line rates to provide a larger effective storage capacity. A host presents a standard interface to external applications, compiles SQL queries into distributable code segments called "snippets" that then get passed to the MPP nodes–originally called snippet processing units (SPUs), now called S-Blades–for processing. The S-Blades contain multi-core CPUs, multi-engine FPGAs, and multiple gigabytes of memory. Since snippet programs are generally "embarrassingly parallel", there is no need for a proprietary interconnect, such as those found on HPC supercomputers. 1Gib Ethernet, along with proprietary network protocols designed specifically for query-based traffic provides sufficient bandwidth to handle typical workloads.

3.3 Summary of Differences between Architectures

The primary differences in HPC architectures and DWA architectures is reflected in the diverging requirements of the supported applications. Here we contrast application requirements for three important components: computation, communication, and I/O.

Historically, computation of floating point operations (flops) is considered the most important quality of an HPC system. Since 1993, the LINPACK benchmark [9], used to calculate the top 500 supercomputers, has been the most common metric used to rate HPC systems. Thus, HPC architects are continually delivering systems with leading-edge CPU performance and parallelism. DWA designers, at least in the case of Netezza, seem less interested in aggregate CPU performance and are more interested in providing the minimum amount processing required to keep up with the disk I/O rates.

In the same way computation is a critical requirement for HPC systems, communication is equally important, and essentially the distinguishing feature separating HPC systems and commodity clusters. The major supercomputing vendors like IBM and Cray use proprietary interconnects to provide this performance. In contrast, DWA architects put much less emphasis on a high-speed interconnect. Computing distributed SQL queries is essentially a streaming computation problem [20] where most of the data is filtered very close to the disk device. DWA systems do not need an expensive proprietary network to get good parallel performance.

The I/O and storage systems are also very different in supercomputers and DWA systems. Supercomputing applications are often write intensive, writing large volumes of simulation results and checkpoint files [5]. DWA applications are typically read-intensive, performing most of their I/O for queries as part of an analysis operation. The I/O system of an HPC is often separate from the compute nodes, as illustrated in Figure 1a, requiring an efficient parallel file system. In contrast, although there is a tremendous amount of aggregate I/O for DWA applications, Netezza is an active-storage [22] architecture that filters and processes most of this data on nodes connected to the storage devices. The devices are independent and do not require a parallel file system for access.

4 An Integration Environment for HPC and DWA

The goal of this work is to explore application workflows that need capabilities of both supercomputers and DWAs. However, a single general-purpose system, designed for both types of applications, does not exist. Instead of trying to force one system to manage both workloads, we explore two ways to connect a supercomputer with a DWA. The first integration is a "loose" coupling that uses a standard Ethernet to connect to a remote Netezza. The second approach is a "tight" coupling that places a Netezza front-end host on the fast interconnect of the HPC system. In this section, we describe the software and hardware modifications needed to support these approaches.

For our experiments, we integrated a Cray XT4 with a small SPUBox Netezza system. Our Cray XT4 consists of a single cabinet containing 94 2.1 GHz quad-core AMD Opteron processors, with 2 GB of memory per core. The nodes are connected by a SeaStar router [2] using a 3-dimensional torus topology capable of 2 GiB/s transfers per link. The service nodes have an additional external 1 Gib Ethernet card that allows connections to/from the machine. The compute nodes of the Cray XT4 use a light-weight kernel operating system called the Cray Linux Environment.

The Netezza SPUBox [1] uses the older generation "Mustang" architecture consisting of a single front-end host and 8 back-end snippet-processing units (SPUs). Each SPU contains a single PowerPC for computation, an FPGA, and a SATA controller for the disk. The host is connected to the SPUs through a 1 Gib/s Ethernet router. An additional 1 Gib/s Ethernet card provides external access to the host node. The host uses a standard Linux operating system and proprietary software, called *NZLib*, that manages processing of code snippets on the back-end SPUs.

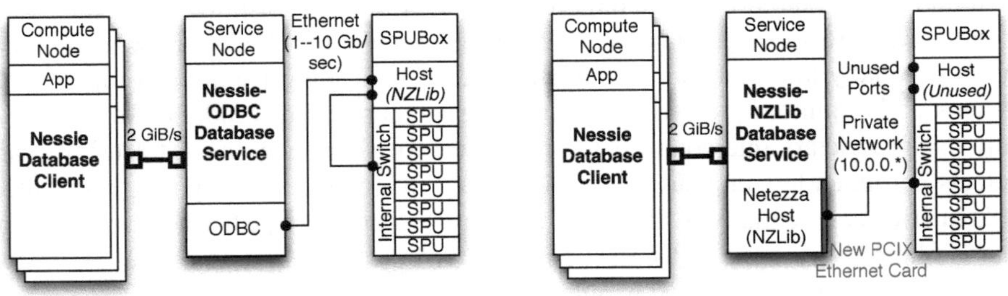

(a) Loosely-coupled integration. **(b)** Tightly-coupled integration.

Fig. 2. Organization of hardware for HPC/DWA integration experiments

4.1 Loosely-Coupled Integration of Cray and Netezza

Figure 2a illustrates the configuration used to integrate the Cray XT4 and a remote Netezza SPUBox. Since the compute nodes of the XT4 do not have access to an external network, we developed a "proxy" database service [19] using the Network Scalable Service Interface (Nessie) [18]. Nessie provides a remote procedure call abstraction, along with RDMA functions to perform direct memory-to-memory transfers between compute and services nodes on the high-speed interconnect.

Our database proxy aggregates and forwards database requests to servers that have connectivity to the external network. The servers, running a full linux OS, use standard interfaces to access the remote Netezza database. Our servers use the implementation of ODBC provided by Netezza.

[1] A commercial version of the SPUBox is now available as the IBM Netezza 100.

4.2 Tightly-Coupled Integration of Cray and Netezza

Although the loosely-coupled approach provides access to a remote database, we anticipate a significant bottleneck between the ODBC service and the remote database. The SeaStar network provides 2 GiB/sec bandwidth per link to the service, but our Ethernet link provides 1 Gib/sec (a factor of 16 slower) from the ODBC service to the Netezza. In addition the Portals interface can achieve nearly full bandwidth of the SeaStar network, but congestion-control algorithms of TCP/IP limit network bandwidth, and overheads in the ODBC protocols further limit performance.

To improve data-transfer rates between the Cray XT system and Netezza, we developed a hardware-integrated solution that allows the host functionality of the Netezza to be resident on a service node of an XT system. Figure 2b shows the system architecture. This configuration allows efficient access from compute nodes to the host through Portals, and we could avoid overheads of software abstraction layers such as ODBC by leveraging the host libraries (*NZLib*) provided by Netezza to interact directly with the back-end SPUs. In particular, we want to leverage the bulk ingest capability called *NZLoad* that is available in NZLib but not in the ODBC interface.

5 Evaluation

To evaluate performance of the different integration schemes, we developed a simple weak-scaling parallel benchmark to generate and ingest 4 MiB of data per client process into a database. The intent is to emulate the I/O behavior of the N-ABLE economic-modeling code. Our experiments measure three different use cases:

ODBC: The loosely-coupled integration described in Figure 2a. We measure time to generate and ingest data into a Netezza database through the ODBC database proxy.

NZLoad: The tightly-coupled integration described in Figure 2b. We measure the time to generate and ingest data through our hardware-integrated platform that uses the bulk ingest NZLoad operation from an HPC service node.

SQLite: A *control* experiment that measures the time to ingest data directly to a shared SQLite database on the HPC parallel file system.

Figure 3 shows combined results of the three different experiments as we increase the number of bytes ingested into the database. As expected, the loosely-couple case demonstrates useful functionality, yet it performs very poorly, taking over 40 minutes to ingest 16 KB of data. This poor performance is due to known issues with ingest using SQL [12]. The issue is that the typical enterprise use of databases assumes that databases are built up gradually over time. Ingesting data using the INSERT command only allows one row at a time to be ingested. Considering each INSERT command is a remote network transfer, it is no surprise this benchmark performs so poorly.

Writing to SQLite files performs much better than remote ODBC, but still starts to degrade rapidly when approaching 1 MB of data. This case suffers the same SQL-interface limitations as the ODBC experiment. In both of these cases, it is the interface, not the hardware that is limiting bulk-ingest performance.

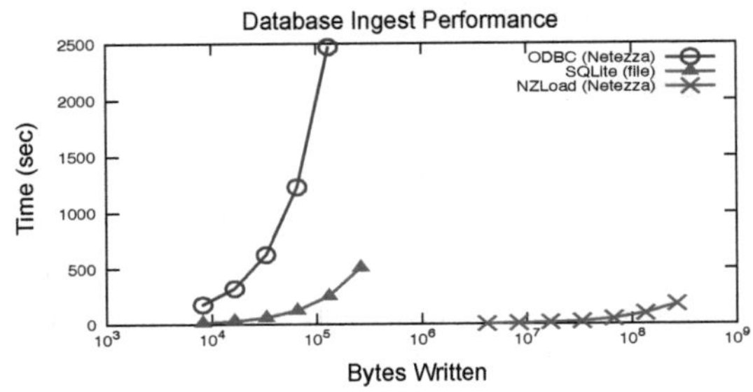

Fig. 3. Ingest performance of the three different experiments

The final experiment, NZLoad, demonstrates a hardware-integration and use of the bulk-ingest capability of the Netezza libraries performs orders of magnitude faster than the other two experiments, achieving an ingest performance of 256 MB in 150 seconds.

The next two figures look in detail at the hardware-integration experiment. To improve performance, our Netezza collaborators suggested multi-threading on the host to increase the number of outstanding requests. Figure 4a shows scaling results of the NZLoad experiment for 1 to 64 client processors, each writing 4MiB to a single server that uses up to 64 threads to send data to the back-end database. The x-axis shows the number of client nodes sending data to the database, and also represents the number of outstanding requests. The plots show a large boost in performance between 1 and 2 threads, but no significant advantage to using more than 2 threads per server.

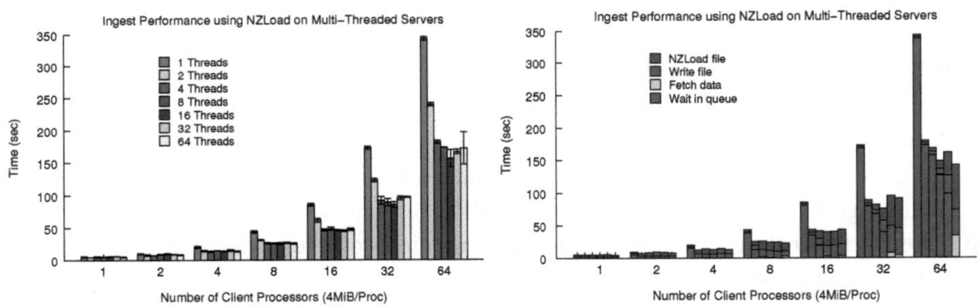

(**a**) Thread Timings. (**b**) Operation Timings.

Fig. 4. Multithreaded ingest performance for hardware-integrated solution. Columns show performance using different number of threads on the service node of the Cray.

To better understand results from Figure 4a, we created a stack plot (Figure 4b) showing the time to fetch data from the client, write data to a file, ingest/load data into the database, and finally the time to wait if the system is busy. The plots show that four threads provides a sufficient level of concurrency to overlap data-transfers and writes with the ingest (NZLoad) to the database. Any more than that has no benefit. This is not surprising given that we are piping all our data through a single network interface. Additional parallelism to the back-end (i.e., more hosts) would likely provide better results. In addition, notice that when the number of threads on the host match or exceed the number of clients, there is no longer any wait time, but the time spent loading, writing, or fetching data increases. This clearly shows a device contention effect.

6 Conclusions and Future Work

Recent interest in using supercomputers for data-analytic operations are causing HPC system architects to explore interesting new designs. In this paper, we propose an integration of two special-purpose architectures: a supercomputer designed primarily for scientific simulations, and a data-warehouse appliance, tuned for analytics jobs.

Our economic modeling application requires rapid ingest into a relational database for analysis. This bulk-ingest problem created serious issues when using SQL-based tools, but showed a clear benefit from a tight coupling that exploited bulk-ingest capabilities provided in the vendor libraries. Another alternative is to explore data-parallel approaches such as LexisNexis DAS, Sector and Sphere, IBM's InfoSphere, and Hadoop. There has already been a good study on using these types of data-warehouse appliances for scientific data analysis [26]. Perhaps similar benefits exist for economic modeling.

Although we propose an integration of two special-purpose machines, it is not clear that an HPC/DWA integration would be difficult with existing supercomputer hardware. For example, an extra partition of "special" DWA nodes, along with Netezza software, could provide capabilities useful for analytics on the fast network.

Although we expect exascale architectures to motivate the integration of simulation and analytics, we have not fully explored the space of possible applications that would benefit from such an architecture. In addition, these new problem domains introduce a number of issues in the operating system, runtime system, and programming models that lead to a possible explosion of research opportunities in the next decade.

Acknowledgements. The submitted manuscript has been authored by a contractor of the U.S. Government under contract No. DE-AC04-94-AL85000. Accordingly, the U.S. Government retains a nonexclusive, royaltyfree license to publish or reproduce the published form of this contribution, or allow others to do so, for U.S. Government purposes.

References

1. Alverson, R., Roweth, D., Kaplan, L.: The Gemini system interconnect. In: Proceedings of the 18th Annual Symposium on High Performance Interconnects (HOTI), Mountain View, CA, pp. 83–87. IEEE Computer Society Press (August 2010)
2. Brightwell, R., Pedretti, K., Underwood, K., Hudson, T.: SeaStar interconnect: Balanced bandwidth for scalable performance. IEEE Micro 26(3), 41–57 (2006)
3. Brightwell, R., Riesen, R., Lawry, B., Maccabe, A.B.: Portals 3.0: protocol building blocks for low overhead communication. In: Proceedings of the International Parallel and Distributed Processing Symposium, Fort Lauderdale, FL, p. 268 (April 2002)
4. Bruaset, A.M., Tveito, A. (eds.): Numerical Solution of Partial Differential Equations on Parallel Computers. Lecture Notes in Computational Science and Engineering, vol. 51. Springer (2006)
5. Carns, P., et al.: Understanding and improving computational science storage access through continuous characterization. In: IEEE Conference on Mass Storage Systems and Technologies, pp. 1–14 (2011)

6. Davidson, G.S., et al.: Data-centric computing with the Netezza architecture. Technical Report SAND2006-3640, Sandia National Laboratories (2006)
7. Deerwester, S.C.: et al. Indexing by latent semantic analysis. Journal of the American Society for Information Science 41(6), 391–407 (1990)
8. DeWitt, D.J., Hawthorn, P.B.: A performance evaluation of data base machine architectures. In: Proceedings of the Seventh International Conference on Very Large Data Bases, VLDB 1981, Cannes, France, pp. 199–214 (1981) (invited paper)
9. Dongarra, J., Luszczek, P., Petitet, A.: The LINPACK benchmark: past, present, and future. Concurrency - Practice and Experience 15(9), 803–820 (2003)
10. Eidson, E.D., Ehlen, M.A.: NISAC agent-based laboratory for economics (N-ABLE^{TM}): Overview of agent and simulation architectures. Technical Report SAND2005-0263, Sandia National Laboratories (2005)
11. Francisco, P.: The Netezza data appliance architecture: A platform for high performance data warehousing and analytics. IBM Redguide (2011), `http://www.redbooks.ibm.com/redpapers/pdfs/redp4725.pdf`
12. Graves, S.: HPC databases: The data ingest challenge. HPCWire (June 2007)
13. Greenberg, D.S., et al.: A system software architecture for high-end computing. In: Proceedings of SC 1997: High Performance Networking and Computing, San Jose, California, pp. 1–15. ACM Press (November 1997)
14. Heroux, M., et al.: An overview of Trilinos. Technical Report SAND2003-2927, Sandia National Laboratories (2003)
15. Kelly, S.M., Brightwell, R.: Software architecture of the Light Weight Kernel, Catamount. In: Proceedings of the Cray User Group Meeting, Albuquerque, NM (May 2005)
16. Maccabe, A.B., Wheat, S.R.: Message passing in PUMA. Technical Report SAND-93-0935C, Sandia National Labs (1993)
17. Negash, S.: Business intelligence. Communications of the Association for Information Systems 13(15) (2004)
18. Oldfield, R.A., et al.: Trilinos I/O Support (Trios). Scientific Programming (August 2012)
19. Oldfield, R.A., Kordenbrock, T., Lofstead, J.: Developing integrated data services for Cray systems with a Gemini interconnect. In: Cray User Group Meeting (April 2012)
20. Plale, B., Schwan, K.: Dynamic querying of streaming data with the dQUOB system. IEEE Transactions on Parallel and Distributed Systems 14(4), 422–432 (2003)
21. Ralston, A., Reilly, E.D., Hemmendinger, D. (eds.): Encyclopedia of Computer Science, 4th edn. Wiley (2003)
22. Riedel, E., Faloutsos, C., Gibson, G.A., Nagle, D.: Active disks for large-scale data processing. IEEE Computer 34(6), 68–74 (2001)
23. Sloan, R.D.: A practical implementation of the data base machine – Teradata DBC/1012. In: Proceedings of the Twenty-Fifth Hawaii International Conference on System Sciences, pp. 320–327 (January 1992)
24. The BlueGene/L Team: An overview of the BlueGene/L supercomputer. In: Proceedings of SC2002: High Performance Networking and Computing, Baltimore, MD (November 2002)
25. Thuraisingham, B.M.: Web data mining and applications in business intelligence and counter-terrorism. CRC Press (2005)
26. Ulmer, C., Bayer, G., Choe, Y.R., Roe, D.: Exploring data warehouse appliances for mesh analysis applications. In: Proceedings of the 43rd International Conference on System Sciences, Koloa, Kauai, Hawai, pp. 1–10. IEEE Press (January 2010)
27. Wallace, D.: Compute Node Linux: Overview, progress to date & roadmap. In: Proceedings of the Cray User Group Meeting, Helsinki, Finland (May 2007)

Investigation of Parallel Programmability and Performance of a Calxeda ARM Server Using OpenCL

David Richie[1], James Ross[2], Jordan Ruloff[2], Song Park[3], Lori Pollock[4], and Dale Shires[3]

[1] Brown Deer Technology, Forest Hill, MD
drichie@browndeertechnology.com
[2] Dynamics Resources Corporation (DRC), Andover, MA
{jaross,jruloff}@drc.com
[3] U.S. Army Research Laboratory, Aberdeen, MD
{song.j.park.civ,dale.r.shires.civ}@mail.mil
[4] University of Delaware, Newark, DE
pollock@udel.edu

Abstract. This paper explores the parallel programmability, performance, and energy efficiency of a recently available Calxeda ARM-based server as a potential energy-efficient platform for computationally intensive applications. A novel OpenCL-based parallel programming model for the Calxeda ARM server is achieved via the use of a higher level STandarD Compute Layer (STDCL) application programming interface and a remote procedure call (RPC) implementation. Empirical measurements of the performance of the platform are obtained and presented using an N-body code executed in various configurations. Furthermore, an auto-tuning technique was developed and analyzed for optimization of the N-body algorithm on a specific architecture.

Keywords: High Performance Computing, ARM server, OpenCL.

1 Introduction

Power consumption has arguably become the single most critical factor impacting high performance computing (HPC) for architectures ranging from large-scale supercomputers to data centers to mobile computing platforms [9,3,6]. It is within this context that ARM processors, which dominate the mobile smartphone and tablet market, are being repurposed as an alternative to the x86 processors that have dominated HPC, desktops, and workstations, for well over a decade. Whereas a modern x86 processor is based on a CISC architecture with substantial per-core capability, ARM processors are based on a RISC architecture designed for low-power operation [8].

Newly developed ARM-based servers, such as those from Calxeda, offer low-energy usage, high-memory density, high-core density, and high-storage density–all qualities that motivate using these servers for HPC applications. However, the

D. an Mey et al. (Eds.): Euro-Par 2013 Workshops, LNCS 8374, pp. 865–874, 2014.

relative core efficiency as compared with x86 CPUs in terms of cost and power metrics remains an open question. The Calxeda ARM servers [5] represent the most direct attempt to date aimed at bringing ARM processors into competition with traditional x86 servers.

This paper reports on exploration into the parallel programmability, performance, and energy efficiency of a Calxeda ARM server using an OpenCL-based approach. OpenCL provides an explicit low-level programming model for co-processor architectures that may also be used to exploit the parallelism of systems with multi-core CPUs treated as abstract OpenCL compute devices. The OpenCL host node is treated normally, while the rest of the nodes are virtualized and treated as OpenCL compute devices through a Remote Procedure Call (RPC) OpenCL implementation. This specialized RPC-based OpenCL implementation permits existing multi-device OpenCL codes to execute across multiple networked compute devices.

Section 2 describes the Calxeda server system used for evaluation. Section 3 investigates the use of existing software packages that leverage OpenCL to provide a novel parallel programming model for platforms like the Calxeda ARM servers. Section 4 discusses the use of an N-body benchmark, including auto-tuning parameterizations, to measure the performance of the Calxeda ARM server. Section 5 provides the evaluation of the Calxeda ARM server. Section 6 presents related work on OpenCL performance. Finally, Sect. 7 closes with conclusions and future work.

2 The Calxeda ARM Server

The Calxeda ARM server experimented for this study was provided by Exxact Corporation and accessible from a remote desktop allowing direct access to a login node connected to the Calxeda system. It was configured with two Calxeda EnergyCards, each containing four quad-core ARM Cortex-A9 system on chip (SoC) devices, as shown in Fig. 1, acting as independent nodes (device nodes); thus, a potential total core count of $2 \times 4 \times 4 = 32$ cores. However, the server that was provided had five device nodes, or 20 cores, configured and accessible for use. Based on documentation, the ARM cores operate at a clock frequency in the range of 1.1 GHz to 1.4 GHz and have access to 4GB DDR3 ECC memory per device node. It is important to note that each SoC interacts exclusively over the integrated network fabric and the quad-socket card is not a shared memory platform like a conventional server motherboard.

Each quad-core node was accessible via Secure Shell (SSH) and presented itself as a standalone node running its own operating system (OS) image, specifically, Ubuntu 12.10. The environment is a typical Ubuntu OS system and included standard development tools, e.g., GCC 4.7, along with most of the supporting tools needed for compiling code. The platform included a baseboard management controller (BMC) that allowed power measurements to be obtained for each ARM device node.

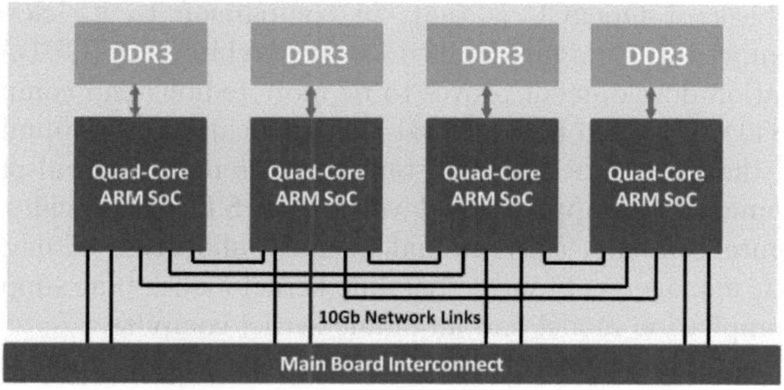

Fig. 1. Block diagram of the Calxeda EnergyCard showing the basic platform architecture of the Calxeda ARM server. Each card contains four quad-core ARM Cortex-A9 SoCs with dedicated banks of 4GB DDR3 EEC memory. Each ARM SoC has an integrated fabric switch with five (5) 10Gb network links supporting a direct all-to-all on-card topology and a total of eight (8) links exported to the main system board to connect with additional cards.

3 Parallel Programming Approach

This investigation leverages freely available open-source software packages to support an OpenCL-based parallel programming model for the Calxeda ARM server. In particular, the CO-PRocessing THReads (COPRTHR) software development kit (SDK) [1] was used to provide libraries and tools for the investigation, including an OpenCL implementation for the quad-core ARM processors, an OpenCL RPC implementation for networked compute devices, and an implementation of STandarD Compute Layer (STDCL).

OpenCL is an industry standard application programming interface (API) for parallel programming of heterogeneous computing platforms [15]. OpenCL provides a portable vendor- and device-independent low-level API for programming parallel platforms. Since an OpenCL implementation for the ARM processor was not available as part of the standard software stack on the Calxeda system, the implementation provided by the COPRTHR SDK was selected to test the ARM processor. In addition, the OpenCL RPC implementation provided by the COPRTHR SDK, designated CLRPC, provided the ability to target multiple ARM SoCs as networked compute devices on the Calxeda platform, which allowed the investigation of inter-device parallelism within an OpenCL programming model.

The operation of CLRPC is outside of the OpenCL standard and warrants discussion. The OpenCL compute capability of any networked device can be exported using a CLRPC server (clrpcd) running on the host node of the device. A clrpcd server will export all available OpenCL platforms on a given host node. An application code running elsewhere can access all exported OpenCL platforms through libocl.so by providing a list of the network addresses for known servers in an ocl.conf file that replaces the standard OpenCL installable client driver (ICD) enumeration.

One drawback of OpenCL is that, in comparison to its closest vendor-supported competitor, Compute Unified Device Architecture (CUDA), its direct use in application development proves to be more tedious and complicated. For this reason, STDCL is used here for host-side application programming. STDCL is an API [4] that leverages OpenCL, but supports more natural programming syntax and semantics for application development. STDCL provides support for default compute contexts, conventional memory allocation of device-sharable memory, event management, and a dynamic kernel loader that supports a more traditional compilation model and an offline kernel compiler.

A particularly significant feature of STDCL used in this investigation is the default context, stdnpu, that leverages CLRPC to provide a single compute context containing all networked compute devices. This feature has no direct equivalent in the OpenCL standard and creates a unique parallel programming model for the Calxeda platform.

4 Auto-Tuning OpenCL N-Body Benchmark

The N-body algorithm is used to solve Newton's laws of motion for N particles subject to an inter-particle force. The algorithm requires the update of all particle positions and velocities based upon the distance of a given particle to all others by calculating a distance-dependent force and then numerically integrating the equations of motion using a fixed-time step. The N-body algorithm provides an excellent benchmark[12] for the evaluation of a computing platform for several reasons. First, the basic algorithm is representative of many real-world computational kernels, and may serve as a proxy for their expected performance. Second, the manner in which the simulation is performed is relatively clean without superfluous computations that would complicate the interpretation of the performance benchmarks. Third, the algorithm provides a simple mechanism of sweeping a single parameter, the number of particles, to drive the system into a compute bound regime because computation and data movement scale as $O(N^2)$ and $O(N)$, respectively. Finally, the simulation is commonly implemented on a range of architectures and provides a convenient canonical algorithm for comparative benchmarking.

Although OpenCL software is portable across many devices, that does not imply performance portability. This investigation included running an auto-tuning OpenCL N-body benchmark that parameterized the kernel in ways that impact performance across different architectures and compilers. The parameters are used to auto-generate kernel source, as opposed to passing arguments, compiled for each unique case. Similar brute force automatically tuning schemes have been used to optimize linear algebra routines in the ATLAS and GATLAS packages for particular architectures.

The kernel parameterization is described below. The parameter *nmulti* is the number of particles updated per thread. This outer-loop multiplicity may allow a compiler to automatically vectorize the computation. The parameter *nunroll* defines the explicit unrolling within the inner loop over particle pair interactions.

The parameter *nblock* is the number of particle positions cooperatively cached by a work-group in local memory for calculating particle pair interactions. This essentially replaces the inner loop over particles with a double loop over blocks of *nblock* particles and a nested loop over the cached particle positions. The parameter *nthread* determines the OpenCL work-group size.

5 Evaluation Study

5.1 Methodology

The software stack supporting an OpenCL-based parallel programming model described in Sect. 3 had never been tested on the Calxeda ARM server architecture. The simplest configuration used to obtain benchmarks involved the execution of an OpenCL benchmark using the CPU OpenCL implementation directly (OpenCL direct). This scenario involves running the host program on the same device node that is also used to execute the OpenCL kernels on up to four cores, and is the conventional model for OpenCL CPU implementations.

CLRPC enables a transparent client-server model to export an OpenCL compute device to another node. Using this scenario (CLRPC remote), a clrpcd server is run on a different device node from that which is used to execute the host program. This configuration is still limited to using up to four cores for the execution of OpenCL kernels.

A variation of the CLRPC remote configuration involves executing the host program on the same device node used to run the clrpcd server, and in turn execute the OpenCL kernels (CLRPC local). The difference here between OpenCL direct and CLRPC local is that in the latter case, the device must incur the overhead of interacting with the local clrpcd server.

All of the above configurations are limited to using up to four cores for executing OpenCL kernels. The STDCL compute context stdnpu, that leverages CLRPC to provide access to all networked compute devices, expands the parallel programmability of the platform by allowing multiple compute devices to be used from a single compute context. This configuration (stdnpu) can be used to study the scaling of the parallel programming model over the entire system of networked ARM SoCs in a Calxeda server, aggregated into a single compute context accessible from a host program running on any node.

Performance measurements reflect results for an OpenCL N-body benchmark based on default code originally tuned for high-end GPUs. This code was modified to develop the auto-tuning benchmark described in Sect. 4. This benchmark was used with different configurations and parameters to explore the Calxeda ARM server platform and the OpenCL-based parallel programming model presented in Sect. 3.

The default benchmark was first used on a single device node with the conventional OpenCL configuration involving a STDCL host program using the OpenCL platform implementation directly (OpenCL direct). The auto-tuning version of the benchmark was then employed to identify the optimum parameters for the parameterized kernel, anticipating that the search would improve the measured performance of the algorithm.

Performance measurements were obtained using CLRPC, which provides a key component for expanding the parallel programmability of the platform beyond a single quad-core device. To address the issue of networking overhead, measurements were taken by running the CLRPC server and STDCL host program on the same device node (CLRPC local) and then repeated by running the CLRPC server on a different device node (CLRPC remote).

Finally, the scaling of the benchmark for 4 to 16 ARM cores was studied using stdnpu, the STDCL default context for all networked compute devices that, in turn, leveraged CLRPC.

Power is measured using the BMC interface for more than the quad-core ARM processor itself and includes other elements of the SoC like the network fabric, global memory, etc. Power data consisted of measurements at idle and under full load while running an N-body benchmark with 32,768 particles, so that the device would be driven well into the compute regime and under full utilization.

5.2 Results

The results reported in this paper are for single-precision floating point computations. The default N-body benchmark was executed with 16,384 particles and nthread=16 using the OpenCL direct configuration and exhibited 983 MFLOPS (million floating point operations per second). With this number of particles, the simulation is driven well into a compute bound regime on this architecture, as discussed more thoroughly below. Examining CPU utilization using the Linux top command showed nearly 400% utilization, indicating that all four ARM cores were utilized at full load. The auto-tuning benchmark was run using the same number of particles and identified an optimized kernel that exhibited 1,094 MFLOPS, a gain of 11.3% over the default benchmark.

Using the CLRPC local configuration, where the clrpcd server and STDCL host program are run on the same device node, the identical default benchmark exhibited 840 MFLOPS. Examining CPU utilization showed that the clrpcd server was running at approximately 350% with the host program using the balance of approximately 50%. With this configuration, the clrpcd server executes the computational load, and the host program drives the computation through RPC client calls. The results provide an indication of the host program overhead incurred when using CLRPC. The reduction in performance (15%) is consistent with the reduction in utilization (13%).

Using the CLRPC remote configuration, where the clrpcd server and STDCL host program are run on different device nodes, the identical benchmark achieved 980 MFLOPS and the clrpcd server showed nearly 400% utilization. This demonstrates that the resource contention found with the CLRPC local configuration can be entirely mitigated when the clrpcd server is run on a separate device node and the CLRPC overhead remains with the host program.

Figure 2 portrays the results for different numbers of particles. Using the OpenCL direct configuration, the benchmark reaches a pure compute regime at around 1,024 particles. For smaller numbers of particles, the performance is negatively impacted by non-compute operations. This reduced performance for small numbers of particles is observed on nearly all architectures and is expected.

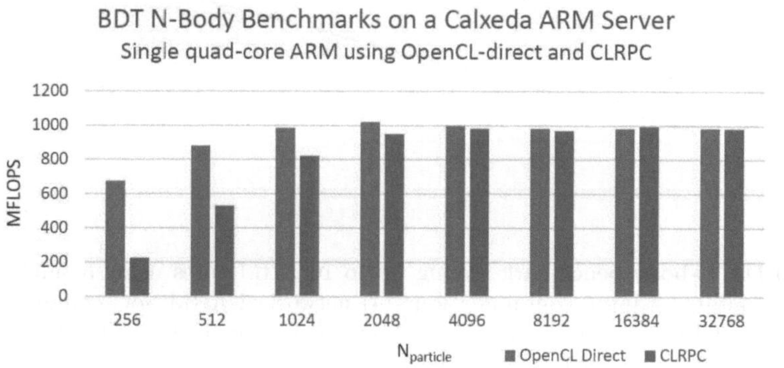

Fig. 2. Performance results for BDT N-body on a single quad-core ARM device on a Calxeda server. Comparison is between the OpenCL direct and CLRPC remote configurations.

Results using the CLRPC remote configuration are also depicted in Fig. 2, where it can be seen that a greater overhead is incurred for small numbers of particles. Not only does the benchmark show that it reaches a compute regime at a slightly larger number of particles by roughly a factor of two, there is a greater decrease in performance as the number of particles is reduced.

Two factors are likely impacting the performance. First, the relative cost of data movement and compute will decrease linearly with the number of particles, being $O(N)$ and $O(N^2)$, respectively. Second, there is is an overhead associated with the CLRPC implementation that will become more pronounced as the computational load is reduced. Nevertheless, the results show that CLRPC can be used effectively for computationally intensive tasks.

The default STDCL context stdnpu containing all networked compute devices, which leverages CLRPC, was used to demonstrate the parallel programmability of the ARM server beyond a single quad-core processor. Figure 3 represents the scaling of the OpenCL N-body benchmark using multiple ARM SoCs up to 16 ARM cores for various system sizes. For the smallest system, scaling is predictably poor because insufficient work is provided per core to mitigate the overhead. However, with a sufficiently large system, the scaling is nearly linear through 12 cores. The deviation from linear scaling at 16 cores is attributable to the overhead described above for the CLRPC local configuration, since the 4th ARM SoC is executing the host program.

Power measurements are displayed in Fig. 4 and indicate a power variance between ARM SoCs that is significant, with a minimum (maximum) idle power of 3.3 W (4.6 W). Under full load, the power increase is reasonably consistent with a minimum (maximum) cost of an additional 0.85 W (1.2 W).

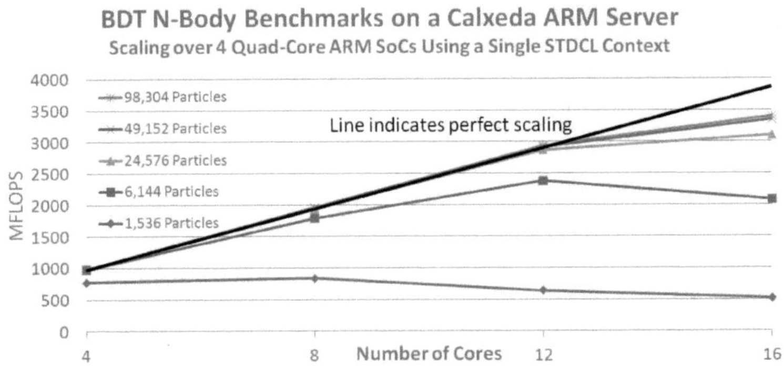

Fig. 3. BDT N-body benchmark scaling up to 16 ARM cores using a single STDCL compute context, stdnpu, containing four (4) networked ARM SoC compute devices. STDCL uses CLRPC to access all of the ARM devices in the Calxeda platform.

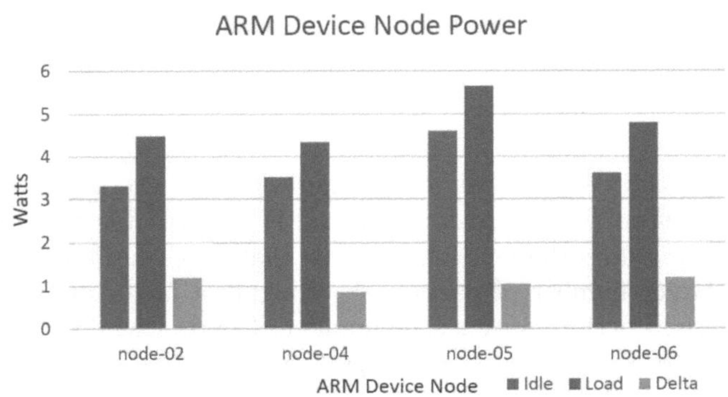

Fig. 4. Calxeda power requirements at idle (blue) and under load (orange) while executing N-body application. The difference between idle and load are indicated by the green bar.

5.3 Analysis and Discussion

The Calxeda ARM server provides a platform that is functionally equivalent to a small cluster of quad-core processors, each running a standard Linux OS. Using an OpenCL N-body benchmark, the ARM processor yielded the computational performance of approximately 1 GFLOP. The ARM SoC device nodes used 3.3 W-4.6 W of power when idle and 4.35 W-5.65 W under full load. Therefore, the power efficiency for this benchmark is approximately 1 GFLOPS/W in terms of processor power and approximately 0.2 GFLOPS/W in terms of total node power. By comparison, using the auto-tuning N-body benchmark on a system with dual Intel Xeon X5650 CPUs (12 cores @ 2.66 GHz) resulted 83.7 GFLOPS with a combined thermal design power of 190 W. Based on this limited scope of power data, it remains difficult to assess the relative power efficiency of the quad-core ARM SoC device since the measured power includes components that do not align with the power measurements of other architectures.

The Calxeda system supported the use of CLRPC to allow OpenCL applications to access any networked OpenCL devices. CLRPC performance shows some overhead for workloads with lightweight kernels, and matches the performance of using OpenCL directly for computationally intensive workloads.

6 Related Work

Others have developed test suites that cover combinations of OpenCL operations, element types, and local sizes to test performance and numerical precision of GPU systems in terms of OpenCL operations [10].

In comparative performance studies between CUDA and OpenCL versions of the same applications, Fang et.al [7] and Komatsu et.al. [11], have shown that performance can be comparable if the kernels are optimized by hand or by compiler optimizations. They also highlighted how automatic parameter tuning is essential to enable a single OpenCL code to run efficiently on various GPUs, motivating the need for auto-tuning for each system and for comparative performance studies. Yao et.al. [16] studied the performance portability of OpenCL across diverse architectures including NVIDIA GPU, Intel Ivy Bridge CPU, and AMD Fusion APU, using three OpenCL benchmarks–SGEMM, SpMV, and FFT. They found that performance portability requires tuning threads-data mapping, data layout, tiling size, data caching, and operation-specific factors. Other studies of OpenCL performance include comparing against OpenMP for multi-core CPUs [14]. Beyond CUDA and OpenCL, frameworks for GPU programming with abstraction include Halide [13] and HIPAcc [2] for image processing.

7 Conclusions and Future Work

To our knowledge, this is the first effort to investigate the use of OpenCL to support a parallel programming model for a Calxeda ARM server. The initial success of applying a novel OpenCL-based parallel programming model that includes the use of a high-level abstraction for OpenCL and an RPC implementation of OpenCL to access networked compute devices demonstrates the potential of this model for utilizing the large number of ARM cores available on a fully configured Calxeda system. Empirical results are obtained for executing an OpenCL N-body benchmark using various configurations and for a range of parameters from which the power efficiency of the quad-core ARM processors could be evaluated. An auto-tuning benchmark was developed that can be used to optimize the computational kernel for a given architecture. Power efficiency results are not sufficient to make a determination as to the energy efficiency of an ARM-based server compared with competing architectures. Future work includes scaling to a much larger number of cores.

Acknowledgments This research was supported in part by an appointment to the Faculty Research Participation Program at the U.S. Army Research Laboratory administered by the Oak Ridge Institute for Science and Engineering through an interagency agreement between the U.S. Department of Energy and USARL.

References

1. COPRTHR SDK (2012), `http://www.browndeertechnology.com/coprthr.htm`
2. HIPAcc - Heterogeneous Image Processing Acceleration (2012), `http://hipacc.sourceforge.net/index.html`
3. Borkar, S.: The exascale challenge. In: 2010 International Symposium on VLSI Design Automation and Test (VLSI-DAT), pp. 2–3 (2010)
4. Brown Deer Technology: STDCL: A Simplified C Interface for OpenCL, revision 1.4 (2012)
5. Calxeda: Calxeda launches the energycore processor; delivers 10 times the performance for the same power (2013), `http://www.calxeda.com`
6. Carroll, A., Heiser, G.: An analysis of power consumption in a smartphone. In: Proceedings of the 2010 USENIX Conference on USENIX Annual Technical Conference, USENIXATC 2010, p. 21. USENIX Association, Berkeley (2010)
7. Fang, J., Varbanescu, A.L., Sips, H.: A comprehensive performance comparison of CUDA and OpenCL. In: Proceedings of the 2011 International Conference on Parallel Processing, ICPP 2011, pp. 216–225. IEEE Computer Society (2011)
8. Furber, S.: ARM System on Chip Architecture. Addison Wesley (2000)
9. Gioiosa, R.: Towards sustainable exascale computing. In: 2010 18th IEEE/IFIP VLSI System on Chip Conference (VLSI-SoC), pp. 270–275 (2010)
10. Jurecko, M., Kocisová, J., Busa Jr., J., Kasanický, T., Domiter, M., Zvada, M.: Evaluation framework for GPU performance based on OpenCL standard. In: ICNC, pp. 256–261 (2010)
11. Komatsu, K., Sato, K., Arai, Y., Koyama, K., Takizawa, H., Kobayashi, H.: Evaluating performance and portability of OpenCL programs. In: The Fifth International Workshop on Automatic Performance Tuning (June 2010)
12. Playne, D.P., Johnson, M.G.B., Hawick, K.A.: Benchmarking GPU devices with N-body simulations. In: Proc. 2009 International Conference on Computer Design (CDES 2009), WorldComp, Las Vegas, USA, July 13-16, pp. 150–156 (2009)
13. Ragan-Kelley, J., Barnes, C., Adams, A., Paris, S., Durand, F., Amarasinghe, S.: Halide: a language and compiler for optimizing parallelism, locality, and recomputation in image processing pipelines. SIGPLAN Not. 48(6), 519–530 (2013)
14. Shen, J., Fang, J., Sips, H.J., Varbanescu, A.L.: Performance gaps between OpenMP and OpenCL for multi-core CPUs. In: ICPP Workshops, pp. 116–125. IEEE Computer Society (2012)
15. Stone, J.E., Gohara, D., Shi, G.: OpenCL: A parallel programming standard for heterogeneous computing systems. IEEE Des. Test 12(3), 66–73 (2010)
16. Zhang, Y., Sinclair II, M., Chien, A.A.: Improving performance portability in OpenCL programs. In: Kunkel, J.M., Ludwig, T., Meuer, H.W. (eds.) ISC 2013. LNCS, vol. 7905, pp. 136–150. Springer, Heidelberg (2013)

Active Data Structures on GPGPUs

John T. O'Donnell, Cordelia Hall, and Stuart Monro

School of Computing Science, University of Glasgow,
Glasgow, United Kingdom
http://www.dcs.gla.ac.uk/~jtod/

Abstract. Active data structures support operations that may affect a large number of elements of an aggregate data structure. They are well suited for extremely fine grain parallel systems, including circuit parallelism. General purpose GPUs were designed to support regular graphics algorithms, but their intermediate level of granularity makes them potentially viable also for active data structures. We consider the characteristics of active data structures and discuss the feasibility of implementing them on GPGPUs. We describe the GPU implementations of two such data structures, extensible sparse functional (ESF) arrays and index intervals. We measure their performance and discuss the potential of active data structures as an unconventional programming model that can exploit the capabilities of emerging fine grain architectures such as GPUs.

Keywords: active data structure, data parallel, circuit parallel, GPU, GPGPU, persistent kernel, index interval, functional array, selection.

1 Introduction

GPUs originated as parallel graphics processing units, but they have evolved into general purpose parallel processors, sometimes called GPGPUs. A GPU contains a moderately large number ($\sim 10^3$) of processing elements that execute multiple threads concurrently. They have been applied successfully to a wide range of scientific applications, which consist largely of data parallel iterations over arrays.

It is important to discover how widely applicable GPUs are because they fit well with current trends in computer architecture, and they provide a good level of granularity. The density of transistors per chip continues to grow, but individual processors are no longer becoming faster. Therefore computer architects are seeking effective ways to use additional transistors to support parallel computing.

A current trend is to reduce the granularity of computation. The granularity of a parallel system relates the size and number of processing elements. Multicore systems have on the order of 10 to 100 processors and memories. GPGPUs have a finer granularity, with a larger number of processing elements (thousands) that are smaller and less powerful than CPUs [5]. Very fine grain SIMD parallel systems, such as the Connection Machine [8], have large numbers of very small

D. an Mey et al. (Eds.): Euro-Par 2013 Workshops, LNCS 8374, pp. 875–884, 2014.

processors. FPGAs (field programmable gate arrays) and CGRA (coarse grain reconfigurable architectures) allow even finer grain parallelism, but they are less portable and harder to program than GPUs. In his Turing Award lecture, Backus argues that finer grain parallel programming models can reduce the bottleneck between a processor and a memory [2].

Applications for GPUs are often organised as a collection of tasks coordinated by the CPU. A task that runs on the GPU is called a kernel, consisting of many concurrent threads organised into several blocks that run on parallel processing elements in the GPU. When all threads have completed, the kernel terminates. A full application will typically perform many kernel launches and terminations. This programming model supports regular parallelism across large and regular data structures.

There is increasing interest in investigating the applicability of GPUs to a broader range of applications. A general discussion of the limitations of GPUs and how to overcome them is given in [7]. One approach is to provide MIMD computations on a GPU, which is essentially SIMD, using interpretation [4]. A cost model for GPU computation is presented in [17].

This paper investigates the application of GPUs to *active data structures* [1], which cause a single operation to affect many elements of a data structure. Examples of active data structures include associative memories and content addressable parallel processors [6]. Active data structures are well suited for "circuit parallelism", such as FPGA or VLSI implementation. These platforms are hard to use and nonportable, so it would be valuable to provide GPU implementations of active data structures. However, there are many challenges in doing so.

The contribution of this paper is an experimental investigation of the suitability of GPUs for active data structures that exploit fine grain parallel computation. We discuss the characteristics of active data structures and the technical challenges in implementing them on a GPU. We then describe the implementation and performance of two experimental case studies: index interval selection and extensible sparse functional arrays. The ESF array algorithm provides operations that have extremely low variance in execution time, making them especially useful for real time applications. To help make the programming techniques more widely available, and to enable others to replicate our experiments, the source code and further documentation are available on the web [13].

Section 2 introduces active data structures, and Section 3 discusses the architectural capabilities needed to implement them. Section 4 describes several active data structures and their experimental implementation on a GPU, and gives performance results. Section 5 concludes.

2 Active Data Structures

An active data structure provides a set of high level operations, where each operation may cause changes to many elements within the structure. This could be simply a software abstraction layer, but it is also possible to use parallelism to implement the operations.

The earliest active data structures were associative memories [6]. A conventional memory identifies each memory element by an address. The fetch and store operations supply an address, and the memory hardware uses a tree of multiplexers or demultiplexers to access the data. Associative memory (also called content-addressable memory) stores words that contain several fields: for example each word might contain (x, y) where the components x and y are bit fields. A memory access instruction provides the value of one of the bit fields (say $x = 147$), and the hardware returns the corresponding value of the other field.

Associative memory can be implemented efficiently with *circuit parallelism.* The memory contains a set of registers, each holding all the bit fields of an element. A dedicated comparison circuit is attached to every register in the memory. When an access instruction provides a value of the x field, this is broadcast ("fanned out") to all the comparison circuits, which determine whether the corresponding element matches. These comparisons are performed in parallel; the time to search n items is typically reduced by a factor of at least $O(\log n)$. Associative memory can reduce communication costs for data intensive applications, with organisation of the data into suitable chunks [10].

The basic idea behind associative memory—to add some logic to each word in a memory, and also to add some logic to the address decoder tree—can be extended further, to powerful "smart memories" that mix memory and computation at a very fine grain. Many applications take this approach, including hardware cache and translation lookaside buffers, database searches, and signal processing. The most efficient platform for such a system is a specialised VLSI design, but the design cost is high and the result is inflexible. It would be valuable to adapt GPUs to active data structures, because GPUs are more cost effective, more portable, and more flexible than custom chips.

3 GPU Capabilities Required for Active Data Structures

GPUs were originally intended to accelerate graphics rendering, a specialised class of algorithm. Because of their high performance and relatively low power consumption, they have been applied to an increasingly wide range of applications, especially in scientific programming.

This does not mean, however, that GPUs are well suited for all kinds of programs. They have several properties that can potentially limit their use for some applications. GPUs offer better support for data parallelism than task parallelism. They have a complex memory model, with limitations in sharing of data and widely varying latency. Synchronisation among threads requires careful programming and can introduce significant overheads.

Many GPU applications are organised as a set of tasks that are coordinated by the CPU. Each task is a function (called a kernel) that is called by the CPU and that runs on the GPU. When all threads in the kernel finish, the kernel terminates and the CPU resumes its computation. Communication between the CPU and the GPU takes place through global memory, which is shared by both systems.

The computation in a GPU takes place in a set of blocks; each block can run a set of threads concurrently. Blocks use different processing elements, so threads in different blocks run in parallel, but threads in the same block may be implemented by receiving very short time slices (one clock cycle) on a single processing element. This hides the latency of memory accesses: if a thread has requested a memory fetch, it is more efficient to allow other threads to execute for a clock cycle rather than stalling the entire system until the data has arrived from the memory. Thus threads can provide parallelism *in effect* even though they may not be truly parallel at the level of the processor clock.

GPUs have a complex memory model, with four or five different kinds of memory. Global memory is accessible to all threads in all blocks, and also to the CPU, but it has high latency. Shared memory is accessible to all the threads within the same block, but not to other blocks or the CPU. Global memory is more flexible but its latency is two orders of magnitude higher than shared memory. Other types of GPU memory, such as constant and texture memory, are not used in our algorithms.

Communication across blocks. The overhead of communication between threads in different blocks is high, for two reasons: (1) threads across blocks must communicate via the slow global memory rather than shared memory; and (2) it is more costly to implement a barrier synchronisation across blocks than across threads within a block. To achieve fast execution, it is necessary to minimise the use of costly communications across blocks, and to do this efficiently where it is necessary.

Persistent shared memory. For efficient execution, it is important to keep active data structures in shared memory. There are two problems with this: (1) threads in different blocks cannot access each other's shared memory, so they can communicate only using global memory, and (2) when the kernel (the function running on the GPU) returns, the contents of shared memory is lost. When inter-block communication is needed, the threads can write data out to global memory, requiring synchronisation across blocks. To achieve persistence, it is necessary to organise the kernel as a long running loop that performs many active data structure operations. In effect, the kernel runs indefinitely. This prevents use of the common program organisation of a sequence of kernel calls. Instead, it is necessary to treat the GPU as a server, and to introduce a concurrent dialogue between the CPU and the GPU (see below).

Synchronisation across blocks. The GPU system provides a primitive barrier synchronisation for threads within a block, but not for threads in different blocks. Active data structures often require multiple blocks, either to gain access to more memory (there is a strict limit on fast shared memory for all the threads in a block) or to increase parallelism.

A common approach for applications that need multiple blocks is to organise the algorithm into sections; each section is initiated by the CPU with a kernel call and runs independently in the blocks. When all the threads have terminated, the kernel terminates, returning control to the CPU. This effectively provides a cross-block barrier synchronisation, and also allows the CPU to assist with communication and any sequential computations that are required.

That common approach is not workable for many active data structure algorithms: it prevents the use of persistent shared memory, it increases overhead, and it introduces a sequential bottleneck. An alternative, which we use in the ESFA system described below, is to use a barrier that operates across blocks [16].

Dialogue between CPU and GPU. Many GPU applications are organised as a sequence of calls from the CPU to a kernel running on the GPU. Data is communicated between the CPU and GPU using global memory and functional arguments and results. If persistent shared memory is required, however, then the GPU needs to run a long-term server: the kernel is effectively an infinite loop that terminates only when the server is shut down. We implement the interaction by running the CPU and the kernel in parallel, with a concurrent protocol using locks to coordinate the CPU and the GPU. First the CPU starts the kernel, which initialises its state (kept in persistent shared memory). The CPU uses a lock to signal that it has a request; the GPU waits on this lock, copies the request, and signals that it has the data. A similar protocol is used by the GPU to tell the CPU that it has a result.

4 Case Studies

We have implemented two active data structure systems on a GPGPU, in order to assess the capabilities of the system and the performance, which are discussed in the following subsections. The system used is running CUDA version 4 on an NVidia GeForce GTX 590, with 512 CUDA cores (16 multiprocessors with 32 cores per mp), and a 1.22 GHz clock speed, with CUDA capability 2.0.

4.1 Index Intervals

Data structures based on *index intervals* [11] support a family of operations on ordered data structures, including selection and sorting algorithms. The algorithms on index intervals are related to quicksort. The idea is to represent explicitly what is known about the location of a value x within the sorted array, rather than using the physical memory address of the value to represent its ordering. Associative searches, rather than indexed addresses, are used to retrieve the data.

Consider an unsorted array $x_0, x_1, \ldots, x_{n-1}$. For any data value x_i, we represent the information that is known about its position in the (unknown) sorted array as a pair (lo, hi), such that $lo \leq j \leq hi$, where j is the position of x_i in the fully sorted array. The (lo, hi) pairs state explicitly the partial information that is known at any time about the data values. Initially nothing is known, so every value has an index interval of $(0, n-1)$, but if the array is fully sorted, then the element x_j will have index interval (j, j).

An operation *improve* takes an index interval, which defines a set Y of elements that have this interval, and refines the interval for every member of Y. This is done in parallel and takes a small constant number of steps, where each step operates in parallel on every value. First an element of Y, called the splitter, is selected. This is broadcast (in parallel) to every element. The elements are then compared (in parallel) with the splitter, and a local flag is set indicating the result. The numbers of elements that are less than (and also equal to) the splitter are counted (using a parallel fold), and this enables each cell to refine its index interval (using a parallel local computation). The entire *improve* operation consists of two parallel folds and two parallel maps.

As shown in [11], index interval sorting has a slightly lower computational complexity than conventional quicksort. Its larger significance, however, is the ability to use the *improve* step just where needed.

4.2 GPU Implementation of Index Intervals

Each array element is stored in one "cell", which is in effect a record of fields operated on by one thread. Parallel fold is used to locate an imprecise index interval, and a parallel map causes every cell to refine its index intervals. Table 1 shows the times for the local computations required by the *improve* algorithm. This includes the comparisons and interval adjustments in the cells, but not the parallel folds.

Table 1. Performance of *improve* step for refining index intervals. N is the number of cells, T is the mean time in microseconds over 1000 measurements, and stdev is the standard deviation.

N	T	stdev
1024	27.5	0.932189
2048	42.2	1.187385
4096	66.3	3.829351
8192	107.2	1.995101
10240	125.9	4.736220

4.3 ESF Arrays

Extensible sparse functional arrays (ESFA) [12] [14] are a complex data structure with demanding computational requirements. It is possible to use imperative arrays in a functional language [9] [3], and there are many algorithms for purely functional data structures [15]. Imperative arrays provide access time of O(1), and it is conjectured that this is impossible for functional arrays on a von Neumann architecture. Nevertheless, ESFA achieves O(1) access time for functional arrays (and several generalisations, including sparse and extensible arrays) using circuit parallelism. Thus the ESFA algorithm is inherently massively parallel.

The algorithm is implemented as a layer of software that runs on a digital circuit that implements a "smart memory". A program can build a collection of ESFA using the *update* operation, which takes an array, index, and value, and creates a new array which is identical to the old one except that it has the specified value at the index. The essential point is that the update is purely functional: update creates a new array but the old one is still available.

It is straightforward to implement functional arrays by building tree structures in the heap, but this means that all operations require a number of steps which is proportional to the tree height. In the best case this gives logarithmic time, but many practical cases have array lookup time that is linear in the size of the array. It is possible to rebalance the trees periodically, but that adds additional significant overheads.

The ESFA system implements every operation in a small constant number of steps. Each step runs on a digital circuit (which can be real or virtual) that has the same topology as a conventional random access memory (RAM). The circuit provides a set of registers for each memory cell, and a tree of logic gates providing access to the cells from a controller. In a conventional RAM chip, the tree circuit is a word multiplexer, while in the ESFA system the tree nodes perform parallel fold calculations. Furthermore, each leaf cell in the ESFA circuit contains a small amount of logic circuitry, enabling every cell to perform a simple calculation on every clock cycle. Typical leaf cell calculations are to compare two natural numbers and set a flag with the result, and to increment a natural number if a flag is True.

ESFA is a powerful application of active data structures. It makes a challenging test case for GPU implementation because each ESFA operation performs a small calculation (a comparison and increment) in every cell in the machine, not just every cell in the data structure referenced by the operation.

4.4 GPU Implementation of ESF Arrays

The GPU implementation requires all of the techniques discussed above in Section 3. We used the lock-free algorithm of Xiao and Feng [16] for synchronising across blocks. We used our own parallel fold algorithm, which is more general than many published algorithms and also makes efficient use of the shared and global memories. We also developed a concurrent algorithm for controlling communication and synchronisation between the CPU and the GPU. The kernel needs to be organised carefully, especially to avoid race conditions and to minimise the scope of conditionals. The program is available on the web [13].

Table 2 shows the performance of the algorithm, as a function of the number of ESFA cells. A number of observations can be made from this data. The total execution time (the T column) grows slowly as a function of the log of the number of cells. The fastest execution occurs with the smallest ESFA memory size, but at the largest memory size (larger by a factor of 512) the execution time is only three times higher. The execution is most efficient at the largest size. Furthermore, the measurements are highly repeatable with low variance.

Table 3 compares the performance of the parallel GPU implementation of ESFA with a sequential simulator. For small data, the overhead of parallelisation makes the GPU slower than the sequential CPU. However, the sequential time

Table 2. ESFA performance on GPU. Each line shows the configuration (k = tree depth, $b \times t$ = blocks × threads, N = number of cells) and the total time T in milliseconds for a run consisting of 50,000 operations (including a mix of updates, lookups, and deletes). For each configuration, the execution was repeated 25 times, and the result of every operation was compared with the result calculated by an executable specification. Thus $10 \times 25 \times 50,000 = 12,500,000$ major operations were performed without error. stdv = standard deviation of T; d = max-min of T. The t column gives the time per ESFA operation in microseconds, and the t_c column gives the time in microseconds per operation per cell.

k	$b \times t$	N	T(ms)	stdv	d	$t(\mu s/op)$	$t_c(\mu s/op/c)$
4	4 × 4	16	5,071.1	32.3	104.0	101.4	6.34
5	4 × 8	32	5,374.3	30.9	99.9	107.5	3.36
6	4 × 16	64	5,606.1	25.9	117.1	112.1	1.75
7	8 × 16	128	6,447.8	26.0	123.7	128.9	1.01
8	16 × 16	256	7,946.3	32.7	122.8	158.9	0.62
9	16 × 32	512	7,994.0	14.0	65.7	159.9	0.31
10	16 × 64	1,024	8,426.2	25.1	101.0	168.5	0.16
11	32 × 64	2,048	12,144.0	35.9	125.0	242.9	0.12
12	32 × 128	4,096	13,424.4	33.5	106.5	268.5	0.06
13	32 × 256	8,192	15,037.2	44.7	183.1	300.7	0.03

Table 3. Parallel speedup, comparing execution time for performing 50,000 operations on the sequential simulator and on the parallel GPU implementation of ESFA. The CPU times were measured one time, the GPU times (taken from Table 2) are the mean of 25 runs. The speedup is $T\text{cpu}/T\text{gpu}$; this is the speedup as a function of the number of ESFA cells, *not* as a function of parallel processors in the GPU.

k	Tcpu	Tgpu	Speedup
4	1,232 ms	5,071.1 ms	0.243
5	2,067 ms	5,374.3 ms	0.385
6	4,046 ms	5,606.1 ms	0.722
7	9,426 ms	6,447.8 ms	1.462
8	24,765 ms	7,946.3 ms	3.117
9	65,193 ms	7,994.0 ms	8.155
10	176,428 ms	8,426.2 ms	20.938
11	534,878 ms	12,144.0 ms	44.045
12	1,866,045 ms	13,424.4 ms	139.004
13	7,228,694 ms	15,037.2 ms	480.721

grows linearly with the size of the data structure because each operation acts on every element, while the GPU time grows slowly.

These results demonstrate how effective GPUs can be for active data structures. Consider an ESFA machine with 8K cells. An efficient sequential algorithm (*not* a simulator) using a tree structure may require an average of 13 RAM accesses to perform an ESFA operation, with additional overhead for loop control.

With fast memory hardware, this would amount to around 0.1 to 1 microsecond. However, if an array is long—say 5000 elements—and the tree is not balanced, the access would require 50 to 500 microseconds. For comparison, ESFA running on the GPU requires 300 microseconds. It is, of course, possible to rebalance the trees periodically, but that introduces further overhead, requires more storage, and increases the variance in execution time. The ESFA algorithm *always* requires a time of 300 microseconds, without any extra overheads, making it valuable for real time applications where each operation must be completed within a deadline.

5 Conclusion

Active data structure algorithms scale well to very large numbers of processors, but they have several characteristics that make them challenging for implementation on GPUs. Key issues include communication and synchronisation across blocks, persistent shared memory, and interaction protocols between the CPU and GPU. We have identified algorithms that solve those key issues. One is a lock-free block synchronisation algorithm by Xiao and Feng [16], and we have developed others (a CPU/GPU dialogue, and efficient and general fold and scan algorithms).

Using these algorithms, we have evaluated the effectiveness of a GPU for implementing active data structures, using two case studies: a relatively straightforward index interval selection/sorting algorithm, and a very complex extensible sparse functional array algorithm. The speedup results compared with sequential versions of the active data structures are excellent, with a speedup factor of 480 on the ESFA algorithm.

There may be sequential algorithms using conventional data structures that are faster on a sequential machine. The key question is: can GPUs provide good enough performance for active data structures to compete well against the best sequential algorithm? The results are encouraging. ESFA on a GPU is sometimes slower than a sequential tree implementation of functional arrays, but in some realistic cases it is significantly faster, unless extra time is taken to rebalance the trees sequentially. Furthermore, the GPU ESFA algorithm has time complexity of $O(1)$ in the worst case as well as the average case. This makes it well suited for real time applications, where predictability, low variance, and a good worst-case time are more important than raw speed. Future research includes investigating active data structures on other platforms with massive fine grain parallelism, including coarse grain reconfigurable architectures (CGRA) and FPGAs.

References

1. Andrews, G.R., Dobkin, D.P.: Active data structures. In: ICSE 1981: Proc. 5th Int. Conf. on Software Engineering, pp. 354–362. IEEE Press (1981)
2. Backus, J.: Can programming be liberated from the von Neumann style? A functional style and its algebra of programs. Communications of the ACM 21(8), 613–641 (1978), doi:10.1145/359576.359579

3. Chakravarty, M.T., Keller, G., Lee, S., McDonnell, T.L., Grover, V.: Accelerating Haskell array codes with multicore GPUs. In: Declarative Aspects of Multicore Programming. ACM (January 2011)
4. Dietz, H.G., Dalton Young, B.: MIMD Interpretation on a GPU. In: Gao, G.R., Pollock, L.L., Cavazos, J., Li, X. (eds.) LCPC 2009. LNCS, vol. 5898, pp. 65–79. Springer, Heidelberg (2010)
5. Owens, J.D., et al.: A survey of general-purpose computation on graphics hardware. Computer Graphics Forum 26(1), 80–113 (2007)
6. Foster, C.: Content Addressable Parallel Processors. Cengage Learning EMEA (1976) ISBN-13: 978-0442224332
7. Gaster, B.R., Howes, L.: Can GPU programming be liberated from the data-parallel bottleneck? Computer 45(8), 42–52 (2012), doi:10.1109/MC.2012.257
8. Daniel Hillis, W.: The Connection Machine. MIT Press (1985) ISBN 978-0262081573
9. Peyton Jones, S.L., Wadler, P.L.: Imperative functional programming. In: Proc. 20th ACM Symposium on Principles of Programming Languages (POPL), pp. 71–84 (1993)
10. Nath, P., Urgaonkar, B., Sivasubramaniam, A.: Evaluating the usefulness of content-addressable storage for high-performance data-intensive applications. In: Proceedings of the ACM/IEEE International Symposium on High Performance Distributed Computing (HPDC 2008), pp. 35–44. ACM (2008)
11. O'Donnell, J.T.: Functional microprogramming for a data parallel architecture. In: Proceedings of the 1988 Glasgow Workshop on Functional Programming, pp. 124–145. Computing Science Department, University of Glasgow (1988)
12. O'Donnell, J.T.: Data parallel implementation of Extensible Sparse Functional Arrays. In: Reeve, M., Bode, A., Wolf, G. (eds.) PARLE 1993. LNCS, vol. 694, pp. 68–79. Springer, Heidelberg (1993)
13. O'Donnell, J.T.: GPU Programming. School of Computing Science, University of Glasgow (2012), `http://www.dcs.gla.ac.uk/~jtod/research/gpu/`
14. O'Donnell, J.T.: Extensible sparse functional arrays with circuit parallelism. In: 15th International Symposium on Principles and Practice of Declarative Programming. ACM (September 2013)
15. Okasaki, C.: Purely functional data structures. Cambridge University Press (1999)
16. Xiao, S., Feng, W.C.: Inter-block GPU communication via fast barrier synchronization. In: IPDPS, pp. 1–12. IEEE (2010)
17. Zhang, Y., Owens, J.D.: A quantitative performance analysis model for GPU architectures. In: 2013 IEEE 19th International Symposium on High Performance Computer Architecture (HPCA), pp. 382–393 (2011)

Architecture of a High-Speed MPI_Bcast Leveraging Software-Defined Network

Khureltulga Dashdavaa[1], Susumu Date[1], Hiroaki Yamanaka[2], Eiji Kawai[2], Yasuhiro Watashiba[1], Kohei Ichikawa[3], Hirotake Abe[4], and Shinji Shimojo[1]

[1] Osaka University
[2] National Institute of Information and Communication Technology
[3] Nara Institute of Science and Technology
[4] University of Tsukuba

Abstract. Collective communication is of great importance in MPI because the execution time of an MPI program is affected by the communication performance it can gain. Particularly these days, when a cluster system composed of multiple computing nodes has become dominant as a large-scale computing system, the execution time of collective communication affects the total execution time of the MPI program. However, in many implementations of MPI, collective communication is developed to make use of unicast-based communication in a repeated and combined way, which may result in inefficient communication. In this paper, we explore the use of a Software-Defined Network, which was originally expected to help network administrators operate networks through central control in a software-programming manner, to accelerate `MPI_Bcast`, a basic collective communication used in MPI. The evaluation in this paper indicates that our prototyped `SDN_MPI_Bcast` is superior to `MPI_Bcast` in OpenMPI in communication performance. Also, the evaluation implies that `SDN_MPI_Bcast` is feasible.

1 Introduction

Message Passing Interface (MPI) [1,2] has been a *de facto* standard API in parallel and distributed computing for around two decades. MPI provides programmers with APIs for point-to-point and collective communication, by taking into consideration possible communication patterns occurring in parallel and distributed computing. Conventional cost-sensitive clusters are usually equipped and configured with gigabit Ethernet switches and famous MPI software, such as OpenMPI [3]. With those combinations, collective communications are implemented as a set of multiple point-to-point communications, which might incur performance penalties caused from packet congestion [4,5].

In this research, we explore a novel method for implementing MPI collective communication leveraging the controllability of interconnect network, brought by Software-Defined Network (SDN) [6,7]. SDN is a new concept of network architecture that enables dynamic control and management in a software-programming manner. SDN is expected to facilitate the daily operations of network administrators. As a proof of concept, we propose an SDN-enabled version of `MPI_Bcast`, the

D. an Mey et al. (Eds.): Euro-Par 2013 Workshops, LNCS 8374, pp. 885–894, 2014.

most basic collective communication, by overturning the conventional assumption that a network is not controllable during computation.

The remaining part of this paper is as follows. Section 2 briefly introduces SDN and then describes the basic idea and approach to MPI Broadcast leveraging SDN. Subsequently, in Section 3, we present the blueprint architecture of MPI Broadcast utilizing the functionalities offered by SDN and then we detail how it is prototyped. In Section 4, an evaluation is conducted to verify the feasibility of our approach of using SDN for MPI Broadcast. Section 5 describes related works. Section 6 concludes the paper.

2 Approach

2.1 Software-Defined Network

Software-Defined Network (SDN) is a new concept of network architecture that separates traditional networking functions into a network control plane (SDN controller) and a data plane (network devices such as switches) [6,7]. Figure 1a shows the layered architecture of SDN. In SDN, a program deployed on the Control Plane works as a SDN controller and is in charge of delivering a set of rules instructing how to deal with network flows to network devices through a Control Data Plane Interface. On the other hand, each of the network devices in the Data Plane is responsible for dealing with network flows according to the rule set delivered by the SDN controller. A promising feature of SDN is that it allows user applications such as MPI programs to interact with SDN controllers.

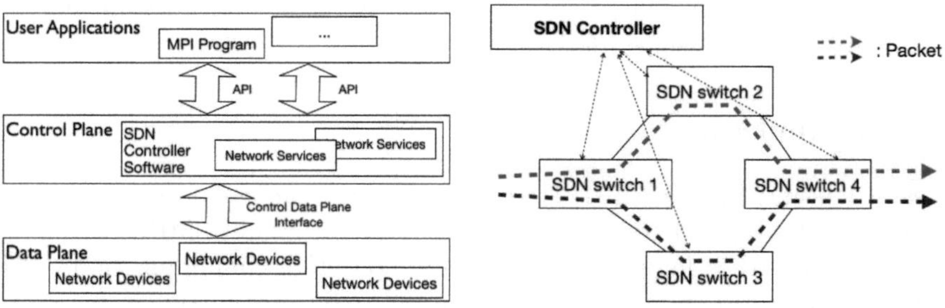

(a) Layered Architecture (b) Controlling Example

Fig. 1. Architecture of Software-Defined Network

From the administrative perspective, SDN is operated as follows. In the case that a network administrator wants to send a specific series of packets to SDN switch 4 from SDN switch 1 via SDN switch 2, all the administrator has to do in SDN is to write and deploy a program as a SDN controller, so that it sends a set of rules describing how to deal with the corresponding series of packets to SDN switches 1, 2 and 4 (Fig. 1b). This behavior is explained from the following SDN mechanism. Under the SDN, whenever the SDN switch receives any packet with which it does not know how to deal, it sends a query in terms of how to deal the packet to the SDN controller. After receiving the packet, the SDN controller informs the SDN switch of a set of rules. In this example case, once the SDN controller installs rules to SDN switch 1, 2, and 4, the specific series of packets is set to flow along the red-arrow path in the figure. Also, in the case that the network administrator wants to set a network flow from SDN switch 1 to SDN switch 4 via SDN switch 3 for another specific series of packets, all the network administrator has to do is to modify the program as a SDN controller.

Currently, OpenFlow [8,9] is a *de facto* standard implementation of SDN. It provides a suite of communication interfaces between the Control Plane and Data Plane [6]. In this feasibility study, OpenFlow is integrated into `MPI_Bcast`.

2.2 Basic Idea Behind the Proposed Solution

The programmability of SDN allows the SDN controller to install a set of rules that duplicate and send incoming packets to specified multiple ports on switches. We approach the SDN-version of `MPI_Bcast`, based on the simple idea that execution time of `MPI_Bcast` can be reduced by duplicating packets on the switch along the data delivery route from a process to remained processes. Specifically, in the case that a process attempts to broadcast data to remained processes, duplicating packets from an incoming port to multiple outgoing ports based on a broadcast tree could lead to the reduction of `MPI_Bcast` execution time. This duplication method is considered to be possible because data on the fly to all remained processes from a source process are identical in MPI Broadcast except for packet headers (Ethernet and IP headers).

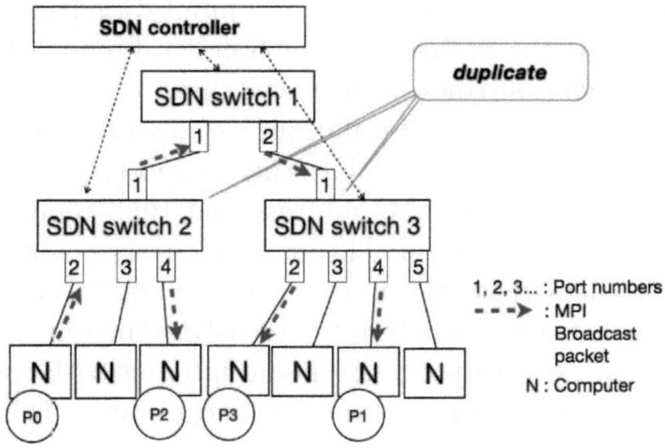

Fig. 2. Basic idea towards SDN MPI Broadcast

Figure 2 illustrates the basic idea regarding how to realize an `MPI_Bcast` using SDN. Assume that 4 processes of an MPI program are running on a computing environment composed of 7 computers, which are connected to a SDN. Also, the figure assumes that Process 0 (P0) is about to broadcast data to P1, P2, and P3. Under this assumption, our proposed method is expected to work as follows.

First, the packet sent by P0 is first delivered to port 2 on SDN switch 2. Then, based on a packet matching rule provided by the SDN controller, SDN switch 2 duplicates and sends it out to port 1 and 4 (respectively for SDN switch 1 and P2). Next, SDN switch 1 forwards data to port 2 (for SDN switch 3) based on the packet matching rule provided by the SDN controller. Finally, SDN switch 3 receives data through port 1 from SDN switch 1. Then SDN switch 3 duplicates data and sends it out to port 2 and 4 (respectively for P3 and P4).

3 Design and Implementation of SDN-Based MPI Broadcast

3.1 Design of SDN-Based MPI_Bcast

In order to realize MPI Broadcast using the proposed method explained in Section 2, MPI processes need to interact with a SDN controller for at least two kinds of information before computation. The following discussion assumes only one process runs on a computing node for simplification.

1. A list of IP addresses of computers, which are used in the MPI Broadcast. The SDN controller needs to understand which computers are used in the MPI Broadcast.
2. A special ID for identifying the target MPI Broadcast packets. The identification of MPI Broadcast packets is required because SDN switches need to duplicate only the target MPI Broadcast packets selectively.

To share the first piece of information between the MPI processes and the SDN controller, a master process of the MPI program is designed to send the list of IP addresses of computers that involve computation to the SDN controller. After obtaining the list, the SDN controller builds a broadcast tree based on it and then creates duplication rules of SDN switches.

To share the second piece of information, we have decided to use a special destination MAC address as an ID. For this purpose, the SDN controller is designed to generate a special MAC address and then send this address to a master process of the MPI program. Through this design, when a process of the MPI program broadcasts data, the process sets the special MAC address into a series of MPI broadcast packets before broadcasting the data.

Figure 3 shows how an MPI program should interact with the SDN controller to realize the SDN-based MPI Broadcast method in detail. The interaction between them takes place as follows.

1. The SDN controller obtains the topology of a network composed of switches and computers, where the computation of the MPI program is performed. Subsequently, the SDN controller waits for the MPI program's connection.
2. All processes of the MPI program initialize the MPI execution environment.
3. After the initialization, a master process of the MPI program sends the IP address list of computers participating in the computation. Then, the MPI program waits for a reply from the SDN controller.

4. After the SDN controller receives the list, it builds a broadcast tree based on the list and the topology.
5. After the broadcast tree is built, the SDN controller generates an ID (special MAC address) for a series of the target of MPI Broadcast packets. Importantly, the ID is assigned to each `MPI_Bcast` invoked in the computation.
6. The SDN controller makes a set of duplication rules, which instruct packets of the target `MPI_Bcast` to flow from a source process to the remained processes on a broadcast tree. The rules are then deployed onto SDN switches.
7. The SDN controller sends the ID for the MPI Broadcast to the MPI program.
8. After a master process receives the ID from the SDN controller, it sends the ID to processes so that the remained processes use it in receiving the target broadcast packets.
9. After the eight steps above, processes can invoke the SDN-based `MPI_Bcast`.

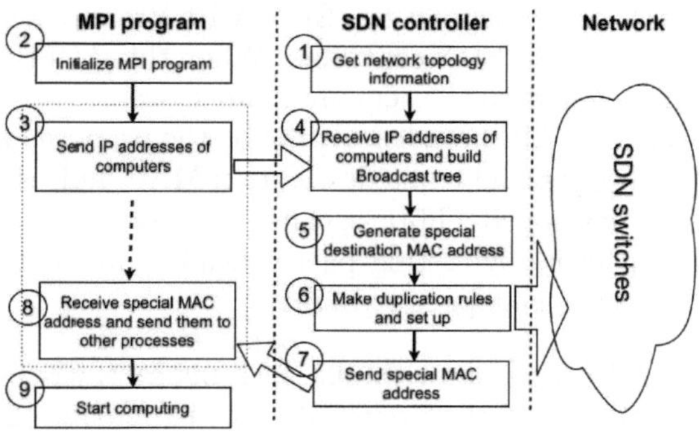

Fig. 3. Interaction model in SDN-based MPI Broadcast

3.2 Implementation of SDN MPI Broadcast

Based on the design in Section 3.1, we have developed the SDN-based MPI Broadcast utilizing OpenMPI version 1.6.3. The prototyped `MPI_Bcast` is composed of two modules; the SDN controller module and the SDN MPI Broadcast library.

SDN controller module. For implementation of the SDN controller, POX [10], which is a development framework for the OpenFlow controller developed in Python version 2.7, has been adopted. POX supports the OpenFlow version 1.0 specification at the time of writing this paper. The SDN controller module has been developed to offer the functions shown in Fig. 3. To understand the network topology, we plan to use an LLDP-based topology understanding mechanism, which our research team has developed in another project [11]. In the current stage of this research, however, the information on network topology is set manually because learning the topology is beyond this paper's scope. For the function of building the broadcast tree, the SDN controller was developed to simply use the minimum number of hops (using the Floyd-Warshall algorithm).

In the near future, however, a more sophisticated method of building the tree is necessary because we have currently assumed for simplification that only a set of MPI programs are executed on a cluster system and thus any background traffic does not exist.

SDN MPI Broadcast Library. The MPI program needs to call `MPI_Init` for initialization and `MPI_Finalize` to finalize the MPI execution environment. The MPI program performs a computation job between these APIs. Taking this execution mechanism into consideration, we have developed a new SDN MPI Broadcast Library called `sdn_mpi_bcast`. This library contains two APIs; `SDN_MPI_Init` and `SDN_MPI_Bcast`.

SDN_MPI_Init: This API is implemented to offer the functions shown in the dotted part in Fig. 3. This API provides MPI programs with the functions of exchanging the IP address list of computers participating in the computation as well as the ID for identifying the SDN MPI Broadcast packets between the MPI program and the SDN controller. When this API is called, a process receiving the ID sends it to the remained processes.

SDN_MPI_Bcast: This API broadcasts data by the proposed method. For this purpose, `SDN_MPI_Bcast` sets up a destination MAC address in broadcasting packets. We have developed a library, called `my_raw_packet`, which can send and receive raw packets by setting packet headers manually. This API has been developed on `my_raw_packet` library.

Importantly, the MPI program with `SDN_MPI_Bcast` is written the same way as OpenMPI. In detail, to use the proposed `SDN_MPI_Bcast`, the developer just needs to replace `MPI_Bcast` with `SDN_MPI_Bcast`.

4 Evaluation

4.1 Experimental Environment

An experiment has been conducted to compare the execution time of `MPI_Bcast` and `SDN_MPI_Bcast` implemented in OpenMPI. Also, we have measured the time required for `SDN_MPI_Init` to learn the setup cost required for our proposed method. Figure 4 illustrates the experimental environment. The experiment was performed on a cluster system which consists of 27 physical computing nodes and 3 OpenFlow switches. OpenFlow switches are 1 Gb/s bandwidth Programmable-Flow PF5240 Switch, and each node has Intel(R) Xeon(R) 2.00 GHz processors. For this experiment, two of three OpenFlow switches were configured to function as two logical OpenFlow switches.

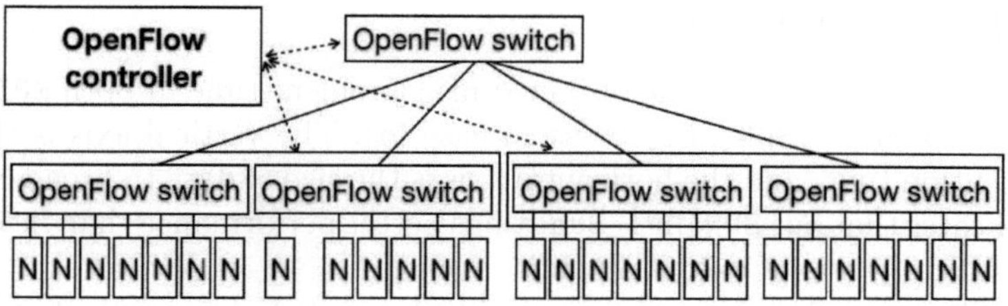

Fig. 4. Experimental environment

4.2 Experimental Method

In this experiment, execution time of our `SDN_MPI_Bcast` and `MPI_Bcast` in OpenMPI was measured and compared through the use of a simple MPI program that just broadcasts an integer array. In this measurement, we have adopted the average execution time spent for broadcast in each of the MPI processes. Furthermore, to obtain execution time, we performed the program 20 times and adopted a average execution time of 20 measurements as the measurement result. A fraction of the MPI program is shown in Fig. 5. `MPI_Wtime`, which returns time in seconds, since an arbitrary time in the past [2] was used for measuring time. The execution time of `SDN_MPI_Bcast` and `MPI_Bcast` in OpenMPI was measured in the following two ways.

```
Initialize MPI execution environment
...
SDN_MPI_Init ( ... ); // For connection with the SDN controller
start = MPI_Wtime ();
MPI_Bcast ( ... ) or SDN_MPI_Bcast ( ... );
end = MPI_Wtime ( ... );
diff_time_on_each_process[] <- end - start // in seconds
average_difference_time = average(diff_time_on_each_process[])
...
Finalize MPI execution environment
```

Fig. 5. A fraction of MPI program used in the experiment

(a) Measure the execution time of MPI Broadcast by running 27 processes for the MPI program, and by changing the data size of the integer array to be broadcast.
(b) Measure the execution time of MPI Broadcast by running the MPI program whose integer array is 4000 in size, and by changing the number of processes.

Furthermore, to investigate the overhead incurred for the initialization process (the dotted part in Fig. 3), we have measured the execution time of `SDN_MPI_Init`. The average execution time of `SDN_MPI_Init` of 20 measurements has been taken.

4.3 Experimental Result

Figure 6a plots two series of the obtained measurement time in both MPI_Bcast in OpenMPI and our SDN_MPI_Bcast in case (a). The vertical axis is the measured execution time, and the horizontal axis is the size of data to broadcast. The graph indicates that our SDN_MPI_Bcast has better performance than MPI_Bcast in OpenMPI in terms of execution time.

Figure 6b shows the measurement result of case (b). The vertical axis is the measured execution time, and the horizontal axis is the number of processes used in the experiment. The graph indicates that the proposed SDN_MPI_Bcast is superior to the MPI_Bcast and also that SDN_MPI_Bcast scales well against process number.

Figure 6c shows the measurement result of SDN_MPI_Init. The vertical axis is the measured execution time and the horizontal axis is the number of processes used in the experiment.

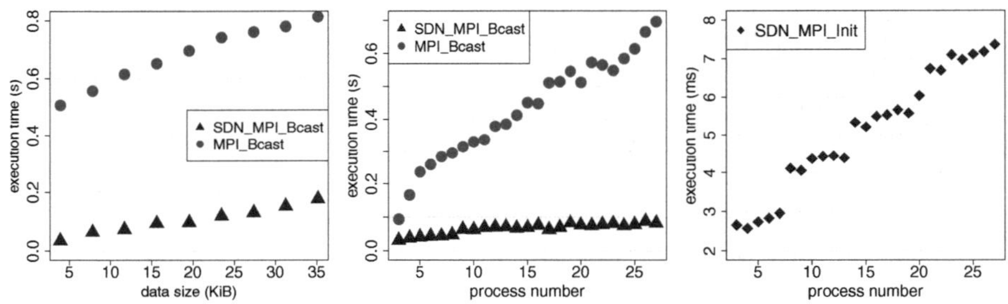

(a) Data size change **(b)** Process number change **(c)** SDN_MPI_Init

Fig. 6. Execution time

4.4 Insights

In case (a), as broadcasting data size increased, SDN_MPI_Bcast had a better performance than MPI_Bcast. Also, the execution time of SDN_MPI_Bcast did not increase as quickly as MPI_Bcast when the size of broadcasting data changed. In case (b), the graph shows that SDN_MPI_Bcast becomes faster than MPI_Bcast as process number grows. The reason can be explained from the fact that MPI_Bcast in OpenMPI uses point-to-point communication repeatedly for a call of MPI_Bcast, while SDN_MPI_Bcast delivers data from source to remained processes along a broadcast tree optimized on the network topology.

In addition, the execution time of SDN_MPI_Init was less than 10 milliseconds when process and switch numbers were 27 and 5, respectively. It could take more time with both the number of processes and switches increased. However, this API has to be called only once in the beginning of the program. Therefore, the execution time of SDN_MPI_Init is not considered a big problem for jobs which take a long time.

5 Related Works

To date, much research related to the acceleration of the MPI Broadcast has been reported. As to MPI Broadcast, several research groups have worked on acceleration of `MPI_Bcast` on InfiniBand, which is a major high-performance interconnect technology available today. Representative examples of such research include [12] and [13]. In these works, to realize `MPI_Bcast` on the top of hardware multicast supported by InfiniBand, the authors have tackled common issues such as unreliability of message delivery, large message handling, and in-order delivery. The experience and expertise reported in these works can be combined with our research from now on. Our research differs from previous research in terms of target interconnect and research motivation. We are motivated to challenge how HPC technology can be changed by regarding the interconnect as a dynamically controllable network resource.

6 Conclusion and Future Work

In this paper, we have explored the feasibility of a high-speed `MPI_Bcast`, or `SDN_MPI_Bcast`, that leverages software programmability brought by SDN for efficient data delivery from a source process to the remained processes of the MPI program. Evaluation shown in this paper implies that `SDN_MPI_Bcast` is superior to `MPI_Bcast` by measuring the execution times of both regarding data size and the number of processes changed. From the result, we believe the use of SDN might be a possible and feasible solution for reducing the execution time of `MPI_Bcast`. At the same time, through this preliminary study, we now recognize many issues to be tackled to realize a practical `SDN_MPI_Bcast`. As described in Section 3.1, we have assumed for simplification that only one process runs on a computing node. However, multiple MPI processes, each of which belongs to a different MPI job, run on a computing node in the usual cases. Although our proposed method allows us to distinguish network flows derived from a MPI job from others, the separation of MPI job groups on a contended environment remains an issue. Finally, how to deal with packet loss should also be considered.

Acknowledgments. This research was partly supported by collaborative research of the National Institute of Information and Communication Technology and Osaka University (Research on high functional network platform technology for large-scale distributed computing).

References

1. Gropp, W., Graham, R., Moody, A., Hoefler, T., Treumann, R., Träff, J.L., Bosilca, G., Solt, D., de Supinski, B.R., Thakur, R., Squyres, J.M., Rabenseifner, R., Supalov, A.: MPI: A Message-Passing Interface Standard Version 2.2. Technical report, Message Passing Interface Forum (September 2009)

2. Gropp, W., Lusk, E., Skjellum, A.: Using MPI, Portable Parallel Programming with the Message-Passing Interface, 2nd edn. The MIT Press (1999)
3. Graham, R.L., Woodall, T.S., Squyres, J.M.: Open MPI: A Flexible High Performance MPI. In: Wyrzykowski, R., Dongarra, J., Meyer, N., Waśniewski, J. (eds.) PPAM 2005. LNCS, vol. 3911, pp. 228–239. Springer, Heidelberg (2006)
4. Rabenseifner, R.: Automatic MPI Counter Profiling of All Users: First Results on a CRAY T3E 900-512. In: Proceedings of the 3rd Message Passing Interface Developer's and User's Conference (MPIDC 1999), pp. 77–85 (March 1999)
5. Rabenseifner, R.: Optimization of Collective Reduction Operations. In: Bubak, M., van Albada, G.D., Sloot, P.M.A., Dongarra, J. (eds.) ICCS 2004. LNCS, vol. 3036, pp. 1–9. Springer, Heidelberg (2004)
6. Open Network Foundation: Software-Defined Network, The New Norm for Networks, White Paper (April 2012)
7. Nascimento, M.R., Rothenberg, C.E., Salvador, M.R., Corrêa, C.N.A., de Lucena, S.C., Magalhães, M.F.: Virtual routers as a service: the RouteFlow approach leveraging Software-Defined Networks. In: Proceedings of the 6th International Conference on Future Internet Technologies (CFI 2011), pp. 34–37 (June 2011)
8. Kotani, D., Suzuki, K., Shimonishi, H.: A Design and Implementation of OpenFlow Controller Handling IP Multicast with Fast Tree Switching. In: Proceedings of the 12th IEEE/IPSJ International Symposium on Applications and the Internet (SAINT 2012), pp. 60–67 (July 2012)
9. McKeown, N., Anderson, T., Balakrishnan, H., Parulkar, G., Peterson, L., Rexford, J., Shenker, S., Turner, J.: OpenFlow: Enabling Innovation in Campus Networks. SIGCOMM Computer Communication Review 38(2), 69–74 (2008)
10. POX Wiki, `https://openflow.stanford.edu/display/ONL/POX+Wiki`
11. Furuichi, T., Date, S., Yamanaka, H., Ichikawa, K., Abe, H., Takemura, H., Kawai, E.: A prototype of network failure avoidance functionality for SAGE using OpenFlow. In: Proceedings of 36th IEEE International Conference on Computer Software and Applications Workshops (COMPSACW 2012), pp. 88–93 (July 2012)
12. Liu, J., Mamidala, A.R., Pand, D.K.: Fast and Scalable MPI-Level Broadcast using InfiniBand's Hardware Multicast Support. In: Proceedings of 18th International Parallel and Distributed Processing Symposium 2004 (IPDPS 2004), pp. 26–30 (April 2004)
13. Hoefler, T., Siebert, C., Rehm, W.: A practically constant-time MPI Broadcast Algorithm for large-scale InfiniBand Clusters with Multicast. In: Proceedings of the 21st IEEE International on Parallel and Distributed Processing Symposium (IPDPS 2007 Workshop), pp. 1–8 (March 2007)

Author Index

MIX
Papier aus verantwortungsvollen Quellen
Paper from responsible sources
FSC® C105338

If you have any concerns about our products,
you can contact us on
ProductSafety@springernature.com

In case Publisher is established outside the EU,
the EU authorized representative is:
Springer Nature Customer Service Center GmbH
Europaplatz 3, 69115 Heidelberg, Germany

Printed by Libri Plureos GmbH
in Hamburg, Germany